Anonymus

Royal Commission on Liquor Licensing Laws

Fifth report (Ireland), minutes of evidence, appendices index

Anonymus

Royal Commission on Liquor Licensing Laws
Fifth report (Ireland), minutes of evidence, appendices index

ISBN/EAN: 9783742810236

Manufactured in Europe, USA, Canada, Australia, Japa

Cover: Foto ©Lupo / pixelio.de

Manufactured and distributed by brebook publishing software
(www.brebook.com)

Anonymus

Royal Commission on Liquor Licensing Laws

ROYAL COMMISSION ON LIQUOR LICENSING LAWS.

MINUTES OF EVIDENCE

TAKEN BEFORE THE

ROYAL COMMISSION

ON

LIQUOR LICENSING LAWS,

WITH

APPENDICES AND INDEX.

VOL. VII. [IRELAND.]

Presented to Parliament by Command of Her Majesty.

LONDON:
PRINTED FOR HER MAJESTY'S STATIONERY OFFICE,
BY EYRE AND SPOTTISWOODE,
PRINTERS TO THE QUEEN'S MOST EXCELLENT MAJESTY.

And to be purchased, either directly or through any Bookseller, from
EYRE AND SPOTTISWOODE, EAST HARDING STREET, FLEET STREET, E.C., and
32, ABINGDON STREET, WESTMINSTER, S.W.; or
JOHN MENZIES & Co., 12, HANOVER STREET, EDINBURGH, and
90, WEST NILE STREET, GLASGOW; or
HODGES, FIGGIS, & Co., LIMITED, 104, GRAFTON STREET, DUBLIN.

1898.

ROYAL COMMISSION ON LIQUOR LICENSING LAWS.

WARRANT.

VICTORIA R.I.

Victoria, by the Grace of God of the United Kingdom of Great Britain and Ireland Queen, Defender of the Faith.

To Our right trusty and well-beloved Cousin and Councillor Arthur Wellesley, Viscount Peel, Chairman; Our right trusty and right well-beloved Cousin and Councillor Victor Albert George, Earl of Jersey, Knight Grand Cross of Our most Distinguished Order of Saint Michael and Saint George; Our right trusty and well-beloved Cousin John Robert William, Viscount de Vesci; the Right Reverend Father in God, Our right trusty and well-beloved Councillor Frederick, Bishop of London; Our right trusty and well-beloved Councillor Sir Algernon Edward West, Knight Commander of Our Most Honourable Order of the Bath; Our trusty and well-beloved Sir William Henry Houldsworth, Baronet; Our trusty and well-beloved Sir Frederick Seager Hunt, Baronet; Our trusty and well-beloved Sir Charles Cameron, Baronet; Our trusty and well-beloved Hercules Henry Dickinson, Doctor in Divinity, Dean of the Chapel Royal, Dublin Castle; and Our trusty and well-beloved William Allen; William Sproston Caine; Alexander Morison Gordon; William Graham; Henry Grinling; Samuel Hyslop; Andrew Johnston; John Herbert Roberts; Henry Riley Smith; Charles Walker; John Lloyd Wharton; Thomas Palmer Whittaker; Alfred Money Wigram; Samuel Young; and George Younger, Esquires, greeting.

Whereas We have deemed it expedient that a Commission should forthwith issue to inquire into the operation and administration of the Laws relating to the Sale of Intoxicating Liquors, and to examine and report upon the proposals that may be made for amending the aforesaid Laws in the public interest, due regard being had to the rights of individuals.

Now know ye, that We, reposing great trust and confidence in your knowledge and ability, have authorised and appointed, and do by these presents authorise and appoint you, the said Arthur Wellesley, Viscount Peel; Victor Albert George, Earl of Jersey; John Robert William, Viscount de Vesci; Frederick, Bishop of London; Sir Algernon Edward West; Sir William Henry Houldsworth; Sir Frederick Seager Hunt; Sir Charles Cameron; Hercules Henry Dickinson; William Allen; William Sproston Caine; Alexander Morison Gordon; William Graham; Henry Grinling; Samuel Hyslop; Andrew Johnston; John Herbert Roberts; Henry Riley Smith; Charles Walker; John Lloyd Wharton; Thomas Palmer Whittaker; Alfred Money Wigram; Samuel Young; and George Younger to be Our Commissioners for the purposes of the said inquiry.

And for the better effecting the purposes of this Our Commission, We do by these presents give and grant unto you, or any six or more of you, full power to call before you such persons as you shall judge likely to afford you any information upon the subject of this Our Commission; and also to call for, have access to, and examine all such books, documents, registers, and records as may afford you the fullest information on the subject; and to inquire of and concerning the premises by all other lawful ways and means whatsoever.

And We do by these presents authorise and empower you, or any six or more of you, to visit and personally inspect such places as you may deem it expedient so to inspect for the more effectual carrying out of the purposes aforesaid.

And We do by these presents will and ordain that this Our Commission shall continue in full force and virtue, and that you Our said Commissioners, or any six or more of you, may from time to time proceed in the execution thereof and of every matter and thing therein contained, although the same be not continued from time to time by adjournment.

And We do further ordain that you, or any six or more of you, have liberty to report your proceedings under this Our Commission, from time to time, if you shall judge it expedient so to do.

And Our further will and pleasure is, that you do, with as little delay as possible, report to Us under your hands and seals, or under the hands and seals of any six or more of you, your opinion upon the matters herein submitted for your consideration.

Given at Our Court at St. James's, the twenty-fourth day of April one thousand eight hundred and ninety-six, in the fifty-ninth year of Our Reign.

By Her Majesty's Command,
(Signed) M. W. RIDLEY.

Royal Commission to inquire into the Operation and Administration of the Laws relating to the Sale of Intoxicating Liquors.

WARRANT.

VICTORIA R.I.

Victoria, by the Grace of God of the United Kingdom of Great Britain and Ireland Queen, Defender of the Faith.

To Our right trusty and well-beloved Councillor, Robert George, Baron Windsor, greeting.

Whereas We did by Warrant under Our Royal Sign Manual, bearing date the Twenty-fourth day of April 1896, appoint Our right trusty and well-beloved Cousin and Councillor Arthur Wellesley, Viscount Peel, together with the several noblemen and gentlemen therein mentioned, or any six or more of them, to be Our Commissioners to inquire into the administration and operation of the Laws relating to the Sale of Intoxicating Liquors.

And whereas one of Our Commissioners so appointed, namely, Our right trusty and right well-beloved Cousin and Councillor Victor Albert George, Earl of Jersey, Knight Grand Cross of Our most Distinguished Order of Saint Michael and Saint George, hath humbly tendered unto Us his resignation of his appointment as one of Our said Commissioners.

Now know ye, that We, reposing great confidence in you, do by these presents appoint you, the said Robert George, Baron Windsor, to be one of Our Commissioners for the purpose aforesaid in the room of the said Victor Albert George, Earl of Jersey, resigned, in addition to and together with the other Commissioners, whom We have already appointed.

Given at Our Court of St. James, the seventh day of May one thousand eight hundred and ninety-seven, in the sixtieth year of Our Reign.

By Her Majesty's Command,
(Signed) M. W. RIDLEY.

WARRANT.

VICTORIA R.I.

Victoria, by the Grace of God of the United Kingdom of Great Britain and Ireland Queen, Defender of the Faith.

To Our trusty and well-beloved Edward North Buxton, Esquire, greeting.

Whereas We did by Warrant under Our Royal Sign Manual, bearing date the Twenty-fourth day of April one thousand eight hundred and ninety-six, appoint Our right trusty and well-beloved Cousin and Councillor Arthur Wellesley, Viscount Peel, together with the several noblemen and gentlemen therein mentioned, or any six or more of them, to be Our Commissioners to inquire into the operation and administration of the Laws relating to the Sale of Intoxicating Liquors:

And whereas one of Our Commissioners so appointed, namely, Our trusty and well-beloved Sir Frederick Seager Hunt, Baronet, hath humbly tendered unto Us his resignation of his appointment as one of Our said Commissioners:

Now know ye, that We, reposing great confidence in you, do by these presents appoint you, the said Edward North Buxton, to be one of Our Commissioners for the purpose aforesaid, in the room of the said Sir Frederick Seager Hunt, and in addition to and together with the Commissioners whom We have already appointed.

Given at Our Court at St. James's, the sixteenth day of April one thousand eight hundred and ninety-eight, in the sixty-first year of Our Reign.

By Her Majesty's Command.
(Signed) M. W. RIDLEY.

TABLE OF CONTENTS.

LIST OF WITNESSES.

Name.		Occupation.	Page.
Mr. D. P. Barton	-	Q.C., M.P., Solicitor-General for Ireland	1
Judge Fitzgibbon	-	Recorder of Belfast	[illegible]
Sir J. Reid	-	Inspector-General of the Royal Irish Constabulary	37
Mr. H. Morell	-	District Inspector, Royal Irish Constabulary, of Belfast	47
Mr. O. W. Leatham	-	County Inspector, Royal Irish Constabulary, of Londonderry	63
Mr. A. Gambell	-	County Inspector, Royal Irish Constabulary, of Cork. (City and E.R.)	70
Mr. U. Bourke	-	Resident Magistrate of Waterford	84
Mr. J. M. G. Foley	-	County Inspector, Royal Irish Constabulary, of Co. Clare	89
Mr. H. Bruen	-	Resident Magistrate of Templemore, Tipperary	97
Mr. J. R. Wigham	-	J.P., Ex-President of the Dublin Chamber of Commerce	103
Mr. F. J. Ball	-	District Inspector, Royal Irish Constabulary, of Tralee, Co. Kerry.	107
Mr. N. M'Cormick	-	General Merchant, of Lismore, Argyllshire	114
Mr. E. G. Swifte	-	Divisional Justice of Dublin	124
Mr. T. W. Russell	-	M.P. for South Tyrone	129
Mr. H. F. Cummins	-	Resident Magistrate of Kilkenny	130
Rev. T. F. Furlong	-	C.C. of Waterford	131
Mrs. Crawford	-	Of Dublin	[illegible]
Mr. T. C. Harrington	-	M.P. for Dublin	165
Sir F. R. Falkiner	-	Q.C., Recorder of Dublin	170
Judge Curran	-	County Court Judge of King's County, Meath, Westmeath, and Longford.	180
Rev. P. O'Leary	-	C.C., St. Finbarr's, Cork	195
Mr. M. A. Ennis	-	J.P. of Wexford	204
Mr. J. Gore	-	Solicitor of Dublin	212
Dr. J. E. Kenny	-	Ex M.P., Coroner of Dublin	217
Mr. M. Healy	-	M.P. for Cork City	223
Judge Orr	-	County Court Judge of Down and Antrim	233
Judge Waters	-	County Court Judge of Cavan and Leitrim	238
Mr. A. Taylor	-	Secretary of the Belfast United Trades Council	241
Rev. M. Ahern	-	C.C. of Ladysbridge, Castlemartyr, Co. Cork	245
Sir J. A. MacCullagh	-	M.D., Ex-Mayor of Londonderry	257
Mr. J. Simmons	-	Secretary of the Dublin United Trades Council	262
Mr. E. D. Daly	-	Chief Clerk of the Dublin Metropolitan Police Courts	263
Dr. J. Hackett	-	County Coroner of Kilkenny	273
Mr. W. Wilkinson	-	Secretary of the Irish Temperance League	276
Mr. D. L. Brennan	-	Chairman of the Dublin Licensed Grocers' and Vintners' Association.	280
Captain R. P. Beamish	-	Brewer, of Cork	307
Mr. D. Donovan	-	Secretary of the Cork Licensed Vintners' Association	315
Alderman J. Dempsey	-	Chairman of the Belfast Licensed Vintners' Association	322
Mr. C. M'Connell	-	Licensed Vintner, of Ballymena, Co. Antrim	331
Mr. W. Moore	-	Licensed Vintner, of Londonderry	333
Mr. A. S. Findlater	-	Chairman of the Dublin Spirit Grocers' Association	339
Mr. M. Shiels	-	Retired Merchant, Representing the Belfast Spirit Grocers	343
Mr. J. O'Brien	-	Secretary of the Cork United Trades Council	345

MINUTES OF EVIDENCE

TAKEN BEFORE THE

ROYAL COMMISSION

ON

LIQUOR LICENSING LAWS.

NINETY-FOURTH DAY.

Queen's Robing Room, House of Lords, Tuesday, March 22nd, 1898.

Mr. H. F. Burton.

22 Mar. '99.

Classification of licenses in Ireland in three classes.

44,660. Is it possible for you to classify, or to put into any kind of categories the different licenses in Ireland?—Yes, I think I can conveniently classify the licenses in three classes. First, there are those licenses which can be obtained only after production of a magistrate's certificate. Of those, there are six in Ireland; first, the publicans' licenses, which comprise a number of varieties; secondly, the publican's occasional license; and thirdly, the [illegible] license for the military and constabulary. Those three are on-licenses. Fourthly, the spirit grocer's license, a license peculiar to Ireland; fifthly, the wholesale dealer's license; and sixthly, the beer retailer's license. The latter three are off; and these are the six licenses in Ireland which require a magistrate's certificate.

44,661. Have the magistrates discretion in granting those?—I will deal with that very fully, if I may, a little later on, under the heads of "Grant," "Renewal," and "Transfer." The second class comprises wine licenses, with reference to which a magistrate's certificate is not necessary, but the magistrates have a power of objection to it—that is the wine refreshment license.

44,662. The wine refreshment house license?—Yes; the wine refreshment house license. The third class comprises those licenses which may be issued without any certificate or consent of the magistrates, and I would mention eight, which practically are all of them: first, the wholesale spirit dealer's license; secondly, the foreign liquor license; thirdly, the wine dealer's license; fourthly, the wine shop license; fifthly, the wholesale sweet dealer's license; these five are off-licenses. And then the sixth, the sweets retail license; seventh, the passenger vessel license; and eighth, the theatre license.

44,663. Do I understand that in all those cases the magistrates' consent, or certificate, is not required?—No, not required in all those cases.

The publican's license; its origin and history. 10 & 11 Ch. I. c. 8.

44,664. I suppose the publican's license would be the most important in Ireland. What would be the general statute regulating that, or what is the history of the statutes which refer to it?—I may as a matter of history mention that while in England the common law right of sale of liquor was first restricted in the reign of Henry VII., I think in the year 1495, in Ireland it was not restricted until the 10th and 11th of Charles I. in 1634, and that statute, of course, was repealed; but it is interesting to consider that it contains and embodies almost all the principles and provisions of subsequent legislation in Ireland, and of the Acts which are now in force.

44,665. The statute of 1634?—Yes, the statute of 1634. It recites the mischiefs which there existed from the excessive number of houses, from the inconvenient and dangerous places in which they were—bogs, and other places—and from the character of the people who kept them.

44,666. Then you do not take any credit to Ireland for having its restrictive legislation applied so much later than in England?—No; I merely mention it as a historical fact. It is only a matter of historical interest. I need not give, I think, that statute; but it does, as a matter of fact, embody the main principles of the law at the present moment.

44,667. But are there no great governing statutes in force now of the present century?—Yes.

44,668. They embody the principles contained in the Act of 1634?—Yes, they do really embody the principles. The law has been changed from time to time, but the main principles of that old Act, hardly improved, are to be found in the present legislation.

Statutes regulating the grant of publicans' licenses. 35 & 36 Vict. c. 94.

44,669. How is the publican's license granted?—The leading statute for the publican's license is the Licensing (Ireland) Act, 1833, and the first six sections of that Act still regulate, subject to some amendments afterwards, the grant of a publican's license in Ireland; and I think it would be convenient, perhaps, if I just dealt with the grant separately, then with the renewal, and then with the transfer. They are three distinct subjects, and I think they can be best dealt with separately. The grant is regulated by that statute, the Licensing Act, 1833. I may just mention the principal amending statutes. They are only, I think, two—the [illegible] (Ireland) Act, 1874, which in sections 9 and 10

17 & 18 Vict. c. 89.

gives the constabulary a locus standi to require notice to be given to them with reference to these licenses.

[illegible]?—Yes, in objections. The Act of 1874, sections 10 and 11, which required the applicant to advertise the notice of application in the local newspapers.

44,671. That is the English Act?—That is the Irish Act of 1874, which is different from the English Act. The English Act of 1872 in the main applies to Ireland, but the Irish Act of 1874 is different from the English Act. It is under that old Act of 1833, amended by these two other quoted sections, that really the grant of the license is regulated, and that particular part of the subject, therefore, is not very complicated.

44,672. Did you mention anything about the advertisement?—Yes; the advertisement is required by the Act of 1874.

44,673. Who is the licensing authority who grant those licenses?—The licensing authority for the grant of publicans' licenses is the quarter sessions in Ireland; and then, in five cities where there are recorders, is the recorder sitting alone—he is the sole licensing authority. That is in Dublin, Belfast, Cork, Londonderry, and Galway.

44,674. How has the recorder come to absorb all the authority of the quarter sessions?—Because he is the quarter sessions in those five places; and he is invested with the quarter sessions jurisdiction, and it is by virtue of that that he is the sole licensing authority.

44,675. But have some of the other justices the right of sitting with him?—Practically not. I speak of my own knowledge of Dublin, as a justice of Dublin. It is a complete sinecure, the office of justice of the city of Dublin; but upon that, with reference to the other cities, perhaps the recorders will be able to tell you if they do anything. As a matter of fact, in licensing, the recorder is the sole judge with no appeal from him, and with nobody sitting with him, in those five cities.

44,676. Outside those five cities, then, the justices in quarter sessions are the authority?—The justices in quarter sessions are the authority, and the county court judge is, by statute, the chairman of quarter sessions, and therefore presides over all licensing sessions.

44,677. So then the recorder presides in both cases?—He does. In the five cities the recorder is also a county court judge of the county in which the city is. That is by custom; and, therefore, in the five cities the recorder sits as sole authority in the city, and as chairman of quarter sessions in the county. In every other county in Ireland the county court judge sits ex officio as chairman of quarter sessions, and presides at those licensing sessions.

44,678. Who is the clerk of the licensing authority?—The clerk of the licensing authority for those justices is the clerk of the peace.

44,679. There is no licensing in counties?—As to licensing in counties, the districts for which those licensing sessions are held, and the places at which they are held, are fixed by order of the Lord Lieutenant in Council, and he may alter them so as to adapt them to local convenience.

44,680. Are there many variations made by Orders in Council?—There are a considerable number. I have frequently seen those Orders in Council—they guide the powers of the Lord Lieutenant to prescribe districts. Then they recite that the magistrates of the locality have represented to him that local convenience will be served by a certain arrangement, and then they prescribe a particular place for the particular district in which it is to be held.

44,681. I suppose at the annual licensing quarter sessions the new publicans' licenses are granted?—Yes, at the annual licensing quarter sessions, which is also fixed by the Lord Lieutenant in Council, and is the Midsummer quarter sessions all over Ireland except in one particular place, Carrickfergus, which is an exception to all rules and to all laws, in which the July quarter sessions is the annual licensing quarter sessions.

44,682. Why is Carrickfergus in that exceptional position?—It is owing to some historical reasons of local charters. It is of no great importance, because it is a town of between 9,000 and 10,000 inhabitants, but it is a curious "fly in amber," if I may so call it. In many matters in Irish law it differs from the other towns and places in Ireland.

44,683. Are the annual quarter sessions the only time at which publicans' licenses can be granted?—

...ow in England and in Ireland.

... do these certificates endure? ... end of the current year, which ... [illegible] on October 10th, and ... [illegible]. Then we come to the

... provisions with regard to ... [illegible] than those with regard ... original licences?—They are ... [illegible] removals are very ... more difficult to follow than ... [illegible], which are comparatively ... before the Licensing Act of ... were subject to all the ... [illegible], and I think, as far as I ... of history, but I believe it is ... every licensee had to run the ... of removal that he had to ... the original grant. The Act of ... and hardships to which the ... [illegible]

[illegible]. When are petty sessions held?—The annual petty sessions is fixed by the Order in Council in the last [illegible] in the month of September.

[illegible]. ([illegible].) Just prior to the Michaelmas quarter sessions?—Yes, just prior to the Michaelmas quarter sessions. At [illegible] it is in June, [illegible] prior to the Michaelmas quarter sessions.

[illegible]. (Chairman.) Is the applicant for removal obliged to attend at petty sessions?—No. The [illegible] section of the Licensing Act of 1874 provides that the applicant for removal need not attend in person at petty sessions in order to obtain the certificate, unless he is [illegible] by the justices or the police to do so by a special [illegible] pursuant to himself?

[illegible]. But if an objection is lodged, he must appear?—Yes. The justices cannot entertain any objection to the [illegible] unless notice has been served on the publican not later than seven days before the sessions.

[illegible]. In the case of a new licence that is not the same?—Yes, there need be no notice of objection [illegible]

Mr. R. [illegible]

Procedure as to removal [illegible] 37 & 38 Vict. c. [illegible]

Mr. D. P. [illegible].

transfers or to emigrate—a new man coming [illegible] of bad character because he did not keep a condition which he had never made, but they [illegible] that on a renewal of an old license it was a moot question whether the justices could or could not. As a matter of fact, I think the justices did so in frequent cases, and there is a pending case of the Dew Drop Inn at [illegible] in the county of Dublin, where the point has been raised, and where, I think, it may be very likely decided in the course of the coming year.

[illegible]. Speaking generally, would the infringement by a publican of conditions laid down by the magistrates not in accordance with the law, amount to a stain on that man's character?—Well, I think, as a matter of practice now, the magistrates do regard it as a matter of character, and they wish, until it is decided to the contrary, to continue to do so. There is a good deal to be said for it. If a man deliberately asks for and accepts a license on certain terms and conditions, and then, having got the license on those terms and conditions, relies on a technical law point to break them, I think there is a great deal to be said from the point of view of the magistrates, that they may regard that as a matter which they will consider in connection with his character.

[illegible]. Even though those terms were not in accordance with the law?—They were terms of honour and not of law, but as a question of law, I may say that this matter is of great importance. It is frequently done in Dublin. The Recorder himself will tell you about it, and it is, in my opinion, a most salutary jurisdiction if it can be legally exercised, because it enables the licenses to be given in cases in which otherwise they would not be given at all by the authority, so that it is far better for the licensees to get them on these terms than not to get them at all, and in other cases it operates in the same way—for instance, in the case of hotels. In Ireland there is no hotel license. The hotel-keeper can only keep an hotel under the publican's license, and the same with a music hall—it enables the authority to prevent a license being refused in a case where it ought not to be so refused, and, speaking generally, therefore, whether it is legal or not, it is not a bad thing for the licensees.

[illegible]. Supposing they had imposed a condition and the condition was broken, would they be obliged to state when they refused the renewal that it was in consequence of this condition not being observed?—They might say that they refused the renewal on the ground of character. They could cover themselves in that way.

[illegible] [illegible]. (Mr. Whittaker.) I should like to ask if it is compulsory on the justices to give this certificate as to character. Is it the law that unless objection is made and substantiated they must do it?—Certainly.

[illegible]. Is there any provision of the law which requires them to give a certificate?—Certainly, in the absence of legal grounds for refusal, there would be a [illegible] to compel them to do it.

[illegible]. Has that been decided?—I do not know that it has been decided, but I do not think in my humble judgment it requires decision; I think that they are bound to do it. They are bound to give a certificate of renewal; unless a valid objection be raised and judicially decided on.

[illegible]. The Excise grant the renewal, I understand, only on receipt of a certificate from the magistrates?—Certainly.

[illegible]. I have not been clear as to whether there is any provision in the law which demands that the magistrates shall give that certificate?—I think that is

Mr. D. F. Browne. — 28 Mar.'98 — Clitheroe's case—contd.

[illegible] decision; too, that in its nature it was not an objection applicable to a transfer, because, to illustrate it, they pointed out this, that, supposing the house was originally licensed, we will say 20 years before, during the intermediate 20 years a number of new licenses are granted. When the house came up to be transferred 20 years after the original license, they said it was not reasonable that the intermediate licenses should be used as an argument against the transfer of a license which was older than any of them, and, in the next place, it was pointed out, by way of illustration, that at the annual licensing sessions there might be other licenses granted which would then and there become previously licensed houses, and the same afternoon or the following morning the transfer would come on, and it would be ruled out, because of licenses granted perhaps five minutes before; because all these houses would become previously licensed houses. Of course this is all reductio ad absurdum, but it was pointed out that because the very house itself was a previously licensed house, and, therefore, it would be an argument against its own transfer. That was one line of argument in that case, namely, that the number of previously licensed houses was not an objection to be made applicable to transfer, but only applicable to a new grant. There was also, I am bound to mention, another line of argument referred to which undoubtedly weighed with the court, and it has been generally admitted by subsequent cases that it weighed with the court. It had been the practice in Dublin apparently —and it was brought before that court that it was so— for 30 or 40 years under the former Recorder, a very eminent man, Sir Frederick Shaw, to treat transfers in this way—that he always acted on this rule, and the court were very much influenced by that fact that properties had been transferred for this number of years upon this basis, and that the courts ought to be very slow to interfere with a practice upon which so much property had become practically a vested interest. That certainly was an element referred to in the decision, and I do not think altogether absent from it.

56,116. (Mr. Young.) This Clitheroe case was a case that was heard after the decision of the House of Lords in Sharp v. Wakefield?—No, it was 20 years before that. I am coming to that, and I will show you the history of this Clitheroe case, because, like the applicant for a new license, its character has been [illegible] from time to time, and the best and the safest way is for me just to tell you what has happened about it, and to show what the judges have said about it since. You will find by that that on the one hand it is a case of great authority, and on the other it is a case which has been subjected to considerable criticism.

56,117. (Mr. Whittaker.) May I ask if I correctly understand you to indicate that the decision was arrived at on the two grounds which you [illegible], but that the judges arriving at that decision thought the law was in doubt?—No; I think it is rather the other way. I think I would rather say this, that the judges, if they had any doubt on the construction, were rather influenced by the magnitude of the property involved, and disinclined, as courts of justice always are, to give a construction to an Act of Parliament, where it is doubtful, which would involve, practically, the confiscation of a great deal of property. I think that influenced them, perhaps.

56,118. That is my point. They doubted the wisdom of the application of it?—I do not think so. I think, on the contrary, they seemed to think that it would have been extremely [illegible] and [illegible] to have refused transfers upon the ground of the number of previously licensed houses for the reasons I have indicated, namely, that it was not fair that an old house, [illegible]

[illegible] of the statute—that on the construction of the statute this particular objection was not applicable.

Mr. D. F. Browne. — Subsequent cases in which Clitheroe's case has been considered. R. (Brannigan) v. Justices of Armagh, 4 L. R. I., p. 271. R. (O'Connell) v. Recorder of Dublin, 13 I. L. T., p. 161. R. (O'Brien) v. Justices of Tipperary, 6 L. R. I., p. 127. R. (Carr) v. Recorder of Dublin, 14 L. R. I., p. 451.

56,119. (Chairman.) Will you kindly pursue the history of that case?—There have been four cases since Clitheroe's case, in which it has been discussed. They are in the Queen's Bench Division, or the Court of Appeal, or both. I will just mention them. I need not go into the details of them all. There is Brannigan's case, which is The Queen v. The Justices of Armagh, reported in 4 Law Reports, Ireland, page 271. Then there was O'Connell's case, The Queen v. The Recorder of Dublin, 13 Irish Law Times, page 161. Then there was O'Brien's case, The Queen v. The Justices of Tipperary, in 6 Law Reports, Ireland, page 127. Then there was Carr's case, The Queen v. The Recorder of Dublin, 14 Law Reports, Ireland, page 451. The two former of these cases were decisions of the Queen's Bench Division, the two latter went to the Court of Appeal. In all these cases the attempt on the part of the applicant was to bring his case within Clitheroe's case, and to escape from the jurisdiction of the magistrates to take into consideration the number of previously licensed houses, and in all these cases the court distinguished them from Clitheroe's case, and held that they were not really cases of transfer at all, although they were very near it, but that they were cases of new licenses really; and, in fact, I think the expressions are used, that they were new licenses masquerading as transfers, in order to bring themselves within Clitheroe's case. In all these cases the court held that the third requirement was necessary, and that the magistrates were entitled to consider the number of previously licensed houses, because, in truth and in fact, they were applications for new licenses, and not really transfers.

56,120. Otherwise, I suppose, if a grant had been given to a house, notwithstanding that the magistrates had taken into consideration the number of previously existing licenses, if that license was once granted that would continue, and there would be no possibility of refusing that house for all time, on the ground that the pre-existing number of houses was more than sufficient? —That is Clitheroe's case, and that is the law still. Then, I think, it would be convenient for the Commission if I were just to read a few of the judgments of the Court of Appeal with reference to that case, and then you will be able to judge what the opinions of the judges are, because a great deal is said about this in a loose way on the one side or the other. There are a few passages only. I will only take the Court of Appeal, because the Queen's Bench Division is a court of coordinate jurisdiction with the court which decided Clitheroe's case, and therefore the other references are not of so much importance, but the Court of Appeal is the important one. In O'Brien's case—that is, The Queen v. The Justices of Tipperary—which I mentioned, Lord Chancellor Ball cited Clitheroe's case, and adopted it without comment. Chief Justice Morris, at pages 134 and 135 of the same volume of reports which I cited, made the following observation. He says: "The "decision in Clitheroe's case was arrived at by the "Court of Queen's Bench when the final tribunal in "this country in such cases." At that time there was no appeal to the Court of Appeal in such cases. "It has been acted on since, and where it "distinctly applies it ought to be followed, but I am "not prepared to extend its operation." Then Lord Justice Barry, at page 135, says: "I think that "Clitheroe's case ought not to be extended, and that "we ought not to go further in interfering with the very "beneficial jurisdiction of the magistrates in restricting "the existing number of public houses on the occasion "of applications for licenses. In Clitheroe's case there [illegible]

Remarks from judgments in the Irish Court of Appeal in O'Brien's case—Lord Chancellor Ball, Chief Justice Morris. R. (O'Brien) v. Justices of Tipperary, 6 L. R. I., p. 127. Lord Justice Barry.

Mr. D. P. Barton.

22 Nov. '98.

[illegible] for any years. He got it renewed every year; then, you see, it was sold and transferred to somebody, and that person coming in wanted to use it as a publican's licence—to have an open bar and to have people come in and to sell liquor to them to be consumed on the premises. Then the Court of Appeal in effect said "Oh, "no; this is not really a transfer; this house was never "used as a publican's house, and we cannot regard this "as a [illegible] house, and the [illegible] regulation must be "applied"; and I think that is a reasonable distinction.

56,157. (Chairman.) That would be in the case of a dormant licence?—Yes.

56,158. But would there be any other case in which it might be possible for a court of first instance to overrule a discretion other than the case of a dormant licence?—There have been such cases, and you can imagine a case arising on eviction. In one of those cases, I think, there was an eviction, and then, by what really was a mistake, the person who got another house got a licence by what you would call in England removal, which does not exist in Ireland. There are no licences so removed in Ireland. That was more or less at the time considered to be a licence in pursuance of the old licence, and the party who succeeded to the original premises did not take out an interim transfer as he ought to have taken out immediately, and then so that [illegible] he tried to get a transfer of the licence which had been on the house in respect of which he was then coming, and when the [illegible] came to be looked into, they said: "No; there has "been some mistake about this; you may have suffered "by it, but there has been no temporary transfer "obtained, and really this is a new licence, although, "no doubt, there had been a long time a licence of this "house." You can imagine that in many ways like that, where there has been an eviction or a bankruptcy, there may be some little hitch in the proceedings, and in all such cases I think the tendency of the court is to keep the rule in Clitheroe's case within the narrowest limits of transfer in the strict sense of the term.

56,159. Supposing a husband had been guilty of misconduct, should he be allowed to transfer his licence to his wife?—Well, I am not certain that that case has arisen, and I should not like to give an opinion.

56,160. (Dean Dickinson.) Have you had many of applications of this kind?—I would not like to say at the moment. It would be a rare case.

56,161. They have been made and refused?—Possibly.

56,162. You were referring to two cases of dormant licences, not where they never operated, and I should describe those as cellar licences. There are others which have fallen asleep, where the holders have [illegible] dormant by going into bankruptcy or something of that kind. We have had three cases of that kind. Those are properly dormant licences?—Yes.

56,163. The other two are what I would describe as cellar licences which never operated at all?—I think that would be perhaps more correct.

56,164. (Mr. Riley Smith.) In Cox's case you say that the licence was dormant. Had Cox been paying for that licence year by year?—Yes, and you will see a little later on a very good reason why people do take out these dormant licences and keep them in Ireland. There is a good reason for it.

56,165. (Chairman.) These dormant publicans' licences?—Yes; which we shall come to later on.

56,166. (Dean Dickinson.) They are certified every year?—Yes. Before I pass from that, the cases I have mentioned are two cases in which the court distinguished the particular cases from Clitheroe's case and held that they were different cases. One case has come before the Queen's Bench Division which, admittedly, is on all fours with Clitheroe's case, which therefore enabled Clitheroe's case to be reconsidered by the Queen's Bench Division, but that was never taken to the Court of Appeal. That case was Smith's case—the [illegible] and the justices of [illegible]—that is the only case I need refer to in addition to what I have done. It is often referred to, and it is reported in the 30th Law Reports, Ireland, page 157.

The case of The Queen v. The Justices of Cavan, in which Clitheroe's case was discussed in the light of the English case of Sharp v. Wakefield. R. (Smith) v. Justices of Cavan, 30 L. R. I., p. 157.

56,167. (Mr. [illegible] [illegible].) Can you give us the date of it?—It was the year after Sharp v. Wakefield, 1892 or 1893. The judgment was given in 1893, I think, but the case came before the magistrates shortly after the decision in Sharp v. Wakefield, and the magistrates held that Sharp v. Wakefield had overruled Clitheroe's

Mr. D. P. Barton.

12 Mar. '96

Decision of the Queen's Bench Division in the case of The Queen v. Justices of Cavan.

behalf of Smith, the applicant, for a Mandamus to compel a transfer to him, and the Queen's Bench granted the Mandamus, holding that Sharp v. Wakefield being a case of a renewal, as, of course, we all know it was, and not a transfer, and having been decided on English statutes, which are quite different from the Irish statutes, did not warrant the re-opening of Chilborne's case, and further that Chilborne's case having been decided by the Queen's Bench Division the Queen's Bench Division would not re-open it, being a court of co-ordinate jurisdiction, and if it was to be re-opened it must be re-opened in the Court of Appeal. It is a very strange thing, but that case was never taken to the Court of Appeal. I do not know how it was. I might just before leaving it mention one or two things in the judgments. In the course of his judgment the Chief Justice quoted the following words of Mr Justice Wills in Sharp v. Wakefield which say that the statutes in the two countries differ. Mr. Justice Wills said, "These statutes, though dealing with general questions, "differ in particulars so important that the decisions "on them given by one of the courts of the two "islands afford no real guide in the case of questions "arising in the sister island." Mr. Justice Holmes, who is now Lord Justice Holmes, used the following words, which are significant. He said; "If this were "the first occasion on which the question was to "be decided, I would be prepared to hold that "the justices had acted within their jurisdiction." In other words, he appears to differ from the decision in Chilborne's case in his own opinion, but he pointed out in the course of his judgment that the case of Sharp v. Wakefield did not touch the point, being a decision on the English Licensing Acts, which were undoubtedly different from the Irish Acts in this all essential particular, that while in England the licensing authority is given a complete discretion in the granting of licenses, and I believe in the renewing of licenses, it is clear that in Ireland the discretion of the licensing authority is limited to some extent, and the question is only how far it is limited. This case was not taken to the Court of Appeal. I tried to inquire why it was, and somebody suggested that it was perhaps because there was not money; but however it may be, the case has never been brought to the Court of Appeal. It rests now as I have stated it, and I think it may be said to be this; that many of the judges have referred to Chilborne's case with a certain amount of, at any rate, doubt and censure, and have expressed an opinion that they would not commit themselves to concur with it; on the other hand, it has been pointed out by the judges that it is a case of great authority, and it is admitted that nobody but the Court of Appeal or the House of Lords can alter it.

Chief Justice O'Brien quotes Mr. Justice Wills' dictum as to the difference between the Irish and English statutes.

Mr. Justice Holmes on Chilborne's case.

Sharp v. Wakefield has no application to Ireland, being decided on a different set of statutes.

56,168. (*Chairman.*) Should I be right in saying that whatever the weight of the law may be as established in the Chilborne case and its successors, Sharp v. Wakefield has not been in any way affected or invalidated by the decision in this case?—No. With regard to Sharp v. Wakefield, as the Irish judges in that case of the justices of Cavan pointed out, even if they were to reverse Chilborne's case in the Court of Appeal, it would not be on account of Sharp v. Wakefield, because Sharp v. Wakefield is on a different set of statutes. It would be only because the judges of the Court of Appeal might take a different view of the construction of the Irish Acts to what the former judges did.

56,169. (*Mr. Young.*) The case of Sharp v. Wakefield has no application to Ireland?—No.

56,170. And the decision of Chilborne's case establishes the principle of vested interests?—That may be said in a popular way. I would not, perhaps, use that phrase as a legal description of it, but certainly to an extent it does.

lord and the personal representatives. The court in a subsequent case of Kelly v. Montague, explained and distinguished the case of Brennan v. Dorney, and held that there is no property in the license apart from the licensed premises. Brennan v. Dorney was reported in 21 L. R. I., p. 353, and Kelly v. Montague, in 29 L. R. I., p. 169.

Mr. D. P. Barton.

56,173. (*Dean Dickinson.*) No inheritance?—Yes, no inheritance and no property. Lord Justice Barry said in Brennan v. Dorney that he could not be understood as even having decided, in Chilborne's case, that there was anything which could be called, in law, a property in the license, and you must remember, of course, that "property" may be used in a popular sense in many ways which are rather loose from a legal point of view and, therefore, you may say you cannot deny that a license renders a house much more valuable—renders it a more valuable property, and that a house with a license renders the people much better off than if they had not got a license. Therefore, in one sense—in the popular sense—it is a kind of property, but the courts have decided that in a legal sense it is not a property, that is to say, it could not be severed from the house with which it is connected and could not be regarded per se as property.

56,174. (*Mr. Whittaker.*) May I ask you if these were Lord Justice Barry's words referring to the Chilborne case. Did he say, "although one or two of the judges "had used the word property, he did not understand "any of them to say that property in the license was "vested; he would have dissented had it been said, "because he did not think there was any property "whatever in the license"?—Yes. I have not the case before me, but from my recollection, I have no doubt those were his words.

56,175. (*Dean Dickinson.*) That would be called in logic a separable accident?—Yes, you will find very little logic in the licensing laws.

56,176. (*Chairman.*) Is that all you feel disposed to say upon this part of the subject?—Yes. I must apologise for going into it at length, but I thought it would be useful to the Commission to have the judgments in these cases which bear on Chilborne's case.

56,177. We do not wish to curtail any of your remarks. Now, as to occasional licenses, how are occasional licenses granted in Ireland?—Occasional licenses are granted in Ireland, I believe, in the same way as in England. They are granted under the Inland Revenue Act of 1862, section 13, and the Inland Revenue Act of 1863, section 21.

Publicans' occasional licenses. 25 & 26 Vict. c. 22, s. 13. 26 & 27 Vict. c. 33, s. 21.

56,178. That is to say, one magistrate may grant an occasional license?—Exactly.

56,179. He need not sit in court?—He need not sit in petty sessions. They may not be granted for more than six consecutive days at one time, and the justices are to specify the hours of opening in writing, and unless the occasion is a public dinner or ball, these hours shall not be earlier than sunrise or later than 10 p.m.

56,180. I suppose they are only granted to those who have a license to sell on the premises?—Quite so, only to those who have a license to sell on. I may mention that occasional licenses are granted to wine refreshment houses, but no certificate is necessary in that case. I merely mention it in passing, because it does not properly come at this stage.

56,181. For how long a time may they be granted?—To wine refreshment houses?

56,182. No, to the publicans?—For six days at a time.

56,183. For six consecutive days?—Yes, for six consecutive days.

56,184. And on each of those days the license must

54,188. Is that with the condition precedent of a magistrate's certificate?—No, not in the case of a wine [illegible] licence.

54,189. The Excise would grant that?—Yes, they would under the Inland Revenue Act of 1864. I may mention that, that down to 1874 publicans in Ireland claimed to exercise the right to sell at fairs and races without an occasional licence. However, by the [illegible] section of the Licensing Act of 1874 this matter was [illegible], and no person can now sell intoxicating liquor elsewhere than upon his licensed premises without an occasional licence, so that if a man wants to sell at fairs or races he must get an occasional licence.

54,190. He must have his house in the district where the fair is held?—Yes. I think I ought to mention there, as it is a matter which distinguishes it from the English law, that there are no provisional licences in Ireland pending building; for example, in the case of an hotel, they do not get a licence in futuro as they do in England. There must be a house.

54,191. These occasional licences enable a man to sell liquor at a place not his own house?—Yes.

54,192. There are exemption orders, as they are called, in Ireland?—Yes, they are very similar to those in England. Under section 11 of the Irish Act of 1874 exemption orders may be made as in England.

54,193. To a man to open his own house till a later hour?—Yes. For example, in Dublin there is one restaurant where they keep open for the theatre-goers till 12 o'clock for supper. That is done on an exemption order.

54,194. Are they granted by the magistrates?—They are granted by the Commissioners of Police in Dublin, and elsewhere by two justices in petty sessions.

54,195. (Vincent de Vere.) In the city of Dublin?—In Dublin the Commissioner of Police, and elsewhere two justices can do it. They must sit in petty sessions.

54,196. (Chairman.) Am I right in saying that an exemption order is for all time unless revoked, whereas an occasional licence is only for a specified period?—I think so; that is the distinction.

54,197. You have no extensions in Ireland?—No, we have no extensions. We have only exemptions, and occasional licences.

54,198. And the exemptions are granted by the police only?—The exemptions are granted by the Commissioners of Police only in Dublin, and by two justices in petty sessions elsewhere.

54,199. ([illegible] Dickinson.) Public notice must be given of that exemption order by its being posted?—I was not aware of that.

54,200. The Act of 1874, I think, provides for that?—I do not know.

54,201. Public notice stating the days and hours for which the exemption order is to be applied for has to be publicly posted?—Yes, I think so.

54,202. (Chairman.) I do not wish to refer to military canteens, but the Canteen Acts apply to the constabulary, and therefore that would come within our jurisdiction, so to speak?—Yes. The military canteens in Ireland are the same as in England under the Act of 1881.

54,203. And the Military Canteen Acts are applied to the constabulary?—No, there is a special Act—the Constabulary Act of 1874, which I believe is only [illegible] by us in Dublin.

54,204. (Vincent de Vere.) There are hardly any separate canteens at all, I believe?—Only one, in the depôt in Dublin. It was for that purpose the Act was passed. That is hardly worth mentioning, but as a matter of fact it does regard to a magistrates' certificate.

54,205. The military canteens are the same as they are here in England?—Yes, the same as they are in England.

46,230. They are general shops?—Yes.

46,231. (Chairman.) Was there any certificate of the magistrate required for the issue of a spirit grocer's licence down to a recent period?—It was not required until 1872. Without referring to these sections, I should just mention the Acts. The Spirit Grocers (Ireland) Act of 1813, the Licensing Act, 1833, and the Spirit Grocers Act of 1845 are the three Acts which dealt with spirit grocers licences before 1872, and none of them required the magistrates' certificate, but in 1872 that requirement was made for the first time.

46,232. In the Act of 1872 was there any distinction drawn of the spirit grocer?—Yes, there was. I have given it practically.

46,233. The "character test"?—Yes. It was first required in the Act of 1872, in the case of certain grants and renewals, that there should be a certificate of good character, and as to the peaceable and orderly way in which the business had been conducted in the preceding year. Then in the Act of 1874, section 9, this was extended to all new applications for spirit grocers' licences, and it was provided that in the case of new licenses the certificate should be as to good character and the suitability of the premises, and, in the case of renewals and transfers, as to good character and the peaceable and orderly conduct of the house.

46,234. Can a new grant be refused to a grocer to sell spirits?—Yes, a new grant can be refused on either of those two grounds, on either character or suitability.

46,235. There is no difficulty which arises about the transfer of spirit grocers' licences such as you mentioned in the [illegible] case?—No, because the two grounds of objection are equally applicable to grant, renewal or transfer. There have been several decisions, and perhaps it will be convenient to mention a matter which I said I would mention, namely, why is it that the spirit dealers in Ireland take out publicans' licences and do not use them. A spirit dealer cannot sell less than 2 gallons; a spirit grocer cannot sell more than 2 quarts. You accordingly see there is a hiatus, and supposing a man were a spirit dealer he could not sell less than 2 gallons, and, in fact, unless he became a publican he could not sell between 2 gallons and half a gallon.

46,236. I think you have a very remarkable case which illustrates the law as to spirit grocers?—Yes, it is Marshall's case. It is a very remarkable case. Marshall, a grocer in the village of [illegible], in north Tyrone, has been for 10 years trying to get a spirit grocer's licence, and four times in the course of that time he has gone before the judges in Dublin, the Queen's Bench, or the Court of Appeal, and different points have been decided in his case. On the first occasion, in the year 1877, it was contended, by those who objected to Marshall's licence, that the objection of the number of previously licensed houses might apply to a grocer, and when that came before the Queen's Bench on application for a Mandamus, that point was not fought, and it went by default. Ever since that it has been assumed that the objection as to the number of previously licensed houses does not apply to a spirit grocer, and that may be said to be the law. The next time, which I think was in 1882, Marshall again tried to get his spirit grocer's licence, and at that occasion his application was for a spirit grocer's and a beer retailer's licence. The magistrates refused both. He appealed to the Queen's Bench only on the spirit grocer's licence and the Queen's Bench and the Court of Appeal held that they could not upset the magistrates' order, because it was a composite one. They had never been asked to give Marshall a spirit grocer's licence only; they had been asked to give him

Mr. [illegible] [illegible] — [illegible] Mar. '98 — [illegible] Vict. c. [illegible]

were in the same position as the two classes I have just mentioned, namely, the spirit grocers and wholesale beer dealers, and they had to get the same certificate with the excise [illegible]. But the Act of [illegible], the Beer Dealers Retail Licences Amendment Act, [illegible] Vict. c. [illegible], too made a very important difference and placed them on an altogether different footing from any other licences in Ireland. The magistrates have an unqualified discretion to refuse the beer dealer's certificate on any grounds, as they may see fit.

The wide discretion of the magistrates in the case of beer retailers.

[illegible]. (Mr. Whitaker.) That is the first application?—Yes, or any application—grant, renewal, or transfer. It is the same as in England. It was an English Act. It is said—but this is a mere rumour, as I may say, of gossip—that the Act was not understood, at the time it passed, to apply to Ireland, and it is mentioned in the Act that it did not apply to Scotland, but as a matter of fact it does apply to Ireland, because every Act for the United Kingdom which does not exclude Ireland applies to it, and so these Acts apply to Ireland; but I think it really passed as far as Ireland was concerned per incuriam, and it was not noticed that it applied to Ireland. It was long before I was in Parliament, and I only speak from what I have heard.

[illegible]. (Chairman.) Of all the licences you have [illegible] requiring, in some shape or other, the magistrates' certificate, the only one as to which the magistrates' discretion is absolute is in the case of the beer retailer?—Yes, the only one.

[illegible]. Are the words used in the statute "Free and unqualified"?—I think the words are "Free and unqualified."

Wine refreshment house licence.

[illegible]. Then we come to the wine refreshment house licence?—The wine refreshment house licence comes in as what I call the second class. I have now done with all the licences that require a magistrates' certificate—six of them. The wine refreshment house licence does not require any magistrates' certificate; but the magistrates are given a power of objection to it. I may mention first what a refreshment house is. A refreshment house is a house, room, or shop, kept by a confectioner or eating-house keeper.

Who may [illegible] a refreshment house [illegible] Excise licence.

[illegible]. He does not sell intoxicants and yet he is subject to an Excise licence?—Yes, he must have an Excise licence. That is in a town of over [illegible] inhabitants he gets an Excise licence as a refreshment house keeper, but not in any other place.

[illegible]. That is the same as in England?—Nearly.

The wine licence for a refreshment house. [illegible] Vict. c. [illegible] s. [illegible]

[illegible]. (Flanagan de [illegible].) Is he subject to the same [illegible]?—Yes. Under the [illegible] section of the Refreshment Houses and Wine Licences Act of [illegible], it is provided that if a refreshment house keeper wishes to sell [illegible] wine by retail, he must make application to the Excise of a very special kind, stating his name, his place of abode, the description and situation of his house, and the net annual value of his house according to the last valuation.

[illegible]. (Chairman.) Then he has to have two Excise licences?—Yes. If in a town with over [illegible] inhabitants, he has to have, first, a refreshment house licence, and then a wine licence. Then the Excise officer serves notice of the application on the clerk of petty sessions and the police. If an objection is forwarded to the Excise officer signed by either the justices in petty sessions, or the police, in [illegible] days the licence is [illegible]. But objections may be made by either the police or the magistrates on eight different grounds. In the case of renewal or transfer, any justice may object to the renewal or transfer, but if he does so he must give fourteen days' notice before the expiration of the licence.

Right of the magistrates or police to object to wine refreshment house licence.

[illegible]. (Sir [illegible].) Then under the refreshment house licence [illegible] he has the right to

[illegible]. (Dean Dickinson.) How are they to be made? In what form?—The Act, as far as I know, says "the magistrates." Does it provide for a majority of magistrates or for one single magistrate?—A justice might do it.

[illegible]. One justice?—Yes.

[illegible]. Supposing they did not agree?—Then it comes before petty sessions.

[illegible]. There is a provision for that?—Yes, he must have petty sessions after the objection is made.

[illegible]. (Chairman.) Any justice may object as a citizen, not as a justice?—As a justice. It is as justice. He is authorised to do so, but he would not be sitting judicially in making the objection.

[illegible]. He might go before his own court and object?—Yes.

[illegible]. One of them he may object?—Not in this case. In this case it would be only one justice. I believe they are the only people authorised to object and the only people who get notice. They are given notice to enable them to object in case they wish to do so.

[illegible]. (Dean Dickinson.) One would like to know how the licence is [illegible] the objection?—As I explained, the matter comes before petty sessions, and it is decided there whether the objection should be entertained there, and I think there is an appeal to quarter sessions, but the thing very rarely arises.

[illegible]. Leaving the Excise to act on the decision of petty sessions?—Yes, I think so.

[illegible]. (Chairman.) Then there are licences which in no sense require the certification by justices?—Yes.

[illegible]. What are these?—First, there is the wholesale spirit dealer's licence for the sale of British or foreign spirits in any quantity not less than two gallons of the same kind to the same person. I may just mention the statutes referring to these. They are the [illegible] Geo. 4. c. [illegible], sections [illegible], [illegible], and [illegible], and the [illegible] Vict. c. [illegible], section [illegible]. You see there that he may not sell less than two gallons, and that is the reason why the wine and spirit dealers take out a publican's licence to enable them to sell smaller quantities than two gallons—between two gallons and half a gallon.

[illegible]. That gives him the right to sell on the premises for consumption?—Not unless he took out the publican's licence.

[illegible]. Do they take it out for the purpose of retailing less quantities?—Yes, and usually they do not use it as a publican's licence, but they take it out for the purpose of retailing off, and it remains dormant for publican purposes. That is the sole reason why it [illegible] that a spirit dealer should go to the [illegible] of taking out a publican's licence, as is very often done. I think there are nearly [illegible] or [illegible] of these, but I am not certain about the number. It is simply to enable them to sell off quantities between two gallons and half a gallon.

[illegible]. Do they ever take advantage of having got the publican's licence for the purpose of selling off, and use it for the purpose of selling on?—They do, and they tried to prove that the other day in a case as to [illegible] and that the licence was not a dormant one. Evidence was given that some wine was taken on, or some beer or ale was taken on, and that was in order to try and prove it was not a dormant licence. Latterly the question has become material, but as a matter of fact these spirit dealers do not take the licence out for the purpose of trading on. They generally take it out in order to pursue their business in those small quantities which they could not lawfully execute under the less than two gallons.

[illegible]. (Mr. [illegible].) As a matter of fact it may be [illegible] there is not a licence in Ireland that would

Mr. [illegible]

[illegible] what a [illegible] The [illegible]

The [illegible]

Mr. D. P. [illegible]. — [illegible] Nov. '96

54,210. When you say the value of the house, is the valuation based on the fact that the licence attaches to the house?—No, I think not. It must be the valuation of the house. I am not quite certain whether the Excise make their own valuation or take the poor law valuation. It would be a matter that an Excise witness could tell you about; but the value of the house asked for, I am sure, must be its own value, because they have to get that before they get the licence in these cases. In fact the magistrates give a certificate to that effect. I may, perhaps, mention the statutes only for the purpose of reference. So far as beerhouses and beer retailers are concerned, it is under the Beerhouses Regulation Act of 1877, section 3, and so far as wine refreshment houses are concerned, under the Refreshment Houses and Wine Licences Act of 1860, section 6.

40 & 41 Vict. c. [illegible] s. 3. 23 & 24 Vict. c. 107, s. 6.

Hours of closing.

54,211. It would be convenient if you would here state the conditions of the licence as regards hours of closing of licensed premises in Ireland?—The main statutory provisions regulating the hours of closing of licensed premises in Ireland are the Licensing Act of 1872, section 25, and the Sale of Liquors on Sunday (Ireland) Act, 1878, 41 & 42 Vict. c. 72.

35 & 36 Vict. c. 94, s. 25. 41 & 42 Vict. c. 72.

Summary of the law regarding hours of closing.

54,212. Could you summarise those?—I summarise the law as follows: I take it in two ways to make it clear. First, I take it by places. Within the Metropolitan Police District of Dublin, and within the cities of Belfast, Cork, Limerick, and Waterford, licensed houses may be opened on Sundays between 2 p.m. and 7 p.m. On Christmas Day, Good Friday, or other public fast or thanksgiving day, between 2 p.m. and 5 p.m.; on other days between 7 a.m. and 11 p.m. That applies to the five cities I have mentioned. Then, secondly, in all other cities or towns where the population exceeds 5,000 inhabitants, on Sunday to be closed during the entire day; on Christmas Day, Good Friday, or other public fast or thanksgiving day they may be open between 2 p.m. and 5 p.m., and on other days may be open between 7 a.m. and 11 p.m. Then, thirdly, in all other places, that is to say, in towns of less than 5,000 inhabitants and in country districts they are closed all day on Sunday; on Christmas Day, Good Friday, or other public fast or thanksgiving day they may be open between 2 p.m. and 7 p.m., and on other days they may be open between 7 a.m. and 10 p.m. Now I will put it in the other way, and instead of places I will take it by days. First, on Sundays licensed premises are closed all day everywhere in Ireland except in the five excepted cities, and there they are opened from 2 p.m. to 7 p.m. Secondly, on Christmas Day, Good Friday, or other public fast or thanksgiving day, licensed premises are closed in cities and towns of over 5,000 inhabitants except from 2 p.m. to 5 p.m., and in other places except from 2 p.m. to 7 p.m.; and thirdly, on all other days of the year licensed premises are closed, in cities and towns where the population is over 5,000, from 11 p.m. to 7 a.m., and other places from 10 p.m. to 7 a.m.

54,213. When you suggested that the Sunday Act provides all over Ireland except the five exempted cities, may I ask you as a matter of experience whether you know of any movement in these exempted cities to have discretion given to the magistrates to close on Sundays, or to modify the hours?—There is no doubt about it from the point of view of the [illegible] who take interest in that point, there is a strong movement to have those cities either altogether included with the rest of the country or have the hours there restricted; but, of course, there is an equally strong movement on the other side. I do not like to express an opinion here as a witness upon it.

54,214. (Dean Dickinson.) Not equally strong, I think?—I dare say not. I would not like to express my opinion on that, but I get resolutions from both sides.

54,215. (Sir Charles Cameron.) On the matter of fact, the Chairman asked you if there was any movement to have the discretionary power?—I am not certain that I have clearly in my mind any definite policy on that point, but you will have witnesses representing the associations who will tell you that. I know in my own constituency I frequently hear of these things.

54,216. I understood that there was what you call a movement for the restriction or for prohibition, but I wanted to know clearly whether you restricted yourself to the Chairman's question as to discretion?—No, I would say nothing about magisterial control.

54,217. (Dean Dickinson.) There is no movement on that question?—I have not heard of it.

Mr. D. P. [illegible]

54,218. (Chairman.) Has as to magisterial discretion?—No, I do not think so. I think they go farther than that.

54,219. Then we come to a question we have had very much to deal with, and that is the bona fide traveller question. I suppose he exists in large numbers in Ireland?—I think I may say that the law in Ireland is exactly the same as in England, and there was a case in 1888, reported in the Irish Reports for 1890, volume 2, page [illegible], a case of Porter, Appellant v. The Queen, Respondent, in which the recent English cases were approved and acted on, and it was pointed out by the court that the persons must be satisfied, where the defendant sets up the defence that he was selling to a bona fide traveller, that the defendant really believed the customer was a bona fide traveller, and that he took all reasonable care to ascertain it, and it was not sufficient that a person should have travelled three miles, but his purpose must be to travel and not to drink. In that the English decisions were [illegible] [illegible] and followed. I may mention that that was a striking case. These were the circumstances, and there has been a somewhat similar case in England, at Southampton. The distance from [illegible] to [illegible] is many miles by land, but much less than three miles by water, and the question there arose whether that navigable arm of the sea was a public thoroughfare within the meaning of the Licensing Acts. The traveller suggested that it was not a public thoroughfare, and that the long carriage route by land ought to be taken to qualify him for his refreshment.

The bona fide traveller.

54,220. Even though he made the short cut?—Yes, but the court held the opposite, and they held that the navigable arm of the sea is a public thoroughfare, and that the man was not a bona fide traveller.

54,221. When you say that the purpose of the traveller must be to travel and not to drink, how is that purpose to be inferred?—The court ought to be satisfied on these points. The onus is thrown on the licensed party to prove or to satisfy the court that he really believed that the customer was bona fide and that he took all reasonable care to ascertain. That is the protection.

54,222. Supposing he asks the question direct, is he compelled to ask the question?—Yes; but I think if the magistrates did their duty they would not accept the mere asking and receiving an answer to that question; but they would in some way gather from the demeanour of the witness and the evidence he gave that he really did believe it, and that it was a bona fide case. That is what they ought to do. I do not say, of course, that it is always is done. I heard it suggested that the law works differently in the three countries. I am not aware that it is worse in Ireland than in England. It may be.

54,223. Then I think there are a few minor points here remaining you would like to draw the attention of the Commission to?—Yes, about the name of the publican being fixed in a conspicuous place upon the premises. The law is the same in Ireland as in England. Then as to the sale of intoxicating liquor to children, the law is the same in Ireland as in England. Then the police power of entering is practically the same. Then the law as to the indorsement of convictions is the same.

Law [illegible] [illegible]

54,224. (Sir Charles Cameron.) With regard to the police power of entry, does that extend to grocers?—Yes. There is power of entry to grocers under the special Acts. Then there is the appeal from conviction. There is an appeal to quarter sessions against any conviction as well as against endorsement of conviction. I have had it suggested that the police ought to have the power of appeal as well as the defendant, but I only mention it as a suggestion that was written to me by a person in authority. They have not got it at present. Then I think that as to the offences it would be more convenient to leave that subject to be dealt with by the police witnesses, who will go into it with personal experience. There are only one or two matters I should like to mention. Prosecutions before the magistrates are mainly under the Licensing Acts of 1872 and 1874. There are a number of old Acts now unrepealed, but the offences created by those Acts are in the main covered by the Acts of 1872 and 1874, so that you may take it that it is an exception when a prosecution is taken under the older Acts. As a rule it is taken under the two modern Acts, but there are

Police power of entry.

Appeal from conviction.

Prosecutions [illegible] [illegible] [illegible].

are points I may mention. There is one important question, and that is the question of the right of arrest for mere drunkenness. As to the right of arrest for mere drunkenness, there is no power given in the Acts of 1872 and 1874. There is a power of arrest for being drunk when in charge of a carriage, and a power of arrest for being drunk under certain circumstances, but for mere drunkenness there is no power of arrest. It has always been, I think, supposed—I always thought so, and I think it is acted on in Dublin—that there is a power of arrest under the old Licensing Act of 1836, section 12, which gives a general power of arrest for mere drunkenness, but I may mention that one of the county court judges has recently decided the contrary, and has held that this old Act is repealed, and that there is no power of arrest for mere drunkenness any longer.

14,237. Have you the words of the Act of 1836?—I can give them to you.

14,238. (*Dean Dickinson.*) No power of arrest for the purpose of prosecution, but a power of arrest for the safety of the person; I have seen the police constantly endeavour to do that?—In Dublin they act on it, and the Crown is taking up this matter, and is going to have the decision of the county court judge—a judge of great authority—tested in the superior court, and the matter settled. The section is section 12 of the Act of 1836. I will read the latter part of the section: "And "every person so found drunk in any street, square, "lane, road, way, or other public thoroughfare or "place, shall and lawfully may be apprehended by any "justice, constable, peace officer, churchwarden, or "overseer as aforesaid, and forthwith carried and con- "veyed before any justice of the peace within whose "jurisdiction he shall be so found, to be dealt with "according to law."

14,239. "So found" does not mean drunk and disorderly?—If he shall be so found.

14,240. (*Mr. Grinling.*) They do arrest for simple drunkenness, do they not?—They do, but they do it not under the recent Acts, but under this old section, and I have pointed out that the question has been raised now in an acute form by one of the county court judges deciding that this former Act is repealed, and that there is no power of arrest for mere drunkenness. The Crown disputes the proposition, and the matter will be brought before the superior courts and settled finally in the course of the following year.

14,241. (*Dean Dickinson.*) Do not the police distinguish between arrest for the purpose of bringing before a magistrate and arrest for the purpose of detaining until the man is sober?—Yes. There is a distinction, but I would rather not go into that. I only mention the well-known point because I know it as a law officer.

14,242. (*Chairman.*) The Act of 1836 has not been formally repealed?—No.

14,243. It is a question of construction?—Yes. I presume the county court judge considered that it had been repealed by implication.

14,244. As to prosecutions. Who prosecutes for offences against the licensing laws?—The police.

14,245. The Chief Constable?—The details of procedure I would rather you would get from the police witnesses, but, as a matter of fact, I think it would be the Chief Constable in the district. There there is only one other matter I should mention, because it would not be complete without. I have said these Licensing Acts cover most of the offences, but it is right to mention one Act. That is the Shebeening Act. That is 17 & 18 Vict. c. 89, ss. 3 and 4. That is an Act for dealing with tippling, and the Act is frequently referred to. I would rather on these police matters that the police should give you the details, because I never appear there, and know nothing about the procedure there beyond theory. As a matter of fact, I think these two are the two Acts in the old law which are most resorted to. The right of arrest for mere drunkenness is under the Act of 1836 and the Tippling or the Shebeening Act, but otherwise the majority of prosecutions are conducted under the Acts of 1872 and 1874.

14,246. That is quite exceptional?—Quite exceptional. I believe it is the only one in the Kingdom. A wholesale beerdealer in Ireland is subject to magisterial control.

14,247. You mentioned with regard to one class of licence magisterial control had been applied for licensing, as you considered it, in Ireland. Was that by Sir Henry Selwyn Ibbetson's Table Beer Licences Bill?—That was the beer retailers. The table beer is a different thing. I may mention that a table beer licence also can be taken out in Ireland, but I did not mention it because it never has been applied for, and I did not want to trouble you with that. It is the beer retailer's licence for the retail of beer in small quantities. The wholesale beer dealer and the beer retailer dovetail into one another.

14,248. You say the table beer licence is not known in Ireland, though you say it is recognised by law?—Well, it is so granted, but never granted.

14,249. Do you happen to know whether the conditions under which a wine grocer's were altered by Sir Henry Selwyn Ibbetson's Act?—I do not. I never took any interest in it, because it never came to us.

14,250. I do not know whether I understand it rightly, but, as I understand you, publican's applications for new licences are considered at quarter sessions?—Yes, at quarter sessions.

14,251. That is totally different from the practice in England?—Yes.

14,252. They are considered at petty sessions with an appeal in England?—Yes, as I believe.

14,253. What is the machinery in Dublin? Are there quarter sessions in Dublin?—In the city the Recorder of Dublin sits alone as sole licensing authority without any magistrates with him. He has absolute authority.

14,254. He grants all new licences?—He usually refuses them.

14,255. He considers them?—He considers them.

14,256. Is there any confirming, as is the case in England, of new licences. A new certificate is not valid until confirmed. Is there any confirmation in Ireland?—None whatever. There is no appeal from the Recorder, and the only way he can be controlled is by a Prerogative Writ from the Queen's Bench.

14,257. The confirming is not an appeal. A new licence granted in this country must, as a matter of course, before a confirming committee?—Quite so. There is confirmation in Ireland of an interim licence. That is confirmed at the annual sessions, but there is no such confirming as you are referring to.

14,258. The confirmation of the interim licence is not by a confirming committee but by quarter sessions?—Yes, by the annual quarter sessions.

14,259. You explained the reason why a wholesale spirit merchant wanted a publican's licence, and you mentioned also that was in consequence of the absence from the Irish licensing laws of the *frequenting* licence such as we have in England?—I believe so.

14,260. In Scotland we were told that the wholesale merchants take out grocers' licences?—Yes, there is nothing of that kind in Ireland.

14,261. You said there are no excise licences known in Ireland?—Not the ordinary retail licences. I have never heard of it; but there may be others. There are a few excise dealers' licences but they never come before the courts. I do not know much about them. Probably some of the other witnesses will be able to tell you.

14,262. (*Mr. Grinling.*) There are some according to the returns?—Yes, something like that. I have never heard them considered in the superior courts of law.

14,263. (*Sir Charles Cameron.*) About the passenger boat licences. What is the condition as to Sunday drinking expressed in it?—I can not quite correctly state that. I have never considered it.

14,264. You mentioned that you had a copy of it. Would you mind putting it in?—Certainly. (*Vide* Appendix.) I have copies of all licences granted in Ireland.

Mr. A. P. Barton.
——
25 Mar. 96.
——
Difference between the beer retail licence and the table beer licence.

Difference between the English and Irish law as to the authority for granting publicans' licences.

The Recorder of Dublin as licensing authority.

No "confirmation" of licences in the English sense of that term.

Confirmation of interim licences in Ireland.

The spirit dealer and the publican's licence.

Excise licences.

Passenger boat licences.

Mr D. F. Barton.

23 Mar. '98

56,255. This form does not give any of the conditions of the licence?—No.

56,256. There is nothing here to indicate about Sunday trading?—There is not.

56,257. You had a case, I think, in Dublin where the "Great Eastern" was on exhibition, and she had a licence, and it was held by some people that she constituted a sort of floating infraction upon the licensing law?—I do not remember that. I think there was such a case, but I cannot remember exactly the result of it. It would arise very rarely.

56,258. You do not know whether the general licensing law makes any provision for the prohibition of sale from a vessel holding a licence of that sort beyond the limits of the land?—I should not like to give an opinion on that without consideration. I have never heard it raised.

Hours of closing.

56,259. As to the hours of closing, you say that there is no geographical distinction in the country, that in all towns above 5,000 inhabitants the hour of closing is fixed compulsorily at 11 o'clock, and in all towns below 5,000 inhabitants it is fixed compulsorily at 10 o'clock?—Yes.

56,260. There is no variety of hours of closing as between grocers or any holders of licences?—No. As to some refreshment house keepers there is a special provision, and it is possible there might be some addition and restriction on them, but it arises so rarely that I do not know that it is worth mentioning.

56,261. Can you tell whether the holders of licences in towns under 5,000 inhabitants, who must shut on Sundays altogether and must close at 10 o'clock on every week-day, get any privileges in the way of diminished licence duty?—I believe not.

56,262. Do they pay for early closing six-day licences?—I believe not. That only applies to people who apply for and obtain a six-day or early closing licence.

56,263. You mentioned that there had been a considerable agitation in favour of the extension of Sunday closing to the five exempted towns?—Yes.

56,264. Can you tell the Commission whether there has been any agitation in favour of earlier hours of closing on Saturdays?—Yes, there has been.

56,265. What support has it had?—Curiously, it has come to me as a member of Parliament. I have heard of the 9 o'clock closing on Saturday as a burning question, in addition to Sunday closing.

56,266. Has that agitation made a distinction between any classes of licences?—I never heard any distinction drawn in connection with that.

Bona fide clubs—A recent Dublin case on the subject. The law practically the same as in England.

56,267. (Mr. Young.) I suppose that owing to your view of not saying anything on matters of policy, you declined night?—No. I can tell you about the bona fide club. There has been a recent case in Dublin about a bona fide club of Lyman v. O'Reilly reported in this year's reports, 1898, vol. 2, page 83, and that is a decision which went at least as far, if not further, than any English case. It was a very strong instance. In that particular case the magistrates had held that the manager under the circumstances was not infringing the law, and the Court of Queen's Bench held that he was. If you like, I will mention what the circumstances were. The manager, who was the landlord of the club, had let the premises to the club as lessees. The club fitted it thereabouts, and handed over in 1895 the management and control to the manager, he to pay all outgoings and to receive all profits. Thenceforward he carried on the club on his own risk, receiving all subscriptions and supplying drink at the club tariff fixed by the committee, and receiving all the profits from the sale of liquor. The divisional magistrate of Dublin held that this was a bona fide club, but the Queen's Bench quashed that decision and held that, according to the English decisions, the test being in whom was the property in the excisable liquor, this man really getting all the profits from the liquor, the property lay in him, and they held it was not a bona fide club. It places the law on the same lines as the English decisions, and it was a strong decision in the direction of controlling clubs.

The registration of clubs.

56,268. Is it your opinion that clubs should be registered?—I should not like to express any opinion on that. I have heard, even from a trade point of view, objections to it. I have heard some people say it would legalise them, but I do not know really. It is a controversial question, and I have not made up my mind about it.

56,269. Is the mode of gra[...] versial question. Is the mode [...] the mode of granting licen[...] opinion satisfactory, or ought [...] I think they certainly ought to [...] be a great advantage if the [...] whether the mode is satisfactory [...] a large one, and I would rather [...]

56,270. Your evidence has [...] I want to know whether I [...] from it. Is this the fact, [...] are concerned, that they [...] first instance by the magis[...] sessions?—Yes.

56,271. With the county [...] except in certain cities?—Quit[...]

56,272. Those cities being [...] Galway?—Yes.

56,273. Where the recorder [...] Cork, in those five cities [...] jurisdiction.

56,274. And is it correct [...] licences is in the hands of the [...] constant licensing petty sessions [...] petty sessions, grocers or [...]

56,275. With an appeal to [...]

56,276. That is in the case [...] of renewals.

56,277. There is no appeal [...] transfer?—In the case of gr[...] licences there is no app[...]

56,278. So far as transfers [...] transfers are granted by t[...] sessions, and what are called [...]

56,279. And these remain [...] quarter sessions?—Till the [...]

56,280. When the magistrat[...] may be, has jurisdiction over [...]

56,281. And all applications [...] whom or by whom granted, [...] annual licensing sessions?—[...]

56,282. May I ask you if the [...] mode of conducting that [...] do not think so.

56,283. Have not you a doubt [...] before one court and then [...] must get the interim transfer [...] all. It may even occur [...] quently the licence must be the [...] is required to get a temporary [...] it is in his interest that the [...] the gap between that time [...] quarter sessions comes round.

56,284. With reference to [...] think I gather from you, [...] opinion that the 5-o'clock sp[...] should be extended to Irela[...] cannot see any reason agai[...] be an anomaly, and they [...] issued, the three grocers' [...] publican's licence when the[...] different and small purposes.

56,285. It would appear [...] it is and the other licence [...] publican's might be. It is a [...]

56,286. And in cases I hav[...] Curiosity, because it is on [...] and probably it would be [...] themselves.

56,287. With reference to [...] licences, would you give [...] power in regard to the regula[...] is a matter of opinion. I [...] of law. I would rather [...] have the legislature, and [...] on their experience.

56,288. Am I correct in [...] Fitzgibbon, was of the opinio[...] refuse, and am I correct in [...] was overruled?—It was [...] to spirit grocers' licences [...] differed from the rest of the [...] with reference to that I [...] with reference to the [...]

[illegible] was of opinion that the [illegible] referred to would exclude [illegible], and that it was [illegible] for the magistrates to take into consideration a chapel, church, or school, or other thing; but the other members of the court were in the majority. He [illegible] of that opinion, I think, in the [illegible] of [illegible] [illegible]

16,[illegible]. I presume you are aware that publicans in England may sell intoxicating liquors and establish a [illegible] established here without a licence. I want to put this to you. That is a [illegible] [illegible]. Are you of opinion that that should be extended to Ireland?—There, again, I should lack the local experience, but in Ireland a publican can get an occasional licence for that purpose.

16,[illegible]. He has to pay for that?—An occasional licence is a very cheap thing. I have no experience with reference to that except knowing the legal requirements. It seems to me an occasional licence meets the necessities of the case.

16,[illegible]. Might I ask you—you may or may not answer—I gave you of the opinion that [illegible] and sports should be [illegible] to [illegible] [illegible] in [illegible] [illegible]?—I certainly do not feel qualified to give an opinion upon that.

16,[illegible]. Ireland is under many disadvantages with reference to the matter, and I thought you would be able to say something upon that?—I think that hardly comes within the Licensing Acts. I know it often comes up in the House of Commons.

16,[illegible]. In England, persons who brew beer for their own use pay no licence under a certain rental, say 8l., and then from 8l. to 15l. they only pay [illegible], and from 15l. to [illegible]l. they only pay [illegible] for a licence?—I never heard of anybody in Ireland who brewed beer for his own use.

16,[illegible]. It is not a duty on beer, it is a licence?—I do not think it is the practice in Ireland to brew beer for their own use. I do not think so.

16,[illegible]. It is not done now in Ireland, but the disadvantage that the Irish people have is that for the national drink they have to pay a large licence for the sale of it; whereas in England for the national drink they pay a small licence?—I have often heard that in the House of Commons, but I do not think it comes under the Licensing Acts.

16,[illegible]. (*Mr. Grattan.*) The grocers' licence is not a large question in Ireland, because out of 16,[illegible] licensed premises there are only about 600 or 700 grocers?—I should think that was about the number.

16,397. And a large number of those are combined with other licences?—Yes.

16,[illegible]. Whereas in Scotland the grocers' licence represents half?—That is a wholly different thing. It is a very large question.

16,[illegible]. (*Mr. Riley Smith.*) Every refreshment house, whether it sells alcoholic liquor or not, is bound to have a licence?—I believe in a town of over 10,000 inhabitants there is the requirement of a licence for a refreshment house, but in no other place.

16,[illegible]. The law in Ireland is different from what it is in England in that respect. In England no ordinary temporary refreshment house requires no licence unless it keeps open after 10 o'clock at night?—I daresay, but I think I am right about that. I do not think the provision is repealed that requires a licence for a refreshment house in towns of over 10,000 inhabitants.

16,[illegible]. In towns with less than 10,000 they still require no licence?—No licence unless they want to retail wine.

16,[illegible]. I see that licences can be granted without a explanation of it that I do not know of, but that it is apparently. It is a curious thing with regard to the law reading, that the law goes against him more than anybody.

16,[illegible]. Apart from any explanation there may be of it, it is the fact?—It seems to be the fact.

16,407. You say that [illegible] take out publicans' licences on the understanding that they will not make use of them?—Quite so—that they will not act them as public-houses.

16,[illegible]. In other words the magistrates make conditions that have no legal force in the eyes of the law?—Quite so.

16,[illegible]. They do that in England at the present time?—I believe so.

16,[illegible]. I do not think myself that it is an objectionable practice, do you?—I only speak for Dublin. I think it is a controversial question, but it strikes me, from what I have seen of the Recorder's [illegible], it is a necessary practice for two reasons. From the point of view of the man applying for the licence, he might be refused, unless he agreed to a limited licence; and where people require a publican's licence for a legitimate and limited purpose, it should be limited to those legitimate purposes and should not be abused. I think there is a good deal to be said for the practice, but it is very doubtful how far it is legal and how it can be enforced.

16,[illegible]. That is when a wholesale trader wants to do a retail trade in addition to his wholesale trade?—That would be the case with the wholesale dealer. It also arises in the case of [illegible] halls and hotels. The Recorder put the condition on the Metropole Hotel in Dublin that they should not use their bar—; forgot the exact terms—as a public-house bar, but only for hotel purposes. That was not only in the interests of temperance, but in the interests of the neighbouring traders, who strongly objected to having a public-house placed near their places of business, and therefore the restriction was for a double purpose; but it was [illegible] to and acted on, and those conditions are always observed faithfully, so far as I know.

16,[illegible]. (*Dean Dickinson.*) He [illegible] on it as subsequent [illegible], so there was some [illegible] of [illegible]?—Yes. It was objected to, but I believe it was finally adhered to.

16,[illegible]. (*Mr. Riley Smith.*) When you say that a condition of that kind has no legal force, it has the force in fact, because if the man [illegible] his word, and has not kept the conditions under which his licence was granted, the magistrates would say We will not renew?—They do that on the ground of character, and that is a question of doubt whether they can do so or not. That question will be, I think, sure to come before the courts shortly as to how far they are entitled to do it, because it has never been raised as an illegal to say, when he comes for a renewal, "You refused to keep "your word, and we regard you as a man of bad character, and refuse to renew." That is the practice at present.

16,[illegible]. (*Mr. Henry Wigram.*) In endeavouring to understand the English and Irish law, there are one or two questions I should like to have cleared up. First of all, am I right in understanding that the day of the annual licensing meetings is under the jurisdiction of the Lord Lieutenant?—Fixed by the Lord Lieutenant by Order in Council.

16,[illegible]. Have you the same provisions for the disqualification of justices that we have?—Practically the same.

16,[illegible]. Then with reference to a new licence. In England anyone may object to the granting of a new licence?—Yes.

16,[illegible]. [illegible]

Mr. D. F. [illegible].

[illegible]

Practice of granting publicans' licences subject to illegal conditions.

Date of Ireland licensing sessions.

Disqualification of justices.

[illegible] of objections to licences.

[illegible]

54,441. On general grounds there is one very important right which is protected in our English law by the 1872 and 1874 Acts, namely, the right of the renewal, which you have not mentioned?—I did not mention it, because I think it is the same as in England. The owner has the same protection. He has power on certain occasions, and it gives the opportunity of getting a transfer on certain occasions.

54,442. May he appeal against a disqualifying order?—I rather think so. Whatever it is, it is the same as in England. I did not think it necessary to draw attention to that, but I do not think there is any difference so far as I know.

54,443. As to these conditions that are imposed, in your judgment would it not be better that they should be laid down by statute?—I daresay it would. I do not like really to express an opinion on that subject at all, because I have never heard it discussed on both sides, but it certainly does seem to be convenient, both for the publican who wants a licence and for everybody, that there should be some way of giving a licence subject to certain qualifications suitable to the particular wants of the particular case.

54,444. From your experience you attach great value to the right of appeal in all these cases?—I attach great value in all proceedings to the right of appeal. I think it is always a powerful and useful check for any court to have an appeal, and entirely apart from it upon those the judge over whom the appeal is, if he is wise, as he usually is. Of course, one must remember there is a strong power by prerogative writ if they exceed jurisdiction or fall short of jurisdiction, but as a general proposition I think an appeal is always a useful thing in legal matters.

54,445. (Mr. Younger.) Do you consider that under the Act of 1872 the penalties for shebeening are quite severe enough?—Well, that is a matter that I think you would get better from the police magistrates and from the police who have to prosecute every day in these cases. I have had a letter from one who tells me the prosecutions are frequently under the early Acts, the Shebeening Acts, very largely for the reason, you say, that the other Act is not sufficiently strict.

54,446. The other Act imposes a penalty of 50*l*. for the first offence, 100*l*. for the second, with imprisonment up to three and six months with hard labour, which appear to me to be severe penalties. I want to know whether you are aware that in Dublin there is a large number of prosecutions for shebeening?—A very large number; a large proportion of the cases are for shebeening.

54,447. Are you aware that the punishments in these cases is extremely light—principally fines ranging from 10*s*. to 1*l*.?—I am not aware of that; but you will have the magistrate who imposes them here, and he will tell you about them.

54,448. It is no part of your business as one of the law officers of the Crown to have supervision of that?—No, they never come before us. As a matter of fact, the Attorney-General is responsible for prosecutions, and I am, but it would not come before him, because that is purely a police matter.

54,449. Any question on the subject should be addressed to the police rather than to you?—Yes, and particularly to the divisional magistrate, who is a most excellent magistrate, and who will be here.

54,450. (Mr. Whitaker.) I think you told us that many of the public-houses in country districts in Ireland are connected with shops?—So I believe.

54,451. Can you tell us whether it is customary to sell drink for consumption in the shops?—I do not know exactly. I am attempted to answer it, but I do not think I have been in any of them. I do not know how far the shop and public-house are separated, but you will get that from local witnesses.

54,452. (Dean Dickinson.) By a low bracket?—There is no doubt about it, the sale of goods and the drinking both go on at the same time, and of course it is open to that observation.

54,453. (Mr. Whitaker.) Did I understand you correctly that the tendency of the courts since the Ottiwell case has been to restrict that decision within the narrowest possible limits?—I should say so—to limit [illegible]

Mr. R. P. Roberts.

14,454. The Act of 1877 raised the rateable value, did it not, of beerhouses before they could have a licence; that is, it raised the qualification?—I think so. It fixed it, if I remember rightly, at £15 and £8.

14,455. That was considerably higher than before?—I daresay. I do not remember what it was before.

14,456. You will be aware that that Act alone closed a very large number of public-houses in Ireland?—It would if it raised the qualification.

14,457. A large number?—I do not know about that, but it would appear likely.

14,458. That Act provided no compensation for those houses that were peremptorily closed in that way?—I am not aware about that. I never heard the subject discussed.

14,459. There is no provision in the Act for mitigation?—Not that I remember. I have only treated the law as I find it. I was called to the Bar in 1880, and therefore, I do not know the law as it stood before. I am not aware whether there had been a similar qualification before that.

14,460. The Act of 1833 gave magistrates a full discretion over off-beerhouses?—A full discretion over beer retailers' licences.

14,461. That put them under a risk or liability to lose their licences which they were not under before?—Certainly.

14,462. There was no compensation provided in that Act?—I do not think so.

14,463. There is one point of rather passing interest. You said you were not aware how it was that that Act came to apply to Ireland?—Yes.

14,464. I will ask you if you are aware of this, that in that Bill when originally introduced Ireland was specially exempted from it?—I was not aware of that. I had the curiosity to look through Hansard in one, when I was preparing to come before this Commission, and I find that the Act passed sub silentio through both Houses, and that only one gentleman made any observation during the whole time; in fact, Hansard throws no light whatever on the policy of the Act. The original Bill you are referring to I did not look at.

14,465. As a matter of passing interest I might point out to you how it was. The Act was brought in by the present Mr Ritchie, and it was blocked by one of the Irish members. During the early hours of the morning he arranged with Mr. Ritchie that if he struck out the word "Ireland" and made the Bill apply to Ireland he would withdraw his block; and he did so, and the Bill passed to apply to Ireland?—I never knew that before. That explains it.

14,466. (*Mr. Roberts.*) First of all as to the absence of the necessity for a certificate from the magistrates for theatre and packet-boat licences. Do you know whether there is in Ireland any strong feeling as to the necessity of a change in that regard. Has it been brought to your notice in any way?—I have been counsel in cases, and my clients always take a strong view on one side or the other, but I never heard the question debated in public.

14,467. You stated in your evidence, I think, that the Act of 1833 really contained the same provisions on which the licensing system of Ireland has been built up?—Yes.

14,468. You also mentioned that that Act recited the evils which resulted from the excessive number of licensed premises?—Yes.

14,469. So that at that time, at all events, that was considered to be one of the principles which would rule the magistrates' discretion with reference to the renewal of licences?—It certainly was one of the grounds of the policy of the Act, because it is the first thing recited in the preamble.

14,470. So that the principle, at all events, of the [illegible] by many that it ought to be universal all over Ireland, and that the county court judge would be a far better authority than the justices at quarter sessions, and I think the general feeling is that a responsible judge would be a better tribunal than a number of magistrates; but I cannot say how far that view is felt all over the country. I have heard it frequently expressed both by members of my own profession and by others.

14,472. If that were so would it not imply that it would be impossible to bring the circumstances of the particular locality to the knowledge of the judge?—I do not think so, because the judge can hear evidence, and the judge is a county court judge in either one or two counties. He goes four times a year round his jurisdiction. He has very fair knowledge of the place and has the opportunity of taking the evidence from the particular place. I do not think that that would be the fault of it. There are other reasons. I daresay the judges themselves would not like it. It would be imposing on them a very difficult and disagreeable duty.

14,473. As to the state of the licensing law in Ireland as to the qualification of the premises; is that considered generally satisfactory?—The only thing I have heard about that is that it ought to be further extended to publicans and spirit grocers. I have had letters to that effect written to me. I express no opinion on it myself. It does not apply to publicans and spirit grocers, but only to the other cases I have mentioned.

14,474. Is there any feeling that it should be raised?—I do not know. I never heard it expressed, but there very likely is. I have not followed the controversy about this matter at all.

14,475. (*Dean Dickinson.*) With reference to the case of Moorhall, I remember that Mr. Campbell, our present member, was counsel in that case?—Yes.

14,476. He argued that the word "suitability" in the Act meant site and structural suitability?—I was not present at the argument.

14,477. What did he mean by "site" if it did not mean position. Supposing the public-house were set up close to a penitential[illegible] or a rifle range, would not that be an objection in respect to the site?—I do not know what Mr. Campbell meant. Whatever he said was in the interests of his client. He is a very astute lawyer.

14,478. That was rather giving away the case, because the objection of site was proximity to either a public-house, or a school, or a place of public worship. That comes under the head of "site," as in the cases I put?—Whatever he did say, Mr. Campbell had some good reason for saying it.

14,479. I am quite sure he had?—I was not present at the argument. I did not hear it.

14,480. (*Viscount de Vesci.*) It is clear under the law, there being no hotel licence, that no hotel could keep a long bar if it chose?—The only licence in Ireland for an hotel is a publican's licence.

14,481. That would enable him to keep a long bar?—It would, if unrestricted in any way, and in many cases it does enable them to keep an ordinary bar, and that is the reason why in some cases—I have known it in my own experience and practice—the licensing authority insists on a restriction so as to make it an hotel licence as far as possible.

14,482. To a certain extent they strain their powers in doing so?—Certainly.

14,483. Will you state whether it is declared in law what are the special reasons for hearing applications for grants of licences at other times than at the Michaelmas licences?—I think I can give an illustration from a reported case. I think it happened at a particular place that they did not hold the annual licensing sessions at the time fixed by Act of Parliament, and the court held [illegible]

State of the law as to the value qualification of premises.

No "hotel" licence in Ireland. Hotels must have publicans' licences.

Applications for new licences "out of" annual licensing sessions.

Mr. D. P. [illegible]

[illegible]

Jurisdiction of magistrates at licensing sessions.

44,485. The constitution of the licensing sessions is the justices resident in the licensing district?—Yes, the same as at quarter sessions.

44,486. The resident magistrate of the district sits on the Licensing Bench?—I believe so. He does not in the county Dublin, but I have never practised before a Licensing Bench except in county Dublin. There the recorder sits with 20 or 30 magistrates round him, and I do not know, but I assume, the resident magistrate could sit if he wished.

44,487. You are not able to state as a fact?—No.

44,488. I think you stated that any justice of the county has a right to object to a licence being granted in any licensing division in that county?—Yes, I think so.

44,489. A justice residing outside the bounds of the licensing district?—In the case for instance that would practically cover any justice of the county.

44,490. Is not quarter sessions solely composed of magistrates residing in the district of quarter sessions?—This is a very delicate subject which one has to be very careful about; but for the magistrates, who have a commission for the whole county, can be restricted in their attendance to particular divisions. In fact, I think it is chiefly regulated by the control of the Lord Chancellor.

44,491. As far as criminal business is concerned, a justice may not serve outside his own petty sessional district?—Because he is appointed to serve at certain petty sessions.

44,492. I am talking of the objection raised to a licence being granted by a justice residing outside the licensing district or quarter sessions district?—I think where it is a question of two persons doing a thing there, they should be in that particular district, but where it is a general quarter sessions sitting, I do not see how you could have all the Bench any magistrate of the county. On the other hand, it is a very extraordinary thing for the Lord Chancellor, supposing any magistrate of the county goes out of his own district under circumstances that become a public scandal, and the Lord Chancellor takes notice of the action of magistrates in Ireland from time to time with reference to this.

44,493. The point is not whether he can adjudicate, but a question whether he is to come off the Bench to object before the Licensing Bench that he does not reside in the district. That is not laid down in the law?—I do not know that there is any limit to the objection. I am not aware that there is. At petty sessions it is more limited. A magistrate is always appointed on a written understanding that he goes to certain divisions only, or perhaps one only.

44,494. I think it is in this way, that he states in his form that he [illegible] that he proposes to attend certain petty sessions, and the Lord Chancellor has the power to prevent him attending others?—Yes.

44,495. I am only referring to a quarter sessions licensing district?—I am not aware that there is any restriction as to the power of objection. There may be, but I do not think there is.

The witness withdrew.

His Honour Judge Fitzgibbon called in and examined.

Judge Fitz-Gibbon.

Position of witness.

44,496. (*Chairman.*) Your honour is the Recorder of Belfast?—Yes.

44,497. And you have been so for some time?—Ten years.

44,498. You are the sole licensing authority for the city of Belfast?—Yes.

44,499. What is the population of Belfast?—Upwards of 300,000. Connected with Belfast it is very peculiar the way the court is situated. Belfast is situated partly in the county of Antrim, and partly in the county of Down.

44,500. As far as county Antrim is concerned, you are county court judge?—I am county court judge of that. Sitting at quarter sessions, of course, I am the chairman of the justices at quarter sessions, and sitting as recorder I am the sole judge in the recorder's court.

Former jurisdiction in Belfast.

44,501. Dealing with licensing matters in Belfast, you act both as recorder of Belfast and as county court judge in presiding over the magistrates of the county?—Precisely. A curious state of things existed previously to my appointment in Belfast. The recorder was in the habit of refusing licences or granting them as the case may be. He, of course, exercised his judgment to act upon the case, and he decided it as he thought right. When he refused the application the same application was brought forward before him sitting with the magistrates as county court judge of Antrim, where the magistrates had control, and the magistrates were in the habit of granting licences which he had refused as recorder. In like manner with reference to the judge of the county of Down sitting in that county, applications which had been refused by the recorder in respect of the portion of Down within the borough, were brought before the county court judge of Down, and the magistrates there were in the habit of granting a licence which had been refused by the recorder.

44,502. Does that state of things continue?—No, that was the state of things that existed when I came to Belfast during the time of my predecessors, who were two very capable and eminent men, and whose decision no person could question the propriety of. Still those decisions of the recorder were invariably [illegible]

and there was an end of it. I took that view of it and I refused, sitting as chairman of the quarter sessions, to entertain the question at quarter sessions, and the matter was allowed to drop.

44,503. Even in licensing cases which had arisen in that part of Belfast that was within the county of Antrim?—Yes, provided it was within the borough. As to any case outside the borough, of course I am the chairman of the quarter sessions, and the magistrates were really the authority.

44,504. Has that decision of yours been questioned?—It has never been questioned. They yielded to it.

44,505. (*Mr. Young.*) Is there no appeal from your decision in the matter of the licensing in Belfast?—None; there is no appeal at all.

44,506. (*Chairman.*) Did you say there were two recorders before your time?—Yes, there was Mr. Otway who was 25 years recorder.

44,507. Were they both sitting at the same time?—No; Mr. Otway was the first recorder and on his death Mr. [illegible] was appointed recorder; and on Mr. [illegible] death I became recorder. There were not two at the same time.

44,508. (*Mr. Young.*) In the case of the refusal of renewal by you, there would be an appeal, would there not?—No, the renewal does not come before me at all.

44,509. (*Chairman.*) When the county of Antrim justices sit, you, as county court judge, are the chairman?—Yes.

44,510. Therefore, you are chairman of that body, and recorder of the body which sits in Belfast proper?—Precisely.

Licensing authority.

44,511. What do you think should be the licensing authority?—Having regard to what was at in Belfast, and the state of things I have just described, it has occurred to me that the licensing authority should be a responsible judge, and that he should be the sole licensing authority. In my opinion, the licensing authority should be the recorder or the county court judge, and in my opinion, the magistrates should have nothing whatever to do with granting licences.

Judge Fitz-Gibbon.

too much consequence, it is better allowed to rest on the opinion of a single judge, the recorder, or the county court judge. Of course we may go wrong, and often, I have no doubt, do.

16,513. In granting or refusing a licence, what are the three considerations by which you are guided?—We must be satisfied as to the fitness of the place, the fitness of the person, and we must have regard to the existing number of public-houses.

16,514. That is as regards publicans' licences?—Yes, and we have no right to grant them unless we are satisfied on those three particulars.

[illegible] publicans' licences refused.

16,515. Has it been your duty to grant many or few new licences, since you have been recorder?—I have granted very few, indeed, and that has arisen by reason of the way Belfast has been crowded with licences granted by the magistrates in the times when the recorder refused them. It has become so full of licences now, that there is no room for granting new licences.

16,516. As that state of things has been altered by your decision, there is no danger of that clashing of authority?—No, not so long as that lasts.

Value and number of public-houses.

16,517. What has been the result of the cessation of the granting of new licences within the limits of Belfast?—The licensed premises have increased enormously in value. The houses are much better conducted and the proprietors are fewer. The system of that appears to me to be the danger of losing the licence or the danger of having the licence marked. The question is whether the magistrates should have any power over them at all, and it appears to me they should not. When once I sat for the Recorder of Londonderry a curious case arose. There was an appeal from a bench of magistrates to the quarter sessions. There were four magistrates on the bench with me. The case was perfectly clear that the magistrates below were right, and when it was heard I turned to the two magistrates on my right hand and said "Of course we should confirm the decision," to which they assented. I then turned to the magistrate on my left hand and one of the magistrates objected; I began to remonstrate with him and point out how clear the matter was, when he said, "I am entitled to my own opinion." I then looked to the next magistrate, and he said, "I will do as Mr. [illegible] does." He was a man who had no opinion of his own. Then the magistrates were equally divided, and I, having the casting vote, confirmed the decision, but the next day one of the magistrates who had acted properly told me that the magistrate who had acted in this way and refused to confirm the decision, said to him, "Do you know what you have "done by refusing to grant that licence? You have "destroyed Mr. [illegible]'s mortgage upon the pro- "perty"; showing, evidently, that the gentleman was considering the private interests of his friends and not the public interest at all.

Action of private interests.

16,518. You have told us you act as Recorder for Belfast, and as county court judge for that portion of Belfast in county Antrim. Do you ever sit in the county Antrim outside the limits of Belfast altogether?—Yes.

16,519. Are you chairman?—I am county court judge of the county of Antrim, and, of course, I sit as county court judge of Antrim outside the borough of Belfast. I have there the magistrates to deal with, and my experience is that the magistrates do not regard much the provisions of the Act of Parliament, which require them to take into consideration the number of public-houses. I find that the magistrates are brought from all parts of the county to sit upon the Bench and to vote on questions about which they know nothing, and in which they have no interest. They live in distant parts of the county and the licence being asked for is in a different place.

16,520. That is one of your governing reasons for abolishing the magistrates as the licensing authority?—Precisely. It is one of my reasons for saying they ought to have nothing to do with it, because these private influences are brought to bear, and they come into districts not belonging to themselves at all to vote.

Appeals.

16,521. You have spoken of appeals under the existing law; there is no appeal from the recorder, is there?—None.

16,522. You would like to see an appeal from the recorder?—Certainly. I am strongly of opinion there should be an appeal. The interests involved are very large.

Judge Fitz-Gibbon.

22 Mar. '78.

16,523. All the same as, as you would make him the only licensing authority?—Yes.

Spirit grocers' licences.

16,524. Do you think the spirit grocers' licence should come within the jurisdiction of the licensing authority as well as the publican's licence?—I would put them on the same ground exactly, and I would give the same right of appeal. The magistrates think they are obliged to grant them, provided the premises are fit, and provided the character of the person is fit. They grant the licences, and they have not any regard at all to the existing number of licences. I should either give them to the same licensing authority as the publicans' licences, or I would give them to the stipendiary magistrate.

16,525. May I ask, so as to be clear in my own mind, what you mean by the stipendiary magistrate?—The stipendiary magistrate is the person who is appointed by the Government to discharge the duty at petty sessions. He is not one of the magistrates appointed without salary. There are a great many magistrates appointed by the Lord Chancellor who have no salary, but there is one person appointed with a salary in Dublin of 1,000l. or 1,200l. a year.

16,526. What would you do with him as regards the licensing authority?—If the licensing authority, in respect of the grocers, was not given to the county court judge and the recorder, I would give it to the stipendiary magistrate, and I would give a right of appeal from the stipendiary magistrate to the recorder or to the judge at quarter sessions.

16,527. The stipendiary magistrate should take cognisance of the three considerations mentioned in the Act of William IV.?—Precisely. I would extend to the grocers' licences the third clause, that he should have regard to the existing number of public-houses.

16,528. Do you think that the spirit grocers' licences are a good or an evil?—They appear to me a very great evil. What happens very often is that the wife of the family gets drink in the spirit grocers' establishment. It is put down to the account under the general head of "groceries" and the husband knows nothing about it, and the wife often acquires the habit of drinking. There is no doubt there is a great deal of surreptitious drinking in those grocers' establishments.

16,529. Do any of these cases come up before you?—Not many of them.

16,530. Have you known of cases of goods having been ordered surreptitiously and put down as groceries?—Not many; very few of them. I do not know that of my own experience personally.

16,531. You know that as a matter of rumour?—I know that is the general opinion about it. I think there are only one or two cases that ever came before me.

Drinking on spirit grocers' premises.

16,532. Have you ever known cases in which the law as to consumption on the premises with reference to these spirit grocers has been violated?—Yes, that has often come before me, for the police have brought them up for selling drink on the premises, and in that way they came up for prosecution.

16,533. What has been the consequence to the spirit grocer on a conviction?—He has been fined.

Endorsement of licences.

16,534. Would any amount of convictions make him forfeit the licence?—No, there is not the marking of the grocer's licence.

16,535. Do you think there ought to be?—I think so. I think the same law should apply to grocers' licences, as applies to a publican's licence.

16,536. Do you think that anybody but the actual owners of the premises should have a licence?—My opinion would be that no person should have a publican's licence unless the person carrying on the business. Of course these licences are held by wholesale dealers. They hold a vast number of these licences, and they put persons in to manage the houses. Of course that tends to a monopoly. If that were not so, and if each individual was obliged to conduct the house which he held, it would remove very much of the objection.

Plurality of licences.

Judge [illegible] — 26 May, '98.

and the licenses being so valuable they would be considered property. It would be in the interest of the persons to conduct [illegible] property.

56,537. You mentioned the word "monopoly," but from the earlier part of your evidence I gathered, perhaps wrongly, you did not object to a monopoly—you thought it raised the character of the house?—No.

56,538. I asked you what was the result of there not being fresh licenses granted in Belfast, and you said it enormously increased the value of the houses and the character of the occupants, I think you said?—Certainly it increased the value of the houses, and the owners became more careful in the management of the houses, and the prosecutions have become very much less.

56,539. Then if monopoly is to exist in Belfast or any other town, why should not the fact of the houses being in the hands of a few people with managers increase the value of the houses and the character of the occupants?—So it would increase the value of the houses no matter in whose hands they were, whether the wholesale dealer had them or the retail persons had them. The number of the houses would be the same, and it would increase the value of the houses, no doubt. What I meant by monopoly is that a wholesale dealer may be the owner of, say, 20 licenses, and he has them all in his own hands, but if you give those 20 licenses to 20 people they are distributed, and it lessens the monopoly. That is what I meant by that.

56,540. You object to the tied-house system?—Yes, that is what it amounts to.

Tied-house monopoly.

56,541. You would object to a great company getting licenses for 20 houses, and putting in 20 managers?—Certainly. I do not mean to say they are not properly conducted—not at all. I have not heard of complaints of that kind about their not being conducted properly. It exists to a great extent in Belfast, the holding of these tied houses, but I have heard of no complaint of any improper conducting of those houses.

56,542. Yet I understand you would give the license to the person actually carrying on the business?—Yes, carrying on the business. Of course when the wholesale dealer has the house he supplies his own goods to the retail house, and of course he can supply whatever the public are willing to accept from him, whereas if they are in the hands of 20 persons they would be all very active and careful to supply the best possible commodity to the public.

56,543. On the ground of social order and of administration of the law, do you or do you not think that a state of things where a great company owns 20 houses with 20 respectable managers would be detrimental to the course of law and order?—Not at all. I am sure they are quite as well managed.

56,544. You would not give the license to the company?—I think it would tend to do away with the tendency to monopoly; but I think the houses would be just as well conducted in one way as the other.

56,545. In that case who would you give the license to?—The individual.

56,546. That is the individual manager?—Yes.

56,547. Would that be with the object of making the person responsible?—The person who is the license-holder is responsible. There must be a householder who has the license, and the householder is responsible for every breach of the Licensing law. If a manager is put in he must be a householder.

56,548. Would you visit on the house the sins of the publican?—No, it is on the individual who is the licensed party. He is the person who is punished, not the house.

56,549. I want to know how you would get—if you wish to get—at the great controlling company?—You cannot get at them at all. The only person liable is the person in whose name the license has been granted who must be a householder. He is the only person who can be punished.

56,550. Therefore after a given number of convictions you would take away the license from the house, and not regard the fact that it was in the possession of a great [illegible] company?—Certainly, you would not look at the company at all, but regard the individual as if he were the owner of the whole concern.

56,551. Have you ever had occasion, sitting as a licensing authority, to overhaul the agreements made between the ostensible tenant and his landlord?—No, never.

Judge [illegible]

56,552. You never ask for them?—No.

Agreements between landlord and tenant.

56,553. Would you see any objection to asking for the agreement to see whether the tenant was tied in a way that would incapacitate him from discharging his duties to the public?—I should have no right to ask that, because the Act of Parliament says that the person who is a householder, if he is a fit person, is the licensee.

56,554. If you suspected there was a tied-house system of a stringent character prevailing, would you do that?—I should not interfere. The law allows that. It is quite settled that these tied houses may be held.

56,555. Some magistrates' benches in England insist on seeing the agreement, and if the agreement is not satisfactory they cancel it?—I never do that. I never inquire at all into anything of that kind.

56,556. Do many retailers in Belfast hold several licenses for different houses in their own hands?—Yes, there are several retailers who hold licenses for several houses in Belfast.

Plurality of licenses.

56,557. Do you see any harm in that?—Yes, because they put managers in to conduct them, and then they cannot exercise, it appears to me, a proper control over the houses.

56,558. I think an application was made to you, was there not, by an individual for a transfer under rather peculiar circumstances?—Yes, there was. That was for the transfer of a publican's license. There was a house in Belfast which had existed for nearly 100 years as a wholesale wine and spirit establishment and in that house there was attached a publican's license. It was necessary for him to have the publican's license because otherwise he could not sell anything under two gallons, and he had the publican's license all the time. The owner of the house died, and a transfer has been asked of the license. It has been violently opposed by the police and several persons on the ground that the person who asks for the license is going to convert it into a public-house with a bar. The person applying for the license is a gentleman from Scotland. In Scotland it was proved before me that he had 22 retail licenses. He has got one in Belfast in another place, and he paid for this license, as it was stated, 4,000l., and he asked from me a transfer of the license. The police oppose it on the ground that he is going to open a public-house. The place is most improper for a public-house, nothing could be worse so. It is not improper as long as he carries on the business that has been carried on heretofore, namely, that of a wholesale dealer, and if he does not open a bar. The first application that was made for the transfer failed because he was resident in Scotland. He then applied again in the name of the manager, and that application also failed because the manager was not a householder in Belfast, and no doubt it will come forward again. The position in which the Licensing Authority is as to this—is this man's 4,000l. to be confiscated, and as the license not to be transferred but he should convert the house into a public-house. It occurred to me then that showed that there should be another kind of license existing in Ireland, and that it should be possible to grant a license to sell quantities under two gallons, but which would not enable the licensee to convert the premises into a public-house. That license does exist in England. It is the three-gallon license that was referred to. They can grant a license for a particular purpose in England, but it cannot be granted in Ireland; it must be a publican's license, and by means of the publican's license he may convert premises which are utterly unfitted for a public-house into a public-house.

Sale of under-two-gallon licenses.

56,559. Even though he has got the publican's license simply for the sake of selling in less quantities than two gallons, that qualifies him to set up a bad public-house?—Yes it does. That appears to me to be a great evil, and for the purpose of preventing that some judges have been in the habit of putting conditions upon the licenses restraining that.

56,560. This gentleman from Scotland who owns these retail licenses in Scotland applied for the transfer of this house to which this publican's license was attached?—Precisely.

[illegible]. And he had paid [illegible] for it?—Yes.

[illegible]. You say the question arose as to whether he should be relieved of the [illegible]?—Whether I should [illegible] his [illegible], or grant a transfer, but he should convert it into a public-house. The police say he is going to do that. He has other premises in the neighbourhood.

[illegible]. What did you do?—He will come up before me again. It is not decided.

[illegible]. The difficulty will remain?—Precisely; but it appeared to me that there would be an independent [illegible] licence altogether different from a publican's licence, or that the licensing authority should be able to put restrictions on the licence.

[illegible]. Then, I suppose, that same difficulty and the same risk of expansion of the house, applies to an hotel or a restaurant?—Precisely. The same thing occurred in respect of an hotel in Belfast. There was an hotel called the [illegible] Hotel, in Belfast, and several times applications were made to me to grant a licence to this hotel. It was opposed on the ground that a public-house would eventually be opened. The situation would be very improper for a public-house, but very suitable for an hotel, and a difficulty arose as to whether it should be granted. It was granted, the [illegible] undertaking not to open a public-house, but, in my opinion, the undertaking was waste paper and worth nothing. It is not binding upon him at all. I think it would be very desirable that the licensing authority should be able to put restrictions on the licence when granted, or a separate licence as existing in England, should exist in Ireland, namely, that it should be possible to grant a [illegible] licence to a wholesale dealer; because it comes to this. Are all the wholesale dealers in Belfast who sell wine and spirits to private individuals to be obliged to convert all their establishments into public-houses and have bars in them? They do not wish to do so, still that appears to be the law as it exists at present.

[illegible]. (*Mr. Young.*) This licence you refer to is the [illegible] licence, I presume?—Precisely.

[illegible]. (*Chairman.*) If an hotel or a restaurant wished to take out the [illegible] licence, would you give the magistrates the right of interfering in their discretion and refusing it?—If it is proper to grant the licence for an hotel or a restaurant, of course it should be granted, but granted in such a way that they could not convert the hotel or restaurant into a public-house. It should be granted subject to a condition that it should only be used as an hotel or a restaurant.

[illegible]. Supposing the proprietor of an hotel or restaurant said he wanted to have a public-house licence by granting which he would be able to use his premises as a thoroughly conventional public-house, would you give the magistrates the power of saying, "No; we "think you ought to be dependent upon the hotel "licence, and should not have the public-house licence "into the bargain"?—Certainly; I think it should be an application for a [illegible] licence to the licensing authority—the recorder or the magistrates. There should be an application for the licence.

[illegible]. As to the hours of closing public-houses, when would you close them?—I certainly would close the public-houses at an early hour on Saturday.

[illegible]. Have you any hour in view?—I would close them at or about 4 o'clock. People get off from their work early on Saturday. They have sufficient time from the time they leave their work to 4 o'clock. That would give them an opportunity of going to the public-house, but when they are allowed to remain longer in the public-house than the result of it is that they go into the public-house and they remain there until 10 or 11 at night, and they spend all their wages, go home drunk, and their families are without their wages, which they otherwise would have but for the public-house.

[illegible]. On Saturday what time do the great works close as a rule—what time does work cease?—Between 1 and 2 o'clock. It would give them a couple of hours for them to frequent the public-house. It appears to me that that would be quite long enough, having regard to the interests of themselves and their families. It [illegible] rather on the families in many cases. I am a

[illegible]. Do you not complain of the *bona fide* traveller?—Yes, at least there is nothing *bona fide* in it. The *bona fide* traveller is a mere password into the public-house on Sunday. There have been several [illegible] before me where the police have interfered, and they detected it, and my experience is that it is a well understood [illegible] between the person entering the public-house and the public-house keeper, "Are you a *bona fide* traveller?" and as a matter of course the doors are opened and he goes in. The person who is the owner of the public-house, when there is a prosecution, is asked, "Did you inquire whether the person was a "*bona fide* traveller?"—"Yes," he says, "I asked him "was he a *bona fide* traveller, and he said he was." They never make any inquiry, but simply ask the question, "Are you a *bona fide* traveller?"

[illegible]. What would you do with the so-called *bona fide* traveller?—I would close the public-houses from Saturday until Monday morning, and I would not allow them to be open upon a Sunday at all.

[illegible]. You do not think that the expansion of [illegible] by cyclists and so on and the [illegible] of [illegible] on Sunday?—No; for as cyclists are concerned they have the means of carrying whatever they require. They can have baskets in front of them, and can carry with them whatever they require. For the sake of the community I am quite an advocate for closing the house from Saturday night to Monday morning.

[illegible]. The licensing authority at present is obliged to confine his attention to the objections raised before him, is he not?—Yes. The licensing authority must state the ground upon which he refuses the licence, and that is taken down by the clerk of the peace who enters it in a book.

[illegible]. If a specific objection is made before the licensing authority must the case be decided upon that objection, or may the magistrates introduce into their decision other considerations?—No, it must be decided on the objection raised, and upon some other [illegible] it may turn out during the progress of the case that other grounds of objection do exist, and the licensing authority has no power to refuse the licence on that ground, the objection not having been made.

[illegible]. Would not that be unfair to the applicant, that in the course of the case being heard, some other point should spring up, and the magistrates should say "We think that is a good objection" and without notice to the parties as to what the specific objection was, the licence should be taken away from him?—No, because that could all be avoided in this way that when an objection was suddenly sprung on the applicant, it would be the duty of the licensing authority to adjourn the case to give the applicant an opportunity to meet the objection. Several cases have been before me where an objection has been made, and where it transpired during the hearing of the case that the licence should not be granted. Still, I was powerless in the absence of an objection, and bound to grant the licence.

[illegible]. Is it your view that the licensing authority in the absence of any opposition, should be able to refuse a licence on the three statutable grounds?—Certainly it should be on statutable grounds. I would not allow the licensing authority to refuse it except upon the statutable grounds.

[illegible]. Who would make the objection in that case that the statutable grounds had been infringed?—If no objection has been made, and it is apparent that the statutable ground does exist, I think that the licensing authority should have power to deal with that matter, and it would be his duty, I think, to adjourn the case, in order that the applicant might have an opportunity of removing the difficulty if he could.

[illegible]. (*Mr. [illegible].*) There are one or two questions I should like to put to you with reference to the question of the licensing authority in Belfast. Belfast, being a large city, you must have a great number of magistrates?—Yes.

[illegible]. Are there some of them on the licensing bench at all?—None.

[illegible]. It lies in the hands of the recorder?—It is all in my hands.

Judge [illegible]. — [illegible]

trained to sit on the licensing Bench. As is usual in this country to allow a number of magistrates to sit on licensing questions, but you would prefer to put it in the hands of one man, namely, the recorder, or the county court judge?—There is no such thing as I intend of adopting any machine to sit along with the recorder. What I would do is this. I would make the recorder or the county court judge the sole licensing authority, but I would also give a right of appeal against his decision to the two going judges of assize.

Appeal from recorder.

54,584. You advocate a right of appeal from the recorder's court?—Certainly. I think it is a very serious thing where such large interests are involved.

54,585. What court would that appeal be to?—The judges go assizes twice a year. Two judges go to the assizes every year, and I would give a right of appeal from the recorder to those two judges and let them decide the case.

Licensing justices unsatisfactory.

54,586. May I ask if the people themselves are satisfied with the present system?—I do not think the public are satisfied with it at all.

54,587. Would they prefer the recorder to deal with the question?—I think the general feeling is that the magistrates should have nothing to do with it.

54,588. Why so?—Because licenses have been granted that should not have been granted at all. As I mentioned in the case of Belfast, where the recorder had refused all the licenses, the magistrates granted them all. Private interests are brought to bear, and magistrates, out of their own districts come up and vote on applications about which they know nothing, and in which they have no interest.

54,589. Surely you would not say of the magistrates of Belfast, that they are men of no minds of their own?—I do not say any such thing. I think they are a very excellent set of men; just as you get in any other place.

54,590. Then why not trust them with licensing questions?—Influences are brought to bear, and men, when applied to, come up from remote districts.

54,591. Why I put that question is, that the highest authorities who have given evidence before this Commission, as far as I remember, have all been of opinion that the licenses ought to remain in the hands of the justices?—That is not my experience in the working of it in Belfast.

The bona fide traveller.

54,592. With reference to the bona fide traveller, you have a number of those to deal with?—Certainly.

54,593. The distances, we have heard, is similar to that in this country? Yes. I think so.

54,594. Do you say that more precautions ought to be taken with reference to the publican asking the question? Then, you say, that he asks if they are bona fide travellers, and they say "Yes"?—That is so.

54,595. But they make no further inquiry to ascertain whether that is true?—No.

54,596. What further inquiry should they make than to ascertain from the traveller himself?—Probably he would give no other answer than that he was a bona fide traveller.

54,597. Then you assume that the man tell an untruth?—So they do, constantly.

54,598. You do not say that to them?—No, you cannot say that to them.

54,599. (Mr. Whitaker.) Are the bona fide travellers a difficulty at Belfast, especially in the vicinity of Belfast?—No, I do not think so.

54,600. They do not go out much in order to get beyond the bounds?—I do not think so.

Connection of drink and crime.

54,601. They are not a serious difficulty?—It is not a serious matter.

54,602. May I ask you how long you have been Recorder of Belfast?—[illegible] years.

54,603. During that time can you give us any indication of the result of your experience as to the effect that drinking and drunkenness has upon crime?—I was for 12 or 15 years Crown prosecutor, and the opinion I formed when I was Crown prosecutor was that three-fourths of the crime was the result of drinking.

54,604. Might I take it that is one of the reasons why you object to any method of licensing which tends to grant licenses freely?—No, I do not say that.

Judge [illegible]. — [illegible]

54,605. I understand you objected to magistrates having the power of granting the licenses, because they granted them much too freely?—Partially. They grant them, in my opinion, where the Act of Parliament provides they should not be granted.

54,606. What I was following that up by was asking you, if your objection to the ready granting of licenses is, that your experience has taught you that it leads to public evils, one evil being that it leads to drinking, and crime follows?—I think it does. I remember the time when I was Crown prosecutor, it frequently occurred that people going along the roads at night could not pass any public-house, but every public-house they came to they thought it necessary to go into to have a drink, and the more public-houses the more drink they had.

54,607. These frequent visits to the public-house, I suppose, end oftentimes frequently in disorder and trouble?—Certainly, and then the crime takes place. They get drink in those public-houses going from one to another as they come along the roads, and then at the final public-house, perhaps, the crime for which the man was prosecuted takes place.

54,608. Therefore it is only fair to state to a considerable extent that crime is the facilities that were provided for obtaining liquor?—That is my opinion.

54,609. You are also the County Court Judge for the county of Antrim, I gather?—Yes.

54,610. In that capacity you will have bankruptcy cases before you, I presume?—That is another jurisdiction altogether.

54,611. Do they come before you?—Yes. The Local Bankruptcy Act made me bankruptcy judge also.

54,612. What I was going to ask you, was whether in that capacity you have noticed the undesirable results of drink?—No, I have not.

54,613. You have not noticed that it leads to bankruptcy?—Certainly not.

Proposed licensing authority.

54,614. (Mr. Yeamans(?).) In suggesting an alteration in the licensing authority, I observe that you do not in any way appear to think that a popularly elected board would be more desirable than the present one?—I have never considered that question at all.

54,615. You have said that a judicial authority would be the better one?—Certainly. I would say a judicial authority and some responsible person, and the threat of a court of appeal.

54,616. I rather take it you would think it would be a rather worse system than the present one?—I do not think it would be a good one at all.

Tied houses [illegible].

54,617. That as to the tied houses in Belfast. You ought to know better than I do, but I am informed that there is no system of tied houses there such as there is in England—that all the publicans in Belfast are the owners of their property, though they may have mortgages from one person or another?—I think there are a great many wholesale dealers who have a great many of the houses.

54,618. Is it not the fact that they simply lend probably a small amount of capital to a man?—Certainly. A great many of them are in the hands of the mortgagees.

54,619. Is it not a fact that in very much the larger proportion of these cases the mortgagees are the banks, and not any brewer?—In several cases that is so, but as to the number I do not know. All I know about them is what I have heard.

54,620. The point I wanted to bring out was this. That these loans, such as they are, when they come on the part of wholesale houses, are loans which can be paid off at any moment by the party who borrows, and therefore he is perfectly free to change from them to anybody else if he is not satisfied?—Yes, but the way the thing is managed, as I understand it, is this. The wholesale dealer enables the retail man to buy the property, and he then gets a mortgage upon the house for [illegible] hundred over it, and of course it is part of the arrangement that his goods are to be taken.

54,621. That may be so, but the publican can pay off the mortgage if he pleases, and go to somebody else?—I think so.

Judge Fitz-Gibbon.

14,623. In that case, he is a free agent?—In that case, he is the owner of the house.

14,624. That is a very distinctly important difference between the systems of tying here, and tying in England?—I know nothing of the tying here.

14,625. Where houses are actually owned by the brewer, and then let to a tenant, you see the difference?—I think it is, as you say, generally in Belfast that it is money that has been lent by the wholesale dealer. He, in fact, buys the house, or gives the money to buy them, and takes a mortgage for his money.

14,626. Assuming he does so, is it not to the interest of the wholesale dealer to deal fairly and liberally by the man who borrows the money, so as to protect his own advance?—I do not say he does not deal fairly with him.

14,627. In what respect is there any objection to this system?—What I have mentioned about a monopoly.

14,628. You know that drapers and people of that sort get money in a similar way from the wholesale houses?—No doubt they do.

14,629. Whatever objection applies to the one applies to the other?—I have no doubt it does.

Early closing on Saturdays.

14,630. You favour earlier closing on Saturday?—I do in the interests of the working-classes.

14,631. Do not you think that if you close the houses so early as you suggest it would lead to a great deal of shebeening?—The police are able to take care of that.

14,632. You have great confidence in the police?—I have the greatest confidence in the police. They are quite on the alert.

14,633. You do not think it would be a serious interference with the liberty of the subject if you would not let him get a glass of beer after 4 o'clock on Saturday?—As you know, all these men are coming from their employers in Belfast, and they have their week's wages and spend them in the public-houses, and go home to their families without any of their wages.

14,634. You do not suggest that that happens often?—I have no doubt it does happen constantly.

14,635. Is pay-day always on a Saturday?—I do not know.

14,636. That is a very important point in connexion with it?—I suppose it is. Saturday is generally the day the work-people are paid.

Licences in excess by the justices.

14,637. (Mr. [illegible].) You told us that you had been rather restricted in the matter of granting new licences because they had been granted too freely, in your opinion, by the justices?—Precisely.

14,638. Does not this case arise. I believe that Belfast is a very rapidly growing town and that new districts may require, in the ordinary opinion of mankind, a new licence though some of the old districts are very much congested with old licences?—Certainly, and in a case of that kind the licence should be granted. I am not one of those persons who say that licences should not be granted. What I say is this: that it is the duty of the licensing authority to have regard to the Act of Parliament which provides that in granting a licence you shall have regard to the existing number of public-houses. If no public-house existed, and if the neighbourhood were suitable and proper for the public-house, it is the duty of the licensing authority to grant a licence.

14,639. Do you ever or does any licensing authority in Ireland to your knowledge use the power of granting new licences in this and those in the old districts where in their opinion there are too many, by requiring what we call surrenders?—That is often done—surrendering a licence in an improper place and granting one in lieu of it in another place.

14,640. That is often done in Ireland?—Yes.

14,641. Is it done in Belfast?—Yes.

Judge Fitz-Gibbon.

16 Nov. 18[illegible]

Liquor licences to other goods.

proper heading, I understand you, of spirits or wine, or beer for groceries. That was one of your objections to the spirit grocers' licence?—Yes.

14,643. And I understand you to say that you had practically few cases?—I cannot say that myself. It is merely from hearsay.

14,644. Have you any idea of the number of cases during the last 10 years, which have come under your notice of that kind?—Very few cases of them.

14,645. Is that the opinion, I think, you said yourself was founded upon rumour?—Certainly.

14,646. May I put this to you. How do you regard a rumour when it comes up before you as a judge from the point of view of evidence. Do you attach value to it?—No.

14,647. Then I shall not be wrong if I say you do not attach too much importance to rumour in this case?—Not the slightest.

Quantities for sale.

14,648. Then the other point was with reference to drinking "on." Under these spirit grocers' licences I understand they can sell in the smallest sized bottle and in open vessels for off consumption?—They can sell anything under two quarts.

14,649. You think the three-gallon spirit licence as it exists in England would be an advantage in Ireland. You are aware under that licence they cannot sell less than a bottle, and cannot sell for consumption in open vessels?—I do not know that at all.

14,650. If that were the case in Ireland, would it meet your difficulty with reference to drinking on the premises?—I am afraid I do not quite understand what you mean.

14,651. If they could only sell under the three-gallon spirit licence, as they do in England, no quantity of less than a quart bottle, and not in open vessels, would it reduce the question of drinking you say goes on under the spirit grocers' licence in Ireland?—I do not see how it would affect it much one way or the other.

14,652. You do not think the fact that you can go into a spirit grocer's shop, and buy a small quantity in an open vessel is conducive to drinking?—In Ireland it is two quarts they can sell.

14,653. The spirit grocer can sell in any sized bottle?—Anything under two quarts.

14,654. In England you can only sell in a closed vessel, and not less than a bottle. I ask you whether you think, as you suggest, that the English licence would be an advantage because that would be a preventive to the drinking on the premises?—That is not the English licence I was referring to. There is a licence in England that enables persons who are wholesale dealers to have a licence to retail.

14,655. That is the licence under which all grocers and wine merchants sell in England?—I do not know that. I was under the impression there was that other licence.

14,656. The restriction is not less than a bottle and not in an open vessel, and I ask you whether you think if that was the practice in Ireland that would do away with drinking on the premises?—No. What I was referring to was that there might to be a licence given for the purpose of enabling the wholesale dealer to sell small quantities. If you ordered a dozen of wine or a dozen of spirits that he should have some licence which would enable him to supply you with those articles.

14,657. That is the point I want to put. That is the licence under which the grocer and every trader for off consumption sells in England?—That does not exist in Ireland.

14,658. But if it was the practice in Ireland?—If it had that effect, I say that would be sufficient.

Early Saturday closing.

14,659. (Mr. [illegible].) You would recommend the idea of closing at 4 o'clock on Saturday till Monday?—Yes.

14,660. Because the working man spends his wages?—Yes.

Judge Fitz Gibbon.

[illegible]

drinking, and having commenced it he carries it on. Whereas on the other days he is kept to his work till nearly 6 o'clock, and then he is tired and goes home, and does not go out to the public-house, and the wages are not spent.

14,663. It is for the purpose of preventing the working man from drunkenness and from the improvident use of his wages that you recommend this, is it not?—Yes.

14,664. Might I ask you are you sufficiently logical as you working to close the public-houses altogether?—No, I do not think so, because we should get like any clubs closed. We like to have an opportunity of visiting them, and I think the working man should also have an opportunity of going to what is his club, namely, the public-house, but I think he should not be allowed to remain there such a long time as to do such mischief to himself and his family.

14,665. I presume you would close the clubs for gentlemen at 9 o'clock?—Well, it is not the same thing. When a working man goes into a public-house [illegible] to get the worse for drink he carries it on his day, and the consequences are very serious that result from it. I am not at all one of those that say that the man frequenting the public-house should not have an opportunity of doing so at all. I think they should.

14,666. Is it possible if you interfere with his liberty upon a Saturday, or unduly in anything, that it might not work well. Is there no way of escaping from that restraint that you propose?—I think we all must be restrained, more or less, in several ways. We are all subject to restraint.

14,667. With reference to that brewer, we have had a number of witnesses before us here, and some of them say, and I think you say, that they are very well conducted?—Certainly.

14,668. That, so far as the public weal is concerned, tied houses are not a disadvantage?—No. It was only on the ground of monopoly, I put it.

Tied houses.

14,669. So far as the public weal is concerned?—I say it tends to monopoly, when one person holds 20 licences. They are confined to that one individual, whereas if distributed over 20 persons, 20 persons would have them.

14,670. The licence itself is a monopoly?—Certainly. That is a monopoly.

14,671. You may know that in Belfast houses are owned not by brewers but by large wholesale spirit merchants and are well conducted?—Certainly.

14,672. And that the articles supplied are as good as if they were not tied?—I cannot say anything about that. I have never tried.

14,673. I thought you mentioned that there is a danger of not the best stuff being supplied?—I do not say that they do not supply the best, it is only an inference.

14,674. May I put it to you, that competition would prevent bad stuff being sold?—Yes, but if the houses are all in the hands of one person, the competition is gone, and it is the competition that ensures the good article. That is the way I intend to put it.

Judge Fitz Gibbon.

14,675. You do not assume that there is any danger of all the houses in Belfast getting into the hands of one man?—I do not.

14,676. The managers of the houses, I presume, have the licence?—Yes. The manager would be a householder, and he has the licence.

14,677. You are not only judge in the county, but you are recorder in the city?—Yes.

14,678. Now, you recommend that the tribunal for giving licences ought to be the judge of the county and the recorder of the city?—Yes.

Proposed licensing authority.

14,679. I may say that probably they could not be in better hands than yours, but may I ask you if the one man is in both places would you still allow him to have the right of giving licences?—The recorder has the sole jurisdiction within the borough of Belfast, and is county court judge for the portions of Antrim outside that borough. It is quite a distinct thing. He is there as county court judge.

14,680. The area of your jurisdiction is very extensive?—Certainly. It is first the borough of Belfast, which has a population of 300,000, and then the county court judge has the entire county of Antrim.

14,681. The question I want to put to you is that if there is one gentleman in those two high positions would you still allow him to exercise the licensing authority in both places?—They are quite distinct.

14,682. But the man is one?—I would allow him to exercise the authority with a right of appeal against his decision to the judges of assize.

14,683. If there is a danger of the judge in the county court being very strict and hypercritical in these matters, and his authority is not only being exercised in the county, but exercised in the borough, it might be very injurious probably to the public weal?—The two places where he would be exercising the authority are perfectly distinct, the one from the other. If he goes wrong, and decides erroneously, I would enable the judges of assize to correct him. I think one individual should not have such a tremendous power as that without any right of appeal, and I think the two judges of assize would be perfectly competent to correct his errors.

14,684. Is there an appeal now from the recorder's court?—No.

14,685. Is there an appeal from the county court?—No.

14,686. Then you recommend an appeal?—Certainly.

The witness withdrew.

Adjourned to tomorrow at half-past 10 o'clock.

NINETY-FIFTH DAY.

Queen's Robing Room, House of Lords, Wednesday, March 23rd, 1898.

PRESENT:

THE RIGHT HONOURABLE THE VISCOUNT PEEL IN THE CHAIR.

The Right Hon. the Viscount de Vesci.	John Herbert Roberts, Esq., M.P.
The Very Rev. M. H. Dickinson, Dean.	Charles Walker, Esq.
Alexander Morison Gordon, Esq.	Thomas Palmer Whittaker, Esq., M.P.
Henry Grinling, Esq.	Sidney Young, Esq., M.P.
Samuel Hyslop, Esq.	George Younger, Esq.
Arthur Jackson, Esq.	

Sir Andrew Reed, K.C.B., called in and examined.

Sir A. Reed, K.C.B. — 23 Mar. '98.

14,587. (Chairman.) You are Inspector-General of the Royal Irish Constabulary?—Yes.

14,588. You have been an officer of that corps for a great number of years?—Yes, for over 35 years.

14,589. You have been Inspector-General for over 13 years?—Yes.

14,590. What is the extent of your jurisdiction?—I have police jurisdiction in every part of Ireland except the Dublin Metropolitan district.

R.I.C. 14,591. What does your force consist of?—The present strength of the Royal Irish Constabulary is [illegible] officers and [illegible] of all other ranks.

14,592. You yourself, I think, have served in subordinate ranks?—Yes. I rose to my present position from a cadet, entering the constabulary in 1859.

14,593. And you have served in different counties in Ireland?—I have served in different counties, and in the city of Belfast.

14,594. You gave evidence before a Select Committee, I think, on the Sale of Intoxicating Liquors on Sunday (Ireland) Bill, 1877, did you not?—Yes. I was in 1877 examined, and also in 1888, 10 years ago next month. I wish to premise, before making any statement of evidence, that any remarks or opinions I express relate to my own police jurisdiction, and do not apply, except upon the general principles of the law, to the Dublin Metropolitan district, of which I have no official knowledge, and can only speak as a citizen and resident in the city of Dublin.

14,595. If necessary you will speak as a citizen and resident of Dublin of the state of things in Dublin?—Certainly.

Statistics handed in. 14,596. I think you have been good enough to hand in certain returns?—Yes; I have handed in certain returns which I have prepared, showing statistics bearing on the subject of the Royal Commission, and which I beg to submit for your consideration. Before going to that, I will hand in, if you will allow me, a small return which gives an [illegible] view of the number of licences. It is a return for all Ireland, excluding the Dublin Metropolitan Police district and cities of Dublin, Belfast, Cork, Limerick, and Waterford, of the number [illegible] Metropolitan Police district is omitted, the number of licensed holding the [illegible] licence only is insignificant. In Waterford city the proportion of licensed premises to the population is highest, Limerick city and Cork city being second and third respectively. In Fermanagh the proportion is lowest. Table II. shows the different kinds of licences held by publicans. Of the total number of licences 80 per cent. hold the seven-day licence. In only two counties (Monaghan and Mayo) are the six-day licences in excess of the seven-day licences. That is an important fact, because in Ireland in these counties the magistrates aimed at having entire Sunday closing as much as possible, and in that way they succeeded in increasing the number of six-day licences, so that they now exceed seven-day licences. I asked for an explanation of why it was, and I was informed, as regards Monaghan, that it would appear the large proportion of six-day licences in the county is due to the action of the county court judge and magistrates, who oppose the granting of seven-day licences with the object of stopping Sunday drinking as far as possible. With reference to Mayo, I wrote to the County Inspector—he is the chief officer of police in the county—and I asked him to let me know how it was that in Mayo the six-day licences exceeded the seven-day licences and he wrote as follows:—"It is, no doubt, singular "that the number of six-day licences should exceed the "number of seven-day licences, but, on analysing the "figures, I find that the great preponderance of six-day "licences occurs in the police districts of Ballaghaderreen and Swinford, which is co-extensive with that "part of the diocese of Achonry which extends into "Mayo. In these two districts there are [illegible] seven-day "licences and [illegible] six-day licences, while in the remainder of the county, including the other seven "police districts, there are [illegible] seven-day and [illegible] six-"day licences. It appears that immediately after the "passing of the 1878 Act, the present Catholic bishop "of Galway, Dr. McCormack, was appointed bishop of "Achonry, and, seeing the amount of intemperance "existing in that congested region and the disorder at "markets, Sundays, &c., in consequence, he exerted "his influence in the cause of temperance, and induced "the publicans to fall in with his views, and those who "[illegible]

Sunday licences.

In Monaghan.

In Mayo.

34,728. You think it has made the people more sober?—I am quite satisfied of that.

34,729. Have you observed, or have your officers observed, any improvement in the towns where the Sunday closing is in operation?—Yes, and I have observed it myself when I was a subordinate police officer in the country.

34,730. What effect do you think the increase of athletic sports and cycling has had on the young men in Ireland?—As regards the effect of Sunday closing in Ireland generally, it has tended to make the people more sober.

34,731. Do you think that the athletic sports and cycling in Ireland have tended to make the young men more sober?—Certainly. On Sundays and holidays they go off for long trips through the country and [illegible] in sports.

34,732. Supposing Ireland were polled with regard to it, what do you think would be the result of that polling, for or against Sunday closing?—I think the people residing in Ireland, outside the five exempted cities—I [illegible] for those—would be in favour of retaining the Sunday Closing Act.

34,733. In those cities that are exempted, do you think there is as much drinking as there was?—I do not think there is as much drinking in the exempted cities as there was.

34,734. What is that owing to?—I attribute it in a great measure to the fact that all the young men and many of the young women go to the country on long excursions frequently on bicycles, and few of the young men who would visit public-houses are to be found in the cities during Sunday.

34,735. We have had a very important suggestion made to us from Scotland, and it has also been made to us with regard to Ireland, that in the exempted towns the authorities should have discretion vested in them to close the public-houses earlier on weekdays, and close entirely on Sundays?—I think that would be an excellent provision if applied to Ireland.

34,736. Not a hard and fast rule that they should do so, but that they should have discretion to do so if they liked?—I certainly would not allow them to further extend the hours. They might reduce the hours fixed by the Legislature.

34,737. And, even in the exempted cities, to close, if they pleased, according to the feeling of the people, the houses altogether?—Yes, I would fix the hours within which limits they might reduce those hours, but I would not allow them to extend the limits.

34,738. Would you allow them to go so far as to close public-houses altogether in the exempted cities?—I should, because the view of the people would be expressed by their local representatives.

34,739. (Dean [illegible].) Would you rather that was done by the discretion of the magistrates, or by statute?—I do not think the magistrates ought to have to do with that. It is a question for the people.

34,740. (Chairman.) My question was, whether you would be in favour of vesting statutory discretion in the magistrates further to restrict the hours, or to close them altogether on Sunday in the exempted towns—discretion by statute?—No; but I would vest the discretion in the corporations. There is an analogy to that in regard to the Prevention of Cruelty to Children Act, [illegible], which enables a local authority to alter the hours during which children may be employed in public-houses, and the local authority there would be the corporation in the exempted towns; and I think the corporation ought to have the power of reducing the hours on Sunday, or to close altogether on Sunday if they were satisfied the people wished for it.

Sir A. Reed, K.C.B. — 10 Sept. '98

licensed houses should be closed at 9 o'clock p.m. Before we go from that, perhaps I may say that in my opinion the hours for sale on Sundays in the five cities should be reduced from 2 to 7 to 2 to 5 o'clock. I made these recommendations 10 years ago.

54,755. You would not leave that to magisterial discretion, of which we talked some time ago, but you would make it a statutory obligation?—I would make it a statutory obligation.

54,756. (*Mr. Whittaker.*) And give the magistrates power to reduce them if they wished?—Not the magistrates, the corporation; I would not give the power to the magistrates. It is a matter that concerns the people. I think the magistrates should not have it.

Municipality familiarly [illegible]

54,757. (*Chairman.*) You suggest the corporation should be put in place of the magistrates for licensing?—No. The corporation have not the power of interfering at present in respect to licensing.

54,758. I thought you were contemplating a new licensing authority. I understand you would give the municipality the power over the hours?—I think the extending still further the closing hours is a matter that really concerns the people very much, and I do not think any magistrate ought to have the power of limiting their liberty in that particular, which is considered very essential by a large number of the community, many of whom are respectable, law-abiding people, who consider they ought to have a certain right which they possess here in England.

54,759. (*Dean Dickinson.*) Should you allow the members of the corporation who were themselves engaged in the liquor traffic to give their vote on the matter?—I do not think they ought to be allowed to vote. That is my view.

54,760. (*Chairman.*) In these five corporated cities the Recorder has the sole licensing authority, has he not?—He has.

54,761. When you say you would give the municipality the power, do you mean you would give the recorder the power?—No, I should give the municipality the power of limiting still further the closing hours in the exempted cities.

54,762. (*Mr. T[illegible].*) On the ground that you think it would be the same power to give to one man?—That would be one of my reasons.

54,763. (*Chairman.*) Do you think there is much illicit sale of spirits in Ireland at the moment?—There is not very much illicit sale of spirits in Ireland, but I consider the law ought to be strengthened in that regard, and I shall submit a recommendation further on.

Illicit distillation.

54,764. Is there much illicit distillation?—No, not much, but I will tell you what the state of the case is as regards illicit distillation.

54,765. Which are the worst counties for illicit distillation?—The worst counties for illicit distillation are the four counties of Donegal, Galway (West Riding), Mayo, and Sligo.

Donegal.

54,766. Perhaps you will deal with them in their order?—In the county Donegal the practice of illicit distillation may now be said to be carried on in two baronies only of this county, viz., the baronies of Inishowen, East and West, that is the northernmost part of the county. Some years ago the practice was extensively followed in almost the entire county, but on the appointment of the present Roman Catholic bishop (Dr. O'Donnell) to the diocese of Raphoe, he immediately took up the question of illicit distillation in that portion of the county included in his diocese. The diocese of Raphoe includes the whole of the county Donegal, except the baronies of Inishowen, East and [illegible]

islands where they used to carry it on very extensively to my own knowledge, and I was engaged in the suppression of it in those islands for nearly five years. There is Owey Island and Tory Island. There is a lot of islands there.

Sir A. Reed, K.C.B.

54,769. There is the island of Arran More?—They never made much poteen there, but they did in Owey Island, and in all the islands between that and Tory Island, along the coast of Donegal county.

Galway.

54,770. (*Chairman.*) Then you come to county Galway (West Riding)?—In this county the practice of illicit distillation is largely carried on, and is confined chiefly to the constabulary districts of Oughterard, Roundstone and Spiddal, more particularly in the neighbourhood of Carraroe, where the inhabitants are most persistent in the making of illicit whisky. The locality, too, favours the making of it, as there are a great many small islands, which are difficult of access, and, in consequence, the exertions of the police in their attempts to suppress the practice is considerably baffled.

Mayo.

54,771. Then county Mayo?—In the county Mayo illicit distillation has been gradually increasing for some years past, the practice being chiefly confined to the constabulary districts of Belmullet, Ballina and Swinford. The chief reason for the increase is that for some years past molasses and sugar have been substituted for malt in the making of illicit whisky. When molasses or sugar are used, the process takes a far shorter time than in the case of malt, the risk of detection being thereby considerably reduced. As a result a large number of people who heretofore would not run the risk of making illicit whisky now engage largely in the practice.

54,772. May I take it that molasses and sugar are almost exclusively used in the production of whisky, that is to say, whisky is made almost exclusively of molasses and sugar in those illicit stills?—Yes, in those counties.

Sligo.

54,773. Then county Sligo?—In county Sligo illicit distillation has in recent years been extensively carried on, and is chiefly confined to the constabulary districts of Easky and Tubbercurry. Some years ago the practice was confined to only to a very limited extent, and one of the chief reasons for the very extensive increase is that a new line of railway has recently been constructed in the county. When the making of the railway commenced in [illegible], large numbers of most of the labouring class came to the locality in search of employment, and having obtained the employment, the making of illicit whisky in the locality, for the accommodation of those labourers, immediately commenced, and has since been carried on. Illicit distillation is also carried on in the counties of Fermanagh, Londonderry and Tyrone, but only to a limited extent.

54,774. Does illicit distillation prevail more in mountainous districts than in other districts?—It does.

54,775. Owing, I suppose, to the difficulty of detection, and perhaps the necessity for drinking whisky?—Yes, and of course they are wilder regions and less populated.

54,776. Would the wet and stormy and tempestuous weather they experience drive the people to drinking whisky? Would the weather in those mountainous districts be an inducement to the people to drink, and the wet boggy land? Would the people be more inclined to drink whisky there than in more favoured parts of the country?—I think there is no doubt of that.

54,777. (*Mr. Gordon.*) Would not the poverty of those [illegible] the purpose of seeking employment at harvesting operations. These young men usually leave Ireland about the month of June, and return in the end of October. In a good many instances, they manage to save a few pounds out of the wages they received in England and Scotland, and a good portion of their savings undoubtedly is invested in the purchase of material and plant for making illicit whisky after their return to Ireland.

54,791. Do you think the practice of making illicit whisky is a profitable one?—It must be profitable, or they would not attempt it, because if they succeed in getting one out of three brewings it pays them.

54,792. Another reason why it would be advantageous would be that they should make it for their own consumption. Is there much illicit distillation for the purpose of consumption in their own homes?—No, it is principally for sale.

54,793. How do they dispose of this illicit whisky?—There are a number of ways of disposing of illicit whisky, and the following may be said to embrace the principal: Illicit whisky is purchased by well-to-do farmers for their own use. It can be bought at about one-half the cost of duty-paid spirits, and in the opinion of people held that illicit whisky, if properly made, is good value for the money paid for it. These farmers usually get their supply from a distance, so that there would be no suspicion attached to them. Some of the small publicans procure the whisky and mix it with Scotch whisky; they then sell it as superior liquor. It is almost impossible to detect it as illicit when so mixed. It is a common custom in mountainous localities in the winter season to have "dances," "balls," "parties," &c. in the neighbourhood. These forms of amusement are largely attended by young people within a radius of [illegible] miles. The illicit distiller takes full advantage of these gatherings, and he attends, having a supply of illicit whisky with him. The market is a ready one, as it rarely happens that the supply of illicit whisky is equal to the demand. In localities where illicit distillation is carried on there are always a number of shebeens, the keepers of which buy large quantities of illicit whisky and retail it. The persons engaged in making illicit whisky, with their families and connexions, consume a large quantity of it themselves.

54,794. Where shebeens exist, I suppose a large quantity of the liquor must be consumed on the premises themselves?—Of course; a shebeen is a house where intoxicating liquor is sold by a person who is not licensed.

54,795. Would you define a shebeen as a place where they make illicit liquor as well as sell it?—No, that is called a still house.

54,796. A shebeen is only where they sell it?—Only where they sell it. They may be selling duty-paid whisky in a shebeen.

54,797. As far as you are concerned, it does not matter whether it is an illicit still or an illicit shebeen?—Of course a shebeen may exist in any part of the country, either Scotland or England. According to my definition of a shebeen it is a house or place where in fact intoxicating liquor is sold, whether the duty is paid or not.

54,798. But both the still-house and the shebeen I am inquiring are illicit?—Certainly; but the still-house is a different place from the shebeen.

54,799. Which gives you most trouble in detecting, the still-house or the shebeen?—We have had trouble with both. There are shebeens in many places all over the country, but the still-houses are principally confined [illegible]

54,791. (Dean Dickinson.) It goes on in a hole in the side of a mountain?—Yes.

54,792. Not necessarily in a house?—Not necessarily. It may be in a house, but it is very seldom in a house, because the householder there is responsible; whereas if it is on the side of a mountain, he can escape and leave the materials behind him. It is a greater risk for any man to attempt to distil in a house because, as I say, the householder is responsible besides the people working it.

54,793. (Chairman.) The appliances for an illicit still are not very great or expensive?—No, they are not very expensive.

54,794. Can you say what would be the general expense of an outfit for an illicit still?—[illegible] would cover the plant.

54,795. What are the utensils used? I suppose there would be the worm?—The still, head, and worm, and of course they have to have barrels and so on for containing the stuff.

54,796. And the molasses and sugar?—Molasses and sugar or malt. They have barley and make it into malt.

54,797. Potatoes?—I do not know that they use potatoes. I have never seen them. When I was suppressing this distillation they always used malt.

54,798. That is the best whisky that would be made out of malt?—The best whisky would be made out of malt. There are three articles used in the manufacture. There is the still, the still-head, and the worm.

54,799. (Mr. Young.) You require about [illegible] per cent. of malt to produce any sort of whisky?—Our work was considerably increased in that regard owing to the fact that they repealed the Act which prohibited the manufacture of malt or the keeping of malt, and any person can keep malt if they like, and unless they are in the manufacture of whisky we cannot seize it.

54,800. (Chairman.) I will reserve the question of special grievances and I will ask you now about the licensing authority. Do you think that the present licensing authority is capable of properly administering the law, or does administer the law properly?—I think [illegible] improvement and radical change is necessary to improve the status of public-houses, and with regard to the licensing authority I certainly think there ought to be some alteration made.

54,801. Would you substitute for the present licensing authority, as we have heard previous witnesses state, the recorders of the cities and boroughs?—I would.

54,802. What would you do in the counties?—I would have the chairmen of quarter sessions the sole licensing authority—the county court judge.

54,803. Sitting alone?—Sitting alone.

54,804. The recorders in cities?—The recorders in cities where there are recorders, and the county court judge as chairman of quarter sessions in the counties.

54,805. Would you have an appeal from either of these to two judges?—I would. I think it would be right to grant an appeal.

54,806. So that you would oust the magistrates altogether?—I would. I think the authority should be left entirely in the hands of the recorder or the chairman of quarter sessions.

54,807. With an appeal to the judges of assize?—It would be only in the case of valuable licences that there would likely be an appeal; but an appeal should be allowed, because the interests involved might be of great magnitude in certain cases.

54,808. [illegible]

Left margin notes: Mr. A. Reed, K.C.B. — Profits. — Disposal of illicit whisky. — Shebeens.

Right margin notes: Mr. A. Reed, K.C.B. — 13 Nov. '96 — Cost of illicit still. — Present licensing authority. — Recorders and county judges to do them. — Appeals.

Sir A. Reed, K.C.B.

persons. It would be quite right, I think, that he should have the power—because he might be ruined in his interests—to have an appeal to a higher authority.

[illegible]. So that you would re-open the whole case before the judges of assize both on fact and law?—I would.

[illegible]. Supposing the recorder or the county court judge granted a new licence, would you have any appeal against his decision on the part of the ratepayers or persons properly interested or the police? In the case of a licence being granted that was objected to by respectable persons, would you allow the police or those respectable persons who might consider they were affected to appeal to the judge of assize?—No; I would not. I think it is the interest of the aggrieved party—that is the licence-holder—that I should consider in appeal with reference to licences. The appeal should go to the judge of assize.

[illegible]. I do not wish to put any opinion in your mouth, but would it not be safer to say that there should be an appeal only on points of law to the judges of assize, and leave the recorders and county court judges without appeal on questions of fact?—As regards points of law, they have an appeal at present. I do not think for such points an appeal is necessary at all, because if there was a point of law raised, as is done very often, the aggrieved person might bring the case before the Queen's Bench if he thought that the county court judge was administering law improperly.

[illegible]. You think, therefore, that some other security is necessary than an appeal on a mere point of law, which exists at present, if you make the recorder sole judge and the county court judge sole judge?—I heard the Recorder of Belfast give evidence, and I listened to his evidence very attentively, and he said that an appeal should lie from him to the judges of assize, and I consider that he means that the whole case should go before the judges of assize. Of course the appeal, I think, ought to lie only in cases of licence-holders and not in the case of new licences.

[illegible]. (Mr. Young.) That is transfers?—Transfers and renewals.

[illegible]. (Lord Dickinson.) There should be no appeal in the case of a new licence?—No.

[illegible]. Either from granting or refusing?—I would only grant the appeal simply in the interests of the person who has invested his money in an established trade, and whose whole property, and in fact fortune, depends on his holding that property. If the licensing judge on an application for a transfer or renewal refused that transfer or renewal of his licence, then he should have the power of protecting his property and going before the judges of assize and appealing to them. The stake being so valuable in his case, that I think he should have the right to appeal to another tribunal to protect his own interests.

[illegible]. On the whole case?—On the whole case; but I would not grant that to the police because it does not so much matter. I may say in [illegible] cases out of 100, so far as the police are concerned, the county court judge or the recorder would in fact do what is right.

[illegible]. (Mr. Young.) That is on a new licence?—Yes.

[illegible]. You simply go for an appeal in the case of a transfer?—In the case of a transfer or renewal, simply in the interests of the aggrieved person.

Canvassing and packing of Benches.

[illegible]. (Chairman.) When the county justices meet, as I understand they do at their [illegible] sessions for the purpose of considering licences and granting licences, have you ever observed that there is a [illegible] [illegible]

my own statement. In the rare instances where a licence was granted, and the police recommended the applicant, I have known the Bench to be packed by interested traders to prevent the licence being given, and it was refused.

[illegible]. How was the Bench packed by traders?—They influenced magistrates to go forward to look after their interests. I can mention the facts of just the case. The case was simply this. In a [illegible] village in Ireland there were two hotels, and they were very well managed, and these hotels wanted to have the monopoly to themselves. A third person came forward and built a house in which he wished to establish an hotel which was needed in the place. It was a great thoroughfare. The police did not offer the slightest objection. They considered it would be very advisable to break down the monopoly of the other two hotels, which were kept in fact by parties related to one another. The applicant went forward for his licence, and there were a large number of magistrates there and in their interest, in his interest in regard to the magistrates who went to support him, and he was refused his licence. He then, in fact, had to canvass and get other magistrates to go forward, and he obtained the licence eventually and has a very good house now, and it is very well conducted, and his house certainly is of advantage to the community and to travellers going that road. I know the house.

[illegible]. I suppose you would pay this tribute to the magistrates that they themselves would like to be relieved of this invidious position in which they are placed as being subject to canvassing. They do not like it, I suppose?—Well, I think a great many of them would be quite delighted to be relieved of it. I have evidence here which, if you like, I will read, being extracts from reports of officers, and also the evidence of the general public on the general canvassing question, which I think most valuable. I do not like simply to confine myself to my own opinion, but I would like to bring before the Commission the important points with reference to this canvassing question, which I think is really a most serious evil in Ireland at present as regards the licensing laws.

[illegible]. Do you think that the magistrates are so impatient of this canvassing that they would like to be relieved of their licensing duties altogether?—I would rather give the opinion of others, because it might be said I had no grounds for it.

Hotel licence.

[illegible]. That will be brought out by one of the Commissioners. I should like to ask you with regard to the hotel licence. Do you think that the hotel licence is given to houses which are virtually hotels for the accommodation of the public with regard to food and drink?—The hotel licence is a mere public-house licence. The hotels throughout Ireland, on the whole, are much improved, but there is a great want, especially in wayside public-houses, where the keepers, in many cases, will not provide any food or light refreshments for respectable travellers of the lower class who cannot afford to go to the hotel. Such travellers often bitterly complain that they can get nothing but intoxicating liquor at such houses. This neglect of the wants of the people of small means, and in humble life, is a disgrace to Ireland. In no other civilised country in the world would such a state of things exist. It is all owing to the fact that no obligation whatever lies upon a publican to supply a weary traveller with anything but intoxicating liquor. The wayside houses, sometimes licensed, have no accommodation for any decent person at all for an hour and rest, and the licensed holders will not furnish a simple cup of tea and a little bread and butter to a weary traveller. The law should compel them to do so on pain of forfeiture of licence at renewal for the improvement of [illegible]. The [illegible] have not considered the wants of men of the middle class or [illegible] class of life who have to go to towns to attend fairs and markets, or who wish to travel through the country and see its beauties and scenery, at such an expense as their purse can afford. There is no provision for that class at all in Ireland. There is provision in Scotland. If we had the Scotch law in Ireland I think Ireland would be a much richer country than at present, but owing to the law in Scotland being so framed, giving certain privileges to hotels and [illegible] hotels, the consequence is that in Scotland there is excellent provision for travellers of all classes, and certainly as good as in any part of the world.

[illegible]. (Chairman.) In connection with that important point it may be useful to ask you, what are the existing licenses, and what changes you propose to make in the licenses? What are the present licenses?—There is (1) the public-house license—an on and off-license; (2) the spirit grocer's license—an off-license; (3) the beer retail license—an off-license; (4) the wine license granted to refreshment houses—[illegible] on and off-license; (5) the [illegible] license granted to publicans and wine license holders—an on and off-license. The great majority of spirit grocers hold also the beer retail license. The magistrates' certificate, granted in annual licensing petty sessions, has to be obtained for these licenses.

[illegible] When you say the great majority of spirit grocers hold also the beer retail license, is the beer retail license on or off?—Off, but they have to go through a separate procedure for each license. These two licenses (spirit grocer and beer retail) ought to be amalgamated and upon one certificate granted by the magistrates, which might be called a grocer's certificate, the holder would obtain from the Excise a license to sell spirits or beer or both by retail upon payment of the duty. This certificate should be granted, not only to grocers proper as defined in the [illegible] section of [illegible], but also to wine and spirit merchants who are not grocers. This grocer's license should enable the trader, grocer, or wine and spirit merchant, to sell spirits in any quantity less than 2 gallons and not less than 1 pint at one time for consumption off the premises, and for the sale of beer in any quantity less than [illegible] gallons or than two dozen quart bottles at one time. All the spirit grocers and beer retailers at present licensed should receive this license. As the law stands now, a merchant who is a grocer cannot legally retail spirits, so as to carry on fully a retail trade without having a publican's license.

[illegible]. A publican's license is taken out, as I understand, by the spirit grocers or the beer retailer in order to enable him to sell small quantities. We have been told that they do take out that publican's license when they have no intention whatever of turning their shop or their establishment into a public-house, but what is your view as to the law. Is a man who takes out a publican's license obliged to turn his house into a public-house. We have heard of divergent [illegible]?—It is now, owing to a recent decision. I will explain that to you. If a trader or spirit merchant in Ireland wants to retail spirits, he has to take out a spirit dealer's license, which is, in fact, also in force in England, which allows him to deal in spirits wholesale; but to retail spirits he has to take out a spirit grocer's license. The dealer's license allows him to sell not less than two gallons; the spirit grocer's license allows him to sell two quarts and under, and there is no covering authority there for the quantity between two gallons and half a gallon. The consequence is, in order to remedy that great defect in the law as regards such and that it would be [illegible] to renew his license, inasmuch as he did not carry out the requirements of the license given to him. That was a great blow to a great many merchants in Ireland, because they were carrying on their trade, as they thought, to their own satisfaction. They did not like to have a bar in their house, and at the same time they carried on their business under the authority of that license that would enable them to sell any quantity of spirits.

[illegible]. [illegible] the law now [illegible] in the law. They have to set up a bar on their premises and go through the form of selling on the premises.

[illegible]. Is it the law as established in the Queen's Bench in Ireland, that if a spirit grocer or beer retailer for the purpose of selling small quantities of liquor takes out a publican's license for that object alone he is obliged by law to erect a bar and turn his establishment virtually into a public-house?—Practically that is the effect of it. The Queen's Bench, of course, considered that the trader did not fulfil the requirements of the license when he did not sell for consumption on the premises.

[illegible]. (Mr. Grimsey.) If I went into a grocer's premises I could compel him to supply me for consumption on—I will read you, if you like, the judgment of the decision. It is Leech's case. Leech's case.

[illegible]. If I go into the premises of a grocer who holds a publican's license for the purpose of selling small quantities, I can compel him to serve me for consumption on the premises, can I not?—Certainly, I think you can.

[illegible]. (Chairman.) It is a public-house?—It is a public-house.

[illegible]. (Mr. Grimsey.) He must?—He must. The public never ask for it because they know it is not the custom.

[illegible]. It can be asked for?—Certainly, I think so.

[illegible]. (Mr. Young.) Notwithstanding the decision of the Queen's Bench, are not these publicans' licenses granted to those who hold wholesale licenses?—They have been opposed, I know.

[illegible]. They are granted in Belfast?—The magistrates may grant them, but at the same time they have been opposed. The application has been opposed on the grounds I have mentioned.

[illegible]. (Chairman.) Are we to understand that if a wholesale dealer in Belfast does take out a publican's license he is obliged to sell against his will for consumption on the premises?—I will read you the substance of Leech's case, which was referred to by the Solicitor-General yesterday. It is a very important case because it has revolutionised the whole matter of law in Ireland in certain cases. It was a case decided on the [illegible] February 1876. It is the case of Leech v. The Justices of the County of Armagh, reported in the Irish Law Times Reports, vol. [illegible], page [illegible]: "Where "premises licensed under a publican's license had not "been in fact used for the consumption of wine and "spirits thereon, in accordance with an undertaking "given by the holder at the time the license was "originally granted, and in that respect the license "had been allowed to lie dormant, it was held that the "justices had no jurisdiction to grant a certificate to "enable the license to be renewed, a condition precedent to such certificate for renewal being that the "premises had been peaceably and orderly conducted, "and here there had been no user at all of the tenure "contemplated by the license."

[illegible]. (Chairman.) I suppose you would be in favour of [illegible]

[illegible] [illegible] [illegible] [illegible] [illegible] 23 May '[illegible] who for granting the licence—I am speaking of the public-house licence before we have the premises passed—and that the applicant should be able to show that he has sufficient capital, as many traders are licensed and start without capital, and in a short time become bankrupt. It would be compulsory that the district inspector should be legally empowered to oppose a licence where necessary and tender his case of objection, otherwise he might not be allowed to do more than give evidence as before. The reason I mention this is, that my proposal is to transfer the whole business to the quarter sessions court. You will come before the chairman of quarter sessions or the recorder in certain cities, and the recorder or the chairman might object to the constabulary officer doing what he does now in the petty sessions courts before the magistrates in certain cases, especially in the cases of some of these localities, and conduct the [illegible].

14,905. As far as the police are concerned with reference to opposing or consenting to these applications, has the chief constable or any officer of police the right of prosecuting?—They are the Crown prosecutors in all the petty sessions courts in Ireland, and they have a locus standi in the case of all intoxicating liquors in the petty sessions courts—that is before the magistrates—but when we come to the quarter courts some county court judges and chairmen of quarter sessions will allow them to appear in cases concerning the police—for instance, in publicans' cases—but others will not allow them.

14,906. Who bears the expenses incurred by the police. Are they a charge on the borough fund?—The expenses of the police are paid out of the Imperial funds by a vote from Parliament.

14,907. The constabulary fund?—The vote of Parliament for the constabulary. We are not paid by local rates at all. We are paid by a vote of Parliament out of the Imperial funds.

14,908. You consider it the business of a police officer to prosecute?—He does it, and has from time immemorial at petty sessions courts. The reason I mention this, of course, was explained yesterday by the Solicitor-General. The spirit grocer's licence, and the beer retailer's licence is granted at the annual petty sessions by the magistrates alone without the chairman of quarter sessions being present, and in that court the district inspector of constabulary would have a locus standi in conducting the case for the police, but if he went before the chairman of quarter sessions he would not, as a matter of right, and therefore he might not be able, in fact, to give the opposition to an application which he might feel it his duty to do owing to the fact that he had not the power to speak.

14,909. Now as to qualification. Is there a qualification for beer retailers and wine sellers?—There is a qualification for beer retailers and wine sellers, namely, not less than 15l. yearly where the population is over 10,000, and elsewhere not less than 8l. yearly.

14,910. Have publicans and grocers got a valuation?—Publicans and grocers have no valuation at all.

14,911. Is there no minimum value required before a man can set up a public-house?—No, none whatever. I can mention to you that in a certain important county town in Ireland there are publicans whose houses are valued at 15s., others at 1l., others at 1l. 10s., and 2l. 4s., 5l., and so on, wretched places quite unfit in fact to be licensed premises at all.

14,912. Why have the licensing authorities granted the licences to houses in that condition?—That is a question that I cannot answer. It is because they like, I suppose, to befriend the applicants. They were, as they would say, a good man and gave him a small property which might give him the means of living. It is the interest of the individual that are considered in most of these cases, and not the wants of the public.

14,913. You would establish a minimum qualification for public-houses and for grocers in the same way as it applied to the beer retailers and wine grocers?—Yes. I would recommend that, that there should be a substantial minimum valuation of the premises of publicans and grocers as there is at present of beer retailers and wine sellers, namely, not less than 15l. yearly where the population is over 10,000, and elsewhere not less than 8l. yearly. I have put it at a low figure because I [illegible]. That would sweep away a good many houses that are now licensed?—Yes, I will come to that. In [illegible] the valuation ought to be [illegible]. That is a very large place, and a wealthy place. I put [illegible] yearly in [illegible] for [illegible] and [illegible]. I would also add another condition with reference to the renewal. At present the conditions of renewal are the good character of the applicant during the past year and the good management of the house during the past year. I would add also the continued suitability of premises, which I consider should be a third condition of renewal. Present traders whose houses are under valuation should be compelled to improve their houses, or procure others, so as to have houses of proper valuation within three years from the passing of the Act. I would thus provide for the existing traders, and thereby give them three years' notice that they might either build new houses on the old sites or get other houses, or dispose of their interests. I think that would be fair. The reason I say that continued suitability of premises should be brought up on renewal is that a man might commence when he applies for a licence in a good house. In the course of time he might allow that house to get out of repair, and become a wretched establishment. The police, I think, should bring under the notice of the magistrates at renewal sessions the fact that, though this man is of good character, and though his house has been properly conducted through the past year, yet his premises are in such a disgraceful condition that the public have no comfort in them. He should be obliged to keep his house in proper repair and order, so that the public might in fact enjoy comfort when they enter his house, and that his monopoly, which is a trust given him by the public, should not be abused.

[illegible]. Coming to the question of occasional licences, do you consider the law is perfectly satisfactory now in respect of these licences?—It is not. I would recommend that no occasional licence should not be granted except by the magistrates in petty sessions, and they should have power to grant such a licence to a publican or holder of a wine refreshment licence to keep his premises open during the night for the occasion of a dinner or ball. With reference to the first, at present the law is that one magistrate out of petty sessions may grant an occasional licence, but the law requires he should be a magistrate acting where the place of sale is situated. That condition is constantly evaded. In fact it is frequently not complied with.

[illegible]. If you abolish, as I understand you wish to do, the petty sessional magisterial licensing authority, who would grant these occasional licences if your reform was carried out?—I did not include in my recommendations the occasional licence which can be only enjoyed for six days. Two magistrates in petty sessions should have the power of granting that licence. At present a licensed trader is in a great difficulty. Supposing he is a man having a splendid hotel, he cannot give a dinner or a ball in that hotel, but he must, in fact, close his bar for the sale of liquor at the usual hour. As the law stands, and, in fact, it is only by the Excise permitting it, that a ball can be given in an hotel which does not, in fact, trespass on the hour at which public-houses should be closed. That is a great defect in the law, and a great want for respectable traders, and the magistrates should have the power of giving that occasional licence for dinners on publicans' premises, because an occasional licence as the law stands, allows only sale in another place than the premises of the publican. Then there is the case of emergency when a petty sessions might not be held for a month, and a case might arise where it might be necessary and desirable for the publican to have an occasional licence granted. I would recommend, as a case of emergency, that two magistrates out of petty sessions might grant this licence with the written consent of the district inspector of the district. Then they would consult the district inspector as to whether the licence was necessary, and on his informing them, he having inquired into the case, that it ought to be granted, they would grant the occasional licence.

there is an evasion of the law and the thing is done above-board.

[illegible]. Provided two magistrates sit together in open court?—In open court.

[illegible]. You would not allow them to give these occasional licences in their own houses separately?—No.

[illegible]. Is that ever done?—That can be done now. It is done by one magistrate at present. He can do it at his own house. The old law was that two magistrates were required, and then there was another enactment passed subsequently, which is last session—I mean magistrates in common. That is the law at present.

[illegible]. He may do that legally sitting in his own house?—Yes. The licence is only for six days.

[illegible]. Without any communication whatever with, or knowledge on, the part of the police?—The police know nothing about it till the whole thing is done, and the licence-holder, in fact, sets up his establishment at the fair or market, as the case might be, or at races.

[illegible]. He is immediately challenged by the police, and then has to produce his authority?—Exactly. They know nothing about it, and they ask for his authority. The hours for sale are entered in the form. The authority is given as a separate form by the magistrate, and he enters on that the hours during which the sale should take place. That is given to the Excise, and the Excise under these hours in giving their licence. Then, of course, the hours of sale may be more extensive than they ought to be. The police authorities have not been consulted, and when the police authorities come and see the magistrates' licence they find that the hours for sale are unnecessarily late, and such as they would have objected to if consulted.

[illegible]. You would return to the old law of two magistrates, instead of one, granting these occasional licences?—Yes. In the old law, as is obtained in Ireland, the presence of two magistrates was required.

[illegible]. Why did they reduce the necessary number to one magistrate?—I do not know.

[illegible]. (Mr. Young.) Do not you very often have a difficulty in Ireland in getting two justices to attend petty sessions?—You can propose, if you like, the stipendiary or paid magistrate. He always attends and you can recommend that the paid magistrate do this.

[illegible]. You would say two justices or the stipendiary?—Yes.

[illegible]. (Vicomte de Fréci.) That is done in other cases?—Yes.

[illegible]. The stipendiary may very often act by himself when it requires two ordinary magistrates?—Yes, in some cases.

[illegible]. (Chairman.) That is another reform you advocate?—Yes.

[illegible]. As to the next reform you advocate, I think we have already elicited that in your evidence as to the hours at which houses in which intoxicating liquor is sold should be closed. You have already said, I think, that they should be closed at [illegible] p.m. on Saturdays, that they should keep closed on Sundays except in the five exempted cities, but in the five exempted cities they should keep open between [illegible] o'clock and [illegible] o'clock p.m., and that was to be a statutory obligation?—Yes. That would relieve Parliament for ever of this disputed question in relation to the five cities, by giving power to the corporations in those cities to still further limit the hours, or to require complete Sunday closing there.

[illegible]. The next reform you advocate applies to bona fide travellers, and I understand you to say the reform you advocated in this case was that the limit should be [illegible] miles instead of [illegible] miles?—Yes.

[illegible]. Then as to the removal of certificates?—My opinion with reference to that is that if the [illegible] [illegible]

Sir A. Reed, K.C.B.

[illegible]

Occasional licences.

Resident magistrates as two justices.

Sunday closing.

The bona fide traveller.

Removals.

Case of emergency.

[illegible]. Your last remark went to this: that you would, speaking generally with some modification in respect of the [illegible] of the [illegible], like to see the age of 16 fixed, below which it should be illegal to serve young persons?—To sell for consumption on the premises; and I certainly should not object to the law as regards limiting the age for [illegible] liquor. The difficulty I had in my mind was the case of a poor sick person wanting a glass of brandy when he or she was ill. If a poor woman had no messenger but her child—if she was alone she would not be able to send the child for it; but, on the other hand, it would be very seldom the case that the poor woman would not have a neighbour who would go and get this liquor for her, which one might require in her illness or necessity. That is only a difficulty I had in my mind about the [illegible], otherwise I should consider that the more young people are kept out of the public-houses the better for them. That is my opinion.

[illegible]. You would not like to fix the minimum age below which a child should not [illegible]?—That is a matter I do not like to offer an opinion upon. My [illegible] would naturally be with that view if it could be done without harm to a sick person, who might have no messenger to send, except perhaps a child who might be under the age that might be fixed by the law if the law were framed in that way.

[illegible]. (Mr. [illegible].) Can you say in your experience whether any great abuse arose in Ireland out of this practice?—Not from my experience, but I have heard of it. I would not call it an extensive abuse, but there are people who have studied the question very closely, and I have heard them say there is to an extent an injury done to the youth by frequenting public-houses for the purchase of liquor and taking the liquor home.

[illegible]. (Chairman.) Should you like to see the licensing authority [illegible] with the power of imposing conditions on the licence?—That is absolutely necessary.

[illegible]. Within a statutory limit, or how?—I will state my view. The licensing authority should have power to attach reasonable conditions to a licence granted by them, which if not complied with should warrant the refusal of the annual renewal certificate. For example, it would be very advisable to require any publican whose house is situated in a town where such accommodation might be needed, or at a distance of three miles from a town, to provide light refreshment for travellers on a journey (such as bread, butter, and tea), and to provide at least two beds for travellers. There are many other useful conditions which if now imposed have no legal effect whatever, and cannot be enforced.

[illegible]. Is it an offence for a grocer to serve liquor for consumption on the premises now?—It is.

[illegible]. Not if he has a publican's licence?—But if he has a publican's licence—but what we call a spirit grocer.

[illegible]. A spirit grocer, not having a publican's licence, may not serve liquor for consumption on. Is there a penalty for that?—There is for consumption on the premises.

[illegible]. Would you make it an offence on the part of the person drinking on the premises?—It should be made an offence for a person to drink intoxicating liquor on a grocer's premises. It is not so now.

[illegible]. You would punish both parties?—Yes.

[illegible]. Would you increase the stringency of the law in respect of drinkers?—I would amend the law as regards drinkers by extending to Ireland the useful [illegible] provisions of secs. 13 and 19 and the definition of "[illegible]" and "drinking" in sec. 37 of the 25 and 26 Victoria, cap. 35—the Scotch Act—which, if you will allow me, I will read. Section 13 of the Public-houses Acts Amendment (Scotland) Act, 1862, is—

"Power to constables, &c., to enter [illegible], &c.

"If any [illegible] [illegible] liquors are trafficked in.

"Penalties for obstructing officers of police, &c."

"or magistrate, or from any chief constable, superintendent, lieutenant, or inspector of police, in any county, district, or burgh, and which they are severally hereby authorised to grant, to enter and inspect any such coffee-house, eating-house, temperance hotel, shops, or places, or any such hotels or vessels within such county, district, or burgh respectively, at any time or times within eight days from the date of such writing, as may be specially mentioned in such writing; and any person who shall refuse to admit, or shall not admit such officer of police or constable into any such coffee-house, temperance hotel, shop, or other place, hotel or vessel, or shall after such demanding his admission thereto, shall thereby be guilty of an offence, and may be apprehended on a warrant to that effect, granted by the sheriff, or by any one justice of the peace, or magistrate, and on being convicted thereof shall forfeit and pay a penalty not exceeding 10*l*., and failing immediate payment shall be imprisoned for a period not exceeding 60 days; and it shall be lawful for any officer of police or constable of any county, district, or burgh, without any written authority, at any time to enter and inspect any licensed inn, and hotel or public-house therein [illegible], and also, where he shall have reason to believe that a breach of certificate is being committed" so as to the rest we have the power already, but the power in the part I have read I think should be extended to Ireland. Then, if you will allow me, I will read the 15th section, which I propose should be extended to Ireland: "*Proof of trafficking in any shebeen.—Persons found in shebeens drunk or drinking may be taken into custody.*"

"In order to warrant the conviction of any person for trafficking in any spirits or other exciseable liquors in any place or premises without a certificate in that behalf, it shall be sufficient, in the absence of contrary evidence, to prove that some person other than the owner or occupant of such place or premises shall at the time charged have been found in such place or premises drunk or drinking, or having had drink supplied to him therein, and that such place or premises is or are by repute kept as a shebeen, or at the time charged contained drinking utensils and fixtures usually found in houses licensed for the sale of exciseable liquors; and every person found in any shebeen drunk or drinking shall thereby be guilty of an offence, and may at the time be taken into custody by any officer of police or constable, and detained in any police office or station house, or other convenient place, and not later than in the course of the first lawful day after he shall be so taken into custody, shall be brought before a justice of the peace or magistrate, or if not so taken into custody, or if he shall have been liberated on bail or pledge, may be summoned to appear before a justice of the peace or magistrate, and on being convicted of such offence shall forfeit and pay a penalty not exceeding ten shillings, and in default of immediate payment thereof shall be imprisoned for a period not exceeding ten days." Then the definitions I would introduce are in question 37.

36,908. I do not think it is necessary to read them if you specify the sections. The provisions of that Scotch Act, you think, should be made applicable to Ireland?—Yes.

Trafficking in liquor.

36,909. Then as to hawking liquor; have you much trouble in in dealing with hawkers of liquor?—We have some trouble. It should be made an offence to hawk any kind of intoxicating liquor for sale. The police are quite powerless to prevent that evil at present. I would extend section 16 of the Scotch Act of 1862 to Ireland—the Act I have already referred to.

on Sunday some magistrates would consider that a valid defence.

Sir A. Reed, K.C.B.

30 Nov. '97

36,910. (*Chairman.*) You would make the delivery within the Sunday closing hours illegal?—Yes, as an offence of the law, even though purchased the day before.

Licences to unmarried women.

36,912. Should unmarried women have licences?—No. I consider that new licences should not be granted to unmarried women who are under 30 years of age. But this should not apply to the transfer of a licence to the widow or daughter of a deceased publican. We find at certain fairs magistrates will grant a licence to unmarried women of 20 or 21, who are not proper persons, and cannot possibly manage the house or control it.

Licences to wives of police officers.

36,913. Should any licence be given to the wife of a police officer or constable?—A licence for the sale of intoxicating liquor should not be granted, transferred, or renewed to the wife of any man while serving in a police force in Ireland. It is forbidden by section 15 of the 3rd and 4th Will. IV., cap. 47, and also by 6th and 7th Will. IV., cap. 13, which is the Act constituting the Royal Irish Constabulary, that a policeman should have a licence to keep a public-house. That law is now evaded by the wife taking out a licence, owing to the change of law regarding married women, and enabling the wife to set up a public-house. She would not set up the public-house at the particular place where the policeman was stationed, but she might in another part of the country, and the consequence is, the policeman when he goes home on leave manages the public-house; and again, the local police may be tempted not to be hard on the wife of a policeman who is carrying on a public-house in the locality.

36,915. Are there many cases in which the wives of constables serving in the police force in Ireland have licences?—There are very few, but we watch them very closely, and try to prevent it.

36,916. (*Viscount de Vesci.*) You have very large powers by moving a man from one station to another?—We do that. We move him to a distant county, but he would get leave, and would go home to see his wife occasionally, and when he goes home he manages the public-house, and the local police have sympathy for the wife of a policeman carrying on a public-house, and may possibly show her more favour than they ought. Of course, I do not say they do. I may mention that in one case where I heard that the wife of a policeman was applying for a licence, I directed the local police to oppose the application, and they did oppose it, but the magistrates granted the licence.

36,917. (*Dean Dickinson.*) What part of Ireland was that in?—It would not be right for me to say.

Endorsement of licences.

36,918. (*Chairman.*) Are convictions now endorsed upon licences?—I have shown you already that about 75 per cent. of convictions are endorsed on the licences.

36,919. You would have all convictions endorsed?—My view on that subject is that all convictions should be endorsed on the licence, and should remain thereon for five years, but it should be left to the discretion of the licensing judge to decide, when applications for renewal of licences is made, whether the licence should be forfeited without regard to the number of convictions recorded thereon.

36,920. (*Dean Dickinson.*) Or without regard to the circumstances under which the endorsement was put on?—Of course the licensing authority should have full power, and should not be bound by the rule of [illegible]. The rule of law at present is that upon the third conviction the licence is forfeited. The magistrate has no power to [illegible] the [illegible].

Sir [illegible], K.C.B. — [illegible] Mar. '98

[illegible], simply because juries would not convict them, the penalty being so severe; and the country there was full of shebeens. In licensing cases magistrates are jurors as well as judges, and they decide as jurors, and they will not ruin a man and destroy him for ever, as they would say, simply because they are obliged to record a third conviction. The consequence is they will take good care not to have a second conviction recorded, lest there should be a third, because in the case of the third conviction, with two convictions already recorded, if the third is a recordable one, the licence is forfeited. The minimum penalty should be fixed for all offences. The reason is this, that the magistrates now will sometimes fine a publican for a serious offence 1s. 6d. or 5s., and of course such a small penalty has no effect, and that without record on the licence either.

[illegible] (Dean [illegible].) Would you fix the maximum and minimum?—The maximum is fixed. Let it be a reasonable minimum, but it ought to be fixed. There should be no discretion in the matter. They may convict or not. If they convict, the minimum penalty should be inflicted.

Form of licence.

[illegible] (Chairman.) When the licence is granted to an applicant, what is stated in the licence? Is he warned as to the offences it is possible for him to commit?—There is no warning whatever. What I would propose is that the licence granted to all retailers should be drawn up in similar form to those granted to such traders in Scotland, setting forth the prohibitions or offences the trader is liable for while exercising his licence, and the clerk of the peace should annually issue, for a small fee, a sheet printed in good type setting forth, up to date, all or the principal actionable clauses providing for offences committed by publicans and others in connection with licensed houses. And the trader should be obliged, under a penalty to have this sheet pasted on a blackboard, or framed with glass (should he so prefer), and exhibited in a conspicuous public place in his shop or bar, in order that he and all others might be constantly reminded of the legal provisions regulating such houses. I regard this as a very important amendment, which, if adopted, would tend much to the better observance of the laws applicable to such houses.

List of offences.

[illegible] The licence would be a very lengthy document?—I do not think it would be so lengthy for the principal chargeable offences. The Scotch do not consider it to be lengthy, but enter on the back of the licence the prohibitory provisions so as to enlighten the licence-holder as to his duties. I am quite satisfied many publicans, especially beginners, offend through ignorance; and, further, everyone requires to be reminded occasionally of some of his professional duties, which, if not kept constantly before him, he might forget. It would be, also, a certain protection to an honest trader to have these laws at hand, to refer to when dealing with the public or the police. I look on that as a very important provision, if it was introduced into law. There is a precedent for this proposal contained in section 2 of 25 and 26 Vict., cap. 41, which requires that—"Every innkeeper shall cause at least "one copy of the first section of this Act, printed in "plain type, to be exhibited in a conspicuous part of "the hall or entrance to his inn." The renewal of the copy yearly would be necessary to enable any additions or alterations of the law, enacted by Parliament during the year, to be made in the sheet, so that it would be brought up to date, for the information and guidance of the licensed person, his shop servants, and of persons entering his premises. In the Factory Acts there is a very similar provision

[illegible] (Mr. Gordon.) I think you spoke favourably to some degree of assimilating the law of Ireland to the law of England, and particularly as to hotels. You have no hotel licence in Ireland as distinct from a publican's licence?—No.

[illegible] You would approve of some alteration in the law which would bring in the Scotch provision which provides for a certain number of lodging accommodation in every hotel. Is that what you desire?—Certainly, I think that would be most conducive to the comfort of a large mass of the people when travelling.

Sir [illegible], K.C.B.

Costs of [illegible] by police.

[illegible] Then there is one point I do not quite understand in your evidence. You stated that the whole cost of the police is paid from the Imperial funds. We all know that is the case, but I think the Chairman asked you what happened in the case of the cost of a prosecution instituted by the police, and costs being given against them. Who would pay them? Would they also fall on the Imperial fund?—Well, of course, if the policeman acted correctly, his expenses would be paid by the State.

[illegible] The State bears all these expenses in Ireland?—Certainly, all the expenses of the prosecution on the part of the police are borne by the State. The expenses of prosecutions by the police are really nothing, so far as the police are concerned. They conduct their own cases. They use ordinary summonses in the cases which are free. They are not charged with these stamps.

[illegible] There are court fees?—There are court fees, but they are not paid by the police. It is little or no cost to the country at all.

[illegible] You do not employ counsel?—When the police prosecute they conduct their own case. No solicitor is employed. It costs the country nothing whatever, so far as the conduct of the case is concerned. In an exceptional case, if the police are worsted, expenses might be given against the police, but that would be a very exceptional case, and in that case the expenses of the policeman, if he were worsted and had performed his duty bona fide and properly, would be paid out of the contingency vote, with Treasury sanction.

[illegible] (Mr. [illegible].) What would be the case with reference to an appeal? That is where the costs come heavy. Who would pay the costs in the case of an appeal? You would have to employ counsel?—We should not employ counsel at all. We have no right of appeal in licensing cases.

[illegible] When the appeal is carried against you?—We get no costs.

[illegible] (Mr. Gordon.) If the costs are given against you in court you would have to pay the defendant's costs. He would have employed a solicitor or agent of some description. Who pays those costs? Would they also fall on the Imperial fund?—It would fall on the Imperial fund. I should say then the policeman did not suffer. I should represent it to the Government in that case, and if the policeman had acted bona fide, and had faithfully performed his duty to the best of his ability—he might not have acted legally, perhaps—but if he had acted to the best of his ability, and bona fide, and was not guilty of any improper conduct, I should certainly represent it to the Government, and his expenses would be paid.

[illegible] You are confident of that—it would be paid out of the Imperial fund?—It could not come out of any other fund.

[illegible] In the English evidence we have often had the point brought up, that the police did not prosecute the cases, because they could not run the risk of costs being given against them?—Our men do not suffer in that way.

14,540. They can be renewed, but there must be a fresh application for each day?—I think that would be very inconvenient, and I think the present arrangement suits our country very well.

14,541. (Mr. Young.) May I ask you this general question. Is drunkenness decreasing in Ireland?—I do not think there is much alteration. The people have perhaps more money than they had 10 years ago with which to purchase drink. I do not think it has decreased.

14,542. Considering the increase in population in the large towns, I do not see by the criminal prosecutions, that there are so many as in former years?—I am considering the country in globo.

14,543. Now in regard to Sunday closing in those parts of Ireland which are not exempted, you say that it has had a beneficial effect?—I think it has had.

14,544. But I think you observed that in the towns not exempted the voice of the people should be deferred to. I understood from your evidence in chief that you would defer rather to the voice of the people with regard to closing the houses?—Yes, I would. There are three parties apparently who are concerned in the Sunday closing question. There are the persons who are opposed to Sunday closing, the persons who are in favour of Sunday closing, and the persons in fact who are indifferent. There is a large section of the people who are indifferent—people who do not use the public-houses, and it does not matter to them whether the houses are open or closed. They are the great bulk of the people; there are also three classes of persons who are in favour of opening public-houses on Sunday, and they are the persons who in fact drop out on Sunday at [illegible] and [illegible] out every day, in fact, in hotels in the large towns. Then there is another class who wish to get fresh liquor for their dinner from the public-house; and there is another class, in fact, who may be abroad during the day or out in the country who would like to get some liquor to have a drink after their dinner. Those are the three classes who use the public-houses.

14,545. Am I right in supposing that those who object are the teetotal classes—in fact, the non-consuming class—who do not want liquor sold at all in any way?—I would not say that. I think it includes more than the teetotalers. There are a great many [illegible] clergymen not teetotalers, and other philanthropists who have the good of the people at heart, and who think the people would be much benefited by having the public-houses closed altogether, besides those total abstainers to whom you refer.

14,546. Am I correct in supposing that that other class except teetotalers are willing to have the houses open on Sundays from 2 o'clock to 5 o'clock, or from 3 o'clock to 5 o'clock? Is it your opinion that the general sense of the people is in that direction?—I should not like to express what their opinion is, and it is because I have a doubt about it that I consider their wishes ought to be consulted, and I do not think it is the province of a police officer to express an opinion on a question like that, which really does not concern us so much, except as regards the peace and good order of a place. As I said before, it is really immaterial to us whether the public-houses of the five cities are altogether closed every Sunday or not.

14,547. How would you consult the people? Would it be by a local vote arrangement?—No, the corporations would decide in their own cities.

14,548. Would there be a plebiscite?—They would do what they liked; they would consult the people if they liked. They are the representatives of the people, and they would represent all classes in their [illegible]

14,551. That is in the rural districts?—Derry is a large city, and Sligo and Galway are large towns. In fact, there are no large clubs in Ireland at all, and we never had a prosecution for a bogus club that I can remember in Ireland. If we had the power which I have asked for we should be able to meet that evil if it cropped up as a result. At the same time it is right for me to observe and I am glad you have brought the point under my notice, that I assume there may be some law with reference to clubs in general extended to England, and I suppose you would extend the same law to Ireland. I think it should be extended so that if you think there is any evil about clubs you would extend the law that you would recommend to be applied to England to Ireland. But even in the present state of the law without that, and if you give us the additional power to enable us to enter houses where we suspect that illegal drinking is carried on, we would be able to meet the difficulty. *Sir A. Reed, K.C.B.* [illegible]

14,552. Now I think you mentioned 9 o'clock as a general hour for closing?—On Saturday evening—that is what I proposed. Early closing on Saturday.

14,553. In Ireland there are many places where they sell only not whisky but groceries. Would not it be very inconvenient if grocers in the rural districts and the small towns were to close at 9 o'clock. Their greatest hour is sometimes about half-past 10 or 11 o'clock—in towns of under 5,000 population it is 10 o'clock, and where the population is that figure or over it is 11 o'clock.

14,554. Would not you be creating an inconvenience by closing at 9 o'clock?—I do not think there would be any inconvenience. I think 9 o'clock would be a very reasonable hour within which every family could make their market on Saturday.

14,555. I think you say that the wives of police officers ought not to have public-houses?—Yes, because really it is an evasion of the fundamental statute under which the force was formed. Owing to the privileges that are now granted by law to married women, they can carry on a separate business in their own name. Licenses to wives of police officers.

14,556. Do you think it has produced so far an evil effect?—It is not very extensive, but it is a difficulty we have to contend with occasionally in the police force, and it is not a good example to have a policeman evading the law through his wife, because he joins the constabulary on the understanding that he will not carry on a public-house, and yet he gets his wife to carry it on in another part of the country.

14,557. I was not thinking of the law that regulates the police, but I was thinking of the public weal. Ex-police officers are publicans to a large extent?—Yes.

14,558. What would be the effect if you excluded the wives?—We have little control over a man when he is pensioned from the force, and we never then interfere with him except for criminal offences. It is only while serving in the force, not when pensioned, the proposal would apply. When pensioned the ex-police have a perfect right to do what they like, and they often set up public-houses, and conduct very respectable houses.

14,559. Then, as I understand your evidence as regards the rules of the service, they ought not?—Only when serving.

14,560. As regards the public, their wives would have as good a right to have a license as the wife of an ex-police officer?—No, because the ex-police officers have no duty to perform with reference to public-houses. They are not brought in contact with publicans. They have given up being policemen; they can engage in what business they like. While a policeman is serving, my opinion is that the law he has to do

Sir A. Reed, K.C.B.

10 Mar. '98

bottle of poteen home with him from the mountains of Donegal?—I have no doubt of it.

64,962. That is how it comes about?—It comes to London. I suppose it is being sent to London to the hut of a lady of Ireland, who brought it to her friends in London. I have known cases when I was a police officer in the country. They used to tell a story of the time of George III. of the King's yacht putting in at Burton Port in Donegal, and taking off some kegs of illicit whisky, which were sent by a magistrate as a present to England. That was the tale. The liquor is regarded as a curiosity.

64,963. But more to the point, the manufacture of poteen is now very much on the decrease. There is very little of it now manufactured?—I would not say it is on the decrease, because it has increased a little lately, I may say. We have to watch it very closely to keep the manufacture down, and employ men specially for the purpose.

64,964. I am very glad that the power of the clergy is invoked for the putting of it down, but may I ask you why it is that the police officers are not able to put it down?—Because the reason is that there is so much profit made by it. As I said before, if they succeed in one venture out of three they make a profit. I should like to make a correction with reference to the remark I made about the royal yacht. Of course, it was a tradition in Donegal, where I was a police officer, that, in fact, a specimen of the liquor made in Donegal was sent over to high personages. I should put it in that form.

64,965. (Mr. Grimsey.) The royal yacht and the royal family are not liable to pay duty, so that there would be no object in smuggling spirits aboard?—This occurred in the time of George III., since 70 years ago. It was a tradition, and I was only speaking of what was supposed to have occurred in the past, and I should guard myself by stating that correction. If I made a wrong impression I should like that to be removed. The tradition about the present of a quantity of spirit to high personages as that it occurred 80 years ago; from time immemorial it has been looked on as a curiosity.

Appeals.

64,966. (Mr. Young.) I think you told you would allow no appeal in the case of the refusal of a licence. There is none at present. Anyone applying for a licence and being refused has no appeal?—No. I refer to an application for a new licence.

64,967. Supposing that a licence is granted next door to someone who is in possession of a licence, he is aggrieved, is he not? Would you not allow an appeal to the holder of a licence who is aggrieved by another licence being granted next door to him?—No, I would not allow an appeal. That I am sure would be considered very carefully by the licensing judges, and if he thought it would be a benefit to the community to establish a public-house, even though it might be next door to a licenceholder, I think he ought to have the power of granting it.

64,968. There is an appeal in the case of a transfer being refused at present?—Yes, I would allow an appeal in the case of a transfer.

64,969. You would not allow an appeal in the case of the application for a new licence?—No, because there is no vested interest there. There is no property vested in the case of a new licence, whereas in the other case there may be a very large amount of property at stake, and the person whose property would be lost or jeopardised by the refusal of the renewal or transfer should have the opportunity allowed him to appeal to a higher authority.

Hotels.

64,970. With reference to hotels, I think you mentioned that you would have some alteration in the way of beverages in hotels for the middle and lower classes?—Yes, I would.

Mr J. Reed, K.C.B.

fettered by any law which really is contrary to the sentiments of the magistrates in Ireland, and which they will not carry out.

26,988. As a witness being able to give an unprejudiced opinion upon the point, I should like to ask you whether your experience is that the licence-holders as a body are as respectable men as any other class of traders in the country?—Certainly; that is my long experience.

26,989. And from your knowledge of Cork, Belfast, Limerick, and Waterford generally, the conduct of the people on Sundays is good?—Yes.

26,990. It compares favourably with the conduct of the people in any other towns you know of equally large proportions?—I think so, and I have visited the [illegible] cities. I am occasionally there on Sunday.

26,987. As to your Table IV., does not it show a very remarkable decrease of convictions for drunkenness in Dublin. During the year 1878 it was 17,000, and in 1887 13,000?—It may be, but I cannot answer for Dublin.

26,988. Still we know that in Dublin a great deal has been done in the matter of improving the dwellings of the poor?—No doubt.

26,989. And you would look upon that as an important factor?—I should. No doubt a great deal has been done to make the poor more comfortable in Dublin, and a great deal is being done.

Habitual drunkards.

26,990. Your Table VI. shows a very large number of persons who might reasonably be classed as habitual drunkards, does it not?—Yes.

26,991. Of course the habitual drunkard is a nuisance to the public, and you may fairly say he is no credit to the licensed trade?—Certainly he is not a good member of the community.

26,992. I do not know whether you have thought of it at all, but could any special treatment in your opinion be resorted to with reference to that class of habitual drunkards? Before you answer that I should like to say that it is stated that in Dublin there are 7,000 habitual drunkards, and that in consequence of that large number, it affects of course very seriously the returns of drunkenness in Dublin. Seeing that large number, would you be prepared to make any suggestion for dealing with them?—Well, it is hardly a question for a police officer to answer. There are homes for inebriates proposed, which is one solution of that difficulty. Then there is binding to the peace on the part of the drunkard, and making some person responsible for his good behaviour for a time certain. That is another remedy. Again, the justices, perhaps, might have the power of longer imprisonment without hard labour, till there is a reformation.

Additional wine and spirit licences.

26,993. I want to ask you two or three questions with reference to that suggestion of yours as to the introduction of the additional [illegible] spirit licence in Ireland, more particularly on the point of magisterial control. The licence in England can be held by a dealer in spirits without any magisterial control at all, so long as he deals only in [illegible] liquors. Are you aware of that?—I am not.

26,994. So that if your proposal were adopted to put these licences under magisterial control, you would have every wine and spirit merchant in Ireland under the absolute power of the magistrates?—As they are at present.

26,995. They are not in England?—They are at present in Ireland. The retail grocers that retail spirits must be either spirit grocers or publicans.

26,996. If you introduce this licence, the largest wine and spirit merchant in Ireland, if he takes that, would have to go to the magistrate, and the magistrate would have absolute power of refusal?—Certainly.

26,997. He has not got it in England except on four conditions, that is, good character, that the place is not the resort of prostitutes and thieves, that there is no misconduct against him, and that the house is suitable. Would not that be sufficient for the same purpose in Ireland? I must point out that there is a distinction in selling for consumption on and off. One is a question of trade and the other a question of public order?—The view I take of that is, that the licensing judge knows the circumstances of the county over which he presides as a judge. He knows the circumstances of every

Mr J. Reed, K.C.B.

Additional [illegible]

locality and he knows everything about it, and if he considers that the number of liquor establishments which exist at the time are quite sufficient, I think he should have power to prevent any more liquor shops being set up in that particular town. It would be a great advantage certainly that the whole power should be given to one responsible judge who would administer the law properly and with that discretion which every judge who holds a high position is presumed to possess.

26,998. I quite agree he should have reasonable control, but supposing there is a large wine and spirit merchant in Belfast, and he takes this additional licence and has to go to the magistrate, and the magistrate is [illegible] [illegible] prejudice opposed to all licences, you put him in the position to refuse that man a licence who is simply carrying on a trade?—If a judge would do that I am quite satisfied.

26,999. He could do so, could he not?—Is that with reference to the renewal?

27,000. This is the case of a new licence, the three-years licence. The view generally is that it is desirable the magistrates should have control of all licences, but the control over a shop simply selling the article where it is not consumed need not necessarily be the same as where it is a place where people resort, and public order may suffer?—My opinion upon the question is, as I have already expressed it, that the procedure applicable to all these licences for obtaining them, or for renewing them, or in fact to transfer them, should be one and the same, and subject to the same rules, and I do not think that any respectable trader would suffer in the slightest way if that rule was established if it was a reasonable application that he made.

The bonâ fide traveller.

27,001. (Mr Johnston.) As regards the travellers who want railroad people they may be divided into two classes, may they not, the one who goes out for the purpose of getting drink, which he could not get in his own town or district, and the one who being out at a distance from his home really requires it for his sustenance?—Yes.

27,002. I suppose everybody would agree that the man who goes out for the purpose of getting it, and really for the purpose of evading the law, ought to have no mercy shown him. You do not want to keep the exemption for him?—No. I think as it stands it casts a serious responsibility on the licence-holder and I think that is very unfair, and I would not alter the law in that way. I do not propose any alteration in the law except as to the distance.

27,003. Do not you think that the case of the bonâ fide traveller—I do not use the expression in its common sense, but in the real meaning of the word—if he is a bonâ fide traveller, who has not gone out for the purpose of getting drink, would be met by the supply of non-intoxicants on one day in the week? Is it such an absolute need to be always drinking that we should keep alive this abuse and this evasion of the law, which is countenanced by the exemption of the bonâ fide traveller?—Then you would abolish the bonâ fide traveller, and not allow a publican to sell intoxicating liquor at all on a Sunday—

27,004. Quite so?—I would not approve of that at all. I think there are a great many men—

27,005. Who would die if they did not get it?—No, but I think there would be a great injustice to the general public. There are a number of young men whom I am always delighted to see going out on a Sunday (instead of remaining in Dublin) on their bicycles, and going 20 or 30 miles into the country and enjoying themselves. That is a great improvement on the former condition of Ireland, and to forbid that man to get his dinner 30 miles from Dublin, and sit down to smoke his pipe and take a glass of beer or a glass of whisky and water, I think would be very cruel. I think it would not be just at all. I have strong respect and regard for total abstainers, and recommend total abstinence in every way I can; but at the same time I think it would be curtailing the man's liberty. I should not care for it, and, in fact, it is my own custom, as a rule, never to take any intoxicating liquor on Sunday, but at the same time that is my practice simply, not as regards the day, but just simply it has never been my habit to take such liquor on a Sunday. It may be a fad of mine, and at the same time I should be very sorry to impose that pleasure on

Mr. A. Reed, K.C.B. 20 Mar. '99

Sunday Traffic.

57,006. Now as to the six-day licences. They are not allowed to supply a *bonâ fide* traveller or anybody else on a Sunday?—They are not. They cannot sell liquor to anyone on Sunday.

57,007. Do you think there is anything in an opinion I have heard expressed in England on high authority that they could be compelled, in spite of their having no licence for the Sunday, to supply the same, and lawfully, and therefore the provisions of six-day licences [illegible] in conflict with the common law obligation to supply travellers?—No, it could not be, for the statute would override the common law.

57,008. You regard the objection as a bugbear?—I think so. The statute law overrides the common law if it is clear and express. That is the previous common law. There may be [illegible] law [illegible] to the statute law by the judges, but the previous common law would be evidently overridden by the statute law.

Hawking spirits.

57,009. (*Mr. Whitaker.*) Is there any hawking of spirits in the rural districts of Ireland?—There is.

57,010. By women?—Yes, occasionally.

57,011. Am I correct in assuming that they buy a gallon or so and hawk it?—I would not say they buy so much as a gallon. They could not carry it with them. They may buy a small quantity and carry it about in baskets.

57,012. That is illegal, of course?—It is illegal.

57,013. Could you suggest any means of grappling with it?—I have suggested it. We have power at present to arrest a person for hawking spirits, but owing to an omission that exists in the law there is no provision made for procedure after arrest. In repealing old Acts and introducing a clause in a new Act to render it an offence to hawk spirits, and gives no authority whatever to the police to prosecute. It gives authority for arrest, but does not provide for procedure after arrest. You have no penalty, and no power to bring before the magistrates, and the consequence is that the provision lies on the statute book a dead letter, but I have suggested a remedy.

Public-houses connected with shops.

57,014. We had an indication yesterday that a great many public-houses are connected with shops throughout Ireland?—Yes.

57,015. Would not it be an advantage to disconnect the public-house entirely from the shop?—I think it would be an advantage, but at the same time I do not think it would be possible to do it. It would revolutionise the whole state of things in Ireland and I could not recommend it because it is a custom amongst the people. If you have the judge the licensing authority and give him the power to impose certain conditions, he could with [illegible] to new licences carry out that principle.

57,016. Is it the fact that when a person goes to a grocer's or a shoe maker's shop it is a very probable that liquor may be sold on another counter in that shop?—It is constantly the case.

57,017. Does not that strike you as being a very great temptation to drink?—It may be so once, and it is, I believe, so since. It is the practice of the country.

Hawking.

57,018. (*Mr. Young.*) Is there any such thing as hawking in the north of Ireland to your knowledge, or in which part of Ireland is there hawking of whisky?—It is done in a small way in every part of Ireland. The police occasionally catch a person hawking spirits—a man or a woman.

57,019. (*Dean Dickinson.*) What do they do?—They cannot do anything at present, except get the name, if they can, and report it to the Excise, and they may prosecute. The Excise may bring them under some licence statute.

57,020. (*Mr. Young.*) Have you any record of hawking whisky in your statistics?—I have not.

57,021. I know the north of Ireland well, and I never met with it in my life?—I have been in the north of Ireland too, and spent many happy years there.

Opinions.

57,022. (*Mr. Whitaker.*) In the question of surrendering the magistrates one of the difficulties in Ireland?—It is a great evil. I have here opinions I should be glad to submit, if it is permitted to me. What I propose to do is to give you opinions, not from my own experience, but the experience of others, and I could give extracts from reports I have here, omitting the names of the [illegible] who write, not also the places, so that they cannot be brought home to anyone. I will read for you these extracts, which will show you the curiosity of the [illegible] that exists at present with reference to the canvassing of magistrates to support an applicant for a public-house licence, or, to [illegible] to support a publican in case he is prosecuted.

Mr. A. Reed, K.C.B.

57,023. I think your strong expression of opinion would perhaps cover the ground?—It may be put more strongly. I really cannot speak too strongly on the subject, and I should like to be permitted to bring out the points.

57,024. Are the magistrates residing outside the [illegible] districts concerned, and thereby induced to come and take part in the proceedings?—Yes; there is canvassing all over the country, and in fact, it is carried on by a system of strategy, consisting on the Napoleonic principle of bringing a large number of forces to converge on one point to carry their view and their wishes with reference to having a licence granted.

Valuation of licensed premises.

57,025. You would probably remember the Act of 1877, which raised the rating value of houses?—Yes.

57,026. Shall I be right in saying that that Act abolished a very considerable number of licences throughout Ireland, and in Dublin especially?—I have no doubt it did. It must have done, certainly. The [illegible] rating must of course cut out a large number of houses.

57,027. There was no provision in that Act, which [illegible] a large number of licences, for compensation?—No.

57,028. Then you suggest a raising of the rating value of other licensed premises?—Of public-houses and spirit grocers.

57,029. That would have the effect of wiping out a great many licensed houses?—I give three years to the present licence holders to get better premises. I would regard a vested interest so far as that is concerned.

Excessive number of licensed houses.

57,030. You think there are too many licensed houses in Ireland?—There is no doubt of it whatever.

57,031. I suppose that has been aggravated by the fact that you have a diminished population?—Not only that, but we have got as much houses for a very much larger population. My view of it is that if the licensing authorities, as far as applications for new licences are concerned, suspended the granting of licences for 5 or 10 years I do not think Ireland would suffer any injury. I give the particulars of the small reductions that had been made by the licensing authorities in Dublin and Belfast within the last 10 years which my police report. I should like to explain that. The public-houses in the Dublin Metropolitan District in 1889 were 943, and the number now in 1898 is 867. The licensing authorities did their very best to reduce the number, but this shows the very small number by which they have been reduced. In the city of Belfast the number in 1889 was 571, and the number is now 540, and I know the licensing authority, whom you had before you yesterday, did its very best to reduce the number of public-house licences, but the reduction has not been very large, for the long period of 10 years.

Licensed houses and drunkenness.

57,032. Would you turn to Table V of the statistics you have handed in to us. At the end of that table, in the two last columns, you give the ratio of licensed premises to population, and the ratio of [illegible] to population in the five cities of Dublin, Belfast, Cork, Limerick, and Waterford?—Yes.

57,033. What I wish to draw attention to is the fact that the last column gives those towns in the order of the proportion of licensed premises to population, and that curiously enough the prosecutions for drunkenness in those towns are precisely in proportion to the number of public-houses in those towns. That is, that where you have the largest number of public-houses in proportion to population, that is, at Waterford you have the largest number of convictions for drunkenness, and every town ranks precisely in the same order?—I believe that is the case.

57,034. That is to say, in Waterford you have [illegible] times as many public-houses in proportion to population as in Dublin?—Yes.

57,035. And you have three times as many convictions for drunkenness in proportion to population?—I believe so.

Sir A. Reed, K.C.B.

37,036. That shows a very close connection between the number of public-houses and convictions for drunkenness in those towns, does it not?—Well, that would be the inference.

Effect of Sunday Closing Act.

37,037. Then I come to one other point. Reference has been made to the decrease in the number of convictions for drunkenness in Dublin. That is in your Table IV. The largest number was in 1878, [illegible]. That was the year, was it not, in which the Sunday Closing Act was passed?—Yes.

37,038. It came into force at the end of that year?—Yes.

37,039. And the convictions after the passing of that Act fell very rapidly?—Yes.

37,040. I suppose I may take it you would find that the passing of that Act, though not the sole cause for the decrease in the number of these convictions, was a considerable factor?—Certainly.

[illegible]

37,041. (Mr. Young.) May I ask, in your opinion, does the number of convictions depend upon the population, is it not the character of the population. In working districts like Belfast and places of that kind, would you expect more convictions than in rural districts, or in cities like Cork?—I would, because there is more temptation in those places.

37,042. And therefore the figures which have been brought before you now have no bearing on the real question?—They have a certain bearing, but there may be other elements.

37,043. A limited bearing?—I think a most important bearing, but at the same time there may be qualifications with reference to the argument.

37,044. (Mr. Whitaker.) I should like to put that to you, that the figures I have been putting before you are purely those for cities?—Yes.

37,045. And therefore I am only comparing cities?—Yes, in the rural population as I have already stated it is not the practice of the people to frequent public-houses daily. In country districts a man might not go to a public-house more than once a month when attending a fair or market.

[illegible]

37,046. (Mr. Walker.) You have expressed the view that it would be in your judgment cruel to deprive a traveller whether on pleasure or business of reasonable refreshment?—Perhaps I might use a better word than "cruel," but at the same time it is a word that came to my mind at the time. I think certainly it would not be just.

37,047. If a law were passed prohibiting his obtaining necessary refreshment would not that be calculated to bring the law into contempt?—Certainly a large number of the public who, in fact, enjoy themselves under the existing law, and legitimately and properly enjoy themselves on a Sunday, would have their liberty curtailed, and would, I am sure, feel that the law was very unjust as regards them.

37,048. Are you of opinion that they would take the first occasion to evade it?—I do not think so. I think myself there would be a strong public opinion against it in Ireland, and I think very justly so, in my humble opinion, if that law were passed. As regards bona fide travellers going a long way in the country to amuse themselves on Sunday and enjoy the country and fresh air, and take pleasant exercise, if they were denied the power of getting reasonable refreshment which they "but I will give you whisky if you want it, or porter "or beer, but I cannot give you food. I am not expected "to supply you with food." In fact there are some of those men would reply in those words, "Just take what "others take going this road, you can have a glass of "whisky for your breakfast or for your dinner, and "nothing else."

Sir A. Reed, K.C.B.

19 Mar '98.

37,049. Is that your experience of the country all over Ireland?—I say emphatically that is the case. They are not obliged in small public-houses to supply food. There is no legal obligation and that is a great defect in the law.

37,050. You previously stated that it is difficult even in the licensed house to get a cup of tea, or bread and butter if required?—In rural districts it is sometimes difficult.

37,051. But is there any demand for it?—There is a demand for it, and now more than ever when you have cyclists travelling all over the country, and penetrating into remote parts of the country, and undoubtedly if small means might to be encouraged to come to Ireland as they are to visit other countries. In fact, excursionists with small means go to other countries because they cannot find any hotels in Ireland in which they can live at a cost they can afford for a day or for a night.

37,052. Do you mean to state that from your own experience and knowledge of Ireland, there is a general custom in all licensed houses outside the cities that they will not supply food or refreshment, but only supply whisky?—No, I never said that, but I said in a great many of those houses they would not. It is not a general custom. In some places they will.

37,053. Is it not contrary to business character or the business mind, that a man who supplies any refreshment should not supply what is demanded?—There is no doubt of it. It would be wiser to do it, but these houses are so wretched—I am speaking of the wild districts of the country, and even some of the towns—that no decent person could sit down for a time or enjoy himself for half an hour, and they have no food. The small publicans have not the money to provide it. Their trade is so small owing to competition, and their condition so wretched, that they have not the means of providing for the requirements of the traveller.

Special conditions imposed on licensees.

37,054. If there was a necessity for this accommodation and they failed to supply it, would not a reminder from the magistracy supply the defect?—Not as the law stands. What influence have the magistrates over them? They have no control over them at all. If they are well conducted and the police cannot show they have misconducted themselves, and they have not broken the law during the year, but have managed their houses such as they are, peaceably and orderly, the renewal of the licence cannot be opposed.

37,055. Is that why you have expressed your opinion that the discretionary power of the magistrates should be increased?—Yes.

37,056. Is that one of the causes that led you to make that statement?—It is; the licensing authority should have the power of attaching conditions to licences to improve those houses, and make these licence-holders perform their duty towards the public. They have a great monopoly, and it is for the benefit of the public and not for the benefit of the publican that the licence is established, and they should discharge their duty to the public, and not only towards the public who drink intoxicating liquor, but to those who merely require food without intoxicating liquor.

Mr. A. Reed, [illegible] 23 Mar. '99

57,064. Have you any special object in that?—Simply that I think there is a large portion of the community who make use of the public-houses in these large cities in the afternoon of Sunday, and that they should be allowed to do so legitimately for dining purposes or for refreshments. I would close the public-houses at 5 o'clock for another strong reason I have not [illegible] already, and that is, 7 o'clock is a very [illegible] hour in those cities for the closing of public-houses. At that hour most people of all denominations go to their place of worship, and it is not agreeable when a man or woman is going to his or her place of worship to meet people coming out of public-houses, sometimes perhaps not as steady as they ought to be, and in fact it would have a better order in those cities if the houses were closed at 5 o'clock, which would be two hours before Divine service commenced, so as to have the streets cleared of any persons who might [illegible] frequent those public-houses.

57,065. Would you approve of their being opened after Divine service?—No, certainly not.

57,066. That is the only reason you advance for the closing of public-houses [illegible] on Sunday?—I have mentioned the principal reasons.

57,067. You speak of closing the public-houses on Saturday night at 9 o'clock?—Yes.

Billiards.

57,068. Previously you had referred to the billiard rooms, and stated that they can keep open billiard rooms, although on the same premises, all night long?—Yes.

57,069. Your opinion is that they should close at the same time as the public-houses close?—My opinion is that the law of England should extend to Ireland in that regard.

57,070. All billiard rooms and all places of amusement or recreation should be closed on Saturday night at 9 o'clock?—Not all places of amusement. I was only referring to billiard rooms. I said that the law of England, which I suppose the people of England consider a very wise and good law, inasmuch as it has been in force from the eighth and ninth year of the Queen's reign, and has never been repealed, should be extended to Ireland. I fancy it must work well, and if applied to Ireland, I think it would be a benefit to our people.

57,071. You are of opinion that the citizens of these cities would approve of that curtailment of the hours?—I do not say that. I really do not know what their view on the question is. I certainly can speak for you, if you will allow me, the opinions of leaders of thought and opinion in Ireland upon these questions, and I have here some papers from which, if you like to hear their opinions, I can read them.

57,072. In favour of the curtailment of the hours on Sunday?—In favour of closing altogether—more stringent than I propose. That is to show that I am a man of quite moderate views.

57,073. You did not express an opinion as to closing every night?—I was speaking of closing Sunday and Saturday only—those two points.

57,074. Is that your opinion and not anyone else's opinion?—With reference to the closing on Saturday night, I am not singular in my opinion as regards closing at 9 o'clock. Some of the leading people in Ireland hold the same opinion. There are persons who know as much about the question as I do.

57,075. With reference to county magistrates attending at licensing sessions, are they summoned?—No, not at quarter sessions.

57,076. How often do they meet?—They are not summoned. They know the day upon which the quarter sessions are held, and they attend voluntarily.

Canvassing.

57,077. Have you any on certain occasions where you believe they are [illegible] they appear in large numbers. Is it unusual for them to appear in large numbers?—They appear in large numbers, especially at the licensing sessions.

57,078. You have given an opinion that the magistrates have been canvassed for licences. Have you any proof of that?—I have very good proof, if I may be allowed to produce it.

57,079. You distinctly say that the magistrates are not summoned by the clerk?—I do not think it is the practice for a summons to be issued notifications from the clerk of the peace that the quarter sessions will be held on such a day, or for the licensing magistrates in the September Sessions for the granting of [illegible] licences to receive notice. They know the day on which quarter sessions are held, and attend voluntarily.

Mr. A. Reed, [illegible]

57,080. (Mr. Johnston.) Whether canvassed or not they come in greater numbers to the sessions for licensing than the sessions where there is no licensing?—They do.

57,081. (Mr. Young.) They get a circular showing the business of the court with all the transfers, and all that is to take place?—There is a publication in Thom's Directory, and in the clerk of the peace office of the dates on which quarter sessions are held.

57,082. (Viscount de Vesci.) An annual publication and advertisement?—Yes.

57,083. (Mr. Walker.) Does a magistrate receive any official communication as to the day for his attendance as a magistrate on the licensing Bench?—I am not aware that he does. Every magistrate in the county knows the date on which the quarter sessions will be held, and if he wishes to attend he can attend, and does attend.

57,084. May not that account for his irregularity of attendance. It may escape his mind for the moment?—I think that is hardly possible.

57,085. (Mr. Johnston.) It never escapes his mind if the licensing sessions, does it?—No. If he is interested, certainly not.

Proposed licensing authority.

57,086. (Mr. Walker.) Can you say, with reference to the transference of the licensing powers from the magistrates to the county court judge, that there has been any expression of opinion or approval on the part of the trade of that change?—I do not know. I certainly never saw their opinion. I only speak as a police officer, and it is the opinion of all police officers whose opinion is of weight—I have consulted a great many of them—that the change should be made, and I also say that I had an open mind on the question till I was asked to come here and give evidence, and I thought myself at first, when it was mentioned to me that the change was necessary, that it would be a great change; but when I read the reports placed before me—energy reports, with those mentioned which I can vouch of if he may wish I should do so—and carefully considered the question, I was thoroughly satisfied and convinced strongly in the view that it is absolutely necessary to make the change if you want to have the licensing laws of Ireland carried out with any effect for the benefit of the people.

57,087. Then, you have no high opinion of the administrative abilities of the magistrates?—Well, with regard to that, I have a great respect for the local magistrates in Ireland. I have been 38 years a police officer dealing with them, and, as a rule, I always find them [illegible] gentlemen, anxious to do what is right, as far as my experience goes, but there are circumstances attending the licensing question which in fact may have led them astray in their view with reference to their duty, and there are influences brought to bear which might have an effect on perhaps the highest minded man if he were placed in the same position, and which might cause him to act and do contrary to what he would do if perhaps he were in an independent position.

57,088. If you have no confidence in the magistrates as licensing justices, why do you ask that these discretionary power should be extended in dealing with these houses?—I propose that the whole authority should be placed in the hands of one judge, that is the county court judge or the chairman of quarter sessions, and in certain towns where there is a recorder, in the recorder, and that is the law at present with regard to Belfast and Dublin, and Galway, Cork, and Derry. It works well there to the satisfaction of every one except those disappointed applicants for licences.

57,089. You testified to the fact that crowds of people on a Sunday leave these large cities and go to suburban districts?—Yes.

57,090. For recreation?—Yes.

57,091. And they require refreshment?—Yes.

57,092. And a very large trade is done by certain licensed houses?—I have no doubt. That is a legitimate trade with the bona fide traveller.

57,093. Does not that present itself as opposed to Sunday closing?—I do not think so. There are exceptional cases and all travellers all through Ireland in the districts where Sunday closing prevails have the privilege of getting refreshments as bonâ fide travellers in licensed houses.

57,094. In your judgment does Sunday closing encourage total abstinence?—People may have as much wine and liquor in their own private houses as they like and drink as much there as they please. I do not want to make total abstainers of the people at all.

57,095. You are not prepared yourself to say just any limit to the age of a child as a messenger sent by its parents to a licensed house?—I am not prepared. I would rather leave that question to you.

57,096. Is not it a question that affects the people more than any one else?—It does. It affects them; but being an official I do not wish to express any opinion on it. As to my own private view, I have expressed it already.

57,097. (Dean Dickinson.) You would not contemplate with approval the placing of the licensing authority in the hands of corporations generally?—No.

57,098. Why, may I ask, do you dream that in one particular, namely, the hours of Sunday closing, the corporations should have control?—Because the wishes of the people on a legitimate subject as regards the opening or closing of public-houses within those limited hours ought to be consulted, and the corporation is composed of the representatives of the ratepayers, and I presume that the ratepayers would make their wishes known to the corporation, and the corporation would consider what their wishes were with regard to those closing hours and would act accordingly.

57,099. Do not you think that the corporations in Ireland have quite sufficient subjects of [illegible], not to say discord, amongst them without introducing another?—I do not know that.

57,100. Do not you know as a fact that there are a large number of persons interested in the liquor trade who are members of the corporations, and frequently the mayor even is a prominent publican?—I believe that is the case.

57,101. Do you think that that state of things would be favourable to the imposition of opportunities for refreshment?—I think that some rule should obtain with reference to those gentlemen who are connected with the liquor trade in any corporation, which, in fact, is provided by the Licensing Acts, to a certain extent, that they ought not to have votes on the question with reference to the fixing of the hours.

57,102. Do not you think an undivided authority such as you advocate in general, subject to an appeal, would be a more satisfactory settlement of all these questions than leaving them to—and to and fro and [illegible] the subject of abuse?—No. I do not consider that point of such moment as regards peace and order, to interfere with the wishes of the people in that regard; I would not therefore place that authority in the hands of one man; if I were the judge, and had that power, I certainly would much prefer that it should be left to the hands of the people, or the persons who represent the people, and who, perhaps, know more about their wishes and views regarding a question which scarcely affects very [illegible] the interests of peace and order in any of these cities.

57,103. Would not you give an opportunity for undivided [illegible] of the members of the corporation which could not be so well tried upon a recorder or county court judge. I am afraid it would be as one of Dickens' characters put it, "a fruitful source of bad water"?—It might be so; but, at the same time, I think it is a practical proposal. Edmund Burke says that all government is carried on by compromise, and that is a compromise that I have proposed. I recommended two years ago the same hours both for Sunday and Saturday. The recommendation has not been put on the statute book up to the present time and you may not be able to carry the other part. You might be able to carry the proposal I make, and I think it would be a fair compromise for Parliament to dismiss the subject for ever and say, "We will hand it over now to the representatives of the people in those localities and let them settle the matter."

57,104. (Fenwick de Fonsl.) I think you have with you several reports from police officers as to the packing of the bench at licensing sessions?—Yes. | Sir A. Reed, K.C.B. | 22 Mar. 98

57,105. You will be able to hand them in to the Commission?—I could not put them in, but I will read you the extracts from them if you will allow me. | Canvassing and packing of Justices.

57,106. Could not they be put in such a form that they could be printed for the private use of the Commission?—I could not do that, because really they are the original reports I have, but I would read you the extracts from them.

57,107. You stated that you did not want to mention the names, but you might mention the names of the places. Could not you make a copy of them without mentioning the names, and put it before the Commission in the same way as it would go upon the record if you read them?—Yes.

57,108. (Chairman.) I understand these reports come from police officers?—Yes.

57,109. And we have your word for saying that they do come from the police officers?—They all come from police officers. (Vide Appendix II.) | Vide Appendix II.

57,110. (Fenwick de Fonsl.) With reference to the question of packing the licensing sessions, from your experience and from the reports given to you, do justices come to the licensing sessions who do not reside within the quarter sessions districts? You are aware that a county may have three or four districts? —Yes, they come from every part of the county.

57,111. Outside those districts?—Outside those districts.

57,112. Knowing probably nothing of the merits of the case in any way?—Yes.

57,113. Is it solely on the ground of the packing of the bench at licensing sessions that you advocate that the licensing power should be transferred to the county court judges in rural districts?—It is.

57,114. You do not consider they treat these questions in a judicial spirit?—Some of them, not all. With regard to that, if you will allow me, I will read the opinions I have here of three county court judges upon that canvassing question which have been published in the press.

57,115. I think those might be handed in to the Secretary without reading them now?—I cannot put them in, because they are newspaper reports.

57,116. Still, we will take it from you you have three strong opinions from three separate county court judges on that point?—Yes, and they are published in the press. | County court judges on canvassing.

57,117. Will you state the purport of them without reading them through? Is it to the effect of what you have stated in your evidence to-day?—It is simply showing the extent of canvassing and the evils that arise therefrom in contemplation of the parties.

57,118. (Chairman.) Who are the gentlemen you refer to?—What is their office?—They are county court judges.

57,119. Of what counties?—I have a judgment of Judge Adams, I have a judgment of Judge Kelligan, and I have a judgment of Judge Overend as reported in the press. If you like I will read the judgment of Judge Adams.

57,120. Is it a [illegible] of the whole?—It is perhaps the best. The subject of canvassing was brought before the judge, and his lordship said:—"He had no hesitation in "stating that he believed the magistracy of the county "were under a great obligation to Mr. Barry for having "brought forward this great scandal of canvassing the "magistrates with reference to the discharge of their "licensing duties at quarter sessions. The magistrates "at quarter sessions were there on a bench of judges, "and their privileges in connection with the discharge "of the licensing laws were just the same as the highest "judge in the land. They were bound by the law to "act upon the evidence and upon the evidence alone. "They were bound to approach a licensing case uninfluenced by any promise, or any other consideration. "If a healthy spirit existed in this country upon this "licensing question no one would have the impudence "to approach any magistrate to canvass him with "reference to the performance of his duty. He was | Judge Adams on canvassing.

Sir A. Reed, K.C.B.

[illegible] Mar. '[illegible]

bound by his oath to his Queen and country to perform that duty without fear, favour, or affection, and that, as he would in any other case, upon the evidence and the evidence alone. No man would presume to approach his honour about a criminal case that was to be tried before that court, but he regretted to say that even he himself had been approached by gentlemen who ought to have known better in connection with a licensing case. No one ever came twice to him. In his honour's opinion this system of canvassing magistrates, which existed throughout the length and breadth of Ireland, was a great scandal, and ought to be made penal by law. To approach any magistrate and seek to induce him, by any influence, to vote in any way, was, in his opinion, to offer to that magistrate a gross insult, and to offer to the law a great outrage. He knew very well what was going on at these sessions and at every other sessions. To show the impudence of an applicant, the clerk of the Crown and peace had got a postcard from a person looking for a licence, saying: "Dear Sir,—Kindly send me a "list of the magistrates of the county until I "proceed to canvass them with reference to this "application." It struck his honour as a great piece of impertinence. In view of this state of affairs it was a matter for earnest consideration whether it would not be well to withdraw the deciding of such applications to the discretion of quarter sessions alone, as he would be disinterested as between the parties, and the case would be decided on the evidence and according to law. The [illegible] of public-houses in the county were a disgrace in their surroundings, as well as a public danger to the peace of the community." That is reported in the "Cork Constitution" of the 7th October [illegible].

57,121. (Mr. Young.) May I ask you if that is confined to one side. May I presume that both sides canvass the magistrates, those against and those for licenses? —I really do not know. I only know, so far as I have observed, that the canvassing is generally on the part of those who apply for licenses.

57,122. Is there no canvassing against them?—Occasionally there may be.

57,123. (Chairman.) There is nothing in these speeches that would show it comes from one party and not from both?—It may have come from both. The canvassing is there. I do not express any opinion as to what source it comes from.

57,124. (Viscount de Vesci.) The speeches refer solely to the question of canvassing on one side or the other?—Yes.

57,125. On the question of the police objections and the question of the site of a house, do they ever object on the score of the house being so situated that it is not sufficiently under the supervision of the police?—Frequently. Police objections.

57,126. Would they object to a licence being given to a house on a country road some miles away from a village or from a police barrack?—They would.

57,127. Has their objection ever been upheld. In your experience has it influenced the magistrates?—I do not know a case. It may be so.

57,128. What is the limit of the authority of the Metropolitan Dublin Police, does it extend over the townships outside?—The metropolitan police district includes Kingstown and the suburban townships. [illegible]

57,129. It extends to the township all round?—Yes, except Clontarf.

57,130. So that a bona fide traveller might travel across the metropolitan district to claim to be a bona fide traveller at a public-house in the constabulary district outside?—He might.

57,131. Three miles would carry him across?—Yes.

The witness withdrew.

Adjourned to Tuesday next, March 25th, at 11 o'clock.

NINETY-SIXTH DAY.

Queen's Robing Room, House of Lords, Tuesday, March 29th, 1898.

PRESENT:

THE RIGHT HONOURABLE THE VISCOUNT PEEL IN THE CHAIR.

The Right Hon. The Lord Windsor.	Samuel Hyslop, Esq.
The Right Hon. The Viscount [illegible].	Arthur Jorrocks, Esq.
The Right Hon. Sir Algernon West, K.C.B.	John Herbert Roberts, Esq.
Sir William Henry Houldsworth, Bart., M.P.	Charles Walker, Esq.
The Very Reverend H. H. [illegible], Dean.	John Lloyd Wharton, Esq., M.P.
William Strachey Caine, Esq.	Thomas Palmer Whittaker, Esq., M.P.
William Graham, Esq.	Samuel Young, Esq., M.P.
Henry Graham, Esq.	George Younger, Esq.

Mr. Henry Morell called in and examined.

D. I. Royal. 57,132. (*Chairman.*) I believe you are Chief District Inspector of the Royal Irish Constabulary stationed where?—At present at Belfast.

[illegible] 57,133. The borough of Belfast has been extended of late years, has it not?—It has. It now comprises a large suburban area.

57,134. What would be the total population including the extension?—Including the extension, [illegible].

57,135. Having risen therefore greatly since 1891?—In 1891 it was [illegible].

57,136. And immediately before the extension?—[illegible].

57,137. Since the extension [illegible] have been added?—Yes.

Decrease of drunkenness. 57,138. Should you say that in Belfast drunkenness is increasing, or stationary, or decreasing?—It is slightly decreasing.

57,139. Judging by the number of prosecutions in 1891?—In 1891 the number of prosecutions, which include both arrests and summonses, was 7,[illegible]. In 1897 the total was [illegible].

57,140. Notwithstanding the increase of the population over which these statistics extend?—Yes.

Causes of decrease. 57,141. To what do you attribute the decrease in proceedings?—One cause is that the police, I think, do not make so many arrests for drunkenness as they did some years ago. If a man under the influence of drink is able to get home with safety to himself, or without annoyance to the public, he is allowed to do so.

57,142. Before that, they were arrested for being simply drunk?—I think in a great many cases they were.

57,143. Is there any other cause to which you attribute the decrease of drunkenness?—The decrease in drunkenness itself, I think, might be caused by three principal reasons. First, the growing use that there is, I believe, of beer and porter in Belfast as compared with whisky; secondly, the efforts of the clergy and temperance societies; and thirdly, the non-granting of new publicans' licences by the Recorder.

[illegible] 57,144. I suppose you would still hold that the working classes spend a good portion of their wages in drink?—They do; I should think a great deal too much.

57,145. Their wages in Belfast, I suppose, are very high?—The wages in the shipbuilding yards are very high indeed, as compared with the wages in mills. I have heard, but I do not know it for a fact, that they do not work full time in some of these yards, simply because they can earn enough money in four or five days to support them for the whole week.

Intemperance. 57,146. As to intemperance among women—what is the condition of that in Belfast?—Intemperance amongst women is increasing. The statistics which I shall hand in show that in the year 1894 there were 1,[illegible] females prosecuted, in 1897 there were 1,[illegible]. In the three years previous to 1894 there were a larger number than that, varying from 1,[illegible] to [illegible], but in the last four years there has been an increase from the year 1894 of something like 10 per cent. Mr. H. Morell. 29 Mar. '98.

57,147. I ask you the same question with reference to women as I did as to the men. To what do you attribute this increase, during the last four years, at all events, of intemperance among women?—First, I think, to the spirit groceries which exist to a very large number in Belfast. The women get credit in those spirit groceries which they will not get in public-houses, and they get drink there when they are getting groceries; secondly, I believe that the larger wages that they are getting in recent years may perhaps account, to some degree, for this; and thirdly, the nature of the employment in mills and factories that these women are engaged in. They live mostly on bread and tea, and I think a very small amount of stimulant affects them. I believe that the stimulant that they prefer is whisky, instead of beer or porter.

57,148. In the case of children below a certain age, is there any intemperance?—There is very little of that amongst what you might call juveniles. I am afraid amongst the very young men—that is from 16 to [illegible] or [illegible]—drinking is on the increase. Juvenile intemperance.

57,149. As to habitual drunkards, whether men or women, what have you to say?—Habitual drunkards are increasing very much in Belfast of recent years. Statistics which I shall hand in show that [illegible] persons were convicted for drunkenness over 100 times, [illegible] of whom were females. This return embraces a period of three years, but of course it is not meant to convey that the persons had over 100 convictions inside the three years. (See Appendix III.) Habitual drunkards.

57,150. What is the highest record of convictions against a woman?—One woman I find had [illegible] convictions. Vide Appendix III.

57,151. Over what period?—She arrived at her [illegible] convictions inside the last three years, but I do not mean that she had been convicted [illegible] times inside the three years. The last time she was released from gaol she was convicted the same evening for being drunk.

57,152. I do not know whether you are able to speak to this; but do you find that amongst persons who are convicted most often for repeated drunkenness, the women exceed the men?—Oh, yes. In this return that I have got there were [illegible] women and only [illegible] men.

57,153. Above how many convictions?—Above 100 times.

57,154. Above the 100 times was there a great majority of women?—Yes.

57,155. When do the number of women begin to exceed the men in drunkenness? When people have

Mr. M. [illegible] — 30 Mar. '98

have [illegible] 10 times or 20 times, to whom he [illegible] [illegible] given, to men or women?—I cannot speak to that.

57,166. At all events, after [illegible] times you say the women greatly [illegible] the men?—Yes.

57,167. What is your suggestion with regard to confirmed drunkards?—I should suggest that after a certain number of convictions extending a number of years, or after a certain number of convictions [illegible] 10 or 12 months, they should be either committed to a home for inebriates, or be liable to six months' imprisonment with hard labour; or, if [illegible] to keep the peace, the magistrates should have the power, which they have not at present, to add hard labour in default of finding bail.

Connexion of drink and crime.

57,168. Do you know any connexion between crime and drink?—I believe that a great proportion of crime is caused by drink, although I cannot [illegible] statistics to corroborate this. I should think there would be over 75 or 80 per cent. of crime caused by drink or traceable to drink, either directly or indirectly.

57,169. Could you say how many people who were arrested for other offences than mere drunkenness are found drunk when they are arrested?—I could not say. I have no return of that.

57,160. Is there any one particular crime in your experience that is directly traceable to drink?—I have obtained a return from the National Society for the Prevention of Cruelty to Children, and it shows [illegible] per cent. of cases in which drink has been an element prosecuted by the Society. (See Appendix III.)

Vide Appendix III.

57,161. Who could trace the [illegible] of that element?—The inspectors of this society, of whom we have four in Belfast, visit all these houses in every case in which they prosecute, so that they know the circumstances of the families, and make their returns to the Society accordingly.

57,162. I suppose their testimony would only go to show that the parents are of drunken habits, not that they were actually drunk when they treated the [illegible]?—Yes. That they were of drunken habits.

Limited certificate for beer.

57,164. I need hardly ask you the cause of this [illegible] drunkenness. To what [illegible] do you attribute it?—I consider it is due to spirits.

57,165. Should you like to say on any [illegible] or [illegible] or whether it is called being granted that the magistrates should have power to limit the certificate to beer and porter?—Yes. I should think that that would be a very good [illegible] in the [illegible] of any new licenses being granted in a country like Ireland, where the population is decreasing.

Drinking shops in Belfast.

57,165. What is the character of the public-houses in Belfast, speaking generally?—The vast majority of the public-houses themselves are nothing but drinking shops, that is, there are no groceries or other goods sold in them.

57,166. Would you advocate the sale of groceries in public-houses?—Not in a large town, certainly not.

57,167. When you say [illegible] should be sold there, you mean food should be supplied as well as drink, in those public-houses?—Yes. I think they should be encouraged, and in many cases compelled to supply tea, and soup, and [illegible].

57,168. Is the supply of food now general in the public-houses in Belfast?—In only three or four cases, I think, is anything of that kind sold in Belfast—that is, in the ordinary public-houses. Of course, there are restaurants.

57,169. But [illegible] or [illegible]?—In some of those there are, but there are very few.

57,170. You think the magistrates should have the power to attach as a condition to the license that they should sell in certain cases not only beer and porter, but whatever they did sell they should have food along with it?—Yes, I should think that would be a good condition to attach.

57,172. So that these public-houses are the only [illegible] places of entertainment of the population?—They are, and they have no attraction in them except drinking.

Mr. S. [illegible]

57,174. You would restrict the sale of spirits, would you, in certain specified houses, according to the discretion of the magistrates?—I was only talking of in the event of new licenses being granted. I do not know that it would be possible to take from them the licenses that they have to sell spirits in Ireland.

57,175. Not when the annual renewal came up?—I do not think so. They have got an interest in their licenses in Ireland, which I do not think they have in England.

57,176. An interest extending for more than one year?—Yes. So long as a licensed house is well conducted, and the premises are suitable, their license cannot be taken from them.

Renewal.

57,177. Is that the law?—I think that is the law in Ireland.

57,178. (Mr. Grosvenor.) It is founded on the [illegible] case, is it not?—Yes; that a transfer of a license cannot be refused on the ground of the number of public-houses.

57,179. (Chairman.) Supposing a full license were granted, if the magistrates, in their discretion, thought that the state of the neighbourhood wanted a restriction of the license to beer and porter, or, at all events, not extending to the sale of spirits, do you think that would not be within the competence of the magistrates under the existing law?—I should think not in Ireland, because the only grounds on which the police have a right to oppose the renewal of a publican's certificate, are the unsuitability of the premises and the manner in which they have been conducted within the past 12 months.

57,180. But suppose one of your subordinate officers were to say, there is an enormous deal of drunkenness in the neighbourhood of this house traceable to the use of spirits in the public-house, would it or would it not constitute a complaint, before the magistrates, which they could take notice of in the annual revision of the license?—Yes, I daresay it would; but I am afraid the magistrates would not act on that unless you could prove that the drunkenness actually originated in that particular public-house.

57,181. What is the opinion of the constabulary force in Belfast as to Saturday earlier closing, or total Sunday closing, or restriction of hours on Saturday or Sunday, or both?—The opinion is that the public-houses should be closed on Saturday at 10 o'clock, instead of 11, and that they should be opened on Sundays from 2 to [illegible], instead of from 2 to 7.

Early closing Saturday, Sunday.

57,182. Is there more drunkenness then in Belfast on the Saturday night?—There is more on Saturday night than on any other night, or perhaps two or three nights.

Drunkenness on Saturday night.

57,183. Are wages paid in Belfast on the Saturday as a rule?—No, they are not. The wages are paid on other days besides Saturday. I thought that might be one of the reasons for drunkenness, but I find that the wages in the large shipbuilding yards are paid on Fridays, and in the mills very often on other days in the week.

57,184. So that whatever may be the cause, do I understand from you that the amount of drunkenness on Saturday night is equal to that of two or three other nights in the week?—Yes.

57,185. Do you know that the state of drunkenness on Saturday night has caused any public inconvenience apart from its example?—I know that trains are very often late on Saturday, and that sometimes the [illegible] the guards [illegible] to the lateness of the trains say that they were late owing to the drunkenness amongst the passengers.

57,186. Is that an official statement of guards of railway trains?—It is no official statement that a manager of the railway gave to me in Belfast [illegible] of amusement, such as dancing and music halls. I think, if possible, they ought to be allowed to keep open till 11 o'clock on Saturday. My reason for that is that I think people, and especially the working classes, ought to be encouraged to frequent a place of amusement, where some other class of entertainment except drink is provided. I think it possibly might keep them out of the public-houses.

57,189. How long would you allow them to be opened? —Until 11 o'clock.

57,190. At what time do the people in Belfast go to bed, if you are able to speak on that question?—On Saturday night they are very late, on other nights in the week most of them are in bed at nine o'clock.

57,191. They have to work early the next morning?—They have to be up some of them at a quarter to six.

57,192. They sit up very late on Saturday, and that is the very day on which you propose to close the public-houses at an earlier hour. Do you think there would be no friction caused by the earlier closing on Saturday night?—I do not think the working class would resent it much. One reason I forgot to mention for the Saturday night drunkenness is the fact that there is no work to be done the following day, and they get out of their work in Belfast by 1 o'clock on Saturdays, and from 1 to 10 ought to afford them reasonable facilities for obtaining plenty of refreshment.

57,193. Apart from the question of obtaining refreshment, do you suppose the working class would like to obtain their groceries from the public-house. They would put off buying them until a late hour on Saturday night. Would they not?—In some cases they postpone the purchase of groceries until the public-houses are closed.

57,194. They would get their groceries at houses which were licensed for the sale of spirits?—They would get them at the spirit groceries?

57,195. As a matter of fact, they do?—I think they do generally.

57,196. So that after the public-houses are closed, if they liked they could get what spirits they liked for consumption off the premises, at all events according to law, at the groceries?—Of course, I would make that apply to spirit grocers as well as publicans; they should be closed at 10 o'clock, certainly.

57,197. Then you would drive the people to get their groceries earlier?—Certainly.

57,198. You would close them all?—I would.

57,199. (Mr. Grinling.) The closing hours at present are the same for both branches of the trade, are they not?—Yes.

57,200. (Chairman.) What would you do with hotels or restaurants as to closing hours?—I think the hotels or restaurants should be opened for the convenience of people who want suppers.

57,201. Hotels with similar licenses?—Yes. I think a restaurant and an hotel should have a separate license. It should not be a publican's licence. It should be a license in which they would be compelled to supply food and beds, and everything of that kind, and the license should be separate from the publican's license altogether.

57,202. If that were carried out, suppose the publican came forward and said, "I will supply beds and food"?—I would raise the license.

[illegible]

57,206. (Chairman.) What would be the percentage of drunkenness on a Sunday compared to the week?—It would be double on a week day to what it is on a Sunday.

57,207. Do you think that any further restriction than what you have mentioned in the hours would lead to shebeening?—I think it might possibly lead to shebeening.

57,208. What is the condition of shebeening now in Belfast?—The number of known or suspected shebeens in Belfast is only 60.

57,209. When you say known ones, how is it that they are not prosecuted and suppressed?—We call a place that has been once prosecuted a known shebeen.

57,210. But it does not continue I suppose?—You may have, and very often have, a second conviction against it, but when we call a place a suspected shebeen, it means that we are not able to prove that it is one.

57,211. A known case of shebeening you might dismiss from your calculations, because presumably the police, I suppose, do their duty, and a known shebeen would be suppressed?—It would. You might practically call them all suspected shebeens.

57,212. You would say that there were 60 suspected houses now in Belfast?—Yes. Of course, the vast majority of these are probably in houses of ill-fame.

57,213. On no particular night or day of the week would they do their business more than others?—I think Saturday night would probably be the worst.

57,214. Would any business be doing in the shebeens on a Sunday as far as drinking is concerned?—I do not think there would be much on Sunday.

57,215. If you opened the houses in Belfast only from 2 to 5 on a Sunday, what would you do with the traveller?—The suggestion I intended to make about the traveller would be that no traveller who had slept the previous night inside the city of Belfast should be able to get a drink, even although he had travelled 5 or 6 miles. — The *bona fide* traveller.

57,216. What would be the extreme radius of the city of Belfast?—The outskirts of Ligoniel, I should think, Balmoral for instance, would be over 4 miles.

57,217. You would not allow any Belfast man to get drunk?—No man who had slept there the night before should get a drink inside that radius.

57,218. It would be rather difficult to identify him, would not it?—I think they are pretty well known to each other in Belfast—the people who frequent these public-houses.

57,219. You do not think shebeens would be increased by the restrictions that you suggest, but what do you say as to drinking clubs?—I do not think drinking clubs would be established in Belfast on account of the disposition of the people themselves. I think the respectable part of the working class in Belfast would not lend themselves to form a mere drinking club, and if a club were established by the rowdy element I do not think it would last long without being interfered with both by the neighbours and by the police. — Clubs.

57,220. Is there any marked absenteeism from work on the part of the workmen on Monday morning in Belfast?—From the enquiries I made and returns I got from mills and factories and also from shipbuilding yards, I find that they attend fairly well on Monday morning. Of course there are a good many more people absent from their work on Monday morning than there are on other mornings of the week. The statistics obtained from one large shipbuilding yard in which — Attendance on Monday mornings.

Mr. M. Morell.

29 Mar. '98

Belfast.

Mr. D. [illegible] — 24 Mar. '98.

most disturbing effect in Belfast both on the attendance at work, and the number of arrests for drunkenness.

Extension of hours in suburbs.

57,223. In the suburbs of Belfast, I suppose, the houses would be open till 11 o'clock now?—That is in the extended area, and from 2 o'clock to 7 o'clock on Sunday.

57,224. They are under the same conditions as to closing as the city itself?—Exactly.

57,225. Their hours were extended when they became part of the city?—Their hours were extended for one hour on Saturday night and allowing them to be open on Sunday from 2 till 7.

57,226. Is it possible for you to trace any effect of that extension of hours?—The time has been rather too short to found any definite opinion on the subject. However, I find that in certain districts in the town where the public-houses are now open later, in the suburban districts—the number of arrests and prosecutions for drunkenness have not increased; but in one particular place, where there are a great many of the working class living and where there are a certain number of mills—I mean Ligoniel—I find that the total number of cases of drunkenness in the three months preceding the extension of the borough was 27, 16 of which were on Saturdays and Sundays. In the three months after the extension the total number of cases of drunkenness were 45, which included 19 on Saturdays and Sundays.

Sunday closing in favour.

57,227. You have said, speaking of your own opinion, you would have advocated total Sunday closing. As far as you are able to gauge public opinion in Belfast, in what way would public opinion be trending towards total closing or restriction, or to leaving it alone?—I think the majority of the people in Belfast would be in favour of Sunday closing.

57,228. (Dean Dickinson.) You are aware there was a plebiscite taken, and an enormous majority were in favour of total Sunday closing two or three years ago? —I believe there was.

57,229. (Chairman.) Would your opinion be formed by the recollection of that plebiscite?—I do not think so. I think, however, if you leave out the other people who are not the working class, the enormous majority of those people would be in favour of total Sunday closing.

57,230. They would not be the people who would suffer?—They would not be the people who would use the public-houses.

57,231. Therefore they would not suffer by the closing if there was any suffering?—No, I think the majority of the people of the working class would be slightly in favour of the public-houses being left open.

57,232. In favour of houses being kept open for some time?—I do.

57,233. Not necessarily from 2 o'clock to 7 o'clock? —No, I do not think they would resent the closing of the public-houses at 5 o'clock on Sundays.

57,234. Would you include among those who are not in favour of total Sunday closing, the Sabbatarian element?—Yes, I would; it is pretty strong in Belfast. In fact, in some cases they go so far as to advocate the putting down of trams and trains on Sunday.

Good conduct of publicans.

57,235. What are the number of licences in Belfast? —The number of publicans' licences is 649 at present.

57,236. What were they in 1891?—In 1891 they were 656, and at present they are 649.

57,237. So that there has been a decrease in the number of licences, notwithstanding the large extension of the population, and of the area of the city?—There is. That is probably caused by hotels having collapsed, and public-houses having been knocked down when they were building new streets, and things of that kind; various reasons.

57,238. Is any of that diminution traceable to the publicans having been prosecuted for breach of certificate?—No; no licences have been taken from them in that period.

57,239. No licences have been taken from anybody in possession of a house?—Not of the publicans—not inside that period.

57,240. That, shortly, the great body of publicans in Belfast would be a respectable body of men and well conducted?—The public-houses are very well conducted, and we have no difficulty whatever in supervising existing licences of publicans.

Mr. D. [illegible]

57,241. I suppose the licences in Belfast are very valuable property?—They are increasing in value every year.

57,242. Increasing in value from their diminution in number?—They are increasing in value mainly on account of no new licences being granted. The recorder has refused to grant, and has not granted, any new licences for a considerable time.

Estimated value of public-houses.

57,243. What can a licensed house be got for in Belfast?—One house I heard was sold recently for 6,000l.

57,244. What is the saleable value of the public-houses?—It is, generally speaking, high, except in some of the older houses along the docks and in back streets.

57,245. Supposing no new licences are granted, as is the practice with the recorder now, and it is a fact that the owners of these public-houses are spending large sums of money upon them, do you consider that the public-houses in Belfast compare favourably with the public-houses in any other part of Ireland?—I do; and I think if the present practice is continued of refusing to grant new ones, they will be the most commodious and the best conducted that there are in Ireland.

57,246. When you say there are 649 licences in the city of Belfast, that includes all licences?—No, that is publicans alone. There are a great many more.

Spirit grocers' licences.

57,247. What would be the number of spirit grocers' licences?—243. That is spirit grocers and beer dealers combined.

57,248. Are they increasing in number?—They are. In the year 1891 there were only 223; at present there are 243.

57,249. Spirit grocers' licences?—Yes, and beer dealers'.

57,250. Could you split them up into spirit off and beer off, or do they hold both?—I include them as one because 90 per cent. of them have the beer dealer's licence as well as the spirit grocer's.

57,251. We have been talking of the grocers that have the spirit licence and the beer licence off. How many publicans sell groceries?—I do not think it is worth taking into consideration. It would not be more than 6 or perhaps 7.

Quality of spirit.

57,252. Turning to the quality of the drink sold in Belfast, should you say that it was generally good, or is it adulterated?—It is good, and it is not adulterated so far as we can ascertain.

Profits [illegible]

57,253. I think you have some suggestions to offer which you think might improve the conditions of things even in Belfast?—Yes. I have made one suggestion already about the supply of tea and food for consumption on the premises. The second one I had was that in case a man was found on licensed premises, or on that of a spirit grocer, drunk, I think the onus of the proof that the person did not get the drink which made him drunk should lie on the licensed person.

57,254. Where does it lie now?—It lies on the police. We have to prove that the publican knew that the man was drunk when he supplied him with drink, or that he supplied him with drink when he was in a drunken state.

57,255. The publican should have to prove the contrary?—Yes; the idea we have is that if a man is found drunk on a man's licensed premises it should be prima facie an offence on the part of the publican.

57,256. Unless he can prove extenuating or rebutting circumstances?—Yes.

Structural alteration of public-houses.

57,257. Who would exercise supervision over the structure of public-houses in Belfast?—The magistrates, I believe, would. It has been decided that a publican has a right to make a reasonable extension of his premises. I think this is a very vague expression to use, "reasonable extension." It might include the opening of a new door in a side street.

57,258. The recorder would take no cognisance of that?—If brought before the recorder, the recorder would refuse permission.

57,259. Supposing a licence had been granted, and before the next annual licensing sessions, the policy [illegible] a back alley, would the recorder refuse the licence?—It would not come before the recorder again, except on the occasion of a confirmation of a transfer. It would come before the magistrates at the renewal sessions, which are held every year, and possibly the magistrates might grant such a renewal, even although the applicant had altered his original licensed premises so as to practically turn them into two public-houses.

37,261. You have the recorder and the city magistrates going on together as a licensing authority?—Yes.

37,262. The recorder alone grants the licences?—Yes.

37,263. And the magistrates of the city renew?—Yes. My idea is that if there is any extension of the premises to be made or an alteration by opening of new doors or anything of that kind, it should be brought before the recorder in the shape of a new licence, and not be brought before the magistrates in the shape of a renewal of an old licence.

37,264. You would like to see one authority substituted for the two?—Yes, I should like to see the recorder substituted.

37,265. And that he should have solely to deal with all licensing matters?—Solely. I think in the first place the decisions that were given would be uniform. As it is at present, the decisions are quite the reverse. One Bench of magistrates may grant one man his licence, and two or three days afterwards they may refuse a licence in which there was probably no difference.

37,266. You think it would not be too much power to give to one man to regulate the licensing trade over a population of 300,000?—It did strike me that it would be a very great responsibility for one man to have. The only alternative idea that I have would be the substitution of some sort of local authority in the shape of, perhaps, the Lord Mayor of Belfast, the two resident magistrates, and, perhaps, two or three of the local magistrates selected by themselves to act as a sort of licensing committee to deal with renewals of licences only.

37,267. Leaving the granting to the recorder?—Yes.

37,268. Why should not the court you have suggested be competent to grant licences as well?—According to the present law the only person who can grant a new licence in Belfast is the recorder sitting alone.

37,269. I am aware of that. I was supposing we had power to deal with the law and make any changes; would you suggest that this court, which you have sketched, should have power to deal not only with the original grant but with transfers and renewals?—I should prefer that they only deal with the transfer and renewal.

37,270. Leaving the grant in the hands of the recorder?—Yes.

37,271. Any alteration in premises you think should be brought to the notice of the recorder, or, if you had this newly constituted court, before that court?—I should be quite satisfied with it being brought before that court, except that, as I said already, it should be dealt with as a new licence, and that licence is only to be granted by the recorder, according to my ideas.

37,272. It depends on what alterations would amount to a new licence. Would not there be some difficulty in saying what amount of alteration constituted a new licence?—There would be some difficulty in that. I think when a man gets a licence for a certain house he should not be allowed to open a new bar perhaps 100 feet up in another street.

37,273. Does he do that now?—There is nothing to prevent him doing it.

37,274. Are there any of those cases in Belfast?—One case of that kind, I believe, occurred, but I think the police opposed it, as far as I recollect, at the renewal sessions, and I think it was only granted to him on the condition that he should shut the door up.

37,275. You would have to define by statute, would you not, what was a reasonable extension; or how would you define it?—I should think that if any extension or [illegible] that that would be necessary to be brought under the recorder's notice. It is the external facilities for getting drink.

37,276. The re-construction would be brought before the court at renewal or transfer?—Yes.

37,277. Continuing your list of suggestions you did, I think, touch upon the bona fide traveller?—Yes.

37,278. Have you any special recommendation to make apart from the six-mile limit, and, I think you said, nobody who slept in Belfast the night before should obtain refreshment on Sunday as a bona fide traveller within the limits of the day?—Yes. In Belfast on Sundays a great number of the working class, that is the clerks and artisans and working men, go with their wives and families to Bangor and other seaside resorts. Those people, in my opinion, are bona fide travellers in the meaning of the Act, but it is a question whether they should be allowed to remain in a public-house longer than would enable them to get reasonable refreshment, unless they were having luncheon or dinner, or something of that kind. It comes, however, a difficult thing to deal with.

37,279. Is it competent for a bona fide traveller to go into a house during closing hours and demand spirits to carry off with him?—There is no reason why he should not get them. I think that should be put a stop to. Any sale to a bona fide traveller should be for consumption on the premises.

37,280. You think the three-mile limit should be raised to six?—Yes.

37,281. What exceptions would you make for railway travellers?—I do not think railway travellers should be entitled to drink at a railway station where they begin their journey unless they are already bona fide travellers. I do not think it is right that a man should go to a railway station, purchase a ticket, perhaps for 1d., to an adjoining station, and constitute himself a bona fide traveller by so doing.

37,282. (Dean Dickinson.) Is the same ticket used over and over again?—I do not know that. However, as far as Belfast is concerned, I do not think that it is very frequently done. We have found out some instances of it, and as soon as it was brought under the notice of the railway people they put a stop to it.

37,283. (Chairman.) I suppose, as a matter of fact, the public-houses in the centre of the city are not troubled with the bona fide traveller?—No; in the centre of the city there are none of the public-houses, [illegible] open for the convenience of bona fide travellers. Of course in the outskirts a very large trade indeed is done on Sunday in supplying drink to people who come from the centre of the town for the mere purpose of getting drink.

37,284. They are not country people who come into Belfast, but Belfast people who go to the outskirts to get it?—Yes, a shifting population from Belfast, who, on Sunday, go to the outskirts. Those people, of course, are not bona fide travellers, but the publicans very often cannot distinguish between them.

37,285. You advocate the extension of the limit from 3 to 6 miles and the prohibition of the Belfast men getting drink?—Yes.

37,285a. What are the number of prosecutions now for bona fide travellers?—They are practically nil. It is impossible to prove the object with which a man went on the top of a tramway to the outskirts of the town. We could not prove whether he went there for business or pleasure.

37,286. If your suggestions were carried out, do you think it would be the matter of proof? Apart from the Belfast people, do you think it would be possible to prove a violation of your new regulations?—I think it would make the publican be more strict than he is at present as to bona fide travellers. I think it is not merely sufficient that he should ask a man who comes whether he is a bona fide traveller, and then serve drink. I think he should perhaps make him sign a book in which he should certify that he was a bona fide traveller, and had travelled the distance.

37,287. (Dean Dickinson.) With the entire and total-

Mr R. [illegible]

[illegible]

The bona fide question.

Railway travellers.

Mr. R. [illegible]

21 Mar. '98.

Hotels and restaurants.

57,289. (*Chairman.*) Would you have separate licences for hotels and restaurants, as Sir Andrew Reed suggested?—I agree with what Sir Andrew Reed stated at the last sitting of the Commission, that a condition of the renewal of a licence to an hotel or restaurant should be that a *bonâ fide* hotel or restaurant business was carried on during the year. I make this suggestion with the object that a licence which is originally granted by the recorder to a person for the purpose of carrying on an hotel or restaurant, should not be permitted to be turned into an ordinary public-house, as has been done in Belfast within the last couple of years.

57,290. Is it common for the hotels in Belfast to have doors in a side street, through which people can come in and drink as at an ordinary public-house bar?—Yes, a large number of hotels have a door, and perhaps two, and some of them have an entrance through a side street. This practically means that where an hotel gets a licence, a new public-house is started. Bars in hotels, I think, should not be for the convenience of the outside public, but for the convenience of the people who are staying in the hotels.

57,291. A separate hotel licence, therefore?—Yes.

57,292. Distinct from a public-house?—Yes, and also a restaurant licence.

Extension of hours.

57,293. Have you anything to say on the subject of occasional licences?—We think that in the country the magistrates in petty sessions, or perhaps, in Belfast, the Commissioner of Police, should have the power to grant to hotel and restaurant keepers, and perhaps also to large publicans, an occasional licence which would enable them to keep open their premises for the convenience of guests on the occasion of large, but necessarily public, dinners, or balls, after closing hours, notice having been served on the police by the applicant.

57,294. Are they not able to get occasional licences of that kind now?—A publican cannot get an occasional licence for his own premises.

57,295. There are no exemption licences in Ireland, are there?—No exemption orders in Belfast.

57,296. What is an exemption order?—That is to enable a publican to practically keep his house open all night, except between the hours of 1 and 5, for the convenience of people going to fairs and markets.

57,297. That licence does not exist in Ireland?—It exists, I believe, in Dublin a great deal, but it is not used in Belfast at all.

57,298. You would not like to see them introduced into Belfast?—No, I should not.

Occasional licences.

57,299. Do you know instances where an occasional licence has been granted in Belfast by a justice of the peace?—Yes, I know of one instance in which an occasional licence was granted out of petty sessions to a [illegible], and the police knew nothing about the occasional licence having been granted for nearly a fortnight.

57,300. It would be competent for him to grant it?—Yes, under the present law.

57,301. Would you restrict occasional licences to being granted by two magistrates sitting in open court at petty sessions?—I should think that occasional licences should not be granted out of petty sessions, if they are to be granted by magistrates at all, and the applicants certainly should be compelled to serve a notice on the police, so that they can give grounds of objection as to granting of the licence if necessary.

57,302. You think the police might be entrusted with the granting of occasional licences?—I think in a large town like Belfast the commissioner of police is the proper person to grant occasional licences.

57,303. Only the chief?—Only the chief. I do not know how it could be worked in country districts. It might possibly be granted there by a resident magistrate. I think the Commissioner of Police in Dublin grants these occasional licences, so far as I recollect.

Clubs.

57,304. I think you have no tangle clubs in Belfast?—No, we have none at all.

Shebeens.

57,305. Shebeens I think you have dealt with. Is there any suggestion in point of law which you would like to make with regard to making the law more stringent?—We consider that in the case of shebeening the district inspector of police should have the power to grant an authority to search any premises which are occupied by a person once convicted of shebeening when he has reasonable ground to suspect that illicit sale is again being carried on; and we think also that a shebeening warrant should last for three months. We also think that the offence of keeping for sale should be included in the third section of the Licensing Act of 1872.

57,306. As to steamer licences, what have you to say?—The steamer licences and railway refreshment licences we find are not abused. The steamer licences, of course, are granted by the Excise.

57,307. You would not wish to see any other authority introduced except the Excise, or an authority co-ordinate with the Excise, in the case of steamers?—If there were any abuses in selling liquor on board a steamer, I do not see why they should not either be under the same local jurisdiction, or why their licence should not be liable to be forfeited by the recorder in the case of anything occurring.

57,308. By the authorities having jurisdiction at the point of departure or arrival?—The port of departure, I should think, would be the place where their licence would be obtained.

57,309. The drunkenness might occur on the voyage?—It might. Most of the people would probably be returning by the same boats.

57,310. Where would these steamers in Belfast ply?—They ply from Belfast to Bangor and back.

57,311. Would that be an easy distance within a day?—Yes, they are daily steamers; at present they are managed by the railway company and are well conducted.

57,312. It would not be an unreasonable thing that the magistrates, or the recorder, or whoever it may be, should have jurisdiction over the licence?—Yes, I think he should.

57,313. As to the publicans' licences, of which we have heard a good deal, which are granted to the wholesale spirit dealers, you would like to see the English custom introduced—the English trader's licence substituted for the publican's licence?—Yes, I think the English trader's licence would probably meet our wishes.

57,314. That is the three-gallon licence?—Yes. I think the traders are very much alive to this question on account of their licences having been opposed at the last annual licensing sessions on the ground that they were not carrying on the ordinary business of a publican. The matter is now being argued, or will be argued before the Court of Queen's Bench. The case has not finally been decided yet.

57,315. Would it be a fact that in these large establishments (and you have some very large ones in Belfast I understand) there is no consumption on the premises?—I think there is practically none at all. If you take the largest place in Belfast, that is Dunville's, it is anything but a large office like a bank. The licence that he holds is a licence for consumption of drink on and off the premises.

57,316. He is obliged to take out a publican's licence?—He is. He pays something like 42*l.* a year for that.

57,317. Is it not 40*l.*?—I think it is 42*l.*, I am not quite sure, something like that.

57,318. Why does he take out a publican's licence?—He takes it out because he cannot supply between two quarts and two gallons without it. The spirit grocer's licence allows him to sell up to two quarts; the wholesale licence only allows him to sell two gallons; so that he cannot sell between two quarts and two gallons.

57,319. He cannot sell between two quarts and two gallons for consumption off?—Yes.

57,320. Would a great establishment like Dunville's care to sell quantities between two quarts and two gallons?—I should think one gallon would be very often sold. I may mention that the objection that the police have to a publican's licence being granted to a wholesale man is this; that there is nothing to prevent the wholesale man at any time turning his premises into an ordinary public-house, whereas it has not been granted for that purpose at all, but for the purpose of carrying on a legitimate wholesale trade.

57,321. There is a legal question, I believe, pending as to whether he would not be obliged to take full advantage of the publican's licence?—Yes.

[illegible]. Turning again to the spirit grocers, I think [illegible] said the number in Belfast was [illegible] in [illegible], and it had increased to [illegible] in [illegible]?—That is so.

[illegible]. What is the opinion of the officers of the Belfast force with reference to them?—The unanimous opinion of the officers and men, and in fact I may say I believe the unanimous opinion of the general public, except those who are interested in those spirit grocers' licences, is that they are the greatest curse that any [illegible] could be. They tend to demoralise the [illegible], and I believe that they lead to carrying on an illegal trade which it is almost impossible for us to put a stop to. We suggest that the licence for spirit grocers and beer dealers should be subject to the same conditions as to grant as the publicans' licences are. In Belfast the publicans' licences are only, of course, granted by the Recorder.

[illegible]. Is there any qualification as to valuation?—There is no qualification for a spirit grocer. A man is of good character, and he has got a [illegible]. The magistrates cannot prevent him getting his licence. They are bound to grant it.

[illegible]. If he has a house and is of good character?—Yes, that is, the premises do not require to be of any [illegible], and the magistrates cannot take into consideration the number of licensed houses already existing as the Recorder can in publicans' licences.

[illegible]. Nor the locality in which it is proposed to be taken out?—The unsuitability of the premises, the character of the applicant, and the number of the public-houses are the three objections that we can make in the case of applications for publicans' licences.

[illegible]. It is a moot point, is it not, as to whether suitability should apply to external suitability or internal arrangements?—I think it has been decided by the Court of Appeal in Ireland that "suitability" does not mean suitability of position.

[illegible]. You have expressed the opinion of the force generally. What is your own opinion, if I may ask it?—My own opinion is exactly the opinion of the officers, and I also go further, and I say that no groceries should be allowed to be sold in any place where spirits or beer is sold. I do not think that these licences should be granted to people who are living on the premises; that is, a spirit grocer's house. If it is necessary at all there should be a house in which spirits are sold by retail for consumption off the premises, and the house should be shut up when the trade is done. There would then be no danger of the great evil that there is going on at present of selling drink to women as "groceries" and putting it down in the bill, as they often do, as groceries.

[illegible]. I will suppose that your suggestion was carried out, and that the spirit grocers' licence was abolished altogether, you would then allow spirit shops, only selling spirits, to be set up in different parts of Belfast, would you?—I prefer that to what they call a spirit grocer.

[illegible]. You prefer that to a mixed trading?—Yes, I would.

[illegible]. But looking to the number of licences now in Belfast, if spirit grocers' licences were abolished tomorrow, should you say it would be necessary, for the convenience of the public, to set up any shops where beer or spirits were sold exclusively?—If the spirit grocers' licences were abolished now, I do not think it would do any harm at all. I think I should make an exception in the case of very large houses in the centre of the town, where the spirit grocery trade and the grocery trade is carried on in a good way; that is in the large houses in which they pay [illegible] [illegible] and [illegible] a year rent.

[illegible]. You would establish a money qualification before a man should deal in the two articles?—I should take the qualification, if the present law is going to be carried out, to [illegible] or [illegible].

[illegible]. If the spirit grocer's licence were kept as at present?—Yes.

there are [illegible] spirit grocers, and there are [illegible] of them in Belfast. I presume the rest of them are in Dublin.

[illegible]. In the agricultural country districts of Ireland, would it be a grievance for the people to have a mixed trade carried on in a small store?—I think in the country districts it certainly would. I think the publican in a country village is the general merchant; he supplies everything; and I do not think it does the harm in a small country village that it would do in a large town like Belfast.

[illegible]. (Viscount de Vesci.) It is very prevalent in country villages now, is it not?—Yes.

[illegible]. But it does not exist in Belfast at all?—Except for the sale of groceries.

[illegible]. (Dean Dickinson.) Have you no co-operative stores in Belfast?—No.

[illegible]. (Chairman.) Can you give us any actual evidence of the evasion of the law by the spirit grocers in Belfast?—Yes. A case occurred recently last week, in which a man admitted that he had put down the porter that was sold on the spirit grocer's premises as tea, and I heard of another instance of the same sort. I do not know of it myself, but I have been told by a magistrate of a case of the same kind which was reported to him.

[illegible]. In recent years?—Within the last two years.

[illegible]. Do you argue from these comparatively few cases which you can cite, that it is probable that the practice exists?—It is not from that entirely. Evidence on this point is almost impossible to obtain, for this reason: there are only two people who can give it, one is the spirit grocer, who naturally will not tell the police such a state of affairs, fearing his licence may be opposed; the other is the woman who buys it. She will not tell, because she will be afraid her husband will hear it.

[illegible]. There being no legal evidence, how is the impression produced on your mind that there is a great deal of evasion on the part of the spirit grocer?—I think the defence that is raised by a spirit grocer in court when he is asked why this liquor was sold for consumption on the premises is invariably that it was a treat.

[illegible]. (Dean Dickinson.) Does the husband ever give information?—I do not think the husband ever gave any information to anybody. I do not think the wife would tell the husband such a state of affairs.

[illegible]. (Chairman.) In the case you are putting the wife and the grocer would be in a sort of partnership or in collusion against the husband?—Yes.

[illegible]. What would be the view of the working classes of Belfast, if you are able to speak to it, as to the suppression of the spirit grocer's licence?—I think the almost unanimous opinion of the working men of Belfast is in favour of the suppression of them. I have never yet heard any man, except a man who is interested in the spirit grocer's trade, say anything but that spirit grocers' licences were a curse. In the return which I sent to a great many of the mills and factories in Belfast I put down this query, "Your opinion as to the suppression of the spirit grocer's licence?" Almost the invariable answer was "We certainly think they should be suppressed altogether."

[illegible]. The magistrates have very little discretion, have they, in granting their part of the certificate to the grocer?—The magistrates have no option in the matter so far as the spirit grocers are concerned if the premises are suitable and the man is of good character.

[illegible]. Then have you formed [illegible] the magistrates, can you, for the great increase of these spirit grocers in Belfast?—Well, I do. I think the magistrates could have made the licence almost valueless if they refused to add it to the beer dealer's licence. They can refuse to grant a man a beer dealer's licence at the [illegible] licensing sessions on the ground of the number. They have that option. They have not done that. The consequence is that nearly every spirit dealer has [illegible]

Mr. H. [illegible]. — [illegible] Mar. '9[illegible] — Evasion of law by spirit grocers. — Abolition of spirit grocers. — Magistrates and spirit grocers.

but I should add to the qualification to the spirit grocer's licence the number of houses. I would allow them to take into consideration the number of licensed houses already existing.

[illegible]. Therefore the mischief to which you object on the part of the magistrates is that in granting their certificate to the spirit grocer they give him also permission to take out the beer licence?—Yes. I think the magistrates should not have [illegible] the facilities when it was within their power to diminish them.

[illegible]. (Dean Dickinson.) You think they do not do what they might do?—Yes.

[illegible]. (Chairman.) Have they power to refuse the sale of spirits?—No; but I do not think a spirit grocer's licence would last for 24 hours if they had not the beer licence with it.

[illegible]. What is the process? A grocer wants to get these licences from the Excise. Does he take out two licences, one for spirits and one for beer?—Yes, he takes them out when he gets the certificate signed by the magistrates; but as a rule he does not take out the spirit licence until he gets the beer licence; that is, he takes them both together.

[illegible]. You think the magistrates might act more severely than they do in refusing their certificate for the beer licence?—Yes, I think they might have backed the recorder up, who has refused to increase the facilities for drinking.

[illegible]. Where are these licensed places mostly situated in Belfast?—They are situated in the back and slum districts. I had a map prepared, which I shall hand in. In this map, in one district off the Falls Road in Belfast there are two what we call hells. The radius of this map from the centre to the extreme of the map is about 300 yards. In this limit I find there are 20 public-houses and 22 spirit grocers, which make 42, dotted all through back streets. I have gone through these streets myself. Some of the houses that these licences are granted to are scarcely fit to live in, let alone to carry on the business of a spirit merchant. Some of them do not pay, I should think, more than three shillings, or at the outside four shillings, a week rent. Other portions of the town are as bad as these. (See Appendix [illegible].)

[illegible]. (Mr. Wharton.) Has a man who holds the spirit grocer's licence to advertise that fact over his door?—Yes.

[illegible]. Conspicuously?—Yes.

[illegible]. I did not know whether he only kept his house as a small grocer's, and then by virtue of the fact that he got a licence sold without advertising the fact?—He is obliged to put over his door the fact.

[illegible]. (Chairman.) What is their turnover with regard to groceries in these small houses?—I should think it is very small indeed. I think it is very small on account of the size of the houses. They have no room for much.

[illegible]. Most of their business is done in beer?—Yes. The other portion of the city I wish to refer to is just the opposite side of the town, a place called Ballymacarrett. In this place the spirit grocers and beer dealers increased in eight years from [illegible] to [illegible], while the publicans' licences, which were granted by the Recorder sitting alone, only increased from [illegible] to [illegible].

magistrate. The Recorder has nothing to do with it in Belfast.

[illegible]. (Dean Dickinson.) Is he the county court judge?—The Recorder of Belfast is the county court judge for the county of Antrim, in which the greater portion of Belfast is.

[illegible]. (Chairman.) Is this the state of things? A magistrate is helpless in refusing a spirit licence to a grocer, but he may refuse a beer licence to him? He has got the discretion as regards beer.

[illegible]. He is bound as to spirits?—Yes.

[illegible]. There are two separate authorities, you say?—Yes.

[illegible]. While the Recorder has sometimes refused the publicans' licences in Belfast, the magistrates give their certificates to the spirit grocer to sell spirits and beer throughout the city?—They do.

[illegible]. And they are increasing the number of them of late years to a great extent?—They are. There is no doubt of that.

[illegible]. Is it your opinion that the good which I suppose you would say the Recorder was doing is nullified by the action of the magistrates?—I consider that is a fact. I consider that the action of the magistrates in attaching a valuable licence like the beer licence to the spirit grocer's licence, when they could have refused it, has demoralised the women in Belfast, and has been the cause of more drunkenness than all the public-houses in Belfast put together—home drinking, I should say, and drunkenness.

[illegible]. Besides enlarging the grocers' licence to restrictions on the points of suitability of their houses and raising their qualification, you would do more, and you would give the magistrates full power over the spirit licence as well as over the beer licence?—Yes; I would add the other condition as to the number of licensed houses already existing.

[illegible]. Could you point us to the statute where the magistrates have power to refuse the beer licence to the spirit grocer, and cannot in the case of a spirit licence?—I think it is in the Beer Licences (Ireland) Act, the 1882 Act.

[illegible]. By the Act of 1882, 45 & 46 Vict. c. 34, it is enacted that "The licensing justices shall be at liberty . . . in their free and unqualified discretion, either to refuse the certificate to any licence for sale of beer by retail to be consumed off, on any ground appearing to them to be sufficient, or to grant the same to such persons as they, in the exercise of their statutory powers and the exercise of their discretion, deem fit and proper."—Yes.

[illegible]. They do not exercise that unqualified discretion in Belfast?—I am afraid they only exercise it as to the granting.

[illegible]. The beer licence, I suppose, in Belfast is more valuable, because I understood you to say that in Belfast the people were taking more to beer and to porter than they were to spirits?—That is so. Of course, the other point of its being valuable is because the magistrates have the power to refuse it, so that it creates an interest in their licence which a spirit grocer has not got. There is no property in a spirit grocer's licence at all.

Mr. [illegible] 13 May '98.

[illegible] have no option in the matter but to grant [illegible] the licence.

[illegible]. If it has been granted in a sort of [illegible] state in the [illegible]?—[illegible] they cannot grant it in the intervening [illegible] in a case of [illegible] circumstances. But at licensing sessions they have absolutely no option in the matter. They must grant it.

[illegible]. (Sir [illegible].) Could you give us the statutory provision which says they have no power to refuse the licence?—I cannot refer to it.

[illegible]. I am asking it as a fact, but I want to know what the authority is?—I will look it up. I cannot [illegible] the section of the Act at present. The [illegible] know that they have got the power, [illegible] that the grounds of objection [illegible] in the grant of a grocer's licence are the [illegible] of the premises and the character of the applicant alone. It is 27 & 28 Vict. c. [illegible], s. 3.

[illegible]. Is it an Irish Act?—Yes. It is section 3.

[illegible]. (Mr. Young.) That question has been argued in the Dublin Courts, and it has been decided that they have no power to refuse [illegible]. It went to the Court of Queen's Bench in the case of the [illegible], I think. In fact, a mandamus was issued compelling them to grant the licence.

[illegible]. (Chairman.) That goes to show that they have no power to refuse a spirit licence at the annual licensing sessions, but at the quarter sessions they have power to refuse, because the [illegible] application is only made upon special grounds?—Yes.

[illegible]. If the special grounds are not proved to the satisfaction of the magistrates they have the discretion of refusing?—Yes, it is [illegible] to them.

[illegible]. [illegible] we have dealt now pretty fully with the grocers. Unless you have other suggestions to make as to the trade as now carried on?—Of course, the trade as now carried on is carried on in such a way as to render a successful prosecution for breach of the law almost impossible. [illegible] and boxes of goods are [illegible] in the shop in such a way that the public can go in behind them, and can drink there. The police cannot see anything of this kind going on from the street, and consequently it is almost impossible to get a conviction against a spirit grocer in Belfast. They have also [illegible] outside the door by which the approach of men whom we detail in plain clothes to try to put down this illegal trade. The prosecutions are very often unsuccessful.

[illegible]. (Mr. Young.) Have the police the right of entry?—Yes.

[illegible]. (Chairman.) The [illegible] give information of the approach of the police?—Yes. We think the fines which are inflicted when a conviction is obtained with a great deal of trouble are not in proportion to the offence.

[illegible]. Would you therefore raise the minimum fine?—I would raise the fine on the spirit grocer and beer dealer [illegible].

[illegible]. What is the fine imposed now?—I think they can fine anything they like.

[illegible]. There is no minimum?—No.

[illegible]. (Mr. Young.) Would it not assist to meet this matter if the spirit grocer were bound to sell only in corked vessels?—A spirit grocer can sell in whatever way he likes, so long as it is consumed off the premises.

[illegible]. (Chairman.) As to these spirit grocers' licences, in whose hands are they? Are they in the hands of large traders and spirit dealers?—I think the great majority of these licences are in the hands of the wholesale trade in Belfast, not in the sense of their being exactly what is known in England as a tied house, but owing to the money for the purchase of these houses having been advanced by the wholesale men with some sort of understanding—I do not know whether it is a condition or not [illegible]—that the liquor shall be bought from that particular wholesale man until the money borrowed is paid up. The reason [illegible]

because I believe that the [illegible] are advancing money [illegible] for the same purpose.

[illegible]. Cannot the magistrates [illegible] which are, so to speak, behind the [illegible]?—The only thing the magistrates could do is to [illegible] a spirit grocer [illegible] his licence would be to [illegible] for not producing it. He is obliged to do so when he is requested, but he generally brings it in a certain time afterwards.

[illegible]. You would impose a fine for the non-production of the licence when he is required to do so?—Yes, the magistrates have that power already.

[illegible]. (Mr. [illegible].) There would be no difficulty, would there, even supposing the [illegible], in the man producing the licence if it were only known that the [illegible]?—There might be difficulty on the day on which he was summoned.

[illegible]. Surely not; the wholesale people would make no difficulty about that if it were known to be a necessity?—I should think they would not, but in some cases there may be some difficulty.

[illegible]. (Chairman.) Is there any practice of adjourning the magistrates' court in favour of the applicant for a beer licence to which you take exception?—The magistrates have on several occasions done so when an application was made at the annual licensing sessions for a new beer dealer's licence. The police have opposed on the ground that the man was not three months in occupation. This is a condition attached to the granting of a beer dealer's licence, which prohibits the granting of this licence until he is three months in exclusive occupation of the premises.

Three months' occupation for beer licence.

[illegible]. That would apply to a grocer?—No, to a beer dealer only.

[illegible]. Would it apply to a grocer wishing to take out a beer licence?—No, it would not. It applies to a beer dealer, and of course to a spirit grocer who wishes to become both. There is this condition, which seems to me to be an [illegible] one (and I do not know the object for which it was [illegible] in the Act of Parliament), of being three months in occupation. The magistrates have frequently on the application adjourned the hearing of the case for a month in order to enable the man to be his regular time in possession. This of course means that the annual licensing sessions are adjourned for a month, as the beer dealer's licence can only be granted then. We think that that condition might [illegible] be taken away; that is, that he should be three months exclusively in occupation.

[illegible]. The magistrates give him time, so to speak, to qualify?—The magistrates say that it is hard on a man who happens to be only two months in occupation, when the annual licensing sessions come, that he cannot get this licence, and consequently they adjourn the hearing of the case until he has been a certain time in possession.

[illegible]. Is it an offence for a man to be found drinking in a spirit grocer's shop?—No, it is not. We consider that it ought to be made an offence.

Drinking on spirit grocers' premises.

[illegible]. It is an offence for the man who serves, but not for the man who drinks. You would impose a penalty on the man who drinks as well as on the man who serves?—I think on both. I do not think that the man who sells should be the only person who should be punished.

[illegible]. Finally, I would ask you as to the annual licensing sessions. Do you observe that there is a very large attendance of magistrates at the annual licensing sessions?—Yes; I notice that at the annual licensing sessions, magistrates attend and sit on the bench whom I very seldom see there at any other time of the year.

Canvassing of magistrates.

[illegible]. Have you any reason to suppose that these magistrates are canvassed to vote for a particular man [illegible] [illegible]?

[illegible]. Can you speak of your own knowledge, or from what you are credibly informed, as to the practice of canvassing the magistrates in Belfast?—I really believe that they are canvassed on both sides.

[illegible]. Is the Recorder canvassed?—No, I am sure [illegible]

Mr. R. Morell. — Mar. '98. — Canvassing.

would recommend that the fact of doing such a thing should disqualify an applicant altogether.

57,413. (Mr. Younger.) What would you do if his friends canvassed?—I would disqualify him also.

57,414. It would be rather hard on him, would it not? Because a man might go and pretend to be a friend of his, when he really did not want him to get a licence?—I presume he could be prosecuted in the civil court, if he did such a thing as that.

57,415. (Mr Graham.) Is it not a matter of fact that when a Bill affecting the liquor trade comes before the House of Commons, the members are canvassed on both sides, by temperance organisations on the one side and parties in favour of the trade?—I do not think there is that same, though, there is any criminal proceeding perhaps, or anything of that kind. The granting of a public-house licence is a different thing from a Bill before Parliament.

57,416. But it may affect the trade just as seriously? —Yes.

57,417. (Mr. Younger.) If you disqualified the trader who applied for a licence, you would have no direct way to punish the man who canvassed against that licence—he would lose nothing unless you punished him in some other way?—I do not think the magistrates should be canvassed by any one.

57,418. The publican who is canvassing, or his friend, has something to lose; the other man has nothing to lose?—A publican has nothing to lose. He has not got anything.

57,419. He has the prospect of getting that which might be very valuable?—Well, yes.

57,420. (Chairman.) I suppose you would say there was a difference between a legislator and a magistrate?—I should think there is.

57,421. I really do not want to argue it, but would not you also say, as the question has been asked you, that a legislator does not deal with a particular case in the same way that it would be dealt with in the case of a magistrate?—I should think that if the practice of canvassing were continued in Ireland, and that if the people got to know that if Mr. So-and-so canvassed his influence, a man would get a licence, it would destroy all confidence in the administration of the law.

57,422. (Mr. Young.) The magistrates are placed in an administrative position, whereas members of the House of Commons are in a legislative position, and there is no parity between the two?—It does not seem to me that there is much.

57,423. It is the business of the magistrates simply to administer the law?—Yes.

57,424. It is the business of the others to create or make the law?—Yes.

57,425. So that canvassing is a different thing in the two positions?—No doubt of it.

57,426. (Mr. Graham.) It is desirable in the one, and not desirable in the other?—I am not familiar with the House of Commons procedure.

Grocers' off-licences.

57,427. (Chairman.) Assuming that the spirit grocers' and the beer dealers' licences are to remain under the present system, do you think that as an improvement of the law, these licences should be granted in a different way to what they are at present, and at a different value to what they are at present? Do you think, for instance, they should be granted at the annual licensing sessions exclusively?—Certainly; I think they should, and of course, as I am suggesting, by the recorder.

Notice of applications.

57,428. Should the petty sessions have notice of what are granted?—Assuming that the law is to remain as it is at present, I think that a notice should be served on

they considered would be the best one or two licences to grant out of three.

Mr. R. Morell.

57,429. Could they not do that now?—I do not think that under the present law there is anything compelling the applicant to serve such a notice.

Habitual drunkards.

57,430. (Mr Algernon West.) You gave us some rather startling statistics about habitual drunkenness, and the number of convictions; and I think you said that you considered the present law perfectly inadequate to deal with it?—I do.

57,431. Then you suggested that power should be given to the magistrates after a certain number of convictions within a certain time to sentence to six months' imprisonment?—Yes.

57,432. Are you of opinion that six months imprisonment is sufficient to cure an habitual drunkard?—I do not think it would cure him, but I do say, that an habitual drunkard is a man who likes six months hard labour; and if he is a man who has got been much in prison but has been able to pay fines, he would find that the six months imprisonment with hard labour is not pleasant.

57,433. Six months imprisonment would have no deterrent effect or curative effect afterwards, would it? —That is a thing upon which I really could not offer an opinion.

57,434. You have not studied the question of foreign countries as regards habitual drunkards?—I have not.

57,435. But you say the present law is perfectly inadequate?—Perfectly inadequate. Of course, the magistrates might have the power of adding a condition binding the man to the peace at the expiration of the time, and if he was not able to find sureties, he should get an additional six months in default of bail.

Black list of habitual drunkards.

57,436. (Provost de Fonti.) Would you be in favour of publishing particulars in the way of habitual drunkards obtaining liquor in any way? It has been recommended and suggested here that a list of habitual drunkards might be distributed to licence holders, and that the licence holders should be prohibited, as far as possible, from selling liquor to them. Would that be feasible in a place like Belfast?—I think in a place like Belfast it might work for some time, but as the town gradually became larger—assuming it got to the size of Glasgow—I think it would have very little effect. I think at present it is a good idea.

57,437. The town is on the increase and likely by absorb all the suburbs?—It has done so already.

57,438. And probably will in the future?—Yes.

Licensed premises and dwelling houses.

57,440. Would you be in favour of a condition which has been attached by the magistrates in Scotland, preventing any interior communication between the private premises of the licence holder and the public-house?—I do not think that would work in Ireland, especially in the country districts. I do not see how a man could be compelled in a poor class of house to separate his dwelling house from the place in which he carries on his ordinary trade.

57,441. I understand that it works this way in Scotland. At the hour for closing, he locks the door; he has to go round by another entry to get to his own part of the house, and he is not allowed to be on the premises during closing hours?—I have already suggested as regards spirit grocers' and beer dealers' licences that they should be absolutely and entirely separate from the dwelling premises, and I do not see why it should not work as regards publicans in large towns.

57,442. You think it might be enforced with regard to public-houses?—I think it might. I had not considered the question before, but I think it might.

[illegible]

57,447. That was a licence to licensed [illegible], that is, of [illegible]. I do not intend to trouble you with statistics as to other places, as to which witnesses will be called. With respect to working men's clubs, you think that there would not be much demand on the part of the working men of Belfast for the establishment of these clubs?—I do not think the working men of Belfast are of the class who would desire them.

57,448. Do you think working men's clubs ought to be licensed, registered, and open to inspection?—That is a question which I have not gone into, but, speaking at present, I should think that they should not. I do not see why the working men's clubs should be put on a different footing.

57,449. I am not proposing that. I hold that there should be equal law for rich and poor. Do you think that all clubs, what we call in London West End clubs, should be licensed, registered, and liable to inspection, and that there should be perfect equality on that point? In that point of view, do you not think it might be right and proper that working men's clubs should be registered, licensed, and open to inspection?—If it were done in one case, I should support its being done in all, but, so far as Belfast is concerned, there are no such things as bogus clubs.

Licences to passenger boats.

57,450. With respect to licences for drinking on steamers, who should be held responsible for allowing drunkenness or the giving of drink to intoxicated persons on board a steamer?—The owner of the steamer, I should think.

57,451. The company?—They have the licence.

57,452. It is very difficult for a company to control it. I suppose they should be held responsible for the misconduct?—Any prosecution that might be instituted would be instituted against the person who had the licence.

57,453. Is the licence held in the name of the company or of the secretary?—Of the secretary of the company.

57,454. Then he is the person who would be responsible?—Certainly he would be.

Public houses not compensated.

57,455. One does see drunken people sometimes on steamers. When those public houses were taken down for the improvement of the town and for the construction of new streets, did the publicans receive compensation in respect of the property—the houses themselves?—They did.

57,456. Did they receive any compensation in respect of the licences?—In some cases they did. They got another licence.

57,457. Were they allowed by the magistrates to transfer their licences to some other part of the town?—Not exactly some other part of the town, but they were allowed by the Recorder to transfer the licences to a place convenient to the district in which the old house had been pulled down.

57,458. Was that done in all cases?—I think it was. No, I think, perhaps, there were one or two cases in which the licence is past, but I am not quite sure about that.

57,459. You cannot mention any instance in which compensation was given by the corporation in respect of the licence?—The corporation did not give compensation for licences.

57,460. But, in respect of the houses, who gave compensation?—The corporation. The licence is not taken into consideration in the compensation that is given.

57,461. Not taken into consideration at all?—No.

57,462. They either lapsed or were transferred?—Yes.

Mr. H. [illegible]. 16 May '98

head constable in charge of the police station, before whom these prostitutes are always brought when they are drunk.

37,484. You are not prepared to charge ordinary drunkenness with the bulk of the serious crimes of the [illegible], such as assault and murder?—I think myself that in very many cases drunkenness is certainly the cause of some of those offences which you have named.

37,485. Would it be your opinion that a man often gets drunk or takes more than is necessary in order to give him courage to perpetrate what he intends to do?—No, I should not say so.

37,486. That is not your opinion?—No.

Supply of food with drink.

37,487. With respect to the public-houses trusted by you drinking [illegible], has it come under your observation that when the [illegible] were established in London the magistrates imposed a condition that they should not supply liquor without certain food; so that, when a customer entered, they forced upon him a small biscuit before they would supply him with drink. Would not that be the case in Belfast if that were enforced?—Do you mean on the publicans?

37,488. Yes. Would not there be subterfuges adopted to evade any law of that kind?—I dare say there would.

37,489. (Dean Dickinson.) Not if they are the respectable men you say they are?—Well, they are a respectable body.

Restaurants.

37,490. (Mr. Walker.) Supposing the public-houses suddenly offered facilities for the consumption of food, would they not claim to be as much restaurants as the other houses that receive that name?—Certainly they would.

37,491. They would all become restaurants?—Yes; but I would cease the houses. I would not allow a restaurant [illegible] to get a license on the same terms as I would a public-house.

37,492. A witness here, speaking from experience, said that a customer may enter a restaurant, sit down and take something trifling to eat, and have 40 glasses of whisky, if he thought proper?—I do not suppose there is anything to prevent him.

37,493. Then, so far as the consumption of liquor is concerned, there is no difference between the two establishments?—I should think in any case such as you mention, of a man going into a restaurant and drinking a considerable quantity of whisky, if that fact were brought to the notice of the magistrates who granted the license they would refuse to renew it at the next sessions, on the ground that it was a drinking shop.

37,494. I am not assuming that it is a case to be found fault with. You do not deny that there is a great deal of consumption of spirits and beer in restaurants?—There is a great deal.

37,495. Why do they ask for the license if there is no trade?—They hold the publican's license at present in Belfast.

37,496. Have not licenses been granted very freely to restaurants in Belfast?—No, I should say not very freely. I only know of one additional license having been granted to a restaurant in five years.

37,497. You are willing to admit that there is really no difference between the two licenses, if they both supply food?—Both should supply food.

37,498. Very often the restaurant drops the furnishing of food and becomes an ordinary public-house?—Yes. My reason for thinking that a supply of food should be given both in restaurants and public-houses would encourage people to go to a place where there are some other attractions besides drink. If a man goes to the theatre he comes out at 10 o'clock at night and finds all the public-houses closed; I think there should be some place to which he could go and at which he could get supper, and, if necessary, drink with it.

Mr. H. [illegible].

37,501. Of course, that is an assumption that it is not possible to get anything to eat in a public-house?—A public-house would be closed according to my proposal at 10 o'clock.

37,502. But still a restaurant which supplied liquor just as freely as a public-house should be allowed to keep open longer?—Yes.

Sunday closing.

37,503. Have you any objection to give the reason of your suggestion that the public-houses should be open on Sunday only from 2 to 5?—I consider that the public-houses being open from 2 to 5 on a Sunday, gives the people a reasonable time to obtain refreshments.

37,504. Do you think they can drink sufficient during those three hours to last them the whole day?—Yes. We also consider that it does not seem right that public-houses should be putting their customers out at the very same time that people are going on to Divine service.

37,505. Under the present condition of things, you allege that there are 60 suspected houses in Belfast, shebeens or illicit places for the sale of drink?—Yes.

37,506. If the hours were curtailed to 3 till 5, would it not be calculated to increase these illicit establishments?—I should think that it would probably increase the illegal sale of spirit grocers' establishments and of shebeens.

37,507. That shows at once that it is a remedy rather to lengthen the hours than to curtail them?—I do not know that it would increase it to any very great extent.

37,508. You have expressed your opinion that the respectable class of workmen would not encourage or connive at establishing, or patronising, or dealing with, or visiting any of these illicit places, and yet you are afraid to trust them with legitimate established houses?—No; I do not think I am afraid to trust them. I do not believe that the majority of working men of Belfast are in Belfast at all on Sunday.

37,509. You do not think that the respectable class of working men require these refreshments? I think where they go, there is outside Belfast altogether, to Bangor, and Larne and other outside places on the Sunday.

37,510. Do you not admit that curtailing the hours is calculated to increase the establishment of these illicit places? You say that respectable working men would not encourage these establishments. Then are they to be deprived because they are more or less of a higher standard? Are they to submit to self-denial more than the class who would readily take advantage of any opportunity?—As a matter of fact, the public-houses are very little used on Sunday in Belfast, and I think we should give the people who are in the public-houses, the barmen and the owners, and everybody else, a couple more hours to themselves on Sundays. That is another reason for it.

37,511. Do you say, as believing it, that holidays are the cause of drunkenness?—I am certain of it. On the occasion of the 12th of July in Belfast, which is a general holiday there, there would be more drunkenness on that day and the next day than there would be on any other two days in the week.

57,516. It had no official sanction?—No, I do not think so.

57,517. (Dean Dickinson.) There were informal returns to the House of Commons?—Yes.

57,518. (Mr. Walker.) You have also given it as your opinion that publichouse licenses in value vary considerably. What do you really think that is due to? Is it due to a stronger feeling of security?—Yes.

57,519. A better order of things; more respect for law and order?—No, I think mainly on account of the non-granting of other public-house licenses.

57,520. We have evidence that restaurant licenses have been granted freely?—Oh, no; I did not say that. I said there was only one restaurant license granted in the last five years. It is the spirit grocers I am speaking of.

57,521. One kind of license has been increased very considerably, and yet the publichouse licenses have increased in value?—The publichouse license is, of course, different from the spirit grocer's.

57,522. Does not that exhibit the fact that there is a stronger feeling of security in the mind of the trade as to the value, and their right of possession?—They always had that feeling in Ireland. The law there is different from what it is in England.

57,523. It was never demonstrated so clearly until the case of The Queen v. Cithero?—Yes.

57,524. You gave your opinion that a drunken man being found on licensed premises, *ipso facto* the publican was guilty of an offence?—It is only a suggestion.

57,525. How far are you prepared to enforce that? A man may come from the street evidently now a licensed [illegible] before anybody can possibly notice him; a constable enters in and discovers him—is that to be treated as a serious offence?—A publichouse is a place meant for the convenience of the public, and I do not think it ought to be made the resort of drunken people coming in from the streets. I think any publican who wished to conduct his place properly would have a person at the door to see that these sort of people did not enter in.

57,526. You would attach a condition that the publican should have a specially appointed person to see that no drunken person entered?—If he wished to conduct his place properly, I should think he ought to do that.

57,527. Do any of the large commercial establishments of Belfast supply refreshments to their boys, in the shape of spirits, beer, and wine?—Do you mean licensed persons?

57,528. No; large commercial establishments?—Where there are employés who live on the premises?

57,529. Yes; are there any?—I could not say. The only ones that I know do not, I think.

57,530. There are large linen establishments at Belfast, are there not?—Yes.

57,531. You know of no instance?—The only instances I can speak of from memory at present are the Bank Buildings and Arnott's, which are two large drapery establishments.

57,532. Do they supply drink or give drink to their customers?—I thought you said employés. The employés do not get anything.

57,533. Have they established a counter or a bar on their premises for the supplying of their boys and their customers?—I do not know of any such case. It would not be allowed in Belfast.

57,534. It is prevalent in London.—If they supplied their customers with drink, I should think it would be a shebeen.

57,535. They may give it to their customers?—It would be practically selling it, because they would not give it to them for nothing.

57,536. (Mr. Green.) Have Arnott's got a restaurant for the use of their customers?—No, but they have a dining-room.

57,537. For the use of their customers?—No; for the use of their employés. Robinson and Cleaver have a restaurant for the use of their customers, but there is no license attached to it—no wine selling.

57,538. (Mr. Hughes.) I have a few questions to put to you arising out of the evidence you have given to us today which I should be obliged if you would answer. I notice that in Belfast you have 449 publicans' licenses granted?—Yes.

57,539. In addition to those you have 445 grocers' licenses?—Yes, that is so.

57,540. That would make a total of licenses granted of 1,094?—Yes.

57,541. In your experience of Belfast, do you find this number in excess of the requirements of the people?—We consider it is greatly in excess as regards the spirit grocers.

57,542. Would you show us in what way you consider the 449 publicans' licenses are in excess of the requirements of the people?—The 449 publicans' licenses we do not consider excessive.

57,543. It is the 445 spirit grocers' licenses?—That is what we object to.

57,544. I notice you have spoken more favourably of the publicans as to the way they have conducted their business in your city?—Yes.

57,545. May I take it that you could not suggest any alteration with regard to the licensing laws in that respect; that those houses are well conducted, and that you cannot suggest any improvement?—No. Except the suggestions I have already made, I have nothing further to add as to how the public-houses could be better conducted than they are at present.

57,546. With regard to the other 445 licenses you have spoken of, you thought they were a great evil in many respects?—We do in every respect.

57,547. There seems to be a disreputable system of selling spirits and beer as groceries?—There is no doubt that that exists.

57,548. I notice that you have only given us two cases out of the whole of that number that could be charged with such an offence?—I have given a reason why I can only give those instances. I consider I am very fortunate in being able to give those cases, on account of the difficulty of procuring evidence on such a subject. The party who commits the offence—if I may call it an offence—the spirit grocer, will naturally give no information to the police. The woman who receives the goods as groceries will certainly not tell her husband and she will not tell the police, so that we have no possible means of getting at it except from police prosecutions that taken place.

57,549. May I ask if the husband does not pay for those groceries?—He does, I presume.

57,550. Is not that a very likely way in which he would come to possession of the facts if he had to pay? He would inquire what he had to pay for if he found it in the book?—He sees it put down as groceries in the total amount.

57,551. There is where you see the deception?—Yes, it is a deception.

57,552. Would it be fair, considering there are 445 grocers' licenses, on account of these two instances to brand the other 443?—Certainly. I think the spirit grocers deserve no word of praise from me because we know from our reports that they evade the law in every other respect, and if they do so in these other respects we have no reason to arrive at any other conclusion than that they are evading the law in this respect.

57,553. One pleasing part of your evidence is that you consider there is a slight decrease in drunkenness in the city of Belfast?—Yes, we do.

57,554. You have ascribed that to three reasons I think?—Yes.

57,555. The first would be that they consume more beer and less spirits?—We think so.

57,556. The next reason you say is the temperance societies?—Yes, and to the efforts of the clergy, and I may say the Salvation Army very greatly.

57,557. The last is that there is no chance of getting a new license—that no new licenses are to be obtained in the city, or very few?—I think there are none; but I do not think that has anything to do with the action of the temperance societies, though they took part in opposing them. I think it is solely on account of the

Mr. H. [illegible]

[illegible]

Liquor charged as other goods.

Decrease of drunkenness.

Mr. [illegible]. [illegible]

19 Mar. '96

57,558. I think there is another great factor that is bringing about temperance, and that is the spread of education?—Yes.

57,559. Do you believe that that has an effect in your city?—I do believe it has.

Connection of drink and crime.

57,560. There is rather a confusing statement in this, and that is, you have attributed crime to the direct outcome of drink, and you have put it that 75 per cent. of the crimes committed in Belfast are due to drink?—What I mean by crime is, of course, offences. You cannot class the offence of drunkenness itself as a crime, but it is still an offence for which the police are bound to arrest.

57,561. I should like to know what test you apply to ascertain whether a crime or an offence that has been committed is the direct outcome of drink?—As I said in my direct evidence there are no statistics available for the purpose. It is almost impossible to obtain any reliable statistics, and the only evidence I can give is derived from the opinions of others.

57,562. May I sum it up as guess-work?—A good deal of it is.

57,563. (Mr. Caine.) Would you not rather infer, if a great number of criminals were drunk when arrested, that drink was the cause of the crime?—If drunk when arrested they would be prevented from committing an offence.

57,564. (Dean Dickinson.) You do not find any temperance people amongst the criminals?—There have been.

57,565. (Mr. Hyslop.) If the father of a family has been convicted for being drunk and afterwards the son commits an offence, will he be charged with having committed that offence through the direct outcome of drink because the father happened to have a conviction against him for being drunk?—I do not think the sins of the fathers are visited on the children in that way.

57,566. Have you some experience of the general licensing system throughout the whole of Ireland?—My experience is more in Belfast. I have served five years in the county of Kilkenny.

57,567. The law is pretty similar throughout Ireland?—It is.

57,568. A previous witness from Ireland gave us some figures with reference to the total number of publicans' licenses as being 17,[illegible], 14,[illegible] holding seven-day licenses?—Those are, I presume, the publicans altogether.

57,569. Yes. I should like to ask you what can be the reason for 14,[illegible] out of this 17,[illegible] holding seven-day licenses while there are only five cities exempted from the Sunday Closing Act?—I could not answer that question.

57,570. (Mr. Whittaker.) They could not serve a bona fide traveller on Sunday if they had not a seven-day license?—They could not. Unless that is the reason, I do not think there is any other reason.

57,571. (Mr. Hyslop.) They contribute in some places a good deal to the revenue of the town?—They have to pay more for the seven-day license.

Sunday closing.

57,572. With reference to Sunday closing, we have had a good deal of evidence this morning, and I think you say it would have a good effect?—Yes, I think it would.

57,573. That is in Belfast?—Yes.

57,574. You think the majority of the people would be against it?—I should think in Belfast the majority would be in favour.

57,575. Would a plebiscite of [illegible] out of [illegible] inhabitants justify an alteration in the law with reference to Sunday closing?—The figures here were taken in 1888.

57,576. The population would not be as large then as it is now; but you have it that the population of Belfast is [illegible], while I find the voters recorded in favour of Sunday closing were only [illegible] out of that number?—That was the point I was going to mention. Before the extension of the borough of Belfast there were [illegible] houses in it. I do not know whether the plebiscite was only taken of the householder, or taken of his family as well.

57,577. (Dean Dickinson.) Householders?—If it was taken of the householders it would be, I suppose, about one third of the number of the householders in the

Mr. [illegible]

57,578. (Mr. Hyslop.) Belfast is one of the exempted cities from Sunday closing?—Yes.

57,579. You would suggest an alteration, that the houses of these publicans should be totally closed the whole of Sunday?—No; we do not suggest that.

57,580. Then you are not in favour of the Bill that is before Parliament at the present time to close them altogether?—No. We are in favour of restricted hours from 2 o'clock to 5.

Sunday drunkenness.

57,581. In your figures you have given for Sunday drunkenness, charged with that offence on that day, 442 cases?—Yes, I think that is so.

57,582. Have you any knowledge of how these 442 cases, where the houses were open, would compare in proportion to population with some other large town where the houses are closed?—I have not; but I should think a witness who comes after me will be able to give you information as to a city in Ireland, Londonderry, where the public-houses are closed, and a comparison could be arrived at.

57,583. If we are to believe in the good effect that this Act of 1878 has produced, we must believe that if you had Sunday Closing in Belfast you would get rid of the whole of these 442 cases?—I do not think you would. If you closed them the whole week, I am sure we should have plenty of work to do in arresting drunken people.

57,584. I find from the statistics that it had in Galway the extreme effect that the closing of public-houses increased nearly double the number of drunken cases on a Sunday. Then the other question I have to put to you is this: There was evidence given by a witness last week that in the counties of Donegal, Galway, Mayo, and Sligo, illicit distillation was very prevalent?—Yes.

57,585. Would you explain the prevalence of these illicit stills when there is a plentiful supply in the houses in the neighbourhood?—I really do not know much about the counties alluded to. I have only been travelling through them, not on duty but on pleasure occasionally. The only reason I could suggest is that the people in these places are so poor that they are very glad to raise money in any possible way they can.

57,586. Might I suggest to you that the restriction of closing these houses absolutely during the Sunday has brought these illicit stills into existence?—I really could not offer an opinion that would be worth much. My own opinion would be that it does not come through that. I should think it is for the reason I say, that the people are so poor that they are driven to their extremity to make a few pence.

57,587. They are so poor that they are driven to evade the duty on the spirits?—It is for the purpose of selling, I believe, that they make this whisky, not for drinking themselves.

57,588. It must be either from the restrictions or for evading the duty. You made a statement with reference to the trains on Saturday, that the trains were frequently delayed by drunken passengers?—Yes.

57,589. Is that a frequent occurrence?—Yes. I am sure it is, especially with the outside trains.

57,590. I thought the trains were not allowed to carry drunken people—that the railway people would not have them?—I think it would be hard lines if they brought them down sober, and they came to the railway station by the last train to get home, that they should refuse to take them in, if they had taken a little too much drink.

Bona fide travellers.

57,591. That is a consideration for the traveller. Now does the bona fide traveller get on?—I think the bona fide traveller gets on remarkably well. I do not think anybody is better treated than he is.

57,592. Do you think it would be a good thing to impose on the publican an increased obligation to put to him test questions with reference to where he is going, and where he has been, and how far he has travelled?—I think if he wants to get a drink the bona fide traveller will get a drink no matter what questions are put to him.

57,593. The question we should is put to him. Do you not consider that sufficient?—I do not think it is enough to ask a man where he slept the night before on open bar [illegible]

[illegible]

17,657. You have a smelt grower's license?—Yes. I

17,635. In England, of course, they are not. Then, I understand further, you think that it would be an improvement if spirits were only allowed to be sold on off-licensed premises in closed bottles?—I do not advocate that, because, as I said before, I think in Ireland certainly the use of beer and porter should be encouraged.

17,636. I was going to except beer—so far as regards spirits and wine?—I think it certainly should be sold in sealed bottles.

17,637. There is an object with regard to beer, because it is an article of low value and has not the same keeping qualities as wine?—It does not keep so long.

17,638. I understand that your contention is that the spirit grocer's licence in Ireland has done a great amount of harm?—I speak altogether as regards Belfast. I have no experience of it in other parts of Ireland.

17,639. What would be the reason why Belfast should have gone so particularly wrong in this respect, because Belfast holds more than one half of the whole spirit grocers' licences in Ireland?—I think the reason it has done so much harm is that it has encouraged drinking habits amongst females.

17,640. On that point may I ask you did you read the evidence of Judge [illegible] last week?—I did.

17,641. I am sure you would like to guard yourself, as he did. When pressed on the question as to grocers entering spirits as groceries, he said he had no positive evidence—that it was rumour?—Yes; I heard that he said so.

17,642. Rumour is rather a dangerous thing in these cases, is not it, to support a statement upon?—Rumour does a great deal of harm in Belfast.

17,643. I understand you would be in favour of transferring the granting of all licences in Belfast to the Recorder?—Yes.

17,644. You think in that way you would concentrate the working of the licensing system in strong hands?—I think, in addition to that, it would add to the uniformity of decisions.

17,645. On the point of convincing the magistrates, it does not do to aim at a too high state of purity in these things, because there is a certain quantity of canvassing that goes on almost all over the world. You admit yourself you have been canvassed?—I do.

17,646. And you were surprised at it?—I was surprised at the man being such a fool.

17,647. You are quite aware it is a common thing where people's interests are at stake that canvassing will go on?—I thought the man a fool to canvass a man whom he knew was going to oppose his licence.

17,648. You think you could frame a law to prevent it?—I would.

17,649. With reference to Sunday drunkenness, can

17,650. You are in favour of giving the magistrates absolute discretion over all licences?—Yes; I wish to transfer it to the recorder altogether.

17,651. You think there is the same remedy for absolute discretion on the part of the magistrates in the case of selling an article simply for consumption away as there is where the article is consumed in a place of public resort?—Yes, I think so.

17,652. May I ask you whether you have ever heard of similar circumstances abroad. For instance, in France every man can sell wine and spirits for consumption away from the premises, and it is not recognised as doing any great harm in France?—The only country which I have any experience of except Ireland is Norway. I have been there, and I made some inquiries when I was there, and I found that the sale of spirits was restricted to four or five houses in the whole of Norway, and there is no crime.

17,653. We all regard the condition of things in Norway as rather abnormal?—I think if we had fewer spirit shops here we should be approaching Norway in the matter.

17,654. As to the conviction of licence-holders for persons being found drunk on their premises, I should like to know in your opinion if the word "knowingly" were removed with reference to that offence, would it help the police?—I do not know that it would help it if the publican was not there himself. He could not be held to be knowingly supplying if it was supplied by his servant.

17,655. Would it not be a protection to the licence-holder as well as an assistance to the police, that that should be made a condition?—I am afraid it would not be of much use.

17,656. Should I be correct in saying that drunkenness on licensed premises is practically unknown in Belfast, and that there have been no convictions for a number of years?—There have been very few at any rate.

17,657. One question on that plebiscite, to get the thing perfectly straight. I understand that the licensed victuallers succeeded in getting by canvassing 25,000 votes. Is that correct?—I have heard it is.

17,658. I am told that the publicans in three days, without canvassing, obtained voluntarily from the shop and shopkeepers 25,000 signatures. Are you aware of that?—No. I was not in Belfast at that time. I am sure both these figures could be collected with some trouble.

17,659. Under the circumstances the 25,000 are entitled to equal consideration, are they not, looking at the means by which these signatures were obtained?—I am sure there are more than 25,000 people in Belfast who use public-houses.

17,660. It rather shows the danger of this argument from plebiscites, does it not?—I really do not know [illegible] the licence, puts him out and supplies a new manager, and the police are not able to get the licence forfeited.

57,673. There is a transfer of licence in that case?— There is a transfer. If there was another conviction during the year there would be probably a forfeiture.

57,674. Is it not an advantage to get rid of the bad manager and to put in a new good manager?—It is a good thing, but it would not be so good as if we could close a spirit grocer altogether.

57,675. I am not speaking of the spirit grocer's, but a publican's licence?—I do not think there are many publicans' licences in the hands of the wholesale men, not any great proportion of them. They are most of them owned by the people who live there.

57,676. I am requested to ask you this. Have you anything to say against the well-conducted spirit grocers in Belfast?—No, I have not. There are a certain number of the larger houses that are undoubtedly very well conducted.

57,677. I presume it is the system you object to?—It is the system of grouping them as they have been grouped in localities and back streets where, in the first place, no supervision can be had over them, by the police, and where the illegal trade can be carried on without interruption.

57,678. Are there too many public-houses in Belfast?—No, I do not think there are, considering the population, but I think there are enough.

57,679. I think you said there was an increase of convictions in Belfast?—I think it is a decrease.

57,680. What I want to draw attention to is this, that for very many years the total arrests in Belfast have been decreasing?—Yes.

57,681. In 1867 when there were only 147,000 inhabitants you had 10,[illegible] arrests?—Yes.

57,682. That continued very much the same until 1871?—Yes.

57,683. When they decreased to 7,[illegible]?—Yes.

57,684. And then they kept rather steadily decreasing until in 1887 there were 4,[illegible]?—Yes.

57,685. Therefore you agree with me, I presume, that there is a decrease of arrests and a decrease of crime?— There is certainly a decrease since 1871 in the number of prosecutions for drunkenness and arrests for drunkenness.

57,686. I suppose, so far as the public-houses are concerned, they are very much the same as they were in 1871. The number then was [illegible], and in 1887 there were [illegible] notwithstanding the increase of the population?—Yes, practically the same.

57,687. So that I presume you are of the opinion that the trade is well conducted in Belfast, and that it has not added largely to the crime of the place?—The publicans' business is carried on as well as it could possibly be.

57,688. Your suggestion is that on Sunday the houses should be open from 2 o'clock to 7?—From 2 to 4 in place of 2 to 7.

57,689. You suggest that on Saturday nights they should be closed at 10 o'clock?—Yes.

57,690. Now in regard to the licensing authority, whether it be for grocers' or publicans' licences, you would confine it to the county court judge in counties and to the Recorder in boroughs, and you would, I presume, exclude all authority on the part of the magistrates?—Well, I should not like to give a definite opinion as regards counties, but as regards Belfast it is my own opinion, and that of all the other officers, that there should be only one licensing authority for all classes of licences in Belfast. In a county it might be advisable that some sort of licensing committee should be appointed, such as I suggested as an alternative in Belfast, consisting of the resident magistrates and a certain number of the magistrates of the county selected out of the whole of them to adjudicate on these licences.

57,691. (Baron Dickinson.) With an appeal to the county court judge?—Yes, I think that would be fair.

57,692. (Mr. Young.) I presume it is not a reflection upon the magistrates, but it is in this way, I presume, that the magistrates in a borough are chiefly merchants?—They are.

57,693. And supposing a wholesale tea dealer sits to grant or refuse licences, he probably has a connection with the person who is seeking the licence?—I should think in the case of the spirit grocer he has not only a connection, but has a very large interest. I do not think a man of that kind should sit.

57,694. So that without being corrupt at all, I presume he is influenced by the considerations of trade?—I am afraid that that would affect a great many of them.

57,695. So that you are distinctly of the opinion that the licensing should be withdrawn from the magistrates of the borough?—I am strongly of that opinion.

57,696. And you are of opinion also that the licensing authority, whether in the borough or in the county, should have the same discretionary power in regard to a grocer's licence as they have now with reference to a publican's licence?—Yes, that the grounds should be the same for a spirit grocer and beer dealer as they are for a publican.

57,697. Do those large grocers who hold retail licences come under the class of what is called domestic licences, if there be such?—I think we have had them referred to [illegible] licences?—I think that refers not so much to grocers as to wholesale whisky merchants. There are only one or two of these grocers that I can recollect at present who hold such a licence and do not use it, and they hold the licence in order to sell the small quantity.

57,698. Is it your opinion that the three-gallon licence, which is known in England but not in Ireland, would be a sufficient substitute for those large grocers who hold this licence, and for the large spirit merchants?— There is another way of meeting the difficulty, which would be that a licence should be granted for the consumption of any kind of drink, no matter what quantity, off the premises alone. That would be practically raising the limit that spirit grocers are allowed to possess from two quarts to two gallons, and make the two licences equivalent. That sort of licence would also meet their wishes.

57,699. (Mr. Gilbey.) They would also be able to sell less than two quarts down to any quantity?— Yes. That is a matter for the traders themselves, and really I am not sure what conclusion they have arrived at. I understand they are holding some meeting on the subject themselves.

57,700. (Mr. Young.) The three-gallon licence will not allow less than a quart bottle to be sold?—Then the licence that I suggest would allow anything. I would suggest simply giving a licence for consumption off the premises in any quantity.

57,701. (Mr. Gilbey.) And in open or closed vessels? —I should think it ought to be in closed vessels.

57,702. It would come down to such a small quantity that it would be difficult to put it in a closed vessel?— I think they would be able to carry it away in some way or other.

57,703. (Mr. Young.) You were asked about Bills before the House with reference to the suspension of licences. Do you think that Sunday Closing Bills should be suspended until after the report of this Commission? There are Bills before the House for Sunday closing, and, in your opinion, should they also be suspended?—I think, perhaps, it would be as well if they waited till the Commission arrived at their report. Of course that is a point I could not give any opinion about.

The witness withdrew.

Mr. Charles W. Langham called in and examined.

57,704. (Chairman.) You are the County Inspector of the Royal Irish Constabulary for Londonderry?— Yes.

57,705. You first of all desire, I think, to hand in a series of tables relating to the city and the county of Londonderry?—Yes.

57,706. What do Tables I. and II. show?—They show [illegible]

Mr. G. W. Leathem.

28 Mar. '98

57,708. The population has of course increased since 18[illegible]?—The population has increased but the number of licensed houses has somewhat decreased.

57,709. The number of six-day licenses bears a very large proportion, does it not, to the whole number of publicans' licenses?—Nearly two-thirds of the whole number of publicans' licenses.

57,710. Then in Tables VIII. and IX. you show the corresponding figures for the county?—Yes.

57,711. Has the population increased or decreased?—The population of the county has decreased. The number of licenses has increased.

57,712. In what direction?—Especially in spirit grocers.

Six-day licenses.

57,713. What proportion does the number of six-day licenses bear to the whole?—Less than one-third of the whole in the county of Londonderry.

Before and after Sunday closing.

57,714. Going back to Table III., what does that table show?—It shows the arrests for drunkenness and shebeening for periods of five years immediately before and after the Sunday Closing Act in the city.

57,715. What has been the effect on Sunday drunkenness in the city, of that Closing Act?—It has decreased.

57,716. Has there been a uniform decrease?—There has.

57,717. And week-day drunkenness, what has been the effect on that?—The week-day drunkenness has decreased 18 per cent. during the first five years after the Sunday Closing Act, and the Sunday 82 per cent.

57,718. Has there not been a great increase in the week-day drunkenness of late?—In the years 1895, 1896, and 1897 there was a slight increase.

57,719. What is the condition of shebeening?—There was a slight increase after the Sunday Closing Act; but that has gone down to vanishing point latterly.

57,720. Then having given us in Table III. the arrests for drunkenness and shebeening for periods of five years in the city, you give, do you not, in Table X. the corresponding figures for the county?—Yes.

57,721. Can you summarise those in the way you have done the others? What about week-day drunkenness?—The week-day drunkenness decreased in the county of Londonderry 14 per cent. during the five years after the Sunday closing.

57,722. Had it increased after the Sunday Closing Act—immediately after?—Very slightly.

57,723. (Dean Dickinson.) Had it been increasing before?—It had been pretty much the same before.

Shebeening.

57,724. (Chairman.) Shebeening increased there too slightly after the Sunday Closing Act?—There was some shebeening in the county of Londonderry.

57,725. What is the condition of shebeening now in the county?—The shebeening cases for the five years after the Sunday Closing Act were 64. For the five years ending December 1897 there were eight cases.

Effect of Sunday closing.

57,726. Would you say as the result of the Sunday Closing Act in county and city that a very immediate and marked effect has been produced?—There has been a marked decrease in both city and county.

57,727. Then in Table XVI. I think you give the results applicable both to the city and the county, do you not?—Yes.

57,728. Arrests for drunkenness for the year ending 31st December 1897, on each day of the week before and after 8 p.m.?—Yes.

57,729. That is applicable to the city and the county?—Yes.

57,730. What I want to know is whether I am justified in inferring from that that those figures show similar results to those which the two previous tables you have quoted show as to the effect of Sunday closing?—Exactly. They show the arrests on each day in the week from midnight to 8 p.m., and from 8 p.m.

57,731. That is the large[illegible] on Saturday the arrests are [illegible] midnight to 8 p.m., and fro[illegible]

57,732. Therefore, compar[illegible] arrests in those tables on [illegible] days, you give the figure re[illegible]

57,733. Against what figure[illegible] those in order?—307 on Mo[illegible] on Wednesday, 227 on Thu[illegible] 511 on Saturday.

57,734. The arrests on the[illegible] are from 8 a.m. on Sund[illegible] Monday morning?—Yes.

57,735. Now leaving fi[illegible] results, causes and effects, [illegible] the cause of the decrease [illegible] and county of Londonder[illegible] Sunday closing is one caus[illegible] Acts of 1872 and 1874; thi[illegible] Secondly, improvement in [illegible] thirdly, increased popularit[illegible] bicycling.

57,737. Now dealing with [illegible] derry as the largest town [illegible] Sunday closing Act applies [illegible]

57,738. It is larger than [illegible] the exempted towns?—Yes.

57,739. Very much large[illegible] larger, and comes up to [illegible] Limerick.

57,740. Do you infer from [illegible] to apply the Sunday closi[illegible] Londonderry to the day [illegible] closing has been working [illegible] derry.

57,741. Do you infer fr[illegible] insisted in, that it would[illegible] houses at an earlier hour [illegible] —I should recommend 9 o'c[illegible]

57,742. Have you any fi[illegible] be advisable?—Table XV[illegible] arrests for drunkenness [illegible] December on each day of [illegible] 8 p.m.

57,743. You think that [illegible] drunkenness arises at the [illegible] double that of any other o[illegible]

57,744. It is double on th[illegible] particular hour, during [illegible] houses closed in the week [illegible] 8 p.m. to midnight were 8[illegible]

57,745. During the same [illegible]

57,746. (Mr. Grindley.) [illegible] a larger population than [illegible] exempt, and Londonderry [illegible] reason why Londonderry [illegible] why?—I do not know, unl[illegible] in Waterford to make it [illegible]

57,747. (Chairman.) Wh[illegible] now in Londonderry?—T[illegible] city, are the Recorder [illegible] application for the hour [illegible] and then in the county it [illegible] the magistrates.

57,748. Therefore in [illegible] Recorder alone at the [illegible] sessions, and also the [illegible] licensing petty sessions?—[illegible]

57,749. To turn to the [illegible] court judge. He is ex-off[illegible] tenant?—He sits as chairm[illegible]

57,750. At the annual l[illegible] Yes.

57,751. Then besides the[illegible] at the annual licensing ses[illegible] —Yes.

57,753. When you say that the police control them, what is the extent of their control?—The police supervise them and see that they do not infringe the law.

57,754. Then as to granting them, who grants them?—In the city, the recorder at quarter sessions grants the publican's licence; then at the annual licensing [illegible] sessions the magistrates grant the other four licences.

57,755. Is the principle different in granting those licences. For instance, as to the publican's licence, what is the principle that guides the Recorder?—The publican is the only man who can sell for consumption on the premises.

57,756. What does the Recorder consider when he grants a publican's licence. Does he consider the character of the applicant?—He considers the character of the applicant and suitability of the premises and the number of existing houses.

57,757. And the fitness of the applicant?—Yes.

57,758. Then he takes three conditions into consideration?—Yes; character, conduct, and fitness of the applicant, fitness and convenience of house or place, and the number of previously licensed houses in the neighbourhood.

57,759. I see in your précis you lay stress on the word "locality"?—Locality would meet the case of Marshall v. The Tyrone Justices.

57,760. Is that the rule now?—It is not the rule now. It is house or place.

57,761. Those are your suggestions of reform?—"Locality" is.

57,762. That is the only introduction you would make?—Yes.

57,763. The only new condition you introduce is that you think "locality" ought to be introduced so as to meet the case we had referred to the other day of Marshall v. The Tyrone Justices?—Yes.

57,764. Do you think that a rateable qualification should attach to all licences?—It should. It is a rateable qualification for the beer retailer. The same rateable qualification should exist for the publican and the spirit grocer.

57,765. The beer retailer has a qualification and the wholesale beer dealer has a qualification?—Yes.

57,766. And also the refreshment house?—The refreshment house wine licence has a qualification of 8l. under 10,000 population, and 12l. for over 10,000 population.

57,767. To whose character does the certificate of those six householders that we have heard of apply?—When a publican comes for renewal at the September [illegible] sessions he brings a certificate from six householders.

57,768. Do you attach much importance to the certificate from the six householders?—Very little. They would be six of his neighbours, in the ordinary way likely.

57,769. Supposing the six neighbours were to enter into recognisances?—That would make them be more careful about giving the character.

57,770. Would you be in favour of that?—Yes.

57,771. Or would you do away with the six householders altogether?—I would require two householders to enter into a bond of recognisances that the publican should observe the licensing laws for the ensuing year.

57,772. That would enlist more people than one in the good conduct of the house?—Yes.

57,773. (Dean [illegible].) Could not the publican enter into another bond with these two people that he would get [illegible] them [illegible] for his behaviour?—He might.

57,774. He would?—He might.

57,775. (Chairman.) There would be a fine imposed on some person?—Some person would have to pay the fine.

[illegible] of convicting and the county court judge spoke of it at last quarter sessions. [illegible]

57,777. Could you tell us what he said if it is reported?—There was a Mr. Lyle who came forward and complained of being convicted, and then the county court judge spoke up and said it would defeat its own object. I will read you his words. Mr. Acheson Lyle said—"What had brought him to the "court that day was the fact that one of the applicants "had had what he asked, and the [illegible] "to come to him and ask him to vote for his application." Then Judge Overend, the county court judge, said—"That as this matter had been broached "he wished the public would thoroughly understand "that the whole magistracy in Derry without exception had set their faces against being asked to "come to quarter sessions or petty sessions to do any "particular thing." Judge Overend's opinion.

57,778. Referring to the tables you have handed in, will you turn to Table No. IV. and Table No. XI. which I think show the number of prosecutions of licence holders both in the city and in the county of Londonderry together with the number of convictions and acquittals for a period of seven years?—That is right. Prosecution of licensees.

57,779. What is the great majority of those offences?—Selling at prohibited hours.

57,780. There is a large proportion in the city, but more in the county I suppose?—No, more in the city. There were 80 cases of convictions in the city and 86 dismissals.

57,781. What was the total number of acquittals?—There were 80 convictions and 81 acquittals in the city.

57,782. What would be the percentage of acquittals in the city as compared with the county?—[illegible] per cent. in the city and 40 per cent. in the county.

57,783. [illegible] per cent. of acquittals on charges of keeping open for sale during prohibited hours?—Yes.

57,784. Does it mean all offences or only selling during prohibited hours?—It means all offences including selling drink at prohibited hours.

57,785. In fact it includes all offences against the licensing laws?—It does.

57,786. Then we have it that with reference to all offences against the licensing laws [illegible] per cent. of acquittals take place in the city, and 40 per cent. in the county?—That is so.

57,787. There is the same police force, is there not?—Two different police forces.

57,788. It is the same body, is it the constabulary?—The same body.

57,789. Acting under the same general orders?—Yes.

57,790. How do you account for that great discrepancy between the city and the county?—I think the magistrates are more particular in the city, and offences come more immediately under their own notice.

57,791. Then two other tables deal with adulteration which we need not dwell long upon, because I understand you to say there is no adulteration?—There is no adulteration except with water. Adulteration.

57,792. Then two other Tables VI. and XIII. deal with habitual drunkards. Will you turn to those. They show the number of habitual drunkards in the city and in the county of Londonderry in 1897?—Yes. Habitual drunkards.

57,793. They include males and females?—Yes. We have those a number of times before the court. There were [illegible] males twice, and 17 females.

57,794. You are taking the habitual drunkards for the year ending the 31st December 1897, in the city?—Yes; that is Table VI. It gives the number of times before the court.

57,795. Will you run over the number of convictions?—There were [illegible] males and 17 females brought before the court during the year—[illegible] males and 6 females, 3 times; 7 males and four females, 4 times; 10 males and 7 females, 5 times; 3 males and 3 females, 6 times; [illegible]

Mr. C. W. Lundbyn.

20 Mar. '98

37,796. Am I right in inferring as I ventured to infer from the evidence of the previous witness, that where you come to the higher stages, so to speak, it is the women that are convicted, and not the men?—That is so.

37,797. Here we have 20 times and upwards no males but four females?—Yes.

37,798. Could you give us any above 15?—I have not got any above 15 in the city.

37,799. Now will you turn to the county?—The county shows a different thing. The women do not drink in the county so much. In the county, Table XIII., twice convicted 41 males and six females.

37,800. From that table it appears as if the women did not attain that bad pre-eminence, but the men?—In the county the men drink and the women do not.

37,801. In the county it is the men who are the habitual drunkards rather than the women?—That is right.

37,802. When you get to the higher grades of convictions those who are convicted five times, six times, seven times, eight times, nine times, and 10 times, in the county are all men and not a single woman?—That is right.

37,803. Whereas in the city we have nine and 10 convictions exclusively women I think?—Quite right.

37,804. (Mr. Gwinn.) Is not that in consequence of living in the city, and not in the country?—In Londonderry we have a very peculiar state of things. There are several shirt factories, and there are some 7,000 women making shirts.

37,805. The habitual drunkards amongst women are mostly prostitutes, if not all?—I do not think that there are many prostitutes in Derry. Those convicted six times and upwards were homeless prostitutes.

37,806. (Dean Dickinson.) The men in the county go to markets and fairs?—They go to markets and fairs without their breakfasts and go into publichouses where they can get nothing to eat.

37,807. Here that the women go to market?—That is it.

Clubs.

37,808. (Chairman.) Have you anything to say about clubs which are referred to in Table XVII.?—We have only three clubs, two in the city and one in Coleraine, social clubs and well conducted. We have no bogus clubs.

37,809. Do you think it is necessary to deal with clubs?—I would suggest that the committee of management, being householders and responsible persons, should enter into a bond of recognizance binding themselves responsible that the rules of the club should be observed. Upon conviction for an infringement of the rules the recognizance could be estreated.

37,810. You would not license those clubs?—No.

37,811. You would register them?—I would register them. The clerk to the magistrates could register the bond.

37,812. (Dean Dickinson.) And you would open them for inspection?—I would open them to inspection in a limited way. The chief officer of police should have statutory power to issue an order to a subordinate to go into the club if he was satisfied of the necessity for it.

Illicit distillation.

37,813. (Chairman.) As to illicit distillation. There is a part of South Derry that is particularly distinguished for illicit distillation?—South Derry has been always more or less afflicted with that evil of illicit distillation.

37,816. (Mr. Young.) How was it you had none in 1894 and 1895?—Because of the injunction of the Roman Catholic priest against it. That was due to him.

R.C. Lept. — The Bishop.

37,817. Is the injunction not still on?—No.

37,818. (Chairman.) The injunction of the priest ended in 1896?—Yes.

37,819. When you say malt was used for potheen, the grain that was spoiled at the harvest was available?—So I am told, in 1895. It was badly saved. Then they make molasses and cheap sugar into potheen.

37,820. In answer to that question we have had some before, I understand, it is necessary to have some amount of grain in the manufacture of whisky?—No. I have some potheen here that was made solely from molasses (producing a bottle).

37,821. (Mr. Young.) Do you mean there was no malt used in the production of this?—So I am told.

37,822. (Dean Dickinson.) Would it keep?—I believe it does not keep more than a few months.

37,823. (Mr. Grinling.) You can make spirit from molasses, but you cannot make whisky from molasses?—I am told that this is made from molasses.

37,824. (Chairman.) I suppose where the police make a raid on the premises where this illicit distillation is going on, and where this whisky is being manufactured, they seize all the materials?—They seize all the kegs and barrels, and I have seen the distillers making a square hole in the bog to put the wash into for fear of the police seizing the barrels.

37,825. Is the wash a palatable liquid?—The wash is the liquid before distillation.

37,826. Has it intoxicating properties?—Very slight. It is something like the hop bitters they sell.

37,827. Is it sold as such?—No, it is not sold.

37,828. If they suppose the police are going to make a raid, I thought they might bottle it off and distribute it, but that would not be saleable?—It is not saleable. They would sell the rubbish after distillation.

37,829. (Mr. Young.) May I ask what the strength of this is?—I could not say.

37,830. I have tasted it and it is simply spirit, it is not whisky?—It was seized by the police in South Derry.

37,831. (Chairman.) According to the police it is whisky manufactured illicitly?—Yes.

37,832. Is there any other kind of drunkenness than by that arising from alcohol in Derry?—There is a good deal of drunkenness arising from ether drinking.

37,833. I think you have a sample of ether here?—I have. That is methylated ether (producing a sample bottle).

37,834. That is the cheapest form?—They get this at about 2s. 6d. a gallon, I understand.

37,835. What would pure ether be a gallon?—Pure ether is 7s. 6d. a pound. It would be about 50s. a gallon.

37,836. (Mr. Young.) Cannot you buy whisky for 8s. a gallon when there is no duty paid?—The people charge the farmers 8s. for that potheen.

37,837. There is no duty. They can produce this for about 1s. a gallon?—I am told they get 8s. a gallon for it.

37,838. (Chairman.) Comparing the methylated ether with pure ether you say pure ether is so much a pound?—It is 7s. 6d. a pound.

37,839. In what shape is it?—Pure ether is a pure liquid, very volatile. It evaporates without leaving

57,843. It was held that getting drunk by ether was not a violation of the pledge given to Father Mathew?—Yes.

57,844. Did the constabulary make a raid against the sale of this ether?—In November [illegible] there was a census taken in the county of Derry and it was found there were [illegible] gallons a month being sold of ether, and then the Government applied the Poisons Act to it. It can only be sold now by chemists. The chemists must label the bottle "poison," and put his name and address.

57,845. The poison is only a label on the bottle?—That is all. Any person can go in and buy five gallons of it.

57,846. And it will not poison him?—It will not poison him unless he takes too much.

57,847. It is not poison in the sense in which arsenic and strychnine are poisons?—No.

57,848. (Mr. Cullen.) Poison in the sense of alcohol, I suppose?—It makes them very stupid.

57,849. (Chairman.) Did labelling the jars or vessels with the word "poison" restrict the sale of ether at all?—For a few years it did, but latterly they have been buying it in large quantities, and taking it home and retailing it.

57,850. I suppose the people find out that it was not what from the label it purported to be?—Yes.

57,851. (Dean Dickinson.) This takes place all within an area of some [illegible] miles?—In an area about [illegible] miles square extending down as far as Cookstown.

57,852. (Chairman.) A person can buy ether, take it home, and retail it without a licence?—Yes. There is no power of search by the police.

57,853. It is not recognised as an intoxicant by Statute?—Not in the Licensing Acts.

57,854. Would you advise that any steps should be taken upon it, or is it important enough to form the subject of a statute?—I think the best thing to do would be to treat it as strychnine or arsenic. It could be then sold only by chemists to persons he knew. He keeps a book, and the purchaser signs his name for the quantity and the purpose for which it is to be purchased.

57,855. You would register the transaction?—Yes.

57,856. (Dean Dickinson.) Now the people who buy it from the chemists retail it?—So I am told.

57,857. (Chairman.) Have you ever known ether used for the purposes of intoxication to have had a fatal effect?—Yes. There was a case in Maghera in county Derry where a woman died on the [illegible] of January last, and the coroner's verdict was that she died from poisoning by ether accelerated by the position of the body causing suffocation.

57,858. Was that pure ether or methylated ether?—Methylated ether.

57,859. Would that be more deleterious to the human constitution than pure ether?—I believe they get speedily drunk. They can get drunk three or four times a day with it.

57,860. Which is the worst to imbibe, methylated ether or pure ether?—I expect the pure ether would be the worst.

57,861. Pure ether would be a more expensive article than whisky itself?—It would.

57,862. And therefore there is no temptation to drink pure ether apart from its effects?—No.

57,863. I suppose the effects of ether drinking are injurious?—There have been cases in the county Derry of a man's whiskers getting burnt after taking a dose of ether and going to light his pipe.

57,864. How long do the effects of this fiery liquid last?—It does not last.

57,865. (Dean Dickinson.) About two hours it is said?—Yes.

57,866. (Chairman.) I will not trouble you to give us a summary of the licensing statistics inasmuch as that has been given us already by the law officers, unless you wish to draw attention to any portion of the evidence you have been kind enough to supply to us with regard to them?—No.

57,867. I do not wish to pass over without notice the tables you have been kind enough to hand in of the statutes. I suppose I might conclude from them that there is great need for consolidation of the law?—Yes, that is why I had them in really. — Mr. C. W. [illegible], [illegible] Sep. '[illegible]

57,868. Codification or consolidation, I suppose?—Yes. — Consolidation.

57,869. Turning to the points in the licensing law which you think show weakness, and which you think might be strengthened, what do you say about these other?—The words "kept for sale" should be added to the offences in section 5 of the Act of 1872. — "Kept for sale."

57,870. You would agree, therefore, with the previous witnesses on that?—Yes.

57,871. As to the sale to children what would you advocate?—It should be illegal to sell to any person under 13 any intoxicating liquor for consumption on the premises. This would repeal an Act of Parliament that makes [illegible] saleable to a child under 13 for consumption on. — Sale of drink to children.

57,872. Then as to the place where the sale to children takes place you would extend that definition to places which had occasional licences granted to them?—Yes. — Occasional licences.

57,873. That you would look upon as important?—Very important.

57,874. It does not apply now?—It does not apply.

57,875. When an occasional licence is in operation any child may be served?—Any child of a [illegible] might go in and get drink.

57,876. Without subjecting the server to a penalty?—Yes.

57,877. Then I think perhaps you have heard the evidence of the previous witness on the question of the power given to the police to arrest for simple drunkenness. You would increase the power of the police?—Yes. The county court judge of Donegal holds that we have no power to arrest for simple drunkenness. — Arrests for simple drunkenness.

57,878. It must be what you style drunkenness and disorderly?—Yes, being guilty while drunk of disorderly behaviour.

57,879. Do you agree that where a person is found drunk on licensed premises the presumption should be against the publican?—Yes. — Punishing drunkenness.

57,880. And the onus of proof should be upon him to show he did not provide that drunkenness, or cause it?—Yes.

57,881. Then you are in favour of six-day licences?—Yes. — Six-day licences.

57,882. You would like to see them further increased?—Further encouraged by increasing the amount of the seven-day licence duty.

57,883. Then with regard to the question of legal proceedings?—The words "or of a resident magistrate" should be inserted so that he would constitute a court of summary jurisdiction sitting alone, or with others. The expression "stipendiary magistrate" does not include a resident magistrate. — Resident magistrates.

57,884. You would add to the stipendiary magistrates the resident magistrate?—Yes.

57,885. The section of the Act to which you refer is section [illegible] of the Act of 1872?—Yes.

57,886. In fact all the suggestions you have made refer to the various sections of the Act of 1872?—Yes.

57,887. Turning to section [illegible] of the same Act which deals with spirit grocers, can an application for a spirit grocer's licence be refused?—It cannot be refused if his character is good and his premises suitable. — Spirit grocers.

57,888. Have you any difficulty in Derry as to the question of the law?—I sent a copy of a letter I had from the priest at Dungiven, and he tells me of a case there where a man applies for a spirit grocer's licence. He has a good house and the man's character is excellent, but his house is [illegible] yards from the Roman Catholic Church door, and the priest objects.

57,889. What happened to the licence—was it refused?—He has applied for it.

57,890. It has not come before the magistrates?—No, and in that case if the magistrates refused the licence he could take them to the Queen's Bench.

Mr. C. W. Leathem. 25 Mar. '98.

37,891. It is a question whether they have power to refuse on those grounds?—It seems they have no power arising out of the Marshall case at Tyrone.

37,892. Do you hold that in the case of a spirit grocer's licence the same objections should hold good which prevail in the case of the publican's licence?—Exactly.

37,893. Would you state those just shortly?—Character of the applicant; fitness and convenience of the house or place, and number of previously licensed houses in the neighbourhood.

37,894. Then I think you would propose to insert the words "or locality" would you not?—Yes, "or locality."

37,895. And in the case of a spirit grocer's licence, would you give the same power of objection as exists in the case of the publican's licence?—Yes. At present only the police can oppose. Any inhabitant of the parish should be able to oppose the same as in the case of a publican's licence.

Value qualification.

37,896. He should have power to object and to state the reason of his objection which the magistrates should consider?—Yes.

37,897. You would agree with the previous witness that you would like to see a qualification applicable to the wholesale and to the off spirit retailers?—Yes.

37,898. The beer retailer, the wholesale beer dealer, and the refreshment-house wine licence, must have a qualification?—Yes.

37,899. You would like to see those qualifications applied, or some qualification applied, to the spirit grocer's licence?—Yes.

Spirit grocers.

37,900. Have you formed any idea of what the qualification should be?—The statute at present states that it should be 8l. under 10,000 population, and 12l. over 10,000 population.

37,901. I suppose it is the poorer class of spirit grocers that need your attention?—The poorer class of house give us most trouble.

37,902. Do you agree with the former witness that it is the beer licence which brings in the profit and not the spirit?—Yes.

37,903. You think the magistrates ought to separate the spirit licence from the other licences?—I think they ought.

37,904. What is the situation of Draperstown?—It is in the centre of the county Derry.

37,905. There was a case, I think, that you wish to call attention to which occurred there at the petty sessions?—Yes, in connection with a spirit grocer. A man applied there in September for a spirit grocer's licence. He had been convicted some years ago of shebeening, and his house was rated at the rate of 10s. a year. The magistrates refused the licence. He appealed then to the quarter sessions at Magherafelt and got the licence.

Transfers to publican's licence.

37,906. Do I understand he got the licence at quarter sessions, though he had been convicted of shebeening in his house, and it was under 10s. rateable value?—Yes.

37,907. Is there any other case you can cite?—There are several cases where men have come up and got a spirit grocer's licence, and then next year applied for an ordinary publican's licence, and the county court judge gives it to them because he considers it a less evil than the spirit grocer.

37,908. The publican's licence would allow him to sell spirits?—The publican can sell beer and spirits.

37,909. What was the principle on which a person who was granted a spirit grocer's licence in Londonderry, and then applied for a publican's licence, had the publican's licence granted to him. Was his former licence taken away?—He gives up the spirit grocer's licence and gets an ordinary publican's licence.

37,910. The magistrates thought that the publican's licence was less detrimental than the spirit grocer's in that case?—Yes, that was it.

Mr. C. W. Leathem.

37,912. Which are increasing most in Londonderry relatively, the publican's licence, or the grocer's licence?—The grocer's licence is increasing, but as soon as they get a grocer's licence then they apply for a publican's licence. The magistrates cannot refuse the grocer's licence if the character is good and the house suitable. Then the man comes up for the publican's licence, and the county court judge says, "We will give you this because it is a less evil than the spirit grocer's."

37,913. That in fact forces the hands of the magistrates with reference to the publican's licence?—Yes.

37,914. You would think that the magistrates were exceeding their duty in granting the publican's licence to a man who had the spirit grocer's licence?—It meant paying for the spirit grocer's licence.

37,915. It gives him a kind of claim for the publican's licence?—It does.

37,916. And you think that the magistrates ought to discourage that idea?—The magistrates cannot refuse the spirit grocer's licence.

37,917. But they can refuse to transfer a spirit grocer's into a publican's?—Yes, they can. The feeling (?) the evil of the spirit grocer's they would rather see that than with an ordinary licence.

37,918. They prefer to grant the publican's licence as the least of two evils in their view?—That is it.

Occasional licences.

37,919. I will not trouble you about occasional licences unless you think you ought to make an observation in connection with them. Do you agree with other witnesses that two magistrates should grant them in open court?—They should be granted by two magistrates with the knowledge of the police and the consent of the committee or the person responsible for the occasion.

37,920. Does not the person who is responsible for the occasion necessarily have notice now?—He may not. There was a case at Coleraine where a publican sold under an occasional licence at some horse-races and the people getting up the horse-races did not want the licence.

37,921. A temperance sporting might be held and a publican might apply for an occasional licence there?—That was the case here. The horse-races were got up by temperance people.

37,922. And for those horse-races this licence was granted by the magistrates?—It was.

37,923. Was the licence in the case of the temperance horse-racing meeting refused by the magistrates in the first instance?—It was refused at petty sessions, and then the applicant went to a magistrate out of petty sessions and got it.

37,924. That of course is a legal proceeding?—It is irregular.

37,925. But not illegal?—Not illegal.

37,926. Then supposing a person gets up sports and a man takes out an occasional licence, though he is not allowed to enter on the ground, he can go to the side of the road and sell the liquor there. Would that be legal?—It would be irregular. The constabulary got up sports at Derry, and a man applied there with his occasional licence and sold outside the sports ground in a public road.

Right of entry by police.

37,927. Have you anything to say as to the entry of premises by the police?—It should be an offence to delay a constable demanding to enter in pursuance of the Act. Constables are delayed admission until evidence of drinking, &c., may have been removed.

37,928. In the case of gambling houses, they take care to hide the dice and the cards before the police enter?—Yes.

37,929. I think you have touched on the closing licence and you would discourage the six-day licence by an increase in the charge for seven-day licences?—Yes.

37,930. I suppose by that means the number of houses which would supply bona fide travellers and others would be lessened?—That would be the object of it.

Mr. C. D. [illegible]

[illegible] May, '[illegible]

17,932. (Mr. Young.) Do you think that the consumption of ether has anything to do with the restrictions that were placed upon the people by Father Mathew, and by the temperance crusade?—It is said that the wave of temperance that existed in the year 1840 gave rise to the use of ether.

17,933. And is was to evade the pledge?—That is what I am told.

17,934. (Mr. Johnston.) You say that arrests for simple drunkenness are not legal, but you can summons the man for the offence afterwards?—We may detain when a person is so drunk as to be incapable of taking care of himself.

17,935. That is the only source of the power to arrest really, the power to detain a man for his own protection?—That is all.

17,936. You can follow a man who is manifestly drunk, and ascertain his name and address, and summon him for the offence of drunkenness?—We can.

17,937. (Mr. Whitaker.) I should like to ask you one question on your table XVI. On the Saturday night from 8 p.m. to 12 midnight, there were [illegible] arrests for drunkenness?—That is right.

17,938. On the Sunday night from 8 p.m. to 12 o'clock there were only [illegible] arrests?—Yes.

17,939. On the Monday night [illegible]?—Yes.

17,940. The public-houses are closed on Sunday night?—They are closed all day on Sunday except to bonâ fide travellers.

17,941. They are closed during those hours from 8 p.m. to 12?—Yes.

17,942. When they are open on Saturday night you have [illegible] times as many arrests for drunkenness as when they are closed on Sunday?—Yes, exactly, a little more.

17,943. Then it would be absurd to suggest, would it not, that the public-houses are not responsible for drunkenness?—I suppose it would be advisable to close the public-houses earlier on Saturday night.

17,944. It is clear that the drunkenness arises from the public-houses, is it not, because when they are open there is drunkenness, and when they are closed there is not?—From that table you would appear to be quite right.

17,945. (Mr. Hyslop.) In table XVI. I see that the arrests for drunkenness are [illegible] on Sunday?—[illegible] is the total in the [illegible] column.

17,946.—Then as they do not get the supply of drink from the public-houses, how does that happen? The public-houses are closed on Sunday?—We suppose there have been bonâ fide travellers who have got the liquor.

17,947. See this number?—It may have been so.

17,948. (Mr. Whitaker.) [illegible] of those are between midnight on Saturday and eight on Sunday morning, and therefore it would be the overflow from the Saturday night's drinking?—Some of them may be.

17,949. Between midnight and eight the next morning they are clearly the people who got their drink on the Saturday night, is not that so?—That is very likely so.

17,950. (Mr. Walker.) Did Father Mathew's Crusade have any lasting beneficial effect?—I do not know personally.

17,951. You cannot answer that question?—I have read a good deal about it. It was very general. It did not only apply to South Derry, it was all over the country.

17,952. It gave rise to an illicit form of drinking that had not hitherto existed?—In South Derry, I am told, it gave rise to ether drinking.

The witness withdrew.

Adjourned till to-morrow at 10.30.

NINETY-SEVENTH DAY.

Queen's Robing Room, House of Lords, Wednesday, March 30th, 1898.

PRESENT:

THE RIGHT HONOURABLE THE VISCOUNT DE VESCI IN THE CHAIR.

Sir Charles Cameron, Bart., M.P.	John Herbert Roberts, Esq., M.P.
The Very Reverend H. H. Dickinson, Dean.	William Walker, Esq.
William Shepherd Caine, Esq.	Thomas Palmer Whittaker, Esq., M.P.
Henry Graham, Esq.	Samuel Young, Esq., M.P.
Samuel [illegible], Esq.	George Younger, Esq.
Albert [illegible], Esq.	

Mr. ALEXANDER GAMBELL called in and examined.

Mr. A. Gambell. — 30 Mar. '98. 57,953. (*Viscount de Vesci.*) You are County Inspector of Cork?—Yes.

57,954. You have been County Inspector of Cork city and East Riding, since the 1st April 18[illegible]?—Yes.

Position of witness. 57,955. What is your previous experience as an officer of the Royal Constabulary?—I have had 29 years and 11 months' service.

57,956. In what parts of Ireland have you been stationed?—In Armagh, Galway, Dublin, Antrim, Kerry, Louth, North Tipperary, Waterford, and Cork, East Riding.

East Riding of Cork. 57,957. Can you state of your own knowledge, how many licensing districts there are in the East Riding of Cork, how many quarter sessions districts?—Three I think, as well as I remember.

57,958. Is there a Recorder of Cork?—The Recorder is the licensing authority for the city of Cork.

57,959. Is he the county court judge outside?—He is the county court judge. He and the magistrates constitute the licensing authority in the East Riding.

57,960. Is he the county court judge of the other Riding as well?—No, there is no county court in the West Riding.

Cork city. 57,961. Will you give the population of the city in 1891?—In 1891 it was 75,345.

57,962. And of the East Riding?—[illegible].

57,963. What is the acreage of the city?—[illegible].

57,964. What is the police force of the city?—Two officers and 1[illegible] men of all ranks; and in the East Riding 11 officers and [illegible] men of all ranks.

57,965. Will you tell us the number of licensed houses of all kinds in the city?—[illegible], of which [illegible] are fully licensed.

57,966. And in the East Riding?—1,1[illegible], of which 1,1[illegible] are fully licensed.

57,967. Will you give the number of seven-day licenses in the city?—[illegible].

57,968. And only nine six-day licenses?—Nine six-day licenses.

57,969. How many spirit grocers are there?—Seven; wholesale beer dealers, 17; wholesale wine and spirit dealers, 14. There are two theatres, eight wine retailers, four beer and wine retailers, and one six-day wholesale and retail wine licence. There are one six-day wholesale and retail beer and spirit licence, and one seven-day wholesale and retail licence.

57,970. Will you give us the figures for the East Riding?—Seven-day licenses, 1,0[illegible]; six-day licenses, [illegible]; seven-day and early closing licenses, 1[illegible]; six-day and early closing licenses, 4[illegible]; spirit grocers, [illegible]; wholesale beer dealers, [illegible]; beer retailers, 3; wholesale and retail beer dealers combined, 5.

57,971. Making in all 1,1[illegible]?—Yes.

Excessive number of licensed houses. 57,972. Will you state your own opinion and that of your officers as to the requirements of the public?—That there are far too many licensed houses.

57,973. What is the proportion in Cork city?—One to 1[illegible] inhabitants.

Mr. A. Gambell. 57,974. And in the East Riding?—The average is one to [illegible] in towns and villages. It varies. In Queenstown, it is one to 1[illegible]; Fermoy, one to [illegible]; Mallow, one to [illegible]; Charleville, one to [illegible]; Mitchelstown, one to [illegible]; Kanturk, one to [illegible]; Kanturk? [illegible], one to 1[illegible]. The last is a very extraordinary case.

57,975. Can you give any particular reason from your own knowledge why there is such a discrepancy in the proportions in these towns?—I really cannot, except as regards [illegible]. The only reason, I think, why there can be so many licensed houses there is that there are [illegible] rather large cattle fairs in the year. It is a small village; I believe there are [illegible] houses.

57,976. There are no other causes except that of the action of the licensing authority. It has nothing to do with the proprietors of the owners?—I am not aware. Fermoy, for instance, is a large military station.

57,977. There is a garrison there?—Yes.

57,978. (*Mr. Whittaker.*) Does the population you have given include the garrison?—I do not think it does; I am not quite sure about that.

57,979. (*Viscount de Vesci.*) Can you give us the average number of troops quartered at Fermoy through the year?—No, I can't say.

57,980. There is more than one regiment there, I think?—Yes; there are artillery as well as infantry.

Low valuation of public-houses. 57,981. Can you give the valuation of the public-houses in Cork?—In a few instances I can. Some of the houses are valued at a low valuation. In Cork there are 11 at a valuation of [illegible] and under, 1[illegible] at a valuation of 10*l.* and under, 1[illegible] at a valuation of 1[illegible] and under. In Fermoy there are 11 valued at [illegible] and under, and 1[illegible] at [illegible] and under. In Mallow 3 valued at [illegible] and under, [illegible] at [illegible] and under, [illegible] at [illegible] and under. In Charleville there are two at [illegible] and under, 11 at [illegible] and under, 11 at [illegible] and under.

57,982. These are the four principal towns in the East Riding?—Well, no, not the principal towns; I take them as instances.

57,983. (*Mr. Whittaker.*) Are these public-houses of all kinds of licenses?—I think they are public-houses.

57,984. (*Viscount de Vesci.*) Public-houses only?—Yes. I got the figures from the Inland Revenue and I asked them for particulars of public-houses.

Structural condition. 57,985. Will you give us your opinion as to what class of houses they are?—As a rule they are fairly good, but some of them are badly adapted owing to scanty accommodation, badly enclosed yards, and back ways.

57,986. Are the back exits very prevalent?—Not very.

57,987. In the city I mean?—Not so very, I think. One hears of them, though, from time to time. I can give you the proportion of good, fair, and bad houses if you wish.

Mr. A. [illegible]

10 Mar. '98.

57,988. Will you give it to us shortly?—In the East Riding, according to returns furnished to me, the houses as regards accommodation generally are 40 per cent. good, 47 per cent. fair, 13 per cent. bad. In the city 73 per cent. good, 26 per cent. fair, and 1 per cent. bad.

57,989. (Mr. Young.) What is meant by "bad"?—As regards structural accommodation generally. I am speaking of the house and its surroundings and general things on licensed premises.

Number of publicans.

57,990. (Father de Fonti.) Then I think you state generally that the result of the excessive number of houses is the creation of a number of needy publicans who are obliged to take up other occupations?—Yes.

57,991. Is it a common thing in the agricultural districts in the East Riding for the publicans to carry on other business in the same premises, besides selling drink?—It is, and in the city too, very much indeed. There are 58 per cent. of the public-houses in the city let out in tenements, for one thing. There are also some of the publicans who are tradesmen, car drivers, and other occupations.

Mixed trade.

57,992. What I mean is, do they carry on other trades in the same shop where they sell liquor?—They do very much in the East Riding. I can give you the figures. Some per cent. in the city and 85 per cent. in the East Riding combine the sale of provisions, groceries, and general goods with that of drink.

57,993. General goods means that a man may be a huckster in fact?—Not so much as selling meal, flour, and general provisions.

57,994. Do you know of any who carry on a drapery business in the same premises?—I do not know of one, there may be.

57,995. You have not gone into that?—I have not. It is generally provisions.

Police supervision.

57,996. I believe you state that it is very difficult to carry on an effective police supervision with such a number of houses?—It is extremely difficult indeed, especially as regards the country public-houses. Some of these public-houses are six miles from a police station, and I know of two instances where they are seven miles away.

57,997. As a matter of fact, I suppose, your men are watched?—They are watched by a large proportion of the publicans; some of them I believe, keep regular scouts for watching the police on Sunday during closing hours.

57,998. It is exceedingly difficult, I suppose, in that case for your men to pay a surprise visit?—Extremely difficult. All sorts of devices have to be adopted.

57,999. Do you employ plain-clothes men at all?—Yes, and men on bicycles; sometimes men on cars. Various devices are resorted to.

58,000. Have you formed any opinion with regard to the area of a public-house whether any condition should be made as to proximity to a police post?—It would be very desirable indeed if it could be done.

58,001. It would be justified?—Decidedly.

58,002. Can you state what distance you would, in your opinion, prefer?—The nearer the better. If possible, within a mile I should say.

Mixed trade.

58,003. I have already asked you about combining the sale of provisions with drink; 85 per cent. of those in the East Riding combine the sale of provisions and groceries?—Yes.

58,004. I think your officers have reported to you strongly against these houses?—Yes. They reported strongly against these houses as tending to the spread of drunkenness, especially among women, and rendering a strict enforcement of the Sunday Closing Act very difficult.

58,005. In what way, with regard to the Sunday Closing Act? Do they find the people on the premises ostensibly with the view of purchasing goods on Sunday?—Yes. People go into these shops; the counter is on one side for the sale of liquor, and perhaps that for the sale of provisions and goods is on the other side. In some instances there is a wooden partition which is movable, and is locked on Sunday, but in other instances there is no such partition, and even where there is, it can be easily opened at a moment's notice, and when the police go into the house, the people found there can say that they are there for the purchase of provisions, and in that way it makes the enforcement of the Act difficult.

58,006. That would be their defence in case of prosecution?—Yes. People who may hesitate about going into a public-house will go without any hesitation into these houses.

Conduct of licensed houses.

58,007. Your next paragraph is a general statement about the way in which the licensed traders keep their houses?—Yes, in general they keep their houses very fairly, but a large proportion of them are inclined to sell on Sunday in contravention of the Act, if they can do so with impunity.

58,008. It is more one for police supervision?—Yes.

58,009. You speak more particularly, I suppose, with regard to the publicans in the city?—They are all the same, city and county.

Adulteration.

58,010. Will you tell us the facts as to the question of adulterating liquor?—My experience is that there is no adulteration of liquor other than putting water into it.

58,011. (Dean Dickinson.) That is dilution, rather?—Yes. One often hears the idea expressed that liquor is adulterated, but my experience, and that of others whom I have consulted, is that it is not.

58,012. (Father de Fonti.) We have heard that already. Will you state the number of cases of late years which have occurred in your district?—88 cases of dilution of whisky by water.

58,013. Have you prosecuted?—Yes. There were prosecuted cases.

58,014. Successfully?—Yes.

Tied houses.

58,015. With regard to the tied houses, what do you say?—There are 84 per cent. of the city public-houses tied, and about 17 per cent. in the East Riding.

58,016. I think you go further into detail on the question of tied houses later on?—I do. The system is spreading rather in the country.

Drunkenness in Cork.

58,017. With regard to the drunkenness in Cork city what do you say?—I have prepared some returns on the subject which I have handed in. There is a good deal of systematic heavy drinking, and a considerable amount of actual drunkenness among artisans and the labouring classes of both sexes in the city.

58,018. Will you give your figures for Cork city, first for three years, 1895, 1896, and 1897?—In 1895 the convicted cases were male, 1,[illegible]; female, [illegible]; total, 2,361. In 1896: male, 1,[illegible]; female, [illegible]; total 2,[illegible]. In 1897: male, 1,[illegible]; female, [illegible]; total 2,[illegible].

58,019. There is no great variation in those three years then?—Hardly any.

East Riding.

58,020. Will you take the East Riding of Cork for the same years?—In 1895: male, 2,[illegible]; female, [illegible]; total 3,[illegible]. In 1896: male, 2,[illegible]; female, [illegible]; total 3,[illegible]. In 1897: male, 2,[illegible]; female, [illegible]; total 3,[illegible].

Habitual drunkards.

58,021. You furnish another table of the number of persons convicted three times and upwards as drunk and disorderly. This is only for the year 1897, I think?—Yes. In Cork city the number convicted 3 times and less than 6 during the year 1897 was [illegible] men, [illegible] women; the number convicted 6 times and less than 10 was [illegible] men, [illegible] women; none were convicted oftener. In Cork East Riding, men convicted 3 times and less than 6, [illegible]; women, [illegible]. Convicted 6 times and less than 10, men, [illegible]; women, [illegible]. None were more frequently convicted.

58,022. You have a table of arrests for drunkenness. Do you wish to put that in now? It is rather long?—I do not know that it is very material.

58,023. Will you state generally where is the drinking mostly carried on?—In public-houses. There is little, if any, home drinking.

58,024. What are the worst days for drunkenness?—Saturday and Monday.

58,025. On what days of the week are the wages paid?—On Fridays and Saturdays.

58,026. Are there any large shipbuilding yards, or anything like that in Cork?—No, there is no shipbuilding. There is a large flax factory, a manure works, four breweries, two distilleries, and large cart yards. Those are the principal things.

Favourite liquor.

58,027. What is the favourite drink of such men?—Porter.

58,028. Not much whisky is drunk?—Not much in the city, there is in the East Riding. Porter and

Mr. A. [illegible]

24 Mar. '96.

whisky are the favourite drinks in the East Riding, I understand.

Female drinking on Mondays.

18,029. With regard to Monday, what have you to say?—It is locally called the women's day. They drink chiefly on Monday, and the men on Saturday. The women have more money on Monday; they pawn the clothes then.

18,030. They pawn the husbands' clothes?—Yes, and redeem the clothes on Saturday night when the husbands' wages are received.

The "small pint."

18,031. What do you state as to the way in which some of the publicans tempt the women to drink?—There is what is called the "small pint" in Cork, and that is an ordinary pint of porter, with a very little poured out of it, and given for three-fourths the ordinary price of a pint.

18,032. They charge 1½d., the cost of a pint full being 2d.?—Yes. I might mention that 25 per cent. of the persons convicted for drunkenness the last three years in the city were women; in the East Riding only seven per cent.

18,033. (*Dean Dickinson.*) Through the greater fondness for drink?—I really cannot account for it; perhaps so; they have pretty good facilities, I think, in the country as well.

Shebeening.

18,034. (*Viscount de Vesci.*) With regard to shebeening, what do you say?—There is very little shebeening indeed. There are 11 prosecutions in three years; at present there are only five suspected shebeens in the city.

18,035. Out of the 11 there were six convictions, and five dismissals?—Yes.

18,036. Can you give any reason for those dismissals?—I cannot. I do not know the facts of the cases. There are five suspected shebeens at present, and no known shebeens in the city.

18,037. What is the difference between a suspected shebeen and a known one? It was stated yesterday, by a witness from Belfast, that a known shebeen was one in which there had been one conviction?—I think that is what is understood by it—where there is almost proof that it is a shebeen. The other is where we have never actually had a conviction or a prosecution.

18,038. Then these shebeens have disappeared altogether?—Yes.

18,039. And the houses are kept properly now?—Yes.

18,040. (*Mr. Young.*) Are these shebeens prosecuted?—No.

18,041. (*Viscount de Vesci.*) Are any of them?—No.

18,042. You come here that there are no bogus clubs?—None.

18,043. You go more fully into the question of clubs later on?—Yes.

Occasions of drunkenness.

18,044. What do you say as to the question of drunkenness in the East Riding?—Country people do not drink except on special occasions, such as fair and market days and holidays, at funerals, &c.

18,045. And at wakes?—Yes.

18,046. You say whisky and porter are the favourite drinks?—Yes, and in the country Monday and Saturday seem to be the days which furnish most of the cases of drunkenness. There is also a considerable amount of drunkenness on Sundays.

18,047. How do you account for that?—It is attributable chiefly, I think, to hurling—they are held very much on Sunday—to football and hurling tournaments, which gather together large numbers of people.

18,048. How do they procure the drink for these Sunday funerals and Sunday meetings?—They get it at the public-houses.

18,049. On the previous day?—No; I should think they get it that day, on Sunday. That is one instance of the bad effects of these combined houses, if I may use the term, which sell drink as well as provisions.

18,050. In your opinion, they are able to go in and carry out drink from these unknown to the police?—Yes; or drink there when the backs of the police are turned. We cannot be everywhere. There is a certain amount of evasion of the Sunday Closing Act, in spite of all our efforts. There is no doubt about it.

18,051. Do they drink much at these athletic meetings?—They do.

18,052. It has been stated here, I think, that athletic meetings are the cause of the gradual increase of drunkenness?—There is no doubt about it that in my district these large gatherings are responsible for a great amount of drinking.

18,053. (*Dean Dickinson.*) Not on the part of the athletes themselves, but the people who come?—Yes, the people who come to a great extent from different places. There are also what are called hiring markets, which gather together large numbers of the labouring classes, and these people are entitled to drink, being *bonâ fide* travellers.

Sunday hiring fairs.

18,054. (*Viscount de Vesci.*) Are these hiring markets held on Sundays?—Yes.

18,055. Is that very prevalent in the East Riding?—Not very prevalent, but there are some of them; I have heard of them.

18,056. Does that happen in other parts of Ireland of which you have knowledge?—Yes. It is very common in Kerry where I have been.

18,057. Take the north of Ireland, the particular part of Ireland. I think you said you were in Armagh and Louth; do they have these hiring markets there on Sunday?—No.

18,058. Is it more prevalent in the south?—South and south-west.

18,059. You state here with regard to the athletic meetings that when the sports are ended then is the time for drinking commenced?—Yes.

18,060. They then go into the public-houses where they can get in without being noticed by the police?—Yes.

18,061. A great many of them, I suppose, claim to come as *bonâ fide* travellers?—They go openly because a great number of them are *bonâ fide* travellers.

18,062. They come from a distance to attend these meetings?—Yes, they go from town to town. One town will challenge another town.

Shebeens in the East Riding.

18,063. With regard to the shebeens in the East Riding. The shebeens I have referred to before are in the city?—Yes. There are 20 what I may call suspected shebeens altogether in the East Riding. I combine the known and the suspected.

18,064. How many prosecutions were there?—Twenty-one prosecutions in three years, out of which there were 17 convictions. There are no bogus clubs in the East Riding. Drunkenness is, if anything, slightly on the increase in the East Riding, but it is very slight.

Crime and drink.

18,065. Do you consider that in crimes classed as outrages a certain percentage is attributable to drink?—Yes. I have had the register in my office examined, and I find that about 17 per cent. of the serious crimes classed as outrages are traceable to or connected in some way with drink.

18,066. With regard to the cases of convictions of cruelty to children, what have you to say?—According to the returns furnished to me, out of 151 convicted cases in three years, 105 are traceable to drink. In that I do not include all dismissed cases, which are also said to have been traceable to drink. Of such cases as assaults, affrays, and disorderly conduct, I should say 50 or 70 per cent. are traceable to drink.

18,067. That is as distinct from the class of crimes called outrages?—Yes.

Truck Act.

18,068. With regard to the Truck Act you have, I think, something to say?—Steps have been taken recently to put a stop to the practice of paying labourers in public-houses, which, until lately, was carried on in a few instances in Cork city.

18,069. That is nothing of great importance, I suppose?—No, it is not.

Clubs.

18,070. Will you be good enough to tell us the number of clubs in Cork city?—There are 22 clubs in the city in which intoxicating liquors are kept for consumption.

18,071. Are they the property of the members of the clubs?—They are. There is one club of a peculiar nature. One is incorporated as a limited liability company. About half the members are shareholders, but having no privileges over the other members except in one particular, that is of voting at the annual general meeting. The profits, if any, are applied to the maintenance of the premises and furniture, and the annual subscriptions are the same in each case.

[illegible]. The other members have no right of voting?—Yes.

[illegible]. It is practically a proprietary club, under the name of a limited liability company?—I think it is, but I am not very clear about the subject. That is the only one that differs from the others, which are ordinary members' clubs.

[illegible]. Of the [illegible] I believe [illegible] are social, and one is political?—Yes. All are properly organised bona fide clubs.

[illegible]. The social clubs are of persons of all classes?—Yes.

[illegible]. Does that include working men's clubs?—I think there is about one only, which can be called a working man's club, the others are of a different social grade.

[illegible]. You can give an instance of one club which was [illegible] dissolved?—Yes, there was one club lately dissolved, and a new one formed in its place. I understand that this new club is lent to a publican, the owner of the house in which the club meets, which is not on licensed premises.

[illegible]a. It is on distinct premises?—Yes.

[illegible]. Are they near each other, or in the same street, for instance?—They are in the same street. They are rather near each other.

[illegible]. You stated with regard to the clubs that some of them are what you call doubtful. Do you believe that a great deal of drinking is carried on in those clubs on Saturday nights?—Yes, there is reason to know that there is. An idea has got abroad that [illegible] [illegible] in these doubtful clubs have [illegible] [illegible] a [illegible] some of the members.

[illegible]. How are the rules observed about admitting outsiders?—I am told rather laxly.

[illegible]. Do they come in as friends of the members?—I think so.

[illegible]. Have you been able to prove any case where they paid for their own drink?—No, I have nothing very definite to go upon in connection with these clubs.

[illegible]. Have the men under you come across frequent cases of intoxication in the case of people going home from these clubs?—Yes, on Saturday nights they have. Police interference has not been found necessary in those cases.

[illegible]. That is because, I suppose, they were going home quietly?—Yes, the other members took them home. I think these doubtful clubs have not called for police interference, but still I think they do some harm to some of the members.

[illegible]. What is the opinion of the licensed traders with regard to these clubs?—They complain about them. They complain of the injury to their business from the facilities for drinking during closing hours enjoyed by these clubs.

[illegible]. Are these clubs open on a Sunday?—Yes.

[illegible]. During prohibited hours?—Yes, and some of [illegible]

[illegible]. Both clubs in the same house?—Yes.

[illegible]. On different floors?—On different floors, and they were [illegible] or [illegible] in their general character. The members, [illegible] in the one case and [illegible] in the other case, were of the labouring class. An [illegible] officer succeeded in buying drink in one club. A prosecution followed resulting in one conviction. Later on the police secured [illegible] convictions. As a result both clubs were broken up, and have not since been re-formed.

[illegible]. These nine convictions were all at one time?—No.

[illegible]. Nine different persons convicted on one night?—Two convictions on three prosecutions.

[illegible]. Brought on at different times?—Yes. If any further details are thought necessary I can give them.

[illegible]. The result is there are no bogus clubs now in the city?—None whatever.

[illegible]. With regard to the administration of the licensing laws, what is your opinion as to the way in which the ordinary justices administer the law?—I must say that I think some of the ordinary justices do not give the police sufficient support in carrying out the provisions of the Licensing Acts. A large proportion of the prosecutions against publicans are dismissed. It cannot well be alleged that the police bring weak cases into court, as the district officers always investigate the facts, and order prosecutions only where they believe there is sufficient evidence.

[illegible]. Are these cases ever submitted to you by your district officers?—Very rarely.

[illegible]. Not often before they begin the prosecution?—No.

[illegible]. Would you give the totals of the convictions and dismissals, first of all for offences against the Sunday Closing Act; the totals will be sufficient?—The total number of convictions of all kinds in three years in the East Riding were [illegible], and [illegible] dismissals.

[illegible]. Taking each offence separately, will you give the total of the offences against the Sunday Closing Act? This is spread over the three years, I think?—Yes.

[illegible]. (Mr. [illegible].) Are these prosecutions all for drunkenness?—No, they are prosecutions of publicans for breaches of the Licensing Acts.

[illegible]. ([illegible].) First of all offences against the Sunday Closing Act?—In the East Riding [illegible] convictions and [illegible] dismissals.

[illegible]. Selling drink to drunken persons, or permitting drunkenness?—[illegible] convictions and [illegible] dismissals.

[illegible]. Other offences against the Licensing Act?—[illegible] convictions and [illegible] dismissals.

[illegible]. The other offences would cover [illegible], and what else?—Selling on week days in prohibited hours, refusing to admit the police, permitting gaming, and various other offences of that kind.

Mr. A. [illegible].

[illegible]

Lax administration by justices.

Dismissal of cases in East Riding.

there any human

be spreading?—The

[illegible] Is there anything in the system of conducting [illegible] houses which would lead men to debate, or supply [illegible]—No, I have never heard that beer, or porter, or stout, was debased. No case of that kind has ever come under my notice, nor have I heard of any.

[illegible] Is it part of the duties of the constabulary, [illegible] to inspect public-houses with regard to [illegible]—[illegible]

[illegible] Samples are periodically taken?—They are. They are inspectors under the Food and Drugs Act, and they take samples for all kinds of food and drink.

[illegible] The men of your force are inspectors?—Yes.

[illegible] Do they do it in plain clothes?—As a rule not; but I have tried it recently in one or two cases. I have not heard the result. It was suggested to me as a good idea, and I tried it.

[illegible] Will you state what was the result of an inquiry you held as to the drift of public opinion as to closing hours?—I interviewed 23 representative persons, chiefly persons of education and [illegible].

[illegible] Any of them connected with the trade?—No.

[illegible] All independent?—All independent. Of these as regards Sunday closing 13 were in favour of total closing on Sunday—that is in the city of Cork—7 were in favour of closing at 5 or 6 on Sunday, instead of the present hour, which is 7.

[illegible] Shortening it by one hour?—Yes; and three were in favour of the present system, 2 to 7.

[illegible] (Mr. [illegible]) Are not these exactly the class of people who do not care whether the public-houses are open or closed?—Yes, but I shall be able to give you the other side also.

[illegible] ([illegible]) These would be persons to be classed as large ratepayers?—Quite so. As regards Saturday closing, of those 23, [illegible] are in favour of closing at hours varying from 6 up to 10, [illegible] of these named 9 as the hour, and one was in favour of the present hour of 11.

[illegible] Will you give us the opinion of the class who use public-houses—artisans, labourers, and factory hands?—I interviewed [illegible] artisans, labourers, and factory hands; [illegible] per cent. were in favour of opening on Sunday as at present from 2 to 7; [illegible] per cent. were in favour of total closing, and [illegible] per cent. were in favour of closing at hours varying from 4 to 6—chiefly 6 o'clock on Sunday, or in favour of the English system of opening twice on Sunday. As regards Saturday night, 78 per cent. advocated closing at hours ranging from 6 to 10. What I mean by that is that some are in favour of closing at 6, some at 7, some at 8, 9, and 10. The great majority are in favour of closing at 9, the present hour being 11; [illegible] per cent. are in favour of closing as at present at 11.

[illegible] Have you taken the opinion of the clergy of the city of Cork of all denominations?—Yes. I have taken the opinion of the three bishops (two Roman Catholic, one Protestant) of one member of Parliament, of the Mayor of Cork, of the President of the Chamber of Commerce, of the president of the United Trades of Ireland, of the Chairman of the Board of Guardians, and some employers of labour, and other representative persons. They are included in the [illegible].

[illegible] What is the opinion of the majority with regard to the present hour of closing on Sundays in Cork city?—Every one, almost, thinks that it is a bad hour, for this reason, that 7 o'clock is the hour when all the churches of various denominations are opened, and the people going to service are liable to meet those leaving the public-houses.

[illegible] Before we leave the city will you give us your opinion with regard to closing hours?—I think opening from 2 to 5 on Sunday would be advisable, and closing at 9 on Saturday night; that is my own opinion.

[illegible] That is on account of the drunkenness at late hours on Saturday night?—On Saturday night from 9 to 11 the drunken cases are almost double, and in [illegible]

[illegible] and 1897. Will you give us [illegible] from 9 to 11 p.m.?—In [illegible], [illegible]; in [illegible], [illegible]; in [illegible], [illegible]; on Sunday for those three years [illegible], [illegible], [illegible].

[illegible] Then I think we may pass to Saturday?—[illegible], [illegible], [illegible].

[illegible] Will you take any one day you like, Tuesday, Wednesday, Thursday, or Friday, and give us the figures for that day?—On Tuesday [illegible], [illegible], [illegible]. On Wednesday, [illegible], [illegible], [illegible].

[illegible] Now we will go to the county divisions, the East Riding?—I did not prepare a return for that.

[illegible] You give us your general figures here as regards the country districts, about the early closing on Saturday. What we have just had is entirely in the city?—Yes. I think as regards the country districts, early closing on Saturday night, say at 9 o'clock, would meet with general approval. Nearly all my officers are in favour of it, and report that the clergy and other representative persons strongly approve of it. There seems to me to be a practical unanimity of opinion on all sides that closing at 9 o'clock on Saturday night would be advisable. I may mention in connection with that that there is no section of the community that seems to be so anxious for it as the labouring men and the artisans, from what I have seen in Cork city. I asked several of them would it be an inconvenience, and their reply was, No, but a great benefit, and a blessing. I was very much struck by it.

[illegible] As to the forfeiture of licences will you tell the Commission how it is evaded?—The section with regard to the forfeiture of licences is sometimes evaded. I will give you a couple of instances of how it is occasionally evaded. The police opposed the renewal of a publican's licence owing to repeated convictions. The renewal was granted. The publican then assigned the premises to his wife, who obtained a transfer, alleging that her husband had left the country. The husband returned directly the transfer was obtained. Another case is this. A publican lost his licence through convictions. He got it back as a new licence immediately on the expiration of the statutory term of disability. Some years later he again forfeited it, and again got it back as a new licence for his wife, without being under any disability in the interval.

[illegible] Are there instances in the city of Cork?—No, in the East Riding.

[illegible] In your experience of other parts of Ireland, have you ever known any instances of the kind?—I cannot remember any.

[illegible] Do you think it is at all customary, or prevalent, to attempt to transfer to a wife?—Not to any great extent. I have known some instances of it. I have two others here. It is done occasionally.

[illegible] In other parts of Ireland?—I really cannot answer for them.

[illegible] Now I think we may go to the suggestions which you wish to make. The first is as to the granting, renewing, and transferring of licences?—I think the power to grant, renew, and transfer licences might well be vested solely in the hands of the county court judges and recorders.

[illegible] The whole business with regard to the granting of licences?—Yes.

[illegible] Will you state the reasons why you think so?—From inquiries which I have made, both personally and through my officers, I must say that I think the system as at present administered is not regarded with full confidence by large sections of the public.

[illegible] Why not?—For one thing a feeling seems to prevail that public-houses have been multiplied to an inordinate extent.

[illegible] Will you first of all confine yourself to Cork city. Do you complain of an inordinate number of public-houses in the city of Cork?—There are an inordinate number no doubt.

[illegible] Granted by the Recorder?—Not, I should think, by the present Recorder at all events.

[illegible] Then they are old licences granted by his [illegible]

Mr. A. [illegible]. 19 Mar. '98. Quarter sessions.

58,195. With regard to the country districts in the West Riding, what do you say?—The licences are increasing only slightly.

58,196. What advantage the magistrates to grant more licences in the country districts?—The magistrates, I have reason to believe, [illegible] of the [illegible] [illegible] of the magistrates have bitterly complained of that, and the Recorder of Cork has made use of some strong expressions of disapproval in connection with that system.

58,197. Speaking as county court judge?—Yes.

58,198. And presiding over the quarter sessions?—Yes.

58,199. The magistrates themselves complain of being overruled?—In a few instances bitterly they have complained.

Recorder of Cork.

58,200. You are satisfied with the way in which, in the city of Cork, the present Recorder administers the law, are you not?—I have no doubt that he administers it properly.

58,201. Does the Recorder as a matter of fact live in or near Cork?—No, his residence is in Kerry.

58,202. But he has a knowledge of the wants of the town?—Yes.

58,203. And thoroughly knows the city of Cork?—Yes, he lives a great part of his time in Cork and in the East Riding within his district.

58,204. Does he live near enough to have a full local knowledge of the circumstances of the case in the East Riding?—I think he does; considering the length of time he spends going round his district, I am quite sure he does.

58,205. Going from one quarter sessions to another?—Yes.

Prosecutions before resident magistrates.

58,206. What is your second suggestion?—I would suggest that the prosecutions against publicans be tried only by resident magistrates, or, failing that, that a resident magistrate should be constituted a [illegible] magistrate, so that he may be empowered to hear cases when sitting alone.

58,207. (*Dean Abdication.*) With an appeal?—Yes.

58,208. (*Viscount de Vesci.*) Are you in favour of an appeal on both sides?—Under the present system I certainly think the police ought to have an appeal, considering the number of dismissals.

58,209. Generally you recommend that the whole of the business of prosecutions against publicans should be tried by resident magistrates on the ground you stated before with regard to granting licences, that magistrates are liable to be canvassed?—Yes.

58,210. They are liable to be brought in and canvassed for a particular case?—There is no doubt of it.

Appeals by police.

58,211. Would you be in favour of granting a power of appeal to the police, or to the prosecution, in cases where they are only tried by a resident magistrate alone, as you recommend?—No, I hardly think so.

58,212. You mean that there should be a power of appeal given to the police if the present system continues?—Yes, should the present system be continued.

Justices to act in own divisions.

58,213. What is your third suggestion?—Justices should be debarred, I think, from voting at licensing quarter sessions outside the divisions in which are situated the petty sessions they usually attend.

58,214. That is to say, you suggest that only the magistrates who live in a particular petty sessional [illegible] should deal with the cases arising out of that petty sessional district?—That was not exactly what I meant.

58,215. That would be too few?—Yes.

58,216. You might not have a magistrate living in a particular district?—If you could be sure of having sufficient magistrates, I think that would be the best system, because they alone know best the requirements of the places; but it might not work practically, for the reason you have stated, that there would not be enough magistrates. What I mean is this, sometimes justices attend annual licensing quarter sessions in different divisions, the result being that they vote not only on applications brought from their own individual districts, but upon those from districts about which they may know very little, or perhaps nothing.

58,217. It has been stated here by other witnesses [illegible] to go and vote, and sit on any quarter sessions bench at the other end of the county?—Yes.

Mr. A. [illegible].

58,218. They can do it now?—I understand so.

58,219. And you wish to debar them from doing that?—Yes.

58,220. You think that only the magistrates who live within the quarter sessions jurisdiction should vote on the question of granting licences in that district?—That is my meaning.

58,221. I think you said that in the East Riding you believe they are three licensing districts?—Yes, as well as I remember there are.

58,222. The East Riding being about half the county of Cork, I suppose?—Yes.

58,223. Then it is clear that only the magistrates who live within the licensing district should be entitled to attend and vote as to the granting of licences, or licensing business generally?—Yes.

Endorsement of licences.

58,224. What is the fourth suggestion; it is as to endorsements, is it not?—Yes. I think in view of the present system that records on licences should be compulsory for a second and subsequent conviction.

58,225. That the licensee should be allowed what is called a first fault?—Yes.

58,226. You think every other conviction should be recorded?—I think so.

58,227. Would you be in favour of retaining the present system of the third endorsement entailing a forfeiture?—Yes, I would certainly.

58,228. Some of the endorsements might be for comparatively trifling offences?—Perhaps in view of that there might be some relaxation. If the endorsement were made compulsory possibly there might be a necessity for some relaxation.

58,229. In other words you would be in favour of a discretion being exercised as to the forfeiture when it came to the third endorsement?—Either that, or extend it, and make the forfeiture liable after three records, and an offence of a recordable nature, instead of as at present, two records, and a conviction of a recordable nature.

58,230. (*Dean Dickinson.*) Or that the magistrates should have regard to the circumstances of the endorsements, as well as the fact?—Yes, perhaps so.

58,231. (*Viscount de Vesci.*) The present system is the magistrates exercise their discretion as to whether they will endorse—as to whether they think the offence is serious enough for endorsement?—They do.

58,232. And the third endorsement entails forfeiture?—Yes, the third conviction of a recordable nature. As well as I remember the law is this, that two recorded offences followed by a conviction of a recordable nature entail forfeiture.

58,233. (*Dean Dickinson.*) The third offence must be of a recordable nature?—It must be of a recordable nature, but whether it is recorded or not does not matter.

58,234. The record in that case is the conviction?—Yes, three records are not necessary.

58,235. Three endorsements are not necessary?—Yes.

58,236. The conviction is virtually a third endorsement?—Yes.

Occasional licences at petty sessions.

58,237. (*Viscount de Vesci.*) What is your fifth suggestion?—Certificates for occasional licences to be granted only in petty sessions, or should that be found to entail inconvenience, I would suggest that they should be only granted on the certificate and recommendation of the district officer of police.

58,238. With regard to the first part of your suggestion, how often do the petty sessions in Ireland sit, on an average?—Fortnightly, and monthly.

58,239. Never weekly?—Very rarely, except in large towns. It might be inconvenient.

58,240. Because of the time that elapses between?—Yes. It might be met in one or two ways either that two magistrates instead of one, as at present, should grant the certificate on the recommendation of a district inspector, or, one magistrate might grant it on the recommendation of a district inspector.

58,241. At present, it can be heard by a magistrate

…should know nothing … result being that … many … and it may be … As a … system … people who have not … All … that licence, goes to … brings it to the … the name of the … then sends the … and goes back the

… punishable offence?— … Licensing Act. I … distance, within the … penalty is that the … the manager of the

… you have two cases … One an order to … and another to sell … the licence, I under- … his own premises, … the part of the law, … ought to be such a … ? as hotel-keeper … a distance, or any- … not get it. That has … not glad you were … be amended so that … licence-holder.

… you suggest that in … premises) from the … —I do.

… is heard, as at … the … or at … necessary to a class … action, and we are

… district inspector or … … through

… that one or the other

… be able, knowing the … state whether they

… question?—I think in … value should be … At present, under … 1877, there is a … of 5l., where … where it is over

… with the seventh … should have the … inspectors or head … be granted a right

… officer brought the … I would restrict … … asking for

… suggestion?—I think … under 16 certainly, … or off the premises … though, that juvenile … It is a matter … notice, that sending … not expose them to … to be avoided.

… question is with regard … I think the distance … should be extended to

… difficulty in proving … selling?—Yes, it is a … deal of difficulty, and …

… is a man in a public- … house have to go by … ?—They have. The

Mr. A. [illegible]

[illegible] Mar. '97.

55,257. Your next suggestion, I think, is as to repealing the Act of 18[illegible], with regard to the entertaining of private friends?—Yes.

Treating friends.

55,258. Do you find that a prevalent thing?—It is sometimes given as an excuse. My suggestion would be to debar publicans from entertaining their friends at their bars. I think it should be restricted to persons entertained by them in their own private premises. I think it might help us to some extent.

55,259. Still that also would be liable to abuse, would it not?—It would. I do not attach very much importance to the suggestion, but I throw it out.

Hours of closing.

55,260. With regard to closing hours, I think you have given us your opinion?—Yes. I think 9 o'clock on Saturday night would be a good closing hour, and that in the city on Sunday they should be open from 2 to 5, instead of from 2 to 7, as at present.

55,261. You would curtail the time by two hours?—Yes. Then, should total closing be applied to the city, it might be well to make the offence of keeping for sale punishable under the first section of the Act of 18[illegible], which carries a penalty of 10l. for the first offence. At present the offence is punishable under the 17 & 18 Vict. c. 89, under which the penalty is only 2l. I think that might be useful in the event of bogus clubs or shebeens being established to any extent.

Keeping for sale.

Sunday closing.

55,262. (Dean [illegible].) You were not connected with Cork in the year 18[illegible], I suppose?—No.

55,263. You have heard of the house to house visitation there, and a vote being taken with respect to the total closing on Sunday?—I have heard something of it.

55,264. The voting stood thus: In favour of total Sunday closing, [illegible]; against total Sunday closing, 1,870; so that there was a majority of [illegible] in favour of total Sunday closing?—I was not aware of the figures.

55,265. You think that if Sunday closing were carried, the action of the police would prevent the development of shebeens and bogus clubs?—I think it would in the long run. We should get them under in the long run, but there might be some difficulty at first.

Small penalties.

55,266. With respect to the maximum penalties, there is nothing to quarrel with in the maximum penalty, but the minimum penalty is left optional with the magistrate?—For what offence?

55,267. For breaches of the licensing law—keeping open at prohibited hours, and so forth—the magistrate has the power of inflicting a very small fine if he pleases?—Yes, for the first offence, but there is a minimum penalty of 1l. fixed for every second and subsequent offence.

55,268. I have seen notice in the newspapers of half-a-crown being imposed?—I am speaking of prosecutions of publicans.

55,269. In those cases the fines are often very small?—Yes.

55,270. And they are accepted as part of the general trade contingency, like the taxes?—Their small fines have no repressive effect.

55,271. Would you be in favour of establishing a minimum penalty in those cases?—No, I would not for the first offence. I think for the first offence it does not matter very much how a man is punished, but for the second and subsequent offences I have recommended that the conviction should be recorded compulsorily on his licence.

Clubs.

55,272. You are not opposed, in the abstract, to the formation of working men's clubs, supposing they are well conducted?—Certainly not.

55,273. Do you think that if working men's clubs were established, they ought to be registered?—As far as Cork is concerned, I see no necessity for legislation in the direction of clubs at all; but, if you register one, you should register all.

55,274. All clubs and of all classes?—Yes.

55,275. Would you approve not only of registration, but of licensing; so that clubs which deal in the sale of intoxicating liquors should pay licence fees just as publicans are obliged to do?—No; I think I should be rather in favour of registering clubs.

of houses?—I think I understand you to say there are markets and fairs?—There is generally a weekly market in a country town, and sometimes a monthly or a quarterly fair; but really, apart from that, I do not see any necessity whatever. Take, for instance, Kenmare. That is a small town of about 1,200 people. There are 61 licensed premises in that town. That is, one licensed premises to every 17 people. There are no manufactures whatever, nor are there any large industries there. The only thing in the nature of an industry is a creamery, which may perhaps employ 20 people; but, in other respects, there is nothing going on, except an ordinary market every week, and an occasional fair.

58,297. There must be a demand for the articles they sell, otherwise they could not keep the shop open?—A good number of them, I fancy, have land as well. At all events, some have.

58,298. You have an objection to any other business being conducted on the same premises with the sale of liquor?—Yes; I am inclined to think that it is not a good system.

58,299. If it were forbidden to conduct any other business in the same premises that wine and spirits, and beer were sold on, that would necessitate in itself a lesser number of houses?—My idea is that there are fully double too many public-houses already.

58,300. True, but you admit that many of these are enabled to gain a livelihood in them by the sale of other articles than wines, spirits, and beer?—Yes, I should think so.

58,301. If that sale is removed, would it not lessen their receipts, and naturally close the houses?—Yes.

58,302. Your view is that houses for the sale of intoxicating liquors should sell nothing else, that they should be established for that purpose and nothing else?—Except, as has already been given in evidence by some witness, that they provide certainly some food, or something besides liquor.

58,303. Ordinary refreshments?—Ordinary refreshments.

58,304. That would be a matter of course, would it not?—As a rule, it is very hard to get anything to eat in some of the public-houses.

58,305. Can you give any just reason for the alteration of the present system, or why it is in any way dangerous to the public?—I think I have said already that it leads to an evasion of the Act on the Sunday.

58,306. That is only with regard to the Sunday Closing Act?—Yes, and I think it also spreads the taste for drink widely. People who may go into these houses to buy groceries and other things without any intention of drinking, are, there is reason to suppose, very often induced to drink when they see the liquor before their eyes, or they are asked to drink by their neighbours who are there—they are treated. I think that, perhaps, especially applies to the case of women—so I have been informed.

58,307. May it not, on the other hand, be a matter of great convenience?—Possibly it may prevent them going into two shops instead of one.

58,308. It is a custom of the country which has grown up for years, is it not?—It has been so for many years.

[illegible]. Does not that indicate that there is a very great necessity for restrictions for the sale of these [illegible] on Sunday?—I do not think so.

[illegible]. You will admit that there must be a demand or otherwise they would not incur this risk?—Of course there is a demand. I think it is not a legitimate demand. I do not see why a man cannot get a few bottles of beer or whatever he wants to get on Saturday and keep it for Sunday.

[illegible]. You think that there is such a demand for the purchase and consumption of these articles as to induce men to try to evade the law to the extent which you have stated?—I do not take quite the same view that you do, because I think that these breaches of the Licensing Acts on the Sunday are caused very much by over-competition, and the publicans are afraid to refuse their customers. In my opinion it really arises a great deal more from that than from any legitimate demand for drink. I do not believe that there is that pressing legitimate demand for drink on Sunday at all. I do not quite see it in the same light that you do.

[illegible]. The customers requiring to drink?—They are very often young fellows who would be very much better without it who are found in these public-houses.

[illegible]. You gave your opinion that there was very little home drinking. Have you any statistics or any proof of that?—I made inquiries about it. It is contrary to the temperament of the Irishman to drink at home. He drinks more for sociability.

[illegible]. Would it not be preferable to preserve that state of things; to purify the house, if it is so dangerous to permit to retail the articles, and to give public convenience for the consumption of them?—That is a view which may be entertained, but I hardly think that the closing of public-houses would lead to home drinking.

[illegible]. You said from your official knowledge that there was very little shebeening?—Very little.

[illegible]. Is not that another testimony to the advantage of having a reasonable number of houses legitimately for the sale of these articles?—I do not think so, because the increase of shebeens applies to the country where the Sunday Closing Act is in force, just as much as it does to the city where it is not in force.

[illegible]. You are of opinion that if you were in your district to restrict the privileges of sale, it would not create more illicit drinking?—I am inclined to think that at first Sunday closing in the city might lead to shebeens and bogus clubs, but I think that eventually the police would succeed in crushing them out. It would, however, be very troublesome. Of course we are quite prepared to do it when the law is changed.

[illegible]. Did you intend to convey the meaning that athletics encouraged drunkenness?—I am afraid they do, in many instances. I am told by my officers that these large hurling and football tournaments, which gather young men in from different parts of the country, are attended by a very considerable amount of drinking when the game is over. Of course I quite hold that athletics, and especially cycling and healthy sports, are very good for the young men of the country; but, as managed at present, these meetings are rather productive of drunkenness. I understand that they are organised to some extent and assisted by publicans.

[illegible]. The meetings are?—So I understand.

[illegible]. Do I understand you to convey the meaning that all these outdoor gatherings for athletic exercises are promoted by publicans simply for the sale of drink?—I understand that they are promoted to a great extent by publicans, and no doubt with a view to the sale of drink.

[illegible]. These sports must be held to some extent on land outside the city. Do the publicans have the privilege of supplying these articles?—No; but when the games are over, their houses are open to all those who are bona fide travellers, and there is a considerable

[illegible]. Then your remedy for that would be to prohibit these athletic meetings on Sundays?—Oh, not at all. When necessary, I would close the public-houses. I did it on that occasion. I had an application made to the magistrates, because we feared a riot. An application was made to them and they closed all the public-houses in the adjoining villages, and we had perfect quietness.

[illegible]. That was upon what may be termed an official and legitimate representation to the authorities as to what was anticipated?—Yes.

[illegible]. So you do not always anticipate a riot simply from the gathering together of young men for athletic exercises?—No; it was only done on one occasion in three years. They are very quiet gatherings as a rule.

[illegible]. You say there are 12 clubs in Cork?—Yes.

[illegible]. And they are open on Sunday?—They are.

[illegible]. All day?—All day, or the greater part.

[illegible]. Is gambling permitted?—I have not reason to think that gambling, at all events such as the police could interfere with, is carried on.

[illegible]. It may not be gambling in a club, but it would be in a public-house—playing at cards or draughts?—I understand that card-playing is general among the clubs.

[illegible]. And they supply drink in any quantity?—Yes.

[illegible]. May not that be a great factor in increasing these statistics in the returns of drunkenness?—I made close inquiries as to that, and I ascertained that the drinking clubs are not traceable to any appreciable extent in drinking in clubs, but I may say that drinking to a view is traceable, I believe, in some of them.

[illegible]. In answer to a question put to you, you acknowledged that the rules of these clubs were very loosely observed?—In a few of them I should say there. On general information, I have reason to believe that the rules as regards the introduction of members is rather laxly observed, but I have no definite or positive information on the subject.

[illegible]. When the public-houses or the legitimate sources of supply are closed, the privileged can enter the clubs and get anything and everything they require?—Yes. There is no doubt that on Saturday nights, after closing hours, there is a great deal of drinking in these clubs, that is, in the doubtful clubs.

[illegible]. You were spoken of the large number of offences against Sunday closing. Do I understand that they were offences by licensees?—All of them.

[illegible]. Are there any prosecutions of the public for purchasing of drink?—There are, decidedly.

[illegible]. Are there many?—In every instance in which there is a prosecution for a violation of the Sunday Closing Act there must of necessity, I think, be a prosecution of persons for being found drinking on the premises.

[illegible]. Are the police as strict in prosecuting those who frequent as they are in prosecuting those who supply?—Quite.

[illegible]. You spoke of the laxity or indifference of the magistrates in dealing on behalf of the cases presented to them; may I ask, have you a very high respect for the magistrates?—Yes; I have.

[illegible]. They are gentlemen appointed by the Crown, are they not?—Yes. Apart from the action of some of them in connection with the Licensing Acts, I have a very high opinion of them.

[illegible]. I take it that so far as the administration of the Licensing Acts goes, you have no faith in them?—In some of them I have not very much.

[illegible]. Still, they are gentlemen appointed by the Crown?—No doubt.

[illegible]. And they are gentlemen of unquestionable position?—They have the position of magistrates, certainly, which is a responsible and a very responsible one.

Mr. A. [illegible]

[illegible]

County Court Judge on [illegible]

[illegible]. We have been told here that the magistrates are [illegible] and [illegible], and I think you have led us to believe that [illegible] is practised in your district, in Cork, and in the country?—Yes.

[illegible]. And then [illegible] has no effect. You have only to ask the magistrates not to punish, and they do not punish. Do I understand that?—In some [illegible] they are open to influence of that kind. I do not for a moment mean to say that the whole magistracy is; but, unquestionably, from what I am told, some are. If you will allow me, I will read a County [illegible] remarks on the subject, at [illegible] Quarter Sessions on the [illegible] November 18[illegible]. "Mr. T. [illegible] Page, J.P., Youghal, said that he would wish to mention that in connexion with the first case on the list two days ago, a [illegible] of the applicant waited on him, and asked him to [illegible] [illegible] the case when it came on in every possible way he could. He had every possible objection to being canvassed. He considered it his duty to [illegible] [illegible] that in public, and let them have their own opinions on it, and to allow of his Honour giving his opinion on the matter." Then—"His Honour said both on public and private grounds he felt grateful to Mr. Page for having mentioned that matter. He was bound to say he was spoken to by others in private, but Mr. Page was the first gentleman who had given him the opportunity of speaking in a public court on this matter. Unfortunately he was aware that the practice of intimidating magistrates was a prevalent one, and it was his (the Recorder's) duty to speak very strongly upon the subject. Anything more infamous than this practice of approaching magistrates for the purpose of influencing them while in the discharge of their business could not be conceived. What would be thought of himself as County Court Judge if he were to allow himself to be spoken to by his friends or others outside the court with regard to the cases that were to be tried by him? What would be said of conduct like that? He did not know, but [illegible] something very severe, but nothing more severe than he would deserve if he indulged in it. A magistrate coming there to sit and hear licensing applications was as much a judge as he (the Recorder) himself was, and if he allowed himself to be swayed by the interests of the applicants in any case he was unfit to hold a commission of the peace. That such canvassing went on as that referred to by Mr. Page is, he was afraid, too true. It was an illegal conduct than he was afraid was growing up, but if a case ever came before him in which it was proved such canvassing was successful, then he would consider it his duty to at once report the matter to the Lord Chancellor and get the person who allowed himself to be thus influenced dismissed from his position of justice of the peace."

[illegible]. Are some of these magistrates in a very [illegible] social position? Do they come under the term of [illegible] magistrates?—I do not think so. I know of none.

[illegible]. Are there any that come under the term of [illegible] magistrates?—I do not think there are.

[illegible]. So that I may take it these justices are gentlemen of position, education, and [illegible] [illegible]?—Some of them, I am informed—I do not know them personally—are of the same social standing as the publicans themselves, a few of them.

[illegible]. You just now said they were not, that they were all of good social position?—I do not think the question of social position was introduced. If I answered that then I did not intend to.

[illegible]. I only want to ascertain from you why it is that these [illegible] as magistrates cannot administer the licensing laws with as much fairness and impartiality as they can administer any other law?—Because they will not. That I suppose is the reason of it really.

[illegible]. You simply say they do not?—They do not. Certainly the Recorder does not seem to think it. [illegible] [illegible] do it.

Conduct of [illegible] houses.

[illegible]. As to [illegible] houses, you were pleased to say that [illegible] houses were better conducted than the [illegible] houses?—Rather better.

[illegible]. (Fitzgerald de Vere.) That there was not very

Licensing Acts, chiefly of the Sunday Closing Act. That is really the offence.

[illegible]. The [illegible] licensee is more careless than the independent licensee?—He is rather worse. I really think there is very little difference, but apparently he is rather more inclined to evade the law as regards closing on Sunday.

[illegible]. Then speaking as an official, are you opposed to the [illegible] system?—I find it difficult to form an opinion on the subject, but on the whole I think the independent house system is rather better.

[illegible]. You would prefer it of the two?—I would.

[illegible]. Do you see any serious results from the [illegible] house system?—For one thing, the [illegible] system completely overrides the portion of the Act which deals with the forfeiture of licenses, and for this reason—the directly a tied publican gets a record on his licence he is got rid of, and another man is put in. That is why a number of licensed houses are kept in existence which otherwise we would possibly be got rid of.

[illegible]. There is no difficulty in transfer?—No, none.

[illegible]. None whatever?—No, there seems to be no difficulty whatever in transfers.

[illegible]. Still, the brewer, if he entrusted his money and property to a manager, would be careful to see he was a man of good character?—He would, and it would be his interest to see to that.

[illegible]. That would be to the public interest, would not it?—It would, but there seems to be an impression, and there is the force, that [illegible], that the responsibility of the brewers should be greater than it is. It seems to me that the tied publican is a sort of buffer between the brewer and the law.

[illegible]. He incurs a very great responsibility?—The tied publican gives security for about [illegible], or from that to [illegible].

[illegible]. As to the hours of closing on Saturday night and Sunday, I understand you have taken the trouble to interview a large number of persons with a view to obtaining their opinions. You stated you had interviewed [illegible] highly educated gentlemen in prominent positions. Who were these [illegible] gentlemen? I think you mentioned bishops?—There were two bishops of the Roman Catholic Church, one bishop of the Protestant Church, one of the Members of Parliament for the city of Cork, the Mayor of Cork, the President of the Chamber of Commerce, the President of the United Trades Association, the Chairman of the Board of Guardians, and [illegible] employers of labour.

[illegible]. And their views were for shortening the hours?—They were.

[illegible]. Was there any one of those that you interviewed that in any way [illegible] the convenience of a publichouse?—I do not think there was one—not one.

[illegible]. If the publichouses or the licensed houses closed on Saturday night at 9 o'clock, would you close all other shops at the same time?—No, I would not. I think really that 9 o'clock is a reasonable hour for people to purchase anything they want.

[illegible]. That may be your opinion. I am asking, would you close all the other shops at the same hour?—No, certainly not.

[illegible]. Would it not be rather dangerous with the [illegible] crowded with people working [illegible] and all the licensed houses closed? Would they not find no outlet to satisfy their [illegible] for these articles?—No. The fact which chiefly weighs with me in advocating the closing of public houses at 9 o'clock is the undoubted fact, from what I can see of the labouring classes and the artisan classes, that they are all most anxious to have them closed. I [illegible] them on that point. Most of them would not be any inconvenience to the working man to close the publichouses on Saturday night at 9 o'clock.

[illegible]. These respectable artisans are members of clubs, are they not?—No, none of them at all hardly.

[illegible]. Are there no working men's clubs?—There is only one I know of in Cork city, and it is quite a newly formed one.

[illegible]. What is the class of people that constitute and support the 11 other clubs?—They are various classes, from the nobility downwards. The [illegible]

[illegible]. The clerks may be looked upon as a class of working men. They are not very high-waged people are they?—No, not very.

[illegible]. May I ask just one question on [illegible]? Is it not possible, and is it not very often the case, that an offence is committed on a licensed house which the proprietor is really powerless to prevent. For instance, is it an offence for a drunken man to come in and sit down on licensed premises?—No, it is not.

[illegible]. Not harbouring?—It is not an offence in Ireland. It has been suggested here by one of the witnesses yesterday, that if a drunken man is found in a public-house, the onus of proof should be on the publican that he did not see him drunk. It is no offence for a publican to have a drunken man on his premises, provided that it cannot be shown that he either made him drunk, or that he provided him with liquor while drunk.

[illegible]. Is it maintained by you, as an official, that if a drunken man is discovered on licensed premises, and the licensed victualler can prove that he was not served there, the licensed victualler is exonerated?—That is the law. It is no offence whatever for a publican to have a drunken man on his premises.

[illegible]. Would you order proceedings to be taken against a licensed victualler, if a man was found drunk and asleep on his premises?—Certainly not. The man himself would be prosecuted for being drunk on licensed premises, but the publican would not be prosecuted.

[illegible]. (Mr. Tenupen.) Have there not been two or three cases of prosecutions of that kind in Cork?—There have been cases of prosecutions of publicans for supplying drink to drunken men on their premises, but not for having drunken men on the premises.

[illegible]. (Mr. Johnston.) Have not you the offence which we have in England of permitting drunkenness?—Yes, that is the offence, and by permitting drunkenness we understand it as making a sober man drunk on the premises—a man goes in sober and becomes drunk on the premises. It entails a prosecution of the publican if a drunken man goes into a public-house and is supplied with drink while in that state.

[illegible]. (Mr. Walker.) With reference to supply to children, you have given your opinion that no child should be supplied for consumption off the premises under 14 years of age?—I think perhaps it would be well. I think it subjects young people to a very great temptation sending them for drink, and I think the parents might fairly go themselves, but I do not press that.

[illegible]. You supplemented that evidence with this remark, that you had not paid attention to it yourself, but it was brought under your notice. It has been a recent matter with you?—Yes. It was brought under my notice in one instance.

[illegible]. Was this one suggested by somebody?—Yes, it was, but I should say, I think myself personally, that it was a suggestion that might possibly be entertained by the members of the Commission.

[illegible]. But they want evidence that there is necessity for it. From your official personal observation and knowledge while in your office, are there many children employed to go to public-houses to fetch beer or spirits or wine for their parents?—As a matter of fact there are. I can give you the statistics if you like.

[illegible]. No, I do not want them. I merely wanted to ask the question, is not this a matter that affects the [illegible]

[illegible]. (Mr. Whitaker.) With reference to the [illegible] of magistrates, may I ask you if you remember about a year and a half ago, Judge Adams at Limerick saying, "That in his opinion this system of [illegible] "magistrates that existed throughout the length and "breadth of Ireland is a great scandal, and ought to "be made penal by law"?—Yes, I have the extract from his speech here.

Mr. A. Gambell.

[illegible] Mar. [illegible]

Judge Adams on [illegible].

[illegible]. You remember he made that statement?—Yes.

[illegible]. That bears out the opinion that the [illegible] is very prevalent and very objectionable?—It is.

[illegible]. (Mr. Tenupen.) Was that speech made in connexion with licensing matters only?—It was made at licensing quarter sessions.

[illegible]. Entirely in connexion with licensing matters?—Yes.

[illegible].401. (Mr. Whitaker.) With reference to [illegible] you have told us the publicans send spies out to look out for the police, and that breaches of the law take place when they can evade the police. What I want to ask is this: Does not that rather suggest that the publicans do not conduct their houses quite in the best way possible and certainly that it is a very bad sign as regards the conduct of the houses. It seems to indicate a deliberate intention to evade the law.

Conduct of licensees.

[illegible]. Therefore, when you say that the licensed houses in your district are, on the whole, well conducted, you do mean us to put some limitations on that general good character?—I do not know whether I stated it in evidence, but I have it in my notes to say they are generally well conducted, with the exception of breaking the conditions of the Sunday Closing Act, which the great majority of them are willing to do if they can do it with impunity. I may also state that I am afraid there is to some extent a giving of drink to drunken men, or else we should not have so much public drunkenness.

[illegible]. Then really the houses are not as well conducted as you would like to see them?—Apart from that they really are very fairly conducted; there is no riotous conduct in public-houses, nor are they disorderly houses or anything of that kind. It is chiefly the sale during prohibited hours, which is very much due to the over-competition consequent on the enormous number of public-houses.

[illegible]. Do you remember some remarks made by Judge [illegible]?—That is the judge whose address I read.

[illegible]. Do you remember that in October [illegible], he said this: "There were a great many houses in the "city as respectable as any in the kingdom, and he "regretted to say there were a great many as dis"reputable"?—I do not quite remember that.

[illegible]. "He thought it a blot on their licensing laws "that such houses could continue to exist. As the "Act of Parliament goes, certificates were required to "be produced from year to year as to their good "conduct; it was perfectly manifest that there was "no difficulty in getting them, and until there was a "radical change in the licensing laws they could not "cope with the evils arising from the liquor traffic"?—I do not remember to have ever read those remarks.

[illegible].407 Would you agree with those generally as being correct?—He had a much better opportunity of knowing those cases than I have. I do not attend the Court; it is not my business to attend the Court.

[illegible]. You told us that the greater portion of the [illegible] [illegible]

Sunday [illegible]

Mr. A. Campbell. — conduct of the applicants, and as to the manner in which the house has been conducted the previous year.

3rd Mar., '88. — 58,413. The suitability of the premises, also?—That is not considered at all at the renewal sessions.

58,414. Do you think it desirable that that should be made one of the conditions?—I think it is, because the premises may lapse into a bad condition.

58,415. The premises may be suitable at the time when they get the license, but afterwards they may become very unsatisfactory?—I think it would be a very good idea.

Heavy drinking on Saturdays. — 58,416. May I take it from what you have stated that there is a very large amount of drinking and drunkenness on Saturday nights in your town, but on Sunday nights it is comparatively small?—Yes. It is small, but you must remember the public-houses are closed—we are talking of the city now—at 7 o'clock on Sunday.

58,417. Did this promote much greater sobriety on the Sunday night than on Saturday?—Yes.

58,418. Showing clearly that the drunkenness comes from the public-houses?—Yes, I should say so, decidedly.

Back-doors, &c. — 58,419. Is it the fact that in a considerable number of the houses they have back doors leading into yards and gardens to which the surrounding people have access, making supervision by the police much more difficult?—Yes. There are a number of houses of that kind, but I cannot give you the actual numbers. I hear of them from time to time, and in case of transfer or whenever the opportunity occurs the police bring the matter before the notice of the magistrates or the Recorder, and try to get these things remedied.

58,420. It would be a great advantage to the police in supervising the houses, if these back doors were closed for trade purposes?—Yes, and I think it would be a great measure if the whole question of the suitability of the premises, and the [illegible] of the premises, and the sanitary arrangements and lavatories and things of that kind, were looked to. I think the matter is not looked sufficiently into perhaps when the original licenses are being granted.

Evasion of forfeiture of licenses. — 58,421. You gave us one or two instances of licenses being transferred to evade after convictions. Do you remember a case a year ago, of Mrs. Catherine Hayes, of South Main Street, in Cork, where there were two convictions recorded on the license, and it had been transferred to the wife?—I do not know of that case, and I cannot speak of that case from experience, but I have given you two other cases somewhat similar.

58,422. In Cork?—No, in the Riding.

58,423. This was in Cork?—Yes. It looks as if in this instance the unprincipled publicans were following the lead of the anti-license system, in transferring in that way when the license is in danger.

Lodgers in public-houses. — 58,424. I think you told us that a considerable number of publicans in Cork, let out portions of their houses or premises to working people—10 per cent.?—I understand it is 10 per cent.

unanimity of opinion that the Sunday Closing Act has acted well, and has reduced drunkenness and improved manners generally.

[illegible]. It took a long time to do it in Cork. It was many years before it had any effect?—That is the opinion generally. Will you permit me to correct a mistake I have made as regards the president of the United Trades Association? I have in my notes here that he says that he [illegible] the majority of the working men in Cork are of his opinion on the subject, that is, as regards the subject of closing on Saturday night, and I have also another statement from an ex-delegate of the Trades Association.

[illegible]. (Mr. *Johnston.*) You were asked as to why justices should be open to private influence in the matter of licensing, and not with reference to other things. The difference is in the large pecuniary interest involved, is it not?—I think not so much that as very often social or local interests perhaps.

[illegible]. That is just my point, that men who would not dream of approaching a justice about some police case, or some minor offence, do so where hundreds or even thousands of pounds may be involved in the decision of the justices?—Possibly that may be one reason, and it would seem as if some justices do not attach very much importance to these licensing questions, and they do not think that these offences apparently are of great importance one way or the other.

[illegible]. (Mr. *Grinling.*) You have told us you have met with no cases of adulteration in Ireland, but they have all been cases of dilution?—Yes.

[illegible]. In those cases where you prosecuted and were successful, what was the nature of the prosecution?—The reducing the strength of spirits.

[illegible]. Beyond the strength specified in the Act?—Yes.

[illegible]. They were not poisons, were they?—No. There is an impression I have met with in many parts of Ireland that licensed traders adulterate their liquors, but I am bound to say that my experience and that of others I have consulted is quite the opposite—that they do not.

[illegible]. I do not know whether you were present yesterday when a sample of what is supposed to be whisky, and was called potheen, was produced, but I presume you would be of opinion that cases like that are hardly cases that require the attention of the Commission?—They are very much confined to particular localities.

[illegible]. You said that the women were the majority of the Sunday drinkers, I understood, and that they went so far as to go to the pawnshop to pawn articles to get drink. I suppose there is no doubt that these women are women of the very lowest class. You would not fairly represent them as respectable artisans' wives?—Chiefly labourers' wives. Labourers and their wives form, I think, the greatest proportion of the people who carry on this drinking. I had some experience in Cork with regard to that, and I found that the labourers are the worst offenders in respect to public-houses.

[illegible]. You have told us in Cork county that the consumption at the present time runs more on beer than on whisky. Is not that a change in the taste of Ireland?—It is beneficial. Porter is the drink in Cork.

[illegible]. A glass of beer?—Yes. I say it is rather [illegible] because whisky in other parts of Ireland is decidedly the national drink, but in Cork porter, and to a great extent through Cork East Riding. I do not know why.

[illegible]. One question with regard to clubs. I think you said there are 10 or 12 clubs and they are all respectable—that they were principally members and social clubs. Do any apply for [illegible]?—I do not think so. There may be exceptional cases but not as a rule.

[illegible]. As to [illegible]-houses, of which according to your evidence, there appears to be a large number in your

Mr. A. [illegible] — 30 Mar. '98

suppose, [illegible] with his [illegible]?—[illegible], I do not think so at all. I think they are perfectly free to buy wherever they like, and they do not consider themselves bound to any person.

[illegible]. It is only a man of independent means that can be free as your suggestion? I do not quite say that either. I am sure there are a number of independent publicans not particularly well off but who are still able to get along. I certainly think that the tied-house system is to a certain extent an indication that the trade is not in a very healthy state, because I do not suppose any independent publican would become tied if he was not going down the hill.

[illegible]. You have got in recent years a large quantity of breweries which you had not before?—I do not know that any of these four breweries are of recent origin. I fancy they have been in existence a considerable time.

[illegible]. I think that the late Sir John Arnott only commenced his large business recently?—Possibly in that instance he may have, but I cannot say because I really do not know, I am only three years in Cork.

[illegible]. I want to say—possibly you may agree with me—that the tied-house system, as conducted in Ireland, is very different from the tied-house system in England?—No doubt. I gather that generally—it is, it seems to me a less pronounced system, and it differs considerably.

[illegible]. With reference to the opinions which you have got from a few people out of a large population, do you attach any importance to those opinions?—I must say that I think I do, speaking of the class of the labourers and artisans that I consulted, for the reason that I went to the factories and places where they work, and I took them as they were. They did not know I was coming. They had no means of making up their opinions before, or being canvassed in any way, and they gave me it apparently from their own minds without any interference on my part, and I think it may be taken as a very fair indication of the feelings of the labouring and artisan class in Cork. I may, perhaps, add that it was taken under conditions that were not at all favourable to the temperance question, because I avoided that part of the city where the temperance clubs [illegible] exist.

[illegible]. You, at all events, found out that the working classes and these [illegible] publicans [illegible] of opinion that these houses should be closed at 9 o'clock on Saturday night?—Yes.

[illegible]. And open from 2 to 5 on Sundays?—Yes, at fairly different hours, varying, I think, from 4 to 8. Some only said 2 to 4, others 2 to 5, others 3 to 6.

[illegible]. May I take it that that is your opinion?—My opinion is from 2 to 5.

The witness withdrew.

Mr. [illegible] called in and examined.

Mr. O. [illegible].

Position of witness.

[illegible]. (*Viscount de Vesci.*) I believe you were appointed a resident magistrate in September 18[illegible]?—Yes.

[illegible]. You were stationed in Donegal for five years, in Bray in the county Wicklow for five years, and you have been 1½ years at Waterford?—Yes.

[illegible]. Previously to being appointed a resident magistrate you were five years, I believe, a legal assistant commissioner under the Land Act, and previously to that ten years at the Irish Bar?—Yes.

Early closing on Saturdays.

[illegible]. You have been good enough to furnish several paragraphs of suggestions to the Commission, and I will take No. 1. Will you give us your opinion as to early closing all over Ireland on Saturdays?—I am in favour of early closing on Saturdays from 8 or 9 o'clock.

Sunday closing.

[illegible]. Then will you give us your view with reference to Sunday closing?—I think as to Sunday closing that the hours are bad hours for closing, they are too late. The houses should be opened from 2 o'clock to 5.

[illegible]. That is in the five exempted towns?—Yes.

[illegible]. You say from 2 to 5. That is a different hour to what you have given in this précis?—Yes.

[illegible]. That is after hearing the evidence that has been given here to-day?—Yes, I wish to correct that.

Endorsing convictions.

[illegible]. Then with reference to the endorsement on licences of convictions?—I would endorse every conviction on the licence.

[illegible]. But you are in favour of giving a power of appeal?—I would give a power of appeal to the chairman of quarter sessions to take off the endorsement, though there should be no appeal against the conviction itself. At the present moment there is a great dislike among magistrates to endorse a licence. I personally do not believe that they object to convicting, but they do not like the penalty of endorsing, because it is such a heavy penalty if there are two endorsements on the licence, and another conviction.

[illegible]. At the present moment what is the nature of the appeal to quarter sessions; is it against the whole conviction?—It would be against the conviction.

[illegible]. You would not only give an appeal against the endorsement, but against the conviction itself?—Yes. I would still leave the appeal in the ordinary way to quarter sessions, but as regards taking off the endorsement, I would give an appeal to the chairman of quarter sessions alone, because in some cases there may be only a technical breach, for which it would not [illegible] the licence.

[illegible]. You are in favour of giving the power of appeal to the chairman of quarter sessions sitting alone?—The chairman sitting alone to have power to take off the endorsements.

[illegible]. That portion of it?—Yes.

[illegible]. And you would allow the appeal against the conviction to the general body of quarter sessions?—Yes.

[illegible]. Will you kindly state your reason for making the distinction between the two appeals?—Because I think there is a great disinclination amongst magistrates to endorse the licence.

[illegible]. You think the chairman's opinion would be to take off the endorsement on appeal entirely from that?—Except in grave cases.

[illegible]. Would you state your view as to the expediency having the power of appeal in cases where the decision of the magistrates was against the prosecution?—I think the present moment the constabulary appear to have no power of appealing against a dismissal under the licensing laws. A considerable number of cases have been given in which magistrates have not convicted and I think that one of their grievances is that there is no appeal from that. As magistrates we feel that though the police may have a very strong case, whether it is true or is not, as presented to us on behalf of the police, there is no strong case made on behalf of the defendant, and we are bound to give him the benefit of the doubt, and there are I have been a considerable number of dismissals. To prevent the idea that there is unfairness amongst the magistrates, I would give the constabulary power to appeal. They have the power under the [illegible] Act of 18[illegible], but no power under the Licensing Act.

[illegible]. Do you agree with the previous witness that there are a great many dismissals in cases that are improper? You have heard the statistics given by the previous witness as to the number of convictions and the number of dismissals?—I think there are some dismissals which are obtained by magistrates being [illegible]; but as to the great quantity of cases, I am afraid he was looking at it from the prosecutor's point of view mostly, and therefore if the police had a power of appeal, and the magistrates had gone wrong in their dismissal, it could be corrected by the county court judge.

[illegible]. Do you agree with the previous witness that the magistrates are lax in the administration of the licensing laws, and too readily given to dismissing cases?—I think that there are some hundreds of magistrates who are in my [illegible] very [illegible] the constitution of the licensing body?—There is no doubt that with the present form of licensing there is a great deal of [illegible] amongst magistrates who are going to sit at quarter sessions. The magistrates who were appointed [illegible] can all sit as long as they sit in their counties, but the magistrates [illegible] are limited in sitting to certain petty sessions districts by the Lord Chancellor.

[illegible]. That is for ordinary criminal business, not for the granting of licenses?—It is the licensing as well as criminal business they are limited to. They can only sit at certain petty sessions.

[illegible]. That is in the case of prosecutions under the Licensing Acts?—Yes.

[illegible]. The question I am asking you is as to the granting of licenses, and what would be the constitution of the licensing body?—I would have the magistrates who usually sit for the petty sessions district in which the house is situated, and the chairman of quarter sessions.

[illegible]. The quarter sessions districts may be made up of several petty sessions districts?—Yes, at present, and the consequence is that magistrates from other districts, perhaps miles away, vote on the licensing questions of which they know nothing and care very little about.

[illegible]. I would put this to you. There may be very few magistrates living in a petty sessions district?—There would always be two magistrates sitting, because there would be the resident magistrate and the county court judge, and if the other magistrates did not attend at quarter sessions there would be still two magistrates to adjudicate.

[illegible]. It would work out in this way, that the application would come up at a quarter sessions district, and the various petty sessions districts would be comprised in that quarter sessions district, but only those magistrates would have a voice who lived in the particular petty sessions district?—Yes, that is my opinion, and, as a rule, I have found the men living in the petty sessions district really acquire [illegible] and know the [illegible].

[illegible]. You do not agree with what has been given in evidence before us up to now, that the county court judge should be the only licensing authority?—I would rather have the county court judge than the present system—than the entire body of county magistrates.

[illegible]. As compared with what you find now I think the more local knowledge is brought in the better.

[illegible]. As a matter of fact, in a great many counties in Ireland the county court judge does not reside anywhere within the county?—Most of them.

[illegible]. They will probably live in Dublin?—Yes.

[illegible]. And come down only for the sitting of the quarter sessions. They would drive straight to the town or come by train straight to the particular town where the quarter sessions are held?—That is the reason that I should like to have the magistrates of the actual petty sessions district associated with him. They could give him the actual views of people really interested in the question of whether there should be a public-house or not.

[illegible]. The object of my question about the county court judge was this. He, you consider, would have local knowledge of the circumstances of the case?—I think he has very little local knowledge and would have very little. In some districts, of course, it would be different. The recorder would be different.

[illegible]. Have in practice [illegible] very much to a casting vote in case of an equal division?—The chairman does not give a casting vote. If it was evenly divided he would give a vote either one way or the other.

[illegible]. You suggest here that if the magistrates are equally divided the chairman should have a second vote?—Yes.

[illegible]. With reference to the *bonâ fide* traveller, you would wish to have him more thoroughly defined?—At present there are certain decisions on it, but in rural districts at petty sessions it is [illegible] hard to get magistrates to follow those decisions, and I think that there ought to be some more definite definition given in the Act as to what is a *bonâ fide* traveller. For instance, it should not apply to persons travelling for drink.

[illegible]. How would you define that? How are you to distinguish a person who travels for pleasure and a person travelling for the purpose of getting drink?—There are many cases in which it is alleged by the police that certain people went out from a town solely for the purpose of drink. There will be reasons given by the defendants as to why they went out, and it should be left pretty much to the magistrates to decide whether these people went out to get drink or went out on the legitimate business for which they say they did.

[illegible]. Do the police find any difficulty in establishing these cases on that particular point?—Very often they find a good deal, but very often the defence breaks down entirely. Sometimes the defence is that the man went out to purchase something, and it is proved he did not.

[illegible]. Then what is your second suggestion?—That people are not to stay in public-houses. *Bonâ fide* travellers are very much accustomed to coming to public-houses for two or three hours of an afternoon, and the ordinary public-house in Ireland supplies no refreshment, but it is simply for the purpose of drink.

[illegible]. You would give the police power if they saw a man going in, to take the time, and prosecute him if he was there unduly long?—Yes, longer than he ought to be there simply for the purpose of refreshment.

[illegible]. Then what is your third suggestion?—That the clause exempting railway stations should be limited so as not to apply to a person drinking at a [illegible] station if he resides within the distance constituting a *bonâ fide* traveller from the station. When I was stationed at Bray it was a common habit for a man to purchase a [illegible] ticket by an early train in the morning at the station, and use that ticket for going in to the refreshment room. The people on the refreshment room did the best they could, but the ticket was used during the whole day, going in and out of the refreshment room. I am not talking of any individual case.

[illegible]. In your experience, you have known it?—Yes.

[illegible]. The man was never a traveller at all, but stayed at the station drinking?—Yes, as long as he had the ticket.

[illegible]. Then what would be your fourth suggestion?—That *bonâ fide* travellers should not be people going in the same town from one public-house to another for the purpose of drinking.

[illegible]. That would throw the onus on the police of following a man and watching him in the street?—Certainly.

[illegible]. They would be entitled to go in and say: "You cannot serve this man, he has been already

Mr. [illegible]

[illegible] May, [illegible]

Chairman's casting vote.

The *bonâ fide* traveller.

Mr. O'[illegible]. [illegible] Mar. '[illegible]

[illegible]. Next with regard to the certificate?—The certificate at the present moment that we have to sign is simply of good character and that the house has been conducted peaceably and orderly during the past 12 months. Very often the police say that the house has not been conducted peaceably and orderly, and the magistrates consider that though the cases that are brought forward are right, it is not a sufficiently strong case to take a man's certificate away and deprive him of his public-house altogether.

The six house-holders' certificate.

[illegible]. I will take the details of your suggestions as you put them before us. First of all, would you say that it would be unnecessary to have the certificate signed by six householders?—That has really come to be a perfect farce. Sometimes they are all in the same handwriting.

[illegible]. Your next detail is that the certificate should be granted on the application of the publican; does that mean that he should appear in court?—No, if he made it a written application.

[illegible]. He has to do that now, and advertise?—He has to send it in for his renewal certificate, but he also has to send in the certificate signed by six householders. I would have the certificate the same as he now sends in, and simply take off the six householders.

Certificate of conduct to be [illegible].

[illegible]. Then the next is:—Form of certificate to be altered so as to make it a true certificate?—If we consider the house has not been conducted well, but that it has not been conducted sufficiently badly to refuse the certificate, I think we should be able not to sign so the certificate. At present we know there are charges against the house, but we do not think the house should be refused altogether, yet we have to sign the certificate that it is of good character and has been peaceably and quietly conducted.

[illegible]. You want a more correct description?—We should have a description of that.

[illegible]. Then the next suggestion is practically what you have just said?—Yes.

Structural condition.

[illegible]. Then the next suggestion is as to the premises becoming unsuitable?—If premises which have been licensed become unsuitable the justices, if it is left in their hands, on the application for renewal, at the same time as they take into account good character and the peaceable and orderly conduct, should take into account whether premises have become unsuitable. I am not alluding to an excess of public-houses, but only to the condition of the structure.

Transfers.

[illegible]. Then with reference to transfers?—With reference to transfers I only allude to a transfer on sale, where a man has sold a public-house the justices should not be bound to grant a transfer if in their opinion the premises have become unsuitable. There are some wretched little public-houses that are sold. For instance there was an instance in a public-house that I know that was sold the other day for [illegible], and the money was not to be paid till they saw whether they got the transfer or not.

[illegible]. In the case you mentioned, from the beginning the premises could not have been suitable?—They may have been suitable, but the suitability should be considered when they come up for transfer.

[illegible]. You do not think that would cause injustice in any way to the persons who have paid for the premises?—The reason I say so is that it would be possible for the man to improve the premises and make them suitable. I am not taking the number of public-houses into account in that.

[illegible]. You would give him an opportunity to put the premises in repair and then let him renew his application for the transfer?—Yes.

Responsibility for acts of servants.

[illegible]. Then the next is as to the knowledge of the acts of servants?—Yes. To be considered the acts or knowledge of the publican. At the present moment the sections are worded differently. There is "knowingly" and "suffering" and "permitting." They are all worded in different ways.

[illegible]. Does the licensing law of Ireland differ from that of England in that respect? Is the holder of a license not responsible for the acts of his servants?—In some cases they are, but the question I wanted to bring forward is this. A licensed person has a house with a servant in possession or a full manager of the business, but does not live on the premises; if the servant or manager infringes the law, for instance, the word "knowingly" is in the section, and it is doubtful if the publican can be convicted; virtually leaving the public-house carry through, if a man takes it under these conditions. There is another case in Ireland where a railway company is licensed all down the line, whether he is bound by the acts of his servants or not, and if he is not you could not get a conviction at all. I do not speak by that as to the servant or anything of that kind, but I want the responsible servant and manager in the place.

Spirit grocers.

[illegible]. With regard to the licenses to be held by spirit grocers and the quantity they are permitted to sell?—If the spirit grocer's license is continued, I think they ought not to be allowed to sell more than the lower one. They are limited now to two quarts and it ought to be more. There are many of the spirit grocers with very substantial houses who have to take out a publican's license to be allowed to sell the intermediate quantity.

[illegible]. Are you in favour of the continuation of the spirit grocer?—No.

[illegible]. Can you give any reason to the Commission for that view?—My impression is, if you take but a rural district that the magistrates of the present moment have no power to refuse a spirit grocer's license if the house is suitable, and the applicant's character is good. A spirit grocer's license in a rural district, to my mind, is a much greater danger than a public-house.

[illegible]. One of the reasons that you object to it is that you find they are very often remote from police supervision?—Yes.

[illegible]. They cannot be properly supervised?—They cannot be properly supervised. Of course, if the spirit grocer's license remains, I should put them under the same terms as to hours as the publican.

Mixed trading.

[illegible]. Then with reference to the premises?—They should be quite separate. It may be very difficult in some of these establishments to arrange it, but there should be no difficulty in the case of future licenses. I think there is a great deal of harm in having a public-house with a drapery counter on the other side. A woman comes in to buy drapery, and Irish people are hospitable, and they offer a treat, and it encourages drink.

[illegible]. The temptation to drink exists?—It increases it very much.

[illegible]. If the public-houses were given a limit of time in which to discontinue any other business on their premises, do you think that would automatically act to diminish the number of public-houses in Ireland, assuming that a limit of time was given, so as not to be brought in peremptorily at once?—There would be a difficulty in altering some of the premises. I think if you were to say there was to be no other business on the premises except a public-house, in most cases of a [illegible] small public-house the business could be made absolutely separate.

[illegible]. Different shops?—Yes, and with a dividing partition down, and two different doors. They would practically become two shops.

[illegible]. I am talking of the large number of small public-houses where they also run a business with a license. Do you find that exists a good deal in small villages?—Yes, I think they would keep to the public-house.

[illegible]. They would give up the other business?—They would give up the other business in those very small places and stick to the public-house.

Valuation of licensed premises.

[illegible]. What have you to say with regard to the valuation of licensed premises?—At present licensed premises are not subject to any valuation, and I think they ought to be under the same valuation as beer-houses. I should say [illegible] or [illegible] in the rural districts, and [illegible] in towns.

Habitual drunkards.

[illegible]. Then with reference to the habitual drunkard?—We find a great deal of difficulty in fixing habitual drunkards. They are fined, and they collect from their relatives the money at once, so that the family are really punished. By habitual drunkards I am not alluding to a man with one or two convictions, but a man with five or six convictions in 12 months, and I think that the magistrates in petty sessions ought to have the power to imprison in the same way as if a man is drunk and disorderly.

[illegible]. Without the option of a fine?—Without the option of a fine.

[illegible]. What number of convictions in 12 months would you consider ought to constitute an habitual drunkard—in a rough way?—Say four convictions in the year.

[illegible]. Would you see any difficulty in rural districts in regard to the [illegible] for obtaining drink by habitual drunkards—I suggest by sending notice to the licence-holders that a certain man should not be served with drink?—I could not give an answer on that.

[illegible]. You have not considered that?—No. I do not think it would do any harm, but I think they would be served with drink.

[illegible]. Then with regard to granting occasional licences?—At the present moment they can be granted by a single justice even if refused by the magistrates at petty sessions. One justice, sitting in his house, can grant an occasional licence, and it has been done where the bench have refused an occasional licence. My idea is that two justices should be appointed at every annual licensing sessions, who should be the two justices to grant the occasional licence in a district whenever wanted.

[illegible]. Two for each petty sessions district?—Yes.

[illegible]. They only should be empowered to grant an occasional licence?—Yes, the only two.

[illegible]. (*Dean [illegible]*.) Together or separate?—Together. Very often a person wants an occasional licence for some time before the next petty sessions, and perhaps petty sessions will fall through in consequence of non-attendance, or the assizes coming on.

[illegible]. (*Vicomte de Vesci*.) How often are petty sessions held on the average in your district?—In Waterford they are held weekly, and three petty sessions are held monthly, and three held fortnightly.

[illegible]. (*Mr. Young*.) In the county?—Yes, and in Kilkenny. I have half of Kilkenny—the southern portion of Kilkenny.

[illegible]. (*Vicomte de Vesci*.) Then with reference to notice to the police of these occasional licences, have you any view to express?—They should certainly let the police know. They should bring the consent of the police to the magistrates when they are getting it signed.

[illegible]. I am assuming two magistrates should be allowed to sit acting together in any place?—Yes, not in court at all, so long as you get the signatures of two magistrates.

[illegible]. They would have to meet together and sit together?—They would have to meet for the purpose.

[illegible]. Have you any permanent exemptions allowed in Waterford?—Yes.

[illegible]. In the city?—It is in the county Kilkenny. It is a fowl market, and the house is opened at 5 o'clock in the morning. I know there was an application before us the other day to allow it to be opened at 3 o'clock in the morning, and we refused.

[illegible]. That is the only one you know of?—Yes. In the county Wicklow, when I was there, there were two or three.

[illegible]. Fairs begin early in the morning?—Yes. I do not think they are numerous there. I could not give a certain answer for the town of Waterford.

[illegible]. (*Mr. Young*.) Is it your opinion that on the whole it would be better to leave all licensing matters in the hands of the county court judge and recorder, and abolish entirely the present authority exercised by the magistrates?—No, it is not my view. I thought I had explained that I would abolish the present system, the whole of the county magistrates meeting to deal with it as a licence, but I should keep it in the magistrates of the petty sessions districts in which the public-house is situated, who are people who know most about it, and the county court judge.

[illegible]. Waterford is a city which has its public-houses closed on Sundays?—Yes.

[illegible]. With reference to the arrests, they have rather increased since this Closing Act was passed? Can you follow me in these figures?—I am afraid I have no figures at all. I have no returns. That is merely a police matter.

[illegible]. Would it be out of place to give you those figures?—I have seen [illegible] [illegible]

[illegible]?—I have only been there a year and a half, and I hardly could say. My impression is that there is a decrease in Sunday drunkenness, but I think that the evil on the Saturday night much more than the Sunday. I think there is much more drunkenness then. That fact I know from my magisterial knowledge, that there are more cases of drunkenness on Saturday night than on Sunday, and more cases of great hardship, because they are the breadwinners who spend the whole of their money.

[illegible]. Statistics do not bear that out?—You will remember, first of all, I have only been in Waterford a year and a half; and secondly, I keep no statistics, of course. I should only have to get them from the police.

[illegible]. In 1874, four years previous to the passing of the Act, convictions for Sunday drunkenness were 1[illegible], and in the year 1[illegible], 10 years after, 1[illegible], and in 1[illegible], 1[illegible]?—That is getting better.

[illegible]. So there is seems to be an increase since the Act passed?—It is a decrease now for the last few years.

[illegible]. I presume the public-houses are well conducted in your opinion?—I think some houses are very well conducted indeed, and some very badly conducted.

[illegible]. You have got no bad houses there?—No, not that I am aware of.

[illegible]. (*Mr. Grindley*.) Your objection to the spirit grocer's licence, I understand, is that in rural places it is difficult of police supervision?—Yes.

[illegible]. That would apply to all licensed premises, would not it?—No, in this way, that magistrates when granting the certificate for a licensed public-house can take into account whether it is wanted in the district. As regards a spirit grocer they cannot take anything into consideration, but are simply obliged to give it, if character of applicant is good and premises suitable.

[illegible]. Subject to good character and suitability of the premises?—Good character and a [illegible] house.

[illegible]. Do not you think the carrying on a shop that is sufficient power to the magistrate?—I think not.

[illegible]. No question of public order can come in?—If it were used solely as a trade, but there is no doubt at all, if once they get the spirit grocer's licence, there is an enormous quantity of drinking goes on on the premises.

[illegible]. I understand the difficulty is the form of the licence as it exists in Ireland. It allows the sale of small quantities in an open vessel?—Yes.

[illegible]. You think that creates a difficulty?—Yes.

[illegible]. Would it get over it if the principle were adopted that applies in England, that is a licence under which all traders come, limiting the quantity and not allowing the sale in open vessels? The quantity in England is a quart bottle for spirits and a pint bottle for wines, and it cannot be sold for consumption on?—I think it would improve the licence that we call the spirit grocer's licence very much.

[illegible]. Would your view as to total magisterial control still hold good under those circumstances? Do not you think, then, that seeing that the premises were good and the parties were of suitable character would be sufficient for that licence?—Personally, I think that whoever the licensing body is, they should have the supervision as to whether they should grant the licence or not. Of course, granting the spirit grocer's licence at present is the thin end of the wedge to get a public-house licence after.

[illegible]. In England we do not know this thing. Your difficulty in Ireland arises from the fact that your licence is such an arbitrary one, that a man is obliged to get a publican's licence to do his trade. With regard to Waterford, do you know the number of spirit grocers there are in the whole county of Waterford?—No.

[illegible]. I think you will be surprised if I tell you that with a population for the county of nearly [illegible] there are only three spirit grocers' licences, so that they cannot be answerable for very much intemperance in the county of Waterford?—No. I was alluding to two licences I am aware of.

Mr. T. Roche. — 30 Mar. '98.

39,405. There are only three in the whole county of Waterford with a population of [illegible]. I was going to put that to you, because the greater means to [illegible] a large amount of [illegible] in connection with drunkenness than one in a little place where one can find everybody to say that is [illegible]?—The worst aspect of the spirit grocer's license I do not think is in a big town. He is more under supervision there, if necessary, but I think the harm it does is where you get a spirit grocer's license in a little outlying place, because there the drink is on the premises and there the temptation to sell to anybody is great.

Endorsement of licenses.

39,406. (Mr. Walker.) One question on the endorsement question. Are you prepared to acknowledge that many offences may occur that would not justify endorsement?—Certainly.

39,407. You expressed an opinion that all offences should be endorsed on the license?—Yes.

39,408. But recognising that many of these are of a trivial character and also recognising the great injury that would be occasioned to valuable property, you would give them an opportunity to appeal?—Yes.

39,409. Can you tell me what purpose is answered by having the license endorsed and then telling the applicant, "I do not believe it is just, so I give you an "opportunity of going to the court of appeal." What purpose is answered by that?—The greater number of convictions would be cases which would be recorded, but a trivial case might arise, as I have known a trivial case to arise in which the man was bound to be convicted, having broken the law, but for some reason or another it might appear to the magistrates that it was a very slight breach of the law by mistake or in some way or another, and all I wanted to do there was this, that there should not be an arbitrary power to take away this man's property for what you might call an accidental breach of the law for which he had no appeal.

39,410. The court of appeal would not be the same authority that had previously endorsed the license?—You cannot have an appeal to the same magistrates who have heard the case. If you do not send it to a higher court you would be asking the other magistrates to reverse their brother magistrates.

39,411. The court of appeal might not remove the endorsement, although it was a case in which those who endorsed it considered it ought not to be there. That is quite possible, is it not?—It is quite possible in any case that the court of appeal might act wrongly. If the legislature gave them the power to take off the endorsement if the offence was only a trivial one, I do not like to presume the county court judge would not act on that and take it off.

39,412. Then, as commissioner says, if it was placed in the three judges in a manner to appeal in case of being an [illegible] and unwarrantable endorsement, they would immediately remove it? It would vary in the case some sitting. He is sitting there as a lawyer.

39,413. Does not that exhibit the weakness of the power of the magistrates to endorse under such circumstances as that?—I am in favour of an appeal in every case. I think it is a great blessing to magistrates to have an appeal if they go wrong, and if they put this on in a case in which it ought not to be done, I do not see why the county court judge should not take it off on appeal.

39,414. Did I understand you to say that you thought the magistrates generally were averse to endorsement in consequence of the very serious consequences attaching to it?—Yes.

39,415. In face of that you would advise that all offences be endorsed?—Yes.

39,416. Would you accept a medium course that, if that were so, they should have the effect so far as injuring the permanency of the license?—I think that there should be an alteration in the law as to the two endorsements, and the one conviction breaking the license.

39,417. We have had men holding high positions—such as county court judges—here before the Commission who have endorsed the same as you have to-day, that though it may be a trivial case, they would have all offences endorsed, but it should only be for the purpose of record, and there should be a discretionary power on the part of the authority as to whether they renewed the license?—That is what I intended to say if I did not say it in my answer to you, that I would alter the present power of legislature and give a power not to forfeit the license on the three convictions, but have a discretionary power with the licensing body when they come to give the certificate whether they would refuse or not.

39,418. You would not make it obligatory to refuse?—No.

39,419. You would not make two endorsements absolute to destroy the license?—No.

39,420. You would give a power of appeal on a first endorsement?—I would give a power of appeal on any endorsement.

39,421. (Dean Dickinson.) You would simply have a record of the circumstances as well as of the facts?—Yes.

The witness withdrew.

Adjourned to Tuesday, April 4th, at 11 o'clock.

NINETY-EIGHTH DAY.

Queen's Robing Room, House of Lords, Tuesday, April 5th, 189[illegible].

PRESENT:

THE RIGHT HONOURABLE THE VISCOUNT PEEL IN THE CHAIR.

The Right Hon. the Viscount De Vesci.
The Right Hon. Sir [illegible] [illegible], K.C.B.
William Abney, Esq., M.P.
William [illegible] Caine, Esq.
William Graham, Esq.
Henry Gourley, Esq.
[illegible] [illegible], Esq.
John [illegible] [illegible], Esq., M.P.
Henry [illegible] Smith, Esq.
Charles Walker, Esq.
[illegible] Young, Esq., M.P.

Mr. John [illegible] [illegible] [illegible] called in and examined.

[illegible] (Chairman.) You are, I think, County In[illegible] of County Clare?—I am.

[illegible] What is your opinion of the licensing [illegible]?—I consider that the licenses should only [illegible] by the county court judge.

[illegible] Do you think the county court judge should [illegible] with the justices of the peace for the [illegible]?—Alone, in the same way as the recorder in [illegible], Belfast, and Londonderry.

[illegible] Do you think that when the county court [illegible] with the county magistrates [illegible] his proper share of influence?—I know in some [illegible] he has no influence whatever. They [illegible] his instructions as to the law of the cases that [illegible] before them.

[illegible] Are the magistrates attached to that particular [illegible] division, or do they come from other [illegible] of the county?—They come from all parts of the [illegible].

[illegible] If the magistrates act as the [illegible] [illegible], do you think the power should remain in their [illegible] of voting at all?—I do not think they should [illegible].

[illegible] You would take away from the magistrates [illegible] power of voting on licensing questions?—Yes.

[illegible] And leave the sole jurisdiction in the hands of [illegible] recorder in towns, and of the county court judge in [illegible] country?—Yes.

[illegible] What would you do with renewals; would [illegible] be under the same jurisdiction?—Yes, and under [illegible] county court judge also.

[illegible] You would leave the county court judge and [illegible] dealing, in fact, with the whole licensing [illegible]?—Unless at petty sessions. Of course I do [illegible] [illegible].

[illegible] What would you leave to the magistrates [illegible]?—The resident magistrate only should [illegible] power to deal with cases of petty sessions [illegible], except under section [illegible] of course, of [illegible].

[illegible] Therefore you would have three, the resident [illegible], the county court judge, and the recorder, [illegible] would be the authorities in different parts?—Yes.

[illegible] You would give to the resident magistrate, I understand, the power of [illegible] in cases of [illegible] of certificates or breaches of licenses?—The [illegible] of adjourning [illegible] cases as to publicans, and [illegible] grocers, and beer retailers.

[illegible] Who would be the prosecutor?—The constabulary.

[illegible] In all three cases?—In all three cases.

[illegible] What would you leave the justices of the [illegible] to do in regard to licensing in the petty sessional [illegible]?—Nothing.

[illegible] You would oust them altogether from having [illegible] to do with the licensing question?—Yes.

[illegible] Assuming that the resident magistrate of the district was sitting at petty sessions, would you let him deal with [illegible] houses, for instance?—Yes, with [illegible] licenses also, and there should be the power of appeal from his decision to the county court judge.

[illegible] Should there be any appeal from the county court judge to any court?—I think it would be hardly necessary.

[illegible] Nor from the recorder?—I do not think there would be any objection to it.

[illegible] Assuming it was thought advisable, to whom should an appeal lie?—From the resident magistrate to the county court judge.

[illegible] And from the recorder, if such a thing were [illegible]?—From the recorder to the judge of [illegible].

[illegible] And from the county court judge to the court of [illegible]?—Yes.

[illegible] Spirit grocers' licenses you would [illegible], I suppose, under the jurisdiction of these three gentlemen in their respective localities, the county court judge, the recorder, and the resident magistrate, would you?—Yes.

[illegible] At present are you of opinion that they are granted [illegible]?—There is too much facility for obtaining spirit grocers' licenses now, in fact they can be obtained without the wish of the magistrates.

[illegible] It is not the fault of the magistrates, but the fault of the law in your opinion?—It is the fault of the law as regards spirit grocers.

[illegible] The only requirements being, as we know, good character and suitability of the premises?—Yes; of course the latter is a mere myth. No opposition could be made on that ground hardly, because I do not see what would be the requirements of the premises.

[illegible] Would you submit the spirit grocer to the same jurisdiction as the publican?—I really do not see why there should be spirit grocers at all.

[illegible] You would abolish the spirit grocers?—I do not see what use they are.

[illegible] I suppose there are not a great many in your part?—There is one in Ennis, and I believe he considers it a grievance that if a customer asks for a gallon of spirits he could not give it to him without [illegible] on two different occasions. He could only sell two quarts at a time. The grievance is that they cannot sell enough. I have heard that he considers that a grievance.

[illegible] You have, I suppose, very few in your county?—I think there is but one in Ennis. I am not aware of any others.

[illegible] In the county Clare generally, are there many spirit grocers?—I think that is the only one in the county. I am not aware of any others.

[illegible] (Mr. [illegible].) And that one is in Ennis, is it not?—Yes.

[illegible]. (*Chairman.*) Do you think that illicit traffic goes on in that gentleman's shop?—Oh, no. It is a most respectable shop.

[illegible]. Excepting that gentleman from all blame, in your view, and speaking generally, have you any experience of the spirit grocer's licences in other parts of Ireland?—Yes; where a man has been refused a publican's licence time after time, he often applies for a spirit grocer's licence, and that enables him to carry on an illicit traffic.

[illegible]. Have you reason to think that that illicit traffic goes on in the spirit grocer's case?—In country places I am quite sure they get it for no other purpose.

[illegible]. What do you say as to the number of public houses in Clare?—In county Clare, there are probably nearly two times as many as are required.

[illegible]. Are they very numerous in the villages or in the towns?—In the town of Ennis there are upwards of 1[illegible].

[illegible]. To a population of what?—I think somewhere between 4,000 and 6,000.

[illegible]. In the villages, are they pretty thick?—Yes.

[illegible]. (*Mr. Grisham.*) The population of Ennis is, I think, between 12,000 and 14,000?—I do not know from memory what it is. I am sure it is nothing like that.

[illegible]. (*Chairman.*) You think the population of Ennis is not 12,000?—Oh, no! Nothing like it.

[illegible]. You said 5,000?—It is nearly 6,000, I should say, as well as I can remember.

[illegible]. (*Mr. Young.*) Is the population getting less every year?—The population of the whole country is decreasing.

[illegible]. But of Ennis?—Yes, it has decreased there also.

[illegible]. (*Chairman.*) You are speaking only of the town of Ennis?—Yes.

[illegible]. Not the petty sessional district?—No; only

was quite unnecessary to have a police barracks where there were no public-houses.

[illegible]. You have made some charges against the administration of the law. Is it your opinion that the justices in County Clare are subject to coercion?—Oh, yes. They are coerced. They are brought long distances to preside at the petty sessions.

[illegible]. Brought by their carriages, do you mean?—Brought by the publican who is being prosecuted.

[illegible]. I want to elicit the full meaning of the word "brought." Do they come of their own free will?—Well, they are conveyed by him, and then I suppose there is a certain amount of moral persuasion used. I am afraid I should say immoral persuasion.

[illegible]. Is there anything else but moral persuasion?—I think some of the magistrates living in out-of-the-way parts of the county, and perhaps under some obligation to these publicans, will not refuse them. They have not the moral courage to refuse them.

[illegible]. There is no such thing, is there, as inducing the magistrates to vote by treating them?—I have heard of a case where, before the case was heard, the magistrate was in the public-house having a drink, and when the case was over he was supplied with more drink. In fact, I may say he was very [illegible] drunk.

[illegible]. Was that within recent years?—It was within recent years, but I may say that the magistrate is dead. I know of several other cases. I know of a case where two magistrates were brought from another county. They happened to be magistrates of county Clare. One of them came on the car with the publican and his solicitor going to the petty sessions, and he and this other magistrate who did not reside in county Clare sat on the bench with two other local magistrates. The case was clearly proved, but of course was dismissed.

[illegible]. Have you any reason to suppose that the particular magistrate who sat on the car took a view favourable to the man with whom he was travelling?—He never attended those petty sessions except when this publican sent for him.

Mr. J. M. O'Fihily. 4 April '78.

drink?—There may be. Probably they are frequented also in other directions, but that would be on the county Limerick side. That is the village in the county of Clare which seems to be mostly patronised.

28,696. Is it within the Barony of Clare?—Yes. I have been informed as many as 150 people have been standing there outside one public-house on a Sunday.

28,697. (Mr. Young.) Are not those houses closed on Sundays in Limerick?—No, Limerick is one of the towns that is exempt, but then they are only open from 2 to 7.

28,698. (Mr. Grimkey.) You say they go to a village where the bona fide travellers go. Does not Sunday closing exist there?—Sunday closing does exist there.

28,699. Then how does the bona fide traveller get served?—Because he comes the 3 miles.

28,700. (Mr. Young.) Do they open their houses for them?—Yes.

28,701. Do they keep their doors open for them?—They generally have side entrances. The houses are so fixed that they have but the one door, and the publican will tell the policeman that he cannot shut the door, that it is the only door he has.

28,702. (Chairman.) There is a collection of 150 people in the course of the day, or at one time, do you mean?—At one time.

Justifying lapse. 28,703. What would you do with the bona fide traveller, then?—I would increase the distance, so that they would have a longer journey to go for the drink.

28,704. You think it is necessary to provide some facilities for the bona fide traveller, if he is really obtaining a drink?—I would eliminate the words bona fide from the Act of Parliament altogether, for I think it is a sham. I think probably there are not 1 per cent. of these bona fide travellers.

28,705. If you call him the 10-mile traveller, he may equally represent that he was a traveller when he was only an [illegible]?—Yes; but I would have it that a traveller going a certain distance might get a drink.

Punishing drunkenness, &c. 28,706. Do you often get convictions for permitting drunkenness on licensed premises?—It is very hard to obtain convictions. I have of course obtained them, but they are very difficult.

28,707. Have you any remedy to suggest?—I would suggest that it should be an offence against public order to allow a drunken person to enter and remain on licensed premises.

28,708. That is to say, the publican should deprive the party he has of [illegible] him out at once if he is drunk?—Quite so.

28,709. And if he does not turn him out and let him outside there, what then?—He should be liable to conviction.

Reg. v. Whitehead. 28,709. (Mr. Young.) Is not that the law now?—No, unfortunately it is not. There was a case of Regina v. Whitehead, decided about five years ago, I think, where it was held that the publican was liable, but then in that case the man was drinking, although he was not supplied by the publican I understand. I think it should be an offence to allow a drunken person to remain at all on licensed premises.

28,710. (Chairman.) Would you make it a primâ facie case against the publican that there was a drunken man on his premises?—I should say that should be quite sufficient to convict the publican, allowing the man to remain on the premises.

28,711. He should be held to have served him unless he could show the contrary?—Yes. At present it must be shown that he served him.

28,712. (Mr. Young.) There have been convictions obtained for allowing persons in a drunken state to remain on premises?—I only know of one case, and I think it must be 15 years ago, in Dublin. In that case I was surprised that there was no appeal.

Young persons in public-houses. 28,713. (Chairman.) Is it a practice in the public-houses or licensed houses of Clare to have waiting or young persons as assistants in the public-house?—That is universal, I think, all over the country.

28,714. Down to what age would children be allowed

should not be allowed into the licensed premises at all as assistants.

28,715. I am not talking of those who come for liquor, but those in the actual service?—That is what I mean. I think it is very demoralising and degrading to have children serving people in a half-drunken state in public-houses.

28,716. Under what age would you not allow any person to be an assistant in a public-house?—I would say 16.

28,717. And as to serving them, would you have that at 16?—I do not think they should be supplied under 16 with drink of any kind to be consumed on the premises.

Recording convictions. 28,718. As to convictions, would you have them all recorded on the licence?—I might draw a distinction between cases. I would certainly have all second convictions and subsequent convictions recorded.

28,719. You would allow a sort of first fault, as they say?—I should not mind the first. I think it should be optional. There may be mitigating circumstances.

28,720. Every offence for which they were convicted should be recorded?—All after the first.

28,721. And that record should be taken into consideration at the annual sessions and on renewals and transfers. Would that be your view?—Yes, certainly.

Adulteration. 28,722. What do you say as to adulteration of liquor?—It is well known that adulteration does exist, but still we have very few convictions.

28,723. Has it come under your notice that the liquor complained of has been analysed?—Yes, we have frequently had some analysed.

28,724. There is a public analyst, is there?—There are public analysts. We were instructed to use very great discretion in sending up samples to be analysed, because out of a large number that had been sent none were found adulterated, unless with water in small quantities.

28,725. (Flemmet de Ford.) There is no cost to the public in sending up these specimens, is there?—I think the analyst is paid by the grand jury.

28,726. He is paid a salary, I think?—Yes.

28,727. (Chairman.) If you found nothing but water in these samples what reason have you for saying that there is adulteration of a more serious character?—I do not understand chemistry well, but I know that there must be some ingredient used which, perhaps, in the course of time dissolves, or is lost.

28,728. Speaking from your experience of what you have seen at fairs, and so on?—That is why I come to that conclusion, because when I have been told of a case in a little village where a fair was being held, the district inspector was taking samples in a tent, and when it became known to the other tents, they threw the whisky all about the fair green.

28,729. Presumably from fear of detection?—Yes.

28,730. Or was it for the reason that it was of such inferior quality that they did not care about taking it home again?—No, they do that also, but on that occasion it was for fear that samples would be taken of their whisky also, and that they would be sent for analysis.

Beer and whisky drinking. 28,731. What is the prevailing drink in Clare; is it beer and whisky?—I think latterly the people are drinking beer very much more, and I think it has a very beneficial effect. There is not so much drunkenness.

28,732. Would beer be coming into favour in lieu of whisky?—I think so, as far as I can understand.

28,733. In the country districts is whisky being gradually excluded or less used?—I think there will be less whisky drunk, and probably more beer.

28,734. (Flemmet de Ford.) Porter, is it not?—Porter.

Civilians drinking in canteens. 28,735. (Chairman.) Have you any complaint, speaking as a county inspector, to make about the frequenting of canteens by the ordinary lay population?—Yes, I would suggest that no people, unless soldiers, or policemen in uniform, should be allowed to enter canteens at hours during which public-houses were

Mr. J. M. G. Fitzp. [illegible]

[illegible] April '98.

whether they have a canteen or not. It is a very small place.

58,738. Is there a canteen in any other part of [illegible] but [illegible]?—[illegible]; it is in Londonderry that I have had experience. I found there that people were [illegible] about the military barracks on [illegible], and when the police were spoken to about it they said they could not help it, that it was not the publicans who were giving them drink. They were getting it in the canteen. I think the plan they adopt is that the soldier gets the money from the civilian who wants to drink, and probably gets enough for a drink for himself. He brings in the civilian then as his guest, and calls for the drinks.

58,739. You would wish that nobody but soldiers should be allowed to enter the canteen?—Soldiers, or policemen in [illegible]. None but soldiers or policemen should be allowed to enter the canteen at the hours when public-houses are closed.

58,740. They would be allowed to enter it, but not for the purpose of refreshment?—It would be impossible, I think, to draw a line. I would not allow them to enter at all.

Mixed trades at public-houses.

58,741. Is it the case that in [illegible], and in Ireland generally, Sunday is a great shopping day?—Not in [illegible], I think, but in other small towns that I have had some experience of.

58,742. The shopping goes on in the public-house, does not it?—Quite so.

58,743. That is to say the publican sells other things besides liquor?—Yes.

58,744. Does he sell flour?—Yes, some of them do.

58,745. I thought the sale of flour was very prevalent in public-houses?—It is in some places, but not as a rule, I think.

58,746. Therefore, when the police see a man or woman entering within prohibited hours, is it the defence that he or she came to buy flour?—Yes, or to buy something else.

58,747. Would you prohibit a publican from selling anything else but drink and victuals?—I think it would be a great advantage if that could be done.

58,748. I suppose it would disturb the habits of the people very much if it were done suddenly?—Yes, I do not think it could be done suddenly on account of the existing rights.

Sunday closing.

58,749. I understand you to be in favour of Sunday closing?—Yes.

58,750. With opening hours?—No, altogether.

58,751. In town and country?—In town and country.

58,752. With the exception of the 10-mile traveller. He should be entitled to enter a house?—Only for the purpose of [illegible] that traveller, and the publican should shut the door while the traveller enters and not allow the door to remain open.

58,753. If 100 people come at once it is hard on the publican to say "shut the door"?—Yes, that would be a difficulty, of course.

Early closing on [illegible].

58,754. As to Saturday early closing, would you close earlier than at present? What are your hours for closing in [illegible] now?—The legal hour is 11, but as a rule they shut much earlier.

58,755. Should you like to see an earlier hour fixed by statute?—I think at 9 for a large town, and 8 for country places.

58,756. I think you have already said that no child under 16 should be served?—Yes.

Opinion of the clergy.

58,757. Do you wish to record any opinions that the clergy in your district have supplied you with?—I

58,761. Have you any means of knowing what would be the feeling of the ordinary classes, for instance?—I think the better and well-conducted ones would be very glad if the houses were closed earlier.

Dr. J. G. Fitzp.

[illegible] of the [illegible].

Canteens.

58,762. (Father [illegible].) You said just now that people were given [illegible] to get drink through the military canteens in Londonderry?—Yes.

58,763. Do you know at what hour those canteens were opened?—No, I cannot say.

58,764. Were you the district inspector of Londonderry at that time?—I was.

58,765. Do you know of any representations made to the military authorities at the time?—I fancy I made a representation myself, but I am not quite sure.

58,766. Do you know if any action was taken by the military authorities in consequence?—I cannot say. I know it lessened considerably. The cause of complaint was lessened before I left.

58,767. You do not know how it was?—I cannot say for certain.

58,768. Your men reported to you that civilians were going in and out of the canteens?—Yes.

58,769. Ostensibly being treated by soldiers?—Yes.

58,770. With regard to the question of distance in rural districts of public-houses from the police barracks, you say that has been a great abuse?—Yes, I consider it a great evil.

58,771. Can you form any opinion as to what distance a public-house should be from a police barracks?—Oh, no, but I should say in general it is a great mistake to give licenses to houses in remote places. It merely brings on drunken habits.

Public-houses [illegible].

58,772. If a police barracks were within a certain distance you would not be opposed to a license being granted on that account simply because it is in a remote district, would you?—If the people required it.

58,773. I am talking more of the question of police supervision; the facilities for the police to supervise the public-house?—Of course if the locality required a public-house I do not think it should be any argument against it that there was no police barracks there; but these public-houses are generally required by the men who apply for them, and not in the interests of the public.

58,774. You spoke of one public-house being five miles away from any police post?—Yes.

58,775. Is that on a mountain, or where is it?—No, there are two or three cases; it is on a line between Londonderry and there.

Licensing [illegible].

58,776. Is there a considerable population round that district?—There is not. I might say that that public-house was granted entirely in opposition to the wish of the local magistrates, by magistrates who flocked to the quarter sessions, evidently regardless of the wishes of the people.

58,777. They were magistrates who came from other parts of the country?—Yes.

58,778. Who did not reside in the licensing district?—No, not many of them in that part of the county at all.

58,779. Would you be in favour of the licensing being solely confined to magistrates residing within the licensing district?—No, I would have it solely confined to the resident magistrate.

58,780. Or the county court judge?—I mean licensed prosecutions.

58,781. I am talking first of all the granting of licenses?—To the county court judge solely.

58,782. You are not in favour of continuing in that way, that only magistrates residing within the [illegible]

I may say that the magistrates do not take the law from the county court judge at all.

28,787. In this case you say a licence was granted at [illegible], and it was doubtful whether it was a licensing district at all?—That is what I have been told.

28,788. The county court judge was presiding there?—Yes, but the magistrates do not mind him.

28,789. I understand you to say that the magistrates do not care for the opinion of the county court judge?—The county court judge has told me that himself, that they will not listen to his ruling.

28,790. What was the county court judge doing at [illegible]? Is it a place for quarter sessions?—It is, but it is doubtful whether they have power to hold licensing sessions there.

28,791. Did he at the time lay down the law and say, "This is not a place to give a licence"?—I cannot tell, for I was not there, but I heard it spoken of. I have known cases where he told me himself that the magistrates were acting illegally, and that they did not mind.

28,792. He told them they were acting illegally?—Yes. They granted licenses [illegible], without allowing the evidence of the police opposing the licence to be heard.

28,793. Surely when a man wishes to apply for a licence it has to be advertised in the local papers?—It has.

28,794. On those occasions was it advertised that they were going to apply at [illegible] quarter sessions for licences?—I do not think they ever deal in that part of the duty. They always employ a solicitor, and he does that part of the work.

28,795. Did they name [illegible] as the place where they were going to apply?—I cannot tell; but of course they would; otherwise they could not apply.

28,796. You are in favour, you say, of the county court judge being the sole licensing authority?—Yes.

28,797. Does the county court judge of Clare reside within the county?—I think not.

28,798. Do you know where he resides?—I think he resides in Dublin.

28,799. He comes down by train from Dublin four times a year to preside at quarter sessions, I assume?—Yes, he does.

28,800. He goes straight to his court, and after the business is over he returns, I suppose?—He does.

28,801. Do you consider that he has the proper amount of local knowledge which would guide him, apart from the evidence given here, to form an opinion as to the necessity for the increase or decrease of licences in any particular district?—Yes. I think Judge Kelly knows the county Clare perfectly.

28,802. He has been a long time county court judge?—Yes.

28,803. Do you consider that he has as much local knowledge as any of the resident magistrates?—I should say he has more than nine-tenths of them. There are a lot of them who have only been appointed within recent years.

28,804. (Mr. Walker.) That knowledge of Judge Kelly would be entirely confined to himself? It is rather special in his case, you think?—From the long experience he has had now in hearing civil and criminal cases at the constantly recurring sessions, of course he has a very good knowledge of the place and people.

28,805. Would it apply to every justice living in [illegible]

28,809. Yes?—I do not. I think it is an advantage, but I do not think it is necessary. Mr. J. M. O'Philip.

28,810. You think it is an advantage?—I do; I think it is an advantage to know the habits and customs of the people. 8 April '99.

28,811. If it is an advantage, is it not necessary?—No, I do not think so.

28,812. In what way is it an advantage?—Well, in knowing the probabilities as to the evidence being true or untrue.

28,813. As to whether the licence is required or not required?—Yes, of course the evidence will be there for or against the requirements.

28,814. You have intimate knowledge, I presume, of all the licensees in the county of Clare, generally speaking?—I have a general knowledge.

28,815. Are they a respectable class of men?—The publicans?

28,816. Yes?—They are a law-abiding, respectable people, as a rule.

28,817. Equally as much as any other class of Her Majesty's subjects?—Yes, in the same rank of life.

28,818. Does rank of life make a difference?—Well, it should.

28,819. You are of opinion that the court of appeal should be constituted simply by the judge of assize?—Yes, and governed in the same way as appeals from magistrates' decisions and other questions. Appeals.

28,820. You would remove from all licensing courts, either in the first or second or third instance, all magistrates?—All justices of the peace. I do not mean resident magistrates, of course.

28,821. The justices of the peace are gentlemen appointed by the Crown?—They are. On composing of justices.

28,822. And they are presumably men of good position and unquestionable character?—I cannot tell.

28,823. You will not admit that they are?—I should not care to give an opinion. Generally, I should say they are.

28,824. But they are gentlemen appointed by the Crown to hold a judicial office. You are not prepared to admit that they are respectable men of good social position?—They are respectable men, but I cannot say that they are of good social position.

28,825. What, may I ask you, do you mean by saying that they are under some obligation to the applicant for a licence; what character of obligation?—It is very hard to tell.

28,826. Why do you make the charge that they are probably under some obligation if you have no foundation for it?—Well, they are neighbours, and some are of the same rank of life, and farmers probably.

28,827. That is all the explanation you can give of it?—There may be other reasons too, but I cannot tell of my own knowledge.

28,828. Then it is from hearsay when you say that the magistrates are under some obligation to the applicants for a licence?—It is what I have been told.

28,829. You have no knowledge of your own, or foundation for a statement of that kind?—No, I cannot say of my own knowledge that they are under any obligation.

28,830. You, personally, are in favour of the constabulary having a right of appeal against the decision of the magistrates if the present system is to be continued?—Yes. Police appeal in dismissals.

28,831. But you also said that the Inspector-General [illegible]

Mr. J. M. G. Foley.

8 April '98.

Does not that in itself prove the necessity for the establishment of houses for the convenience of these men?—I do not think so.

38,837. You think that large crowds of men wanting refreshment should be told they cannot have it?—I think these people go there merely for the purpose of drinking.

38,838. True, but they require it; they wish to purchase it?—I do not see why there should be any requirement about it.

38,839. Are you in favour of prohibition—entire prohibition of the sale of these articles?—Certainly not.

38,840. You are in favour of prohibition on Sunday?—I am, on Sunday.

38,841. Country and town?—Country and town.

Permitting drunkenness.

38,842. With respect to drunkenness on licensed premises, you say the simple fact of a drunken person being discovered on the premises is *prima facie* evidence of permitting drunkenness?—I do.

38,843. How would you deal with the case where a drunken person entered the premises, and before there was time for discovery, a constable stepped in and saw that person?—I think that would be a fair defence for the publican.

38,844. Your *prima facie* case of a person being found there would fall to the ground?—I do not consider so.

38,845. It is a circumstance that is often occurring—a very common occurrence for a drunken person to walk into a house, and until he is discovered he cannot be removed?—It may be. If the house were crowded it would be easier for a drunken person to get in without being seen.

38,846. Do you admit that that would not be a proper case for a prosecution?—If it were clearly proved that the publican was not cognisant of the man being there I consider that that would be a good defence.

Children employed in public-houses.

38,847. As to service in public-houses, I did not catch the age you suggested?—I think 18.

38,848. Of course you are aware that for years, and hundreds of years, young people have always served?—They have no wages [illegible].

38,849. Have they not in all the United Kingdom?—There has been no prohibition.

38,850. Can you point to any instance where wrong has been the result of it?—No, I cannot.

38,851. It is a fear alone altogether, is it not?—Well, it may be.

38,852. You have no reason to suppose, and no proof to show, with regard to the young people, the children of the licensee, grown up under his roof, standing about his house to serve customers, that any immorality or anything really wrong has been done to these children?—I have no proof.

Adulteration.

38,853. As to adulteration, you say, "I believe there "is mixed in some ingredients which dissolve, and in fact, "tend to adulterate." What proof is there of that?—I have none.

38,854. Is it hearsay?—No, but large numbers of samples have been taken of whisky where it was [illegible] there was adulteration, and comparatively very few samples were proved to be adulterated. Of course it might be that the very new whisky might be the cause of people becoming suddenly stupefied from the small quantity as they take.

38,855. Will you express an opinion that it is possible for an [illegible] of such a dangerous character as this

38,859. Can you mention any case where a sample has been taken and this ingredient discovered by analysis of the ingredient, but where there was adulteration, in the majority of cases I understand the adulteration was simply water.

38,860. Can you mention a case where anything else has been discovered?—No, I cannot.

38,861. You had some conversation with the Roman Catholic Bishop, and he gave it as his opinion that a great improvement in the habits and [illegible] and general conduct of the people had been gradually taking place?—Yes.

38,862. (Mr. Hyslop.) I should like to have your opinion with regard to this. With regard to premises that are licensed you have stated that the rateability of those premises is a myth?—Yes. That is as regards spirit grocers. Of course where the liquor is taken off the premises for consumption it is immaterial as to the premises.

38,863. That remark was confined to spirit grocers?—It was.

38,864. It did not apply to the [illegible]?—No, nor to the publicans.

Valuation of houses.

38,865. What do you mean by saying that the rateable value of those premises, but for the [illegible], would not amount to more than 10*l.*? Is that so with regard to spirit grocers?—Yes. I have no doubt it is. I do not know of a case. The only place I spoke of was a very good house that I know of in Ennis.

38,866. With regard to the fully licensed house, what is the qualification? Is it a rateable one?—It is not.

38,867. Then the rateability and the fitness of the place has no meaning at all?—The magistrates quite ignore that when the police oppose.

38,868. With regard to the magistracy, are the licenses granted or renewed by the resident justices of the peace, or by the county court judge?—They are granted by the county court judge and magistrates.

38,869. (Chairman.) Mr. Hyslop asks you as to whether when you spoke of qualifications you were not speaking of spirit grocers. There is only one spirit grocer in Ennis, and that is the only one in the whole of Clare, I understand. My question was directed to what are the qualifications of the public-houses?—There is no qualification required.

38,870. You gave us an instance of a great number of public-houses the united qualification of which amounted to 30*l.*?—Yes, I gave 10 public-houses, and the total Poor Law valuation was 3*l.* 1*s.*

38,871. (Mr. Hyslop.) With regard to those public-houses, I think the Act of 1872, extended in 1874, made it imperative that all licensed property should be of certain structural dimensions, otherwise the license could not be renewed?—That is entirely now in the hands of the county court judge and the magistrates.

38,872. Can you tell us how the Irish people have evaded that law?—I do not think that that is the law. I do not think there is any regular qualification as to the premises.

38,873. It is perfectly plain that the Act meant at that time that all licensed property should be put into repair, and except certain exemptions provided for [illegible] and travellers, and that it should be of certain structural dimensions approved of before the license could be renewed?—Well, it is never acted up.

38,874. I think in the county of Clare there are 611 public-houses? That is the figure given here?—I am not sure of the number.

38,875. Does that 611 include [illegible]

keep open till 11. They are very early people in Clare. As a rule the poor people go to bed very early.

[illegible]. It appears that the publicans there are doing exactly what you wish, they are closing before the hour allowed to them by the Act of Parliament?—Yes, as I say.

[illegible]. I think you said to one of the Commissioners that you did not study the requirements of the people with regard to Sunday closing?—No, I do not think I said that.

[illegible]. The words were these I believe; that with regard to closing houses altogether on Sunday, and driving people to become bona fide travellers, you did not think the requirements of the people ought to be studied?—Oh, no, I do not think I said that.

[illegible]. That is precisely the answer you gave to one of the Commissioners, that you would not study their requirements; you did not think they required anything and said that I did not think because a person travels three miles he requires to get a drink.

[illegible]. You have also said you think they require something during six days of the week?—I did not say I think they required it, but I think they have a right to get it if they wish.

[illegible]. If they require it six days a week, is not it rather strange that they should hunger and thirst during six days, and neither hunger nor thirst on the seventh?—Sunday, of course, is an idle day, and if the people have nothing to do, and the public-houses are open, they will probably go there and drink. On week days they do not frequent the public-houses unless they happen to be at fairs, or markets, or something like that, and even then they have improved wonderfully in that respect. They generally go home earlier from fairs and markets.

[illegible]. I wish this question to apply specially to the licensing. How are the houses generally conducted in your district?—Throughout the whole county the more respectable houses are very well kept. Of course the poorer classes, particularly, when they get a chance, will sell on Sundays.

[illegible]. But there are very few convictions for infringement of the law?—That would not be correct, because many cases that are clearly proved are dismissed.

No public-house, no police.

[illegible]. (Mr. Roberts.) In reference to what you said about the district in the county of Clare, where there is no public-house, and where you did away with the police barracks, do you trace a direct connection between the necessity for the police and the facilities for drinking?—Yes.

[illegible]. That has been your experience as a police officer?—It has.

[illegible]. Not only in Clare, but elsewhere?—Yes.

Spirit grocers.

[illegible]. As to spirit grocers' licenses, of course in Clare, as has been brought out, there are not very many of that kind of license existing?—No.

[illegible]. But you have had experience, I take it, of the working of that license in other parts of Ireland?—I know of a case where I opposed a publican, and the magistrates refused to grant him a license, and then he got a spirit grocer's license.

[illegible]. That practically enabled him to carry on the same trade?—It did.

[illegible]. Would you be in favour of some restrictions of this kind being placed upon these licenses, that they should only be granted in towns say of a certain population, of 5,000 or 10,000 inhabitants?—Yes, I think that would be very good. I may say that opinion generally, so far as I can understand, is rather against spirit grocers.

[illegible]. Because of the known evils resulting from the license?—Quite so.

[illegible]. (Mr. Cadon.) Would you be in favour of abolishing them altogether?—I would. I do not see what use they are.

Hours of closing.

[illegible]. (Mr. Roberts.) You are in favour of Sunday closing?—Yes.

[illegible]. One or two questions as to the hours of closing. Take Saturday, for instance. Would you be in favour of an earlier closing hour on Saturday?—Yes.

[illegible]. What hour would you think?—I think in Ennis it might be nine, and in towns of that size, say over 5,000, and in other towns 8. That is the opinion of the leading, the rector, and the Presbyterian clergyman to whom I have spoken on the subject.

Mr. J. M. O. [illegible]

[illegible]

[illegible]. In the country districts I think in the latter you favour an earlier closing on Saturday, and in towns of considerable population, 9?—Yes.

[illegible]. As to Ennis, it has been brought out in your evidence that some of the licensed premises close before 11 o'clock?—I have never observed it myself, but I believe they close about 10.

[illegible]. With regard to the other days of the week, Monday to Saturday, would you be in favour of closing all through the country earlier than 11?—They do close at present at 10.

[illegible]. Would you be in favour of having an earlier closing hour than 10 o'clock?—I never thought of it. I do not think it would be necessary.

County court judge as licensing authority.

[illegible]. As to the question of granting new licenses, it has been put to you that the county court judge has no local knowledge?—That he might have no local knowledge.

[illegible]. That coming from Dublin four times a year he has not the necessary local knowledge?—Yes.

[illegible]. Is it not a fact that after some years of experience he must gain practical local knowledge as to the circumstances of each district?—Yes. I might say with regard to that, that of course where a county court judge has no experience of the county he could easily have the assistance of the resident magistrates.

[illegible]. As a matter of fact he hears the local evidence from the police on the one side, and from the applicants, the publicans, on the other?—Yes.

[illegible]. And if he were not satisfied he could adjourn the date, I suppose?—He could.

[illegible]. And make personal inquiries?—Yes.

[illegible]. Is that ever done?—I have heard of it being done, but it is many years ago.

[illegible]. At all events there is no practical difficulty in the way of his acquiring the necessary local knowledge?—No, I do not see how there can be any.

The bona fide traveller.

[illegible]. As to the bona fide traveller, you have been asked as to the difficulty in regard to opening and shutting the door when there are a large number of supposed bona fide travellers wanting to get into a public-house say 150?—Yes, it is quite impossible.

[illegible]. If your suggestion as to the 10-mile limit were carried out, is it at all likely that there would be that number often congregated at the door of a public-house?—No, but now that bicycles are so much in vogue I fancy that those who would walk three miles heretofore would ride on bicycles.

[illegible]. There is one point I should like to have your opinion upon. Is it the case in Ireland that so-called bona fide travellers take liquor away with them from public-houses?—I know of one case recently which was reported by the district inspector, where two so-called bona fide travellers knocked a man up at one o'clock in the morning, and they got drinks from him and then took away half-a-pint of whisky. A short time afterwards the patrol coming up found the two drunk a short distance from the public-house.

[illegible]. Were they proceeded against?—They were.

[illegible]. And convicted?—No, the magistrates dismissed the case.

[illegible]. Would you be in favour of a suggestion which has been made more than once before the commission, that is that the publican should have a book and enter the names of the so-called bona fide travellers?—I think it would be a very good plan—the names and address.

[illegible]. (Mr. Cadon.) On this question of bona fide travelling, do not you think it would be much simpler to repeal the clause altogether and get rid of the bona fide traveller?—If a man had to travel on Sunday a long distance I do not see why he should be deprived of having a drink if he was accustomed to take it. I certainly he would find it a great hardship to do without it.

[illegible]. (Mr. Roberts.) I think you said you were in favour of abolishing the term?—Yes, because it is a fraud.

[illegible]. Again, on Sunday closing, I think you gave evidence in 1888 before a Select Committee of the House of Commons?—I did.

Sunday closing in Londonderry.

[illegible]

Limerick.

[illegible]

Spirit grocers.

[illegible]

The *bona fide* traveller.

[illegible]

22,970. I thought I understood you to say that a resident magistrate probably should be employed in that way?—No, but I said that where a county court judge has no experience of the county, it would be [illegible] to have the resident magistrate sitting with him on the bench, and he might consult him on any question he wished.

22,971. Then you would do away entirely with the position which the local magistrates now have in the county?—Yes, unless under section [illegible] of the Licensing Act.

22,972. With regard to the adulteration of spirits, you do not know of your own knowledge that there is any adulteration?—No; it is only the complaints that I have heard, and rumours that I have heard about it. I know nothing about it.

22,973. You are aware that there is what I will call a common notion or a vulgar notion in the country, that persons getting drunk must really take something besides whisky. There is a common notion that there is adulteration going on, but you do not know that of your own knowledge?—I do not.

22,974. You are aware that there are very cheap whiskies?—There are. I think that those new whiskies are very injurious.

22,975. You have not analysed them, and you do not know the quality of the whiskies?—No; I know nothing about it.

22,976. It is simply hearsay?—Yes; there are a few other matters that perhaps the Commission would wish to hear my upon. There is the description of the houses that are licensed at present.

22,977. (Chairman.) Their structural arrangements?—Yes.

22,978. Is this in Tuam?—I will take Kilrush.

22,979. Where do these particulars come from, or are they official statistics?—Yes; they are from the district inspector. In Kilrush the population is 5,[illegible]. There are [illegible] public-houses in it.

22,980. What is the character of those houses?—There is one held by a man named John O'Neill, of Vandeleur Street. This man was a cooper by trade, the house consisting of a workshop 21 feet by 17 feet, and a kitchen 14 feet by 13 feet, on the ground floor. There were three bedrooms on the ground floor 18 feet by 14 feet 6 inches, 17 feet by 10 feet 4 inches, and 14 feet by 9 feet 6 inches. There was a yard 17 feet by 30 feet in which there was a piggery, and a wall round it 9 feet high. The entrance to the yard was through what was the workshop, and what is now the public-house. That license was granted at the quarter sessions in October. The yard is practically open to the adjoining houses.

22,981. That is to say, it is only separated by a 9-foot wall?—That is all; and it is impossible in consequence to exercise any police supervision. There have been two successful prosecutions there since the license was granted in October.

22,982. Prosecutions for what?—For illicit trading. Almost all those cases are for breaches of the Sunday Closing Act.

22,983. What were the premises entered?—I cannot tell you. Most extraordinary efforts have to be made by the police in order to get into the houses without being seen. It is generally a strange policeman, if he [illegible] to get, a policeman from another part of the district, and in plain clothes.

22,984. The same man who has been twice convicted in this house still keeps the house?—He does. Then there is Mary O'Shaughnessy, of Moore Street. She has a house the frontage of which is 14 feet. The entrance to the yard is also through the shop, that yard is common to three houses.

22,985. The shop is now the bar?—Yes; that is the only room. That house, I am told, is closed at present, in order to evade the creditors.

22,986. Have you any other instance?—There is a very bad case in Kilkee also. A man named John Hickey had a licensed house there. He is a prize-fighter.

22,987. A prize-fighter in practice?—Well, he gives exhibitions. He had been prosecuted on several occasions, and he became bankrupt. He then got the license transferred to his wife, and she remained in occupation of the house. Last October she procured a small dilapidated house in the same village, and she applied for a publican's license.

22,988. She disposed of the first house?—She did; and then she got the other. She transferred the license.

22,989. The license did not continue to the first house, I suppose?—It did, I presume so.

22,990. She sold it with the license attached?—Yes. She then applied for a license for this house, and she was beaten only by the casting vote of the chairman, the county court judge. He remarked that it never gave him so much pleasure; as to give the vote for the licensing of such a house would have been a disgrace. In January, at the next quarter sessions, she again applied for a license for this house. It was still in a dilapidated state, and the license was opposed by the constabulary. The judge said that it was unsound, it was illegal to grant a license at all, and that it would be a scandal to grant it. Nevertheless, the license was granted by a majority of the magistrates, many of whom never attend the quarter sessions unless for purposes of this kind.

22,991. (Mr. Walker.) In the case you first mentioned of the cooper's house, was that license obtained simply for the purpose of working the bar and supplying on Sunday?—Oh, no; certainly not. I do not allege that at all.

22,992. Do I understand you to say that since it obtained the license last October, two prosecutions have taken place for Sunday trading?—Yes.

22,993. Do I understand from that, that the principal source of revenue was derived from Sunday trading?—The principal revenue, in the majority of those wretched low public-houses, is derived from Sunday trading.

The witness withdrew.

Mr. Hugh Burke called in and examined.

22,994. (Chairman.) You are, I believe, a resident magistrate in the county of Tipperary?—Yes. Mr. H. Burke.

22,995. You have some suggestions which you are willing to offer us as to the present licensing system. First of all, I suppose, you would be of opinion that it is necessary to codify the existing Acts?—Yes. They are rather complicated.

22,996. There are many English Acts, are there not, which apply to Ireland?—Frequently. I do not think they are identical. They differ, I believe, in some small instances.

22,997. Those small discrepancies between the two Acts cause great confusion and difficulty, do they?—Yes, a certain amount.

22,998. I suppose there is the usual confusion in the way of later Acts amending and supplementing preceding Acts which applies not only specially to Ireland but also to the United Kingdom?—Yes.

22,999. As to the present licensing authority in Ireland, are you satisfied with it?—No, I do not think it is at all satisfactory in its results. Licensing authority.

23,000. You are speaking now of the country, I understand?—Yes.

23,001. We know that in the country it is the county court judge sitting with the magistrates?—Yes, in quarter sessions.

23,002. Who are the petty sessional magistrates, and what concern have they with the licensing question?—Not with the actual granting of licenses except in the case of beer licenses and grocers' licenses, but as regards spirit licenses they have not anything to say to the granting of new licenses; only to the renewal at the annual licensing day.

23,003. A new license and a transfer is only granted by magistrates at the annual quarter sessions?—Yes, practically that is the only time; they can apply at the

10,008. In the eight years you have been in the county of Tipperary as a resident magistrate, has the population greatly decreased?—I fancy it has. A good many people emigrate from there.

10,009. Has the number of public-houses increased or decreased?—It has largely increased. I have a list here of new licenses that were granted in the year 1880. These are the only new licenses that were granted—they are not old ones renewed. There are 31 in the year 1880; in 1881 there were [illegible]; in 1882, 37; in 1883, [illegible]; in 1884, [illegible]; in 1885, [illegible]; in 1886, [illegible]; and last year, 1887, there were [illegible] new licenses granted.

10,010. (*Sir Algernon West.*) Is that only in Tipperary?—In the county of Tipperary.

10,011. (*Chairman.*) Were they publicans' licenses?—They were.

10,012. No grocers' licenses are included in that number?—No. These are the ordinary publicans' licenses.

10,013. The population of the county of Tipperary in the year 1881 is stated here to be 173,000 odd?—Yes.

10,014. You do not know what it is estimated at now?—No. In 10 years before it was 190,[illegible], that is in 1871. It was nearly 20,000 more.

10,015. It has been as many as 400,000 odd?—Yes, 40 years or 50 years ago. I may say these figures that others may be slightly misleading. These licenses, though they are called new licenses, in a few instances, only amount to renewals or transfers. There are certain circumstances under which publicans have to get a new license instead of a transfer, but that would only amount to a very small percentage of them. I should think 10 per cent. would be a large estimate of it.

10,016. Ten per cent. would be a large deduction to make for those which are technically new licenses, but really transfers?—Yes.

Number of licensed houses.

10,017. You say that the public-houses are excessive. You came eight years ago, but perhaps you can speak to 10 years ago. Do you consider that 10 years ago there was a sufficient number of public-houses in Tipperary to serve the public?—I am sure there was. It is the universal opinion. I never met anybody who was not of the same opinion.

Proposed licensing authority.

10,018. What body would you substitute for the present licensing authority?—It would be hard to say, I think. Probably the county court judge, or perhaps with him there might be one or more resident magistrates associated.

there should be no trade carried on at all in conjunction with it in the same house at any rate.

[illegible]. You would let the present houses which carry on this [illegible] trade gradually die out, or would you name a certain number of years after which they must adapt themselves to your new reform?—It would be rather a strong measure, I think, but it would be a good thing in the end.

[illegible]. It would be a good thing if it could be fairly done without injury?—Yes.

[illegible]. There is no qualification, as you know, for a public-house in Ireland?—No.

[illegible]. Do you think a qualification should be affixed?—I think so, certainly.

[illegible]. What would, in your view, be the minimum qualification?—It is hard to put it at a sum. I think there is a limit now for spirit grocers' licenses. I think it is [illegible] or [illegible].

[illegible]. Some qualification like [illegible] or [illegible] would be, you think, a reasonable [illegible] as the minimum qualification for a public-house?—I think so.

[illegible]. There, again, as to those houses which you say combine the sale of liquor and the sale of groceries, you think it would be a hardship to abolish them; but it would be a hardship, I suppose, to raise the qualification of those licensees up to [illegible] or [illegible]. How should we get out of the difficulty?—There are a sufficient number of public-houses already in the country, and I think that being the case, if any more licenses are granted, they should be under much more strict conditions.

[illegible]. You would leave the present [illegible] houses to die out?—Yes, I think so. I think it would be a rather large order to abolish them. There are such a very large number of [illegible]. If they received compensation it would be a heavy tax.

[illegible]. What hope of reform is there if these [illegible] houses are to be allowed to continue for all time?—I think a great many of the badly-conducted ones might be extinguished by having compulsory recording of the convictions on the licence which would, after three convictions, extinguish a licence.

[illegible]. You think they have rendered themselves liable under the present law, though not under the present administration of the law, to have their licences withdrawn?—I think a great many of them would be extinguished.

[illegible]. In the case of appeals, would the magistrate mark "dismissed" on the case, or say "the case is dismissed"?—They use the word "dismiss"?—Yes.

[illegible]. In the case of a "dismiss," should you think there should be a right of appeal on the part of the complainant?—Yes. I think it would be a good thing, because sometimes I think a miscarriage of justice [illegible]. There are cases, I am afraid, which are dismissed owing to the [illegible] of the [illegible].

[illegible]. And you think that a person who has a grievance against the [illegible] should have the right of appeal?—I think the complainant should be in the right to appeal.

[illegible]. Who would be the complainant?—The police prosecute in nearly all offences under the Licensing Acts. There is an appeal given to the complainant under a good many [illegible] Acts, and Acts of that sort, and I do not see why it should not be so in this case.

[illegible]. What is a "dismiss"? That the case is not proved, or what?—There are two sorts in the Petty Sessions Act. It may be dismissed without prejudice—there may not be witnesses in attendance, [illegible] that may occur which may prevent it going on, and instead of adjourning it, it is very often dismissed without prejudice. It does not prevent a man being tried again for it if it is dismissed without prejudice, only if it is dismissed on the merits.

[illegible]. Do you think the resident magistrate might be substituted in many cases for the two justices whose presence is required before a certain act can be done?—I think it would be very useful in many cases. In a good many instances there are cases that require two magistrates, and very often there is no second magistrate there, and there is a great deal of inconvenience caused to the parties who come there to have their cases heard, which cannot be heard if there is only one magistrate, whereas a resident magistrate is obliged to attend, and he is always there.

[illegible]. I suppose the reason for requiring two justices was that it was thought the discretion could hardly properly be vested in one, but you would not hesitate to give that discretion to one resident magistrate?—I do not think so. The Licensing Act says one stipendiary or two justices, so that it is vested in one in a good many instances, only a resident magistrate in Ireland is not what they call a stipendiary magistrate.

[illegible]. One stipendiary is equal to two magistrates?—Yes.

[illegible]. At all events, you would give one resident magistrate the power of doing that for which two magistrates are required now?—I think it would save a great deal of inconvenience.

[illegible]. As to the *bona fide* traveller, of which we have heard a great deal, what would you do with him? Would you abolish or restrict him?—I should be in favour of enlarging the limit to five or six miles instead of three, otherwise I think the present law would catch any infringement.

[illegible]. You think he should insist opening a house after prohibited hours as a *bona fide* traveller?—I think if he is a *bona fide* traveller he should be entitled to get refreshment.

[illegible]. Notwithstanding that the house at that hour is closed to the public?—Yes.

[illegible]. Do you think it would be a hardship that a *bona fide* traveller should be made to [illegible] himself to the same hours as the ordinary public are confined to on Sunday?—I think so. On Sundays the public-houses are not open at all in the country, and if he were confined to the same hours as the public he would not be able to get anything on Sundays at all. I think it is only in the cities that public-houses are open for certain hours. In the country they are not open at all.

[illegible]. He should have a right to get refreshment at any house in the country?—At any house that was licensed.

[illegible]. Any house that had a seven-day licence?—Yes, of course.

[illegible]. He has a right to obtain his refreshment now at any house that has a seven-day licence, has he not?—Yes.

[illegible]. Apart from the question as to whether a publican is under an obligation to serve any customer at all, the *bona fide* traveller has a right as regards Sundays to be served when other customers have no right?—Yes, at any time he can be served as long as the house is in force.

[illegible]. It would not meet with your view, I understand, that public-houses in the country should be

[illegible]

Mr. [illegible]

[illegible] April '[illegible]

Resident magistrate for two justices.

The *bona fide* traveller.

Mr. H. Bruce.

1 April '98.

59,071. Do I understand that in Ireland no public-house is open on Sundays, throughout the county districts except to the bonâ fide traveller?—That is so.

59,072. ([illegible].) No resident in a country district can get a supply?—No. There are certain exemptions which apply only to certain cities.

59,073. (Chairman.) In England, as you know, the public-houses are open on Sundays during certain hours without reference to the bonâ fide traveller?—Yes.

59,074. In Ireland outside the exempted towns all houses in the country districts are closed except to the bonâ fide traveller?—Yes.

59,075. Does not that make it a still greater hardship upon the publican if he cannot serve an ordinary customer during any hour on the Sunday? He is obliged to wait on his premises till the chance bonâ fide traveller turns up; or is that his principal trade? Does he get his greatest profit on that day?—I do not know. Different localities differ very much, of course, in a great many places there are practically no bonâ fide travellers.

59,076. You could not say what would be the feeling of the publicans, as to whether it is a hardship to be kept on their premises?—No, I do not suppose they would object if they could sell.

Persons found drinking on unlicensed premises.

59,077. In the case of selling intoxicating liquor without a licence, a person who is found on the premises and presumably drinking cannot be had up, can he?—I think under certain circumstances he cannot. If there is an information sworn, and a search warrant issued, and then people are found on the premises, that would be different.

59,078. It is only in the case of a search warrant being issued, and persons being found on the premises where unlicensed sale is going on, that they can be apprehended?—Yes, or at least made liable.

59,079. Do you think any change should be made under these circumstances? Do you think it desirable that persons found on unlicensed premises and apprehended should be liable to a penalty?—They should be liable. It seems to be an omission in the Licensing Acts. It is provided for under the Shebeening Acts.

59,080. You think it has crept in per incuriam, as they supposed it to be a bit of negligence?—I should think so; I think it would be a good thing to have such a provision.

59,081. You think it would be advisable that, in the case of an illegal sale where the house is not licensed, everybody found on the premises should be apprehended whether there is a search warrant or not, and should be liable, on being found guilty, to a penalty?—Yes.

Public-houses and population in Tipperary.

59,082. (Mr. Young.) May I take it that there has been a tremendous decrease in the population of Tipperary?—A very large decrease.

59,083. During how many years?—I have the accounts of the various censuses here since 1841. In 1841 there were over 430,000, and they decreased regularly every 10 years to 173,000, which was the last census.

59,084. I think those figures are pretty nearly correct during the last 10 years. There are 173,000 at the present time, against 199,000 10 years ago?—199,000, I think is probably it. Practically, that is so.

59,085. You admit that this is a very extraordinary diminution in the population?—It has been going on ever since 1841, which is as far back as I have taken the figures. I think it is pretty general in most parts of Ireland.

59,089. I suppose there are no manufactures going on in the county. Probably it is in consequence of there being no manufactures that the people take to public-houses as a means of living?—There may be something in that. No doubt it is very profitable.

Mr. [illegible]

Licensing authority.

59,090. As to the remedy for this state of things, do you think there is any fault with the licensing tribunal?—Yes, I think it is unsatisfactory.

59,091. If you changed the licensing authority, would you diminish the number of houses that are not suitable?—It would be a very big thing to do to reduce the numbers, and if they had to be compensated, the ratepayers would have to pay a great deal of money, but it would be a good thing for the country if they were diminished.

59,092. At all events, you are of opinion that the increase should not have taken place?—Certainly, I am.

59,093. And you are of opinion that it is in consequence of the leniency of the magistrates?—Certainly.

59,094. You are of opinion that the tribunals for granting licenses, and for renewals and transfers of licenses, should be changed?—I think there has not been much fault to be found so far as the renewal of licenses goes, but as to the granting of new licenses I think it decidedly calls for reform; that there should be a new licensing authority.

59,095. And that is owing to the magistrates sitting with the county court judge?—If the county court judge had been sitting alone there would practically not have been any new licenses granted. There is no demand for them in the country.

59,096. With regard to petty sessions, does a resident magistrate sit in every court?—Practically in every court. He has to attend every petty sessions in his district.

59,097. Would you allow him any power to grant licenses, or would you not confine it entirely to the county court judge?—The reason that I propose a resident magistrate as well, is that of course it is possible that if there was only one man to grant the licenses he might be a man of very decided views on one side or the other, and there might be some difficulties in the way.

Power to grant licenses, under [illegible]

59,098. You would allow an appeal?—If there is an appeal given, of course that would obviate that difficulty.

59,099. Would you recommend an appeal?—Well, I do not know. If there was a larger body than the county court judge, if the licensing body consisted of more than one man, I do not know that I should recommend an appeal.

59,100. I do not think I have got it clearly from you that you would abolish the power of the resident magistrate in petty sessions?—The petty sessions have no power to grant publicans' licenses.

59,101. But they have the power of opposing?—Yes. I think I would leave it as it is, with an appeal to the new quarter sessions licensing body. If the new licensing body at quarter sessions were changed, I think the appeal to that body would be sufficient to obviate any miscarriage of justice which might occur at the petty sessions.

59,102. That is presided over entirely by the county court judge?—At present it is presided over by him, but it consists of all the local magistrates as well.

59,103. Would you continue that system?—No.

59,104. At the present time, there are six houses [illegible] better for the people, and conducive to good order?—I do not think so. I would rather see them closed altogether.

59,109. Do you not find that in consequence of their being closed altogether, the people resort to back-door work?—They do, no doubt, but I think they would in any case.

59,110. If they were publicly open, they would be open to the cognisance of the police, and subject to public opinion; but now the people drink in a sneaking way. Are you not of that opinion?—I think the drinking that is pointed at, which they used to carry on on Sundays, is excessive drinking, and I think they would not have time for excessive drinking in the two or three hours allowed by law.

59,111. (Mr. Ormsby.) I gather from one of the replies which you have just made, that your view is that any forcible reduction of licenses must be accompanied by compensation?—That is only my own view.

59,112. And that that compensation would come out of the ratepayers' pockets?—I suppose so.

59,113. You think, perhaps, that the money of the ratepayers might be spent in a great many worse ways than that?—Well, I do not know. That is rather a large question. I think it would be a good thing for the country, but I do not think it would be very popular.

59,114. On the question of the qualification of premises, I think I understand that in Ireland there is only one class of license where the question of qualification of premises comes in, and that is the off-license to retail beer?—I think in the case of the spirit grocer's license there is a limit in the qualification, too; but I am not certain whether that is all.

59,115. In the case of the off-license to retail beer, the qualification is 15l. in cities with more than 10,000 inhabitants, and 8l. elsewhere. Do you think that acts to a certain extent as a check upon an inferior class of houses?—I think it would do so, but practically there are very few beer dealers licensed in Ireland.

59,116. Is the rating qualification a better guide than the rental qualification in that respect?—I have not considered that question.

59,117. At any rate, if there were a rating or a rental qualification of a reasonable amount, it would practically shut up those small houses that we have heard of, some of which are described as unfit for human habitation?—Yes.

59,118. Would not that do away with a great deal of the complaint which at the present time arises against such class of licensed holder? It would be a means of improving the character of the houses?—I think so. That is why I should recommend it.

59,119. With regard to Tipperary and this question of the large decrease of the population, the number of houses has rather increased. What is your opinion as to the state of temperance in county Tipperary, taking the last years from 1880 to 1888? Would you say that the residents in Tipperary are more temperate than they were ten years ago?—I really have no statistics to go upon; but, merely from my own observation, I should say there is perhaps a little less intemperance now.

59,120. That rather goes to show that the question of the number of houses, after all, has not a great deal to do with the question of intemperance?—Not directly, perhaps.

59,121. On the point of these very small and inferior

59,122. It acts rather unfairly on the residential shopkeeper, does it not?—I do not quite understand in what way.

59,123. (Mr. Sprigge.) I understood you to say you would suggest a new licensing authority, and that probably would be the county court judge?—Yes. | Mr. H. Bruen. 9 April '89. Proposed licensing authority.

59,124. Would that be for all license purposes?—Yes, for all sorts of licenses.

59,125. For the granting of a new license?—Yes.

59,126. And the removal of old licenses?—When I said all licenses I meant beer-dealers' licenses and spirit grocers' licenses, and those things which are sometimes granted at petty sessions; but, as to removals, I think the present way of giving a certificate of removal acts fairly well.

59,127. That is, by the justices in petty sessions?—Yes.

59,128. Then you agree to that?—I think so; with a final appeal to the newly constituted licensing body at quarter sessions.

59,129. You would like an appeal from the petty sessions to the quarter sessions?—Yes.

59,130. I understood you to say that that appeal should only be for the complainant; that he only should have the right to appeal?—(On the question of appeal by the complainant.) I was referring more to cases of offences against the Act at petty sessions.

59,131. Even that being so, would it not be fair to allow the defendant also to have a right of appeal?—The defendant has it now always in every case, but at present the complainant has not.

59,132. In the case of all licensing questions being delegated to the county court judge, how would that act with regard to the question of temporary transfers?—I think that might be left to the petty sessions, as at present.

59,133. Temporary transfers?—Yes.

59,134. (Mr. Graham.) As far as I can understand, there is no statutory rateable value required for public-houses in Ireland, is there?—Not at present. | Value qualification of premises.

59,135. Nor apparently for grocers' licenses?—I think there is for grocers' licenses. I am nearly sure there is.

59,136. I find by the 10 Vict. c. 4, s. 8 there is a statutory rateable value for beer retailers' licenses?—Yes.

59,137. Where a grocer holds a beer retailer's license the same statutory limit of value applies?—Yes; I am nearly sure that the spirit grocer's premises have to be of a certain valuation, as well as those of the beer dealer, but I am not quite sure.

59,138. I do not think it is so. In the case of a public-house and in the case of a spirit grocer, the magistrate is required to consider, amongst other things, the fitness and convenience of the house?—Yes.

59,139. But no particular value is specified?—No.

59,140. As a matter of fact, many public-houses are rated much lower than the limits for retail beer-houses, are they not?—They are.

59,141. The limit for retail beer-houses where the population is less than 10,000 is 8l. a year, and over 10,000 15l. a year?—Yes. There is a list here of the valuations of the public-houses in the town of Thurles, and there are 23 under 10l., but I have not got them made out under 8l.

59,142. I see from the returns supplied to us that,

59,146. Do you think it is a desirable state of things that publicans should continue to be licensed without requiring a fixed rateable value?—No. I think in future any new premises that are licensed should be above a certain valuation.

59,147. (*Mr. Walker.*) In respect to the county magistrates, as at present, it is stated that they grant licenses and are very lenient to offenders. You are not prepared to deny that they act conscientiously in the discharge of their magisterial duties, are you?—I do not quite understand the question.

59,148. It has been implied here that the licensing magistrates have been, to use a mild term, somewhat lax in discharge of their duties. Are you prepared to say that they are not conscientious in the discharge of those duties?—I think they allow themselves to be canvassed before cases come on. They very often hear the cases out of court.

59,149. And that influences their judgment on the Bench?—I do not think anybody could approach a case quite unbiassed if he had heard all the facts outside, on one side.

59,150. Can they prevent themselves from being canvassed?—I should think it rested with themselves.

59,151. Does it necessarily follow that if they are canvassed, that would guide their deliberations and decisions?—Of course it depends upon each particular man; but I should not think it a desirable thing that anybody in a judicial position should hear a case before it came before him in court.

59,152. You are not prepared to say that you believe them to act conscientiously in the discharge of their licensing functions?—I think they give licenses very often when they are not required.

59,153. You will not say yes or no to the question?—I do not quite understand the question. Do you ask me whether I consider they always act conscientiously?

59,154. Yes?—Well, I do not know. As far as their lights go, I suppose they do.

59,155. (*Provost de Vesci.*) You act in Queen's County as well as in Tipperary, I think?—Yes.

59,156. Speaking from a comparison of the two counties, are the licenses as excessive in Queen's County as they are in Tipperary?—There is not the number of magistrates in Queen's County to grant the licenses that there is in Tipperary.

59,157. Is the number of licenses excessive in Queen's County in the same proportion as in Tipperary?—I do not think so. I have not the statistics for Queen's County. There has not been the same number of new licenses granted lately that was formerly the case in Tipperary. I did not get the statistics; but I can see there are quite enough.

59,158. With regard to the mixed trade being carried on in a licensed house, do you think it would be possible without great hardship to require the holders of existing licenses to do away with those trades, on condition that they had a limited time, say three years, given them?—I have no doubt that they would consider it a great hardship.

59,159. In your opinion, would it be a great hardship?—It would interfere very much with their business, I think.

59,160. With their profits?—With their profits.

59,161. Do you think it would automatically aid in the reduction of the number of licenses?—I have no doubt it would. It would have the effect, no doubt, of reducing them very much.

59,162. Which do you think they would give up by preference, the license or the ordinary business? In other words, which is the more profitable?—The license, no doubt; but still it is a question whether they should not be compensated for it.

59,163. You stated that you are in favour of the county court judge and the resident magistrates being the licensing authority?—Yes; I think two.

59,164. Do you think the county court judges would have sufficient knowledge of the requirements of the districts, living as they do in many cases away from the district?—At present in Ireland it does not make very much difference. It is not like England, where the population is increasing and more public-houses are required. As far as it goes at present, I think they know enough about the requirements of the district. In Tipperary, and in those parts, they do. I cannot speak as to other parts where the conditions are altering. [illegible]

59,165. Do you not think it would be possible to devise some other means by which local magistrates should have some authority, either by confining it to magistrates residing within the licensing district, or by having committees of magistrates?—I do not think it would work in that way. I think there would be the same objections to confining it to local magistrates that there are now.

59,166. In fact, you think the number of magistrates who are likely to be influenced are the majority of the magistrates of the county in which you have experience?—Of the magistrates who attend, certainly.

59,167. There are a great number who do not attend at all?—Yes.

59,168. (*Sir Algernon West.*) I think your evidence and that of the witness who preceded you was very condemnatory of the present licensing authority in Ireland?—Yes.

59,169. You both recommended that that authority should be transferred from the magistrates to the recorder or to the county court judge?—Yes.

59,170. Would that be a practical suggestion to make; because the very moment that you are giving local government to Ireland you are taking away the authority of the magistrates?—That is a question of policy.

59,171. I only wanted to lead up to this question: is there no other suggestion you can make as to somebody being added who would represent the people of the country?—You mean a more popular body?

59,172. Yes?—You would not have a more popular body, I think, than the present one; and it has not been found to work very satisfactorily.

59,173. You cannot suggest anything better than the existing one?—No, I do not think so. I think it is quite in a very small part of Ireland that there is this unsatisfactory state of things. I do not think it is general over the whole of Ireland.

59,174. You think that Clare and Tipperary are rather peculiar in that way?—I believe so. At the same time, no doubt, it shows a weakness in the system.

59,175. I want to clear up one matter about the *bona fide* traveller. The *bona fide* traveller, as I understand, has a right to demand refreshment from a publican?—Yes; at any time. [illegible]

59,176. Supposing the public-house is closed when the traveller arrives, may he not knock up the landlord and insist on having refreshment?—I suppose he may. I do not know his common law rights exactly.

59,177. What remedy would he have against a publican whose premises are closed? Would he have any?—That is a question of common law. I am not a lawyer, and I am afraid I could not answer that. I do not suppose that the publican would offer any objection to supplying him.

59,178. Of course he would not, in any event. In remote villages, where there is a chance of a *bona fide* traveller, the poor publican is bound to stay at home all day, on the chance of a *bona fide* traveller coming and demanding refreshment?—Well, he has the privilege of selling drink under his license, and I suppose there are certain disadvantages too. I believe in England an innkeeper is obliged to supply anybody who comes; and I do not know that that does not apply to the case of a public-house in Ireland. I do not know of a decided case in which the question has been tried.

The witness withdrew.

Mr. John R. Wigham called in and examined.

Mr. J. R. Wigham.

39,179. (Chairman.) You are a justice of the peace for the county of Dublin?—Yes.

39,180. You have been engaged in trade in that city for many years?—Yes.

Position of witness.

39,181. You are the ex-president of the Chamber of Commerce of Dublin?—Yes.

39,182. And, as some of us know already, you are a director of several large companies in Dublin employing a large number of men?—Yes.

39,183. Have you any connexion with the townships in the neighbourhood of Dublin?—I am chairman of the Blackrock Township, which is a township very close to Dublin.

Public feeling.

39,184. So then what with those engagements to which you have referred, and the fact that you have been a member of the council of the Royal Dublin Society, you are able to speak with very considerable experience of the state of public opinion in Dublin, and perhaps, too, in Ireland, as to the effect of the Sunday Closing Act?—Yes, I think I know the minds of a great many people upon that subject.

39,185. Would you say that opinion trended in favour of the maintenance of the provisions of that Act?—I think so. I can say without the slightest hesitation that the balance of opinion is in favour of the maintenance of that Act and of including the exempted cities within it.

39,186. You think public opinion goes in the direction of including the exempted cities within the provisions of the Act?—To extend the Sunday Closing Act to all Ireland as it extends to Scotland.

Early closing on Saturdays.

39,187. Then would you close public-houses on Saturday at an earlier hour than at present?—Yes, there is a very strong opinion on that subject that public-houses on Saturday nights in Ireland should be closed much earlier than they are, in order that the working men may have their wages given to their families without having the temptation to spend them in drink.

Plebiscite in Dublin.

39,188. There was a so-called plebiscite taken in Dublin, was there not, in the year 18[illegible] with reference to the question of Sunday closing?—Yes, there was, and there was a very large majority in its favour.

39,189. You think that that majority would be maintained?—I do, if there was a poll taken in Dublin. The figures then were 34,039 for, and 8,117 against.

39,190. Have there been public meetings in the city with reference to the extension of the Sunday Closing Act?—Yes, many public meetings have been held. I have attended many of them, and I think on some occasions I have been in the chair, and those meetings were enthusiastically in favour of the continuance of the Sunday Closing Act and of early Saturday night closing.

39,191. So far as you are able to speak for the men in your employment in the works with which you are connected, would you say their feelings would be in favour of the extension of the Act?—I think so, not only the people I have spoken of, who belong to what may be called the richer classes of society, but the working people with whom I am acquainted, some [illegible] of whom are employed by the companies with which I am connected, and I think if they were polled also they would be of the same mind.

The bonâ fide traveller.

39,192. Holding to those views with reference to Sunday closing, do you think that the provisions for the bonâ fide traveller impair the operation of those Acts?—I think that the bonâ fide traveller is a mere myth, a mere sham. He comes and invades my township to a most uncomfortable extent and causes great disorder. In the township of which I am chairman they come on a Sunday there to the number of 1,400 or 1,500, and sometimes it is computed at as many as 2,000, and they are so numerous and so boisterously unpleasant, that ladies cannot go there without fear of insult; and so great is the crowd there sometimes that the public-houses door cannot be shut, and the drink is handed over the people's heads and taken in the open air. I have not myself seen that, but I can testify to the great disorder which I myself have seen on a Sunday evening owing to the so-called bonâ fide travellers, who are really not bonâ fide travellers, but people who come there four miles from the city to get drink.

Mr. J. R. Wigham.

6 April '88.

39,193. You do think that the provisions for the supposed convenience of the bonâ fide travellers do interfere with the due operation and full effect of the Sunday Closing Act?—Yes.

39,194. You speak of the effect in Black Rock. What do you say as to the other townships in the neighbourhood of Dublin?—Black Rock is the one I know most of, but in Kingstown, which is a very large township, I have seen also on Sunday evenings, perhaps in a minor degree, what I have seen in Black Rock and in Dalkey too; but it is a singular thing that the townships on the north side of Dublin are not included in the exemption of Dublin. It seems a very strange anomaly that on the north side there is no such thing, and on the other side these townships are exempted in the same way as is Dublin.

39,195. How was it that the suburbs of Dublin came to be so unequally treated as compared with the suburbs of other towns?—I think that has to do with the fact that the southern townships are in what is called the Metropolitan Police District; the northern townships are not so, but are in charge of the constabulary. Therefore I think perhaps that is the cause of the difference; but I feel it to be a very strange thing that whereas the other exempted cities besides Dublin are exempted simply as cities, and the exemption extends to them as cities, yet in Dublin the exemption extends not only to the city of Dublin, but to those townships on the south side of it which have a very large population and which are the very places that the Act should extend to.

39,196. Was there any public agitation in favour of their being included in the exemption?—I do not remember myself; but I have heard that the thing was done through a mistake; that instead of saying "the Municipality of Dublin," it was put "the Metropolitan Police District," which means a very different thing.

39,197. That extends, I suppose, 10 or 12 miles out?—Ten miles outside the city.

39,198. In the southern direction?—In the southern direction, and not at all in the northern direction.

39,199. The whole of this great area was exempted, therefore, from the operation of the Sunday Closing Act?—Yes.

Number of public-houses in Ireland.

39,200. Speaking generally of Ireland, if you are able to speak so widely, should you say that the public-houses were in excess of, or behind, the requirements of the public?—So far as I have seen, and so far as I have heard, I should think the public-houses were in excess of the requirements of the people in most places. For instance, there is a little town I have had to go through sometimes, called Cahirciveen, down in Kerry, and every house, I think, certainly every other house, is a public-house, and we find, wherever we travel, that very much the same thing is the case, perhaps not to the same glaring extent as in Cahirciveen.

Chilberry's case.

39,201. The licensing authority, which may has to consider applications, are not able to take into account the necessity for a public-house in any district?—They are not. The same law that applies to England does not apply to Ireland in that regard. In England, I understand, and I suppose it is so, that the licensing authority are at liberty to consider the needs of the neighbourhood when they establish public-houses, whether another public-house is really wanted; but in Ireland, on account of a case called the Chilberry case, in which the Courts ruled that the magistrates had no such jurisdiction, they are restricted from considering the needs of the district at all. They must consider the character of the applicant, and the suitability of the premises, but they are not allowed to consider whether there are any more public-houses wanted there.

39,202. So that in the case of renewals and transfers of licenses you would like to see full discretion given to the magistrates to refuse to renew or to refuse to transfer in consequence of the already sufficient or more than sufficient number of licenses in the district?—Yes, we would desire that.

59,203. Was there ever a law in Ireland which required the magistrates, before they granted a renewal or transfer, to consider the supply of public-houses in the neighbourhood already existing?—There was a law in the time of George III.

59,204. The reference you have given is the 48th George III., cap. 10, section 7?—I believe that is so. There was a law which, if it were in existence now, and in practice, would give the magistrates discretion as to whether any new public-house should be put in addition to those at present in a particular district.

59,205. That was repealed by implication, I suppose. It was not formally repealed, was it?—I am not sure.

59,206. Then do you think that the magistrates were not influenced in their decisions by the potential value which is attached to the house in consequence of its possessing a licence?—No, I do not know that I would go that far, but I have found on the bench of magistrates a good deal of discussion and consideration given to the fact of how much a man may have spent on his premises, and whether it would not be very unfair to deprive him of a licence considering how much money he had spent. I do not say they put that in their precise terms as an official matter, but they do talk about it, and it has a large consideration.

59,207. I never meant to hint anything more than that. In considering whether a licence should be forfeited or not they take into consideration the enormous value, and think it would be a severe punishment if that monopoly value were forfeited. That is what I mean?—Yes; that has passed through their minds and entered into their deliberations.

59,208. Do you think that a grocer should have power to sell spirits?—I think not. I have seen very great evils arising from what we call spirit grocers' licences, chiefly with reference to women servants who go in to buy groceries, and who get drink, and form drinking habits probably in consequence.

59,209. If you object to a grocer selling liquor, do you object to a publican selling groceries?—I do not know that. That is a different thing. A respectable grocer's shop is one into which anybody can go, and I have it on record in there not thinking at all of liquor, and then when they are there under the plea of buying groceries they perhaps get drink. In the other case of public-houses, if a person goes into a public-house he is supposed to go in for all in connection, drink and everything else.

59,210. I understand from the previous witness that it was the practice of publicans to sell goods of all kinds, drapery, groceries, and everything else?—I believe they do in many parts of Ireland.

59,211. Not in Dublin?—I think that is not the case in Dublin.

59,212. It was to those cases I was referring when I asked you, if you would object to the grocers selling liquor, would you object to the publicans selling groceries?—I think there is hardly such a thing in Dublin as the publicans selling groceries.

59,213. You think that no grocer should have a licence to sell liquor on the premises?—I do. I am strongly of that opinion.

59,214. Do you mean for consumption on the premises?—Yes, consumption on the premises.

59,215. (Mr. Grimley.) There is no such thing. There is not a grocer's licence to sell for consumption on?—A spirit grocer's licence which enables the people to get the drink on the premises.

59,216. It is against the law. They may not drink it on the premises?—If I have made a mistake I am sorry for it. I never myself went into a grocer's shop for the purpose of getting drink, but I have understood that in these cases of servant women, they went in there, and it was not to take away liquor but to drink it.

59,217. That would be an offence against the law, and would forfeit the licence?—I do not think so. I think the spirit grocer's licence enables the grocer to sell it.

59,218. (Chairman.) I think you are misinformed?—I am only saying what I believe.

59,219. No liberty is given to a grocer or to a spirit dealer to sell for consumption on the premises. The liquor may be bought on the premises, but has to be taken out of the house before it can be consumed, otherwise it is an offence against the law?—I remember one case at the moment, of a very respectable family grocer's shop in one of the large streets of Dublin, and I was there talking to the proprietor, and I found in the back shop a kind of bar, and the people getting drink there—drinking money.

Mr. J. A. Ryan.

59,220. (Mr. Grimley.) I think I can explain that. There are many spirit grocers who hold a publican's licence combined with that other licence. Do you know the circumstances of the licence?—I know very little about them; I did not come to speak on that as much as my own experience.

59,221. (Mr Young.) In fact what you said cannot be the case except against the law?—They may have publicans' licences. Perhaps that would be the explanation of it.

59,222. (Mr. Grimley.) Your charge is against the spirit grocer's licence?—What I meant was that respectable servants go into what appear to be grocers' shops, and are able to get drink there, no matter what kind of licence it is, which is a bad thing.

59,223. To consume on the premises?—Yes.

59,224. Then that is consumption under a public-house licence. Otherwise it is against the law?—Probably that may be so.

59,225. (Chairman.) In the case of penalties for drunkenness, do you think the existing penalties are sufficient?—We have some—I have, of us who have looked into that matter—that the wives who have to pay the fines when their husbands are fined are put to great difficulty in doing so. They have to pawn their own and their children's clothes, and a state of things worse than the absence of the father of the family, if he were confined by imprisonment for his drunkenness, arises to these poor people. I think it would be better to imprison him than to fine him. A fine is sure to be paid, and paid at the expense of those who could not afford it.

Penalties for drunkenness.

59,226. You would not give him the option of a fine?—I would not.

59,227. As to clubs. Have you formed any distinct view as to any classes of clubs and the necessity for reforming them, or do you think abuses exist?—I do not know much about clubs; but I should have thought there was no difficulty in having them registered and under the care of the police, and if disorder arose in any of those clubs or in any club, that the police should interfere and prosecute the proprietor or the manager.

Clubs.

59,228. If you were to give the police power to enter any club if they had reasonable ground for suspecting that irregularities were prevailing within it, what would be the necessity for registration?—If it is applied to every club there need be no registration.

59,229. Turning back to the licensing authority, did you hear the evidence of Sir Andrew Reed, the Inspector General of Constabulary?—I was not here, but I read his evidence.

59,230. What do you think about his suggestion of the new licensing authority?—I very much agreed with what he said about having but one licensing authority. Though I am on the bench of magistrates myself, I have seen so much of what I call a packing of the bench, and have suffered so much annoyance and vexation, that I do not think it is a good system. I should much rather that a man above all reproach, a man who could not be approached in any way, were put in possession of the necessary power, such as the recorder.

Proposed licensing authority.

59,231. That the recorder should sit alone and be sole judge of the licensing law?—Yes, I would give an appeal from his decision certainly.

Appeal to judge of assize.

59,232. From the recorder?—Yes, to the superior court.

59,233. To the judge of assize?—Yes.

59,234. With reference to the county districts, should you like to see the county court judge empowered to deal with licensing matters, instead of the magistrates?—Yes, that the county court judge in the country and the recorder in cities should sit without the assistance of the bench of magistrates.

59,235. In petty sessions what would you do?—I do not know much about them. They do not apply to [illegible] in Dublin. The magistrates are paid magistrates there.

[illegible]. (*Sir Algernon West.*) Your opinion is that there are too many public-houses, I think, in Ireland for the requirements of the people?—Yes, speaking generally, I think so.

[illegible]. You would like the power now given to English magistrates extended to the licensing authority of Ireland?—With reference to the suppression of public-houses I should.

[illegible]. Have you formed any idea as to how you would deal with the publicans who were suppressed for the benefit of the public, as to compensation?—I do not know that I have thought very much about that. I think that compensation perhaps ought to be given, or something of the kind should be taken into consideration; or they should be given some reasonable time to clear out, or something of that kind.

[illegible]. You have not gone into the question?—No, I have not thought much about that, except that one does think that they owe some compensation to the poor ratepayers who have suffered by the drinking usages they promote.

[illegible]. (*Vincent de Vere.*) You state that you are much troubled at Black Rock township with the *bona fide* travellers on Sundays?—Very much.

[illegible]. I think you also stated that the southern townships of Black Rock and Kingstown are within the area of Dublin for the purpose of being exempted?—They are.

[illegible]. Then how do these *bona fide* travellers come in, before 2 o'clock and after 7?—The houses are shut in Dublin and shut in these townships also, because they come under the same rule as Dublin, but the people come in from the surrounding parts on the Sunday to get drink when they cannot get it in the county. The public-houses in the county are closed altogether under the Sunday Closing Act, and these houses are open, and then besides that the people call themselves travellers. The houses are shut both in Dublin and in Black Rock by the law at 7 o'clock, but these people come down in considerably large numbers, call themselves travellers because they have come four miles by railway at a cost of 4d. by a return ticket, and demand drink and get drink and make a perfect pandemonium in the streets.

[illegible]. Practically they without the hours on Sunday?—Practically it comes to that.

[illegible]. Is the Recorder of Dublin the licensing authority in the townships?—No. The townships are in the county, and therefore the county bench of magistrates are the people who regulate licences for the county; but the recorder is our chairman.

[illegible]. As a county court judge?—Yes, as a county court judge.

[illegible]. That is for the southern townships of Black Rock and Kingstown?—For the whole county, but in Dublin city the recorder alone sits.

[illegible]. Do you consider that in the townships the licensed premises are increasing or diminishing?—I am not quite sure about that. I think they must be increasing, judging from the number one sees.

[illegible]. You have not gone into it?—No, I have not.

[illegible]. (*Mr. Walker.*) I understand you to say you would close, if you had the power, all licensed houses on Sunday, both in town and country?—I do not know

[illegible]. The statement you made was that the crowd was so great that they could not serve the liquor but handed it over their heads?—You will find I immediately added that I had not seen it myself.

[illegible]. Do you personally believe it?—I do, because I am credibly informed of it.

[illegible]. Is not that evidence that a necessity arises for houses to be opened for the supply of this want?—No, I do not think so.

[illegible]. The mere fact of crowds of great inconvenience to themselves jostling each other in order to get the drink is no indication that necessity compels them to obtain it?—The crowds I speak of are a great public evil and ought not to be allowed to take place.

[illegible]. If the houses were closed in Dublin the same as in the country, would not that crowd be likely to increase?—They are closed in Dublin.

[illegible]. Are they not open from 2 to 7?—They are closed at 7 o'clock.

[illegible]. If they were closed altogether would not the crowd be likely to increase?—I do not know that it would. If the houses in the country are shut as well as in Dublin, I think there would be no place for the crowds to go to drink.

[illegible]. Would you deprive the traveller of refreshment?—I would let the traveller, if necessary, get such refreshment as the traveller wants, including his bed and his rest and his food; but I think it is a very different thing having places open for drinking only.

[illegible]. I understand you to say these crowds were *bona fide* travellers?—They call themselves *bona fide* travellers.

[illegible]. I ask you again, if you had your wish and all the houses were closed, whether that crowd of *bona fide* travellers would not be likely to increase?—No, I think not at all. They come there to drink.

[illegible]. Are you of opinion that closing the houses would stop the desire for indulging in wines, spirits, or beer?—I think that if the houses were closed by law, whether the desire existed or not, people could not get the drink, and therefore would not come and create that kind of nuisance that I have just been describing.

[illegible]. You admit the rights of the *bona fide* traveller would remain?—I think, certainly, the people should get food and every refreshment that is necessary; but that is a different thing from drinking only.

[illegible]. Have the public-houses in Dublin externally and internally very much improved during the last 20 years?—I do not know, I never go into them.

[illegible]. You have no experience of licensed houses?—No, I have not.

[illegible]. Have you ever visited a licensed house?—I do not think I was ever in one in my life.

[illegible]. You know really nothing about them?—I know this, that I see as much what is in there as when they turn out I object to—the disorderly drunken people that come out of them so frequently.

[illegible]. Do I understand you to say you would inflict the penalty of imprisonment for the first act of drunkenness?—I did not say the first act. I think, perhaps, that is a matter of detail, but I do think that imprisonment would be a more merciful punishment to drunken persons than the system of a fine, for the reasons I gave, that it falls heavily upon the family.

[illegible]. Are you in favour of the establishment of Clubs

Mr. J. R. Wigham.

3 April '99

Sunday closing

Mr. J. R. Wigham.

8 April '98.

Canvassing and packing bench.

59,277. (*Mr. Hughes.*) On certain occasions you complain of the packing of the bench?—Yes. I have seen it myself.

59,278. In answer to a question which was put to you by a Commissioner I think you said you are a total abstainer?—I am.

59,279. Was the bench packed by a majority of total abstainers or the other side?—In the cases that I have in my mind now the bench seemed to be packed for the purpose of granting a licence, and the complaint was made on those occasions by magistrates who did not incline to grant the licence, that they had been troubled and persecuted by people praying them to come there and vote for this particular licence.

59,280. If it had been packed with magistrates that were not inclined to grant the licence, would you then have considered it a grievance?—I do not think there should be canvassing either way, and canvassing leads to packing. No later than Tuesday, if you happen to have read our papers, you would have seen that our Recorder, who is a man very much respected, was so much annoyed at what he considered the canvassing, that he would not go on—I was not present on that occasion, but it appears in the newspaper—he considered the canvassing was so glaring that he adjourned the case, and was apparently very much annoyed about it. He adjourned the case till Friday, and said he would let this Commission know about it, as that you see your Commission is known as a useful body to appeal to.

59,281. (*Mr. Young.*) On that bench would you personally have contended for a licence, whether it was proved it was needed or not?—I could not say that till I knew the circumstances of the case.

59,282. You were on the bench and heard the circumstances stated there by the advocates for and against?—In this particular case that I mentioned I was not present.

59,283. It was at Kilmainham, was it not?—Yes, on Tuesday last.

59,284. If you had found there was a necessity for that public-house would you have voted for it?—If I thought there was a necessity, certainly.

59,285. But if you thought there was no necessity?—If I thought there was no necessity I should have voted against it.

59,286. You are, I understand, a total abstainer from choice?—I suppose it is from choice; my real reason is for an example.

59,287. Would you interfere with another man's choice if he desired to have wine, beer, or ale?—Certainly not. I would interfere with nobody.

59,288. Would you provide public-houses in which he could get these commodities?—I would not provide them.

59,289. Then you would interfere with his rights?—Not at all. Other people may provide for him, but I would not. You asked me if I would.

59,290. Would you promote a Bill to interfere with their rights?—I do not exactly understand the bearing of that question, would I promote a Bill?

59,291. Yes, for interference with their rights?—I think whatever their rights are they should not be interfered with. I would not interfere with any man's rights.

59,292. You admit that all those persons who want ale or beer have a perfect right to drink ale or beer, and they have a perfect right to be afforded facility for drinking ale or beer. Would you promote a Bill which would interfere with their rights, I want to ask you?—I would promote any Act of Parliament or any Bill, or I would do anything I could, that would prevent the public from being injured by those people exercising what they consider their rights.

Mr. J. R. Wigham.

The witness withdrew.

Adjourned to to-morrow at half-past ten.

NINETY-NINTH DAY.

Queen's Robing Room, House of Lords, Wednesday, April 6th, 18[illegible].

PRESENT:

THE RIGHT HONOURABLE THE VISCOUNT PEEL, IN THE CHAIR.

The Right Hon. the Lord W[illegible].	Samuel [illegible], Esq.
The Right Hon. Sir Algernon West, K.C.B.	[illegible] W[illegible], Esq.
William [illegible] [illegible], Esq.	Thomas Palmer W[illegible], Esq., M.P.
William Graham, Esq.	[illegible] [illegible], Esq., M.P.
[illegible] [illegible], Esq.	

Mr. F[illegible] James Ball called in and examined.

[illegible]. (*Chairman.*) I believe you are district inspector of the Royal Irish Constabulary, and are now stationed at Tralee?—Yes. Mr. F. J. Ball. 6 April '[illegible].

[illegible]. You have had experience, I think, in various parts of Ireland?—Yes, for about [illegible] years.

[illegible]. Have you had much experience specially in connexion with the trade in liquor?—I have had a [illegible] [illegible] all my service, and for the last [illegible] 11 years I have given special attention to it in [illegible] of things that came under my notice [illegible] the peace of the district.

[illegible]. You are good enough to hand in returns [illegible] to the Tralee district?—Yes.

[illegible]. Perhaps before handing them in you will [illegible] them as far as they need explanation. They [illegible] clear, but will you summarise them?—I have [illegible] a return relating to the Tralee district. The [illegible] about [illegible] miles by [illegible] miles. There are [illegible] eight ordinary stations, and also [illegible] [illegible] for the special protection of individuals. [illegible] strength of the district force are district inspector, [illegible] a head constable, [illegible] sergeants and acting [illegible], and [illegible] constables. The strength of Tralee [illegible] is a head constable, [illegible] sergeants and acting [illegible], [illegible] constables. The population of the sub-[illegible] attached to that station is [illegible]. In the [illegible] there are [illegible] six-day licences and [illegible] seven-day licences, making a total of 11[illegible].

[illegible]. One hundred and seventeen to a population of what?—The population of the town of Tralee is [illegible], and the whole of these 117 houses are in Tralee. [illegible] makes an average of about 1 to [illegible] persons. [illegible] there is the sub-district of Abbeydorney, a small [illegible]. The strength of that is a sergeant and four [illegible]. The population of the sub-district is [illegible]. [illegible] are in the sub-district four licensed houses—[illegible] six-day licences and two seven-day licences. Two [illegible] licences are in the village of Abbeydorney, and [illegible] others are in the village of K[illegible], which is about [illegible] away. The population of Abbeydorney is 107, [illegible] there being two houses there is here an average [illegible] is [illegible]. The next sub-district is [illegible]. It is a [illegible] post for the protection of an individual who [illegible] a farm and gave evidence in a murder case. There [illegible] public-house in that sub-district. Then there is [illegible]. The strength there is a sergeant and four [illegible]. The population of the sub-district is [illegible]. [illegible] are in the sub-district five public-houses—[illegible] and four seven-day licences. The population of the [illegible] is [illegible]. The five public-houses are in the village, [illegible] [illegible] 1 to every [illegible] persons. Then there is [illegible]. The sub-district strength is a sergeant [illegible] four constables. The population of the sub-district [illegible]. There are three seven-day licences. The population of the village is [illegible], and, all the public-houses being in the village, that is an average of 1 to [illegible] persons. Then there is [illegible]. The strength of that is a sergeant and five constables. The population of the sub-district is [illegible]. There are [illegible] licences, all in the village, one six-day and five seven-days. The population of the village is [illegible]. That leaves a public-house to every [illegible] persons. Then there is [illegible], which is more or less a small fishing village near a pier. The strength there is a sergeant and four constables. The population of the sub-district is [illegible]. There are two public-houses seven-day licences. One of these is at [illegible], and one is at a small fishing village about a mile away. The population of [illegible] is [illegible], so there is one public-house to [illegible] people there. The next is [illegible]. That is a protection post. There is no public-house in that sub-district. Then there is [illegible]. The strength there is a sergeant and four constables. As a rule there are only a sergeant and three constables there. The population of the sub-district is [illegible]. There are three seven-day licences in the sub-district, and one of these is in the country about a mile and a half from [illegible].

[illegible]. There are only two questions which occur to my mind upon these figures. When you give the population, as compared with licences, you only include the town or village in which they are situate?—Yes.

[illegible]. But the town or village, as I understand from these figures, supplies a large district round?—To a certain extent, but in most cases the people living in the sub-districts get their supplies in the large towns, such as Tralee.

[illegible]. You have excluded Tralee?—Yes.

[illegible]. There are very few public-houses, or licensed houses in the country districts, are there?—There are three of them, I think, altogether.

[illegible]. I think you set down four, one in the country?—In the Abbeydorney sub-district there are two in the country. In the [illegible] sub-district there is one in the country, and in the [illegible] there is one in the country. That is four altogether.

[illegible]. There are four in the country?—Yes.

[illegible]. And these four supply a considerable population, do not they?—They supply the people living more or less all round them. There are small shops attached in all cases.

[illegible]. Therefore, when you give us the proportion of licences to the population, you ought to take into account, ought not you, the whole of the country district as well?—I went on the principle of some evidence which I had seen had been given here, of giving the proportion as regards the population of the town, because in large cities, of course, the houses supply people from a distance who may come in, and I went on the same principle.

Mr. F. J. [illegible]

6 April '98

Porter the [illegible] drink.

supply not only of the village but of a considerable country district around?—As a matter of fact they do supply people around.

[illegible]. What is the drink mostly, whisky or porter?—In some parts of the country porter is the main drink, and in other parts they drink a good deal of whisky. I have had a good deal of experience of the working of the Act in the Fermoy district in Cork and in the Tralee district in Kerry; and I should say in both those districts porter is the staple drink. In one village in the Fermoy district I was told by the sergeant there was not a single glass of whisky to be got in any public-house in the village—that none of the people drank anything but porter. In one place they only drink one brewer's porter.

[illegible]. Would that preference for porter be in consequence of any adulteration of the whisky, or the inferior quality of the whisky?—No, I should say it is from an acquired taste. They draw a distinction between one porter and another, and they acquire a taste for a particular one.

Adulteration.

[illegible]. Speaking generally of the Tralee district, and Kerry generally, has any adulterated whisky come under your notice?—Not in the county Kerry. As a rule, there are very few prosecutions for adulteration of whisky, because the samples sent up very seldom show any adulteration on which a prosecution could be had. I have had a sample. In any case that I had acquaintance with it was adulteration with water only.

[illegible]. If the samples sent up prove absence of adulteration, what are we to conclude as to the general character of the whisky so sold?—Notwithstanding the absence of any adulteration as shown by analysis except by water, I am firmly convinced that other adulteration is used, for this reason; I have frequently seen men after fairs and markets in a state of intoxication approaching madness, which I do not believe could ever have been caused by ordinary intoxication by liquor. I have been told by them in the morning, when they were in custody after committing a serious assault, that they had not the vaguest recollection of what had taken place the night before. No men were more astonished than these men were, and no men more aggrieved their action. They seemed for the time to be absolutely unaccountable for their actions. I ascribe that to some adulterations; and I know by general repute it is ascribed to some adulteration which has not as yet been detected.

Recipe for adulteration.

[illegible]. I think you are qualified to give us a recipe for the adulteration of whisky?—Yes, I can give a recipe which was obtained under peculiar circumstances. A very large fair is annually held in a certain county. If necessary, I can give the name of the county and the place. It is attended by people from all the country around, and the fair day is looked upon as a sort of holiday for servants and workpeople. The owner of a public-house in that place was in jail awaiting his trial on a charge of manslaughter. He had got a son who worked a farm, but took no part in the management of the licensed premises, and while the father was in jail on remand, the son came there to see him, and, in the presence of the governor, got from the father the recipe for preparing the whisky for the fair which was about to be held. That recipe was this, two gallons of new whisky, one gallon of rum, half a gallon of [illegible] ([illegible] spirits of wine), [illegible] gallons of water, and one drachm of sulphate of copper.

[illegible]. Do you consider that a harmful compound?—I do not know what would be the effect of that whole composition, especially the sulphate of copper.

[illegible]. At all events, you would not like to drink it?—Certainly I would not drink it knowingly. I believe sulphate of copper is more or less a poison.

[illegible]. Is Sunday a quiet day in Tralee?—It is [illegible] a quiet day, but there is a market for [illegible] buying [illegible].

Mr. F. J. [illegible]

Sunday [illegible]

[illegible]. Every Sunday?—Every Sunday. In other parts of the country servants and workpeople are engaged for the year—usually about the spring.

[illegible]. Is it true that the public-houses are open as shops in Tralee on Sunday, as we have heard they are in some other parts of Ireland, and that the shopping is done in those public-houses, and that, of course, as we may suppose, drinking goes on at the same time?—Some of the houses, in fact, nearly all the public-houses in Tralee, and nearly all the average class of public-houses, and lower classes of public-houses, carry on a mixed business. Sunday is used both in Tralee and in the villages but especially in the villages, as a shopping day; people buy their groceries and their flour, and while getting groceries and flour, if the coast is clear, and a constable is not within view, they can get a drink, and conceal the traces of it.

[illegible]. (Mr. Young.) Is Sunday closing in force there?—It is; but on account of the construction and situation of the premises, in many cases Sunday closing is a farce there, do what the police can.

What takes place.

[illegible]. (Chairman.) Should I be exceeding the truth by saying that in Tralee public-houses are open all day on Sunday?—That would not exactly describe it. They are practically open all day. There are so many people about who can claim to be travellers that the doors are practically kept open. As regards the sale in places where a mixed business is carried on, that matter was referred to Mr. [illegible], Q.C., a good many years ago, and the police have been to a great extent [illegible] by the action taken by the magistrates on the opinion he then gave, that the mere fact of having the door open will not justify convictions. You must satisfy the magistrates that there was a sale or an intended sale. In practice it is very hard to satisfy the magistrates of that, and the result is that we cannot get convictions.

[illegible]. Should you like to see the separation of the ordinary business from the public-house proper?—Certainly; there should be no connection between the licensed part and any portion in which other business is carried on, especially on Sundays.

There [illegible]

[illegible]. They might be on the same premises then?—I should have no objection to their being on the same premises if one was divided from the other, so that you could, at closing hours and on Sundays, entirely close off the licensed premises. I have endeavoured to get that carried out wherever I had a conviction against licensed premises. I opposed the renewal of the license unless they entirely shut off the bar from the other part of the premises, so that on Sundays, for example, the liquor part would be entirely shut off. In many cases it was quite exposed to view.

[illegible]. You think that change could be effected without too violent an interference with the habits of the people?—I think it might in many cases, but in some others it could not.

[illegible]. Were you successful in the appeals that you made?—I was indifferently. I opposed the renewal wherever I had a conviction. I always raised the point as a question on the question of [illegible] of premises, and I got it carried.

[illegible]. (Mr. Young.) Is the Sabbath Day Observance Act not in force in Ireland?—It is, or rather it is nominally in force; that is all I can say of it.

[illegible]. These persons could be prosecuted, could they not?—The Sunday Observance Act is an Act which we have not the enforcement of. It is an Act which the police are directed not to enforce except under some circumstances; for instance, carrying on games which may lead to disorder or riot, but as to selling things on the Sabbath we have nothing to do with the enforcement of that.

Mr. P. J. Bell.

[illegible] to put up shutters or blinds obscuring all the bar, I withdrew the opposition. At first when I tried that, I was opposed on it; it was insisted I had no law for it, but I carried my point, and I have ever since insisted on that.

Trade of the public-house on Sunday.

40,329. Seeing that so much business is done on Sunday in Tralee, should I be wrong in saying that Sunday is one of the most profitable days for the publican?—It is, on account of the illicit traffic. It is not necessarily so; the ordinary shop business done on Sunday would not lead to much profit to the publican. It is the illicit traffic that does.

40,330. Illicit traffic under the guise of shopping?—Yes, and under no guise at all, simply dropping in and getting a drink. The illicit traffic done under the guise of shopping in Tralee itself is comparatively small; in the villages it is a good deal.

40,331. You made an attempt, did you not, to ascertain the state of the license in a certain town?—Yes, in the town of Fermoy.

Condition of public-houses in Fermoy.

40,332. What is the population?—It is 4,4[illegible], and the number of public-houses is [illegible].

40,333. Do these houses do a large business on Sunday?—Like every other town I have known.

40,334. I suppose they are very small houses?—Some of them, others are good sized houses; some are very fine establishments, and these are well-conducted.

40,335. They would do comparatively little business on the week-day?—On the week-day I visited every single house there, and examined the premises, and in many cases when I required some alterations to be made the publicans complained of the expense on the ground that they were making next to nothing on the premises, that there was so little business going on.

40,336. There being very little business going on on the week-day I suppose no new licenses have been granted?—On the contrary, frequently applications were made, and I had great difficulty in keeping down the licenses. I got some rejected, but others were occasionally granted.

40,337. Were these houses to which the new licenses were granted structurally or sanitarily fit for a license?—As far as I recollect, not. None of them was what I call suitable considering the size of the town, but a great number of those already licensed were in an utterly worse position. Some were so bad that when visiting them I could not stand in the yard to make my notes. I had simply to glance round and run into the house, I could not stand the stench. In some of them I had to pick my way through liquid and filth running all along the yard. I do not know how people live in them. I was two days on the duty, and after I came away from the houses on each day I had a headache.

Rise of competition.

40,338. Then there is great competition for business, I suppose, among these small houses which are compared together in those comparatively small towns?—Great competition.

40,339. What effect has that on the quality of the liquor or the conduct of the trade?—I should say the effect is that the quality of the liquor supplied is inferior, and as they cannot compete with the better class of public-houses during open hours, most of their business, and the business which makes it profitable for them to remain open, is done after hours and on Sundays.

Public opinion in Tralee.

40,340. Coming to the general state of public opinion in Tralee, should you say it was adverse or favourable to the publican?—I should say that general opinion there, except amongst the very much more respectable and some of those who are strongly opposed to drinking, is that they do not much care one way or the other, others who wish to get a drink would be very strongly in favour of things being left as they are.

Relations of the magistrates and publicans.

40,341. If you are willing to give us your impression of the magistrates' bench, what should you say was their attitude towards the publicans?—From what I

40,342. Has it ever been realised by the magistrates themselves or by the clergy [illegible] an extent that the magistrates there took very [illegible] account about it. He was a resident magistrate. He openly commented on the Bench about what he saw going on when he saw the way cases were dealt with, and the action of certain magistrates. He openly, in the presence of the court, asked several magistrates when they came in, "Well, gentlemen, what is the job to-day?" There was one particular magistrate—one of those thus present—who openly would tell the sergeant to go out and get another magistrate "because Mr. So-and-So and I can never agree." I saw published some time ago, and I have got here a copy of a very strong letter written by the Most Reverend Dr. O'Dwyer, Bishop of Limerick. It deals with a licensing case in Limerick. I also have a copy of a letter written in connection with that written by Dr. O'Shaughnessy, one of the magistrates present at the hearing of the case.

Mr. P. J. Bell. — 8 April '02. — Conversing.

40,343. Protesting against convicting?—He deals first with a case that had been tried at petty sessions.

40,344. Who did?—The Most Reverend Dr. O'Dwyer, in which it appeared to him the evidence was very clearly strong, and which was dismissed. He deals with the evidence for the prosecution and with the evidence for the defence, and gave his opinion very strongly about the defence. He then went on and dealt with sentencing. He said: "If it were a mere mistake of judgment in a difficult case I could understand it; but I know of my own personal knowledge that, as a rule, the magistrates are canvassed, and the Bench is packed for the trying of such cases. As soon as ever a publican is detected he and his friends run for days before the petty sessions, going around the houses of the magistrates to influence their judgment, and get them to sit on the Bench the following Friday as partisans instead of judges. This is a most intolerable and shocking state of things, and it raises the question, if we are to have any hope of dealing successfully with what is the most colossal evil amongst us, whether the right thing would not be to have every such case taken out of the hands of the unpaid magistrates, and confined to officials such as the magistrates of Dublin, who would deal independently in the administration of the law. Recently this abuse of Sunday drinking has gone so far that the Director of the Confraternity of the Holy Family felt it his duty to go before the magistrates and appeal to them to put it down. There was then for some time a display of zeal on all sides, but already they have flagged, with the results to which I have called your attention this evening. A publican was recently fined £1, and with an independence that was most delightful, the magistrates screwed up their courage to mark the penalty on the back of his license. They further, with great [illegible], refused a certificate for the renewal of the license of petty sessions. All that gave us great hope that a new era was going to begin, but [illegible] feelings when we learned that that same license, which was so justly forfeited, had been transferred by the same magistrates to the relative of the man convicted, and that the trade is being carried on by the same family, who must have laughed very heartily at the very profitable farce in which they and the magistrates had played so remarkable a part."

Letter from Bishop of Limerick.

40,345. What was the date of that letter?—11th October 1893. It was written to the "Munster News," in Limerick.

40,346. Do you think any reform has taken place since then?—I have not had personal acquaintance with Limerick, but judging by some of the reports I have seen in the papers, I should think it has had some effect. There is a letter from Dr. O'Shaughnessy, one of the magistrates, dealing with the same case, in reply to the bishop's letter.

Letter from Dr. O'Shaughnessy.

40,347. Is it to the same effect?—It is dated the 14th October 1893, and is written to the "Limerick Chronicle."

40,348. Can you give us the [illegible]

Mr. [illegible] 6 April '[illegible]

"removed from our jails, reformatories, industrial "schools, and penitentiary, these institutions in a "very short time would be all emptied, and as a "consequence the overtaxed ratepayers of Limerick "would be materially benefited."

Trading and [illegible] the bench.

[illegible]. Speaking from your own personal observation, have you ever seen cases in Tralee which would warrant you in coming to the belief that the magistrates were [illegible]. I will say in a [illegible] manner [illegible] here. If the Commission wishes, I can give actual facts. I can quote what evidence was given in certain cases, and what was the result of those cases.

[illegible]. I do not mean you to re-try the cases, but do you know any instance of anything taking place which was [illegible]?—I can state certain facts that were proved, and I can state the action taken by the magistrate. I can also state something observed by a constable as regards, I might call it, packing the bench. There was a trader in Tralee who carries on a very respectable business and occupies a good position there. He supplies liquor to a great many of the country publicans. What came [illegible] publicans were for hearing he was frequently seen to [illegible] late [illegible] and [illegible] up [illegible] to certain magistrates who were on the bench. A magistrate in Tralee told me that he had given up attending the sessions on account of the way in which he was so constantly canvassed by publicans beforehand when a case was coming up. Another magistrate told the same thing to a constable. I think that during the last year and nine months or so I have seen that magistrate on the bench only twice, and I do not believe he has ever acted in a public-house case. Then on another occasion there was a public-house case up for hearing which had to be brought on four times before a definite order could be got. This was what was observed by the police. The owner of the public-house [illegible] for him. A certain magistrate lived not very far outside the town. The day was very wet. A covered car belonging to the publican went out and brought this magistrate in, and dropped him at the court. It then drove down to the houses of two other magistrates; the constable was watching; it went to four magistrates; the constable was watching, and some of those magistrates were brought up to the court.

Justices brought in by publicans.

[illegible]. That only goes to show that he gave the magistrate a lift on a wet day?—Yes. He went and brought them in specially; that is the view I take of it.

Favour of a publican, &c.

[illegible]. What was the action of those magistrates?—I can tell you what the result of the case was. I can tell you, if it is required, what the facts were which were put before the magistrates. The result of the case was this. On the first occasion there were [illegible] magistrates present; the case was marked "No rule." It was then brought on again; there were eight magistrates present and it was marked "No rule." It was brought on a third time, there were nine magistrates present and it was marked "D.W.P.," that is, Dismissed without prejudice. (See Appendix VII.)

Vide Appendix VII.

[illegible]. Were those four magistrates who were brought up present on each occasion?—I believe they were. One of them was present once; two of them were present on each of the four hearings; one was present three times, and one was present three times.

[illegible]. What was the ultimate result of the case?—On the fourth hearing there were seven magistrates present, and it was dismissed on the merits.

[illegible]. What was the charge?—The charge was having open for sale, and for selling on Sunday. I can, if required, give you what the facts proved were. I have the police report here. The facts proved were these. This was a house where the Society of Foresters [illegible]

of the premises, although a man who drank a good deal and paid no attention to his business, was a very [illegible] person. We found it very difficult to get [illegible] there, but still, on the [illegible] October 18[illegible], he was fined [illegible] and recorded. I am only dealing with cases [illegible] occurred within five years before these proceedings. On the 2nd October 18[illegible] he was fined [illegible], and on the 12th April 18[illegible] he was fined [illegible] and the case was recorded. There are used to [illegible] about the premises, and they were frequently seen going away in the [illegible] more or less under the influence of drink and [illegible]. The police visited the premises on Sunday [illegible] July 18[illegible] at 9.15 p.m.

[illegible]. Is this the Foresters' meeting room?—Yes. Mrs. Brennan was in the bar. There were three persons standing at the counter, the back door was open, and there were three men standing in the [illegible], quite close to the bar. One of the men lived in Tralee, another lived some distance beyond the three-mile limit from Tralee, and the third lived some distance from Tralee. There were also three men with the publican. He said he had invited them in—they were living about the place and the publican was drunk.

[illegible]. Was that proved before the court?—Yes. The constable asked Mrs. Brennan, the publican's wife who came out, what the men were doing there, and she said her husband had invited Doolan, and that the two Ryles were travellers. The constable told Mrs. Brennan that William Ryle was not a traveller, and she said that he was.

[illegible]. How was this connected with the meeting of the Foresters—were these men Foresters?—No, but this is dealing with the case which was brought on four times, and I thought you wished to get the facts proved before the magistrates?

[illegible]. This is a previous case?—It is the case which was brought on four times and was finally dismissed on the merits. I was about to give the facts.

[illegible]. I thought the gravamen of the charge against this house was that there was a Foresters' meeting taking place there on a Sunday?—That is a matter to which I will refer later on as the question of not allowing any societies to meet in licensed premises.

[illegible]. Then we are not dealing with that Foresters' case now?—No, not at all. Well, the constable told Ryle that he was not a traveller, that he did not live three miles from Tralee. Ryle said he thought he was a traveller; the publican's wife put the liquor into his hand after that statement was made and told him to drink it, and he drank it. Ryle was examined for the defence as one of those travellers, and he was asked whether Mrs. Brennan had asked him any questions before she went to get the drink, and he said she had not asked him any question, that nobody had asked him whether he was a traveller until the constable came in and said he was not a traveller. Under the [illegible] section of the Act of 1874, if it were proved that the publican took reasonable precautions and honestly believed that the man was a traveller he was entitled to sell him liquor without being held responsible. It was proved in this case, on the evidence of the woman's own witness, that she asked no questions before supplying the drink, and that even after the constable said that the man was not a traveller she gave the drink into his hand and insisted on his drinking it.

[illegible]. What was the result?—The final result was that that case was dismissed on the merits, although there was evidence that she had not asked a single question before supplying the drink, and that the man was not, as a matter of fact, a traveller.

[illegible] sessions at [illegible] an application for the licence was made there, the police opposed, amongst other grounds alleging that this was not the sessions at which it should be made; that it ought to be made only at the annual licensing quarter sessions. It happened that at this particular quarter sessions the hearing of licence applications did not come on on the usual day, and did not come on until three days afterwards. There were three magistrates present, and during my acquaintance with the place, extending to seven years and [illegible] months, I had never seen three magistrates on the bench, and I was aware that they lived, some of them, [illegible], or [illegible] miles away. They attended on the first day and they remained there, staying at an hotel during the three days. Finally, when the case came on on the third day it was refused on the ground that it was not the proper sessions and the magistrates went away. These three magistrates were [illegible] in straightened circumstances, and the general belief and report was that they had received [illegible] expenses for attending there and remaining for three days at an hotel—that they could not afford to do it otherwise. That came on afterwards at the proper sessions at [illegible]. There was then the largest attendance of magistrates I ever saw at [illegible]. There was not room for them on the bench; they were standing on the steps of the bench closely packed; they were standing in the passages, and there was at least one down in the body of the court apparently taking no part in the proceedings at all. The magistrates took the evidence in a [illegible] of cases and they retired to consult. When they were retiring a relative of one of the applicants rushed over to the magistrate who was down in the body of the court, and apparently not acting with the rest, and in my hearing said to him: "Are not you a magistrate? Go and vote." He got him by the shoulders and pushed him on before him up the passage until he pushed him with a final push into the midst of the magistrates who were retiring, and this magistrate went in with the others. The licence in that particular case was granted there that day.

[illegible]. Apart from the question of licences, take the case of offences, have you ever known cases leniently treated for offences which in your opinion were grave?—I have known numbers of them. I have several cases here which I will give.

[illegible]. Will you give us a striking case?—I will give a couple of rather strong cases. First, I may tell you of a case which occurred in my district a short time before I went there. I was informed officially of it by the sergeant. A detection was made for selling a short time before opening hours, I think about a quarter to 7 on a week day. Well, it was not a very serious case, because I do not attach so much importance to sales during closing hours on the week days as to sales on a Sunday, and the police would have been quite satisfied if they had got a conviction without pressing for any [illegible] punishment. The case could not be defended; no attempt was made at a defence, and there was a practical admission and plea of guilty. The magistrates said it was a very mild case, and they would only fine 10s. It was pointed out that there had been a previous conviction, and that there was no power to fine less than 20s. They did not think the case was sufficiently serious to merit a penalty of 20s., and they were discussing as to what they should do. Just then another magistrate drove up who had not been in court before. He came almost galloping to the court door, he came in to the room, and without having heard a single word of the evidence given in the case he took part in the discussion after the magistrates had decided to convict, and when they were discussing about the penalty, he took part in the discussion and got the magistrates to dismiss the case.

[illegible]. That was told you by your predecessor?—By my sergeant, who began the prosecution, and the sergeant told me that the magistrate had afterwards told him that he attended the court on a letter of [illegible] received from a magistrate in another petty sessions district to attend and do what he could for the publican. I will now give what is even a stronger

Mr. F. J. [illegible].

[illegible] April '[illegible].

about the house. The man Collins was then produced, and he swore he had gone there to get change of a shilling, in order to pay part of the shilling to a man living in his house to whom he owed money for work done. In reply to questions from me he admitted that he only wanted the change of a shilling; that he got no drink; that he did not ask for any drink; and that the man for whom he wanted the change wanted to go out there and buy some things in shops. I called his attention to the fact that this was after 11 o'clock on a Sunday night, and I asked him, "What did the man want to buy at that hour?" He said he did not know, but there were things sold at that hour; he denied that he knew anything about the jug in which the porter was found; he denied that he was standing near it. Then an old man was produced whom the constable had not seen, but who, it was alleged, was upstairs when the constable called. He swore that the jug of porter which the constable found was the remains of three or four gallons which had been got the night before for seven or eight of them to drink, and that a short time before the constable came in this had been put in that jug by himself and had been taken out into the yard. I cross-examined him and asked him, Did he expect any bench of magistrates to believe that seven or eight men living in that house-way and having got in three or four gallons of porter on the Saturday night would have left a single drop of it after an hour, let alone 24 hours? and he said he did expect them to believe it. I asked him then was it a fact that there was froth on the porter, and he said there was. I asked him, "How do "you account for the fact that froth was on this porter "if it were porter that was got before 11 o'clock on "Saturday night?"—that is 24 hours before. His explanation of that was this, that if you add soap and water and put that into porter and stir it up you can put a new head of froth on it. He was ordered off the table. There were only two magistrates on the bench; one a resident magistrate, and the other a magistrate who supplies the man Flynn with flour and meal. I thought after the exhibition the witness had made of himself there ought to be no difficulty about getting a conviction, notwithstanding things that I knew before, but the other magistrate would not agree to a conviction, and there being only two present, we could not get a conviction.

59,769. And the case was dismissed?—I asked to have it adjourned as the bench was divided, and it was adjourned for the attendance of other magistrates. The following court day we got a conviction. The publican appealed, and the conviction was upheld on appeal; the county court judge condemning the defence very strongly. This old man was produced the second time to prove about the soap and water; he was very much under the influence of drink, and was ordered off the table, and did not complete his evidence. We got the conviction affirmed. I could give numbers of other cases of the same class.

Other cases available.

59,770. I think that will be sufficient, unless you have anything of a different character?—They are all of much the same stamp, but I can give heaps of them.

59,771. Would this house which you say has a six-day licence be open on a Sunday for the sale of other things than liquor?—It might be not exactly open, but people might be passing in and out. In some places they do not keep the door open. If the police find them there they say they come for tea or sugar.

Sham trading in public-houses.

59,772. There would be nothing irregular in a person going into a house at 11 o'clock on a Sunday night in the case of a public-house with a six-day licence if he [illegible] this particular grocer's?—My own opinion upon that is very strong. I do not believe such a case should be permitted at all, because if a man is allowed to go in there and get what he calls a box of matches, in one half minute he can get a drink unless the licensed portion is entirely shut off, and in most of these cases it is not shut off.

up take the law from him on any point, but in some cases they will not do it.

[illegible]. He has a casting vote, I suppose?—No, he has not. There is a decision on that point.

[illegible]. (*Sir Algernon West.*) He has equal powers to other magistrates?—The only thing is, if they take the law from him he has a power in that way; but in many cases they will not.

[illegible]. And he is powerless?—Practically powerless. Sometimes if he takes a very strong line he can in a sort of way excite the magistrates ashamed of going against him. I heard from a county court judge of one case which was conclusively proved. It came before him on appeal. It was not a licensing Act case. There were two magistrates present who had not attended the court before. The case was absolutely proved beyond doubt, and when he turned to these magistrates he said, "I suppose we have nothing to do but to affirm." "Oh, well, I am not at all satisfied," says one of these men—a salmon had been found in a man's boat—"I am not at all satisfied that we have "sufficient evidence to prove that it was the man who "put the salmon into the boat himself." "Well, I am quite satisfied," said the county court judge, "and I will confirm the conviction"; and without asking their opinion at all he confirmed the conviction.

[illegible]. (*Chairman.*) Are public-houses very much congested; are they very near together in Tralee?—They are; and in some cases if a man was blindfolded, and put standing in the centre of the street, and spun round a couple of times, and started off in no particular direction, I do not suppose he could go 20 yards without striking the door of a public-house.

[illegible]. That would not apply to the country?—It applies to other towns almost equally.

[illegible]. But not to the country?—Not to the country. There is one [illegible] to which I make reference, where a street is about 50 yards, or it might be 40 yards, long. It is so narrow that two carts cannot pass—one cart must be almost on the footpath, and, if a dray, one wheel would have to go on the footpath. There were [illegible] public-houses in the street; one has been bought out and extinguished within the last three months.

[illegible]. Are there enough wayside public-houses in the country to supply the legitimate wants of the travelling public?—I should say that there are far too many of them. These wayside public-houses act as traps for men who are half drunk coming home from markets or fairs.

[illegible]. You are not speaking of Kerry now?—I am speaking of any part of the country.

[illegible]. But not Kerry?—I can give a case in Kerry.

[illegible]. I understand that in the district of Tralee, for instance, there were only four houses in the country, as compared with a larger number in the town itself?—Yes.

[illegible]. How far does that scarcity of public-houses extend in Kerry, in the country?—There are only four in the country in the Tralee district. In one direction, there is a place called Fenit, seven miles from Tralee, and there are two public-houses a mile apart at Fenit; and in that seven miles there are three public-houses, so that a man leaving Tralee to go to Fenit may have drinks from three public-houses on his way.

[illegible]. Was not Fenit one of the cases which you gave?—I mentioned Fenit a while ago.

[illegible]. Did not you give it to in your statement?—Yes. Spa is direct between Fenit and Tralee.

[illegible]. What do we understand by the district of Tralee; what area does it cover?—About 16 miles by 12.

22,412. And that transfer wipes the slate clean, wipes the slate so far as regards the licence; it has a good and correctly [illegible] so far as regards the transferee. The conduct of the previous tenant during the licence could be urged against the renewal, but in practice in Ireland the magistrates will not act upon it. It can only be raised on renewal. As regards the question of forfeiting the licence the fact of previous convictions is wiped out when there is a change of tenancy. The only way in which it has effect is where it is recorded against the premises; but in that case it is only the second and every subsequent conviction against such particular owner [illegible] that you must have two convictions recorded against such owner before it will enable the magistrates against the house itself.

[illegible] Therefore practically they have the power of making it a condition that the licence should be a six-day or a seven-day licence?—They would have the power if they exercised their powers in a wrong way. They have a very great deal of power if they would only exercise it in a firm and reasonable spirit.

[illegible] You would be of opinion, I suppose, that the public-houses should be apportioned to the requirements of the public?—Most certainly—to the requirements of the public, not of the publicans. The latter is the point usually taken into account.

[illegible] Would you be of opinion that the granting of a licence confers a monopoly upon the licensee?—Yes, it confers a monopoly of business on him.

[illegible] Do you think he should pay for it?—I think he should, in proportion to the value of the monopoly.

[illegible] Do you think he should pay down a lump sum or should pay a certain sum each year?—At present he pays in an indirect way by the licence duty; but what I should propose would be that if it were decided to take any steps to reduce the number of licensed premises and so interfering with the rights of individuals, that could hardly be done without compensating those individuals. On the other hand, it would be hardly fair that the compensation should come from the public rates, and the only other source would be to have it come from those who derived a direct advantage by the reduction in the number of public-houses. The monopoly they have hitherto held would be made still more valuable, and it would be well worth their while to pay a higher licence duty for that monopoly, and whatever was the sum of money expended which bought out a certain number, it could be repaid at a yearly interest by the publicans who got the whole of the business.

[illegible] Those publicans who were left and who had the great monopoly, would they not have a tremendous claim for compensation, supposing in their turn they had to be abolished?—I should think that the [illegible] ought to set things straight, that it would be only [illegible] at two or three times. Once the effort is made it should be an effort that would do for all time, and that after that strong measures should be taken to prevent the granting of any licence except the local requirements actually required them.

[illegible] I am thinking of a case in which a man has

words intro-
the lawyer to
my persons

[illegible] to have a right of appeal in certain cases against the decision of the magistrates. Upon that I and other Commissioners have asked the question, Do you not think that would put the commissionary in a very invidious position as regards the magistrates? What is your view on that point?—I do not think that at all, and for this reason. We have at present the right of appeal in revenue cases, and I do not see why [illegible] in a revenue case should not have the same effect as an appeal in a licensing case as far as putting the magistrates and the police at variance with each other. But I can go further than that. We have at present a right of appeal against the grant, renewal, or transfer of a spirit grocer's licence, a wholesale beer dealer's licence, or a retail beer dealer's licence, and I do not see why we should not have the right of appeal against the grant, renewal, or transfer of a publican's licence, and if we have I do not see why we should not have a right of appeal against a dismiss[illegible]

39,469. Do you ever exercise your right of appeal in the case of renewals?—We have no right of appeal in the case of renewals.

39,470. In the case of a new licence?—We have no right of appeal except in the case of a spirit grocer, a wholesale beer dealer, and a retail beer dealer.

39,471. In the case of the spirit grocer, or the beer retailer, do you ever exercise your right of appeal against a decision of the magistrates?—I have never had to do it. So far as I remember I never had to deal with spirit grocers, and I have only had to deal with wholesale beer dealers, a couple of them, and I never had any complaint to prefer against the way in which they conducted their business.

39,472. I understand you to be of opinion that in the case of orders of magistrates dismissing a case the commissionary should have the right of appeal?—Yes, I say we have the right of appeal in those cases, and I do not see why we should not have it in the case of a public-house.

39,473. You would like to have the right of appeal in the case of the grant, transfer, or renewal of a public-house licence?—Yes, a grant, renewal, or transfer, or dismissal of a complaint.

39,474. (Mr. Young.) To which court?—It would come before the court of quarter sessions from the petty sessions court. Taking the law as it stands at present, of course the appeal from the grant would have to go to the sessions. The appeal from the renewal would be from petty sessions to quarter sessions, and at present we have practically an appeal from a transfer. It is first granted by the magistrates at petty sessions and comes up for confirmation at quarter sessions.

39,475. (Chairman.) You would have an appeal by the commissionary against the renewal of a publican's licence?—We have no power of appeal at present.

Mr. F. J. Hall.

8 April '98.

[illegible]. What I complain of is that they do not appear to support the police when the cases are brought.

Conduct of prosecutions.

59,460. Do you find in cases that come before the Court that your police sergeants are a match for the trade solicitor employed on the other side?—Not at all. Some years ago the practice was to let the constable, or sergeant, who made the detection prosecute. I found that what appeared to be a conclusive case failed, and I took the matter into my own hands, and I conducted all the prosecutions. After, I think, two or three years a general order was issued that the district inspector should prosecute in all such cases, but I had been doing it for three years before the order came out, and ever since then I have conducted all the prosecutions myself. You cannot expect a sergeant to cope with a solicitor acting for the defence in such cases, and a magistrate would not accept from a sergeant what he would accept from the district inspector in the way of evidence or argument.

59,461. Is it customary for you, supposing circumstances happened that made it desirable to employ a solicitor to prosecute?—We never do. The only case in which it is done is some peculiar case. A report is made and the official crown solicitor is directed to attend to represent the police, but I never had a case where he attended under the Licensing Act to do so. I have always conducted the cases myself.

59,462. With reference to the action of the police in these prosecutions, you have given an interesting table extending over a considerable period of time of prosecutions by the police and convictions obtained?—Yes.

Percentage of convictions.

59,463. Would you explain that table pretty fully?—There was a table prepared for the Commission, which was handed in by the Inspector-General, relating to the whole county, and I looked over that and took out some particulars relating to a particular petty sessions district. I have, as I have already said, had no difficulty, or practically no difficulty, in enforcing the Act where I had a fairly strong bench to deal with, because if there was a fair percentage of convictions the police got encouraged and attended to the duty, and we had other cases, and then the publicans began to be more careful and there was not much trouble, but if the bench did not properly support the police, the police did not care about bringing cases and having them dismissed, and they became careless. Looking over the returns—I [illegible] to five years—I [illegible] out the number of prosecutions and convictions.

59,464. What five years?—It was 1893, 1894, 1895, 1896, and 1897.

59,465. What happened in 1893?—In 1893 at the particular petty sessions there were 31 prosecutions and 12 convictions, showing a percentage of 38·7. Immediately after that there were a number of new magistrates appointed, and in the second year there were 37 prosecutions and 12 convictions, being a drop to 32·3 per cent.

59,466. That was in 1894?—Yes, then the next year there was a change of resident magistrates and there were 43 prosecutions and 34 convictions, or a percentage of 79·0.

59,467. You say a new resident magistrate came on the scene?—Yes, then in the fourth year, 1896, there were 48 prosecutions and 33 convictions, or a percentage of 68·7.

59,468. There was a great diminution?—Yes, then in the fifth year there were 27 prosecutions and 15 convictions, or a percentage of 55·5.

resident magistrate who was there that year, and who only remained for about a year altogether, was a very [illegible] gentleman; and when he saw the way things went on on the bench he expressed his opinion very openly and very forcibly on the bench on several occasions, and it went so far on this, that on different occasions, when he saw certain magistrates come in he would say, "Well, gentlemen, what is the job on to-day?" and that would be said openly so that it could be heard by people in court. Then, when one particular magistrate continued sat alone with the resident magistrate it frequently happened, when only the two of them were present on the bench, the resident magistrate would turn to the sergeant, and in a loud tone of voice tell him to go out and look for another magistrate. "Mr. [illegible] and I can never agree," and the sergeant would have to go out and hunt up another magistrate and bring him in. I am also informed that when taking the votes of the magistrates after the hearing of a case, he first commenced by asking the opinion of magistrates who were regarded as [illegible] in their judgment, and then, having got their opinions, he then took the opinion of the others in such a sort of way that they either did not dissent, or could not dissent, from the opinion of the others, and convictions were had. When the police found that they got convictions it made them keener, but when they got a good case, which was laughed out of court on a most ridiculous defence, they thought it was not worth their while to be bringing up cases and be made laughing stocks of, and they ceased to take much trouble about it.

59,469. But that forcible action of the resident magistrate did drive up the percentage to 79 per cent.?—That is what was explained to me, and I believe it was a thing that took place in open court as I was informed. I was not there at that time.

59,470. That practice of the resident magistrate is not continued?—There was a change of resident magistrate since that. At first when I commenced proceedings there I had as many as eight cases on one Sunday, and I got six convictions; but after that some very strong cases were dismissed, though I brought them on two or three times. I have the records here of some of those cases.

Behaviour of individual police.

59,471. Do you find as a rule that you are supported by the men of the constabulary force?—I suppose there is a difference in their character as to their energy?—Yes, some men are more energetic than others; but my experience during my service has been that the particular duty has been regarded by the police as a most unpleasant duty, and I think that that feeling arises from the fact that they have not been properly supported by the bench. I have always found that the duty was properly performed only by men who were naturally energetic, or by active men who were pushing their [illegible] for promotion and wanted to bring themselves prominently under notice.

59,472. Are the men permanently stationed at one particular place?—No, they are constantly removed. A man may be two months or five years in a place, or I have known them to have ten years; it all depends upon what way he gets on there, and partly on the requirements of the service. A man must be particularly energetic to discharge the duty properly and must be a very intelligent man because he must be very sharp the moment he enters a house to observe quickly anything at all tending to bear on the case, otherwise he may have his case knocked by a legal defence, whereas, if he had been very sharp and observed all that took place and made notes immediately afterwards, his own evidence might be [illegible]

[illegible] Some of them are [illegible] of the "corner boy" class. They get up and point blank contradict the [illegible] or points upon which the [illegible] cannot be [illegible] by reason of [illegible] or a want of observation. There must be deliberate perjury on one side or the other, and when a constable finds that the magistrates accept the evidence of these [illegible] ... against his own evidence [illegible] in the case, [illegible] can hardly expect he will be very keen about bringing up other cases, especially when the [illegible] for the defence in the discharge of his duty [illegible] ... suggest that there is anything improper [illegible] ... [illegible] the constable and suggest by the line of [illegible] that he has made an unfair act on these premises, and that he is wilfully [illegible] ... and practically deliberately perjuring himself. Some of the constables will feel very sore about this, and when they find, on the top of that, their case is dismissed, and the magistrates have practically told them that they do not believe them on their oath against some of the corner boy class and the publican who is practically interested in the result of the case, it cannot be wondered at that a constable will not be very keen on bringing up a case of the sort.

[illegible] Do you know any cases, except those in which it might be inferred from the magistrates' conduct that they did not believe the case, in which they have directly told the police that they have perjured themselves?—No. I think you have slightly misunderstood the reference in my statement. I have known cases where the magistrates have [illegible] directly characterised the evidence for the defence in that way; but I have never known the magistrates to allege that against the police. But [illegible] it might be suggested, inasmuch as they did not accept their evidence.

[illegible] Apart from the cases in which by inference it might be supposed that the magistrates did not believe the police, did you ever know the magistrates directly to say that they did not believe the evidence of the police?—No, I never did.

[illegible] (Mr. Young.) As an Irishman, I am rather ashamed of the revelations which you have made to-day?—I could give you much stronger cases.

[illegible] The character of these magistrates is certainly very bad?—I do not mean to say that what I have told applies to all the magistrates of Ireland. There are a large number of the magistrates of Ireland who rarely attend over me at all. I speak only of certain ones.

[illegible] I hope it is only peculiar to Kerry?—No, I should say it is; I know ever the same thing in other places.

[illegible] You seriously think that the magistrates have been doing their duty as all [illegible] is a matter of opinion. If they consider it their duty I certainly do not consider it their duty in the way they have done it. I have felt strongly [illegible] I cannot close my eyes to the facts.

[illegible] Many of these magistrates are men of long experience?—Some of them are, but not among the ones I am dealing with. There are some of them but are men of [illegible] [illegible] them have [illegible] by their [illegible] that they have sound business judgment and capacity, but they do not, [illegible] if you judge by results and [illegible] they were acting perfectly straight, [illegible] to weigh evidence.

[illegible] The hypothesis is that they can to be [illegible]?—Certainly, that is what I directly charge.

[illegible] Do you not think that is a very extraordinary charge against the magistrates of the country?—I do not make the charge against the whole magistracy of the country; I make it against certain magistrates. I do not say they are all the same.

[illegible] With these decisions to which you have taken objection, I presume the county court judge does not [illegible]?—Unfortunately that is one of the things we [illegible]?—The county court judge has absolutely no more power there than any other magistrate; he has one vote, and each of them has one vote. I have known him to take a strong line in expressing his views about the law to the magistrates.

Mr. F. J. [illegible]

[illegible] April '[illegible]

[illegible] (Mr. [illegible]) Does the county court judge preside?—Yes, he is chairman.

[illegible] (Mr. Young.) Has he ever complained about this matter of being over-ridden on his vote?—I have seen it frequently represented in the papers, and seen very strong remarks by different county court judges, and I have had conversations with some county court judges who all spoke much in the same way.

[illegible] You have only one county court judge in Kerry?—Yes, I have had to deal with Kerry, but I have seen newspaper reports of proceedings at quarter sessions in adjoining counties. Co. Kerry.

[illegible] Your evidence is only with regard to Kerry?—No; my evidence deals a great deal with Kerry, but also with part of the county Cork.

[illegible] In mitigation of the conduct of the publicans might I ask you if, especially, Kerry is not a very romantic and beautiful county?—Parts of it have got very fine scenery, but other parts have got no scenery to speak of. It is very wild and uninteresting.

[illegible] You have an enormous quantity of tourists?—About Killarney you have, but not about the part I have spoken of. You have no tourists, in the ordinary sense, about Tralee.

[illegible] They have to pass through many of these towns to Killarney?—I think the majority as a rule go direct to Killarney, and as a rule go away direct. Sometimes they tour round the south of Kerry. A few may come through Tralee, but very few.

[illegible] They bicycle through the country?—Very few, but the bicyclists are not the ones who lead to the violation of the Sunday Closing Act at the public-houses in Tralee. Sunday drinking.

[illegible] When [illegible] and tourists go out do not you think that they should have their ordinary wants ministered to, such as the supply of beer and ale?—Yes, and I have not the slightest objection to their getting it. What I object to are the persons not entitled by distance [illegible] or how to get it. I have no objection to men travelling getting drink if they want it, but what I object to is the people within the town spending Sunday after Sunday drinking. I had a case where a man's wife came on a Sunday and complained to the police that her husband had gone and got drink in a public-house; the police went out to get evidence on which they could take it up. In the other case the man's wife came and complained that her husband was drinking, but that on try and keep him at home she had had to send out eight times on one Sunday her little daughter round about it to a public-house to get drink for him. I made inquiries and prosecuted and got both publicans convicted, and that is the sort of [illegible] I want to put down.

[illegible] You will always get these exceptional cases?—Unfortunately it seems to be the rule in the cases I have had to deal with of this Sunday drinking. I complain more about Sunday drinking than anything else.

[illegible] It is rather off the line I intended to take you upon, but supposing you had had the houses open from 2 o'clock to 6 o'clock on Sundays, would you not have obviated a great many of these evils?—Unfortunately, I do not think so, because the class of people who do the drinking will not have their thirst quenched in the hours of 2 o'clock until 6 o'clock on a Sunday. Their thirst goes on the whole day and the whole night.

[illegible] You have no experience of that and consequently you could scarcely say that that would be the case?—I have the experience that their thirst goes on from Saturday night to Monday morning, and continues there until Tuesday.

Mr. F. J. [illegible]

— 6 April '98 —

County court judge as licensing authority.

[illegible]. At all events I suppose you would consider that if the licensing laws were administered by the county court judge, or by a resident magistrate, it would cure many of the evils of which you complain?—It would. It was suggested yesterday that a difficulty might arise from the county court judge not having local knowledge, but I do not think that enters into the question. The county court judge has to give his decision not on local knowledge but on sworn evidence given before him, and the only way that local knowledge can come in, if at all, would be in forming an opinion as regards the relative credibility of the witnesses, but the very same difficulty would arise as regards a judge of assize. The judge of assize going round the circuit to the assizes can judge the relative credibility of the witnesses, and it does not require local knowledge to enable him to decide criminal cases and give his judgment upon them, and I do not see why the county court judge should not do the same.

Perjury in licensing cases.

[illegible]. I think I gather from you that you have a very poor faith in the credibility of the people?—No, I should be sorry to say so, but there are a number of cases against publicans brought up and, from the evidence I have heard given, I have very little faith in the credibility of those particular people, and my opinion is certainly supported in this way. I have had cases time after time in which the evidence for the defence was, if you believed it, conclusively strong, but we got convictions and the publican did not appeal. I think the only inference you can draw from that is a tacit admission that his evidence was perjured. I have never seen a class of case in which such gross perjury is wilfully committed as in cases under the Licensing Act I am sorry to say; but I have known cases of publicans standing up where they would not defend the case—they admitted their guilt. I have known cases where a publican might have put in a defence supported by perjured evidence if he would have taken his oath, but he would not do it, and wherever a publican admits his guilt and comes into the court I have always left the case in the hands of the magistrates and have not pressed for a penalty. Then I have known cases—but they are rare—where the witnesses listed on the summons have declined to come forward to support the case the publican was making. They declined to perjure themselves, but unfortunately those cases are very rare too.

[illegible]. I am an Irishman as well as you are. I do not think that that is a characteristic of the country?—It is not characteristic of the country, but it is unfortunately of some of the people.

[illegible]. What you are saying about this county and the people [illegible] would lead any one who was listening to you to suppose they were a very degraded people?—Unfortunately what I have expressed about their credibility, or the credibility of some of them, has been over and over again in my hearing expressed by the county court judge and sometimes by the judge of assize for the county.

[illegible]. You may point to one or two instances and from these instances you may come to a very false conclusion?—I have [illegible] and only some cases, but I have other cases I have not used at all. If you wish, I can give you the facts and you can form your own opinion whether the opinion I have expressed is just.

Crime in Kerry.

[illegible]. Is crime very prevalent in that county?—It depends on what you call crime.

[illegible]. Is there more crime in that county than in the other counties of Ireland?—As I say, it depends upon what you call crime. In this country [illegible] understand as crime ordinary offences against the criminal law, but in Ireland a good deal of the crime there arises more or less in connexion with the land question, and the majority of the cases of crime in that county are indirectly connected with either drink or the land question. You have not many cases of larceny or [illegible] in that county, as far as I have known it, of crime connected with drink, or with land disputes.

[illegible]. I conclude from the nature of your evidence that there ought to be the convictions [illegible] of crime. The magistrates being so very [illegible], and the people having conducted themselves in so dreadful a manner, I should have expected a great number of convictions. Can you say whether there are more convictions in the county Kerry than in any other county in Ireland?—I would not say that there is a larger quantity of crime, but what I have been speaking about as regards the action of the magistrates has no direct bearing at all on ordinary crime. I am dealing now with these magistrates in a particular class of case. These magistrates may act as independently as anybody else in regard to any other charge. I am dealing with these cases having [illegible] the Licensing Acts.

[illegible]. Do you suppose that these magistrates have not a clear conception of their duties in regard to this matter?—I presume they have, but I cannot say from what I have seen that they act as if they had.

Sunday closing.

[illegible]. Now you are still for Sunday closing the entire day?—I think I would leave the Sunday closing very much as it is at present. I think I would exempt the larger towns.

Early closing on Saturday.

[illegible]. And the Saturday night closing?—I think that it would be a good thing—I would not insist on it as a sine qua non—if the houses were closed an hour earlier on Saturday night. There is too much tendency for the men to remain drinking on Saturday night and spending their wages, and then the drink is wanted on the Sunday, and that necessitates drinking on Monday, and very often the men do not get to work till Tuesday.

[illegible]. You say they drink a great deal of porter?—I should say the greater part of the liquor drunk in Kerry is porter, and I think in a great part of Cork.

[illegible]. Are there many breweries there?—There is no brewery in Tralee. They get their porter from Cork, and they get Guinness's, but a great deal of Cork porter is drunk there.

Adulteration.

[illegible]. One question about adulteration. You described the sort of compound which you said is used. You have not analysed it yourself?—No.

[illegible]. It is something you have heard?—That is a recipe which was given by a publican to but one in the presence of the governor of a gaol, the publican being confined in the gaol.

[illegible]. What has occurred to me as difficult for me to understand is that this compound is cheaper than whisky?—I presume it is, or the publican would not find it profitable to sell it.

[illegible]. Do you know the price of sulphate of copper?—No, I do not.

[illegible]. So far as I can understand it, there is no compound of this kind would be so cheap as whisky, and therefore I have a difficulty in coming to the conclusion with you that there is such a thing as adulteration?—Unfortunately a good many people think whisky is too dear, but if a publican can make what he calls whisky cheaper than he can buy what is understood to be whisky, he makes a greater profit.

[illegible]. We have not had that before us in any serious [illegible]. You are sure that the Irish people seem to want a thing so adulterated in addition to their other inferior qualities?—I can hardly think you are asking me the question seriously.

[illegible]. Why?—Because it is beyond the possibility of doubt, and I do not mean to say the Irish people only are accepting it.

[illegible]. You do not know it yourself?—I have seen certificates for it.

39,553. That is not adulteration?—It comes under the Food and Drugs Act. You can convict if it is brought below a certain strength—25 per cent. under proof for whisky and 35 per cent. for brandy and gin, I think it is.

39,554. (*Mr. Grubb.*) As to the inefficiency of the magistrates, has there within a recent period been any large addition made to the magistracy in Ireland?—In what respect, because I do not speak of its inefficiency.

39,555. The fact that they do not administer the law. I think you put that very strongly?—Yes, I cannot put it too strongly.

39,556. I ask you on that point whether that for a series of years, but there been a large addition made to the magistracy of Ireland within recent years?—There was an addition made. I cannot say to what extent, but there was what I should call an appreciable addition made, and I may say that, as regards these details I have spoken of in particular, a good deal of what I complain of has arisen since then.

39,557. Were the magistrates who were appointed at that time a similar class of men or men of equal standing and responsibility with the men who had occupied the position of a magistrate before that period?—A great many were not. A great many of them were men of no pretence to social position. Some were ordinary farmers connected with people all round the locality. Some were men of business whose business was entirely dependent upon the people in the locality. Some of them were doctors who, of course, have a great interest in keeping in with the people.

39,558. Should I be saying more than I ought if I say that the appointments in those cases were to a great measure a political matter?—I do not think it is for me to express an opinion about that. I am dealing with what I have seen, and I do not like to express an opinion as to how the thing was done.

39,559. (*Mr. Young.*) Do you mean to say that it is only during the last two or three years that the evil has arisen of which you complain?—No, I do not mean to say that, but I mean to say it has been intensified during the last three or four years.

39,560. I should conclude from your evidence that it is the late magistrates who have been the cause of your complaint?—I do not mean to suggest that at all, but I do suggest that a number of those have acted in that way, but some of the older magistrates have acted in a similar way.

39,561. Then may I say that you do not know of any distinction with reference to the later appointments? You speak as if you charged the late appointments?—I make no charge at all, and I have only stated what I have seen, and some of the later appointments are often mixed up with some of the older, but unfortunately a great number of the old style of county magistrates rarely attend petty sessions at all, and some of those who most frequently attend are ones who are said to be there for special purposes.

39,562. (*Mr. Cobes.*) The old magistrates neglect their duty altogether?—If you like to put it in that way, a large number of the county men rarely attend petty sessions.

39,563. (*Mr. Grubb.*) Is that a current assumption? Is it not rather than that a class of magistrates have been appointed of a different status altogether, and the magistrates who were in the habit of administering the law and who were of a different class do not feel satisfied at the conjunction of the two classes?—It is very possible, but I cannot enter into what has been passing in their own minds.

39,564. Taking the whole of Ireland as the law stands now, it does not require any very great or serious change does it?—It does under existing circumstances.

39,565. And those circumstances are that you dispute the efficiency of the administering power of the law?—Yes. If the means of putting the Act into force were efficient, the present law would be sufficient.

39,566. That is my point?—Yes, practically sufficient.

39,567. Therefore you have no very great suggestions to make in the way of changes in the law?—Yes, I have a great number. I can give you about 25 of them. I have a list of them here. (*Vide* Appendix VI.)

39,568. I want to get some general idea of county Kerry. I have asked you about the law generally in Ireland; but as to county Kerry, that, how long have you been connected with it?—Since August 1896; but a great deal of my evidence relates to other places, particularly county Cork.

39,569. You have been able to form a good opinion as a resident in county Kerry, as far as the state of the temperance question is concerned during your service, as to whether there is much drinking there?—I have a very fair idea.

39,570. Should you say that there, temperance has increased or decreased within the last 10 years?—I do not know anything about county Kerry before August 1896; but I can tell you what I have observed. I went there in August 1896, and very often I went out to bonâ fide places in the country on Sunday afternoon, riding out on a bicycle, and on my return I met Sunday after Sunday a larger number of people drunk, or under the influence of drink, than I have ever met on Sunday in any other place before, and quite as many, if not more, than I would ever meet on a fair day. I gave that evidence before the Intoxicating Liquor Committee in opposing the grant of licenses, that I saw more drinking in Tralee and about it on Sunday than I ever saw anywhere else in Ireland.

39,571. You are referring to the Sunday now?—My main complaint all through is about Sunday, and I attach most importance to that.

39,572. Do not you think if [illegible] facilities were given it would meet the difficulty?—I think the opinion of Sir Andrew Reed was that the houses should be opened from 2 till 5, but if you drive the people out of doors you do these things which you have described?—I do not wish to place myself in conflict with anybody. I simply give my own opinion, and let other people give theirs. I am only responsible for my own opinion.

39,573. (*Mr. Whitaker.*) How long has the overlooking of magistrates and their unsatisfactory action, as the result of it, been an evil in Ireland?—I cannot say exactly how long it has been an evil; but, as far as I recollect, it first came prominently under my notice about five or six years ago, and time after time it has occurred it has again and again come under my notice.

39,574. Has the law, in your judgment, been efficiently administered in Ireland with reference to licensing?—I can only deal with the places I have actually served in. I take it that those places may be taken as a very fair index of what goes on in other places, and as regards what I have had personal experience of, I have found some courts support me strongly; then, later on, I found perhaps in some courts which had supported me there was an alteration in the Bench, and my hands became powerless; but where the magistrates do support the police in a fair and reasonable spirit we have not much difficulty.

39,575. With reference to Sunday closing, you think the hours should remain as they are in the extended areas.

Mr. F. J. Ball.

5 April '98.

Need for alteration of the law.

Vide Appendix VI.

Sunday drinking in co. Kerry.

Overlooking.

Sunday

Mr. F. J. Bell.

6 April '98.

10,577. In the district where you have had official experience, where the Sunday Closing Act has been in force, you approve of the Sunday closing?—Yes.

10,578. And your suggestion as to large towns really refers to districts where you have not had official experience?—Yes, I should simply leave what I do not know about as it is.

Reduction of licenses.

10,579. (*Mr. Sprigg.*) With reference to Tralee and the county, I think you stated that there are 117 licensed houses?—In the town of Tralee 117 in existence.

10,580. I understood your answer to be, that they ought to suffer a great reduction—that they are in excess of the requirements?—Largely.

10,581. In reducing that number would you be in favour of allowing the licensees to reckon any money they may have invested in their businesses by compensation or otherwise?—I do not think it would be at all fair to interfere with the vested rights of any licensed persons without compensating them on the principle I mentioned in my direct evidence.

Adulteration.

10,582. With reference to this question of adulteration of spirits, I understood you to say that you had had two cases of adulteration come under your notice?—I cannot say the number—perhaps about three or four prosecuted in my district.

10,583. You mentioned two?—I am not sure I limited it to two. I mentioned two cases I had at present pending—two cases of the improper use of an occasional licence.

10,584. By law publicans are allowed to dilute spirits to 25 degrees under proof?—Yes, and 35 degrees in the case of gin.

10,585. Am I right in saying that a reduction of the spirits to 25 degrees would be dilution?—Yes.

10,586. And do you call adulteration?—I do not call it. That is the way the law stands. I take the law as I find it.

Sunday drinking.

10,587. The greater proportion of drunkenness you complain of you meet with on Sundays?—Unfortunately there is a great deal of it after a fair or market, but except for a fair or market the most drunkenness I see is on a Sunday.

10,588. In the division of the county and the town you supervise, you say that the greater proportion of drunkenness occurs on Sundays?—I did not quite put it in that way.

10,589. I understood you to say so?—No, I said when out on Sunday afternoons in the country on my bicycle I met more persons drunk, or under the influence of drink, than I had before met on any other day before—quite as many if not more than on a fair or market day.

10,590. In that part of Ireland the Sunday Closing Act applies?—Yes.

10,591. I am curious to know how it is so much drunkenness occurs in the county and the town when the public-houses are shut up by law. Where do the people get their supplies?—Because publicans sell after hours on a Sunday, and we cannot control it. A number of the houses are so situated that it is practically impossible to control the sale of drink unless there is a police constable at the door of the house.

10,592. You have stated that in a street of 45 yards there are 13 public-houses?—There were 22; there are now 11.

10,593. Would it not be possible for one officer to stand at the end of a street and control it?—You must post a constable in every street and every lane over all Tralee, and post him there all day, and to do that you must increase the district force in Tralee by 40 or 50 men.

10,594. (*Chairman.*) I understood you to say that as these public-houses do other business than sell liquor, there is no presumption?—That is another difficulty. A person may go in, and if the police come in they may say I came in for a pound of tea, but while in there they may have got their drink. You must post a man at the door of every public-house to prevent it.

10,595. (*Mr. Sprigg.*) Are you in favour of the Sunday Closing Act in Ireland?—I put it as I put it a little while ago, that I would leave things as they are under the Sunday Closing Act excepting the exempted cities.

39,608. In both borough and county?—I think so. I am not certain about boroughs. I have had to deal with counties there.

39,609. I should like an answer upon that point?—I meant told you what I do not know. I have only had to deal with counties, and that is not a matter that comes under my personal knowledge, but from general knowledge I believe the appointments are made on the recommendation of the Lieutenant of the county. About boroughs there is this: It is open to the town commissioners to nominate two or three of their number. As a general rule, the chairman of the town commissioners is a magistrate.

39,610. Who do they submit the nomination to?—To the Lord Chancellor. The chairman is, as a rule, appointed, but I have known cases where a commissioner who was not chairman was appointed and held office for three years.

39,611. What is the qualification of those men selected to be justices of the peace?—The town magistrates I speak of had not jurisdiction under the Licensing Act. They only acted under section 13.

39,612. The selection must be bad to begin with, because you have told us to-day that the majority of the magistrates in your county at large are not fitted?—I did not say that.

39,613. You said that they were not fitted?—I beg your pardon; I did not. I said the majority of the magistrates who attend the court.

39,614. Were wholly unsuited for the administration of the licensing law?—I did not put it in that way, but that inference may be drawn from the facts I gave.

39,615. You have stated to this Commission that the bench has been so packed that the magistrates have been standing on the stairs, and yet there was a majority against?—That particular case I referred to was in the county Clerk.

39,616. That would show they were enlisted for the purpose of carrying out the licensing law?—You may draw that inference from the facts I have told you.

39,617. You have also told us that they were so impecunious that they could not pay their hotel bills?—I did not say that. I dealt with those magistrates in particular that I was aware were in straitened circumstances.

39,618. Does not that prove what I say?—No. Your question as you put it was that I said the whole of the magistrates were so impecunious that they could not pay their hotel bills.

39,619. I say some of them, but that shows that they were [illegible] ... as regards those, that they were in straitened circumstances, and I am quite satisfied they could not afford to spend three days in a country place stopping at an hotel unless their expenses were paid, and it was generally stated and believed that they were paid what were called travel expenses. That was supposed to cover more than their actual cash out of pocket.

39,620. I should like to know from you with reference to the body of men selected to serve as magistrates on the bench, what is the qualification you would apply at a [illegible] position?—You would have to ask the Lieutenant of the county that. As far as I know, no qualification is laid down. It is a matter of his discretion; application is made by influential people, and he may consent to some and refuse others. I am aware of one case where a man who ought to have held a good social position, but who did not come to his own [illegible] ...

39,621. You will admit it is so?—It is so, but arising from nothing connected with the licensing Acts.

39,622. It applies to your district equally as well as to other districts of Ireland?—As I have said, I have only had acquaintance with Tralee since August 1896, but I take it they are much better off now than they were before, because their rents have been reduced. It has nothing to do with the Licensing Acts.

39,623. Is it your opinion that it is to the benefit of a landlord to make his customers excessively drunk?—No. I do not, but from what I see going on, he regards it as up his benefit to sell as much drink as he can, no matter what the result to his customers may be.

39,624. True, but if he were to add to the drink a deleterious ingredient that had the effect of rendering his customers incapable, would that be to his advantage. Would not that stop the consumption of liquor?—That would depend on a thing about which I cannot express an opinion. If the drinking of one glass of such liquor rendered his customer incapable, the publican would lose, but if the customer could drink as many glasses of that liquor as he could of the good liquor, then the publican would gain considerably by the adulteration.

39,625. With reference to the question of endorsement, you expressed an opinion that it would be desirable that every slight offence should be endorsed?—I said no such thing.

39,626. That every offence should be endorsed and that endorsement should remain throughout?—No. What I suggest as advisable is that the present law which provides that a conviction within five years should have effect for all purposes should apply irrespective of any transfer that is the renewal may have taken place from one licence-holder to another.

39,627. That is the exact question I asked you. That is your opinion?—For the period of five years.

39,628. Then if a bad tenant who has committed an offence, and had the licence endorsed, is succeeded by a good tenant, that tenant should carry his predecessor's guilt with him?—Yes; and according to two English decisions that is the law at present. There are two cases I can quote upon that.

39,629. You say that is your opinion, and that is all I desire to elicit from you?—Yes.

39,630. Would not that be calculated to deter any respectable man—a man of capital and business ability—entering upon the possession of one of those houses where the licence was so endorsed?—To a certain extent it might, but supposing that he bought the blemished licence, he paid that licence for a smaller price, and if he commits no offence, he does not run the risk of losing it.

39,631. I want to ask a question as to your special qualifications. You said when you requested certain repairs and alterations, you were met by the statement that they could not afford it. Is that part of your official duty. Have you power to request certain alterations or additions to be made?—It is part of my duty to take those steps within the Licensing Act for the enforcement of the Act, and when I visited these premises I found that they were quite unsuitable for having the law properly carried out. I found that there was only one door in one case.

39,632. Would you kindly answer my question. Have you the power to compel alterations?—I have not. I have power to request it to be done, and in case it is not done, I can lay it before the magistrates, and it was to enable me to do that I visited the houses.

39,633. In answer to the Chairman, you expressed an opinion that the magistrates should have a discre-

Mr. J. J. Bell.

6 April '98.

Endorsement of licence.

Alteration of premises.

39,641. (Chairman.) You come here with the precise and specific object of rebutting a statement made by Mr. McDonald, in answer to question 39,[illegible], where he says: "We have in our own neighbourhood the islands of Lismore and Tiree, the property of the Duke of Argyll, who allows no licence on them, and it is quite a well-known fact that when the Lismore men come to Oban to market, they invariably, without exception, go back drunk and take large supplies of liquor with them. It has become quite a proverb in Oban, the Lismore men going home drunk on market days; and at Tiree, when the steamer calls, a large number of men go out in boats, and buy whisky from the stewards of the boats." That is the statement which you wish to modify or refute?—That is so.

39,642. Are you a native of Lismore?—Yes.

39,643. Have you lived there some time?—I have lived almost all my days there.

39,643. What do you say to that statement?—I say that Mr. McDonald told what was not right when he made that statement.

39,644. There were some licences in Lismore, were there not, some little time ago?—Yes, there were licences within 40 years.

39,645. So long ago as that?—Yes.

39,646. Was there much drunkenness, so far as you can recollect, on the island at that time?—As I have heard it said there was a good deal at that time.

39,647. Within your own memory have there been licences?—There were two licences within my own time.

39,648. They have been closed?—Yes, the last was closed about 22 years ago.

39,649. Have you noticed any change in the habits of the people in consequence?—A great deal, and especially in the young generation.

39,650. Then do you say that that statement that Mr. McDonald made before this Commission has been much observed upon in Lismore?—Yes, very much. The people felt it very much.

39,651. You simply deny it?—Certainly I deny it.

39,652. I suppose you are not in a position to deny that when the Lismore men come to Oban they might get drunk there, and be sober when they get back?—There is only one way of getting back, and that is by the steamer, and it must be upon there. I have seen cases of drunkenness, but very few.

39,653. Therefore you contradict the statement that they invariably go back drunk?—Yes, he says, "without exception." I say that I can prove that that is not the case.

39,654. What is the number of inhabitants on the island of Lismore?—About [illegible].

39,655. So far as you can testify from your observation, when the men who go to Oban to market come back they are sober?—Yes; as I say with the exception of very few.

39,656. On some occasions I suppose?—On some occasions, perhaps on a market day, I have seen two or three, I know them all, and I have seen only perhaps one or two, and perhaps once or twice a year.

39,657. Would the captain of the steamer corroborate what you say?—Yes, he would be the very man that could do it as well as other men in Oban—well-known men, such as Mr. Cameron, the auctioneer that carries on the market there.

39,658. I understand you not only to dispute the statement but to deny there is any truth in it except on those few occasions of which you speak, and the few individuals whom you have seen there?—Exactly that is it.

39,659. (Mr. [illegible].) Do you know that there was a letter in the "Scotsman" not very long ago on the subject. Has that come to your knowledge?—I never saw it in the "Scotsman."

39,660. The statement I understand there is, that the refusal by the Duke of Argyll to allow a public-house in Tiree, and another place which is mentioned, has caused [illegible]?—I do not refer to Tiree; I do not know much about Tiree, but I know Lismore. Part of Lismore belongs to the Duke of Argyll.

39,661. You do not know about that letter or any correspondence that followed it?—No.

39,662. (Mr. [illegible].) Is there any desire whatever on the part of the people of Lismore to have a public-house on the island?—None whatever. If a plebiscite were taken it would be found they would not want it.

39,663. By a large majority?—Yes.

39,664. Do you think anybody would vote for it?—It is possible. There is hardly anything but what somebody would support it.

39,665. The great bulk of the people of Lismore are against having a public-house on the island?—They are against it.

The witness withdrew.

39,737. You are speaking of beer off-licences?—Yes. It is only in the particular case of beer off-licences that the Act applies.

39,738. (*Mr. Hayden.*) I understand you to say that you believe the Sunday Closing Act was a partial failure in Ireland?—What I intended to say was that the evil of intemperance requires further checking and that the present law in that direction has proved insufficient.

39,739. That is my meaning, that the present Act has proved insufficient and therefore a partial failure? —Yes, the present Act as part of the whole legislation.

39,740. I also understood you to say you would extend the hours of closing on Saturdays?—Yes.

39,741. The evidence as to the question of payment of wages has been in the direction that Saturday is the day on which wages are paid. Does Dublin differ from Belfast in that respect?—I do not know what the day is in Belfast.

39,742. We have been given to understand that the wages are principally paid in Belfast on Friday?—I think in Dublin they are chiefly paid on Saturday.

39,743. In that case you would have to close the houses on Friday as well as Saturday. If the men are not to be trusted with the money they have earned you would close the houses on Friday as well as Saturday? —I am rather assuming that in the great majority of cases the wages are paid on Saturday, and then the Saturday half-holiday comes in also.

39,744. To what time would you [illegible] the sale on Saturday?—I suggest—it is more or less an arbitrary suggestion—a knocking off of two hours. I think if they could get drink up to 9 o'clock on Saturdays that should be sufficient.

39,745. Would you leave it to the discretion of the magistrates?—That was what the Chairman put to me, but I would make it a matter of legislation, as it is now.

39,746. Referring to the same authority I quoted before, Mr. O'[illegible], of Dublin. He says: "I would "close public-houses at 9 o'clock but for this fact, "which I think a most serious one, because you are "dealing with the habits of the people." Do you agree with that?—I do not exactly know what that means as it was developed. I suppose he means that the people make their purchases on Saturday nights.

39,747. He states that?—I suppose he means they are exposed to a particular temptation when making their purchases.

39,748. The custom in Dublin has been that the working people shop on Saturday nights, and the shops of the butcher and the grocer are kept open till 12 o'clock for their convenience?—Yes. I do not propose to interfere with that custom, but I mean that the people should not be able to get drink after 9 o'clock.

39,749. Then comes the question as to going to those places where drink is sold. How would you prevent their going to grocers' shops and various shops where drink is sold along with other commodities?—The grocer cannot give them drink for immediate consumption, unless he has a publican's licence, without breaking the law. They have only off-licences. The spirit grocer's licence is an off-licence.

39,750. (*Mr. Whitaker.*) Should I be correct in saying that your view as to Sunday closing was that so far as it had gone it had been beneficial, but you think it ought to be extended a little further?—I think that is it.

39,751. (*Mr. Grimley.*) With reference to your suggestion as to the increased magisterial control over the spirit grocers' licence, the largest wine merchants in Dublin, and in fact all over Ireland, trade under that licence, do not they?—Yes, I believe they do.

39,752. You put an extreme case of an application for a licence in respect of a [illegible] [illegible], [illegible] licensed houses; but taking the case of old family wine merchants, would you think it necessary that they should go to the magistrates except under the [illegible] present conditions, would not you consider those sufficient?—The magistrates should have a discretion. I think that in such a case as that, where a house has an established reputation, the magistrates should have a discretion.

39,753. If you send a man to the magistrates with reference to what he is to sell, you put him in an invidious position from the trader's point of view. The law of England is different to that of Ireland. A man trading under an English off-licence can sell wines and spirits immediately he gets his licence without magisterial control at all?—Yes.

39,754. Would you see any objection to that?—There is a good deal of breaking of the law, I am afraid, by the spirit grocers. I do not know whether it is so in England or not.

39,755. Does not it rather arise from the anomalous state of the licences. Under the spirit grocer's licence they are restricted in the quantities they can sell, and the result is they are driven to a publican's licence? —Yes.

39,756. A great deal of complaint made against the spirit grocer's licence has nothing to do with the licence, but with the class of the law under which he carries on his business. I think that is a fair statement, is it not?—Yes.

39,757. (*Mr. Young.*) May I ask you do you think that spirit grocers should be confined to the sale only of bottled liquor?—I think it would be a considerable safeguard against their breaking the law if they were so confined. That would limit them necessarily to carrying out the restrictions of their off-licences if they sold in bottles only, but if they can sell a glass of whisky of course they can easily break the law.

39,758. You would recommend then that spirit grocers should only sell under seal—bottled liquor?—I do not know that I would go so far as to recommend that without consideration; but I think the question is worthy of consideration, and it would certainly meet one difficulty.

39,759. If the latter was confined to a half pint and closed vessels, would it meet the requirements of the trade?—I do not know exactly what the requirements of the trade are.

39,760. (*Mr. Grimley.*) It would give the trader a fair chance of carrying on his business, and would meet the requirements of the public regarding the off-licence —do not sell it a spirit grocer's licence—[illegible] the sale in sealed vessels or closed vessels, and the [illegible] was half a pint?—I say that that would be a desirable change from my point of view, because it would help to prevent the breaking of the law which occurs in a great many cases by spirit grocers providing their customers with drink on the premises.

39,761. That would give an opportunity of preventing drinking on the premises?—Quite so.

39,762. (*Mr. Young.*) May I take it you strongly recommend that?—I think it would be, as far as I can see, a desirable reform.

39,763. With reference to clubs you recommend that they should be registered?—I do not think I said that.

39,764. (*Chairman.*) Your evidence was rather in the opposite direction?—I recommend that the police should have a large discretionary power under the warrant of the Chief Commissioner of Police for entering suspected clubs.

39,765. (*Mr. Young.*) Do you think that that would be effective in preventing bogus clubs?—I do, or in deterring them.

39,766. You would recommend, I think, that imprisonment should be imposed for a third offence of drunkenness?—Yes, after the third.

39,767. Is that for the sake of reform or what other view do you take of the matter?—It is very hard to reform a drunkard, but at any rate as a punitive measure I think it would have a deterrent effect. I think people who do not mind paying fines would not like to go to prison for a month.

39,768. You think the penalty at present is not sufficiently large?—I am inclined to think that, because these people come up over and over again before us— the same people.

39,769. I think it is the opinion of many that if they were imprisoned—that is, the habitual drunkards—for two or three years it would be a great advantage to themselves and probably would be a deterrent?—Yes, of course that means compulsory total abstinence for the time, and it is perhaps not improbable that people who undergo that would reform.

The witness withdrew.

Mr. [illegible]

6 April '98.

Sale in sealed vessels.

Clubs.

Penalties for drunkenness.

ONE HUNDREDTH DAY.

Queen's Robing Room, House of Lords, Tuesday, April 26th, 1898.

PRESENT:

THE RIGHT HONOURABLE THE VISCOUNT PEEL IN THE CHAIR.

The Right Hon. the Viscount [illegible].	[illegible] Johnson, Esq.
The Right Hon. Sir Algernon West, K.C.B.	[illegible], Esq.
Sir William Henry Houldsworth, Bart., M.P.	Charles Walker, Esq.
Sir Charles Cameron, Bart., M.P.	Thomas Palmer Whittaker, Esq., M.P.
The Very Rev. H. H. Dickinson, Dean.	Samuel Young, Esq., M.P.
Henry [illegible], Esq.	George Younger, Esq.
[illegible], Esq.	

Mr. Thomas Wallace Russell, M.P., called in and examined.

Mr. T. W. Russell, M.P. — 26 April '98. — Position of witness.

59,770. (Chairman.) You are, as we know, Member for Tyrone?—For the Southern Division of that county.

59,771. You are a resident, I believe, in Dublin?—Yes.

59,772. Have you been for many years connected with the Irish Temperance Party?—I was Secretary and Parliamentary Agent for the Irish Temperance Party for 21 years.

59,773. The Sunday closing movement, with which you are very well acquainted, originated in what year?—In 1866.

Irish Sunday closing in Parliament.

59,774. As we know, five towns were exempted from the operation of that Act?—Perhaps I might say that the movement first took Parliamentary shape in the year 1871. On the [illegible] May 1876 a motion was carried against the Government by a majority of [illegible]. A Select Committee sat in 1877, over which Sir Michael Hicks-Beach, the present Chancellor of the Exchequer, presided. The [illegible] on that Committee proposed to exempt five large towns—Dublin, Belfast, Cork, Limerick, and Waterford—from the operation of the Bill. The Government were defeated on the Select Committee by [illegible]. Then the Bill was introduced by Professor Smyth in 1878, and as a matter of policy the Government amendments were accepted; the five towns were exempted, the hours of sale being reduced by two hours. The public-houses were closed on Sundays in these five cities at 7 o'clock instead of at 9, as previously. An amendment was accepted making the Bill experimental for four years. That is a point I wish to put before the Commission. That was not a Government amendment; it was an amendment moved by Mr. Collins, then member for [illegible]; and the promoters of the Bill desiring to have it passed, accepted that amendment.

The Act experimental.

59,775. From that date to this, that Act appears in the Expiring Laws Continuance Bill?—Yes. I should [illegible], if it is desired, to give the first results as shown in the Parliamentary Returns.

59,776. I should like to ask you first why was it passed as such that it should be only an experiment for four years?—The reason was this. The Irish opposition to Parliament was very small; I think only 11 Irish members voted in the division against the Bill, an overwhelming majority, something between 50 and 60 voting for it all through. There was more than one all-night sitting. The feeling, however, was very strong indeed. The temperance party were so confident of the success of the Bill, that they accepted that amendment in order to get the Bill through on the last day of the Session. It only passed on the last day of the Session of 1878.

59,777. The fact that it was made an experiment for four years was rather a question of expediency than of settled policy on the part of the majority of members, was it not?—Quite so. If the temperance party had opposed it, the Government would not have accepted it; but time was so precious, and it was so risky, that, acting on my own advice, the members supporting the Bill in the House of Commons accepted that amendment.

Mr. T. W. Russell, M.P. — Permanency favoured by Chief Secretaries.

59,778. In favour of that Bill, you have had, among [illegible], have you not, from several Chief Secretaries?—Previous to the expiration of the four years a very large deputation waited upon Mr. Forster, who was then Chief Secretary for Ireland; I think that was in November 1881. The Parliamentary Returns showing the results were placed before the Chief Secretary. His statement practically amounted to this—I have the exact words—that the Government would on no account allow the Bill to lapse; that if it were not made permanent by a private member, the Government would certainly put it into the Expiring Laws Continuance Bill; and he said there could be no doubt of the success of the measure, and, what to him was more important, it had not gone ahead of public opinion. Sir George Trevelyan as Chief Secretary for Ireland in the year 1883 introduced a [illegible] Bill, covering the five towns, into the House of Commons. It was not passed. Mr. Arthur Balfour, when Chief Secretary in 1888, declared to a deputation of which I was a member that the matter was one past argument altogether; and Mr. Morley, who has been Chief Secretary since, has declared over and over again that he looks upon the matter in the same light as his predecessor, Mr. Arthur Balfour.

The exempted towns.

59,779. The Bills that were before these successive Chief Secretaries included the exempted towns?—Yes; but I think, in passing, I ought to say this, that in 1888, while Mr. Balfour was Chief Secretary for Ireland, the Bill was referred to another Select Committee over which Mr. Justice Madden, then Attorney-General for Ireland, presided. There again Mr. Madden, then the Attorney-General, introduced precisely the same amendment that Sir Michael Hicks-Beach introduced in 1877. These amendments were rejected by that Committee also, by a larger majority. I myself was a member of that Select Committee.

The Select Committee of 1888.

59,780. What were the amendments?—The amendments were to exclude from the operation of the Bill the five exempted cities. Mr. Madden was defeated in the Committee by a larger majority than that by which Sir Michael Hicks-Beach was defeated in 1877. While the Committee was sitting, I myself had charge of a Bill for shortening the hours of sale on Saturday night. That was carried in the House of Commons by 178 to 102, and referred to Mr. Madden's Committee. The report of the Committee was to this effect: "The Committee have considered and amended "the Bills referred to them, and now report them as "amended to the House. In view of this report the "Committee recommend, first, that the Act of 1878 be "made perpetual and extended to the five cities now "exempted from the full operation of the Act." I feel bound to say that the Government, so far as it was represented upon the Committee, opposed the inclusion of the five cities, although it was carried against them. The Government Opposition was to exclude the five cities and to shorten the hours of sale from 8 to 9. "Second, that the qualifying distance under the bona "fide traveller provisions should be extended to [illegible]

Mr. F. W. Russell, M.P.

"miles. Third, that all houses for the sale of intoxi- "cating liquors in Ireland should be closed at 9 o'clock "on Saturdays." That was the result of the Bill which had been referred to them, which the House of Commons had sanctioned by carrying the second reading; therefore I wish the Commission to understand that whilst Mr. Balfour and Mr. Morley, with other Chief Secretaries, have spoken in favour of the Bill, I believe they have always spoken with a view of having at least three hours' sale in the five exempted cities. These gentlemen are not here, and I know the exact facts, and I believe if the Bill had come to a Committee of the House of Commons the Government would have moved such an amendment.

Hours of [illegible]

39,781. What were the hours they would be in favour of?—Two to 5 o'clock was Mr. Madden's proposition— it is now 2 to 7. Previous to that it was 2 to 9, and previous to that 7 to 11. It has been reduced from 11 to 7. I may say that the Bill as sought to be amended by Mr. Madden was the policy of the Government from 1882 to 1892 beyond all question, and they were quite ready to pass it and to support it in that shape.

Irish Sunday closing [illegible]

39,782. What happened to the Bill in 1893?—In answer, a private member's Bill has to run the chances of the ballot. In some Sessions it got to a division, in others it failed, but on no occasion that that Bill has been before the House of Commons has it failed to secure a substantial majority of the House of Commons and a very considerable majority of Irish members always, with the exception that on the last occasion there was a majority but it was not so large as on previous occasions.

39,783. What is the condition of that Bill now?—The condition of that Bill is that it is the First Order of the Day to-morrow week, but the time of the House has been appropriated for the Irish Local Government Bill, and I am afraid that the Bill, so far as this Session is concerned, is dead. On the last occasion, although Mr. Arthur Balfour spoke for the Bill, he explained that the majority of his colleagues thought that it ought not to be passed in view of the fact that the Royal Commission was now sitting; and I think that argument would be still stronger now, seeing that the Commission is actually engaged in taking Irish evidence.

[illegible]

39,784. Are you prepared to say that there is no material change of opinion in regard to that Bill?—I am quite clear about that. I should say that it has passed out of the range of an electoral test question. Since 1877–8–9 and so, when it was in that position, Irish politics have become very intense, and very bitter, and the Irish political mind has been occupied with other and very different questions.

[illegible]

39,785. This feeling you say has been expressed, and is generally held, with reference to Sunday closing, and you say that that extended in some degree to the Saturday early closing movement?—Only more so. As a matter of fact a great many of the opponents of Sunday closing, and I should say many of the trade themselves, were greatly shocked at the results of late Saturday night drinking, and were very hard in their declarations that it was from Saturday night drinking and not from Sunday that most of the harm proceeded. Magistrates and others—police magistrates of Dublin, for example—were very strong indeed that the Saturday night drinking was infinitely worse than that on Sunday.

39,786. Have you any declarations by magistrates or others with reference to Saturday early closing?—Yes. I can give the declarations of the Dublin magistrates and others before Mr. Madden's committee, and before Sir Michael Hicks Beach's committee. Perhaps I may refer to it afterwards.

39,787. I will take your word for it that they were in favour?—Yes, but I should like to put them in. You will take it at all events from me, that I am quite clear that all over Ireland the feeling is very strong for early closing on Saturday night. Of course the hour is another matter. People will differ as regards the hour for closing, but as regards earlier closing, you will find that magistrates, and priests, and clergymen of all the churches feel the evil of Saturday night drinking so much, that they are even stronger against that than the other.

39,788. There was a house-to-house canvass taken in the five exempted cities, was not there?—That was on Sunday closing.

Mr. F. W. Russell, M.P.

14 April '88.

Canvass in the five cities on Sunday closing.

39,789. Was any canvass taken as to Saturday early closing?—No. These canvasses were taken when the Sunday closing question was the great question, and we referred to it in comparison with the Saturday early closing. I could give the facts as regards the canvasses. They were carried out under my own personal superintendence, and I can give the figures for each of the places.

39,790. And the conditions under which the canvass was made?—Certainly. I was personally responsible for the whole canvass in the five towns.

The ballot papers.

39,791. What was the form that the canvass took? What were the questions asked? It was not a personal canvass. It was by writing or printed ballot?—What we did was this. We prepared a number of practically ballot papers, upon which we asked this question: "Are "you in favour of the entire closing of public-houses in "Ireland on Sundays?" There was a column "Yes," and a column "No," and they were directed to put a cross in either of the columns, just as they thought fit.

Result of the canvass of heads of families.

39,792. What was the electoral body?—We took the heads of families in the five exempted cities. Probably I had better give the Commission the results. In the first canvass there were 74,[illegible]——

39,793. (Dean Dickinson.) In Dublin?—No, in the whole of the five exempted cities. In the canvass there were [illegible] in the affirmative.

39,794. (Chairman.) I presume a large canvass— taking the exempted cities together, and taking them singly—did not reply at all?—Yes. Perhaps I may give the figures with regard to the 1888 canvass. In Dublin there was a total vote of 35,733 heads of families. There voted, "Aye," 34,[illegible]; "No," 8,117.

Dublin.

39,795. What proportion would 43,[illegible] householders bear to the total number of householders in Dublin?— The population of the Metropolitan Police District— because the 1888 canvass covered the Metropolitan Police District as a whole—is about 3[illegible] or 3[illegible].

39,796. (Sir Algernon West.) That includes the townships?—Yes. It goes down as far as Killiney, which is 12 or 14 miles down, but it does not touch Clontarf, which is only 3 miles from Dublin.

39,797. (Chairman.) Are you able to say the total number of houses in Dublin?—It was not merely householders, it was heads of families. There are not self-contained houses in Dublin. The working class do not live in self-contained houses as English working men do. They live in tenements. Many a house would have 14 families in the house, living in different rooms, and therefore householders would give a wrong impression. It was simply we did our best to get at the widest suffrage that we could, and we instructed the canvassers to canvass the heads of families.

39,798. I suppose you could not say from recollection as to whether the majority of votes were given in the more congested districts of Dublin, or in the better quarters?—I have a very clear recollection of that. In the better quarters a considerable number of householders declined to vote, on the ground that they were not concerned, and that it concerned more the people living in the poorer districts.

39,799. (Mr. Whitaker.) Do the figures which you have now given us of the total vote refer to that wider field of the 320,000?—Yes. Then in Belfast there was a total vote of 50,[illegible]. Of these 33,411 voted aye, 1,[illegible] voted no. I may say that in Belfast there was not nearly the same difficulty in the canvass, because the working classes there mostly live in these self-contained houses, and not in tenements. In Cork the total vote was 11,[illegible]. There voted aye, 9,[illegible]; and no, 1,[illegible]. The whole population of Cork at that time was about [illegible]. Then in Limerick the total vote was 6,[illegible]; aye, 5,[illegible]; no, [illegible]. Waterford total vote 3,7[illegible]; aye, 3,[illegible]; no, [illegible]. Making a total vote of 90,[illegible], an affirmative vote of 76,[illegible], and a negative vote of 13,7[illegible]; or a majority of [illegible] in favour of total Sunday closing.

Cork.

Limerick.

Waterford.

39,800. (Chairman.) Can you tell us the number of ballot papers issued?—I could not tax my recollection.

39,801. There were a number who did not vote at all? —There must have been.

Mr. T. W. Russell, M.P.

[illegible] April '98.

Method of canvass.

[illegible]. The great majority of the population therefore did not record their vote?—We did not ask a plebiscite. We did not put it in the shape of a petition to Parliament for every adult to sign. We asked what we considered the responsible heads of families. Of course, we might have done otherwise. We might have had a plebiscite, but that was not the form it took. Whether right or wrong, we took the heads of families, and it was a very difficult matter to carry out. There were a large number of people excluded altogether. If you take the population of Dublin, the police is a large body; the army is a large body; the hospitals cover an a large number. There was a large number of excluded [illegible]. It was considered at the time that, taking the difficulty of the operation into account, there was a very large vote indeed.

[illegible] (Dean Dickinson.) Who took out the papers?—They were, not employed; mostly ex-policemen of the Royal Irish Constabulary—very reliable men. The papers were left one day and collected the next.

[illegible] (Chairman.) Were the ballot papers accompanied by any remarks representing the particular views of the temperance party?—The canvassers were employed by the Sunday Closing Association. Their instructions were to leave the paper without note or comment, and [illegible] that they were to call for it the next day. They called for it the next day, and took it up as it was signed.

[illegible] (Mr. Whitaker.) Will the number of persons to a family in Ireland be about the same as in England —will it come out at about five?—I should say it was a little more.

[illegible]. You do not know from the census?—I went into all that with the Chief Secretaries; but I cannot tax my recollection. At all events, I feel bound to say that [illegible] heads of families is a very large number.

[illegible]. (Dean Dickinson.) There would be not more than [illegible] heads of families dividing it by five?—No. If you include the members left out deliberately.

[illegible] (Chairman.) However, you insist on the fact that it was not a plebiscite?—It was not intended to be.

[illegible]. (Mr. Young.) How do you know that no one voted except heads of families?—I examined the papers personally every night as they were brought in, and tested them by every possible test. They were laid out for public inspection in the city of Dublin, and they were laid openly before the Members for the City of Dublin who were opposed to the Sunday Closing Bill.

59,810. (Chairman.) The voters put their crosses and their names?—Their crosses and their names.

59,811. (Mr. Whitaker.) Was more than one paper left for a family?—No.

59,812. Therefore, there could only be one vote for each family?—That is all.

59,813. (Chairman.) There were no means of distinguishing male from female voters, I suppose?—No. As far as I am personally concerned I think that the women heads of families had much more interest in it than the men. We certainly made no effort to shut out heads of families who were women.

Arrests on Saturday drunkenness.

59,814. Are you able to give us any evidence as to Saturday drunkenness which you mentioned just now?—I am.

59,815. Taking towns with a population of 10,000 and upwards?—Yes. I have here a rather remarkable Parliamentary Return. The return which I am about to quote was obtained by Mr. Meldon, who was then Member for County Kildare. It gives the arrests for drunkenness on Saturdays in the 19 towns with a population of 10,000 and upwards, and the hours at which they were made. I think 1877 was the date. The figures are very suggestive, and it is for that reason I have brought it before the Commission. In Dublin the hours were not given in the return, but there were [illegible] arrests for Saturday drunkenness in the city of Dublin in that year. In the 19 towns with a population above 10,000 the arrests took place as follows:—From 8 a.m. on Saturday morning to 9 a.m. there were 7; from 9 to 10 there were 18; from 10 to 11 [illegible]; from 11 to 12, 60; from 12 to 1, 67; from 1 to 2, 74; from 2 to 3, 117; from 3 to 4, [illegible]; from 4 to 5, [illegible]; from 5 to 6, [illegible]; from 6 to 7, [illegible]; from 7 to 8, [illegible]; from 8 to 9, [illegible]; from 9 to 10, [illegible]; from 10 to 11, [illegible]; from 11 to 12, [illegible]; from 12 to 1, [illegible]; from 1 to 2, [illegible]; and so on until it gets down to 10 again.

Mr. T. W. Russell, M.P.

[illegible]. The largest number took place between 11 and 12?—Yes, but the figures rise from 8 to 12 in a very alarming way. These are the returns of these 19 large towns. I think it was on that return that the agitation for Saturday closing was pressed.

[illegible]. Is it not a remarkable fact that for every hour there is a progressive increase except in one or two instances?—Yes. I think the whole thing very remarkable.

[illegible]. Some hours of the day the working man would, I suppose, be at their work, yet there is a steady increase of arrests for drunkenness?—You must bear in mind that a very considerable number of workmen are paid on Friday night, not all, but a very considerable number, and they have been paid on Friday night with the very best intention of endeavouring to [illegible] the Saturday evil.

[illegible] Would Saturday be a half-holiday?—Yes, with working men largely. The point I lay special stress upon is that the contention in Ireland with all who are interested in this matter is that the real evil is done during the late hours on Saturday, and these figures, in my opinion, bear out that proposition almost beyond argument.

[illegible]. (Mr. Whitaker.) Do these 19 towns include Dublin?—I mentioned that the hours were not given, but that the total of arrests in Dublin for Saturday was [illegible].

Saturday drunkenness.

[illegible]. Can you give us the total for the 19 towns?—The total arrests for drunkenness in these 19 towns during the year 1877 were [illegible]; that is in the 19 towns with a population of 10,000. The Saturday arrests were [illegible].

[illegible]. (Mr. Young.) Is not this at a great distance? Could we not get nearer to the present time than 1877?—I quite agree. I do not think it will lessen the force of the figures at all; and I think the Commission would do well if it were possible to get a Parliamentary Return bringing them down to date. I produce this to show the evidence upon which the agitation for Saturday early closing was founded; and I think the figures are very strong.

[illegible]. (Sir Algernon West.) Are these arrests only for drunkenness; or are they accompanied by any other crime?—This is drunkenness and drunkenness and disorderly conduct, which generally follows in Ireland I am bound to say.

[illegible]. (Chairman.) In some of these towns are not these special Acts which enable the police to arrest for simple drunkenness?—Yes. There are two charges in Ireland, simple drunkenness, and drunkenness combined with disorderly conduct. Our people are very excitable. They drink whisky more than beer, and drunkenness is very often allied with disorderly conduct of some kind or another.

[illegible]. (Dean Dickinson.) Nearly one-third of the whole arrests in those 19 towns were on Saturday?—Yes.

[illegible]. (Chairman.) Would these figures you gave us be simple drunkenness, or drunk and disorderly?—As the Parliamentary Return is headed, it is: "Summary of arrests for drunkenness on Saturdays."

Absence of working-men's clubs in Ireland.

[illegible]. (Mr. [illegible].) I suppose in these 19 large towns there are a good many workmen's clubs, are not there?—I am sorry to say not. With the exception of Dublin and Belfast, I do not know a working-men's club in any of the 19 towns.

[illegible]. If there were, I suppose a great deal of that drunkenness might be attributable to those clubs?—But if the clubs are not there, it cannot be. With the exception of Dublin, I do not know where there are any working-men's clubs.

[illegible]. (Dean Dickinson.) There are not many in Belfast, are there?—No; I know one, but I rather think that is conducted upon principles that would not produce drunkenness at all events far afield. The club system has not taken hold in Ireland. The Irish people are rather a family people. There are no political clubs, in the sense that there are in England. They spend their time more at home than in clubs. As a matter of fact it cannot be from club drinking because they do not exist.

39,530. (*Chairman.*) Do you think the absence of [illegible] is in any way owing to the fact that there is a very large and frequent opportunity of getting drink in the ordinary licensed houses?—No, I cannot say that. I would say that the absence of drink [illegible] among the ordinary working classes in Ireland is due to a national characteristic. They are more [illegible] people than [illegible] people.

39,531. (*Mr. Whitaker.*) The public-houses are closed on Sundays, are they not, in all but the exempted cities?

39,532. That would have produced claims, if the closing of public-houses produced them?—Certainly. It has not done so.

39,533. There are much fewer arrests for drunkenness on Sundays?—I have the returns here.

39,534. There are, as a matter of fact, fewer?—Yes.

39,535. That shows that it does come from the public-houses?—I have no doubt of that.

39,536. (*Mr. Fenny.*) Could you give us the names of the 15 towns?—The names of the towns are Dublin, Belfast, Clonmel, Cork, Drogheda, Dundalk, Galway, Kilkenny, Limerick, Londonderry, Lurgan, Newry, Queenstown, Waterford and Wexford.

39,537. (*Chairman.*) You cannot give us the figures on Saturday later than 1878, but are you able to say whether there is a strong public feeling, or not, as to the necessity of this present proposal for earlier Saturday closing? Has that ever been tested?—I have not the slightest doubt that all over Ireland amongst all classes of the people the proposal to shorten the hours on Saturday meets with universal approval.

39,538. There have been some public meetings in Ireland, have not there, held against Saturday earlier closing?—There have been publicans' meetings, and public meetings, held against the Bill that is now before Parliament; and on that question I should like to say this, during my time, which expired probably about 1884—I came into Parliament in 1885, and things are not different since—not more than a dozen public meetings had been held in Ireland against this whole proposal. One of them was held in Limerick. The Mayor gave the Corporation Hall. The Mayor presided. The Rev. Edward O'Dwyer, who was then Catholic curate of Limerick, and who is now the Bishop of Limerick, went to the meeting. The resolutions proposed by the trade were rejected, and the amendment moved by the present Bishop of Limerick was carried by an overwhelming majority in favour of the Bill. That is in a Catholic city where Catholic agitation has not the slightest hold. In Cork in my time a meeting was convened on the same question on Sunday. That meeting was upset and resolutions carried against the proposal of the promoters of the meeting.

39,539. You are now speaking of Saturday closing?—I am speaking of the Bill as it is now before Parliament. There has been no agitation for Saturday closing pure and simple. It has been combined with this Bill.

39,540. Has there been any public agitation against the proposal to close earlier on Saturday?—Not that I am aware of. Of course the agitation is in favour of the Bill.

39,541. You cannot say whether the agitation was directed against Saturday earlier closing, or against Sunday closing?—I will tell you what really did happen. While the Sunday closing movement was being pressed a considerable number of people who did not see their way to total Sunday closing were very largely in favour of Saturday closing; but when Saturday closing came anything at all, it must be a statutory declaration that cannot be got behind. The publican body in these five large towns, and in all these large towns, is a very powerful body generally, and their influence is very great, both in the local politics, municipal politics, and in Imperial politics. Any local authority would be subjected to very great pressure undoubtedly; and therefore if any change is to be made, it ought to be a statutory change.

39,542. Even in the case of total Sunday closing in the five exempted cities?—I am a member of the Government, and I came here mainly for the purpose of giving facts, and I should like to avoid questions of policy as far as possible, but upon the question of permissive legislation versus statutory and direct legislation I have no hesitation in giving my opinion.

39,543. Has there been any evidence on the part of the exempted towns from any public action that they have taken, that they would be in favour of investing the corporation, or some other licensing authority, with a discretion?—None whatever. That would be universally opposed.

Licensees and early closing on Saturdays.

39,544. But they would not be opposed to giving them statutory powers within defined limits?—I believe if the question of two hours earlier closing on Saturday were submitted even to the trade themselves—I have the evidence of their secretary before Sir Michael Hicks-Beach's Committee—the evil is so appalling that the publicans themselves would realise it. They are not men who delight in drunkenness, on the contrary they have no desire to see this shocking form of drunkenness on Saturday night. I am certain that a very large number of the publicans would be in favour of a reduction of the Saturday night hours. Then, if I may go back, there are Parliamentary Returns showing the result of Sunday closing, which I think would be of great value to the Commission.

Returns on result of Sunday closing.

39,546. Can you hand them in or give us a summary of them?—I will give a summary. When the experimental Act had run three years, and the question of renewing it became a public question, Parliamentary Returns were ordered.

39,547. What year was that?—These returns were dated from October 13th, 1878, when the Sunday Closing Bill came into operation, until the end of the year 1881. That was 3½ years the experiment had run when the returns were ordered. From October 13th, 1877, to April 13th, 1878, six months before Sunday closing, there were 2,306 arrests in the total Sunday closing area. I distinguish it from the exempted cities. Six months after it came into operation, from October 13th, 1878, to the 12th April 1879, there were 7/7, a reduction of 1,637 arrests, in the six months. For the year ending April 12th, 1878, before Sunday closing there were [illegible] Sunday arrests excluding the large towns. For the year ending April 12th, 1880, after Sunday closing, there were 1,610 arrests, a reduction in the year of 2,714 arrests. In the year ending the 12th of April 1881, after Sunday closing, there were 1,682 arrests against 4,344. This was a reduction of 2,662. Then going to the exempted cities, the results from October 13th, 1877, to April 12th, 1878, before Sunday closing, were 1,694; for the six months after it there were 1,589. For the year previous to Sunday closing there were [illegible], for the year after it, 3,132. For the next year [illegible] and 3,716. These figures show on the aggregate that since the Sunday Closing Act came into operation in October 1878 to April 23rd 1880, there have been 7,093 fewer arrests for drunkenness where entire Sunday closing exists than there were in the corresponding periods before the Sunday Closing Act was passed, and in the exempted towns in the same period there has been a reduction of 2,[illegible], or in the whole of Ireland in the 3½ years a

Saturday closing. May I add one or two. Mr. Charles J. O'Donel, the Chief Magistrate, said before Sir Michael Hicks-Beach's Commission: "I apprehend "they may, at all events, earlier on Saturday. "At present it is 11; and as it would be better not "to do the thing too violently, I should say 9 o'clock "in the summer and 7 in the winter." Mr. Woodlock, his colleague, said: "I would close them on Saturday "evening, certainly not later than 7 o'clock, and "possibly earlier." The Recorder of Dublin said: "I should be very glad to see the hours shortened on "Saturday." Captain Talbot, the Chief Commissioner, said: "I should strongly recommend the closing of "public-houses on Saturday at an earlier hour." When I proposed to bring forward this the statement of the secretary of the Licensed Vintners' Society (that is the trade organisation in Dublin), Mr. Michael Dwyer. He is dead now, but he and I have had many a battle here. He was a man of outspoken humour. He said this: "I can say that much for them (the publicans) "that if the inconvenience and if the scenes of drunkenness "which undoubtedly do exist much more on Saturday "night than at any other time can be put a stop to "by any reasonable sacrifice on their part, I think I "could almost undertake for them that they would be "willing to consent to that sacrifice." In regard to the question as to simple drunkenness, the arrests for ordinary drunkenness in 1876 were 83,[illegible]; in 1877, 8[illegible],483; in 1878, 88,761; in 1879, 79,008; and in 1880, 79,[illegible]. That is general drunkenness. I think that is all I have to say as to Saturday and Sunday.

20,367. (*Sir Charles Cameron.*) The reduction would appear to be pretty much governed by the amount of the reduction on Sundays?—Yes.

20,368. (*Chairman.*) You just now mentioned bogus clubs. Is it your opinion that the police are competent to deal with bogus clubs or do you think it is possible that further legislative facilities should be given for their suppression?—My impression is that the Dublin police have been able to deal with them pretty satisfactorily, and they exist nowhere else.

20,369. They exist nowhere else than in Dublin?—Not to my knowledge, and I have a pretty extensive knowledge of the country.

20,370. Turning to a peculiarity of Dublin and of Belfast, I understand that in Ireland the spirit grocer is almost exclusively confined to Dublin and Belfast?—That is so.

20,371. How is that?—The freedom with which public-houses were obtained all through Ireland in many places amounted to what is practically free licensing. Take the case of a town like Castleisland, in the county of Kerry. I suppose it has not a population of more than 3,000, but in the main street it would puzzle anyone to get a house that was not a public-house. The magistrates have acted on the principle that another one will not matter. They are at every door.

20,372. How is it that, as we have been told, the spirit grocers, as to whom some abuses have been alleged, are confined almost exclusively in Ireland to Dublin and Belfast? Is it a fact that that is so?—That is a fact. They were confined largely to Dublin and Belfast, because the licensing authority in those two cities—the two recorders, Sir Frederick Shaw, the first in Dublin, and Sir Frederick Falkiner, afterwards, and the recorder of Belfast—would not grant new public-house licenses unless a very strong case was made for it. These spirit grocers are made up of two classes. First of all there is the family grocer who has not a public-house license. He takes a spirit grocer's license, which is sufficient for his trade. He does not wish to have consumption on the premises and the spirit grocer's license suits him. That is the first class and it is a small class. Then there is the grocer who is disappointed in getting a public-house license. This is a question of fact. There were 694 spirit grocers in Ireland in 1880; three-fourths of these were in Dublin and Belfast. Of the 372 in Dublin in that year the police authorities reported that over 90 were engaged in illicit traffic and they give the number of prosecutions against them. I want to distinguish the respectable family grocer from the disappointed publican, who simply gets his grocer's license and strives to do a publican's trade.

20,373. Am I right in saying that a spirit grocer can only sell legally off the premises?—Yes.

20,374. I understand that publicans are also grocers, and therefore a publican who happens to be a grocer,

Mr. T. W. Russell, M.P.

20 April '97.

Prohibition of beer licensing in Ireland.

and every one interested in moral reform of any kind would welcome some plan by which they could all be dealt with alike.

20,885. Why I asked you the question about giving absolute discretion to the licensing authority was this. I suppose you would be of opinion that with regard to spirit grocers, for instance, and spirit licences generally there is absolute free trade now?—I am very much afraid that is opposite to that, and so free trade has no free licensing. Of course free trade means no licensing at all, but free licensing in many parts of Ireland is absolutely the rule.

20,886. A licence to any applicant?—Yes, under whatever pretence, it amounts in many parts of Ireland to free licensing. That is not so in the north or in some parts of the midlands, but in the southern districts it amounts to that. The words of Mr. Ritchie's Bill as to the beer dealer's certificates are rather interesting on that point. Mr. Ritchie, who is now the President of the Board of Trade, in the year 1882 introduced a Bill to prevent beer dealers who could get their certificates in precisely the same way as the spirit grocers can in Ireland. That Bill says: "Whereas by the Beer "Dealers Retail Licences Act, 1880, it is provided that "the Licensing Justices shall be at liberty to exercise "their discretion respecting the grant of certificates "for such additional licences for sale of beer by retail "off the premises as are therein referred to, and that "certificates for such additional licences shall be "granted." And then it goes on to say: "Notwith- "standing anything in section 8 of the Wine and "Beerhouse Act, 1869, or in any other Act now in "force, the licensing justices shall be at liberty in "their free and unqualified discretion either to refuse "a certificate for any licence for sale of beer by retail "to be consumed off the premises on any grounds "appearing to them sufficient, or to grant the same to "such persons as they, in the execution of their statu- "tory powers and in the exercise of their discretion, "deem fit and proper."

The beer-retailers Act of 1882 in Ireland.

20,887. Was Mr. Ritchie's Bill extended by amendment to Ireland?—It is very curious. The Bill undoubtedly dealt with an English Act, the Wine and Beerhouse Act.

20,888. Will you give us the purport of Mr. Ritchie's Bill?—There was a class of beer dealers in England who, as I understand it at the time, and I was in the lobby, and responsible for the alterations that were made for Ireland, could get their licences from the Excise.

20,889. (*Mr. Whittaker.*) Without going to magistrates?—Yes. I am not so certain of my ground as to the English law, but my recollection is that this class of beer retailers were entitled to get their licences from the Excise without going to the magistrates at all. Mr. Ritchie introduced this Bill to bring them all under the magistrates. There was a good deal of feeling about the beerhouses in Ireland at the time. I asked Mr. Ritchie to get the Bill extended to Ireland. He extended the Bill to Ireland by simply striking out the words in the last clause, which was: "This Act may "be cited as the Beer Dealers Retail Licences (Amend- "ment) Act, 1882, and shall not extend to Ireland or "Scotland." He struck out the words "to Ireland" and left it standing, "This Act shall not extend to Scotland." The Bill dealt with an English Act, but to make everything certain they said: "Notwithstanding "anything in section 8 of the Wine and Beerhouse Act, "1869," which is an English Act, "or in any other Act "now in force," and the Irish Courts held that the insertion of the words "or any other Act now in force," covered Ireland, and that the Bill is applicable to Ireland. But it is practically useless, because the magistrates who grant the spirit dealer's certificate will not refuse the beer dealer's certificate.

up to 8l., and in a city or town of 10,000 inhabitants it had to come up to 15l. The Bill was very drastic indeed. It paid no respect to vested interests. It used the words, "a grant or renewal of the certificate," and at the election after the Bill became law, the Excise licensing authority in Dublin, 300 beerhouses were closed at one swoop in the city of Dublin.

20,890. (*Mr. Whittaker.*) Did the Bill provide any compensation?—It did not.

20,891. (*Chairman.*) That was a much stronger step than was taken in England in the year 1869?—In view of the importance of it, I think I had better read the section of the Bill. I see I have not the Bill here, but I know the expression "grant or renewal." I was present at the moment. The whole beerhouse interest was smashed in the city of Dublin by that Bill.

20,892. Who were the owners of these beerhouses?—The most wretched people. They were in cellars and in garrets. It was a shocking state of things.

20,893. They were not in the hands of brewers?—Not at all. There is nothing like a tied-house system in Ireland. The great firm of Guinness & Co. boast that they have not a tied house. I do not suppose that there are 50 tied houses in the whole of Ireland. The brewers have nothing to do with them.

20,894. Were there no indignation meetings held on behalf of these 300 dispossessed beerhouse keepers?—No.

20,895. (*Mr. Walker.*) They were not dispossessed by statute, were they?—Yes, they were.

20,896. (*Sir William Houldsworth.*) In what year was that Act?—It is the 40 Vict. c. 4. I think it was in 1877. It is practically a Bill of one clause. It says this: From and after the 1st day of July 1877, it shall not be lawful "for any officer of Excise in Ireland to "grant a licence or transfer of a licence for the sale of "beer, ale, or porter to be drunk or consumed else- "where than on the premises where sold, or to grant a "renewal of an Excise licence so aforesaid to any "person whatsoever in respect of any premises, unless "upon the production of a certificate that such pre- "mises with premises belonging thereto and occupied "therewith, if any, are rated for the relief of the poor "at a sum of 8l. or upwards."

20,897. (*Mr. Walker.*) That is an attempted qualification?—The effect of it was this: that 300 men who were in statutory possession of premises were disqualified.

20,898. (*Chairman.*) If they had chosen to raise their qualification, could the magistrates have refused the continuance?—I do not think so, if the houses had come up to the statutory requirement.

20,899. (*Dean Dickinson.*) They could not have raised the valuation without a change of premises?—Most of them could not. As I have said, they were cellars.

20,900. (*Mr. Whittaker.*) They had a licence under certain conditions?—They had.

20,901. The magistrates absolutely refused the renewal of the licence on the same conditions, and wiped them out?—Yes, I was present.

20,902. Without any compensation whatever?—Without any compensation whatever. It was a very drastic Bill, no doubt.

20,903. (*Chairman.*) What gave point and vigour to it was that that section was held to be retrospective in its operation?—Certainly. It was one of the most drastic measures I have ever known passed.

20,904. And so it was made applicable to renewals?—It was.

[illegible] the [illegible] of the [illegible] and the [illegible] of the [illegible] to the same.

39,907. So far as Sunday closing goes, there has been no agitation in any of the [illegible] districts for repeal? You have had the same experience in Ireland in that respect that we have had in Scotland, I suppose?—There has never been in any of the Sunday closing areas the slightest symptom of public opinion against the measure.

39,908. Have the publicans themselves become reconciled to it?—The publicans of the country have joined the publicans of the towns in resisting the present Bill, but that is all.

39,909. That is to say, they joined in resisting the extension?—And the Saturday night early closing.

39,910. But they have made no effort to repeal the Sunday Closing Act?—None whatever.

39,911. Was there been any movement in favour of early closing generally in Ireland?—The only matter that I know about that was before the Duke of Westminster's Committee. There was evidence given on that subject; and one of the recommendations of that Committee was that public-houses should be closed an hour earlier on every night of the week.

39,912. A statutory closing?—A statutory closing.

39,913. (Mr. Young.) I think you said that the desire for Sunday closing in the five excepted cities has been growing?—I do not think it is wonderful. It has passed away as a question at elections and all that kind of thing. It used to be a test question at elections, but it has passed out of that condition.

39,914. Your evidence has been very clear, but I think that you will admit with me that the statistics are confined to a very meagre detail?—I feel that difficulty, but, of course, the Commission can alter that very readily.

39,915. Your statistics are almost confined to 1877 and 1871. I only remark that from those periods to the present time the population of the country has greatly decreased and there are many altered conditions existing?—The population has undoubtedly decreased, but I am not very sure that some of the altered conditions have at all tended in the direction of temperance.

39,916. Do you not admit that intemperance has decreased during that long period?—I think so. I think the returns will show that.

39,917. Do you not admit that there may be a great difficulty now in our coming to a conclusion on your figures as to the state of the country at the present moment?—I put in the figures, of course, subject to all the drawbacks of date. I myself do not believe—and I watch these returns very carefully—that the general returns of drunkenness as regards Saturday night arrests, will be substantially altered. If you had the returns for last year I am not sure that they would not be increased. I think Saturday night traffic is becoming an increasing evil.

39,918. Yes, but that, of course, is purely a matter of opinion?—It is a matter of opinion which the Commission could can verify by calling for returns.

39,919. Do you think it is a satisfactory way of ascertaining the minds of the population of a great city to send out ballot papers from a temperance society? In sending out those ballot papers, did not you put on them many other things besides the simple questions?—I think the question was substantially what was on the paper. I cannot tax my recollection as to every word.

39,920. You have not got a specimen of the ballot papers?—I have not.

39,921. On those ballot papers was there not a homily?—There may have been, but it is 20 years ago.

39,922. About happy homes, and all that?—I am sure there was nothing about that. I will not at 20 years' distance tax my memory to say that there was absolutely nothing on the paper but the question; but so to my knowledge, I am sure there was no such thing.

39,923. I am not complaining. I only put it to you that if you were going to ascertain exactly the minds of a population, you would go at the matter in a very different way, would you not?—This was only one of the methods that we took. In addition to that, we had a petition to Parliament signed by everybody in Dublin, and we had great public meetings in Dublin and in all those places. This was only one of the methods out of many that we took to elicit public opinion.

39,924. You may or may not have arrived at a proper conclusion?—Of course that is a matter of opinion.

39,925. I think you will admit that it may not be an accurate way of taking the minds of the people. Why I say so is this. In Belfast, after that canvass was made, I think there was a petition got up and sent to Parliament against the Closing Bill?—Yes.

39,926. And it was signed by many thousands more than appeared on the canvass?—Yes, and the same is true in Dublin. I examined the petitions in the vaults of the House of Commons here, and I found my own name 15 times in the Dublin petition, and the name of the late Mr. A. M. Sullivan on almost every page.

39,927. Do you not admit me to discount the value of the canvass?—No. I will not admit you to say anything of the kind. I simply say this, that so far as the temperance party was concerned at that time, this was one of many methods that we took to elicit public opinion, fairly and honestly. As to the value of our work, that was for Parliament to decide, not for us.

39,928. You got 72,000 people to sign these ballot papers out of a population of 300,000 inhabitants?—Yes.

39,929. You agree with me that you are not quite sure that in the signing of those petitions there were not more names than heads of houses?—A matter of that kind must, of course, be undergone with precautions, and what I say is that individually in all those five cities (Mr. A. M. Sullivan was my chairman at the time) we endeavoured to carry out this work as fairly as it was possible to do it. That we might not be deceived in some cases, that people might not sign who ought not to have signed, I am not here to say. It was submitted in every test. The opponents of the Bill had the whole 40,000 papers before them. They were submitted to every test, and I have never yet heard of a single successful test being applied against them.

39,930. (Dean Dickinson.) The papers were not scattered broadcast, but given individually to the heads of houses?—Yes, and collected the next day. I do not claim perfection for it, but I do say this, that the temperance party endeavoured to elicit public opinion, and the opponents of the temperance party never made any effort to elicit it at all.

39,931. (Mr. Young.) I think you expressed an opinion that there should be total Sunday closing?—I have not expressed any opinion. Of course, everybody knows what my opinion is, but I am here under some difficulty. The truth is I am, I suppose, the only person now living who could give the facts I have now given, but I am sure the Commission will recognise that on a question of policy I ought not to be pressed.

39,932. Suppose I put it to you that the official witnesses, and in fact the experts in the matter of ascertaining the condition of crime in the country who came before us, are generally of opinion that there should be open public-houses from 2 to 5 o'clock, is it your opinion that they have a right to understand that that would be good for the community?—Well, I should like to see the evidence and to know the witnesses. If you tell me that the police are in favour of reverting to the sale of drink and against Sunday closing, it is a matter of very great surprise to me.

39,933. (Mr. Graham.) This question of Sunday closing resolves itself more or less into a question of expediency, does it not?—Well, I should not quarrel with that.

39,934. Where you find that a very large proportion of the population—I will say the mass of the artisans particularly—have strong views opposed to entire restriction, you would attach great weight to it?—Those views, however, would have found their expression in Parliament.

39,935. You do attach considerable importance to the voting that has taken place from time to time with reference to the Sale of Intoxicating Liquors (Ireland) Bill, I understand?—Yes. I attach some importance to it, of course.

39,936. The last time that it came before the House was on May 12, 1897, was it not?—Yes.

39,937. Is it a fact that the majority for the Bill on that occasion was 89?—Yes.

39,938. As against 99 in a previous division?—Yes.

Mr. T. W. Russell, M.P.

28 April 1897.

Sunday closing.

Irish Sunday closing in Parliament.

39,939. Of course it is very important in a question concerning Ireland, above all other countries—more so than Scotland or England—that the feeling of the Irish people should have expression in this matter?—Yes.

39,940. Looking at the votes given by the Irish members, I find that on that occasion the number of votes given by the Irish Nationalist members in favour was 16, and against 23?—Yes.

39,941. That does not show that, so far as the Irish members are concerned, on a question peculiarly interesting to Ireland, a majority were in favour of the restriction sought to be imposed?—It strikes me as rather a peculiar method of dealing with the Irish vote that you should take the Irish Nationalist vote and exclude the Irish Unionist vote.

[illegible] of absolutely [illegible] tending to bogus clubs was claimed by her to commence?—That was at the time when bogus clubs were rather giving trouble. I have had experience of Cardinal Cullen and Cardinal M'Cabe, who were both Archbishops of Dublin, and they were both in favour of this legislation. Cardinal Cullen was one of the founders of the Association. Archbishop Walsh has come to Dublin since I left. I can quite understand Archbishop Walsh saying that if bogus clubs were to be allowed to prevail there was no use in interfering with the licensed trade. My case is that the police have [illegible] dealt with them, and the magistrates have backed them up. Outside Dublin they do not exist; and they have been brought under control in Dublin.

[illegible]. I gather that you are in favour of the extension of Sunday closing to these exempted cities. I must be here to [illegible] out very clearly that there is a great weight of opinion behind, that if you extended it the result would be bogus clubs and shebeens and other improper and illicit places?—You will be very much astonished when I tell you that it was entirely owing to my influence in 1878 that the cities were exempted. The temperance men were resolutely opposed to the acceptance of the Government amendment in 1878; and I was almost alone in advocating that the cities should be exempted. I do not say what my opinion is now, but as a matter of policy I [illegible] to them. I have no [illegible] on this question. I [illegible] that things cannot be carried [illegible] in [illegible] or [illegible] [illegible]; it is quite impossible. Anyone who has spent 10 or 12 years in the House of Commons knows that. It is a case where the legitimate wants of the people must be attended to. Those wants should be supplied with due regard to the public interest and welfare. That is my case.

[illegible]. Suppose, for a moment, the adoption of Sunday closing in the exempted areas did result in the production of bogus clubs and shebeens, do you not think that, as a matter of policy, greater evils are likely to arise from drinking in bogus clubs than in a public-house under the supervision of the police?—That is a hypothetical question which I am prepared to answer when it comes about, but I would rather not answer it now; it is pure hypothesis.

[illegible]. I take it that it is only the abuse of drinking and not the use of it that you object to as an evangelist?—What does it matter what I object to as to the use or abuse of drink? I am here as a public man, not as [illegible] drinking. I have my own views about it, but what do they matter? If I were a drinker it would not alter one figure or fact which I have quoted to-day. I am really giving my opinion as a public man, and not as a [illegible] at all.

[illegible]. Do you consider that if a man is moderation [illegible] beer or [illegible] or anything of the kind, say he takes a pint of beer to his dinner and a glass to his supper on days in the week, he ought not to be at liberty to get it on the seventh?—If that were the whole case I am sure you would not be sitting here to investigate the question.

[illegible]. You quoted 19 cities, and gave your statement of drunkenness. Were those 19 cities taken [illegible]?—It is a Parliamentary Return of the only towns with a population of 10,000. Saturday night drinking is considered a greater evil in the towns than in the country; and Mr. [illegible] took a population of 10,000 as the [illegible].

[illegible]. If you take the five exempted cities, which [illegible] a population of [illegible], the average number of Sunday arrests was only [illegible] or 1 in every [illegible]. That does not seem to be a very extraordinary amount?

[illegible]. (Mr. [illegible].) You are quite clear that Sunday closing has not produced Sunday clubs and shebeens?—As to bogus clubs, certainly it has not; as to shebeens, there has been some difficulty. The old Act dealing with shebeens had the offence "keeping for sale." The Act of 1872, which has practically taken its place, does not [illegible] to the offence of "keeping for sale." The difficulty the police have is this, that under the old Act the penalty of "keeping for sale" is a very small one, and they prosecute under the new Act of 1872. The difficulty of proving an act of sale in a shebeen is very great. If you had 100 bottles of beer in a person's house, and all the machinery of drinking, the magistrate will come to the conclusion that he was keeping that drink for sale. But where you have to prove the actual sale the thing is very difficult. That is a drawback to the law.

[illegible]. There has been no special outbreak of shebeening?—No.

[illegible]. And no bogus clubs?—Mr. [illegible] was absolutely right when he said that the Act had in no way gone beyond public opinion.

[illegible]. May I ask you if before the Act was passed it was predicted that these results, shebeening and bogus clubs, would follow?—The predictions were most alarming. There were a great many things to happen that have never come about.

[illegible]. As these predictions have been utterly falsified with regard to the closing that has taken place, is it a fair assumption, is it not, that you must not attach too much importance to such predictions?—I am never troubled about predictions about anything. I wait for the facts.

[illegible]. With regard to the present Sunday Closing Act, may I ask you whether since 1878—during the last [illegible] years—any Irish member has opposed the renewal of the present Sunday Closing Act?—No, and even Irish members who say that they are opposed to the Bill as it now stands, including Saturday night, declare that they would not oppose a simple renewal of the present Act. That is never contemplated.

[illegible]. May I take it that you could not have a stronger indication of Irish opinion than the fact that throughout the whole of the Irish members not one single member has been found in [illegible] years to oppose the renewal of the Sunday Closing Act as it now stands?—It has been brought in in the Expiring Laws Continuance Act every year, and it has never been opposed. There is no member who has made a motion or introduced a Bill to do anything of the kind.

[illegible]. With regard to the [illegible] vote. Do I understand you that that vote was influenced to some extent by the fact that this Commission was sitting?—Mr. Arthur Balfour made a speech. He had stated when he was Chief Secretary that the day for argument had passed, and he stated in the House of Commons that with his views upon the question, and with his knowledge, he [illegible] vote for the Bill, but that his colleagues held very strongly that no legislation ought to take place while this Commission was sitting; and that is a [illegible] and a reasonable ground to take. That, I have no doubt, accounts for the diminished number of the English vote. From circumstances that do not lie known to the members of the Commission, the attendance of the Irish Nationalist members is exceedingly [illegible]. It is exceedingly difficult to get them to come for measures of this kind. Undoubtedly great efforts were made I suppose on both sides; I am aware that there were on the Opposition side, and notwithstanding those efforts, only [illegible] Irish members could be found to vote against the Bill, including Saturday in the towns, and everything.

[illegible]. (Mr. [illegible].) Your [illegible] does not account for the [illegible] of the Irish [illegible]

Mr. T. W. Russell, M.P.

[illegible]

Sunday closing and clubs, shebeens, &c.

Keeping for sale.

Renewal of the Sunday Closing Act not opposed.

Sunday closing in Parliament.

Mr. T. W. Russell, M.P.

[illegible]

59,994. (Mr. Walker.) Do I understand you to imply that the House of Commons was influenced by the fact that this Commission was sitting, and that they did not so strenuously support the measure as they otherwise would have done?—I cannot state that. Mr. Arthur Balfour, speaking for the Government, said that he, owing to his views, voted, but that his colleagues held a different opinion, as the Commission was sitting. It was a very reasonable ground to take.

59,995. If there existed in the minds of those charged with this measure the desirability of paying respect to this Commission, why did they bring it forward at all?—The promoters of the Bill had not the same view that the responsible Government had. I have been speaking of the Government, not of the Members of the House of Commons. Of course the position taken by the Government would influence a certain number of their supporters. I think it is a perfectly reasonable view, and one that there is a great deal to be said for.

59,996. Does not the mere fact that the measure did not receive the support last session that it did the previous session indicate that the desire for Sunday closing is not so strong as it was?—I have been explaining to the best of my ability the abstention of votes that would have been given for the Bill on perfectly rational grounds by the Government. I am not prepared to admit that that shows any failure of interest in it.

59,997. (Dean Dickinson.) Or change of opinion?—Or change of opinion.

59,998. (Mr. Walker.) Change of opinion on the part of the Irish electors?—Oh, no.

59,999. The fact remains that the measure was not supported last session in the manner that it was on the previous occasion?—It remains that the majority for the second reading of the Bill, in consequence of Government abstention, was [illegible]. That fact remains, and there was an Irish majority for it notwithstanding.

[illegible] Act

60,000. This Act of 1877 related to the beerhouses. I think it is rather a misnomer, as it was, for beerhouses to be carried on in a cellar or one room?—They got beerhouse licences.

60,001. They were simply Excise licences?—Yes. Of course they were obtained for consumption off the premises, and the whole of it was consumed on the premises.

60,002. I want to obtain from you an admission, if I can, that these, what you term beerhouses, which were carried on in one room, or in some dirty cellar, did not incur any expense in their establishment?—Not a farthing.

60,003. They merely got a cask of beer and sold it?—They were the most wretched places you could imagine, I have been through them.

60,004. Therefore in the strict sense of the term there was no confiscation where no expenditure had been incurred?—There was confiscation of the man's income, whatever that was.

60,005. (Chairman.) And some of them, I suppose, had been licensed year after year for a long period?—I cannot say for a lengthy period, because they were constantly prosecuted for breaking the law; but they were there in possession of a licence, and that licence was [illegible] in the ordinary way, and Parliament said it shall not be renewed except on conditions.

60,006. (Mr. Walker.) It was an Excise licence that anyone could obtain?—Quite so. It was not got from the magistrates in the way of a publican's licence.

60,007. It was not a magistrates' licence?—Yes, it was statutory.

60,008. It was not brought into existence by custom, was it?—Not at all.

60,009. Can you give me the date when Parliament were unanimous to carry on business in such a manner?

60,010. There shall be a valuation of 15l. in cities, and 8l. in country places?—Yes. The Act under which these beerhouse licences were granted was the Beer Retailers', Spirit Grocers', and Wholesale Beer Dealers' Licenses Act, 1864.

60,011. Parliament permitted persons to take out Excise licences, and sell beer in any small or dirty cellar?—That was so.

60,012. There was no confiscation if they occupied premises of the value you state. They still held their licences. Is that so?—You say there was no confiscation. I should imagine that there are many publicans with valuations of 8l. even in small wretched places. I do not know that the Commission would be prepared, if Parliament said no licence shall be granted to a publican whose valuation was not 8l., to say that there was no confiscation there.

60,013. You told the Commission that you had been, I understand, for 21 years secretary, or Parliamentary agent, of the temperance party of Ireland?—Yes.

60,014. Does that, in other words, mean the teetotal party of Ireland?—Oh dear, no. The Sunday closing movement was largely financed by non-abstainers. There was no distinction of that kind.

60,015. What do I understand you to mean by the temperance party of Ireland?—I mean exactly what I said. The temperance party was a party of good citizens, irrespective of personal habits, combined to bring about reforms of the law that they considered for the welfare of the people.

60,016. The temperance party, as you represent it, were not teetotallers?—Not all, and not nearly all.

60,017. (Dean Dickinson.) Nor one-half?—Not one-half.

60,018. (Mr. Walker.) Are you yourself opposed to the existence of this trade under any circumstances?—No, not under any circumstances. If you ask me my opinion, as a politician, upon that, I am prepared to go with public opinion, and not one step further.

60,019. When the plebiscite was taken?—It was not a plebiscite. I guarded myself against that.

60,020. It was a house-to-house visitation?—It was a paper to be signed by heads of families only.

60,021. So that if there were in some instances 14 families in a house, would you leave 14 papers there?—Yes; 14 families in different rooms.

60,022. An officer was charged to discover the head of the family?—Yes.

60,023. I suppose he made a return that he had done so?—They made a return every night to the [illegible].

60,024. They left the paper?—They left the paper.

60,025. The signature was sufficient with a cross?—Yes.

60,026. Are you in possession of the number of the papers that were returned signed simply with a cross?—No. The papers that were counted were signed as required, by the signature of the party, and a cross.

60,027. Then you are not prepared to say what number of the papers were signed simply by a cross?—There were none counted unless the signature was attached with the cross.

60,028. Would that indicate that those who signed those papers were uneducated?—The vote was largest in the parts where the district was poorest.

60,029. Would you mind answering my question. Did simply being signed by a cross indicate that those persons were uneducated, and unable to sign their names?—I have not admitted that they were sent in without a signature at all.

60,030. (Mr. Whitbread.) You did not count any that were not signed?—No.

60,031. (Mr. William [illegible].) That was

[illegible]. But you will admit that there is a strong desire, as we have had evidence here, on the part of crowds of men waiting to obtain refreshment on a Sunday when the houses are closed?—Yes. I will tell you what I saw with my own eyes. I have seen people who were recovering from a late Saturday night debauch going out to the "Fox and Goose" on the [illegible] Road [illegible] on Sunday morning, when the [illegible] public-houses were shut, in order to get drink. My view of that is this, and this is not a question of policy at all, that if the overwhelming mass of the people decide that that convenience shall not exist, the opinion of the overwhelming mass should prevail against the desires of those men recovering from a Saturday night's debauch.

[illegible]. That is, that the law should be absolute in favour of the majority, notwithstanding that there is a large minority?—It depends on the character of the minority. I should also add that I consider the law to be a great educative power in this matter, and that the duty of Parliament is to make it easy for those people to do right, and a little difficult for them to do wrong. I would go so far in the way of paternal Government as that.

[illegible]. I understand you to express yourself in favour of entire Sunday closing?—The Chairman put that to me, and I think he saw it might [illegible] the principle that I have laid down. I would rather not express that. Of course nobody can mistake what my position is. It is perfectly well understood in the country. I say frankly that I have always held that the country and these large towns differ. I have always held that the circumstances differ, and I am not prepared to spoil the ship for a [illegible] of tar; and I am not prepared to lose a substantial gain because I cannot get all I want.

[illegible]. As a principle of policy would you like large towns exempted?—No, I do not say exempted, but I have my own views as to how they should be treated. I would rather the Commission would not press me upon a question of policy which is vital.

[illegible]. I take it you are of opinion that the closing of public-houses earlier on Saturday evening meets with universal approval. May I ask you what you mean by universal approval?—I think I might qualify that a little. I speak of public opinion generally. I should imagine all the responsible men in those large towns would welcome it. I am certain that the clergy of all the churches would welcome it, and that public opinion on a whole would support it. I must not be understood to say there would be no opponents. There would be to anything; but I am satisfied that the magistrates and the police are committed to it.

[illegible]. Would you close all other shops at the same time?—Oh, dear, no. Why should I do that?

[illegible]. Do you decline to answer the question?—No. The shops are not limited to hours by law now.

[illegible]. No, only it would be a strange sight to see the streets thronged with people marketing and all the houses of refreshment closed?—I should say it would be a very happy sight for a great many people, and a very happy thing for the wives and families who have to do the marketing.

[illegible]. You say: "I am aware the responsible

Mr. T. W. Russell, M.P.

24 April '97

diminished. Excepting, perhaps, in those large areas surrounding the big towns, the evil has been unsatisfactorily dealt with. I drove on an experiment round county Wicklow myself last year [illegible] going back to 18[illegible], and I was perfectly astonished to see the order prevailing. There was no attempt to evade the Act at all, even in that beautiful county, which is the resort on Sunday of tourists.

60,057. You have known instances where the police have brought forward evidence to show that a man had been drinking in other public-houses than the one in which they found him, and were able to secure a conviction, and that that man has not been a bonâ fide traveller?—Yes. As a magistrate myself, I have sat on appeals at Kilmainham where [illegible] bonâ fide travellers have come up, and the Recorder of Dublin has always dealt in a legal manner with them. It is a real evil, because the magistrates and the police have come to believe, I do not know how, that the mere travelling three miles gives the right to get drink.

Mixed trades on licensed premises.

60,058. With reference to the carrying on of other trades on licensed premises, are you of opinion that that is a temptation to drink?—Of course, if you take the original idea of what a public-house was intended to be, it was not intended to be a grocer's shop. It was intended to be a house of entertainment for travellers. That was the original conception of the licensing laws. The Commission must judge for themselves whether a woman on Saturday night going into a public-house for the purchase of groceries is not exposed to temptations to which she ought not to be exposed by having drink sold at her elbow. Of course, there is a difficulty in dealing with a new [illegible] that the evil is done.

60,059. Do you know of other trades besides that of grocery being carried on in the same premises?—Yes. Drapery, ironmongery, and in many cases a post-office.

60,060. Where the goods are sold at one counter, and the liquor at another?—No, where they are sold at the same counter.

60,061. If a limit of time were given to the holders of licenses who carry on other trades, and they had to take their choice between surrendering the license or the trade, do you think that would be advisable?—That, again, is a question of policy, and I think the Commission would have the greatest difficulty in dealing with it, seeing that it is an established rule, and that 12,000 out of 18,000 houses are carried on now in that [illegible] way. My view of all these licensing questions is that you cannot go ahead of public opinion, but that you must carry it with you.

60,062. Do you think public opinion is in favour of continuing the present system?—No, but I think if there were anything like a general order that these two trades were to be separated it would cause a very great deal of friction and trouble and perhaps a great deal of loss to the publicans. I think there would be great difficulty.

60,063. You do not think if a limit of time were given that a very large number of these smaller public-houses might be discontinued automatically?—That affects more the valuation than the joint trade.

60,064. I am directing my question to the fact of the evil of the carrying on of the two trades under the same roof?—You must take it that it exists, and it is for the Commission to take the responsibility of finding a remedy.

60,065. You have not given any opinion with regard to the constitution of the licensing authority. Do you wish to state anything as to that?—I would rather not. I know what it is myself, but I would rather you give an opinion.

60,066. (*Dean Dickinson.*) You are aware that licenses are granted with great facility in Ireland, are you not?—They have been.

60,067. (*Sir Algernon West.*) Will you tell me why Derry is excluded from the exempted cities?—Mr. Charles Lewis—afterwards Sir Charles Lewis—was member for Derry at the time, and he made it impossible to exempt Derry, although Derry has a larger population than Waterford.

60,068. Would you object to giving the Commission your views upon compensation?—I think that would be taking me into ground which I am absolutely precluded from entering upon.

60,069. I think you said they would compensate you?—I voted for Mr. [illegible]'s scheme in the House of Commons, but I should be obliged to the Commission if they would not press me upon that.

60,070. (*Mr. Young.*) In a small village in a rural district, is it not convenient that the two trades should be carried on together in one house?—Convenient. For what?

60,071. Convenient for the public?—Very convenient for the publican.

60,072. The farmers all round come in and they want their tea and various other articles, and they want their liquor as well. May I put this to you, that the grocer could not live by selling tea, he could scarcely live by selling drapery, and it is necessary for him that he should combine other trades?—Is it your case that a man can only live in Ireland by selling whisky? Surely it has not come to that.

60,073. Is it not necessary that there should be a combination of trades, for the sake of the trader and for the sake of the public?—I do not think there is any necessity about it.

The witness withdrew.

Adjourned for a short time.

Mr. [illegible] F. C[illegible] called in and examined.

Mr. [illegible] F. C[illegible].

Position of witness.

60,074. (*Chairman.*) You are a resident magistrate stationed at Kilkenny?—Yes.

60,075. You have been resident magistrate I think for several years?—Yes, for the last 16 years.

60,076. What is your district?—My district comprises almost the entire of the county Kilkenny with the exception of a small portion just at the end which belongs to Waterford, and it also extends to a portion of the Queen's County.

60,077. It includes therefore a great number of petty sessional divisions?—It includes 15 different petty sessions districts and two borough courts, or two courts under the Towns Improvement Act.

60,078. It comprises an area of what extent?—Of something over 1,000 square miles.

60,079. You have acted besides in other counties?—I have also acted in the county of Cork; I was stationed there for some time; and in Kerry I was also stationed for over five years. I have acted also in several other counties.

60,080. Do you attend 15 different petty sessions?—Yes, I do.

60,081. Are they held at different times?—They are nearly all on different days. One would be the first Monday and the first Tuesday, and so on.

60,082. Fortnightly and monthly?—Fortnightly and monthly, and some weekly.

60,083. (*Viscount de Vesci.*) Mostly fortnightly?—No, mostly monthly in my district.

60,084. (*Chairman.*) Besides attending petty sessions you also, I think, attend quarter sessions?—Yes, as an ordinary justice.

60,085. Can you state what is the jurisdiction of petty sessions. What do they deal with?—The court of petty sessions consists of the justices of the peace and the resident magistrate. It deals with almost all cases under the Licensing Acts; it deals with the granting of spirit grocers' licenses and beer dealers' licenses, the [illegible] wholesale beer dealers' licenses and retailers' licenses. It deals also with transfers, with certificates of [illegible]

[illegible] an appeal lies from their decision to the [illegible]?—Yes, in all cases an appeal lies from [illegible] to the quarter sessions.

[illegible] as to the constitution of the quarter [illegible]—The quarter sessions court consists of the [illegible] judge at the [illegible] sitting as chairman [illegible] magistrates of the division and the resident [illegible], and it deals with all appeals from petty [illegible], the confirmation of transfers and [illegible] of new licences.

[illegible] from the decision of quarter sessions [illegible] appeal?—No, there is no appeal.

Do you object to the mode of granting of [illegible] or beer licences or [illegible]—I should consider the granting of all these [illegible] the licensing authority I shall suggest, and [illegible] permit me, I will deal with that a little later.

When we come to your suggested reforms?—

No objection can be taken to the granting of [illegible], except on the ground of the character of [illegible] and or the suitability of the premises?—Yes, as regards spirit grocers and [illegible] beer [illegible], but as regards beer retailers that is [illegible] with the magistrates. With reference [illegible] of new licences an objection can be [illegible] the ground also of there being a sufficient [illegible].

In the case of transfers, the only objection

are houses such as were referred to a short time ago. The accommodation largely consists of merely a bar [illegible] by a [illegible], and shut off by that [illegible] either from the small shop or from the ordinary living rooms of the house.

Mr. E. F. [illegible]

26 April '98

63,108. Then when you say that the houses are fully licensed houses, are we to understand that there are public-houses in the ordinary acceptation of the term?—Yes, certainly, the ordinary every-day houses.

63,109. Do they conform to one's idea of a pure and simple public-house?—Oh dear no. I did not intend to convey that. There are very few pure and simple public-houses. These houses are largely run in connection with small grocers' establishments but not as a [illegible] grocery establishment in any sense.

Constitution of courts.

63,110. Are they mere drinking shops or public-houses where refreshments might be obtained as well?—No, not refreshments. They have no such thing as refreshments in the vast majority of cases. Of course there are exceptions.

63,111. ([illegible]) There are one or three [illegible] in the city of Kilkenny?—Yes. I am not referring to those but I am referring chiefly to the lower class public-houses to which attention has been called.

63,112. (Chairman.) Do you observe any change in the drunkenness of the last few years, either in the county or the city?—There is practically no change so far as I can detect. If there is any change at all it would be in a decrease of drunkenness. All the same, there is a vast amount of drunkenness.

Great prevalence of drunkenness.

Mr. [illegible] Gunning [illegible] April '99 — there are no refreshment houses or breakfast houses of any kind open, and it naturally arose that with the drink there, under the people's noses (if I may use the expression), they [illegible] drink at a time they ought not to have it, and when they have had no food; and I have known several cases myself of persons who have taken no food up to 3 o'clock in the day, though they have been up all night, but they all had drink.

60,126. Up to 3 o'clock in the day?—Yes.

60,126. They have had opportunities of getting something to eat before 3 o'clock?—Yes. They would have lots of opportunities, but they commenced by drinking. My point is, that if they had not had the drink before them at that early hour, and had had a reasonable hope for their breakfast, they would have gone to their breakfast and taken food, but with the temptation to drink before them—urged on their [illegible] naturally [illegible] to it.

60,127. Is it peculiar to Kilkenny that these [illegible] exemption orders should be granted?—I have never known it anywhere else.

60,128. They do not come up for revision for a twelvemonth?—That is so. When I went to Kilkenny first the number of exemption orders—that is, 11 years ago—was very large indeed. I cannot give the number, but I think the majority of the houses had exemption orders. I urged on the magistrates the desirability of doing away with them.

60,129. By that [illegible] of exemption orders you might violate the whole operation of the licensing laws?—Entirely. The only hours that you cannot grant an exemption order for are between 1 and 5 o'clock in the morning, but you may grant exemption orders for any other times you like.

Occasional licences.

60,130. In this connexion what do you say to occasional licences? Are they granted with some latitude?—Yes, but occasional licences are not given for the fairs and markets. They are chiefly given in connexion with race meetings and [illegible] meetings and things of that kind. They are given with certainly a considerable amount of freedom.

60,131. Are they given in anticipation of the coming year?—No, only for a special occasion, and they can only last, under the law, for three days.

60,132. They may be renewed, may they not?—Yes, they may, but it is not so. They are granted only for those occasions, and granted within definite hours.

60,133. Therefore you have not so much complaint to make of occasional licences as of the exemptions?—I make no complaint of the occasional licences, but I think exemption orders are granted in the most unnecessary manner, and I think they contribute very much to the amount of drunkenness.

Price of whisky [illegible] quality.

60,134. You touched on the quality of the whisky just now; what is the price of it?—Whisky is sold in Kilkenny, or advertised for sale in Kilkenny, at 12s. 6d. a gallon. Now the duty is 10s. 6d. per proof gallon, and it can be reduced by 25 per cent. of water. I have calculated that the actual duty on the gallon so reduced would be about 8s. 3d.; that would leave 3s. 3d. to pay for the actual cost of the whisky, to pay for all expenses attendant on it, and to provide a profit. When I mention that the price of the best whisky fresh from the still, such as that produced by Messrs. John Power and Son, and John Jameson, is from 4s. to 5s. a gallon, the inference is very [illegible] as to the quality of the material provided for 12s. 6d.

of pints of porter," but when I pressed them on the point it generally turned out they had had a glass of whisky also, and the frequent saying with regard to that by the police was, "Well, sir, it is the whisky that has done it, and not the beer or porter."

Mr. [illegible] Gunning

60,141. It is difficult to say if a man takes two pints of porter and one glass of whisky what has operated most deleteriously?—That is certainly so, but I think there are very few persons that two pints of porter would make drunk, and when you have the circumstanced fact that they have become drunk, and then they had had two pints of porter and a glass of whisky, it being admitted that two pints of porter would not do it, I think the other inference is clear. I do not think with regard to the beer and porter supplied there is any such ground for complaint with regard to it.

Use of beer and porter spreading.

60,142. Is the use of beer and porter spreading as compared with whisky?—I think it is.

60,143. Saturday is a half-holiday?—Yes.

60,144. The wages day is not necessarily Saturday?—No, but it frequently is.

60,145. They are paid on Friday night?—Friday night.

Sunday drunkenness.

60,146. Do you think on Saturday night there is an increased amount of drunkenness?—Unquestionably. There is more drunkenness on Saturday night than any other night in the week. I have no statistics whatever on the point, though I did at one time, when I had to give evidence before a Commission, get statistics which unquestionably proved it. I think Mr. T. W. Russell stated them here to-day, but the facts of police summons show it very clearly. Monday is our [illegible] court, and on the Monday there are a great many more cases coming up than on any other day.

60,147. Saturday being a leisure day, and there being money in their pockets, the temptation is to take more drink than is necessary?—Quite so.

Number of licensed houses in Kilkenny City.

60,148. Do you think the number of licensed houses is adequate, or excessive, or below the need?—Largely excessive. In my opinion the great evil in my district and in Ireland as I know it, is the excessive number of the public-houses. In Kilkenny we have a public-house to every 100 of the population.

60,149. Are you talking of fully-licensed houses of all kinds?—All kinds of licensed houses, but as I have said already, you may take them all as being practically fully-licensed houses.

60,150. Are there no grocers' licences?—I cannot recall one at this moment. I think there is one now.

60,151. (Mr. Gunning.) Licensed quite recently?—Yes. That is the only one I can recollect.

One public-house to [illegible]

60,152. (Chairman.) Taking licensed houses, there is 1 to every 100 of the population?—Yes, including women and children in the city of Kilkenny, and in the county of Kilkenny, there is 1 to every 218 of the population. At the last licensing sessions in Kilkenny I heard the responsible officer of the constabulary there swear that, in his opinion, 50 per cent. of the existing licensed houses in the city of Kilkenny would be ample for the requirements of the place.

60,153. That is in your opinion that the licences are too many by half?—Yes.

60,154. That 50 per cent. are unnecessary?—Yes, I consider 50 per cent. are unnecessary, and as I say, I heard the responsible officer of the constabulary swear that in his opinion 33 per cent of these existing houses and according to my recollection, there were 54 public-houses there. He described it accurately when he said you would find it difficult in going up the main street to find a house that was not a public-house.

60,159. Is the proportion excessive now?—I cannot tell you now what the proportion is. I should think probably it has decreased a little. The magistrates were very anxious to reduce the number when I was there.

60,160. How did it come about that Castleisland was so pre-eminently favoured as to public-houses?—I cannot tell you.

60,161. (*Mr. Grubb.*) Where do you get the figures from with reference to Castleisland of the proportion of licensed premises to population?—I was there for five years.

60,162. The statistics we have show 1 to 129 of the population?—They may have taken a different region altogether to what I did.

60,163. It is Castleisland, Co. Kerry?—That is the Castleisland district, because the population of Castleisland itself, according to the last return, was under 1,500.

60,164. (*Chairman.*) You are talking of the village of Castleisland?—Yes.

60,165. (*Mr. Grubb.*) We must distinguish between the town and the district?—I am dealing purely with the village of Castleisland.

60,166. (*Mr. Young.*) They sell to the neighbourhood?—Of course they do. They will sell to any person that will buy from them.

60,167. (*Chairman.*) When you speak of Castleisland being the most drunken and lawless place you have known, you are speaking of the village with a population of 1,450?—I am speaking of the village and of the general district.

60,168. (*Mr. Grubb.*) It has 15,000 population?—That is the district all round.

60,169. When it is stated that there is 1 to 30 in the village of Castleisland, that conveys a wrong impression. It is the statistics of a district?—It might to a certain extent convey that unquestionably, but not more than it would as regards the town I think.

60,170. (*Sir William Houldsworth.*) Still it is true of the village of Castleisland, as I understand?—Most absolutely true at the date I speak of 20 years ago. I cannot tell you now because I am not there, and I did not look into the matter. I merely mentioned the fact.

Magistrates' ambition to reduce number.

60,171. (*Chairman.*) Where do you look for reform?—Well, I should like to see the public-houses reduced in number and improved in quality; and I believe that if you reduce the number you will improve the quality.

Reform cannot be carried out under present licensing authority.

60,172. Do you think that those two reforms you have indicated can be carried out under the existing licensing system?—No, I think not. I should alter the existing licensing authority; and I wish to guard myself in what I say now against making any reflection upon the magistrates in the discharge of their duty. I do not mean to impute to them any intentional wrong doing as regards the licensing. I merely consider that from the circumstances of the whole position, they are not the proper tribunal.

60,173. Do you think they are acted on by their local associations?—Yes, I think they are acted on by local associations—some of them; and I know some of them are approached, and that they yield to the pressure.

60,174. You think they are influenced by their relationships, social or family relationship?—Some of them might be by family relationship in the case of some applications.

60,175. We will talk of the system and we will not single out any particular magistrate. Are there any licensing ... of magistrates there, but the vast majority of magistrates never give a thought to the licensing question. It is not that they mean to do wrong, but they are just a unsuitable tribunal.

Mr. W. F. Considine.

21 April 1897.

Lavish granting of new licences.

60,176. Do they readily grant new licences?—Yes, with the greatest facility. There is no trouble as a rule in getting a licence.

60,177. Can you give us any figures to prove the increase of licences?—No, I cannot, but I thought I heard Mr. Russell read out the figures, and I think he said there were 16,000 at one time and 18,000 now.

60,178. What district are we speaking of?—I think of the number of public-houses in Ireland.

60,179. I am confining myself as much as possible to Kilkenny?—I cannot give you figures on that point.

Proposed licensing authority.

60,180. As you find fault with the present system, apart from those who administer the present system, would you create a new licensing authority?—Yes, I would constitute as the licensing authority, the county court judge, and if it be deemed advisable, I would suggest the addition to him of the resident magistrate of the district. I would suggest the resident magistrate because he has a large amount usually of local knowledge which would possibly prove useful in the case of conflicting testimony.

60,181. You would exclude the magistrates or justices altogether?—Yes, I would.

60,182. You would let the county court judge sit with the resident magistrate to hear all cases?—I would transfer to him all these licensing applications, or rather the power of granting all licences that is at present vested in the petty sessions court, and I would make him the licensing authority for the granting of new licences, and for the granting of exemption orders. I would leave the granting of occasional licences in the hands of the present authority, or as has been suggested, to one in the hands of the resident magistrate.

Trial of licensing offences at petty sessions.

60,183. You would leave very little for the petty sessions to do in the way of licensing?—I would leave nothing to petty sessions, except to deal with offences, of course, but as regards granting licences, I would place it entirely in the hands of the new licensing authority.

60,184. Why do you stop at leaving them jurisdiction for offences?—I would leave them to try those the same as they would try a case of assault. They would deal with drunkenness.

60,185. Do not you think the same bias would come in there, in your judgment?—No, I do not think so. They are acting there as jurors, and my experience is they act fairly.

60,186. Supposing there was a charge against a man of permitting drunkenness?—I do not think they would act unfairly.

60,187. You think they would exercise a fair discretion?—I do.

Convicting before the end of offences.

60,188. Have you ever known cases where there has been an offence tried before a magistrate, and the magistrate has been convicted in respect of that charge?—I have heard of cases of the kind, but I have never known one myself. I do not think the magistrate would probably mention it to me. Any magistrate capable of being convicted in a matter of that kind would probably keep it to himself. I have heard statements, but I have never heard some of it myself.

60,189. My difficulty would be this: if the magistrates are so unfit to deal with ordinary licensing cases, why should they be entrusted with the very delicate affair of adjudicating on offences against the licensing laws?—One is merely the granting of these licences. As I have said, I do not think they have ever considered carefully the question of licensing at all, and are not conscious of doing any wrong by either granting according to their view or refusing a licence, but to deal with a case of an actual offence is another matter altogether.

Mr. M. F. Considine.

20 Apr. 1898.

licences, and everything with reference to those offences? —Yes.

60,191. That is to say, that in the latter case you do not think that [illegible] is at all prevalent in endeavouring to [illegible] the magistrates with reference to a criminal offence?—Yes.

60,192. In the other case of granting licences there is a great prevalence of canvassing?—Exactly. I have not known magistrates canvassed as regards their dealing with offences.

60,193. (*Chairman.*) You have heard of one case, but you do not know of any?—Yes, I have heard of a case, but I never knew one to my knowledge.

60,194. Constituting this licensing authority in the way you propose, and transferring to them all licences except occasional licences, and leaving all jurisdiction over offences to the petty sessional divisions, comes to be your reform so far?—Yes, up to this point.

Reduction of licences by purchase.

60,195. Then as respects renewals?—At the present moment renewals can only be opposed on the ground of the character of the applicant and the manner in which he has conducted his house within the previous twelve months. I should be disposed to extend to Ireland the power of objecting to renewals on the ground of the unsuitability of the premises and the unnecessity for the existence of the house, but I would not go to the extent of making that a ground for the absolute rejection of the licence or rather refusal of the renewal, but I would suggest the court that would be the licensing authority, on being satisfied that the premises were not suitable and the house was unnecessary, to grant a certificate to that effect, and on that certificate being granted, the justices should bring that matter under the notice of the county council at its next sittings, and the county council should be empowered, not compulsorily, but should be given the option of buying up that licence at a price to be arranged; and in the event of a disagreement about price, that price to be fixed by a Government arbitrator, and the money for that purpose to be advanced by the State, in like manner as it is at present advanced under the Labourers Acts.

Scheme for purchase, compensation, &c.

60,197. Then, however often a licence should be renewed, you would leave it to the licensing authority to say: "This particular year we think that the licence "is not required, though it has been apparently "required in past years"?—You must remember I have gone on the basis that there are a great many, too many public-houses—houses that are absolutely and entirely unnecessary, and I should leave it to the licensing authority to say that the house is unnecessary and unsuitable. I should make that a combined finding.

60,198. I am putting myself rather in the position of a publican whose licence has been renewed year after year, and at last the authority comes down on me and says: "The last five years we have renewed your licence, but in the sixth year we think there are too many, and we select you for extinction"?—To a certain extent it would come to that, but they would only take the cases of the houses that were both unnecessary and unsuitable.

60,199. You would consider the suitability?—Yes, and then I do not take it away from him except with compensation.

60,200. With an ultimate reference to a Government arbitrator?—Yes, a Government arbitrator in the case of disagreement—in case they cannot settle the price. It would be the thin end of the wedge as regards local option, of course.

60,201. Supposing the county council declined to enforce on the publican the improvement of his premises?—Quite so, and if he did not carry out the order the licence should lapse. Then I would give power of appeal against these refusals to renew and orders and certificates to the judge of assize.

60,202. You see no objection, supposing the system of the county councils in taking up the licensing question with the other duties appertaining to the county council?—All they have to do is to decide whether they will buy up the house or not. They have not any judicial authority of any kind in the matter. After all what questions more largely concern the community than the licensing question.

60,203. I believe you have an alternative plan to that, failing the county council and the licensing authority?—Failing any change of that kind, I should be disposed to limit the number of public-houses—I am proceeding on the basis that there are a great deal too many in the population—and to place a minimum valuation on the houses. Of course that would not affect existing houses. It would be only in the case of new licences.

60,204. By what process would you reduce the existing number of houses to the number you think is required for the population?—In the case of cities and towns, or villages of 1,000 inhabitants, I would fix the number at 1 to every 200 of the population.

60,205. By what process would you reduce the number to one to 200?—It would have to be done by the gradual extinction of licences as they dropped out.

60,206. Supposing the proportion is one to 100, and you wish to reduce it to one in 200, where would you begin, or how would you select a particular house?—You must wait till it drops out of itself, unless you adopt the system of buying it out as I suggested. I see no way of getting rid of public-houses except by waiting for their extinction, unless you adopt the principle of buying them out in some shape or form.

60,207. Do you think buying out the public-houses and reducing the number to what you may think the proper proportion, would be popular in Kilkenny?—I am sure it would not meet the views of the persons who hold houses, but I do not think the people would have the least objection to it.

60,208. (*Mr. Whittaker.*) Would it be as popular if they had to pay the money?—The sum would be so small that it would make hardly any difference.

60,209. (*Mr. Young.*) You propose to take the money out of the Consolidated Fund [illegible] originally.

60,210. If you took it from that fund the people would not feel it much. It would be [illegible] from them that they were paying for that at all?—Under the Labourers' Acts the sums are repayable in a certain number of years, and a certain percentage goes to establish a sinking fund.

60,213. You would propose to put the burden on the locality in question, would you?—Certainly.

60,214. (*Chairman.*) You would not make those licensees that are left pay a higher sum for their continued existence?—No, I would not. Nothing more than they would be required to pay in the ordinary course of taxation.

60,215. You would not increase the licence duties?—No, I should not.

60,216. If it be true that a licence puts a large sum of money in the hands of a licensee, in the case of his getting a new licence you would not make the sum go to the public instead of to the owner of the house. Supposing a house has not got a licence, if a licence is [illegible] would meet you with this objection; I have already paid [illegible], you are now going to extinguish me?—I do not think I proposed that.

[illegible]. To bring about a gradual reduction you would be quite firm on the way of not granting any new licenses?—Certainly. I would grant no new licenses until such time as the number had been reduced to the proper level, which would take a long time unquestionably. I only suggest that as an alternative scheme. I should prefer the first one myself.

[illegible]. So that the reform must necessarily be gradual?—Yes. I think that is an advantage, and you do less harm to any vested interest that may exist.

[illegible]. Are convictions frequently endorsed on the licenses?—No, the convictions are endorsed very seldom indeed on the licenses, and I think it is a great [illegible] in the administration, because the endorsement, [illegible] in the event of future [illegible], carries no penalty. In the event of [illegible] it does, and a very grave one. I should suggest that all second convictions or the second and any subsequent conviction within 12 months of a previous conviction should be endorsed on the license compulsorily and should not be within the option of the magistrates at all, but they should necessarily endorse.

[illegible]. [illegible] that you have now got a court according to your proposal, in which you put nature considerations, namely, the county court judge and the resident magistrate should you [illegible] to [illegible] on the [illegible] every offence of which a man is convicted, and then allowing the court constituted as you propose to decide as to whether there is such an accumulation of offences as to warrant a forfeiture of the license?—That is repealing section 30 of the Act of 1872. I have no objection to doing that under these circumstances.

[illegible]. You would not make it compulsory on the court to endorse a license in the present technical sense, and carrying with it the present technical consequences of endorsement? Would you constitute the court [illegible] such as I say, and give them the power you have mentioned, I see no [illegible] for doing so.

[illegible]. Would you raise the minimum fines for offences?—Yes, under certain conditions. In the case of a person found on licensed premises within closing hours I would make the minimum fine 10s. I have reason to believe, from matters that have come to my knowledge, that in many cases it is the persons seeking the drink that are at fault rather than the publican. They want drink, and they urge the publican, who is [illegible] up with them by local [illegible] that he cannot refuse, and he opens his house and sells at a wrong hour. I should make the penalty on persons found on licensed premises within closing hours 10s., and then a minimum penalty of 10s. on all persons who falsely represented themselves to be *bona fide* travellers.

[illegible]. Would you increase the maximum penalty in the case of a publican serving drink to a drunken person?—Yes. I would make the minimum penalty there 40s. with endorsement, and also in the case of any publican permitting drunkenness on his licensed premises.

[illegible]. If a person were found drunk on licensed premises would you give the presumption against the publican?—Yes, I would make that *primâ facie* evidence of the fact that the man had been supplied with the drink there that made him drunk. At the present moment, as the law stands, you have to prove the drink was got there. I should make it presumptive evidence of the fact that drink was got there.

[illegible]. Do you think there is any change of opinion in Kilkenny since Sunday closing?—No. I am quite clear that all are in favour of Sunday closing, and also to a large extent in favour of Saturday night closing.

[illegible]. Earlier closing on Saturday night?—Yes; 9 o'clock on Saturday night. Nine is the hour I have usually named, and it appears to me to be the hour when all persons can have completed their purchases, and after that it is rather for drinking than anything else that the public-houses remain open.

[illegible]. As to the *bona fide* traveller, we have heard about extending the radius which constitutes him a *bona fide* traveller?—There is a tremendous diversity of opinion with regard to that; but I think on the whole the opinion is in favour of extending the radius.

[illegible]. You do not think that the prevalence of opinion is in favour of extinguishing him altogether, and letting him be served when the other members of the public can be served if houses are opened on Sunday?—The houses are not open in the country districts on Sunday.

[illegible]. You would put the *bona fide* traveller in a better position than that of the ordinary public?—Yes. I certainly would if he were a *bona fide* traveller. But I should be very particular in requiring him to show that he was a *bona fide* traveller. I would suggest that you should make the radius five miles.

[illegible]. It is a hypothetical question, but supposing Sunday closing were not prevalent in the country, should you think it a hardship on the *bona fide* traveller that he should be admitted to the same privileges as ordinary men and no more, and get his drink in the hours when the houses were opened?—If he were a *bona fide* traveller I think I should.

[illegible]. I will not press that, because you have Sunday closing?—Yes. On the question of the *bona fide* traveller, Mr. [illegible] mentioned here that until recently the prevailing notion of the magistrates was to go on the basis that a man could only claim to become a *bona fide* traveller where he had travelled three miles, and then only could he set up his claim. That is unquestionably so; but the decisions are that if a man has travelled three miles from where he slept the night before, by the ordinary public route, and has not done it for the purpose of seeking drink, he is a *bona fide* traveller.

[illegible]. How can you prove that a man has not been in search of drink?—That is the question. That is the effect of all the recent decisions, and not only that, but that once he has become a *bona fide* traveller he does not lose his status, and he can go from one house to the other drinking the whole afternoon so long as he remains outside the radius.

[illegible]. Can he admit other people to the same status as himself?—No, he cannot.

[illegible]. He cannot treat the people in the village to which he comes?—No.

[illegible]. (Mr. [illegible].) Is that quite settled in Ireland?—Yes. It is settled so far as this, that I have heard it laid down repeatedly by the county court judge in my own district.

[illegible]. (Chairman.) Have there been many offences recently against the Sunday Closing Act in Kilkenny?—No, there has been a remarkable falling off within recent years in offences against the Sunday Closing Act within the county and city of Kilkenny. I only mention now what has been told to me by persons—the police and others—and they say they attribute it largely to the establishment of clubs. There are no such things as bogus clubs in Kilkenny, that is, established for purely drinking purposes; but at the clubs people have facilities for obtaining drink they would not otherwise have, and they no longer trouble the publicans on Sundays.

[illegible]. To evade the stringency of the Sunday Act they set up what are practically drinking clubs?—No. I do not mean to convey that. They did not set up clubs, some of them in connection with athletic movements and so on, and these clubs were then turned into ordinary clubs of an ordinary character, where they have their billiard tables and their ordinary amusements, and they have attached to them also drink or drinking bars. They were not established for the purpose of drinking clubs.

[illegible]. But they were brought into being by the Sunday closing [illegible]?—Well, that may be possibly so, but I would not like to say with any certainty they were. They were started chiefly as athletic clubs and for other purposes, not with a view to drink, but drink became attached, and I daresay, very possibly, that if it were not for Sunday closing the drink would never have been attached, but they would have remained a kind of reading-room. I should be sorry to say that with certainty.

[illegible]. You say they are not bogus clubs. Is admission easy to them?—It is very easy, and the subscriptions is very small. I am told that subscriptions, at all events in one or two cases, is [illegible] a week, and that persons are admitted with a great deal of readiness there as guests, and, it has been stated to me,

Mr. [illegible] — [illegible]

Sunday [illegible]

Offences against Sunday closing in Kilkenny County and City.

Clubs.

61,269. Do you think from his personal knowledge of the agricultural districts of Kilkenny he himself can know or have any idea of the public necessities for obtaining drink of his own personal knowledge?—No, I do not think he would know much of that from personal knowledge.

61,270. In fact he would not have the same means of forming an opinion as an ordinary magistrate has?—Certainly not.

61,271. (Chairman.) Do you think that would be an advantage or a disadvantage?—I think he would have evidence before him to enable him to form an opinion. A judge when he tries a case knows nothing about it when he starts.

Mr. H. F. Chamber.

60,280. Is there a [illegible] up these clubs, or may a person pay a subscription of [illegible] a week, and be a member [illegible] by payment of the [illegible]?—I cannot absolutely say.

60,281. That is what is meant by a bogus club?—I believe that is not so. I believe these are regularly constituted clubs.

60,282. Mr. Russell seemed to think there were no bogus clubs anywhere except in Dublin and possibly Belfast, and they had been suppressed by the police?—I do not think they are bogus clubs. In my opinion they are not. There may be odd ones to which people come in and drink improperly.

60,283. That would not be allowed in properly constituted [illegible] clubs?—It would not if they were very particular. I have heard of cases in properly constituted clubs.

Occasional licences.

60,284. As to occasional licences, surely it would be [illegible] for the [illegible] judge to be expected to [illegible]? Whom would you propose to give the issuing of occasional licences to?—I do not think I should be disposed to disturb the present arrangement, that is, that the magistrates of the district should do it; but if you like, you might give it to the resident magistrate only, but that would create a considerable amount of inconvenience, because the resident magistrate may live a considerable distance away from where these licences are required, and possibly the resident magistrate might be away on leave and the adjoining resident magistrate acting for him.

60,285. Would not there be a difficulty in taking away the licensing authority from the magistrates and giving to the ordinary magistrate the power to grant occasional licences?—They have it at present.

60,286. But would not there be some inconsistency in the [illegible] proposal in taking away the licensing authority from the magistrates altogether, and giving them exceptional authority as to occasional licences? Would not that be inconsistent?—An occasional licence is intended to meet a temporary necessity which temporarily arises.

60,287. You would not approve of a single magistrate giving the occasional licence in his own drawing-room or study?—That is what he does at the present moment, but I would have it given at petty sessions.

60,288. Would not the inconvenience of waiting for petty sessions be as great as the necessity for applying to the resident magistrate?—It would. You must have inconvenience, I am afraid, in all these cases.

Exemption orders.

60,289. Also exemption orders. Will you explain what is meant by those?—An exemption order is to permit the opening of premises for the sale of drink at an hour that is earlier than the proper hour. The proper hour is 7 o'clock.

60,290. And later?—Well, I have not known them given as [illegible] later.

60,291. Only to open earlier?—Yes.

60,292. Do you approve of these exemption orders?—No, I am entirely against them. I think I said so very distinctly to the Chairman.

60,293. Would you allow them to be ever granted under any circumstances by any authority?—Yes, I would permit them to be granted by the county court judge if the necessity for it arose. I would not debar a person having it altogether.

Number of public-houses to population.

60,294. With regard to the proportion of public-houses to population, is it quite fair to include the children in that population? Ought not the proportion to be really larger? Supposing out of 150 you exclude 50 or 60 as being children, and [illegible] of public-houses, that would leave the proportion 1 to every 60, or 80 or 90?—It would.

60,295. Practically, it is not quite a fair thing to take the number of public-houses in proportion to the whole population, including infants, but the proportion to the adult public-house frequenting population?—You would find it rather difficult to arrive at that.

60,296. Out of the 150 there would not be more than 50 who would resort to a public-house under any circumstances, and then the proportion would be 1 to every 50. If you take such a principle as eliminating the [illegible] community, it would not be 1 to 150 but 1 to 50 or to 60?—Quite so.

60,297. That would make a considerable difference in the calculation?—Yes.

60,298. I see one place in Ireland where the proportion is 1 to every 11?—That would be Castleisland that I have mentioned.

Mr. H. F. Chamber.

[illegible] April '98.

Sunday closing and clubs.

60,299. (Mr. Walker.) You expressed an opinion that the [illegible] of closing the houses on Sunday did not give rise to the establishment of clubs. Did I understand you to express that opinion?—I said that the [illegible] clubs did not, I thought, arise from that cause.

60,300. Have you ever known a club established where they did not sell drink or where drink was not supplied?—An ordinary club—never.

60,301. You testified to the great difficulty at the present time there is officially to control the appetite to obtain drink or the desire to obtain drink during illegal hours, speaking of the *bonâ fide* traveller?—Yes.

60,302. If the licenses were still further restricted on Sunday, would not that difficulty be increased?—I am afraid I do not quite follow you.

60,303. The houses are now open in the exempted towns from 2 o'clock to 7?—Yes.

60,304. At the present time you speak of the great difficulty of bringing under control the sale of excisable liquor during the hours that the houses should be closed in respect of the *bonâ fide* travellers?—Yes.

The *bonâ fide* travellers.

60,305. They give a good deal of trouble. You have testified to that?—Yes.

60,306. It brings about a scandal in the neighbourhood where it takes place—the drunkenness of persons from the fact of the *bonâ fide* traveller having obtaining drink?—I do not know that I did say that. I have no recollection of having said it.

60,307. You complained of the large number of persons obtaining drink during prohibited hours as being *bonâ fide* travellers?—I told you there was less drinking now on Sundays than there used to be, and less infractions of the law. I do not remember having made any complaint of the kind.

60,308. Then you have no fault to find with the present system of supplying *bonâ fide* travellers?—Yes, I have. I think it a fact that persons are supplied with drink who are not in my opinion *bonâ fide* travellers. I do not think the mere fact of a person walking for 3 miles proves that a person is a *bonâ fide* traveller, though it does under the present law so long as he does not do so for the purpose of drinking.

60,309. Is there any drink supplied on Sunday?—Yes, I think there is.

60,310. Is it excessive in your view?—Yes, it is. I think persons obtain drink on Sundays who ought not to.

60,311. Exactly. Then that occasions considerable trouble to the officials?—I suppose it does to a certain extent.

60,312. It has been stated here by officials, and I understood you to testify to the same thing yourself?—I have never experienced any trouble with regard to it.

60,313. But the officials do?—I suppose they do. I do not know what the police may have to say about it. I have nothing to do with the police.

60,314. If the houses are still further restricted and closed at 5 o'clock instead of 7 on Sundays, will not the difficulty be increased in controlling this trade?—I do not speak at all with reference to exempted towns. I have never had any trouble up there, and I do not express any opinion whatever with regard to the exempted towns. I am dealing here with country districts and places like Kilkenny, which is not an exempted town.

60,315. You have been dealing with the *bonâ fide* traveller?—Yes.

60,316. I ask you if there is further restriction in Kilkenny whether it would not be likely to increase the difficulty of controlling this?—That is to throw greater work on the police. I suppose to a certain extent it would.

60,317. If you take away the privilege of the magistrate to grant an occasional licence in his drawing-room, as put by the Reverend Dean, does not that imply a doubt of his *bonâ fide* conduct?—It might be taken in that way, but I do not mean to put it in that way. What I say is that really doing what is practically a judicial proceeding in his own drawing-room is not the proper thing. I should rather see it done in a more formal way by an application to sessions.

Mr. W. F. [illegible]

[illegible] [illegible] has been done for ages, has not it?—I [illegible] to [illegible] till it is [illegible].

[illegible] That has always taken place throughout the length and breadth of the land?—It has.

[illegible] And it occurs at the present time, does it not?—Certainly.

[illegible] Endorsement of a conviction.

[illegible] You expressed the opinion that all offences committed should be endorsed on the licence?—No, all offences. The opinion I expressed was that every second or subsequent conviction for an offence within 12 months of a previous conviction should be endorsed on the licence.

[illegible] Is not that the law now?—No, certainly not. It is entirely optional with the magistrates to endorse offences, and I have seen persons convicted of a [illegible] offence.

[illegible] You would make it compulsory on a second offence?—For a second or subsequent offence within 12 months of a previous conviction.

[illegible] The house being sold and a new landlord coming in, would you have that endorsement [illegible] on the licence to the new landlord?—The landlord would buy the house as it stood.

[illegible] The endorsement to remain on that licence as long as it exists?—Not at all. By the action of the law [illegible] at the end of five years it disappears. An endorsement only operates for five years.

[illegible] You will grant that the more respectable the tenant of the house the better it is for the public?—Certainly.

[illegible] In your opinion would that act as a deterrent to men of capital and respectability purchasing a house with an endorsement on the licence that [illegible] to [illegible]?—Yes, I am sure it would. It would act as a deterrent to any one.

[illegible] Do you think that it is fair that a respectable well-ordered man should suffer for the misdeeds of [illegible] predecessors in those premises?—He would not buy, I take it. Under those conditions if he did he would buy for a small sum.

[illegible] Would you endorse it in order to make it legal to destroy the house?—No, certainly not; not for that purpose. I am afraid we are at cross purposes. I am willing to tell you what I can on the subject. If a person is acting badly in the conduct of his house, and the licence has been consequently endorsed, that man, I think, is [illegible] the same position as a person who has property and chooses to [illegible] it. If he sells his property subsequently, having [illegible] it, he would not get the same amount for it as he would get if it was not [illegible]. In like manner with regard to the publichouse licence. If it is [illegible] with endorsements it would not fetch the same sum in the market.

[illegible] But you are [illegible] the morals of the people to a commercial [illegible] by that suggestion?—I do not quite see that, if you will explain how I am doing so.

[illegible] [illegible] not the fact that getting rid of a bad landlord is a great benefit to the public?—Yes, I should think so, decidedly. You mean a bad publican?

[illegible] Yes. Is it not to the advantage and benefit of the public?—Yes.

[illegible] Is it not what all authorities desire?—Certainly.

[illegible] The mere fact of getting rid of him is not [illegible]. You do not want to saddle the licence to a respectable man with all kinds of endorsements?—If what you desire is that the licence should pass to a respectable man free of all these endorsements, if you establish that he is a thoroughly respectable man, I see no objection to doing so.

The [illegible] of [illegible] [illegible].

[illegible] You expressed an opinion that you yourself wished to cast no reflection whatever on the conduct of the licensing magistrates generally?—Yes, that is that I do not wish to charge them with intentional [illegible].

[illegible] Do you charge them with unintentional [illegible]?—Yes. I charge them with granting licences with far too great freedom and to persons who ought not to get them.

Yes, and, if you will permit me, I will give an example that came under my own notice at the last licensing sessions. There was a man who had a licence in the outskirts of [illegible]. The house was a wretched [illegible], [illegible] though it was a full licence, that is a licence to sell beer, spirits, and everything for seven days, he only took out a licence to sell it [illegible] for six days. In [illegible] of his having died and the house passing to the hands of another man, it became necessary for the other man to obtain a new licence. He could not get a [illegible], and so it came up for a new licence. It was opposed on the ground, in the first place, that it was unnecessary, and in the second place that the premises were unsuitable. It was admitted, even by the applicant, that the premises were [illegible] and entirely unsuitable, and he produced a plan of a new house that he was about to build there, the date of the plan being that of the day before the licensing sessions. It was suggested that it would be quite time enough to [illegible] that house when it existed, but the magistrates gave the licence to the man for that [illegible] house, or rather they gave it for a bad house which was to be turned into a good house; and though that was since last October, not one single [illegible] for the new house has yet been drawn. [illegible] [illegible]

[illegible] I do not wish to enter into that?—I merely [illegible] it as an illustration of the way in which the thing is done.

[illegible] You desire to take away from the magistrates the licensing power?—Yes, and this is a sample of it.

[illegible] Would it meet with general approval that the control of this great interest should be placed in the hands of one man?—I am sure the magistrates would be very glad to get rid of it—the vast majority of them.

[illegible] Has there been any expression of opinion by the magistrates to that effect?—There has been no general consultation on the point, but I have spoken to a great many of them, and they have said that to me.

[illegible] With regard to the character of the licensees in your district. Are they respectable men?—The vast majority of the publicans are, certainly.

[illegible] They are not permitted to hold a licence unless they are proved to be of fit character?—No.

[illegible] You said all crimes are referable to drink, and perhaps you will explain that?—Crimes of violence.

[illegible] You qualify it by saying crimes of violence only?—Yes, and I said so before.

[illegible] Then as to [illegible] orders. Do I understand you to say they are granted and held good for so long a time?—Yes.

[illegible] And that that is the cause of much drinking without food?—Yes, to some extent.

[illegible] That if there was no permission to sell [illegible] liquor at fairs and markets the man would not have instead of drinking beer?—If the publichouse were not open at an hour when no other place is available.

[illegible] Your complaint is simply that it opens at least [illegible]. Is that so?—You misunderstand me. I am not talking of occasional licences, but exemption orders, that is, power for the publican to open his house at an earlier hour than 7 o'clock in the morning. I object to that.

[illegible] It is common in London at the markets?—I do not dispute it.

[illegible] You say, then, that it causes a man to drink to the extent that he cannot take any food?—No, but I say when a man was to drink in the morning before he has taken food it will have a far greater effect on him than if he had eaten food.

[illegible] Do not they sell food at those places?—[illegible].

[illegible] Have whatever [illegible] will not say that whatever, possibly they do. I have never been in these [illegible].

[illegible] The customer is a free agent, and is not compelled to drink unless he likes?—No; but food is the exception and drink is the rule, that is so the [illegible].

—I imagine it is the combined half-holiday and having money.

[illegible]. That is the day they receive their wages?—Yes.

[illegible]. There must be a cause for more drinking and drunkenness on Saturday. Is it due to the half-holiday and receiving their wages on that day?—Yes.

[illegible]. (*Dean Dickinson.*) Or is it due to the prospect of a rest on Sunday?—I do not think that enters into their [illegible] as it is done.

[illegible]. They are not required to get up early in the morning?—No; I think it is facility and money that does it.

[illegible]. (*Mr Walker.*) You said you heard a responsible officer say that 25 per cent. of the public-houses would be sufficient?—Yes.

[illegible]. He spoke to that from his experience and knowledge?—Yes, of course. I can give you his name if you like.

[illegible]. (*Mr. Young.*) If you regard the justices who are, I suppose, appointed by the Lord Chancellor, as an unsuitable authority, I suppose you would consider that any authority popularly appointed would be a still more unsuitable authority for licensing?—Yes, I should for granting licenses.

[illegible]. The case you spoke of a minute or two ago is it not at all inconsistent with what we have in England—what is called a provisional license, or licensing a house that does not exist, on plans?—I do not know anything about that.

[illegible]. You used very strong expressions about it, and it occurred to me you perhaps did not know that that is a provision of English law?—I did not.

[illegible]. Therefore, perhaps, you might modify those expressions if you knew it was so. Do not you think it a desirable thing that the justices should have the right and power to license from plans?—To satisfy as to extent (?) of the house is erected under certain conditions the license would in due course be granted.

[illegible]. Or would not, as the case might be?—Quite so.

[illegible]. It is a very wise provision in the law?—I think so.

[illegible]. It may prevent the erection of a house which the justices do not want to license. When it is erected without this particular condition, the man comes with an air of injured innocence appeal, and gets a license that they do not wish to grant?—That is the case frequently with us.

[illegible]. You would agree it would be a wise thing to engraft that provision on to the Irish law?—I think it would be a good thing. This was not a case of provisional licensing, but granting a license to what is really nothing more than a wretched hovel, and admittedly so by the applicant, on the faith of a house that was to be built in the future, and which has not yet been commenced.

[illegible]. It is bordering on the same principle of law?—Yes, it is something like it.

[illegible]. One word about endorsements. After the last endorsement you would make every offence an endorsable offence?—Within 12 months of a previous offence.

[illegible]. You would have no regard to the triviality of the offence, would you?—I do not know. I think they may have.

[illegible]. Take the case in which a publican might be quite properly convicted for the default of his servant who had acted contrary to his orders. Do you think that should be endorsed, if the magistrates thought it was a very trivial case?—No, I should not care to see an offence of that kind endorsed.

[illegible]. You would qualify that?—Yes; but it is difficult to draw the line.

[illegible]. It is reasonable it should be drawn?—As far as possible I should like to see it done. I should like to see trivial offences excluded if it could be done.

[illegible]. (*Mr. Grimshaw.*) Your suggestion is a proportion of five licenses to 1,000 population, as it not?—Yes.

[illegible]. If you take that with reference to Kilkenny, as a place you know, of course, thoroughly, has it occurred to you the number of licenses it would give for the whole of Kilkenny?—Yes, about 55.

[illegible]. Then taking your own suggestion, that only 25 per cent. of the licenses are necessary, you would reduce then the number of licenses in Kilkenny to one-third, and it would bring it down to 25?—I did not make that suggestion. I told you that was given as the last October licensing sessions by a responsible police officer, but I did not say it was my idea.

[illegible]. I was going to ask you, with your knowledge of Kilkenny, do you think 25 licensed premises would be sufficient to carry on the trade?—I think it would be rather too much of a reduction. I would not favour more than I have said, about half of the existing licenses. I did not mean to convey that was my idea.

[illegible]. A reduction of that kind would necessarily lead to two things. First it would put the trade in the hands of a monopoly?—It is practically so now.

[illegible]. It would make it still more so?—It would.

[illegible]. Like all monopolies there is a certain disadvantage to the public in connection with it. Do you think the public get so well served with the article, because you have said you attach importance to the quality?—I think they would be served better than they are now.

[illegible]. When you have done away with competition?—The competition is excessive, and I think it is that that leads to a great many of the existing evils.

[illegible]. What was the price of that whisky you spoke of?—[illegible]

[illegible]. Have you gone into a calculation at all, when you have added the duty and the price of the article, how far it is possible to sell at that price?—One of the Commissioners put me in mind of another whisky, which I called patent whisky, which can be sold at a much cheaper rate. I know nothing about that. Pot-still whisky is the great Irish whisky, and I was calculating on that basis.

[illegible]. You attribute a large amount of intemperance to an inferior article, but the price would hardly support that?—The price of it might not, but no doubt the general belief amongst all classes is that the whisky sold is inferior.

[illegible]. I understand you that a large number of new licenses have been granted last year at Kilkenny?—There have been a good many new licenses granted.

[illegible]. As a matter of fact according to our return in 10 years there has been an average of less than one license granted in the city of Kilkenny each year, in a population of 11/400?—I am very much afraid the population also is diminishing. I wish it were not so.

[illegible]. Nineteen licenses in 10 years does not imply the grant of a number of new licenses?—No; but I think it is 19 too many.

[illegible]. It is not a question of the number, but you do not want to see new licenses granted at all?—I should have no objection to new licenses when you have obtained a proper level, but I believe the excessive number of existing licenses is responsible for much of the evil that at present prevails.

[illegible]. (*Mr. Young.*) Did I understand you to say that the granting of new licenses was in the hands of the county court judge alone?—No; it is in the hands of the magistrates at quarter sessions.

[illegible]. And the county court judge?—With the county court judge as chairman.

[illegible]. That is not so in many other counties in Ireland. It is simply the county court judge?—I think in no country district.

[illegible]. In the county of Antrim it is simply the county court judge, and in the borough it is the Recorder. In the city of Kilkenny in whose hands does the granting of licenses lie?—In the hands of the magistrates with the county court judge as chairman.

[illegible]. You simply want to abolish the power of the

Mr. H. F. Considine.

—

[illegible]

40,398. (Mr. Whitaker.) The county court judges do not grant the new licenses in Ireland?—Mr. Young says so.

40,399. Not the new licenses?—I do not know of it.

40,400. (Mr. Young.) In the case of new licenses, the local magistrates sit with the county court judge, but that is not so in many of the other counties in Ireland. In order that there should not be too much power placed in the hands of one man, would you agree with me that there should be a selection made in each county of a limited number of local magistrates with the county court judge, for the purpose of granting licenses?—How would you make the selection?

40,401. That is a selection that should be made by the magistrates [illegible] a certain number, say eight or four, or whatever number should be determined upon, and on whom the responsibility should be, with the county court judge, of granting the licenses. And that selection should be annual?—I think I would prefer to leave it as I suggested. I think you would find a great deal of difficulty in getting suitable men there, not but what there are plenty of suitable men, but I think they would shirk it to a large extent. They would find it a very disagreeable and invidious task placed on them, and I think they would prefer not to do it.

Licensing committee of justices.

40,402. (Viscount de Vesci.) Why should they find it more invidious than the English licensing authority?—I think they would in this way. In England you have got a vast population—a large teeming population; and really the owners of one town are not known to another, as in Ireland. Our population there is very limited, and every person knows almost everybody else.

40,403. (Mr. Young.) Would you allow me to read this to you:—"In the county of the city of Dublin, and "the cities of Cork, Belfast, and Londonderry, and in "the town of Galway, the authority for granting "publichouse certificates is the Recorder sitting at "quarter sessions"?—Yes.

40,404. You say it would be hard to get six or seven local men to sit with the county court judge so responsible as to take the responsibility of granting licenses?—I do not think you would get the really good men to do it. That is what I think. If you could succeed in getting a tribunal of that kind, by all means do it. All I ask is a perfectly independent tribunal.

40,405. Do you mean out of the enormous quantity of magistrates created in a county you would not get six or seven first-class men that would act in the thing?—Certainly, of course you would if the first-class men would act, and a great many more than six or seven.

Valuation of premises.

40,406. With reference to valuations in Ireland, may I take it that the valuation of houses is lower in Ireland in regard to size and accommodation than what a similar valuation would represent in England?—I could not tell you that. I do not know.

40,407. It appears to many here that the very low valuation in Ireland is an indication of the [illegible] of the house. The low valuation does not always indicate that the house is bad?—Well, I think in the majority of cases a [illegible] valuation means a very indifferent house.

40,408. Is the rental in Ireland about twice or three times the valuation?—That I cannot tell you either. I do not know.

40,409. You may take it from me that the rental of the house is generally always double or more?—That may be. I know nothing about house rents.

40,410. I presume you do not know much about distillation?—Nothing.

40,411. You have said that the whisky sold at 12s. 6d. is an indication of the [illegible] of the article?—Certainly, if it be pot-still whisky.

40,412. What I was going to ask you is this. Are you sure that the distillers in Ireland sell whisky at 12s. 6d. to the traders?—No. I am not talking about distillers at all. I say that the whisky man in Kilkenny advertised whisky at 12s. 6d. a gallon. What price he gets it from the distiller at I cannot tell you.

40,413. You mean his retail price?—You can hardly call it retail. I do not suppose he would sell it retail at that. He would sell a gallon at that.

40,414. What is the strength, do you know?—It is passed by according to law not more than 25 per cent. under proof. If it is, it is an adulterated article.

40,415. The fact is he would have a good profit if you look into it?—I have worked it out, and I can give you the figures. Taking the price at 12s. 6d. and the duty at 10s. 6d. a gallon, he can reduce it, as I have said, by 25 per cent., and that would bring down the duty to 8s. [illegible] per gallon. That will leave him 4s. 6d. to supply the whisky, pay the expenses, and leave him a profit.

40,416. It is a very large percentage—4s. 6d. profit?—I did not say it was 4s. 6d. profit. He has to pay for the whisky yet.

40,417. That would leave 3s. 9d. for what is called short price?—I am not up in the terms. It leaves 3s. 9d. to pay what I have said.

40,418. That is the price of the whisky itself without the duty?—It would leave him 3s. 9d. to pay for the whisky, to pay expenses, and leave him a profit.

40,419. If you are not able to say what strength this is sold at, it is not an indication that the article is bad?—I must assume it is not sold under the lawful strength, and that is 25 under proof. You think I am wrong in assuming that? Possibly I am.

40,420. You may sell it at any strength if it is labelled. You forget that, probably. You may put a drink on a bottle and sell it at 50 per cent. under—if you [illegible] it on the article he is selling.

40,421. You do not know [illegible] that that is the case?—I have never bought the 12s. 6d. whisky, so I cannot tell you, but I have every reason to believe it is not done.

40,422. In Ireland, as a rule, really bad whisky is not sold. The fact is that the whiskeys are generally sold throughout all Ireland, and no better whisky is made?—You are perfectly right. No better whisky is made than that whisky, I believe, though I am not a whisky man myself.

40,423. I have had considerable experience of Ireland, and I differ from you altogether when you say that bad whisky is sold even in county Kilkenny?—It depends on exactly what you take me to convey. If you take me as conveying that the whisky sold throughout Ireland as Irish whisky is bad whisky I do not say so, but I say the whisky sold in [illegible] publichouses, call it what you will, is bad whisky.

The witness withdrew.

Adjourned to tomorrow at 10.30.

ONE HUNDRED AND FIRST DAY.

Queen's Robing Room, House of Lords, Wednesday, April 27th, 1898.

Present:

THE RIGHT HONOURABLE THE VISCOUNT PEEL IN THE CHAIR.

The Right Hon. the Viscount de Vesci.	John Herbert Roberts, Esq., M.P.
Sir Charles Cameron, Bart., M.P.	Charles Walker, Esq.
The Very Reverend H. H. Dickinson, D.D.	Thomas Palmer Whittaker, Esq., M.P.
Henry Grainger, Esq.	Samuel Young, Esq., M.P.
[illegible], Esq.	George Younger, Esq.
Andrew Johnston, Esq.	

The Reverend T. F. Furlong called in and examined.

Rev. T. F. Furlong.

Sphere of work.

60,424. (*Chairman.*) You are, I think, a native of the city of Waterford?—Yes.

60,425. Your ministrations lie in what part of Ireland?—In the city of Waterford itself, including the cathedral parish. That has been so for the last eight years.

60,426. You were, I think, resident for some time in Dundee?—Yes, my first mission was in Dundee for six years.

60,427. Where there is a very large Irish population?—We calculated that the Irish population there was [illegible]. I was an assistant to a curate there.

60,428. Turning to Ireland, you held the curacy of Passage?—Yes. After being recalled home into the diocese of Waterford, I was placed for three years in the curacy of Passage East. It is a village on the harbour, about six miles from Waterford.

60,429. Therefore your experience may be said to have been gained both in Scotland and in Ireland?—Both in Scotland and in Waterford.

Sunday closing in Ireland.

60,430. Has the bishop of your diocese ever expressed any opinion on the question which we are now considering?—Yes. The bishop of the diocese of Waterford, Dr. Sheehan, has been for a long time mixed up with the temperance movement in Ireland. He is well known as a strong advocate of the closing of public-houses on Sundays—if not of closing altogether on Sundays, at least of a considerable reduction in the hours in which public-houses are allowed by law to be open in the exempted cities. He is also most anxious that public-houses in the cities and towns throughout Ireland should be closed at a much earlier hour on Saturday nights.

60,431. Would those opinions be shared by the clergy generally in their individual capacity?—Yes. Those views are held by all our clergy so far as I am aware. I have spoken to many of them on the subject, and the views I have stated as being the views of the bishop are the views generally of the clergy. I may mention that I have spoken to a number of clergymen not of our own church, and they are equally anxious with us that Sunday closing should be carried, and that the movement in favour of the earlier closing of public-houses on Saturday nights should be also carried.

Effect of Sunday closing in Dundee.

60,432. Your experience in Dundee enables you to speak of the effect of Sunday closing in that city?—It does.

60,433. What is your opinion of it?—I have always considered that the closing of public-houses in Dundee had a most healthy effect morally and socially upon the people. I could not help contrasting the conditions of things in general in Dundee, and the state of the streets with the condition of things, and the state of the streets in our towns in Ireland where public-houses are open on Sundays.

60,434. The streets of Dundee being very orderly?—Very orderly, particularly on Sunday evenings. It was my custom after my evening service to walk through a considerable part of the town, and I have pleasure in stating that I never witnessed the smallest disorder in passing through the streets, and I have met very large crowds coming, I should think, from different places of worship, or people taking recreation. There was never any disorder or disturbance of any kind.

27 April '98.

60,435. Dundee, speaking from recollection, is rather favourably situated for outdoor recreations; there are plenty of parks and recreation grounds, are there not?—Yes, there are two or three parks. Then there is a promenade by the river.

60,436. The population would be rather of a rough kind, would they not?—Yes; the population is 180,000.

60,437. Rough factory hands employed in the jute manufacture?—Yes, the staple trade of Dundee is the jute trade.

Public-houses in Waterford.

60,438. Turning to Waterford, what do you say as to the number of licensed houses in Waterford?—I have got returns from the police in relation to the number of houses and I shall be able to give them to you. There are 137 public-houses, pure and simple, where nothing but drink is sold.

60,439. You mean fully licensed public-houses?—Fully licensed. The grocer licence houses are 91.

60,440. (*Mr. Younger.*) Are those spirit grocers?—Yes.

60,441. (*Mr. Grainger.*) Is that for the county of Waterford or for the city of Waterford?—The city of Waterford.

60,442. (*Mr. Young.*) I think those 91 are fully licensed houses?—I am giving you the returns which I got from the police. The number of wholesale and retail beer dealers is [illegible]. That makes the total number of licensed houses in Waterford 237.

60,443. (*Chairman.*) In this return which has been laid before us Waterford city is bracketed with Waterford police court?—Yes.

60,444. Do you wish to speak of the Waterford Police Court District as well, or are you speaking only of the city proper?—I asked the head constable for the number of public-houses in the city of Waterford, and this is the return which he gave me.

60,445. According to the return, the public-houses in Waterford city and Waterford police court district is 223, and the spirit grocers are 7; beer retailers' licences, 8; wholesale beer dealers, 1; total of all licences, 11. Would you agree with those figures?—I can only give you the figures I have got.

60,446. At what number do you put the grocers' licences?—Where groceries, &c. are sold, 91; the number of wholesale and retail beer dealers is 9.

60,447. Are you speaking now of public-houses which do a trade in grocery, or the shops proper which do a trade in drink?—I am speaking of houses that are publicly known as grocery establishments, and have a licence to sell intoxicating drinks for consumption on the premises.

60,448. (*Mr. Grainger.*) They are not spirit grocers then?—I think they are both the one and the other.

60,491. Then what are we to do?—I think the evil would be considerably mitigated by simply prohibiting the sale to children of intoxicating drinks in open vessels. If it were legal to purchase drink only in closed vessels, one source of temptation to intemperance would be considerably removed.

60,492. (Dean Dickinson.) But if the cork was easily taken out?—Yes, but then the child would have to provide himself or herself with a [illegible].

60,493. (Chairman.) You would not prohibit altogether the sale off the premises in open vessels?—Personally I would, but there I see the amount of inconvenience that might be caused.

60,494. Therefore you would draw the distinction between children being served, and the ordinary public being served?—Yes.

60,495. You would raise the limit of age up to which children are entitled to be messengers?—I would. There is not the same danger I think for a child 13 or 14 years of age as there is for a child of 7 or 8, because the child of 13 or 14 has heard in school and in the church instructions upon intemperance, while the child of 7 or 8 has heard nothing as a rule, being too young.

60,496. I am reminded that there is no limit in Ireland below which a child may not be sent as a messenger?—I do not think so.

60,497. You would advocate a limit?—Yes, an age limit.

60,498. And also a limit at which a child should be served in the public-house for his own consumption?—Yes.

60,499. Are there many clubs in Waterford?—There are five clubs with bars attached to them for the dispensing of excisable drinks.

60,500. With bars the same as in a public-house?—Yes, practically the same.

60,501. Have you any idea what are the terms of membership of these clubs?—They pay an annual subscription.

60,502. A very small one?—Barely under a guinea, I think. For a working man that would be large enough. A couple of guineas in some of the clubs.

60,503. Would there be any limitation of age?—There is, I think. In some of the clubs no member is admitted who is not over, I think, 18.

60,504. Do these clubs keep open on a Sunday?—

60,505. Mostly young men?—Mostly young men. Young men principally from the shops, drapers' assistants, and so on.

60,506. Are they large premises?—Yes, they are fairly good premises. Objection could not be raised against them on that score, I think.

60,507. Is there any sleeping accommodation?—No, not that I am aware of.

60,508. What do you propose in order to remedy the state of evil which you say exists in these clubs?—It is a very difficult question to tackle, because men will have their clubs, and you will hardly have a club unless there is a bar attached to it. It is hard to know what to suggest in relation to these clubs.

60,509. Why should there be a bar attached to every club?—Because the expenses in running a club are pretty high, and it appears that it would be practically impossible to keep the club open if money was not made at the bar to support the club.

60,510. Why should not the members be served as in an ordinary club without having an objectionable technical publichouse bar?—I do not know.

60,511. (Dean Dickinson.) Is that bar open to the public?—No, but I think a member can bring in his friends and treat them there.

60,512. (Mr. Tennant.) Do you happen to know whether these are members' clubs or proprietary clubs?—They are members' clubs.

60,513. (Chairman.) Is there any carrying away of liquor off the premises in these clubs?—I do not think so.

60,514. (Dean Dickinson.) When a member introduces one of the public, does he pay or does the member pay?—The member pays.

60,515. Or appears to pay?—I do not think there is an abuse in that way. I hardly think an Irishman would bring a friend into his club and ask him to pay for his drink.

60,516. (Chairman.) Is there any provision made in the club for a man getting dinner there?—I do not think there is for getting dinner, but I know that at the bar of some of the clubs they can get cold meats at any time, and coffee and tea, and temperance drinks are availed of considerably in some of the clubs.

60,517. The class of young men who frequent these clubs would be, you say, shop assistants?—A great many. In one club particularly, called the [illegible] days, Saturdays, and fair days, who would not be seen going into who would not probably visit a those grocers' shops and get drink

[illegible]. You are aware, no doubt, the passing of the Spirit Grocers' [illegible] passed in the Irish Parliament by [illegible] should not be tempted to go into houses, and so get, as it was thought, [illegible]?—Yes.

and I would suggest the appointment of two other [illegible] men, who would have no connexion whatever with the trade.

[illegible]. Who would appoint them?—I would leave that to the executive.

[illegible]. (*Dean Dickinson.*) The resident magistrate of the county, do you mean?—The resident magistrate who presides at the bench of the city. I would include him.

[illegible]. Would you include the resident magistrate of the county to sit with the resident magistrate of the city?—I do not know that he would be able to understand the local classes.

[illegible]. Could not he be informed by the resident magistrate of the city of the facts?—Yes, but if you had a man appointed from the city he would know the requirements of the city, and it would be much better.

[illegible]. (*Chairman.*) The resident magistrate would have jurisdiction both in the city and county?—Yes.

[illegible]. You think the present existing body of magistrates, owing to the system under which they administer the law, are so open to canvassing and other undue influence, that they themselves would like to be relieved from their duty?—I am sure that some would; most of them I should think.

[illegible]. Would you be in favour of a high license duty?—I would, because it would have the good effect I think of keeping the poorer class publicans out of the trade. I think there are seldom serious or frequent charges where you have an independent man engaging a public-house.

[illegible]. If you raise the license duty very high and secured a better class of men, what would become of the [illegible] class of men who at present hold a [illegible]?—Some regulation could be made by which they could die off gradually.

[illegible]. You do not think they would be driven to keep shebeens or other illegal places?—I made inquiry from the police as to the number of shebeens in the city of Waterford, and I was told there were [illegible] suspected shebeens, and most of those that were suspected had been convicted. I have since learnt from some of the [illegible] men in the city, who are in a position to know, that there are considerably more than [illegible], and more than double the number.

[illegible]. (*Mr. Young.*) Would not that sense of [illegible] [illegible] very much worse if you restricted the licenses to the number you desire?—Not if the police were more active and vigilant.

[illegible]. (*Chairman.*) Do you think the police at present do act with sufficient vigilance?—I think they do not. The police are a very estimable, [illegible], and intelligent body of men, but I think they do not exercise sufficient zeal or watchfulness in relation to the administration of the licensing laws. I know that the difficulties in the way of their doing so are enormous.

[illegible]. Is there any feeling among the police that, apart from actual offences committed, the supervision of public-houses is hardly a matter which falls within the duty of the constabulary?—They are being so much used as a military body in Ireland that they, perhaps, forget what their real duties are.

[illegible]. Have they enough leisure time to look after the public-houses?—They have plenty of leisure time, no doubt of it, very often too much leisure time.

[illegible]. (*Chairman.*) You think the payment by [illegible] might be attended with danger?—It might.

[illegible]. Are you in favour of the Government taking any active interest in temperance questions?—Decidedly. Nothing is done in the way of promoting temperance among the people by the Government.

[illegible]. You would wish the Government actually to interfere?—Yes, firstly by some right legislation all round, and then by positive encouragement; for instance, if the Government would help in sending round lecturers who would be qualified to speak upon the evils physically and socially of intemperance.

[illegible]. Could not that be done by local organisations?—It is, to a considerable extent, but our country is a poor one, and we find it hard to raise funds.

[illegible]. (*Dean Dickinson.*) Is it not done in the national schools of Ireland?—It is, because the clergy visit the national schools, and during the half hour's instruction often speak on the subject, but that is not sufficient; that is only amongst children.

[illegible]. Books are provided in the national schools on temperance?—They are, but that is for children. I am speaking now of the difficulties all round.

[illegible]. (*Chairman.*) You think the whole burden of dealing with the question now rests with the clergy?—The question of promoting temperance is to my mind left too much to the clergy and occasional lecturers; and frequently in the church the people are exhorted to temperance, but more might be done to attract people to temperate habits by the establishment, for instance, of technical schools, if we had such in our country, or the giving of lectures of a popular kind. There has been an advance in that way of late years, but it is hardly sufficient.

[illegible]. (*Mr. Young.*) Is it legal control or moral control you speak of?—I think there is sufficient moral control exercised by the clergy of all denominations. I would advocate legal control of a more stringent character than we have at present.

[illegible]. Would you close the houses all day on Sunday?—Certainly; and if possible I would close the public-houses at 9 o'clock every evening in the week. I do not see why they should be open from 7 o'clock until 11.

[illegible]. Are the clergy of your church quite of your views there?—I cannot speak for the clergy of Ireland. I can speak only for those with whom I come in contact, the clergy of the city of Waterford; and all are in favour of closing public-houses on Sundays, and earlier closing on Saturday evenings. I spoke to some of the clergy in the districts in the smaller towns, and they advocate the same policy.

[illegible]. Then they are abstainers?—Personally [illegible].

[illegible]. You recognise the legality of the trade, and the necessity for the trade, do you?—Yes, you have to do that I think.

[illegible]. Your views are for the better regulation of the trade, I presume?—Yes; it is a necessary evil.

[illegible]. Are these the two suggestions you have to make?—These are the suggestions I have to make.

[illegible]. They are the only suggestions you make; closing on Sunday, and closing every night at 9 o'clock?—And I said more right legislation all round, and encouragement on the part of the Government of [illegible] to the public [illegible] giving of lectures.

[illegible]

Rev. T. F. Furlong.

[illegible] April [illegible]

Temperance education.

Sunday and early closing.

Temperance education.

Rev. T. F. Furlong.

17 April '98.

40,599. Do you think the serious crimes of the country are committed in drunkenness?—I am morally certain of it.

40,600. In countries where there is very little intemperance do you not find there is crime quite as abundant as in Ireland?—I do not know what the peculiar failings of these people may be; I am speaking only for Ireland.

40,601. I think if you were to inquire into the history of those countries where there is more temperance—some of the continental countries, where you scarcely see a drunken man—you would find that crime is quite as prevalent as in Ireland. Intemperance includes petty offences which can hardly be called crimes. Perhaps being a little disorderly in the street you call crime?—No; disorder in a small way I would not call a crime.

40,602. The serious crimes of the country are not committed in drunkenness?—Many of the serious crimes are. Manslaughter I consider as a serious crime, and I think nine out of ten manslaughters have their origin in intemperance in Ireland.

40,603. Take forgery?—I think forgery is a rare crime in Ireland.

40,604. In fact, drunkenness incapacitates a man for very serious crime?—I think it stimulates a man to very serious crime.

40,605. I think that the clergy, with the very best intentions in the world, attribute too much to the use of alcohol?—I suppose that is a personal opinion of yours?

40,606. Yes?—I may give my personal opinion, I suppose?

40,607. Certainly?—My personal opinion is that we do not. Unfortunately we have too much experience of it in our towns and cities in Ireland.

40,608. Are there many persons taken into custody on Sunday?—Yes, a considerable number.

40,609. Are there more than what you would ordinarily expect in a city?—I do not know that I can answer that question. I might answer it in this way, that before the magistrates on Monday there is a large number of cases for drunkenness. If the public-houses were closed you would not have half so many I should think.

40,610. Are they merely taken into custody for being drunk, or drunk and disorderly?—I think drunk and disorderly go together.

40,611. Oh, yes?—Generally speaking it is so in Ireland. If you take up the papers recording the proceedings of the police court you will find that in nearly every other case of drunkenness it is "drunk and disorderly."

40,612. One would think that the strong moral influence which you exercise upon the people might produce a change?—Yes, but we know a good deal of the workings of human nature; it is the study of our lives; and we find something else is required besides moral influence. That is beneficial in theory.

40,613. Then the clergy really invoke the power of the law?—They have to do so from time to time. I have had to do so myself where I found men under the influence of drink, or where I found publicans abusing the law.

40,614. You do not say that there is more crime in Waterford than in any other city of the same size, do you?—I do not think there is. You speak of Ireland?

40,615. I say in Waterford?—Comparing Waterford with the other cities of Ireland, do you mean?

40,616. Yes?—I do not think so.

Clubs.

40,617. As to these clubs, are you for abolishing the clubs?—I should be very glad to see the clubs abolished. That is my own personal opinion, but I know that young men will have these clubs.

40,618. The respectable classes have got clubs, have they not?—They have.

40,619. You would allow the same liberty of course to a poor man?—I would allow him the same liberty, certainly.

40,620. You speak of the quality of the whisky that is consumed as being very bad?—Yes.

Quality of whisky.

40,621. You do not know anything about it personally of course?—No.

40,622. Do the working men go and ask what sort of whisky they drink?—Very often they can. If a medical man is called to the bedside of some of these working men, he will often see whisky in a bottle there. He will know from the very smell of it that it is not old enough for consumption.

40,623. Do you know what age it ought to be before it is consumed?—I see good Irish whisky advertised as six years old.

40,624. (Mr. Grinling.) On the point of Irish whisky, you suggested that the bad quality was occasioned to some extent by a blend of Irish and Scotch being sold?—Yes, I understand there is a considerable amount of blending of Scotch and Irish whisky.

40,626. Which of these two is the bad constituent?—I hope it is the Scotch.

40,627. Another suggestion of yours is the employment of special detectives for looking after the houses?—Yes.

40,628. Do not you think that rather savours of introducing a system of espionage on the trade?—Yes, but for a great evil you have to use very stringent means.

40,629. Do you think in Ireland that a system which involved really paid spies to watch the trade, and that the police should handle by the law, would be desirable? Do you think it would be consistent with Irish feelings?—I think the better class of people in Ireland would be very glad to see legitimate means used for the detection of abuses on the part of publicans.

40,630. The question would be whether that would be legitimate?—You may call detectives paid spies if you like. I call them detectives. They are appointed by the law to do their duty.

40,631. With regard to these five clubs, do they supply on Sunday?—They do.

40,632. It evidently shows that there is a class of people who will get drink under any circumstances if you were to close all the houses?—Yes, but many of the young men who go into those clubs would never think of taking drink on Sunday, although the drink is there.

40,633. You have heard of the danger which has been pointed out over and over again, that if you close all the legitimate places for supplying these things you will drive them into clubs and shebeens?—I have heard of that.

40,634. You do recognise that there is the danger?—I do, certainly.

40,635. Therefore, if you can limit the trade within reasonable limits, it is far better than preventing it being carried on altogether. You do not want a hunted trade?—No.

40,636. That is what the club and the shebeen is?—Yes.

40,637. The legitimate trade is usually far better than that?—It would be, of course.

40,638. As regards these five clubs, I suppose they are only the ordinary means of supplying the members. It is a company. If their members are entitled to have wines and spirits and beer on the premises they must have a counter for the purpose?—Yes.

40,639. They are nothing worse than, I suppose, the ones we heard of in the House of Commons?—Not at all. I do not object to them on that at all.

40,640. (Mr. Younger.) Waterford is one of the excepted cities?—It is.

40,641. In 1878 was the limit of opening time from 2 to 7?—Yes.

40,642. Can you tell us whether that had any reduction or effect on the arrests for drunkenness on Sunday?—I made inquiries and I was told there was a reduction in the number of prosecutions since the limit of time from 2 to 7.

40,643. To any great extent?—I think to a considerable extent.

40,644. The entire number of arrests was given here by Sir Andrew Reed, in a statement made before the Commission, as 179 in 1897. That is an average of [illegible] you got that considerably [illegible] a very large number in relation [illegible]

[illegible] that under these circumstances [illegible] and prudent to entirely [illegible] Sunday afternoon?—I think so, [illegible]. There is not much [illegible] in Waterford; there may [illegible] like Dublin and Belfast where you [illegible] of people passing through.

[illegible] figures, you have the very [illegible] is no great amount of drunken-[illegible] comparatively very few [illegible] the people and that facility [illegible] Do you think it [illegible] entirely [illegible] perhaps go where they might not [illegible] there could be a great many more [illegible] on Sundays than there are [illegible].

[illegible]; we can only take the figures [illegible] are drawing deductions from this [illegible]

[illegible] from these figures [illegible] that the [illegible] and the [illegible] you [illegible] of the state of matters in [illegible]?—I am only giving my own [illegible]

[illegible] to bear it out?—Well, I [illegible]

[illegible] only [illegible] whether these clubs [illegible] were established after the [illegible] on Sunday?—I know they [illegible] the restriction of hours.

[illegible] the result of that in any way. [illegible] do not think so. [illegible] political spite in Ireland. [illegible] in connexion with the [illegible].

[illegible] of the condition of Dundee?—Yes.

[illegible] you had no experience whatever [illegible] Dundee before the Sunday Closing [illegible]

[illegible] you [illegible] that state of [illegible] before?—No.

[illegible]) Are you aware that drunken-[illegible] in your city?—I think it is [illegible] comparing the city of Waterford now [illegible] twenty-five years ago, there is less [illegible] among our people.

[illegible] years probably it will disappear [illegible] be disappearing ourselves [illegible].

[illegible]) You have told us that there [illegible] number of public-houses in Waterford?

[illegible] been suggested to you that there [illegible] amount of drunkenness because of [illegible]

[illegible] you if you are aware of a [illegible] that in Waterford [illegible] far more numerous in proportion [illegible] than in any other of the [illegible]

[illegible] in any county in Ireland?—Yes.

[illegible] there are also more arrests for [illegible] Waterford than in any other of the [illegible] in any of the counties in proportion [illegible] Yes.

[illegible] the public-houses in Waterford are [illegible] numerous in proportion to population [illegible]?—Yes.

[illegible] the arrests for drunkenness are [illegible] numerous in proportion to population [illegible]

[illegible] to think that the large number of [illegible] increase the drunkenness?—Yes.

[illegible]) In reference to the suggestion [illegible] to moving temperance [illegible], I [illegible] is this, that there is a [illegible]

60,667. You think there is a necessity for more information to be disseminated through the country?—Yes, it would encourage those working for temperance, and it would be a great encouragement to the people at large.

60,668. (Mr. Walker.) I think you admitted that drunkenness had decreased in Waterford?—The consumption of drink may be as large, but I think it is spread over a greater number of people.

60,669. May I take it as the answer that drunkenness has decreased in Waterford?—Visible drunkenness has in my experience decreased.

60,670. What do you mean by "visible"?—As far as you can see by the streets.

60,671. Has it decreased in the percentage?—There is a decrease in the percentage, I think.

60,672. Then drunkenness really has decreased in Waterford?—It has.

60,673. Then does not contain the statement that the large number of public-houses in Waterford has brought about an increased state of drunkenness?—I do not know that the number of public-houses in Waterford has increased very much the last 25 years. That is as long as I can remember.

60,674. There has been no variation in the number of public-houses in Waterford for 25 years?—Not very much, I think, as far as I can remember.

60,675. Have you made any inquiry as to whether, relatively to other towns and cities in the United Kingdom, a larger number of houses increases drunkenness, and a smaller number of houses lessens drunkenness?—No, I have made no inquiry.

60,676. Would you be surprised to find that statistics prove the contrary to what you in your answer expressed to Mr. Wh[illegible]?—I should be surprised.

60,677. The fewer houses the more drunkenness?—I should be very much surprised.

60,678. Then I may take it from you that, in your judgment, both individually and officially, drunkenness has decreased in Waterford?—Yes.

60,679. You expressed an opinion that the licensed trade was a necessary evil, and is being [illegible], and also necessary that it should be surrounded [illegible] proper protection?—It should be.

60,680. Do you consider that the clubs are surrounded with proper protection. I mean morally?—They are, morally, yes.

60,681. I understand you to say that when the legally established houses are closed the clubs are supplying any quantity of drink?—To the members, yes.

60,682. And to the members' friends?—A member has the privilege of bringing in his friend.

60,683. And in many instances no limit is placed upon the number?—I do not know if the rules of the club make any regulation of the kind.

60,684. Have you yourself any practical knowledge of clubs of this character?—I have. I was at the establishment of one club, and advocated very strongly [illegible] no bar, except a temperance bar, attached to the club. Representations were made by those who were establishing the club, that it would be practically impossible to keep the doors open if they were not allowed to sell intoxicating drinks to the members.

60,685. You have intimate knowledge of the rules that govern these clubs?—I cannot say that I have an intimate knowledge.

60,686. Have you seen any rules that govern these clubs?—I have.

60,687. Are you prepared to say there is not a rule that gives permission for a member to take into that club as many visitors as he pleases?—I cannot say the [illegible] limit is placed by rule as to the number of [illegible] member may introduce into the club.

60,688. You are prepared to admit that they may take in visitors?—Yes.

60,689. And that they keep open, or supply drink up to midnight when the legally established houses are closed?—Yes.

Rev. T. F. [illegible]

17 April '9[illegible]

Drunkenness in Waterford.

Clubs.

Rev. F. F. Furlong. [illegible]

60,691. Have you anything to say otherwise than that they are a respectable class of men?—All round I would say of the publicans in Waterford that they are a good respectable class of men.

60,692. They are not permitted to hold a licence until they have proved their respectability before getting the licence I understand they are bound to do so.

60,693. If you were asked, are the licensees a respectable well conducted class of men, what would be your answer?—I should say that they were, all round.

60,694. And that they were fit and proper in every respect to enjoy the privileges, or to have the responsibility of occupying a house of that character?—Yes.

Sunday closing.

60,695. If the hours of opening of public-houses were further restricted on a Sunday, what is the opinion as to whether it would give rise to an augmented number of clubs, shebeens, or other illicit modes of sale?—I think if the hours were restricted you would have no illicit clubs or shebeens, because you have the public-houses open from 2 to 7. If you have them open from 2 to 5 they give quite sufficient time for any man to get drink legitimately. The men who visit public-houses on Sundays are not the class of men who would visit clubs.

60,696. Are you of opinion that the statutory restriction would destroy the desire to consume these articles?—I do not think so.

60,697. Would any man's legitimate thirst seek means of obtaining that which he requires?—Man's desire is one thing; the temptation placed before him is another thing.

60,698. Is it not calculated to give rise to the existence of illicit places of sale?—I do not know.

Prosecutions of publicans.

60,699. (Dean Dudleston.) Have there been any prosecutions of publicans within your knowledge in Waterford?—There have been.

60,700. Have there been many?—In reading the papers almost every week there are cases of prosecution.

60,701. You would not include those convicted publicans among the generally respectable class?—I said "all round." The exception is those who are prosecuted.

60,702. You said in answer to Mr. Whittaker that there was a certain relation between the large number of public-houses and the large amount of intemperance. There is a larger number of public-houses in proportion in Waterford to other cities, and consequently there is a larger amount of intemperance?—There is a larger amount of temptation to intemperance.

Habitual inebriates.

60,703. It is reported to have been said in the House of Commons the other day that there are no inebriates in Ireland. Is that your belief?—I wish it were true.

60,704. Do you think it is not true?—I am positively certain that it is not true.

60,705. Of course I mean habitual inebriates?—Yes.

60,706. You think there are habitual inebriates?—I know some of them, unfortunately.

60,707. Is it your belief that it would be a good thing to extend the establishment of homes for inebriates to Ireland. You know the question has been before the House of Commons of the establishment of two classes of homes for criminal inebriates and for non-criminal inebriates, and Ireland is not included as yet in the provisions of that Bill. Do you think there is any reason why Ireland should be excluded from that Bill?—I think there is no reason why it should be excluded. I think it would be a good thing for Ireland to include it.

60,708. You think it would be a grievance to Ireland if it were not included?—Well, we have so many grievances there is no use adding to them.

60,709. You think that there should be a treatment for those inebriates?—I do.

60,710. And not always as criminals?—No.

60,711. But as persons who need to be protected and pitied and reformed?—Yes.

60,712. Do you attribute the excessive number of public-houses to the want of moral courage on the part of the magistrates?—I would not say that. Rev. F. F. Furlong.

60,713. How do you account for it?—Before some of the present magistrates were appointed we had the same number of public-houses that we have at present.

60,714. Has there, in your experience, been an increase lately?—There may have been an increase of four or five public-houses in the last six years, but no very appreciable increase the last 20 years.

60,715. Your official experience is the last eight years?—Yes.

60,716. You stated that you are in favour of the county court judge sitting with the resident magistrate and two other persons, I think, as the licensing authority?—Yes.

60,717. Would you select those from the general body of magistrates by co-option or how?—My idea is that they should be appointed by the State.

60,718. From among the magistrates or from outside the magistracy?—If you appointed them from the magistracy you are likely to have the same difficulty and danger, that the local men will be directly or indirectly connected with the trade.

60,719. Or subject to influence?—Subject to influence.

60,720. Can you state what proportion of persons holding publicans' licences carry on other trades?—No, I cannot tell you that.

60,721. Do you know of your own knowledge that they carry on other trades except that of selling groceries, such as drapery?—No, we have no such thing in the city of Waterford. We may have one or two cases where the husband is a draper, and his wife or daughter may be attending to a public-house, but it is only in very few cases. There may be two or three. Mixed trade premises.

60,722. In those cases is the sale of drink carried on upon the same premises?—No. In such a house there is only the sale of drink.

60,723. The wife holds the licence for a separate house?—Yes; or they may live over the house, but no other goods will be sold in the house. There is no such thing in the city of Waterford as a draper selling drapery goods and intoxicating liquors in the same shop.

60,724. Can you speak at all for districts outside the city of Waterford and county of Waterford on that point?—I cannot, but from my own knowledge I think it is exceedingly rare that anything else except food would be sold in a public-house.

60,725. Except in the case where they sell groceries?—I look upon that as food.

60,726. Not sold for consumption on the premises?—No. In what I call public-houses, pure and simple, no food as a rule is provided, and that is I think an evil.

60,727. Not for consumption on the premises?—Not for consumption on the premises.

60,728. Are there no what are called restaurants in the city of Waterford?—Yes, but those restaurants, I think, as a rule, have no licence to sell intoxicating drinks.

60,729. They are temperance restaurants?—Temperance principally. They are more like confectioner's shops, where you get a cup of tea or coffee and a sandwich.

60,730. You stated that, in your opinion, the police are slack in the administration of their duties?—Yes, but I think there is room for more zeal and activity on the part of the police. Police.

60,731. Do you attribute to that slackness the large number of drunkenness—the unprosecuted drunkenness?—No, I do not attribute the number of drunkenness to the slackness of the police.

60,732. In consequence of the slackness of the police that there were a large number of drunkenness?—Yes, there are a large number of drunkenness, but I think it must be said for the police that they display commendable activity in bringing up the drunkards.

60,733. On that point they are not slack?—Certainly not.

Rev. T. F. Furlong.

60,736. The police themselves may have men in plain clothes, have not they?—They have.

60,737. Do you know the class of shebeens; can you divide them into classes. Do many of them keep a large quantity of drink for sale on the premises?—I do not think a large amount of drink. I do not suppose they would have more than four or five dozen bottles of porter, for instance.

60,738. Do you know cases where they have even less?—There might be.

60,739. You do not know of your own experience?—I do not.

60,740. (Chairman.) You mentioned a case where the husband kept the draper's shop, and the wife held a licence?—I did not say a draper's shop. I said the husband to [illegible] the city of Waterford [illegible] be a draper's [illegible]—and his wife would carry on a public-house.

60,741. (Vincent de Vesci.) I understand it was two different shops?—Yes, the husband may be a draper's [illegible].

60,742. The husband would go out to attend to his business during the day as a draper's assistant?—Yes.

60,743. Are there many licences granted to married women in Waterford?—I could not say.

Rev. T. F. Furlong.

11 April '99.

Licences to married women.

The witness withdrew.

Mrs. Eugenie Crawford called in and examined.

Mrs. E. Crawford.

Sale of drink to children.

60,744. (Chairman.) I think you wish to direct your evidence to the special question of the frequentation of public-houses in Dublin by children?—I do.

60,745. You are a member, and, if I mistake not, President, of a total abstinence association?—Yes.

60,746. In combination with other associations which have pretty nearly the same object in view?—Yes.

60,747. What would those be?—The Committee that requested me to come forward represents four associations: the Catholic Women's Temperance League, the Dublin Women's Total Abstinence Society, the Rathgar Branch of the Irish Women's Temperance Union, and the Dublin Women's Methodist Temperance Union.

60,748. You have been chosen a representative of these four associations to come and give evidence before this Commission?—I have.

60,749. Does the practice of frequentation of public-houses by children exist to any large degree in Dublin?—I believe it does, as the result of observations that we have made.

60,750. You hand in, I think, some tables which illustrate that observation?—Yes. (See App. VIII.)

Children frequenting public-houses.

The [illegible] figures, &c.

"His mother was an habitual inebriate; his father who "was of sober habits, therefore as soon as possible sent "this child to be brought up, away from her example, "into the country. Returning home, when but six "years of age, the propensity for alcohol soon manifested "itself; for then, discovering a bottle of whisky "provided by his mother, he helped himself freely to "its contents, became speedily drunk, and thence- "forward tippled, whenever he could, for two years. "A few days before admission to the hospital, he ab- "stracted a bottle of port wine, which he had finished "all but a glass or so when discovered. After this "bout he fell into a drunken sleep, in which he nearly "died, and subsequently becoming delirious, was "brought to the hospital. He then exhibited all the "symptoms of delirium tremens, understood perfectly "what was said to him, but shook like an aspen leaf "on being spoken to, and tried to hide under the bed- "clothes, complained of imaginary assailants, and "showed abject terror of the other children in the "ward. His glance was distant and staring, pupils "dilated, skin cool and clammy, tongue moist and "furred, abdomen natural, temperature subnormal, "pulse 140—weak and somewhat irregular. He was "put on suitable treatment, and on the following day

Mrs. E. Crawford.

Mrs. E. Crawford.

27 April '98.

60,766. I want to trace the causes of the intemperance of the children, and my question is whether you can trace the intemperance of these young children to any particular shop or to any particular effect of the system of the trade?—I do not think we can trace it to anything more than the habit of being sent for drink, and, of course, hereditary tendency comes in.

60,767. They might be sent innocently to a grocer's shop for grocery and get drink there, might not they? —As a rule children would not be supplied with drink unless sent for the drink.

60,768. They might be sent for drink under the guise of going for groceries; is that ever the case?—I should not think so. They are sent for groceries to the public-house, but they are also sent for drink.

60,769. Speaking more generally, do you see any evil in the combination of the two trades?—I do see a great deal of evil.

60,770. You cannot trace to that system any particular evils as affecting juvenile intemperance?—Excepting in this way: that when children are sent to fetch groceries they are surrounded with the influence of a public-house. On the very counter there is often a glass of liquor. I have gone in myself just to buy groceries, to see the surroundings, and I have stood at the counter, and there has been a jug of whisky and water, or a glass which had been just used, beside me, and there have been women drinking on one side of me, and a little child standing looking at the women at the counter.

60,771. In a grocer's shop?—Yes, in a shop where I bought candles. I went in to buy some for the sake of observing the surroundings.

60,772. It was not a public-house?—Yes, it is a public-house. In Dublin almost universally the public-house and the grocer's shop are one.

60,773. At the same counter grocery and intoxicants are sold?—Yes.

60,774. And when the child went in to get groceries, she saw on the table whisky in jugs, in open vessels?—Persons drinking at the counter. Usually the drinking is [illegible], but it is [illegible] at the counter.

60,775. That is at a regular public-house?—Yes.

Private bars.

60,776. Are there such things as private bars in those houses?—There are in a great many public-houses.

60,777. I mean a public bar in a somewhat private part of the house?—Yes, that has been a subject that has been considered very important as bringing out the facilities for women's and even ladies' private drinking. I have myself found a great many places where the hall door, which to a casual observer would look like an entrance to a private dwelling, was used for drinking purposes. There was no board saying "private bar." "Private bar" is often put up, but in those houses there is nothing to distinguish it from the dwelling house. There is a great deal of drinking in the halls of what appears to be the entrance to the private dwelling-house.

Poor relief in public-houses.

60,778. Before we go to the statistics is there any custom in Dublin of distributing tickets for poor law medical relief in public-houses, or any houses where intoxicants are sold?—It is very usual. The guardians have the distributing of them before the medical relief —that is for the medical men to attend the applicants at their own houses; but so many of the guardians are publicans and the public-house is a familiar place to

60,782. (Chairman.) Would it be possible that they should be distributed only at the relieving officer's office?—Yes, at the dispensary, that those holding public-houses should be prohibited from having the distributing.

60,783. I suppose in many cases the publican is a guardian?—Very often.

Children frequenting public-houses. (See Appendix.)

60,784. I believe you hand in a return showing the number of children under 13 who entered public-houses on Sundays between the hours of 2 and 3 o'clock, do you not?—Yes.

60,785. Did members of your association watch these houses and count the number of children who went in? —They did. There were 80 observations made by 43 different persons. That is, there were 80 [illegible] tabulated which were made at different times by 43 different persons in respect of 58 different public-houses.

60,786. Was one person told off to watch every public-house?—Sometimes there were two, and sometimes there was one.

60,787. At all events on 80 separate observations were taken?—Yes.

60,788. The total number of children entering those 58 public-houses while they were under observation was how many?—3846.

60,789. That included children who went there with vessels as well as those who went there without vessels? —Yes, we observed both, because on account of the practice of selling groceries we believed it would be well for us to find out how many went simply to fetch drink, and how many might go for other purposes; and we found that 2,344 went with vessels and 1,[illegible] without vessels. I should observe that on 13 occasions those without vessels were not counted, and this gives the average of children entering lower than it actually was.

60,790. (Mr. Young.) Over what period of time is that?—We commenced our observations about the 17th October and I think our last observations were at the end of February. They extended over the winter-time months at all events.

60,791. (Chairman.) The length of observation is given. It extended, roughly speaking, from an hour down to 17 minutes?—Yes, we sometimes observed for 15 minutes and sometimes for an hour. The average length of observation was really 47 minutes.

60,792. (Dean Dickinson.) Why does December come after February?—It just happens that the first table [illegible] out lady sent in her observations too late. It was a little mistake in the tabulating.

60,793. (Chairman.) It would be a little misleading, would not it, to take the final statement as the result, because we do not know what was the time during which this particular house was under observation, but I think your first table tells us that pretty clearly. As I understand it, the length of observation in that case was 60 minutes, and the number of children was 22 who went in with vessels, and came without?—I have it down that the average length of observation between 2 and 3 on Sunday was 37 minutes.

60,794. That is the average, but there is so much uncertainty in averages that I wish to take special cases of observation?—On the 12th February one who observed for 60 minutes.

60,798. Not with their parents?—Not with their parents. Very often two or three children go in together to keep each other company. We did not count children who went in as if to play.

60,799. And you did not count a child who went in with an adult?—No. We did not count infants that were carried in. We did not count children who ran in and out. We observed that the children ran in and out to play in the public-houses as if they were quite familiar there, and quite happy there, but we never counted those children. We took care only to count those who went on business.

60,800. (Dean Dickinson.) On errands?—Yes.

60,801. (Chairman.) Do you think any encouragement was given to these children by presents of sweets being handed to them over the counter?—We observed nothing of the kind.

60,802. It was only external observation?—We had no reason to believe there were any inducements offered. Occasionally I have seen children coming out eating biscuits or sugar. We thought it was a very natural thing for a kind-hearted person to give a little child a biscuit, and we did not make anything of that; we were not aware of any bad purpose offered to children.

60,803. That rather points to the fact that they do get some little present when they go into those places?—We did not observe such a custom.

60,804. To summarise your Sunday observations, your total number of observations I think were 45 between 6 and 7?—Yes.

60,805. What was the total number of children entering in those hours?—2,746.

60,806. And during those 45 observations?—Yes.

60,807. The average length of observations was what?—45 minutes.

60,808. The average number entering in during 45 minutes was what?—The average number entering in was 61.

60,809. And the average number during 60 minutes?—We made out that that would make an average per hour of 82.

60,810. Do we gather from these statistics that there is any particular hour at which the entering into public-houses is more frequent than at other times?—Yes, between 2 and 3 on Sunday, and between 6 and 7 on Sunday evening, because they are the hours immediately after, and immediately before closing. It seemed as if there was a higher average on Saturday afternoon as well.

60,811. Presumably, therefore, the greater number of messengers entered the public-houses during those hours?—Yes.

60,812. Those were the hours during which child messengers would be most likely to be made use of, would they?—I think so.

60,813. (Mr. Grinling.) I suppose the reason for entering between 6 and 7 would be that the houses close at 7, and therefore they naturally go at that time if at all?—Exactly; to bring home drink.

60,814. (Chairman.) That is the conclusion you draw from these statistics that you would prohibit children from entering public-houses?—We would wish to do so.

60,815. Up to what age?—The suggestion that I make is that the law which prohibits the sale of drink should be extended to including. That law prohibits the sale of drink to children for their own consumption under the age of 13, or spirits under 16. I might also [illegible]

"should be extended to the supplying to them of "intoxicating drink in any licensed house for any "purpose whatever." And the other resolution is from the Police Aided Children's Clothing Society, of which the Commissioner [illegible] is president. The terms are the same.

Mrs. E. Craigford

— 7 April '99

60,816. As to the proportion of boys to girls. In these statistics do you give the proportion of girls to boys?—No, we do not. It was considered of no importance for they were all young children, but we have seen children going in apparently of the age of 3 or 4.

60,818. (Viscount de Vesci.) One question just to bring out again what you said before. You are of opinion that the fact of the mixed trades existing, groceries being sold on the same establishment, throws greater difficulties in the way of limiting the sending of children to public-houses?—Of course it does, because necessarily children may be sent as messengers for things other than drink.

Mixed trades in public-houses.

60,819. You would admit it is absolutely necessary that children should be sent to fetch groceries?—I think amongst the poorer people it is very necessary. I am aware of the difficulty, but the fact seems to us so very grave that so far the difficulty has to be faced, for the children are being educated up to be drunkards.

60,820. You say in your précis that the mischievous nature of such an arrangement is apparent, and the evils resulting from it will continue so long as household groceries can only be procured at the public-house?—Perhaps I should say they are generally purchased in the public-house, because in Dublin it is a rule that in the poorest districts every public-house is a grocer's shop and is described as a family grocer's, and I think this has even a greater influence on young women in encouraging drink amongst them than amongst children, because young women sometimes go who would be ashamed to go into a public-house. Having to go for their household necessities, that feeling is completely broken down, and while waiting for their goods they can have a drink.

60,821. For that reason the association with which you are connected is in favour of prohibiting the sale of other goods besides drink on the same premises?—They would think it very desirable.

60,822. (Dean Dickinson.) With regard to the society you referred to last, the Police Aided Clothing Society, that arose from the fact that children were seen almost naked in the streets, arising from the circumstance of their parents pawning the clothes given to them?—Yes.

Police Aided Clothing Society.

60,823. (Chairman.) Do you know that?—Yes.

60,824. (Dean Dickinson.) Then to prevent that repeated pawning for drink on the part of the parents the Police Aided Clothing Society was established to clothe the children, placing on the clothes indelible marks, and warning the pawnbrokers against receiving those clothes in pawn?—Yes.

60,825. And prosecuting the pawnbrokers in case they were received in pawn?—Yes.

60,826. In order to prevent the patently disgraceful fact of children running about the streets half naked, or nearly altogether naked?—That is so, and also kind-hearted people giving clothes encouraged the drink, for the clothes went to the pawnbrokers and then the money went to the publican.

60,827. I wanted to bring out for the information of the Commission that that society originated in the too frequent habit of parents pawning the clothes of the children?—Yes. It has worked well in Edinburgh and [illegible]

[illegible]. Relief means a visit?—Yes, medical relief.

[illegible]. (Mr. Walker.) They have to go to the guardian at his public-house to get the ticket necessary for medical relief?—The poor person goes to the house of a guardian to get that ticket, and they have a habit of going to the public-house.

there must be relieving officers to whom I have spoken of it as a particularly mischievous practice, and said that some of the guardians hold it to be so mischievous that they were using their efforts now to prevent it.

60,871. How many visitors would a guardian have?—He would give them to anybody he was satisfied was a suitable applicant—a person too poor to pay for private medical attendance.

60,872. The guardians look to appeal to the suffrages of the people to become a guardian?—Yes.

60,874. If this was such a very objectionable practice, or had such a very bad effect on the people, would it not very soon come to the ears of the electorate? Would not it be your duty, as representing your constituents, to put it before the electorate?—There are a great many customs that are injurious, and there has not yet been any fuss made about them.

60,875. I can only say this, that the guardians are appointed by the electorate, and if you placed before the electorate that the guardian is a licensed victualler or was guilty of improper proceedings from your point of view, would not that prevent his being re-elected?—No; we could not think of calling it an improper proceeding from a guardian's point of view.

60,876. It is not improper?—Certainly not. He is only fulfilling his duty as a guardian. I am not finding fault with the publican who distributes these tickets, but I only say that the practice is considered mischievous, and if there was a law to prevent the going to a publican to obtain medical relief it would be desirable, but I am not attacking him as the publican, who may do it out of kindly motives.

60,877. (*Mr. Hyslop.*) There is one question I should like to repeat with reference to the figures that you have given. You have given 1,544 children with vessels and 1,301 without vessels. What is the inference your society would draw with reference to those children who entered those houses without vessels?—Very frequently we have thought it quite possible there might be bottles. We have often seen a bottle, which is not a vessel, but the children might have been sent for any other purpose.

60,878. You seem to have had a meaning when you gave the figures of the children who entered a public-house without a vessel or without anything to lead you to a conclusion?—Our meaning was this, that in our city there are other reasons for the children entering. They may be going to buy groceries. The children might be sent for a lawful purpose to buy groceries, but we consider it none the less an evil that they should be mixed up with the public-house.

60,879. I take those figures as referring to public-houses. I did not think your remark here applied to grocers at all?—All those public-houses are grocers' shops. All the houses that we watched have also a grocer's shop attached to them. In every one of the instances you will see written up family grocers, tea, coffee, and everything that is in a grocer's shop will be in those public-houses.

60,880. With reference to children entering a public-house, there are a variety of causes that might lead them there. It is not unusual to send for a postage stamp, and there are other things children are sent for to a public-house besides fetching beer and spirits?—That is why we were particular to count those who did go to fetch beer and spirits.

60,881. I should like to ask you another question with reference to this child drunkard. May we accept the paper you have read with reference to that case as a doctor's certificate?—This is a pamphlet already published.

60,882. Is it the doctor's certificate of the case?—Yes, I think it is the medical report of the case read before the Medical Association.

60,883. Is that signed by the doctor?—His name is to it.

60,884. I want to know if he signed the paper—if he has given it as a certificate of the case?—He read this paper himself.

state of affairs before the public as an exposé of the mischief to the children.

60,886. Giving this very distinctive statement of the case of this boy, it represented a large number of others, and in fact in this pamphlet there are [illegible] cases reported, and not only by Dr. More Madden but by Sir Francis Cruise, another very eminent man. There is a case reported by him here, and I have letters from Sir Francis Cruise and Dr. More Madden on the subject expressing their opinion of the great mischief of children getting drink. They are both eminent men.

60,887. (*Mr. Roberts.*) I notice in the pamphlet containing the address of this eminent doctor in Dublin, Dr. More Madden, that he states a case based on his own experience on page 6. He points out that on one occasion, and that unfortunately not an exceptional one, "I saw three children, all under 10 or 11 years of age, "reeling drunk out of a public-house in one of our "leading thoroughfares on a Sunday afternoon. One "was unable to stand unaided. Another was vomiting "at the door of the gin-palace, and was using filthy "improper language." Apparently, therefore, he had personal experience of what he was talking about?—Yes.

60,888. There is one question I should like to ask you upon this table. Mr. Hyslop has asked you why you made a distinction between those with cans and jugs and those without. I want to ask you whether it is likely that a large proportion of those not apparently having cans or jugs would be buying groceries on Sunday night? Is Sunday night the usual time for sending children to buy groceries for family purposes?—I do not think it is usual, but in the poor neighbourhoods they do get bread, candles, and the like and sugar at any time. They might have done so, but I think it is just as probable they were carrying drink, but I believe they did not receive it in a vessel. We were careful not to take a note of it, and we thought it wise to make the distinction.

60,889. (*Mr. Whitaker.*) If two children went together from the same house one would carry the jug, or whatever it was, and the other would be without?—Yes.

60,890. That would account for some of them being without vessels?—Yes. Sometimes three would go together. They like going.

60,891. (*Mr. Crossley.*) I think you stated that you did not count the children who went together; if two went together you counted them as one?—We counted one carrying the vessel and one without.

60,892. (*Mr. Whitaker.*) I understand they were not counted when they went in twos?—No.

60,893. (*Chairman.*) Or when they went in and out of the house?—No, we did not count those children, or few such going on a Sunday.

60,894. (*Mr. Whitaker.*) Then I think you told us that there was an arrangement in many houses by which, if customers went in at what appeared to be a private door, they found facilities inside for the supply of liquor?—Yes.

60,895. May I gather from that that a great many people who go into public-houses are ashamed of going in, and like to find some way where it will not be known they are going into public-houses? Is that the reason for those private doors?—I think so. Perhaps I may say how I was led to find out about these private doors—it might answer your question. It was a lady of a very good social position who had got under the power of drink. She was trying to make a struggle against it, and a friend of my own who was trying to help her in that way observed her turn the handle and go into what seemed to be the private dwelling-house of one of these houses—I have a picture of it here—and when she came out my friend asked her why she had gone in there, and she said, "That is a private way; "you do not suppose that I would stand at the bar "with other people." She was a lady in a very good social position, and one that we should like to protect. The mischief of this is that they offer such facilities for ladies and others privately drinking, and because they are scarcely open to police supervision. The policeman would hardly turn the handle of a dwelling-house and go in. I have myself been in since of those places.

60,896. May I take it that this trade about what

Mrs. R. Crawford.

[illegible]

because everybody should try and prevent that lady. I have two pictures here of these private doors. They are only just the hall doors of the dwelling-house.

60,897. Would you allow me to look at them?—Yes (handing in same). One of them is in one of the very low neighbourhoods of Dublin inhabited by the [illegible].

60,898. (Viscount de Vesci.) Is that the private entrance door?—It seems to be the entrance to the dwelling-house.

60,899. (Mr. Roberts.) Is this the door on the left-hand side?—There is a little step indicating it—the hall door. There was indication that it was a bar. Very often, in other cases, "private bar" is written up.

60,900. (Viscount de Vesci.) Does the licence in that case attach to the whole building?—I believe there is nothing illegal in it. I believe it is perfectly legal.

60,901. (Dean Dickinson.) The drink was sold in the hall?—Yes.

60,902. That is not totally included in the licence?—I do not think it makes any matter, whether it is illegal or not.

60,903. (Mr. Whitbread.) The publican evidently knows that these people who use these places would be ashamed to go in the ordinary entrance?—I think so.

60,904. He provides facilities for them to do secretly what he knows they are ashamed of doing?—It looks like that.

60,905. Does not that strike you as a reflection on the moral character of the publican?—It seems very bad.

Child messengers to public-houses.

60,906. (Mr. Graham.) However much one may agree with you as to the desirability or undesirability of children being sent to public-houses, you do recognise that there are great difficulties surrounding the question?—I do.

60,907. And, as a lady engaged very largely in philanthropic work, you have met with difficulties?—Yes.

60,908. Take the case of a working man—because a case very often clears up these difficulties. He goes to work, say, at 7 o'clock and comes home at 12 o'clock to his dinner. The wife is employed in tidying up the house, and in many cases has work to do besides. The man comes home to his dinner, and part of his dinner, as I suppose you would agree, is a pint of beer. The wife is engaged in cooking and preparing his dinner and doing the housework. She has a child, say, of 13 years old. Do you think it would be possible entirely to do away with the use of that child as a messenger?—I believe it is difficult at present, but I think the danger and mischief are so very great that the difficulty should be met.

60,909. Your view is that you would like to do anything within reason to discourage the use of the child for these purposes?—I would.

60,910. You do admit there are circumstances and always will be circumstances where it is impossible to avoid it?—From inquiries amongst some very respectable working women that I know very well I know that they have the habit of sending their children to the public-houses for groceries, and that is one of the mischiefs that one must call attention to, that in the poorer neighbourhoods there is nowhere else to send them than to the public-house, and I know women who object to it very much, but they are forced to send their children to the public-house.

62,929. They have nothing to do with consumption at?—Not with what we call a spirit grocer's license in my mind.

62,930. (*Sir Charles Cameron.*) They are licenses for consumption on?—Yes, on the premises.

62,931. You know in other parts of the kingdom the grocer's license does not permit of consumption on the premises?—I do.

62,932. I suppose even that would be a great practical reform that you would advocate?—The abolition of the spirit grocer's license.

62,933. The abolition of licenses to grocers permitting sale on the premises?—Yes.

62,934. A restriction of grocers' licenses to selling off the premises?—At present the restriction on spirit grocers' licenses is to sell entirely off the premises. If you mean not granting a publican's license to a man who has a grocery establishment we think that would be very desirable.

62,935. (*Dean Dickinson.*) The separation of the two?—Yes, very desirable.

62,936. (*Sir Charles Cameron.*) That is a very strong point in your opinion?—Yes, especially in dealing with young women, the wives of the working classes.

62,937. There is another point. In other parts of the kingdom in connection with the issue of publicans' licenses—that is for sale on the premises—the authorities are very careful about the number of entrances and so on. In many places they will not permit back entrances and they regulate all those things very carefully. That does not appear to be the case in Dublin. Has any representation been made against those private entrances?—I am not aware that any representation has been made.

62,938. You say they are so common that you have seen yourself some of them?—Yes. It is very common to have the drink in back, and they have it announced by the words "private bar" on the hall door in every case, but in the cases I specially allude to there was no such notice on the hall door.

62,939.—You said that you had letters from Sir Francis Cruise and Dr. More Madden?—Yes.

62,940. Have you any objection to handing them in?—No. The letters were addressed to Miss Barrett, the sister of Professor Barrett.

62,941. (*Dean Dickinson.*) Who has a Home for children?—Yes. Miss Barrett wrote to Dr. More Madden asking if he had anything further to state on this subject, and he replied:—

"[illegible] Merrion Square, Dublin,
"March 21st, 1902.

"Dear Madam,

"In reply to your letter of to-day, I return the questions you sent me, which I have answered as far as I could. I need hardly say that I fully sympathise with all efforts to diminish alcoholism amongst children. But I fear that it would be impossible for me to add much, if anything, to what I have already written on this subject. In a paper published some time ago by the Temperance Publication Society (of which I enclose a copy), you will find an abstract of my views on this question, and of some of the cases on which those opinions were founded. If you think any of these likely to be useful in the evidence you are preparing for the Royal Commission they are at your disposal.

"Believe me, dear Madam,
"Yours very faithfully,
"Thos. More Madden.

"Sending—are quite out of my power."

62,942. It was in that way you got Dr. More Madden's paper, from which you cited the cases?—No, we had got the facts of Dr. More Madden's observations before that. The case was written just before I came away, and I have also one from Sir Francis Cruise.

62,943. (*Dean Dickinson.*) Will you give us that letter?—Yes. Sir Francis Cruise writes:—

"Merrion Square West,
"Dear Miss Barrett, Dublin.

"Nothing is more necessary in the great struggle against intemperance than to restrict children from all intoxicating drinks. I dare say you have read in Dr. More Madden's paper on this subject a case which I contributed illustrating this point. Children, unlike animals, appear to have no inborn taste for alcohol. Dip a finger in toddy or punch and you will see the youngest infant suck it greedily, while the brute will turn from it in disgust. In my opinion no alcoholic drink should be given to a child, unless as a medicine or under competent direction. Not alone does it risk their complete demoralisation, but it is injurious to the physical development of children, injuring the nervous system and digestive organs, and laying the foundation of liver and kidney disease.

"I remain, yours faithfully,
"F. R. Cruise.

"P.S.—I have put but in a few words my views touching children and alcoholic drinks, and I enclose a slip from 'The Tablet,' a Catholic paper of position, on the subject."

62,944. Sir Francis Cruise is one of the most eminent doctors in Dublin?—Yes.

62,945. (*Sir Charles Cameron.*) You have quoted the case that Sir Francis Cruise refers to?—Yes.

62,946. In connection with these visits of children to public houses, I suppose the vessel that you refer to would be a can for beer?—Usually a can, but I have sometimes seen children carrying away small bottles—what they call naggin bottles, or half-pint bottles—and those observing saw children drink from those half-pint bottles.

62,947. The usual use of such a vessel that it would indicate beer or spirits?—I have seen little children getting small bottles, and the bottles had whisky in them.

62,948. Have you visited any of these children's homes?—No. We did not wish in taking these observations to do anything of that kind, because we simply wanted to prove that phase of the question—the drinking. We did not follow it up.

Mrs. [illegible]

17 April 1902.

Child messengers to public houses.

The witness withdrew.

Mr. Timothy C. Harrington, M.P., called in and examined.

Mr. T. C. Harrington, M.P.

62,949. (*Chairman.*) You, as we know, are Member of Parliament for the Harbour Division of Dublin City?—Yes, since 1885.

62,950. You sat previously for Westmeath?—Yes.

62,951. You have acquired a considerable knowledge of the licensing laws and their operation?—Yes; for that time I have had considerable experience through all Ireland, but of course I am most intimate with Dublin; and it is rather to Dublin I should wish to direct my evidence chiefly.

62,952. Do you think that in Dublin we have gone as far as we could in the direction of limitation either on Saturday or Sunday?—I am afraid any further limitation will rather increase than diminish the evil of drunkenness. I have observed that every time a Royal Commission is sitting and every time a Sunday Closing Bill is on the point of passing there is an increase both in the number of arrests for drunkenness and in the number of clubs, some of which are generally regarded as [illegible].

62,953. Could you summarise your objections to any further restriction?—I should put them under four heads. First, I say it is exceptional legislation, and I do not believe with reference to Dublin, and I think with reference to Ireland generally, that any case is made out for exceptional legislation in the matter of the licensing law.

Exceptional legislation.

62,954. May I say, with regard to that, that you are aware that the whole system of law is in that sense exceptional with reference to the licensed trade, and therefore by itself it would not be a weighty argument?—That is so. The whole system is exceptional, but I am speaking of its being exceptional with reference to one particular district or one particular country. I say the case of Ireland does not present any feature which requires exceptional legislation in the matter of temperance. I do not believe, taking the city of Dublin, that the people are any more given to drunkenness than they are in any of the other large cities of the United Kingdom.

[illegible] England and Wales, and therefore the [illegible] we would realise by bringing Dublin [illegible] of the other countries?—Yes, to some [illegible], not in all.

[illegible] you kindly pursue your reasons?—I [illegible] of respectable public-houses kept [illegible] supervision by the police, where the orders [illegible] to occur and where the publican has a [illegible] he has to defend and has a great in-[illegible], will lead to the increase of drinking in [illegible] of a much more dangerous character [illegible] and to morals. I do not believe [illegible] closing of public-houses on Sundays [illegible] diminish—it may to some small extent [illegible] amount of drunkenness in the streets [illegible]. I do not believe it will to any [illegible], for I think the facilities for [illegible] will remain whatever you do, and the [illegible] drunkenness are likely to be quite as great. [illegible] for opposing any further legislation [illegible] the working population, for whom the [illegible] chiefly intended, there is really no [illegible] demand for it. I am aware that there [illegible] active temperance societies in Ireland, [illegible] elsewhere. They have a special capacity [illegible] themselves. They appear in different [illegible] places and in another. They are a tem-[illegible] in one place and a philanthropic associa-[illegible], and they pass various resolutions; but [illegible] general body of working people I see no [illegible] demand for increased restriction.

[illegible] any longer"?—All I can say is the practice in the police courts is entirely in contradiction of that, because the charges of the police made day after day is simple drunkenness, and undoubtedly men are every day charged, and these cases are reported to Parliament as cases of drunkenness in the public streets. Mr. F. C. [illegible]

60,963. I may say the authority was the county court judge of Donegal, and I only thought it necessary to refer to that as an expression of a legal opinion. You do not agree to that?—I do not agree to that. I have seen people arrested for nothing excepting the mere appearance of drunkenness in the public street, men whom I considered perfectly capable of going to their homes.

60,964. Therefore the disparity which appears in the statistics between the drunkenness of Dublin, and some other cities may be in part owing to the fact that the police are more active, and arrest people for simple drunkenness, where in other towns they would be let off?—Yes, and so far as I can understand the activity of the police is their discipline. At the present time every policeman in Dublin is, I believe, supposed to have five cases a month. That does not mean cases of drunkenness, but every policeman is supposed to show a certain amount of activity. Drunkenness and the police.

60,965. I suppose it is not an injunction to the police from any superior authority that they must show ten cases per month?—I think it is. I understand that a circular has been issued to the Dublin police. I hope, if the Reverend Dean disputes my evidence——

60,966. (Dean Dickinson.) I do not dispute it. I do—

Mr. T. D. [illegible], M.P.

[illegible]

it is only the skilled artisans in Dublin who knock off for the half-holiday on Saturday.

60,884. (Chairman.) But are they paid their wages on the previous day?—Some are, but not all. In a great many working establishments they are paid their wages on Saturday, and in some cases the men are working a distance out of the city, and they have to travel home. They have to work till 6 o'clock on Saturdays—the unskilled labourers and those engaged in discharging vessels along the quay. They are a large proportion of my constituency, which extends on both sides of the river.

Mixed trade in licensed premises.

60,885. (Viscount de Vesci.) With regard to the shopping part of the question, you think it would be impossible to organise the trades in Dublin [illegible] so that they could do it. Practically you would have to revolutionise the whole trade in Dublin as it exists. I may say that with regard to some working men, it would be impossible for them to get their marketing done by 9 o'clock on Saturday. They return a distance of two or three miles from their work. Then they take supper and clean themselves and turn out to do business, often with their wives, and if you close the grocers' shops at 9 there, you do not give them an opportunity of doing it, and then they have to buy the drink and keep it in their houses. Many of these houses only one or two rooms, where it would be open to all members of the family. I doubt whether you would do anything better by having it exposed to the children in the house than having the children going out for it on Sundays.

Clubs.

60,886. (Chairman.) What is the rule amongst the great mass of the working population in Dublin? What hour do they go to bed?—They do not go to bed, I think you may take it, till after 11 o'clock certainly. I may say that I visit a good deal in my own constituency, and I see clubs in full working order, and there up to 1 and 2 o'clock on Saturday nights, and I think those clubs are a much greater evil to social life, and a greater injury to those men and their families than the public-houses, where the wife can find out the husband if he is there, and where she can go in herself, or a member of the family can go in and find him.

60,887. How would you deal with the clubs?—That is a great difficulty. I think it would be very hard for the Legislature to draw a line between the clubs that ought not to be interfered with and the other clubs that ought to be.

60,888. It would not be difficult for the Legislature to draw a distinction between a bona fide club no matter in what class of society it may be, and a bogus club?—That would be very easy, but I mean this. If you limit it by the payment of subscriptions—if you put the subscriptions at a certain rate, it would be very hard on the working man to increase the subscription he should pay to his club, and if you once allow them at a low subscription, you open the door to the establishment of a number of bogus clubs.

60,889. I only meant to imply that the amount of the subscription would be a presumption against the legality of the club?—Yes, that is so; but then the danger is that you would get one kind of legislation for the wealthy man able to pay a good subscription, and shut out the working man, who ought to have his club to meet his friends socially.

60,890. You would not abolish the clubs?—No, I do not think you can abolish them. I think that would be strongly resented.

Mr. T. C. Harrington, M.P.

8 April 1898.

[illegible] than can be done by throwing the clubs open to the inspection of the police, but I think every class of society will regard that strongly. If you have a working-man's club open to the inspection of the police, you must, if you want to be consistent, throw the gentleman's club open quite as much, and I think you will find the gentlemen will strongly resist such interference with them, and the working men would follow their example.

60,994. Do you think the working men would resent the police entry, because they would think it would be a different thing in their clubs to what it would be if the police went into the Carlton or any other of the great clubs?—I am afraid there would be a strong opposition in Ireland to giving the police any further power of entry to their clubs or houses than what they have at the present time, or what they can get by swearing information. To some extent, of course, the political condition of the country and political questions enter into this, and it would excite strong opposition to give them further power of searching.

Increased arrests for drunkenness.

60,995. (Sir Charles Cameron.) You mentioned that when a Royal Commission was sitting with a Sunday Closing Bill to the front, you had a notable increase of the statistics of drunkenness in Ireland. Has there been anything of that sort in connection with the present Commission?—I do not think we have the statistics. There is no legislation proposed in connection with the present Commission now.

60,996. This Commission has been sitting for over two years now?—I have not got the figures which deal with it, but it is quite possible there may have been.

60,997. You mentioned a Commission, but it appears it was not a Commission but a Select Committee to which the Bill was referred?—Yes, it was a Select Committee, and legislation was regarded in Ireland as pretty certain at that time. Everybody in Ireland believed at that time that legislation was sure to follow. There was one matter I did not mention in answer to the Chairman, if you will permit me to give it now. There was a point referred to by Mr. Russell which I should like to direct the attention of the Commission to. He spoke of the vote of the Irish representatives on the question of Sunday closing, and seemed to think the Irish vote was one of importance. I have taken out the figures of the Irish vote. Taking the division on this question in 1879 for the Sunday Closing Bill, the ayes were 245, the noes 81; the majority 164. The total Irish vote then was 66, and 50 were for the Bill and 16 against. In 1881 the majority in favour of the Bill was less, though the vote of the House was larger. The total Irish vote was 65, the ayes being 54, and the noes 11. Now I come down to 1888, when the total majority was 59, the Irish vote being 27, there being 16 for and 9 against. When you come to 1893 the total majority for the Bill was only 33, and the Irish majority for the Bill was only 1. The Irish vote was larger than it had been in preceding years. The figures were 33 for, and 32 against.

Irish vote on Sunday closing.

60,998. (Mr. Grinling.) The figures I have are, for the Bill 34, and against it 33?—You are speaking the Tellers in. The Tellers are excluded in my figures.

the police are very active and they have a great many prosecutions, but these clubs do not keep any large supply of drink. They get in a small supply just before the prohibited hours come in to operation, and so there would the police seize any very large quantity in the place, and if they can get a publican who will be in collusion with them, or a spirit grocer who will be in collusion with them, they will find some means of being illicitly supplied during prohibited hours.

Mr. T. C. Harrington, M.P.

61,004. You spoke about clubs being open at 1 or 2 o'clock on a Sunday morning; were those drinking clubs?—There are some clubs connected with labour and trade organisations, some are connected with politicians' organisations, and various social clubs at which they have bars set up specially for the purpose of drinking.

Clubs.

61,005. They have no regulations, so far as you know, as to an hour at which the bar should be closed?—Some of the better-class clubs close their bars at 11 o'clock nightly on Sunday evenings and all night, and close the clubs practically, but some of the others do not.

61,006. Those clubs are open on Sundays?—They are open on Sunday. I should think they would not be open only that we have the public-houses closed on a portion of the Sunday.

61,007. The hour that you spoke of was 1 to 2 o'clock on Sunday morning, that is, after Saturday night?—Yes, they are open at that hour, and I think a very considerable proportion of the arrests for drunkenness on Sunday come from those clubs.

61,008. You say they drive a particularly brisk business on Saturday nights?—When the public-houses are closed, because the members themselves and their friends are much more likely, if they meet a friend, to bring him to a club and give him a drink, when the chances are they would go into a public-house if the public-house was open. The danger is that they remain longer in the club than they would in the public-house.

61,009. We were told by a witness, I think yesterday, that the police had been reasonably successful in dealing with bogus clubs in Dublin. Are you aware of prosecutions?—I am aware of several prosecutions, and you will find that the statistics of drunkenness went down considerably. In 1893 the police commenced a series of prosecutions against bogus clubs, and I think the existing law was certainly strained as far as it could be stretched to meet the case of these bogus clubs.

Police prosecutions of bogus clubs.

61,010. You mentioned that you are a barrister, and therefore I thought we might get some definite information on that point. I attended the sessions I referred to where the bogus clubs were dealt with in Dublin. The difficulty in either party was that there is nothing against the clubs existing, and no legal definition of bogus?—It was chiefly under two heads; first of all, that persons who entered those clubs obtained drink who were not members.

61,011. Paid for it?—Yes, paid for drink who were not members. It was not paid for by a member of the club, and the police were able to satisfy the magistrate on that evidence that the club was a bogus club.

[illegible]. At the present time twenty three [illegible] numbers of clubs, for the reason that they can get a drink on Sunday before the public-houses are opened, and on Sunday night after the public-houses are closed; and the further you extend repressive legislation the more you will increase these clubs, or the more [illegible] [illegible] clubs [illegible] within the law, and which you cannot deal with under the [illegible] of bogus clubs. Some clubs in Dublin have found it necessary, from the [illegible] of persons to entertain their friends, to pass bye-laws prohibiting any member from entertaining a resident of Dublin during the hours at which the public-houses are closed.

61,014. (*Mr. Young.*) I think you have said that arrests for drunkenness were on the decrease?—I think drunkenness in Ireland is very largely on the decrease, and will be as the social condition of the people improves and as the means of employment are extended. One circumstance which leads very largely to the diminution of drunkenness in a city like Dublin will be the improvement of the dwellings of the poor. A working man who has only one apartment where his whole family is, six or seven children and his wife, when he has done his work on a Saturday evening, or when at home on Sunday, unless he is a particularly domestic man, does not care to remain in that room sitting with the whole of his family during that time, and naturally he is quite likely to go out, and if he meets a friend will meet him in a public-house. I think if you improve the dwellings of the poor you will keep men at home. If you make their condition of life in their homes much better, you will largely diminish drunkenness, and I think drunkenness is being largely diminished in that way in Dublin.

61,015. I might fairly say that your evidence is very important because you have had a large experience, as I understand?—A very large experience. I think my evidence will be the evidence of all the Members for Dublin. I do not think any Member for Dublin is in favour of any further prohibition of the public-houses in Dublin. I am not authorised to speak for them, but I think that is the feeling of all the Members for Dublin.

61,016. (*Mr. Grinling.*) Your objection to the further limitation of the hours either on Sunday or Saturday is that it would be exceptional legislation?—It is exceptional legislation, for which, to my mind, no case has been made.

61,017. When you say that, you mean class legislation?—To some extent class legislation, and to some extent exceptional, because you deal with Dublin differently from what you deal with any other large city.

61,018. Then if it is class legislation there is all the more reason why the class who would be affected by it should have a preponderating voice in the decision?—I think so.

61,019. It would be no use [illegible] to submit it to the people not affected by the action of the prohibitors?—My idea is that the whole temperance movement in Ireland, or what I may call the demand in favour of further restrictive legislation, comes from people mainly who are entirely opposed to the sale of intoxicating drink of any kind. They only go in for the restrictions because they think it is as much as they can get, but the great body of them are totally opposed to the drink sale altogether. I think it is largely a question of social life. I have always been a strong and healthy man myself, and I have a good constitution, and I have never found the necessity for drink; but I should not like to impose it on everybody else, and I should not [illegible] [illegible] [illegible] or habits by [illegible], and I

61,020. I think your opinion is confirmed by the evidence of Mr Mallon, the Assistant Commissioner of the Metropolitan Police for Dublin. He was asked whether they arrested in Dublin for simple drunkenness or whether the persons must be disorderly or not, and his answer was "No"?—He ought to be a good authority.

61,021. He also says: "We can arrest for simple drunkenness"?—They do.

61,022. You say as regards the police having more extended power, or exercising more extended power, that would account for a large amount of what appears to be excessive drunkenness?—Of course, and you may take it in connection with these cases of breaches of the licensing laws, such as permitting drunkenness on licensed premises. A policeman goes into a public-house and sees a person under the influence of drink in a public-house. His first step is to prosecute the person who has been under the influence of drink there. That is certainly arresting or prosecuting him for simple drunkenness, and in order to bring the charge home to the publican, he first summonses the person whom he alleges to be drunk.

61,023. That important item in the question of drunkenness in Dublin is shown by these tables of the Dublin Metropolitan Police. I see there is a heading of "Drunkenness not combined with any other offence"?—Yes.

61,024. And the number is 4,821 for the last year that the table is for; 5,[illegible] for 1883, and 5,[illegible] for 1884?—That is so.

61,025. That must be a large proportion?—It is. From my experience of the police court the larger proportion of the cases that come before the police court are cases of simple drunkenness, and very few are cases of habitual drunkenness unfortunately.

61,026. If the action of the police was the same in Dublin as in other towns, the state of affairs would put a much more favourable aspect on it?—The statistics would be much better.

61,027. Then on the point of Sunday closing, Mr. Mallon was again asked this question (No. 1[illegible]), "I think you say that you consider the Sunday Closing Act of 1878 brought clubs very much into existence. (A.) It has been observed by the police officers and others, that as the Sunday Closing Law was passed the clubs sprang up into existence"?—I say from my knowledge of the country that a club with a bar was absolutely unknown in the rural districts in Ireland until the Sunday Closing Act of 1878. I did not know of the existence of a club in any rural district in Ireland until the Sunday Closing Act was passed.

61,028. Then he was asked, "As to the 23 bogus clubs you talked of, are they in the city of Dublin or outside," and he answers "All within the city proper"?—Yes.

61,029. There is no question about the fact of a certain amount of drunkenness being due to the different action of the police, and a certain amount of drunkenness being due to bogus clubs existing?—Undoubtedly.

61,030. Taking the exempted cities, I think the five cities are Dublin, Belfast, Cork, Waterford, and Limerick?—Yes.

61,031. Are you acquainted with the Parliamentary Return which was prepared in April 1877?—Yes, I have got it here.

61,032. Would it be correct to say that that return shows that these five cities embrace a population of [illegible]?—Yes.

61,033. Can you tell me what the average number of

Mr. F. C. Harvey, Esq., M.P.

[illegible] April '[illegible]

Sunday closing.

Mr. T. C. Harrington, M.P.

22 April '98

very much the same. In the rural districts where the Sunday Closing Act exists a large number of young men gather in from the country. They have a football match or some amusement in the neighbourhood of the town, and they have the right to go in and get drink in those cases, and in addition to that a large number of surreptitious drinkings go on. A number of people not qualified at all as *bona fide* travellers undoubtedly are allowed to and evade the vigilance of the police and get drink.

Early closing on Saturdays.

61,038. Going back to the question of exceptional legislation, take the case of Saturday closing. Would not the proposal to close at 9 o'clock on Saturday night entail a great amount of inconvenience on the class chiefly concerned?—To my mind, in the city of Dublin it would alter the complexion of the entire city. Take the case of a man in Dublin. At the present time a man leaving a theatre in London can turn in with a friend and get refreshments after the performance is over, but in Dublin, unless the theatre is over before 11, he is absolutely prohibited from that. But if you impose an additional closing at 9 o'clock on Saturday night, for the few people who abuse the privilege and for the few people who get drunk you inconvenience the whole of the population.

Irish vote on Sunday closing.

61,039. Reference has been made to the voting that has taken place formerly on the question of the Irish Sunday Closing Act, and on May 11th, 1887, which was the last occasion, you gave us the particulars of the numbers. Is it a fact that year by year comparatively there has been a weaker support of that Bill on the part of the Irish members?—That is so, of course due to the fact that the Irish members see that without the operation of further restrictive legislation temperance is going ahead and drunkenness diminishing.

61,040. Is it reasonable, considering the great improvement there is at the present time on social questions particularly, that it should be left to the Irish people; and if you cannot secure a preponderance of Irish votes on the subject, may it not be assumed there is not a strong case to put forward?—I do not think there is. My belief is that the question of further restriction is being pressed by persons entirely opposed to drink of any kind. I do not think it is wise for persons to legislate for persons who take drink, and that is why I, as a teetotaler, am chary of imposing restrictions on persons who do not live in the same manner as I do, and may drink in moderation, and may regard it as necessary for their condition, which I should not.

61,041. On that question of drunkenness it was put to you that your argument was a large one from a legal point of view, and you added to it voluntarily that you yourself are a total abstainer, and I believe you have been so through all your life?—All through my life I have never touched anything in the shape of spirituous liquor.

61,042. As an opponent of these restrictive measures, is it not reasonable to say that in you we have a man who has no strong opinions, and no interest in the question; and that, if anything, your view would lead you in exactly a contrary direction, and therefore your evidence must necessarily be far less biassed than the evidence of people who are practically living on agitation on the subject. Is not that a reasonable view to take?—That is so. I do not like to say the people are living on agitation on the subject. I do not make that charge against the temperance reformers, but I say there is a great deal of intolerance and there is a good deal of what they do, and I think a great deal of exaggeration in some of their statements. I do not wish to reflect on any particular statement, but for instance, take the evidence given here to-day of the fact of 63 children going in the course of an hour into a public-house. That seems to me a great exaggeration, for that means one child every minute.

61,043. (*Dean Dickinson.*) Many?—Yes.

61,044. Why not?—Well, I know Dublin pretty well.

61,045. So do I?—And I have not the slightest hesitation in saying that such a thing is absurd. One child may go in from a family bringing two or three other children of the same family with it. The older child goes out having charge of two or three other children, and then a person who wants to exaggerate the case, and to make the case big—supposing a society employs a person specially to take these statistics, and the man sees one child going in from a family accompanied by three or four others, it is a case of immediately multiplying by four. If the child goes in for a biscuit—and biscuits are sold in these shops, and it is a common thing for a working man to give his children a penny to buy biscuits—if they go in to buy biscuits they are set down as going in to buy drink themselves. I think that that does no good either to a cause for temperance or anything else.

61,046. (*Mr. Grimley.*) Let me remove your impression. I used the words "live on agitation," and you very kindly—and I quite endorse the view—put it in a form which I regret I did not put it in, that is to say, they are people to whom this is a hobby?—Undoubtedly.

61,047. And they are more or less impressed with the importance of it. When I said "live on agitation," I hope you will accept it that that was the meaning I wanted to convey?—I quite agree with you. My general belief is that the temperance reformers are the most intemperate advocates I have ever met on public questions.

61,048. (*Mr. Whitaker.*) When they go for their biscuits with the penny do they take a jug with them?—They do not always take a jug with them, that is quite true. They are undoubtedly going for drink if they have a jug with them.

The witness withdrew.

Adjourned till Tuesday next, May 3rd, at 11 o'clock.

ONE HUNDRED AND SECOND DAY.

Queen's Robing Room, House of Lords, Tuesday, May 3rd, [illegible].

PRESENT:

THE RIGHT HONOURABLE SIR ALGERNON WEST, K.C.B., IN THE CHAIR.

[illegible]

The Very Reverend [illegible]

[illegible]

Mr. [illegible] HARRINGTON, M.P., recalled and further examined.

Mr. T. Harrington, M.P.

3 May '98.

[illegible]. (Mr. Whittaker.) You suggested to us last Wednesday that inquiries by means of Commissions, and also the prospect of legislation on Sunday closing in Ireland, increase drunkenness and the arrests for drunkenness, and [illegible] the number of [illegible] and [illegible]?—It increased [illegible] and [illegible], and [illegible] in [illegible] was represented by an increased list of drunkenness also.

Committee of 1888.

[illegible]. I should like to go back to the Commission of [illegible] for a moment. You will probably remember that that Committee was asked for by Mr. [illegible] at the end of the session of [illegible]?—Yes.

[illegible]. It was asked for by the opponents of the Sunday Closing Bill under the belief that they could show that it was working unsatisfactorily?—I really do not remember the circumstances under which it was asked for, of course I take it from you.

[illegible]. That was so. What I want to suggest to you is this, that a Committee being asked for by the opponents of the Bill, why should that lead to increased drinking, because would not they expect that the Sunday Closing Bill would be [illegible] on the result of their inquiry?—I do not think the public looked upon it from that point of view. The one thing which they had regard to was that a Select Committee of Inquiry was sitting inquiring into the question; that the Government of the day had given its sympathy to that Committee of Inquiry, and that there was every probability that the inquiry would report in favour of further restrictions, and that the Government would carry out those restrictions. The attitude of the Government, as well as of the Committee of Inquiry, was, of course, an element. It is the [illegible] of legislation which, I suggest, increases [illegible] and illicit drinking.

[illegible]. I gather from that that it was the opinion of the people in Ireland that inquiry into the working of the Sunday Closing Act would lead to recommendations that it be extended and its stringency increased?—The object of the inquiry was to recommend further restrictions.

[illegible]. The inquiry was asked for by Mr. [illegible] on behalf of the opponents?—With the history of the asking for it I am not conversant. I did not know that Mr. [illegible] took a strong view.

[illegible]. I cannot say how he voted, but I looked at the attitude he took. The inquiry was granted in the following session. In connection with that I suppose you are aware that that Committee reported that the Sunday Closing Act had very considerably diminished drunkenness?—Yes, I am aware that the Committee so reported, but I may say I do not quite agree with the conclusion at which the Committee arrived. I think the improvement in the social condition of the country had more to do with the diminution of drunkenness than the Sunday Closing Act had.

[illegible]. You are also aware that they reported this,—I will read the words—"that none of the evils which were predicted by some persons as likely to ensue from the passing of the Act have been proved to have arisen to any appreciable extent"?—My recollection of the operation of the Sunday Closing Act in Ireland is that a very great amount of [illegible] [illegible] between the police on the one hand and the publicans on the other, and a very deplorable state of demoralisation generally as to [illegible], has certainly followed upon the Sunday Closing Act.

[illegible]. That kind of thing was predicted before the Act was passed?—My experience is that it has very generally occurred.

[illegible]. The Committee specially appointed to inquire into it, consisting of members of all sides of the House, reported that these evils had not resulted. That was so, was not it?—I think so. It is, as you have said, the finding of the Committee.

[illegible]. I will take you a little further. There were on the Committee two members of the House of Commons nominated by the paid secretary of the Licensed Victualers' Association of Ireland, Mr. John O'Connor and Mr. [illegible] [illegible]?—I [illegible] say that, but I know both members were friendly to the trade interest.

[illegible]. Mr. Biggar stated in a debate in the House of Commons at the earlier time he (as the Whip of the Irish party) selected them as the nominations of the paid secretary of the Licensed Victualers' Association?—I am rather surprised at the statement that Mr. Biggar selected them for that purpose, because he was one of the most strenuous opponents of the trade in the House.

[illegible]

41,0?? The convictions are the serious matter; the difference between prosecutions and convictions is not very great?—No.

41,0??. In 1890 the convictions were 8?0 in Dublin; in 18??, ???; in 18??, ???; in 18??, ???; in 18??, ???; in 1897, 7??. I wanted to come back to 1890 and 1897 afterwards, because the Chief of the Police in Dublin gives a special reason for it. I go back now to 18??, 18??, 18??, and 18??. In 18?? the convictions were 3??; in 18??, ???; in 18??, ???; in 18??, ???—nearly double?—Yes, these were the years following immediately on the restrictive legislation, and, of course, the number of shebeens had considerably increased, as I have said.

41,0??. And the drunkenness went down enormously. I have quoted the figures?—Not so low as at the present time. Drunkenness has been steadily going down, but not so low as at present.

41,0??. In 18?? the arrests for drunkenness on all days in Dublin were 7,???; last year, 6,???—In 18?? they were 13,000.

41,0??. Yes, but they were down during this very period?—They may have been down for one or two years, but undoubtedly the decrease on the whole has been steady. In 18?? it was the highest number that had been reached for ?? years, except in 18??.

41,097. When the shebeens were flourishing, the convictions for drunkenness were smaller?—I do not accept that proposition.

41,???. It is the fact, from the figures?—Are you speaking of prosecutions for shebeens? That is a very distinct thing from shebeens. There may be shebeens and yet there may be no prosecutions for shebeening. There may be successful shebeening. That is a different proposition altogether from speaking of the shebeens producing high statistics of drunkenness.

41,???. When the Committee sat on this question of shebeening, and they were discussing the Report, Mr. John O'Connor moved to insert these words: "Yet "[illegible] witnesses testified to the existence of shebeening." A vote of the Committee was taken upon it, and the only members who would support that were the two representing the trade, and an English member, who was in the trade himself. The other eight members of the Committee voted not to add these words to the Report?—And the authorities justified the action of the two members by immediately instituting prosecutions in Ireland against shebeens; and a very vigorous campaign against shebeens followed.

41,1??. There have been fewer prosecutions every year steadily since then?—You cannot say that in face of the fact that there were 3?? last year, and ??? the year before.

41,1??. Except the last two years. During the last two years the chief of the police has put on a special sergeant and constable in each district to look after [illegible] matters, and the sale of drink, has he not?—I cannot say. I am not conversant with everything they do.

41,1??. He states so in his annual report, which is printed and circulated in the House of Commons?—I am aware that a great deal more rigour has been shown in the supervision of publichouses, inspecting people at the counter, challenging them, speaking to them, questioning whether they are under the influence of drink or not; a good deal of that activity has been carried on during the last two years. I think it is rather a questionable policy. I do not approve of it, I think, except where they have clear evidence of men getting drunk in public-houses. It is very apt to interfere largely with the persons who are allowed to keep their houses open.

41,1??. You are aware that the police authorities state that the shebeens are mainly brothels?—I have not heard that. Some of them are, but I would not accept that as the general character of them.

41,1??. That they are largely in one district only?—Yes.

give you the figures. The total number of arrests in in Dublin are ?13. I am speaking of Sunday arrests. Of these, ??? were effected when the publichouses were closed; ?? were arrests between the hours of 8 a.m. and 2 p.m. They cannot be traceable to publichouses, unless there is surreptitious drinking in the the public-houses. Fifty-five took place between ?? at night and 8 a.m. on Monday morning. I do not see how they could be in any sense traceable to publichouses. Anybody who knows Dublin knows perfectly well that if a man comes out of a public-house drunk, he cannot avoid the police from 7 in the evening till 12 at night. He could not go ?? yards in Dublin without meeting a policeman. Then there are ??? arrests, which took place between 7 p.m. and ?? at night. That I regard as by no means a good division of the [illegible]; for I think if the hours were taken from 8 to ?? it would be better. I think one hour after the houses are closed is a good time to judge the result of the opening of the houses on the habits of the people and on drunkenness; but to take 7 o'clock as the hour at which the houses should close, and to make one period between that and ?? o'clock at night, I do not think would enable you to arrive at any proper result. I do not think you are able to judge. A large number of the later arrests from 8 to ?? cannot be traceable to publichouses, but all those that may take place between 7 and 8 may very fairly be traceable to publichouses.

41,1??. Mr. Harrel, the Chief Commissioner of Police in Dublin, dealt with this point before the Commission of 18??. If you allow me I will read you what he said, because it quite refutes the view you have been putting before us. He said, "A man is not always arrested "just after he has taken the drink which made him "drunk. To set down all the arrests after 11 o'clock "on Saturday night as attributable to illicit drinking "would not be fair. On the contrary, a man who has "got the drink at 10 o'clock may not be arrested till "midnight, and the same thing will occur till 1 o'clock "in the morning." Later on, referring to Sundays, he is asked "How long after closing do they go on?" He says "For two or three hours there are still many "arrests on Sunday night, after 10 or 11." Then he was asked, "But it is possible that many of the "Sunday night arrests have arisen from the facilities "of getting drink in an illicit form." This is the answer: "Many of them may, but I would not say that "the arrests made after the closing hour on Sunday "night arise generally from drunkenness, where the "drink was got in an illicit form." His opinion differs from yours?—No, we have common ground to a certain length. I quite agree that a number of the arrests which take place after the closing of publichouses may be traceable to publichouses, and, give it possibly to them, but I should take an interval of an hour as a very fair time to divide the margin between the two, and I think a man who leaves the publichouse under the influence of drink, who walks about and gets no other drink but in drink, and who knows the police, may be fairly presumed not to get drunk in a public-house; and if he is arrested after that I think his arrest may be traceable to drinking in some other place besides the public-house.

41,107a. That is not Mr. Harrel's opinion?—He goes to a certain extent with me.

41,108. I think you told us that Sunday in Ireland is much more of a holiday than in England; sports are held?—Yes. In accounting for the difference in the statistics between the two countries, there were two circumstances which I mentioned. There was the power of arrest in Ireland for simple drunkenness, which is not the case in England. Then there was also the fact that the inhabitants of Ireland spend Sunday more out; they do not remain in their houses so much. They have sports, football matches, hurling matches, and various amusements, which we have not in this country.

41,109. In spite of the fact that this is a holiday time, and they have sports, and people are at liberty, and it is the day after pay day, arrests for drunkenness are only one-third as great on Sunday as on Saturday?—I think

Mr. T. Harrington, M.P.

8 May '96

Sunday of the drunkenness.

Sunday in Ireland.

Mr. T. Harrington, M.P. — 3 May '99

[illegible] that indicate that when the public-houses are closed altogether, throughout the greater part of Ireland, and for a considerable portion of the day in the excepted cities, it does reduce the drinking and the drunkenness very materially indeed?—Undoubtedly if the public-houses are closed, you must reduce the drinking. That is a matter that does not require any elaboration, and to some small extent you will reduce the drunkenness. But the position I take up is this, that the improvement [illegible] in drunkenness does not justify your interference with the general body of the public, who may take drink in moderation. That is my whole position. The improvement is so small that it does not justify your interference.

Sunday closing and drunkenness.

41,111. I do not wish to argue that point, but only to get at the fact that there is a very large reduction of drunkenness on Sunday as compared with the Saturday and Monday, and Sunday being a holiday is just the time when, if the temptations were available, the drunkenness would take place?—The [illegible] are as large on Sunday as on other days. I think if you compare other days in the week with Sunday you will find that some of the other days in the middle of the week the drinking is smaller. Take Wednesday.

41,112. On Wednesday it is more than double what it is on Sunday. Friday is the lowest day, and that has more than double the arrests of Sunday. Saturday has the most, Sunday the least, Monday the second highest, and then they drop away to Friday, but the lowest point reached when the public-houses are open is double what it is on Sunday. So that does not carry out your argument, does it?—It carries out my argument to this extent, that I believe the improvement which you spoke of in the Sunday drinking is largely due to the improvement in the condition of the people; but I do not know anywhere in Ireland where a man who desires to take drink on Sunday cannot get drink and become drunk if he likes. He has only to travel a distance of 3 miles. He need not travel that at all. He can get [illegible] drink in a public-house. If he is anxious to continue it as a habit he can join with others in establishing a club, and he has got it all Sunday if he likes.

41,113. Surely if the diminution of drunkenness and drinking on Sunday were due to the improvement in the condition of the people that would have told on Saturday and Monday as well?—I rather think it has. I think the diminution has extended all round.

41,114. There are more than three times as many arrests on Saturday or on Monday?—But it has told all round on all the days of the week. My contention is that the decrease in drunkenness covers the whole week.

41,115. My point is that the comparatively fewer arrests on Sunday is due to the fact that there are not the facilities that there are on other days?—Of course if you diminish the facilities, to a certain extent you will diminish drunkenness, but the extent is very small in my mind.

Clubs.

41,116. On the question of clubs, I gather that your contention is that the Sunday closing and restrictions tend to develop clubs?—Yes.

41,117. You are no doubt aware that the clubs are the fewest where the Sunday closing is complete?—Of course that is so in the rural districts of Ireland, for Sunday closing is only in the rural districts of Ireland; they have not the clubs that they have in the towns.

41,118. Sunday closing is in all the towns except five?—Yes, but they are the smaller towns.

41,119. But there are fewer clubs there?—I cannot take that. In proportion, to the population of course there are, because the working men are fewer. They have not the opportunities of banding together. There are not the wide facilities, and the same facilities for establishment of clubs in the rural districts that there are in the cities; but that does not at all touch the question.

41,120. A regular working man's club?—All the working men's clubs by no means have bars. Facilities for drink are not given in a great many that I know, but in the rural districts of Ireland, of which I have a good acquaintance, such a thing as a club with a bar was absolutely unknown until the Sunday Closing Act passed.

41,121. Dublin has 44 clubs, has it not?—It has a great many more than that.

41,122. That is the number reported to us by the police?—There are a great many more than that.

41,123. Do you suggest that the police do not know of these clubs, and that you do?—I doubt very much whether the police know of these clubs.

41,124. Do you know of them?—I know a good deal of them. My constituency is very largely a working man's constituency. I have examined it very closely and I believe there are a great many more than 44 clubs in Dublin.

41,125. Are you likely to know better than the police of the existence of clubs. They report that there are 44?—I think the number is much higher than that. That is my impression.

41,126. In Bradford the number is 43. The great increase in the clubs in Ireland has been during the last 10 years, has it not?—Yes.

41,127. During the first 10 years, after the passing of the Sunday Closing Act, there was a very small increase in clubs, I believe?—In the rural districts after the passing of the Sunday Closing Act, there was an increase, not a very considerable increase, but I think I may say that since the sitting of the Select Committee of 1888 clubs have extended very largely.

41,128. Are you aware that during the last 10 years clubs have increased more in England in proportion than they have in Ireland?—I do not know. I have not examined the question in England at all.

41,129. In the City of London they have multiplied fourfold during these 10 years. My point is that the influence which creates a club is evidently more at work in the City of London than in Dublin, and we have not got Sunday closing in the City of London. Therefore it cannot be Sunday closing that creates clubs?—I do not know from what your statistics are derived; whether the police are speaking of legitimate clubs, which they do not attempt to interfere with, or whether they include bogus clubs which they have been prosecuting, because, most undoubtedly, if they include bogus clubs, their statistics ought to be much higher.

41,130. They give every club of which they have any knowledge whatever throughout the whole country, and if there is a bogus club, and they acknowledge its existence, they must be prosecuting it. My contention is that there are a large number of bogus clubs of which the police do not take cognisance.

41,131. That is a little wide of our present case. The authorities in giving us these returns also point out some of the technical difficulties which they experienced in prosecuting them?—Yes, I have just mentioned in my evidence the difficulties are very great.

41,132. You seemed to think that there was [illegible] necessity for special legislation regarding liquor in Ireland?—And there was no necessity for further restrictions.

41,133. You think that they do not drink excessively as compared with other countries?—I dispute the proposition which seems to be so constantly before the House of Commons and the country, that we are a drunken race of people in Ireland. I say that the statistics look high, but it is due to the different system in which the law is administered in the two countries. Take, for instance, the arrests for simple drunkenness. A question was put to me on Wednesday with regard to that. I have since looked at the figures, and I find in the police statistics that the total arrests in Dublin for 1896, which is the last year for which we have [illegible] is considerably less than the people of Great Britain, is it not?—I am not quite certain. I take it from you, of course.

61,138. In connection with another question, which we will not enter upon, it is generally considered, I think, that the people of Ireland, taking Ireland as a whole, have only about one-twentieth part of the wealth of Great Britain?—Yes.

61,139. On that basis the people of Ireland spend 45 per cent. more per head on liquor in proportion to their means than the people of Great Britain do?—Perhaps in some measure that is accounted for by the class of drink which they take. They have different tastes, and they have different kinds of drink. I have not quite been sufficiently able to answer you. They take stronger drink in Ireland, and consequently there [illegible]. I think the disposition to take strong drink is diminishing in Ireland. Beer and other light drinks are taken more extensively.

61,140. Would not that indicate that if by legislation we could diminish the amount of drinking in Ireland, it would be an advantage?—If you could diminish the amount of drinking, certainly it would be an advantage. My position is that those who take up the temperance question in Ireland are not pursuing it from the point of view of temperance but the point of view of total abstinence from drink; that they want to prevent any person who wishes to have a drink from taking it. The restriction which they seek is only a step in the direction in which they would go of closing up public-houses and drink altogether. It may be a very good condition of things, but I am not prepared to force my opinions upon every one else. As I have explained, I am a teetotaler, but I would not like to force anybody to be a teetotaler because it may suit me. I do not know why there ought to be any interference with anything except drunkenness. It is the abuse of drink which I think the public has a right to take cognisance of, and the legislation to provide for. I do not know why there should be any special legislation, because persons may take drink when other persons may not think it desirable for themselves.

61,141. I should occupy another half-hour if I were to enter on a discussion of that, and therefore I do not do so?—I only explain my views. It may seem somewhat inconsistent that a man who is a teetotaler himself should take up the line I take up.

61,142. It does not matter what the aim and object of individuals may be. The statistics clearly show that the restrictive legislation of the past has reduced drunkenness in Ireland, and has not, as you have suggested, set up an extra number of clubs?—That is your contention; it most certainly is not mine. My contention is that the improvement of the social condition of the people of Ireland is going steadily on, and is diminishing drunkenness, and that without any interference of Parliament or the Legislature, as that social condition improves, there would be a still further diminution in drunkenness.

61,143. I venture to suggest that the social improvement is the result of the diminished drunkenness?—I do not think so. I know the social condition of the people. Apart from that it has been improved almost 50 per cent. in the last 20 years in Ireland. Their living has been improved, their clothing has been improved, their habitations have been improved; and all that is certainly not due to the Sunday Closing Act. We consider it due to some action of ours, the Irish representatives, quite independent of that.

61,144. (Mr. Grindley.) With regard to the number of clubs, you were asked whether the number of clubs was 64 in Dublin?—Yes.

as far as I know, in the trade. I am speaking of Dublin. No demand has been made to extend the hours on Sunday I think, but in the rural districts I think there is a great difference of opinion as to whether it is a useful thing to close up certain public-houses, and, in some of the villages, and allow persons who travel three or four miles to have drink when others cannot. I am not sure that on the whole the Irish people would not prefer to leave the question as it is, rather than to reopen it.

61,145. I am referring particularly at the moment to the view of the trade in Dublin, with which no doubt you are acquainted?—Yes.

61,146. I suppose you represent their views here?—I think so.

61,147. You are authorised to do so?—No, I am not at all. My constituency is a mixed constituency. I am not authorised to represent them in any way. Since I represented Dublin, and before, when I represented a constituency in the centre of Ireland, where the Sunday closing question was a very strong question with the clergy, my views have been always precisely the same on that question.

61,148. I think you stated that you had peculiar means of knowing the real view of the trade?—Of knowing the real views of the working men of Dublin, the "trades." I think I used the "trade." If you mean the liquor trade, I mean the tradesmen.

61,149. You stated that so far as the trade in Dublin was concerned, they did not desire any further restrictions, nor did they desire any further extension?—I have never seen any demand made by them for any further extension of the hours.

61,150. The view of the trade as to further restrictions is a very natural view, is it not?—I think it is. Of course men who have paid very large sums of money for their houses, and have invested all the savings of their lives in them, naturally enough resent any restriction which is likely to deprive them of their property. I may say also, from what I know of them, there could not be, generally speaking, a more respectable body of men than the publicans who have the trade in Dublin. They stand at the very head of the commercial men of Dublin.

61,151. You admit that it is a natural interest view which they take?—Certainly.

61,152. (Mr. Hayden.) I believe that the constituency which you represent in Dublin is principally a working man's constituency?—Yes. My constituency is the largest in point of size and population, and is very largely a working constituency. It is the Harbour Division, extending on both sides of the river for a considerable distance.

61,153. The question upon which you have given evidence is the question of Sunday closing. That has been in existence for some 20 years?—Yes.

61,154. May I ask you if you were in the House when that Bill was passed?—No. I came to the House in 1885.

61,155. It was passed in 1878?—Yes.

61,156. Efforts have been made from year to year to extend the Act, I think, by including the exempted cities?—Yes.

61,157. It was thought wise when the Act was passed that these cities should be exempted?—Yes.

61,158. Containing a large population?—Yes.

61,159. The Bill of 1878, I think, was passed on a Saturday?—I do not remember.

61,160. You, perhaps, cannot remember how many

The general body of the peasantry of Ireland have had their social position improved, I should say, 50 per cent. within the last 20 years. They are a different class and a different peasantry; and that certainly I do not attribute it to the Sunday closing.

61,163. You think the great changes in the social condition of the people are due to other causes than Sunday Closing?—Yes; and those causes are still in operation, and will [illegible]. I think the social condition of the people will in the next few years improve very much more. I may say the improvement in the housing of the poor has a very great deal to say to it. A working man living in a small room, with his whole family around him, having very often only the one apartment for the whole of his family, has not the same inducement to spend the whole of his Sunday and his time in that house which he would have if he had a better house and [illegible] accommodation. Naturally enough, men in that position have had, in the past, to go out and meet their friends and often to go into the public-house. I think that as you improve the houses of the poor you will very sensibly diminish the disposition to go to the public-house. That has taken place largely in the rural districts of Ireland, where labourers' cottages, with three or four compartments, have been built for the agricultural labourers, and in the towns of Ireland there is a very considerable improvement in the housing, especially in Dublin.

61,164. Might I suggest that education has had a great deal to do with the change?—In my opinion it has had a great deal to do with it.

61,165. I should like to take for a moment the question of Sunday closing in Ireland as it is, and to compare the excepted cities. Can you tell us what were the arrests for drunkenness during 1897 in the excepted cities on Sundays?—They were 1,830 in the year. I have got the figures for the rest of Ireland.

61,166. How many would that be on each of Sunday of the year?—It would be one in every 34,080 of the population, and if you take into account what I have in mind, that the greater portion of these arrests are for [illegible] drunkenness, not drunk and disorderly, which would not be arrests at all in this country, the proportion is still further diminished to one-third.

61,167. What is the total population?—The total population of the police districts of the cities, because the police districts extend beyond the cities, is [illegible], I think.

61,168. Is the five excepted cities there is a population of some [illegible]?—Yes. When I speak of the population of Dublin, Kingstown, and Blackrock, I mean Dublin, the police district which extends beyond the city.

61,169. Have you taken out the proportion of the arrests in the [illegible]?—The total arrests in 1897 for these five cities were 1,830. [illegible] was the highest; it stands at the head, and though it is the highest for the whole year, it means only two arrests on the Sunday all the year round. That is not an alarmingly large number.

61,170. These are the statistics with regard to the excepted cities, and these would compare favourably with the rural districts where the Act is in operation?—I think so.

61,171. Is it your opinion that further restrictions would not conduce to increased sobriety?—That is my opinion. A man who wishes to get drunk would have sufficient facilities to do so, no matter how you restrict him. My chief objection to further restrictions is the class of drunkenness which it begets. I think if a working man is driven to keep drink in his house, or to have recourse to shebeens for it, it is a much more dangerous and demoralising description of drinking than his having recourse to a public-house with a friend, where we know the public-house must be well-conducted, and where it is under police supervision. I cannot regard anything as more dangerous than the carrying of drink on Saturday night, and bringing it into the family, and keeping it before the children. That I should regard as a most deplorable result of further restriction. Those people have no wine cellars, they cannot store it away; it is in the presence of the children; and if there is an objection to a child going into a public-house on Sunday to bring out beer for the Sunday dinner, there ought to be tenfold more objection to having the drink under the child's nose [illegible] produce those conveniences, there can surely be no use in restricting the licensed houses or shutting them up?—No. To my mind there is none. My idea is that the legislature should be rigid in enforcing the law in regard to drunkenness, to punish the man who gets drunk, and to punish the publican who makes him drunk; and I think that there that the law ought to be vindicated. But I think the closing of the public-houses, and the taking away of the liberty of a man who is not given to excess, is not the way to settle the question.

61,173. Would the closing of public-houses earlier on Saturdays, in your opinion, produce any ill effects?—I think it would be a most dangerous experiment. My opinion is that the closing of public-houses earlier on Saturday nights would lead to any amount of illicit drinking. If you could guarantee that the people would go home at nine o'clock and go to bed, it would be all right; but I am afraid you could not effect that.

61,174. (Mr. Young.) If there be a slight falling off in the arrests on Sunday in consequence of diminished hours does it follow that drunkenness in the people's dwellings does not take place as on other days?—What I should be chiefly afraid of would be the drunkenness in the dwellings. I am much more alarmed at the prospect of introducing drunkenness into the home than having it outside, because I think it leads to much more demoralisation. I think the effect of a father coming home drunk is bad enough on the children, but I am afraid the effect would be worse if they were looking on the spectacle of his getting drunk in his own home, with the dangerous tendency of his offering them drink and getting them to share in his demoralisation.

61,175. (Mr. Whitaker.) The Report of the Committee in 1888 was that that trend of things did not occur?—I am not very conversant with the Report, but I know if you impose restrictions it will occur, and to some extent I am sure it has occurred.

61,176. (Mr. Walter.) I think you informed the Commission that you were a total abstainer?—Yes.

61,177. Therefore it is only right to assume that you do not come here as an advocate of the publican, but more as the friend of the public?—I come here not as an advocate of any one party. To a great extent, I am here because I do not share in the imputation made upon my country that we are a drunken people. I came here to resent that. That is my reason for being here at all. I think that has been pushed too far against our people.

61,178. Although a total abstainer yourself, you are not an enemy of moderate drinking?—No; I am not a man who would go in for the abolition of all drink. I meet a lot of good fellows who can take their drink and who do not drink to excess. If all people drank moderately without drinking to excess, I do not know why there should be any interference by the law at all.

61,179. You would not support prohibition?—No; certainly not.

61,180. Would you endorse this? This is a Report by Mr. Fortescue with regard to the liquor legislation of the United States. "The prohibition has but "brought nothing but dissension. Almost every house "has become a bar-room, and every young man has "his bottle, so as to return the hospitality of his "neighbour." That is a state of things you would not like?—That is precisely what I should be afraid of. I regard that as much worse than two friends meeting and going into a public-house and having a drink, making the public-house their club, to a certain extent.

61,181. He further says: "I found five young men "the other night, who only two years ago had never "tasted liquor"—that was at the period of the prohibition established in the State of Georgia—"in a "deplorable plight, each with his bottle in his hip "pocket. I had occasion to enter the room of a "friend, and found there six of the town known young "men of [illegible] drunk and asleep, while upon the "table stood six empty bottles." That is a state of things which you would probably contemplate in Ireland should further restrictions be imposed?—Yes; and from a short experience of America, I may say I found where prohibition is in full force that there is

Mr. T. Harrington, M.P.

8 May '96.

41,182. Would you be inclined to consider that the present restriction on Sunday is an infringement of the liberty of the subject, or, that it certainly would be so if it were further extended?—I think so. I do not see why Sunday is selected. We have got that stated view with regard to Sunday in Ireland which exists in the other portions of the United Kingdom. It seems to me as if this Sunday legislation had been forced upon us by a class who do not properly understand our views on the question. We really do not see why Sunday is taken above all other days. Of course temperance reformers say they take Sunday because the working man is idle, and they want to save his family from his extravagance; but these reformers would shut up public-houses altogether, and abolish drink altogether. That is my view of them. I think the whole temperance question is being pushed from the point of view of total prohibition, though they do not go to that extent, because they cannot get it.

41,183. Was not the second reading of the Irish Sunday Closing Bill of last session passed by the Scotch vote?—Well, it was not passed by the Irish vote, but I do not remember the figures. There was a majority of [illegible] on the Irish vote.

41,184. Had it not been for the Scotch vote the Bill would have been thrown out by a considerable majority?—Yes.

41,185. The fact that the members were so evenly balanced shows that there was a very large minority opposed to the Bill?—That is so; and that minority is becoming larger every year as the Bill is discussed in the House. The majority by which the Bill was carried last time was the smallest majority by which it has been carried in my recollection.

41,186. (Mr. Whittaker.) Is not there a very well-known reason for that?—If you know it, you might suggest it. I do not know what it is. My reason is, that the Irish members have appreciated that the necessity for further restriction is not so great as they took it to be some time ago, and that the condition of the people is improving without that restriction.

41,187. Is it not because of the much more intimate relations that have grown up between the Irish members and the trade?—No, I do not think so. I do not know that any more intimate relations have grown up, for this reason: That in recent years the Irish members have divided into different parties on nearly all public questions. Those who went upon a very old bill [illegible] are [illegible] now, and I think it would be the other way.

41,188. Is it not because there is a division, and that one of the sections has practically become the trade party?—I do not think so. I do not know what section you mean. The section I did belong to has been considered to be friendly to the trade, but it only consisted of 10 members; that would not make a very appreciable difference. Some of the 10 are very strong temperance advocates. Mr. Redmond was, I believe, vice-president of the Temperance Alliance.

41,189. (Mr. Walker.) Is it your opinion that the opposition to a measure of this kind is increasing daily in Ireland?—My impression is that the opposition to it is increasing.

41,190. Is it increasing among the classes in Dublin whose circumstances this measure interferes with?—I think so. I think those are the only parties who ought to be regarded on the question. I think it is the men who, to some extent, are in such a position of life that they would have to use public-houses, whose opinions ought to be taken into consideration, and not those who never did and never will use them.

41,191. I gather from your evidence that you have had very considerable experience as a barrister in the law courts, and, generally speaking, as a politician among the classes in Dublin affected by this measure?—Certainly.

41,192. As the result of that intercourse and knowledge, you say that the opposition to this measure is very considerably increasing?—It is. I think you may take the fact that I, representing as I do, a constituency over 11,000 voters, came to give evidence upon the [illegible]

41,193. Would you be disposed to endorse the statement of Mr. Justice Crompton when, in charging the grand jury at Cardiff, he said: "But there is no doubt "at all about it, that there is less drunkenness where "there is more drink than there is where there is more "restriction"?—It is a very general proposition, and I should like to know the circumstances to which it was applied before I endorsed it.

41,194. Charging the grand jury, he says, "I want "to know why the people should not be allowed to take "a quiet glass of beer on a Sunday as well as on any "other day"?—That is precisely my position. My view is that the legislature ought to punish excess and that the laws ought not to be stringent for the punishment of offences; but that it is wrong in principle to prevent the use of drink unless you are going to abolish it everywhere and in all social circles. If you allow the gentleman to have his wine today, you must allow the workingman to have his pint of beer. If the one goes to excess, I think he ought to be punished quite as much as the other. Equal legislation is what I go for.

41,195. If this measure were passed and the [illegible] shebeens and clubs would very naturally increase?—I think they would very largely increase. [illegible] their influence is very demoralising, and much worse than any drinking that can take place in public-houses.

41,196. From your knowledge of the world generally, and speaking as a total abstainer, you are of opinion that a well-conducted public-house, with a proprietor responsible to the authorities, is certainly preferable to any such places as clubs or shebeens?—Most certainly. I know a good deal of the circumstances of the public-houses in Dublin, and I should think that 90 per cent. of them are certainly most excellently conducted. I know the men at the head of them, and I know that no persons could be harder on drunkenness than they are, both with regard to the servants in their own employment and as to allowing anything like drunkenness on their premises. That is my knowledge of the trade in Dublin.

41,197. Do you think it is desirable that the physical condition of the premises where the trade is carried on should be improved?—I know we are very careful in Dublin about the condition of the premises. I am the Recorder of Dublin here. I have the honour of appearing very frequently before him in his court. He is very particular as to the locality where the public-houses are situated and as to the physical circumstances of the houses themselves. He is most rigid about preventing any increase of public-houses, and he is extremely rigid about allowing public-houses to be placed where any of the working men's dwellings have been erected, where they might catch hold of the working men and [illegible] demoralisation amongst them. If ever he is disposed to grant a licence to any body, it is by granting him to exchange a licence in a low locality where it is likely to do harm, and giving an extension or privilege to some publican situated in a respectable portion of the city.

41,198. There has been very considerable attention directed to this improvement in Dublin of late years, I believe?—Yes, and I may say the Recorder is unremitting in his endeavours to improve the city in that respect.

41,199. I believe the licensed houses in Dublin have, physically and [illegible] speaking, very considerably improved during the last few years?—I think they have.

41,200. That you consider is an advantage to the public?—I think so.

41,201. It increases the value of the houses and increases the responsibility of the proprietors?—Yes. Very few proprietors in any respectable position in the trade in Dublin are ever brought into the police court. There are in the trade in Dublin men who have never had a complaint against them.

41,202. The more respectable the man, the better his house is conducted?—Yes.

41,203. And the stronger the guarantee to the authorities and the public that it will be well conducted?—Yes.

Mr. T. Harrington, M.P. — 4 May '97.

[illegible] from my experience of the court, I think a discretion ought to be allowed to the magistrates. There are very often cases [illegible] of a mere technical breach, as to what might be considered the law drawn by the magistrates. A man may be summoned by a policeman for opening his house five minutes before the time. It may be owing to a difference in his clock. There is a case in my mind in which I appeared professionally one or three weeks ago. I was defending a man whose [illegible] had been prosecuted for opening five minutes before 2 o'clock on Sunday. That was a case certainly where it ought to be at the discretion of the magistrate, if he felt himself compelled to impose a fine, not to record that fine on the licence. The evidence of the licence would be taken as evidence of misconduct against that person on any future application. I do not think it ought to be so, and I think the magistrates ought to have a discretion. They are really the best persons to judge whether that record ought to be placed on the licence or not.

41,[illegible]. Seeing that the magistrates have a discretion, and that in their discretion they endorse the licence, should not that be only a record of that proprietor's [illegible], and not carried any further when he disposed of the property, and a respectable man entered into possession? Should not he have a clean sheet or a clean bill of health?—Yes, it certainly ought not to be brought on to the new man, because the party who goes in is the innocent party. It is not the premises that are licensed. I do not think the record of one man ought to be put on another. I think that would be unfair. I think generally the authorities do not interpret the law so very rigidly as that they would punish the incoming man for the record of the outgoing man, unless he was associated with him. Supposing the incoming publican had been the foreman of the outgoing man, he would then perhaps be entirely responsible for the management of the house, and the authorities would rightly hold him as being to some extent a party to what had taken place; but, generally speaking, my impression is that the authorities do not interpret the law so very rigidly as that.

41,[illegible]. True, but that would be discovered on enquiry into his character?—Yes.

Clubs.

41,[illegible]. You say that you have had some experience of the nature of clubs. Have working men's clubs in Dublin, as they have in England, a drinking bar and a counter, just as in any public-house?—No, not precisely as in a public-house. Generally speaking, the bar is at the end of the smoking room. Men sit down and talk, and the bar is generally at the end of that room, and they are supplied from the bar, except in the reading room. My experience is that where books and newspapers are kept drink is not supplied, but it is supplied in the billiard room, or in the smoking room.

41,[illegible]. Can a member of a club take a friend, or two or three friends, and go to that counter and ask for drink?—Yes.

41,[illegible]. And pay for it the same as in an ordinary public-house?—Yes, he treats the same of the friend in the visitors' book as he enters the club.

41,[illegible]. So far as the consumption of drink and drunkenness is concerned, it is quite as likely to emerge from that as from the public-house?—I think a very considerable proportion of the Sunday statistics of drunkenness in Dublin do come from those clubs. A great many of those arrests after 8 o'clock on Sunday night are, I think, traceable to them.

41,[illegible]. That would in itself be evidence of the fact that if the hours were still further restricted, these clubs and illicit places would flourish?—I should think they would extend. I may say with regard to some of these clubs in Dublin, we have had instances where men who have themselves been connected with the law, police constables, for instance, who have very often become the [illegible] of these clubs. They know the law very well, and they are able to draft the rules in such a manner that the authorities are not able to pick a hole in them, and they have led the way in defeating the authorities in establishing these clubs in Dublin.

41,[illegible]. Should you be willing to endorse the opinion [illegible]

very small, and that the means of obtaining liquor away from the locality are very limited.

Mr. T. Harrington, M.P. — The bona fide traveller.

41,[illegible]. With reference to the bona fide traveller, a [illegible] mile radius has been suggested. That would be absurd, would it not?—I think it would be perfectly absurd.

41,[illegible]. If a man went [illegible] miles, he would be exhausted?—If he walked [illegible] miles to have a drink he would be a fool.

41,[illegible]. A man riding [illegible] miles would not be exhausted?—Not so much.

41,[illegible]. Therefore he would not require refreshment so much as a man walking four miles?—I think the bona fide traveller question and the Sunday closing merely shift the drinking from one locality to another. In my opinion it does nothing more than that. During the hours public-houses are closed in Dublin, within three or four miles in the outer police district, under the same authority, you have public-houses open the whole day, with a man standing at the door, who challenges everyone: "Are you a bona fide traveller? "How far have you come? Where did you sleep last "night?" and the man answers the questions and passes in. I see no advantage in carrying out the law in that manner.

Licensing authority.

41,[illegible]. Do you desire to express an opinion as to whether the present licensing authority in Ireland should be changed?—My impression is that the present licensing authority works very well. I have heard some witnesses making recommendations. One witness, I think Father Furlong, recommended that two resident magistrates should be appointed to sit with the county court judge as the licensing authority for the county, with two other persons. The whole question comes in, who are the two other persons going to be?

41,[illegible]. (Dean Dickinson.) He said two resident magistrates, two persons who may be resident magistrates, and two others?—I beg your pardon, I think he did. He said two resident magistrates, two others, and the county court judge.

41,[illegible]. (Mr. Walker.) Your opinion is that the present licensing authority is satisfactory?—Sometimes it is subject to abuse, but I think any system you have will be subject, more or less, to abuse. Sometimes there is canvassing going on among the friends to try and get a licence. That canvassing will go on whoever is the licensing authority. On the whole it is found that the magistrates coming from different districts of the county know the local requirements, and I think it is in favour of their knowledge of the local circumstances that they have been put on as helping the licensing authorities.

41,[illegible]. Canvassing is a very common thing in all phases of life, is it not?—Among members of Parliament I know it is very common.

41,[illegible]. (Dean Dickinson.) The canvassing of members of Parliament is a totally different thing from the canvassing of men who are sitting in a judicial position. You are not supposed to be sitting in any judicial position as members of Parliament?—I am afraid that in all countries of the world, and in all circumstances of life, canvassing will more or less go on, even with regard to judicial matters. I am not by any means in favour of it. I do not maintain it.

Total abstainer.

41,[illegible]. You said several times that you are, personally, a total abstainer?—Yes.

41,[illegible]. You defended yourself from the charge of inconsistency in some of your present evidence in that position?—No, I do not think there is any inconsistency at all, nor even a suspicion of it.

41,[illegible]. Is it not a fact that you represent a constituency, the larger proportion of which consists of publicans?—I should think a large proportion of my constituency does consist of publicans, and we have some temperance societies too.

41,[illegible]. Do answer my question?—I have answered your question, but I am entitled to add to the answer that, if the temperance societies were so strong in the constituency, and the feeling in favour of temperance was so very strong, then, if I were having regard to the views of my constituency, I should not be here at all.

Mr. T. [illegible], M.P.

[illegible] [illegible]?—There have been [illegible] from the [illegible] bodies through the representatives of the working men.

41,227. The trades unions?—Certainly.

41,228. What trade?—The Amalgamated Trades Unions of Dublin.

41,229. I have never seen or heard of any public meeting of working men in opposition to Sunday closing?—Resolutions have been frequently passed by the Trades Council of Dublin, representing all the organised trades bodies of Dublin, and evidence was given before the [illegible] Committee in 1888 by representatives of that body, on behalf of that body, against further restriction.

41,230. I asked you, was there any movement on the part of the working men generally in Dublin?—No, I do not think there has been any organised movement on the part of the working men against it, for this reason, that the working men know if you allow further prohibition they will easily have their remedy in these clubs and places where they can get drink; and, as a matter of fact, the trades council that passed that resolution has a bar in its own trade room.

41,231. You state, by way of explaining something in Sir David Harrel's evidence, that Sir David Harrel was only a short time acting as Commissioner of Police?—In 1888 he had been only a short time.

41,232. Are you aware that Sir David Harrel held for 10 years the office of Chief Commissioner of Police in Dublin before he was made Under Secretary for Ireland?—We were speaking of Sir David Harrel's evidence in 1888. At that time he had not been many years in charge of the police in Dublin.

41,233. He had been at least four?—A year or two I think. My impression is that Sir David Harrel was appointed in 1886 or 1887.

41,234. Is it not a fact, as proved to you by several witnesses, that the number of Sunday arrests in the five exempted towns is exactly three times as much in proportion to population as in any other of the towns of Ireland non-exempted?—That may be so. I do not know the exact figures, but I should take it that that would be precisely the case, because in the large cities where you have a large population thrown together, it is likely that the numbers would run higher than in the rural districts where the population is scattered.

Arrests for simple drunkenness.

41,235. You trace the number of arrests in Dublin to the fact that the arrests there are [illegible] made for simple drunkenness?—Yes.

41,236. And you [illegible] from the calculation at least 3,000 which were to be struck off as cases of simple drunkenness?—Yes.

41,237. Are you aware that under the Act of 1874, which is the Act by which the police are guided, there is no arrest for simple drunkenness? These are the words: "Every person who is so drunk as to be incapable", he must be drunk and disorderly in the public streets, or drunk and incapable of taking care of himself?—That is not the law in Ireland. It is a legal question, and I will answer it. The reason I interrupted you was because you had [illegible] the law in the commencement of your question.

41,238. Let me read the clause: "Every person who "is any highway, or any public place, whether a "building or not, is so drunk as to be incapable of "taking care of himself, may be detained by any con-"stable until he can with safety to himself be dis-"charged, but if so detained he shall be summoned in "due course, and [illegible] for such offence." That is [illegible]

[illegible]. But the magistrates in Ireland [illegible] [illegible], and they are, as Mr. Barton explained to the Commission, bringing a case into the superior courts to establish the fact that the law was wrong, and arrests are taking place as a matter of fact at the [illegible], and in every other district in Ireland, under the old statute of 1836, which is still in operation, for simple drunkenness. Mr. Barton distinctly stated in evidence here and an opportunity of referring to it, because I spoke to him on it—that the magistrates did not agree with Judge Walsh, and were bringing a case into Court to upset his decision. If you look at the heading of the Police Returns you will see, "Drunkenness not "associated with any other offence." These prosecutions are taken under the Statute of 1836.

41,239. We will pass from that to another question. What did you state was the number of bogus clubs in Dublin?—I did not state the number; the number of clubs given to me was 51.

41,240. The whole number of clubs in Dublin, clubs of all sorts, was stated by Mr. Mellon to be 50, and of these 50 clubs he said there were only a dozen irregular drinking clubs; and he said there were in Dublin three proprietary clubs which are illegal, as he stated. The number of 51 or 51 included clubs of all kinds?—I find it very difficult to distinguish between what is a bogus club and what is a club which is really allowed by law. I do not think Mr. Mellon would attempt to draw the line of separation between them.

Clubs in Dublin.

41,241. I pass to another and more important question. You stated last Wednesday in your evidence that every policeman in Dublin was supposed to have five cases in a month; every policeman was supposed to show a certain amount of activity. In [illegible] question, [illegible], (Chairman.) "I suppose it is not an [illegible] to the "police from any superior authority that they must "show five cases a month?" You answer, "I think "it is. I understand that a circular has been issued to "the Dublin Police. I hope if the Hon. Dame disputes "my evidence—(Dame [illegible].) I do not dispute "it, I deny it." And then you ask me to ask the Commissioner of Police. I have asked the Commissioner of Police, and I have seen the circular which you refer to, and the circular asks the number of arrests made. The object of the circular is stated to be this, and it is this, and I have the authority of the Assistant Commissioner of Police to make that statement to the Commission. The object of that circular is [illegible] to discover in what districts the policemen has the most arrests made, in order that the duty of the police may be fairly equalised, and a man who is in a very quiet district may be sent to a more troublesome district, and the man who has had a very great deal of trouble may be relieved for a short time by an exchange into some quieter district. That was the object of the circular, it was in order to ascertain the character of the district, and the amount of the policeman's trouble, that the circular was issued. That puts a totally different complexion on it. You stated that as a matter of information, but you had not seen the circular and I have, and that was the object of it, and I am authorised by the Commissioner to state so [illegible]?—Will you allow me to explain. I do not think you have quite shaken my view as to what the purport of the circular is. My impression of the circular was gathered from a policeman who came to speak to me on the [illegible] about it, and who was to me an utter stranger.

Dame police and Sunday [illegible].

41,242. You heard that from a discontented constable?—I do not think that the man who spoke to me was a discontented constable, but I took his interpretation of a circular directed to him requiring him to do a certain duty as on the whole likely to be the best impression as to the effect which the circular produced

Mr. T. Harrington, M.P.

[illegible] May '98

41,244. There is not a word of that in the circular?—(No answer). If this circular was read to you also, if the superintendent has to report on his slips the policemen who have not five cases a month, I make you a present of the term circular; I do not mind whether you call it a circular, or what you call it, the effect of this on the country which Father Furlong spoke to as being necessary on the part of the police, would be very great. He wanted to bribe them by giving them a portion of the fine. That is the reason I drew attention to it. My contention is that the police are stimulated to activity without giving them portions of the fine, and that they are constantly reminded of the necessity of bringing up cases of that kind, whether you speak of the police in Dublin or throughout Ireland.

41,245. The Commissioner of Police authorises me also to say that the absence of offences is taken as evidence of the efficiency of the policeman, and the quietness of the neighbourhood, brought about by his vigilance?—I have the very highest opinion of the Commissioner of Police, of the Assistant Commissioner of Police, and of the police themselves as a body. I do not believe in any country in the world there are better men.

41,246. Do not you think I was bound to vindicate the character of the Commissioner who you say was most responsible, and you proposed to bribe the police under his charge?—I made no such allegation, and there is no man in the world who would be more slow to make an allegation of bribery against him than I would. On the contrary, I resented very strongly the suggestion of a witness here that the police ought to be bribed, and I believe the police in Ireland would themselves resent it quite as strongly, and would repudiate the idea that they ought to be bribed for the execution of their duty. I believe they are incapable of it.

41,247. Did you use the word "bribed" just now?—No. I spoke of a witness, that is Father Furlong, who suggested that they ought to get a portion of the fine inflicted on the publican, or the person who is drunk.

Mixed trades in public-houses.

41,248. (*Viscount de Vesci.*) You are opposed to any interference with the mixed trades?—Yes. So far as I know Dublin I do not think you could very well interfere.

41,249. Are they mostly grocers?—A large body of them are.

41,250. Provision merchants generally?—Yes.

41,251. Do you know from your experience of Dublin, particularly in your own division, what proportion of the provision merchants do not hold licences. Can you form any idea without giving the figures?—A large proportion of them hold spirit licences, spirit grocers, and there is a general complaint in Dublin that the spirit grocers' licences are granted too easily. It is not the licensing authority, and the Recorder, who has the granting of them, and there is a general feeling of [illegible] that the spirit grocers' licences are becoming too common.

41,252. I am talking of those who sell "on." Do you consider that there are a sufficient number of provision merchants, who do not hold licences, to supply the wants of the inhabitants of your division which can [illegible] during the prohibited hours, say after the closing hours on Saturday, and during the closing hours on Sunday?—I do not think so. I think the number of provision merchants, grocers who do not hold licences, is exceedingly small in my division.

Clubs.

41,253. (*Sir Algernon West.*) In talking of the resolutions which have been passed by trades associations in Dublin, I understood you to say that they themselves have a bar in their own rooms?—I spoke of one trade association of the Trades Council representing all the trades of Dublin; I spoke of them as passing a resolution against the operation of the Sunday Closing Act, and I said they spoke as the representatives of all the organised trade bodies, but as a matter of fact in their own trade hall they have a club.

41,254. You draw a distinction between a club that is a legal club and one that is not?—Yes; it is not an illegal club at all. All the members have to pay their subscriptions, and it is very rigidly and carefully carried on.

41,255. (*Viscount de Vesci.*) Is it not only a long bar, but they sell provisions?—It is a club with billiard tables and rooms for amusement.

41,256. (*Sir Algernon West.*) They only supply members?—Only to members, or visitors introduced by members.

41,257. The visitors do not pay for these refreshments?—No, that is the distinction between a bogus club and a real club.

The witness withdrew.

Sir FREDERICK RICHARD FALKINER called in and examined.

Sir F. R. Falkiner.

41,258. (*Sir Algernon West.*) You are Recorder of Dublin?—Yes.

Position of witness.

41,259. Will you tell the Commission how long you have held that office?—I have completed my 21st year. I have served more than 21 years in the office of Recorder of the City of Dublin. In the year [illegible], I think, the duties of the county court judge, or chairmanship, as it was called, of the county of Dublin, were imposed on the duties of the Recordership. I have been chairman of quarter sessions, or county court judge of the county of Dublin, since 1880, and I have been Recorder of the City of Dublin, the old office, from 1876.

41,260. You held that office during the Committees of 1877 and 1888?—Yes, and I had the honour of being examined by them, before Sir Michael Hicks Beach's Commission in 1877, and before the Committee of the House of Commons presided over by the present Mr. Justice Madden, then the Solicitor-General for Ireland, in 1888.

Sunday and early Saturday closing.

41,261. I think you would be ready to give your opinion to the Commission on the subject of Sunday closing, and Saturday early closing?—Speaking of the matter from large experience, I think it is perhaps the most important question. There are very large and widely [illegible] topics connected with the general administration of the licensing law, but I, who view this subject of early Saturday and Sunday closing not from a temperance or from an anti-liquor point of view, but as a great social question, think that this is by far the most important of the questions with which those who are interested in social welfare of the people have to deal—I mean as connected with the licensing law. I may state that the evidence which I ventured to give when my experience was small in 1877, which was confirmed in 1888, has never had anything to shake it in the interval, and that looking at the matter, as I think we ought all to do, from the point of view of the welfare of the people in these democratic days, I think it is of vast importance, if we can, to save, so far as legislation can do it, the wages of the wage earner, and prevent them from being mortgaged at the beginning of the week.

41,262. You think that is the case now?—I know that it is in very many cases. The people have not got thrifty arrangements, I am sorry to say—less than they have here. The wages are paid usually on Saturday. The temptation to spend on Saturday evening—for our people are very social, very fond of congregating together—is very great. On the Sundays, the second day of the acquisition of the wages, there is of course all the freedom of the day, and great temptation also to spend. The consequence is that amongst a large class—and I say this from my knowledge of things I know—the rest of the week in vast numbers of the tenement houses of the city of Dublin the people are in misery, a misery which cannot be overstated, and so it goes on a dreary round in all the 52 weeks of the year.

41,263. You attribute that to the vast amount of wages that are spent on drink?—Yes. I wish to say that I very often hear the taunt, which we all have heard, Why should not a working man have his glass of beer? I say, certainly, why should not he have his glass of beer, or his glass of whisky, which is what they call a glass of beer in Dublin; but I say he ought not to have 7*d*. or 1*d*. if he cannot pay for them, and if the result is a bare misery, [illegible] and [illegible] children, and his wife [illegible] into a [illegible] prematurely, for that is what is happening.

61,874. Should you be afraid, if there was any more legislative restriction, that it would lead to home drinking?—That is a matter which can only be answered by experience. I think the legislature ought to be careful and wise. May I refer to the last public utterance on that subject? It only comes from a [illegible] source, no doubt, but an important one. At the late meeting of the General Synod of the Church of Ireland, in which there are representatives from every part of the Irish world, there was a resolution passed unanimously—I will show you how it touches the question as soon as I have read it:—"That the Bishops, clergy, "and laity of the Church of Ireland in General Synod "assembled, call upon the Government and legislature "to carry into law during the present session of Parlia- "ment the Sale of Intoxicating Liquors (Ireland) Bill, "which provides for making the Irish Sunday Closing "Act permanent, extending its provisions to the five "exempted cities, closing all the licensed premises at "[illegible] on Saturday nights, and extending the *bona* "*fide* traveller distance to six miles, in accordance "with the recommendations of the Select Committee "of the House of Commons, and as public opinion "has been unmistakably expressed in favour of this "measure, this Synod trusts that the Government and "members of Parliament will no longer ignore the "wishes of the people of Ireland in this matter. That "the General Synod strongly urge the Government "not to introduce any business in the House of Com- "mons on Wednesday, the 4th of May, that will inter- "fere with the second reading of the Sale of "Intoxicating Liquors (Ireland) Bill; and that copies "of this resolution be sent to His Excellency the Lord "Lieutenant of Ireland, the Chief Secretary for "Ireland, the Right Hon. the Marquis of Salisbury, "the Right Hon. A. J. Balfour, and the Right Hon. "Sir William Vernon Harcourt." As I was going to say, I happened to be present when that resolution was passed. I did not take any part in it. I was making an attendance to the Lord Primate. The reason I mention it is that Mr. Justice Madden, who was Solicitor-General, and chairman of the Committee of the House of Commons of 1888, took part in the debate which ended in that resolution. He referred to his experience as chairman of the Committee of 1888, and he said that a Bill had been brought into the House of Commons on the lines that are indicated in that resolution, namely, a total closing on Sunday in the city, as well as early Saturday closing, and the increase of the distance in the *bona fide* traveller clause, that he on the part of the Government was prepared, if the matter had gone on, to endeavour to carry through a clause or amendment qualifying that to the extent of reducing the hours on Sunday, not not entirely closing, and he said his reasons were those which were suggested in the question which you have been good enough to put to me, namely, that the wrench might be too great, and the consequences of a too severe restrictive legislation so severe that he thought it was wiser to be more tentative. He did not like, however, to fall to the evidence that he had heard, nor give before his own Committee in 1888; and he reminded me that I had spoken to the same effect before that Committee. Well, I adhere to that. The sense of the General Synod, however, was to pass the matter as one of principle, and that would logically mean entire closing on Sunday. Though I should be very glad if the people could have it, for the reasons I have mentioned, because it would save more of their wages, yet I think it would be too great a wrench; and if I may venture to say so, I think legislation in dealing with social matters and the habits of the people, ought to be cautious, and not to seek to do too much at once, remembering that the laws of this country have been always tentative, and have endeavoured to represent and to mirror the wants and the wishes of the people as these change from age to age.

surprised. It occurred to me at once, though I allowed the applicant to take the place in the chair, to which he went very triumphantly, and to be examined, that something must have occurred to warrant this, and I said, "Before you are examined I must ask you a "question. Upon your oath, Sir, have you canvassed "the Bench?" He was very much taken aback, and he said, "Well, I believe I have asked them to [illegible]," which he then turned into two or three. I said, "I "must ask you another question: Are any of the gentle- "men whom you have canvassed sitting at the Bench "with me now?" He hesitated, and he said, "I will "not answer that question." "Well, then," said I, "I "propose to adjourn. I will not, if I can help it, allow "this to be decided by this tribunal under these cir- "cumstances. My authority is limited. I propose "now to adjourn this question till April, when "people may be sitting about it and I will put "that to the vote as to whether it is to be ad- "journed until April, and if I am overruled upon "I will retire from the Bench to-day. I will not "proceed to hear the case, I will not allow this "question to go before a tribunal upon which it is "admitted there are (I will not say how many) gentle- "men who have been canvassed, and who came here "to pledge themselves to the applicant." That is the way I answer the two questions. It illustrates the utterly fluctuating character of the decisions that will be given if you have got what is the general tribunal, and though I am perfectly satisfied if the whole juris- diction be taken from me, for I do not want it, I do say that it is a lamentable thing that under the guise of a magisterial or a judicial inquiry one man is to get what his neighbours have been refused year after year.

61,277. You have told us the objections to the present system. Have you any suggestions to make as to what would be a better licensing authority?—If I were to say that I think the sole authority is a good one it would be very much as if I were expressing satisfaction with my own authority which I wholly disavow, but speaking as impersonally as I can I do think it will be far better if you have regard to the far reaching consequences that the decision should be judicial, that it should not be uncertain and fluctuating, from session to session, and from day to day. I will give you another instance of the fluctuation, if I am not wearying you. There was another case also at Kilmainham. There were present something less than 40 magistrates. A case again on application which was very strongly objected to, and upon a vote as to whether he should be given a new licence the magistrates were divided 18 to 18. I gave a vote, which made the 19th vote, making it 19 to 18. Almost immediately afterwards the counsel who was applying for the licence came back to me, and he said, "We have ascertained that a gentleman has improperly "voted here amongst the Bench who is not on the com- "mission of the justice for the county at all, his "commission is confined to the city," and that was so. I turned round to see whether I could get the Bench again, but the Bench had changed. Many of those who had been sitting with me only 10 minutes before were gone, and I found that I could not fairly get the matter to a second vote. That made it 18 to 18. Then it turned out curiously enough that the case was upon the opposition to overthrow the application, and not, as you might suppose, on the part of the applicant. In other words, it came under the section that has often been before you, as doubtless the 3rd and 4th William IV.— which says: "and if the objection shall be sustained." The consequence was the objection was not sustained, as there were only 18 to 18, and they were obliged to go up to the Queen's Bench Division, and to have it

small grocer's or haberdasher's, or even a bootmaker's shop and sold for licences, at great value freely. But, as time went on, and it was found these things were becoming so valuable, the licence that was granted for a small licensed holding house was then applied to it in an altered circumstances when it ought to be turned into a gin palace, and the consequence was the drinking power, not only in quality, but in quantity, was so great that it was acknowledged by every responsible person—the publicans among others—that the licenses in the city of Dublin were excessive, and accordingly I came to the conclusion that I would not grant a new licence at all, except under very special circumstances, unless the applicant assured me that in asking to increase the volume of liquor drinking in Dublin he was prepared to reduce it in some other direction. I said if you are asking for this very great luxury, and you want this monopoly and very great advantage, which will increase drinking in the city of Dublin, are you prepared to reduce it in another direction? I found that in this way I gave a lot of new licences by putting upon the applicant the necessity of purchasing and closing, in the nature of removals, licences of a small character in objectionable places; and it has worked well. In 1896 I was questioned in the connection by a gentleman I think representing the licensing interests, who said, "Are not you accused of "trafficking in public-houses?" and I said, "I am very "glad you asked me that question, because I will tell "you exactly what I do." I mentioned what I have had the honour of stating to this Commission. I showed them that I never did what I say was done some time ago here, by the County Council, I think, in London (somewhere in England I know) where a licence was granted to a man on his paying a large sum of money to a charity. The Queen's Bench Divisional Court most properly held that that was wholly illegal, and that the County Council went outside of their authority in doing it. That was trafficking in public-houses, because it was asking a man to pay a fine, or to give to a charity entirely outside, and outside their jurisdiction. It is so far accepted that the explanation I gave to him was satisfactory that two of the members of that Commission, the present financial secretary of the Local Government Board Mr. T. W. Russell, who was one of the members of the Committee, and Mr. Timothy Healy, Member of Parliament, representing different views, each brought in a Bill before the House of Commons to vindicate that very system, namely, providing generally as one of the provisions that new licences ought not to be granted increasing the facilities for drinking except where there was by the applicant a reduction in some other direction.

61,278. That Bill was not passed into law, was it?—It was not. Each of the Bills, I believe, was blocked in the usual, but there was a general consensus that it was fair and reasonable, and I may tell you it has worked very satisfactorily ever since. I said I only granted new licences when there was some corresponding reduction of drink; but the other ground upon which I gave it is when the person asks under very special circumstances and gives an undertaking that he will use the licence where he gets it for that purpose only. For example, when a man asks for an hotel, when a railway company are opening a restaurant, when a new [illegible] had to opened, and things of that kind, I think there it would be a sort of paternal exercise of my authority if I were to say, "No, you shall not have any "new licence." I should like to give a little explanation here, because there is a great confusion about the words "conditions" and "undertakings." It was decided by a very eminent Lord Chief Justice in England—Lord Chief Justice Cockburn—and the Court of Queen's Bench, over which he then presided,

Sir F. R. Falkiner.

1 May '9[illegible]

[illegible]

Licences on special undertakings.

Sir P. R. Falkiner. 8 May '97

"ordinary bar," I could not impose a condition upon him, and I say to him, "I cannot grant you this "unless you choose to voluntarily give an undertaking "to use it in a particular way." I hope I make myself understood as to the difference between a tribunal imposing a condition and a tribunal accepting a voluntary undertaking, given under special circumstances. This has worked well. A man gives an undertaking, say, for an hotel, that he will not open an ordinary bar so as to injure his neighbours, or to increase the sale of drink. He gives an undertaking that he will only use that as a restaurant, say, along with food, like the old taverns. The sanction for that undertaking is, that hitherto if a man breaks it, or is said to break it, the matter is considered not by me, but at the annual licensing renewal sessions, and if he is found, for he is regularly watched, to have broken the undertaking which he has given to a tribunal of the country, and on the faith of which he has been given a large grant, the magistrates have hitherto invariably refused to renew his licence. There is an appeal to me from the refusal of the magistrates, and, in the case of one or two hotels that I might mention, to which I had given a licence, as I have said, on the undertaking to use it in a certain way, upon the allegation that it had been used contrary to the undertaking, the magistrates had in each case refused the renewal, and the cases were brought before myself upon appeal, and I granted them, because I did not think there was in each case an intention to break the undertaking, but that there was just the temptation of perhaps using it a little loosely, and accordingly I restored them on a renewal of the undertaking. That has worked well. Now this is very important. In a late case

Leach's case.

in the Queen's Bench the matter was talked of incidentally—it was a case from the country known as Leach's case. In that case they held that a man could not get his renewal though he was well conducted if he had not actually used the licence during the year. One of the judges used this expression, that conditions were illegal, and that a man could not be punished for breaking them, and I think the judge went so far as to say that he thought that an honest man might break an illegal undertaking. The result of this appeared in the case of a man, who having given a solemn undertaking to close one of his houses on Sunday under circumstances which I will mention, deliberately broke that undertaking, and he pleaded [illegible] those dicta of the judge I mentioned. The result of the Sunday Closing Act is [illegible] was rather [illegible]. It had the direct result of establishing a set of open houses in the county in which they were all supposed to be closed, in this way. Just outside the three-mile boundary from the city of Dublin the thirsty souls who could not go into a Dublin public-house until 2 o'clock started off in hundreds just to the three-mile limit, and as bona fide travellers pushed in

Travellers outside Dublin.

150, I think, as many as 200 or 300 were found going into a house which under the Act of Parliament was closed—all going in as bona fide travellers. The case came before myself and the magistrates at Kilmainham. I should say there were two prosecutions against him for trading on Sunday. He pleaded the bona fide traveller. The only evidence that was given was that on each of these 200 or 300 thirsty souls coming in on Sunday the person behind the door asked three catechism questions, "Are you a bona fide traveller? What is your name? Where did you sleep last night?" And on the three questions being answered, "Yes, I am a bona fide traveller." "What is your name," answered according to whether he liked to tell the truth or not. And "Where did you sleep last night?" If it answered it is three miles off—"Come in and "to get in presumably to drink, and I therefore hold that you did not bona fide believe that "these were in good faith travellers." We were then to affirm the decision of the magistrates, when he said, "Well, that is a great difficulty; I have got another "public-house on the other side of the street, which is "inside the boundary, and I will close this one on "Sundays altogether if you will let me off." This came quite voluntarily from himself, and accordingly the magistrates forgave him. There had been the

Sir P. R. Falk.

Hotel licences.

[illegible]

rendered conviction on his licence. They forgave him, and he kept his promise; he worked as a single public-house, which clearly answered his purpose, and this year he has renounced in breach of his undertaking which he then voluntarily gave. The magistrates before whom the matter came refused the renewal on the ground of bad character, and I affirmed it. Now I believe the question is to be raised, and it is of the utmost importance to have a clear understanding about it. If I cannot give faith to a voluntary undertaking given by an applicant before me, I am paralysed in this jurisdiction—I cannot exercise it. If a man comes and says, I want this for a particular purpose, I do not want to use it in competition with my neighbours at all; I want it for a special purpose, and it is given for that special purpose and a man is to be allowed after he has, I would say, cheated a tribunal of the country into giving him a large monopoly—if he is allowed afterwards to break his word, I say that nothing can be more unsatisfactory than that result will be, and the proper jurisdiction on the subject is taken away from me the [illegible], for I cannot work without it. I will mention though upon that subject that a short time afterwards I had a very respectable and well-conducted communication from one of the organisations that represent the licensing business in Dublin, in which they went so far as to say they wholly disavowed any desire on the part of the trade to allege that these undertakings did not bind them to law as they did in honour and good faith.

Spirit grocers and the trade.

61,274. (Sir Algernon West.) You were going to tell us something about grocers' licences and your views with reference to them?—Yes. I would begin by stating a matter of fact, that very early in my career as Recorder the publicans interest raised the question as to how much illegal work was done by the grocers. They had reason to believe that these rights of selling under our licences were infringed by the grocers, and the temperance party joined with the licensed interest, and at a licensing sessions before me a man was produced who had been sent round to try the question, rather called here a "spy," that is, a person sent for the purpose of making the experiment—and he swore he had gone to 17 of these grocers' houses, who only had off-licences, and had only been refused drink in two of them in the county. Though I do not think that is at all a fair representation of the average breaking of the law—I think it is enlarged at the same time I think there is no doubt that, taking the country altogether, there is a good deal of that sort of illegality. The temptation is enormous to some of those people when everybody comes in to drink at their [illegible] to make the money easily when nobody is looking on, and I have had a good many cases before me in which it has appeared that they have broken the law—the spirit grocers particularly. That being so it raises a question of how far on the general subject it is desirable that there should be magisterial control over the granting of these spirit grocers' licences. They are in some respects peculiar to Ireland, as you know. That is to say, there is not exactly the same licence in England as the spirit grocer's. The law is very inconsistent as it stands on that subject. Of course with which I think have been brought before this Commission by the very able evidence of the Solicitor-General for Ireland—the case of a man named Marshall and a man named Morgan—goes to the extent that the magistrates must give the certificate unless there is a legitimate [illegible], and the only legitimate [illegible]—that is, the only legal [illegible]—is the police, and they went so far as to decide in Morgan's case that though the justices had before them on the admission of the man himself a condition of the premises, which showed the premises, in their opinion, to be unsuitable, yet, nevertheless, the magistrates could not act upon that, and were forced to give, in the face of the very evidence that they had from the man's own cross-examination, a certificate under their hands of the suitability of the premises and as the character of the applicant. It is altogether [illegible] for this Commission in any recommendation they make and then for Parliament to consider whether that is a satisfactory state of things, that is to say, that there should be no magisterial control over the spirit grocer's licence at all. I may mention to you the reason I thought it right to speak of it was this. I have nothing to do with the granting of these spirit grocers' licences, they only come before me as the Court of Appeal from the Dublin magistrates sitting in petty sessions, but the matter was brought before me lately in a rather remarkable way. A man applied before me by way of appeal from the magistrates for a grant of a spirit grocer's licence and of the beer licence, that is to say, the beer licence. He had been refused. Two magistrates had sat, and he had been refused on the ground of character. There were then appeared. The house in which he asked to carry on this business was in a [illegible] street in Dublin. His application was vehemently opposed by a publican on the other side of the way, and the publican, who was examined before me, made this very striking case. He said: "I bought my public-house "opposite to this house just three years ago; I gave "[illegible] for it, and I bought it upon a distinct state-"ment made at the auction that the house opposite, "which had been a spirit grocer's some years before, "was not and could not be used as such." He said, "I gave fully 1,000*l.* for my public house more than I "should have given for it if I had known there was a "grocer's immediately opposite"; because he did the business of a family grocer and a publican himself. On further inquiry it transpired that the owner of the house in respect of which the man was applying had kept this as a spirit grocer's, and had also owned the publican's opposite, and in order to enhance the price of the public-house had instructed the auctioneer to state that the spirit grocer's opposite could not be used as such. As soon as ever the owner—it was a woman, the widow of the former proprietor—had effected this sale and got 4,000*l.* for the public-house she proceeded, in breach of her promise, to open the house as a spirit grocer's, relying on this law that they must give it to her—that there was no legitimate [illegible]. The magistrates, however, refused to grant it to her on the ground of character, because they considered that that was a breach of good faith, and therefore they would not certify to her character, and she then sold it to the unfortunate man who applied before me on appeal from the magistrates' refusal to give a licence to him. He said, I am perfectly innocent in the matter; I know nothing of the previous transaction; I have bought this house, and spent also 100*l.* on it, which for a small man like him was a large amount, putting the premises in repair. Then, when it came before me, I found myself in this rather absurd position. I had complete control over the matter in so far as it was an application for drinking on the premises, but, according to Marshall's case, I had none in the case of the spirits, and the same was the position before the magistrates, but there the police—that means the Crown really certified, and he said he would not be prepared to say he had yet. He answered in a manly way I thought, and he said one of his reasons for wishing to come to town from the country was finding it difficult to carry out the law there. He was then asked in the usual way: "Will you swear you have not broken the "law many times?" and he said, "I will not give "you any answer to the subject at all." Now that was alleged as against the man's character, and I confess it appeared to me to be a very hard case, because a man was asked, and had never been convicted of anything, and who was perfectly innocent of any knowledge of the sale connected with the house which I have mentioned to you that [illegible] the Commission. I thought it very hard to condemn him on the matter of character. It is only very lately, and I mentioned at the time that well considered I advised him to apply at the next licensing sessions to try the matter over again. I said I did not like to overrule the magistrates who had refused to give him a certificate of good character, though I rather liked the honest manner in which he admitted that perhaps the law might have been broken previously, but I thought it was not a judicial thing to condemn a man for that kind of thing on a mere admission of his own. There the matter rests, but I think that it is well worth your consideration whether there ought not to be something like a judicial control in the case of the granting of these licences. As I tell you, in remote places where they are not subject to police supervision it is almost impossible to carry out the law—to prevent a man who has an off-licence from using it as an on-licence—almost impossible—and, as I have told you, in Morgan's case, which was a very remarkable case, it appeared that on the man's own evidence the premises were not suitable, and also in Marshall's case, the ground upon which the magistrates, who were overruled by the Court of Appeal, refused was because it was not subject to police supervision, being such a distance from the police barracks as well as being near a school, and the Court of Appeal held that on the ground that the phrase "suitability of premises" had added to it the expression, "suitability for sale." That touches on another part of your function here—I mean the uncertainty of the language used in these Acts, and the necessity there is, or the expediency there is, for consolidating and for new and clear language being used, because you can hardly read the statutes, and believe it was really intended that suitability of premises in one set of statutes should mean one thing, and suitability of premises in the other statutes should mean a different thing, and there is no doubt whatever in the case of suitability of premises with reference to the granting of an on-licence, you can consider all these collateral circumstances, condition of the neighbourhood, and all that, whereas in the other case of the spirit grocers, you can only consider whether they are suitable for sale. That table is suitable for sale. It is hard to know what is unsuitable in that respect, and therefore it seems to me to be very well worth consideration whether there should not be some magisterial control over the granting of these Dublin spirit grocers' licences.

42,878. Now, is the administration of licensing in Ireland satisfactory?—Well, that involves the question of the Clitheroe case that you have heard a good deal about, and it is not at all for me to say whether it is satisfactory or not; but I think it is very important in view of possible future legislation that there should be a very clear understanding of exactly what the difference between the English and Irish law is on the subject—I mean that the question might arise at any time before Parliament as to what compensation should be given in case the legislature undertake to diminish the number of public-houses and so forth, and the amount of the vested interest is a very important one, that public men should have it taken both financially as well as connected with the magisterial question.

Sir F. R. Falkiner.

6 May 1897.

Language of Licensing Statutes.

Clitheroe's case.

Mr F. E. [illegible]

6 May '98

The bonâ fide traveller.

[illegible]; but that was only [illegible] till the quarter sessions [illegible].

61,277. (Chairman.) I understand you to be in favour of closing all public-houses on Sunday. Am I right in that?—No. I said that I thought the general opinion [illegible] was represented by the resolution of the General Synod was in favour of it, but that personally I think it would be too dangerous [illegible] a sudden [illegible] to alter the habits of the people, and it would be wiser [illegible] the [illegible] to [illegible] the more moderate course.

61,278. The reason I asked the question is this, I suppose you would be of opinion that if Sunday closing were carried out throughout all Ireland the difficulty of the bonâ fide traveller would be increased?—Yes, partly that, but also I think that to close all the houses in the city of Dublin would be too great and sudden a wrench in the habits of the people.

61,279. Assuming they were closed, what facilities would you give to the bonâ fide traveller for obtaining refreshment on Sunday. Would you give them any or none?—I think there ought to be a licence granted in the nature of the old tavern licence from which the whole thing grew, because originally the old drink licence was [illegible] to the [illegible] I should like to have an opportunity of saying a word upon that—and it all grew out of the innkeeper's licence.

61,280. You would give the magistrate's discretion as any [illegible] house should be open for the supply of the bonâ fide traveller on the Sunday?—I think so. I think there ought to be some places. For instance, there are people who come to Dublin who have no home, and no place to get their dinner, and I think it would be too severe a [illegible] to say they should have no power of getting it.

61,281. It would be a great privilege conferred on the house that was opened when others were not permitted to be opened?—No doubt there is that monopoly, and it is a very hard thing to deal with it.

61,282. (Mr [illegible].) It would arise in the case of townships. They would have to select one house in the [illegible] for the bonâ fide traveller?—I think the judicial aspect of it would be this, to consider, not the individual, but the wants of the neighbourhood, and [illegible] as they could be [illegible] how many were required. It would have to be [illegible], but the exceptional privilege being given for the benefit of the public, and for the licensed person, the benefit of the public would be the [illegible] of granting.

Suggested [illegible] licence.

61,283. Could it be provided for as it is now in Scotland, by only allowing hotels to serve the bonâ fide traveller, and not the ordinary public-house?—Yes, that is what I meant, that they should be in the nature of the old innkeeper's licence.

61,284. On one side of Dublin going towards the townships it is easy enough to get a house of the kind you have described, but going out further towards the mountains it would be difficult to find a house of that kind, would not it?—Like all social questions it is a question of compromise. You would have to judge each case on its merits, and what would be for the advantage of one set of people would be for the disadvantage of the others. You could only act in each case according to justice.

61,285. Sitting as Recorder, your licensing authority is confined to the city only and does not extend to the Metropolitan Police district?—No.

Recorder and county justices.

61,286. You said you were in conflict rather with the body of magistrates with reference to a licence they gave just over the boundary, where you as Recorder inside the boundary had refused the licence?—I am glad you have given me an opportunity of saying that I did not at all [illegible]—[illegible] I was misunderstood—[illegible] within the [illegible] of the county, and the cases are tried chiefly at Kilmainham.

Mr F. E. [illegible]

61,287. That is the quarter sessions district for the townships?—Yes.

61,288. What I wanted to ask is this: Are the licences in the townships excessive as compared with the licences in the city in proportion to population?—I think they are not at all in the same disproportion, because they have grown up in later years. They have all been since that system adverted to earlier [illegible] under which magistrates [illegible] and even [illegible] gave licences to small people almost for their asking for them in the beginning of this century. Those houses have remained in the city, but that system was abolished before the modern Victoria period, in which the Dublin suburban districts have grown up.

Licensing [illegible] Dublin county.

61,289. You stated there were four licensing districts in the county of Dublin, are there four quarter sessions which grant licences?—Yes, there is a northern rural district which I visit occasionally. The business is very small there, but at Kilmainham, in the southern district of the county, the licensing matters chiefly are dealt with.

61,290. You have occasionally a large number of magistrates attending—as many as [illegible]?—Even [illegible].

61,291. At one district quarter sessions?—Yes, during part of the day.

61,292. Were they drawn from all over the county or were they mostly residents within the district?—It is impossible to give precise information, but of course the larger number came from the more metropolitan parts because there is a larger population, but I think the rural districts are represented also. The last Governments have very much enlarged the number of justices of the peace. Mr. Morley made a large number, and a good many have been made by the Unionist Governments.

61,293. Do you find that, having the full body of magistrates there, there is want of uniformity of practice from one session to the other?—I should not like to say [illegible] any difficult [illegible] of getting a vote from the majority. They crowd into the grand jury box; they are all sitting over the clerk of the peace and the officers; they are in the petty jury box, and it is very hard to take the poll.

61,294. Do you think that the area is too small, or would you extend the area of the licensing authority to the whole county, assuming you maintained the present system of the magistrates being the licensing authority. At present, there are four licensing sessions for the county Dublin but would you have only one licensing sessions for the whole county?—I think the practice that we have adopted is a very excellent one, that is to say, that it should be annual, and that is what we called the adjournment [illegible] but exceptional cases should be taken. As I have told you, that has worked very well, and the magistrates have kindly allowed me to say when the exceptional circumstances are, but I have [illegible] occasional cases in which they overruled me upon it.

Licensing [illegible]

61,295. My question is directed to this—whether you would have only one session, a county session—instead of having quarter sessions districts?—The district question hardly comes in. I think Kilmainham is an excellent place for the portion of the county it represents; that is to say the whole of the metropolitan part of the county outside the city itself. I think that is excellent, and I do think it would not be a good thing to entirely take away the power of the magistrates to deal with exceptional cases at the sessions; but I think it is wholly and entirely objectionable that an off [illegible] should be allowed to act as if they were an annual sessions and exercise an absolute discretion.

[illegible] any man ought to get what another man is refused because he has contravened [illegible]

41,[illegible]. By [illegible] you mean that as Recorder you would sit as sole authority perhaps associated with [illegible] magistrates?—Yes, I should like to have [illegible].

41,[illegible]. What kind of assessors would you prefer? It has been suggested that the resident magistrates should sit?—I should like to have persons who were known to have [illegible] and entirely unconnected with either party or with any "[illegible]" persons who were perfectly fair. I should like to have a couple of assessors with me.

41,[illegible]. It has been suggested that the resident magistrates should be the assessors of the county court judge?—I think they would be excellent.

41,[illegible]. Would you have anybody else selected from the body of magistrates as assessors?—I have not thought enough on the subject to say.

41,[illegible]. I am not talking of county Dublin now, but taking the counties generally. Have the county court judges sufficient knowledge of the local [illegible] of the [illegible] independently of the evidence that may be brought before them?—I think they nearly all have. They may not the first year of their sitting.

41,[illegible]. You think they acquire it?—They are a very able body of men in Ireland, and most of them have been Queen's counsel of eminence, and they get the local information very soon.

41,[illegible]. It was stated by a witness here the other day that in the city of Dublin—I do not think she stated it was frequent—there were cases where private bars were set up in the backs of some of the licensed premises, where they had a separate private entrance, and that women who were ashamed to go in a public bar could be admitted at the private bar and would enter there. Have you any knowledge of that or has that been brought before you?—No; not exactly that; but at the time of the new licenses I ventured to speak of I have very often been asked to look into the undertakings they offer in [illegible] objections made by the police, or by the temperance party, or by [illegible] [illegible] publicans on the subject. As a rule I [illegible] the judicial responsibility myself of deciding these [illegible] questions. It would be very [illegible] to do so, because I should then have to exercise a sort of supervision over them afterwards; but when objections are made I generally refer it to a [illegible] of the opponent and the applicant and they come to an agreement among themselves, and when that agreement is arranged a [illegible] is registered with the clerk of the peace and becomes a record of the court, and it is on that that the magistrates act afterwards as a question of whether a man has broken his undertaking or not.

41,[illegible]. (*Dean Dickinson.*) Do you not think that if the public-houses were closed on Sunday, there are many in Dublin who would see to the establishment of coffee houses and places of refreshment of that kind to provide the working man and travellers with what was necessary and healthy for them?—If the [illegible] was carried out, and there was a total closing, you may be quite sure that all sorts of [illegible] [illegible] would spring into existence, [illegible] and illegitimate.

41,[illegible]. And they would be frequented and used so that they would pay, because they cannot be kept up unless they pay?—The destruction of the one means of obtaining refreshment would give an opening to the others.

41,[illegible]. And induce them to do it?—Yes.

41,[illegible]. You have a large acquaintance with the police of Dublin in your court. Have you any reason for suspecting or believing that any pressure is put on the police to maintain their zeal by a certain number of arrests, or anything of that kind?—I never heard it suggested till the other day, and, if I may venture to make an observation on what I heard in the room, I would humbly suggest it would be a very desirable thing to know the actual document which was considered today as emanating from the police. It should speak for itself like any other legal document.

41,[illegible]. I want to have had that today, but I have got leave from the Chairman to [illegible] that so when I get it [illegible]. If I had had it today I would have handed it in, and it would have saved a good deal of trouble?—I know that, as a matter of fact, the police do not [illegible] arrest a man because he is drunk in the city. They sometimes are taken kindly by him and will take him home, and all that sort of thing. I am not prepared at all to say that [illegible] jurisdiction policemen will not arrest everybody they can.

41,[illegible]. That was another point. You think, as a matter of fact and practice, the arrests for simple drunkenness are not common?—I am not able to speak to that, because I only indirectly know them. I have to speak generally, but I do not believe for one moment that any sort of espionage exists as has been suggested exists, and that the men are desired to make up a certain number of cases in order that they may make rows, like the old Neapolitan [illegible]. I do not believe it for a moment, having regard to the characters of the authorities who have been at the head of it.

41,[illegible]. It is only fair to Mr. Harrington to say he made that statement on hearsay information?—On the information of what is called the "Man in the street."

41,[illegible]. (*Mr. [illegible].*) What kind of license did you refer to when you stated that you imposed conditions on the applicant?—Forgive me for [illegible] out, I did not say "conditions." I never impose a condition, I take undertakings.

41,[illegible]. I understood you to say you imposed certain conditions, and that afterwards the applicant had broken those conditions—that he had made a pledge that he would only use his house for certain purposes?—I have spoken in vain if I did not try to explain the difference between an undertaking and conditions. I have no right to impose a condition. It has been so decided [illegible] years ago by Lord Chief Justice [illegible], but I do take from applicants asking for a license undertakings that they will use that license in a particular way, and there is all the difference in the world between the two in the legal sense, and, I should have thought, in a popular sense.

41,[illegible]. My question is whether the justices, in granting or renewing a license in Ireland, have greater authority than in this country?—I have again said that I have never imposed conditions.

41,[illegible]. It is laid down that no condition can be imposed on the granting of a license?—No condition can be legally imposed. You cannot say to a man "I give you this on the condition of it being an hotel only." That is one of the [illegible] [illegible]; but I can say to a man who is asking for an hotel license and says I only want it for that, I will not grant you a general license because I cannot impose a condition, and then he knows the position, and he therefore always applies voluntarily to use it as an hotel, and undertakes to use it so only.

41,[illegible]. That is what you suggest with reference to the conditions?—Yes, and I am very emphatic on it, because that is the whole difference.

41,[illegible]. With reference to the entire Sunday closing in Dublin, you think that would be too great a [illegible]?—As a practical man, I should be afraid to do that.

41,[illegible]. You would allow it to remain as it is now?—I should shorten the hours.

41,[illegible]. On Sundays?—Yes, I think three hours ought to be quite enough, or two; and that is what Mr. [illegible] [illegible] said the other day at the Synod, that that is what he [illegible] was on behalf of the then Government in [illegible].

41,[illegible]. What hours would you have the houses opened, taking into consideration the convenience of the people?—I should say from [illegible] to [illegible], which would be three hours, or [illegible] to [illegible]. That is for the ordinary public-houses. Besides that I would allow a certain amount of [illegible] licenses.

41,[illegible]. You think that would not be too great a restriction for the people?—I think not. I tried to give my reason for wanting to [illegible] the people [illegible] their wages at the beginning of the week.

41,[illegible]. If you allowed the houses in Dublin to remain open as at present you would allow the other four exempted cities to have the same privilege?—I do not like to say anything about the other exempted cities. I do not know anything about them, and if I can give any evidence at all of any value I wish to confine it to the places where I have had actual experience.

41,[illegible]. You must know that at present there are five exempted cities?—Yes, I know that.

Sir F. R. Falkiner.

[illegible]

Licenses on special undertakings.

Sunday hours of closing.

Sir F. R. [illegible].

[illegible] May '[illegible]

61,[illegible]. Would you allow the same privilege to the other exempted cities that you suggest for Dublin?—I know that they are exempted, but I have not information on which I could say whether I think it is a wise thing or not. I am not able to answer whether I think it is wise or not.

61,[illegible]. It seems rather odd for a person to wish to give Dublin the privileges which the other cities have not?—[illegible] I should wish to speak of things I know, and not to speak of things I know not.

61,[illegible]. Perhaps then only be one matter in the question. We are under the impression that you came here to give general evidence with reference to Ireland?—No. I will tell you anything I think I am able to give you an answer about.

Clubs. 61,[illegible]. With reference to clubs, can you suggest any restrictions to be placed upon them?—I think I was asked that question in [illegible]. I think it would be a good thing if whatever restrictions in the way of licenses [illegible] put upon a working man's club should be made to go right along through the whole of society. If there be any licence required in the case of a working man's club, I do not see why the gentleman's should not be subject to the same conditions on the principle of perfect equality.

61,[illegible]. What would be the wisdom of closing the licensed houses against the public and allowing clubs to remain open?—By taking care that clubs should be only reliable, true, and bona fide clubs.

Early closing on Saturdays. 61,[illegible]. (Mr. Roberts.) On the question of the hours of closing, when you gave evidence in [illegible], I think you spoke in favour of an earlier closing hour on Saturdays?—Yes.

61,[illegible]. Would that be your opinion still?—Certainly. I think it is almost more important, but at all events it is quite as important as the Sunday question.

61,[illegible]. To what extent would you go back in the way of hours on Saturday?—I would shorten them as much as I could consistently with not interfering with the reasonable power of the people to purchase groceries on Saturday—I mean excluding liquor.

61,[illegible]. Would 9 o'clock be too early in your judgment?—I should be very glad to see them closed at 9 o'clock; but I rather think that that is a question on which the police authorities might give better evidence as they see more of the people in the evening than I do. The only thing I can say is that the more you can curtail [illegible] speak for the people, and on that ground only—the wages of the people on Saturday evening and on Sunday the happier and the better for them, in their social [illegible] and in their homes.

Chairman's [illegible]. 61,[illegible] (Mr. Whitaker.) I only wish to put one question to you (and I do not wish you to enter into it at any length) in order to understand the bearing of the [illegible] case, with which you were so prominently [illegible]. I have not quite gathered whether your individual opinion is that it is extremely desirable that some such case bearing on that point should be taken to the highest court so as to get a final decision upon it. Is that your opinion?—I think, on public grounds, it is desirable. I should be very sorry to give my own opinion, but I think it is a very important thing that the nation should understand how far there really is a different law in Ireland and in England.

61,[illegible]. You do not consider it quite satisfactory that it should be left to the present somewhat [illegible] position?—It is too long and too technical to go into at length, but perhaps you will allow me to say a word [illegible]

[illegible] as he is bound by a whole set of [illegible] obligations and penalties of all sorts, and the law [illegible] he should be the real owner of the place, and I do not [illegible] if he has merely a nominal interest.

[illegible]. It is almost impossible in any [illegible] to find a man carrying it on who is the real owner. There are [illegible] of that sort, whether public-houses or other places of business?—You are quite right, and that is the reason I say I feel very [illegible] [illegible]. I have only done so in three or four cases. The last is one [illegible].

[illegible]. Do not you think a man of that class, having given [illegible] only for a house, and probably that [illegible] [illegible] but a [illegible] interest in seeing the business carried on properly? Do you think he would rush the [illegible]?—I have been led to this by finding a lot of cases of premature bankruptcies. It has been done by [illegible] the value and holding out to these young men, who would give their lives to be the owners of a public-house, [illegible] to give inflated prices. The reason why I came to the conclusion that the man was not fit, having regard to his position to hold the licence, was in consequence of want of real interest.

[illegible]. My information is that it must act as evidence before you that the money was lost by some [illegible]?—It was.

[illegible]. Does not that go to prove that the [illegible] thought it a good risk?—The [illegible] would put almost every pressure on the man to make money. If you knew of the cases that have come before me of the [illegible] in the publicans' [illegible], in consequence of the giving of these inflated prices, you would understand what I mean.

[illegible]. I quite agree that the prices are inflated [illegible]?—I am glad you have asked me the question, because I think that what I do is a subject, and ought to be [illegible] in evidence.

[illegible]. (*Mr. [illegible]*.) Referring to the two conditions under which the spirit grocers' [illegible] is granted, the goodness of character and the question of suitability of premises, I understand the difficulty you see is that suitability of the premises alone is not sufficient?—The Court of Appeal have held that the question of suitability refers only to the structural [illegible] for sale.

[illegible]. If that was enlarged so that it covers suitability of environment and surroundings, would that meet your objection?—It would meet one of the objections.

[illegible]. If a house was built on the immediate doors of a church or school, you would like that brought within the question of suitability?—Yes, certainly.

[illegible]. That is a recommendation you would like the [illegible] to [illegible]?—Yes. The other question would remain, whether there should not be [illegible] further [illegible] in being allowed to consider the [illegible] of [illegible] which, for a great many years, it was supposed you could do. It was only in [illegible] case they [illegible] you [illegible].

[illegible]. I [illegible] the words you used were that the temptation was [illegible] in the case of [illegible] to break the law. That arises a great deal from the character of the houses and the fact that the [illegible] in Ireland [illegible] in small quantities under his [illegible]. If that did not exist, [illegible] the temptation would be [illegible], would it not?—Do you mean if they were not allowed to sell in small quantities?

[illegible]. If they were not allowed to sell in open [illegible]?—Yes, that would modify the difficulty.

they find the [illegible] of the [illegible]. At the same time I think that you cannot [illegible] them, but that the [illegible] of the [illegible] would enable him to [illegible] by which he could break the law if he wanted to.

[illegible]. (*Mr. [illegible]*.) Have you frequent instances of publicans becoming bankrupt in Dublin?—I think not. They are respectable [illegible] people generally. I have not a word to say against them; they are [illegible], and, as I have told you, they support me in carrying out the undertakings. It is only in an exceptional case that they break it.

[illegible]. (*[illegible]*.) They are not [illegible] to be bankrupt?—Yes. There are cases, of course, but I do not think at all, if you ask me, that there are many more in their case than in the case of other trades.

[illegible]. (*Mr. [illegible]*.) I suppose you agree with me that a [illegible] in the [illegible] is not a new development in this country?—Would you allow me to close my evidence, partly in answer to that, by mentioning what I had intended to refer to, namely, this subject of early closing on Saturday and on Sunday, and to refer to the fact that legislation in that direction, if recommended by you, is not so new [illegible] as some people think it would be. I refer to the statute of 1815, the year of Waterloo, 55 George III., and this is pertinent to what you have just said. The preamble of that Act is: "To grant certain duties of excise upon licences, and to discourage the 'inordinate use of spirituous liquors in Ireland.'" I beg [illegible] to say that that is my policy, but I emphasise the adjective to discourage the "inordinate" use of spirituous liquors in Ireland. In the first place it established Sunday closing. There are things not generally known, and, secondly, it provided that nobody could hold a licence except he gave security that he would keep a victualling house, and, in terms, during the time such licence should be in force. That was as to the qualification for it. Then, thirdly, in two or three sections it provided, under penalty, that no wages were to be paid in public-houses to artificers or [illegible]—and those are the people I want to save, if I can. There is a penalty imposed for paying any [illegible], [illegible], servants, or labourers, and furthermore the Act provides that no [illegible] of spirits were sold in less than one pint—which was afterwards changed to two quarts—could be [illegible] if credit were given, and that is the law at present.

Mr. F. M. [illegible].

1 May '[illegible]

Provisions under Act of 1815.

[illegible]. I am glad you have referred to that, because I am anxious to know the specific cure for the condition of things of which you complain. You really have pointed out what you think are some of the remedies?—Yes. May I add to my answer, to make the history of it more clear, that the provision requiring the houses to be [illegible] for a licence was [illegible] afterwards by the 6th George IV., that is 1825. By the [illegible] section of that Act it was provided that no excise licence should be granted for the sale of beer, cyder, or perry by retail to be consumed on the premises of the person applying for such licence to any person who should not produce the certificate of the justices to keep an inn, alehouse, or victualling house, and that continued the law till the big Act of 3 and 4 William IV., and in that Act, without referring at all to the particular clause, it gives a different rule with reference to the granting of licences; and, incidentally, the old qualification of keeping a victualling house was removed, not by special enactment, but by implication.

[illegible]. I want to put one or three leading questions in order that I may get your summary. You acknowledge this to be a necessary and legitimate trade?—Of course I do.

Sir F. R. Falkiner. — 1 May '96.

tive legislation and restrictive judicial decision in Ireland, unless it be practical, and unless it aims at dealing with things as they are. If I may refer to myself, I exercise my criminal jurisdiction very elastically, according to what I see the circumstances in the city are, and if I consider it necessary to inflict a severe punishment I give it; but if I find I can be lenient I am so.

61,259. Are the public-houses the root of the evil of excessive drinking in your opinion?—I think it would be unfair to say the public-houses are; but I think that the intemperate use of liquor is a very great disadvantage, and as a large portion of that comes through the public-houses, to that extent I think so, but not otherwise.

61,260. You are of opinion that the carrying on of the business on the public way as we have it seems to you a disadvantage but, on the contrary, is conducive to order?—Certainly.

61,261. Do you agree with me, that if you improve the condition of the people in their dwellings and elevate them by education, you will lessen intemperance?—Yes. Every improvement in the progressive advance of the people makes restrictive legislation less necessary.

61,262. Is that process not going on now in your experience?—Yes it is, but, as Lord Tennyson says, there are retrogressions, and there are retrogressions constantly revolving round each other, and severing dragging ... in the road, but the general trend is in the way of improvement.

61,263. Are you of opinion that you can cure the evils of which many of us complain by stricter legislation, or do you depend also upon the advance of civilisation?—I depend a great deal more upon the advancement of civilisation. There is a very hackneyed expression that you cannot make people sober by Act of Parliament, which, like a great many truisms, is very true, but if pressed too far is very false. That is to say, that you can never make people sober by bidding them be sober by Act of Parliament any more than you can make them honest by the Ten Commandments, but that is no reason for repealing the Ten Commandments or to deny the morality they have forced from there through all the ages, and so I may say that restrictive legislation will never of itself make people sober any more than the penalty laws will make men honest, but we think they will help.

61,264. (Mr. Whittaker.) They may prevent them from getting drink?—They may restrain them.

61,265. (Mr. Fenwick.) So with reference to restrictive legislation, you would as soon establish a society for the prevention of theft as a society for the prevention of drunkenness? —No, I do not think it is necessarily so. There is a very fine society for the prevention of theft called the Dublin Police.

The witness withdrew.

Viscount PEEL in the Chair.

His Honour Judge CURRAN called in and examined.

Judge Curran. — Position of witness.

61,266. (Chairman.) I believe you for some time were engaged as counsel in licensing cases?—Yes.

61,267. After that you were appointed divisional magistrate in the metropolitan district of Dublin?—I served for two years.

61,268. You then became a county court judge?—Yes, for King's County and the counties of Westmeath, Longford, and Meath.

61,269. By virtue of that office you became chairman of quarter sessions in those counties?—Yes. The county court judges in Ireland are also chairmen of quarter sessions.

61,270. You have some experience, too, of a county that was in a very disturbed state when you went there?—Yes, I went at the request of the Government to Kerry for five years, while it was in a disturbed state. Then I returned to my present district.

61,271. You acted there as chairman of quarter sessions?—Yes, but I am now in the same district I commenced in.

61,272. You returned to your old district, and you are chairman now of the quarter sessions of the four counties?—Yes.

61,273. As we know, the county court judge presides at quarter sessions with the magistrates?—He as county court judge sits as sole judge, but presides with the magistrates at quarter sessions.

61,274. Therefore you can speak for the five counties of Kerry, Longford, Westmeath, King's County, and Meath?—Yes.

Excessive and increasing number of public-houses, &c.

61,275. What do you think generally as to the number of public-houses in Ireland? Are they adequate, or excessive, or sufficient?—I have always been of opinion that the number of public-houses in Ireland is out of all proportion to the necessities of its inhabitants.

61,276. I am afraid as the population of Ireland is decreasing the proportion has become greater?—The population is decreasing, I am sorry to say, but the number of public-houses, except in a few isolated instances, is increasing, and where the number of public-houses has decreased, I am sorry to say the ratio is just as bad, because the population has gone down.

61,277. Do you say that the houses have increased in number?—Yes.

61,278. They have not only remained stationary where the population has decreased, but where the population has decreased the licenses have been increased?—The licenses have increased considerably in number.

Judge Curran.

61,279. Does that apply to any one of your counties in particular that you have spoken of?—It applies to the counties over which I preside now, and also to Kerry.

State of the law.

61,280. You would, perhaps, admit that the licensing law in Ireland is in a very complicated condition?—The law is very complicated. I agree with all that has been stated by the Solicitor-General and other witnesses as to its being complicated, but the digest given of it by Mr. [illegible] in the abridgment of the law in Vol. 2, Blue Book is remarkably clear and accurate.

Administration of law by Justices.

61,281. Would you say that the law as administered by the licensing authority in quarter sessions was so complicated that they could not understand it?—No. I think the law to be administered at quarter sessions in granting licenses is very easy, and easily understood. There is no difficulty at all about it. We have one or two Acts of Parliament to deal with, and there is no necessity for a man to be a judge to be able to know what the law is.

61,282. So that the magistrates do not act up to their powers?—No. The duties at quarter sessions are evaded by magistrates, in my experience, and the granting of licenses, so far as they are supposed to act judicially, has become, so far as a large body of magistrates are concerned, if I may use the expression, a large farce. I have prepared here statistics showing the number of public-houses and the population in each town and village of the five counties in which I have referred. (See Appendix IX.)

(See Appendix IX.)

61,283. Can you give us any particulars that you think salient from those returns?—Yes. I have here a return from Longford, and I find that in Longford town there are 4,70[illegible] inhabitants and 53 licensed houses, 38 seven-day and 15 six-day licenses and two off-licenses, and it may throw some light upon the ratio of the public-houses to the number of other houses in a town like Longford containing 4,000 inhabitants, if I just show you this map. This is a map of the town of Longford, and the houses marked red are public-houses (producing same). (See Appendix X.)

(See Appendix X.)

61,284. What is the length of the street?—It is a town of something under 4,000. That will give you an idea of the number of public-houses in the town of Longford, and this is a pretty fair specimen.

61,285. (Mr. Grimley.) This is a difficulty that has cropped up rather frequently. I find Longford is [illegible] here with a population of [illegible] and [illegible] public-houses?—That is the Longford district.

61,[illegible]. But you say [illegible] public-houses?—In the town.

61,[illegible]. In addition to the [illegible]?—There are [illegible] public-houses.

61,[illegible]. That is to a population of [illegible]?—That is the petty sessions district. I have given you the return [illegible] of the town. The return supplied in the book is the population of the petty sessions district, which, of course, is much larger.

61,[illegible]. There are only [illegible] public-houses to the [illegible]?—There are [illegible]. There must be some mistake in your return.

61,[illegible]. (Chairman.) Are you able to say that that [illegible] of public-houses, as shown on this map, has [illegible] of late years [illegible] have been granted?—Yes, in Longford.

61,[illegible]. In the town of Longford?—Yes, in the town of Longford. Not very long since the owner of a [illegible] shop near the Court House applied for a licence, and the magistrates, who had time after time refused licences in the town of Longford on the ground that the number was excessive, all [illegible] on this day and granted the gentleman his licence, the result of which is [illegible] that next to the Court House is a [illegible] shop, and [illegible] who go in there to buy [illegible] on one side of the shop can turn to the other side of the shop to get a drink.

61,[illegible]. Do you know many cases where a licence has been refused at the ordinary annual sessions, and applied for and granted at a particular session before a [illegible] court of magistrates?—Yes, [illegible] they [illegible] be [illegible]. I may say that there are some magistrates who go from quarter sessions to quarter sessions to vote for every licence. There are other magistrates who will not fairly and properly attend in every case until a friend of theirs comes up, and they vote for that friend.

61,[illegible]. It is not illegal to go from one quarter sessions to another in the county?—It is not illegal; but it is [illegible] in the case of a licence.

61,[illegible]. Do they ever go from petty sessions to petty sessions?—I have no jurisdiction in petty sessions, but I hear that they do. I have been [illegible] informed they do; but there are some magistrates, I must admit, who are always [illegible] in each of the four counties.

61,[illegible]. (Mr. [illegible].) Have you any who make a [illegible] of voting against the grant of any licence?—No, I have not, but I have gentlemen who come forward and try cases on the evidence before them. I have some who come to vote for any licence, and behind my [illegible] to vote for the licence.

61,[illegible]. (Chairman.) Should you say there is much [illegible] of magistrates by applicants?—In a very great measure. It is [illegible], the amount of [illegible] that goes on, and I say that the magistrates are themselves to a very considerable extent to blame for it.

61,[illegible]. Would you go so far as to say that the magistrates canvass one another?—Over and over again I have found magistrates canvassing each other. I have known many cases where it has been done behind my back on the Bench, and I have heard them say, "Won't you vote for that man?"

61,[illegible]. That might be only an interchange of their judicial opinions, might it not?—You may put it in that way, but I know myself I very recently met a magistrate at one of my sessions, and he asked me what time would the quarter sessions be on [illegible] day. I told him. Then he asked what time would the licensing be on, and I asked him, "Why?" "Because," he said, "[illegible]," mentioning a brother magistrate, "who is "an old friend of mine has pressed me very hardly to "vote for a friend of his who is up for a licence." He came and voted for him. He came in late; he did not hear the case, but he voted for the man, and of course I could say nothing; but time after time I have found that to occur, so that you can scarcely put it down to an interchange of their opinion on the Bench.

against a licence, and a brother magistrate of his who was behind you on the Bench said to him, "What do "you mean by that, did not you promise to vote for "the licence before we came into court"? That is [illegible] to [illegible]. It occurs time after time.

61,[illegible]. Did you, when he asked that question, [illegible]?—I did. I told him it was a very improper thing to do, and I ordered him off the Bench, because he was the landlord of the premises for which the licence was sought.

61,[illegible]. (Mr. [illegible].) That was a legal disqualification, of course?—Yes, but I did not know he was behind me.

61,[illegible]. The Chairman rather wanted to know whether you ordered him off on account of what he said?—I could not order him off the Bench for that. I told him he had no right to be on the Bench as landlord.

61,[illegible]. (Chairman.) Have you left the Bench yourself?—On one occasion in Kerry—about [illegible] in the [illegible] the [illegible] were applied for a licence. It was very strongly opposed by the local magistrates, but magistrates came in from all parts of Kerry, [illegible] and [illegible] miles away. I myself saw them driven in, [illegible] the [illegible], who was the applicant himself. It was just like an election. They came from all parts. Some of the magistrates had been not [illegible] there [illegible] days before that, and they all came in, and so satisfied was I that it was a [illegible] that I stood up and said; "Gentlemen, I refuse to preside over "such a pack of [illegible]"; and I retired from it.

61,[illegible]. What happens to the Bench then if you retire?—They had to [illegible] each other in the [illegible]. They had no head, and so they went about their business.

61,[illegible]. In the absence of the county court judge, or, as on that occasion, if you leave the Bench there is nobody to take your place?—I had no other means of showing my horror of what was taking place.

61,[illegible]. (Mr. [illegible].) There is no power to elect a temporary chairman?—No; I am by Act of Parliament chairman.

61,[illegible]. (Dean [illegible].) Have you ever known bribes to be offered?—I do not like to go into that question. I have heard it said that they were, but I should not like to go into it.

61,[illegible]. (Chairman.) Do you think the magistrates [illegible] in the judicial part of their functions?—[illegible] They look on it as a bit of patronage. They boast of the fact that they came in to vote. I remember sitting in one of my counties on one occasion and a Deputy Lieutenant came up to me and said; "Judge, what "time are the licences on?" "What do you want to "know for?" "I want to vote for [illegible], a friend of "mine." I said to him he could come on, but he never came afterwards.

61,[illegible]. You think the present licensing authority [illegible] a bad one?—It could not be worse. That is my experience [illegible], and I have been over [illegible] years acting as chairman of quarter sessions.

61,[illegible]. It could be made better?—It could be, but it could not be worse than it is now, and that is my experience of an [illegible] number of magistrates all through these counties.

61,[illegible]. How would you improve it?—I should not give it to the chairman alone, because a chairman of quarter sessions is just as likely to get wrong on the [illegible] questions as any one else; but I think you could not have a better tribunal than the chairman and [illegible] magistrates sitting at the quarter sessions in [illegible].

61,[illegible]. What would you do with the Recorder? Would you let him sit alone?—I do not like to say anything about the Recorder because he is here, though I may say that I approve thoroughly of everything that he said here to-day, but the Recorder has been doing alone and doing very well sitting alone.

61,[illegible]. Your [illegible] in the chair is doing very well; but is the Recorder of a city, do you think, more to be trusted than a county court judge?—No. I would not trust a county court judge, and I would not trust a Recorder on a licensing question, because each has his [illegible] [illegible]

Judge Curran.

8 May '98.

in Dublin. It would be impossible to get two resident magistrates to act in the city of Dublin, because there are no resident magistrates in the city of Dublin. There are for the county but not for the city.

61,415. It is fortunate though there are no resident magistrates there that you say the Recorder is above all suspicion and an excellent judge?—No, I am only speaking of the present Recorder. I do not say a future Recorder would be above suspicion.

61,416. How would you introduce the resident magistrates if there are none?—Unless you appointed one of the divisional justices to sit with him—the position I occupied before I was chairman of quarter sessions—then you would have the same court.

61,417. (Dean Dickinson.) The resident magistrates in Dublin would be only the stipendiary magistrates—the divisional magistrates of police?—That is all.

61,418. (Chairman.) Would the divisional magistrates be competent to sit with the Recorder in Dublin?—He would if an Act of Parliament were passed. You could do anything with an Act of Parliament.

61,419. Would you get a good man from amongst the divisional magistrates?—Yes. The divisional magistrates are first-class men. I will not say anything of the fact that I was one myself, but at the present moment they have been Queen's Counsel, and they are all efficient men.

Appeals.

61,420. Constituting the licensing authority in the town and country in that way, would you have any appeals on questions of fact?—No, not on questions of fact, because you could not have the two judges of assize to sit to hear a publican's appeal. One judge of assize hearing the matter of fact, would be open to the same objection as the chairman, because it might be the case of a man having peculiar notions about licenses, and a judge of assize is just as liable to have impressions, or false impressions, about the ground for the granting or refusing licenses as the chairman of quarter sessions; and the chairman of quarter sessions, it was mentioned here to-day, thoroughly knows the county. I may say I know every man, woman, and child in my four counties now.

61,421. You would have an appeal lie, on a question of law, to the judge of assize?—To the judge of assize going the circuit—on law only. I do not think you could have a better tribunal than the one I have mentioned.

Law infringed by small publicans.

61,422. I suppose you do not bring any indictment against the publicans at large of Ireland?—No. The publicans at large of Ireland are a most respectable body of men, and I say that in the presence of the Dean, but, on the other hand, there are a number of them—small men—who only live, and can only live, by breaking the law.

61,423. It is competition that does the mischief?—Yes. There are many small houses, and it is impossible, having regard to the decisions in the Glasgow case, to get rid of them; and they do all the mischief, because the respectable houses in Dublin and in the country never break the law.

61,424. (Dean Dickinson.) Do you think there are a large number of small ones?—A very considerable number.

61,425. (Chairman.) How do they live when they go before the magistrates?—It is impossible to detect them unless you had four times the number of police in the county. It is impossible especially to detect outlying houses. The police are very watchful, but, with reference to these outlying houses, the owners of which break the law so frequently, they have watchmen, and the moment a policeman's shadow is within half a mile of the house everything is square and right.

Serving drunken persons.

61,426. Is it a common practice in Ireland that drink is served to drunken persons?—It is, I am sorry to say. If you could get rid of the serving of drink to drunken or half-drunken persons you would get rid of what, in my experience, is the cause of nine-tenths of the crime in Ireland.

61,427. There are very few charges of that kind laid before the magistrates, are there not?—Very few, [illegible]

unless he could show he was there without his knowledge or consent; otherwise, you will never stop them from giving drink to drunken people. A man is found drunk on the place, and the owner swears he gave him no drink, that the man dodged in. It is always proved to a certainty that nobody gave him drink, and the result is, no conviction.

61,428. You would throw the onus on the publican?—Yes, I should increase the minimum penalty. You might break all the laws dealt with in all the other sections without breaking the moral law. There is no moral harm in giving a glass of whisky to a man on Sunday, not a bona fide traveller, but there is moral harm here.

61,429. Have you known of convictions taking place of publicans for serving drink to a drunken person?—I have.

61,430. What is the penalty that is inflicted?—Very small.

61,431. (Dean Dickinson.) Would you substitute imprisonment or suspension of license for fine?—There should be some severe penalty, because, really, if no licensed person gave drink to a drunken or half-drunken person you would get rid of all the prosecution, or a good part of the intoxication, throughout the country. It is horrible, coming in as I have to a large town like Tralee on a market day, to see the number of people all going out in their carts—women, children, and men—drunk and still getting drink in the outlying public-houses.

61,432. (Chairman.) And the offence of serving drink to a drunken person is the subject of endorsement on the license?—Yes, it is; but it has led to this. By the Act of 1872 the magistrates were obliged to endorse them; but by the Act of 1874 they got a discretion. The result is they very seldom, if they do inflict a penalty, endorse the license, and that is the only thing the licensed trader fears. He would make up in a couple of Saturdays the amount of the fine easily.

61,433. Do you propose to compel the magistrates to endorse?—Yes. I think, except in some isolated instances it would be better for them to have a discretion to acquit in a case like that mentioned by Mr. Harrington this morning, where a man was summoned for selling five minutes before the time. It would be better, almost, to acquit in a case like that; but in any case in which they think they ought to convict they ought to endorse.

61,434. Looking at the class of magistrates as you have described them to-day, I suppose rather than endorse they would acquit?—I am supposing that the magistrates are gentlemen who do their duty efficiently; but I am sorry to say that at the trying of publicans' cases, or charges against these small publicans, the same amount of canvassing, and the same amount of interest is made, and the same jobbery goes on that we find at the outset of the granting of licenses.

61,435. My question was directed to this point. Looking to the constitution of the Bench in each county, and looking to the social relations of the parties, do not you think, rather than take away a man's license by endorsing, they would acquit him?—They do it now, under any circumstances, probably they would, but they do it now. I can instance a case that occurred very recently. A man was summoned for permitting drunkenness. The police proved the man was drunk, and there were two magistrates for a conviction, and two for an acquittal, the result of which was that it dismissed; and when the court was over, one of the magistrates who was for acquittal stated to the district inspector, in the presence of his sergeant, that now that the case was over he had no hesitation in saying that, after all, the man was drunk. They had decided on the case on the ground that he was not. The case came on on the following court day, and the two magistrates who had been for an acquittal turned up, and they tried the case. It was objected that they had already made up their minds, and then the district inspector stated to the magistrates what the latter had stated on the previous day. He denied it, and said that he believed the police had perjured themselves in the case, and dismissed it then and there.

[illegible]

Dublin. The working men in Dublin dine about 2 o'clock—on an average between 1 and 2 o'clock. I think he is entitled to get refreshment, and it is better not to have it in the house. I agree with Mr. Harrington there, but I should be entitled to have refreshment if he takes a walk.

Judge Carton.

3 May '98

61,451. Would you like to see the hours 2 to 5?—I think 2 to 5 would give him ample time for drinking.

61,452. Why should the *bona fide* traveller have his refreshment at other hours besides those?—I think there is a great deal in that view. I have never looked at it from that point of view. I do not think he ought.

Restriction of hours for travellers.

61,453. I can see that if you establish Sunday Closing for the whole of Ireland the difficulty of the *bona fide* traveller is rather accentuated, but if there are certain hours during which the houses are open, then let the *bona fide* traveller take advantage of those open hours and leave the publican free for the rest of the day?—If it was the case of a real *bona fide* traveller I should keep the houses open at all times, because a man might travel on bicycle 40 miles and come in during closing hours and then not be able to get any drink on Sunday; but whether you have a limit of 4 or 5 miles, I should think it would be quite right to say, if you want drink, you must go to the country or take a walk between 2 and 4.

61,454. Or you might license particular houses on the line of route which *bona fide* travellers frequent, for the purpose of supplying drink to them, within certain hours?—It was suggested that that would be the case when the six-day licenses were established, and that the seven-day license would be taken for the purpose of enabling the *bona fide* traveller to get drink; but, I am sorry to say, there are very few six-day licenses, comparatively speaking.

61,455. I gather you have not a very high opinion of the *bona fide* traveller?—No, a very low opinion.

61,456. Do you think any abuse arises from the spirit grocer's license?—I was two years a magistrate, but [illegible] months of that time I was engaged in the Phoenix Park investigation. Therefore I was only 18 months sitting as a magistrate of Dublin, and, during that time, I came to the conclusion—I am only speaking from what took place 17 years ago—that a spirit grocer's license costs a very high figure; it is higher, as a rule, than the publican's, and the small spirit grocers could not pay it without selling drink to be consumed on the premises; it would not pay them to take out the spirit grocer's license unless they sold over the counter and illicitly.

Abuses of spirit grocers' licenses.

61,457. Do you mean that in a great town in Ireland a man could not live on the sale of groceries?—In the small shops he could live by the sale of groceries, but he could not pay the same duty as a spirit grocer. He could not get a sufficient sale of spirits.

61,458. (*Dean Dickinson.*) He must break the law?—Yes.

61,459. (*Chairman.*) Are you in favour of abolishing the trade?—No; I think that the spirit grocer's license in large shops is a very proper license, but in small shops it is merely an inducement to break the law. In the case of the large shops I think it is a fair enough license, because you are almost sure they would not sell illicitly. That raises the question that the Recorder referred to with reference to the grant of spirit grocers' licenses. Having regard to the present law, the suitability of the premises has been held to refer to the structural suitability of the premises only.

61,460. We know that a "[illegible]" property, as it is called in England, sells not only drink but groceries and other things; that is the shop which the poor classes resort to?—Yes.

61,461. I am not talking now of grocers' licenses, but of publicans who in addition to their trade in drink sell other goods. Would you like to see the trade separated in this case?—Certainly I should, if it were possible. I doubt it very much, but I certainly should like to see it impossible for a man who perhaps has a haberdasher's shop or a meal shop to hold a publican's license.

Mixed trades in public-houses.

Judge Curran.

4 May '98.

for the sale of intoxicants? If a man goes in he may say, I came in for groceries?—They cannot know. There is the same difficulty with regard to those other shops.

61,464. And yet you would forbid the combination of the trade in the grocer's shop, but allow the combination to go on in the publican's?—No, I would not allow it either in the publican's case. I think the publican ought to be kept to selling drink for consumption on the premises. There is no other way of detecting illicit sales, except it is known that the man can sell nothing but drink to be consumed on the premises.

61,465. Looking at the habits of the people and the long time this practice has been in vogue, would it be possible in the present state of public opinion to say to the publican: You shall sell nothing else but pure intoxicants and food?—It would be very difficult to say that.

New licences obtained by canvassing.

61,466. Are many new licences granted in your experience?—Whenever a man can get a friend of his to intercede with his brother magistrates for him, or canvasses properly, he can get a new licence. I have been on the Bench myself where there has been a large batch of magistrates, and I have seen the solicitor and his client before me crossing round the bench of those they expected to vote, knowing very well what the result would be long before the case came on.

61,467. Is objection taken on the Bench that there is already a sufficient supply of public-houses in a district?—I have known gentlemen come in to oppose—I am not speaking of the last appointments—a large number of persons who was applying for a new licence in a town, and immediately in the list before that applicant there were two or three others, and those magistrates voted against them first on the list, on the ground that there were too many licences already existing in the town; and when it came to their friend they voted for their friend and gave him the licence. That is the system that goes on all over Ireland. I am not alone giving you my own views or my own opinions, but many clergymen have told me that is their opinion.

Stipendiary includes resident magistrate.

61,468. Turning to a point of the interpretation of the law with reference to magistrates, you have mentioned the stipendiary. Does the term "stipendiary" apply to a resident magistrate? Is the resident magistrate a stipendiary?—I will refer you to the section. It is the 61st section of the Licensing Act of 1872, which says:—"The court of summary "jurisdiction, when hearing and determining an "information or complaint, other than in a case "where the offence charged is that of being found "drunk in any highway or public place, or any licensed "premises, shall be constituted either of two or more "justices of the peace in petty sessions sitting at a place "appointed for holding a petty sessions or of a stipendiary "magistrate." Now at the time that Act was passed it was supposed that that would include a resident magistrate in Ireland, but the Court of Queen's Bench in Ireland have held that the word "stipendiary" does not include a resident magistrate in Ireland, the result of which is that a resident magistrate in Ireland can in publicans' cases hear only ordinary drunken charges when sitting alone.

61,469. Do I understand that the word "stipendiary" was used in the Act of Parliament when there is no such thing as a stipendiary magistrate in Ireland?—The stipendiary there the Court of Queen's Bench held referred to the English stipendiary and not to the Irish resident magistrate; so that that would be an important point of legislation if such a power were given to the resident magistrate, because frequently he has to adjourn the cases, when he has no magistrate sitting with him, for a brother magistrate to attend.

61,470. (*Dean Dickinson.*) The expression "stipendiary magistrate" is not in common use in Ireland?—No, it is resident magistrate.

61,471. The resident magistrate is a stipendiary?—The resident magistrate is the same as the English stipendiary.

61,472. (*Chairman.*) With reference to the reform which you think would be brought about by the term "stipendiary" being made to include a resident magistrate, may I ask does the resident magistrate ever sit alone?—He sits alone but he can only sit in a hearing case under the Acts of 1872 and 1874 to hear ordinary charges of drunkenness, because it requires two magistrates or a stipendiary. He is not a stipendiary, and therefore a second magistrate is required.

61,473. If you made that change as the legal term you would give a certain increased authority and power to the resident magistrates?—It was intended originally he should have that power. A section simply finding that the word "stipendiary" in the 61st section should include a resident magistrate in Ireland would obviate the difficulty.

Judge Curran.

Renewal applications for licences.

61,474. You have sketched a new licensing authority altogether, but supposing your reforms were not carried out and the existing licensing authorities were maintained, would you make any change in the system of applying for new licences? The 13th section of the Act of 1872 deals with the mode of applying for a new licence. It was intended that you should only apply at the general October sessions for a new licence, but then it went on to say that in case the magistrates saw fit they might grant a licence at the intermediate sessions. More than once it has occurred where a man has applied before me at the October sessions and has been refused by a majority against the vintner, the minority have appeared at an intervening sessions and granted the licence.

61,475. You would only allow, except in special cases, applications for new licences to be granted at the annual sessions in October?—I should think no man having applied at the October sessions should apply till the following October, and no man should have the power of applying during the year who could have applied at the preceding October sessions.

61,476. After the lapse of what time would you allow an application to be made again?—I do not complain of their making applications at the October sessions when all the magistrates are there, but the minority has frequently come in at an intervening sessions and granted the licence.

61,477. So that you would say the application should not be less than annual?—Yes.

Wakes.

61,478. I do not know whether you can suggest anything with reference to wakes, which in your statement of your evidence you allege to be a fruitful source of intemperance?—It is very bad, and if it could be put a stop to in the way I suggest it would be an immense good to Ireland.

61,479. What do you suggest?—You have all heard of the waking system in Ireland. No sooner is the breath out of a man's body than one of the next-of-kin, or some friend, rushes off to the nearest grocer's, or publican's, and orders in three or four gallons of whisky. That is the very best—sometimes it is considerably more. If he had to pay for that whisky he would only order in perhaps a quart, but from three to nine gallons of whisky are ordered in, and the whole country round is not drunk upon this whisky which is obtained upon credit. I should put an end altogether to these wakes, and the clergy have done as far as they possibly can to the contrary, that is by insisting that the body should go to the church at night, but still the drinking goes on.

61,480. Your statement is that the drink is obtained at the public-house on credit?—Yes.

61,481. Not paid for at the time?—They have no money. The publican gives it on speculation of being paid out of the wreck, or by the man who orders it. The whole country side is set drunk with the whisky.

Proposed amendment of Tippling Act.

61,482. (*Dean Dickinson.*) That practice exists only in one religious community?—Yes, but what I do suggest, and it would do an immense good in Ireland—and I have had a great deal of experience of the undoubtedly results of wakes—is that if a man supplies whisky on credit to anyone for the purpose of being used for a wake he should be in the same position as the man who supplies drink over the counter on credit under the Tippling Acts, that he cannot recover the amount.

61,483. (*Chairman.*) The remedy would be that they would stint the money together?—They would not have it.

61,484. Is not it so ingrained in the habits of the people of Ireland to drink at a wake?—Because as a rule they get the whisky on credit. They would have no drink if they did not get it on credit.

61,485. (*Dean Dickinson.*) Is it not much discouraged by the Roman Catholic priests in Ireland?—It is. The Catholic priests discourage it, and insist, wherever they can, on having the body brought into the church. That does away with it to some extent, but the drinking [illegible] on. The amount of whisky ordered is [illegible] terrible as I see in the cases that come before me. Seven or eight gallons are ordered for the wake of a man who would not [illegible] a quart when he was alive.

61,686. (Mr. Young.) I think that is only confined to a few counties of Ireland?—No, in the four counties over which I now preside, and in Kerry, it is very frequent. I cannot speak of other counties.

61,687. (Chairman.) Can you speak of Meath?—Meath, Westmeath, Longford, and King's County. I wish to impress that on the Commission, because I know myself the enormous amount of good that would do in putting down drinking in Ireland, and I am positive about this, that nine-tenths of the crime in Ireland is directly due to whisky.

61,688. You object to the habit and practice, but you think you can stop it by enacting that there should be no credit allowed?—No credit allowed for the whisky supplied to a wake—that the man should not be able to recover for it. At the present moment under the Tippling Acts a man cannot recover for drink sold over the counter on credit. If the same law were applied to whisky sold for the purpose of a wake I should guarantee a very serious diminution in the amount of intoxication in general in the county.

61,689. (Mr. Young.) May I ask you if the clergy have referred to any case where a wake has been held in King's County?—That I have not heard of. I could not tell you that, but I know this, that they are doing their best to put it down and they cannot, and I say this would put it down.

61,690. (Chairman.) Do not the spirit grocers sell their goods on credit?—Yes, but the small spirit grocers would not have power to sell over a certain quantity.

61,691. A number of people might go to them and each buy a small quantity, and those small quantities would make up a large amount?—When I say spirit grocers I should include the sellers of spirits as well as publicans.

61,692. (Mr. Young.) With reference to this licensing tribunal you suggest that it should be the resident magistrate with the county court judge?—Yes.

61,693. Would you not consider that two or three of the local magistrates should be associated with them?—That would be going back to our present system. How would you select two or three magistrates?

61,694. They might be selected by themselves. You would wipe out the magistrates altogether?—No, I would not. It is only fair to say that apart from the drink question nothing would be better than the way the magistrates generally throughout Ireland do their duty. They run riot over the drink question, but apart from that nothing could be fairer than the way they perform their duties.

Judge Curran.

6 May '96.

61,695. I want to take your opinion on this suggestion that where the licensing comes into a place two or three local magistrates should be invited to associate themselves with the county court judge?—I should have no objection at all.

61,696. You spoke of County Kerry, and of the magistrates in County Kerry, as being very anxious to give licenses wherever asked [illegible]. May I ask you is County Kerry not a peculiar county in that regard. Do you think that applies to other counties—that the local magistrates override the opinion of the county court judge in granting licenses. Is that peculiar to Kerry, or does it apply to other counties?—It is not peculiar to Kerry.

Wakes.

61,697. Now with reference to these wakes, may I suggest to you that they are scarcely known in the North of Ireland?—You are very good people up there, a good deal better than we down in the South, but you at the same time have a few faults.

61,698. I suppose you acknowledge they are disappearing year by year even in your counties?—I am sorry to say they are not.

Permitting drunkenness.

61,699. You referred to a person being found drunk on licensed premises, and you said you would make the licensee liable. Do you not think that there is a great difficulty in knowing exactly whether a man is drunk or not on premises. There might be great difficulty on the part of the licensee in knowing exactly at what point the man was drunk?—Neither a publican nor a policeman ought to have any difficulty in knowing when a man is drunk. There is no difficulty at all if they like to open their eyes.

61,700. Is it not illegal at present to have a drunken man on the premises?—No. It is illegal if you permit drunkenness, which is a very different matter, and I wish it were illegal to have a drunken man on the premises. It is illegal now to permit drunkenness, but what the meaning of that word is I cannot make out.

61,701. You say that if a man is found drunk on the premises it is not an offence?—No, unless you show that the publican permitted drunkenness, that is to say, gave him drink to make him drunk, but if a man is drunk the publican may say, I did not know he was drunk at my house, I did not see him drunk, though half-a-dozen may prove he was so.

The witness withdrew.

Adjourned to to-morrow at 10.30.

ONE HUNDRED AND THIRD DAY.

Queen's Robing Room, House of Lords, Wednesday, May 4th, 1898.

PRESENT:

THE RIGHT HONOURABLE THE VISCOUNT PEEL IN THE CHAIR.

The Right Hon. the Viscount de Vesci.	Andrew Johnston, Esq.
The Right Hon. the Lord Windsor.	John Herbert Roberts, Esq., M.P.
The Very Rev. [illegible], Dean.	Thomas Palmer Whittaker, Esq., M.P.
William Stevenson Caine, Esq.	Samuel Young, Esq., M.P.
Alexander [illegible], Esq.	George Younger, Esq.
Henry [illegible], Esq.	

The Rev. Patrick O'Leary called in and examined.

Rev. P. O'Leary.

4 May '98.

61,502. (Chairman.) You are, I believe, a priest in West Cork?—In the city of Cork.

61,503. In the western division of the city?—In the south side of the city of Cork, within the city.

Position of witness. Female intemperance in Cork.

61,504. What is your opinion, from your experience as to female intemperance?—I have been living for 19 years continuously within the city of Cork, and I believe that one of the worst aspects of the drink evil is that which concerns women, and especially married women.

61,505. From the effect that their drunkenness has upon their offspring?—From the effect that it has upon themselves and the effect which it has upon their homes, the home life being scattered and destroyed to a very great extent, and in many cases altogether, the woman who should regulate the house and be the angel of the home, losing her influence with the family, there being no respect for her authority or guidance once the family know she is intemperate.

Women's public-houses.

61,506. Where do you think these women get the drink?—They get the drink chiefly in public-houses, and they go to a shocking extent to a certain number of public-houses, because in various parts of the city of Cork there are numbers of houses that are noted as women's houses. While I must admit that there are a great many publicans in Cork who would not sell drink to intemperate women, and particularly to those who are notably under the influence of drink, I regret to say, from an intimate knowledge of the subject, that a great many publicans sell drink without the least scruple to intemperate women and women who are scarcely free from drink and unable to take care of themselves.

61,507. How is it that these houses have come to be called women's houses?—Numbers of women may be seen in these houses, as still happens, on Monday mornings about 11 o'clock, and on Saturday nights considerable numbers of women there, with infants in their arms, some of the infants getting porter to sip from their mothers, other women bringing children by the hand and remaining for hours in public-houses, and any passer-by can see that some public-houses are far more remarkable for this kind of trade than others. In fact, within the past three or four weeks I have gone late at night through certain streets in Cork, and I have been shocked by finding literally rows of women of various wearers, several of them intoxicated, others sitting on benches in front of the counters or the bars, and evidently the majority of them being married women, mothers of families, the homes thus being neglected, the children allowed to roam about without any parental care, perhaps to beg or to steal, because, as a rule, the children of such parents are greatly in need of protection through the sad circumstances in which they are brought up and the want of parental care and the bad example.

Rev. P. O'Leary.

Drinking during prohibited hours.

61,508. Do you think they get the drink within prohibited hours?—They get the drink at the ordinary opening hours, as a rule. They are intoxicated in the drink shops. They come into the streets intoxicated in many cases, and the police authorities, as I know well, pay no attention whatever to that particular end of the drink seller by which he is guilty of complicity in the act of the drunken person in supplying drink.

Intemperate parents and cruelty to children.

61,509. Are you connected with the Society for the Prevention of Cruelty to Children?—I have been connected with it for 11 years, and for five years I have been president of that society in Cork.

61,510. What is your opinion as to the parents of the children who come under your care?—With regard to the parents, I have had careful examinations and inquiry made into all the cases. Last year, for example, we had 112 cases under supervision. It was only in one case that we could find that intemperance was not at the bottom of this course of cruelty. In that case there was a dispute between a father and mother, and jealousy, I believe, was at the bottom of it, and because of that the children were neglected and very badly treated, but in all the other cases, which involved cruelty to nearly 300 children, it was simply the result of gross habitual intemperance on the part of the parents.

61,511. On the part of both parents?—Intemperance of both, very often of only one. As many as 30 mothers were brought before the society last year—a great many brought into court—and a great many convicted. And that is what we desire to do in all cases. A great many get time for improvement. Month after month cases are adjourned to see if there is any hope of improvement. Clergymen are asked to take an interest in them, because we do not wish to punish if we possibly can avoid it.

Police returns and mothers' drunkenness.

61,512. Are the women who are brought up for cruelty to their children ever convicted of drunkenness?—I want to show that the police returns really give a very poor index to the extent of intemperance, for that particular reason. I have made inquiries from the inspector of the society, from the secretary who deals with every case individually, and from the clerk in the office, and I find, to my surprise, that very few of the cases that have come before our Society for the Prevention of Cruelty to Children have at all been prosecuted by the police for drunkenness or disorderly conduct. They are habitual drunkards, who are able, because of the habit they have contracted, to walk home, and though they do not disturb public order, they disgrace and destroy their homes and families.

61,513. They would not come within the cognizance of the police, would they?—They would not, as drunkards or as disturbing public order, because—I regret to say—I have it from the authorities in Cork that the police do not take up women unless they disturb public

Rev. P. O'Leary. 4 May '98

order, or unless there is some danger to the individual. If he can be taken home by a friend, or gets home himself, he is not arrested.

41,514. Do you trace cruelty to children to the vice of intemperance in the parents?—To that, and to that alone. I will illustrate it in this way: I have met the fathers in prison. They come under my jurisdiction in gaol. They are as anxious as any people could be about the welfare of their children. They really feel heart-broken while in gaol because of their conduct, and because of the suffering they have brought on their families; but while they are addicted to drink, when outside, they simply have lost their nature through it. In the same way, in the female prison, mothers take their babies with them. They are obliged to do so by the law. If they are convicted of cruelty they may take their babies to prison. They absolutely dote on those little children. Nothing could be more touching than their affection for their children, but when given to drink out of prison, they simply forget the very existence of those children.

41,515. You were chaplain, I think, in the Cork prison for some years?—I have been chaplain for 8½ years.

41,516. When you say you trace cruelty to children to the vice of intemperance, what do you say as regards ordinary crime?—With regard to ordinary crime, I have gone into that thoroughly, and, having gone into it myself, I inquired last week from the governor, who has had 30 years' experience, and the deputy-governor, who has had 25 years' experience. The governor was in two prisons in Ireland, and the deputy in several prisons. Their views, to my surprise, perhaps, corresponded exactly with my own, because, after all, I felt that I had opportunities of knowing the sources of crime better even than the governor, because prisoners throw off all reserve in their relations with the chaplain. They simply tell at once the source of their crime and the nature of their misfortune, and they have no hesitation in doing so. As the result of my observation, I have had no hesitation in coming to the conclusion that 80 per cent. of those imprisoned in the Cork gaol owe their misfortune to drink.

41,517. You do not think that they wish to try to curry favour with the chaplain by making out their position to be better than they really were?—I do not think so at all. Every evening there are visitors to my house, mothers and sisters and wives who sometimes have come long distances from the country. Their story is always of the saddest kind. They say "John" or "Patrick was the best son or the best husband in "the world till he got addicted to drink." "Well," I say, "He is in good for larceny." "Oh, but it was "simply that he took up with drinking companions, "got addicted to drink, and then he became addicted "to these other vices."

41,518. What do you say as to the conduct of the police generally in dealing with cases of drunkenness and punishing the guilty?—With regard to the conduct of the police generally, I must say I have been greatly disappointed. I have taken a very special interest in this work, because I really feel greatly concerned about the condition of the working people. I am anxious to have intemperance stopped. I want sobriety. I have adopted certain means to secure it. I have never advocated, in public or private, prohibition or anything of that kind, but I want to secure sobriety, and I may say the police might help us considerably if they did their duty, but I do not think they do their duty. I say that emphatically. I think they fail considerably in the discharge of their duty. At the same time I say that the present county inspector in Cork is as anxious as any man could be to discharge [illegible]

41,520. Is it, or is it not, too much to expect of the police, with their other duties, that they should suppress the vice of drunkenness, or do you think the Royal Irish Constabulary have not much to do?—I am quite certain that they could do an enormous amount of good in stopping this evil if they chose, without really very much additional trouble to themselves, and I will illustrate it by instances that came under my own notice. I have certain localities which were becoming demoralised by illicit sale on Sundays. I applied to the county inspector for a stranger to go, if necessary, in disguise. The county inspector immediately complied with my request on more than one occasion. I believe there was hardly a single visit that was paid by this man that did not prove most effectual. On some occasions he actually discovered publicans selling to people who had no right whatever to get drink, and who made no claim to be travellers at all. On other occasions he saw crowds running away from the public-houses, thus clearly demonstrating that the illicit sale was going on, and that those who were receiving the drink wanted to save themselves.

Special inspectors for public-houses.

41,521. Do your remarks point to the opinion that you would employ strange policemen or detectives?—I would employ them for the simple reason that the police do not fulfil their duties. I have been for years in a populous district in Cork, and there are only perhaps two or three policemen in those barracks that can be trusted to do their duty, and in two of the districts illicit sale was going on habitually, and none of the police ever interfered or took the least step to put a stop to it. At my request it was stopped effectually by one man, for a long time together, at certain periods. Even one man stopped it. He succeeded in detecting and punishing on some occasions. The general result of his visits was that the publicans got afraid to practise this illicit sale, so that there was the greatest possible improvement noticeable for a considerable time afterwards.

Illicit sales by publicans.

41,522. Do you believe that publicans in Cork very often sell within the prohibited hours?—I believe they do. I have often asked people myself—unfortunate victims of drink. I have met them in various places, at various hours, in prison, and other places. I have put the simple question to them, have they much difficulty. They say, "That depends. Some publicans "will not give it, and others will; but we have not "much difficulty as a rule." I said, "Have you been "refused drink in those places where you think you "can get it?" "Yes;" they say, "if we have no "money, but if we have the money we have very "little difficulty in getting the drink." I know myself from my experience of portions of the city that illicit sale during prohibited hours is going on very generally indeed.

41,523. You have given us your opinion, of course, very generally, of the police. What should you say as to the general body of the publicans in Cork? Do they habitually, as a body, break the law?—I say that a very large proportion of them break the law without scruple. I would not like to say exactly the proportion, but I certainly think a very large proportion are anxious to break the law, and they actually do so when they can. They are afraid to a certain extent. They are watching. They have scouts out. I know publicans who have trained their children to act as scouts, thus, of course, demoralising them, having them posted here and there observing the police. I have known them to make use of corner boys to watch for them on Sundays, and if the police are seen in the distance, word is given to the publicans.

Permitting drunken-

41,524. What happens to a drunken man if he is past the limit of sobriety in one of these houses? Is he [illegible]. An ordinary [illegible] by, like you on that [illegible], [illegible] a [illegible] of this sort, a drunken woman turned out of the house, would it be competent for the [illegible] to prosecute that publican?—It would not be competent.

[illegible]. The [illegible] would not [illegible] the [illegible]?—No. I presume I would have no [illegible] at all in the matter. The police should prove that that publican made a sober person drunk, or gave drink to a person actually drunk already. The police must give actual proof of that.

[illegible]. If the law were altered, and if the fact of a drunken person being found in a house, or turned out of a house as you describe, was prima facie evidence against a publican, you think there would be greater facility for conviction of the publican?—That would leave no excuse to the police, and I wish to say that the police at present excuse themselves on that very ground. They say, "What is the use of our bringing forward "these cases? We must prove that the publican "actually gave drink to the person while drunk, or "made a sober person drunk." They could prove it very often, but I say it would be very well if even the [illegible] were taken from them, which they make use of, then it is difficult for them to prove it.

[illegible]. In your experience does payment of wages in public-houses prevail to any great extent in Cork?—The payment of wages has been very generally made in public-houses with regard to a certain class of labourers called quay labourers, it prevails to a certain extent amongst other labourers also, but chiefly amongst the quay labourers, and there are in Cork, on an average, employed on the quays about 600 or 700 every week. Their life is of a precarious nature. They may get 9s. or 8s. or [illegible] a week some weeks; other weeks very little. I have been trying to make out an average, and I think they would earn over [illegible] a week each.

[illegible]. When they come to have their wages paid at the end of the week, do I understand you to say that money is stopped out of wages due to them for the drink they have drunk in the course of the week?—They have got the drink in certain public-houses, and of course it is stopped out of their wages. The men who hold the public-houses in which they are paid in [illegible] are their paymasters and employers by arrangement with the merchants. The merchants have these publicans acting as [illegible] or employers of labouring men for them. They pay their wages or give employment, as the case may be, to the quay labourers in the public-house.

[illegible]. Would what we call in England the ganger be the publican?—He would be the publican in some cases. It was most demoralising. As a proof of its demoralising effects, we had as many as 30 quay labourers out of a total of [illegible] before the Society for the Prevention of Cruelty to Children last year. The practice has been going on for the past 30 years I am told. I referred to it publicly last October, but no notice was taken of it by the authorities. I declared that it was a breach of the law of the Truck Act. At the last annual meeting of the Society for the Prevention of Cruelty to Children I referred to the matter again, and brought it under the notice of the county inspector in a very formal way. The police authorities did not seem to think it was their duty to look after the matter at all; they thought that it belonged to the duties of the inspector of factories. However, I said it was illegal, and I was determined that it should be put a stop to. It was demoralising. These unfortunate men believed they would have no chance of employment unless they became habitual customers of those public-houses.

[illegible]. Tom is [illegible] to paying their wages in [illegible]?—Yes.

[illegible]. Which is illegal, is it not?—This practice was quite illegal.

[illegible]. The publican could not recover at the end of the week the sum for the drink that he had supplied on credit, could he?—No, he could not.

[illegible]. He stops it from their wages?—Yes. The county inspector got the order from the Government to have it put a stop to, but I must say that it happened so generally along these quays in Cork that it was most demoralising. Anybody could know the effect of it through looking at the condition of these unfortunate men, and hearing the complaints of their families, as I know it from the information brought to our society.

[illegible]. There must be considerable employers of labour in Cork who are in no way connected with the publicans [illegible]. What do they say to this practice?—I called on a couple of them, and they told me they would put a stop to it as soon as ever they could make arrangements for the payment of the men elsewhere. I waited for some months, and I found from the men and mothers of these men that they were still paid in public-houses. I took the matter then into my own hands and warned the authorities. I believe that the men whom these merchants employ as gangers, or heads of a certain number of men, at one time had not public-houses at all, but they have got them as a very shrewd and wise plan for [illegible] custom, and the merchants did not like to get rid of them when they had had in their employment for years.

[illegible]. As to the evils you have pointed out connected with the drink, I think you said in the earlier part of your evidence you believe that these evils were intensified by the fact that an habitual drunkard transmitted the habit to his children. Is that so in your experience?—Yes. I have given some reasons why the evil is bound to increase unless the State takes the necessary steps to check it. I have given the inordinate number of public-houses, the increasing number of grocers' licences, all trying to extend the market and to vie with one another in pushing on their sale; the formation of tippling [illegible] with [illegible] here and there through the land; and the transmission of it to the children. I do not know whether a craving for drink is directly transmitted to the children, that is a matter of opinion, but certainly from my observations the children of habitual drunkards have a very low species of morals, very little self-control, and they inherit very great nervous weakness, so that they are easily liable to fall very early victims to intemperance once they take to it; and I find from experience that it is almost a miracle, and a miracle alone, that will save them once they have taken drink at all.

[illegible]. You have said, speaking generally, that the police neglect their duties. What do you say as to the [illegible]?—With regard to the magistrates, the police, of course, assert, as one of the reasons for their apathy, that they are not encouraged by the magistrates. Now, I should like to guard one thing while this is pretty clear, and the conviction has been formed in the public mind that the magistrates are not at all to be trusted in the administration of the law in this matter, that conviction has been formed upon [illegible] of facts which have come before the public year after year, such as witnesses who came before this Commission have [illegible], and as a result a great many dismissals have taken place where cases were brought before the magistrates. In the case of prosecutions for illicit sales, I think there have been [illegible] convictions in Cork in three years, and [illegible] dismissals. The police had a strong case to comply with those cases, and yet there were as many as [illegible] dismissals. That, of course, gives some justification to the statement of the police that the magistrates do not encourage them. At the same time I believe that the police are actuated by other motives as well, namely, the desire to be popular with the publicans who live around them. That is the chief reason, and the want of encouragement given by the magistrates.

[illegible]. What is the number of the police in Cork?—I do not know the exact number.

[illegible]. I suppose the circumstances under which a policeman would do his duty would be very embarrassing to these people, that is to say, he would find himself very unpopular in the immediate neighbourhood and among his own associates?—Yes, he would find himself very unpopular, and of course they do not like that. The instinct of popularity is as strong in them as in everybody else.

[illegible]. Are the public-houses in Cork let out to lodgers?—Yes, there are as many as [illegible] let in tenements, and in many of these houses there are as many as five or six families living in different apartments.

[illegible]. With communication with the bar?—In most cases there is communication with the bar from within the house. I have known cases where there was no communication with the bar within the house, but I have known of illicit sale being carried on indeed by letting vessels down from the windows, and by an arrangement with the publican the drink was put into the vessels, and the practice carried on at any time when the people wished. Of course these people living in tenements claim to have a right, they are tenants of

Rev. P. O'Leary.

The evil dealt of [illegible] [illegible].

The police and the [illegible].

Public-houses let to [illegible].

41,556. Would you endorse that opinion?—There might be other safeguards, but I prefer it very much to the present system.

41,557. Supposing all the houses were closed in Cork on the Sunday, do you think, or do you not think, that the working classes might say, "We are deprived of "the same opportunities as other classes"?—They would have the same opportunities, as a matter of fact, as all other classes.

41,558. Except that they would not be able to go to their own clubs?—If [illegible] they might, if they choose, get in a bottle of stout or beer on Saturday night, and if they could not be trusted to keep it, that proves the necessity for some grave and stringent measure to be taken to save them.

41,559. You do not think there is the same necessity of feeling in regard to local Sunday closing as to other Saturday closing?—There is not, owing to the [illegible] that people have with regard to bogus clubs and shebeens; but I find that there is no tendency in Cork to form bogus clubs. I have known of two. It is a remarkable fact that those who formed, or attempted to form, these clubs were [illegible] of mine, whom I know in prison as soldiers of Her Majesty's gaol. Amongst the respectable working people there is no such tendency whatever. These clubs were quickly crushed by the exertions of a single policeman within the past couple of years.

41,560. Is it the habit of the bishops of your church [illegible] or to enforce in any way pledges upon children?—They do not enforce them, but on the occasion of administering confirmation throughout the country they put before the children the advantages of keeping from drink on the score of so many misfortunes to them in after life, and so much sin. They ask them if they choose freely to pledge themselves to total abstinence. As a matter of fact the children practically all do take the pledge on that occasion. I have taken very special note of it. We find that a vast majority of them take drink afterwards, and in many cases very soon afterwards, and break that pledge; and that is accounted for chiefly by the practice of their parents and neighbours sending them for drink, and the publicans selling them drink. I would not have drink sold to any child under 16 years of age, either to consume on the premises or to take away.

41,561. You would raise the age from 13 to 16?—Yes, and I would not allow them to take it away either, because I maintain that the law in that respect is simply a fraud. They may go outside the door into a lane, or into a field, and consume it themselves, after having stated to the publican that they want the drink for a neighbour, a mother, or father; and as a matter of fact I have known several children to be taken to the infirmary in an unconscious condition. The doctors have had to have recourse to [illegible] to restore them to consciousness. I believe they got the drink in that way.

41,562. You would allow no child to be served either for consumption on, or consumption off, under 16?—On or off under 16. I think it is the cause of intemperance amongst mothers. I know several women who have become addicted to drink, and the neighbours know nothing whatever about it, because those women get the children round by giving them a few pence to bring them drink habitually.

41,563. Do you think imposing fines upon drunkards who have broken the law by being drunk and disorderly is of any avail?—I think fines are not of any avail as we see them ordinarily in the police court, simply because it is not the drunkard who is punished but it is his family. He does not mind it. He is master of the situation. The wife, or mother, or sisters, or relatives will pay the fines, and the man is free to go on as before.

Rev. P. O'Leary.

4 May '9[illegible]

No tendency to bogus clubs.

Sale of drink to children.

Uselessness of fining drunkards.

Rev. F. O'Leary. 4 May '9[illegible].

the police in these cases, at all events, cannot complain that the magistrates have not co-operated with them, because there were only four dismissals in three years, and 13 convictions for complicity in the Drunkards Act.

[illegible] Increase and necessary number of licensed houses.

41,5[illegible]. Do I gather that you think there is a superabundance of public-houses in Cork?—Yes, twice as many as are required, I should say.

41,5[illegible]. Are they being added to?—Yes. In the last [illegible] years there has been an addition of [illegible] or [illegible] ordinary public-houses, and I think about [illegible] other shops selling drinks, such as spirit grocers and [illegible]. I know there have been [illegible] or [illegible] ordinary public-houses added.

41,567. Within [illegible] years the population must have seriously decreased in Cork?—Very much decreased. The numbers are [illegible] [illegible] in Cork from January 18[illegible] to January 18[illegible], and the increase in ordinary public-houses is 21, while other shops selling drink have increased by about [illegible].

41,5[illegible]. Do you think that if the laws were properly enforced as they stand, that would tend to diminish the number of licensed houses in Cork?—As things stand, the law will not be enforced, because the law gives facilities for its own violation.

Furnishing drunken men.

41,5[illegible]. If the law were made more stringent, what security would you think that the law then would be administered with any greater stringency than now?—For instance, there are evils which are very remarkable, supplying drink to drunken people. To my mind, on the part of the man who does it, that is as bad as, or worse, than the evil is on the part of the man who gets drunk. It is more deliberate and more wilful in every way. That practically escapes [illegible]. Make the law simple, so that sort of [illegible] crime will be put a stop to. Make it clear, and let it be punishable to allow drunkenness on the premises at all. Let that be prima facie a case against the publican, and let the conviction be recorded on the licence, and in that way, by stringent measures, the number of public-houses might be decreased by some of them being abolished.

Licensing authority.

41,570. Are you contemplating a continuation of the present licensing authority, or would you like to see that changed?—I should like to see that changed, and that might indirectly diminish the number of public-houses.

41,571. That is to say, the county court judge should be a person, and sit alone in country districts?—Yes. I think he would be far more independent of those influences which prevail than the ordinary magistrate would be.

41,57[illegible]. You would not have anybody sitting with him; not a resident magistrate, or any selection of magistrates?—That would be a matter of opinion.

41,573. Would you see any objection to giving to the county court judge or Recorder, alone in city and county, all renewals of licenses?—No, I should leave it to those alone. There might be a right of appeal given perhaps to a higher tribunal if people felt aggrieved.

41,574. An appeal on questions of fact?—An appeal because of any grievance that the parties might have.

Habitual drunkards.

41,575. You are aware that there is a Bill now before the House of Commons for dealing with inebriates?—Yes, I have heard of it.

41,576. Do you know of any of its provisions, or speaking generally, without reference to that particular Bill, do you think a Bill providing for the detention of inebriates is likely to be a general remedy?—I do not think it would do the least good. It might be some good to individuals if they were detained long enough in these homes, but I say the wide-spread and general evil would go on all the same, the crop of inebriates would be appearing year after year, and certainly I think it would be an unwise proceeding to deal with effects while leaving the cause untouched; just like as a pestilence breaking out, there would be very little wisdom in providing hospitals for the sick and dying as long as the plague spot was allowed to remain open from which the pestilence proceeded.

41,577. But they still would have the hospitals?—Yes. Unless the evil be dealt with at its source, the other proposal would have very little wisdom in it.

41,578. You cannot contemplate such a state of things as that there should be no inebriety, as at present constituted, no such thing as a confirmed inebriate, and you must deal with him somehow. You do not think you can extirpate the inebriate by any legislation?—Of course there will always be inebriates.

Rev. F. O'Leary.

41,579. For these people, as far as it goes, you think an inebriates' home, or place of detention for a long period, would be a useful measure?—I think it would be useful, but I mean it would not be the part of a wise man to form such a plan as that of dealing with the evil alone; treating effects while leaving causes untouched.

41,580. (The [illegible] de Vesci.) I think you said that the county inspector or the police authorities in Cork, received instructions from the Government to take steps in the case where wages were paid in public-houses on the quays?—Yes.

Wages paid in public-houses.

41,581. Had he never taken steps of his own accord?—It was at my instance.

41,582. You represented it to whom?—To the county inspector.

41,583. I think you said he received instructions from the Government to take steps?—He made an application, after I spoke to the county inspector, to Dublin Castle, as I understand, and as the result he wrote to me to say that the Government had acted in order to have the practice put a stop to.

41,584. Surely it was not necessary for him to apply for leave to do this?—He felt that probably it was not his business at all, that it belonged to the inspector of factories to look after it. I spoke to several constables, the head constable and others, and they were perfectly ignorant as to the state of the law on the matter.

41,585. He was not aware that he had power as a police authority to take the steps?—No, he was not.

41,586. Have any private individuals taken steps to prosecute in these cases?—No.

41,587. Nor societies?—No. I exposed the matter twice, once in October, and again at the annual meeting of the Society for the Prevention of Cruelty to Children, because it was forced upon my mind by the fact that so many as [illegible] young labourers out of [illegible] were brought before the Society for this unnatural crime.

41,588. Then the police authorities were fully aware of the breach of the law before you called their attention to it?—They did not understand that it was illegal, I think.

Administration by the police.

41,589. I think you cited another case where, at your request, he sent a plain clothes policeman to one particular quarter of Cork?—He sent a plain clothes policeman to certain districts just bordering upon the city.

41,590. Which you called his attention to?—Which I called his attention to.

41,591. It had not been his habit to do that before?—It had not. He complied at once with my request; and he gave certainly then a genuine desire to put a stop to the demoralising practices that I complained of there in Cork.

41,592. You say that there is a certain amount of slackness on the part of the police. Do you attach blame to the constables on their beats for not going into public-houses to see if drunken persons are on the premises?—I think that duty is not done at all, scarcely.

41,593. (Dean Dickinson.) With regard to prosecutions, you said that you could not yourself prosecute; that that devolved on the police?—Yes.

41,594. In Dublin I prosecuted myself, and personally served the summonses on two publicans in my own parish, and prosecuted them without the aid of counsel or solicitor, and successfully. One was deprived of his licence, and the other was convicted, and has behaved better since?—I am very glad to hear it.

Prosecuting drunkenness.

41,595. I have walked into public-houses, and cautioned the publican: "If you let that man come in when he is drunk I will serve you with a summons to-morrow." Why cannot that be done in other places?—I have done a great deal of that myself. I have gone into houses, and I have spoken to publicans who were supplying drunken people. I have said, "You are doing very wrong; you are breaking the law"; and their reply to me was, "If we do not serve them, others will"; then showing the terrible nature of the competition between them. "It is our way of living; we do put out, there is all the [illegible]," and various explanations of that kind were given, showing that they did not realise at all their obligations not to supply drink to drunken people. I have myself succeeded in stopping a great deal of it in that way.

41,[illegible]. I know you have done a great deal of that in Cork, but I suggest, respectfully, that it is possible for where there [illegible] to prosecute?—Yes; I am very glad of it. It would be a very [illegible] matter for a clergyman to undertake things of that sort.

41,[illegible]. On the question of inebriates you are aware that that Bill as it at present stands before the House does not include Ireland?—So I understand.

41,[illegible]. Do you think that concurrently with other means of prevention, that method of cure or dealing with inebriates, on the understanding that the term of detention is long enough, ought to be extended to Ireland?—Yes, I think so; but what I find is this, that a great evil ought to be dealt with at its source, and that it is [illegible] of remedies that will be more effectual, simply to deal with it by putting up houses for inebriates.

41,[illegible]. Do not you think we are bound as much to undertake the cure of disease as the prevention of them?—I think prevention is very much wiser.

41,[illegible]. Of course it is, but sanitary measures do not take the place of hospitals?—It is a very important thing in itself I admit.

41,[illegible]. I only wanted to draw out from you as an Irishman interested in that question, your feeling that that Bill if it is passed into an Act ought to be extended to Ireland?—Yes. I would welcome the thing, no doubt.

41,[illegible]. There ought to be a strong expression of opinion from Ireland to those who have the conduct of that Bill that Ireland should not have the prevention of being excluded from it?—Yes.

41,[illegible]. (*Mr. Roberts.*) Have you been a considerable number of years in Cork?—19 years.

41,[illegible]. I suppose you have had the best opportunity of knowing the inner life of the people, the working classes of Cork?—Yes, I have seen them in a very intimate way indeed. I have visited them from house to house every evening practically for the past 19 years when they come home from their work, and when they can be seen at their leisure time, and all their circumstances thoroughly known and understood. That has been my practice closely for the past eight years.

41,[illegible]. Is it a fact in Cork that the greater number of public-houses are in the working class districts?—Yes; they are located very much among the working people, and at the bridges where the working people pass to and fro to their work.

41,[illegible]. You agree that the fact that the public-houses are placed in such positions produces special temptations to the working classes as they pass to and from their work?—They are a constant temptation to them. With any people's social tendencies, the social instinct being strong in them, these public-houses forming a network around them are a temptation which they really can hardly resist.

41,[illegible]. In reference to the society in which you are interested, the Society for the Prevention of Cruelty to Children, do you remember whether the number of cases that you have in a year is considerable?—We have had 1,[illegible] cases for the past seven years, those involving the well-being of 3,0[illegible] children. They vary. In some years we have 170, in other years [illegible].

41,[illegible]. There is one small point I wish to ask you about in reference to illicit sale on Sunday in Cork, to which you refer. Would that refer to shebeening?—No. There are a few. There are, I believe, [illegible] or [illegible] suspected shebeens in Cork, but if they carry on an illicit sale it is on a very small scale.

41,[illegible]. Then what you chiefly refer to by "illicit sale" is sale in prohibited hours?—Yes, and to drunken people; that is one of the worst forms of the evil in my mind.

41,[illegible]. Cork is an exempted city under the Sunday [illegible]

one other practice. It is on the part of a number of men known as lumpers. They are charged by merchants, or captains of ships, to unload a cargo. These men give their word to a certain publican to supply drink to the men who are engaged in loading or unloading the ship during the week, and I have had very sad complaints from members of the families of these poor labourers that when the week's end came they had very little wages for their families, because it was spent on drink during the week in that way; drink given on credit, through the word of the lumper or man who had charge of loading or unloading the ship, by the publican.

Rev. F. O'Leary.

4 May '98.

41,[illegible]. Do you know, or has it come under your experience, that there is any gambling going on?—Yes, there are certain houses in which unquestionably gambling is carried on to a very great extent. The houses are very well known to the clergy. I have known men go from one end of the city to the other, married men, leave their homes and families, and go home in the morning, having spent the greater part of the night gambling in certain public-houses. I am sorry to say in some of those cases I had clear proof that the police were aware of the gambling going on, and paid no attention to it. I spoke to clergymen in whose districts those houses were situated, and the clergymen told me it was the case; the police knew all about it, and they could not get them to interfere.

Gambling in public-houses.

41,[illegible]. You know, as a fact, that the police were informed of these places?—So the clergy told me. The wives and mothers to my knowledge, have gone to the districts where those public-houses are located, and waited until midnight for their sons and husbands to come out, and they came out perhaps after midnight under the influence of drink, having been gambling previously in those public-houses. I have known the sad history of those facts from the members of the families.

41,[illegible]. With reference to total Sunday closing, you have indicated your view that the best practical step at present would be to shorten the hours on Sunday?—My own view is to close them on Sunday. I think it might cause some inconvenience to individuals, but at the same time the advantage would greatly counterbalance those inconveniences. I have seen on Sundays, quite recently, numbers of women with their little children in their arms in public-houses, [illegible] along before the bars under the influence of drink; young girls too going into the streets under the influence of drink, while a very sad and strange contrast was presented by respectable people going to their places of worship with their little children looking on at this, the young people being scandalised, and possibly some of them might get demoralised by the sights they see. I think that demoralisation is a terrible social evil, and that if some inconvenience followed by closing the public-houses, a greater part of this demoralisation would be put a stop to, at all events, so far as it concerned women and children, I think it would be totally stopped, and there would be great advantage from Sunday closing.

Sunday closing.

41,[illegible]. Your personal view is in favour of total Sunday closing?—Yes. As far as the personal inconvenience to the working man goes, I have seen multitudes of working men enjoying themselves without touching alcoholic drinks on Sundays, and if they were drinking at ordinary consumption it would be a very different story indeed. I have seen large numbers, under my own control, in Killarney and other places. They were not exclusively teetotalers, but a great number were—perhaps the majority. They enjoyed themselves thoroughly. They took their meals with them in little baskets, and many of them [illegible] or their drives, as the case might be, and they enjoyed their outings. They were back in time to catch the train, whereas if they were ordinary excursionists they would have spent most of the day in the public-house, become riotous in the evening, given trouble to the railway officials, and perhaps injured the windows of the railway carriages, and so on. I think myself the inconvenience to individuals would be very slight indeed, and that they would, after a very short time, find that it was a blessing instead of an inconvenience.

41,[illegible]. At all events, from your experience of the country districts in Ireland, total Sunday closing has [illegible]

Rev. P. O'Leary. 4 May '98.

under?—I am quite sure that the present county inspector has taken the matter seriously in hand. I have the pleasure of knowing him, and I know his views about it.

61,617. And he has practically stopped it now?—Yes.

61,618. Do you think if you had entire Sunday closing there would be any large attempt to re-establish shebeens?—I do not think so at all. I have asked working men themselves, and they say [illegible] working men has the least desire for anything of the kind. They would be very glad if the temptation were removed from them.

61,619. And if there were any attempt at re-establishing shebeening in Cork, under Sunday closing, you have sufficient confidence in the chief constable that he would very soon crush it out?—I feel he would, and he feels it himself, and he has stated so before this Commission.

61,620. The question of shebeening does not affect your mind in the smallest degree in advocating Sunday closing?—To some extent it does, but I really would not consider the matter as comparable to the advantages.

Wages paid in public-houses.

61,621. (Mr. Whitaker.) With reference to the payment of wages in public-houses, and also the [illegible] of money due, that is obviously illegal under the Act of 1883, which applies to Ireland?—Yes. I know it was quite illegal.

61,622. Then why not prosecute these men?—The fact was I did all in my power, and the authorities did not seem to know anything about it. The county inspector knew nothing of the practice until I brought it under his notice. The police knew of it, but they did not know it was illegal. They told me so.

61,623. Have they put it down now?—Warning was given to those who were practising it, but I do not know whether the warning has been effectual.

Publicans supplying drinking persons.

61,624. You have spoken of the condition of the women who spent their time in the public-houses, and you have spoken of the men spending the money there, which is obviously wanted for their families and children. The publicans who supply liquor to these men and women, and take their money, must know as well as you do what is the condition of those people. Does not that indicate to you some strange lack of moral sense on the part of the publicans?—Their moral standard is very low, I think, on the part of many of them at all events. I know when they go into the trade they may be as respectable as others, but I do believe that the trade tends to demoralise them. They [illegible] at and have things that naturally tend to lower their moral sense.

61,625. Do not you think anybody with decent [illegible] would decline to make a living by getting it from people in such a condition, [illegible] they are not responsible in any sense who get money from such unfortunate creatures. I have gone myself into public-houses and dragged out women who were prosecuted for cruelty to children. They [illegible] actually opposite those publicans who were supplying them with drink. They knew them as well as they knew their families. They knew they were in jail for cruelty to children. They were supplying them with drink while actually drunk. Not only were they drunk, but they were habitual drunkards, neglecting their families. I have dragged them out of the houses myself personally, and remonstrated with the publicans for supplying them, and I do not know how they can claim to be respectable in any sense if they do things of that kind.

61,626. Does not it indicate the degrading nature of the whole business?—Well, I do not say the whole business, to be accurate; but the abuses are very general, so general that they have grown to be a [illegible] evil, eating into the very vitals of the nation.

Objections to tied houses.

61,627. Have you any views as to tied houses; do they prevail in Cork?—Yes, I have known several tied publicans myself. I have known some of them obliged to give up the business through the competition and the keen struggle for existence amongst them.

61,628. Do you think the introduction of the tied houses in Cork tended to intensify the competition, and also show the evils of the system?—Yes. I explain it in this way. A tied publican must accept the terms of the brewer, if he wishes to get a licence from the brewer, because it is practically the property of the brewer. He must accept the terms of the brewer. He will not get as many terms as [illegible], according to his sale, and he will not get [illegible] premises for the licensed, or [illegible], or the prices that others may get for a certain amount of sale, and he feels that he must make certain returns to the brewer regularly. Otherwise he may be put out, and another man may be put in. On the other hand there is the difficulty with the police authorities if he continues to [illegible] illegal sale, to which he is very often driven by necessity, because [illegible] no law. So that he is placed in a tight corner, and his difficulties are enormously increased by the fact of having a tied house. An independent licence-holder can deal with any brewer he likes.

Rev. P. O'Leary.

Inducements to sell.

61,629. I understand you to say just now something about prizes and premiums being given for quantities sold?—Yes.

61,630. Do you mean the brewers give them?—Yes, and gratuities to barmaids.

61,631. All tending to force the sale?—All tending to push the sale as far as possible.

61,632. (Mr. Younger.) Can you give any specific statement of the charge you make against the brewers of Cork?—What charge is that?

61,633. That they bribe people?—I do not say "bribe," but I say they give them gratuities and that prizes are offered for a large quantity sold.

61,634. You can give no specific instance?—I do not want to give names, but I know individuals who got them.

61,635. You know the names of the brewers who gave them, I suppose?—I would not say that I do know that. I do not know which porter is sold by the people who got prizes. I did not inquire into that.

61,636. It is quite possible that these gratuities may have come from other sources altogether?—Not at all. I have had the information from people who received the gratuities.

61,637. That that was the source from which they came?—Yes.

61,638. You have told us that there is a very strong [illegible] feeling in Cork in favour of the Intoxicating Liquors (Ireland) Bill, which is before the House of Commons at present?—Well, there is a very strong feeling with regard to one part of it, that is the Saturday early closing.

Trades Council and Sunday closing.

61,639. Is it, or is it not, the fact that quite recently there was a resolution passed by the United Trades Council of Cork, which I suppose represents a very large body of tradesmen there, against that Bill?—The United Trades Council is elected once a year, representing the trades in a general way, but it would be unfair to say that in this particular matter the act of the council represents the views of the members, because they were not elected specially to represent their views by the [illegible].

61,640. Can you tell the Commission whether it is not the fact that only a week ago the city council of Cork passed a resolution against that Bill by a majority of [illegible]?—I may revert to your first question, because I did not completely answer it. I have here the statement of the United Trades Council, and the [illegible] of the several speakers on that occasion are all based upon opposition to Sunday closing, and that alone; there is not a word in them about Saturday night closing.

61,641. At the Trades Council?—At the Trades Council.

61,642. It was a unanimous resolution all the same, was not it?—It was a unanimous resolution against the Bill in globo, which was perfectly legitimate if they objected to any part of it.

The city council.

61,643. With regard to the resolution passed by your town council by such a large majority, that I do not think [illegible] in the same way that the other did—I think it limited itself in a very much more reasonable way. It said that there were certain provisions of an objectionable nature in the Bill, and because of those provisions they opposed it. All the opposition [illegible] from six men who were opposed to it. In those [illegible] men in the town council of Cork, as many as [illegible] were publicans.

Rev. P. O'Leary.

4 May '9[illegible]

[illegible] —Well, I speak under correction [illegible] ... [illegible] ... from unfortunate victims of ... pledge their clothes in order to [illegible].

[illegible] ... in the mayor of Cork ... the mayor of Cork, as you ask.

[illegible] ... Of course I quite understand ... trade is greatly felt in every ... The trade has its ramifications everywhere. ... [illegible]

[illegible] ... I do not think much importance was ... people of Cork.

[illegible] ... (Dean Dickinson.) How do the members for ... —Both members for Cork ... on all occasions.

[illegible] ... They voted for it?—Yes.

[illegible] ... The importance of the ... to a great extent, yes.

[illegible] ... What is the hour you fix for Saturday early closing? ... great importance in Saturday ... very important. It is a most ... working people ... I think that it is a very important ... Commission, that working men ... on Saturday night they get ... the least ... of ... and they ... really remain hour after hour until ... whereas, if they were closed ... go home as readily as they [illegible].

[illegible] ... my question ... I think. ... what hour you have in your mind ... for closing on Saturdays?— [illegible].

[illegible] ... paid on Saturday generally?— ... at ten o'clock on Saturdays.

[illegible] ... would not entail any inconvenience, the houses being closed at ... to the fact that a large number ... articles ... inconvenience ... facilities for getting goods of ... think it would be a ... in purchasing useful commodities ... their time in the public-house.

[illegible] ... as regards Sunday closing, you ... to the extreme step of ... there would be difficulties in the ... it personally?

[illegible] ... view you would not believe the [illegible]

41,661. What is the largest number of separate families that you know of in one house?—I have heard of as many as six families, five or six; they vary.

41,662. What would be about the size of the public-houses?—They would be houses in the centre of the city; large houses.

41,663. Would the families occupy more than one room, or one room only?—Some of them perhaps one and some two.

41,664. Have you the Public Health Act in operation in Cork?—Yes.

41,665. Could not the officers of the Public Health be able to prevent that?—I suppose it would be against the Act if they were in excess of the number allowed by the Act.

41,666. Your evidence appears rather to show that all the police machinery, the machinery of the magistrates, the machinery of the public officials seems to be at a standstill. It is an extraordinary state of things for a large city, is it not?—I would not say the public officials connected with the Health Acts were failing in duty, because I have no knowledge really of how they act in the matter.

41,667. If you have got this large number of lodgers in a public-house the closing hours would fail altogether because the licence-holder can supply at any time to the lodgers in the house, can he not?—Yes. They cannot legally supply to them, but at the same time of course they do.

41,668. I think they can legally supply the lodgers in the house?—Not to tenement holders I think.

41,669. (Dean Dickinson.) They are not hotels?—They are not.

41,670. (Mr. Grimley.) This, as I understand, is the Act, s. 9, 35 & 36 Vict.: "None of the provisions "contained in this section shall preclude a person "licensed to sell any intoxicating liquor to be consumed "on the premises" (that surely must be a publican or an hotel keeper) "from selling such liquor to "bona fide travellers or persons lodging in his house."?—I am not an authority on the legal question, but tenement holders are not lodgers.

41,671. Out of those [illegible] publicans that you have in Cork, I suppose there are a large number whom you would regard as respectable traders?—Yes, certainly.

41,672. I rather want to remove from the minds of those who read your evidence that you came here with a desire to brand the whole trade?—None whatever.

41,673. The question put to you was that there were associated more or less positively with an immoral trade injurious to the public. Your answer would not support that?—No, not at all. A large number of them are endeavouring to conduct their business very well.

41,674. There is no reason to brand them as separate traders?—I did not mean to do it for a moment.

41,675. (Mr. Young.) I think you said the wages were paid on Saturdays?—Yes, that is the usual thing, I believe.

41,676. Would you be surprised to know that the largest employers of labour pay on Friday?—I know Mr. Hall pays on Friday. Days for paying wages.

41,677. I will read them to you: the Great Southern and Western Railway Company, the Clyde Shipping Company, the Cork, Brandon and South Coast Railway Company, the four breweries, the Cork Distillery Company, the Cork Steam Packet Company, and the

Rev. F. O'Leary.

[illegible] May '[illegible]

Pudding [illegible]

41,650. With regard to [illegible] paying, I do not think you used bribes, but certain sums of money?—Not bribes by any means.

41,651. To the gentleman, are you sure that it was not in the form of discount? Because in buying large quantities of any commodity you probably may get discount in proportion to the amount you buy; was not it discount?—As it was represented to me it was simply a premium given for a large amount of sale, an unusual amount of sale made during the year.

41,652. That is exactly what it would be, because in purchasing commodities you get discount in proportion to the amount?—I suppose it would have the same effect.

Female drunkenness.

41,653. With regard to drunken women, one is surprised to hear that that is so prevalent in Cork. From your large experience do you think the Cork women drink more than in other places?—I do not wish for a moment to say that they are worse than other people, but I believe that in the cities the women drink far more than they do in the country districts, or country towns, for the simple reason that the facilities are greater in the cities and then the sense of shame which is very strong in every woman, at least unless the woman becomes demoralised in some way, keeps them from drinking in the country districts and country towns, but does not prevent them in the cities because they can escape public notice, whereas in the country every one's actions are more or less noticed by the public. People are more on a pinnacle in the country towns and districts than in the cities. Again, in the cities they get facilities from children bringing drink.

41,654. You do not mean to say that the excess of drinking appertains to women in Cork in a peculiar degree?—I do not say that for a moment, but it is, I suppose, pretty much on a par with what happens in other cities.

41,655. What proportion of women among the operative classes drink, one or two per cent. do you think?—I think a great many more.

41,656. But you do not know exactly?—Of course I have been through the houses of the working classes in Cork a great deal, and I believe that until the society over which I have charge made a great reformation in the matter, drinking among women was very general indeed. At the same time it is not our function so much as it is the function of the government to put a stop to the social evil. It would be the acme of irony to expect us to keep the people sober while the State gives every facility for the spreading of indulgence in drink.

Connexion of drink and crime.

41,657. Of course you have great experience in prison life, and the habits of the classes whom you have brought before us to-day. Does that very fact not lead you to believe that the condition which you describe is more than what another man would ordinarily expect?—The experience which I describe as coming under my notice in connexion with the prison is more than would fall under the notice of ordinary people, because my opportunities are very much greater than those of ordinary people for discovering the sources of crimes of various kinds.

41,658. That being your own view you probably compared the position, do you not?—I compared my views with those of the governor of the Cork gaol and the deputy governor. Mr. Andrews, the governor, has had [illegible] years' experience and he fully agrees with my view. The chaplain of the female prison, whom I consulted, holds precisely the same view. I asked him about the unfortunate class, the females condemned who were leading immoral lives, and he assured me, what I really believe to be the case, that there was not one of them who did not owe that sad condition to intemperance, and that in reality they hated the life because of its nature, but that they come from intemperate homes, or else they have got into the habits of drinking themselves in youth; sometimes coming from intemperate homes they have to walk the streets, and are exposed to temptation, and their reformation is rendered impossible, because when they leave prison they fall back into the old drinking habits.

Sunday and early closing.

41,659. Do you think the closing of public-houses at an earlier hour on Saturday, and closing them entirely on Sunday, would prevent those evils which you describe?—I believe it would prevent a great deal, because the people would go home before they got into that intoxicated state; they would save their wages to

The law is very plain, but quite inadequate, about giving drink to people who are intoxicated. The police might do a great deal, but it seems to me that the law should be so adequate that the police would have no excuse but to do their duty in the matter.

41,698. I am trying to account for the laxity of the police, as you describe it, and I want to know from you, do you think that if it were not a military force in Ireland matters would be otherwise?—I do not think so. I think the reason which I give would operate in both cases. There is the question of popularity, and the influence of the trade, and there are [illegible] that if the police do not cease to give annoyance they may find themselves in trouble. I have known certain efficient policemen to be [illegible] in that way by publicans. The influence of the trade of course being so strong, the police generally would shrink from being too efficient or very efficient.

41,699. With regard to the publicans themselves, may not they exercise great control over the people with regard to these habits?—Certainly.

41,700. They are trusted at present as [illegible]?—Who are?

41,701. The publicans?—I would not say so by any means.

41,702. If they were trusted with more confidence, would they not act in a better manner than they do?—That is to say, if you give them more freedom of action.

41,703. Have more confidence in them. It is like the government of a country, you require to have confidence in the people. If you place confidence in the publicans and treat them as you would do other members of society, do not you think that you would really have a better class, and higher notions of duty?—I think they have been trusted with too much laxity altogether on the part of the agents of the law and the magistrates. They have had too much liberty. That liberty and that confidence which you speak of have been dealt out in too large a measure to them. They have had a great deal to do with forming the habits of the people, but in a wrong direction, and if they got more liberty they would certainly intensify the evil.

41,704. You are thinking of putting more restrictions on, I presume?—Entirely.

41,705. (*Mr. Gordon.*) In reply to the Chairman you gave us the number of additional public-houses which you have in the city. Who is the licensing authority in Cork—the Recorder?—Yes.

41,706. Is he the sole authority?—Yes.

41,707. And yet during the years you have been there he has granted all these additional licences?—The present Recorder has not increased the number at all; he has been only some few years in Cork. It was done before his time by different Recorders.

41,708. I ask simply because we have been told that if we had a judicial licensing authority the administration of the law would be much more severe, but it does not seem to be so in Cork?—It does seem to be so at present, certainly.

41,709. Under the present Recorder?—Yes.

The witness withdrew.

Mr. [illegible] A. [illegible] called in and examined.

41,710. (*Chairman.*) You are, I believe, a merchant carrying on business in the foreign timber trade in Wexford?—Yes, for the past 27 years.

41,711. You are also a justice of the peace for the county?—I also hold Her Majesty's commission of the peace for Wexford County. I am a visiting justice for Wexford County Prison, a governor of Wexford County Infirmary, Chairman of the Wexford Dispensary Committee, and I am connected with several other public and charitable societies in Wexford in honorary positions, in which positions I have studied the question of the present licensing laws as referring to the county of Wexford, and I have formed opinions in connexion with that question.

41,712. Speaking with that experience, what is your opinion as to the granting, renewal, and transfer of licences?—I consider that the present law with regard to the issue, renewal, and transfer of licences is unsatisfactory, and capable of very considerable improvement.

41,713. What do you say as to the granting of licences? [illegible] consider that the condition of the law in that respect is unsatisfactory.

41,714. Then you considered renewals and transfers?—I speak especially as to the grant when I say that I consider the present condition of the law unsatisfactory.

41,715. Is it the practice in County Wexford for the magistrates of the county generally to go into a particular petty sessional division and vote?—In the county of Wexford the granting of licences for all portions of the county is dealt with at two annual licensing sessions. The issue of licences for all the north district of county Wexford is dealt with at the licensing sessions of Enniscorthy, held in November of each year.

41,716. My question rather was with reference to the business ordinarily transacted at petty sessions; whether the magistrates of the county generally think themselves justified and have established the practice of going into the particular petty sessional division from all parts of the county, so as not to leave the jurisdiction to those magistrates specially attached to that petty sessional division?—No, that is not so. If the licence is granted at petty sessions, it is granted only as a temporary measure, to hold good until the annual licensing sessions comes on in November. At that annual licensing sessions the case must be heard, and unless the licence is then granted, the grant made by the petty sessions magistrates as a temporary measure does not hold good. It must be confirmed by the annual licensing sessions.

41,717. I understand you would like to confine the jurisdiction to the petty sessional division?—Quite so. With regard to the present hearing for the granting of licences, I can give a case in point. The town of Wexford has a population of 11,[illegible]. All licensing applications in connexion with that town are dealt with at the town of New Ross, 23 miles distant, which is the place at which the annual licensing sessions for that district is held. At that annual licensing sessions very few magistrates of the Wexford bench attend. In fact, I think, generally speaking, I am the only resident present. I have never seen more than two members of the Wexford bench present on these occasions. The result is that all licences applied for—all renewals, transfers, and applications in the town of Wexford—are dealt with at the town of New Ross by a body of magistrates, generally from 20 to 30 in number, who have no local knowledge.

41,718. You object to the magistrates of the county of Wexford collectively dealing with all cases of applications arising within the county, and you would limit the exercise of the jurisdiction in those applications to the petty sessional division in which the application arises?—Quite so. With regard to the proposal to confine the licensing authority solely upon county court judges in the rural districts, and upon Recorders in the cities, I hold that that proposal is open to this objection: that, in the case of county court judges, their want of local knowledge would of necessity cause that their decisions would be very largely based upon information supplied to them by the local constabulary.

41,719. If you object to the county court judge sitting as sole licensing authority, whom would you have to sit with him?—My suggestion is, that the county court judge should preside at the hearing of these cases, possessing a casting vote, and that associated with him should be the resident magistrate or magistrates for the district, and the county justices for the petty sessions district within which the premises proposed to be licensed are situated, excluding from participation in the voting all magistrates who are outside the petty sessions district in which the premises proposed to be licensed are situated. I would wish to point out that

Rev. P. O'Leary. 4 May '88. [illegible]

Mr. [illegible] A. [illegible]

County court judge as sole licensing authority.

Licensing by petty sessional divisions.

Mr. M. A. [illegible] 4 May '96.

the result of that would practically mean, that in the hearing of these cases the bench dealing with the case would consist, instead of as at present of 20 to 30 individuals, of not more than one or two, but who would have local knowledge. It would consist of the county court judge, the resident magistrate, and probably two, or at the most three justices belonging to the petty sessions district, and the powers of the county court judge to give a decision would be enormously greater than under existing conditions.

61,720. Would you always be able to get the resident magistrate to sit on that point?—I think so, speaking for the county of Wexford only. With regard to that county, I feel certain we should always have the resident magistrate present; in my experience, he invariably attends.

Wexford P.S.D.

61,721. What would be the number of magistrates in the petty sessional division of Wexford?—The petty sessions district of Wexford is one of the largest in the county. It contains 15 magistrates. That includes the town of Wexford, which has, roughly speaking, a population of 12,[illegible], and it is the most important.

61,722. They go down to what number?—They go down to seven or eight in some of the small districts. I have a record which I will hand in later of the different petty sessions districts in county Wexford, 12 in number.

61,723. Whether the magistrates were 15 or seven, you would like them made to sit with the county court judge and the resident magistrate, would you?—Yes, because I find that in practice the total number of magistrates never would sit. I have never known anything more than a certain percentage of magistrates sit on any of these cases.

61,724. (Mr. [illegible].) You are talking of magistrates resident within the petty sessions district?—Magistrates sitting and acting for the petty sessions district.

61,725. Who habitually sit at petty sessions courts?—In Ireland we have different petty sessions districts, and when a magistrate receives the commission of the peace he is appointed for a petty sessions district. He has power, if he so chooses, to sit outside that district, but it is not customary. It would be contrary to custom altogether for any magistrate in Ireland to sit outside his own petty sessions district.

61,726. (Chairman.) As I understand you, the advantage of your plan is that whereas the county court judge now, whatever may be his individual authority or individual right to authority, is swamped by the opinion of the other magistrates, if he sat with the resident magistrate and a small body of, say, six magistrates, he would have a preponderating authority, or at least guide the court in matters of necessary and discretionary?—I believe that on a bench composed as I have suggested, there would be no abuse whatever of the intentions of the legislature with regard to the issue of licenses.

61,727. I think you told us that the applications of the town of Wexford are dealt with at New Ross?—Yes; that is 23 miles distant. There is a provision in the Licensing Acts that a publican or intending publican applying for a license must give notice in the local papers.

Licenses in Co. Wexford.

61,728. What is the population of Co. Wexford?—112,[illegible].

61,729. What is the number of licensed premises?—[illegible]. They are distributed among the twelve petty sessions districts in the manner indicated in the Return which I beg to hand in.

61,730. Do you consider that the number of licensed houses throughout the county Wexford is adequate, deficient, or excessive?—I consider that it is vastly in excess of the requirements of the population. I think so especially in view of the fact that Ireland is not situated similarly to England in this matter. In England the population is increasing by leaps and bounds, in Ireland it is rapidly decreasing.

Decreasing number of licenses.

61,731. Notwithstanding that decrease of population, have you had any new licenses granted recently?—We have; but though we have had some licenses granted, we have had some others extinguished. I should say that the number of licenses is rather the normal quantity. I have a return of the number of licenses granted in the town of Wexford during the last 10 years. In the year 1886 we had in the town of Wexford [illegible] licensed premises; in the present year we have [illegible]—a decrease of two. During the intervening period the numbers have risen to [illegible] on one or two occasions, and then have reverted to [illegible]. They have now dropped to [illegible].

Mr. M. A. [illegible]

Objection to mixed trades.

61,732. You probably heard the evidence of the previous witness. I do not want to go over the same ground again, but generally do you see any objection to the combination of the trades?—I do; I see the greatest possible objection to the combination of the trades, and I suggest that no license should be granted in future with respect to any premises except those which are intended solely for the sale of drink and for food which may be supplied on the premises to bonâ fide travellers.

61,733. Turning from the county to the town of Wexford, what is the population of the town?—[illegible].

61,734. What is the number of licensed premises?—At present [illegible].

61,735. How many of those licensed premises carry on the mixed business?—Of those [illegible] licensed premises, certainly [illegible] carry on the mixed business of a grocery and publican's business. I believe, as a matter of fact, that [illegible] carry on that business, but I cannot speak with certainty; there are two cases as to which I am doubtful. Certainly, [illegible] of the houses in Wexford carry on the mixed business, and there are only two or four which are absolutely confined to the publican's license. One of them is the local hotel.

No spirit grocer in Wexford.

61,736. Have you reason to think that Wexford is exceptional in that way, because we have heard of a different state of things in Cork?—I think Wexford is exceptional in that way. In the town of Wexford we have no such thing as a single spirit grocer holding an off-license. In other towns and cities they exist to a large extent; but in the town of Wexford there are absolutely none. There are two establishments in Wexford, very respectable licensed traders—who as a matter of fact do not sell over their counters for consumption on the premises, but all the same they hold publican's licenses and they could be compelled by an intending purchaser to do so. They do not wish to do so, and as a matter of fact they do not do so, but they could be compelled to do so.

Proposed value of licensed premises.

61,737. What do you say as to the valuation of the houses either in the town or the county of Wexford?—I think a large number of houses exist which are altogether too small and inferior in character to carry on the business of publicans, and I propose that the Poor Law valuation of any future licenses in the urban districts should be at least [illegible], and in the rural districts at least [illegible].

61,738. Do you think that that would extinguish a great number of existing houses?—I only propose that with regard to the issue of fresh licenses. I do not wish to make proposals with regard to vested interests. I think that that would raise the question of compensation, which is a very large question.

61,739. How would the existing system die out? It would be perpetual, would it not?—The existing system, I believe, would gradually die out. If fresh licenses were not granted on the conditions which at present exist, I think the present system would gradually die out.

61,740. It would be a very gradual process?—Undoubtedly it would; and I should be strongly in favour of a more rapid process if I considered it practicable, but the question would be one of considerable magnitude. There are many suggestions that I might embody in my evidence, which would strike [illegible] as very excellent suggestions in themselves, but which it would not be practicable to carry into effect.

Six-day licenses.

61,742. Are there very many six-day licenses in Wexford?—The number of six-day licenses in Wexford at present is [illegible], and there are [illegible] seven-day licenses. In the year 1886 Wexford contained [illegible] six-day and [illegible] seven-day licenses. At present the number is [illegible] six-day and [illegible] seven-day—showing an increase of six seven-day licenses. These six seven-day licenses have been obtained at the New Ross annual licensing sessions, and the reason for the applications for these six seven-day licenses has been in connexion with the question which I shall refer to later on, under the head of bonâ fide travellers, where disorder has arisen in Wexford in connexion with football teams and sporting men generally visiting the town on Sundays.

Proposed abolition of seven-day licenses.

61,743. Do you consider the [illegible] seven-day licenses are sufficient to provide for the needs of the bonâ fide traveller?—I consider that they are altogether in excess of the requisite number. I hold that no seven-day various other matters. A large portion of the time of the police is occupied in Ireland, and I suppose it is elsewhere, in looking after unmuzzled dogs. They have multifarious duties to perform, and I hold that the number of police available for superintending the licensed premises is totally inadequate. Although I consider the police supervision to be inadequate, and a number of publicans to [illegible] free from the commission of illegal actions, I do not impute to the constabulary much fault in that respect; because I hold that it is beyond their power to cope with the number of licenses.

61,732. Am I right in saying that your opinion would be that the governing condition of the state of a particular county or city is the number of licensed houses and the proportion of Royal Irish Constabulary to those supplied?—Quite so. As an instance of that I might cite the town of New Ross. The town of Wexford has a population of 11,[illegible], and the number of licensed premises is [illegible]. New Ross has a population of [illegible] and has two licensed houses more than Wexford. It has [illegible] licensed premises. Enniscorthy has a population of [illegible], and [illegible] licensed premises. It is within the knowledge of every inhabitant of the county of Wexford that the number of violent deaths and fatal affrays and drownings, and things of that kind, which occur in the town of New Ross, are vastly in excess of such occurrences in the town of Wexford, although the town of Wexford has double its population; because the town of New Ross has two thousand [illegible] more than the town of Wexford with very little more than half the population, and has a smaller police force. I believe this to be the cause of the state of New Ross, which is, as I have indicated, very much inferior to that of Wexford as to law, order, and sobriety.

61,733. Speaking generally of the publicans in Wexford as a class, what should you say of their character?—I should say that a large number of publicans in Wexford, the larger grocery establishments, do their business well, and have a desire that their business should be conducted in the manner that the law intends. I have, myself, heard some of the leading publicans of the town of Wexford express a desire that the Sunday Closing Act should be in operation. They say they have no wish to sell on Sundays. I have heard the leading publicans say that. That remark does not by any means apply to the entire body of publicans in Wexford.

61,734. I am not talking at this moment of Sunday closing, but with regard to their general character?—A certain portion of the trade in Wexford conduct their business in an admirable manner; but there is also a large number who do not conduct their business in by any means a proper manner.

61,735. You are a frequent attendant at petty sessions, are you not?—I am a very frequent attendant. As a matter of fact, I believe that I am the most frequent [illegible] at the Wexford bench, my attendances each year [illegible].

considered that on the Sabbath day it was a most disgraceful state of things. It came under my observation, also, that a large number of those whom I saw outside the public-houses, and in the public-houses that I looked into in passing by, were men of the country labouring class, and it led me to the conclusion that, the Sunday Closing Act being in operation in the rural districts outside of Waterford, all the thirsty souls in the rural quarters had flocked into the city to indulge in drink there, and thus the fact of the Sunday Closing Act being in operation outside Waterford helped to concentrate the evil of the exemption of the city itself from the provisions of the Act.

61,773. Therefore, would you advance the extension of the Sunday Closing Act?—Most decidedly. I advocate the extension of the Sunday Closing Act to the five cities. I do not profess to speak with reference to any of the cities as to personal observation, except Waterford, though I have been in the other cities on Sundays occasionally. Still my observations have not been sufficient to justify me speaking of them; but I fail to see why the population of the other towns larger should entitle them to exemption from the law that governs the rest of the community.

61,774. Now, in Waterford, can you see any valid reason for its exemption?—I see every reason, on the contrary, for its inclusion, in the Act.

61,775. Turning to earlier Saturday closing, what is the feeling in Wexford, in the county or in the town?—The feeling is strongly in favour of earlier Saturday closing. A public meeting was held in the town of Wexford for the purpose of advocating Sunday closing and earlier Saturday closing. The attendance comprised all classes of the community, but the great bulk of the attendants were working men, and the attendance at the meeting was very large. It was held in the Town Hall, which is not a large building admittedly, but it was the largest public room in the town, and the attendance was so large that they overflowed the room and the stairway, and were in the street outside.

61,776. What was the feeling of that meeting, was it in favour of 8 o'clock or 9 o'clock?—It was unanimously in favour of early Saturday closing.

61,777. At what hour?—The hour advocated was 9 o'clock, and the latest dealt with in the resolution placed before the meeting was 9 o'clock.

61,778. Would you be in favour of 9 o'clock or a still earlier hour?—I believe a still earlier hour would be more in the interests of public order; but at the same time I do deprecate anybody holding extreme views on any question, and I think the hour of 9 o'clock would be most reasonably an hour to make trial of at first, and if Saturday closing at 9 o'clock were found to work satisfactorily after a few years, I consider it would be ripe for consideration then whether a still further decrease of hours would not be necessary or desirable.

61,779. Do you think that the same early hours should apply to the town and country?—Certainly, but more especially to towns.

61,780. Would you have a different hour in the country to the town?—No, I think the same hour would be sufficient for country and town, but I think the evils arising from Saturday opening are greater in the town than in the country, because in towns the working men get their wages paid on Friday nights in some cases, and on Saturdays in others, but Saturday is the great market day for the working men. They are about the town, and it is most desirable that they should not be carousing up to the verge of Sunday morning.

61,781. I think you have already desired to provide for the convenience of the bona fide traveller, and therefore [illegible] resort on Sundays through the summer months.

Mr. M. A. [illegible]

4 May '98

61,782. Would you make it an offence for the bona fide traveller who had not travelled six miles, and who misrepresented the matter to the proprietor of an hotel or to the man who served him?—I would impose a penalty on both.

61,783. But how in the world is a publican living 6 miles off to know whether a man has actually travelled 6 miles?—I admit is one of the difficulties that exists under the Act, but any publican would know the locality in which he lives very well. I should not have any difficulty if anyone questioned me as to the distance of any given point in the vicinity of Wexford, from say the centre of the town, in knowing whether it was 6 miles or 5 miles from that point.

Limitation of hours for travellers

61,784. If I have apprehended you rightly, you are in favour of opening one-third, or somewhere about one-third, of the licensed houses for the accommodation of the bona fide traveller?—My idea is that it would be desirable not to have nearly so many as that open.

61,785. A certain number at all events?—Yes.

61,786. Would not that number supply any reasonable requirements of the bona fide traveller, if they were open not the whole day, but say from 2 to 5 or whatever hour might be fixed?—Certainly I should be strongly in favour of that.

61,787. So that for the rest of the day the publicans would be at liberty to enjoy his Sunday holiday?—I should be strongly in favour of limiting the hours during which the bona fide traveller might be served to reasonable hours.

61,788. In the county of Wexford could you name a reasonable hour in the afternoon. I suppose it would be, say, from 1 o'clock?—I should say in the county of Wexford that it would be a reasonable limit to impose to allow the bona fide traveller to be supplied between the hours of 2 and 5.

61,789. And houses specially licensed for their accommodation?—Specially licensed for their accommodation.

61,790. Do you recognise that a great evil is caused by the bona fide traveller now, and that he impairs the operation of the Sunday Closing Act?—I do, decidedly. I believe it is very difficult for even well-intentioned publicans to discern altogether who is a bona fide traveller, and who is not.

61,791. I am not talking of the difficulty on the part of the publican, but of the fact of the bona fide traveller having a statutory right to demand refreshments. Does not that impair the operation of an Act which says all houses shall be closed on Sunday?—It does, decidedly.

61,792. Whether you have a 3 mile limit or a 6 mile limit, the abuse of the bona fide traveller denied, that will be the same. Whatever limit you have, 3 miles, 5 miles, or 7 miles, the bona fide traveller will always be a menace to the due administration of the Sunday Closing Act?—That is so, but the effect of the extension of the limit from three to six miles will be that you will have a much smaller number of bona fide travellers to deal with than you have under the 3 mile limit, because a number of men will proceed especially from town on foot, and from country districts into town on foot. Three miles is a short distance for a man to walk, and they will come in especially for the purpose of getting drink. I am aware that in England magistrates have held—at Nottingham, I think—that where men made a practice of leaving the town of Nottingham to proceed to beer shops just outside the 3 miles limit they were not entitled to be supplied because they were not bona fide travellers; they were

Mr. M. A. [illegible]

4 May '98.

Endorsement of convictions.

be *bona fide* travellers, should be [illegible]. I would look on it as unreasonable that a man who went with his family into the country on a day's holiday from a town or city should be debarred from procuring some reasonable refreshment if he was in the habit of taking it, but at the same time I regret that such a privilege as a *bona fide* traveller should exist. I should like to say, if you will permit me, that with reference to publicans' licences, and with reference to the records on the licences of publicans of convictions, the police in Ireland find such an extreme difficulty in procuring evidence, for the reason I have already stated of the unwillingness of people to come forward and proffer evidence, and in procuring convictions of publicans for breaches of the law, that I think in all cases where a publican is convicted for a breach of the law, a record on his licence should follow as a matter of course, even in a case where it may be proved to the satisfaction of the magistrates that such breach of the law occurred without the knowledge, connivance, or consent of the publican. There may be exceptional cases of respectable publicans where a young assistant, his son, or some one of that kind, without his knowledge or consent, may possibly break the law.

61,795. Every conviction should be recorded on the licence or kept in other record, but not necessarily three of those convictions entailing forfeiture?—Yes. I would make three convictions entail forfeiture, so long as it was quite clear to the magistrates hearing the case that the publican himself had cognisance of the breach of the law.

Forfeiture through endorsement.

61,796. Have you ever known three convictions endorsed on a licence and forfeiture resulting?—Yes.

61,797. Have you ever known it in practice?—Yes. A case has occurred in the county of Wexford within the past few months in the town of Gorey, which is at present the subject of litigation. The magistrates at Gorey have forfeited the licence there, but the case is at present being litigated on some technical grounds. The police applied to have the house closed, and proceeded against the publican for opening his house for the sale of drink after three convictions had been obtained against him.

61,798. Do I understand you to say there is an appeal on a point of law from the decision of the magistrates?—This occurred at Gorey, in the north of the county, in a district I do not quite know myself—I have simply read the case in the local papers; but in this case I think the publican had transferred, or sought to transfer his interest in the house to another member of his family.

61,799. And the question is whether it is a *bona fide* transfer or not?—Yes, some question of that kind arises, but on a matter of fact the police applied, and the magistrates at petty sessions sustained the objection in this case.

61,800. Evidently the attention directed to this case shows it is a very rare case?—It is a rare case.

61,801. You have never known any other case?—No, I think not in my experience. I have heard of other cases. I know of other cases that have occurred, but in my own experience I cannot speak of them. I know of houses in the country which have been closed in the past for that reason. I should like to make another suggestion with regard to the applications for publicans' licences. At the annual licensing sessions it has been the custom for people seeking a licence to bring forward an application, and when that application is defeated and refused at the annual licensing sessions they bring forward the same application the next sessions, and following sessions, and bring it forward year after year in the hope that on some occasion they may find the Bench more liberal in its views regarding licences than on others. I suggest that a man who brings forward an application for a licence which is refused should not be permitted to bring forward a similar application for reasonable period, say for three years after, unless under totally different conditions, such as in a case where the premises are held not suitable, and there has been a reconstruction of the premises or something to alter the conditions, but a man should not bring forward an application session after session for a licence that has been refused on one or two occasions. I wish to detail in particulars of a case of the description that came within my own knowledge, a case of a man who applied for a licence, and I believe this licence that I speak of comes under the category to which you have just been referring. I do not wish to speak with absolute

Repeated applications for a licence.

certainty, because I am not sure on the point, but I believe it to be the fact that the house was deprived of its licence on three convictions in the past. The owner of the house applied for a licence—the case to be practical that licence—and it was refused on that occasion. He then let the house on lease to a tenant with a covenant in the lease that in the event of the tenant succeeding in procuring a licence the rent of the premises should be increased by £1 annually. Since that time the tenant and the landlord combined have made every effort to procure a licence for the premises, and they applied on four different occasions; on each occasion, when the circumstances of the lease was spoken of by the intending publican and his solicitor, they have withdrawn their application.

61,802. At what interval have they applied?—Every year. There were two applications in the year 1893, they applied again in 1894, 1895, 1896 and 1897, and I presume it is extremely likely they will make a further application in the November of 1898. I wish to hand in a explanatory memorandum [illegible] that case.

61,803. (Mr. Young.) You said in the county of Wexford that you had several meetings for the closing of public-houses on Sundays and Saturdays [illegible] meeting I spoke of. I spoke of the town of Wexford only.

61,804. Was that a meeting got up by the inhabitants?—Yes. The meeting was presided over by the Roman Catholic Bishop of the Diocese of Ferns, and was attended by the Protestant Rector of Wexford, and by clergy of all denominations and the inhabitants generally.

61,805. I understood you, with regard to indictments of publicans, to say that you would not allow the young man in the shop or any person to be called as a witness except the police?—No, that is not my suggestion at all. I deprecate a proposal that the onus should be thrown on the publican of proving. A suggestion has been made by some people who are rather authorities on the subject, that in the event of a man being found drunk on licensed premises the onus should be thrown on the publican of proving that he was not supplied with drink there. I deprecate that method of dealing with the question, because I believe that, if adopted, that would lead to the perjury which, I regret to say, exists in other cases, because if you threw the onus on the publican of proving that the man was not supplied with drink on his premises, the temptation is great, in the case of a publican of low character, to swear that the man was not supplied on the premises, and to put his assistants in the box to swear that also.

61,806. From what source does the indictment come?—This is not an existing law. It is simply a suggestion which I say I do not approve of, because I say I believe it would lead to that state of affairs.

61,807. In the case of a man being drunk on the premises, where does the indictment originate?—As the law stands at present, with reference to a man being drunk on the premises, the police must prove the sale of drink to that man, and the difficulty arises in proving that.

61,808. It remains entirely with the police, I think?—Quite so.

61,809. Have you perfect confidence that the police will always do right?—Police are human, as well as anybody else; but taking the police force of Ireland as a whole, they are a very exemplary and well-conducted body of men.

61,810. I think your suggestion would place the whole importance of the indictment with the police?—No. My view is that the fact of a man being found to be on licensed premises for a certain period of time—

61,811. Found by whom?—Found by the police.

61,812. Exactly?—The fact of a man being found to be on licensed premises for a certain period of time, and being drunk, that should be sufficient to procure a conviction, because it would be the duty of the publican not to permit any drunken man to remain on the premises; and to my own knowledge some of the respectable publicans of the town of Wexford are in the habit, if a drunken man should enter their premises, of immediately sending for the police to remove him.

61,813. Do you leave the evidence for the conviction entirely in the hands of the police?—Certainly not.

61,814. Would you not allow other evidence to be brought up?—Most decidedly.

61,815. I understood you would not allow the young men in the place to be examined?—I should not be inclined to allow the young men in the place to give evidence. I should not be prepared to adopt a system which would permit the young men, serving as assistants on licensed premises, coming forward and tendering evidence with reference to a matter of fact whether the man was supplied with drink on the premises or not, because that is a point upon which it would be utterly impossible for the police to give evidence on the other side.

61,816. It is a matter of fact we want to ascertain, and if you leave it in the hands of the police alone, and do not take the evidence of the young men at all, how do you ascertain whether in fact or not the man was served?—I say it is the duty of every publican, it should be the duty of every publican, not to supply drink to a drunken man, and on the other hand it should be his duty not to allow any drunken man who may enter his premises in a condition of drunkenness to remain there. It is his duty to immediately eject that man from his premises or call in the police to do so; and failing his putting the man off his premises in a reasonable time, the fact of his failing to do so should found a conviction against him.

61,817. If you allow only the police to give evidence, and not the persons there who ought to know, surely you place too much reliance on one source of authority?—I think you misunderstand me. What I suggest is this: I have given you what my idea is with reference to the present course of procedure, but a proposal has been made, which I have stated I do not agree with, that the fact of a man being found drunk on the premises, even if he had only momentarily entered the premises at the moment, should throw on the publican the onus of proving that he did not get drunk there. I object to that, but I hold that the publican should be placed in such a position that it would be his duty to allow no drunken person to remain on his premises, and the fact of a man being on licensed premises for a certain length of time, and being there found drunk on the premises, the consequence would follow without further evidence that he got drunk on those premises, because it would be the duty of the publican to eject him from there if he entered against his will in a condition of drunkenness.

61,818. (Mr. [illegible].) Could you tell us whether the Sunday Closing Law, if I may use the expression, of the bishop of the diocese, or the legislative Sunday Closing Act, had the best effect?—The Sunday Closing Law of the bishop of the diocese, in my opinion, had the best effect with reference to the Roman Catholic population, but that did not apply to anyone except the Roman Catholic population, and in districts where the Roman Catholic population would not be in the great majority, as in the county of Wexford, it would not have the same beneficial effect.

county court judge in exceptional cases concerning a fine, I think there should be then an appeal to the judge of assize.

61,820. With regard to the limited number of 7-day licenses, to which you have referred, would you be in favour of dispensing not only the [illegible] condition, but a condition as to having bedroom accommodation?—Yes, with regard to any new licenses, but with regard to existing licenses it would create a difficulty.

61,821. I am speaking only of new licenses?—Decidedly. With regard to bedroom accommodation, I would suggest that nobody should get a license who did not have ample bedroom accommodation; and it should not be a dormant accommodation, to say that they have so many bedrooms and could provide them, but they should be bedrooms furnished, and in a condition for occupation.

61,822. With reference to the police, do you hold any view as to the desirability or otherwise of granting licenses to persons who have been members of the Irish constabulary [illegible] [illegible] to the granting of licenses to any ex-members of the constabulary force, not on the ground of the character of those men, but because I believe it would be in the public interest undesirable for that reason. There is a very salutary regulation at present in the Irish constabulary force, to the effect that a constable marrying in a town or district is removed from the district in which his own or his wife's relatives reside. He is not permitted to reside in that district, in order that nothing in the nature of favouritism should be shown by him to friends of his; and for the same reason I think it would be undesirable that any ex-constabulary man should hold publicans' licenses, because, whether the members of the constabulary would or would not favour them, the opinion in the public mind would be to the effect that they would be favoured; and in Ireland recently one of the judges of the High Court gave a very strong expression of opinion in the case of a magistrate in the county of Galway who sat on the bench during the hearing of a case with reference to [illegible]. He took no part in it, but he sat on the bench, and the judge commented strongly on his conduct, and stated that the Irish were a suspicious people, and that though his motive in the matter was no doubt perfectly bona fide, and that he did not influence the decision of the bench in any way, it was undesirable that the people should be led to suppose that justice could be tainted in any way, and for the same reason I think the members of the constabulary force should not be granted licenses.

61,823. The last question I have to ask you is simply this. From your experience as a magistrate, would you say with reference to the [illegible] clause that a large percentage of the crime of the country is due to drink, and believe that if it were not for drink our gaols would be practically empty. I am a visiting justice of Wexford Prison. My avenue gate is directly opposite the prison entrance, and as a matter of fact I am constantly within the prison. I am called upon by

Mr. [illegible]

anything of difficulties of that kind?—In the town of Wexford the question arose some time since. I was on the bench when it was adjudicated upon. A publican was charged with opening and keeping open for the sale of drink his licensed premises on Sunday during closing hours. The facts were that certain men, bona fide travellers, were found on the man's premises and he had the door leading into his premises left open, and he had not any one at the door to discern between bona fide travellers and members of the general public. We convicted that man on the ground that, having opened his premises, it was his duty to admit bona fide travellers, and only them, and he should have kept his door shut, and opened it on a knock or request for bona fide travellers to be admitted.

61,527. This publican complained that it was not always possible to keep the door shut any more than put one at a public meeting?—We held it was his duty to have an attendant on his door to prevent that, and that he did it at his own risk—that if he admitted anyone not a bona fide traveller, keeping his door open, he took on himself the risk of being convicted of an offence.

Perjury in licensing cases.

61,528. I had not an opportunity of asking Judge Carson yesterday a question, which he said I might ask him, but I might perhaps put it to you. Is it quite a part of the recognised duty sometimes of publicans' assistants to swear their employers through any charge? Is it part a condition, or term, of the wages paid?—As a matter of fact, very few cases of that description have come under my observation. The great majority of cases that have come under my observation are cases in which either a publican or a shebeen-keeper has been charged with selling drink. The publicans during closing hours, or the shebeen-keeper, with the sale of drink, and the witnesses who have been brought up in those cases, in my experience have been chiefly men found on the premises, and accused of being on the premises; and in cases of that kind I think it is very desirable and very efficacious—and I suggested some time since to my brother justices that it would be a desirable plan to adopt—at the beginning of cases of this description to have the witnesses on both sides out of court. We now have adopted the practice of putting the witnesses on both sides out of court, and the result is that men who come up to swear falsely with reference to the sale of drink to them, or the supply of drink at improper hours, do not have the advantage of hearing what has been sworn by the previous witnesses, and the discrepancies in the evidence are generally very striking.

61,529. I think you have cast the fact that the proportion of public-houses in Wexford to population is about one to 116?—The proportion of public-houses is greater. There are 84 public-houses in Wexford.

61,530. That would be about 1 to every 48 of the population?—Yes.

61,531. (*Viscount de Vesci.*) Is there a quarter sessions court held in the town of Wexford?—Yes.

No licensing court at Wexford.

61,532. You allege as a grievance that you have to go to New Ross on licensing business?—Yes. It is a grievance with reference to the town of Wexford.

61,533. Have you taken any steps to have the quarter sessions court in Wexford constituted a licensing court?—No steps have been taken, because the evil would go the other way. If the quarter sessions court were held at Wexford, applications from the town of New Ross, another important town, would be heard at Wexford.

61,534. Is there any reason why both courts should not be licensing courts?—I think it would be a decided advantage to have both courts licensing courts.

61,535. I think the Lord Lieutenant is the person who constitutes a licensing court, is he not?—Yes; but as the present arrangement stands the licensing court for the south of Wexford is held at New Ross, and for the north of Wexford is held at Enniscorthy. New Ross is on the borders of the county. The river Barrow only divides New Ross from the county of Kilkenny; and with reference to the county of Wexford, in the north of the county, 5,[illegible] acres are included in the district of Carnew, county Wicklow. That is one of the petty sessions districts in the south of the county of Wicklow, extends into the county of Wexford, and takes in 1,[illegible] acres in the district of Carnew, and a portion of the Newtownbarry district runs into the County Carlow.

61,536. You suggested that the licensing authority should be composed of the county court judge, the resident magistrate, and the magistrates of the petty sessions district in which the applicant resides?—In which the premises proposed to be licensed are situated.

Proposed licensing authority.

61,537. The magistrates you suggest would be those who reside in that petty sessions district, or attended the petty sessions court?—I should not confine the suggestion absolutely to be those who reside, because in one or two cases I know of, magistrates will sit in a petty sessions district they do not reside in. The reason of that has been that in some of the rural petty sessions districts in the county of Wexford there has been a difficulty in procuring a sufficient number of magistrates to attend petty sessions; and to remedy that state of affairs on the appointment of a new magistrate, he has been assigned to one of those petty sessions districts to strengthen the bench there, and he would not in that case reside there.

61,538. Without special permission he is not allowed to sit in a petty sessions district out of which he resides?—As a matter of fact a magistrate for the county of Wexford can sit at any petty sessions district in the county, and his decision in any case on which he adjudicates would be valid and binding; but it is contrary to custom, and what is considered proper in a magistrate to do, that he would run the risk of being deprived of his commission by doing so.

61,539. You suggested that an applicant who has been refused a licence should not be allowed to apply again for three years, but I think I understood you to say that where the cause for which he had been refused had been removed, then he might apply again?—Quite so. In case a man applied for a licence, and the cause for which he was refused was the unsuitability of his premises, he might reconstruct them.

61,540. Or in case of a diminution in the number of other licensed houses?—Quite so, in a case of that kind.

The witness withdrew.

[illegible] in connection with the [illegible] case—[illegible] the [illegible] of [illegible] which I should [illegible]. The Solicitor-General for Ireland made some reference to that case, and he was asked by one of the members of the Commission as to why it was not proceeded with. [illegible] I have been supplied with a letter of indemnity signed by two citizens of Dublin, one of whom has since died and the other is still living. [illegible] The Court of Queen's Bench granted a [illegible] [illegible] particularly the Irish Society for the Prevention of Intemperance, [illegible] the justices. The names of the four justices are here, but it is not necessary to mention them. I have the original letter of indemnity, indemnifying those gentlemen against all [illegible] and expense in the matter, even if the case should be carried to the House of Lords. [illegible]

[illegible] I think we have heard the Acts [illegible] which regulate the sale to children. Would you be in favour yourself of restoring the age of 16?—Yes. [illegible] The last Act has reduced the age from 16 to 13. I suppose they considered that boys and girls [illegible] [illegible] under 13 [illegible] they should not be allowed to enter a public-house for any purpose.

[illegible] I suppose it would complicate the law to say that [illegible] between 13 and 16 [illegible] "for consumption on the premises" were eliminated it would meet the case.

[illegible] I think it would complicate the law for the publican to interpret if he had to discriminate between 13 and 16. It would add to his difficulties, would it not?—I suppose it would in some way add to his difficulties.

[illegible] How would he know in one case whether a child was 13 and in the other 16? [illegible] a better way [illegible]

[illegible] I am only asking your opinion. The expression "consumption on" occurs in all the three Acts, I [illegible]

[illegible] How as to the minimum penalties in respect of the [illegible] against the Licensing Acts. Do you think they are too low?—I do. I think that the penalties for the prevention of the [illegible] are probably heavy enough, but it ought to be entirely revenue, plus [illegible] [illegible] I think, for instance, that a fine of [illegible] for selling to a drunken person or selling to a child under 13 is not adequate punishment to a publican, and I think it would be [illegible] [illegible] substantial minimum sum should be fixed, and the maximum.

[illegible] With reference to the sale of drink to children, would you see any other amendment of the law to be desirable in the way of knowingly allowing?—Yes. The Act of the [illegible] Act, the last Act on the subject—says: "Every holder of a licence, who knowingly sells, or allows any person to sell, any description of intoxicating liquors to "subsequent offence." In the Act of [illegible] I think the penalty for the third offence was [illegible], but here they have reduced it to [illegible] forty shillings, and, of course, [illegible], for any subsequent offence.

[illegible] With reference to the words "knowingly" and "allow," you think it would be doubtful whether [illegible] would make the [illegible] liable?—I do. I think it has been ruled by the courts in England that, to convict [illegible] on the part of the licensee, and allowing to sell, or permitting to sell, would, I think, be interpreted by the courts in the same way.

[illegible] We have had a good deal of evidence about the [illegible] of the [illegible] and the [illegible], in the view of [illegible], to separate the trades. What is your opinion upon that?—I think that we ought to [illegible] as much as possible from temptation. I believe that many persons, and in fact, I know from my own personal knowledge from intimate acquaintance with many, that they go into the family grocer's to purchase groceries, and they drink before they come out [illegible] [illegible] it would be an advantage, that when a person went into a public-house he should know where he was going to [illegible] great improvement.

[illegible] Are there many licensed grocers who have the right of selling off only in Dublin?—There are a few, but I do not altogether object to the spirit grocers having the right to sell off, provided that they are not allowed to sell anything on draught or in an open vessel. I think generally the trade in Dublin is combined. There are, of course, a good many gin palaces.

[illegible] I am talking of the ordinary grocer who gets a licence to sell off only. Are there many of them in Dublin who may not sell for consumption on the premises?—I do not think that there are many.

[illegible] I am not talking of what you call rightly the publican grocer, but the grocer with a shop to sell off?—I do not think there are many of that class.

[illegible] Speaking generally of the public-houses in Dublin, what do you think as to their number? Are they excessive?—I think that we have at least three or four times too many public-houses in Dublin. I take, for instance, Thom's Directory, which is looked upon as a very good authority in this matter, and if you take Great Britain Street, a street that I am very well acquainted with, according to Thom's Directory there are in the street [illegible] houses and of these [illegible] houses are licensed, so that would be [illegible] over one in every [illegible] houses.

[illegible] What would be the number of persons in a house?—The houses are let in tenements largely in that street [illegible], and probably there would be on an average, I should say, eight persons to a house.

[illegible] Not more than eight in a house?—I do not think so—[illegible] because the under parts of the houses are generally shops and it is not [illegible] the upper parts are let in tenements [illegible] Great Britain Street is [illegible] largely as other streets.

[illegible] You have one public-house to every [illegible] in that particular street?—Yes. Then I will take Dorset Street. I do not take these streets because they have more public-houses in them than other streets, but merely because where I do business is Rutland Square, and these streets I have named are the boundaries of the square. In Dorset Street there are [illegible] houses, and of these [illegible] are licensed houses, or more than one in [illegible]. The houses in this street are let in weekly tenements also. Then if I take Capel Street it contains [illegible] houses, of which [illegible] are licensed houses, or more than one in [illegible]. I should mention that amongst these licensed houses I have included a place called the Trades General Insurance, as they have a large bar there. Of course they call that the Trades General Club, but actually it is a genuine public-house, but of course for the trades that are members of the club there.

Mr. [illegible] — 4 May '[illegible] — Penalties [illegible] — [illegible] trade in public-houses. — Excessive number of licensed houses in Dublin.

63,[illegible]. Then take Belfast?—Belfast had 1,1[illegible] licensed houses, and according to what I suggest it would have 41[illegible].

63,[illegible]. Then take Waterford?—Waterford has [illegible], and according to my plan it would have 44. Then Clonmel has 1[illegible] licensed houses, and allowing one to each 100 families it would have [illegible].

63,[illegible]. I suppose as a matter of fact in fixing the Poor Law valuation, the licence is never taken into

61,895. Then am I right in saying that the total number of people who alighted from the tramcar was 300, and of these 150 the great majority went into the public-house?—The great majority; in fact, I should say there were 150 of them.

61,896. What time did it take to get from where the tram started to Clontarf?—About 12 minutes, if so much, scarcely 12.

61,897. Did you see in the case of any of these people who you say were not bonâ fide travellers, any test imposed on them?—There was a person that stood at the door, and every one that came to the door he said something to them; what he said to them I do not know, but I did not see any person refused admission. I spoke to the head constable, and he told me that that Sunday was nothing exceptional, that it was the same every Sunday of the year.

61,898. Can you speak of any houses advertising the fact that they are just at the limit of three miles?—Yes, there is one house known in Dublin as "Nancy Hand's." The proprietress was a Nancy Hand. It has since passed into other hands, and the name is Nolan. I have a cutting here from the "Evening Herald" of the 23rd January 1898, and the particulars run as follows:—"Nancy Hand's, Phœnix Park, open for bonâ fide travellers on Sundays, all drinks of the best quality; don't forget 'The original Hole in the Wall'; cyclists well catered for." Then he signs his name. I may state I visited that place last Sunday week in order to see what the catering he had was. I could get nothing in the place except whisky or porter, or intoxicating drink. He had mineral waters. I asked for tea or coffee, but he had none. He said he kept none, but he intended to erect a place to supply it.

61,899. The notice that at the advertisement put do you object to, and the limit of three miles [illegible] to the terms of it?—In the first place I think it is a proof that what they want people to go there for is not as bonâ fide travellers but to drink. The great inducement there is "All drinks of the best quality," and the only drink you get when you go is whisky or porter. Tea should be obtainable as well as the other.

61,900. The legislature has thought to say that a three-mile traveller is a bonâ fide traveller, with some conditions attached. What is to prevent the publican putting in an advertisement such as you have described if you extend the limit to seven miles?—There is nothing to prevent them doing it, but it would not be so likely to be availed of merely to get a glass to the house than a [illegible] three miles.

61,901. The point of your objection is that they ought, if they are bonâ fide travellers' accommodation houses, to sell something more than mere drink?—Yes, that is mainly my point.

61,902. Would you be in favour of closing the public-houses during the entire day on Sunday throughout Ireland?—Yes, the entire day. Of course from what I say at the end of my evidence, in my suggestions it will be found that I do you wish to deprive bonâ fide travellers or [illegible] of legitimate refreshment. As a bonâ fide traveller myself I should like to get refreshment, but I am sorry to think, and in fact I know it from having tried it, that it is very difficult for anyone as a traveller of temperance to get refreshments in those parts of Ireland on Sunday in anything like a reasonable way. Public-houses do not supply legitimate refreshment other than drink, and, of course as of intoxicating drink is the only refreshment a bonâ fide traveller is to get.

61,903. They should set up in their own range of licensed victuallers, and sell viands as well as drink?—I think so.

61,904. Having closed the houses all through Ireland on the Sunday, would you allow a bonâ fide traveller, assuming him to be such, to knock up a publican at any hour for the purpose of obtaining refreshment?—No, I would not. I do not think that would be necessary. The railway companies of course provide for their stations, and I think I would allow them able to open his house for the accommodation of bonâ fide travellers during three, four, or so many specified hours of the day?—No, I would not say that. I would say, perhaps, from 12 o'clock in the day, until, perhaps, 7 in the evening, a bonâ fide traveller should be admitted to obtain refreshment, but there that refreshment should not be drink only.

61,905. I am not dealing at the hours during which the houses should be opened for bonâ fide travellers. Would not the publicans themselves rather like a restriction of hours during which the house should be open, rather than be kept open the whole day?—I think there is a great deal to be said from that point of view, but the publicans themselves at all events are opposed to Sunday closing, and I gather from that that as they are opposed to Sunday closing, they would be anxious to keep open. I think if they are anxious to keep open, though the law would make them close, they should be made to attend to the requirements of the public.

61,906. You would not allow any houses, supposing Sunday closing prevailed all over Ireland, to be open for the reception of bonâ fide travellers?—No, I should not. I would only allow properly constituted refreshment houses to be opened.

61,907. Under the licensing magistrates, or the licensing authority, whatever it might be?—Yes.

61,908. I think you have already spoken about what you consider the undue extension of the Dublin Metropolitan Police District with reference to the exemption from Sunday closing?—Yes, I think that even supposing that Sunday closing be not made compulsory all over Ireland, and that Dublin still continues one of the exempted places, the right to open any from 2 to 5, instead of from 2 to 7, should only be allowed to extend to the municipal district; and I would not go further on the south and south-west of Dublin than to the north; that is, the townships should be excluded altogether.

61,909. Do you wish to hand in a memorial with reference to that subject?—Yes.

61,910. Will you state shortly by whom that memorial was signed?—I have a memorial signed by 13 Roman Catholic Bishops of Ireland; by 13 Protestant Bishops; by the Moderator of the General Assembly, the Vice President of the Methodist Conference; by 15 of the nobility; 33 Members of Parliament; 1,[illegible] clergymen; 1,[illegible] magistrates; [illegible] medical doctors; [illegible] poor-law guardians and town commissioners; and 1,[illegible] merchants and employers, making a total of [illegible].

61,911. In favour of what specific thing?—In favour of Saturday early closing over the whole of Ireland and entire Sunday closing.

61,912. I suppose temperance and religious bodies have passed similar resolutions?—They have. The memorial is also signed on behalf of 87 large public meetings, and temperance and religious bodies representing thousands of people.

61,913. As to occasional licences?—With reference to occasional licences, I think the wording of the statute is worthy of Mr. Gilbert [illegible]. The 26th and 27th Vict. cap. 33, section 12, empowers the Inland Revenue Authority, wherever they should consider it conducive to public convenience, comfort, and order, and with the consent in writing of two justices of the peace, and so on, to grant an occasional licence. Well, I think granting a licence for the sale of intoxicating drink at an Irish fair is just as likely to contribute to order as sanctioning a handful of lawyers amongst school boys would be to contribute to order in a school. The very idea of coming to the conclusion that giving drink to our people at fairs and markets would contribute to order seems to me to show that whoever frames the [illegible] must either be entirely ignorant of our people or without a conscience.

61,914. The statute required the consent in writing, did it not, of two justices of the peace?—It is one justice now. That section I have read will require the consent in writing of two justices.

Mr. J. Gee.

4 May '[illegible]

Licence for a total abstinence fête.

[illegible], in my humble judgment, is very much abused by the magistrates.

61,918. Have you known cases where in the case of a total abstinence excursion an occasional licence has been given for sale on the ground where they themselves were advocating the principles of total abstinence?—Yes. The Dublin Coffee Palace, which was got up by the Dublin Total Abstinence Society, gave an excursion some years ago to Drumree, in the county Meath. When they arrived at their destination they found a public-house almost in full swing outside the grounds on the road. The hon. secretary, Mr. Wilson Farr, wrote a letter to the papers the following day, and I have a copy of the letter if the commission wish to hear it. He remonstrated with the police, but they told him they could not interfere; that the publican had got an occasional licence from a magistrate, and they had looked at the licence and did not even know the magistrate who signed it.

61,919. Has any further abuse sprung up of not only having one local justice to sign, but that one justice not residing in the petty sessional division where the application is made?—Yes, and Dublin Castle found it necessary, in the year 1874, to issue a letter to all the magistrates of Ireland with reference to that very practice. This letter appears in Mr. Sergeant's book, which is a book on the licensing laws specially prepared for Irish solicitors, and if you will allow me I will read the letter.

Suggested reform.

61,920. Perhaps you will tell us what it is, or read the pertinent part of the letter?—The point of it is this, that it had come to the knowledge of the authorities that magistrates not acting within petty sessional districts were in the habit of granting licences outside their own districts, and they were forbidden to do it in future. That is the substance of the letter.

61,921. Do you think it would be an improvement to go back to the two justices and enact that they should sit in a public court?—Yes, I think that the magistrates in a petty sessions should be applied to for these occasional licences. Of course there might be some circumstances arise in some districts where this would be very inconvenient, and probably the resident magistrate, or it might be the county inspector, might then be empowered in those cases to grant them.

Suggested classification of licences.

61,922. I am now coming to your suggestions, and first of all you would divide the licenses into classes?—I would. At the present time there are very many licenses, some of which, of course, I would not at all interfere with, but I would divide the retail licenses into five different classes.

Classification.

61,923. Will you state them?—First, the public-house licenses for the sale of spirits and other alcoholic liquors. All these licenses I would make six-day licenses only, and I would make it imperative on the licensee to have [illegible] food—for sale, but I would allow him to sell no groceries, tea or sugar, or anything of that sort—nothing but these drinks and prepared or cooked food.

61,924. Do you think you could bring about that change in the existing mode of dealing in Dublin?—I think it would be possible to do it. No doubt it would cause some considerable inconvenience, but I think it would be possible to do it.

61,925. Then secondly, you would have a refreshment house license?—Yes. I do not mean the refreshment house as at present constituted by Act of Parliament, but I would give a refreshment house license. I would not allow the licensee to have a public bar, but simply a supply bar. Any persons taking their dinner or refreshments in the place might require drink, and I would allow them to be supplied from that bar, but I would not allow drink to be sold there as a beverage except with food.

61,926. Would you give these seven-day licenses?—A certain number of them in each district I would allow a seven-day license to suit the requirements of the bona fide traveller. Then with regard to beer licenses, I think it would be a good thing if we could introduce the drinking of beer, instead of the drinking of whisky into Ireland, and with that object properly constituted and decently got up houses at a certain valuation. I would allow a beer-house license, but not to sell

[illegible]

The witness withdrew.

Adjourned for a short time.

The Lord Wimborne in the Chair.

Dr J. E. Kenny called in and examined.

Dr. J. E. Kenny. [illegible]

41,940. (*Lord Wimborne.*) You are, I believe, the Coroner for the city of Dublin?—Yes. I have occupied that position for [illegible] years next July.

41,941. Previously to that what were you?—I had occupied the position of dispensary medical officer for [illegible] years on the North Quay. That was my earliest appointment; and subsequent to that I was visiting [illegible] to the North Dublin Union, and finally became the Coroner. These positions were all more or less [illegible] one to the other.

41,942. In those capacities, I suppose, you became [illegible] acquainted with the habitations of the people?—Very intimately, as [illegible] nobody else [illegible] would do. The dispensary doctor [illegible] of the family life. He [illegible] at all times and in all [illegible] places.

41,943. What was the class which your attention was [illegible] specially directed to?—The working class, especially the poorly paid amongst the working class. Artisans very frequently belonged to the class, and would not come under my supervision [illegible], but where the dispensary officer would have to attend [illegible] in the case of persons who do not belong to a class that would earn at least [illegible] a week.

41,944. You also, I think, sat for [illegible] years as a Member of Parliament?—I was a Member of Parliament [illegible] years. I sat for the College Green Division of the City of Dublin, which includes my old dispensary district and the North Union Workhouse.

[illegible]

Dr. J. E. Kenny. 4 May '98

which I refer. That drives them into the public-house for social intercourse with their fellows, that being the only place where there is anything like warmth or comfort, where they can sit at night in a climate like ours. If a man wants to meet his fellows he cannot invite them to his room, and the only place he can go to is the public-house.

Conduct of public-houses.

61,857. What is your opinion from your experience of the way in which the public-houses are conducted?—I think they are very well conducted. I think those that are ill-conducted form an exceedingly small percentage of the whole. I think the publican's interest is distinctly, as far as I can observe, to conduct his house well. Great evils fall upon him if he does not, but they seem to me to be very well conducted taking all in all.

Workmen's clubs.

61,858. Then I will pass on to the question of workmen's clubs?—Until recent years there was very little done in the way of workmen's clubs in Dublin. There are a couple of old-established workmen's clubs which are [illegible] in the working classes. There is one on Wellington Quay called the Dublin Working Men's Club, and another in Capel Street, which is practically the Trades Hall. These are tolerably old institutions, and well conducted, and they do a great deal of good; but six or seven years ago a wave of bogus clubs seemed to come over the city, and they did incalculable evil. They were not clubs in any true sense of the word. They were got up merely by persons who could scrape a few pounds together, and who got a few friends into a room, called it a club, asked their friends to join as members, generally without any payment whatever, but if there was any payment it was quite a small one. Then on and after the first time, and they introduced universally their friends without any club regulations into these places, and made them simply illicit public-houses. They became illicit public-houses in the worst sense.

Results of drinking in clubs.

61,859. Do you know of serious cases that have resulted from drinking in these clubs?—I do. In 1893, I think it was, my attention was first directed to them in a case which came before me officially. It was the case of a man found hanging in his room. The evidence showed that he hanged himself while suffering either from excessive drinking or delirium tremens. I could not make out exactly where he had got the drink, but the evidence in that case came out quite accidentally. The poor widow said that he had gone to Mr. [illegible]'s public-house, in the neighbourhood, and was refused drink there, and had gone to another and been refused, and then she said he went to the club and got drink there. Then I asked where the club was, and I found it was down a blind alley, in a most miserable and dilapidated dwelling, and it consisted of a room or two rooms, one off the other, and there was no restriction whatever for admission to it. She described having been there on a Sunday often, and said that she had seen the hall full of people, women and children, with cans in their hands, waiting to get served in their turns with porter or whatever drink they wanted. Then I got other witnesses in my court who proved to me that they had been admitted into this club, without any restriction whatever, that simply a friend went there, and they went in, and in most cases the friend was not a member, but if he was he had not taken any steps to, but walked in to drink with him, and they could drink there as long as they pleased.

Bogus clubs stamped out in Dublin.

61,860. Did you direct the attention of the police to this club?—I did, and immediately proceedings followed, and then the whole matter was enquired into, and I think latterly there are very few bogus clubs in Dublin. I think they have been stamped out very largely.

61,861. You think there are very few now existing?—I think very few, and carried on necessarily now in such a way as not to attract the attention of the authorities to them. I regarded them as really flaunting the authorities in the way they carried on their business, and they did not seem to care. They took no precautions apparently. Now, if they exist, they must take precautions, and not flaunt the police officers, but there are no prosecutions going on at the present moment. At least I do not hear of them.

61,862. Do you think that the present power of the police is sufficient to deal with these bogus clubs?—I think quite sufficient.

61,863. (Mr. Cokey.) What was the nature of the prosecution. Was it prosecuted as a shebeen?—For the illicit sale of drink. I forget the terms of the prosecution.

61,864. Why do you call it a club, it was simply a shebeen?—They called it a club. They called it the Denmark Street Club. It was in an alley off Denmark Street. Denmark Street is a dilapidated street, and this was a dilapidated alley, and I think it was called the Denmark Street Club.

61,865. It was purely a bogus club?—Yes.

61,866. And immediately on prosecution it collapsed?—It collapsed completely. There was no defence.

61,867. Have these clubs disappeared from Dublin?—Very largely.

61,868. They are easily dealt with if the police are vigorous?—They are, very easily. I believe there is power for the police to deal with them at present. I am very jealous of affording more power to the police. Mr. Field and I had a Bill when I was in the House, with reference to clubs, for the purpose of generally establishing workmen's clubs, to try and suppress at once the evils which flow from bogus clubs, that is to say, to encourage the formation of workmen's clubs, but destroy the possibility of a bogus club. We never got it to a second reading, of course.

Dr. J. E. Kenny.

Is closing public-houses.

61,869. (Lord Windsor.) Do you think it would encourage the respectability of the inhabitants, taking Dublin from your experience, if the public-houses were confined to the best conducted?—I think any ill-conducted public-house is a very great evil and should not be allowed to exist, and a public-house, as I take it, is that: it is a house of entertainment conducted, and must necessarily be conducted, under certain restrictions; those restrictions are very good restrictions, and necessary. I say, then if the conditions are not fulfilled, I think the public-house should be closed, because then I think it would become an evil, which I do not think it is now.

Coroner's cases due to drink.

61,870. Then within your experience as Coroner, do you think that a large proportion of the deaths coming under your cognisance are directly due to drink?—No. A percentage of them are, undoubtedly. I have kept, not officially but for my own instruction, and for my hereafter, registers of my own and I have gone over these registers, and I find that I have held since I was appointed coroner, 1,788 inquests, and I have dispensed with 1,000 other cases besides, though I did not think inquests necessary. Out of these cases in which I held the inquests, I found 34 cases in which the death was distinctly attributable to drink, and six in which the evidence was doubtful but leaned distinctly to the side of drink being the cause. I would like to define what I mean by that. I am speaking now, you will understand, not of the verdicts. Juries do not like, when they can help it, to append to their verdicts that drink was the cause of death. They think it casts a slur on the dead, and on the relatives. Whenever they can avoid it they do so, but with reference to the verdicts returned I would not be at liberty, as coroner, to put in drink on the verdict, but in my own mind of the cases where I believed drink was the cause, though the jury might not have found a verdict that drink was the cause, I have included every case in which the evidence showed that. For instance, such a case as this: a man in charge of a horse and cart, it is proved he had taken drink and he falls off the cart, and the wheel goes over him, and he is carried into the hospital dead; or a woman goes to bed who is known to have been drinking the night before, and the child is found smothered in the bed beside her in the morning. These, in my opinion, are deaths directly due to drink, and I include these cases, and the number is what I tell you. There are only 34 in which it was distinctly proved that drink was the cause in that sense, and six which, although doubtful, I think ought also to be included.

61,871. Were you able to trace in any case of those cases specially where the drink came from?—I made every endeavour to do so in all cases, and I shall continue to do so, but I have never been able to satisfactorily find out. It has been an exceedingly difficult thing to do. The witnesses you have to deal with are very shifty. They are generally related with the [illegible] themselves, and they will not give their friends away, and I have found it impossible to fix what I call the guilt—for I think it is a very guilty act to give drink to a man under the influence of drink—I have never been able to fix one case in a legal sense. I have had

Dr. J. F. Kenny.

strong suspicions of certain public-houses that the man had got drink there when under the influence of drink, but I have never been able to fix a single case in which it was brought home so that you could found a prosecution on it.

41,972. Not drink served by the publican?—I have never been able to prove that in one case a drunken man, or a man under the influence of drink a little short of drunkenness, was given drink in any of these cases by a publican. I have never been able to do that, though I have had my suspicions of a house from time to time, but not a very large number.

Early closing on Saturdays.

41,973. I do not want to pass over anything of importance, but I will come now to the suggested earlier closing of public-houses on Saturday night?—I do not think that that will meet the evil of drink at all; the public-houses are open from seven in the morning till eleven at night for six days a week, and from two to seven on Sundays, that is 104 hours. Now, assuming that the evil of drink arises from the existence of public-houses it seems to me a ridiculous and inadequate remedy to curtail them two hours on Saturdays and Sundays, that is to cut four hours off 104 hours. As regards the earlier closing on Saturday I am aware there is a reason given why they should be closed (but so far as Dublin is concerned it does not seem to me to apply)—that is, the payment of wages. Wages are not paid by the large employers, generally speaking, on Saturdays. They are paid mostly on Fridays. It is true that a good number of small employers, that is persons who have a few employees, will pay on Saturday, but if so they are paid early in the day, and not late at night on Saturday. Therefore I do not think that what is alleged to be the reason why the public-houses should be closed on Saturdays more than any other really applies, inasmuch as wages are not generally paid on that day; but as to the adequacy of the remedy whether wages are paid on that day or not, if the evil arises from the public-houses then it is an absolutely inadequate and a ridiculous remedy.

Sunday closing.

41,974. Then with reference to Sunday closing?—I am totally opposed to Sunday closing. I think seeing the conditions of life of the poor to which I have referred, and that this refers as well to people of a better class than mere labourers, the artisans themselves, and even the small shop-keeping class, it would be a hard thing for them if they wished to get drink on Sunday, that they should not be allowed to get it; and whether they have three hours or five hours in which to do it I do not think it makes the smallest difference. A person who wants to drink will drink as much in three hours as if the sale were spread over five hours if he has the predisposition to do it.

The bona fide traveller.

41,975. Then with regard to the bona fide traveller?—I have been also puzzled to know where he comes from. It seems to me an absolute absurdity—the bona fide traveller. It seems to me absurd to call a person who goes into the country to take a walk a bona fide traveller. I think the name ought to be done away with and that he ought to be called an excursionist. A man who takes a little excursion in the country ought to be allowed to get refreshment if he wants it.

41,976. Would you be inclined to extend the present limit?—I am rather disposed to extend the limit a little, but viewing it from that point of view I do not hold any very strong opinion on it. If a man goes three or four miles in the country he wants refreshment as much as if he went five or six miles, and it is exceedingly difficult to draw the line, but he ought not to be called a traveller at all.

41,977. (Mr. Quinn.) Would not that logically take you to unrestricted Sunday sale?—Certainly. I always face up to the logical consequences, and I think it does bring it to that, to an unrestricted sale. I am referring to large centres of population. It is not necessary in the country.

41,978. Does not that logically lead you to the opening of public-houses on Sunday for something like the same number of hours as upon week-days?—Not necessarily to keep them open. You get it by knocking and declaring yourself an excursionist. You need not keep the public-house open at all. That places them in the neighbourhood if you open the public-house.

41,979. You still keep the bona fide traveller restriction?—Yes, but under what is the real name for it. It is the name giving a name that does not attach to it at all.

Dr. J. F. Kenny.

8 May '98.

Prosecutions of bona fide travellers.

41,980. (Lord Windsor.) With reference to the prosecution of the bona fide traveller?—I have no personal knowledge, but I have seen in newspaper reports of cases, etc., as I have understood them, they have conveyed the impression to my mind, that it has always been the publican who has been prosecuted, but in very few cases the bona fide traveller, or the gentleman who signs out not to be a bona fide traveller, and who has given a false information. I think it is throwing too much on the publican to say to him, "You must be cognisant that A. B. lives three miles from you," and if A. B. comes and says "I do live more than three miles from you." Under that clause, as I understand it at present, he has to know that that is an untruth, and that the man lives only two and three-quarter miles away, and you expect the publican to know that. The man making the representation is the party I would prosecute, and I would throw the onus of proof on his shoulders to show that the publican knew who he was.

Remedies for excessive drinking. 1. Better housing.

41,981. I come now to the remedies you suggest for excessive drinking. Perhaps you will kindly take them in the order you have given them in your précis?—I have spoken of Dublin as to the dwellings of the poor being the main cause of drinking in that city. I will mention this, that if I lived under the conditions in which I know the poor of the city of Dublin live, and such large numbers of them—in fact a good proportion of the city of Dublin live under the conditions I referred to—I am very much afraid, though I have never cared for alcohol, that I should consume something very like a tipple before the end of my life. Improving the dwellings of the poor would be my first remedy. But there is beyond that the question of education. Compulsory education ought to be enforced in Dublin;

2. Compulsory education.

it is not enforced there, and a large number of the younger generation is growing up without instruction, and so far as one can predict their future it must be a miserably prospective. They are growing up the street-corner boys and prostitutes, a great number of them, and they are, occasionally employed by their parents in some trivial employments in the streets, but in reality they are, whereas the Compulsory Education Act would clear them off from the streets and give them a chance. I do not believe that reading and writing will do everything, but it will give them a chance in life. These creatures have no chance in life because they have not the first rudiments of gaining a livelihood, and I would give them a chance in that way. If it does not do everything—and I am perfectly aware it does not—it will go a considerable way in that direction. That is the first thing I would recommend, that is to say, a very rigid enforcement of the Compulsory Education Act. The Act of 1892 is so imperfectly framed, that the Corporation—they are not to blame for this—have never been able to put it into execution, because they have no means under the Act of paying the inspectors. The Act was very badly drawn, so that it failed in Dublin, and an Act is wanted immediately to amend it in that particular, so as to make it operative.

41,982. It is not the fault, in your opinion, of the authorities, but of the Act itself?—I think not. They were very willing and actually went ahead to take the first steps for appointing a school committee; but when they came to see how they would carry out the Act there was nothing in it to enable them to levy a rate. I have a very strong opinion on that. That is the first thing to be done. The next in order would be the

3. Formation of real workman's clubs.

formation of real workmen's clubs. My point is that if the public-house is an evil it is an evil because it has no competitor, and you want to have something in competition; one of the things would be bona fide workmen's clubs under proper regulations, and with such powers of visiting on the part of the police as might be deemed just under the circumstances without interfering with the liberty of the subject, or without having any open privileges that might be misused. I do not say the police would misuse them, but they ought to be of that character that they could not be misused.

41,983. That would include all clubs, I suppose, not only working men's clubs?—Yes, whatever regulations you make for workmen's clubs, you must make general for every club. The next, I think, in order is this: There

4. Libraries, reading-rooms, &c.

are three or four libraries in Dublin, but they do not at all meet the great want. I think there ought to be an extension of reading-rooms and lecture-rooms, and I am very strong on that subject, that in a climate like ours, and it applies as much to England as to Ireland, except that we have more rain with us, we have no places of resort whatever on a rainy night. But the [illegible] as [illegible] to get some [illegible] or [illegible] after a day's work, and he has no place at present. Even if he [illegible] a club it would not answer the purpose in summer weather. There are no covered spaces in the nature of winter gardens, not necessarily very elaborate winter gardens, but I suppose they might be originally a public square which might be covered in or roofed over and have open sides to it, and in that coffee stands, and so on, might be erected for those who liked to use them. Then they could meet each other in the fresh air and under cover from the weather. On a greater number of nights with us there is more or less rain. There are more wet nights than dry nights, and on a wet night a man is confined either to his room with his family about him, or he gravitates into the public-house. If he has no club he must go to a public-house or must stay at home. I hold a strong opinion on this, that the local body ought, under the Local Government Act, to have power to provide such places as those.

41,[illegible]. I suppose that would be a municipal thing paid for out of the rates?—Certainly. I would have no objection to private [illegible] doing it, but if private enterprise does not do it or private charity, it ought to be the duty of the community to do it. I have spoken of the [illegible] dwellings, but there is one point I have not mentioned, and that is that it ought not to be possible under the law for a tenement to be let without provision for the separation of the sexes. In most of these tenement dwellings to which I refer there is no possibility of it. You have a man and his wife and growing daughters and sons, and there is no possibility of the separation of the sexes in those dwellings. No tenement ought to be let which has not provision for that. I have seen it carried out by a private individual in Dublin, and he did it well, and told me he made money out of it. I saw in my old dispensary district one side of a [illegible] street in which a gentleman who bought more than merely to drag the rent out of his tenements, set about it and has, even with the poor facilities at his disposal, made exceedingly comfortable [illegible] dwellings out of those houses, in which he did make a provision (so far as it is in [illegible]) for the separation of the sexes. He simply, where he [illegible] a single room, [illegible] off an angle of it and made a separate room of it, and had other improvements which added greatly to the comfort of the tenants. He told me he never had one vacant, and practically could get what rent he liked for them, but he never asked more than a reasonable rent. This is the only case I know in which that has been done, and it was [illegible] successful and paid him very well. Then with regard to public-houses as they exist at present, I remember in my boyhood's days there was no standing-up bars, which is an innovation, and I think a recent importation rather in imitation of the American system. The old places where you could go in and sit down and talk and chat, did not lead I think to drinking so much as standing-up bars,—that is to excessive drinking. A man who stands at a bar and knows that his place is to be taken up by somebody else is inclined to take too many drinks one on top of another. I think publicans ought to be encouraged to give refreshments other than alcoholic drinks, in fact I go so far as to say that they ought to be made to afford facilities for tea and coffee and for light refreshment as well as alcoholic drink.

41,[illegible]. And make their premises suitable for that?—Yes; and also to have simple games. I look to what anyone's experience is, who has travelled a little on the Continent. You go into a café in Paris or Brussels, and you see men sitting down in these cafés—they are nothing but public-houses—and they can get tea and coffee, and play dominoes and draughts, and sit there, and you seldom see a man under the influence of drink.

41,[illegible]. Generally speaking, in your opinion, am I right in saying that it is more important to look after the [illegible] of the premises, and the manner in which those premises are conducted than to the question of curtailing the hours?—Yes, far more. I think it is far more important to see they are suitable and carried out properly, with restrictions to be carried into effect, than to curtail the hours. I do not think the number of hours is the evil. I may say, generally speaking, I have a great objection to long hours, but they apply as much to [illegible] in any other way as to publicans. I do not like to see [illegible] worked as hard as a man is who is 16 hours on his legs at work, but that applies not merely to the publican but to provision dealers, because the provision dealer is open as late as the publican and later. On Saturday night in Dublin, small provision dealers are open till 1 o'clock.

41,[illegible]. (*Mr. Cowan.*) Do I rightly summarise your view about the earlier closing of public-houses in three or four words, that as to the suggested earlier closing of public-houses on Saturday, admitting for the sake of argument that they are the great evil alleged, you think it absurd to say that the curtailment of the hours by two would by any means be an efficient means of coping with the evil?—I do.

41,[illegible]. You do not think that drinking resulting in drunkenness takes place within those two hours on Saturday nights?—I do not think it does. Any persons who are paid their wages on Saturday are paid earlier in the day, and all the working classes have a half-holiday. The drinking does not commence at all late at night in those places.

41,[illegible]. But it goes on till late at night?—That is by a different class. In my opinion, those who drink late in public-houses on Saturday nights are not the working men but the clerks in small employment who do not belong to either. I believe they belong to a different class.

41,[illegible]. Do you not think the amount of drinking in the last two hours is very large by those who begin drinking earlier in the afternoon and get under the influence of drink and remain in the public-houses?—I do not think so at all. I do not think a man ought remain that number of hours in a public-house. I do not think he would be permitted to.

41,[illegible]. He would be permitted to remain there as long as he had money to spend?—I do not think so, not in a respectable house.

41,[illegible]. (*Mr. Younger.*) Provided he was sober?—Yes, he must be sober. If he was drinking from two o'clock or from three or four o'clock till seven or eight o'clock in the evening he is not likely to be sober at the end of that period.

41,[illegible]. (*Mr. Cosier.*) Do not you think there is more drunkenness on Saturday in Ireland than on any other day?—I do not think so. I have heard statistics cited, but I do not know myself of my own knowledge.

41,[illegible]. You attach great importance to statistics of a public nature which are properly taken?—I do, but statistics do not tell you everything.

41,[illegible]. Have you seen a return that was given to the Select Committee on the Sunday Closing Acts (Ireland) in 1888?—I am not acquainted with it myself.

41,[illegible]. You may take these figures as correct. They were furnished by the Royal Irish Constabulary Office in Dublin Castle. This is "A return showing the "number of arrests on each day of the week for "drunkenness or drunkenness combined with any "other offence, and the number of convictions, in the "under-mentioned years." It begins with 1874, and goes on till 1887. I will give you the figures for 1887 day by day for all Ireland, with the exception of the town of Belfast and the cities of Cork, Limerick, and Waterford, and the Dublin Metropolitan District. On Sunday there were 1,[illegible] during the year—taking the round figures—Monday, 6,[illegible]; Tuesday, 4,[illegible]; Wednesday, 4,[illegible]; Thursday, 7,[illegible]; Friday, [illegible]; and on Saturday, 11,[illegible]; so that you see the smallest amount of drunkenness is on Sundays, and the largest amount of drunkenness is on Saturdays, nearly double the average of the rest of the week?—I take it these figures are correct, but they surprise me. I cannot understand the reason. There is a strong reason why with the Catholic population Saturday should not be the day for drinking. The religious practices take place on Saturday.

41,[illegible]. Then is it the Protestants who take the opportunity of going to the public-house?—As a matter of fact all those religious people come nearly without exception on Saturdays. There are other holy days, and the eves of those holy days are days of fast, but every Saturday in the year, except a holiday itself, like Christmas Day or some day of that kind, or Easter Sunday, would be a day the evening of which would be largely employed by the working classes, who are very religious, in their religious practices, and I cannot see how they can combine the two—going into a public-house and the chapel at the same time. I have been in chapel myself on a Saturday evening.

[illegible]. If the whole population go to chapel on Saturday night, why should you keep the public-houses open?—It is another class that goes to them.

[illegible]. As to the [illegible] that Saturday [illegible]. It is [illegible] the same in all the large towns. If the [illegible] Roman Catholics are all at chapel on Saturday evening [illegible] themselves to [illegible] and do not use the public-houses, it is clear that the lowest and worst classes of the population, [illegible] all the [illegible] of the [illegible] are [illegible], are in the public-houses during those hours when the rest are at chapel?—Possibly.

[illegible]. Is not that a reason why the public-houses should close at that time?—I do not think so—I do not think that is a conclusion to be drawn from it.

[illegible]. You think it is a good thing to keep the public-houses open for the lowest class of the population?—I do not. I do not think it is a good thing for them to drink at all—quite the reverse.

[illegible]. You do not think that a large proportion of the deaths coming under your notice as coroner are directly due to drink?—I know a large portion are not.

[illegible]. Do you not think that drink is largely contributive. [illegible] not [illegible] in these [illegible]?—[illegible]. That is my opinion; but as a matter of opinion, I tell you in my opinion far more people die prematurely from over-eating than over-drinking.

[illegible]. We are not inquiring into that?—Only if you ask me can I [illegible] tell you the other. It is a well-known fact [illegible] physiologists over-eating is a far greater evil, and a more universal evil. I am happy to say it is more universal because it is more [illegible] thing to endure.

[illegible]. How long have you been Coroner?—Seven years next July.

[illegible]. Do you [illegible] your predecessor Dr. [illegible] Whyte?—Yes.

[illegible]. He was Coroner for [illegible] years?—I think so, for that time.

[illegible]. Do you think he is as much entitled as yourself to give trustworthy evidence on this question?—Quite as much, provided he took the same precautions.

[illegible]. And he say how far cases coming before a Dublin Coroner are directly due to drink. He had [illegible] years' experience, and you have seven?—I know he did not keep what I keep.

[illegible]. You have not access to his private papers?—No, but I have inquired into it.

[illegible]. Are you his executor?—No, but I have inquired and found he did not keep the same record.

[illegible]. He seems to have formed a strong impression. He appeared before the Select Committee on the Sunday Closing Acts in Ireland, much in the same way as you have appeared before us today, and I am going to read you one or two questions that were put to him, and ask you whether you agree with them. He was asked:—"Taking the facts as they exist, what should you say was the cause of most of the crime and misery in Dublin?—(A.) Drink, unquestionably, without doubt. (Q.) You have a great many cases come under your cognisance during the year?—(A.) I have. (Q.) Are you able to say, from your personal experience in your official capacity, what are the main evils with which you have to deal?—(A.) Do you mean with regard to homicide only, or with regard to deaths from all causes? (Q.) I am speaking of cases which come generally under your notice in your capacity as coroner for the city?—(A.) I think drink is the preponderating cause." Do you think so?—No, I do not at all, and I will give you the best [illegible] I think disproves that conclusively. The most frequent cause of death coming before a coroner, I am sorry to say, is [illegible] and [illegible] of children. I have had a percentage—I have not made it out exactly—of either [illegible] or [illegible], but take it at the lowest figure. It is absolutely [illegible] per cent. of my cases. That is a large proportion, and not one of those cases has been due to drink. In every case the history is [illegible] and it comes to the question of the dwellings of the poor and there being [illegible] given. Here is the mother's evidence in these cases:—"I went downstairs with a bucket to empty the slops, or carry up water from the yard, there being no tap in the room; I was only absent two minutes; on coming up the stairs I heard a cry; I rushed up and found my child in flames on the top of the stairs." That is the history in [illegible] cases out of [illegible], and in not one of them have I found that drink was the cause. Now there is one of the [illegible] [illegible] with me, and drink does not enter into it.

Dr. J. E. Kenny. 4 May '88

[illegible]. I do not dispute your statement at all, but I may bring in comparison with your evidence the evidence of a gentleman of [illegible] years' experience as coroner?—Do not take me as being unable in any way [illegible] should be taking before him, as that is not [illegible] to the fullest [illegible]. He was a great friend of mine. I do not agree in his views, but there is one portion of them which you have read which comes entirely to refer to criminal statistics—the first portion. That is with regard to Sir Frederick Falkiner's evidence in which he is speaking of criminal [illegible]. There is nothing I have said against that. I say yes, that a great deal of the crime is due to drink, because those who drink are more likely to be [illegible] than those who do not.

[illegible]. Mr. T. W. Russell, who was examining Dr. Whyte, led up to this definite question and said: "I am speaking of cases which come generally under your notice in your capacity as coroner for the city"; and then he gave this specific reply: "I think drink is the preponderating cause." Dr. Whyte was not a teetotaler, and he said he had got here by the [illegible] statistics go against that, and I have taken them in an abstract way without trying to spell anything out of them. I take them as they stand.

Coroner's cases due to drink.

[illegible]. I daresay you are aware that you differ with most of the coroners in the country on this point?—I do not know that.

[illegible]. They may not have kept statistics?—I do not think from what I know that they do.

[illegible]. Is it not the kindly habit of coroners to avoid as far as possible verdicts suggesting drunkenness as a contributory or principal cause of death with a view to avoid pain or disgrace to the family?—It is on the part of juries, but not on the part of the coroners.

[illegible]. On the part of juries it is [illegible], as I told the Chairman, there are cases that I considered directly due to drink outside the verdict of the jury, and it is the [illegible] I myself made.

[illegible]. It is your own personal impression of each case?—And I might recommend the jury to find that drink was the cause, but they do not do it. That does not [illegible] the [illegible]; the coroner has a right to show what the [illegible] of the evidence is, and recommend the jury that they ought to find so and so, but I have no right to coerce them provided they find the facts [illegible] on the evidence.

[illegible]. Is it not a fact that coroner's juries also are very [illegible] alive to the [illegible] of [illegible] [illegible] with [illegible] companies and burial clubs?—[illegible] [illegible] but [illegible] to [illegible] what I think is right, but there is a [illegible] [illegible] with regard to the [illegible] [illegible]. The [illegible] of [illegible] are [illegible]. They are [illegible] as a general rule. In my own [illegible] I have had [illegible] that to be the case when you have special juries. When you get a [illegible] jury and you take a man from the street he is very likely to be of a different class to the [illegible] jury, but the jury I get are [illegible]—they will not attend to my [illegible], and I do not [illegible] them to do it unless there is some [illegible] in the [illegible]—I am at all disposed to [illegible] as to [illegible] any [illegible].

[illegible]. Up to a certain point Dr. Whyte is in some agreement with you when he is asked what his greatest [illegible] is, and he says, "I suppose I have held about [illegible] inquests and about [illegible] cases in which I did not hold inquests"—[illegible] statistics are [illegible] with [illegible].

[illegible]. Then Mr. Peter M'Donald asks him: "But I think we must [illegible] you to [illegible]. Out of the [illegible] how many cases had you where death arose from excess of alcohol?—A. I have no return of that, I [illegible]

Dr. J. E. Kenny. 5 May '98.

"what's the verdict of the jury, I cannot tell you the number, but I suppose not above a dozen such recorded verdicts. I had [illegible] [illegible] [illegible] speak of the last [illegible] connected with drink in four [illegible] cases where no record of drink appears at all. For instance, a man was kicked or [illegible] out of a public-house in Tyrone place, and he died. He was a confirmed drunkard; he received a kick in the [illegible] causing a rupture of the [illegible] and an extravasation of [illegible] [illegible] [illegible]. Clearly that was a case of death by drink, but there was no word of it recorded because he was found to have heart disease. Q. But it is the fact that you have only 11 out of the [illegible] deaths recorded as arising from drink?—I am merely giving them to my impression; it might afterwards turn out that I had less or more." Then he went on to say in a long series of answers to other questions, that it was his conviction that in a very large number of these cases that came before him as coroner, drink was a strongly contributive cause to the death?—I have gone on a different principle. My practice has been different. I have put down in my own books what my impression was and not the verdict. I have guarded the source of error. He did not put down, and said so, that drink was the cause where the jury did not find that drink was the cause; but I have. In such a case as that the verdict of heart disease was a wrong verdict, in my opinion, and it should have been homicide against some person or persons unknown.

Days for paying wages.

62,022. With reference to Friday and Saturday payment, is it not the case that the best employers pay on Friday?—All the best employers do.

62,023. And practically all the worst employers—the employers of occasional labour, the class of the community which largely contributes to the drunkenness of Dublin, pay on Saturday, or whenever they get the money to pay their men, but mostly on a Saturday?—I think so, but I am assuming that that is the case, that a great number of the small employers—they are just as respectable men as the others—may not be able to collect their money to pay before Saturday, and may [illegible] it till the last moment; [illegible] [illegible] that is the case that a good deal of the wages are paid by them, they do not form the bulk of the employers by any means.

Bad dwelling-houses and drink.

62,024. When Dr. Whyte was asked to tell the Commission what, in his opinion, was the main cause of that poverty and misery, his reply was "The main cause is the drinking; their wages are wasted in that way, and they cannot keep their houses comfortable"?—I agree with that, that a great deal of misery of the poor is due to drink. What is the cause of their drinking? That is a different thing, the fact remains, that a good deal of the wages of the poor is wasted on drink, and a good deal of the money of the poor [illegible] out of that, and my evidence is that what I put down as the cause is not the cause.

62,025. You think their drinking habits are [illegible] largely due to the lives of the poor?—Yes. I am afraid I should be a tippler myself if I lived under their conditions.

62,026. You know these tenement houses? Do you find the teetotallers in any of them?—Yes.

62,027. Many?—A good many of them I am happy to say are teetotallers, and if you go down to Church Street, that is a street in the middle of the poorest district in Dublin in which a great movement has been made by the clergy, and with which the publicans, so far as I know, are thoroughly in sympathy; there you will find a number. You would be surprised to find the number that fill the Temperance Hall in Church Street of teetotallers and sympathisers with teetotalism.

62,028. Do not you find that their houses are better?—Of course.

62,029. And they generally have two rooms?—I do not know that. I am afraid very few [illegible] of the teetotallers have two rooms. They cannot afford it. [illegible] [illegible] in that class of life is the great [illegible] thing I know.

62,030. It is the same in London. It is the most serious question we have to deal with?—It is dreadful. The poor man cannot get decent accommodation under a rent which is prohibitive, and breaks the back of he tries to pay it.

62,031. I will put to you three or four plain questions, the same questions that Mr. John O'Connor put to Dr. Nicholas Whyte, and in every case he answered them in the affirmative?—I hope you will not prejudice me by saying how he answered them.

Dr. J. E. Kenny.

62,032. The first question is: Are you in favour of the Sunday Closing Act being continued in operation?—That is for the whole of Ireland?

Sunday closing for the whole of Ireland.

62,033. As it now stands?—Yes. I am in favour of that.

62,034. You agree with him on that point?—Yes.

62,035. Are you in favour of its extension to Dublin?—No.

Dublin.

62,036. Would you explain. The rural districts do not want public-houses, nor do they in little villages. Anyone can go into his neighbour's cottage, and is always going to bed early in the country. His life is in the open air for all the week, and on Sunday he has no need of the public-house in the same sense as a dweller in the city. I should like to say that in city life, as civilisation goes on, wants are engendered—a want of something stimulating, not necessarily alcohol, but some stimulating thing to overcome the great [illegible] of labour under which we groan and sweat. It does generate wants which are satisfied by alcohol, unfortunately. They ought to be satisfied by anything else which would come within the grasp of the masses, but alcohol is not treated as a scheduled poison. Treat it as a poison if you like and do away with it, but so long as there [illegible] and it is an article of food—definitely to a considerable extent—I say that so long as alcohol is looked upon from the point of view that the great portion of humanity do look upon it as a [illegible] as well as a stimulant, it will be taken by them to relieve what they think they want, though they may be under a wrong impression. A man feels he wants something, and finds that alcohol, for the moment relieves that craving, and he goes to alcohol, it being within his reach. If it were a scheduled poison he could not get it, but not being a scheduled poison he can get it. But if the public [illegible] that a pint of beef juice or a wineglassful of beef juice would stimulate him there he would never take alcohol at all.

Difference between town and country.

62,037. You are also opposed to Saturday night closing?—I am opposed to the proposed curtailment. I think it is quite inadequate if the evil be what it is, and that you would in no way modify it. It would be like cutting off a lion's tail to make him a less dangerous animal. If it be a lion then do not treat him by cutting off the end of his tail.

Early closing on Saturday.

62,038. I want to cut his teeth and his claws?—That is a different thing, but that seems to me to be the wrong end of the tail.

62,039. (Mr. Younger.) You know it to be the fact that the Temperance Hall in Church Street, my colleague has alluded to in his cross-examination, has to a large extent been created by money supplied by the publicans?—I do not know that as a fact, but it does not surprise me at all to find it so stated, because publicans are exceedingly charitable men.

Publicans and the temperance hall.

62,040. It shows that it is their interest so far as possible to get rid of drunkenness in their customers?—I think the worst enemy of the publican, and the worst enemy of himself or his neighbour is the drunkard. I detest him, and I am greatly afraid I should treat him very drastically if I had the power.

62,041. You seem surprised at the figures Mr. [illegible] gave you, but they were rather misleading. The arrests for drunkenness in 1878 in Dublin were 17,[illegible], but when I tell you on the strength of Sir Andrew Reed's figures that the arrests last year were only 8,[illegible] or one-half of the number, that would tally with your experience?—Yes. If I understand rightly the total arrests for drunkenness in Dublin were 8,[illegible].

Drunkenness in Dublin.

62,042. Yes, as against 17,[illegible] in 1878?—There is a great diminution.

62,043. What I want to put is this. We find though your predecessor's experience with reference to the causes of death in the [illegible] he held, may to some extent have been accurate, this process which is going on proves almost so conclusively that your [illegible] experience is equally accurate?—I am quite satisfied with my own experience. I take very accurate observations of these things.

[illegible] Your observations are borne out by the [illegible] figures for arrests during the year [illegible] as compared with the time when your predecessor was in office?—Yes. I should like to say with regard to that, that I never had any notion of being examined here. I was not thinking of this Commission. My [illegible] are going on from the moment I was appointed. I like to get these things for my own satisfaction from other points of view—the [illegible], a medical point of view.

[illegible] Your experience extends over a long period before you were made coroner?—I may say that I am a practising physician, and Dr. Whyte never was. Dr. Whyte never practised as a physician but I do.

[illegible] (Mr. [illegible].) In your experience as a public officer you see a good deal of what is generally known as the seamy side of life?—Indeed I do, a great deal of it.

[illegible] Coupling that fact with what you have told us as to your beliefs as a teetotaler, I gather that you have come to the conclusion there has been more harm, even in the cause of temperance by exaggeration possibly than anything else?—There is nothing I have said to bear that construction, but I must say the most intemperate people I know are temperance advocates. I have always told them perhaps this will answer your question, that they were beginning at the wrong end. I am as much a temperance advocate as any man living, but I say they begin at the wrong end entirely in the closing of public-houses. That is my view.

[illegible] If you can imagine yourself placed in the position, that you had the power of dealing with this question and the two remedies you had suggested to you were restrictive legislation, very frequently suggested of an [illegible] kind, and such plans as you have sketched out of [illegible] and sanitary improvement, which would you consider the most reasonable?—Before I did a single penny's worth of restrictive legislation I would give the fullest play to the [illegible] I have mentioned, and if then I found that these were not effectual, and if they established, as they would establish one way or the other, that the public-house was an evil, I should not hesitate to grapple with that for a moment.

[illegible] Though you do not use these articles yourself your experience and your knowledge of mankind tell you that they always will be consumed?—I do not believe [illegible] will ever be made sober by Act of Parliament. I believe education, and those other things, will ultimately make a considerable improvement. There will always be a residuum unfortunately handed down by this generation and the generations that have gone before, because the largest factor in [illegible]—heredity is the chief item in the drinking propensity?—As a practising physician, I know that.

[illegible] I think additional importance is due to what you have told us with reference to your experience of the number of inquests you have held, because your experience is not simply based on what verdicts the jury have returned?—No.

[illegible] The impression was rather endeavoured to be conveyed to [illegible] that a jury were likely to be [illegible] by the circumstances under which they gave their verdict?—I do not think it is [illegible] for juries not to add drink to their verdict when there are other specific causes for the death. I think that is quite [illegible]. I think I have made that clear that I am not led by that. I put my note in the case not as to what the jury found, but what I believed was the case.

[illegible] Therefore when you tell us that a very small number could be traced directly to drink, it is reasonable that considerable importance should be attached to your statement?—I was taken by surprise at the smallness of the numbers myself.

[illegible] It is very frequently stated that the cause of suicide and of crime is largely due to drink. May I ask you, does not your experience go to show that a very much larger proportion is due to misery and poverty?—I do not think I have studied the question from that point of view as to whether a large number of suicides are not due to drink. That is not the case. The number of suicides in Dublin is singularly small. Some time ago in consequence of a return I wanted myself, for another purpose, I got a return, two years ago, of the average number of suicides. It extends to the whole kingdom, but it was my duty to compile it for Dublin and I compiled for five years the number of cases in which a verdict of suicide was returned, and in which insanity was found to be the cause, and I found it was as follows: taking the 5 years, [illegible]; that is an average of 10 per year. It is a most extraordinary thing year after year, that is the average. In those cases drink was not the cause, except in a very small proportion. In some cases it was simply due to an hereditary taint of insanity. In one case certainly [illegible] was the cause of the suicide. In those cases the jury did not find that at all. I was [illegible] of it on the medical testimony myself, from the [illegible] of the witnesses, but the verdict was simply insanity. There was not any very large proportion of them—I do not think more than 4 out of the 49 I so compiled—in which the cause of the insanity was drink. One of them was the case I referred to, with reference to the [illegible]. That was clearly due to drink. The man hanged himself and was not known in the ordinary sense, though I think all such persons ought to be treated as insane. I have a strong opinion upon that.

[illegible] One of your suggestions is the improvement of the dwellings of the working classes?—Yes. Improvement of dwellings.

[illegible] Do you contemplate that that can be done by the municipal authority?—I do. It is to be done in the active sense by the municipal authority, and in the passive sense by the proper sanitary authority compelling the owners of houses to construct them properly and give accommodation. All houses that are unsanitary ought to be compulsorily closed at once, and then the owner has the option left to put it in good condition or else leave it altogether.

[illegible] You would prefer to see it as far as possible done by private enterprise?—I should like to see all these things done by the owners of the property themselves.

[illegible] Do you know that in London within the last few years a scheme has been started for finding lodgings for the working classes?—I have heard of it, but I do not know the details.

[illegible] And I think it is a fact that any man can go and can get a comfortable lodging with all the conveniences of a [illegible] room, reading-room, and accommodation for cooking if he wishes, and his expenses so far as lodging is concerned are 6d. a night, and even with that 6d. they return 5 per cent. to the shareholders?—6d. a night is far beyond what the class I am speaking of in Dublin could pay. They could not pay 6d. a night.

[illegible] Not so much as 3s. a week?—It is absurd. 3s. a week out of a man's salary whose average wages are perhaps 14s. or 15s. is quite impossible.

[illegible] This applies to single and not married men?—A single man could do it, but that does not apply to families. I am happy to hear the thing done there. I think it is a step in the right direction; but it would not touch the misery of the dwellings of those I refer to. It is an excellent thing for [illegible], they could afford to give 3s. a week.

[illegible] I only mention it because from your experience, Dublin seems to be pre-eminent in the lack of accommodation?—It is the worst housed working class in the world.

[illegible] You have a large class of people there herded together, and provided no proper means of ventilation or amusement, or anything else?—Exactly. I ought to say this, that I hope I am not being taken as assuming that the charge against Dublin of being a drunken city is true. I do not believe it is true. It might be assumed I was taking that to be the case. The drunken cases are made up of the same persons appearing over and over again. There is not a large proportion of the workmen in Dublin who are drunken at all. They are very few, but not drunken.

[illegible] What does your experience as a coroner suggest as the best means of dealing with the class that come up 20 or 30 times?—I would treat them as lunatics distinctly. I would have institutions for them in which they should be treated, not as lunatics, but not the ordinary lunatic asylum. That is Sir Charles Cameron's Act in Scotland made compulsory. Habitual drunkards.

Dr. J. E. Kenny.

6 May '98.

62,665. You would treat them as criminal lunatics?—Not as criminal. No lunatic ought to be treated as a criminal lunatic.

62,666. Not in cases of constantly repeated offences?—No. He is a lunatic, not a criminal. It would be the same if you treated a man as a criminal whose lunacy happened to be that of a kleptomaniac. He is a diseased man and never ought to be treated after he has committed a crime as an ordinary criminal.

62,667. A place of that kind would simplify [illegible] of escape, would it not?—I think it would. All those things would.

Housing of the poor in Dublin.

62,668. (Mr. Young.) Is not the condition of Dublin very different from the condition of almost every other town so far as artizans' dwellings are concerned?—So far as Ireland is concerned.

62,669. Am I right in saying that there is very little prospect in Dublin of having self-contained houses for artizans?—At present.

62,670. In consequence of there being so many deserted large houses which were built for people who have now gone to live in the suburbs?—I think that is so. I think it is the tendency to leave houses of the class you speak of, and let them get into a state of dilapidation, and become uninhabitable, that largely tend to stop the movement of building new houses which would be proper ones. They cannot make them really good without an expenditure, which, in my opinion, would come very near the expenditure of erecting new dwellings on a proper plan.

62,671. The English Conservatives think it very extraordinary that we should not have self-contained dwellings for the poor; but you agree with me, it is the deserted condition of the large houses, and the condition of Ireland altogether?—Yes, perhaps as everyone knows, with us all roads lead to Rome, and all this comes to Home Rule with me. If we had the dealing with all our own affairs we should alter it altogether.

62,672. (Mr. Cator.) Have not the Municipality got the powers already?—Not to the extent that they ought to have them, and they are watched by a class in Dublin of a most worthy people who being opposed to Home Rule look with too critical an eye on the actions of the corporation, though they do not damage, [illegible]

62,673. (Mr. Young.) There are streets of large houses deserted?—Street after street.

62,674. And you have to put eight or ten families into those houses?—You have to put a family into each room on an average.

Sunday closing.

62,675. I did not hear your answer to Mr. Cator with reference to closing on Sunday. Did I understand you to say you wanted the hours open from 2 to 5 on Sundays?—My answer was that I think the present regulation was a very good one. That is, 2 to 7. What I said was this, that I did not think it would be any use curtailing the present hours by two hours; that is, cutting off the two hours.

Counter-attractions to the public-house.

62,676. Have you any free libraries in Dublin?—There are free libraries, but not enough of them. There are three free libraries in Dublin.

62,677. There is a little difficulty that has occurred to me, when you say there is nothing whatever given to the poor of Dublin that can compare with the public-houses?—I was speaking in general terms. In certain localities where these libraries are, they are very good, and they do produce good results wherever they are. That is my belief, but not founded on statistics.

62,678. Certainly there is a want of public amusements in Dublin?—I think it is the most melancholy country in the world. There is no amusement for a man who has not plenty of money in his pocket. It is the natural gaiety of the people that keeps them alive. They belong to the Mark Tapley school.

The witness withdrew.

Adjourned till Tuesday, May 10th, at 11 o'clock.

ONE HUNDRED AND FOURTH DAY.

Queen's Robing Room, House of Lords, Tuesday, May 10th, 1898.

PRESENT:

THE RIGHT HONOURABLE SIR ALGERNON WEST, K.C.B., IN THE CHAIR.

The Right Hon. the Viscount [illegible]	[illegible] Esq.
The Right Hon. the Lord [illegible]	[illegible] Esq., M.P.
Mr Charles [illegible], Bart., M.P.	Charles Walker, Esq.
The Very Rev. H. M. [illegible], Dean	Thomas [illegible], Esq., M.P.
Henry [illegible], Esq.	[illegible] Young, Esq., M.P.
Samuel [illegible], Esq.	[illegible], Esq.

Mr. Maurice Healy, M.P., called in and examined.

62,979. (Sir Algernon West.) You are the Member for Cork?—Yes.

62,980. You have something to tell this Commission as to your views on the question rate which we are inquiring?—Yes.

62,981. Are you of opinion that the public-house licences in Cork—or would you deal entirely with Ireland—are more than are necessary for the wants of the people?—Enormously in excess of any rational view of what would be the reasonable requirements either of the city of Cork or of the country.

62,982. Is that all over Ireland?—All over Ireland, so far as my knowledge goes.

62,983. Would you then be opposed to the granting of any new licences?—Certainly.

62,984. Would you be in favour of diminishing the existing number of licences?—Where possible.

62,985. When you say "where possible," would you leave it in the discretion of the licensing authorities to do so?—My view would be that the granting of new licences, which will be constantly sought, should be made conditional on the extinguishment of two or three licences, or as many licences as the licensing authority should think fit—the number to be calculated having some relation to the value of the new licence given. I believe that system has been tried in Dublin, and has produced excellent results there, and I should be glad to see it tried in other parts of Ireland.

[illegible]

Mr. M. Healy, M.P.

18 May '98.

put into a public-house on a weekly tenure, or, as is very commonly done, on a monthly tenure, it is idle to say that that publican can take an interest in the house or his business, as will induce him to conduct his business on legal lines. There is a great temptation on a publican so situated to push the sale of drink so as to satisfy the brewer or concern under whom he holds his tenure. I think that necessarily leads to evil.

62,102. Would you particularise the evil that it leads to?—I should say the illicit sale of drink.

62,103. Would you think any provision should be made in any new law to prevent this tied-house system?—It is a very difficult question. I do not think that any mere agreement enabling a covenant to deal with a particular brewer illegal would have any effect whatever, because my view is that the power of the brewer in cases of that kind does not arise so much from the covenants. It arises from the insecure tenure of the publican which places him at the mercy of the brewer, quite irrespective of any covenant to deal exclusively with the brewer.

62,104. Therefore, if these covenants or agreements were put before the county court judge on his granting a licence, you would think that that would not prevent the system of tied-houses?—I think not. I think it would be quite ineffective to prevent it.

62,105. You see no way, then, of remedying it?—Yes, I see a way.

Suggested remedy.

62,106. Will you tell us what it is?—I would compel the licensing authority to see that the publican has such a tenure of the public-house as gives him a substantial interest in the house and business. I would not allow a licensing authority to grant a public-house licence to a publican with a tenure on a monthly, or weekly, or even a yearly tenure.

62,107. Are you yourself a teetotaler?—Yes.

62,108. Do you take an active part in the movement?—There is not a very active movement in Ireland, I am sorry to say, to take part in. I have always been a supporter of the temperance movement so far as it has existed in Ireland.

Sunday closing.

62,109. Would you be in favour of closing public-houses on Sunday in all the big towns?—Certainly. I think that would be a most beneficial change in the law.

Early closing on Saturdays.

62,110. And earlier hours on Saturday?—That would be a still more important and a more beneficial change.

62,111. Do you know what the feeling generally is in Ireland on that subject?—I cannot pretend to say that the feeling in Ireland, taking the people as a whole, is strong either on one side or the other; but I am certain of this, that there would be no strong feeling against such a change in the law.

62,112. You think it would practically be adopted without any ill-feeling?—I am certain of that. I am certain that apart from trade interests, there would be no serious objection on the part of any large section of the population to such a change in the law as I have indicated.

Effect of Sunday closing.

62,113. Do you think the results of Sunday closing so far as it has gone have been satisfactory?—I think in the country districts Sunday closing has made a very great and a very significant change for the better.

62,114. And there is a great diminution of drunkenness?—Yes.

62,115. Does the drunkenness on Saturday nights proceed from the payment of wages on that day, mainly, do you think?—I should suppose so, coupled with the fact that the artisans very commonly, in cities [illegible]

towns where a movement for the extension of the boundaries of those towns was a actively opposed [illegible] because it was apprehended that an extending the boundaries would bring the population over the [illegible] limit, and would thereby enable licensed houses to be kept open an hour later than otherwise would have been the case.

62,116. The great disadvantages arise from the present state of the law as regards *bona fide* travellers?—I think everybody admits that the three mile limit is very evaded.

62,117. Would you extend that limit?—Certainly.

62,118. Have you any definite ideas as to what limits you would put?—I should say at least six miles, and as much more as the legislature would allow.

62,119. What do you say as to the proof that a man was a *bona fide* traveller?—I think it would be very difficult to import into any statute rules which would be effective on that point.

62,120. Therefore you think it had better be done by extending the number of miles beyond which he may get his drink?—Yes.

62,121. As to convictions of offenders against the licensing laws, have you any views upon that, as to whether these offences should be endorsed on the licence?—I have sometimes thought it would be interesting to get a return of police prosecutions showing results, and enabling a comparison of results to be made as those police prosecutions as between licensing prosecutions and other prosecutions. I think it would be found that the failures to convict in the cases of licensing prosecutions are enormously greater than in any other class of police case.

62,122. Then you would be in favour of all offences against the law being endorsed on the licence?—I certainly would be in favour of making the existing law more stringent than it is on that point. Whether you would go to the limit of compelling the magistrates in every case to endorse in a defensible manner. It might lead to magistrates being reluctant to convict in a great many cases if you made the law very stringent. Certainly the existing system on that point is not satisfactory. My opinion is this; at present the presumption is rather in favour of not endorsing, except in cases of a bad character. I would reverse the presumption, I would make the presumption rather in favour of endorsing unless extenuating circumstances were shown.

62,123. Have you any other point which I have omitted, which you would like to bring before the notice of the Commission?—I think those are the principal points.

62,124. Have you no general observations to make?—No; nothing occurs to me at present.

62,125. (*Sir Charles Cameron.*) I gather that you are strongly in favour of putting the licensing power, or the granting of new licences, in the hands of the Recorder?—I am in favour of abolishing the grant of new licences. I wish to make that perfectly clear. I am in favour of no compromise with the present system at all.

62,126. You are in favour of abolishing new licences and only granting them in return for the extinction of old ones?—Quite so.

62,127. In fact, the plan of the Recorder of Dublin?—Yes. It is a curious point that in cities having Recorders, I think the Recorder is the sole licensing authority. I do not know whether by statute or common law.

42,134. Then you are strongly of opinion that great good has resulted from Sunday closing?—I am perfectly satisfied of it.

42,135. And you see no practical obstacle to the extension of Sunday closing to the excepted towns?—None whatever.

42,136. So far as earlier closing has prevailed in these smaller towns, you consider its result has been an unmitigated good—closing before 11?—Certainly.

42,137. You would like to see that extended?—Quite so.

42,138. What do you say as to there being any agitation for the abolition of Sunday closing in the districts in which Sunday closing prevails?—I have never heard of it. Of course naturally there is always a trade objection to it.

42,139. But no popular objection to it?—No.

42,140. Do you happen to know whether it has had any effect in giving rise to an increase of shebeens and illicit trading?—Nothing of the kind.

42,141. Therefore you do not agree with previous witnesses?—I do not believe there is the smallest connection between the existing Sunday Closing Act and the existence of shebeens. I believe that shebeens where they exist are quite as common in the towns—for instance, in Dublin, where you have Sunday opening—as they are in rural districts, where you have Sunday closing. As long as you have any restrictions on the sale of drink, so long you will have establishments that will endeavour to evade the law.

42,142. (Mr. Whittaker.) So long as you have a big duty, too?—No doubt.

42,143. (Sir Charles Cameron.) Do you suggest that there is any necessity for legislation for the prevention of bogus clubs or the licensing of clubs? Have you considered that point?—It is generally used as an argument against temperance people that they never say anything against clubs. I am quite prepared to support any proposition on the subject of clubs, but I cannot say that I consider there is any serious grievance in the matter of clubs which the existing law has not dealt with. There was a great outbreak, as no doubt the Commission has heard, of bogus clubs in Dublin two years ago, and the police put them down very effectively with the existing power. In Cork, in the past 12 months there was an attempt to establish a couple of bogus clubs, and the promoters received got a very short shrift from the magistrates, and there has been very little heard of bogus clubs ever since.

42,144. You do not attach much importance to the assertion that has been made, that the law will require to be strengthened to prevent evasion on the part of clubs which might technically comply with the requirements of a club, but which were established simply for the purpose of evading the restrictions of the Licensing Acts?—I should be glad to see some limitation with regard to individuals [illegible] together for the purpose of having at their disposal a house where they could get drink at all times. I think the present state of the law on that point is objectionable.

[illegible] by licensing authority. 42,145. (Mr. Young.) How would you carry out your views with regard to the buying up of old licences? Imagine a person making an application for a new licence, what would the licensing authority say?—They would say to him: "Sir, you ask us for a new licence "—a very valuable privilege, having a commercial "value. What do you propose to give for it?"

42,146. He would have to go and buy up some of the licences in the town?—Certainly. I would not say necessarily in the town; I would not suggest a very limited area in which he could extinguish the licences. I would give him the county if that were thought desirable.

42,147. Does not that allow a monopoly to remain in the hands of those who are in possession of it?—What is the present system but a monopoly? True. If there is to be a monopoly in the city of Cork for the sale of drink, I would sooner have that monopoly in the hands of 200 persons than in the hands of 500 persons; I think less evil would result.

Mr. M. Healy, M.P. 26 May '98.

42,148. Is it your idea that the licensee who wants to sell should simply make his bargain with the owner?—I do not express any opinion about a licensee selling. My view was about the man who was looking for a new licence.

42,149. I do not see how the thing would work, the buying and selling?—I assure you it has worked admirably in Dublin. It has been going on in Dublin for 20 years as far as I know, and nobody has suggested that it has created any difficulty.

42,150. One could understand a licensee wanting a transfer and giving up the old licence and getting a new one. Your system simply would mean buying and selling on the part of the present holders?—I do not quite follow you.

Tied houses. 42,151. What do you mean by tied-houses; do you mean that the houses are owned by the brewers?—Mostly—owned or leased.

42,152. Do they simply put managers in?—Oh, no, not nominally managers—really that is what it comes to, but nominally the persons who are put in are tenants on a very fragile tenure.

42,153. Are you sure that it is not in this way, that the owner of the licence gets the loan of a certain amount of money and that ties it?—I do not at all suggest that there is only one method of tying a house. I say, so far as I am aware, in the city of Cork the other plan, I think, prevails to a great extent, the brewers in a great many cases own the house and puts in a tenant. Of course the other system also prevails, and prevails very extensively in the county of Cork.

42,154. But you would not desire to prevent that; you would not interfere at all with a man having a loan on a house, would you?—I think I would scrutinise very closely any transaction between a brewer and a publican which placed the publican in a position of being ready to sell a certain quantity of drink if he was to preserve his status in the house.

42,155. (Mr. Younger.) Do you suggest that there are agreements between brewers and publicans in Cork, one of the provisions of which requires him to sell a certain quantity of beer?—Brewers are not so foolish as to draw agreements in that form, but that is the substance of the transaction—that rather is the effect of the transaction than the form of the transaction.

42,156. You do not suggest there is such a clause as that in the agreement?—Any such clause, of course, would be absurd.

42,157. (Mr. Young.) In all lines of business you will find the same mode of tying. A grocer is tied practically to the man who supplies him if he has got a bill or an overdraft?—That is not to push the sale of that in a manner injurious to the community. The cases are not parallel.

42,158. You make this trade an exception to other trades?—Certainly, as the existing law does.

Sunday closing. 42,159. You advocate total closing on Sunday?—Certainly.

42,160. You do not agree with the expert witnesses who have come before the Commission. I think every one has the idea that the hours should be limited—that it should be at least two hours on Sunday—you are differing from that?—So far as I have expressed disagreement with the evidence of any witness I, of course, disagree with it.

42,161. You do not think it would lead to the purchase of liquors on Saturday?—I am sure it would not.

42,162. And the consumption of those liquors on Sunday?—I am positive it would not.

New licences. 42,163. (Mr. Grubb.) Your view is, that no licensing authority is necessary, because no new licence

Mr. [illegible] M.P. [illegible]

[illegible],168. Suppose the population shifts in consequence of the striking of [illegible] in different districts?—That is the mistake which arises from comparing the conditions in England with the conditions in Ireland. In Ireland you do not have these conditions. You do not have localities growing up, and you do not have the population shifting, and I would make my legislation for Ireland in accordance with the conditions which exist there.

[illegible],169. You have that condition in Belfast. You have 270,000 inhabitants now, and about 30 years ago you had a very small number?—Does anyone seriously suggest that there are not enough public-houses in Belfast?

[illegible],170. You would make no provision at all for an [illegible] of population?—I would make provision for that case when it arises. Parliament sits once a year, and is supposed to legislate from year to year for the country.

[illegible],171. Then the only provision for granting a new licence should be the being able to buy up some existing licence?—Certainly.

[illegible],172. What would be the effect of that? Of course, competition would run up the prices, would it not?—I should not think so.

[illegible],173. You do not think when there was such a restriction that you could not get a licence, and a licence was actually wanted, that there would be competition amongst traders to get it?—Oh, competition for a licence, certainly.

[illegible],174. And that would force up the value of the licence?—Unquestionably.

[illegible],175. By your system of legislation you, first of all, compel the trader, if he wants to carry on his trade, to pay a high price for the right to carry it on?—I do not think that that can be said, in view of the fact that you have at present a very large number of licences. None of the holders of those licences would have to pay anything.

[illegible],176. Surely your suggestion amounts to this, that if a man gives a large price for a licence, then he has a definite right in the licence—he has paid for it?—Quite so, but at the present time I say there is a great excess of licences over the number required.

Vested interest in [illegible]. [illegible],177. Imagine that a man has paid under your principle 1,000*l.* for a licence, surely you recognise that then you have created a certain amount of vested interest in the licence?—Certainly, and the law at present gives the publican in Ireland a vested interest in his licence.

[illegible],178. You would be prepared to recognise that the licensed trader under those circumstances, if you abolished his licence was entitled to compensation?—At present the Irish publican has what the English publican has not, he has a vested interest in his licence with a right to have the licence renewed every year, except in the case of misconduct. Nothing of the kind exists in England.

[illegible],179. You see no circumstances under which compensation would be reasonable where licences are abolished?—Certainly, if I made a man pay 1,000*l.* for his licence, I should think it a hard case to take it away from him without paying him for it.

Tied houses. [illegible],180. On the point of tied houses, do you not think that tied houses have restricted the trade, and that evils have sprung from that restriction?—Restricted the trade in what way?

[illegible],181. You say that the system of tied houses has put an inferior tenant in?—"Inferior" is a strong word. I say it puts in a tenant who is practically the agent of the brewer, and who has no substantial interest in the licence.

[illegible],182. Does not that go to show a state of things which applies to all these recommendations, that the extreme restrictions all meet and is evil?—I do not follow you.

[illegible],183. You are opposed to the system of tied houses. I presume no one would give very big prices for these licences if there were anything like open competition?—Of course a tied house, with the very extensive licence which the publican has, would be practically of no value in the publican's hands. It is of great value in the hands of the brewer.

[illegible] [illegible],184. (*Mr. Johnston.*) You dropped an expression to the effect that it would be unimportant what the licensing authority was if they were restricted from granting a new licence without something like an equivalent in the shape of a surrendered licence?—That is my view.

[illegible],185. Do you not think there is a very great responsibility involved in the discretion of deciding what would be an equivalent? Would it not be open to a licensing authority, if they were not a judicial body, to consider that as an equivalent which other people might think a very poor equivalent indeed?—I think I would put a scale in the Act of Parliament. I think I would take into consideration the value of the two premises. For instance, if a public-house were being opened in an important street in large, good premises, the licence to the house would, of course, be a good deal more valuable than a licence in a small wretched house in a back street. I think I would establish a scale of valuation.

[illegible],186. Still, there are so many circumstances affecting the value that it would, in any case, have, as it seems to me, great discretion to the licensing authority?—Some discretion at any rate. My view is that the question of the licensing authority would then become comparatively unimportant. I do not suppose there would be any objection if you wished to leave it, as I propose to leave it entirely to the county court judge or Recorder.

[illegible],187. You are aware that the surrender system has been adopted largely in many licensing divisions in England, and with very beneficial effects as it is generally considered?—I was not aware of that, but I am glad to hear it.

Sunday closing [illegible]. [illegible],188. (*Mr. Younger.*) I suppose your desire for Sunday closing arises from the fact that you think a considerable number of evils arise from the existing system of opening on Sundays?—I think so.

[illegible],189. Do you happen to know what the existing figures are—the that recent figures we have in connexion with the arrests for drunkenness on Sunday?—I do not attach the smallest value to statistics about the arrests for drunkenness.

[illegible],190. You attach no value whatever to them?—None whatever.

[illegible],191. Will you tell me why?—Because the number of arrests for drunkenness bears very little relationship to the number of cases of drunkenness.

[illegible],192. Can you explain why that is?—Because a policeman does not arrest a drunken man unless he is a bad case.

[illegible],193. The Irish police, however, are entirely controlled by one authority throughout Ireland?—Certainly.

[illegible],194. So that you do not know the difference there that we see in England with regard to police regulations about matters of that sort?—If the suggestion is that the central authority in Ireland exercises an intelligent control over the action of the police in licensing cases, I do not accept it.

[illegible],195. I am not talking of licensing cases but of drunkenness on Sunday?—I include that in the category of licensing cases.

[illegible],196. You say that the central authority exercises no control?—None whatever in a matter of that kind.

[illegible],197. And there is no general regulation with regard to arrests, with regard to that particular crime, throughout Ireland?—I should doubt it.

[illegible] [illegible],198. I think you also said that in Cork the only real objection to the Sunday Closing Bill arose from the trade opposition?—The only substantial objection.

[illegible],199. I suppose you are aware that quite recently the traders' council passed a resolution against it, and that the corporation of Cork by a very large majority passed a similar resolution?—Quite so.

[illegible] [illegible],200. Do you not regard those as factors of any consequence in the consideration of the question?—I consider, in the first place as regards the corporation, the corporation represents a limited constituency. The constituency of the electors for municipal purposes in Cork is 7,000, whereas the parliamentary constituency is about 20,000 within the bounds of the city. In most of the wards political parties are pretty evenly balanced, and the value of a drink trade vote is very great. I think if I were a corporator and wanted to stay in the corporation, I should probably like to please the person who had those votes.

[illegible] (*Mr. Whitaker.*) I understand you that the franchise is a much more limited one for the municipal vote in Cork than for the parliamentary vote?—Much [illegible].

[illegible] That means, of course, that your corporation is elected by fewer persons?—Much fewer.

[illegible] Therefore, when the Cork corporation passed a resolution against the Bill now before Parliament, that did not represent the opinion of the people of Cork in the same way as the action of the parliamentary representative?—Of course the corporation is not elected on any issue of that kind. The question of Sunday closing or Sunday opening is never debated at all at the municipal elections.

[illegible] As you have put it, the vote being close in many of the wards, publicans can turn the scale at the municipal elections?—Unquestionably. If you have a [illegible] franchise, that gives the vote to every publican. I once described the existing municipal franchise in Ireland as a publicans' franchise.

[illegible] It would seem, then, that the working men have to a very small extent the vote for the municipal franchise?—To no extent.

[illegible] Therefore that vote of the corporation could not be said to represent them in any form whatever?—Certainly not.

[illegible] With reference to the increase in clubs during recent years, do you think that has to any extent arisen from the fact that there has been some increase in the number of political parties in Ireland, and that each political party has in some of the larger cities desired to have its own club?—Unquestionably within the last [illegible] years the tendency of a particular party is to meet its political objects by forming a club.

[illegible] When you have a split and two political parties amongst the Nationalists, each one would have its own club?—That would be the tendency.

[illegible] (*Mr. [illegible]*) Referring to the streets as not being a true test for drunkenness, I suppose you mean not only that those streets do not show the drunkenness of the country, but that there is a great deal of drunkenness goes on outside the eye altogether?—I think that is so. I should expect that that would be so not merely in Ireland, but in England also. I did not wish to suggest that there was any distinction in that matter between Ireland and England.

[illegible] As to Sunday closing, you are in favour of increasing the three miles to six miles as one condition. Would you also be in favour of limiting the number of Sunday licenses for *bona fide* travellers?—I should be in favour of limiting the number of licenses for every-thing. Really the last place I would expect to find a *bona fide* traveller is in a public-house.

[illegible] As to early closing on Saturday, I do not think you mentioned the hour that you would be prepared to recommend for earlier closing on Saturday nights?—The proposal in our Bill was [illegible] o'clock; I should personally be glad to see it [illegible] o'clock.

[illegible] You have expressed the view that the practical way of reducing licenses is by a system of [illegible]?—Yes.

[illegible] There would be another way, that is, you might give the licensing authority the power of refusing the renewal of existing licenses if they thought the needs of the neighbourhood did not require it?—Well, that would be a strong proposal in the case of a trade which has at present a legal right to the renewal, and I think the [illegible], perhaps, it might take a little longer—would work out quite as well in the end. If I have a right by law to renew my license every year, I think it would be a wrong thing for Parliament to take away that right without some compensation. It would strike most people as being [illegible].

[illegible] (*Mr. [illegible]*) I think you expressed yourself as being of opinion that the existing licenses were greatly in excess of the requirements of the people?—Enormously; scandalously.

[illegible] You would reduce them where it was practicable?—Yes.

[illegible] In reducing those licenses I have no doubt you refer to licenses which are in congested districts, or is it all over the country?—Of course most of them are in the towns, but really, literally the country is beginning to be peppered all over with licenses in rural districts.

[illegible] Would you be in favour of any of these licenses that are taken away being used as a new license in a new place?—That, I think, is my suggestion. I said that I would fix an area, perhaps a large area, such as the county, and give the applicant for a new license the privilege of [illegible] the compensation for the purpose of acquiring licenses which he was to surrender as an equivalent for a new license.

[illegible] I understand you to use the word "abolish." If with regard to any of these licenses it was found for the public good and for the convenience of the public that a license should be continued, you would allow that license to be used in some new district where it was required?—No. I would not allow one new license to be given for one old license. I do not think that would carry out my purpose at all. I would insist on having at least two licenses surrendered before I gave any new license.

[illegible] Are you in favour of local veto?—I cannot say in Ireland that I am. I have not considered the matter very attentively, but I cannot say that in Ireland I am in favour of local veto.

[illegible] You made a remark with regard to placing the licensing power of granting and renewing licenses in the hands of the county court judge, or it might be of the Recorder. Would that harmonise at all with the principle of local veto?—As I understand, the principle of local veto is that the locality decides whether there should be any licenses, and if so, how many. Of course, that is somewhat inconsistent with the existence of any licensing authority.

[illegible] It is to give the people the power of saying whether they will have a license or not?—Yes.

[illegible] And you spread it over a very wide area if people have the whole power. How would you narrow down the important question of granting these licenses and removing them to one or two men?—I do not see. If you are to have a licensing authority, how is it to be composed of a mass meeting; I think you must limit it in some way.

[illegible] With regard to the diet-house, I understand you to say that whether it was a tied house or whether it was a free house, you would have a license [illegible], or a *bona fide* tenant?—Certainly, with a substantial tenant.

[illegible] With regard to the endorsement of licenses, I think you said you would have every license endorsed for any offence whatever?—I did not go quite so far. I said I would have the presumption in favour of endorsement instead of against it, as it is at present.

[illegible] Then may I say that you would have the license endorsed for the first offence?—That would depend on the offence. I think there might be cases in which I would not endorse it for the first offence. If it were a bad case I would endorse it, unless there were extenuating circumstances.

[illegible] If it were to become statute law that the first offence would cause an endorsement, you could not help yourself, could you?—You could easily draw a provision that the magistrate was to endorse the license unless he considered the special circumstances of the case warranted him in not endorsing it.

[illegible] In that case you would make it discretionary by a provision?—Yes, discretionary, but pointing in a particular direction.

[illegible] (*Mr. Whitaker.*) The endorsement would take place unless the magistrates ordered otherwise?—Certainly.

[illegible] (*Mr. [illegible]*) With regard to clubs, I think you say that at one time you had a good number of these clubs in Dublin?—I read of it. I do not profess to have any special knowledge of Dublin.

[illegible] You believe the police have sufficient power to stamp them out?—They did stamp them out. Whether the police require any additional powers I would leave to the police, and if the police ask for them I would give them.

[illegible] The other kind of clubs—the better class of residential clubs—you would not interfere with?—Well, really, I think that the comparison of the ordinary respectable club with the public-house is largely used. No gentleman would [illegible] together such drunken people amongst them.

[illegible] We cannot assume that they are drunken people at these better-class clubs?—As I say, and that

Mr. M. Healy, M.P.

16 May '98.

to the protection you have in a better-class club against drunkenness. The [illegible] of the club cannot be preserved if you have drunkenness in it, so it is to the interest of every member of a respectable club not to permit drunkenness.

62,233. You are aware that these clubs sell to their members wines, spirits, and beer precisely as any public-house does?—Exactly, except that the profit goes to the club.

62,234. As a temperance man, would you advocate any restriction?—As a measure of precaution, and to set an example, I should have no objection whatever to [illegible] restrictions on the sale of liquor in clubs; but I do not believe that any serious evil exists in the case of respectable clubs.

62,235. (Mr. Walter.) You have stated to the Chairman that you are a total abstainer?—Yes.

62,236. Probably from that circumstance you have not much sympathy with the licensed victualler?—I suppose a man's own habits [illegible] influence his opinions. I should say that would be a fair assumption.

Prohibition.

62,237. Are you in favour of prohibition?—I do not think prohibition is within the range of practical politics in these countries at present at any rate. I would consider that matter when it arises.

62,238. Then your answer would be judged by the circumstances of the day?—True.

62,239. I ask for your opinion?—My view on that point is that prohibition in the face of strong popular feeling against it would be more likely to be mischievous than beneficial. I think it is just as dangerous to legislate in advance of public opinion as to legislate behind it. I should be glad to see public opinion in these countries so advanced that it was possible to make a proposition of that kind practicable.

62,240. May I take it then you are in favour of prohibition?—I am not in favour of prohibition in the present circumstances.

Tied houses.

62,241. As to tied houses, you consider that a person holding a tied house is [illegible] to sell as much beer as possible?—That is my view.

62,242. Do I take it as your answer that if it were a free house he would not care to sell any beer at all?—I do not lay down any such absurdity. [illegible] he has [illegible] to sell beer. It is only a question of whether you will aggravate his natural tendency to do so by a system which places unnatural pressure upon him.

62,243. Is that in accordance with ordinary human nature that you are seeking to do others good in your own [illegible]?—I should not expect to find any tendency of that kind largely amongst licensed traders.

62,244. Can you tell me what has given rise to that opinion in your mind, that a tied house would be compelled by some influence to sell as much beer as possible?—I think if I were in the position of being a [illegible] bound to a brewer, and the traveller came round week by week and examined my sales book, and said, "Mr. [illegible], your sales " are very short this week; now there's [illegible] over " the way, he has sold so much. Really we are " expecting better from you,"—if I were a publican in that position, I think I would look about me, and see if I could not improve my sales.

62,245. Then you would have no evidence of such a condition in an agreement or anything of the kind to that effect?—I am sure no such agreement exists.

62,246. You say that from the very simple fact of holding a tied house he is compelled to sell considerably more beer than otherwise he would sell. I want to know upon what practical knowledge which you possess you make that statement?—I think, under the circumstances that I have mentioned, if I was the publican of the way on a Sunday morning and a brewery [illegible] came along, I should probably be [illegible].

62,247. Could you give any reason why, as a free man, he should not seek to do business as though he held a tied house?—I have pointed out to you that he has no inducement which the ordinary publican has not. If the ordinary publican has, as he ought to have, a substantial interest in his business, it is his interest not to break the law and run the risk of forfeiting his license.

62,248. Then do tied-house tenants break the law?—I should say so.

62,249. Are they not punished for it?—Sometimes.

62,250. Are not they removed?—The tenant is removed, but not the license.

62,251. Does the license belong to the tenant?—To ask if a tied-house license belongs to a tenant is rather a contradiction in terms. It belongs to him technically, but not substantially.

62,252. May I take it to be your opinion that the more value the occupier imports into the business the better the security or guarantee for the protection of morals?—I think so.

62,253. The better the class of men, and the more respectable the man, the better it is for the public generally?—By all means.

62,254. Have you anything to say in reference to the general conduct and character of the licensees of your district?—There are a very large number of prosecutions for breaking the law.

62,255. Have you anything to say as to their character?—I think the remarks I have made carries its own meaning.

62,256. There are a large number of prosecutions. Are they out of proportion in Cork to any other city of Ireland?—I do not say that Cork is worse than any other city in Ireland. I should be glad to think that Cork was better. I am a Cork man and a Cork member. I should be very sorry to run down Cork publicans.

62,257. Are not licensees, so far as you know them, as respectable a class of men as any other class of Her Majesty's subjects?—I am sure Cork publicans are as respectable as Irish publicans generally.

62,258. As any other class of men?—There is no word in the English language less capable of accurate definition than the word "respectable." You remember Carlyle's definition of a respectable man as a man who kept a gig.

62,259. With reference to Sunday closing, you stated to the Chairman that the feelings were not strong either one way or the other?—I do not think there is much feeling on temperance questions in Ireland. We are too fond of politics in Ireland.

62,260. That is your statement as to the feeling?—Yes.

62,261. You accept that?—By all means.

62,262. You stated that you yourself would have Sunday closing?—Yes.

62,263. If you had it in your power you would have Sunday closing over the whole of Ireland?—Certainly.

62,264. Do you consider yourself qualified, being a total abstainer, to determine that the houses should be closed on Sunday?—Admirably.

62,265. When, according to your statement, public opinion is equally divided?—I did not say that public opinion was equally divided. I said there was no public opinion on the question. I did not at all say that there was public opinion against.

62,266. What do you mean by "feeling"?—I made no statement which could in any way imply that there was feeling against the Sunday closing of public-houses. I should be sorry to do so, and I do not believe it.

62,267. Is it not a fact that [illegible] Irish members voted for it and [illegible] against it, and is not that being pretty nearly equally divided, and did not they represent public opinion or public feeling?—An Irish member represents an Irish constituency for all purposes. In Ireland, I am sorry to say, we do not conduct parliamentary elections on temperance questions. A man is elected because he is a Parnellite or an Anti-Parnellite—on some high question of that kind.

62,268. You admit that public opinion in Ireland is almost equal as to Sunday closing?—I did not say so. I said there was no public opinion, speaking roughly, on temperance questions in Ireland. I expressed the opinion very strongly that there was substantially no feeling against Sunday closing outside the trade.

62,269. Do you say that there has been no public opinion on temperance questions expressed in Ireland?—I did not say there was no public opinion, or if I did I should correct myself. I say there is not much public opinion on these temperance questions in Ireland. [illegible] thoughts are not turned very much in that direction.

62,270. Do you admit that public opinion, taking it how you like, is not utterly equally divided as to this question of Sunday closing?—I do not admit anything of the kind.

62,271. Do you admit that there is a large minority?—I do not.

62,272. You will not deny the test of the vote in the House of Commons?—I will not deny the test, certainly. The division lists would confound me if I did.

62,273. With reference to the *bona fide* traveller, you are of opinion that the three miles limit should be extended to six miles?—Yes.

62,274. Have you any other qualification of your own to suggest for the *bona fide* traveller?—The qualification of the *bona fide* traveller, in my judgment, is that he should be a *bona fide* traveller.

62,275. Take the case of a fully grown man—an adult, taking a walk out of the city of Cork three miles?—I think it is ludicrous to say a man that walks three miles is a *bona fide* traveller. It is enough to make one laugh.

62,276. It would take him nearly an hour, and if his system were exhausted it would require a stimulant?—All I can say is, if my system were likely to be exhausted after a three-mile walk, I would stay at home.

62,277. Would not it be regarded somewhat as an attack on the freedom of the subject?—All laws invade the freedom of the subject. The essence of any law is that it restrains human freedom.

62,278. Is not it a great restriction of the freedom of the subject that he should not, after walking three miles, be permitted to partake of some refreshment if he so desires?—I do not think the average man would feel it very much.

62,279. With reference to endorsement, what did you mean when you said "I think it would be interesting to have a return on the licence"? Is that all the purpose you had in view?—That observation did not relate to endorsements, I think. I said it would be interesting to have a return of police prosecutions of all kinds, showing the number of convictions, and enabling a comparison to be instituted as regards the proportion of convictions comparing licensing cases with non-licensing cases.

62,280. You are a solicitor?—Yes.

62,281. Have you practised in the licensing courts?—Very little.

62,282. Are you not aware that all offences are recorded, whether licensing offences or any other?—I am afraid we rather differ as regards the meaning of "recorded." If you mean recorded in the sense that the magistrate writes down the conviction in a book, he certainly does that; but I understood when recording was referred to, what was referred to was the special record referred to in the Licensing Acts—a record on the licence.

62,283. I only asked the question following your own line of evidence. I am quite prepared to keep the old endorsement of the licence if you like, but you said you thought it would be interesting to have a return. Is that the only motive you have for suggesting that all offences should be recorded on the licence, merely that it would be interesting?—I assure you my remark about the return had no reference whatever to the record on licences. I was answering a question by Sir Algernon West as regards whether the present tribunal for the hearing of licensing offences was a satisfactory one.

62,284. Having an offence, whether a slight or a severe offence, recorded on the licence, and on the day for renewal that licence presented to the magistrates, would it not be intended to act as a deterrent to the magistrates renewing the licence?—I did not express [illegible]

a remark; giving the magistrate power, if he thought there were extenuating circumstances, not to record. At present the presumption is rather the other way. The tendency of magistrates under the existing law is not to record. I think the tendency should be the other way.

Mr. M. Healy, M.P.

[illegible] May '97.

62,285. The law at the present time gives a discretionary power to the stipendiary magistrate?—Which I think he exercises wrongly. When I say wrongly I do not mean wrongly in point of law but wrongly in the interests of public policy.

62,286. He is a responsible officer of the Crown placed there for the purpose of discharging his duty. You do not wish to impugn the acts of the magistrates?—I am discussing the law and not the acts of the magistrates.

62,287. You would give discretionary power, and I reply to you that the law does give a discretionary power to magistrates?—I would rather point out in the law how that discretion ought to be exercised in the normal case.

62,288. If a licence were endorsed, and the man gave up the house and the licence passed to another man, would you still continue the endorsement or let him have a clean sheet?—I should not allow the mere transfer to wipe out the endorsement *ipso facto*. I think that would be a wrong measure.

Transfer after endorsement.

62,289. You would not allow the transfer to wipe out the endorsement?—No.

62,290. Should it remain in perpetuity?—I believe the present limit is five years, and I certainly should not be in favour of cutting down that limit.

62,291. You state in your opinion that the more respectable the man the more salutary the law, and the more worldly wealth the better for the public?—I think so.

62,292. Is it at all feasible that a man possessing those qualities would seek to purchase a property already damaged by his predecessor who had suffered for his offences?—It is his look-out if he chooses to buy a damaged property.

62,293. Do you think it is for the public benefit?—I think it is for the public benefit that a breach of the licensing laws should be punished. That is the first proposition. You may qualify it afterwards if you like.

62,294. If a man commits an offence he should be punished. I ask you if that endorsement under which the man has been punished and compelled to get rid of his house should remain on the licence, with all its terrors to the new tenant, who may be a good respectable man?—The man is not compelled to get rid of his licence.

62,295. You decline to answer my question?—I do not. That is not a fair representation of my observations. I am pointing out that your question involves an erroneous assumption.

62,296. Shall I put it again?—Yes, correcting the erroneous assumption.

62,297. I say that a licensee being endorsed a man is compelled to yield up his premises?—I say that he is not. He is not compelled to yield up his premises because there is an endorsement.

62,298. Assuming he does give it up. He would be anxious to commence it, and probably if he did, as you have previously stated, the owner of the property would compel him to give it up. It is only natural to assume he would yield up his licence?—That is not my experience in Ireland. A man does not give up his licence for one endorsement.

62,299. How many endorsements does it take to make him give it up?—My experience is he does not yield up his premises till the law takes them from him.

62,300. That is different from what it is in England. I put the question to you presuming he did yield it up, or sell it, and would you say that his successor should still carry forward the offences of his predecessor?—That is to say, shall the man who has a damaged article to sell be allowed to sell it as if it were not damaged? I should not allow him to do so.

62,301. [illegible]

Mr. [illegible] M.P. — [illegible] May '98

you made that statement?—No, I made no such statement. That would involve an argument against all [illegible] on the sale of drink, which certainly is the last thing I should have dreamed of advocating. I [illegible] have conveyed any meaning [illegible].

[illegible]. Did you not say you will have an illicit [illegible]?—Certainly not. I said the contrary.

[illegible]. Did you say this in relation to clubs, "I do [illegible] very great harm is done in clubs?"—[illegible] legitimate clubs, I think.

[illegible]. Put in the word "legitimate." You say there is no great harm in a legitimate club?—I think so.

Clubs.

[illegible]. What do you call a legitimate club or an illegitimate club?—A legitimate club is a club formed for the purposes of social intercourse, and not for drinking.

[illegible]. Are there such clubs in Ireland as clubs formed entirely for social intercourse and no drinking permitted?—I did not say no drinking permitted. I [illegible] for the primary purpose of social intercourse.

[illegible]. Have you any knowledge of any club in Ireland where no drink is permitted?—There are such clubs.

[illegible]. Have you any knowledge of these?—Certainly. There are political clubs in Ireland where no [illegible] of drink is permitted—[illegible], very [illegible] clubs, that would not dream of permitting the sale of drink.

[illegible]. The majority of clubs sell drink?—Quite true.

[illegible]. And sell drink at all hours?—Quite true.

[illegible]. When the public-houses are closed?—Yes.

[illegible]. In your judgment is drink sold in clubs less injurious than drink sold in properly and legally conducted houses?—Not a bit.

[illegible]. (Mr. [illegible].) Are you aware that in those tied houses to which you have referred they are not restricted to sell only the particular beverage as to which there is a restriction?—I am quite aware of that, and I rather [illegible] the importance of the restriction on the sale of liquor. I said expressly that I thought the chief evil in tied houses was not the restriction binding the publican to one particular brewer's liquor.

Public opinion and Sunday closing.

[illegible]. (Dean [illegible].) You said there was not a very strong opinion about Sunday closing in Ireland. Do you remember that in Cork there was a large majority on a house-to-house canvass in favour?—Yes. When meetings are called they are well attended. In the past two months I have attended two large meetings in the city of Cork, chiefly attended by working men, and all in favour of Sunday closing.

[illegible]. Do you know, on the other hand, of any large meetings of working men against Sunday closing?—Certainly not in Cork.

[illegible]. Nor in Dublin. Are you aware also there was a large majority in Dublin?—I believe so.

[illegible]. Perhaps you are also aware there is a very [illegible] society called the Irish Society for the Promotion of Temperance, which consists of clergymen and laymen of all denominations?—Yes, and it does a great deal of good.

[illegible]. They are at present carrying on a very vigorous movement—a crusade they call it—in favour of Sunday closing?—I am quite aware of it.

[illegible]. Is not that public opinion?—[illegible]. I only [illegible]

you will express yourself in favour of it?—I shall be happy to do anything I can in that direction.

[illegible]. There have been a great many witnesses before the Commission who seemed to think that there can be no more [illegible] licensing authority possible in the case of Ireland than the ordinary magistrates had acted. I think [illegible] infinitely worse.

Mr. [illegible] M.P. — [illegible] May '98

[illegible]. What would you suggest?—I think you could invent a worse. That is a very strong proposition. It is quite sufficient, I think, for me to say that I do not consider it an ideal body.

[illegible]. Then you think that giving the licensing authority to the county court judge, with perhaps the addition of the local [illegible] of two or three resident magistrates, with an appeal to the [illegible] judge, would be sufficient?—I should think that the county court judge would make a good tribunal. I should not add any resident magistrates to him, but I must add that even in a county court judge I would not confide, in the present circumstances of Ireland, the power of granting a new license except on the condition of other licenses being surrendered.

County court judge and appeals.

[illegible]. Would you not give a right of appeal on matters of law to the [illegible] judge?—On matters of law, yes.

[illegible]. I only meant that the resident magistrate would supply a [illegible] judge with the local information?—I think legally there would be an objection to that. The court is supposed to act on evidence, and I think a lawyer would say it would not be competent for a resident magistrate to offer what would practically be evidence from the Bench. I think it would be better, if making any change at all, to leave that power in the hands of the county court judge.

[illegible]. With an appeal on a question of law to the [illegible] judge?—Yes.

[illegible]. ([illegible].) You do not attach importance to that knowledge?—The court is not supposed to act on local knowledge, but on evidence. It would be very mischievous if you had a legal tribunal supposed to act on knowledge in its own breast. All legal tribunals are bound to act on sworn evidence.

[illegible]. Are these tied houses in Cork tied to local brewers?—Yes.

Tied houses.

[illegible]. All of them?—All of them.

[illegible]. With reference to your suggestion about the grant of new licenses, would you like us to lay down any standard of proportion of licenses to population at all?—I do not think it would be necessary at all. I should go on reducing the licenses till a state of things arose which required the intervention of Parliament again.

Reduction of licenses by surrender, &c.

[illegible]. You have stated that you think no new license should be granted unless on condition that the applicant could prove that he had purchased up one or [illegible] licenses?—Not one or [illegible]. I should not allow a new license to be granted merely because one license was purchased up.

[illegible]. You stated two or three?—At least two, and as many more as you like.

[illegible]. You would leave it to the discretion of the local licensing authority how many licenses he should require to be extinguished before granting a new one?—Yes, subject to what I have said, that I would provide in the Bill [illegible] in the nature of a [illegible] on [illegible] of [illegible].

[illegible]. Only on that—not on population?—Not on population at present.

some specific number of licences?—I should lay that down very strictly.

62,245. Shall you are not in favour of laying down any standard of proportion of population?—I do not think the necessity for that would arise at present, because I conceive that if the system I have advocated were put into operation it would take many years before the licences were so reduced that you would have at all to consider the element of population.

Mr. M. Healy, M.P.

10 May '99

62,246. In fact, you would be contemplating future legislation?—Yes, but it would be in the very distant future.

The witness withdrew.

His Honour Judge Orr called in and examined.

Judge Orr.

62,247. (Sir Algernon West.) You are county court judge for county Down and half of Antrim?—Yes.

62,248. How long have you held that office?—In 1891, seven years ago, I was appointed county court judge of Monaghan and Fermanagh. In 1897 I was transferred to county Down, and at the commencement of the present year a small portion of County Down was taken from me and added to the district of the Recorder of Belfast, and in return for that half of Antrim was given to me.

62,249. From your experience have you come to the conclusion that the state of the licensing law is very confused?—Hopelessly confused.

62,250. And would require consolidation?—Codification to a large extent.

62,251. Will you tell the Commission what, from your experience as county court judge, are the reasons that have induced crime in Ireland?—I have not the slightest hesitation in saying that nearly all the ordinary crime I have had to do with has been created directly or indirectly by the public-houses.

62,252. Therefore you have a view, I suppose, as to the number that ought to exist?—Yes. The number of public-houses at present is very excessive.

62,253. Are you talking of your own district?—Principally of my own district; but generally from my knowledge. I may give an instance that happened me when I was county court judge of Fermanagh. There is a little village in Fermanagh called Derrygonnelly where the population by the last census was 650. There were ten public-houses there—that is, one for every 65 men, women, and children, and in addition to that there were, if I recollect rightly, either one or two spirit grocers.

62,254. What is your view as to the possibility of diminishing these licensed houses?—I think that if the case of Ulnhurst was overruled by Act of Parliament it would be possible gradually to diminish them, and perhaps stamp out the bad ones. Ulnhurst's case was decided in 1877 by the Irish Court of Queen's Bench as it then existed, and it decided that in the case of transfers the licensing authority could not take into account the existing number of public-houses; that is, in other words, that a transfer must be granted as a matter of course. That decision took the profession very much by surprise, and it has been disapproved of very much by the succeeding judges. I think if it was overruled so that the licensing authority could take into account the existing number of houses in the case of transfers, gradually without injustice to anyone, the number would be properly reduced. In many of the towns of Ireland—in fact, in some of them—the population is decreasing, though that is not so in my district. In my district it is increasing, but in many parts it is decreasing, and what would not have been at all excessive 25 or 30 years ago would be quite excessive now. I think the licensing authority ought to have the same powers in cases of transfer that they have in cases of new licences.

62,255. You say whether the licensing authority should [illegible]

[illegible] has only come to the conclusion that the present licensing authority is a very bad one.

62,258. Would you allow the licensing authority to be the county court judge only?—Certainly.

Appeals.

62,259. With any further appeal?—Not of what we call an appeal in Ireland; I would give no appeal to the judge of assize. In the sense in which the term appeal is used in Ireland, it means a rehearing, and if you give an appeal in that sense to the judge of assize, you would make him the actual licensing authority, because in every case in which a licence was refused there would be an appeal as a matter of course. The expense is small and the licence is valuable, and there would be certain to be an appeal in those cases, and I think there would be an appeal in most cases where either the temperance people or the police or anyone else was opposing; so that practically you would make the judge of assize really the licensing authority, and I think the county court judge must be much better acquainted with the county than the judge of assize. The county court judge has four quarter sessions every year. In addition to that, he is the revising barrister, and has to revise the voters' lists for the parliamentary franchise, and will have to revise the lists for the new county councils, and that takes him to every part of his county particularly. He must know his county better than the judge of the high court, who only goes there once every two or three years; but I would give an appeal in this sense, that if any question of law arose, I would make it compulsory for the county court judge to state a case, not for the judge of assize, but for the Queen's Bench Division. At the assizes the appeals are hurried; everyone is in a hurry to go to the next town. There is no library, and counsel cannot properly prepare themselves. It would be far better to have the question quietly and properly argued in the Queen's Bench Division, and I would make it compulsory for the county court judge, if any questions of law arose, to state a case.

62,260. That would be the only instance in which you would allow an appeal?—Yes.

62,261. (Dean Dickinson.) Do you mean compulsory when asked?—Certainly. If not asked there would be no need.

Evils of Sale without food.

62,262. (Sir Algernon West.) You have, I think, some views as to the necessity for publicans supplying solid food?—Yes. I think a great deal of the mischief is done in this way. My districts are principally rural, and I am acquainted with people coming into market, perhaps starting very early in the morning and getting a very small breakfast, going the whole day without any food, and when business is over, going into the public-houses and drinking bad liquor. I think if the food were there they would take it and then the liquor would not do so much harm.

Adulteration.

62,263. You do not mean adulterated liquor but coarse or new liquor?—I mean adulterated liquor.

62,264. Adulterated with anything except water?—

62,268. Then what do you say about the spirit grocers' licences?—I think the spirit grocers are the greatest evil in Ireland. The law at present as regards spirit grocers is perfectly absurd. It has been the subject of decisions in the Queen's Bench Division, and I must take the law to be correct as laid down by them, and it comes to this that the licensing authority, which is the magistrates at petty sessions—not the county court judges—have no discretion at all. It has been decided that they cannot take into account the unfitness of the premises with reference to their local surroundings. It has also been decided that the magistrates cannot inquire whether the applicant is really a grocer or whether he is not, that that must be left to the Excise. The result is that unless the police can show the applicant is of bad character—which they never can—the spirit grocer's licence goes as a matter of course. That the consequence of that is that every one who cannot get an ordinary licence immediately goes and takes out a spirit grocer's licence, and the number of them is increasing enormously, and many of them are in remote country districts far from police barracks and in very low and wretched houses, and there is not the slightest doubt an immense amount of illegal tippling goes on in them.

62,269. In Ireland spirits are sold in open vessels by grocers?—In bottles.

62,270. And also in open vessels?—I am not sure—it is possible. There is nothing in the Act of Parliament to restrict that that I know of.

62,271. We have had evidence that that is the case in Ireland differing from what it is in England. Then also though you would therefore wish to see the law altered very much, you would not propose to abolish grocers' licences?—If I could, I would; but I do not hope to do it.

62,272. You think the law ought to be altered?—I think at any rate the licensing authority, whoever it may be, should have absolute discretion whether a spirit grocer's licence should be granted or not without giving any reason at all for the refusal.

62,273. Have you any views about Sunday closing, and ordinary closing hours?—As regards Sunday closing, I am not in favour of closing in the five excepted towns altogether. My view is this, that if you have closing altogether, you would produce a greater evil than the one you diminished, because you would give tremendous impetus to shebeen houses and bogus clubs.

62,274. Would you therefore be content with shortening the hours on Sunday?—On Sundays I should be quite content with shortening the hours, say to 7 o'clock. I think it would be of the greatest importance to have earlier closing on Saturdays.

62,275. Do you think that the Sunday closing in the country districts has had any ill effect, that is to say, has produced illicit trading?—From evidence given before me, and from what I have heard on various occasions, I am sure it has. I am sure there is a great deal of illicit trading in houses that ought to be closed.

62,276. Would you be in favour of merely re-enacting the hours in the country districts?—I do not know. I think perhaps the best way would be to keep the law as it is at present with the simple change of having an earlier hour to close on Sundays in the five excepted cities. That probably would be the best way out of it.

Will certainly pay on Friday, and I think a good many others do too.

62,277. (*Sir Algernon West.*) Have you seen in your experience any difficulty from the present provision about the *bonâ fide* traveller?—That does not come before me. I have never had cases before me, but I was listening here while Mr. Healy was under examination, and I agree with him that it is most grotesque to call a man who walks 3 miles a *bonâ fide* traveller.

62,278. What limit would you put?—I should put 10 miles as a minimum.

62,279. Would you put any other restriction on the *bonâ fide* traveller beyond the distance?—I do not see what else you can do. If you call him a *bonâ fide* traveller it is for somebody to find out whether he is or not. That is always the difficulty the magistrates have in dealing with these cases. The law is that a man who walks 3 miles for the purpose of getting drink is not a *bonâ fide* traveller, but if he walks 3 miles without the intention and goes thirsty and takes a drink he is a *bonâ fide* traveller. The magistrates have to determine upon the evidence before them what category he comes under.

62,280. As to the quality of liquor sold in public-houses, have you any suggestions to make?—If I have been correctly informed, there is this very bad deleterious whiskey sold in many places, and I would enforce the provisions of the Food and Drugs Act very much more vigorously than they are, and make it compulsory on the police to have periodical visits of the public-houses from time to time, and make raids on them and take samples, watch the people who were bringing the regular consumers, and make sure they were helped out of the same vessels, and have that analysed. I am perfectly sure a great deal of good would arise if that were done.

62,281. Have you any other suggestions to make that I have omitted asking you?—I think I should like to say a little more about the licensing authority at quarter sessions. I think it has been before the Commission already that there is a great deal of canvassing amongst the magistrates. I have read the evidence on that, and I can only say as regards that that I agree with it. I do not think these cases are what I may call judicially determined. When cases do come before a court the court should be entirely ignorant of everything before the case comes on, and the cases should be decided entirely on the evidence given in the court. It is very desirable to have a little local knowledge to aid in analysing the evidence, but at the same time the court should be decided on the evidence, and I do not think that is done—in fact, I am sure it is not done. There is a great deal of canvassing goes on amongst the magistrates.

62,282. Do not the magistrates accept the guidance as a rule of the county court judges?—I find they never do. Then there is another thing, that the court as at present constituted is quite unworkable from its size. In the county Tyrone, according to Thom's Directory at the beginning of this year, there were 103 magistrates. That is one of the counties of which I am the judge. In fact, there are so many magistrates that we have not a full supply of grand jurors at quarter sessions, because the quarter sessions being the magistrates' court, a magistrate cannot be a grand juror in it, and the result is that I never have a full [illegible]

[illegible] with the other witnesses that have [illegible], that the power of licensing should be [illegible] the county court judge alone; but if [illegible], I would suggest, as an alternative, that [illegible] in Ireland should be compelled to do [illegible] I understand the magistrates in England do [illegible], that is elect a licensing committee, that [illegible] should have a [illegible] to it, and let the magistrates for that district [illegible] a certain number of their own body, say 6 or 10, [illegible] to form a [illegible] licensing committee. That would be a very [illegible]. It would be more under the influence [illegible] the county court judge, and I think the best men would be elected, and [illegible] of them, by the [illegible] them after time, and having [illegible] of the county court judge before them and [illegible], I think they might [illegible] to [illegible] judicial principles in their decisions. At the same time, that is only an alternative. I should rather [illegible] the county court judge alone.

[illegible] (Thomas de Vesci.) I do not quite understand [illegible] evidence about transfers. You would [illegible] as to granting [illegible] may explain, perhaps, what the law is. The statute is the Act of William IV.—one of the principal Acts—and it is stated that certain persons may oppose on the ground of the unfitness of the premises and the existing number of public-houses.

[illegible] That is the granting of new licenses?—That [illegible] was granted and applied to all [illegible] of premises, the [illegible] or bad character of the applicant, and the number of previously granted licenses in the district. That was the law which applied both to new licenses and transfers down to the year 1877. In the year 1877 the case of [illegible] against the Recorder of Dublin was tried before the Queen's Bench Division in Dublin, and they decided that in [illegible] transfers as opposed to new licenses, notwithstanding the words of the section, the magistrates could not take into account the existing number of licensed houses, and that therefore no opposition could be made by the police or by anybody else on that ground. As I have said, that took the whole ground [illegible]. It has to be followed because the decision is there, but a similar case came on a good many years afterwards before another Queen's Bench Court, when all the other judges had died or had gone, and though they held themselves bound to follow [illegible] case they highly disapproved of it. What I should propose is that an Act should be passed enacting that [illegible] case should no longer be law, and that the magistrates should have the same discretion in granting transfers which they have in granting new licenses. I do not think it would work any harm, because transfers generally take place after a man's death, when his [illegible], or somebody wants to transfer a license, and I do not think there would be any hardship in saying that the vested interest, which you say you have, was only the result of a sort of an accident by reason of this [illegible] decision, and you shall have no vested interest.

[illegible] Then the effect of that would be that you would cause a person to remain a licensee who no longer wished to pursue the business?—Then let him give it up if he likes.

[illegible] It would be a question with him whether he gave it up or asked for a renewal, if he continued it at his own convenience?—Or [illegible] his chance.

[illegible] (Dean Dickinson.) You have recommended an elected body or a selected body of magistrates from the other magistrates?—[illegible] by their brother magistrates.

[illegible] From your knowledge of Ireland generally do you think in all parts of Ireland that would work satisfactorily?—I only propose that as an alternative to giving the sole power to the county court judge, which I am clearly of opinion is far the best thing that could be done.

[illegible] And in one place you mentioned there were [illegible] inhabitants and 10 licensed houses?—Yes.

[illegible] What was the character of those licensed houses—were they public-houses?—Yes, all public-houses.

[illegible] No grocers' licenses?—As well as I recollect there were either one or two grocers' licenses in addition.

[illegible] Then there were [illegible] ordinary public-houses?—Yes; [illegible] licenses.

[illegible] Did those licenses combine any other business?—No.

[illegible] Their only living was obtained from selling liquor?—So far as I know.

[illegible] You have spoken of the great number of public-houses; do they all get a living?—Well, they all exist and they all go on, and if a man wants to transfer a license and sell it he can always get a purchaser.

[illegible] Is not that a proof that there is a necessity for a class of house of this character?—I think not; I think it is a proof that there are far too many facilities for getting drunk.

[illegible] The fact that all these licensees are getting a living, paying rents and rates, and are good citizens, obeying the law, is no proof that they are required at all in the country?—I do not think so. I do not think there is any requirement for people to be habitually [illegible] every fair or market-day, which is what [illegible].

[illegible] You would not permit a license to be a transferable property?—I should not make it transferable as of right. I would give the licensing authority a discretion to say whether the particular license should be transferred or should not, and if he had that power he would be able to weed out a great many undesirable houses. In the past licenses have been granted to houses which should never have had a license at all; houses where there is a communication with a [illegible] yard, so that the people can get from one house to another, which makes it impossible for the police to exercise proper superintendence. There are a great many things of that sort, and I think if the licensing authority had full discretion in these matters, in the course of time you would find all those bad houses weeded out and a better class and a smaller class substituted.

[illegible] Would not this law operate against the better class you are speaking of as well as against the inferior class?—I do not think so.

[illegible] Is it likely that you will get a better class of men if you offer no facilities for ordinary commercial [illegible] of trading?—I think if it became known that the people with good houses and good accommodation are most likely to obtain licenses, you will have people of that sort applying for them.

[illegible] But you say they are to be left to the mercy of one man and his discretionary power, whether he allows a transfer or not?—I think it is what we call a judicial discretion; it will be exercised on judicial principles with regard to [illegible] and the evidence before him, and the wants of the neighbourhood.

[illegible] Is an absolute power in the hands of one man calculated to create confidence in the administration of justice, generally speaking?—I do not know. I can say that there could not possibly be less confidence in anything than in the present tribunal.

[illegible] You say the present licensing authority is very bad. May I ask in what respect?—From what I have explained, and as has been detailed by previous witnesses, an immense deal of canvassing goes on amongst the magistrates, and many magistrates—I do not say all, far from it, but a large number of magistrates—have pledged themselves to vote for a particular license before they come into court at all. I say that is wrong.

[illegible] Are you of opinion that the canvassing is a very bad thing?—I think it is the destruction of or- [illegible]

Judge Orr.

[illegible]

Transfers.

Licensin[illegible] authorit[illegible]

Canvass[illegible]

… are judicial functions … beforehand and pledges … f action that is very

… you brought the magis- … attended in such large … in fact, you could get … ad you could not agree … at court. Is that what … ay are out of touch … ng during all round you … with you or you with

… e words after detailing … ppened, as in England, … they would be more … y court judge. If they … fluence of the county … but by a committee of … at place I do not mean … of the county court.

… ?—Possibly, but then … you do not intend. … ould have a small body … ol of the county court … be head and be able to … the law who; but … r question I may state … that it would be better … t judge than have a … magistrates.

… to charges against the … here in England the … on their magistrates, … s for them, and I do … proper administration … trates. Therefore I say … it is these gentlemen

61,434. Can you point to an instance where the discovery has been made of any injurious substance or liquids being mixed with the liquor?—I have already said I have very little personal knowledge on the subject, but I am perfectly sure if the Food and Drugs Act were carried out instances would soon be forthcoming.

61,435. Do you charge the authorities with not carrying it out?—It is not carried out so energetically as, in my opinion, it ought to be.

61,436. Is it carried out in London?—To some extent it is carried out everywhere, but I think it should be better carried out.

61,437. Out of 400 samples in one instance I can refer to, one sample was found to be adulterated?—I am very glad to hear it.

61,438. Is it fair to the licensees to make the statement when you say it is only based on rumour?—It is more than rumour. If, as a matter of fact the stuff is not adulterated, it will do the licensees no harm.

61,439. It prejudices them. You, as a county court judge, surely should not make statements unless you have some foundation to rely on?—I consider I have a very strong foundation. I cannot say I can point my finger to A.B. or C.D. as the persons who have done it, but from what I have heard all my life I believe it is done, and you have had evidence of it before to-day.

61,440. And rumour is all the authority you have?—Of course, that is so.

61,441. You spoke of the case of two men entering a public-house at 8.30, and at 10.30 they had not any money left?—No, I said one had 1s. left and the other had his wages.

61,442. What was the amount they had when they entered?—One had 10s. and the other 7s.

61,443. What was the character of the drink they

Judge [illegible]. — be closed two or three hours earlier, so that they should not have an opportunity of doing it.

62,451. Was not that a matter for the police? Do you bring that as a charge to support the abolition of public-houses?—I do not want to abolish public-houses at all. In fact, I think they are necessary evils.

Licensing [illegible]. — 62,452. (Mr. Roberts.) As to this alternative licensing authority, you suggest the permanent licensing committee of magistrates acting with the county court judge, would it not be likely that at all events in some degree these magistrates would be liable to similar influences to which they are now liable?—It would, and I must repeat again I only suggest that as an alternative. I would abolish the magistrates altogether, but so far as I know the English people, I do not think they would like that. The English people have got that respect for old established institutions that they would not like to abolish the magistrates and to trust the thing to more officialism, and therefore as an alternative to the present system which is so unwieldy, I would have that. I think the committee I have suggested would be an improvement.

62,453. You are no doubt aware that some of the witnesses from Ireland have advised the county court judge or Recorder as the only authority?—That is what I advise, too, and if I had my own way in the drafting of the Act of Parliament, that is what I would do. Whether it would be done or not is another matter.

[illegible] — 62,454. You have referred to carrying the [illegible] to the highest [illegible]?—No. I have suggested it should be [illegible] by Act of Parliament, that is to say, that if any legislation ensues on the report of this Commission that should be provided for.

62,455. But it would be all important to carry out the results that you say are desirable in Ireland with reference to the diminution of licensed premises, to make some change with reference to the licensing authority, would it not?—I think that is of the utmost importance.

Licensing [illegible]. — 62,456. That lies at the root of the matter?—It lies at the root of the whole matter, and I must repeat again that I would, like other witnesses, give the exclusive authority to the county court judge. In Dublin, Belfast, and, I believe, Cork, the Recorder has it—those are the three largest towns—and it is done much better there than it is done in the counties.

62,457. Together with the resident magistrates?—I would not have resident magistrates at all.

62,458. I should like to ask you whether it is a fact, as is the opinion you have expressed with reference to the number of licensed premises, that it is not only your opinion but the general opinion in Ireland?—So far as I have been able to ascertain, it is. All the people I have conversed with, my brother county court judges, and police officers, and [illegible] clergymen and country gentry.

62,459. It is not a debatable point?—I do not think it is.

Reduction of licenses. — 62,460. And the drink problem in Ireland also resolves itself into the best way of reducing the number of facilities for drinking in Ireland?—To a large extent I think it does. Of course you cannot make people sober by Act of Parliament, nor will you make them sober by largely reducing the number of houses; but I think that by reducing the number of houses you would largely reduce the temptation to drink, and thereby diminish the amount of drunkenness. I should think the ordinary Irish small farmers and peasants in their own homes are sober people. One seldom hears of their drinking when at home; it is when they get into fairs and markets, and their business is over, and they have somebody's hands, and the question is where are the [illegible] hands to [illegible] it in.

62,461. In your ordinary experience in other cases that you try before you judicially they are very often appealed, I suppose?—Yes, of course they are.

Judge [illegible]. — 16 May '[illegible]

62,462. And I should think your decisions occasionally are reversed?—Of course.

62,463. Why should you be less likely to err in dealing with licenses than with ordinary cases?—It is not the same thing at all. If you give an appeal in that case it means a rehearing, and if you give an appeal to the judges of assize you make them the licensing authority in reality, because it is an absolute certainty that in any case where a license is refused there would be an appeal, and in most cases I think where the license is granted there would be an appeal too. If that is done you might as well cut out the county court judge altogether. I think there would be an appeal in every case.

62,464. You do not suggest that you are going to refuse every license?—No; but whether I granted or refused, there would be an appeal.

62,465. Do you think so? Would there be an appeal against the grant?—I think there would in those cases where there was an opposition.

62,466. You are talking of new licenses?—Of course, new licenses.

62,467. You are not talking of doing away with the right to appeal on the question of refusal to renew?—No. Renewal only comes before me by way of appeal. I am the appeal court in cases of renewal. Renewals come before the magistrates at petty sessions. If the party who applies for a renewal is refused, and he thinks wrongly, he can come before me.

62,468. Am I to understand that the whole of the evidence you have given as to the new licensing authority has reference entirely to the grant of new licenses?—To new licenses and transfers.

Renewals. — 62,469. You do not propose to interfere with the magistrates' present privileges as to renewals?—No, not at all, because they are bound down by principles which they must follow.

62,470. I do not think that was made quite clear?—I wish to make that perfectly clear. I said at the beginning of my evidence that I would not interfere with the present system of renewals in any shape or form. A man is entitled to a renewal if he can get the certificate of two justices that his house has been properly conducted during the previous year, and any objection that anyone has to his renewal must be stated and he must have notice of that, and if he is not given notice of it at the time the licensing sessions come on, the case must be adjourned for the purpose of enabling him to prepare his defence, and then if he is refused his renewal and he thinks wrongly, he can appeal to me at quarter sessions. So that he has full protection, and I would not interfere with this in any shape or form.

62,471. So that you are only interfering in the case of new licenses and transfers?—Yes, and spirit grocers.

62,472. The transfer is an important question, is it not?—It is an important question.

Licensing authority. — 62,473. And so that you would claim to be the sole authority?—Yes.

62,474. We have had county court judges, who suggested that that would be rather a serious responsibility?—I think if one takes the office one should take the responsibility too.

62,478. One question with reference to your objection to the decision in the Clitheroe case?—You would like to see that overridden by an Act of Parliament?—Yes.

62,479. That case was decided 20 years ago?—21 years ago, in the year 1867.

62,480. A large number of the public-houses at this moment must have been bought by people who considered they had a vested interest under that decision?—They must.

62,481. Do you think it would be reasonable to pass such a drastic Act of Parliament as that and interfere with the vested interests these people have acquired in these houses on the assumption that the law is what the Judges of the Queen's Bench Division have declared it was?—That raises the question of compensation, which is another matter altogether.

62,482. That is an important question in connection with your proposal. Would you approve, in such circumstances as that, of compensation being awarded to a man whose licence was taken away through no fault of his own?—That is a question I have not thought of. I must say.

62,483. Surely it is at the very root of your proposal?—I do not know that.

62,484. It is the first principle of making a proposal of that kind, to consider the interests of those in possession of it if they are in possession under the authority of the law?—Perhaps it would be fair, if a man did not get a transfer, to give him some compensation. I do not know, but I think the power of granting would be very sparingly used.

62,485. Now you are begging the question?—Yes, to some extent. I suppose it would come to this, that compensation would have to be given.

62,486. (*Mr. Golding.*) Your objection to the spirit grocer's licence in Ireland, I understand, is not so much to the licence itself as to the mode of granting it?—It is to the impossibility of refusing it.

62,487. Not to any special evil arising from it?—Yes. I think the spirit grocer's licence is a bad thing.

62,488. You are no doubt aware that with the extreme teetotal party it has been a very strong point, this attack on the grocer's licence?—I am not aware at all that it is one of their very strong points.

62,489. If you read teetotal literature you will see that it is so?—I never do.

62,490. Perhaps you would recognise that there is a certain amount of diplomacy in it. It is an attack on the weaker portion of the trade?—I have been looking at it as rather the other way, that the spirit grocer is a part of attack on the licensing trade.

62,491. There is an old saying of a celebrated leader to the effect that if you cannot attack the enemy as a body, attack them in sections, and therefore you would attack the weaker section?—The reason that I object is that the licensing authority, which in this case is the magistrates, have no discretion at all. In my own knowledge so-called spirit grocers have been established in wretched little hovels, nobody being able to prevent it, far away from police barracks and supervision.

62,492. That objection would be the same in every trade carried on in unsuitable premises, and under unsuitable conditions?—I think the spirit trade is different to all other trades.

62,493. Do not you think that this question of the evils of the grocer's licence has become with the extreme teetotal party more of a shibboleth than anything else, that you have only got to use the expression "grocer's licence" to get it attacked immediately?—I do not know, because I have never communicated very much with the teetotal party, but I know that all the other

62,496. Your knowledge would come from those districts?—My judicial knowledge comes from those districts, but I have other knowledge.

62,497. You are speaking judicially on this subject?—Principally. Of course I have my knowledge as an individual besides.

62,498. I do not want to traverse your opinion unnecessarily, but I would put it to you that you did not know what the powers of the licence were with reference to the sale in small quantities and "off," and that is an extremely important question in forming an opinion on the licence itself?—They can sell up to two quarts not to be consumed on the premises.

62,499. I understand you did not know really that the spirit grocer can sell in small quantities in open vessels?—No, I said as far as I knew there was nothing in the Act of Parliament to prevent him, but I did not know whether, as a matter of fact, he did.

62,500. Speaking of the two counties you represent, would that change your view at all? In the county Monaghan, speaking roughly, there is a population of 86,000?—I am not in Monaghan now.

62,501. I am going to take those two counties of Fermanagh and Monaghan because I understand you came here to speak with reference to those two counties?—I was there six years.

62,502. Speaking roughly, there is a population of 86,000 in the county Monaghan, and in that 86,000 there are five grocers' licences, and three of those are in Monaghan itself?—Yes.

62,503. I think you used the words that the spirit grocers' licences had increased enormously. Do those figures support that statement?—As far as they go they do not; but you will find other places where they do. In Belfast I understand there have been 250 additional spirit grocers in a short time.

62,504. I want to deal with places you represent?—If the law remains as it does at present, how many spirit grocers' licences do you think you will have in Monaghan in 10 years to come?

62,505. Do not you think the fact of whether the trade will pay or will not will regulate the number?—It seems to me every man who sells spirits makes money.

62,506. Then take Fermanagh with a population of 72,000, two grocers' licences in the whole county of Fermanagh?—Is that so?

62,507. Do you think that is a very enormous increase?—That cannot be a very enormous increase.

62,508. Could you say anywhere beyond Dublin and Belfast where this class of licence has enormously increased?—Those are the principal towns, and that is what was principally running in my mind when I made the statement.

62,509. I only want as far as possible to suggest to you to have an open mind on the subject. The entire number of spirit grocers' licences is 744 for the whole of Ireland, and if you except Dublin and Belfast you have got about 23 licences of this class for the whole of the rest of Ireland. Is it possible to say that a great amount of evil can result in Ireland from these 23 distributed over the whole country?—It is not so bad there as in the big towns, but I am sure of this, that the people are only beginning to find out the virtues of the spirit grocer's licence. It is only recently it has been decided that the magistrates must grant the spirit grocers' licence, and I think if the law remains as it is so that the number of spirit grocers all over the country will be tremendous, because any man refused an ordinary licence will take a spirit grocer's as a matter of course.

Judge [illegible]

but the original application goes to the petty sessions, and I cannot get evidence about them at all.

62,214. Really, so far as present licences are concerned, you have not much experience of the bad effects coming before you?—There have been a certain number of appeals. I know the law and I have been reading the cases on the subject.

62,215. You are not where they are. Yours is a rural district?—I know some applications have been made in very improper places that have come before me on appeal.

Licensing authority.

62,216. With reference to the licensing tribunal, do I understand you to say that you would like not only the county court judge, but in addition, probably, three or four local magistrates yearly elected?—I proposed that as an alternative to giving it to the county court judge alone, but after all, like the other witnesses who have been examined, I would rather have the county court judges without adjuncts; but if that is not done, then I should prefer to have a small committee of magistrates selected by themselves for each town.

62,217. Do not you think it would put rather too much power into the hands of one man if you put it in the hands of a Recorder or county court judge? Would it not be better to have elected yearly by the magistrates of the county, say three, four, or five magistrates yearly to sit with him?—I think the county court judges and Recorders, from their legal training, look on this from a more judicial point of view, and they are more inclined to go entirely on the evidence and on what is proved to them as to the wants of the neighbourhood than gentlemen, no matter how respectable or intelligent they may be, who have not had legal training, and I am of opinion with all my brethren—of course, you cannot expect perfection in this world—that the county court judge alone would be the best tribunal in the interests of the public.

62,218. The judges are human?—They are only human, of course.

62,219. The other course, I think, would be more agreeable to the public?—I am only giving my own opinion. I do not wish to dictate to anybody else.

Transfers.

62,220. With reference to transfers of course you would put those transfers under the same licensing authority?—They are; but I would give the licensing authority the same discretion as in the case of a new licence. My principal reason for that is what we all unfortunately know, that the population in many parts of Ireland is decreasing, and therefore a number of licences not excessive 30 years ago would be excessive now.

Judge [illegible]

[illegible] May '98

62,221. Supposing there was a trade carried on in an inferior house, you would in all cases, if there was a transfer sought for better premises, give the transfer notwithstanding the quantity of houses in the district?—I should as far as possible in the exercise of judicial duty try to ensure that the trade was carried on in good suitable houses in the hands of respectable men of good character. That would be the governing principle. I would subordinate everything else to that.

62,222. In the county of Derry you have no bad houses?—Not that I know of. I never heard of one.

Statistics of drunkenness.

62,223. In the county of Derry drunkenness is decreasing?—I cannot tell you that. I have no statistics.

62,224. That appears from the number of arrests yearly?—I do not think that the arrests are very much of a test. There is a great deal of drunkenness with reference to which there are no arrests at all. If a man is not absolutely incapable, or if he is with his friends who will take care of him, the police never arrest at all. They are satisfied with summoning him afterwards.

The six householders certificate.

62,225. On renewals there are six householders who must certify. Do you approve of the continuance of that?—Yes. I have already said that I would make no alteration in the law as regards renewals at all. I would allow a man, so long as he can get the certificate that he has conducted the house properly, to renew.

62,226. Is it necessary for six householders to certify?—I think it is desirable. I do not say that if one were making the law for the first time that one would select six as the number, but finding six there I do not see any reason to change it.

Excessive number of licences.

62,227. It is not in the county where you are now, but in Fermanagh and Monaghan you referred to an excessive number of public-houses in Derrygonnelly?—I gave that as an instance.

62,228. Might I ask whether those houses were not in the centre of a large or extensive rural district—from which enormous quantities of people come? Were they not for the supply of a large area?—There is a very large area beyond it with no other town or village, but I am not aware that the fairs were very large there. There at the time that there were 280 people and 10 public-houses.

The witness withdrew.

Judge Waters. 18 May '97.

[illegible] in patent and [illegible]. There is no [illegible] of it at all. I may state that I myself have been canvassed. I have been asked to grant a license to A.B. or C.D. or some particular person. That has occurred three times in my experience.

[illegible]. Then if these things happened to you it is more probable they occur largely to the magistrates?—As I have said, my opinion is that the canvassing of magistrates is patent and notorious. It has taken place on the bench beside me, and when I have been sitting on the bench I have heard the magistrates canvassing and [illegible] with each other, or one man having an interest in a particular applicant or license and canvassing his brother magistrates to vote for him.

County Court Judge as sole authority.

[illegible]. A good many Commissioners have asked the opinions of previous witnesses whether they think there would be any objection to putting the power in the hands of one man. What do you say to that?—I do not know that there would be any objection. The law at present has put into the hands of the county court judges jurisdiction that reaches the [illegible] of human life to a far greater extent than giving a license to a man to carry on a public-house. I can send a man to penal servitude for his life, I can dispose of property [illegible] to the extent of [illegible] with land valued at [illegible]. The law [illegible] that jurisdiction to me; and I think it is not saying too much when I say that it appears to me that that is just as important as granting a license to a person in a small village.

[illegible]. You have had a long experience, and therefore your opinion is of great weight?—I have been [illegible] years sitting on the bench in Ireland.

[illegible]. You think public opinion would not be against giving the power, such as it is, to one judge?—It is very hard for me to say. I think that if Ireland were polled to-morrow there would be an immense vote in favour of reducing public-houses, and doing anything that is possible to prevent them from increasing in the future. However, that is a [illegible] opinion, to which I would not attach any importance. I have seen on the bench, in the administration of the law at present, proceedings in respect to which I think I do not use too strong a word when I say they were scandalous. I have seen cases such as this. One man applies for a license in a small town. He is objected to by the police on the ground that an additional public-house is not required there, and a number of justices perhaps will vote, [illegible], in number to refuse that license. That applicant, perhaps, had no friend on the bench. Then another case comes up a few months afterwards, the same objection is made, and the men who voted against the man a few months ago because his house was not necessary, vote for the other man because they have been canvassed, or because they are friends of his.

[illegible]. Do you think the magistrates themselves would resent the licensing powers being taken away from them?—That is a matter of opinion. Perhaps they would be hurt. I do not know.

Adjourned for a short time.

[illegible] in the Chair.

Renewals.

[illegible] (Mr. [illegible].) In your evidence you suggested that there ought to be a new tribunal entirely for the granting of licenses. What is your opinion about the existing tribunal which has the privilege of granting renewals in sessions?—Renewals are granted, as a matter of course, by justices at petty sessions, unless some objection is made.

[illegible]. Transfers are granted by whom?—In the first instance, by the petty sessions, and the petty sessions are only able to grant what is called an interim transfer that holds good to the next quarter sessions.

[illegible]. Do you propose any alteration with reference to that system?—No.

Transfers.

[illegible]. Only with reference to new licenses?—Only with reference to new licenses. Generally speaking, there is no difficulty about transfers, unless any question is raised as to the character of the man who applies for the transfer. That, so far as my experience goes, is the only circumstance that raises any question at all. Generally speaking, as regards transfers, they pass off without any discussion whatsoever, just as a mere matter of right.

[illegible]. Have you any opinion with reference to the question of appeals from the single judge who would sit in the new court?—I have not thought about that at all.

[illegible]. You do not think an appeal would be necessary?—I do not think so.

[illegible]. So long as the [illegible] responsibility is confined to the granting of licenses?—Yes.

[illegible]. (Mr. [illegible].) I think you want to confine the licensing laws to the county court judge, and the Recorder in cities?—That is the granting of licenses.

Judge Waters. 18 May '97.

Transfers.

[illegible]. And the transfers as well?—Yes, but as I have already said in the case of transfers it is an exceedingly rare thing that any question at all arises, because the house has already been licensed and therefore that puts an end to anything about the fitness of the house, and the only case in which any question could arise is if objection is made to the character of the new man, which very seldom arises.

County authority.

[illegible]. I think you were asked in cross-examination, whether you thought the county court judge should be made the licensing authority, and it was objected that there would be too much power in the hands of one man, and I think you said you had [illegible] as important to deal with as the granting of licenses?—So it appears to me.

[illegible]. But this granting of licenses is a very different sort of thing from the administration of law. Would it not be better to have some of the local magistrates with you who have a knowledge of the [illegible] of the country?—I have already expressed my opinion on that point that I think it would be better not. In anything that I said, of course, I did not speak of magistrates universally. I know a great many magistrates who exercise their jurisdiction with the greatest care. But on the other hand I mean my [illegible] is looked upon as a part of the judicial jurisdiction as to which it is not necessary to exercise any conscientious consideration, but it is looked upon as a thing in which the justices may administer the law by favour.

[illegible]. (Dean [illegible].) A bit of patronage?—Quite so. I wish again to guard myself. I do not mean to say that it is to be applied to all justices. On the contrary, I know some most highly conscientious, most honourable gentlemen to whom I would entrust the matter with as much confidence as to any county court judge.

[illegible]. (Mr. [illegible].) Does not it arise from this, that what is everybody's business comes to be nobody's business, and does not come to be a responsibility?—Possibly.

[illegible]. What I want to know is this, whether three or four magistrates appointed by the [illegible] of the county, who would sit with the county court judges, would not feel the responsibility of their position as much as the judge would?—I hope so.

[illegible]. And it would alter the condition of things very much, would it not, in your opinion?—I really have never considered that matter. I would not wish to offer any opinion about it.

[illegible]. Your present opinion is to take away the power entirely from the local magistrates?—Yes.

Canvassing.

[illegible]. Are they canvassed?—Most unquestionably. Perhaps you did not hear me say that I have been canvassed myself. Thinking it was so common and so right a thing to do, persons were not ashamed to come to ask me to vote before I had heard the case in court at all.

[illegible]. Are they as impervious as you are to this sort of solicitation?—I can only speak for myself.

[illegible]. I know your county well, and they are very respectable magistrates?—Highly respectable gentlemen, some of them.

Drinking in Cavan and Leitrim.

[illegible]. Do not you think in your county drunkenness is on the decrease?—I really am not able to form an opinion upon that. I believe the Irish people generally have the character of being drunkards. I believe they deserve the exactly opposite character. I speak now of the country that I know of, the counties of Cavan and Leitrim. I think the people are remarkably sober. They go to a fair and get the drink there. They cannot sell a pig, or a cow, or do any business without having several treats over it, treats on one side or the other. Treats are the ruination of these people. A man will not taste a drop of drink from that till the next time he goes in, and I believe that really the peasantry of Ireland are a remarkably sober people.

42,564. It is the kindliness of their natures to be generous to each another when they meet?—It is a matter of [illegible] more than anything else, perhaps, springing from what you say.

42,565. In your time as county court judge, have public-houses increased?—Yes, they have; but I have only a [illegible] knowledge and I speak from a [illegible] recollection. I have no details as to the number there are, but to my own personal knowledge I know they have increased in several of the small towns in Cavan.

42,566. And that is owing to the granting of new licences?—Yes.

42,567. Which were granted by the local justices?—Yes. They took it all in their own hands. I do not recollect an occasion on which I voted on the granting of a licence.

42,568. You are simply chairman?—I say to the justices, "You are accountable for the peace of the county, as you depends [illegible]"; and I leave them to vote as they like.

42,569. You want to alter that condition of things?—I do. For instance, in this respect. The law says that applications for new licences must be made at the licensing sessions. The licensing quarter sessions in Cavan and Leitrim are the October sessions. A man applies in January for a new licence. I have told the magistrates over and over again—I do not apply this to one county or the other, and I want leave you entirely in the dark as to what I am pointing out when I say to the justices, "The law is that the applications should be made at the licensing sessions in October," and I tell them that my view of the law is that they have power under the law, notwithstanding that, to grant a licence at any other sessions than the licensing sessions. I tell the magistrates that my view of the law is that they ought not to grant a licence at any sessions other than the licensing quarter sessions, unless there be some exceptional circumstances in the case that render it just and proper to do so. They disregard that altogether, and a man coming up, who has come back from America, or has got [illegible] from America, and has got a house, applies for a licence, and if he has got enough friends on the bench, they give it him without any question at all. For a long time I went through the form of asking the justices in the first instance, "Do you think there are any exceptional circumstances in this case?" and their view as to the exceptional circumstances seemed to be so different from mine, that I gave up the practice in the end as a futile proceeding, and I now just simply ask them, "Are you in favour of giving the licence or not"?

42,570. You have Sunday closing?—Yes.

42,571. Does it work well?—I cannot say. I have only experience on the bench.

42,572. Have you any drunkenness on Sunday?—I do not know.

42,573. Any arrests?—I cannot say. I do not know. All the [illegible] with reference to arrests will be with the police, and I do not know about it at all. I simply see them quoted in the paper sometimes, but I do not know anything about them.

42,574. (*Dean Dickinson.*) Do you think that, as is proposed in the Bill now before Parliament, that for drunkenness there ought to be provision for two classes of inebriates, the criminal inebriates, and those simply become inebriates where there is no crime connected with it?—I think that distinction should be always held between them.

42,575. Do you think that the Bill on the whole ought to be extended to Ireland?—I should be very glad that it should.

42,576. The reason I asked the question is because I want to bring it out plainly that the whole weight of opinion of the Irish witnesses is in favour of the extension of that Bill?—I should be very glad to have it extended to Ireland, hoping for the best that it would be of some use.

Judge Waters.

10 May '98.

Habitual drunkards.

The witness withdrew.

Mr. Alexander Taylor called in and examined.

42,577. (*Viscount de Vesci.*) You are Secretary to the Belfast United Trades and Labour Council?—Yes.

42,578. And you have a fairly extensive knowledge of the working classes and have had an opportunity of knowing their opinions on most subjects affecting their interests?—Yes.

42,579. Will you state what their opinions are with reference to the number of public-houses and spirit grocers which are permitted in working-class districts?—I believe the opinion of the working classes is that too many licences are licensed in the working-class districts of Belfast.

42,580. As compared with the residential portions of the town and city of Belfast?—Yes.

42,581. You think that the residential portions have not the excessive number that you think there is in the working-class districts?—That is so.

42,582. What do you think would be the result of a poll of the working classes in Belfast regarding the number of public-houses?—I believe the number would be considerably lessened in the working-class districts.

42,583. If they had a voice in the issue of licences?—Yes.

42,584. Have you anything else you wish to say with reference to the undue number of public-houses?—No, except with reference to spirit grocers.

42,585. Would you tell the Commission what you have to say with reference to them?—Spirit grocers are regarded with more abhorrence than the public-houses, and the general opinion is that they are the most potent cause in the demoralisation of women, and lead to drinking amongst women who go under the cloak of buying groceries and purchasing cheap groceries, and purchase drink.

42,586. Is that a fact in your opinion that groceries are sold cheaper in those houses than sold between?—Slightly.

42,587. You think that is done for an inducement to go and deal there?—I decidedly do. I think it is to allure women to them.

42,588. The result being what?—That women get into the habit of deceiving their husbands by going ostensibly to purchase groceries and purchasing drink, and children are also educated in the art of deception.

42,589. Do the women run up accounts at these shops?—In some of them I know they do. I do not know about all.

42,590. Do you believe they get liquor put down to them under the head of other commodities?—Yes. It is quite a common practice to get liquor put down as "goods."

42,591. Generally?—Yes.

42,592. Not specifically under the head of any particular groceries but under the head of "goods"?—Yes.

42,593. Will you say what your opinion is with reference to children?—Children are sent to these houses, I believe, more frequently than to ordinary public-houses for drink, simply because they may be going for some groceries and can purchase drink along with them, and this leads to the father being very often deceived in that way, and leads to a great deal of [illegible] in the home and discomfort.

42,594. Do you believe that the children are served in these houses with drink?—When sent by their parents for it.

42,595. You are talking of the spirit grocer?—Yes.

42,596. Not the ordinary publican who sells other goods besides drink?—I believe the same practice obtains with the ordinary publican who sells other goods, but in Belfast there are not a great number of them in proportion to the population.

42,597. They are not so prevalent as in other parts of Ireland?—I do not think so.

Mr. A. Taylor.

Children [illegible] [illegible].

Mr. A. Taylor. 30 May '97.

62,598. What you speak of more particularly is the spirit grocer?—Yes. He generally sells tea, sugar, and tobacco.

62,599. And ought to be suppressed altogether?—Yes.

62,600. Children are sent, you say, to fetch away drink from these grocers, besides bringing home groceries?—Yes.

Abolition of spirit grocers.

62,601. On that head is there anything else you wish to add for the information of the Commission?—Yes. I think it would be a great advantage if the spirit grocer's licences were entirely abolished, and I think it would also be in harmony with public opinion in Belfast. I am certain that at least 90 per cent. of the working men of Belfast would vote for the abolition of the spirit grocer's licence.

62,602. They would vote for the abolition of the mixed licence?—Yes.

62,603. Has any poll ever been taken of the people of Belfast, to your knowledge, regarding the spirit grocers?—No, I have never known it.

Sunday and early Saturday closing.

62,604. On the general licensing question?—Yes; many years ago there was a poll taken, and a very large majority was in favour of Sunday closing.

62,605. Total Sunday closing?—Yes.

62,606. Your opinion is that Saturday early closing and total Sunday closing would conduce to the general diminution of drunkenness. Will you state what hours the houses ought to close on Saturdays?—I think 9 o'clock would be a reasonable hour. I have observed that there is a deal more drunkenness after 9 o'clock, and a great many more drunken people to be seen in the streets after that hour; and, besides, it would allow certain men that have been drinking to get home with the residue of their money, and their wives could make purchases at other shops, and that would allow other shopkeepers to get closed. Some have to open on Sunday morning.

62,607. On what day are the bulk of the working classes paid their wages in Belfast?—Fridays and Saturdays, some on Thursday.

62,608. But the bulk?—The bulk, I believe, on Saturday.

62,609. (Mr. Whitaker.) Saturday is the market day?—Yes.

62,610. (Viscount de Vesci.) What time do the factories close on Saturdays?—The ordinary workshops half-past 1; the shipyards and foundries close at 12.

62,611. Are they paid their wages just before the hour of closing?—The ship-yards are paid on Friday, and, I believe, the foundries are principally paid on Saturday, but I am not quite sure. I know the mills are largely paid on Saturday.

62,612. Up to what hour is this increase of drunken people to be seen on Saturday?—Up to half-past 11 a great number of people are to be seen drunk.

The bona fide traveller.

62,613. What effect does that have under the bona fide clause?—I believe that this conduces to a man getting up early on Sunday morning and endeavouring to obtain drink illicitly, and those that cannot do it on account of the surveillance of the police, go to the three mile limit, which is actually within the borough of Belfast now.

62,614. What is the area of the borough of Belfast now?—I should think it would extend to about four miles.

62,615. Then it is possible to obtain drink even within the extent of the Borough of Belfast?—Yes.

62,616. What you state is that the men will drink to a late hour on Saturday evening, and then these men would go out under the bona fide clause on Sunday morning and get more drink?—Yes.

62,617. Can you give us any information as to the numbers of these bona fide travellers on Sunday?—Yes. I have frequently seen them coming down one of the leading roads in Belfast—the Antrim Road—just after the church hour and immediately before the houses would open in town, and coming from a house that is known as a bona fide traveller's house, drunk and unseemly insulting respectable people, and I have seen the police having to interfere; but, of course, these are what are generally called the rowdy element.

62,618. Will you state the feeling of the citizens and working classes of Belfast with reference to Sunday closing?—I believe the majority of the working classes are decidedly in favour of Sunday closing, and in proof of that I would mention the result of the first plebiscite that was taken years ago, and the great number of public meetings that have been held on the subject, because a considerable portion of the working classes are members of temperance societies, and, of course, all those are favourable. Again, in all the Protestant churches at least resolutions have been passed in favour of Sunday closing, and I have never known a public meeting convened against it in Belfast.

Mr. A. Taylor.

Sunday closing.

62,619. How does it affect the publican's assistants?—Their hours are extremely long, and I think even out of sympathy with them a great many men, who perhaps would not be averse to taking a drink on Sunday, to give them a holiday would be disposed to favour Sunday closing. I have frequently heard working men declare that they were in favour of Sunday closing, owing to the long hours the publican's assistants were compelled to work.

62,620. Men who otherwise were not total abstainers?—Yes.

Payment of wages in public-houses.

62,621. Now will you give your opinion as regards the payment of wages in public-houses. What evidence can you give with regard to that?—So far as I have actual knowledge of it, I do not think the payment of wages in public-houses in Belfast is very general, but there is certainly one very flagrant instance of it, that is a violation of the spirit of that Act. There is a firm of stevedores who also own three large public-houses. Is it necessary to give the name?

62,622. I think you had better not give the name, but state the general facts?—These stevedores are in virtual command of the whole work of the docks. They employ between 400 and 500 men. The men are paid in the yard that adjoins the public-house, and they are kept waiting there frequently for hours for their wages, and, of course, the temptation to drink is very great. I may say that to men casually employed, of course, it is a very heavy temptation to them, and they can obtain drink on credit as a sort of lien on their wages during the day. They wait there for sometimes hours after work at night, and I may say this has been felt to be such an injustice to these men that the matter has been discussed publicly in Belfast. The paper that is established under the auspices of the Belfast Trades Council, the "Belfast Citizen," has had several articles written under the name of the Secretary of the Dockers, Mr. Michael McKeown. A resolution was also passed by the trades council condemning the system, and a deputation was appointed, of which I was one, to wait on the Harbour Commissioners asking them to issue licences to stevedores and to give no stevedore's licence to any man who was a publican.

62,623. Is there any entrance from the public-house into this yard?—Yes, it has a door adjacent.

62,624. The men have to go out of the yard into the street when waiting for their wages to get in the public-house entrance?—Yes.

62,625. Neither the yard nor the place where they are paid are actually within the bounds of the licensed premises?—I believe that is so. I am not absolutely sure, but they are quite convenient and adjacent.

62,626. But you cannot say for certain they are within the actual limits of the licensed premises?—I could not.

62,627. In your opinion does it come within the purview of the law, the practice that goes on now of paying in this yard adjoining the public-house?—I think it can scarcely come within the law because it will be pretty well known, but it is certainly a violation of the spirit of the Act.

62,628. Have the police in any way taken action with reference to the matter at all?—Their attention has been directed to it, but I have never heard of any prosecutions.

62,629. What is the result of that—have you heard?—I have not.

62,630. You stated that this firm have got three public-houses?—Yes.

62,631. Are the other two at all adjacent?—No, they are not convenient.

62,632. Not for the docks?—One is a mile from the docks, or more. I am not sure where the third one is, but it is the one adjoining the docks we are complaining of.

62,633. Are there any other facts you wish to bring before the Commission on this particular subject of the payment of wages at public-houses?—No, I do not think I can add anything.

62,634. Does the system of paying wages in that way prevail anywhere else in Belfast?—I have no direct

Mr. A. Taylor. 16 May '98

they would not want it, but, not being so, they will put it somewhere. You say 14 per cent. would be for the abolition of the spirit grocer's licence, and I ask you, would they goods, meaning to the public-house?—I think I stated that the objection is, because of the deception practised. They would know when they were sending a child to the public-house what it was going for. They are used to the spirit grocers ostensibly for groceries and they bring out a bottle.

62,675. What evidence have you to support that statement?—The experience of 15 or 20 years.

62,676. Your own personal experience?—Yes, my own personal experience.

62,677. Can you produce anything in the shape of a public expression of opinion that would support it?—Yes. I have known the spirit grocer's licence to be opposed, and action to be taken in a working-class neighbourhood, which is rather an uncommon thing with reference to a spirit grocer's, and simply because of the disfavour with which they regard it.

62,678. With reference to the question of deception, your idea is that the practice goes on largely in those places of booking beer and spirits, or porter and spirits, as "goods"?—Yes, in some of them.

Liquor charged as other goods.

62,679. Surely, if they wanted to practise deception, they would not say "goods," but they would say sugar, for instance?—They may vary it. I have known goods to be put down. I have actually seen it myself.

62,680. Are you quite sure what you have seen is not in a statement of a supply for a time, and they were rendering the statement which has gone in under the heading of "goods"?—No.

62,681. It seems a little extraordinary, because when you want to deceive, you generally use the term that will deceive best. If you booked whisky as "sugar" you would deceive, but booking it as "goods," you do not?—Well, it would take a large amount of sugar to represent a small amount of whisky.

62,682. Speaking of Belfast, I believe there are a large number of the spirit grocer's licences distributed over the residential quarters of Belfast, are there not?—I am aware of it.

Position of spirit grocers.

62,683. Of course, you are aware that in Ireland you can only carry on your trade under the spirit grocer's licence or publican's licence?—Yes.

62,684. You are aware that there are large traders in Belfast carrying on that trade?—Yes.

62,685. I could name 20 houses, and you would recognise them all, probably?—Not in the residential districts.

62,686. In the best quarters of Belfast. I only want to put it that the statement you are making is condemning a body of respectable tradesmen. I do not say there may not be some where the licence has got into the wrong hands, but there is a large class of respectable traders in Belfast who carry on that trade properly, surely?—There may be.

62,687. And you do not know them?—I do not know of them. I have never heard them spoken of as a respectable body.

62,688. Though you are connected with a trades council representing 12,000 members, and can speak for 85 per cent. of the working population of Belfast, you do not know a respectable grocer's licence in Belfast?—I have never heard them spoken of as a respectable body.

62,689. (Mr. Young.) I suppose you represent yourself. Are you sent here to represent anybody?—I am here to give my opinion and my experience, I presume.

Position of witness.

62,690. By whom are you sent?—I expect I am invited by this Commission that wishes to investigate.

62,691. In Belfast are you commissioned by any society, or any persons from Belfast, to come to represent public opinion there?—No, I am not commissioned by any person in Belfast or any society in Belfast.

Liquor charged as other goods.

62,692. Now how many instances do you know really of goods being put down in the place of whisky as you suggest?—I have known of several and heard of a great many.

62,693. Did you ever really examine them?—Yes.

62,694. How many more?—I have not kept count, but if you ask them I am prepared to say third, and [illegible].

62,695. You say there was a plebiscite taken vote in Belfast, when the working people of Belfast expressed their opinion in favour of Sunday closing?—Yes.

62,696. Are you aware that there was a petition from the publicans of Belfast with 1,000 more signatures than appeared on the plebiscite—that there were in favour of it?—No, I am not aware of it.

62,697. The petition was signed by many more than what appeared on the plebiscite?—I heard of the petition, but I never heard of the exact number. I heard of it being in the public-houses on a Saturday evening, and a large number of signatures being got to it.

62,698. Did you ever hear that there were a great many more signatures to the petition than what appeared on the plebiscite?—I did not.

62,699. (Mr. Whitaker.) As secretary to those trade councils you may be considered to occupy a representative position, I suppose?—Yes.

62,700. Was there a municipal election last November in Belfast?—Yes.

62,701. Were six labour members elected at that time?—There were.

62,702. Was attention drawn to the fact before the election, and published in the papers, that these labour members were all in favour of Sunday closing and earlier closing on Saturday night?—Yes. There were questions issued asking their opinions regarding the subject, and I understand all the labour members were favourable.

62,703. And the labour members who replied that they were in favour of this Sunday closing and early closing on Saturday night were, at the municipal elections, elected?—All elected.

62,704. We may take that as an indication of public opinion, may we not?—It certainly evidently did them no harm.

62,705. Have public meetings frequently been held in favour of Sunday closing and earlier Saturday night closing in Belfast?—Frequently.

62,706. Has there ever been a public meeting against it?—I have never known of a public meeting against it.

62,707. (Mr. Young.) In consequence of the questions put by Mr. Whitaker I will ask you this. I have in my hand here a paper edited by you, called the "Belfast Citizen," in which there is an article dated April last, written by yourself, I suppose, on the very question of these municipal elections, in which this language is used: "These, says the report,"—that is the United Trades and Labour Council Report—"were all elected on the labour ticket, they did not "owe their commencement to the advocacy of any "political or religious creed—they sought to be "returned as direct labour representatives pledged to "oppose jobbery, to safeguard the public health, to "uphold the rights of labour, and to secure for the "municipal revenue money that is at present appropriated by private individuals and companies. This "programme commended itself to the electors of "Belfast, and completely triumphed over the petty "parrot cries." Will you tell me where any reference whatever to Sunday closing or temperance comes in that?—You are quite right. There was no reference so far as the programme was concerned, but there was a reference as to the questions were asked. Questions were asked by our organisation in Belfast of each candidate, and sent to each candidate, were they favourable to Sunday closing and early Saturday closing. We were favourable to it.

62,708. Those who were elected?—Those who were elected.

62,709. It was not at all a test question at the election, I suppose? It was not made so by you because you say so?—It was not made by us, but I have no doubt it influenced a large number of votes in our favour. I know I was worked for by a temperance body.

62,710. Is it not misleading, holding the position you do, and holding the views you do in the temperance party, you do not say so here?—It is not at all misleading.

The witness withdrew.

Adjourned to to-morrow at 10.30.

ONE HUNDRED AND FIFTH DAY.

Queen's Robing Room, House of Lords, Wednesday, May 11th, 1898.

PRESENT:

THE RIGHT HONOURABLE THE VISCOUNT [illegible], in the Chair.

The Very Rev. H. H. [illegible], Dean.	John [illegible] [illegible], Esq., M.P.
William Allen, Esq., M.P.	Charles Walker, Esq.
William [illegible] [illegible], Esq.	Thomas Palmer Whittaker, Esq., M.P.
Henry [illegible], Esq.	[illegible] Young, Esq., M.P.
Samuel [illegible], Esq.	George [illegible], Esq.
Andrew Johnston, Esq.	

The Rev. Michael Ahern, R.C.C., called in and examined.

The Rev. M. Ahern, R.C.C.

43,711. (*Viscount de Vesci.*) You are the curate of Ladysbridge, Castlemartyr, county Cork?—I am.

East Riding of Cork.

43,712. I believe that you propose to speak of the East Riding of county Cork?—Yes, principally the East Riding of county Cork.

Excessive number of public-houses in Cork.

43,713. Will you give the Commission your opinion as to the number of public-houses?—I strongly believe that the public-houses in the whole county are three or four times too numerous.

43,714. What is the proportion in the East Riding?—The proportion in the East Riding has been given as 1 to 71.

Composition of the population.

43,715. Do you accept that proportion as being correct?—Yes; but to fully understand its significance, we must take account of the composition of the population, and also of its character. In Ireland, owing to emigration and to enlistment for the army and navy and the police force, we possess to a large extent but the old and young, so that a ratio of public-houses to the inhabitants, which in England would be barely sufficient to satisfy the needs of the people, would in Ireland be altogether excessive, because of the number of males between the ages of 20 and 35 who have left the country.

43,716. What is the state of public opinion as to women drinking in public-houses?—There is a very strong public opinion against women being seen drinking in public-houses at all in Ireland, and I am of opinion that if it were left to the people to determine how many public-houses would be necessary to satisfy the reasonable requirements of the community they would not take account of females.

[illegible]

43,717. What is the practice of the Roman Catholic bishops?—The Roman Catholic bishops when confirming the children give, with the approval of the parents, a total abstinence pledge which binds them until the age of 21.

43,718. Meaning by that if the parents objected they would not administer the pledge?—The parents not only permit them to administer it, but earnestly desire them to do so.

43,719. I suppose there are no instances where the parent objects?—I do not know any instance where a parent objected. Even before children are confirmed at all they come and ask the priest to administer the pledge binding them till 21, and I think this shows that in the opinion of the people, the public-houses of the country are not, or at all events ought not to be, provided for the minors.

43,720. This pledge binds the children until the age of 21?—Yes.

[illegible]

43,721. What is the usual age they go up to be confirmed?—From 9 to 12 or 14. That much of the women of women drink in these public-houses, but that is regarded as one of the natural consequences of the conditions of publichouses in the country, and especially of the objectionable character of some of them, inasmuch as they carry on other trades with the liquor trade on the same premises.

The Rev. M. Ahern, R.C.C.

11 May '98.

43,722. It is the case that the majority of public-house licensees carry on other trades?—It is.

43,723. Is it mainly to sell groceries, or other things?—Yes, general groceries. Some have a meal and flour business, and generally all kinds of businesses are connected with them.

43,724. The majority of the mixed trades are in provisions?—Yes. That gives women, of course, a plea for entering such houses, and it protects them from the influence of public opinion. For instance, quite recently I saw a farmer's wife having a man and a very young boy into a public-house. This house was a general grocery and meal-seller's establishment, as well as a public-house. On returning from the premises I remonstrated with her on the impropriety of bringing a young child into the public-house to drink, and she immediately answered me that the reason she went in was to pay a little bill. She said her only reason for entering the public-house was to pay a bill. Then I have it also on the authority of a person who lived for about two years in one of those houses, that on fair days and market days especially a large number of women drink in them. There is another reason also

Refreshments elsewhere than in public-houses.

why women in Ireland drink in public-houses, and that is the difficulty of getting other refreshments, such as tea and coffee, in other houses, and they believe that it would be rather beneath their position in life to enter the small houses in which those provisions are kept. They are of a very low character, and the farmers' wives do not go in there, and the consequence is that they enter the public-houses, and very often take porter there for their lunch or dinner.

43,725. Do you mean by that that the inferior grocers do not have licenses in the shops they object to go into?—They have not got licenses. Then there is also a reason why boys break their pledges before they come to the age of 21, and another reason is, of course, the great difficulty in getting other refreshments in these public-houses.

43,726. Would you be in favour of compelling the publican to have other refreshments besides intoxicating liquors?—Yes, I should like him to have other refreshments as well. I should prefer, of course, that there should be an opportunity for other bodies to carry on exclusively the business of supplying temperance refreshments, but if that could not be done, I would have the public-houses in Ireland supply other refreshments, such as tea and coffee, and especially milk. These young boys, when they go to the fairs and markets, must take something, and when they enter the public-houses they will get nothing except temperance drinks or distasteful liquors. The temperance drinks which are kept in the majority of these little houses in the villages in Ireland and small towns are of a very inferior quality and very unpalatable. I have taken them frequently myself, and they really are unpalatable. Therefore they must either take the strong

62,730. Is there any reason why purely temperance houses should not be started in these villages in Ireland? You say that facilities ought to be given to have the temperance houses?—Certainly.

62,731. What difficulty is there in having them?—From the very fact of there being such a number of public-houses in the villages there is no room whatsoever for the other houses.

62,732. You have, I believe, a return of the proportion of public-houses to males over 20 years of age?—Taking the principal towns of Ireland, I find that the proportion of males over 20 years of age to the total population is only one-fourth and that holds good also with reference to the villages.

62,733. You live in a village yourself?—I live in a village. Then if we look at the [illegible] of the [illegible], I find that a large percentage of them are over the age of 60.

62,734. Are you also acquainted with the county Kerry?—I am not acquainted with the county Kerry, but I have some extracts from the [illegible] of the judge of county Kerry with reference to the number of public-houses.

62,735. Is that Judge Shaw?—Yes.

62,736. We have had the evidence about Kerry?—In the principal towns the proportion of the public-houses to males over 20 years is about 1 to 12. It varies, of course, in the different towns. In Queenstown it is 1 to 20, and in Mitchelstown it is 1 to 9 or 10; in Mallow it is 1 to 14, and in the whole county the public-houses are as 1 to 14, including the city of Cork. Then if you come to the villages, the proportion in many of the villages is as 1 to 8 or 9.

62,737. Is that in the portion of the county you know the best, the East Riding of Cork?—Yes. Of course this proportion shows to what a frightful extent the villages and the small towns are overcrowded with public-houses, especially when taking into consideration the feelings of the people with reference to Sunday, and with reference also to [illegible], that they ought not to enter public-houses, or public-houses ought not to be [illegible] by them. That really is a very strong feeling in Ireland so far as I am acquainted with the public feeling and opinion. Then I should like to give an instance of the proximity of these villages. For instance, I live in a village myself, the village of Ladysbridge, and I will take a circular tour around. I will start from that little village and come back to it again. In the village where I live, we have four public-houses, one for every 25 of the inhabitants.

62,738. How many houses are there in the village—can you form any idea?—I did not count them.

62,739. Can you give us an approximate idea of the number of houses?—Perhaps it will be 40 or 50, I should think.

62,740. And there are 4 licensed houses?—Yes. I have a photograph of the village here, where the houses are shown (producing same). Then 4½ miles to the east of Ladysbridge there is the village of Ballymacoda, which has 4 public-houses. There is 1 for every 22 of the inhabitants, and 1 for every 6 of the males over 21 years of age. Then 4 miles to the north of Ballymacoda is Killeagh. There there are 6 public-houses, 1 for every 44 of the inhabitants, and 1 for every 12 males exceeding 21. Then north of Killeagh 3 miles is Mount Uniacke, where there are 3 or 4 inhabited houses, 2 of which are public-houses, and a mile from there is another public-house, and then away from it in the contrary direction, we come back again to Ladysbridge, and it is only 3 miles from Killeagh; but 2½ miles to the west of Killeagh is the village of Mogeely, with 2 public-

[illegible] otherwise come home sober and [illegible], to remain out late and get intoxicated. I am authorised also to say that this is the experience of the Bishop of [illegible], and of his priests, and is I believe, so far as I have been able to find out, the opinion also of the other priests of the county.

Public [illegible]

42,744. You attribute that to the excessive number of public-houses?—Yes; I myself can bear witness to the extent of the evil. For a few years past, whenever I happened to be in a village on the occasion of a fair in a neighbouring town, almost invariably I looked to see whether any horses and cars were drawn up at the public-houses, and I do not remember a single instance of passing by one of those villages of an afternoon or evening of the day on which there was a fair held in some neighbouring town, that I did not notice from 1 or 2 up to 17 or 20 horses and cars outside the public-houses, and perhaps 4 or 5 miles away from the town at which the fair was held. The fair is generally over about 2 o'clock, and the majority of the people leave the fair for home in very good time.

42,745. They begin at a very early hour?—Yes, and the people are generally coming home from about 12 o'clock, but then they [illegible] on their way at the different public-houses. It is the custom when they travel in company to treat one another at those different houses, and they go into almost every one they meet from the time they leave the fair till they come home; and the result of that is that a large number of these people do not reach home on fair days till midnight. I have frequently myself heard cars coming from the fairs [illegible] as late as 10 and 11, and sometimes up till 12 o'clock at night.

42,746. Do you find in consequence of that there are many charged by the police of being drunk in charge of a horse and cart?—No, I never knew any charged by the police on those occasions.

42,747. It is usually treated as an aggravation of an offence to be in charge of a horse and cart, if a man is prosecuted for being drunk?—Certainly. I remember one evening noticing some of those cars at a public-house, and I went on my bicycle to a fair field, which was 3 miles away, to see whether many of the country people remained at the fair-place after the fair was over. I did not see anyone. They had all left. I then rode to another village, which was about [illegible] miles the other side of the town, and there I found two horses and cars outside a public-house with the people inside drinking, and they were very [illegible] and could easily be heard outside. I [illegible] [illegible] up the village from which I started, and there were the horses and cars still outside the doors of the public-house.

42,748. The principal drinking is on the way home?—On the way home, and numbers of accidents occur in those [illegible], and some of these accidents [illegible] fatal. I have known some of those to [illegible] fatally.

[illegible]

42,749. Do you state that the police do not do their duty in taking notice of these offences?—I do not say that with reference to the fairs, but I have often noticed the police in the village, and these horses outside the public-houses without a single person in charge of them, and the police never noticed it.

42,750. That is an offence against the law?—I believe it is, but what I have to say with reference to the police applies principally to races and popular [illegible]. On those occasions they very seldom arrest a person for being drunk, except the case is so strong that they could not possibly overlook it. I have seen them taking persons home on those occasions. And once I asked a constable why it was that persons whom he would arrest on other occasions, he would on the occasion of a race or regatta, allow home, and he said such were the instructions issued to the police.

42,751. Were those persons summoned afterwards?—They were not summoned.

[illegible]

42,752. Your suggestion is that they see these facts, but do not take any further steps?—That is so. Then the multiplication of public-houses causes a great deal of drunkenness on the occasion of races. When the people are returning from the races, they also go to these public-houses and remain out very late. I remember on one occasion going to some public-houses about 6 miles from the race-field, to see whether there were many people drinking in them, and I noticed that they were filled with men, and that most of those I saw were heavily under the influence of drink. I would not say they were drunk, but they were heavily under the influence of drink. Then I asked the opinion of some friends whether those races were generally got up and organised by publicans, and of the [illegible] replies which I received, [illegible] said that they were promoted by publicans.

The Rev. [illegible] P.C.C. 11 May '[illegible]

42,753. Are these the athletic sports?—Small country races. I do not mean the large races, but these are the small country races.

42,754. (Mr. Young.) Horse races?—Yes. The funds are subscribed to principally by the local publicans and the brewers, but the stakes are so small, and the class of horses that run there are so very inferior, that I believe they serve no other purpose whatever but to bring the country people there for the purpose of drinking.

42,755. (Vincent de Vesci.) Does that apply also to athletic sports?—And also to athletic sports.

Liquor consumed in the villages.

42,756. Then will you tell us about the amount of liquor disposed of in some of those villages?—In some of those villages there is a large quantity of liquor disposed of. I know of one village in a very poor district, and it disposes of 1,[illegible]l. worth of drink annually.

42,757. That is amongst all the public-houses in that district?—There are four public-houses in that village.

42,758. (Mr. Younger.) How do you arrive at those figures?—I happened to meet the brewer's man who was bringing the porter to this village, and I asked him for an estimate of the average number of barrels of porter he carried to the village every week, and he gave it me.

42,759. Then that 1,[illegible]l. is mainly porter?—Principally porter. There are some few pounds worth of [illegible] drinks included, but it would be principally porter.

42,760. (Vincent de Vesci.) Do the people drink far more porter than whisky in the country districts?—Far more porter. In that same parish there is another village in which there are four more public-houses, and I should think that in the second village there is at least [illegible]l. worth of porter sold, so that from that parish about [illegible],000l. goes yearly in strong drink.

42,761. Is it a thickly inhabited parish?—Part of it is fairly thickly inhabited, but not very.

42,762. By small farmers?—Yes.

Overcompetition and illegal sales, &c.

42,763. Now, will you give us your opinion as to the overcompetition and its effect on selling during prohibited hours?—The number of public-houses prevents the publicans from refusing drink to persons who ask for it during prohibited hours, because they are afraid of losing their customers.

42,764. You attribute that to over-competition?—Over-competition. I have seen one [illegible] a publican refuse drink to some persons who applied for it, and they went straight away to the next publican's house and got it, and of course the publican who will give drink to those persons on the Sunday will get their custom on the Monday as a rule. So that if a person tries to really carry on his business properly in Ireland, it is very hard for him to make a living out of the sale of intoxicating liquor.

42,765. In the case of those men, all those people claimed as bona fide travellers?—No, they were not bona fide travellers. They were simply from the neighbourhood.

42,766. It was illegal drinking?—Yes.

42,767. They were turned in one of the other houses?—Yes. At all events they were allowed in, and I presume they were served.

42,768. Is there a police station in that village?—No, there is not. There is a police station about a mile from that village.

42,769. It is patrolled, of course?—Yes.

Administration of law by justices.

42,770. Will you pass on to the conduct of the magistrates?—I hold the magistrates responsible for the [illegible] of public-houses, and I believe there is [illegible] evidence, though much of it is necessarily of a circumstantial nature, to show that they have abused the power conferred on them by law, in granting, renewing, and transferring licences, and I believe that their [illegible] in this respect, as also in connection with breaches of the licensing laws, discourages the police from enforcing those laws, and encourages the publicans and the public to evade them, and it is calculated to

Licences granted contrary to evidence.

62,772. Do the police often object?—The police very often object, and the clergy often object.

62,773. Do the clergy appear in court?—I have cases where the clergy have appeared.

62,774. Have you yourself appeared?—I have gone to court to object to the grant of a licence, but the case was not called.

62,775. Have you yourself on more than one instance appeared to object to a licence being granted?—Only in one instance.

62,776. Have you been present in court when applications have been dealt with in other cases?—No, but I have read those cases in the press, and I have taken a note of them, and I can refer to them.

62,777. You state, in a general way, that licences are granted in spite of the objections made by the police and the clergy?—Yes, in many cases. I say that the police and the clergy are, of course, the best judges as to whether a licence is necessary in a locality, and that if the magistrates were really determined only to grant those licences that are necessary, they would take into account the objection raised by the police and the clergy, and on the strength of it, they would refuse the licence, especially seeing that in very many cases—in the whole of them—there is no person appearing from the community asking for those licences, except the publican or his friends.

62,778. The applicant does not adduce evidence in support of his application?—No.

62,779. The only evidence they have before them is the evidence of objections by police and clergy?—Yes.

62,780. In the face of that, you find the licences are granted?—They are granted often in spite of those objections.

Canvassing. Offer of a Cork brewer's agent.

62,781. Will you give your opinion, as to the facts, as to the canvassing of the magistrates. Is it the case, from your experience, that magistrates are canvassed beforehand?—Certainly. I can give evidence, including one in which a canvasser called on myself. He wanted me to use my influence with some magistrates who were living in a parish where I then was, to go about 50 miles to vote for a licence for a friend of his. I said that it was altogether unreasonable to expect magistrates to go so far away, and he said that distance made no difference whatever, that he himself was authorised by a brewer to give 5l. by way of defraying expenses to any magistrate whom he could get to go and vote for the licence.

62,782. Was that a local brewer?—A local brewer.

62,783. Of the city of Cork?—In the city of Cork.

Indication of corrupt influence.

62,784. Could that allegation be supported by other evidence, do you believe?—I have no other evidence to support it, except that a case occurred in Macroom last year, in which the chairman of the quarter sessions stated that one of the magistrates on the bench had received a postal order in a letter asking him to vote for a licence, and that postal order, which was for 10s., was enclosed apparently for the purpose of defraying his expenses. I should also mention that I know a case in which a private person frequently applied for a licence for his house, and was each time refused by the magistrates by a large majority. Then a firm of brewers made the application, and it was granted to them by a large majority. The licence was granted in a little village in which there were only seven houses, and there was already one public-house in the village.

62,785. They granted a new licence in a village in which there was already existing one licence?—There was one licence already existing, and this was a second.

62,786. They gave it as a tied house to a firm of brewers?—Yes.

62,787. (Mr. Younger.) Might it not have been because the magistrates thought, in their judgment, that the firm of brewers would look better after the firm, that the magistrates granted that public-house, not because it was necessary, but because some influence was brought to bear on them by the brewers. That is my opinion.

62,788. (Viscount de Vesci.) You are not prepared to bring evidence to support that?—No.

62,789. To go back to the first case just mentioned, where 5l. was offered to a magistrate, that was by a person who represented himself to be an agent of the brewer?—He represented himself as an agent from the brewer. He was a commission agent going about the country selling goods.

62,790. A traveller?—A sort of traveller.

62,791. For that particular firm?—No, not for that firm, but he represented himself to me as being authorised by the firm to give this money, and he said he had the money in his pocket.

62,792. Was that fact brought before the county court judge in any way at the next licensing sessions?—No. I afterwards wrote to the public press, and mentioned the case in the press.

62,793. You state you wrote to the public press about this. Was any attempt made to refute your statement?—No, there was no attempt made whatever to refute it.

62,794. There was no answer to the allegation?—No.

62,795. Did you mention the name of the firm?—No, I mentioned no names whatsoever.

62,796. (Mr. Younger.) Exactly. It is nobody's business to pick up an allegation of that sort?—I mentioned no names, but the press commented on this letter of mine.

62,797. (Viscount de Vesci.) Did you write this to a Cork paper?—To three Cork papers.

62,798. Circulating in the city of Cork?—There are only three circulating in the city of Cork, and I communicated the fact to each of the papers, and I mentioned that it was a Cork brewer, and there was no contradiction whatsoever of it. I might mention that a person, who made an application, though I referred to his house, and he wrote to me to ask me to write to the papers and say this application did not apply to his house—that this offer of money did not apply to his house. I replied and said I would do nothing of the kind, and I did not do so. I should also mention that when I wrote this letter, it was just the day after a licensing sessions had been held at Macroom, and I mentioned in the letter that, as far as I could make out, this offer was made with reference to one of the applications which came before the court, and which was refused by the magistrates, and I said that if the other magistrates all over the county followed the example of the Macroom magistrates, that we should soon hear no more about canvassing.

62,799. How long before the licensing sessions at Macroom had this communication been made?—I believe it had been over 12 months.

62,800. A year before?—Yes, I expect 12 months before.

62,801. Now will you pass to the question of the renewal of licences?—The necessity for annually renewing the licence and the power of objecting to such renewals were, in my opinion, evidently intended by law as a means of weeding out badly-conducted public-houses, and of protecting the public from being injured by them; but the practice of the magistrates, so far from having any restraining power on unscrupulous publicans, is calculated to encourage them to evade the law, for, as a rule, there is no distinction made at the renewal sessions between those who offend and those who do not. The certificates of all are signed in globo.

62,802. What happens when objections are raised?—Objections had been raised by private individuals at the Cork Licensing Sessions of 1898, and it was decided that as this person had no right whatever to object, and the consequence of that decision was that publicans were enabled to sell illegally.

[illegible]. The police do object in some of these cases? —They do, but their objections are, as a rule, paid no attention to. For instance, I have for the past five or six years very carefully read the proceedings at the different licensing sessions, as reported in the press, and what I have stated is the opinion I have arrived at. I never remember reading a case of a badly-conducted licence being extinguished on the result of an objection to its renewal, and last week might have escaped my notice. I wrote to the different district inspectors of the constabulary in the county asking whether they remembered to have succeeded in this respect. They all replied. Four said they had no case of opposition to renewals; three said they had succeeded, and the remaining [illegible] said that although they had frequently opposed renewals they never remembered to have extinguished a licence at one of the sessions.

[illegible]. Did any give the grounds on which they objected?—None, but many of them expressed the opinion that it was a forlorn hope to attempt to extinguish a badly conducted house by objection to renewal.

[illegible]. Now will you give us your view as to transfers?—The facility with which magistrates grant them is in my opinion a great encouragement to badly-conducted publicans and calculated to render the police remiss in enforcing the law. I could give cases in which licences with records against them have been transferred from the mere nominal holder to the person who had actually conducted the business when the breaches of the Licensing Acts took place.

[illegible]. They conducted the business as manager?—At one spot under the tenant, the tenant living in the house. For instance, there is the case of a husband transferring to his wife, a man transferring to his son-in-law, a sister transferring to her sister. These cases appeared in the public prints, and I have some of them here.

[illegible]. Is it a common thing for a husband to transfer to his wife?—I believe I have three cases of it here. One occurred at Middleton last year. The publican had been frequently fined, and the amount of fines paid by him was 10 guineas, and at the same time there were two records on his licence. He was permitted to transfer the licence to his wife, and he himself went to gaol. Since then I understand there has been another conviction against the wife. This wife was the manageress of the public-house before the transfer took place.

[illegible]. Then as to the practice of the magistrates with reference to breaches of the law?—For the last six years I have carefully read such cases of the kind as appeared in one of the Cork newspapers, for the express purpose of observing how the magistrates dealt with them, and the general rule seems to be to dismiss the case when the publican gives a direct denial to the charges brought against him. This practice enables a bad publican to defy the police.

[illegible]. Do you find that the police in consequence do not prosecute?—They are discouraged from prosecuting. I do not say they do not prosecute, but I say the practice is calculated to discourage them from doing so. I know a case in which a priest has frequently complained of a publican giving drink to drunken persons. The police have had the publican prosecuted for it more than once, but he always contradicts what the police say, and the magistrates dismiss the case.

[illegible]. You allege they take the publican's word against the word of the police?—Yes. On the last occasion, when the publican was brought before the court the resident magistrate publicly protested in court against the decision of the majority of the Bench. There is also is calculated, I believe, to tempt those who are prosecuted for violating the licensing laws to give false testimony.

[illegible]. To commit perjury, in other words?—Yes. Any person who reads the newspapers and pays any amount of attention to the decisions of the magistrates with reference to these breaches of the licensing laws, would see that whenever a publican directly contradicts the police as a rule he is dismissed. Consequently, this practice in its very nature must stimulate the unscrupulous publicans to perjure themselves in order to protect their business and in order to carry on illegal sales.

The Rev. M. Ahern, R.C.C. — 11 May '[illegible]

[illegible]. It is the fact that the constabulary patrol usually in pairs?—Yes.

[illegible]. There must be many cases where the police produce two witnesses—where there are two policemen to give evidence?—I have read many such cases.

[illegible]. Do the magistrates take the word of a single publican against the word of two policemen?—Yes, they generally take the word of the publican and some person in the house, or some person found drinking on the premises, and then they say there is a conflict of testimony, and they give the benefit of the doubt to the publican; but what I complain of principally is that the magistrates in these cases do not seem to wish to weigh the evidence, and they are prepared very often to take the evidence of corner boys and to attach to it as much weight as they would attach to the evidence of the most respectable man to be found in the police force, and I need not tell you that must be very humiliating to the police.

Reluctance to endorse licences.

[illegible]. Now, with reference to endorsements on licences. Can you give us the practice of the magistrates with reference to that?—They seem to have great difficulty, and to be very reluctant to endorse the licences at all. I have been told of a case in which they decided to put a second record on the certificate, but they were appealed to not to do so, as the publican had promised to sell it. They complied, but the publican did not sell, and soon after was convicted again, and was only fined. Had the second record been put on, the last conviction would have extinguished the licence. I remember a case where there were two records and a re-ordainable prosecution.

[illegible]. This is a case you know of yourself?—I heard of it at the time. I was living in the town, and I inquired of the constabulary, and verified the report I had. The publican made no defence. If, when the case was tried, the licence was bound to be endorsed, and thereby forfeited, but, to save it, the magistrates continued to adjourn the case from time to time for eight or twelve months or more, until one of the records dropped outside the five years' limit, and then they adjudicated on the case.

[illegible]. That is a serious allegation against the conduct of those magistrates, and that you believed to be true?—I believe it to be true. It was publicly reported in the town where I was. I was not in court when the case came on, but I happened to be in the town at the time. It was in the parish where I lived, and when I decided to give evidence before the Commission, I went to the constabulary and asked whether this report I then heard was true, and they told me it was. A constable who was in court said that it was.

[illegible]. (Mr. Young) Who told you it was true?—The head constabulary.

[illegible]. (Vincent de Vere) The man concerned in this prosecution?—Yes.

[illegible]. (Mr. Young) Did the inspector tell you or one of the men?—Two of the men.

[illegible]. (Vincent de Vere) The responsible man—a sergeant of constabulary?—Two of the constables; but it was an understood thing at the time when I was in the town; there is no doubt whatever about it; it is a real fact, and that licence is still in existence.

Sunday closing.

[illegible]. We will now pass to the question of Sunday closing?—With reference to Sunday closing, my experience is that very few publicans observe the Sunday Closing Act strictly. The majority of them, especially in villages and at cross roads, I consider do their principal trade on Sundays, and were the Act properly enforced a large number of them would derive little or no profit from their business.

[illegible]. Are there many public-houses in the East Riding which are situated any distance from a police station?—A large number of them are. In the little village where I live, the public-houses of the village are about a mile from the police station. Then the police station has charge of four villages, and the furthest away is between four and five miles—over four miles.

[illegible]. What is the force of police?—I believe there are four policemen—a sergeant and three men—at the station.

The Rev. M. Ahern, R.C.C.

11 May '88

[illegible]. They have to patrol all that country ?—Yes, and they cannot be here and there.

[illegible]. Five miles in extent ?—Yes.

[illegible]. (*Mr. Younger.*) I suppose they have no stated times for coming to these places ?—No.

[illegible]. Nobody knows when they will turn up there ?—Certainly.

Opinion of clergy on Sunday closing.

[illegible]. (*Viscount de Vesci.*) You are in favour, and you state that the majority of the clergy of the country are in favour of the total Sunday closing ?—Yes.

[illegible]. I understand that you really fix the responsibility more on the magistrates than on the police for the non-observance of the Sunday Closing Act ?—Certainly. I fix the responsibility principally on the magistrates. There is an opinion amongst the clergy that some of the police are remiss in enforcing the Sunday Closing Act, but they do not say that all the police are, or that they are remiss in all cases, but that certainly some of them are. All are agreed that the superior officers of the police, from the head constable upwards, are most anxious to enforce the Sunday Closing Act, but it is certainly thought some of the rank and file, from one reason or another, have no disposition to enforce it, or a reluctance to enforce it.

Police and enforcement of the law.

[illegible]. Is that in consequence of not being able to get their cases ?—That is my opinion.

[illegible]. Not being properly supported by the magistrates ?—Yes. I remember a case that came under my own notice where two constables came towards a public-house, at the door of which there was a horse and car standing, on a Sunday. One of the constables moved on past the public-house; the other approached the door and knocked; the door opened, and there was not time for more than one word between the constable and the person who opened the door, and then he also passed on; he did not go in at all. I know that constable to frequent the house on week days at very late hours, and I have seen him frequently inside it.

[illegible]. Did you bring that to the attention of the authorities ?—I brought it to the attention of the sergeant, but I did not mention the name of this policeman—I did not like to injure him; but I spoke to him and I told him, if it occurred again, I should report it to the authorities.

Police watched by publicans.

[illegible]. Are the police watched ?—Yes, the police are watched, and I have a photograph here of the publicans on a Sunday at the door watching the police (*producing photograph*).

[illegible]. Do they employ men besides to watch the police ?—I believe they do so in the towns; at all events, I have been told that they do so. I know very well there are men in the country engaged by the publicans—whether paid or not I do not know—to watch the police. I have seen them. I also produce photographs showing the character of some of these publicans in Ireland (*handing in same*).

[illegible]. (*Mr. Younger.*) There is no legal proof on the face of these photographs that they are watching for the police ?—I know the persons perfectly well—both of them—and I know they are there for the purpose of watching the police.

[illegible]. (*Mr. Grindlay.*) Could not you get the policeman take the photograph when coming in ?—The moment he appears, the men disappear.

[illegible]. (*Mr. Cosens.*) Is the whole population outside the public-house ?—This is on a week day with nobody at all about.

Adulteration.

[illegible]. (*Viscount de Vesci.*) Will you give us your opinion with regard to adulteration ?—There is a general idea among the people that publicans mix something with the whisky which enables them to add a quantity of water to it, which gives the mixture a hot biting taste. I have inquired of many with reference to it, and that seems to be the opinion of all; but the common expression amongst the people is that this mixture is not spirit—that it is something else, but, whatever it be, it is very injurious to those who drink whisky.

[illegible]. Do you know of any cases where the police have prosecuted for adulteration ?—No, I do not.

[illegible]. Or taken samples for the purpose of analysing ?—No, I do not know of them.

[illegible]. Is it the duty of the police to do that from time to time ?—Yes, it is.

[illegible]. To take specimens of drink ?—Yes. I have been told by many persons to whom I mentioned the fact, that the publicans have a special bottle very often prepared to offer to the police when they ask for a sample, and that the vessel in which this mixture is contained is hidden away in some part of the premises under the counter or in some place where the police will not see it. That is what I have been told by more than one. A gentleman once assured me that he got a glass of whisky in a low public-house, and that although he had been accustomed to drink whisky, and had only to cross the street from the public-house to his own house, the moment he entered the latter he felt intoxicated and had to take to bed. I have myself seen persons who having taken drink could not be described as drunk. I could only describe them as mad. They were able to walk.

[illegible]. You attribute that to the deleterious mixture put into the liquor ?—Yes.

[illegible]. They do not do that with porter ?—No.

[illegible]. It is only spirits ?—Yes.

[illegible]. You state that the majority of people drink porter ?—The majority do, but you will meet with a few who drink nothing but whisky. An old publican assured me that all the publicans in the large town where she had carried on business made their own whisky.

[illegible]. Made it up ?—Her expression was: "Made their own whisky."

[illegible]. (*Mr. Younger.*) Do you mean made it from the beginning ?—Mixed it—prepared it. She told me that one of the reasons she broke down in her business was, in her own opinion, that she was not able to make this mixture.

[illegible]. You are not suggesting that they smuggle it or have a still ?—No, but mix something with it by which they are enabled to add a large quantity of water.

[illegible]. You said a glass of it made a man intoxicated. What is meant is it for a publican to sell a man liquor one glass of which will make him intoxicated ?—The bad liquor would not make the low-class man intoxicated, but would make a gentleman intoxicated. I am speaking of the lower classes accustomed to drink whisky and bad whisky, and a glass of whisky which is adulterated would not affect them as it would affect the gentleman accustomed to drink good whisky.

[illegible]. Our information certainly is to show that if a gentleman goes into a public-house where this drink is sold and asks for a glass of whisky, he does not get that at all ?—No, nor the police if they go in and ask for it.

[illegible]. (*Viscount de Vesci.*) If the police go in for the purpose of taking a sample you say they have a special bottle ?—I have it on the authority of a good many persons.

[illegible]. (*Mr. Grindlay.*) When the police go in, as a rule they do not go in uniform for that purpose ?—I believe they do.

[illegible]. I thought they generally went so that the publicans did not know ?—Sometimes they go in uniform and sometimes they do not.

[illegible]. If they do not go in uniform, what is the use of that special bottle ?—I am only mentioning what I have been told; that they keep a special bottle, and I always understood that the police go in uniform, as a rule. Sometimes they go in plain clothes. I should like to give one other instance. A gentleman told me that he himself had seen this mixture, and he said that one glass of it added to a 10-gallon cask of whisky would enable the publican to add 5 gallons of water.

[illegible]. (*Mr. Younger.*) Which would reduce the strength of any whisky in the cask to such an abnormal extent that a man would be breaking the law by selling it. Do you know that ?—Certainly.

[illegible]. It would be so weak with 5 gallons of water added, that it would do nobody any harm ?—This mixture is of such a nature that it would still have this biting taste.

[illegible]. (*Viscount de Vesci.*) Will you now give us your suggestions with regard to the licensing authority. Who do you think ought to be the licensing authority to consider for granting licenses ?—For granting and renewing licenses, I think the licensing authority ought to be the county court judge.

[illegible]. Who ought to deal with the cases of prosecutions?—The resident magistrates. I believe that this is also the opinion of the clergy. They seem to be unanimous in believing that a change ought to take place, and that the licensing authority ought to be transferred from the magistrates to the county court judge.

[illegible]. What is your opinion with regard to appeals?—I believe that an appeal ought to be given in all cases from the Recorder and county court judge to the judge of assize.

[illegible]. That is in the case of granting and renewing licences?—Yes.

[illegible]. Then with regard to prosecutions?—With regard to prosecutions I should also give an appeal.

[illegible]. You think there ought to be an appeal by the police in the case of a dismissal?—Certainly.

[illegible]. What is your opinion with regard to the further issue of new licences?—I think that a law should be passed suspending the further issue of new licences because the country is at present overstocked with public-houses.

[illegible]. What means would you adopt for lessening the number of existing licences?—I should like a Bill to be introduced to diminish the actual number of public-houses, but failing the passing of such a Bill I would be in favour of lessening them indirectly by making it obligatory on the licensing authority to grant no new licence until the applicant had either bought out or otherwise extinguished three other licences. This rule is observed in Limerick city, and I understand that the number of licensed premises in the city has been reduced. Last year I remember seeing in the paper that an applicant had to buy out two public-houses, and extinguish the licenses before he received a new licence.

[illegible]. Then with reference to disqualifications?—I would also disqualify from being again licensed, except on the condition I have just mentioned, any house which has allowed its certificate to be dormant or die out from bad trade. I remember cases where houses were offered for sale and no one in the town or neighbourhood could be got to buy them. The houses were then closed up, and after a while some brewer or wholesale dealer in Cork rented these houses and obtained licences for them. Then I would also disqualify from ever being again licensed any house which forfeited its certificate from repeated convictions.

[illegible]. Then with reference to records?—I would oblige the licensing authority to record every conviction, after the first, and make these records tell against the house as well as against the licensee.

[illegible]. Then as to the bona fide traveller?—I would extend the bona fide traveller distance to 6 miles, and punish with a severe term of imprisonment without the option of a fine any person falsely representing himself as a bona fide traveller, because in many cases I understand the publicans are prepared to pay part of the fines, and thereby of course encourage persons to represent themselves as bona fide travellers who really are not such at all.

[illegible]. Then as to Sunday closing?—I would make Sunday closing permanent and extend it to the exempted cities.

[illegible]. What would you do with reference to the hours on Saturday?—I would close the houses earlier—about 9 o'clock. I would mention with reference to early Saturday night closing that the opinion of the clergy—the Bishop of Cloyne and the clergy of his diocese, and the clergy of the whole county—is unanimous as to earlier Saturday closing.

[illegible]. What hour would they recommend?—About 9 o'clock.

[illegible]. Then, lastly, with reference to habitual drunkards?—I think habitual drunkards should be imprisoned and never fined at all, and that the term of imprisonment should be increased with each offence.

[illegible]. After a certain number?—Yes. I think if imprisoned for a certain time it would have not only a deterrent effect but a curative effect, because when fined they do not suffer themselves at all, but their family suffer very much. I remember cases of very hard drinkers, what you might call confirmed drunkards, and I have seen them when they kept the pledge for six months to twelve months for 18 months and two years sometimes. The difficulty seems to be to keep from drink for the first six months, and I think it would have a good effect on them if they were imprisoned for a time. It would strengthen their nerves, and help them to overcome their taste for drink.

[illegible]. (Dean Dickinson.) With reference to your last answer do you think that all habitual inebriates without any distinction should be considered as criminals and sent to prison?—No—only those who have been convicted.

[illegible]. Of what?—Of drunkenness, and appear frequently before a court.

[illegible]. Drunkenness is simply in such a case—it may be a sin, but unless the drunkenness is associated with some criminal action ought they to be dealt with criminally? Have you not known cases of persons who from heredity or some other reason got into the habit of inebriation, who ought not to be treated as criminals and sent to a common prison?—Certainly.

[illegible]. Have you seen the Bill which is now before the House for dividing the inebriates into two classes—criminal inebriates, and those who ought to be treated as objects of pity and subjects for reformation?—I have not seen the Bill, but I have heard of it.

[illegible]. Do not you think that there ought to be some such classification?—Certainly I think there ought to be, but I was referring to those cases of habitual drunkards who appear before the police courts in Ireland.

[illegible]. There are many cases of domestic inebriation which do not come before the police courts at all?—Certainly there are; but I do not refer to them.

[illegible]. You think that the Bill with that qualification ought to be extended to Ireland?—Certainly.

[illegible]. With reference to the supervision of the police, is it impossible that the police with their barracks four or five miles away can be everywhere to supervise all the public-houses in a district on Sunday?—Practically impossible.

[illegible]. The only remedy for that would be, do not you think, a failure to prevent any public-house being licensed that does not come within the purview of the police?—I think it would be a very good thing to pass a measure of that kind.

[illegible]. (Mr. Walker.) I think you are a priest in Holy Orders of the Catholic Church?—Yes. Position of witness.

[illegible]. May I ask if you are a total abstainer?—I am.

[illegible]. You have gone over nearly every point in connection with the licensing system, and I think you have dominated the whole of it. Do you speak for yourself or do you speak collectively for the Catholic community of the district in which you live?—I speak for myself.

[illegible]. Entirely?—Not entirely. I speak for the clergy on certain points, and I have referred to their opinions when those points came under notice. Some of my opinions are personal, and others of them are shared by the other Catholic priests of the diocese with me.

[illegible]. Are you prepared to say that the whole of what you have stated here to-day is approved and shared by the Catholic community and the religious teachers?—I could not say so, because I did not consult the community on these points. I do not know whether the whole Catholic community shares my views. I expect many of them do not share them.

[illegible]. (Mr. Graham.) Do you think the great majority share your views?—I think, so far as the licensing authority is concerned, the great majority share my views.

[illegible]. (Mr. Walker.) Should I be right in interpreting what you have said to mean that you are directly hostile to public-houses?—No, by no means. I only want the public-houses to be properly conducted, and that the number of them should be so proportioned to the population that they would supply their reasonable wants and no further.

[illegible]. Have you not charged here to-day the publicans as being guilty of serving drunken people and generally encouraging drunkenness?—No. I made a distinction between the low class of publicans and the others; and I say there is a low class of publicans in Ireland who are habitually guilty of that offence of serving drink to drunken persons. Proportion of low licensing publicans.

The Rev. M. Ahern, C.C.

[illegible] May '98.

62,894. Are the low-class publicans in a majority?—A minority.

62,895. A very small minority?—I would not say a very small minority, because they are being increased every day [illegible] owing to competition.

62,896. What is the relative proportion?—I could not tell you.

62,897. You are certain it is not a small minority?—I am certain from my own observation.

62,898. From your observation, take any place you like to mention, how many houses would you say are not since any others [illegible]?—In some places in the country perhaps one might say a quarter of them, or a little in some places, would have no objection whatever to serving a person who was under the influence of drink.

62,899. These men are licensed?—They are.

62,900. And they have gone through the ordeal of inquiry into their character and approval by the police authorities?—I do not know that their character has been inquired into or was inquired into when they got their licences.

Inquiries into character.

62,901. Is a licence granted to a man without inquiry into his character?—I have known of licences granted to men whose character was proved in court to be bad.

62,902. You may have known it, but the authorities did not know it?—It was proved in court.

62,903. I ask you if it is not an official custom to inquire into the character of a man applying for a licence?—I do not think so. As a rule, there is no inquiry held into the character of an applicant for a licence.

62,904. It is stated by the officials that that is not so?—The police might inquire into it officially, but I have known the police to object to licences because of the character of the applicants, and I have seen it stated in the papers that the majority of the bench granted the application. I remember one case that occurred not very long ago at Skibbereen. It was proved that the applicant and his wife were bound to the peace at the time the application was made, and when a vote was taken of the magistrates, 10 magistrates voted to give the licence and 11 against it.

62,905. Have you ever visited a public-house yourself?—Yes, I have sometimes.

62,906. I suppose you consider that part of your religious duty, do you not?—On holidays I think it part of my religious duty to enter some of the houses in the parish where I live.

62,907. Then you have only visited them for the purpose of discovering some [illegible]?—Of discovering whether persons were inside who were under the influence of drink, and asking them to leave and go home if I found them, because if they did not leave and remained there till late at night, I know, from experience, the result would be rows on the way home and various accidents; and I might mention with reference to that fact, that I entered once a public-house and there was a young man visibly under the influence of drink, staggering about from side to side, and I asked the publican not to give him any more drink. The publican refused to me on my suggestion and gave him drink before me, and he certainly was not a person who ought to have received drink. If he had not got it there he would simply have gone to the next house.

62,908. You are speaking to single instances that have come under your notice. Do you know the Rev. James M'Keown, C.C., Member of the Royal Irish Academy?—I do not know him.

62,909. He delivered a discourse on April [illegible] in this year—that is only a short time back—in St. Michael's Church, [illegible], and he said this:—"Some people "blamed the publicans for supplying liquor to the "low-class drunkard; he regarded this as a fallacy to a "certain extent, because no publican would go to the "street and take a man into his house to get drunk. "Therefore, no man could be forced into a public-"house to drink. Those who could use God's gifts in "moderation and every want to excess, might without "sin continue to do so; and although it was a "supremely good thing to be a total abstainer, he, for "one, would not insist that the man or woman who "could use these gifts in the proper way should take "the pledge, but to those who go to excess in the use "of intoxicating drinks, and who know their own "weakness, he would say that they were bound under "pain of grievous sin to take the total abstinence "pledge." Do you agree to that?—I must take exception to the first part of the paragraph. I should like to know whether he was speaking from his own experience or arguing from theoretic principles.

62,910. That is a discourse on temperance?—He thinks they ought not to get them in, but the question is, do they get them in? It would be right not to do so, and it is so theory intended not to do so; but taking things as they exist I know of my own experience they do give them drink when they come in, and that is a very marked distinction.

62,911. You do not object to the public-house?—No, I do not object to the public-house.

62,912. You would certainly prefer the public-house as a legally established house for the sale of these goods than an illicit place called a shebeen?—Certainly.

62,913. You would consider that the latter is more demoralising?—Certainly. I speak only personally. My own personal view would be to lessen public-houses as much as I possibly could, but taking into consideration the feelings of the people and their opinions with reference to intoxicating drink, I would not for a moment deprive them of public-houses so long as their present way of thinking about or regarding strong drink so predominant.

62,914. Is it your opinion that the physical character of the houses should be improved?—Certainly it should.

62,915. Are you prepared to bear testimony to the general respectability of the proprietors?—Of the majority of them.

62,916. The great majority?—Of the majority of them, I would not say the great majority.

62,917. With reference to the action of the magistrates, you alluded to the public declaration that they had abused—I think those were your words—the powers entrusted to them?—Those were my words.

62,918. Of course, as magistrates, they possess a discretionary power?—As magistrates, in certain cases, but not in all cases.

62,919. We are speaking of the licensing laws?—Yes, I believe that with reference to the granting and renewing of licences they have not a discretionary power. I saw it stated by the county court judge of Limerick, and I believe it has been also stated here before the Commission, that in granting a licence they must take into consideration the character of the applicant, the necessity for the house in the neighbourhood, and the suitability of the house. There is no discretion there, and they have no right to grant the licence if the character of the applicant is bad, if the house is not a suitable one, or if the house is not required in the neighbourhood.

62,920. I understand you to say that, when a charge was made against a publican it was met by a denial?—Yes, that is with reference to the breaches of the licensing law.

62,921. And the evidence being conflicting, the magistrates dismissed?—Yes.

62,922. There was nothing wrong about that—no abuse of power there?—What I blame them for is for attaching so much importance to the evidence given by the earliest [illegible] of the town, as to the evidence of the most respectable members of the constabulary force.

62,923. That is your construction of it. As magistrates they have the right to hear the testimony, and properly dispose the testimony of any man?—And I have cases [illegible], but there have occurred where though the weight of evidence was altogether against the publican, and cases have occurred and have come to my knowledge where those [illegible] have sworn in favour of a publican, and then admitted afterwards to the police that they took a false oath, and they did not believe it was perjury to do so, because they injured no person in doing it.

62,924. And that is sufficient justification for your saying they have abused their powers?—No; my justification for saying that they abused their powers relates principally to the granting, renewing, and transferring licences, also to permitting [illegible], and being influenced by canvassing and for everything [illegible]

[illegible] of the [illegible] on points of law, and in many other points.

[illegible]. How can you prove that they have been influenced by canvassing?—The evidence is circumstantial, but taking it as a whole it convinces me that they have been canvassed and have yielded to it. First and foremost the very fact of canvassing being practically universal throughout Ireland shows to me that canvassing has been a success. It never would have been practised at all so extensively if it did not succeed in bringing magistrates to court and getting them to vote for or against licenses, as the case may be.

[illegible]. Did I understand you to imply that a magistrate could be bought for 5l.?—I did not say so. What I said was, this offer was made to a magistrate for the purpose of defraying his expenses.

[illegible]. He offered him 5l. to pay expenses?—He said to me he had 5l. to give to any magistrate.

[illegible]. (Dean Dickinson.) You said magistrates?—Any magistrates—as many as he could get.

[illegible]. In the plural?—That is the sense. He used the words "any magistrate," and I understood him to mean any number whom he could influence to come and vote for this licence were to get from him 5l. apiece.

[illegible]. (Mr. Cullen.) Did any magistrate take the 5l.?—No.

[illegible]. (Mr. Walker.) May it not have been idle talk?—This gentleman was a relative of mine and came, probably, to use me to get my influence to bear on those magistrates.

[illegible]. The gentleman that wanted to bribe the magistrates was a relative of yours?—The gentleman who was authorised by the brewer to give the money happened to be a relative of mine, and came to call on me, I suppose, simply because he was a relative.

[illegible]. (Mr. Cullen.) With a view to getting your influence for the license?—To get my influence to bear on the magistrates to vote for it.

[illegible]. (Fineman de Vere.) He was asking you to canvass the magistrates?—Yes, and he would give the 5l. to cover their expenses.

[illegible]. (Mr. Walker.) Are you prepared to prove this?—I am prepared to prove what I have mentioned to the Commission is true.

[illegible]. That a relative of yours was the agent of the brewer and with a commission for bribing the magistrates to the extent of 5l.?—I did not use the word "bribe." What I am prepared to prove is that a gentleman who represented himself as an agent of the brewers called on me to get my influence to bear upon certain magistrates, and said that he would give those magistrates 5l. to defray their expenses if they went and voted for the license.

[illegible]. Are you prepared to say in your judgment any magistrate would accept the 5l.?—I do not know, really, I could not say, because I have never known a case of the kind. I mention only the fact.

[illegible]. In what way does that justify you in saying that the magistrates have abused the powers entrusted to them?—I do not bring forward any one fact, and on that fact alone base that conclusion, but I bring forward a number of facts.

[illegible]. On an idle statement coming from the lips of an unscrupulous-minded man, you would attach so much importance to it as to say that the magistrates, as a body, have abused their powers?—No. With reference to the gentleman who called on me, I know he did not tell me a lie.

[illegible]. Was that sufficient justification for your statement?—That alone is not a sufficient justification, but I have not based my statement on that fact alone. I have given a lot of statements on which I base the conclusion.

[illegible]. (Mr. Cullen.) You bring that 5l. case forward to show the strong pressure that is put by unscrupulous people on the magistrates, do not you?—Yes.

[illegible]. You do not base your view on that?—I bring it forward to show there is any amount of influence brought to bear on the magistrates.

[illegible]. You made this statement in public?—Yes.

[illegible]. Did you name the man in public?—No.

[illegible]. No notice was taken?—No.

[illegible]. You did not name the brewer?—No.

[illegible]. (Mr. [illegible].) Are you aware that there are only four brewers in Cork, and that these four brewers are people supposed to be of the highest standing and respectability?—Yes, I am aware of that. I always understand it. (The Rev. [illegible] Ahern, P.P. — [illegible] May '[illegible].)

[illegible]. Do you suggest for a moment to this Commission that people of the highest standing would do a thing of this sort?—I do not know whether they would or not. I only state a fact that occurred.

[illegible]. The fact being that a third person altogether suggested to you a certain thing. You have no proof that that man was telling the truth?—I cannot prove that; but I can say that he had the money in his pocket and would pay it out. He had the money in his pocket, and would give the money if I would get the magistrate to go and vote for the license.

[illegible]. (Mr. Walker.) Have you stated as a charge or complaint against the licensed houses that they do not supply any temperance drinks?—I did not say they did not supply any temperance drinks, but I said the class of drinks they did supply was of a very inferior quality in the majority of the houses. I know that from my own experience. The lemonade and ginger beer is generally made in small local establishments and is of a very low character. (Temperance drinks in public-houses.)

[illegible]. They are the best that the market presents?—Of course, some of the houses have very good temperance drinks. They get them from Cork and Dublin.

[illegible]. That at once does away with the charge. I understand you to say that the publicans do supply temperance drinks?—Of some kind, as a rule.

[illegible]. Then there is no charge against the trade that they do not supply temperance drinks?—Not temperance drinks, but refreshments, such as tea, coffee and milk.

[illegible]. Is there any demand for it?—I have often heard persons say they have asked for milk and been refused it.

[illegible]. And not tea and coffee?—Some would also ask for tea and coffee—[illegible]. I have heard them say that it is a great hardship on them.

[illegible]. Have you any practical experience that a number of people have gone into a house and demanded tea and coffee and been refused?—They have never asked for it, because they know it is not to be had.

[illegible]. If there was a demand there would be a supply?—I do not think there would be a supply, because they can make more profit out of the strong drink than tea and coffee, and it is not so troublesome.

[illegible]. One word upon this. I do not know whether to describe it as a Catholic ordinance or Catholic rule that young people on being confirmed should be compelled—if that is the right word to use—to take the pledge?—No, they are not compelled. (Children and the pledge.)

[illegible]. They never refuse?—They never refuse, and the bishop sometimes questions it from the altar, and the people often mention it too, that if the parents have any objection whatever, the pledge would not be administered to the children.

[illegible]. The pledge is administered as an order of the Church?—Not as an order of the Church at all; the Bishop, of course, will administer the pledge, knowing it is the desire of the people he should do so.

[illegible]. I understand you to say this was another charge against the licensed individual, that by some means or other he induced these young people to break the pledge?—It is the fact that so many since the young people break the pledge about 18 or 20 simply because they cannot get any refreshments such as tea or coffee when they go to fairs and markets. The only refreshment will then consist either of these temperance drinks to which I refer, or this strong drink.

[illegible]. Is that a just charge against the licensed [illegible]?—It is, and I charge them as being responsible for these people breaking, and very often (especially) as they do not keep proper temperance drinks to give them, and in many cases by giving them, as a non-intoxicating drink, drink that is intoxicating.

[illegible]. You acknowledge they do sell temperance drinks?—They do, but of a very inferior quality, and they know very well these young men will not ask for these drinks very often. They will ask for a non-intoxicating kind of wine, and the publican will say:

The Rev. [illegible], C.C.

[illegible] May '98.

"This is a [illegible] term, it is a temperance "[illegible]; it is the League of the Cross where there is no "harm in it"; and from the fact of it being called "League of the Cross ..." they will take it, and when they come home at night they find themselves [illegible], and they say they have got their pledge broken, and next day they take strong drink.

Sports, &c., organised by publicans.

42,964. These matter always to promoting athletic meetings. Do you object to athletic meetings?—No, certainly not; but I object to the number of public-houses which makes it impossible to hold any kind of popular amusements without very grave consequences following from it. I am altogether in favour of amusements of all kinds, but in Ireland we cannot encourage them simply because of the irrational multiplication of public-houses.

42,965. Are there not any influential wealthy people in your district?—Not very many in my present district.

42,966. Not sufficient to interest themselves to organise these meetings instead of the licensed victuallers?—No, there are none.

42,967. Somebody must organise them?—Yes. It is generally supposed they are organised by the local publicans.

42,968. Do you consider that that meeting is morally tainted simply from the fact that it is organised by a publican?—Not because it is organised by a publican, but because it is held close to a public-house.

42,969. Is the public-house on the corner of the field?—Generally it is in a village, and the field where the athletic sports are held is the field next to the village, and all day long there is drinking going on.

Adulteration.

42,970. One word as to adulteration. The witnesses that have preceded you have all spoken about the adulteration of spirits. You all acknowledge that there is no adulteration of beer, and beer is the most consumed. As to spirits, you have an idea that they are adulterated?—Yes.

42,971. What justification have you for saying that?—I am only giving the opinion of the people round about, and I went to the [illegible] in Cork, and one of them told me—he did not know what I intended asking him about, but he said he was a good judge of whisky because he always drank it—and he told me the publicans kept two bottles, one bottle for respectable persons who came into the house to drink, and another bottle, or a cask, for a man such as himself.

42,972. Would not that be very easy to put such a matter to the test?—I do not know whether it has been put to the test or not.

42,973. This has occupied the minds of officials, and now it seems to occupy the minds of the clergy, and yet with all their zeal they have been unable to discover what this adulteration is?—It is represented by the people of the country that what this thing is is kept very secret; it is a sort of mysterious thing to their estimation; it can be got from the distillers, and the distillers alone, and very few persons would be allowed to see it.

42,974. This adulteration can be procured from the distillers?—Yes, that is what I have heard—that the distillers keep it and it is got from them.

42,975. Now as a clergyman taking about in the world, and with all classes of people, do you give the slightest credence to such a statement as that? Do you think you can?—I am inclined to think there must be some foundation of truth in it.

42,976. You know very well that the Excise officer is always about the distillery?—This may be some kind of spirit. I remember once seeing in the town of [illegible], large placards upon the walls. I cannot recall to mind just now what the words of the advertisement were, but I remember distinctly it advised the people not to drink their whisky except they had a certain kind of spirit in it—to see that the publicans put this spirit in before they drank the whisky. What that spirit was I do not know.

42,977. That is all you can offer in support of the statements that spirits are adulterated with some deleterious agents?—I am only giving the opinion of the people round about. They tell me the whisky they get has a very burning taste.

42,978. Do you really consider that you are justified in coming here and giving evidence on statements of hearsay from other people. Why do not you inquire into it yourself?—Most of these statements are yet based on hearsay.

The Rev. [illegible], C.C.

42,979. You say, "I am told so and so, and I am told this"?—The persons who told me said they had themselves taken the whisky and it was of a biting taste. Another told me he took a glass of whisky and it made him drunk. I have seen, myself, persons under the influence of drink, having taken whisky, who could not be described as intoxicated but simply maddened. The appearance of their eyes would frighten a person.

42,980. (Mr. Caine.) Is not whisky capable of producing that effect?—I do not know—not that sort of effect I found in them. I have seen persons drunk under the influence of whisky, but these men were able to walk about and talk to you, but there was a wild stare on their face, and you could imagine they were capable of committing any crime whatsoever.

Excessive number of public-houses.

42,981. (Mr. [illegible].) You have stated to us that in the East Riding of Cork they have three times too many public-houses?—That is my opinion.

42,982. Then do you think that three out of every four might be taken away without any detriment or inconvenience to the public?—I think so.

42,983. You have also given us the number of houses in villages in the East Riding, and you have given the number of the male population to each public-house?—The male population over the age of 21.

42,984. Now there is a licensed house there to every 21 persons of the male population?—In some places a licensed house for every 21, in some 23; but I think, in these villages you have, as a rule, a public-house for every five males over the age of 21.

42,985. I understand there were two houses in one particular village, and therefore you would have one public-house to 40 males over 21 years of age?—Not over 21, not in any of the villages I mentioned. I believe in a small town you would find that.

42,986. What did you mean when you made a statement that there was a house to every 21?—Twenty-one of the whole inhabitants, but one to every five or six of the male inhabitants over the age of 21.

42,987. These houses are kept open for business, are they not?—Yes.

42,988. Do you wish to suggest that they can be kept open as places of business with 21 customers to each house?—No. What I object to is that they make their principal living by illegal sales.

42,989. I want you to answer that question. This is the number you have given to maintain these two public-houses?—That is the number in the village, but there on the Sundays persons come in from all parts of the country towards the village, or outside the public-house, and simply because of the number of public-houses in the village the publicans are driven to sell illegally to these people during prohibited hours; whereas if there was only one public-house in the district the publican would be able to make a living by a respectable trade, and be able to refuse drink to those people who come for the mere purpose of getting drunk, not because they want it, but for wanting to an idle day, and they stroll for a mile to the public-house and get a drink.

42,990. Are these houses, then, maintained in the position of business houses by an outside population?—Partly, and the publicans and their families are also supported by other trades.

42,991. If two public-houses can be kept in existence in a village with a population of 41 customers, certainly Ireland is in a more prosperous condition than I ever hear of?—I have made no statement of the kind. You must remember that the vast majority of the public-houses in Ireland have other businesses as well as the publican business. In the village where I live, for instance, there is one publican a smith, another a farmer, another a harness-maker, and another has a general grocery business. They are not exclusively dependent for their subsistence on the profit of the publican's trade.

42,992. (Mr. Caine.) In many cases the profits are only pocket money for the wives?—Very often that is the case.

have been drinking there. They sometimes go in to see whether they are drunk, and if there is a row in the public-house they very often go in and bring the publican to order for permitting disorderly conduct on his premises. The Rev. [illegible], P.C. 31 May '98.

63,608. Then are we to believe that the clergymen simply act as a spy?—Nothing of the kind. They go in there for the purpose of keeping order where the police are not in the neighbourhood.

63,609. One question with regard to Sunday closing. The city of Cork is an exempted city with reference to Sunday closing?—Yes. Sunday closing.

63,610. The houses there would be open while in the rural districts of which you have given evidence they would be closed entirely?—Yes.

63,611. Is it your opinion that the Sunday Closing Act has been a benefit to Ireland?—Yes, and in my opinion a very decided and great benefit.

63,612. You think it has been a great success?—A great success and would be a still greater success if it were enforced properly.

63,613. With reference to the district you have been speaking of to-day I should like you to reconcile that statement with the suggestion you have made that the bulk of the publican's trade is done on Sundays?—Certainly.

63,614. And yet you sit there and tell us the Sunday Closing Act is a great success?—Yes, it has been a great benefit in spite of all the abuse, for this reason, that before the passing of the Sunday Closing Act the people were accustomed to stay in the public-houses all day long on Sunday, and get drunk in the evening and fight going home. There is nothing of that kind now.

63,615. With Sunday closing?—Before Sunday closing. I am comparing the condition of the people at present after Sunday closing with the condition of the people before Sunday closing was enacted, and I say, comparing their condition, there is a very great improvement brought about by Sunday closing.

63,616. (Dean Dickinson.) They only do it on the sly now?—Yes. They must drink very hurriedly, and drink as it were with fear and trembling. They have not time to get drunk, and very few do get drunk; but to see the benefit of Sunday closing at present you have only to compare the condition of small towns and villages on Sundays with the condition of those places on holidays when the country people come in and sit down in the public-houses all day. On holidays there is fighting and quarrelling going on very frequently, but you see very little of it on Sundays. A sergeant assured me once, the majority of his cases with reference to assaults in his district were all cases that occurred on holidays when the public-houses were open, and those people gathered from all parts of the country and sat down and drank.

63,617. (Mr. Quinn.) I understand it is your opinion that there is a considerable number of low-class public-houses in your district and that it would be well for the general benefit of the community if they were closed?—Yes. [illegible] public-houses.

63,618. The persons who keep these houses sell drink without judgment and indiscriminately to anybody who is prepared to pay?—Not all.

63,619. I am speaking of the low-class public-houses?—Yes, most certainly do.

63,620. You think that the magistrates as a whole are biassed in favour of the publicans?—That is my opinion based on their action at court.

63,621. There are many of these low-class public-houses where persons who do not want to drink intoxicating liquor, find great difficulty in getting refreshment of any kind?—Yes.

63,622. It is very difficult to get a meal in them?—Practically impossible.

63,623. That is to say the great number of licensed victuallers in your district do not keep victuals at all?—I believe the whole of them do not, so far as I know.

63,624. Their trade is simply a bottle or two of whisky and perhaps a cask of beer?—Yes.

63,625. And very few of these small public-houses where they are so numerous as you have named are able to make enough to maintain the family in comfort out of the profit of their public-house, and they are obliged to have land, or some other trade?—Yes.

The Rev. M. Ahern, R.C.C.

14 May '98.

Question of the clergy.

43,026. Taking your evidence on the whole and generally, are you prepared to say that in your opinion the great majority of the priests of the diocese agree with it. Supposing you brought this before a conference of priests of your diocese and you proposed a series of resolutions based on your evidence, would you expect to carry those resolutions?—I should expect to carry them.

Licensing authority and constabulary.

43,027. (Mr. Young.) A question or two about the Bench. Has there been any marked deterioration in the Bench in your district of recent years?—I cannot answer that question; I have not been very long in the district.

43,028. You bring a pretty serious charge against the magistrates in your district which I do not dispute at all, and I want to ask you whether things are worse recently, or better than they used to be?—I have not considered that question and really I cannot give an answer.

43,029. It is a fact that a few years ago a large number of new magistrates were added to the Bench?—Yes.

43,030. Has that been satisfactory?—I have heard some say they were responsible for a good deal of the laxity practised amongst the magistrates; that those men recently appointed are more connected in different ways, through business interests, with the people living in the neighbourhood, and they are more liable to be influenced than others would be. I have heard that frequently stated.

43,031. And in point of fact the Bench is not so good as it used to be and not so independent?—As far as I know, it seems to be almost liable to be influenced in favour of or in opposition to a licence.

43,032. You would therefore desire an alteration in the Bench?—I would.

Drunkenness arising from public-houses.

43,033. You complain of a good deal of disorder in your neighbourhood arising from public-houses?—Not merely disorder. I make complaint of evil consequences of many kinds different from disorder.

43,034. Is it not notorious in your part of the world that a good deal of disorder arises from poteen?—No, not in the district where I am. We have a large number of accidents arising from excessive drinking, a good deal of violence from excessive drinking, and I attribute that to the multiplication of public-houses on the roads leading from the towns where fairs are held, and principally to the public-houses that stand about a mile or a mile and a half outside the town.

43,035. You do not suggest that the people generally are a drunken people?—By no means, and I think there is a great improvement in that respect in the habits of the people, and I attribute it all to the Sunday Closing Act. They do not stay now in the public-houses sitting down drinking all day, even on fair days, but they simply stand at the counter and take their drink and go; whereas, before the Sunday Closing Act came into operation, it was a common practice to sit all day in the public-houses, and that practice extended to the fairs as well. They went into the public-house, called for their drink and remained drinking. When the Sunday Closing Act did away with that practice on Sundays it was done away with also at fairs.

Adulteration.

43,036. One question with reference to the adulteration of whisky. You have told the Commission, in answer to cross-examination, that the distillers themselves supply the adulterant which you complain of?—One gentleman told me that the distillers supplied it—only one.

43,037. From any ordinary commonsense point of view, do you think it is the least likely a distiller would supply an adulterant which is going to seriously interfere with the sale of his own article?—I really do not know. Looking at it practically, I imagine he ought not to do so.

43,038. It is not a question of ought; would he not be a fool to do it?—Persons may do things that they ought not to do. Many persons do things that reason and other motives should compel them not to do.

43,039. Only it would be short-sighted policy on the part of the distiller?—If detected, I should think it would be.

43,040. But irrespective of that. You say one glass of this adulterated liquor is sufficient to knock a man over?—That is what I have been told.

43,041. Then the distiller would only sell one glass, whereas if he supplied ordinary ingredients he would sell two or three?—I cannot say. I only state the fact, that this seems to be the case. It is believed by people to be a fact; and whether the distiller would be a fool for doing so, I cannot say. I only state the fact.

The Rev. M. Ahern, R.C.C.

Adulteration.

43,042. I do not say there may not be adulteration. I am only suggesting to you some unlikeliness of your testimony, that the distillers supply the adulterant, which appears to me to be an extremely foolish thing for him to do?—It would seem to be a foolish thing, but it would seem he is doing so, and has done so, according to some.

43,043. (Mr. Young.) Do you think you could supply the Commission with a sample of this mixture?—I do not think I could succeed in supplying a sample of it. It is very hard to get a sample. It is almost impossible for any ordinary person.

43,044. Is the same mixture sold in every public-house—is there a patent for it?—I really have not seen the mixture at all. I am only stating now what I have been told by a number of persons.

43,045. Are the ingredients which compose this mixture well known?—They do not seem to be well known at all. They seem to be some mysterious kind of thing.

43,046. The mystery, I suppose, is confined to the publican?—The publican and the distiller, according to my information.

43,047. Do the distillers or the merchants who sell the whisky all sell the same sort of mixture?—I really would not say.

43,048. I am quite sure you do not think the story very credible. You scarcely believe the story?—I believe there is a mixture of some kind, and I am thoroughly persuaded of it. What the mixture is I do not know; but it is well known that there is some ingredient that is mixed with the whisky that is sold in the ordinary public-houses in Ireland, and that the whisky sold there is of a very bad quality.

43,049. I assume from your evidence that they drink a good deal in your division of Cork, and do not you think it marvellous that they should not know whisky from that composition you describe?—They do not drink so much whisky in my district, but those who do take whisky declare so it is like vitriol. They compare it to vitriol.

43,050. At all events it is hearsay to you?—Yes; but I must also declare that those who told me about these things have said that they themselves got that whisky.

43,051. It would solve the mystery very much if you could give us a sample of this whisky?—I fear I could not succeed in getting a sample of it.

Decrease in number of public-houses.

43,052. Your evidence, I think, means that you have too many public-houses in your district?—It amounts practically to that.

43,053. So that your opinion is that if you diminish the number of public-houses you would diminish the consumption of liquor?—Certainly, and many of the evil consequences that follow from the existing consumption of liquor.

Good by reduction.

43,054. If you had six public-houses in a village and you abolish three, do you suppose thereby you would lessen the consumption?—Certainly I do. It would lessen the temptation to drink, and thereby would lessen the existing consumption. I remember a case myself where there was a public meeting being held on a Sunday about four miles away from a village where there were four public-houses. One of these public-houses was so situated that persons coming from the north towards the meeting were bound to pass its door. The publican had closed his house for the day and he himself had gone to the meeting. Knowing this fact, I watched the house for some time—for half an hour—to see what those persons would do who applied at the door for drink, and found they could not get it. During the half hour about three or four horses and cars drew up at the door at different intervals. The occupants dismounted, knocked at the door, and finding they were not admitted, they remounted and drove on to the meeting. They did not turn to the next public-house which was only about 50 or 60 feet distant, but in an opposite direction. They simply got on their cars, drove to the meeting, and did not mind about the refreshment, showing clearly that the very fact of having to pass that public-house was a temptation for them, and that they yielded to the temptation, and that if that public-house had not been there they would never have thought of asking for a drink, even though the other public-house was only a short distance away from the road.

42,055. If there had been only two public-houses surely it would have been the same, they would have knocked at the door and tried to get in?—Perhaps one of those public-houses would not have been at that corner. The public-houses at present being so numerous they guard every road. There is one at each side of every road almost, wherever there is a village, so that it is impossible for any person to come into the village without passing one or more public-houses. I have been told by a person very fond of drink, that the very fact of seeing a public-house open is a temptation to him to go in and have a drink, and one person told me that in order to avoid entering a public-house when he had taken the pledge, he had to run across the door to avoid yielding to the temptation.

42,056. I think Sunday closing in your county is a failure?—I look upon it as a great success.

42,057. Is it not a failure?—It is not a perfect success.

42,058. Do not you say that they drink there without being detected by the police?—I admit all that.

42,059. Do you not come to the conclusion that it would be better really to keep the houses open?—I regard the enforcement of the Sunday Closing Act as partly a failure, but the Sunday Closing Act itself is a success, and I judge of its success by the consequences it has produced. I do not care how the people get drink, provided there is not drunkenness and rioting as a consequence, and drunkenness and rioting are certainly very much diminished by the Sunday Closing Act in Ireland.

42,060. As to the magistrates who have been made lately, you have heard that it is owing to them that there are so many public-houses?—No, I have not heard anything of the kind.

42,061. I thought you said you heard that it was the magistrates who were recently appointed?—I have heard that they are more liable to be influenced than some of the other magistrates, because the older magistrates were more independent of the people; these are much mixed up with the people, and are liable to be coerced. In fact, they depend, many of them, for their means of living, on the people.

42,062. That is rather a reflection on the last appointments?—I do not think so at all. I think that is merely a reflection on the system generally, because this system of increasing magistrates had existed long before the late appointments took place, but it was never publicly adverted to till, I think, then. Might I conclude my evidence by reading a letter which I received from the resident surgeon of one of the hospitals in Cork with reference to early Saturday night closing. I saw it stated by the Bishop of Limerick that in one of the hospitals in the city of Limerick the residents were kept up till 3 o'clock on Sunday mornings dressing wounds, the result of Saturday night drinking, so I wrote to the resident surgeon in charge of the South Charitable Infirmary in Cork, to ask whether he noticed any difference between the number of casualty cases treated in the hospital on Saturday nights and early Sunday mornings and those treated there the other nights of the week, and his reply was as follows:—

"South Charitable Infirmary and County Hospital,
"Cork, April 28th, 1888.

"Rev. M. Ahern, C.C.,
"[illegible]

"Dear Sir,
"In answer to your inquiry as to our Saturday night and Sunday morning casualty list, so far as my experience goes, formerly as resident student and presently as house surgeon, I have no hesitation in saying that the numbers treated are double those treated on other nights of the week, and these cases, in the immense majority, are primarily due to alcoholic intoxication. Indeed, on that night the resident rarely gets to bed before 3 a.m. Hoping that your efforts in the direction of Saturday night closing will be crowned with abundant success,

"I am,
"Very faithfully yours,
"John Berry, M.D.,
"House Surgeon."

The Rev. M. Ahern, C.C.

11 May '88.

Reduced cases on Saturday night through drink.

The witness withdrew.

Sir James Acheson MacCullagh called in and examined.

Sir J. A. MacCullagh.

42,063. (Examined by ...) You are, I believe, a justice of the peace for the city of Londonderry; you were mayor of the city for three consecutive years, 1882 to 1884; you are a doctor of medicine of Dublin University; you were resident medical officer of the Derry City and County Infirmary, and are now medical officer of the city of Derry No. 1 Dispensary, and you have also been in private practice as a physician and surgeon in Derry since 1877?—Yes.

42,064. Did you attend at petty sessions regularly, and during the years when you were mayor did you preside almost daily at the police court?—Yes.

42,065. Will you be good enough to give your views as to the licensing authority?—I think the licensing authority should be left to the county court judge, the same as it is left to the Recorder in cities. It works very well in Derry with the Recorder being the sole licensing authority and the magistrates not having anything to say to it. I believe that the same practice should be followed in the counties in Ireland.

42,066. Have you experience of licensing business outside the city of Derry?—No, except from the public press.

42,067. Are you a magistrate of the county?—No.

42,068. You are not called upon to sit as one of the licensing authorities of the county?—No.

42,069. Will you state your view with reference to the granting of occasional licences?—Occasional licences at present are granted by one magistrate, who is supposed to be the custodian of petty sessions. They are granted irrespective of the permission or otherwise of the people who are promoting the sports, or other things for which the occasional licence is asked. My idea is that the written consent of the organisers of the entertainment, or the sports, or whatever they may be, should be obtained, and then at least two magistrates should grant the licence.

42,070. The promoters of the sports should be parties to the application?—Yes.

42,071. And should two magistrates always sit?—At least two magistrates should sit.

42,072. I believe at present the occasional licence can be granted by a magistrate in his own house?—Yes.

42,073. With the cognizance or without the cognizance of the police?—Without.

42,074. Where, in your opinion, should the two magistrates sit to grant occasional licences?—If in a town in the petty sessions court, or if in a village they should sit in the police barracks. That would be a convenient place.

42,075. Do you know of instances where occasional licences have been granted against the wishes of the promoters of the sports?—I do. We had some sports some years ago—in fact, very large sports—and did not wish to have a licence, and tried to prevent it, but it was of no avail. It was granted by a magistrate without asking the promoters at all about it. We informed the police that we did not wish to have a licence, but it was of no effect, and the police could not interfere.

Occasional licence against local feeling.

42,076. You were one of the organisers of those sports?—Yes.

42,077. Within the limits of the city of Derry?—Yes.

42,078. Were they in private grounds?—In athletic grounds belonging to a club.

42,079. Were not you able to prevent the entrance of the persons to whom the licence was granted into the grounds?—He got an occasional licence capable ...

Mr J. A. M'Cullagh.

11 May '98.

63,080. Just outside the grounds?—Yes.

63,081. Close to the entrance, I suppose?—Yes.

63,082. Have you anything more you wish to say with reference to the granting of occasional licences?—No. I think that if the proprietors' consent were asked, and, perhaps the police consulted, and a couple of magistrates sitting, the licence would probably be given to persons who would carry on and conduct the licence in a proper manner.

63,083. Not only should the promoters of the sports be parties to the application, but notice should be given in every case to the police?—Yes.

Canvassing before petty sessions.

63,084. Then with reference to the canvassing of magistrates to attend at petty sessions?—There is a great deal of canvassing. You are asked to attend at petty sessions when a case is coming on.

63,085. Take the case of prosecutions?—In the case of prosecutions, I think it would be well it should be made a penal offence to ask a magistrate to attend. I do not at all say that there are any inducements held out to magistrates to attend, and I know that the magistrates in the city of Derry object very much to being asked to go, and that they would consider it an advantage if such a thing were stopped altogether.

63,086. You would make it a penal offence?—I would.

63,087. Is it a common practice in the city of Derry, in your experience, for magistrates to be canvassed?—The magistrates are very often asked when prosecutions are coming on.

63,088. What is the number of magistrates in the city?—I think 40 or 42.

63,089. Is there one court for Derry?—One petty sessions court. It sits twice a week.

63,090. Is there a mayor's court besides?—Yes, there is a police court every morning, but that is for cases of drunkenness or assaults, or anything of that sort occurring.

63,091. The petty sessions twice a week would clear up arrears of prosecutions of licence holders for breaches of the licensing laws and so forth?—Exactly.

63,092. In your opinion are magistrates influenced by this canvassing at all?—In some cases I know that the canvass compels a large number of us to not to go to the courts on the day we are asked to attend, in consequence of having been asked.

63,093. That is the result of having been canvassed. Do you think there are magistrates who would not otherwise attend, but do attend in consequence of being canvassed?—No, I would not go that far.

Canvassing as a penal offence.

63,094. What kind of penal offence would you make it? How would you propose a man should be punished for canvassing magistrates?—It would be a difficult thing to lay down.

63,095. There might be various kinds of canvassing that would be perfectly innocent?—If a man is summoned for a breach of the Licensing Acts, and meets a magistrate and asks him will he come to the Bench that day, I am afraid that would not be innocent.

63,096. That would be the person immediately concerned, but take the case of a person unconnected with the defendant. Would you necessarily punish him if a man said, "My friend is going to be summoned"?—Personally I think it would be a great advantage if it could be prevented.

63,097. Have you any other suggestions to make with reference to the question of canvassing magistrates?—Of course when applications are coming on for the grant of a spirit licence we are asked to attend, but we have nothing to say except to transfers.

63,098. The Recorder is your sole licensing authority?—Yes, except for a transfer; and the Recorder sits alone.

63,103. What do you say with reference to evidence?—On the appeal there is new evidence allowed to be brought up. It is for that reason that I think no appeal should be allowed, because the evidence is perfectly obtainable at the primary hearing. New evidence has been produced in cases, and brought before the Recorder, and the magistrates' decision has sometimes been upset.

63,104. Do you know whether it is a common practice to bring new evidence up on appeal in other parts of Ireland before quarter sessions in country districts?—I believe so.

63,105. In the country districts the appeal is to quarter sessions, the county court judge, and the magistrates?—Yes, the county court judge is the chairman.

Endorsement of the licence.

63,106. Then with reference to endorsements?—I think endorsements of all offences should be entered on a register or that when a house is coming up for a licence or transfer the exact character of that house should be distinctly before the authorities. The law at present is that the third conviction forfeits, but I do not say that because a licence has been endorsed, perhaps once or twice, that that should necessarily confiscate it. I think it would be well to have a register of the convictions on the licence.

63,107. How would you deal with the question of the forfeiture of the licence?—Of course the law would have to be changed in that respect.

63,108. What should you suggest—that it should be left to the discretion of the magistrates what class of endorsements should entail forfeiture on the third conviction?—No. All convictions should be recorded on the licence. Sometimes the conviction might be a very small or a slight one, and unless it was a serious endorsement I do not think it should forfeit the licence.

63,109. In other words, you would classify the endorsements?—Yes.

63,110. (Dean Dickinson.) Would the fine be the measure?—Yes.

63,111. (Viscount de Vesci.) Or according to the gravity of the offence?—That would be, necessarily, the fine also.

Habitual drunkards and restraint.

63,112. Then with reference to the habitual drunkard?—That is a very difficult question, but I have no doubt whatever that if there was some way of dealing with people, at first, who are becoming addicted to drink, and have been convicted several times running, that cures might be effected in these cases if there was some way of isolating them and treating them.

63,113. Are you speaking now from your experience as a medical man or a magistrate?—As a medical man.

63,114. What specific suggestions can you make?—There should be, I think, some homes of detention or some place where they could be sent. You might have central ones—three or four in a place like Ireland where they could be sent and detained for three or six months and treated and looked after. I believe in several instances, where people have become hopeless drunkards now, they would have been saved if that could have been carried out.

63,115. You would do that without the consent of the friends or of the person affected as a penalty?—I should.

63,116. And you would confine them in specific homes of detention?—Yes. At present it is done over and over again after they are convicted.

63,117. Can you state how many convictions, in your opinion, should constitute an habitual drunkard?—At present 3 in the 12 months would.

63,118. You would maintain that standard?—Perhaps for the isolating that might be too few, but half a dozen within the 12 months ought to do it at any rate.

63,119. [illegible]

Deemed [illegible]

[illegible] past, since 1873 [illegible] denominations have been [illegible] public-houses in every way [illegible] working men have been [illegible] of temperance, and I believe [illegible] help considerably to decrease [illegible] better-class houses that are being [illegible] that he has had a good deal to

[illegible] a great deal of building in

[illegible] working men's houses are more

[illegible] working men's clubs temperance [illegible] coffee-rooms, with billiard [illegible]

[illegible] are around there?—No, no

[illegible] temperance refreshments?—No.

[illegible] reading-rooms and amusements?—Yes.

[illegible] clubs of the ordinary kind in [illegible] are sold?—There are two.

[illegible] of those working men's clubs?—[illegible] is a county club and the other [illegible]

[illegible] a great deal of the decrease to [illegible] associations?—Yes.

[illegible] is one other cause?—Yes, a [illegible], the late Father [illegible], in [illegible] large and very successful Catholic [illegible] which has done an immense [illegible] about three years afterwards a [illegible] was also started amongst the

[illegible] temperance association a branch of [illegible]?—I do not think so.

[illegible] of her own?—Yes, simply in the

[illegible] state your views with reference to [illegible] Sunday closing has been of great [illegible] think the opinion of most of the [illegible] Sunday closing should be continued. [illegible] closing hour on Saturday would

[illegible] do you suggest on Saturday?—I [illegible] o'clock.

[illegible] you represent public opinion [illegible] of the earlier closing?—Yes, on [illegible] at 9 or 10 o'clock, but not very [illegible] do not think that would be the

[illegible] means of obtaining the opinion [illegible] who are public-house on this [illegible] closing and so forth?—Yes, I think [illegible] would be in favour of it, my [illegible]

[illegible] in the week are the wages paid in [illegible], which are the chief business [illegible] on Fridays; the builders and [illegible] at half-past 2.

[illegible] shipyard?—We have not a shipyard [illegible] working at present.

[illegible] do the tramcars close on Saturday?

[illegible] reference to the *bonâ fide* traveller? [illegible] in my opinion, and also in the [illegible] number of the people of Derry, [illegible], I think, should be increased to

[illegible] the size of the city of Derry now?

[illegible] many public-houses outside the [illegible] the city of Derry?—There are

[illegible] roads?—Yes.

[illegible] believe that the *bonâ fide* traveller [illegible] those? Have you noticed yourself [illegible] Sundays in those suburban public-[illegible] of the exact 3 miles?—I do not [illegible] any houses exactly within the [illegible] 4 or 5 miles, to which

there is no doubt people who wish to drink go on Sundays to drink.

63,147. You believe a lot of men go only for the purpose of obtaining drink?—Certainly.

63,148. Do the young men of Derry bicycle much?—Yes, there is a good deal of bicycling.

63,149. Do they go for excursions into the country?—They do, but I do not wish it to be thought that I say that the bicyclists drink, because I do not. I consider that bicycling has done a great deal to the cause of temperance.

63,150. Do the people of Derry make excursions out of Derry for a considerable distance in the country?—Yes. There is a boat running during the summer a little way down the river, about 10 or 12 miles, and there are two or three places the people go to by train, 6 or 8 miles down.

63,151. Do they sell drink on board the excursion boat?—Yes.

63,152. (*Dean Dickinson.*) They go down for 1*d.*?—No, it is 1*s.*

63,153. (*Viscount de Vesci.*) What suggestion would you make besides extending the limit? You say you would extend it to 6 miles?—Yes. I think that if a register was kept in each of those public-houses, and each person going in had to give their name and address, it would ensure in a measure that there were all *bonâ fide* travellers.

63,154. The licence-holder should keep the book?—Yes, he should keep the book.

63,155. And enter information given him by persons applying for liquor?—Yes, and that should be open to the inspection of the authorities at any time.

63,156. You think that would be a check on persons applying?—Yes. I think large numbers of people who think there is no harm in going in and getting drink, would not do so if they thought their names and addresses were entered.

63,157. Then take the question of children as messengers to the public-house?—At present children are served at public-houses with liquor to be taken away. I think it would be advisable, certainly in towns, if no child under 13 were served with drink for any purpose whatever, either for taking away or any other purpose.

63,158. At the present moment there is no check upon it. A child of any age can go in?—And be served with drink to be consumed off the premises.

63,159. In your opinion, do you believe an evil arises with reference to the drinking of women in consequence of children going to public-houses?—Yes. I think a large number of women who are drinking and tippling send their children who would not go out and go to the public-house.

63,160. They would be ashamed to go in themselves, but do not hesitate to send their children?—They do not hesitate to send their children, and tipple away at their own homes.

63,161. What is your opinion with reference to the spirit grocer's licence?—I think the spirit grocer's licence should not be issued at all.

63,162. What is the nature of the majority of the licences in the city of Derry?—Ordinary public-houses.

63,163. Are they public-houses pure and simple, or do they carry on any other trade?—Yes; a large number carry on grocery business as well.

63,164. Do you say the majority do or not?—The majority—mixed, as, the spirit grocers' licences.

63,165. I am talking of public-house licences?—Yes.

63,166. Do they carry on other trades besides selling provisions?—No, not as a rule.

63,167. (*Mr. Young.*) Would you not think it advisable to have an addition to the county court judge, say three or four elected local magistrates?—No, I would not. I think the county court judge would be the best authority, sitting by himself.

63,168. Would you commit the whole authority to him?—I would. It is done in the cities a little, I believe, good effect, and with satisfaction both to the publicans and the public.

63,169. Are the local magistrates satisfied with it?—In the city of Derry they are certainly.

Mr. J. A. McCulloch.

14 May '98.

Boat excursions.

Register of travellers.

Selling drink to children.

Abolition of grocers' licences.

Licensing authority.

Sir J. A. McCullagh.

11 May '98.

63,170. Would it not be more satisfactory to have, say, three elected local men sitting?—Personally I think not, and I think the view would be in favour of the county court judge being the sole authority. I think every person, publicans and others, is satisfied with the decisions of the Recorder in the city of Derry, and I believe in the other cities.

63,171. It is possible you might have a county court judge or a Recorder with very extreme views on questions in relation to the liquor laws. Would it not be a safeguard to have at least two or three others elected?—For myself, if I were a publican, I would prefer the decision of the county court judge, even though he had those views. I believe his position would be such as to rise above all that.

Spirit grocers.

63,172. (Mr. Grundy.) Would you state what are the grounds of your objection to the spirit grocer's licence?—The grounds are, that people will go in and buy drink in a spirit grocer's who would not go into the public-house and buy it. I have no objection to people going in and buying drink when they want it, but I think the people who are tippling and drinking, and go into the grocer's and carry away drink from there, would be ashamed to go into the public-house and buy their drink there.

63,173. Is your objection to the fact that they can go to the spirit grocer's, and can buy in open vessels, and therefore practically the trade is much the same as the public-house trade?—Yes, it is, practically.

63,174. I suppose you would recognise that in a large city like Londonderry there are a number of respectable spirit grocers who carry on the trade legitimately, and meet the requirements of a certain class of people?—Not with the spirit grocers in Derry.

63,175. I was rather surprised when you spoke so emphatically about abolishing the spirit grocers, because the population of the county of Londonderry is about 152,000, and you have only 17 spirit grocers to that population of 152,000. They would not appear to be the element of much mischief?—There are only six in the city itself.

63,176. In Derry, with a population of 33,000, there are three actual spirit grocers only?—I think it is three beer dealers and six spirit grocers.

63,177. That is an entirely different licence?—Yes.

63,178. Do you know the three traders who hold those spirit grocers' licences?—No, I cannot say that I do.

63,179. You could not tell us the standing of them?—I could not. If I heard their names I probably would.

63,180. You would agree that so far as the spirit grocer's licence is concerned, if it carries out the object it is supposed to do, that is, to supply the middle and upper-class households with goods for consumption at home, there can be no great question of temperance connected with it?—No.

63,181. Recognising that people do drink wines and spirits and must get them somewhere?—Yes.

63,182. And the spirit grocer would not be the worst place in the world to get them?—I think they can get them at a respectable publichouse.

Clemency.

63,183. (Mr. Walker.) With reference to the clemency of magistrates I think I understand you to say that the simple fact of controversy had no influence on the magistrates?—I do not think it does.

63,184. They can prosper in any such interference as that?—I think any length does. I think that the most influence that it has is that the magistrates very often stay away when they are asked to go.

63,185. The previous witness this morning condemned the magistrates, and said that they had abused the power entrusted to them. You are not prepared to endorse that?—I am not at all prepared to endorse what the previous witness said.

The one final licensing authority.

63,186. Presuming that the legislature took the licensing authority from the magistrates and placed it in the hands of one man, do you think that would be as sensitive as it would be if placed in the hands of a number?—I do. I think as a barrister from practical experience I believe it is quite as safe at present in the cities or safer than in the country.

63,187. You think that the predisposition on the part of the official would have no effect on his administrative action?—I do. I do not think it would have the slightest effect on the men acting as judges.

63,188. It might give a colouring to his action if the judgment was trembling in the balance—his predisposition might turn it the other way to decency?—I do not think so.

63,189. That is not human nature?—Our own Recorder is a man who is rather in favour of temperance, and I think there is no absolute feeling that he is absolutely impartial, both on the side of the public and the publicans.

63,190. We are dealing with the whole United Kingdom here, and [illegible] it from that point of view, generally speaking, one could not understand, a man may be of such a strong character as to rise superior to everything, but looking at it from a national point of view, do you still think it is desirable?—I still think when it has worked as well in the cities it would work quite as well in the counties of Ireland.

63,191. You are one of opinion that there is more capacity in one man?—It is in that instance.

63,192. You are speaking of immense pecuniary interests, and those men who may be appointed would have to deal with those interests, and undertake a great responsibility?—Yes.

63,193. You think they would be better placed in the hands of the men officially appointed?—Yes, of the county court judge of the county.

Endorsements on licence.

63,194. I understand you to say that endorsements on the licence should not have a penal effect?—When I suggested it that all endorsements should be put on the licence. It might weigh very hardly if that was done.

63,195. Three endorsements at the present time confiscate the licence?—Yes, if under this category.

63,196. It is quite possible that there might be three endorsements of a very slight character with comparatively endorsement, but you would not have that destroy the licence?—Certainly not.

63,197. Therefore, you would wish it to be left discretionary in the power of the magistrates, when the applicant applies for a renewal of a licence?—No, I think all endorsements should be on the licence, but it is quite possible to make certain endorsements penal as they are at present.

63,198. Then you would have to have them discriminated?—Yes, you would have to change the law on the point at present.

63,199. Change the law altogether?—Yes.

63,200. Now you, in your mind's eye, what kind of offence should involve the loss of the licence?—The [illegible]—any very serious offence—[illegible] serious offences as at present.

63,201. What would you call a serious offence?—An offence for which the penalty was a large penalty, and for which the magistrates might inflict a penalty of, say, 3l. or 4l.

63,202. Here's a pecuniary punishment. What we regard as a serious offence in the trade, as a house being used as a brothel?—Yes, certainly.

63,203. Or the landlord being convicted of any serious crime?—Yes, that would still stand as I say.

63,204. Would not that be quite sufficient?—That would be of itself quite sufficient.

Causes of decreased drunkenness.

63,205. You spoke as to the decrease of drunkenness. You acknowledge drunkenness has decreased?—Certainly.

63,206. In your opinion has drunkenness decreased all over Ireland?—That I could not say. I can only answer for the place I know of.

63,207. Is it the county you are speaking of?—No, the city and neighbourhood of Derry.

63,208. It has decreased in the city of Derry, and it would be right to assume that that is indicative of the whole of Ireland?—I could not say that.

63,209. You do not know the statistics that apply to that?—I do not.

63,210. You have been good enough to say that this has been due to several causes. The first you put was Sunday closing; the second, better education; third, working men's clubs, and the influence of the clergy and athletic exercises?—Yes.

Mr. J. A. M'Cullagh.

[illegible]. You say that all these causes are devoting a much better moral state?—Certainly.

[illegible]. Would not this apply to every town and village throughout the United Kingdom?—It would.

[illegible]. Where the same influences were at work?—Yes, if the same influences were at work, certainly.

[illegible]. And we may draw a conclusion from this that the publican has nothing whatever to do with it; but if the various authorities exercise and discharge their duties it would naturally bring about a better state of things?—It certainly would.

[illegible]. In respect to serving children you would [illegible] the age of supply to any one either for on or off consumption to 16?—Not under 16, certainly.

[illegible]. Of course you will admit this is legislation for one class only. You would not, personally, require a [illegible] for [illegible], for [illegible]?—I am afraid it is so.

[illegible]. You are now speaking of legislation for a class, without knowing perhaps quite whether it would meet the approval of that large class?—I quite admit it might occasionally be a hardship, but I believe that the good that would be done to the greater number would counterbalance that hardship.

[illegible]. This would be a matter for the legislature?—Certainly.

[illegible]. It has nothing whatever to do with the publican?—No.

[illegible]. (*Dean Dickinson.*) Mr. Walker has laid stress on [illegible] or five potential causes which have led to the improvement of the people in respect of temperance?—Yes.

[illegible]. You agree with him?—Yes.

[illegible]. And he has cleared the publican from all participation in these ameliorating causes. He says nothing of all this is due to the publican. Is not that so?—So he said.

[illegible]. Then the amelioration of these habits of the people is not due to the publican according to Mr. Walker. Is not that so?—Yes.

[illegible]. All these [illegible] cannot tend to counteract the influence and [illegible] of the public-house. Is that what you say?—Yes.

11 May '[illegible]

The witness withdrew.

Mr. John [illegible] called in and examined.

Mr. J. [illegible].

[illegible]. (*[illegible]*.) I believe you are the secretary of the Dublin United Trades Council?—Yes.

[illegible]. You have held that position for about [illegible] years?—Yes.

[illegible]. Is the council composed of [illegible] delegates, representing [illegible] labour organisations, the maximum number of delegates in any one case being [illegible]?—Yes.

[illegible]. There is one body, I think, that is not represented on the council, the bricklayers and stonecutters?—Yes.

[illegible]. Are they in agreement with the views you come here to represent?—Yes.

[illegible]. Do you represent your own views here to-day, or the views of the Trades Council?—The views of the Trades Council. I have a resolution, passed at the last meeting of the Trades Council, authorising me to give evidence.

[illegible]. When was that passed?—Last Monday evening.

[illegible]. Authorising you to appear here?—Yes, on their behalf, and on behalf of the bodies they represent.

[illegible]. What has been the policy of the Trades Council up to the present in reference to matters affecting the administration of the licensing laws?—Since [illegible] the Trades Council have passed resolutions on various occasions protesting against any alteration in the existing licensing laws.

[illegible]. Will you state what resolutions and on what dates they were passed?—In March [illegible], July [illegible], April [illegible], and May [illegible], and subsequently on Monday night last.

[illegible]. These were occasions when legislation of a restrictive character was brought forward?—Yes.

[illegible]. What was the tenor of the resolutions passed on those occasions?—The first resolution reads thus, on the [illegible] March [illegible]:—"That we, the "members of the Trades Council, regard the Bill now "before Parliament for the total closing of public-"houses on Sundays as a further attempt to abridge "our liberties, and if it becomes law will tend to "demoralise our people by the promotion of shebeening, which at present does not exist to any great "extent, owing to the facilities afforded for legitimate "refreshment by the regular licensed trade, and that a "copy of this resolution be forwarded to the four city "members and the Dublin Corporation." Then another resolution was passed in June [illegible] to the same effect, and another on July [illegible]. Prior to that the President of the Dublin Trades Council in that year came to give evidence against the passing of the then proposed Sunday Closing Act, and the Trades Council passed a resolution that the trades delegates comprising the council heartily endorse the evidence given by their representative. Then on the [illegible] of July [illegible], a resolution was passed emphatically protesting against an alteration of the existing law, and on [illegible] April [illegible], the following resolution was carried with two dissentients:—"That we protest against the closing of "public-houses in Ireland on Sundays and Saturday "early closing, as we believe it to be an uncalled for and "coercive measure, and to call on our representatives "in Parliament to oppose the Bill." Then on the [illegible] of May [illegible] a resolution was passed similar to the previous one, and then on last Monday night this resolution was adopted:—"That this Trades Council, "composed of representatives of the organised trade "and labour bodies of the City and County of Dublin, "reaffirms the resolutions adopted by the council on "the [illegible] March [illegible], and on the [illegible] June [illegible], "endorsing before the Select Committee, and also "July [illegible], and the [illegible] April [illegible], protesting against "any further restrictions on Sunday and Saturday "nights in Ireland, and that the council now hereby "authorises Mr. John [illegible] to present copies of "this and all previous resolutions to the Royal Com-"mission on the Licensing Laws in the course of his "examination on the [illegible] inst. (Signed) [illegible] "Chambers, Chairman."

[illegible]. Was due notice given of these resolutions being passed?—Due notice.

[illegible]. Was there a full attendance of the council on these occasions?—The council generally have a full attendance of delegates, but the average attendance is somewhere between [illegible] and [illegible] delegates.

[illegible]. Was there a meeting besides the resolutions passed by the Trades Council?—Yes, in [illegible] there was a meeting held in the Phoenix Park, and subsequent to that there was a meeting in the Rotunda. I am not quite sure whether it was subsequent to or previous to the meeting in the Park. It was attended by the trades of Dublin.

[illegible]. With reference to what particular legislation was that meeting in the Park?—It had for its object a protest against the proposed passing of the Sunday Closing Bill.

[illegible]. Will you state your view, as representing the Trades Council, as to the state of licensing regulations, first as to Sunday?—Their views are practically embodied in these resolutions, and they believe that any alteration of the existing law with reference to Sunday would produce very bad effects indeed.

[illegible]. (*Mr. Whitaker.*) An extension would?—An extension would.

[illegible]. (*Chairman.*) Or curtailment?—Yes, by the encouragement of shebeening and the promotion of further bogus clubs, of which there are a number still in Dublin.

[illegible]. (*Dean Dickinson.*) Them?—There are more than that.

[illegible]. (*Mr. Whitaker.*) Do you mean an increase of the hours would cause evil—an curtailment of the hours.

Mr. J. Simmons. 11 May '98.

[illegible]. You said so [illegible]. Would [illegible] of hours?—I think if the hours were curtailed, to say 8 o'clock, it would be a hardship on the people, and consequently they would obtain the drink elsewhere by illegal methods, whereas now I believe the people are perfectly satisfied so far as the public are concerned.

[illegible]. (Viscount de Vesci.) You consider that five hours is the proper allowance of time that should be given on Sundays?—I think so, and so do the other delegates to the congress.

Shebeens, [illegible] in Dublin.

[illegible]. What is your view as to the main cause of the drinking that goes on on Sunday? To what do you attribute the drunkenness that prevails on Sunday night?—I believe most of the drunkenness which prevails at the present time is due, to a very large extent if not entirely, to the fact that drink can be obtained in a great many of the streets of Dublin otherwise than in licensed houses.

[illegible]. From shebeens or from public-houses?—From shebeens.

[illegible]. Do you attribute it only to shebeens?—Yes, and to some clubs. I know that women [illegible] at street corners—I have positive knowledge of the fact—with liquor on their person, soliciting passers by to purchase it from them.

[illegible]. Have there been prosecutions by the police for this?—No.

[illegible]. Do you believe that the police are aware of this practice?—I do not believe they are.

[illegible]. What do you say with regard to the returns that have been placed before the Commission by the Assistant Commissioner of Police?—I believe that the drunkenness referred to in these returns has not been produced by drinking in regular licensed houses.

[illegible]. What do you attribute it to?—I attribute it to what I have said before—to shebeens.

Bogus clubs.

[illegible]. To any extent to the clubs?—And to bogus clubs.

[illegible]. How do you define a bogus club?—I define a bogus club as a club in which there is no library, no [illegible], no rational amusement in the shape of papers, [illegible] or [illegible] and such like, and these bogus clubs in some instances have nothing but a dirty pack of cards. That is the only game they have, and the members, or so-called members of the club, sit over them night after night, Sunday night after Sunday night, and do nothing but drink.

[illegible]. Have you yourself at any time been personally present in a bogus club?—I have, for the purpose of seeing what it was like.

[illegible]. How were you admitted?—I was admitted by a supposed member, who introduced me.

[illegible]. (Mr. Whitaker.) Have you lectures and libraries in the public-houses?—No.

[illegible]. (Viscount de Vesci.) Did you have any refreshment when you visited that bogus club?—I had.

[illegible]. Was it paid for by the member?—It was paid for by the member.

[illegible]. In no case were you called on to pay yourself?—No.

Shebeens.

[illegible]. What have you to say with regard to the return of the prosecutions for shebeening?—I believe that these prosecutions, no matter what they are attributed to, are mostly to be attributed to the shebeens; that is to say, the drunkenness from which prosecutions arose.

[illegible]. The prosecutions for shebeening [illegible] [illegible] to [illegible]?—Yes. There may be some drunkenness due, of course, to public-houses; but, I think, it is not fair to attribute the whole or the majority of it to public-houses.

[illegible]. What do you say as to the action of the police with regard to these shebeens?—I believe the police are powerless. They do, in some cases, secure convictions; but, I believe, there are a number of cases which have not come to their knowledge.

[illegible]. Do you believe that if further restrictive legislation was imposed on Saturday or Sunday it would be followed by an increase of shebeens?—I think so, and that is the general opinion of the working classes.

[illegible]. What is the character of these shebeens as a rule? Do many of them keep a large amount of liquor for sale on the premises?—They are low [illegible] houses.

[illegible]. Do they keep any amount of liquor on the premises, or just so about so much as is wanted for the day's consumption?—They do not keep any amount, but they are able to purchase it. They keep it at a distance in other houses and are able to purchase it in small quantities.

Mr. J. Simmons.

[illegible]. They bring it in for the day's sale only?—Yes.

Mixed trades in public-houses.

[illegible]. Now with regard to Saturday night closing. What is the fact with regard to the mixed trades? Do many of the public-houses carry on a mixed business?—Yes, a great number.

[illegible]. Groceries and provisions?—Yes, sometimes provisions.

Hours of working people on Saturday.

[illegible]. Will you state your view with regard to the habits of the working classes purchasing on Saturday from that point of view?—Their habits are that they generally market late, especially in congested districts or populous districts such as Thomas Street, Earl Street, George Street, and Queen Street. The people generally market up to 9 and 10 o'clock, and sometimes up to 11.

[illegible]. When are the wages paid as a rule?—In some cases they are paid on Thursday. In some cases they are paid on Friday, and in others on Saturday.

[illegible]. When do the majority of the trades pay?—The majority of the trades are paid, I think, on Friday.

[illegible]. As a matter of fact, are there not a sufficient number of provision stores and grocery shops in Dublin who do not hold licenses?—I think the majority of the grocery shops hold licenses.

[illegible]. You think there is not a sufficient number of grocery shops to supply the wants of the working classes?—No, they are not distributed sufficiently well.

[illegible]. If the hours were restricted on Saturday to nine o'clock, what would be the effect on the working classes?—I think it would be a hardship on the working classes. There are many cases in which respectable artisans' wives are not sufficiently well able to go out in broad daylight to do their marketing, and they prefer to do it a little late, after twilight.

Habitual drunkards.

[illegible]. What have you to say with regard to habitual drunkards?—I think there ought to be a home for inebriates. I think that is the only place to cure those of what I call a disease, because it certainly is a disease. We have a Maison de Santé in Dublin that works very well, but you have to pay very dearly for inebriates to go in there.

[illegible]. Do you say there is an inebriates' home in Dublin?—There is an institution called the Maison de Santé which is a sort of hospital for inebriates, but they have to be paid for pretty dearly, I think [illegible] to [illegible] a week.

[illegible]. (Dean Dickinson.) Do you mean the one at Charlemont Street?—Yes.

[illegible]. That is not for inebriates?—I have known confirmed drunkards to go in there.

[illegible]. It is a general hospital?—Certainly, one can be [illegible] treatment.

[illegible]. (Viscount de Vesci.) They went into this place?—Yes, to get cured. Their family sent them in.

[illegible]. They have to pay there?—Yes, very smartly.

Sunday closing.

[illegible]. (Dean Dickinson.) You say that abridgment during of the hours on Sunday would be a hardship on the working classes?—I think it would.

[illegible]. Then you think that during these five hours on Sunday these public-houses are very largely used by the working classes?—Not very largely.

[illegible]. They are largely used?—They are not largely used say at 3 or 4 o'clock.

[illegible]. Why should you think it a great hardship unless they are used by the working classes?—That is during the dinner hour of the working classes, which would range from 3 to 4 o'clock.

[illegible]. What would constitute the hardship on the working classes, if they do not frequent these houses on Sunday, in the reduction of the hours?—I think if a respectable man takes a walk for a distance from Dublin after his dinner and comes back and finds the public-houses closed at 5 o'clock or earlier than 7 o'clock, it would be a hardship that he could not get refreshment.

[illegible]. It is because they are used by the working classes, and yet you say that drunkenness on Sunday is not to be attributed to the public-house?—I believe it is to be attributed to shebeening.

[illegible]. Do you think the alcohol sold in public-houses has the peculiar property of being non-intoxicating?—No, I do not say that.

[illegible]. You say that these houses are used by the working classes, and yet you say that the working class intoxication is not due to the public-house. Therefore it must be that the alcohol sold in the public-house has the peculiar advantage of not being intoxicating?—I believe if they do not get it in the public-house they will procure it elsewhere.

[illegible]. (*Mr. Younger.*) You probably believe that in a public-house they are not allowed to get more than is good for them, but a shebeen is uncontrolled?—Yes.

[illegible]. (*Dean Dickinson.*) I see in Mr. Mallon's evidence he was asked: "Are there many shebeens in "Dublin?—(*A.*) There are. They are all or nearly all "confined to one locality. That is the one district in "which the houses of ill-fame are all located, and "shebeens are generally associated with houses of ill-"fame." Do you say then that all those who go to shebeens are accustomed to frequent houses of ill-fame on Sunday?—I differ from Mr. Mallon on that. I believe that shebeens are distributed over a larger area.

[illegible]. You think your knowledge of the city is to be compared with the knowledge of the Assistant Commissioner of Police?—I do not say so, but I have knowledge of the fact that they exist in other places than that division. I have it from authority I have no reason to doubt.

[illegible]. Mr. Mallon says there are at least a dozen drinking clubs he suspects, and he mentions there have been prosecutions, and several prosecutions, of a large number of shebeens. Do not you think the police could deal with the shebeens if they were multiplied?—I believe that shebeening is carried on, and the police cannot get at the bottom of it.

[illegible]. Do you think the liquor drunk in shebeens is more deleterious than the liquor drunk in public-houses?—I do believe it.

[illegible]. You want, in the interest of the trade, to confine the sale of liquor to the public-houses?—I believe it is very demoralising to get it in a shebeen.

[illegible]. By whom was that meeting in the Phoenix Park organised?—It was organised by the existing Trades Council.

[illegible]. Who are the prominent movers in that Trades Council?—One of the late presidents was Mr. R. [illegible] Richardson.

[illegible]. What was his business?—A printer.

[illegible]. What is Mr. Chambers' business?—A saddler.

[illegible]. Does this council fairly represent all the trades of Dublin as a whole, or does it predominantly represent the trade of the liquor sellers?—It represents all the trades of Dublin with the two exceptions I have mentioned—the stonecutters and bricklayers. There is one society of stonecutters in it, but the Dublin stonecutters are not affiliated with it now.

[illegible]. Do you publish a report?—Yes, there is an annual report published.

[illegible]. And a subscription list?—Yes.

[illegible]. Could we see that subscription list so as to know by whom the Trades Council which moves in the interests of one special trade is supported?—I have not got it with me.

[illegible]. Could you supply it or could it be obtained?—I could send it to the Commission. There is a register kept of the affiliated trades in the Trades Council.

[illegible]. It would be interesting to know what trade it is that contributes most to the support of that society, because the trade that is most interested, so far as it appears, is the one trade of the publicans?—The publicans are certainly not allied with the Trades Council.

[illegible]. Not connected with it?—Not connected with it.

[illegible]. (*Mr. Ockney.*) Are the brewers' workpeople in it? Is there any union amongst the brewers' workpeople?—Brewers' labourers.

[illegible]. Have they a union?—They have.

[illegible]. And they are affiliated?—Yes.

[illegible]. (*Dean Dickinson.*) Did you ever know of any public meeting in Dublin held of working men to protest against Sunday closing and the early closing?—I remember the working men meeting at the Park. *Mr. J. [illegible]* 11 May '[illegible]

[illegible]. Not in the city of Dublin?—As you know, the Phoenix Park is very adjacent to Dublin.

[illegible]. I have never known a public meeting of working men being held in Dublin against Sunday closing, and I have spoken to large meetings of working men in favour of Sunday closing?—This meeting was held for the purpose of denouncing the Sunday Closing Act.

[illegible]. (*Mr. [illegible].*) The Rev. Dean has said or implied that you are here in the interests of the publicans, is that so?—I am not. Position of witness.

[illegible]. Not in the slightest degree?—Not in the slightest degree.

[illegible]. Then an assumption of that kind is entirely out of place?—Out of place.

[illegible]. The Rev. Dean also asked you when you expressed an opinion that further restriction as to Sunday closing would be injurious and inconvenient to the working classes, do the working classes throng these houses during these hours, or were the houses largely used? I suppose you meant to imply this, not that these houses were filled all those hours by men, but that if they wished abroad and wanted refreshment you saw no reason why they should be deprived of it at a later hour than 5 o'clock?—I said so. Sunday closing.

[illegible]. That is what you mean to imply?—Yes, that is what I did say.

[illegible]. The working classes do not drink in public-houses especially, any more than any other class?—No.

[illegible]. They go in for what they require, they have it and go away?—Yes.

[illegible]. You hold a very important position, and you no doubt have great knowledge and experience of the habits of the working classes?—Yes.

[illegible]. You are quite qualified in every way to express an opinion here as to what they would like and what they would dislike?—As the delegates of the Trades Council think.

[illegible]. With reference to the question of the serving of children, you probably know that there is a very strong feeling on the part of the temperance people, and they have evidently discovered that it is most demoralising for a child to enter a public-house. What have you to say as to whether any restriction should be placed on the age?—I seldom see children sent to a public-house for dinner drink under, certainly, 13 or 14 years of age, and I should be certainly disinclined to have a child sent under 14. Selling drink to children.

[illegible]. You would leave the age limit to 14?—I should say so.

[illegible]. Then you are in favour of the prohibition of sending children?—I think that it would only lead to the elevation of children's morals to limit drink of any kind under 14 years of age.

[illegible]. (*Mr. Whitaker.*) The trades unions of Dublin desire shorter hours for working people generally, I suppose?—Yes.

[illegible]. Have they made an effort to secure shorter hours for the people working in public-houses?—We have several times applied to the grocers' assistants to become affiliated to the Trades Council with a view of improving their condition, and they have declined to do so. Shorter hours for [illegible].

[illegible]. Have you made efforts to secure shorter hours for people working in public-houses?—No.

[illegible]. None?—No.

[illegible]. Nor to stop Sunday labour?—For the simple reason I have told you, that they have refused to cooperate in any effort.

[illegible]. Have you made any effort to get the persons employed in public-houses to co-operate with you?—We have.

[illegible]. What have you done?—We applied to them to become affiliated to the Trades Council, and they declined.

Mr. J. Simmons.

15 May '97.

63,235. That is the tavern?—Yes.

63,236. Have they a tavern?—Yes.

63,237. And the union declined to co-operate with you?—They declined to co-operate.

63,238. Would respectable working men go to shebeens?—No, I do not think respectable working men would go to shebeens.

Sunday closing and shebeens.

63,239. Then the closing of public-houses would not drive the respectable working men into shebeens?—What I do say is, that a respectable working man would be deprived of his reasonable drink, for the general drink of the working classes is draught porter, and draught porter bought at 3 o'clock would be unfit for use in a couple of hours.

63,240. You said it would increase the number of shebeens?—Yes.

63,241. I gather from you, that the respectable working men would not be driven into shebeens, because they would not go to them?—There are others, besides respectable working men, who, if they could not get a public-house, would not go to the shebeens.

63,242. The respectable working people would not?—I do not believe the respectable working people would.

63,243. Am I to take it, the working people you represent would not go to those shebeens if the public-houses were closed?—All the people I represent are not respectable.

63,244. They are not all respectable?—It is very hard to find a respectable community without some exceptions.

63,245. With reference to these shebeens, are you aware that before the Sunday Closing Act was passed which did reduce the hours in Dublin, there were far more convictions for shebeening and illegal hawking than there have been since?—That is, before 1878?

63,246. Yes?—No, I am not aware of that.

63,247. That is the fact. Are you also aware that the convictions for drunkenness in Dublin on Sunday have diminished considerably since the passing of the Sunday Closing Act?—I believe there is a lot of undiscovered drunkenness.

63,248. Would not that have been the case before?—I have seen men myself going through the streets on Sunday absolutely drunk, and yet there were no arrests.

63,249. Might not that have been likely to have been the case before 1878 as well as after?—It might, but they are able to get it now.

63,250. Does not the fact that there have been a smaller number of convictions for shebeening since Sunday closing than before rather go against your conjecture that the reduction of hours of sale promotes shebeening?—I believe shebeening is carried on by a more subtle process, namely, that to which I refer by the sale of drink in the public streets. I was solicited myself by a woman at the corner of the street.

63,251. The convictions are for shebeening and hawking as well?—I do not remember to have seen that have [illegible] or to have heard of it.

63,252. You say you do not suggest any extension of the present hours?—I should not suggest any curtailment of the present hours.

Hours of opening on Sunday.

63,253. I ask you if you would suggest any extension of the present hours. Would you have them open later?—No, certainly not, I think people are perfectly satisfied with 7 o'clock.

63,254. Then might I ask you, what was the meaning of the phrase used in the resolution you read to us—the first one passed in 1896 where they refer to a further attempt to abridge their liberties? What does the word "further" mean there? Does that mean that the Sunday Closing Act already in existence was an attempt to abridge their liberties?—Yes, I believe the intention of the framers of the resolution was that.

63,255. Objecting to that Act?—Yes, I believe so.

63,256. Although it has been proved to be very beneficial?—I cannot say that it has been very beneficial.

63,257. You do not suggest any departure from it?—No.

Mr. J. Simmons.

Drink and poverty.

63,258. In remarking that the women drop into on Saturday night, did I understand you correctly to say that some of the respectable workers were doing so and did not care to go out till dark?—Quite so, under circumstances over which they have no control—large families, &c.

63,259. Do you think that drinking has anything to do with that destitution?—In the majority of cases, I think high rents and large families have to do with it.

63,260. Perhaps you have not read it, but I may mention an instance that the Recorder gave us here when giving evidence the other day, of men who carrying 30s. would give 15s. to their wives and keep the overplus themselves. Does not that seem to indicate there is a leakage considerably greater than the rent?—I have a very high opinion of the Recorder, but I certainly think the Recorder is sometimes very hostile in his views with reference to the working-men, and I know the working-men themselves, after some of the utterances of the Recorder, have very little confidence in his professions of respect for them.

63,261. Have you anything approaching a club in connection with your Trades Council?—We have.

63,262. Is there a bar in that club?—There is, and one of the finest libraries in Dublin, started by Mr. John Mallon himself and the secretary of the late Lord Lieutenant, who gave us a subscription towards the management of the club and the library.

Sunday clubs.

63,263. (Mr. Young.) Might I ask you whether it is not notorious that the league clubs in Dublin on Sundays are only used to any extent when the public-houses are closed?—Quite so.

63,264. And between the hours of 2 and 7 they are practically deserted?—Yes.

63,265. That shows that the respectable working classes in Dublin prefer to use the public-houses if they get the opportunity?—Yes.

63,266. Do you think that state of matters would be aggravated by further restriction?—In my opinion it would, and in the opinion of those I represent.

63,267. (Mr. Allen.) What percentage of the workers in Dublin are there in trades unions?—I speak for my own trade, and I suppose there are 1,300 in the trade union, and I do not suppose there are 100 outside.

63,268. That is in your own trade. What will be the average taking it all through?—I believe that will apply to all trades. Of the bricklayers I would say the same. I do not believe out of 600 bricklayers there would be 50 outside.

The Trades Council.

63,269. These are all affiliated to the Trades Council?—Yes, amongst the bricklayers.

63,270. You think there is almost a unanimous opinion throughout these trades as against any further curtailment of the hours?—So much so that, on any of these resolutions that have been adopted by the Trades Council, not a single voice has dissented from the trades bodies.

63,271. (Mr. Grimston.) You come here with the direct authority and sanction of your Trades Council?—Certainly.

63,272. May I ask if you are a teetotaller?—No, certainly not.

63,273. If you came here not representing your council, but as a teetotaller, would you expect the Commission to attach much value to your evidence?—I cannot say, of course, what the opinion of the Commission is.

63,274. (Mr. Young.) How long have you been secretary to the Dublin United Trades Council?—Since 1885.

63,275. Twelve years?—Yes.

63,276. You really do represent the opinion of the vast bulk of the working men of Dublin?—Yes, on this question.

63,277. How many league clubs have you in Dublin?—I cannot speak with exactness, but I understand there are 30.

63,278. Mr. Mallon admits he knows of 13, but you say there are many more?—Many more.

ONE HUNDRED AND SIXTH DAY.

Queen's Robing Room, House of Lords, Tuesday, May 17th, 1898.

PRESENT:

THE RIGHT HONOURABLE THE VISCOUNT PEEL IN THE CHAIR.

The Right Hon. the LORD WINDSOR.	ANDREW JOHNSTON, Esq.
The Right Hon. SIR ALGERNON WEST, K.C.B.	JOHN HERBERT ROBERTS, Esq., M.P.
The Very Rev. H. M. DICKINSON, Dean.	HENRY RILEY SMITH, Esq.
WILLIAM SPROSTON CAINE, Esq.	CHARLES WALKER, Esq.
HENRY GRAHAM, Esq.	THOMAS PALMER WHITTAKER, Esq., M.P.
SAMUEL HYSLOP, Esq.	SAMUEL YOUNG, Esq., M.P.

Mr. EDWARD D. DALY called in and examined.

Mr. E. D. Daly. 17 May '98.

63,879. (Chairman.) I believe you are Chief Clerk of the Dublin Police Courts?—Yes.

63,880. Both the defaults and the summonses of the licensing laws in that capacity come under your notice?—Frequently, for the last 36 years.

63,881. Have you noticed any habitual drunkards in the course of your experience?—The number of habitual drunkards is difficult to speak of. I have noticed repeatedly most aggravated cases of habitual drunkenness. If I might make two observations that would apply to the whole of my evidence, I should like to say this. First, I want to say that, coming from Dublin, as I do, and being about to speak of what seems to me very shocking instances of aggravated misconduct from drunkenness, I wish to guard myself against any misapprehension that my observations are directed to the whole of the Dublin working men, the majority of whom, so far as my information goes, can drink without abusing it, as I do myself. The next observation I should like to make is that I should like to call the attention of the Committee to the fact that no suggestions of mine are intended as any substitute for the great work carried on by the Temperance party. The point I wish to impress on the Committee is that the suggestions I wish to bring forward would be a great aid to all the moral influences that are directed to promote sobriety, and in that view I am glad to be supported by the heads of one of the great Roman Catholic temperance bodies in Dublin, the Capuchins of Church Street, who carry on a branch of the League of the Cross, and who are resident philanthropists in one of the depressed districts of Dublin. They say and they think, and they have supported me on the platform in saying, that if such suggestions as I intend to bring before the Committee were legally adopted, their efforts to promote temperance in Dublin would be seriously supported.

63,882. Having the advantage of your views on the general subject, what is your opinion of the habitual drunkard,—is he more of a plague abroad or at home?—He is more of a plague at home, so far as I see, than abroad. Might I suggest that in bringing my views before you I should like to give you some figures as to the conditions of Dublin which have forced those views upon me?

63,883. What are the causes for drunkenness in Dublin?—The causes for drunkenness are figures upon which I do not base my views. I think they are unreliable as indicating the extent of drunkenness. I should like to call your attention to the [illegible] of Dublin as compared with other Irish towns. More than half the [illegible] crime of all Ireland passes through the Court with which I am connected; that is to say, [illegible] cases out of [illegible] for the whole of Ireland.

63,884. To what do you trace those cases mainly?—Partly to [illegible] conditions, and to a very large extent to intemperance. I should like also to say that taking the latest judicial and criminal statistics, I find that in 1896 out of 1,[illegible] simple larcenies committed in all Ireland, 1,374 were committed in Dublin. Putting aside breaches of licensing, drunkenness, and so forth, various offences per 10,000 of the population were for Dublin 72, for Belfast 7, for Cork [illegible]. In the same year Dublin sent every 1,000 persons [illegible] by indictment, Belfast 1[illegible], and Cork 1[illegible]. A gentleman whom I know, who is acquainted with both Belfast and Dublin, tells me that there are no such slums in Belfast, and I presume in the rest of Ireland, as we have in Dublin. Might I show the Committee a map of the Dublin police district with the [illegible] coloured around it, and the city district in the centre [illegible]?

63,885. You say that slums are one of the causes of intemperance and crime in Dublin. Do you maintain that there are such a large number of public-houses in Dublin as compared with other cities that it is a serious factor in the production of crime?—I do not think that is so potent a factor as the other social conditions. In Dublin we have a very large number of the population living in houses occupied by more families than one. I should say the number of houses occupied by from 4 to 17 families accommodate about 100,000 of the population. That indicates that the poor in Dublin are abnormally collected together in tenement [illegible] [illegible] from respectable centres into which only the [illegible] and where he goes there he is not helped by the law.

63,886. When you find a drunken person under those conditions I suppose his condition acts upon his children and his wife?—It does. It acts particularly [illegible], and the point I want to call the attention of the Commission to is that aggravated cases of drunkenness in such areas cannot be dealt with at all efficiently by the mere power of arrest and fine under the Licensing Act.

63,887. What are the usual fines for drunkenness?—Do you mean as put in practice?

63,888. Yes?—Five shillings or seven days, and 10s. or seven days, represents about the average.

63,889. But the fines sometimes go down below 5s., do not they?—Not frequently of recent years.

63,890. Would you raise the minimum?—I would. I was going to suggest that that applies to one branch of the question that I will touch on later, the penalties under the Licensing Act. Would you allow me to mention now, as regards the slums of Dublin, the figures bearing on it?

63,891. Will you give us the number of public-houses? Everybody admits, I suppose, that the overcrowding of the people, and the wretched condition in which they live, is productive, at all events, of intemperate habits. That we can quite understand. Are there such [illegible]

Bad housing the poor.

Penalties for drunkenness.

Mr. E. D. Daly.

17 May '97.

for drink so to be [illegible] temptation?—So far as I see the distribution of drunkenness in the C division—that is that little space in Dublin—are the biggest, and the public-houses are not more numerous in that particular division where drunkenness is concentrated. As I said before, I think the social conditions and the unprotected state of the industrious husband—the absence of sufficient happiness against him—are the most potent and at the same time the most neglected features.

63,392. Should you say that in the parts of Dublin where the population was most congested there are more public-houses there in the richer and more sparsely inhabited divisions?—Certainly; in the city of Dublin, in the centre, there are more public-houses than in the suburbs.

Sober wife of a drunken husband.

63,393. I want to know what remedy you would adopt to prevent the drunkard from scandalising himself in public or from committing those cruelties on his wife and children in private to which you alluded?—If you ask me that question I would begin by dealing with him in his family relation. The crueltest wrong that comes before me is the position of the sober mother who is trying to help to keep her children and trying to earn money for the household, and who has the results of her industry appropriated without redress by her habitually drunken husband.

63,394. You think the present law is not sufficient to protect her?—I think the present law is not sufficient to protect her in humble life. In rich life it is, because either party can always take civil action against the other, who, presumably, holds property. In humble life there is no such means by which the wife can protect her separate property.

63,395. I suppose in the cases you mentioned the poor woman would not have much property to protect?—She would have most material property to protect. She has her week's earnings, she has [illegible] and instruments by which her bread is earned, and which benevolent people frequently give her. She has other things besides her separate property for which she is entitled to protection, that is the clothing of her children. All these are unprotected at present against the misappropriation of the drunken husband who lives with her.

Protection by order of the magistrate.

63,396. Assuming a drunken husband, how would you set about giving her protection without subjecting her to too much cost?—I propose giving her protection by taking what one sees ordinarily are two things—first her earnings, her separate property, anything that she has purchased or directed to be purchased by them, the wearing apparel and school requirements of her children or the children, and their earnings, if any, such as the earnings of a little newsboy, tools, instruments, and appliances entrusted to her, and not entrusted to her husband by people who try to help her. I propose, if the husband took these away and sold them for drink, then she should have power to go and represent to the magistrate that her husband was an habitually intemperate man, and on the basis of doing that, that the magistrate then should have power to give her an order protecting those things, and that the effect of the order should be to practically extend the provisions in the Married Women's Property Act which prohibits her from using any criminal remedy; that she should then have power to go to the police court and get a shilling summons against the husband either for damaging her goods or for misappropriating them.

See Appendix XI.

63,397. When I said the poor woman had not much property to protect, I suppose you may take it that the head of the family would be the wage-earner; the great bulk of the wages would be contributed by the man?—No, that is not so in the cases of which I am speaking.

63,398. (*Dean Dickinson.*) You mean, [illegible] and sewing machines?—Yes, and children's earnings.

63,399. (*Chairman.*) So that in those cases you would give sufficient protection to the woman for her property which was for her sole and separate use, if her husband was convicted of habitual drunkenness?—Yes, if she proved to the magistrate that he was an habitually intemperate man. It is right to say that I have several instances which I can give you even within the last couple of months where women have come to the court and asked for redress, and been told that they could not get it.

63,400. In those cases which you speak of have those husbands been convicted before the police court, or is it a case of habitual inebriety at home?—Habitual inebriety at home, these self-degenerate habitual drunkards, is a man who is astute enough to avoid arrest.

Mr. E. D. Daly.

63,401. Therefore how would you arrest him in his own house?—The remedy I proposed was that the wife should have power to get a summons against him, and that he should be brought before the magistrate to account for having damaged or misappropriated her property.

63,402. Apart from any violence that he might have used, if he was an habitual inebriate and spent her wages, would you punish him for that? Would you punish him for drinking at home and squandering away his wages?—Until the intemperate habit results in some definite overt act, I am not inclined to suggest punishment.

Present penalties for repeated drunkenness.

63,403. With regard to those habitual drunkards, the open and overt drunkards who come under the notice and cognisance of the police, is the punishment upon those sufficient, do you think, after repeated cases of drunkenness?—No, the power of punishment is utterly insufficient. There are utterly no restrictions for the habitually intemperate man. I am not thinking of the casual drunkenness of the habitually sober man.

63,404. Would you imprison them without the option of a fine after a certain number of offences on the part of the drunkard?—I would consider that discretion.

63,405. By imprisoning the drunkard after three, four, or five convictions, you would save the family from the risk of his interference with them?—I would not only deter his drunkenness as far as punishment can deter it in respect of his own family, but I would make him an example to his class and deter others from becoming like him.

Disproportion of fines.

63,406. Turning to the important case that you have opened, of fines for different offences, do you consider that the fines under the licensing laws are well arranged and suited to the particular offences for which they are inflicted?—I think the fines under the licensing laws are badly arranged. There are no exemplary fines for exemplary offences as distinct from the fines for mere breach of trade regulations. I will give you examples if you wish.

63,407. Take the case of harbouring prostitutes in a house. We will suppose a bad case; what would be the penalty?—The maximum for the first offence is 10l.

63,408. Would not it be competent for the magistrate to take away the licence in that case and to refuse to renew the licence?—Do you mean at the annual sessions?

63,409. Yes?—I think the magistrate's discretion as to what constitutes good character is very large. If a magistrate came to the conclusion that that particular offence made a man a bad character he might refuse to renew the licence.

63,410. Your point, as I understand it now, is that comparing one offence with another, the fines are ill proportioned?—Yes.

63,411. That the 10l. is an inadequate fine?—As compared with 2l. for selling drink to a child, or as compared with 10l. to save a trader, who has the temptation, happens to have his house open a little after hours.

63,412. The fine in all cases being a maximum of 10l.?—For the first offence, as a rule, it is a maximum of 10l.

63,413. Therefore in the case of more heinous offences, harbouring prostitution, permitting drunkenness, what would you say?—Do you mean what should I suggest?

63,414. How would you class that offence? Would you class that among the more heinous offences?—I would. Offences of a trader who directly conduces to drunkenness or vice I would single out and visit with increased severity.

Compulsory endorsement of the licence.

63,415. Having raised your fines for offences, would you endorse all those convictions upon the licence?—I think the compulsory endorsement is almost more important than merely raising the fine—the compulsory endorsement, I mean, in those aggravated offences. I do not think courts of summary jurisdiction will carry the power of optional endorsement out efficiently. There was only one recorded in Dublin in 1896 and three in 1897. There was only one recorded, I believe, by the figures, in Manchester for the whole year, and one recorded in Birmingham in the whole year.

[illegible] drunkenness, the power to give the police the right to enter [illegible] what the facts actually are should be [illegible]. Mr. [illegible] Daly

[illegible] 17 May [illegible]

63,437. Do you think registration or licensing would by themselves be a protection?—By themselves I think not.

63,438. Would you prefer registration to licensing, or vice versa?—[illegible] I prefer is to base the attack on these [illegible] upon the ground of [illegible] and disorder. The remedy.

63,439. You would not subject a respectable working man's club to the constant danger of invasion by the police?—Certainly not. If I were a working man I should resent [illegible] any right of police [illegible] so long as I conducted myself properly.

63,440. Therefore how would you protect that bona fide and respectable club?—It would be protected by the condition I attach to the right of entry. Where there is [illegible] that habitual drunkenness is carried on in a club, I think the police, in the interests of the community, ought to have the right of entry, in a rich man's club as well as a poor man's club. Police entry under conditions.

63,441. If there was sufficient evidence [illegible] to show that there were habitually drunken people on the premises?—Yes, or disorder, or a large [illegible] of drink [illegible] with disorder.

63,442. A [illegible] has been [illegible] lately—in fact a Bill has been before Parliament for dealing with inebriates. Have you studied the provisions of that Bill?—I have looked over it. The Habitual Inebriates Bill.

63,443. If I may ask your opinion upon it, do you think it adequately deals with the evil?—[illegible] a [illegible] help, but I do not think it adequately deals with the evil. I should like to give you one case in point which occurred the day before yesterday. A man was brought to me by one of the [illegible], who told me that it was a remarkable case. I questioned him. I am not giving this as an exceptional case, but as [illegible] man [illegible] to be a type. His story was this. He did not tell it me in these words. He said: "I am a bricklayer; I am in good "work. I married my wife 34 years ago, and about [illegible] "8 years she took to drink. Since then my life has "been"—he said "a hell," and I suppose it was true. He said: "I am fond of her, and I do not like to punish "her. I want to get her cured. The thing has come "to such a pass that my employment is [illegible], and I "went up to the [illegible] three weeks ago and offered to "pay them to take care of her, and was told there was "no power to take care of a person [illegible] ad-"dicted to drink. I then talked to her"—(these were his actual words)—"like a clergyman, and I induced "her last Saturday to take the pledge. She made all "sorts of promises, and on Saturday I gave her a pound "for the housekeeping. On Monday I found the money "all gone, and she was lying dead drunk; and I have "now come to the police court to ask if the law will "give me any help." I explained to him that there was no [illegible] for such [illegible] in Ireland; and he went away saying: "I am going away with a "sad heart, because if a man is [illegible] in any "class of life and willing to pay for it, he ought to "get some help." I got the [illegible] of [illegible] hospital in the [illegible] the day before yesterday. He told me [illegible] that, in his opinion, a [illegible] in Ireland for an Inebriate Act. The Act you have asked me about while it will be a help, will not [illegible] the poor [illegible] who came up to the police court where he [illegible], because a condition of applying is that he should [illegible]; and in a large number of cases it will be hopeless to ask a man as the condition to consent to go under compulsory detention, and give up his whisky and tobacco for a long period.

support the children, and there is no power under the existing law to force the drunken parents either to pay a contribution or to punish them for not paying it. That sets a premium again on the intemperate parents as compared with the other parents. [illegible]

63,444. What remedy would you suggest for that state of things?—The remedy falls under the general considerations that apply to the distinction between a civil remedy and a criminal remedy. I suggest that criminal procedure should be applied to force drunken people either to work and pay contributions or go to prison if they will not.

63,445. You would relieve the ratepayers and throw the expense of maintaining the children by law on the drunken parents?—Yes. I may mention, perhaps, that in Switzerland they take a man of that kind who will not pay contributions to the maintenance of his children and they put him into a workhouse, and make him earn the contribution.

63,446. Are the fines in Dublin progressive fines? Would a man who had been brought up five times for drunkenness be fined a larger sum than a man brought up for the first time?—As a matter of practice, that remedy only comes up occasionally, and in every large city it will never crop up more than occasionally, because of the difficulties of identifying the man who has been repeatedly convicted before. No magistrate notices. Penalties for repeated drunkenness.

63,447. But surely there must be some notorious cases in Dublin, as elsewhere, of men and women who are habitual drunkards who are well known, not only to the police but to everybody in the town, are there not?—There are some cases.

63,448. In these cases are the penalties progressive?—They are. In those cases the magistrates, where the man is charged by the police for a third conviction, will put on in many cases 20s. or a month.

63,449. What is the maximum fine and the maximum imprisonment in lieu of fine?—The maximum fine for repeated drunkenness, no matter how often it happens, is 40s. That is not enough of a punishment for repeated drunkenness, because, as a rule, the wife has to pay it or she will get black eyes when he comes out.

63,450. In default of payment, what is the maximum imprisonment?—One month—only in default of payment.

63,451. (Dean Dickinson.) When you spoke of protecting orders, you did not bring out that there is a distinction between the case of England and Ireland. In England there is such a power of obtaining from the magistrate a protection order?—That is so. I did not bring that out. Protection orders to wives of drunken husbands.

63,452. You want a similar protection order available by the wife or by the husband in Ireland?—Not similar. I think there is a considerable amount of objection to the, so to speak, extended divorce jurisdiction given to the police court in the English Act 28 & 29 Vict. c. 39.

63,453. I mean the protection orders simply?—I do not think the English Act protects the separate property while they are living together. I want an Act to do that.

I say, if I were a working man, it is important and [illegible] with liberty that the police should be kept out of private premises unless I [illegible] myself, and if I do [illegible] myself there are ample [illegible] for them to get an entrance.

[illegible]. If a policeman does come into a house it is a presumption against the house that there is a reasonable suspicion of [illegible], whereas if it is a customary thing to have a half-yearly visit, then there is no [illegible] attached and no [illegible] attached to the house. That is another point of view which the working man might look at?—Quite so. I could not say I am competent to represent the feelings of the workmen. If I were a working man myself I should resent intrusion by the police so long as I conducted myself properly.

[illegible] Would not you resent it more if a policeman came in only on the suggestion that you were misconducting yourself?—No. If I act so as to give reasonable grounds for that supposition, I have a right to be subjected to the inconvenience of entry, and I could be.

[illegible] You remember, of course, what was called the Dalrymple Act. It was proposed by Dr. Dalrymple to make detention of an inebriate compulsory, of course on medical evidence and satisfactory proof of the fact?—Yes.

[illegible]. That Act was spoilt by the omission of that clause, leaving it voluntary. Would you propose that the non-criminal inebriates should be subject to a compulsory detention on satisfactory evidence of their habitual [illegible]?—The only thing that makes me pause is the use of the word "[illegible]." I propose that in the case of every man who comes before a magistrate in a police court, when the magistrate has reason, from his antecedent knowledge of the case or facts that are brought to his knowledge, to suspect that he is a [illegible] inebriate, the magistrate should have power to call in a medical assessor, and upon due inquiry send that man for curative treatment.

[illegible]. Your experience is of course largely connected with police cases?—Yes.

[illegible]. My knowledge of facts outside the police courts is that there are inebriates, even perhaps in the position of ladies, who never go into a police court, people of refinement and education and of no fault except that one which is many a [illegible] than a fault. Would you not provide for the detention of inebriates of that class, not in prisons, not as criminals, and not mingling with criminals?—I would indeed, subject only to the condition that they should not be sent to the asylum by any private authority.

[illegible]. Of course, but sent by a recognised authority and on sufficient evidence?—Quite so.

[illegible]. In the case of the criminal inebriates, it would be necessary, but do not you think besides being curative it ought to be preventive and reformatory—preventive in the way of deterring others, and reformatory as regards the individual inebriate?—It is necessary to [illegible] up the two, because the preventive side of it, I think, would apply best to those who go before the magistrate?

[illegible]. Do not you think that all imprisonment ought to have if possible the reformatory element in it also?—That is the reformation of the individual.

[illegible]. Yes?—I think so. That is the meaning of the [illegible] treatment.

[illegible]. Then in order to bring about that there must be the detention for more than three months. You cannot reform an inebriate in three months, or even in six months?—No. There must be prolonged detention, but how prolonged would depend on the authority.

[illegible]

"[illegible] of the weak [illegible] in the Licensing Laws, and "[illegible] the [illegible] were paralysed in their efforts "by defects in the present state of the law."

[illegible]. Then you do speak on temperance platforms?—If by on a platform you mean such as is devoted to temperance entirely, I speak on such platforms whenever I can.

[illegible]. In answer to the Chairman, you said the drink was almost a plague at home than abroad. May I take it from that that anything that induces home drinking is more demoralising and more dangerous than frequenting legally established places for the consumption of liquor?—Unless the present law is amended so as to deal with home drinking, I am afraid I agree with what you say, that there is great danger in driving it to home.

[illegible]. Again, in reply to his Lordship, you said, speaking of drink, "I do not think it is such a factor as the other [illegible], such as the wretched [illegible] conditions of the people." Did you mean to imply that?—The other condition that was in my mind then was the want of deterrent legislation against the [illegible]. I think that is the most potent factor at present. To weigh the difference between the extent to which public-houses, and industrial conditions, and the absence of alternative enjoyments create the evil, I find a very difficult question.

[illegible]. Do I take your answer to be, that drink is not in any way the only factor in the demoralisation of the people?—Drink is not in any way the only factor.

[illegible]. And that some is due to the present insanitary condition of the houses of the poorer classes?—I did not say that above was due, but a great deal is due to that condition of the houses of the poorer classes.

[illegible]. You also said just now that the want of proper amusement is another cause?—It is another, and a potent cause; that it is more than another I cannot say, they all contribute.

[illegible]. But drink no more than any other cause?—Again I say, I cannot say more or less. They all contribute. To my mind the importance I attach to deterrent legislation is that no one seems to be thinking of that [illegible] cause, and trying to meet it.

[illegible]. I do not know whether I am right, but I understood you to say that the public-houses are not so [illegible] where drunkenness most abounds, is that so?—That is my recollection. I think the public-houses in Dublin are most numerous in the [illegible] or [illegible] division, and I think the drunkenness is most [illegible] in the [illegible] Division.

[illegible]. And that is correct?—I think so.

[illegible]. One word as to the club question. You say that the constable should have a right of entry where reasonable evidence had been presented to him that drunkenness took place. Is that your view?—The drunkenness took place is [illegible] habitually [illegible] by people who do not live in them. You [illegible] the [illegible] together.

[illegible]. But people do not reside at clubs, do they?—No, I am directing my attention to what they call bogus clubs.

[illegible]. I take your answer to be then, that the constable or the police should have the right of entry where they have reasonable evidence that drunkenness was permitted?—No, a constable should have no right of entry into my own house if I choose to get drunk in it.

[illegible]. What do you mean by "on reasonable evidence"?—I said that where a constable has evidence that particular premises are frequented by [illegible] not residing there, and in connection with that condition drunkenness takes place, then he should have a right of

Mr. [illegible] Daly.

17 May [illegible]

[illegible]

Drink and other causes of demoralisation.

[illegible] of public-houses and drunkenness.

Clubs.

Mr. D. D. Daly.

11 May '9[illegible].

is it ?—The usual fine. The maximum provided in the Act is 10s.

[illegible]. The question was put to you that the fine in recent years was much smaller, and you said not very ?—Because originally, years ago, when I was a boy, it was very frequent to have only 1s. and costs fines.

Result of fines for drunkenness.

[illegible]. I may take it that in previous years the fine for the first offence would be 5s. 6d. ?—2s. 6d. or 5s. [illegible] was a most usual thing.

[illegible]. Then you have raised it now to 5s. ?—It is rare to find a less fine than 5s. or four days, or 5s. and seven days.

[illegible]. Has the raising of the fine to 5s. proved to be any good—has it had any salutary effect on the number of cases ?—The number of cases is very difficult to compare, unless statistics [illegible] too much; but in the 1887 Report, Mr. O'Donnel, my late chief, gave evidence, in which personally I thoroughly concur, that the raising of the fine even to 10s., which was the usual fine for years and years, did not affect drunkenness a bit.

[illegible]. Then does it follow that if you raised the fine to 15s. or 20s. you would have the same result ?—I do not think 15s. would be much good. What I think is—I am speaking of habitual inebriates, not of casual drunkenness of men who are habitually sober—but so far as the habitual inebriate goes, who is idle and loafing and lives on his wife, I do not think any fine is [illegible] good. What he wants is imprisonment. Fines are a very trivial remedy, because they react on the wife much more than imprisonment does in that class. Imprisonment, as a rule, means the imprisoning of a man who is not earning.

[illegible]. Speaking of that division of your city which is most productive of drunkenness, you say that there are there the smallest number of public-houses ?—That is my impression. I have the book here; I can show you.

Home drinking.

[illegible]. Then that would lead you to say that the secret drunkenness at home is much more than the open drunkenness in duly licensed public-houses ?—What strikes me is that in every large city the poor are gathered together in close areas, and the drinking that occurs there is much more [illegible] than the drinking that can occur anywhere else.

[illegible]. In this drunken division is the drink supposed to be had from clubs or unrespectable places ?—Mostly from unrespectable places—what are called shebeens.

Clubs.

[illegible]. I notice that you say that you would not have interference with the working man's club ?—I would have no interference.

[illegible]. By the police or otherwise ?—If I were a working man myself—though I cannot speak for the sentiments of the working man—I should resent any breaking down of the line between privacy and intrusion, unless I misconducted myself; and if I did misconduct myself, as I point out, by habitual drunkenness, there would be no difficulty, I think, in giving the police the right of entry.

[illegible]. You would, I suppose, permit the drink to be supplied to those clubs ?—Certainly. I am thinking of clubs where they would be brought to eat or where they did not drink, as I do myself, without getting drunk.

[illegible]. Then, if you refused the admission of the police into clubs that are not licensed in any sense, what would you do with the licensed trade of a public-house ? Would you also refuse the interference of the police with the publican ?—No, I would not. A publican does not assume that his premises are private premises. If a man wants to go to a public-house, he is understood to go to a house that is open to the public. I am speaking of premises which a man chooses to carry on as private premises. The only restriction that comes to me, which I would impose on them, would be that I would not allow any drink to be supplied to be carried away and be consumed elsewhere. I would confine them to the use of drink for themselves on their own premises.

[illegible]. Why should you treat the publican with greater severity than the keeper of a league or other club ?—Upon the ground that I have stated, that the one purports to be public premises, and the others purport to be private premises.

Drink in the slum areas.

[illegible]. (Mr. Roberts.) With reference to the slum areas which you have described, if you could imagine no drink being sold in it, what effect would that have upon the area ? What would be the result of that class of change upon the condition of life in the neighbourhood ?—It would turn them all into teetotallers. I think it would be a good thing. Teetotalism, in my mind, is good where there are exceptional circumstances of temptation. I am altogether in sympathy with the temperance efforts of people like the priests of whom I spoke, who are trying day by day to persuade people in the slum areas to be teetotallers.

Mr. D. D. Daly.

Drinking, cause or effect of bad housing.

[illegible]. (Mr. Johnston.) Following up the last question, perhaps it might be summed up in this way: if drinking is partly produced by bad dwellings, it is equally true that bad dwellings are produced by drinking, is it not ?—To a large extent, that is true.

[illegible]. The one thing reacts on the other ?—Yes.

[illegible]. It is difficult to say which is cause and which is effect ?—To a large extent.

[illegible]. They are both cause and both effect ?—To a large extent that is true; but the most preventive cause of drinking resides in the individual. It is the fault of the individual, and I want different legislation to deal with the individual himself.

[illegible]. Whatever the cause of drinking, its effect is to produce miserable homes, insanitary surroundings, [illegible] accommodation, and all those evils of which we have heard ?—Has it [illegible] in that direction. It is not the sole cause of that condition.

Female inebriates.

[illegible]. With reference to the law and the protection orders for married women, you want to have something of the same sort in Ireland as there is in England ?—I want to have something different. In Ireland the objection on the part of the clergy—and that is a potent factor in reference to Ireland—is that there is too much of the divorce court in the English Act. I want simply an Act that will protect the separate property of the woman or the man, in [illegible] life, without separating them.

[illegible]. You are aware that the use of these protection orders in England has almost ceased since the Married Women's Property Act ?—I was not aware of that, but I fancy it would be accounted for by the fact that the Married Women's Property Act of 18[illegible], as I read it, affords no provision for separate protection unless you leave the husband or wife out.

Power to obtain [illegible].

[illegible]. But you know that it has done for all women what the protection orders did for the particular women who obtained them. Perhaps we need not pursue that. Is there no power to commit to prison in default of distress a parent who does not pay what he is ordered to pay for the maintenance of his children in an industrial school ?—In Ireland there is none. There have been enterprising cases of failure to recover contributions from people.

[illegible]. You can order them ?—You can order them, and you can levy a distress to enforce them, but an habitual drunkard has no goods.

[illegible]. In default of distress is there no power of imprisonment ?—Not in Ireland.

[illegible]. (Dean Dickinson.) If a wife or child go into the workhouse, the workhouse guardians have the power to prosecute, have they not ?—I understood Mr. Johnston to ask me with reference to enforcing contributions towards the support of children in industrial schools.

[illegible]. (Mr. Johnston.) In industrial schools or reformatories ?—You are quite right, Dean, as far as regards the case where a man deserts his wife.

Bad, [illegible] effect.

[illegible]. (Mr. Haley Smith.) Following up my colleague's question about miserable dwellings, do you find that the greatest tendency to drunkenness is where the population is badly housed ?—Where the population is badly housed, and where alternative enjoyments such as ground in well-made life are impossible. I think that is where you find drunkenness most. The Liverpool, Manchester, and Birmingham tables which describe arrests by occupations conclusively show that, I think.

[illegible]. It would almost follow that poverty and misery lead to drink, as much as drink leads to them ?—In answer to one of the Commissioners I said that they were all contributing causes, but I cannot say which is most.

[illegible]. I gather that you have no complaint whatever to make as to the condition of the licensed houses in Dublin ?—No; I think that the majority of public-houses, that is to say, licensed for consumption on the premises, are undoubtedly well conducted.

[illegible] Would you allow every man who had got suitable premises and good character to have a licence? —No. On these questions of trade limitations I do not like to offer any direct opinions. I have not thought that matter out. What I want to press on the Commission is, what I started with, the need of deterrent legislation against the [illegible] in both cases.

[illegible] As far as I understand your evidence it is this, that you want to deal with the drunkards, not to make any alteration in the licensing laws?—I do not want so much any alterations in the licensing laws, as far as I am concerned; I leave that to the temperance party. To my mind the [illegible] [illegible] the public-house; the public-house did not [illegible] the [illegible]. I want to deal with the individuals in whom the [illegible] is [illegible].

[illegible] You do not think that any alteration of the licensing laws would meet the [illegible] of intemperance? —No alteration that is confined to trade limitations alone will make people sober.

[illegible] Your view is better housing of the working men, and better sanitary arrangements?—That would be the cure; but I am not thinking of the cure. I am only thinking of what an Act of Parliament can do, and an Act of Parliament can help all these cases.

[illegible] I have a slight difficulty which I hope you will clear up with regard to greater penalties for drunkenness. If you inflict additional penalties on the drinker he will cease to be a bread earner, and what will become of his family?—The class of drunkards on whom I propose to inflict greater inconveniences are not as a rule bread earners, and it will be a relief to the wife and children to have them supported at the public cost, and not at their cost, for an interval.

[illegible] I think I understood that in Dublin, on account of so many large houses being converted into dwellings for families, you have a great deal of drunkenness because of the [illegible] state of the houses, and the condition in which they are placed. These people come up from time to time as drunkards. Would you send them, say a year, to prison, or for a longer time than the law permits at present. The working man comes up repeatedly to the court, and he is sent for seven days. If you send him for a year what becomes of his family?—I do not think we can be thinking of the [illegible] man. I never proposed to send a man for a year but where seven days would be adequate; but where there is complaint that he is a diseased [illegible], that is to say that the craving has got beyond the power of his control, I think the magistrate should have power to call in a medical opinion, and if it be so, if it be a disease akin to lunacy, I think short sentences are useless, and nothing will do but to prolong the sentence to give him a chance of being cured.

[illegible] What becomes of his family?—They will probably be better off than if he had been allowed to [illegible] at home, where the wife, in addition to supporting the children, would have to support him.

[illegible] You are aware that drunkenness is decreasing in Dublin?—I am not sure of that. I [illegible] figures with regard to drunkenness especially, for obvious reasons. Drunken arrests are mainly at the instigation of the police. Arrests for other crimes are at the [illegible] of the public as well as the police; and the police action is liable to vary from so many causes that it is difficult to say how far the actual arrests for drunkenness represent the extent of drunkenness.

[illegible] Are temperance societies doing much for the reformation of the people?—A great deal. I believe but for the temperance work the drink problem would be in a far worse condition than it is, owing to the defects in the action of the State.

[illegible] (*Lord [illegible].*) Referring to the habitual drunkard in his own house there is only one question I should like to make clear. I understood you to say that you would not like to punish the habitual drunkard unless he committed some overt act?—I think I am inclined to say that. I think in married life if either the husband or the wife fall into serious habits of intemperance it ought to be left to moral influence, such as the moral influence of the home and friends, but when the husband goes beyond that state and inflicts direct injury on his wife or his family, then I think the law ought to interfere.

[illegible] That is the point I wanted to make clear; in your opinion misappropriation of his wife's property should constitute such an overt act?—Certainly.

The witness withdrew.

Dr. JOHN HACKETT called in and examined.

[illegible] (*Chairman.*) You are Coroner for the County and City of Kilkenny?—Yes.

[illegible] And have been so for several years past?—Yes; I am also surgeon of the county infirmary, and physician to the workhouse hospital.

[illegible] In the course of your professional duties you have therefore been brought into contact with the poor classes, and the working classes?—Very intimately.

[illegible] Do you agree with the last witness, so far as your experience goes, as to the housing of the poor?—The housing of the poor, I think, has a very demoralising effect on their habits and customs where it is deficient and insufficient. When the accommodation is bad, and the surroundings are in an insanitary condition, I think it has a very deleterious effect on their moral tone.

[illegible] I do not notice to say that the medical officers can cure that entirely, but the medical officers have a distinct duty to perform. Have they not performed it? —They have in a great number of instances tried in Kilkenny to improve the condition of the poor classes, and the corporation, in a certain measure, has helped them, but there remains a great deal to be done. The corporation have [illegible] three schemes of building model houses for the poor.

[illegible] Two schemes are already in operation?—Yes, with very beneficial effect.

[illegible] And one is now being carried out?—One is now being carried out.

[illegible] From the experience of the two, has it answered financially?—It has, fairly well. They at present lose money by it, but after a time it will be a considerable gain. They have borrowed the money, and they pay off the capital and interest at the same time.

[illegible] So that you think on the whole, do you, that the habits and customs of the people are improving?—They are.

[illegible] You think that has been owing, not so much to a restriction on the sale of liquor as to the general improvement of houses and sanitary arrangements?—Yes. In one division of Kilkenny in which I was medical officer for a great number of years the houses continued to be bad. Recently I have gone into practice amongst the poor in another division of the town in which the housing is considerably better, and there I find that the sobriety and the general conduct of the people bears a very favourable contrast to that of those who are badly housed.

[illegible] I suppose in the lower quarters of the city with which you are acquainted there is a great deal of drunkenness?—There is a considerable amount of drunkenness.

[illegible] Are there many public-houses?—Not in that immediate neighbourhood, not in the actual lanes, but in the streets adjoining there are.

[illegible] Are you of opinion that there are not too many public-houses?—I do not consider that there are.

[illegible] Do you know at all what the proportion of public-houses bears to the population?—I do not exactly know the number, but I know there are a very considerable number of public-houses.

[illegible] But you do not advocate reduction in the number?—I do not. I think it is more important that they are well conducted, and that the drink supplied is of a class that would not be injurious.

[illegible] Are you of opinion that the State has reached a point of interference with the trade beyond which it ought not to go?—I think there ought to be a restriction put on the description of drink sold. I think if a law were passed, which some time ago was attempted by the Member for [illegible], that no spirit should be sold younger than three years, it would be a step in the right direction as regards the pot still whisky, and as regards the patent still whisky I would certainly label that, and make the same distinction as is made between margarine

[illegible]

and better, so that when a man wanted to drink patent still whisky he would know that he was getting that article.

43,576. Therefore you would advocate a better kind of liquor for the Irish people?—I would.

43,577. [illegible] whisky?—[illegible] and porter.

43,578. As you go so far in asking the State to interfere with the actual quality of the liquor sold, should you like to see the State say there shall be no whisky sold?—I should like to see that the porter and ale sold was not adulterated; that it was of a good class.

43,579. Do you believe that the present whisky that is sold is adulterated?—I believe that the whisky sold is new young whisky. I do not believe that it is adulterated so much as people think, but I believe that it is the young whisky, containing the [illegible] fusel oil and other things, that does the harm, and leads the people to violence. It is not the amount they consume, but the quality of the drink which they take.

43,580. Like the other opinion you have just expressed, that you think the public-houses ought not to be reduced in number, even in the poorer districts, I suppose I may take it that your opinion is against any further restrictions or limitations on Sunday drinking?—As to Sunday drinking, I think that if the public-houses are open between two and five o'clock, and people are allowed to have drink with their dinners, it would lead to no abuse. I think that the closing of the present Act leads to a great deal more harm than if people are allowed to drink openly, and without restriction.

43,581. Therefore you would like to see all over Ireland the houses open on a Sunday from two to five?—From two to five.

43,582. Do you think that would meet the public requirement?—I do. I saw that done in England, to a certain measure, and I thought it a very sensible procedure. I have seen in police cases where the Sunday Closing Act was violated, very conflicting testimony, and it made an impression upon my mind that there must have been perjury on one or the other side to a great extent.

43,583. That being your view as to Sunday hours for drinking, what should you say to earlier closing on Saturday?—I think, from the habits of the people in Kilkenny, it would interfere greatly with the ordinary supply of their households for Sunday. I would be inclined to limit the hours of trading to 10 o'clock on the ordinary week days. I would not interfere with Saturday night closing.

43,584. You would allow the houses on Saturday to be open to what hour?—Until eleven o'clock.

43,585. All over Ireland?—Yes.

43,586. Speaking as a clergyman, and from your experience as a [illegible], do you trace the cases which are brought up before you to drink?—I do not. I find that there is very little drink in connection with the cases I have to deal with. There are some, but not very often.

43,587. As to deaths, you do not know them to be due?—I do not trace them to drink.

43,588. Speaking from your experience otherwise than as a [illegible], are you able to speak to the connection between crime and drink at all?—Oh yes.

43,589. Apart from your experience as a coroner?—A great number of the violent crimes committed are in connection with drink, and I ascribe that to the quality of the drink supplied.

43,590. Should you say that the percentage of deaths due to drink that have come before your notice is very low?—Very low.

43,591. You would not say whether the drink entered into the causes of a number of deaths that came before you?—It sometimes does, but in very few cases. Sometimes a man drinks too much at a fair, and in driving home his car overturns on him. That has occurred sometimes in my experience.

43,592. That would be a case which you would put down as directly attributable to drink, though the car killed him?—Yes.

43,593. I think we have had some evidence as to [illegible] orders in Kilkenny?—Mr Coughlan, in his evidence here, as well as I remember said there were 11 [illegible] orders.

43,594. Do you agree with that statement?—I do. I think they are too numerous. I think that no [illegible] order should be granted to anyone who would not simply lead to these poor men engaged at the fairs and markets carry, so that they might have the option of having food as well as drink. I very often find the countrymen going to a fair in the winter have to travel very early a great number of miles, and when they get no chance of having food and only get drink, it affects them, and causes them to get drunk very easily.

43,595. On the number of reported cases of drunkenness that come year after you go to recall the apparent number of cases of individual drunkenness?—Yes, there are some habitual drunkards who are very frequently convicted.

43,596. That raises the question?—I submit the question [illegible].

43,597. Have you any definite figures by which to base that statement?—Yes, a witness before the Committee [illegible] three years ago said that there are 27 habitual drunkards in Kilkenny. 17 of them were convicted between three and five times in the year, and the remainder were convicted over five times and under ten.

43,598. Out of the large number of arrests for drunkenness, I suppose that would operate to a very [illegible] extent with reference to the increase of the cases [illegible]?—The average would be about six.

43,599. Turning from that point to the remedy, do you think any special provision should be made for these habitual drunkards?—Yes, I have a very strong opinion on the matter. I think the only way of dealing with them is by stringent legal measures making it more feasible and easy than the present law permits. The habitual drunkard should, in my opinion, be put under restraint for a considerable time. It should be feasible that that should be accomplished without the present [illegible] machinery. During my practice, on some occasions, I have met habitual drunkards who are willing to be put under restraint, but when the question came of their signing their own imprisonment, when they were asked to sign a document empowering the law to imprison them personally for two years, or two or three occasions they have refused to do so. I never could get them, even though they consented to sign the document when I produced it before them. By the present law I understand they must sign it themselves, and they always have refused. So that if habitual drunkards could be like [illegible] to put under restraint, I think it would have a very deterrent effect on those who are inclined to become habitual drunkards, and probably a corrective effect on those who are put in inebriate homes.

43,600. You would put that compulsion upon them whether they were criminal inebriates or not?—I consider it a form of lunacy when a man gives way to drink like that. He is irresponsible, and he simply ought to be treated like a lunatic, and put under restraint.

43,601. Apart from that view the Bill, I understand, provides for two classes, for criminal inebriates and others who are not criminal inebriates; compulsion is applied to the one, and personal [illegible] is required in the case of the other?—I would make it compulsory in every case.

43,602. I see you mention again the point of adulteration of whisky. You do not lay so much stress upon the fact of the adulteration of whisky, but you think it is the young whisky which causes the mischief?—I do.

43,603. Which is the worse, pot still whisky or patent still whisky?—If the pot still whisky is kept a sufficient time, of course, it loses all the fusel oil, and becomes perfectly harmless, or comparatively speaking so, whereas the patent still whisky, if it is sold very shortly after manufacture, is very injurious. I consider the patent still whisky the worse.

43,604. Is there anything in the manufacture of pot still whisky as distinct from patent still whisky which makes it more necessary to keep it in one case than in the other?—I am informed that keeping patent still whisky does not improve it.

43,605. Therefore you would, if you could, restrict the people to pot still whisky, and keep it a certain number of years?—I would not allow it out of bond younger than three years.

43,606. We have heard of some crime, I think, in Kilkenny?—Yes. It is a very difficult question to deal with.

Rev. J. Blackett. 17 May '77.

Habitual drunkards.

Pot and patent still whisky.

Crime.

Dr. J. [illegible]. 17 May '[illegible]

[illegible]. Are they frequented [illegible] on the Saturday and Sunday nights?—They are.

[illegible]. Is that one of your reasons for thinking that we have reached the limit of restriction on Sunday and Saturday nights?—It is. Before the Sunday Closing Act was known in [illegible] there was only one club. Now there are, I think, six.

[illegible]. I suppose you would think that you cannot prevent people associating together in a club, and drinking when they get there; but would you not be of opinion that the police can deal with any disorder in those clubs, and put them down, if illegal practices went on within them?—I should hesitate to have any police interference with clubs. It is like interfering with a private house.

[illegible]. You would not even register them?—I do not know what remedy to suggest.

[illegible]. Suppose they were made to comply with certain conditions, or at least, if they did not comply with those conditions, that they should not be registered, and get the advantages of registration?—I think there is some remedy necessary.

[illegible]. Would that at all be a remedy?—I think it would in some measure be a remedy.

[illegible]. That if they broke the conditions of registration they should be left to the action of the police at any moment?—Yes.

[illegible]. As [illegible] a bogus club; would that meet your view?—I am very tender about having any interference with the liberty of the working man any more than with the liberty of the [illegible].

[illegible]. Interference with clubs [illegible] at all [illegible], of [illegible], related to rich and poor?—Exactly.

The bona fide traveller.

[illegible]. Lastly, as to the bona fide traveller, what have you to say?—I would extend the limit [illegible], and I would punish more the traveller who made a [illegible] representation than I would the publican, taking it for granted that the publican was imposed on.

[illegible]. You would raise the limit to what, 5 or 6 miles?—I would certainly raise the limit to 5 miles.

[illegible]. I take it your view rather is that you look not so much to restrictive legislation as to the improvement by education and by [illegible] advancing, and by all the other [illegible] which civilisation can bring to bear upon the people?—I think that is the proper way of dealing with the question.

New whisky and drunkenness.

[illegible]. (Mr. Young.) Do you think that mostly the drunkenness arises from the use of new whisky?—No, I do not, but I think a great deal of the violence of the drunken man arises from drinking young whisky.

[illegible]. I think you have undertaken to say that patent still whisky should not be used?—I did not. I say that patent still whisky should be labelled so that the man who drank it would know that he was drinking patent still whisky.

[illegible]. Your idea is that it is inferior?—I think so.

[illegible]. And that it contains a great quantity of fusel oil?—It contains some substances that are more [illegible] to the body than the pot still whisky.

[illegible]. (Chairman.) If pot still whisky improves by keeping why is it impossible for patent still whisky to improve by keeping?—The process of [illegible] drives off the fusel oil at the time in the case of the patent still whisky, but it leaves the other deleterious substances.

[illegible]. Fusel oil is driven out, but a worse spirit remains in?—Fusel oil is the worst of all the [illegible] substances, but there are others.

[illegible]. We have been told by some witnesses that it is the fusel oil which has the mischief?—Yes.

[illegible]. You say in the patent still whisky the fusel oil is driven out, and its place is taken by a worse element?—There are other elements. I do not say a worse element.

[illegible]. (Mr. Young.) Are you a chemist yourself?—I am not.

[illegible]. You only hear that patent still whisky has some fusel oil and is more dangerous?—I did not say that.

[illegible]. You think that pot still is the best whisky to drink?—I do.

[illegible]. How do you arrive at that conclusion?—I have arrived at it from practical observation.

[illegible]. You do not happen to know that actually in patent still whisky there is little or no fusel oil whatever?—I read that.

[illegible]. And probably you do not know that it is in pot still whisky that you will find such large quantities of fusel oil?—That is the reason I wish the legislature would prevent its being sold until the fusel oil has evaporated.

[illegible]. The fact is that there are the properties if you keep it for many years that make for the improvement of the article. Patent still whisky has got little or no fusel oil, and is less dangerous to drink when new than pot still whisky. Probably you do not know that the most dangerous whisky of all to drink is the pot still when it is new?—I know it is dangerous to drink.

[illegible]. But the patent is not, because it does not possess the fusel oil to any extent. You probably only know about the different sorts of whisky; you do not know yourself?—I do know.

[illegible]. You have told the Commission that it is the drinking of patent still whisky in which the danger lies?—I think all young whiskies are bad.

[illegible]. But that the least dangerous is the drinking of patent still when it is new, and that the pot still whisky ought not to be drunk till probably it was five or six years old?—Certainly not under three years old.

[illegible]. For the good of the people probably patent still is the very best thing they can drink?—In drinking pot still whisky, if it is not under three years old, I know I am not drinking anything that is very injurious, but the alcohol it contains.

[illegible]. (Mr. [illegible].) Is that injurious?—Yes; in excess.

[illegible]. (Mr. Young.) Probably you do not know that bad whisky at first will grow worse and worse, and that it has to be made good at first in order that it may get better and better. Temperance is on the increase in your town?—I consider that it is.

[illegible]. And you do not want really any alteration of the laws?—Except those that I suggested.

[illegible]. You wanted the hours to be open on Sundays, probably, from 5 to 7, or 5 to 9?—No; I said from 2 to 5.

[illegible]. And you do not want earlier closing on Saturday nights?—I think not. That is my opinion.

[illegible]. (Mr. [illegible].) With regard to your suggestion as to not allowing whisky to be sold under three years old, have you thought of any plan by which the public would be secured, supposing that was the law? How would you propose that the public should know that it was not under three years old?—The means would be that no whisky could be taken out of bond unless it was three years old. That would be a guarantee.

[illegible]. (Mr. Young.) What amount of money would you suppose as damage to the country; how many millions would you require to store it?—That is very immaterial to my mind compared to the health and the absence of violence and drunkenness in the country. I think no matter what amount of money would be lost, the benefit accruing to our country by taking these proper measures would be counterbalanced.

[illegible]. (Mr. [illegible].) Are you aware that it would increase the price of whisky very much?—I am sure it would.

[illegible]. There is the loss in strength and loss in bulk?—And the tying up of capital for such a length of time.

[illegible]. The interest on the money. Do you not agree with me that it is a very revolutionary idea to suppose that it must be bonded three, four, or five years?—Yes, I do; but I think that the health of the people and the welfare of the country is very much more important than any loss which will accrue to the country.

[illegible]. We have had a very first-class [illegible] witness before us, Mr. [illegible], one of the first chemists, probably, in the three kingdoms. He tells us that alcohol does not disappear from the article by being kept. You can get drunk as easily on a six years' old article as on a two years' old article?—In my opinion the drunkenness arising from the six years old article may not develop the amount of violence that it would if it were a two years' old article.

they were in a position to get on Sunday what they required?—In some cases, yes.

[illegible]. (*Mr. Whitaker.*) May I ask you if you have come all the way from Kilkenny to tell us that nothing [illegible] be done there on this question except to label [illegible] whisky, and give [illegible] facilities for drinking on Sunday afternoon?—Well, I did not come all the way to give that information; I came here to tell you what my experience of the Sunday Closing Act was, and of the [illegible] of the people, and the causes of those [illegible].

[illegible]. With reference to what you have said about clubs in Kilkenny, you say they followed Sunday closing?—Yes.

[illegible]. Is there a single club in existence in Kilkenny that was started during the first eight years of Sunday closing?—There is.

[illegible]. What is its name?—The [illegible] Club.

[illegible]. That was in existence before Sunday closing?—The Working Men's Club.

[illegible]. Which one?—It is called the Working Men's Club.

[illegible]. When was that started?—I think that was started subsequent to the Sunday closing.

[illegible]. Was it started within eight years after it?—That I could not tell you.

[illegible]. Can you name one that was?—I know that before the Sunday closing these clubs did not exist.

[illegible]. My point is that for eight years afterwards they did not?—Well, they exist at present.

[illegible]. Just so. If it was Sunday closing that produced the clubs, it would have produced them within eight years?—It is possible.

[illegible]. Are you aware that there has been a greater increase in clubs in England during the last 10 or 15 years than in Ireland?—The population is so much greater, I should not be surprised.

[illegible]. But there has been a great increase in the clubs?—Yes.

[illegible]. It shows that there has been a movement to open clubs, altogether apart from Sunday closing, does not it?—But I think that those clubs would not have been opened but for the Sunday closing.

[illegible]. You cannot name one that was opened within eight years?—Well, they are in existence now.

[illegible]. Just so. They were open a considerable time after Sunday closing, which indicates that they were [illegible] to another cause, does not it?—It is possible, but I do not think so. The impression left on my mind [illegible] is a [illegible] established that they are open since then.

[illegible]. (*Mr. Cairns.*) Have you any evidence to show that these clubs were started to provide for Sunday consumption?—I have no evidence to show that.

[illegible]. They are open on week-days as well, are not they?—They are.

[illegible]. (*Mr. Whitaker.*) With reference to repeated convictions, you seem to desire to minimise the number of convictions for drunkenness by conveying the impression that the number was very much increased by persons who are frequently convicted?—Yes.

[illegible]. Are you aware that seven out of eight of the cases of persons convicted in the year for the city and county of Kilkenny are not convicted more than twice?—I do not know anything of the county. I can give no opinion about the county.

D. J. Kerbet.

17 May '98.

Clubs and Sunday closing.

Convictions for drunkenness in Kilkenny.

Dr. J. [illegible]. 13 May '97.

63,688. How many of them?—There are three or four [illegible], without referring to the class of abandoned women.

63,689. That would be 84 (sic)?—I gave you the statistics of Mr. Higgis, which were given before the Commission. He was then mayor of the city, and he stated there were 22 habitual drunkards.

63,690. How often were they arrested?—He said that 17 of them were arrested between three and five times, and the balance were arrested between five and ten times.

63,691. You have about the same proportion as in the county, and the figures come out there that seven out of eight of the total arrests are only arrested once or twice at the most. That does not seem to bear out your contention, does it?—If you say the proportion is the same, it does not bear out my contention.

Number of public-houses and [illegible].

63,692. You think there are not too many public-houses in Kilkenny?—I think there are a great number.

63,693. But there are not too many, I think you said?—I do not think there are too many.

63,694. You have 1 for every 160 persons?—So I understand.

63,695. You are probably aware that Mr. Considine said there were double as many as there ought to be?—I understood that he said that.

63,696. Fifty per cent. of them were unnecessary. You are aware that he said that?—I lay more importance on their supplying good drink than the number of them.

63,697. You would admit, I suppose, that he is in a position to form an opinion as to whether these houses are necessary or not?—He may form an opinion that other people would not form.

63,698. But he has good opportunities of forming an opinion?—Yes.

Prevalence of drunkenness in Kilkenny.

63,699. You tell us the condition, from a temperance point of view, or non-drinking point of view, is improving very much in Kilkenny?—We consider it is.

63,700. Are you aware of what Mr. Coggridge said?—No.

63,701. Do you agree with this. The Chairman asked the question: "Do you observe any change in the "drunkenness the last few years, either in the county "or the city?" Mr. Considine answered: "There is "practically no change so far as I can detect; if there "was any change at all, it would be a decrease of "drunkenness; all the same, there is a vast amount of "drunkenness." That does not seem to indicate very much improvement, does it?—There is a decrease.

63,702. He thinks there is a decrease, but still a vast amount of drunkenness. You do not agree with that?—My impression is that there is a decrease.

63,703. Do you agree there is a vast amount of drunkenness?—There is a considerable amount.

63,704. With reference to the dwellings: if a man spends on drink more than would pay the rent of a decent house, and as the result lives in a miserable unsanitary place, is it reasonable to say that his drunkenness is the result of his living in that miserable hole?—I consider they react one upon the other.

63,705. If he spends what he would pay for a decent house on drink, that is the first cause?—If you put a well-disposed man in insanitary surroundings he will gravitate towards drink from the very fact of living in those surroundings.

63,706. Will not a well-disposed man, who does not spend his money on drink, avoid insanitary surroundings by having a decent house?—It is very likely he will.

Position of witness.

63,707. (Mr. Graham.) Your experience is based upon your residence in Kilkenny?—Yes.

63,708. And you do not even desire to speak of the county?—No; my position as confined in a great measure, excepting the supervising position, to the city.

63,709. Your views are really based upon your observation of the town?—Yes.

63,710. You do not speak for Ireland in any way?—I do not.

it, almost a great many bogus clubs being established subsequent to Sunday closing.

Dr. J. [illegible].

63,712. You have not read the evidence on that point?—No, I have no personal knowledge of it.

63,713. I suppose you are aware that a Bill has often been introduced into the House of Commons dealing with the alleged flaws in the Sunday Closing Act, but it has not been passed?—I am not aware.

63,714. (Mr. Hughes.) In your official capacity as coroner, there can be no doubt as to the answer you gave with regard to the cases that came under your notice, that a very small number are directly traceable to drink?—That is exactly my experience.

Early closing on Saturday nights.

63,715. You are also of opinion that any further legislative restrictions upon the curtailment of hours during Saturday, and the total closing of houses on Sundays, would not improve the condition of the people to the extent that is generally supposed?—I do not think it would. I must qualify that answer by saying that there is very little business done after 10 o'clock at night on the ordinary working days in Kilkenny, and I think that, considering the employés, it is a cruelty that they should remain up and the houses open after 10 o'clock when there is no business done. I think if the houses were closed at 10 on the ordinary nights it would be a great relief to the people employed in those houses.

63,716. But it being the custom of the working classes to do their shopping on Saturday nights?—It has been for a number of years; hence I think it would be a hardship to close earlier on Saturday nights.

Drink on premises.

63,717. You have no knowledge how those figures which you have given with regard to lunacy would apply to ex-paupers; whether the great proportion of paupers charged before the prison courts is traceable to drink?—I have no figures to give in that connection.

63,718. I see that you are medical officer for the union workhouse?—Yes.

63,719. You will have some experience there. Of the paupers in that house what proportion do you think is directly traceable to drink?—There are some cases directly traceable to drink, but not a great number.

63,720. You have never made any test of the question?—I have not, but it is from my own observation.

63,721. It is frequently stated that from 70 to 80 per cent. of them are due directly to drink. That would not be your experience?—I do not think it is nearly so. There were a greater number in years gone by.

Clubs.

63,722. With regard to these clubs there can be no doubt about this, that in 1870 there were no working men's clubs in Kilkenny?—None, as well as I remember.

63,723. And now since 1870 you have an increase of those clubs up to six?—I think six is the correct number.

63,724. May I ask if they are permitted to keep open during the whole of Sunday?—They are.

63,725. And they all supply drink?—Four of them do.

63,726. And two do not?—Two do not.

63,727. What are they?—One is a dramatic club and the other is a labourers' club. They have no bar. They have a bagatelle room and newspapers, and they have no drink.

63,728. Then we are to understand that in those two clubs no drink whatever is supplied?—None.

Early fairs.

63,729. (Mr. Walker.) One question as to the fairs. You say the chief cause of complaint is that the licensed houses do not supply food?—In those houses.

63,730. At what time are they open?—I think 4 o'clock in the morning, as well as I remember.

63,731. How far, as a rule, do the men travel that frequent those fairs. They bring cattle, I presume?—They bring cattle, I daresay, from a radius of 12 miles. I sometimes see them coming in the night previously, the men who come a greater distance than that. They generally drive them cattle to a fair to my own knowledge from a radius of 8 miles round, the morning of the fair, starting about 12 o'clock the night before.

63,732. Is it not the custom of those men to travel

[illegible] Is not it a general rule for workmen, when they are going out to work, to take their food with them?—[illegible] going to take do so not, as a matter of fact.

[illegible] Would not it be considered an improvidence, on the part of the men going to travel all night, to take nothing in the way of refreshment?—I think it is a very foolish one, and [illegible] the first thing they do is to drink a glass of very bad whisky the first thing in the morning, [illegible]

[illegible] It is not improvidence on the part of these men to drink this whisky, is it?—No, it is not, but they have had a very hard night's work, and they have to go a long, tedious, slow journey, and the first thing they do, as a rule, is to drink the whisky.

[illegible] Is it not right to assume that the fault lies with the men entirely?—Yes.

[illegible] Why should not they provide themselves with food to take with them during the hours of the night?—If they had common sense they would, I presume.

[illegible] Have you any practical knowledge of the spirit trade, the trade in alcohol?—I have no practical knowledge of it.

[illegible] Then you do not presume to be a judge of the [illegible] and [illegible] of alcohol?—I do. I can form a very good estimate of the character of it.

[illegible] That is, I suppose, from [illegible]?—Yes.

[illegible] You have spoken of adulteration, or [illegible] you have spoken of adulteration; what do you mean by it? On what basis is your information?—From inquiry I find that, as far as I can make out, it is young whisky diluted with water which is sold, and which makes a great many of the people who drink it very violent and [illegible].

[illegible] (*Dean [illegible]*) Not the water?—Not the water, no; it is the young spirit.

[illegible] (*Mr. Walker.*) Do you call young spirit adulterated spirit?—I do not say it is adulterated. I did not use the word adulterated, but I consider it the cause of a great many of the violent acts of those people who drink it.

[illegible] Have you any reason to believe that German potato or [illegible] spirit is used very much?—I have heard that it is so.

[illegible] Have you heard, also, that [illegible] quantities of this spirit are imported into this country?—I have heard that.

[illegible] And that in itself is a very coarse, crude, objectionable spirit?—It is.

[illegible] (*Mr. Young.*) It is not imported into Ireland?—I have heard that it is imported into Ireland.

[illegible] (*Mr. Walker.*) You have also heard, probably, that this German spirit is not so good or [illegible] as whisky produced from English malt?—It is not.

[illegible] You were asked just now whether, in speaking of the moral condition of Kilkenny, you did not speak for Ireland generally. I presume you are an Irishman?—I am, and I confine myself to my own personal belief as much as possible.

[illegible] Still you know something of your own country?—I do.

[illegible] The evidence you have given us here, and the knowledge you state you possess, would have a [illegible] relevance, a [illegible] reference to the whole of Ireland, would not it?—I daresay it would.

[illegible] As to these cheap dwellings for the poor, I think I gather from your evidence that the chief cause of the [illegible] of the poor in Kilkenny is bad [illegible] and bad places to live in?—Where these conditions exist I have found the most drunkenness.

[illegible] Is that the condition of Kilkenny?—I say where these [illegible] exist in Kilkenny, in those quarters I have always found the people more demoralised and more drunken.

[illegible] If it were possible by some means to afford the whole of the poor people of Kilkenny, or any other town in Ireland, clean, decent, and good sanitary dwellings, to put a picture that would be a grand measure to improve the moral condition of the people?—That, with other conditions added.

[illegible] Would that in itself do so?—That in itself would tend in the right direction, to make them more temperate.

[illegible] (*Dean [illegible]*) How long do you think it would take a decent house to be converted into a house of an opposite character by being inhabited by a drunkard? To put it shortly, which do you think is [illegible], to improve the tenants or the tenements?—I think if you put a fairly temperate man into a bad locality with bad surroundings, he will very soon become an intemperate man.

[illegible] You said where the dwellings are worse the drunkenness is most, and it is just as true to say the converse?—They very often go together.

[illegible] Do you think it would be for the benefit of the working classes in Kilkenny, or anywhere else, that all shops where necessaries of life are supplied should be open for the greater part of Sunday?—I do not.

[illegible] That the working men should be free to buy necessaries of life whenever they wanted them on Sundays?—I think if they were open for a limited time it would be better.

[illegible] All shops?—No, not all shops.

[illegible] Why should there be a special exemption from the usual law which closes places of business on Sunday to the interest of the working classes and employes? Why should there be a special privilege extended to liquor sellers?—Because I think that men who are inclined to drink will, by any means, no matter what the law provides, get drink, and I think it is a great deal better for them to get it openly and above board than by running the risk of having [illegible] in [illegible].

[illegible] Would a larger number of people get drunk if the public-houses were closed? If the opportunities of getting it openly were taken away, you think a larger number might get it covertly. My question is, would a larger number of people, on the whole, get drunk on Sundays, if there were no facilities for getting drunk?—I think the larger number would get it if there were facilities for getting it.

[illegible] Of course, [illegible] might be increased, but the amount of drinking would not be increased by diminishing the facilities. Do not you think, or has your [illegible] any experience of clubs (for you only have experience of fact), that besides Sunday closing there is a distinct return by the establishment of such clubs; first, to escape from the [illegible] of houses; secondly, to escape from police supervision; and thirdly, to escape from the necessity of paying licence duty. Are not these sufficient motives for the establishment of clubs apart from Sunday closing?—No doubt it is a remarkable thing that these clubs did not exist until Sunday closing was established.

[illegible] The first-mentioned did not come into existence till eight years after Sunday closing. You would not say, if a man got something after being in a [illegible] eight years, it was due to [illegible]?—I do not think that is an analogous case.

[illegible] As to late shopping in Kilkenny and elsewhere. Does not the necessity for poor women going late shopping on Saturday night, come from the fact that they wait for the [illegible] of their husbands bringing any money, or anything for the house, to them from the public-house?—I do not think so. My impression is that they make a sort of pleasure of the business of shopping on Saturday evening.

[illegible] My experience of Dublin is that poor women have to wait for the chance of finding a few pence in their husbands' pockets after they come home?—That would not hold so much in Kilkenny, I think, because the principal employers in Kilkenny pay their wages on Friday. Some of the principal employers pay the wages at [illegible] o'clock on Saturday.

[illegible] Mr. Whittaker brought out the fact that the proportion of public-houses to population is 1 to 169. Do not you think it would be fair to deduct 60 from that 169 as [illegible] of the children and women who do not frequent public-houses, and that would give 1 to every 60 or 90?—My idea is to improve the [illegible] supplied.

[illegible] Apart from that, it leaves the actual proportion of public-houses to the public-house frequenting or drinking people at 1 to about 60?—Yes. I do not think it makes so much difference. I think if a man wants to

Mr J. Harbon. 17 May '98

[illegible]

61,770. [illegible]

61,771. [illegible]

61,772. [illegible]

61,773. [illegible]

The witness withdrew.

Mr. W. W[illegible] called in and examined.

61,773. (Chairman.) You are Secretary of the Irish Temperance League?—I am.

61,774. [illegible]

61,775. [illegible]

61,776. [illegible]

61,777. [illegible]

61,778. [illegible]

61,779. [illegible]

61,780. [illegible]

61,781. [illegible]

61,782. [illegible]

61,783. [illegible]

61,784. [illegible]

61,785. [illegible]

61,786. [illegible]

61,787. [illegible]

61,788. [illegible]

61,789. [illegible]

61,790. [illegible]

62,791. In this case the police were on your side?—Yes.

62,792. Had the police not served the notices?—The police had served the notices, but all the applications were [illegible].

62,793. As the notices had been served, why were not you allowed to state your case in opposition to the renewal? The notices had been served not by you but by the police?—Practically it was owing to the [illegible] of the [illegible], and I will come to that later on. Then, as a contrast to that, last year we appeared at the annual licensing sessions at Belfast on the [illegible] [illegible] a number of renewals. We did not serve notice, but [illegible] we appeared and asked that the objection should be taken down and, if the parties were not represented in court, the renewals should be adjourned for the purpose of the magistrates' clerk bringing them into court and hearing our objection. It happened in the course of the [illegible] that the police had served notice.

62,794. As they had in the first case?—Yes, as they had in the Cork case, but the police had not served what might be called legal notice, that is to say, they had called at those premises and told the [illegible] people that they were going to do this, and that they would serve notice upon them, but the applicants took advantage of the police not having served legal notice, and said that the police had no right to oppose.

62,795. That is a fair objection?—Quite fair as a legal objection, but it was not a legal objection in this case, because some years ago it was held by the Court of Queen's Bench, that if the person was in court, then though he had not been asked to come he was before the court and the court had a right to deal with the case, and in this case every one of those who were being opposed were represented in court by solicitor or by [illegible].

62,796. The notices had been legally and formally served?—No. I heard the district inspector say he thought it was very [illegible] on the part of those people, because they had been a little [illegible] [illegible].

62,797. Still it is advisable for the police to comply with the strict letter of the law?—Quite so.

62,798. Then you complain as the law recognises the fact that the inhabitants of a district have a [illegible] interest in the existence or non-existence of a public-house, that there is no effect given to that right on the part of the public [illegible] in the case of renewals.

62,799. How would you say the law recognised the right of the inhabitants at present?—Even in the case of renewals it is recognised that any person may in open court make objection, and that the court "may"—it is not "must"—but may then adjourn the sessions so as to bring the person opposed before them by a notice from the clerk.

62,800. In these two cases you have mentioned in Belfast and Cork, it would have been competent to the Court to say that notices have not been served, but we will adjourn the case so as to enable notices to be served. Would that have been competent?—Quite competent, but the difficulty is that in very few cases will you get a bench willing to do that, because even in the case in Belfast we asked them to do that and they refused, but a few minutes afterwards they adjourned a case, or agreed to adjourn the case, so that an applicant who could not be there or had not his [illegible] there, or something else, might be heard at the adjourned sessions, but they would not do that for us who were opposing.

62,801. Might it not be said on the part of the magistrates that it was not for them to remedy a defect of legal procedure on the part of the police, and if they had chosen not to serve the proper notices the case fell to the ground?—Clearly so; but that did not apply in our case, because we had not the power of serving legal notices.

62,802. I am talking of the police. You wish you had power to serve notices?—We do. We think it would be only right that we should.

62,803. Would you leave it competent for anybody to serve notices, or must it come through some recognised body?—I think it must be any person who could sign a legal notice.

[illegible] 62,804. (Chairman.) Where there is a [illegible] [illegible]?—In the case of a renewal at the present time any person can appear and object, and they do not require to be an inhabitant of the parish or anything else. If you do not mind I will give you an illustration of an [illegible] case. Some years ago Mr. T. W. Russell happened to be in a court in the county Kildare I think it was. They were renewing the licenses. A case was called on and a man said in a very [illegible] tone—"All right, I am here." Mr. Russell looked round and said—"Who is that?" to some one. He said—"Why, that is the fellow whose licence has been called." "Oh," says Mr. Russell, "I object." The presiding magistrate said—"Why?" "Because he is not a fit person. He is drunk—here in court." The man was then brought into the box, and the renewal was refused. He appealed to the Court of Queen's Bench, and they held that although he had not been summoned, and though no notice had been served on him, the fact that he was in court was quite sufficient. He was before the court, and that was all that was necessary, and they refused to grant him a licence.

62,805. I should have thought being in flagrante delicto was enough to justify the court in refusing him. Was he drunk?—He was drunk.

62,806. The fact of his being in court dispensed with the necessity of course?—Quite so. I give that as an illustration. The court held that Mr. Russell was a good objector, though he resided in Dublin, and this happened in the county Kildare.

62,807. You think it should be competent for you as representing your society—not saying it at all offensively—to swoop down on a place and make your objection though you had no connection with the place locally?—Quite so; but not as representing my society, only as an individual.

62,808. As an individual not connected with the place?—Quite so.

62,809. It would be competent for you living in Cork to go down to Belfast and object to a particular licence being renewed to you, not being a ratepayer or in any way connected with Belfast?—That is held by the court as the reading of the law, as representing a society. It is not acknowledged that a society has any right to oppose. It must be the individual.

62,810. (Mr. O'[illegible].) You would have to establish good ground for the objection when the case came on?—Yes. All we could do would be to ask the magistrates to adjourn so that they might hear the objection.

62,811. (Chairman.) What do you want, if I may put it in that way? Do you want the temperance league or the temperance society to be qualified to appear in any part of Ireland just as an individual may?—Yes, at all. I do not think it would be fair that it should be. I think it must be an individual, and, indeed, I have refused on many occasions where the inhabitants have not had the moral courage to oppose themselves to go down and take the case out of the fire for them. I said if there was no one in the place who had the moral courage to oppose, I did not think a person from a distance was called on to do so.

62,812. A little time ago you used the expression that you had a police court missionary?—Yes.

62,813. Would any of those missionaries be competent to appear and oppose?—Yes. He would be an individual.

62,814. It would come to the same thing. He would be one of your servants or one of your ministers?—Yes.

62,815. And you would easily instruct him to oppose?—Yes.

62,816. You would lose nothing by not being competent to appear in your corporate capacity?—We would lose nothing, only I think it would appear invidious that a society should have the right, although of course the Society for the Prevention of Cruelty to Children and the Society for the Prevention of Cruelty to Animals do appear officially. Still I think it would be better not to ask for it.

62,817. As to uniformity of procedure in the Irish courts, do you consider there is lack of uniformity?—A very great lack. I do not think it is necessary, but I have several newspaper cuttings here showing flagrant cases in which the police have opposed the renewal and yet the magistrates have granted the renewal; but I think perhaps you have heard evidence on that.

62,818. As to the application of an Act in Ireland, would one court hold the Act was applicable, and another court hold that it was not applicable? How there [illegible]

Mr. W. [illegible]. 17 May '98.

any case of that kind?—There is a case which I wish to direct special attention to, to show how we are handicapped in the matter. In [illegible] the Beer Dealers Amendment Act of Mr. [illegible] was passed, and in the Dublin court it was immediately acknowledged as extending to Ireland; but it was not until [illegible] that we were able to get the Belfast court to acknowledge that it extended to Ireland, and then only when the Lord Lieutenant was induced to send the following letter to the clerk of the court:—"I am directed by the Lord Lieutenant to inform you that His Excellency's attention has been called to certain cases in which beer dealers' licenses have been granted at Belfast otherwise than at the annual licensing petty sessions, contrary to the Beer Dealers Licenses Amendment Act, [illegible]—[illegible] and [illegible] Vict. c. [illegible]. His Excellency is advised that this Act extends to Ireland, and that under it certificates for licenses for the sale of beer to be drunk off the premises can only be granted at the general licensing sessions and not at any other time."

[illegible]. It was 17 years before the Belfast licensing court recognised the application of that Act to Ireland?—Yes.

[illegible]. What happened in the other parts of Ireland. Did they apply it?—There were very few places where there were any of these licenses. I have not the actual [illegible] here.

[illegible]. In Dublin?—In Dublin and Belfast there have been a large number, but in other parts of Ireland there were very few licenses taken out under the Act.

[illegible]. The law was in that state of uncertainty for 17 years?—Quite so, although we had been repeatedly drawing the attention of the different authorities to it, and it was only when I wrote simultaneous letters to Sir Andrew Reed, the Attorney-General, the Lord Chancellor, and the Lord Lieutenant, and I got replies from all of them saying it did not belong to their department but it belonged to some other department. I wrote back to each of them telling them that I had written to all of them and they all said the same thing, and I hoped something would be done.

[illegible]. From your answer am I to understand the certificates for the sale of beer off have not been granted in Belfast except at the annual licensing sessions?—Yes.

[illegible]. In what year was that letter?—[illegible].

[illegible]. Then from [illegible] to now you have got into the legal state of things?—Practically so. Two months after that an attempt was made to still carry out the old system, but the resident magistrate drew their attention to it, and then one of the solicitors who was applying said he did not wish to embarrass the court, but he wished it clearly established that they could not be granted because certain applicants that had come to him had said that if he could not get it for them, such and such a solicitor could get it for them. But it is now universally recognised.

Law as to spirit grocers unsatisfactory.

[illegible]. What is your experience of the law as applicable to spirit grocers?—The law with reference to spirit grocers is in a most unsatisfactory condition.

[illegible]. Is the law unsatisfactory, or the existence of the licensed grocers unsatisfactory, in your opinion?—Both.

[illegible]. Have they been increasing in Ireland?—They have been increasing in Belfast very much. According to a return presented to the House of Commons on the [illegible] of February [illegible], moved for by Mr. [illegible], it appears that during the previous ten years [illegible] new spirit grocers' licenses had been granted, and to show that these could not possibly have been wanted, [illegible] of that number had lapsed. Then during the three years previous to February [illegible] there had been [illegible] prosecutions.

[illegible]. In Belfast alone?—In Belfast alone.

The magistrates and trial of licensing offences.

[illegible]. Against the spirit grocers?—Yes, against the spirit grocers, but in these cases there had only been [illegible] convictions obtained by the police although there had been [illegible] prosecutions.

[illegible]. Was that small percentage of convictions owing to the weakness of the cases?—Not at all in my opinion. It was quite a usual thing to hear a solicitor say when the case was coming up, "Ah, we must keep that on awhile; this is a bad bench," or to hear the police saying, and you would hear them saying quite openly in court, "Ah, we shall not get any convictions to-day," owing to the constitution of the court. Of course one can draw their inferences from it, and indeed, looking down reports of cases in the police court, when you see who was there on a particular day, you could almost tell what the decisions would be.

[illegible]. Who do you think should be the court in the case of licensing prosecutions?—The resident magistrates.

[illegible]. And the Recorder in Belfast?—The Recorder, I think, should deal with the granting of all licenses, but it would multiply his duties too much to try prosecutions for breaches of the licensing laws, and I think the resident magistrates would be quite capable. There are two resident magistrates in Belfast, and it would be quite easy to arrange any [illegible] a special time for hearing licensing cases, and the two resident magistrates might sit there.

[illegible]. You would not make the same man deal with the granting of licenses and then attend to some of the prosecutions of offences against the law?—I think not.

The law as to spirit grocers.

[illegible]. You would introduce the resident magistrate?—On that point, for dealing with offences against the licensing law. Then, on the other hand, I would say these licenses are much too easily granted and too easily obtained. The decision in the Marshall case has led to a very great evil, and to show the very anomalous position in which it is situated, there were four judges in the Court of Queen's Bench. Three of them held for the larger interpretation, to put it roughly, of the suitability of premises as the Spirit Grocers Act to as the other portions of the Licensing Acts where it applies to publicans. One judge held for the more restricted interpretation of it, practically that it should only apply to the suitability of the premises for the purpose of sale—the structure. It then went to the Court of Appeal, and three judges held with the one in the Court of Queen's Bench, and one held with the three. So that eight judges have heard the case. There have been four on one side and four on the other, and I think it a most [illegible] thing that the Government should have left it in that position and not have taken it to a higher Court.

[illegible]. I suppose it will be taken?—I understand not.

[illegible]. Then at present the only conditions are the suitability and character?—Suitability of premises as premises, nothing to do with surroundings.

[illegible]. Not as to the requirements of the neighbourhood?—Not as to the requirements of the neighbourhood.

Attitude of clergy towards the spirit grocer.

[illegible]. What is the attitude of the clergy towards these spirit grocers?—The clergy object to them very strongly—that is the clergy of all denominations. I would say that there is a real alarm amongst the people, and yesterday I happened to be in the lobby of the House of Commons, and two leading officials from Belfast holding responsible positions came and spoke to me, and said: "You are going to give evidence to-morrow; "we hope you are going to tell everything you can "against these spirit grocers, they are such a curse to "the community." Nothing could be stronger than the language that is used by everybody.

[illegible]. Were these clergy?—No, these were officials.

[illegible]. (Mr. [illegible].) Will you say what officials they were?—I will; only I would rather not give names.

[illegible]. Were they police or not?—I will tell you who they were, and their names, but I think they should not be put on the notes.

[illegible]. (Chairman.) What is their position or what office do they hold?—I do not suppose they would object, only I think it would be as well that they should not be subject to any annoyance.

[illegible]. (Mr. Young.) Were they government officials?—The one was the clerk of petty sessions and the other the town clerk, but if you do not object I would rather their names were not put on the notes.

[illegible]. (Chairman.) The opinion they stated to you yesterday in the lobby of the House of Commons is, I understand, confirmed by the expressed opinion of the Bishop?—Yes, I would like to give you that; but I will tell you why I do not like to put their names on the notes. It is because I will not give the opinions of any one unless I have asked their permission—unless it is something taken from a printed document—and I have asked their permission to mention their names.

[illegible]. We will take it from you that two gentlemen in the official positions you have described did express that opinion to just yesterday?—Yes. Then a [illegible] the most Reverend Dr. M'Alister, the Roman Catholic Bishop of Down and Connor, in his Lenten pastoral said: "A new and, in my opinion, a very dangerous "source of temptation is being developed in the multi-"plication of spirit grocers' licences I refer to "intemperance among women and girls, and to family "drinking, one of the worst sources of intemperance "and incident to [illegible]."

[illegible]. Dr. M'Alister is not Bishop now?—No, he is dead, but that was in his [illegible] pastoral, and I may say that in conversation with the most Rev. Dr. Henry, he has endorsed that [illegible] emphatically.

[illegible]. (Mr. [illegible].) What would be the date of that expression of opinion?—The Lenten pastoral was in [illegible]. That would be issued immediately before Lent.

[illegible]. (Mr. [illegible].) Might I ask you if that is Dr. Henry's opinion, the present Bishop's opinion?—Yes, and he has authorised me to say so. I have had conversations with him before, but I did not like to use it without his authority, and he gave me his opinion on that and some other matters and said I could use it. He authorised me to do so. I have [illegible] other [illegible] here from the last Lenten pastorals of the different Bishops with reference to intemperance and so on.

[illegible]. (Chairman.) To the same effect?—Yes; some very strong indeed, and also with reference to drunkenness generally.

[illegible]. Would you like to see then the control of these grocers' licences put under the absolute discretion of the licensing court?—Yes, and also that the inhabitants should have the same right to oppose an application as they have with reference to applications for publicans' licences, and that the authority to grant them should be the same as it is for publicans' licences.

[illegible]. Either the Recorder or the county court judge?—Quite so.

[illegible]. Is there any limitation now upon the value of these houses?—None whatever, practically.

[illegible]. You would fix a minimum valuation for a spirit grocer?—Yes; I would fix a minimum valuation. I do not think that a spirit grocer's licence should be granted unless to large respectable premises.

[illegible]. You have no objection in principle to the mixed trade?—Yes, I have, but I recognise that there are very many people who think that there should be an opportunity of obtaining spirits so long as they are sold otherwise than at the publichouse, and whilst I may have strong opinions, one has, in making recommendations at any rate, to deal with things as they are rather than [illegible] that they might wish.

[illegible]. What would you raise the minimum valuation to?—I think [illegible] in the country and [illegible] in Belfast and large places of that kind.

[illegible]. Speaking as a practical man, would you consider that as an effect of that valuation you would sweep away a great number of the existing licences?—Yes, I forget the number, but I should say it would sweep away seven-eighths of them.

[illegible]. Do you think it would be a feasible plan?—I do, and I think it would be equitable and right, because almost every one of these spirit grocers' licences that have been granted, have been granted simply because they had to be, and not because any one thought they were required. The Recorder has refused to grant publichouse licences for a very large number of these. Then they apply for a spirit grocer's licence, and on getting it they go and take out what is termed a kitchen licence.

Belfast now than there were in 1872, although the population has increased, I suppose inside the old area where that would apply, to perhaps 150,000

[illegible]. The Recorder has frequently, I understand you, refused a publican's licence. In that case what does the applicant do?—He then almost invariably applies for a spirit grocer's licence.

[illegible]. And invariably gets it?—Invariably gets it. There is no power to refuse it.

[illegible]. Except on the ground of character?—Except character. Then a few months afterwards, or at the next annual licensing sessions, under the last regulation, he applies for a beer retailer's licence, and though the magistrates have the absolute power to grant or refuse that particular kind of licence, they generally say: "He has a spirit grocer's licence, what is the use of refusing this?" They do not always, but generally that is the line that is taken.

[illegible]. So that they add on to the spirit grocer's licence a beer retailer's licence?—They do. I should say it is the experience of the police, and the experience of those who are living in the poorer [illegible] where these are granted, that unless the applicant can get the beer licence, the spirit grocer's licence is of comparatively little value to him.

[illegible]. They have the power as [illegible] Mr. [illegible]'s Act to refuse the beer licence?—They have, but they very seldom do.

[illegible]. But if the consequence of refusing the beer licence is to make the spirit grocer's licence of no value, why do not they act in that way, and check it if they think it an evil, the spirit grocer's licence [illegible] with the magistrates, not with the Recorder.

[illegible]. You say that the beer licence gives the real value to the house, and that without it the spirit grocer's licence would not be of so much use. The magistrates can under Mr. [illegible]'s Act of [illegible], in their full discretion, refuse to grant a new licence, and my [illegible] question was, if they can refuse the beer licence, and so take away the value of the spirit grocer's licence, why do not they do so?—I might perhaps just say what I heard at the last annual licensing sessions when I was present; I heard a police officer, and not in a whisper, say, "Ah, well, it is very "little use. The Bench will grant everything."

[illegible]. Have you ever known a case, for example, where the Recorder had refused the licence to an extension of premises he had thought undesirable, and the applicant has then acted in the way that these other applicants have done and got a spirit grocer's licence?—Yes. There was a case where the Recorder had refused on five different occasions to grant an extension of particular premises, because the original licence was in a [illegible]. The purpose was that the applicant wished the licence extended to—he had to apply for a new licence, for it was more than doubling his premises—even in the front street; he would then have been able to extend into the front street, but the Recorder refused it persistently. He then applied for a spirit grocer's licence for these particular premises. He got it, and then he, at the annual licensing sessions, was unanimously granted a beer-dealer's licence.

[illegible]. When the Recorder sits in the court with the county magistrates, what happens then?—We know certain instances where the licences are pretty sure to be granted, but at other times sessions they are not; but as you heard from Judge Orr in the County Down, that is the worst place, for there will be as many as [illegible] magistrates coming from all parts of the country, and some entirely outside the county, in fact some coming so far that they have to come the previous night. The whole [illegible] with reference to the [illegible] [illegible]

Mr. W. Wilkinson.

17 May '98.

Beer retailer's [illegible] added to spirit grocer's licence.

Action of magistrates as to beer retailer's licences.

Mr. W. [illegible]

[illegible] May '97

a publican's licence, and the magistrates in petty sessions granted him the spirit grocer's and beer retailer's licences. It has been transferred to other parties since, but still, the grocer's licence and beer dealer's licence were granted. Even at the last quarter sessions held just a few days before the exhibition of the borough he applied again and he was again refused the publican's licence. That house has given a great deal of trouble to the police, and I have it from the authorities, that they have had to increase the number of police in the station, and yet they find it almost impossible to get a conviction.

Drinking next to spirit grocer's premises.

62,872. It gives trouble to the police from the fact that liquor is consumed on the premises?—Consumed on the premises and near the premises. There was one particular case where an appeal was taken to the Recorder, the magistrates deciding that there had been consumed just close to the premises. This case illustrates the great difficulty of interpreting the Licensing Act.

62,873. (Mr. [illegible].) In what district was this case?—I have no objection to mentioning it. It was on the [illegible] Road, the case of a licence held by Dougherty, formerly granted to [illegible], close by the [illegible] and the level crossing of the railway. The Recorder held that although the manager was looking out through the window and saw the men drinking, he not being the owner, the law was not broken.

62,874. He was not put up the owner of the house?—Yes. The words are these. Mr. M'Grath, on behalf of the appellant, that is the licensee, submitted the case was one in which privity and consent contemplated, as the Act of 1872, should have been on the part of the licensee and not on the part of the servant or assistant. Then His Honour Judge Fitzgibbon said: "There is no evidence that there was privity or consent on the part of the owner. There's a penal clause, and it must be by consent of the licensed person. No evidence has been given that that was so. In my opinion the present case is not distinguishable from the case set up by Mr. McGrath. The decision was reversed."

62,875. In whose name was the licence made out at that time?—At that time it was held by Dougherty.

62,876. And the man looked out of the window?—No, his assistant.

62,877. If you supply liquor to be consumed off the premises, and the men purchasing it take it off the premises, is it an offence under the law of Ireland, on the part of the publican who sells the liquor, if the men take the liquor 10 yards off the premises and consume it there? How is he to know if they go round the corner and consume it within 10 yards of the house?—I think it is quite possible that it should be proved that some one in his employment was privy to it, but I think that if an assistant supplied the liquor and the men went back two or three times and got more liquor, and the assistant looked out of the window and saw them drinking it outside, that the licensee should be held responsible for the act of his servant.

Responsibility for acts of servant.

62,878. Am I to take it to be the law now, that if a spirit grocer's assistant breaks the law to any degree or any extent, because he is not the owner of the house therefore no penalty can be inflicted upon anybody?—I think, reading Judge Fitzgibbon's judgment—and I must say he is a very careful judge, and very particular in following precedents—he lays it down here that this is a penal clause, and, I think, it must be only in cases where it brings about something very serious, and where it is mentioned in a particular clause, a penalty can be inflicted.

62,879. Would the assistant escape altogether?—Yes.

62,880. And the owner would be free from any kind of charge?—Quite so. In point of fact all the man who owns the premises has to do is to stay in the back kitchen and make the assistant do the business, and you cannot prove he is privy to it.

[illegible] law by spirit grocers.

62,881. You would like to see the law altered to make any assistant throw the responsibility on the owner, unless he had done it maliciously?—Unless he did it maliciously, the owner should be held responsible if his assistant does it. In connection with that particular licence, to show how the law is evaded, on one occasion a gentleman who was riding on the top of a tram past it saw the people inside drinking. He had this information conveyed to the police, and I may say it was conveyed through myself. That evening as he was going home the blinds were drawn down about 18 inches so as to hide the view of the interior from the tram, and they have been kept in that way ever since.

Mr. W. [illegible]

62,882. In the case that was seen by the man on the top of the tramcar, what happened?—Nothing, because he was not prepared to come forward as a witness, and, therefore, the police could not proceed. All he was prepared to do was to give the information that such practices were going on.

62,883. He might, if he had liked, have come forward and sworn to it?—Quite so, but there is a strong objection, I find, in Ireland against being what they call an informer. They do not like anything in the shape of that, but, I think, it bears out what one of the resident magistrates said on one occasion in Belfast, that those spirit grocers' licences were practically obtained with the full intention and purpose of not adhering to the law. He stated that [illegible] as his opinion from the bench.

Property depreciated by proximity of licence.

62,884. Have you ever heard any complaint from owners of property that the granting or renewal of licences interfered with the value of their property?—Yes. We have had applications by owners of property who had terraces of houses in different parts of the city, and they have said: "I hope now you will offer the greatest possible opposition to that application; I have had experience of a public-house near some property of such and such a place, and if that licence is granted it will make a very great loss to me."

62,885. Turning from the owner of the property to the occupiers of the property, have you had any remonstrances from them as to the existence or continuance of a licence in their neighbourhood?—Often they have come to me and begged me to try and get a licence stopped; that it had so deteriorated the district that if it were not stopped they would have to move from it.

Evidence as to the wishes of locality.

62,886. Do I understand you to say that the inhabitants collectively have no right of appearing before the court?—No, and I think that is hardly fair. At present a solicitor appears in court, and the clerk will only take down one name, although the solicitor may be instructed by 50 or 100, and in some cases by almost every inhabitant within a radius of 100 yards. There is no way of bringing that fact before the court unless by bringing all these people and putting one after the other into the box. I think that if a memorial is signed and any petition is prepared on oath to certify that these names and addresses are bona fide, and that he has obtained them, that ought to be accepted as legal evidence of the wishes of the locality with reference to whether the licence should be granted or not.

62,887. I suppose, as a matter of fact, the solicitor can generally inform the bench if it is the fact in a particular case that he does represent the whole, or a large percentage, of the population?—Yes, but then the solicitor for the applicant immediately jumps up and says: "I object to this altogether; this is not legal; we do not receive memorials here; this is waste paper: put it under the table."

62,888. You would wish legal sanction to be given to a memorial presented by a percentage or any number of parishioners?—Yes, but I think it should be presented on oath. I do not think that an ordinary document with nobody to verify it should be taken.

62,889. You would have everybody who signed it come up to swear?—No. I think if one credible witness is prepared to swear he was a witness to the signing of those names that should be sufficient.

62,890. Signatures are easily obtainable?—Yes, and that is why I would guard it in some way, because I think it would be hardly fair to put in a long document without being verified.

Map of Belfast.

62,891. Before we go further I should like to ask you with reference to this map of Belfast you have handed in what are the red dots along the sides of the streets?—They are licensed premises.

62,892. Grocers and publicans?—Grocers and publicans.

62,893. Are they distinguished?—They are not distinguished. That is as they existed three years ago.

62,894. (Sir Algernon West.) Then I see a few blue dots?—Those will be wholesale ones.

The bona fide traveller.

62,895. (Chairman.) I do not want to go over the same ground at all unnecessarily as we have gone over with other witnesses, but as to the bona fide traveller would you like to raise the limit?—I think the limit

[illegible]

62,909. You object, I gather from what you have said, to the spirit grocer combining his grocery or other trade with the sale of intoxicants. Do you also object to the publican combining his publican's trade with the sale of [illegible] and [illegible] and other goods?—I do, and perhaps, if you will allow me, I might mention that last night I got a telegram from the secretary of the Grocers' Association in Belfast, in which they confirmed a conversation I had with them. I wrote to say that I must get anything in writing, and they wired me that they [illegible] objected to these spirit grocers on account of many of them selling goods at a lower price than what they can be legitimately sold at to make a fair profit, because they are [illegible] to make a profit over the drink.

62,910. (Mr. [illegible].) That is the unlicensed grocer versus the licensed grocer?—This is the unlicensed grocer, but I think it only fair to put it in saying that they have taken the trouble to send it to me. That is their objection that they are handicapped in the legitimate grocery trade.

62,911. ([illegible].) What would be the proportion in Belfast of unlicensed to licensed grocers?—I am afraid I could not give that. I should say that of people who do a fair grocery trade there would not be more than one in eight who were licensed—that is who do a fair grocery trade, because many of these spirit grocers do not profess to sell groceries. They have a few practically empty [illegible] and perhaps a [illegible] or [illegible] up there, and a little pepper in one old case, put in [illegible], and that enables them to obtain the licence and that is all they care about; but they are there for the purpose of selling intoxicating drink to be consumed off the premises, and on the premises when they can escape detection. With reference to the mixed trade, I have from a good many sources, but more from ministers of religion and from town missionaries and others, very strong representations about the evils that result from the publican's business being mixed up with the other businesses, and from some country districts I have been told that there are villages where you cannot buy even a loaf without going into licensed premises to buy it; it is impossible to send a child or [illegible] to get any article without having to go into a licensed place.

62,912. I suppose the custom of mixed trades in the case of the publicans is a custom rooted in the habits of the people?—I think it has originated in the case with which publicans' business could be [illegible] and the desire on the part of everyone to be equal with his neighbours.

62,913. Do you think you would cause a dislocation of trade generally if you were to prohibit a publican from dealing in anything else but [illegible] and drink—[illegible] proper, [illegible] grocery?—The question has been before my mind, and during the last few months I have been over a great part of Ireland, and in some of those small towns I have looked to see how it would work, and I find that in many of them the drink trade is very small indeed, and that if they were brought to change between the two it would simplify matters very much, because one man would be a publican and do a good trade at it—make a living at it, and another man who was a baker would make his living at the bakery, because he would get some of the trade—selling bread and so on—that the former publican did.

62,914. So that the separation of the trade would enable the [illegible] of the respective branches to make their own living?—Yes, and to do their business much better than what they do at present, and more to the advantage of the people. With regard to that, if you would allow me, I would read a heading of a bill in a particular place, the name of which I would rather not mention.—"Family grocer; tea, wine, and spirit "merchant; commercial hotel proprietor; posting and "livery establishment; general hardware merchant; "leather and shoe findings; iron and [illegible] [illegible] "and [illegible]; agent for the [illegible] [illegible] "Company, and for chemical manures. Lime for sale "at 1s. per barrel for cash." That shows the very wonderful complication there is of businesses in these places.

Mr. W. Wilkinson.

17 May, '98.

the place was to be a restaurant. Before long, all signs of a restaurant have disappeared, and it has become simply an ordinary public-house, but the magistrates had no power of acting in regard to that. The licence would not have been granted originally by the Recorder, only that he considered it was to be a restaurant, and as he has often expressed it, he thinks it wise to encourage restaurants being established. Under the 43 & 44 Vict. c. 20, subsection 8—that is an Inland Revenue Act—provision is made for a reduction of the licence duty, provided that the restaurant keeper agrees not to have an open drinking bar, and that the sale of spirits is only an auxiliary to his other business; and there are similar provisions for hotel-keepers. That is optional with a restaurant keeper or with an hotel keeper at present when he goes before the Excise to pay his licence duty.

63,916. As I understand, you would give the magistrates a discretion to impose such conditions as these compulsorily on the applicant?—Quite so.

Payment of wages in public-houses.

63,917. We heard something about the payment of wages in public-houses from a previous witness. Do you hold that that custom prevails at all in any part of Ireland with which you are acquainted?—It prevails just as much now as when it did some years ago when we called attention to it, but there are some difficulties, and especially in the case of Messrs. Harland and Wolff's business. I have the authority of the manager to say anything I like about it, so that it is no breach of confidence or anything of that sort. They employ a ganger or a head of a squad. He employs the men under him. Harland and Wolff pay that man a lump sum to be distributed amongst the men. Harland and Wolff have provided places for these gangers to repay in, but they do not use them, and they go to the public-house and use that. The police say that the Act as it is drawn does not cover the case because these gangers are practically employed by Harland and Wolff, and Harland and Wolff do their part of the business by paying on their own premises, and that is simply an arrangement amongst the men to devote the money in the public-house, but the result is the same.

63,918. If that is the state of the law, if a contractor was forbidden to pay his men in a public-house, if a sub-contractor—the man to whom the contract was sub-let—chose to do it, he might escape scot free?—That would be the inference, but I think there should be something done to make that perfectly plain.

63,919. Are the dock labourers in Belfast the victims of this system?—They are the worst victims because of their occasional employment and having to hang about, and the men who employ them have licensed houses, or had—I believe they have been sold lately, though I am not sure whether they have passed out of their hands or not—the men hang about the office which is next door to it, and it is very difficult to deal with them, and it could only be dealt with by the Harbour Commissioners passing a bye-law as they have in Liverpool.

63,920. Do you know any other town in Ireland where that custom prevails, or there is an abuse of the payment of wages in that way?—I do not know particularly of my own knowledge to the same extent, but I am told it does prevail in Limerick and Cork.

Post offices at licensed premises.

63,921. Are post offices conducted on licensed premises to any extent?—Yes. I find according to a return which Mr. William Johnston got, in answer to a question in the House of Commons, that there are in Ireland 344 sub-post offices on premises licensed to sell on the premises, and 30 on premises where the licence is for consumption off the premises.

63,922. The great majority is where there is a licence to sell on?—To sell on. The figures are very remarkable, because in England there are only 35 on-licences; in Wales only 8; in Scotland only 20; but in Ireland, 344.

63,923. There are cases where there is an on-licence and a post-office?—Yes.

63,924. Can you give us the number of cases where there is a post-office and an off-licence?—In England, 202; in Wales, 13; in Scotland, 11; and in Ireland, 30. I have often had complaints from my friends about this, and I have always told them that their proper course was to get up a memorial to be sent to the Postmaster-General.

63,925. What has the Postmaster-General done? He has received some memorials I suppose on the subject?—He has, and in several instances he has had the premises divided.

63,926. At the same time, notwithstanding your representations, I understand you to say in Ireland there is a total of 370 instances which are at the same time post-offices, and houses either with the on-licence or off-licence?—Yes. One reason why I wished to bring it before the notice of the Commission was, that I think the Postmaster-General should have it remedied without waiting for individual protests from the people, for in many places they do not like—although they object to it very much—to write so that their neighbours should not be allowed to continue it in this way. I know it is very cowardly on the part of the people, but still it does exist.

Rate collectors' offices in public-houses.

63,927. Would you like to see the licensing authority modified or changed?—I would. Would you allow me to mention that there is another grievance in connection with this matter, and that is that collectors of rates often have their offices at public-houses. That has been brought to my notice by a couple of letters I have just received about that very thing, and the great annoyance to persons having to go and wait in a public-house for the purpose of paying their rates. With regard to the licensing authority, I think that the county court judge, or the Recorder, should be the sole licensing authority, and if it would not be wearying the Commission too much, I would mention several instances which I consider flagrant instances of the canvassing of the magistrates, and pressing them to very considerable annoyance. There was one case in which I thought it necessary to instruct our solicitor to raise an objection to the composition of the bench with reference to some members having an interest in brewer concerns, and one gentleman, a director of a bank, shortly afterwards got up and said to the Recorder, "Well, I will take your advice," and the Recorder said, "I think you are wise." He went out. I had occasion to go to the hall of the court to send a message, and a man and woman rushed up to this gentleman and said "Oh, sir, surely you are not going to go away; our case has not come on yet." He replied: "I am very sorry, but,"—pointing to me he added—"they have threatened to fine me £50, if I sit in any of these cases." The woman then exclaimed: "Oh dear! we shall not get it then." Then there was another case at one of the quarter sessions last October in County Down. There was brought into the office to me the original letter of which we took a copy, and omitting names it is as follows:—

Canvassing.

63,928. Do you know that the letter was sent to a magistrate who was on the bench?—That letter was sent not to a magistrate, but to another gentleman asking him to use his influence with the magistrates. It is to illustrate the way in which the thing is worked.

63,929. (Mr. Young.) What town was that in?—The quarter sessions were held at Newtownards. I do not wish to give the names, because I do not think it would be wise unless the Commission insists upon it. Newtownards was where the case was to be heard. The letter is this:—

"B———

"27th September 1897.

"Dear Sir,

"As you are already aware my renewal application for spirit licence will be heard on 13th of next month, and I understand from Mrs. A——— that you do work for D———, Esq., and if so I will be very much obliged to you if you can secure his vote for me, and any others you can influence.

"Thanking you in anticipation,

"I remain,

"Yours truly,

C———."

63,930. (Chairman.) Is not that a letter that any ignorant person would have written thinking the bench were open to influence?—Exactly so, and that is just it. Everyone thinks the bench is open to influence, and it is according to the amount of influence you can command whether you can have a licence or not, and not according to the justice of your claim.

63,931. We do not know what the result of that letter was, and whether this man did use his influence?—He said he would not do anything of the kind; that he was not going to be made a cat's-paw of to do anything of that kind.

63,932. So far, then, it is to the credit of the person concerned. He refused to be the medium of the promise?—Yes. Then there is another case in which the following letter was sent out by the manager of a bank. It was in 18[illegible]:—

"[illegible] Banking Company, Ltd.,
"—— Branch, [illegible] January 18[illegible].

"Dear Sir,
"At last sessions an application was made by Mr. J. [illegible] for a transfer of a licence from Mr. [illegible] for premises in [illegible] Street. You were good enough then to vote for the licence, but owing to some legal [illegible] the application was, on the second day of the sessions, refused. The objections to this licence have all been got rid of now, but I will esteem it a favour if you will kindly attend at the sessions here, on Friday next, and give the applicant the benefit of your vote.
"The bank are interested in the case, having sold the premises.

"I am, dear Sir,
"Yours faithfully,
"—— Manager.

"——, Esq., J.P."

There were circumstances connected with that that I am personally aware of, but I think it is not necessary to detain the Commission with it. Then in 18[illegible], at [illegible] quarter sessions, two new licences were granted, although there was a [illegible] by [illegible] of the inhabitants. Two of the magistrates voting for them lived [illegible] miles off, and the other was one of the landlords of one of the houses. On this occasion County Court Judge [illegible] said to the solicitor who was instructed by the League to oppose: "There is no use in opposing licences here; you should go to the legislature and get the power of granting the licences transferred from the present body. In fact the magistrates did not wish to [illegible] it, but, having it, they cannot refuse the applications."

[illegible]. (Mr. Young.) Were not you entertained in the lobby of the House of Commons by two Belfast men yesterday?—Well, it was hardly that.

[illegible]. (Chairman.) Are you a magistrate?—No, I am not. Then at [illegible], in the county Tyrone, two magistrates actually removed a licence which had been refused at quarter sessions. It was quite illegal to do so, but the licensee having got his licence it could not be opposed.

[illegible]. Two magistrates granted a licence which had been refused at quarter sessions?—Yes.

[illegible]. That is, from your point of view, a snub to the quarter sessions?—Yes, but it shows how the magistrates act in these matters. There are several other cases.

[illegible]. That was not legal, was it?—It was not legal, but the man had got his licence.

[illegible]. In an illegal way—the licence was still a legal grant?—Yes.

[illegible]. (Dean Dickinson.) Could it not have been upset?—No.

[illegible]. Not on appeal?—No. That is [illegible] we were advised. A case was submitted to counsel, and there is a [illegible] counsel [illegible] it at the moment—that only that he having the licence still in his possession, and having paid the duty, it could not be upset.

[illegible]. (Mr. Grinling.) Why, when the Irish Temperance League got such a good case as this, did not they take action? Here is a case which there is no doubt about?—We are taking action and bringing these facts before the Commission. The fact is that the magistrates of Ireland do not look upon the licensing court as a judicial body in any sense. It is only as a place to confer favours on their friends.

[illegible]. (Dean Dickinson.) A kind of patronage?—Yes.

[illegible]. (Chairman.) That is rather a sweeping assertion of yours, that the magistrates throughout Ireland do not look upon granting licences as a judicial act. Have you ever heard any of them say [illegible]?—Yes. Of course I do not mean to say that that applies to every magistrate in Ireland. I am speaking in the general sense. On one occasion a number of us were standing together and remonstrating, and there was a magistrate there who had been lately appointed, and he said, "It is all very well for you fellows talking, but "the others [illegible] had their turn at granting licences to "their own [illegible] and [illegible], and it is little enough "we should now have a chance of giving our friends a "turn." That is how it is looked upon by the vast majority of the magistrates.

[illegible]. (Mr. Young.) You say you were told that?—By a magistrate.

[illegible]. (Mr. Whitaker.) You heard him say it?—He said it to myself.

[illegible]. (Chairman.) Then I think the Recorder of Cork said something on this subject?—The Recorder of Cork had made some very strong observations on one occasion with reference to drunkenness in Cork. That was in the year 18[illegible]. The present Recorder, when he was appointed, said he would administer the law very rigorously, and in the first case that came before him where he suspected that it was not a bona fide application on the part of the person who was applying, he pressed them very hard as to the legal [illegible] and so on. I was sitting in the court, and a young fellow, apparently a clerk, sitting near me called over the man who looked after the houses belonging to a brewery there, and told him he had better not go on with the case [illegible] was down, for as he could not swear he was in possession of the premises, and so on. They had a considerable conversation, and eventually the man who looked after the houses said "All right, we will "have the case postponed, and we will make it all "right to-morrow." The case was postponed till the following day, and the documents were forthcoming and he went into the box and got the licence.

[illegible]. Do I understand you to infer a charge against the court that they purposely postponed the hearing of that case?—Not at all. The point I wish to make is with regard to the tied-house system.

[illegible]. That is a different subject altogether. I asked you for your opinion as to whether any magistrate had expressed the opinion contradictory of what you say you have heard—and no doubt you have heard it—as to the magistrates not regarding cases in a judicial spirit. Have you dealt with that?—Yes, I quoted one case and I thought that was sufficient. This other case is an illustration of the evils of the tied-house system. You asked me about the Recorder of Cork, and it was in connection with that that it came up. My point is that licences are kept in existence by brewers and wholesale men that otherwise would not be renewed because the trade had gone from them, and they are kept up in this way by [illegible] [illegible] [illegible] to an [illegible] for licences, so that if afterwards the traffic should happen to be diverted in that direction, or there is an improvement of the street, they might possibly become valuable. I have several in Belfast that were kept that way.

[illegible]. Do you see any objection to magistrates in the court saying, If you will surrender [illegible] it may be, according to the value of the licence, we will grant you a licence in another place?—So long as the court is satisfied that a licence should be granted in that other place.

[illegible]. And so long as the court is satisfied that the value offered is sufficient?—I should leave it entirely with the court, but I think, of course, it would be a very good way of getting rid of old houses and shutting them up, but then the [illegible] of Belfast, I [illegible], will not always act in such cases, for I remember where they offered to surrender, and he said, What I am asked to do is to shut up practically one door in a [illegible] public-house, and another one in a place where it is not [illegible], and open a new public-house in a residential working-class district. I will be no party to doing anything of the kind.

[illegible]. I suppose he would be entitled to say, Here are six open doors. I will close all six and open one door in another part of the city. Would not that be for the benefit of the city as a whole?—It might, and I should be quite satisfied to leave anything of that sort to the county court judge and recorder.

[illegible]. You would not agree with one witness who stated he would have nothing to do with that sort of barter or [illegible] [illegible] of that kind, namely, the exchange of one licence for another?—Well, we must recognise that the liquor business is in existence, and when we are dealing with regulating it, I do not think it is any use bringing in ideal principles, which perhaps many of us would like to see carried out. In regard to the granting of licences, there is one other point I should like to mention, and that is, in the year 18[illegible], in county Donegal, when the [illegible] railways were being made, there were [illegible] new licences granted, notwithstanding the opposition of the police, and in several cases of the inhabitants, and many of those were not granted at the annual licensing sessions. Then in the county Mayo, which is always looked upon as a congested district

Mr. W. Whitaker.

17 May '98

The Recorder.

Grant of new licences for surrender.

Large granting of new licences in Donegal and Mayo.

Mr. W. Wilkinson.

17 May '98.

and steeped in poverty. I am sorry to say, from 1880 to 1890, according to the Registrar-General's returns, no fewer than 200 new licences were granted in that one county—in the period from 1870 to 1890 inclusive.

Occasional licences and the principle of the Bench.

62,953. Then with regard to occasional licences, are [illegible] licences freely granted in Belfast?—Not very freely, but still the police and the authorities and the public are placed at a very great disadvantage. I know one recently where it had run two months before the police knew it was in existence, though it was practically renewed from week to week. There is very great difficulty in opposing them. We did in Belfast successfully oppose one, but it cost a great deal of money, and it was after a great deal of trouble and expense. We went to the fountain head, the Commissioners of Inland Revenue, and they decided as follows:—"The Commissioners of the Inland Revenue are of opinion that a licence so requested is not one of the kind contemplated by the legislature when they provided for the issue of occasional licences, and they would not be justified in granting it."

Occasional licences.

62,954. (Dean Dickinson.) Was that in connexion with athletic sports?—No; it was in connexion with an exhibition in Belfast for the purpose of raising funds for a temperance hall, a working man's institute, and the temperance people objected to it.

62,955. (Chairman.) The Commissioners of Inland Revenue gave that opinion?—Yes, they upheld the objection of the temperance people.

62,956. Why were the Commissioners of Inland Revenue brought in?—It is they who grant the licence.

62,957. Do they grant the occasional licence?—They do.

62,958. Without the magistrates?—There used to be one magistrate to sign a certificate, but the absolute discretion lies with the Inland Revenue whether to grant it or not. It is not obligatory on them to grant an occasional licence even though the applicant should obtain the signatures of two magistrates.

62,959. I thought occasional licences were granted in Ireland by two magistrates sitting together, or one magistrate in his own house?—They grant a certificate which is presented to the Inland Revenue authorities.

62,960. They must endorse it?—They then grant a licence.

62,961. They must grant it?—Not necessarily.

62,961a. They do?—Of course they usually do.

62,962. In this case, though the magistrates had granted the occasional licence, objection was taken, and the Commissioners of Inland Revenue were referred to and said the magistrates had acted ultra vires?—Not quite so.

62,963. Against the spirit of the Act?—Practically it came to that.

62,964. (Mr. Young.) I think that the law of Ireland is that it must be a publican who asks for an occasional licence, and in the case at Belfast it was not so; and your temperance people took care to come up to London, and explain the whole matter to the Excise?—Yes, but in the meantime the applicant had made that matter right by not applying himself, but by applying in the name of another person who was a publican; and what the Commissioners held in this decision was not on the application of the man Coulter, but the application of the publican who had given him authority to appear for him.

62,965. (Chairman.) In this case, contrary to their general usage, the Commissioners of Inland Revenue acted on moral grounds, and said it was not likely that this licence was wanted for an exhibition promoted by the Temperance League?—It was not promoted by the Temperance League. We opposed.

62,966. It was promoted in the interests of temperance?—For a temperance hall.

62,967. They said it was not likely that an occasional licence for the use of the people attending the festival or the meeting would be applied for by the promoters of the movement?—Not quite. They told us they could not refuse it on such grounds; that they had nothing to do with morals.

62,968. How was it against the spirit of the Act?—They said the spirit of the Act was to grant an occasional licence for a short period, but this was to extend over a number of months, and they said it was not intended that an occasional licence should be renewed week after week for a long period. Of course the matter, as you can quite understand, was fully argued, at first with the Assistant Secretaries, and then with the Commissioners.

Mr. W. Wilkinson.

62,969. I thought it had to do with a somewhat frivolous application on the part of a publican to have an occasional licence at a temperance meeting. It had nothing to do with that?—Practically nothing. Had they to be influenced there to some extent.

62,970. (Mr. Young.) I attended a deputation to Somerset House, and there was a strong representation on the part of the temperance people of Belfast that this ought not to be granted, seeing that the proceeds of the licence were being applied to temperance purposes?—Yes, I met you there.

Occasional licences to be granted only in open court.

62,971. (Chairman.) What change do you think should be made in the granting of occasional licences?—I think that they should be granted in open court after the police have been notified, as is proposed by the applicant for a new licence under the 33rd and 34th Victoria, chapter 167, sections 12 and 14. Of course, it would have to be slightly altered in the wording, but it would be the same principle as is involved in that.

62,972. Occasional licences should only be granted in open court?—Yes.

62,973. Would the Commissioners of Inland Revenue require to have any hand in it?—I mean the authorising certificate of the magistrates, so that the State would be given time; and the police having been notified previously, they would say whether they thought it was a case that ought to be granted or not.

62,974. Then on this circular the Commissioners of Inland Revenue would have their consent as a matter of course?—They might, or I would leave it with their discretion, as at present.

62,975. They never have refused except in this single instance?—No. I should say that the deputy chairman said to us that it was a most extraordinary revelation, almost, to them, that they were licensing authorities. They said they never had thought of it before, and they could not understand why the legislature should have left such a duty on the Commissioners of Inland Revenue.

62,976. Then may I ask you whether you would retain the Commissioners of Inland Revenue in any sense, or make the granting of the occasional licence so public that it must necessarily come to the knowledge of the Commissioners of Inland Revenue?—Quite so. It would come to their knowledge in the way I am mentioning. The application would be made to them, and they would serve a notice on the police, and also on the licensing authority that an application had been made, and then it would be tried in open court, and on the certificate of the Bench the licence would be granted.

Householders' certificate.

62,977. Then with reference to the certificate, about which we have already heard a good deal, by six householders as a condition precedent to the granting of a renewal of a licence?—I think there is a great principle involved in that certificate, and I should be sorry to see it done away with, but I think that the law should be amended, so that it would be the duty of the police to verify the six householders' certificate, so that the applicant should be compelled in court to declare that they were *bona fide* signatures obtained, and also that they should be open to the public to inspect, which they are not at present.

62,978. In the case of a renewal of a publican's licence, is the certificate of the six householders required?—Yes.

62,979. That, surely, must have degenerated into a mere farce?—Practically it has. I have known cases where they have been filled up from the directory.

62,980. If there is a principle involved in it, you would like to retain the custom?—Yes, I think it ought to be retained.

62,981. The principle involving the connection of the neighbourhood?—Yes, quite so, that the house has been properly conducted during the year. The people are the most interested in it.

62,982. (Dean Dickinson.) They generally get six good customers to certify?—I think in most cases they could not obtain them, that is, men prepared to certify that the place had been properly conducted.

[illegible]

The witness withdrew.

Adjourned to to-morrow at [illegible].

ONE HUNDRED AND SEVENTH DAY.

Queen's Robing Room, House of Lords, Wednesday, May 18th, 1898.

PRESENT:

THE RIGHT HONOURABLE THE VISCOUNT PEEL, IN THE CHAIR.

Sir Charles Cameron, Bart.	[illegible] Smith, Esq.
The Very Rev. H. H. Dickinson, Dean.	Charles Walker, Esq.
William Stevenson Caine, Esq.	Thomas Palmer Whittaker, Esq., M.P.
[illegible], Esq.	Samuel Young, Esq., M.P.
[illegible], Esq.	George Younger, Esq.
John [illegible], Esq., M.P.	

Mr. W. [illegible] recalled and further examined.

[illegible]

[illegible]

Saturday afternoon, and during the whole of Sunday. By referring to the returns for drunkenness in that year, we find that whilst in Dublin there was an increase of [illegible], in Belfast there was a decrease of 413, and an increase the following year. During the period of these riots I frequently during the daytime visited the scene of them. I was in conversation with employers and so on—that is, grocers and drapers and men who were not associated with the licensed trade, and I was conversing with them on the great loss of trade. In every instance they laughed, and said, "Oh, we have "no reason to be concerned with. We have taken more "ready money since the public-houses were closed "than ever we took in the same period before."

44,015. These are the unlicensed grocers and drapers you are speaking of?—Yes.

44,016. What effect had it upon those who had a mixed trade?—If they could not necessarily shut off the bar they had to close entirely. Of course, the police did not cover it can with the present enactment, but with such enactment as there was it resulted as I have said.

44,017. Do I understand you to imply that there was more money available, and that that money, instead of going to the public-houses, went into the ordinary shops apart from those for the sale of intoxicating liquor?—Quite so. I, of course, wished to elicit fully from these their opinion, and said, "Well, but how do you make "that out? The people cannot get short in the "evenings here when the riots are on." "No," they said, "but you see they cannot get to the public-houses "to spend their money; and when it comes to Satur-"day afternoon and they have plenty of money they "come to us, and they have not only paid their back "debts, but they have money to spare to buy little "extras or luxuries."

44,018. Do you think there is any feeling among the publicans in Belfast themselves in favour of earlier Saturday closing?—Yes. There is a feeling in favour of entire Sunday closing, and also of earlier Saturday closing. On one occasion, in the Lobby of the House of Commons, when I was canvassing for our Bill, a gentleman who was over here as representative of the Licensed Vintners' Society and myself were talking together, and I said, "Well, it is an strange thing for a "man like you to hold the opinions which I know you "do in favour of closing on Sunday; and yet here you "are opposing this Bill." "Well," he said, "you "know, Mr. Wilkinson, we are in an association, "and, being there, we are bound to act together, and "to defend our interests, whatever our private opinion "may be the other way or not." Other publicans have come to me and said somewhat the same; and, only recently, some publicans have been writing to the Belfast papers saying that they are in favour of Sunday closing.

44,019. But that cuts both ways. If people were forced, so to speak, to vote according to the views of their associations, what notice have you of finding the real, genuine, individual opinion of the component parts of these associations—if you say there is a sort of constraint put upon them?—It is only from their coming to me, or my speaking them in the street, and their telling me that they are in favour of it; of course, we would not canvass them, because they would not put it in writing.

44,020. I understand that these people, of whom you speak, are in favour of the Intoxicating Liquors Bill which is now before Parliament?—Yes.

44,021. What are the provisions of that Bill?—To close from 9 o'clock on Saturday night until 7 o'clock on Monday morning throughout the whole of Ireland, and to extend the bona fide travellers distance to 6 miles.

44,022. (*Baron Dowse.*) And Sunday closing?—That includes Sunday closing—from 9 o'clock on Saturday night to 7 on Monday morning throughout the whole of Ireland.

44,023. (*Chairman.*) But leaving the exempted cities as they are?—No; throughout the whole of Ireland. That is, closing at 9 o'clock on Saturday night for the whole of Ireland, and altering the law in the five cities to make it entire closing on Sunday.

44,024. Have there been any public meetings held at Belfast in favour of entire Sunday closing and earlier Saturday closing?—Yes; public opinion in Belfast, I think, has been thoroughly tested. For many years we have held public meetings, and only recently we had two very large ones in the Ulster Hall. We have also had a very large number of open-air meetings. I have a sample of the bills to show that they are perfectly open. They read, "Working men of Belfast: Are you "in favour of closing public-houses on Sunday and "earlier on Saturday night? Assemble on Tuesday "next, the 5th June, at the New Road School, at 7.30, "and speak for yourselves. Let the publicans know "that they are not the authorised defenders of your "rights, as they state they are". And so on. There are bills issued for open air meetings and district meetings, so that we ascertained the opinion of the people thoroughly on it.

44,025. Resolutions were proposed, I suppose, at these meetings?—In every instance resolutions were proposed and carried, practically unanimously.

44,026. Was there any dissent?—There might be one or two, nothing more.

44,027. (*Mr. Young.*) By whom were these meetings got up?—By the Irish Temperance League and the people in the locality. The people in the locality come to the Irish Temperance League and say, "We want to "get up a meeting; will you help us to do so?"

44,028. (*Chairman.*) While there is some doubt in some people as to the desirability of Sunday closing, should you say there is any doubt in the same way as regards earlier Saturday closing?—No, I do not think there is.

44,029. Not even among the Roman Catholic clergy?—No.

44,030. When I say "even," that is because they did express some doubts?—No. Only recently, the week before last, I think, I had an interview with Dr Henry, the Roman Catholic Bishop of Belfast. He had expressed his desire to see Lefroy, but as I wished to quote them here, I went and told him I was coming, and asked him had I his authority for saying so, and he said "Yes," that he had not changed the views that he had publicly expressed, and which were published in the Belfast newspapers some time ago. He considered that earlier closing on Saturday night would be most beneficial, and, in his opinion, was even more important than dealing with the Sunday. He thought they ought to be closed earlier than 10 o'clock; if 9.30 could not be accepted he would say 9 o'clock in preference to 10. In his opinion he thought it would be better for the present to allow two or three hours' opening in the middle of the day on Sunday. This was his declared opinion to me, and he authorised me to make any use I liked of it.

44,031. When did he express that opinion?—Shortly after he was appointed Bishop. This interview was at the beginning of this month—within the last few days.

44,032. You have attended meetings, I believe, in large cities and towns in Ireland?—Yes. I have attended meetings at Cork, Limerick, Galway, Dublin, and Belfast, in conjunction with the Secretary of the Irish Association in Dublin, and he has attended at Wexford, Naas, Athlone, and other centres. I may say that there have also been meetings held in smaller towns as well.

44,033. Have the Roman Catholic Bishops ever presided over any of these meetings?—The Roman Catholic Bishop presided at Limerick, at Galway, at Wexford, and at Waterford; and at Naas and Athlone it was the Administrator of the parish who presided.

44,034. Were there any counter meetings on the other side?—None. No such thing is attempted in Ireland as to hold meetings in opposition to the Bill, unless meetings are got up by the trade.

44,035. You canvassed the five cities themselves, did you not?—Yes. In connection with that canvass questions were asked; I think it was when Mr. Russell was giving evidence in regard to the forms, and so on. I have a number of the original forms brought out of our office from Belfast that were issued in 1882 showing the names signed, and everything else.

44,036. Has there been any canvass since 1882?—No. I have here a paper showing how the canvass was made up. Here is each street taken with the votes for and against, and checked by two persons.

44,037. Have you any means of knowing whether the majority of these signatories came from the poorer districts of the city, or not, in the five exempted cities?—In Belfast there was a larger proportion in favour of entire closing from the working-class districts than from the better-class districts.

Mr. W. Wilkinson.

18 May '88

Early Saturday closing.

Opinion of Dr. Henry.

Public meetings in other parts of Ireland.

The canvass of heads of families in exempted cities.

Mr. W. Wilkinson.

13 May '98.

The ballot papers.

64,038. You issued your papers to the heads of families, did you?—Yes. Perhaps I might read one of the papers. This was in 1882, at the time the Act was about to expire. We have had other evidence, which I will give, as to the opinion being the same. "For "householders, and heads of families only. (This "paper will be called for.) Closing of all public-"houses, beer shops, taverns, and spirit groceries on "Sundays in the borough of Belfast. House-to-house "canvass, 1882. The Irish Temperance League having "resolved to ascertain the opinion of the householders "and heads of families in the borough of Belfast on "the Sunday closing question, respectfully request "that you will kindly fill up the following form." Then follow the names of the officers of the association. "Are you in favour of the entire closing of public-"houses, beer shops, taverns, and spirit groceries on "Sundays in the borough of Belfast?" "Yes or no." Then comes the name and address. "If you are in "favour of Sunday closing, place a cross in space headed "Yes; if opposed to Sunday closing, place the cross in "the space headed No. Please sign your name." And on the reverse side we give us the facts for Sunday closing, the consumption of spirits and beer in Ireland in 1877, 1878, 1879, and 1880, and the arrests for drunkenness in Ireland in the same years.

64,039. That was issued on the ballot paper?—On the back of it.

64,040. An argument in favour?—This is the wording: "Results of Sunday closing. The Sunday closing Act "came into operation in the year 1878. Attention is "[illegible] requested to the following statistics taken "from Government returns." We do not say whether they are in favour or against; we ask attention.

64,041. (Mr. Younger.) Do you state in that the reduction of the population which had taken place in the meantime?—No. This only extends over three years.

64,042. (Chairman.) Did you think it necessary to put that statement on the back of the ballot paper. Would not that, in the case of a Parliamentary election, be thought an infringement of the freedom of the elector. If you had just before an election a ballot paper showing the reduction of crime during a Liberal, and during a Conservative Administration?—Well, it might; but these were facts taken from the Government Returns; and we thought it was not unreasonable that we should place them facts before the people.

64,043. (Mr. Graham.) I take it it was a means of canvassing, really, was not it?—I do not know. You could hardly call it a means of canvassing.

64,044. You said just now that you were canvassing in the lobby of the House of Commons, and so I imagined canvassing was commonly practised by your society?—Oh, yes, we canvass Members of Parliament very freely, and use every influence we can to induce them to vote on the side we think right.

Result of the voting.

64,045. (Chairman.) What number of returns were sent in to these ballot papers? How many people voted out of the total population? It would be better if we could have better later figures than 1882?—I have none. I can give some figures with regard to Parliamentary elections. There were 20,000 voted in favour of the entire closing—that is, of course, for the city of Belfast—4,000 voted against. That showed a majority of the papers filled up of 16,000. At that time the population of Belfast was a little over 200,000. This, of course, included the inmates of the workhouse and other institutions. Taking five to a family—I take five, although it has been stated here that six or seven possibly would be a more accurate estimate for families in Ireland—that would be 40,000 families in Belfast, and of these, roughly speaking, 24,000 voted yes. Supposing all those who did not vote who were practically neutral were added to those who had voted against, it would still give a majority of 8,000 of the entire householders of Belfast in favour of the Bill.

64,046. When you say you included the workhouse, would there be a considerable number of people in the workhouse?—I should think somewhere about 3,000.

64,047. (Mr. Young.) There are about 4,000 there?—I am speaking of 1882.

64,048. (Chairman.) Do you know how the inmates of the workhouse voted?—They did not vote at all. I am deducting them from the population.

64,049. I thought you said the ballot papers were sent to them?—No. That is the reason I say that the population included them, and therefore we are entitled, if we like, to deduct them from the population.

Mr. W. Wilkinson.

64,050. Roughly speaking, as I understand, out of 40,000 heads of families a clear majority, and something more than a majority, voted in favour of Sunday closing?—Yes, that is the position.

Result of Parliamentary election, Belfast.

64,051. Twenty-four thousand out of 40,000?—That is so. Well, then, I might mention that in 1885, when the franchise was enlarged, and the cities were sub-divided, Dr. Seeds stood in opposition to Mr. William Johnston for South Belfast. Mr. William Johnston, of course, was known as a strong temperance man. Dr. Seeds favoured the publican interest. Mr. William Johnston received 3,610 votes, and Dr. Seeds received 971.

64,052. (Mr. Young.) That was not a temperance question?—Dr. Seeds was a Conservative, and so was William Johnston.

64,053. The one was an Orangeman, and that is a strong element there?—They were both Orangemen.

64,054. (Chairman.) You think it did turn on the temperance question?—I am quite satisfied of it. The strong [illegible] that any man should come forward for Belfast in the interests of the publicans, and think he had any chance of getting into Parliament as a Conservative. Therefore they turned very much to Mr. Johnston, even although they might have favoured Dr. Seeds.

64,055. Would not the publican interest in Belfast be able to muster together more than 900 votes on a test question, such as you state that election turned upon?—This was a division of Belfast—South Belfast.

64,056. In that division they would have commanded, probably, would they not, more than 900 votes?—I think not—not in that division—there are other divisions in which they could.

Petition against the Bill.

64,057. (Mr. Young.) At this time was not there a gentleman in Belfast who objected to the mode in which these papers were filled up and the way in which it was done altogether, and did he not offer to take a plebiscite of Belfast and give 1,000l. to an hospital if it were found that the majority of the people were for Sunday closing? Were not letters placed in the "Belfast News Letter," and was there no answer and no one to take them up? Is not that a fact?—I could not say it was a fact. If you say it was, no doubt it was so.

64,058. This gentleman said that this mode of taking the plebiscite in Belfast was a fictitious mode, and done by the teetotalers, and that they themselves filled up the papers in many instances, and not the heads of families, but all sorts of persons—Sunday school teachers signed them; and the gentleman offered 1,000l. if it were proved to be the fact that the majority of the inhabitants were for Sunday closing?—I do not remember it as you describe it at all.

64,059. (Chairman.) Following that line of examination, were there any petitions against the Bill?—There were.

64,060. Were those petitions examined?—They were.

64,061. What was the result?—There were petitions against the Bill in the year 1888, presented, professedly, from 15,000 inhabitants of Belfast. The late Lord Plunket, Archbishop of Dublin, and the late Mr. Henry Wigham and myself examined them.

Petition against the Bill of 1888.

64,062. Was there a petition against the Intoxicating Liquors (Ireland) Bill as it is now before Parliament?—Yes, as it is now before the House of Commons. It was at that time before the House of Lords. We spent some days in carefully examining the petition from Belfast, and we found, in the first place, that it was headed as a petition from the inhabitants of Belfast and the Province of Ulster. Then, when we came to examine the addresses of the people, we found that many were Dublin, some Ballinasloe, some Boyle, some Fleetwood, Glasgow, Bombay, Stockport, Ashton-under-Lyne, Edinburgh, United States of America, Italy, &c., &c. Many of these I knew to be forgeries, and a large number of them were fictitious, because we took the trouble of taking the Directory, and in the better-class streets that were given, where the people do not move very freely, we could not find any trace of the people at all.

64,063. How many of the 15,000 signatories did you eliminate?—We did not eliminate any, because in the House of Lords they do not take any notice of petitions in the same way as they do in the House of Commons.

64,064. I should have thought for your own purposes it might have been useful to ascertain who were [illegible] and who were *bona fide* signatures?—The petition was so stained with beer and spirits that we looked upon it as perfectly useless to go any further with it. It was utterly valueless.

64,065. Do you mean naturally stained?—Yes, it had been got up in the public-houses in Belfast.

64,066. (*Dean Dickinson.*) Did you expose that?—We did.

64,067. Where?—In the newspapers.

64,068. (*Mr. Younger.*) There was no secret made about it at the time. The petitions lay openly in the public-houses, and were signed by people who went there?—Yes.

64,069. (*Chairman.*) I understand the gravamen of your charge to be that this purported to be a petition from Belfast and Ulster [illegible] reported in the newspapers in Belfast and as reported in the proceedings of the House of Lords, it was a petition presented from inhabitants of Belfast.

64,070. Was that at the head of the petition itself?—No, it was not. Even the heading was not properly quoted. The heading was "Petition from Belfast and the Province of Ulster," but then it was [illegible] in the newspapers as being "inhabitants of Belfast."

64,071. That was not the fault of the people who drew up the petition, was it?—People who have a petition presented usually interpret those who present it as to what it is. Then further the heading of the petition was not attached to the signatures at all. It was evidently added afterwards.

64,072. There was another petition which at the same time came from Dublin, was there not?—There was. It purported to be signed, as reported in the newspapers, by 10,000 working men of Dublin. One of those working men was T. W. Russell—at least that was the signature that was there, and there were other names that we could see at a glance were not genuine.

64,073. (*Dean Dickinson.*) He told us of that; that his and Mr. Wigham's names were signed several times?—We brought him to see it from the House of Commons when we came across his name. Then it was headed as coming from inhabitants of Dublin, and the counties of Dublin, Wicklow, and Kildare. So that these petitions were practically worthless.

64,074. (*Chairman.*) There is a rule in the House of Commons that some names must be written upon the same bit of paper on which the petition is written?—Yes, and I was surprised to find that there was no regulation with regard to the petitions whatever in connection with the House of Lords. They appear to be treated as just so much waste paper, and thrown away.

64,075. Do I understand you to say that the House of Lords received a petition, though there were no names written upon what I may call the heading of the petition?—That is so.

64,076. It would not have been received in the House of Commons?—Lord Plunket mentioned it to the House of Lords to some of the officials; they said: "We have so very few coming here we never take any notice of them."

64,077. I suppose there is a record of them, is not there? They print the petitions in the House of Lords as in the Commons?—I think not. I think it is only in the proceedings that they are mentioned. I do not think there is a clerk [illegible] as there is in the House of Commons.

64,078. (*Dean Dickinson.*) You said Lord Plunket and Mr. Wigham questioned them?—The time of an inspection. Might I mention that I have quite a number of letters and personal representations from the added area in Dublin in regard to the effect of Sunday opening. In November last the boundary of the city was extended, and of course all the public-houses in the added area were allowed to open the same as in the previous area. I cross-questioned a number of the people with regard to it, when they complained of the disturbance, and so on. I said, I have asked the police, or town the police [illegible], and there are very few more arrests for drunkenness, and they said, We think the police, perhaps, are right in that, and we do not blame them. It is not a question of arrests for drunkenness, but it is the [illegible] and the inconvenience to people who go out for a quiet walk, meeting men and boys coming out of the public-houses, and in a state fit for the police to arrest them, but yet in such a state as to make a great deal of annoyance and a great deal of disturbance.

Mr. W. Wilkinson.

13 May '98

64,079. (*Chairman.*) Were the results of your ballot ever canvassed by the other side as you canvassed these petitions of the working men of Dublin; where they ever sifted by an avowed opponent?—No. We published it that they were there to be examined by anyone who liked. We had a room specially set apart for the purpose, and had them all laying out in piles, and [illegible] of each pile, in this way (*showing a bundle of the forms*), so that it could be examined, and anyone who likes to look at them will see they are every one signed in the ordinary way. They are witnessed where they are signed by the canvasser. I may mention in connection with that, Mr. Ewing said they were tainted, the men who conducted the work are teetotallers necessarily. In the first place, we employed all the Liberal agents and all the Conservative agents who were willing to take the work, without question as to what their habits were or what their opinions were. I thought that they would be the men who would know the districts better than anyone else.

The canvass in Belfast.

64,080. Were they paid?—We paid them 1*l.* or 30*s.* a week. In some cases the man was a sort of superintendent, and we gave him 30*s.* a week. They worked only a certain number of hours in the day; they could not work the whole day, and night was no time to do it. We sent them out two by two, so that the one would be a check upon the other, and we took every possible precaution to have it fairly and honestly done as a test and without prejudice.

Irish Temperance League.

64,081. (*Mr. Walker.*) I think you told the Commission that you were Secretary to the Irish Temperance League?—I am.

64,082. May I ask you why you desire to disassociate yourself, in giving evidence here, from that temperance league?—I do not wish to do so.

64,083. Did not you just now express yourself as desirous of so doing?—No.

64,084. I understood you to explain to his Lordship that you wished to say that your evidence here was not at the instance of the league?—You must have misunderstood me. His Lordship, I think, put the question, the opinions of your association are so and so, meaning what I was saying, and I said that I had not submitted my statement of evidence to my committee or to my association, and that, therefore, it could only be taken as being my evidence, as secretary of the society of course, but I do not wish to make them responsible for everything I say.

64,085. You are a paid secretary?—I am a paid secretary; I make my living by it.

64,086. It is owing to the financial position of the league that you have been enabled to travel all over Ireland to gain this experience?—Yes.

64,087. And yet you wish to disassociate your evidence from any responsibility for the league?—No, I do not.

64,088. Are you editor of the "Irish Temperance League Journal"?—I am not.

64,089. Are you responsible in any way for the matter that is inserted in it?—Only as publisher. I am responsible, as publisher of it, for any libel that might be in it.

64,090. You are perfectly cognisant of anything and everything that appears in the paper?—No, I am not. As an instance, I may mention that I got a letter yesterday calling my attention to something that was in it, and I had not read it. That was for this month.

64,091. Do I understand you to say that, as secretary of the league which has attached to it a paper called the "Irish Temperance League Journal," you never read its pages?—I never said anything of the kind.

64,092. You are not cognisant of anything that is inserted in its pages?—No, I did not say that. I contribute to it, and, if I happen to be at home when it is going to the press, I usually have a look over it.

64,093. Who writes its leading articles—do you have anything to do with that?—Sometimes I would write a leading article, but not often, not more than, perhaps, once in the twelve months.

64,094. It is very extravagant in the language sometimes?—You might think so.

Mr. W. Wilkinson.

1st May '97.

64,095. You do not? May I read a passage from this journal? Speaking of the Duke of York, you say —— ?—Excuse me, I did not say it.

64,096. Well, the journal?—Yes.

64,097. Speaking of the Duke of York, it says "That "young man who, if spared, will one day occupy the "throne of the United Kingdom, does not exhibit as "much wisdom and public spirit as we should like to "see in the heir presumptive to the British throne, in "taking under his wing the licensed victuallers." That was, I presume, in consequence of his taking the chair at the Licensed Victuallers' Asylum in London?—It was.

64,098. Do you think that is a decent and proper thing to put in a paper?—I do not think there is anything wrong about it.

64,099. (*Chairman.*) You did not write it?—I did not.

64,100. (*Mr. Walker.*) Still you are Secretary of the League?—Yes.

64,101. You are committed to some extent to what appears in this paper?—If it were a libel I should have to stand an action, as being the publisher.

64,102. The league is established to endeavour to bring about prohibition of the trade?—I will read you our constitution.

64,103. It states at once?—I think it is better to be perfectly accurate as to the wording: "The object of the "society shall be the suppression of drunkenness by "moral suasion, legislative prohibition, and all other "lawful means."

64,104. The league has a very large staff?—No, not very large.

64,105. Does it employ any paid lecturers?—It does.

64,106. How many?—Three.

64,107. Are you quite sure of the number?—At the present moment three is the number.

64,108. And they are paid a salary?—And they are paid a salary.

64,109. They meet with approval in proportion to the degree of zeal and energy they display in the discharge of the duties for which they are paid?—I do not quite understand that question. It might apply to the committee, or it might apply to the public.

64,110. I am speaking of the lecturer?—The public of course approve of them according to the zeal and ability they display.

64,111. I say he is a paid lecturer, and in proportion to his zeal, and the energy he displays, and the success he has from your point of view, so he is approved?—Naturally I should say so.

64,112. It is his duty wherever he goes to stir up opposition against this trade?—It is his duty wherever he goes to stir up public opinion in favour of temperance.

64,113. And in opposition to this trade?—If you put it that it must be in opposition to the trade to produce temperance, then of course it is.

64,114. You have a large staff of clerks also?—No, not very large. I can tell you what there are in the office.

64,115. Is it supported by voluntary contributions?—Yes.

64,116. Have you ever had a very large donation presented to you by one individual?—No, I do not remember anything of a very large amount.

64,117. Do you know of a sum of 500*l*. being presented to the league for the purpose of Sunday closing by a Mr. Hill?—No; he never presented more than 50*l*. to us.

64,118. He did present that?—He did—one year. He was to have come to our annual meeting, but he was lying ill in bed and sent us a cheque for 50*l*. and hoped it would compensate for his absence. We were very glad to receive it, but we were sorry that he was ill.

The League coffee stands in Belfast.

64,119. You referred to the coffee stands in Belfast, in the street; it was a concession from the Town Council to permit those stands to be there. Do you pay any rent?—Yes.

64,120. [illegible]

Alderman Dempsey, moved that the question of the rent should be reconsidered, and there was only one other gentleman, the gentleman who seconded, prepared to support him. So that the committee evidently thought that we were paying quite enough.

R. W. Wilkinson.

64,121. Is the late Lord Mayor of Dublin a temperance advocate?—No, I think the Lord Mayors of Dublin are usually publicans.

64,122. Then you cannot answer the question?—The present Lord Mayor of Belfast in speaking of Sunday closing a few days ago wrote: "All classes in Belfast, "including some publicans, desire to see the public-"houses closed upon Sundays."

Sunday closing.

64,123. Did I understand you to say that there had been no strong expression of disapproval of Sunday closing by the working men in any part of Ireland?—I was speaking of Belfast at that time. I think when I used that particular expression that is what I was thinking of. It is quite true that there has not been anywhere in Ireland a legitimate expression of protest by anybody against the present Sunday Closing Act.

64,124. I have a cutting here from the "Saturday Herald" of Dublin, as to a meeting of the Waterford Trade and Labour Council. It says, "The secretary "stated he had much pleasure in moving: That this "council, representing the various trades and labour "bodies of the city and district, while deprecating the "excessive use of alcoholic drinks, is strongly opposed "to the Sunday and Early Closing Bill, as it is of "opinion that if this Bill was carried into law it would "injuriously affect the industrial interests of this city; "furthermore, we are of opinion that the crushing of "legitimate trade is highly dangerous to public "morals of the city in opening up a new path for vice "by tending to create the nefarious practice of shebeen-"ing. That copies of this resolution be sent to the "Chief Secretary for Ireland, and the city and county "M.P.'s"?—I think that you are mixing up two things. I am speaking of the present Sunday Closing Act; you are speaking of a Bill that is at present before Parliament.

64,125. What is the difference?—The one is an Act of Parliament, and the other is a Bill which has not been passed.

64,126. This is a protest against any further restriction of the hours of closing on Sunday and Saturday night?—Exactly.

64,127. You admit that?—I admit that that is there, but I do not admit that that reflects the opinion of the working people of Waterford.

64,128. (*Mr. Whittaker.*) Your statement was that there had been no declared disapproval of the existing law as to Sunday closing?—Quite so.

64,129. What Mr. Walker refers to is another thing altogether?—It is a proposal for that restriction.

64,130. (*Mr. Walker.*) But you have also advocated further restriction—closing altogether from 9 o'clock Saturday night until a certain hour on Monday morning?—I have.

64,131. Then you do not recognise this as being of any importance?—It is of some importance.

64,132. Is it not equally important as anything passed by any temperance body?—It is not of equal importance to the opinion of the Roman Catholic Bishop, the Protestant Bishop, of their clergy and the clergy of all other denominations, and to the expression of a public meeting called for the purpose in the town hall where the Lord Mayor supported the resolution on behalf of entire Sunday closing.

64,133. I think I understood you to say that you had had some conversation with publicans, and they had expressed to you their approval of entire Sunday closing?—That is so.

64,134. Of course you know that the trade organisations have presented resolutions to the Government opposing Sunday closing?—Yes.

64,135. Those would be exceptions to the general rule?—Well, they might be exceptions.

64,136. Are you prepared to say that the great body of the licensed victuallers in Ireland, or even in the city of Belfast, are in favour of entire Sunday closing?—I suppose if they were absolutely free they would be almost equally divided.

bound by the majority in that association to an [illegible].

64,158. Do all of them belong to the association?—No.

64,159. Those who do not belong to the association would be in favour of Sunday closing, is that your view?—No, I would not say that.

64,160. Have you any memorials sent to the responsible Ministers of the Crown objecting to any further interference with their trading?—I remember a short time in the lobby of the House of Commons a gentleman was there representing the association and representing similar complaints to these. I said to him, "What is the use of your coming here when personally, as you have told me over and over again, you are in favour of entire Sunday closing?" "Well," he said, "I know, and it would be a good thing for me if I could get entire Sunday closing. I do not want to be open; but so long as the majority of the trade want to keep open, I am bound to go with them."

64,161. Is that fair evidence, merely the ordinary gossip and conversation of one or two men?—Take it for what it is worth. I do not wish to attach special importance to it.

64,162. You are in favour of removing the control of licensing questions from the magistrates to an appointed officer?—To a legal authority.

64,163. What has been suggested here in the city recorder and in the county districts the county court judge?—Quite so. I approve of that.

64,164. Do you share the opinion that has been expressed here, that the magistrates generally have failed to realise their responsibility in the discharge of their duty faithfully?—I do most emphatically endorse that opinion.

64,165. Have you read that on the 12th May, in the House of Commons Mr William Johnston said he desired to dissociate himself from the opinions expressed by his two friends. So far from the magistracy being abolished, he believed that the men who filled the positions had discharged their duties hitherto most conscientiously, and he should very much regret if a paid magistracy were substituted. Let say, in your judgment that is not so?—In my judgment it is the reverse.

64,166. (Mr. M'Lindon.) Was Mr. Johnston speaking with reference to licensing at that time?—I do not know at all; I never heard of it before.

64,167. (Mr. Walker.) He was speaking on the Irish Local Government Bill, and there is a portion of that Bill that has reference to licenses?—I do not know.

64,168. (Dean Dickinson.) Mr. Johnston was speaking of the substitution of a paid magistracy all over Ireland for the present magistrates, not of licensing at all?—I do not know.

64,169. (Chairman.) You do not know the circumstances under which that speech was delivered?—I do not know anything about it.

64,150. (Mr. Walker.) You spoke of 220 prosecutions and out of these 135 convictions. By that statement do you imply that the magistrates failed to do their duty?—I did.

64,151. That if they had done their duty, in your judgment, the people prosecuted ought all to have been convicted?—No, I did not say that.

64,152. Would it bear that interpretation?—Decidedly not.

64,153. Why do you imply that the magistrates failed to do their duty; in their discretionary power and ordinary common sense they may have dismissed it as to the charges made?—You never sat for two hours in the Belfast Police Court, or you would not ask that question.

64,154. You spoke of the facility which was permitted, and how easy it was for a commercial-traveller to obtain a spirit license?—I hardly put it that way.

64,155. Should they be licensed if it was shown that they supplied food to the people?—Yes, decidedly.

64,156. Did you not complain that that is merely a blind to get the license?—Yes, I have cases in my [illegible]

64,157. That is a practice that you, of course, object to?—I decidedly object to it, and, I think, provisions should be made so that it could not be done.

64,158. A great deal has been said here to the effect that the licensed victuallers of Ireland established in the country districts, and also those places where little are held, do not supply food. Is not that an indication that there is no demand for food even in the rest [illegible] [illegible]?—Not at all.

64,159. (Mr. M'Lindon.) It does also show that the licensed houses are mere drinking shops?—That is so.

64,160. (Mr. M'Lindon.) It also shows that there is a demand for drink and there is no demand for food?—No, not at all. There is the demand for food.

64,161. Even in licensed houses?—If they do supply food, there is the demand for it.

64,162. Are you of opinion that the publican neglects his business to the extent that he refuses to supply an article which he could make a profit out of?—The trades are so mixed up in Ireland that in these towns there are very few pure publicans. It is a grocer with a publican's license, a draper, a [illegible], a barber, in the larger places, a man who sells newspapers and tobacco, and so on. It does not lend itself very well to adding a restaurant.

64,163. Is not supplying food a fair charge of complaint against the licensed victualler?—I do not know that I usually made it as a charge.

64,164. I ask is that do not say that you can make it. Do you consider it a fair charge of complaint against the licensed victualler for not supplying food?—We have no licensed victuallers in Ireland. They are vintners. If he was a licensed victualler, then I consider it would be his duty to supply food. I have suggested changes which I think would bring it about that food would be supplied.

64,165. (Mr. Dunlop.) You have been pleased to put in evidence the contest which took place in one of the divisions of Belfast to elect a Member of Parliament?—Yes.

64,167. The minority vote, I think you said, was something like about 800?—Yes.

64,168. Would you give the number of registered voters in that division?—I do not think I could supply that at the moment, but in addition to the other [illegible] that I mentioned there was a Liberal candidate and he received 120 votes.

64,169. The importance is attached to the minority vote?—You see the majority vote was 3,615. It is the very great disproportion that I drew attention to.

64,170. Of course in the division it is common property. The number of registered voters is generally on the list and anyone could have them?—Yes, but I have not it here.

64,171. (Chairman.) Dod's Parliamentary Companion would give it?—Dod's Parliamentary Companion would not represent 1898. We have grown so much since that.

64,172. (Mr. Dunlop.) With regard to the petitions that we have heard of. They were got up, I understand, in hospitals against [illegible] licensed purposes?—So I understand.

64,173. You have characterised them as containing a great number of forgeries?—Yes.

64,174. I heard a question put to you whether you could prove that they were forgeries?—Oh, yes.

64,175. You can?—Oh, yes.

64,176. What test have you applied?—I have being in the case whose name was there, and he said he never signed it.

64,177. That is one case only?—There were several. I took a list of a number of names, and when I returned to Belfast I went to these and asked them if they had signed it, and they said no.

64,178. As to these petitions, when they are sent to the House of Commons, do you say they would result to no notice at all?—Except one, the House of Lords.

64,179. All petitions, I understand, go before committee?—Not in the House of Lords, I understand.

Mr. W. M'[illegible]
16 May '98
No food supplied in public-houses.

Parliamentary election in Belfast.

Petitions against Sunday closing, &c.

Mr. W. Wilkinson. 16 May '98.

day's journey?—30 miles, and I had a letter yesterday, and I have a newspaper here in connection with it, where he partly mentions two magistrates drove a considerable distance, and then drove on the car with the publican who was to be brought up, and they did the best they could for him when on the bench; they brought out of the party concerned [illegible] to which the man was bound.

Canvassing of magistrates.

64,181. Your opposition to the magistrates, I understand, is principally because they are canvassed?—No, not principally.

64,182. That is one thing?—That is one very strong matter. Because they do not act judicially.

64,183. Is the system of canvassing very prevalent in Belfast?—It is, but not so bad about Belfast as it is in some other districts.

64,184. Do you think it would be more reprehensible to canvass a magistrate than for you yourself to canvass a Member of Parliament?—I suppose that is what a Member of Parliament is for. We make the Members of Parliament for that.

Opposition to the Belfast coffee stalls.

64,185. With regard to those stalls that have been put up in Belfast for the supply of coffee and tea and food; were those first of all put up through a public demand on the part of the people?—Yes.

64,186. Not an enterprise or scheme of any particular party or syndicate?—No. It was not at first intended in any sense as a commercial undertaking.

64,187. It has been a very money-making scheme?—It has not been yet. We are very well satisfied with it, and intend continuing it.

64,188. You think there was no demand for such stalls by the public?—Yes, there was the demand, but not the supply, and it was to supply that demand that we established them.

64,189. Would that demand not really come out of the fact that you closed the other public places—that you had closed the public-houses against the public, and during the time that they were closed they required these places?—No, not at all.

64,190. I understood you yesterday to say so, that you had met with very violent opposition from a part of the trade?—We did not try to close them up so much as they have tried to close us up.

64,191. What was the opposition that the trade offered to you against these stalls?—When the Commission was appointed to inquire into the misdeeds of the Belfast Corporation—I cannot give the exact date—one of the complaints that was brought against the Corporation was that they had granted these sites to us, and the chairman, after listening a little bit, said, "What is all this about?" and they said, "Oh, you know, your honour, it is this outside here." He said, "Is it that place that you pass coming in here every day?" and they said, "Yes." "Oh well, if the Town Council have never done anything worse than that we will forgive them. What is the next?" Then they got up a deputation to the Corporation, and tried to use all means to get us removed. They started it. Two publicans undersigned it. There were five publicans in the immediate neighbourhood, and none of the others would sign it. They said it was no use; it was absurd. That fell through. Then they did get a deputation up in a general way, and went before the Harbour Commissioners, and also before the Town Council, and asked them to remove us.

64,192. Is it not a fact that the only opposition they offered you as to the promoters of that scheme was sending a deputation to the Harbour Commissioners to say that the [illegible] was entirely [illegible], that he was very heavily rated and taxed, and these people were allowed to have these places at a nominal price, say 1s. or so a stand?—No, that is not the fact. It is a fact that they did do that, but it is not a fact that that is all they did.

64,193. If it is denied, I must ask his Lordship to allow me to read the paragraph which appeared on the 15th September 1896?—Before you read it you will notice the answer I have given. The assertion to which you put it is that that is the only thing they did. I say they did that, but they did a great deal more. I acknowledge they did that, but I say they did a great deal more.

64,194. (*Mr. Roberts.*) I suppose you have had the opportunity of testing public opinion upon these temperance questions all over Ireland generally?—All over Ireland.

64,195. Do you move about from place to place almost constantly?—I have travelled something like 20,000 miles since the end of January.

Sunday and Saturday closing.

64,196. So that you are in a position to speak of the prevailing opinion in all parts of Ireland upon these points?—I think so.

64,197. I want to ask you a question as to the present condition of Sunday closing. I understand you to say that there was no real difference of opinion in Ireland as to the present law on Sunday closing?—Practically no difference of opinion.

64,198. With regard to earlier closing on Saturday, the overwhelming opinion of the country was in favour of earlier closing?—That is so.

64,199. But when they come to the question of the present Bill dealing with the exempted towns you have said that the clergy, the Presbyterian and the Episcopal denominations, and the majority of the Roman Catholic Church, were in favour of total Sunday closing?—Yes, and all other denominations.

64,200. But that some of the Roman Catholic clergy are not so sure of the matter?—They were not so sure of what the result would be.

64,201. The Bishops rather favour a gradual limitation of the hours of opening on Sunday?—I believe so.

64,202. That was a matter of opinion?—A matter of opinion and only a matter for experiment.

64,203. You are perhaps aware that some of the police authorities in Ireland have given it as their opinion that if this Bill were passed they would be able to carry it out without any increase of illicit drinking in the places?—Yes.

64,204. If they had certain powers?—Yes; and I put that question to several leading police officials. I said: "Well now, you think it would be better to let them have an hour or so; are you afraid of the result?" "Oh, not at all," he said; "whatever law you pass we will see that it is enforced, and we have powers enough to see that it is carried out and that there is no increase in drinking or drunkenness."

64,205. One question as to the Irish Temperance League. That includes, I think, all religious denominations, does it not?—It does.

Public opinion. [illegible]

64,206. As to the public meetings which you refer to as having been held in favour of Sunday closing, do you say they were attended by working men?—Yes; and some of them were comprised almost entirely of working men and held in the district where working men reside, the open-air meetings especially. I addressed one last year where they calculated that there were nearly 3,000 present at an open-air meeting and the vote was unanimous.

64,207. What is the result of your experience of the majority of the working men of Ireland with reference to Sunday closing; are they in favour of it themselves?—As far as Belfast is concerned they are very largely in favour of it, and almost unanimously, except those who are in the habit of indulging to excess on Saturday nights, and who, of course, would like to be able to get a hair of the dog that bit them as early as possible on Sunday. I have in my hand a letter from the manager of one of the factories, only an instance of others.

64,208. In Belfast?—In Belfast. He says "Everybody agrees, Roman Catholics and all." That is in favour of the Bill. I do not wish to speak so emphatically of the rest of Ireland, because I am not so intimately acquainted with it.

64,209. With the other exempted towns?—With the other exempted towns, and my opinion is from information I have derived from people in those towns, that the majority in every case is in favour of entire Sunday closing.

Sale of drink to children.

64,210. We have heard a good deal from other witnesses as to the serving of drink to children. Have you anything to say to that in regard to Ireland?—There has been so much said, and especially after what Mr. Simmons said as representing the Trades Council of Dublin, that I do not think I need put in the picture of children going to public-houses and so on; but I should like to mention that at a meeting in Belfast of the [illegible] on Monday, 28th February, this year, the following resolution was adopted: "That a representation should be made to the Licensing Commission to have a clause inserted in any new licensing Bill prohibiting the sale of intoxicating liquors to

Mr. W. [illegible] — 10 May '[illegible]

"children under [illegible] years of age, even for the purpose "of carrying off the [illegible]."

64,211. Was that carried by a large majority of the [illegible]?—It was carried [illegible]: at least, without dissent. Even the [illegible] who were present and who were members of the trade, I must say, supported the resolution. Some of them spoke in support of it.

Barmaids. 64,212. Have you anything to say in reference to the [illegible] of barmaids, which [illegible] out of your personal experience?—In Ireland, in some places there are very few barmaids; there are not many in Belfast, but in Cork I have had very strong [illegible] made about the barmaid [illegible], and also in Limerick. I have been urged—in fact [illegible] for not taking up the case, as it is one of the worst things possible, and I have the letter from a person who was engaged in the trade.

64,213. At Cork?—No; this is in the north of Ireland. He is not engaged in the trade in the town he writes from. "The employment of women in public-houses "I consider this will be the first [illegible] to further "the temptation [illegible]. I say this from many years' "experience as a policeman, and now as a publican "both in England and Ireland. Women will not "frequent the houses kept by men so much, nor will "men remain so long to get the women for drink."

64,214. From your own experience, do you think that there is an evil which ought to be seriously considered?—I think barmaids should not be employed at all.

64,215. (*Dean Dickinson.*) They are not allowed in America?—I believe not.

64,216. (*Mr. Roberts.*) Do you think public opinion in Ireland would be in favour of what you suggest?—Yes, especially amongst the clergy. They have spoken very strongly about it.

[illegible] 64,217. My last question is to ask you whether you have anything to say as to the police frequenting public-houses when off duty?—Yes. Some few years ago the regulations of the police were altered, and although they have canteens in their principal barracks, they are allowed, when off duty, to frequent public-houses. I [illegible]—I have [illegible] and [illegible] it beyond a doubt—that it is most detrimental to the younger men who have not got thoroughly into discipline, as they frequent some houses where there is a [illegible] which is known as the policeman's [illegible], and they go there and spend their time off duty which, of course, does not make them inclined to look after the publicans so strictly as they would do if they had not gone there.

64,218. What is your suggestion?—I think on the police force now, they should not be allowed to frequent public-houses for the purpose of social drinking.

64,219. (*Mr. Gates.*) Would you make it illegal to supply a policeman, in or out of uniform?—Well, hardly. I think that would be putting too much upon the publican. I would hardly go that length.

64,220. How would you carry out your recommendation?—As far as Ireland is concerned all the Inspector-General has to do is to say that they are not to do it, and they must not do it.

64,221. It would be an offence on the part of the policeman, and not on the part of the publican?—Yes.

64,222. (*Mr. Roberts.*) A recommendation to the police authority you mean?—Yes.

64,223. (*Dean Dickinson.*) A policeman can get a [illegible] amount of liquor in the canteen of the barrack?—Yes; that has been expressly provided for.

64,224. In order to keep them out of the temptation of going to public-houses?—Yes. Of course it may be that the police authorities think that it is a good thing that certain policemen should be allowed to go to public-houses to see what is going on, in a confidential way, when they are off duty. I do not know.

[illegible] 64,225. (*Mr. Gates.*) Has there to your knowledge been any organised agitation or other sort of public opinion in Ireland against the Sunday Closing Bill?—There has not.

64,226. It is part of your business in life, I suppose, to keep track of everything that goes on in Parliament with regard to the Sunday Closing Act in Ireland?—It has been so for many years.

64,227. Have there been any petitions sent from Ireland, from the trade or anybody else, against these [illegible] proposals to amend the Sunday Closing Act?—There have been petitions sent by the trade and petitions got up by the trade.

64,228. Are they of appreciable magnitude?—No.

64,229. The general trend of public opinion in Ireland, in your opinion, is strongly in favour of the proposed amendment of the existing Sunday Closing Act?—Yes. To a great extent I differ from what Mr. [illegible] said, and I think I have a better means of judging, [illegible] the country all over. My opinion is that at the present moment the feeling in favour of this Bill is stronger than it has been for the last 10 or 12 years.

64,230. Have there been any petitions for the repeal of the existing Sunday Closing Act?—Not that I know of. There was, of course, an effort on the part of Mr. John O'Connor in 1887, but it came to nothing.

64,231. And there has been nothing done for the last 10 years?—Nothing.

64,232. That was an organised trade opposition?—Yes; it was quite understood that Mr. John O'Connor was a salaried official of a brewery.

Meals in public-houses. 64,233. I should like to ask you, as bearing on some evidence you gave just now, do you think it would be an improvement in the Irish Licensing law if it were made compulsory for publicans to supply meals; not lodging, but simply meals?—I should not like to make any proposition which is not practicable, and I do not think it would be possible to carry that out.

64,234. Bread and cheese, for instance?—I was thinking of meals, but then I knew what it would come to, that it would simply be a bit of cheese on the counter and a biscuit so as to comply with the law.

64,235. You know well enough that in country districts in Ireland if a passer-by stops at a public-house and wants a meal he [illegible] get [illegible] anything, not even a potato?—Quite so, and therefore I made the suggestion that in connection with the [illegible] of travellers there should be a special licence issued for hotel-keepers, and that they should be bound to supply refreshments to travellers.

64,236. Of course any building, licensed or unlicensed, that is open for the accommodation of travellers comes under the Innkeepers Act?—Yes.

64,237. I do not propose that public-houses should be brought under the Innkeepers' Act, but it would be to my mind an advantage if every person taking out a publican's licence in Ireland were compelled by law to supply food as well as drink to any person demanding it?—I do not think that that would be a great hardship, seeing that they get such a valuable monopoly.

64,238. I myself have [illegible] it in Ireland lately by going into a number of country public-houses and asking for something to eat, and being unable to get even a potato. If you happened to hit their particular meal time you might get a share of it, but they simply say, "We have no food and we cannot give you anything"?—I have experienced the same difficulty myself.

64,239. If it were only to compel them to have a loaf of bread and a piece of cheese it would be something?—I think that might be carried out. I was thinking of a [illegible].

64,240. No—tea and bread and butter, or any other sort of food?—Yes. I mean say that in Ireland they are much worse off in that respect than you are in England.

Convening of magistrates. 64,241. (*Mr. Whiteley.*) We have heard a great deal as to the providence of convening of magistrates in Ireland. May I ask you if you have convened magistrates?—No.

64,242. You have never done so at all?—Never.

Sobriety and early closing in Belfast. 64,243. You gave us some interesting evidence as to the closing of public-houses at Belfast, through the riots, and the great diminution of drunkenness which there was in the result of that, and the great improvement in the trade done by the shopkeepers during that time?—Yes, that was so.

64,244. That would rather suggest, would it not, that while there are bad public-houses are worse?—There is no doubt about that.

64,245. I think you referred to a case where a publican objected to closing up a private door, because it would necessitate his wife and children going through the public-house?—Yes. The point was that a publican was ordered out of the premises he was in, and he took

Mr. W. Williams.

16 May '98.

Side doors, &c.

premises a little bit further down the street at a corner. We did not oppose the granting of the licence absolutely, but we did oppose it because there were a number of side doors to the street, that is, it would have made two or three public-houses, practically. Eventually the applicant agreed to close up all the doors but one at the back, and one solicitor was insisting on that being done; he said, "Now I must have a bell-door: would you like to have your wife and children going through a public-house?" And I think if publicans do not like their wives and children to have to go through a public-house to get to their houses, other people's wives and children should not be compelled to go into a public-house for a post-office or for buying other goods.

64,246. The fact that the publican did not like his own wife and children to pass through the public-house is a very useful indication of what the publican really knows the public-house to be, a most undesirable place?—I think that every publican will own that it is a most undesirable place for anybody who wants to be decent.

Irish Temperance League.

64,247. (*Mr. Younger.*) I do not know that it is very material, but I think, in answer to Mr Walker, you said the largest subscription you had received for your campaign was 50*l*.?—No. He asked what the Irish Temperance League had received from a certain gentleman.

64,248. Mr. Hale?—Yes.

64,249. And you said 50*l*.?—Yes.

64,250. The "Temperance League Journal" calls it 250*l*.?—No, excuse me, it does not.

64,251. "Mr A. F. Hale, who has contributed 250*l*. to "the special Sunday Closing campaign"?—That is not the Irish Temperance League.

64,252. That is the "Irish Temperance League Journal," is it not?—Yes, but that was contributed to a special campaign committee, not to the Irish Temperance League.

64,253. I do not know that it is material, only I wanted to give you an opportunity of correcting it if it were wrong?—I intended explaining where the 250*l*. had been given to, but, of course, I had to answer Mr. Walker's questions. He gave 250*l*. to Irish Sunday closing.

Sunday closing in Belfast during riots.

64,254. With regard to the riots which Mr. Whitaker suggests are bad and public-houses are worse, is it not the fact that during the existence of those riots the police were very chary about arresting people, and that they had far too much to do to arrest drunken people, when people of much greater importance were required to be put in limbo?—The police had very little to do in the latter part.

64,255. You would hardly suggest that during a riot state a policeman would take much trouble about the mere arrest of a man for drunkenness?—Yes, as a, in Belfast what leads to riot is the mere saying "To hell with the Pope," or "To hell with King William" during the riots, when the man is a little bit the worse for liquor, party feeling runs so very high. Therefore during those times of riot the police would arrest men under the influence of drink whom in other conditions they would allow to find their way home.

64,256. Even, although under such circumstances of tumult it is convenient to arrest people who are not really doing any serious harm in order to avoid inflaming the populace?—We deal with things in a very drastic way in Belfast. When there is anything of that sort they do not wait to think whether it would have that effect or not, they believe prevention is better than cure, and that it is better to run the man in before he has caused a disturbance than to arrest him afterwards.

64,257. (*Dean Dickinson.*) A sort of striking of matches in a powder magazine?—Quite so.

64,258. (*Mr. Younger.*) So that you think the drunken people received the usual attention at that time?—A little more.

Sale of drink to children.

64,259. With regard to the resolution passed about the supply to children. Was that resolution on the agenda paper of the meeting which passed it?—Oh, yes.

64,260. Intimation was given of the resolution?—Yes, a meeting was especially summoned for the purpose of considering it.

64,261. Had you anything to do with that resolution?—I was not aware that it was to come before the magistrates at all.

64,262. You had nothing to do with the drafting of it?—Nothing whatever.

Mr. W. Williams.

64,263. It was suggested by the magistrates themselves?—Yes. At the same time, lest it should be misunderstood like the other question, I will give the history of how it came about. The Lord Mayor presided at the annual meeting of the Irish Temperance League in the Ulster Hall, on the [illegible] January 1898, and a resolution was passed at that meeting requesting him to summon a meeting of the magistrates to take action. The Lord Mayor did not communicate with me afterwards, neither did any of the magistrates; nor did the clerk of the police court; nor was I aware that it was coming on until I saw it reported in the newspaper on the morning on which the meeting was held. I may say I felt a little bit annoyed, because I thought I could have framed a resolution a good deal stronger if they had only given me the chance.

64,264. You are aware, however, that the police—I think the name was Inspector Morell, stated here that they had never had any case of abuse, so far as he knew, of this grocer system?—I do not remember it.

64,265. It seems also a curious thing (my information may not be correct) that the magistrates never sent any intimation of that resolution to the traders in Belfast. Do you happen to know whether that is so or not?—I do not know anything at all about it.

64,266. It seems a curious thing that they should have taken the trouble to pass a resolution of that kind and not intimate it to the trade?—You see the resolution is just very similar to what was passed in England.

64,267. Still it had a very important bearing on that question?—The resolution is only that they should communicate with the Royal Commission. I did not know that even the clerk of the police court took the trouble to send it here.

64,268. (*Mr. Grierson.*) You have attended a very large number of meetings of the Commission of late, have you not?—I have, ever since the Irish evidence came on.

64,269. I suppose I shall not be saying anything offensive if I say that you hold a kind of watching brief for the Irish Temperance League?—Decidedly.

Spirit grocers.

64,270. You have had an opportunity of hearing the questions that have been put repeatedly on the subject of the spirit grocer's licence?—I have.

64,271. As your evidence is more or less a repetition of the evidence we have had beforehand, it is really unnecessary that I should go into those points again?—Well, that is for you.

64,272. If I did I should not be likely to produce any impression upon you, should I?—Well, I do not know.

64,273. I am confining myself to two or three questions. Your evidence, I think, shows that it is not only a spirit-grocer's licence, but the licensed trade generally in Ireland you are opposed to; the whole of the trade?—Perhaps it is hardly fair to put it exactly in that way, but I do not see the point exactly. I do not wish to be misunderstood.

64,274. You did go so far as to say—speaking of the spirit-grocers, the law by which the licence was arranged was bad, and that the grocer himself was bad?—Not in every case. I did not say in every case.

64,275. Practically that was your evidence, that the law with regard to the spirit-grocer's licence was bad, and the trade was a bad one; that is a fair statement, is it not?—Yes.

64,276. (*Chairman.*) If I recollect rightly, you were speaking of the grocers when I asked you if you saw any objection to the mixed trade, and you thought it a bad system, and the law which applied to it was also bad?—Quite so.

64,277. (*Mr. Grierson.*) I understood you differently; that the law which governed the spirit grocer's licence was a bad one?—Yes.

64,278. And that the spirit grocer's trade was a bad one?—I did not use that expression.

64,279. I understand now you qualify that to a certain extent, and you say you would like to draw a distinction between the respectable members of the trade and the portion of the trade that your remarks principally applied to?—Decidedly. I do not think everybody should be condemned because members [illegible] associated with them, or being in the same trade, or living in the same street, happens to be a bad man.

[illegible]. You referred to the remark of a bishop in [illegible]—one of the Roman Catholic bishops—where he said there was a lamentable increase of spirit grocer's licenses?—Yes, that was Dr. [illegible]

[illegible]. Do you think he knew, or do you yourself know, what was the lamentable increase during the years there were?—It was very great. I gave the numbers.

[illegible]. Can you give them for us? May I give them to you? In [illegible] as the whole of Ireland there were 575 spirit grocers' licenses?—We are speaking of Belfast, except [illegible].

[illegible]. No. I am asking about the whole of Ireland?—He was speaking of Belfast, and I wish to confine myself to that. I think you will find that at least [illegible] of them were in Belfast.

[illegible]. I am afraid we have no means of [illegible] that at the moment. I will treat it simply as the spirit grocers' licenses in Ireland. The increase between [illegible] and [illegible] was from 575 to [illegible] for the whole of Ireland?—Yes, but it is not fair to treat it in that way, because it is a special evil in Belfast.

[illegible]. I quite admit that. I only want to get my point, that is, the increase for the whole of Ireland. Would it be reasonable to describe that as a "lamentable increase"?—If it were spread all over Ireland, I would not use that expression; but if it were in Belfast alone, and the Recorder had refused almost every one of those applicants a publican's license in his discretion, I think it would be very lamentable.

[illegible]. I think you have heard during the time you have been attending here, the reasons assigned why the spirit grocer's license has increased largely in Belfast and Dublin, have you not?—I have heard of many reasons.

[illegible]. The general assumption is that if you refuse all other classes of license and this particular license only can be got, necessarily there will be a large increase in that number. That is a reasonable explanation, is it not?—Yes.

[illegible]. (Mr. Young.) I think you said the feeling was stronger for Sunday closing in Ireland now than formerly?—I said it was more expressed.

[illegible]. But you do not say that there is a greater number of people for Sunday closing in Belfast than before?—There are quite as many as ever there were.

[illegible]. How do you know that?—By the readiness with which public meetings are attended when announced; by the unanimous resolutions passed at them, and also by the fact that the trade cannot get up a meeting in opposition unless of their own particular members and their friends.

[illegible]. They do not try. What class of people are you associated with in Belfast, is it the church-going people?—Yes, and those who do not go to church.

[illegible]. Do you come into contact now with the operatives and labouring classes?—Yes, very considerably.

[illegible]. Are your meetings held at the Young Men's Christian Association?—No.

[illegible]. Where?—In the Ulster Hall, on the Custom House steps, and in the open spaces up by Ewart's mills and elsewhere. We have held them out at Ballymacarrett, and at the entrance to [illegible] and Wolff's works.

[illegible]. At all events they are temperance meetings?—There are [illegible] [illegible], but they are [illegible]

[illegible]. Have you large numbers of Roman Catholics coming to your meetings?—I have a letter here from a Roman Catholic clergyman in Belfast.

[illegible]. I dare say, but could you answer my question; have you large numbers of Roman Catholics coming to your meetings when held in different places in Belfast?—I could not answer that question, because we never ask a man coming to our meetings whether he is a Roman Catholic or a Protestant.

[illegible]. (Chairman.) What were you going to say when, in answer to Mr. Young's question, you said you had a letter?—From a Roman Catholic clergyman in Belfast.

[illegible]. Would that be an answer to the question of the Commissioner?—Yes, I wanted to show that there is a very strong feeling amongst the working-class Roman Catholic people of Belfast in favour of our Bill. This is a clergyman in a district that is almost exclusively inhabited by working-class people. Mr. Young will know the district very well—the Falls Road District.

[illegible]. To what effect is the letter?—That he is most heartily with us in the matter.

[illegible]. (Mr. Young.) Does that clergyman say it was with reference to Sunday closing?—In favour of the Bill as it is before Parliament.

[illegible]. When you say that public opinion in Ireland is stronger for Sunday closing, may I draw your attention to the last that [illegible] year, when the Bill was before the House, it [illegible] to be [illegible] [illegible], the test in the House of Commons last year proved that really the tendency was in the other direction?—No; almost the [illegible] proved that there were more prepared to [illegible] the Bill than there had been when it was before the House previously, but [illegible] that there were fewer prepared to vote for it. I am quite aware of all the manipulation that went on, and that produced that result. I must not enlighten you on that.

[illegible]. (Dean [illegible].) Were not there 40 Irish members absent?—Yes.

[illegible]. (Mr. Young.) May I point this out: that there was an election in Belfast where a man called Turner, who was an [illegible] of public-houses and connected with public-houses, stood in opposition to a teetotaler?—He did.

[illegible]. He was one of the most popular men in Belfast, and one of the most leading [illegible], but, to the surprise of everybody, the publican was within [illegible] of getting in, and there never was such a thing before?—Do you say there was surprise?

[illegible]. I am asking you this; is not the tendency rather in the other direction in Belfast, when you find out these examples which I have pointed out to you?—Of course it is a very delicate thing to speak of a man's popularity or otherwise. I had better be perfectly open. The other candidate was Sir James Haslett. An Episcopalian had been wanting for that division. There is always a certain amount of jealousy between the Presbyterians and Episcopalians in Belfast. Mr. Turner was an Episcopalian, and a great many of the Episcopalians were annoyed that the Conservative Party should not have done what they think they ought to have done, and put up an Episcopalian to succeed Sir William Ewart, instead of a Presbyterian, Sir James Haslett. The result was that you might say there was a half among the Episcopalians, and they would not come out to [illegible] [illegible] Haslett. You know that as well as I do.

Mr. W. [illegible]

16 May '98

Sunday closing.

Sunday closing and Irish M.P.'s.

Mr. W. [illegible] — [illegible] May '98

64,810. (Mr. Young.) [illegible]? —No, I think not.

64,811. [illegible] a section of a political party in Ireland [illegible] to what you call the publicans' interests. That is so in your opinion?—Yes, they have, [illegible]. Not a single one of that party voted for us, although three of them had on [illegible] candidates [illegible] on the back of the Bill.

Sunday closing, [illegible] Irish M.P.'s.

64,812. We must not speak of the motive. The motive, according to you, was not a very good one, if I may say so. Therefore I would not [illegible] a question. You do not know what the motive was?—Yes, only if members want to be elected to the House of Commons they must take a certain course; just as in England certain men [illegible] support the trade; I do not wish to impute any improper motives in the course of history.

64,813. One section has gone over; well?—But the first time the English trade thoroughly allied themselves with the Irish trade so far that the whips were [illegible] signed by English brewers, as well as by Irish members of Parliament, against the Bill, and every possible effort was made. Up to that time we, the temperance party, had not been [illegible] the [illegible] so very much. Many of our members [illegible] "Now, look here, the measure you can show me that this Bill is likely to pass into law I am prepared to defy the publicans, and I am prepared to vote with you. In the meantime I do not want to have my life made miserable by having constant [illegible]."

64,814. (Mr. Young.) Does it not show that the tendency of public opinion at all events is in the other direction, as manifested in the House of Commons?—I think not at all. It simply shows that the liquor trade is better organised in Ireland than ever it has been before, and is prepared to resort to any means—legitimate means, of course.

64,815. (Dean Dickinson.) Were there not 48 abstentions from voting altogether on that question in the last division?—Something like that.

64,816. The total number is 103; there were 48 abstentions?—Something like that. At the General Election in 1892 the publicans' party [illegible] a [illegible], and this is one paragraph of it: "[illegible] such men as T. W. Russell, Thomas Lea, William Johnston, William Redmond, W. J. Corbet, Thomas Healy, John [illegible], and Jeremiah Jordan."

64,817. (Chairman.) We do not want to go into the minutiae of the [illegible] process. Do I understand you to say that your explanation is that the opponents, for some reason, were there [illegible], and the supporters of the Bill, considering that there was no real danger, did not give themselves the trouble to go up?—And the other point, which is very important, that we could not obtain an assurance from the Government that if we carried the second reading they would carry the Bill through. They had [illegible], and we were bound to let our friends know it that the Government declined to support us until after this Commission had reported.

64,818. (Mr. Young.) May I ask you is not your evidence very [illegible] history. You give us some statistics about 1888, when the city of Belfast was very much smaller than it is now. Since 1888 we have had an enormous influx of English and Scotch, and various people, to the works, and the population is now [illegible]. Do you think that any evidence you present to us is quite up to date. Would you rely upon them?—I believe they are a fair indication of the opinion of the people at the present time as tested by these public meetings last year and this year.

64,819. In fact you only got [illegible] votes by hard pushing, and by sending your canvassers through the people, and putting down their names?—Nothing of the kind. We neither pushed nor [illegible] in that town, nor did we put down their names.

64,820. At all events there are now about [illegible] inhabitants, and you would not rely upon the plebiscite of that time?—No, I do not rely upon that alone. That is the present work, and we worked up from that to the present time.

64,821. Do you represent the league in Ireland?—There are a good many leagues in Ireland. I do not wish to be misunderstood, and I do not want to put something past on the notes which might be thought to mean something else.

64,822. It is interesting to know whom we are examining. Do you represent the league here?—I am a Secretary of the Irish Temperance League.

64,823. Do you speak for them?—So far as it is possible for me to do so. As I have explained, I have not submitted what I have said here to my committee, nor to anyone else.

64,824. There have not been [illegible] in Ireland appointing you to represent them at this Commission?—No, we never thought of such a thing.

64,825. Then it is rather your own individual opinion that you have given?—It is not my own opinion when it is the result of inquiries from a great number of people in every condition of life. You cannot call that my personal opinion.

64,826. I have before me a statement of your accounts, and you pay out yearly [illegible]; salaries, [illegible]; and you pay for [illegible], for the League Journal, [illegible]; and for the London Temperance Hospital, a charitable thing, you pay [illegible]—out of this [illegible]?—We did not pay anything——

64,827. It is here at all events. "[illegible] there, [illegible]"?—Will you say what year that is?

64,828. This is for the year 1896?—Have you the full account, the debit and credit?

64,829. Yes?—I am afraid you have not studied it.

64,830. (Dean Dickinson.) You spend [illegible] on the direct objects of the society, and [illegible] you gave as a donation outside the society?—No, not at all.

64,831. (Mr. Young.) "London Temperance Hospital, [illegible]." Is that correct?—That is money handed to us for the London Temperance Hospital by collections.

64,832. (Mr. Carter.) There is a debit and credit entry for that amount?—Yes.

64,833. It is not paid on your resources at all?—No.

64,834. (Mr. Young.) You hold meetings throughout Ireland?—Yes.

64,835. Are not the same speakers to be found in several places all dotted round the country?—Not always.

64,836. Do not two or three start from Belfast with a [illegible]?—No, we usually go straight on.

64,837. Is the object of this league to find out all the faults and the crimes that have been committed in the country?—Not at all.

64,838. What is the object, then, of the association?—"The object of this society shall be the suppression of drunkenness by moral suasion, legislative prohibition, and all other lawful means."

64,839. Is your object the suppression or the regulation of the trade?—Both, or either, or anything that in our opinion will produce sobriety.

64,840. But is your main object the suppression of the trade?—No, our main object is to make Ireland sober. That is what we are aiming at.

64,841. You do not agitate for the shutting up of breweries and distilleries. If your object is of any use to this Commission, it must be for the regulation of the trade. Do you come here to make any suggestions for the better regulation of the trade?—I leave it to the Commissioners whether I have or not. It is for you to judge. I have tried, but I may not have been able to do it.

64,842. Not my your object is to crush the trade?—Excuse me, I did not say anything of the kind.

64,843. Are you dissatisfied with everything connected with the liquor trade? Are you satisfied with any of the rules or regulations by which the trade is conducted?—As long as the trade is to be continued I am quite satisfied that the licensing of it should be in the hands of the [illegible] in Belfast and the [illegible], and in the hands of the county court judges throughout the rest of Ireland.

64,844. You want a change in that land [illegible] clause?—Yes. I think everybody owns that he is a bona fide [illegible].

64,845. You want the refreshment rooms of the railway stations closed, except when trains go out and come in?—That is the law at present.

64,846. No, they are open all day?—No.

Mr. W. Wilkinson.

Railway [illegible]

64,347. Then you do not want any alteration?—I do not see why they ought to be open at all.

64,348. You want, then, to close the refreshment rooms?—I think they might be closed with very great advantage.

64,349. (*Chairman.*) I thought you told us that apart from the fact that a great number of people come in, took a 3d. ticket, or whatever it was, and then availed themselves of the advantages of the refreshment rooms provided by the railway company?—Quite so.

64,350. (*Mr. Young.*) You object also to general tenders, especially if liquor is included. Do you object to grocers, drapers, and whisky?—Yes, all mixed up together.

64,351. I am only pointing out the tremendous number of objections that you have. You object to the mode in which the renewal of licenses is conducted. You say that it is very unfairly in the public?—Yes.

To six householders' certificates.

64,352. You object to the six householders' certificate? —Oh no, I do not.

64,353. (*Chairman.*) On the contrary you wish expressly to sustain them as embodying a principle?—Yes.

64,354. (*Mr. Young.*) Have you not said that these are forged sometimes?—I have said so.

64,355. Did you ever see six householders' names forged to a paper?—No, because we are not allowed to see them.

64,356. You said to his lordship that you knew of forged certificates?—Yes.

64,357. Did you see them?—I did not see them, but the man who gave the names down to the publican one of the signatory, told me that he had done so, and he is a man whose word I would thoroughly credit.

64,358. But it was hearsay?—And I asked the police, and they told me, "Oh yes, it is a common thing; they are often all in the one handwriting." I verified it by asking the police.

64,359. Do not you think that any publican could get six men to give him a certificate?—Not if the names were to be published. Nor can the man swear openly that the house has been conducted in an orderly manner during the previous twelve months.

64,360. And the police say that that is done?—The police do to the best of their ability, but it is impossible for them to get it done. The result would be that in every case where a house had been a great nuisance it would be impossible for him to get two men who would in the same street to sign it and certify that, if those names were to be published. That is, they would not be prepared to certify what was not true, if other people knew they were the parties who had done it.

64,361. It is a reflection on the licensing tribunal, because they ought to examine these papers?—Excuse me, the law says they have nothing to do with that, and they have nothing to do with them whatever.

64,362. The police never see them?—No.

64,363. Who sees them?—The Excise. The certificate is a sheet about this size, and the heading is, of course, in the usual way, and then the six householders sign, and then there is a space for the justice to sign underneath. The superior courts have held that the justices have nothing to do with those six householders, and neither have the police. It is only when the completed forms goes before the Inland Revenue that it is their duty to see that there are six names there, and that they are the justices' names, and that is all, without verifying their correctness at all.

64,364. I am only trying to point out how dissatisfied you are with everything. You say the magistrates do not faithfully perform their duty; they look upon some of their functions not as judicial?—No, I would rather have it put exactly, or as accurately as possible, what I said. In regard to the granting of licenses, I said, they did not look upon it as a judicial act. I think those are the words I used.

64,365. Yes; and you are dissatisfied with the granting of occasional licenses as well?—Yes.

64,366. I suppose you are opposed really to any sort of licenses, are you?—Not at all. As long as the trade is continued it must be regulated;

64,367. You say that you know of tobacco licenses being kept open by licensees for a purpose?—Grocers or wholesale merchants, yes.

Mr. W. Wilkinson.

14 May '96

64,368. You know of that?—Yes.

64,369. In Belfast?—In Belfast. I do not think I ought to mention the houses, but I can do so.

64,370. You object to the practice of canvassing, and you are opposed to grocers' licenses, and you give only one isolated case of the abuse of the grocer's license in a suburban district?—It is typical.

64,371. You say that the publicans object to coffee stands, and you refer to the opposition they made with regard to coffee stands?—Yes.

The League coffee-stands.

64,372. Was it purely and simply because they were coffee stands or because you were only giving to the Corporation a very small sum for them?—Quite so. As I mentioned yesterday, the Corporation or the Improvement Committee said that they would pass a resolution that any other responsible ratepayers could have suitable sites on the same conditions as the Irish Temperance League had them; and one of the deputation objected and, "That is not what we want at all," and then someone said, "What do you want?" "We want them put out of that."

64,373. How much do you pay for your coffee stand?—I understand Alderman Dempsey is coming up, and he knows all about it. He is a member of the Corporation. I may as well tell you that we pay 1s. a year for the ground. We expended upwards of 100*l.* on putting up the building. The building is here (pointing to a photograph).

64,374. Did you ever pay a shilling a year for any one of them?—Yes, I said so at the commencement.

64,375. A shilling a year?—I believe it was one shilling a year at first. A nominal rent was put upon them, because they looked upon it as a philanthropic undertaking, and did not think we would make any money out of it.

64,376. Some of the inhabitants of Belfast thought you ought to pay the rates of the town rather more than one shilling a year?—That is a long time ago.

64,377. You represented here that there was strong opposition to those coffee stands. I want to show that it was not because they were coffee stands, but because you were paying 1s. a year for what probably you should have paid 5*l.* or 6*l.*?—At this time we were not paying only 1s. a year. I have explained that one of the deputation let out the meanness of the opposition by saying they would not be satisfied for other inhabitants to get the same privileges, but they wanted us "out of that."

64,378. There is another thing you object to, the sessional solicitor should not be employed in prosecutions?—Oh, no; he should not be employed in the defence in licensing prosecutions.

64,379. I have only gone over this to show how dissatisfied the teetotallers are with everything. I suppose you admit that you are dissatisfied with everything connected with the trade?—Oh, no.

Sunday closing.

64,380. With regard to Sunday closing, will you allow me to point out that the late Bishop McAlister said: "I would prefer to see the Act of 1878 adopted in "rural districts, but the extension of Sunday closing "to large towns where it is usually accompanied with "shebeening and legally drinking, would not, in my "opinion, tend to promote sobriety or morality"?—Yes. I did not say that he said anything to the contrary of that.

64,381. Is it your opinion that you should interfere so much with the working man as to prevent him from having his drink on Sunday, if he so desired?—

64,382. You will not answer that question. Would you interfere with the working man, if he so desired, having his glass of beer on Sunday?—That is assuming the ordinary working man does want to get it, which we deny.

64,383. To prove he does, there are as many as 40,000 people who use public-houses in Belfast on Sunday?—Yes.

64,384. Would you desire to take away the means of gratifying the legitimate desire to have his beer, wine, or whisky on that day?—We want to have public order and sobriety.

Mr. W. Whitaker.

19 Nov. '98

64,385. You will not answer any questions ?—I believe that the vast majority of the working men and the vast majority of those who are public-house frequenters in the week would prefer that they were closed on Sundays.

64,386. There are more than 20,000 people in Belfast who never go to church, and would it not be more desirable that you should devote your energies to them ?—I do not know that I need answer that.

Sunday and early Saturday closing.

64,387. (Mr. Charles Cameron.) You mentioned that you answered that the feeling in favour of Sunday closing was increasing. That is your belief ?—That is my belief.

64,388. I want to ask you your opinion as to the progress that is being made in connection with Saturday early closing. Is that increasing ?—The feeling throughout Ireland is practically unanimous in favour of Saturday early closing.

64,389. Do you think that the feeling in favour of earlier closing on Saturday is making as much progress as the feeling in favour of Sunday closing ?—I believe so. I think it has rather interfered with the strengthening of opinion in favour of entire Sunday closing, owing to this fact, that the publicans really [illegible] to a compromise, and they say that closing earlier on Saturday night would really produce better results, and, as Mr. Young has indicated, send more people to church on Sundays than closing entirely on Sundays would do.

64,390. You think the opinion in favour of early Saturday closing is, in fact, outstripping the opinion in favour of Sunday closing ?—I scarcely say yet. There is one point that I have been asked to mention which I have not done, and that is that the Theatres Licensing Act of 5 and 6 William IV., c. 38, is really not applicable to anywhere but Dublin. I think that there should be some other form made applicable to the whole of Ireland, so that theatres and music halls could take out a licence suitable for them, rather than be compelled to take out a publican's licence. Then I should like to hand in a Bill which was prepared by the late Mr. Biggar in the year 1883, immediately before his death, and which he introduced into the House of Commons as a result of the Commission of Inquiry in 1888, in which he proposed that the hours of opening should be from 8 o'clock in the morning to 9 o'clock at night throughout the whole week.

Mr. W. Whitaker.

License, theatres, and music halls.

64,391. (Mr. Walker.) Was there any division taken on that Bill ?—Unfortunately, Mr. Biggar died before the day came for the second reading, and when it was brought up by Mr. Leamy, in his place, it was talked out.

64,392. (Chairman.) What were the names at the back of the Bill ?—Mr. Biggar, Mr. Jordan, Mr. Arthur O'Connor, Mr. Leamy, and Mr. [illegible].

The witness withdrew.

Mr. Daniel L. Boyle called in and examined.

Mr. D. L. Boyle.

Position of witness.

64,393. (Chairman.) You are a member of the Dublin Corporation ?—Yes.

64,394. And are Chairman of the Dublin Licensed Grocers and Vintners Protection Association ?—Yes.

64,395. And you are otherwise connected with associations on behalf of the liquor trade ?—I am on the executive body of the Central Committee of the Liquor Trade of Ireland.

64,396. The larger body to which you belong deals with public questions which effect, or may be held to affect your trade ?—Yes.

64,397. What is the Central Committee of your association, how is it composed ?—The Central Committee is an organisation to which is affiliated all organisations belonging to the licensed trade throughout the country.

Tied houses in Dublin.

64,398. Taking the licensed houses in Dublin what number are tied and what are free ?—I think as far as I know we have not more than two tied houses in the sense in which it is understood in England ?—There are perhaps 20 partially tied, that is, tied through loans, to brewers.

64,399. In the case of those which are partially tied to brewers in consequence of a loan, are they obliged to get their liquor from that brewer ?—Sometimes altogether. And in some cases a certain quantity.

64,400. Would you say that the tied house system was increasing or not ?—I should say decreasing, because the firm of Guinness does the very great proportion of the trade in Dublin, and they have got out of the tied-house system altogether. They have not a single tied house.

64,401. And there is no attempt of any other great brewery companies competing with them and tying the houses ?—There is no sign of that.

64,402. (Mr. Fenwick.) Is that because money is less difficult to get in Dublin for the purpose ?—The money can be obtained in other ways in Ireland. I think that is the principal reason.

64,403. From banks ?—Yes.

64,404. Because there is a security in the licence that is not supposed to exist here ?—Yes, we are protected by the Callinan case, and the banks lend on the security.

64,405. (Chairman.) Do the distilleries own any houses ?—I do not know of any instance of a distillery owning a house in Dublin or about Dublin.

64,406. There are no houses under pecuniary obligations to distillers in Dublin ?—I do not know of any. It must be to a small extent, or I should be aware of it.

64,407. Has the number of retail licensed houses in Dublin increased or decreased of late years ?—Slightly decreased, I should say. The present Recorder, when anyone is asking for any increased facilities, such as extension from six to seven day licences, makes it a condition that some other licence must be cancelled; that is, a person asking for some of these facilities must buy up licensed premises elsewhere, usually at the back places in the city, where he considers it is not desirable to have public-houses.

Mr. D. L. Boyle.

Not licenses granted by Recorder.

64,408. Speaking as the representative of your trade do you object to that system of surrender ?—No. On the contrary I think that has increased the respectability of our trade. It has brought these houses out of objectionable places into an important open street where they are constantly under police supervision and the supervision of the general public.

64,409. You would be in favour of the reduction of the small and less respectable houses and merging them and setting up if necessary a better public-house with a full licence in another part of the town ?—I see no reason to be opposed to it. Also in the case of extensions where premises are small and are considered too small for the custom they get, in some cases there is an alteration granted and the Recorder requires a licence to be cancelled. I think there are some houses in Dublin where there have been as many as three or four licences given up in order to get additional facilities.

64,410. The value of public-house property, I gather has increased of late years ?—Yes, considerably. I think 150 per cent., that is in 20 years at all events.

Increase in value of licensed property.

64,411. Have there been any causes which have specially brought about that increase in value ?—Yes, I should say the decision in the Callinan case in 1877 or 1878. From that time the value of property has been constantly on the increase. And there was a further impetus given to it by the case of Smith v. The Justices of Cavan. The reason, I think that the prices have gone up is, that the facilities for borrowing are much greater; the banks look on it more in the nature of a commercial transaction to lend money on licensed property in Ireland.

64,412. You hold that the Legislature has recognised a vested interest in their property ?—I wish to state that public money has been lent on that security. That is the security of the bankers.

64,413. It has been lent on the security of these public-houses, which have increased in value in consequence of this recognition by the Legislature of a vested interest in these houses. Would that be your view ?—Yes, that is my view.

64,414. Does the Recorder ever enquire into the money interest of the money position of the applicant for the licence ?—Yes, he usually inquires into it.

Financial position of applicant.

Mr. R. L. Burge. 23 May '98

64,415. Do you object to that proceeding on the part of the Recorder?—We have not objected to it until he has come to refuse a licence very recently owing to the amount of money that the party taking the licence had in his own right, of his own property.

64,416. Then, I presume, you would be against the court, whatever it might be, [illegible] by the money [illegible], which would put [illegible] the [illegible] between the applicant and the brewer, or the distiller, or whoever it might be?—We do not admit the right of the Recorder to interfere in that matter.

64,417. Supposing the Recorder had the view that it was necessary in the public interest that houses should be free, and that the ostensible licensee should be the owner of the house, and in the course of carrying out that principle he inquired into these relations, would you think he was straining his power?—

64,418. Supposing the Recorder thought it was contrary to public policy that there should be what might appear to him [illegible]—I do not mean it in an offensive sense, of course—relations between the ostensible licensee and a large brewer, and he thought he was entitled to inquire into their money relations, should you think he was acting beyond his power?—I do not refer to the case of brewers because they are gone with us, but in the case of bankers we strongly object to it.

64,419. You think there is no right in a public officer to inquire into who is supplying the money?—I am entitled to put the opinion of the late Attorney-General, who is recognised to be perhaps the principal authority on licensing matters in Dublin, The MacDermott, Q.C. It was to the effect that the Recorder had no right in the particular case to do so, because the applicant had [illegible] of his own money, and he was [illegible] the law too much with reference to the [illegible] of the applicant. It was on the ground of the [illegible] of the applicant that the licence was refused, and he looked at it as a matter of unfitness that this applicant should only have [illegible] of his own.

64,420. Will you give us the opinion?—Yes. I will read it to your Lordship. "I do doubt the decision of "the Recorder in the case of Thomas Henley to a lot "[illegible] and [illegible] [illegible], [illegible] the [illegible] of "the Vintners Association. In my opinion the "Recorder's view was wrong in point of law. I am of "opinion that the unfitness mentioned in section 4, "5 & 6 William IV., does not include such considerations as the [illegible], or prudence or imprudence, of "the applicant in borrowing from a bank. That a "bank trusts and keeps him shows he is a person of "credit. His [illegible] to the bank gave him a real "and strong interest in [illegible] the licensed house "a success, and it is difficult to see why or how a line "can be drawn between that, or [illegible] as a collection of "'Sharers.'"

64,421. Supposing the Recorder found that this is [illegible] [illegible] this house so hampered with debt that it is impossible he can discharge his duty to the public, that he will force the sale and resort to illicit practices for the purpose of paying off this heavy debt that hangs round his neck, would you think that was a wrong thing on the part of the Recorder?—In that case he would be backed by the opinion of the bankers that they thought it was a sound commercial transaction or they would not lend their money, and it is lent at a fair [illegible] rate of interest, not an exorbitant interest.

64,422. Supposing it was a brewer who lent the money and whose object was to push the sale of his own goods?—I do not know about the case of the brewer.

64,423. (Dean Dickinson.) That opinion of the Attorney-General was not an official opinion of the publican had permitted drunkenness?—Yes, it would be very hard, because he might have got it without being observed by the assistant or the proprietor. We have had instances in Ireland where publicans have been convicted where there was no proof whatever that the man had been supplied with drink, and where the publican and the people in the shop and the assistants swore he had not.

64,427. I suppose as a matter of fact, it is generally the other way, that in proportion to the vast number of [illegible] for drunkenness there are very few instances of the conviction of the publican for serving a drunken man with drink when he must have done it?—It is not for the want of strict supervision in Dublin. The other [illegible] night an Inspector and a sergeant visited my house at [illegible] minutes to 11 and walked all through it, also on the previous Saturday night. This is not at all exceptional. It is equally so with my neighbours. So that I say on that ground it is impossible we can be spreading drunkenness where this strict supervision goes on.

Police watchings to publicans.

64,428. I complain side by side with that strict supervision there is [illegible] [illegible] [illegible] by the police on behalf of the publican, and in this way that if a constable sees a drunken man enter a house he would think it his duty to go and warn the publican that the man who had gone in was drunk?—I have never known it to be done, but I have known cases to the contrary where the policeman has followed a drunken man and on his own evidence waited outside till such time that he would be likely to have obtained drink, and then he went in and prosecuted and got the publican fined. We complain that that state of affairs should exist, because we believe it is the duty of the police to protect the publican.

64,429. Do you say the constable saw the man go in drunk, then he waited till he came out in the same condition and then swore that his drunkenness was caused by the serving of drink to that drunken man by the publican?—That is so. In different parts of Ireland it has occurred, notably in Cork. I have here the report of a case at which it says: "Constable McHugo "deposed he saw three persons enter defendant's "premises, several one man drunk, but waited for the "lapse of some minutes till he thought the man would "be supplied with drink. On cross-examination he "admitted that he did not think it was his duty to go "in and warn the barmaid not to give him drink, "though he could easily have done so; fined 10s. and "costs; not to be recorded."

64,430. (Dean Dickinson.) How long did this drunken man remain inside the publichouse?—I am not aware.

64,431. Long enough to be discovered by the publican if he was wide awake?—I am not aware.

64,432. (Chairman.) The publican was fined 10s.?—Yes.

64,433. Was there any evidence besides that of the policeman?—I do not think so. Then there was another case in Cork: "Acting-Sergeant Madden deposed to "seeing three persons enter defendant's house, one "of whom was drunk. He waited till he thought they "would be supplied, then went in and found a drink "in front of the drunken man. On cross-examination "he thought it was not his duty to go in and warn the "publican not to supply this person. Head constable "Smith then remarked that if such a rule were observed "by the police, they would be told that they were "interfering with the publican's business. Fined on "[illegible] November 1897, and fined 1l. and costs. Not to "be recorded."

64,434. (Mr. Whitaker.) It amounts that the publican

Mr. D. L. Bergin.

13 May '98.

Shebeens in Dublin.

and put into barracks unoccupied?—That is so, and it is a very great hardship.

64,437 (Chairman) Are there many shebeens in Dublin?—Yes there is one division in which they are very numerous—in the C Division of police and it is in this division that the drunkenness is greatest.

64,438 What about the public-houses there?—The public-houses are much less in comparison with the other police divisions.

64,439 Do I understand you to account for the existence of these shebeens by the comparative fewness of the public-houses in the C division?—The C division is peculiarly situated at present with regard to the other divisions. It is the worst division of the city. The A division, a few years ago, was very bad, but the corporation have been working in that division to a great extent to provide better houses for the poor. They have cleared out three or four areas that were considered very bad slums, and in place of those at present there are some very good dwellings erected. I know of one instance where there was [illegible] Meath Street a place called Crab Alley, full of thieves and vagabonds of every kind. Where that was now stands Grey Square, a very fine square, and called after one of our most respected citizens.

64,440. In that C division, should you say that the number of licensed houses that now exist are inadequate to the legitimate supply of the population?—I do not really know. It goes to show that the public-houses are not responsible for the vice and drunkenness that exists in that particular division.

64,441. What I want to know is whether you think the number is so small that shebeens have been created by the paucity of the legitimate public-houses?—No. I should say that it is principally on account of the poorer people living there, and the worst houses of the people being in this particular locality. It is in this particular division that the corporation have not yet come to operate with the scheme of providing better houses.

64,442 So that the police will ultimately deal with these shebeens?—They seem to be doing their best, but they do not have a very good effect.

Penalties for shebeening.

64,443. Would you increase the strength of the law in the case of shebeens?—I think it would be well that in many cases there should not be any option of a fine, for the accused escapes at any rate.

64,444. Would you increase the presumption of law against persons found in the shebeen where there was evidence that illicit sale or illicit consumption had been going on?—I would rather deal with the shebeen-keepers. These people keep the shebeens in rooms. They have so many of them, and when a fine is imposed they are very often gone away before it can be enforced.

64,445. Would the shebeens of which you speak in the C Division manufacture illicit whisky on the premises, or would they only sell whisky which had been made elsewhere?—I do not suggest any illicit manufacture.

64,446 Only the sale of whisky that has not paid duty?—No, I do not think so.

64,447. Only selling without a licence?—Yes.

64,448. The whisky would not be illicitly made?—Of course it would be the very cheap whisky. These people buy the cheapest they can get, and for that reason it is not good. There is nothing too cheap or inferior for these places.

64,449 It would be in the wild and mountainous districts where shebeening would exist for the manufacture of whisky? It would be most likely to find its way into such places.

64,450. It would find its way into the towns?—It would be more likely to find its way into unlicensed places.

64,451. That is what made me ask whether the whisky had paid duty?—In Dublin, I should say, it has.

64,452. The obverse infringement of the law is the selling without a licence?—Yes, entirely so, I think.

Sunday closing.

64,453. Would you be in favour of total Sunday closing?—No. My own opinion, of course, is, that I would not favour Sunday closing, and I would like to say also, that so far as the public opinion of the city can be taken, as far as there are any means of taking public opinion, it goes to show that the men who use public-houses in Dublin are nearly altogether against it.

64,454 Would you say there was any feeling amongst the publicans themselves, we have heard there is, that they would not greatly close their houses, but that it would be a great relief to them?—I have never heard such a suggestion at all. There may be one strange person in every section of the community.

64,455. You do not know such a strange thing as a publican who is in favour of closing his public-house on a Sunday?—I do not know the man. There may be such a man, but he is a curiosity.

Early Saturday closing.

64,456. Would he be an equally rare person who would be in favour of earlier Saturday closing?—Certainly.

64,457. The trade generally, so far as you are able to speak for it, would be against any extension of Sunday closing and against earlier Saturday closing?—Certainly.

The bona fide traveller.

64,458. Would they wish to repeal the existing Sunday closing as it applies to Ireland?—In the event of any further change in the law with reference to the bona fide traveller, they would think it very desirable in some country districts that public-houses should be open for two or three hours, because I believe that if the limit distance that at present applies to the bona fide traveller were extended we should have a greater increase of illicit drinking in the city.

64,459. You have a belief in the honesty generally speaking of the bona fide traveller?—Well there is a good deal to be said on both sides I may say.

64,460. What was in my mind is what a previous witness stated, that he was a "bona fide humbug"?—That is not always the case. I would not go so far as to say that.

64,461. There will be a large percentage of people who [illegible] represent themselves as bona fide travellers?—It is very hard to say who is a bona fide traveller. It is reasonable when a man is walking on a Sunday if he takes in a circle of six or seven miles, that half way on his journey he should be entitled to take a drink.

64,462. Speaking as the representative of your trade, would you like to see the limit extended?—No, I should say not.

64,463. You would like to see the three mile limit preserved?—Yes. I think that any extension of the three miles will be followed by much more illicit drinking, unless as I state the public-houses are open for two or three hours on Sunday.

Clubs.

64,464 We have had evidence, I think, that there are several clubs in Dublin of a doubtful character?—Yes, there are. Mr. Mallon stated that there are at least 12, and I should say there are more. These clubs that you speak of are only open when the public-houses are closed. In the winter time for instance, on Sunday nights, the gas is not lit in them till after 7 o'clock. I think that goes to show that although they may be able to keep within the law, with reference to their rules and regulations, it is entirely a drinking club they are open and for the purpose of defeating the law.

64,465. Have they sprung up within the last few years?—Within the last 15 years. They were unknown in the city before the Sunday Closing Act—completely unknown.

64,466. Did they spring up immediately after the passing of that Act? No, they sprang up gradually. It appears the people did not quite understand their powers exactly as the establishment of these clubs, and they also became more numerous when they were threatened with complete Sunday closing.

64,467. Then speaking as the representative again of your trade you would object to these houses as being practically public-houses without restrictions of a public licence imposed on them?—They are carried on entirely as drinking places at the present time. I think they should not be allowed to be carried on without the other elements that belong to a club, such as proper furniture and reading rooms, and such things as that.

64,468. Would you reduce them to the same status as the public-houses and license them?—No, I would not say so. I would say that there should be registration, and that the police should have the means of obtaining a right of entry by application to a magistrate.

64,469. They have that now?—Yes. The police know very well when a club is being carried on illegally, but they are liable to keep within the law by going through [illegible] certain forms, and they are carried on entirely for the purpose of drinking.

64,470. In those clubs which are open during the closed hours of the public-houses is there any sale off the premises?—Not to any great extent I would say.

64,471. Is there any consumption off—is the liquor carried off?—Not to any extent, I should think.

64,472. To some extent?—Yes. The complaint is that the evil of them is that they have the means of [illegible] the same as a public-house is. They are not under the [illegible] that we are, and anyone going into these places can [illegible] there and get drunk, whereas they cannot get drunk in a public-house under the strict supervision that we are subject to.

64,473. You say that the increase in clubs and these [illegible] has been of a [illegible] marked character during the last [illegible] years?—Yes.

64,474. What class of clubs are they. What class of society frequents them—the working classes, or those of a superior social standing?—The working classes—[illegible] principally, I would say.

64,475. I suppose in the actual City of Dublin there is no such thing as a *bona fide* traveller traffic?—Not [illegible] the limits of the city.

64,476. If an offence is committed and a so-called *bona fide* traveller is convicted of misrepresentation is he alone punished, or does the publican ever come in for punishment?—In [illegible] and altogether [illegible] it has been the publican that has been punished, no matter what precautions he has taken to find out whether a man was a *bona fide* traveller or not, and even in cases where the *bona fide* traveller has admitted he deceived the publican the publican has been fined [illegible].

64,477. I suppose it would turn on the question whether the publican ought to have been deceived?—The man was asked where he slept the night before and he said he slept in a certain street in Dublin, whereas the man was a native of Kingstown, [illegible] miles from where this public-house was, in Blackrock. He stated he slept [illegible] in Dublin. It would be a [illegible] thing to state that the publican could not have had any knowledge of where he lived.

64,478. Notwithstanding that, the publican was fined?—Yes.

64,479. What amount?—[illegible]

64,480. What was the traveller fined?—I am not sure that the traveller was fined at all. He stated that he lived at [illegible] Street, Dublin, and stated the [illegible] to the police officer, and swore that he wilfully deceived Mr. Murphy, the publican, when before the magistrate, and, notwithstanding that, Mr. Murphy was fined [illegible].

64,481. And the traveller escaped?—My information does not [illegible].

64,482. He could hardly have escaped, would he?—They have very often escaped till recently. Recently the magistrates have taken notice with the travellers [illegible] than they did before.

64,483. What is the usual fine imposed on the [illegible]?—[illegible]. We think it should be much more.

64,484. What would be your view about the mixed trade about which we have heard so much, that is publicans carrying on other trades in the public-houses?—[illegible] of the trade of Dublin is a mixed trade. Nearly all the public-houses in Dublin sell groceries—there are a few that do not. Except only in the centre of the city they all sell groceries as well as drink.

64,485. You would not, as representative of the trade be in favour of separating the trades?—It would be a very great hardship on the trade. It would upset the whole [illegible] of the trade in the city of Dublin, and the people are brought up to this class of trading. They give their orders for groceries and drink all at the same time.

64,486. Would you defend the mixture of the trades on the ground that the liquor business itself was not remunerative?—No, I would not say that. In country places one of these trades would not be self-supporting. In Dublin it would be self-supporting.

64,487. Would it be too much to say that in cases where the mixed trades are carried on, the liquor trade could not stand by itself, and the grocery, and [illegible] trade could not stand by itself, but the combination of the two enables the man to get a living?—That is so in many cases. In a city like Dublin each would certainly be self-supporting.

64,488. Turning to the administration of the law, are you satisfied with the way in which it is administered?—I think there is general satisfaction in the city of Dublin.

64,489. Satisfaction with the sole jurisdiction by the Recorder?—I should be wrong if I said that they were not satisfied with the jurisdiction of the Recorder in the city of Dublin, but there is principally wrong to the decision in the [illegible] case. The Recorder seemed to be inclined to interpret the law against the interests of the licensed trade previous to the decision in the [illegible] case.

64,490. Should you like to see the sole jurisdiction exercised by the Recorder within the city extended to the county court judge outside the city?—There is a great difference of opinion, even amongst the members of the trade.

64,491. Should you say that the desire is at all general to see the administration of the licensing law in the hands of a county court judge?—The view is not at all that it should be.

64,492. You do not agree with the opinion that has been expressed that in a great number of cases the magistrates do not act in a judicial spirit, but act both either and not [illegible]?—I think they have acted very fairly, and in that respect I should be supported by my experience as a member of the executive of the [illegible] Committee. When we receive complaints from country traders we submit to them a form of statutory declaration which they sign before a magistrate, asking them test questions as to the *bona fides* of the case they ask us to defend, and when we find that it is a case of harsh or harassing prosecution or of a frivolous nature we defend these people, and in [illegible] per cent. of these cases we have been successful.

64,493. I do not quite follow that. In those cases do the magistrates inform the trade?—No, we ask the trader to make a statutory declaration of his case, and I can submit a copy of it to the Commission, ([illegible]). The questions that are asked to test the *bona fides* of the applicant are on one side, and then it is declared before the magistrate to be true.

64,494. That is issued by the trade?—Yes.

64,495. This is with the design of ascertaining whether it is a case that your association for trade protection should take up?—Yes.

64,496. You say you are very particular in examining the case beforehand, and getting answers to all these questions before you embark on the defence of the case before the magistrates?—Yes, but we have taken up a great number of these cases—I daresay thousands—and in [illegible] per cent. of the cases we have been successful, which shows that the complaints must be coming with considerable [illegible]. We have legal advice before we send men to defend these cases.

64,497. I do not quite see it. Because the magistrates have decided in your favour in a large percentage of cases which you have defended, therefore you say the magistrates are impartial?—Because we have had legal advice before we have undertaken to defend them.

64,498. (Mr. [illegible].) You say that it is because you have taken such care to see that the case had a *bona fide* defence, and great care not to defend a man who has been breaking the law wilfully, and the evidence is such as to prove your contention?—Yes, and we have in all these cases had legal advice before we took steps, and as I say in [illegible] per cent. of the cases we have been successful.

64,499. (Chairman.) Do I understand that the statement and the answers to the questions which you have referred to a statutory declaration made under the Statutory Declarations Act, and signed by a magistrate?—Yes, that the statement made by the applicant for assistance is true.

64,500. That statutory declaration has to be signed and attested by a magistrate?—Yes. That is for our guidance, to show that we are not going into the business to take up any frivolous cases.

64,501. This statutory declaration is not attested by the magistrate who ultimately hears the case?—Not necessarily, any magistrate. He merely asks if the declaration is true. It is declared before a magistrate.

Mr. D. L. Sharpe.

19 May '99

64,502. It is only a statement by the magistrate that this man has made this affidavit before him?—Yes.

64,503. It does not imply that the magistrate thinks the statement is true?—No.

64,504. What I asked you was, whether the magistrate who signs this attestation of the declaration having been made, can not know the man?—No, it is merely an attestation, that the man believes the statement to be true.

Vexatious prosecutions of publicans.

64,505. He may be on the Bench of course?—He may be. There there is a great complaint in country districts that the publicans are summoned a long distance away, and very often when they arrive there is only one magistrate to hear the case, and they are put to two days' legal expenses for going there again; also the magistrate in many instances is not turned till the day previous to the petty sessions sitting. That is a great hardship as the man have not got the opportunity of making their defence.

64,506. In a very great number of those cases you undertake to defend. In your conversations of opinion that the prosecutions are of a harassing and vexatious character?—That is so.

64,507. By whom?—We find that the police in the country districts take a dismissal very badly, and are likely to follow up such a publican. Upon having obtained a dismissal they like to follow them up in a rather vexatious way.

64,508. They do not like to be beaten?—They take a beating very badly.

64,509. Supposing the summons is dismissed and the case held to be frivolous, are there any costs given?—No, it is dismissed without costs, and that is thought to be a great hardship, and is a great cause of complaint.

64,510. In the case of summonses against licensed traders, by whom are the summonses issued?—In the Dublin district they are not issued until they have been ordered by the Commissioner or Assistant Commissioner of Police. In many instances in the country places they are issued by the sergeant of police, and the number of frivolous cases that have been repeatedly brought before us goes to show that there is not a wise discretion exercised in the issuing of these summonses.

64,511. You do not make any complaint in Dublin against the Commissioner or Assistant Commissioner of Police?—No, it is in the country districts where it is in the hands of the constabulary.

64,512. The Commissioner or his subordinate makes a careful investigation into the case, but a police sergeant prosecutes in the country districts?—Yes, where the constabulary are in authority.

64,513. Then you think that the magisterial action removes any evil that you see in that system, or do you wish to see any reform introduced?—No, I do not know that there is any reform necessary with reference to that.

64,514. You are satisfied with the action of the magistrates in dismissing frivolous cases?—Yes, but we believe that many of these cases would not go so far as the magistrates at all if there were careful supervision on the part of the constabulary.

64,515. That is what made me ask you where you would locate your reform?—We think that the district inspector should have supervision of these summonses before they are issued in every case, as in Dublin such supervision is exercised by the Chief Commissioner or Assistant Commissioner.

64,516. In the country districts does it rest with the constable himself to take out the summons or not?—In many instances we think that the frequency with which these frivolous prosecutions take place goes to show that the supervision is not careful.

64,517. Are you sure that the district inspector in the country districts does not have control over the issuing of summonses and the institution of proceedings?—If he does it must be in a very loose way. It would not be possible they would allow so many frivolous cases.

64,518. You have admitted that the inspector in Dublin exercises very careful supervision?—That is so.

64,519. But if the inspector there does have (as I believe he has) control over the issuing of these summonses, you think in the country he exercises very small supervision?—I think so. It seemed to us, because there are no complaints of frivolous prosecutions in the city of Dublin as compared with the country districts.

Mr. D. L. Sharpe.

No loss of licences through inefficient management.

64,520. Before we come to spirit grocers, is there anything I have passed over you would wish to state?—I would like to mention with reference to the reduction of licences that in 44 years' experience I have not known a single licence to be taken away owing to the misconduct of the trader in the city of Dublin. There has been no reduction of licences on that ground.

64,521. Is that owing to the care having been exercised before the these endorsements have been made?—No, I have never known any one have to remove on that ground either.

64,522. You have never known these endorsements made on the licence?—I do not think I have.

64,523. (Mr. Whitaker.) Do you mean us to gather from that that the publicans of Dublin have, during that period, been model men?—That they have conducted their licences well.

64,524. (Chairman.) There must have been a great number of objections?—I mean the losing of a licence, not the transfer. I have never known a licence to be transferred because the Recorder went in ... on account of the number of records on the licence to ... the law.

64,525. Have you known a tenant to be removed from a house where there was a prosecution hanging over him?—I have not known any such case in the city of Dublin.

Spirit grocers.

64,526. Then, turning to the question of the spirit grocers, do you think the administration of the law as regards the spirit grocer should be put on the same footing as the law with reference to other retailers?—I think they should have the same form of application as publicans—that they should give due notice of their application.

64,527. Would you give discretionary power to the magistrates in the case of the spirit grocers' licences, the same as with reference to publicans?—Yes. I should like to see the law assimilated, that is, with reference to future licences. Any change in the law should not affect licences already licensed.

Illegal drinking ... spirit grocers.

64,528. Do you think there is any prevalent idea in Dublin that a great many illicitly conducted spirit grocers exist?—Yes, there are a considerable number that badly conducted in that way; they sell drink on the premises. I must not be taken as stating that there are not very respectable spirit grocers in the city of Dublin that do not do anything of the kind, but their licences are held under similar conditions to those who do trade illicitly.

64,529. Would you be of opinion that some of these spirit grocers' licences are taken out by people solely for the purpose of illicit sale?—I believe in many instances they could not support themselves without that trade.

64,530. What does the licence say on the face of it as to their selling? Does it compel them to sell in open vessels?—I do not know that it compels them to sell in open vessels, but they do sell in open vessels.

Sale only in closed vessels.

64,531. There is no condition on the licence that they shall sell in open vessels?—I am not able to say.

64,532. But the respectable spirit grocer does not sell in open vessels?—No, he does not, and I think if that were made the law generally, the illicit trading would very soon die out.

64,533. Your remedy would be that they should sell in closed vessels, and sell not less than a certain quantity. Would you say half a pint or a pint?—Half a pint would be sufficient to put an end to the illicit trading.

64,534. Do these shops keep taps?—Yes, every facility for drinking on the premises.

64,535. A bar?—A bar and taps.

64,536. In the spirit grocer's?—In the spirit grocer's.

64,537. How do you differentiate them from an ordinary public-house?—By their writing over the door in small letters the word "at" and the word "off." That represents the only difference, but to the passer by there is no difference whatever.

Wholesale beer dealers.

64,538. In the case of the wholesale beer dealer's licence, I understand that these are granted only at the

Mr. D. A. Boyd.

[illegible] licensing sessions. Is that so?—That is so, and it is considered a hardship in the case of [illegible] a chance to apply if they cannot obtain an ordinary [illegible] license to sell beer to eat.

64,[illegible]. You would be in favour of the license being granted by the excise authorities in those cases without any intervention of the magistrates?—Yes, in the same way that spirit dealers licenses are now granted.

64,[illegible]. (Mr. Grimsby.) I believe you wish to state that there can be no cause of complaint against the quality of the liquor kept for sale in Dublin?—I believe [illegible]. The liquor sold in the public houses in Dublin is chiefly manufactured in Dublin and it is recognised to be of a very high quality. Nearly all the porter sold in Dublin is manufactured by Guinness.

64,[illegible]. You would like also to say that the houses in Dublin, in your experience, are well conducted?—Yes, I believe so.

64,[illegible]. Any [illegible] conducted house would receive sympathy or assistance from the respectable members of the trade?—No, nor from any of the public.

64,[illegible]. On the point of Sunday closing, I believe you wish to refer to a return which was made to the House of Commons; would you tell us what it shows?—It shows that one in every [illegible] is all that is arrested as representing the drunkenness in the [illegible] cities in Ireland on Sundays, and that is a very small number.

64,[illegible]. The proportion is very small?—Yes.

64,[illegible]. In places which comprise a population of [illegible] there was only one person in every [illegible] that was arrested for Sunday drunkenness?—Yes.

64,[illegible]. With reference to the spirit grocers, I take it your evidence is this, that where a license is in proper hands and conducted as the original [illegible] was, there is no ground of complaint?—They are most respectable houses. There is never any complaint against them for breaches of the law.

64,547. A good deal of the complaint with reference to drinking on the premises arises from a special condition of the license, the being able to sell in open vessels?—I should say so.

64,[illegible]. So far as your part of the trade is concerned, you would like to see that altered, and that the sale should be in closed vessels, limiting the quantity to half a pint?—Yes. I believe that would prevent any illicit drinking going on in those houses.

64,[illegible]. With those changes, you are aware of no objection to the spirit grocers' licenses, so far as the Dublin trade is concerned?—Except that I should like to see the conditions of applying for those licenses [illegible].

64,[illegible]. (Mr. Roby Smith.) I suppose the society you represent have come merely for the legitimate [illegible] of your trade interest?—It is entirely a protection [illegible].

64,[illegible]. You are in no way a political organisation?—No. We never allow politics to be discussed, no matter how [illegible], at any of our meetings.

64,[illegible]. It is fair to say that your members have no wish to evade their responsibilities in any way, but [illegible] to conduct their business in every way in conformity with the law?—That is the general desire and the [illegible] in our business also.

64,[illegible]. You have already told us that you do not give any [illegible] to the [illegible] of a licensee who has wilfully [illegible] the law?—No. We are very careful not to give assistance to any one who does wilfully break the law, and I think I am right in stating that the Recorder of Dublin complimented us on that when giving evidence here.

64,[illegible]. Am I right in saying that, as proof of that, nine out of every ten cases you have taken up you have won?—Yes, all over the country.

64,[illegible]. It has often been suggested that if a customer enters a licensed house and orders a [illegible] beverage the proprietor receives him with less favour than if he orders a glass of spirits or a [illegible] of beer. Is that your opinion?—I think the contrary would be the case. We have more profit on mineral waters than on whisky or beer.

64,[illegible]. There is no foundation for the suggestion that pressure is put upon anyone to take alcoholic drink against their will?—I have never known it to be done, but I have often known the contrary.

64,[illegible]. In fact I may say that yours is a business establishment, and you do not mind what you sell so long as the transaction leaves a profit?—Provided it is properly sold, for the proper conduct of the house.

64,[illegible]. You simply supply the public with what they require?—That is so.

64,[illegible]. (Mr. Whitelaw.) With reference to the point of the good conduct of the trade, I suppose you are aware that [illegible] convictions were obtained against licensed persons in Dublin last year?—If you say so, I dare say it is right.

64,[illegible]. And there are about [illegible] licensed persons in Dublin?—Not so many in the city proper. The police district is very different.

64,[illegible]. That means 1 in [illegible] were convicted for breaches of the law last year?—It is hardly fair to take it in the way of considering the ordinary licensed house. Many of these convictions have arisen over the *bona fide* traveller question. The Dublin police district embraces nearly all the area affected by the *bona fide* traveller.

64,[illegible]. Still there were [illegible] convictions?—As I state, many of them—in fact, I should be inclined to say the great majority of them—arose from the dispute over the *bona fide* traveller point.

64,[illegible]. Still there is the fact. How many persons connected with the trade have you on the Dublin Corporation?—At a rough guess, I should say about 14 out of 60.

64,[illegible]. (Dean Dickinson.) [illegible]?—I should deny that.

64,[illegible]. (Mr. Whitelaw.) Should I be wrong in saying there are [illegible]?—I should say so.

64,[illegible]. I have got the names of [illegible] before me?—[illegible] license holders?

64,[illegible]. No, connected with the trade?—I do not know where you would carry what you say connected with the trade.

64,[illegible]. I have four aldermen?—Would you read me the names.

64,570. Burke, Mulligan, O'Reilly, and [illegible]?—These are four publicans.

64,571. These are aldermen. Then I have the councillors. First of all, [illegible]?—He is not a publican.

64,572. He is connected with the trade?—A spirit grocer.

64,573. Then, John P. Smyth?—A publican.

64,574. Doyle?—Yes.

64,575. [illegible]?—Yes.

64,576. O'Reilly?—No, he is not a publican.

64,577. He is connected with the trade?—Yes.

64,578. [illegible] Smyth?—He is a family grocer, not a publican.

64,579. (Dean Dickinson.) He has a publican's license?—He does not sell drink as a publican. This is the first time I was aware he had a publican's license.

64,580. He has a publican's license over the door?—Unless you had read it you would not know it.

64,581. (Mr. Whitelaw.) Then, Phillip [illegible]?—A publican.

64,582. Daniel Tallon, Lord Mayor?—Yes.

64,583. Robert [illegible]?—Not a publican.

64,584. Connected with the trade?—An hotel proprietor, or he is connected with an hotel—a large confectioner and wine merchant.

64,585. Then, William Ireland?—Not a publican, but connected with the trade.

64,586. (Chairman.) Are these members of the Corporation?—All members of the Corporation.

64,587. What is the total number of the Corporation?—60.

64,588. And [illegible] of these are in the trade?—Only 14

Mr. D. A. Boyd.

10 May '98.

Bona fide traffic.

Quality of liquor sold in Dublin.

Sunday closing.

Spirit grocers.

Treating.

Convictions against licensed persons.

Dublin Corporation and the liquor trade.

Mr. D. L. Boyle.

18 May '98.

64,590. (Mr. M'Mahon.) I am reading you the names and you have admitted them so far?—I thought you wanted to make out they were publicans.

64,591. They are in the liquor trade?—Some of those men differ from the publicans on many trade questions.

64,592. Still they are in the liquor trade?—Yes.

Dublin Corporation and the liquor trade.

64,593. My point is this, that is an enormous proportion as compared with the number of people in the trade in Dublin on the Corporation, is it not?—I do not know that it is.

64,594. Twenty-two out of 60?—I am speaking for my own trade and I do not think, considering the great interests there are in the publicans' trade in Dublin, they are over represented.

64,595. It is much larger than any other trade?—It is much larger than any other trade and the representation is larger.

64,596. It is a much larger proportion of representation than any other trade?—The interests of the trade are much larger than any other trade.

64,597. Perhaps you are not aware, but I would suggest there is not a single town in England where such a number of publicans are in the Corporation in proportion to the number of members?—I do not know about that.

64,598. My point is this, that the Dublin Corporation seems to be practically dominated by the licensed trade?—I could not say that. For [illegible] years I have only known three had mayors publicans.

64,599. (Mr. Walker.) These councillors have received the suffrages of the citizens?—Yes.

64,600. They are all publicly elected?—Yes.

Mr. D. L. Boyle.

64,601. Then if those citizens thought otherwise, or considered it desirable, they would not elect them to the town council?—I suppose not.

64,602. In your judgment, do you think that gentlemen connected with the licensed trade are in every way as fit and well qualified to discharge local government duties as any other citizens?—The public seem to think so.

Selling drink to drunken persons.

64,603. One word as to drunkenness. Is it not within your experience that an offence may be committed, and the proprietor of the house may be powerless to prevent it under the present law with reference to selling to drunken persons?—Yes, that is what I have stated in the observations. A man without the knowledge of the publican gets on to licensed premises in a tipsy state, and the publican can be prosecuted for having him there, and it has happened in some instances.

64,604. It is quite possible and probable, within your experience, that a drunken man can so present himself on entering the house that no one can detect him?—That is one of the greatest difficulties at present in the carrying out of a licensed house. It is almost impossible, at busy hours.

Liquor's dilution.

64,605. (Sir Charles Cameron.) You spoke about the drink sold in these shebeens in Dublin, and you said they got the very worst possible liquor?—The very cheapest article.

64,606. Have you any reason to think there is much adulteration of the drink sold there—that they manufacture this whisky?—I would not say so. I do not think that there is any adulteration going on, I think the cheap article is bad enough.

The witness withdrew.

Adjourned to Tuesday, May 24th, at 11 o'clock.

ONE HUNDRED AND EIGHTH DAY.

Queen's Robing Room, House of Lords, Tuesday, May 24th, 1898.

PRESENT:

THE RIGHT HONOURABLE THE VISCOUNT PEEL in the Chair.

The Right Hon. Sir ALGERNON WEST, K.C.B.	HENRY GRINLING, Esq.
The Very Reverend H. H. DICKINSON, Dean.	SAMUEL HYSLOP, Esq.
WILLIAM ALLAN, Esq., M.P.	ANDREW JOHNSTON, Esq.
EDWARD NORTH BUXTON, Esq.	JOHN HERBERT ROBERTS, Esq., M.P.
WILLIAM SPROSTON CAINE, Esq.	GERALD WALKER, Esq.
ALEXANDER MORISON GORDON, Esq.	HAROLD TENNANT, Esq., M.P.
WILLIAM GRAHAM, Esq.	GEORGE YOUNGER, Esq.

Captain H. PERCY BEAMISH called in and examined.

Captain H. P. Beamish.

64,607. (Chairman.) You are here as representing the Cork brewers, I believe?—I am.

Position of brewers.

64,608. Are the majority of houses in Cork tied or free?—The majority of houses are tied.

64,609. Brewers have acquired the property in them?—They have acquired the houses in many cases, as well as the licences, and they let them on short terms as a rule to the tenants.

Tie for beer given a [illegible]

64,610. Therefore, between the licensing laws on the one hand, and the commercial arrangements, if I may call them so, on the other, there is a good deal of complication in the administration of the law?—A good deal.

64,611. As to the agreements which brewers enter into between themselves and the licensees, do you consider that the brewers have taken this course on account of [illegible] conclusions arrived at, or supposed to be arrived at, by the Irish judges, so as to protect their own interests?—They have endeavoured to do so. The result has been an exceedingly complicated state of things.

64,612. On what terms are the houses let to the occupiers?—Chiefly on short terms.

64,613. Who pays the rates and taxes?—I believe the brewer pays the rates and taxes.

64,614. Does the rent that the brewer gets leave him a pretty large margin of profit, or the reverse?—I say the brewer pays the head rent, rates and taxes, and it leaves him a very small margin of profit.

64,615. A very small margin of profit, looking to the rent that he can get for the house?—Looking to the rent that he receives from the tenant.

64,616. Do you mean to say that it is not a profitable business for a brewer to buy up houses?—It is profitable in the way of the disposal of his goods, but in no other way.

64,617. That is to say, it is easier to dispose of his goods to a particular house?—Precisely.

64,618. Does the tenant in all cases covenant to deal exclusively with the brewer?—He does, in these letting agreements.

64,619. For all articles?—Only for the articles manufactured by the brewer himself.

64,620. But the brewer manufactures a good many articles now, does not he?—He manufactures, in Cork, only ale and porter.

Tying an old custom in Cork.

64,621. Not mineral waters?—No. Perhaps I might mention that this custom of tied houses is a very ancient one in the city of Cork. I have a deed here which is dated over 100 years ago.

64,622. Do I understand by that, that that particular house has been tied to a particular firm for that time, and has been in the hands of a succession of the same family?—Scarcely that. It merely was brought forward to show that the system of tied houses is a very old one in the city of Cork. It is an old custom.

Captain H. P. Beamish.

24 May '98.

64,623. Besides covenanting to get all his articles from the brewer, what else does the tenant covenant to do?—He covenants to pay his rent, and he covenants to maintain his licence without forfeiture and to conduct his house in a proper manner.

64,624. Does he give any security for his good behaviour?—He does in many instances.

Length of tenancies.

64,625. What are the lengths of leases; for what period?—They are exceedingly various. They range from a monthly tenancy up to a year, or a term of years.

64,626. I think you just now inferred, though not perhaps absolutely stated, that the same family continues for a long time as publicans of the same licensed houses?—For three or four generations.

Goodwill.

64,627. Is goodwill recognised?—In the majority of cases it is not recognised. There is a firm in the city of Cork that recognises goodwill to their tenants.

64,628. It has been known, has it not, that large prices have been paid for goodwill?—Considerable sums have been paid for tenant right in very short terms.

64,629. What sort of prices are given for goodwill; what is the common range of prices?—They have given from 40l. up to 600l.

Property in the licence.

64,630. Taking the case where the brewer has purchased both the house and the licence, does any complication arise from the landlord being in that particular relation?—There is very considerable legal complication as regards control of the licence.

64,631. Do you consider that in that case, where a brewer has purchased the house and the licence, the law courts of Ireland have recognised any property in the brewer?—There is a very celebrated case in the Irish Court of Queen's Bench called the Clifford case, in which Chief Justice May said that existing vested interests could not be expropriated, even with a legitimate object, without compensation.

64,632. Do you consider that that legal dictum or decision has been confirmed by any English courts?—English judges appear to hold that a licence is the goodwill, without which the business cannot be carried on.

64,633. That is a business, is it not?—Precisely.

64,634. If you have no licence you cannot act under the licence?—The tendency of that is, that it would be useless for the brewer to purchase a house on which he has no profit, unless it were for the purpose of securing his trade.

64,635. Would you go so far as to say that the law courts of Ireland have recognised a licence as a property to be assigned as a property?—Well, they have; but

Captain E. F. [illegible]. 24 May '98

the decisions in the Irish courts appear to have been exceedingly contradictory.

64,636. Do they recognise the consistency, so to speak, of the licence with the house? Can you assign a licence without assigning the house to which it is attached?—Such has been the custom, and many transfers in Cork have recognised that custom for a great number of years, but the present Recorder of Cork does not do so.

64,637. In the case of a licensed publican, what has been decided as to the nature of the property in the licence which he holds? Has it been held to be personal property?—It has been dealt with as personal property.

64,638. Not as freehold property?—Not as freehold.

64,639. But there is rather [illegible] against the idea that it is a permanent property, is there not?—The whole law of licensing is so complicated in Ireland, so administered by these different contradictory decisions, that it is very difficult to answer the question.

64,640. You have given us cases in which you say the judges have decided that there was a property. Have any judges of great eminence given a contrary decision?—Lord Justice Barry has said that though he admitted that some of the judges in giving judgment in the Cilthorne case did apply the word "property" to a licence, he (Lord Justice Barry) did not think that there was any property in a licence.

64,641. On the other hand you think the English judges have decided that there is a kind of property in a licence?—Precisely; a kind of property.

64,642. Is there any case which you wish to bring before us of a judge, in any case that came before him, laying down that rule of law?—In the case of The Queen v. The Justices of [illegible], Mr. Justice Mellor is reported as saying: "I see nothing unreasonable in the case of a house already licensed in limiting objections to those affecting the personal character of the applicant." And in Garrett v. The Justices of Middlesex, the English judges decided that occupants of licensed premises were entitled to the renewal of the licence, though the licence expired and stated [illegible] did not require a renewal. The property in a licence is also recognised by section 15 of the Licensing Act, Ireland, 1874.

64,643. Though the licence of the house does not require the renewal of his licence, that licence can be transferred as property?—It has been absolutely done in the city of Cork by the Recorder. He has declined to listen to the objection which the man has raised to the transfer of his licence to another man, and he has transferred it for him.

64,644. How can the transferee be put in a better position than that of the licensed [illegible] licensee?—Because when the party who is licensed has for valuable consideration parted with his licence to the lessee, and afterwards declines to transfer that licence to another man, he has been in certain cases compelled to do so.

Perversity of licensing law.

64,645. That is rather a dangerous doctrine is it not? Does not that imply that the lessee can override, by a special agreement with a lessor, the spirit of the law, which requires an annual licence to be renewed, and that he regards the licence once granted as granted in perpetuity?—In the Cilthorne case the other principle appears to have been so completely introduced, that they now grant their renewals as a certainty, or almost as a certainty.

64,646. Personally speaking, on behalf of a great association, should you hold that a licence once granted cannot be cancelled?—It can be cancelled for misconduct.

64,647. I put misconduct out of the question?—Certainly.

64,648. Supposing it is cancelled for misconduct, does the licence then revert from the licensee to the house, and can the house never be bereft of its licence?—No, that is not the sense of the law at the present moment, but that is what we think ought to be the case, in order to simplify what is an exceedingly complicated position at the present moment.

64,649. (*Mr. Cohen.*) Do you think that the custom of an individual court of justice, as at Cilthorne, overrides the law, and overrides the specific enactment?—The Cilthorne case was decided by the Irish Court of Queen's Bench. It was not a local matter.

64,650. I thought it was Cilthorne in England?—No.

64,651. Do you contend that that alters the law in any way?—I do not attempt to contend anything of the kind. I merely say that a custom which has regulated the disposal of the properties of Cork for many years has recognised an indirect property in the licence to the man who has purchased it.

64,652. Now you use the word "indirect," which considerably qualifies it?—Of course, the whole thing is most confused.

64,653. (*Chairman.*) You do not contend that a licensee once having got a licence is entitled to it for all time, but you do contend I understand, that a house once invested with a licence has a right to it in perpetuity: is that your contention?—If the licence has been purchased by the owner of the house from the licensee for a valuable consideration, what we claim is that it should follow the house; and what we are anxious for is, that the law should be brought into accordance with the custom which enables that to be done. That is my case. Practically, that has been carried into effect—locally, I mean.

64,654. I do not wish so much to argue the question, but I should like to ask you whether you consider that the legislature has laid down a distinct series of statutes, and that because behind the back of the statutes—I mean nothing offensive—a great quantity of commercial arrangements have sprung up, those commercial arrangements are to override the express wish of the legislature as declared in repeated statutes?—Certainly we could not contend such a thing as that for a moment.

64,655. Does not your evidence rather point to that? —It does point in that direction most decidedly, but in Ireland we are somewhat differently placed from the case of a licensee in England.

64,656. Does the Recorder of Dublin ever make it a condition before a licence is granted that licences in other parts of the city shall be surrendered?—He does.

64,657. Do you object to that plan?—The number of licences throughout Ireland is unquestionably too large as it is.

64,658. And, therefore, a good method of reducing them would be to surrender four, five, or even six licences in a congested part of the district for a new licence in a suburban or a new quarter?—I should not like to bind myself to the number, but I think that a change in that direction might be beneficial in some degree.

64,659. The number is unimportant in itself; the only question is, whether the good answers to the one, or the one to the good; whether the value is equivalent? —Yes.

64,660. You would say that?—I should say that the number of licensed houses, particularly in some of the cities, is too large, and that, as the Recorder of Dublin often does, calling upon some of these licences to be extinguished, is beneficial to everyone.

64,661. I was rather looking to the value of the thing proposed to be set against a new house. I suppose the Recorder would not admit the surrender of three or four temporary houses in a poorer district for the purpose of granting a licence to a full public-house in a better district?—I really do not know what his plan is in that respect.

64,662. You do not yourself, speaking on behalf of your association, object to the system of suppression and transfer, or suppression and creation of a licence?—Provided it is done under fair regulations.

64,663. (*Mr. Younger.*) I suppose each case would, in that particular principle, be treated on its own merits? —Each case would be treated on its own merits.

64,664. (*Chairman.*) Suppose a number of houses in a congested district had been practically left by the diminution [illegible] have been closed. I suppose the Recorder would take into consideration the fact that those houses were evidently not doing business, or they would not have been closed. Do you know any case like that?—If a house is closed the practice of the Recorder of Cork is to decline to renew the licence. He will not allow it to go on.

64,665. Of course, he would not accept it as one of those houses to be surrendered against the granting of a new house?—I could not answer that. He has not called for any suppression of licences.

Captain J. P. [illegible]

64,666. Are you of opinion that no amount of offences by the manager, if there is a manager, or by the licensee, or by the tenant, whoever he may be, would possibly warrant the taking away of the licence from that house?—There are no managers in the houses in Cork. The brewers do not put in managers.

64,667. Whom do they put in?—They put in monthly tenants, or quarterly tenants, or yearly tenants, or six-yearly tenants as the case may be. They put in no managers. There is one solitary exception in the case of one of the brewers in Cork, where a manager has been put in as a trial, but it is only as an experiment. Practically, there are no managers in Cork.

The man goes, the house remains.

64,668. Would you agree with a former witness who said that the man can go, but the house cannot?—That is the form in which those that I am connected with are anxious that the law shall bear on this; that the man may go, but the house remain.

64,669. And that, though a house might have acquired a notoriously bad character from a succession of not only incompetent, but I will assume, vicious, misbehaving, bad tenants, the magistrates should not be entitled to say, this house has got such a reputation, that we will refuse to license it any longer. I put an extreme case to illustrate what I want to draw out?—My answer to that would be that the brewer would be very short-sighted who would permit the tenant to remain in one of his houses, if he had the power of getting him out under such conditions.

64,670. (Mr. Younger.) And that if he did he should lose the licence for the house?—Certainly.

64,671. (Chairman.) Suppose a tenant has committed an offence which brings him under the cognisance of the magistrate, he might introduce the endorsement upon the licence. Who suffers in that case?—The first endorsement, of course.

64,672. I am talking of the endorsement entailing forfeiture?—Before it comes to that point, the brewer immediately gives notice to his tenant that he must leave the house and that the licence must be transferred to another tenant. In order to prevent that very thing the short tenancies, these monthly tenancies have been adopted in order to give the owner of the house the power of being able to dispossess the tenant who is breaking the law and is endangering his licence.

64,673. When the brewer puts himself in the position of the law?—The brewer gives notice to the tenant, the tenant has to go, and he calls upon the tenant to transfer his licence over to another tenant who will not transgress the law.

64,674. What happens to the man who has sinned?—The man who has sinned goes out of the business altogether—there is no more about him. He leaves the house and transfers his licence.

64,675. He is punished by the brewer instead of being punished by the law?—Because the brewer would be punished by law, by the loss of the licence, if he did not do so.

64,676. No; I understand you to say the brewer cannot lose his licence?—That is our contention, that we wish should be established, but as the law stands the brewer runs the risk of the house no longer having a licence.

64,677. Is there no penalty on a brewer? Is it conceivable that a brewer should sin like a tenant?—Your point is, supposing the house were constantly ill conducted, and that the brewer appointed a succession of ill-conducted tenants. Certainly in that case there ought to be a punishment on the brewer.

64,678. What kind of punishment?—The law as it stands has not given us an opportunity of thinking that out at all.

Licence to belong to the brewer.

64,679. Would you like to see the licence made out to the brewer, and not to the tenant?—I should like the licence to belong to the brewer and to the brewer's house, and I should like that a brewer, if he were to put ill-conducted tenants into that house who would be likely to break the law, should suffer some penalty which would prevent his doing it in future.

Changes of tenancy.

64,680. Are there many changes in the occupants of the houses that belong to your association?—Not as a rule. Of course, you would not get rid of well-conducted tenants, but I ask you as a fact whether you find there is a considerable change among the tenants of your houses?—Not a great many.

Captain J. P. [illegible]

24 May '98.

64,681. Then you think that an existing licence should be capable of being transferred to another house, provided that the transfer did not increase the number of existing licences?—And that there was no objection to the character of the incoming tenant.

Disqualification of justices.

64,682. Have you anything to say about the qualifications of magistrates adjudicating the licensing courts?—We consider that as all magistrates interested in the manufacture or sale of intoxicating liquor are prohibited by law from acting in licensing cases, the same prohibition should be extended to biassed opponents of the liquor trade, such as admitted supporters of the total abstinence cause.

64,683. (Mr. [illegible].) How would you define an admitted supporter of the temperance cause?—It would be very easy to define it in any part of the world, because they are very clear.

Provisional licences.

64,684. (Chairman.) I suppose the brewers, or whoever is the party interested, occasionally apply for a provisional licence, do they not?—We do.

64,685. Before the house is built?—The existing state of the law in Ireland as regards that we consider to bear very hardly on Irish brewers, because in England before a brewer invests his money in the erection of a house he can ascertain whether, when the house is built, he will obtain a licence for it, but that is not the case in Ireland. He must run the risk of building the house, and then apply for a licence or a transfer of a licence.

64,686. Is there no method of the magistrates considering the specifications for a house, and saying: Yes, this appears to comply with all the necessary qualifications for a licence?—No, that is not so in Ireland. We should wish to see that provision of the English Acts applied also in Ireland.

64,687. But suppose in the course of an erection of a new house, there is a departure from the specification, what power would you give the licensing authorities then?—I would give the licensing authorities the power of declining a transfer or the grant of a licence.

64,688. Can they do so now by law?—At the present moment, I do not know, because the question never arose in Ireland. We never can go to the magistrates and say we propose to erect the house according to certain specifications.

Conditions imposed upon licences.

64,689. I suppose you know cases in Ireland where conditions have been laid down by the magistrates, and where they have afterwards been infringed?—I do not know any case in Ireland where a new house has been built according to certain specifications laid down to meet the requirements of the magistrates, and where they have undertaken to give the licence on that being done. It is not the custom. It is not the law in Ireland.

64,690. Is it the custom for the magistrates when they grant the licence to say there shall be no long bar?—They do make certain conditions. They are more particular with regard to back entrances and back doors, and places which would prevent the police having a proper supervision of the place.

64,691. But apart from that, as to the actual construction of the house and facilities for drinking, conditions are frequently imposed, are they not?—I could not answer that from my own knowledge.

64,692. Would you say that the conditions which magistrates now impose are not according to statute?—They do not impose conditions on the erection of new houses, because we do not go before them until the house is completed.

64,693. Supposing a house has been granted a particular licence, and in the course of the year fresh developments take place in the house, the magistrates consider, when the case comes up for renewal at the annual licensing, that the original compact has been departed from?—Of my own knowledge I could not answer that.

64,694. You contemplate cases in which not only is

[illegible]

Captain E. P. Bagwell.

64,726. Have you ever had any complaints?—No complaints whatever.

64,727. Have you ever heard of any complaints from the public that they cannot get the particular kind of liquor that they like?—None, that I have heard.

64,728. You can conceive such a case, I suppose?—Certainly; but the competition between the different rival breweries is quite sufficient to correct that.

64,729. What I was pointing out was the great and increasing power of brewers, that they might secure a whole district and only sell their own liquor, whatever they may choose to sell, in that particular district—a deal conceivable?—Quite so.

64,730. They might have no interest in pushing off their beer which might not be wholly to the taste of the public?—Quite so.

64,731. Do you think that might be?—It is quite possible.

64,732. And that their interest in selling an article palatable to the public would not be so great as their interest in getting rid of a particular kind of liquor which they sell?—In that respect I think you have slightly misunderstood me. When I say that a district may belong to a certain extent the property of a brewer, I do not mean to say that he would in that district put a different class of manufacture from what he would in any other district.

64,733. No, I was not implying that?—That I do not wish to imply. The brewers of Cork give the same manufacture at the same price to all their people.

64,734. To put a case crudely and roughly; suppose a powerful brewery company had got a whole district in its hands, and suppose they decided to sell only Guinness; that they were interested in the sale of Guinness; some people might want to have Beamish; they could not get it. I put that as a result. Should you say that was for the good of the district?—It is so very extreme a case that I can hardly conceive it.

64,735. But you can conceive of a case in which a brewery has got hold of a district?—I can, certainly.

To alter statement of Rev. by an agent on behalf of a brewer alleged to by the Rev. M. Ahern.

64,736. I do not wish to omit anything that you wish to make. Is there any other point you would like to mention?—There was a statement made here by a Roman Catholic clergyman, the Reverend Michael Ahern, a Catholic curate, of Ladies Bridge, near Charleville. He appears to have repeated on more than one occasion, two or three times very distinctly, that a bribe of 5l. was offered by one of the Cork brewing companies to the magistrates. We should wish to have an opportunity to individually contradict that, because there are four brewers, and he did not mention the name of any brewery. I think it was on the (46th) day—the 11th May.

Denied by Cork brewers.

64,737. Do you say it was stated that a bribe was offered or accepted?—I do not think he went to the extent of saying it was accepted. I have not a copy of the evidence. What he stated was that a canvassing agent had the authority of a brewer to offer the money he wanted for the support of the justices to the particular licence, and he appears to have repeated it two or three times with very great strength.

64,738. (Mr. Younger.) But without any proof of the statement at all emanating that?—None. As I say, there are four brewers in the city of Cork, and I have been requested by letter by two of them, and Mr. Murphy represents a third firm, and I represent the fourth, to give the statement the most emphatic denial. Mr. Lane writes: "As far as this brewery is concerned the "statement is absolutely false." Messrs. Arnott write: "We challenge the statement made by the Reverend "Michael Ahern, Catholic Curate of Charleville, in his "evidence before the Royal Commission, namely, that "magistrates were bribed by a Cork brewer, and desire "to say that so far as we are concerned it is absolutely "untrue."

64,739. (Chairman.) This gentleman states it from his own experience. He says: "I can give instances, "including one in which a merchant called on myself "and wanted me to use my influence with some of the "magistrates who were living in a parish where I then "was, to go about 15 miles to vote for a licence for a "friend of his. I said that it was altogether unreason- "able to expect magistrates to go so far away and he "said that distance made no difference whatever, that "he himself was authorised by a brewer to give 5l. by "way of defraying expenses to any magistrate whom "he would get to go and vote for this licence"?—It is a very strong statement, and it is one made of course personal knowledge. It only concerns the one brewing firm in the city of Cork there are four practically in doing that, and there he must bring out the name of the man that was supposed to have been represented by that canvassing agent. He would have to state who it was. I have read you letters from two of the firms. Mr. Murphy, who is here, says, with regard to bribing magistrates, his firm had never done such a thing, or authorised its being done by any of his agents. As regards canvassing, on two occasions when applications were being made for licences in districts in which, in his opinion, they were required, and when it came to his knowledge that a strong canvass had been made against the granting of the licence, he asked some of his friends to attend, and if they considered on the evidence that the licences were required, to vote accordingly—that is to say, to see fair play.

64,740. You will observe that his statement is, not that a direct 5l. note was offered for a person to vote in a particular way, but that the brewer offered to defray the expenses, the distance being no object, up to 5l., if he would go and vote in a particular way; that is the allegation?—That is the allegation. That allegation is distinctly denied by Messrs. Arnott and Co., distinctly denied by Messrs. Lane, it is distinctly denied by Mr. Murphy, and on the part of my own firm I can give it an equally distinct denial. I can go further than that, and I can say that we have never attempted to influence magistrates in any way whatever with regard to licences.

Canvassing.

64,741. You would admit, I suppose, that magistrates were greatly canvassed in Ireland?—They were, most undoubtedly.

64,742. You, of course, and your associates, I am sure, repudiate the idea of any kind of canvassing?—We should be very glad if all canvassing should be absolutely punishable by law—canvassing on both sides; that is on the total abstinence side as well as on the brewer's side. We consider it to be grossly unfair.

64,743. It depends on how you define canvassing?—It is very difficult, of course.

64,744. Would a petition got up by the inhabitants to say that they objected to a licence being put into a particular district be canvassing the magistrates?—No, I should not think it would be.

64,745. (Mr. Younger.) I suppose you mean private canvassing?—Personal, private canvassing.

The charges against the Cork brewers.

64,746. (Chairman.) Private personal solicitation?—Precisely. Mr. Murphy states, and I may state the same, that no premium to encourage the sale of drink is given to any licensed, or publican; and I may go so far as to say that the firm that I represent will not even give what are called the usual Christmas boxes. We do not give anything at all to these people. I was anxious for the opportunity of being able specifically to deny that charge, and now it remains for the Rev. Mr. Ahern to state publicly who the brewer was that did it, and then, of course, we must proceed further in the matter.

64,747. (Dean Dickinson.) The priest from Cork said that this was given by way of paying travelling expenses, not as a bribe?—Yes.

64,748. You do not mean to say that witnesses who come here and are paid their travelling expenses are bribed?—No, but that is quite a different thing.

64,749. How is it different?—I should look upon it in the light of a bribe if I offered to pay magistrates the travelling expenses.

64,750. (Chairman.) I am bound to observe that it is for the purpose of defraying the expenses of any magistrate whom he could get to go and vote?—Precisely.

64,751. It is something more than paying travelling expenses for a judicial investigation?—Yes.

Property in a licence.

64,752. (Dean Dickinson.) With respect to the Property Clauses case, a question was asked you by a Commissioner opposite; was there any adverse opinion expressed upon that matter as to the property in the licence. There was a very strong expression on the opposite side. One of our chiefest judges, Lord Justice FitzGibbon, said "Where a licensed person holds "licensed premises with his connexion, of the devolu- "tion of this from him in certain specified ways, but not "otherwise, the licence may pass from the premises by "way of transfer; but when the connexion between "the person and the premises is determined, and the

[illegible]

Captain [illegible] Burnish. [illegible]

64,[illegible]. You have said that it is your opinion that there are too many public-houses in the city of Cork. Did I rightly gather that?—Quite so.

64,[illegible]. What would you say in relation to the result of that fact. We have had a considerable amount of evidence given here by police authorities and others as regards the city of Cork that there is a great deal of drunkenness arising from that fact. What is your opinion about that?—I think that the result is more [illegible] to the unfortunate struggling holders of these licenses, where the house has an extraordinary small trade, there [illegible] to be the [illegible] [illegible], because these men have [illegible] got the means of making more than an extremely precarious livelihood. In the case of some of these holders of licenses in Cork their sales are so extremely small that their livelihood must be an extremely precarious one.

64,7[illegible]. And they are, in your opinion, [illegible] to that way to push their trade?—As I told you before, not being a publican myself, I could not answer that question.

64,7[illegible]. I have before me an extract from what was said by the Recorder of Cork in reference to this matter, in which he says, addressing a jury in 18[illegible]: "This sad "list of offences, as I have said, is exceptional. When "I looked through the calendar it at first occurred to "me that that great and steady increase of crime might "possibly be due to want of employment in the com"munity. I have carefully gone through the cases to "see if I could account for it, but I cannot. On the "contrary of the cases to be disposed of [illegible] "are the result of drunkenness. This is a curious state "of affairs in this city." I suppose you generally would not deny the truth of that opinion?—I have not gone into the statistics of drunkenness myself, and I must leave that to others who have done so with much greater care. I should not venture on an opinion.

Gilmour's [illegible] [illegible] [illegible]

64,7[illegible]. (Mr. Cavan.) In the matter of the Gilmour case, you seem very familiar with it, and no doubt you have read the summing up of the different judges in the case?—I have not. We only know that it is a case which appears to have had very great influence on the licensing authorities in Ireland in general terms, but not being a technical lawyer myself I have not gone into the particulars of the case at all.

64,7[illegible]. Will you allow me to inform you of one or two very simple statements made by the judges in giving the decision. Lord Justice Barry, one of the judges who decided the Gilmour case, said "he entirely "[illegible] that he, for one, in Gilmour's case ever "decided directly or indirectly that a licence obtained "to privilege the sale of liquors in a public-house "would properly be described as property. Although "one or two of the judges had used the word 'property,' "he did not understand any of them to say that a "property in the licence was created. He would have "dissented had it been stated, because he did not "think there was any property whatever in the licence." Do you agree with Lord Justice Barry in that expression of opinion?—Not being a lawyer, and the state of the law as regards Irish licensing being rather obscure in my opinion, I cannot state to you what my opinion as to the truth has really is.

64,7[illegible]. It is not a [illegible] statement, it is a very simple one, and you are quite capable of understanding it, I am sure, from the clear evidence you have given to us to-day?—Judge Miller [illegible] that there was a property in a licence in [illegible] O'Brien. We also have it that Chief Justice May, in giving his judgment, said: "Existing vested interests should not be extinguished "except with a legitimate object without compensation." In giving judgment, Lord Justice Barry said that he did not think there was any property in a licence, though he admitted that some of the judges, in giving judgment in Gilmour's case, did apply the word "property" to a licence.

64,7[illegible]. But then he goes on to use the expressions that I quoted, which are very important indeed?—They are.

and Justices Ball, Deasy, and FitzGibbon, all these judges—I am now giving their very words—expressed their opinion that Gilmour's case ought not to be extended, and that they "ought not to go further in "interfering with the very beneficial jurisdiction of "the magistrates in restricting the existing number of "public-houses on the occasion of applications for "licenses." Do you agree with the legal opinion thus expressed by these distinguished judges, or are you still not a lawyer?—I am still not a lawyer.

Captain [illegible] Burnish. [illegible]

64,7[illegible]. You lay down the doctrine, which is often quoted with regard to a public-house, that the man may die, but the house exists. Is not the house really the brewer?—When I say the house exists, I mean that, judging by the ordinary rules of human nature, a man will not go commercially contrary to his own interests. It is not the brewer's interest if he has a large sum of money invested to run that into ruin.

The [illegible] may die, but the house exists.

64,7[illegible]. If a man has a public-house in a [illegible] district, a district which is inhabited largely by [illegible] and bad characters, he has to make his living out of the customers he can get; do not you think that greater responsibility rests upon the brewer who draws the bulk of the profits from the sale of drink under such circumstances, than rests upon his servant, or even upon his licensee, whom he puts in as a [illegible] or tenant, as you described just now? Do not you think that some moral responsibility ought to rest upon the brewer, who is practically the house, if the house owns?—I think that that moral responsibility is felt by the brewers. That is my experience; but I [illegible] they [illegible] up to it in all cases.

64,7[illegible]. You seem to have a considerable knowledge of [illegible] [illegible]. It is human nature sometimes to [illegible] responsibility, and not to live up to it?—Yes, that may very easily be. That is a question to which really I do not think I should be called upon to answer yes or no. My own idea is that it would be better for public policy that the conduct of the house should be more thrown on the brewer.

64,7[illegible]. That is just what I wanted to get out?—That is my idea.

64,7[illegible]. I am quite content with that answer. You made use of an expression which rather impressed me. You expressed your opinion that the number of licenses in Ireland is considerably too large?—I did not say in Ireland, I said in Cork. I do not know all about Ireland.

Excessive number of licensed houses in Cork.

64,7[illegible]. Why is the number too large?—Because I think that there are a number of very small impoverished houses that it is not good should continue to exist; that, with very small sales indeed, and who are themselves so impecunious that they are very difficult indeed to manage.

64,7[illegible]. The houses are very difficult to manage?—Well, the [illegible]—the occupier of the house—is.

64,7[illegible]. And you think they tend to a considerable amount of drunkenness?—That, I cannot tell you.

64,8[illegible]. Why do you object to these small houses?—I object to a man being placed in the way of temptation to do anything that should tend towards illicit action, by his being so exceedingly poor.

64,8[illegible]. And you think to [illegible] tend to that action?—I think human nature generally would tend in that direction. I do not myself know of my own personal knowledge that such is the fact, but, reasoning from analogy, I should certainly think so.

64,8[illegible]. Is it not rather the tendency of [illegible] of brewers to crush out these smaller houses? Why is beer or whisky which is sold in a small house any more deleterious than when sold in a big house?—Of course it is not more deleterious in one house than it is in another. I am speaking of the class of men who inhabit these impoverished houses.

64,8[illegible]. He only sells all the whisky and beer he can, the same as you do?—That is perfectly right. What we do [illegible] [illegible] a [illegible] [illegible] [illegible] are able to do

64,806. What would you do with this large number? —That we must leave in the hands of the legislature. It is not for us to suggest.

64,807. You are here to suggest, if you have any suggestions to make?—If they will give us some relief from the chaotic condition of the licensing laws in Ireland, that is the point that we press for.

Disqualification of justices.

64,808. You propose to disqualify teetotalers from sitting on the bench?—Certainly if brewers are disqualified.

64,809. But if you are going to disqualify teetotalers, would you disqualify those who drink alcohol?—Oh, my goodness, no, not in my opinion.

64,810. A teetotaler is simply a person whose habit of life is not to drink?—A man may do what he likes as regards his own personal habit of life, but if he wants to force his opinions upon the community at large, that is quite a different thing.

64,811. But the teetotaler does not want to force his opinions?—A brewer is supposed to force the sale of beer on the community. The man who advocates total abstinence is anxious to prevent anyone drinking anything but water.

64,812. Not at all?—Well, any alcoholic drink.

64,813. Can you point to any proposal for legislation that has ever been brought before Parliament in your time which indicates anything of the kind?—Do you mean the exclusion of total abstinence advocates from the bench?

64,814. No. You say you wish to exclude men who are total abstainers from the bench?—Not total abstainers, very strong advocates of the local abstinence. [illegible] I wish to be excluded from the bench, in the same way that those who are interested in the sale of liquor are now excluded.

64,815. Would you exclude a medical man who delivered lectures [illegible] the use of alcohol for dietetic purposes?—That is a point I have never considered.

64,816. If you have these strong opinions as to the [illegible] of [illegible], surely you should consider what they involve on the other side; you must be fair all round?—I should wish to be fair all round, so far as [illegible] [illegible] [illegible] of the subject to be in. But [illegible] [illegible] [illegible] [illegible] [illegible] [illegible] the purpose of rejecting every licence that comes before them, and every renewal of a licence that they can possibly get rid of, I say that such men as those are so strongly biassed that they ought to be excluded from the bench, just as much as a brewer.

64,817. That is clearly a reprehensible action if anybody packs the bench for a distinct purpose. I should [illegible] [illegible] [illegible] [illegible] [illegible] [illegible] or for other purposes, but you are proposing a very sweeping change in the law. If your recommendation means anything it is that you think that this Commission ought to recommend to Parliament that total abstainers should be disqualified from sitting on the bench?—Not total abstainers. Let a man do what he likes himself, but those who are so strongly opposed to the sale of any alcoholic liquor whatever should be as much excluded from the bench as the brewer or the distiller who makes it.

64,818. (Mr. Younger.) I suppose your point really is this, that you object to placing this licensing power in the hands of people who are very zealous, and who have declared themselves publicly to have very extreme views on that question?—Quite so.

64,819. And you consider them unfit to judge, exactly as you would object to a judge who had very strong opinions on the [illegible] from sitting upon cases which were brought before him for the purpose of enforcing those laws?—Precisely.

64,820. That is your principle, I suppose?—Exactly so.

Dual licence.

64,821. We rather gather from your evidence that you favour the principle of dual licence?—I scarcely clearly understand what the meaning of the dual licence is.

64,822. A licence attaching to the owner, and a licence attaching to the occupier of a house?—I think it would be an excellent plan, subject to the details being able to be worked out.

64,823. Whatever interest either had in the licence would be represented by the particular certificate, and there would be less difficulty about it than there is at the present?—Far less, provided that the details could be carried out satisfactorily; that is, that the house should remain licensed, but that, as I understand it, the licensing authority should have the power of depriving the tenant of his licence to sell in case his conduct was not what it ought to be.

64,824. Of course, you do not for a moment complain that a thoroughly bad tenant should be continued with the privileges?—Certainly not.

64,825. If a ship went unseaworthy you would not punish the captain but the owner?—Yes.

64,826. And to that extent the owner of a public-house would require to see that, so to speak, it was seaworthy? —Yes.

Tenancy of licensed houses.

64,827. (Mr. Burton.) I understand you to say that the tenant who loses a licence is subject to a money penalty as well as to the loss of his position under an agreement with the owner of the house?—The agreement with the owner of the house as regards the licence is that in case the conduct of the tenant were such that he was deprived of the licence, and the licence endangered or broken so that there would be no further [illegible] of it to anyone else, he or his executors would make good to the brewer through whom he obtained that licence the value of the licence to a specified sum. That acts as a deterrent on the tenant from evil courses or endangering his licence badly.

64,828. That is a stipulation primarily in the interest of the brewer, or whoever may be the owner?—Absolutely, because the licence would be comparatively speaking valueless to the brewer if it were deprived of the licence.

64,829. Incidentally is it not the fact that it is in the public interest as well?—Certainly so.

The licensing authority.

64,830. (Mr. Yerburgh.) I think the questions are pretty much exhausted, but I want to know your view with regard to a licensing authority. Would you be content simply with the recorder in boroughs, and the county court judge in counties, without having associated with them local magistrates?—So far as I can gather the views of those for whom I appear, they would be content with the same licensing authority, if provision were made to prevent magistrates from voting out of their own Petty Sessions districts. The county of Cork in which I live is a very large one; it is the Yorkshire of Ireland. In certain cases magistrates have been known to travel from one extreme part of the country to another to vote at licensing sessions, either for or against the renewal or the granting of new licences. I think that is a very great abuse, and that the local magistrates, the men who attend the petty sessions of any particular district, are the best judges of the requirements of their own district.

64,831. To satisfy the public mind, and not to put too much power into one man's hand, would it be advisable to appoint yearly some three local magistrates to sit with the recorder or the county court judge?—It might be a very good plan, but I think the Recorder of Cork is perfectly satisfactory as a licensing authority in the city of Cork. I was speaking just now of the county licences.

The tied system in the Cork district.

64,832. With regard to the tied houses, do not you think there is a line wanting: we have neither the name of the brewer, nor the name of the house owner, nor the name of the lessee?—No, I presume the evidence I have given to-day will show that. We shall find out then who it is.

64,833. The brewers of Cork are a very intelligent people; do not you think it would be a very clumsy way of bringing it out to do it?—I should say absolutely clumsy. I cannot conceive a brewer doing such a thing.

64,834. Printed [illegible] it would be a very clumsy way of doing it?—I should say extremely so.

64,835. Might I ask you are the houses in Cork chiefly owned by brewers?—The majority of the houses in Cork are what we call tied houses. Some of them are owned by the brewers, who own both house and licence, and in other cases they have advanced money on the houses. The great majority of the houses in Cork are tied houses in one form or another. The tie is a very old thing; it has been in existence over 100 years.

64,836. Why I refer particularly to it is that it is almost peculiar to Cork in Ireland. Tied houses are

Captain J. F. [illegible]. 14 May '78.

[illegible] houses in any other place in Ireland?—So I am told.

64,837. With regard to the tied houses, the houses are entirely the brewers; or do you find out a man wanting money, and do you lend him money, and in those cases are they tied, or are they absolutely the property of the brewers with a manager placed there?—We have no managers, practically. There is only one case of a manager, and that man was tried as an experiment by one firm of brewers, and it is not said that they will go on with it. They are tenants on short leases in the case where the brewer owns the house. In other cases the brewer lends a sum of money on mortgage, and in that manner ties the house.

64,838. May I ask is the licensee the servant of the brewer?—How can he be the servant? If he repays his mortgage the brewer ceases to have any control over him whatever.

64,839. He is so far a servant that if he does not buy his beer of him he has to leave the place?—If he does not buy his beer from the brewer, certainly, if he is selling in the brewer's house.

64,840. In your answer to a question put by his Lordship you said it was quite possible that there might be a great monopoly by a brewer buying up the whole of the houses in a place?—In a particular district.

64,841. Do you suppose that that is probable?—Such things might be. I cannot really tell you as to the probabilities and improbabilities. His Lordship asked me a question, and I had to give him the answer, "It is possible."

64,842. With regard to the article supplied in your tied houses, I suppose the competition regulates the value given absolutely, and there is no danger of inferior beer being supplied in a tied house, is there?—None whatever.

64,843. Because it would not be your interest to do so?—Certainly not.

64,844. Are they as well conducted houses as the free houses?—My idea is that they are better, because there is more control over them.

Property in a license.

64,845. With regard to property in a license. That being peculiar to Ireland, I want to make it clear what the position of the Irish people is. At any time was there any doubt as regards the property in licenses in Ireland—at any time in your recollection, or in your historical knowledge?—It was always recognised that practically the license was the property of the man who purchased it, that is who paid down money to the [illegible] for the license, and it was so dealt with by our Recorder of Cork after practice. He dealt with the license as being the property of the man who purchased it. I mean, if you put it in another form, who advanced money on it.

64,846. Was there any doubt on the part of the people of Ireland as to whether they did or did not possess property in their licenses?—I cannot answer for the whole of the people of Ireland; I can only answer for the inhabitants of the city of Cork, and it was always decided by the magistrates of the city of Cork that a license was an article which was capable of being sold, and so it was treated.

64,847. Am I right in saying that in the year [illegible] one of your brewers had that matter tested?—I have the deed in my possession here if you wish to see it. It is between Daniel [illegible], of the city of Cork, brewer, of the one part, and Edward [illegible] and William [illegible], both of the city of Cork, merchants, of the other part. This was dated the [illegible] September [illegible]. It is a deed tying the house.

64,848. Do you know if there be any statute directly opposed to the frequent decisions of the Irish courts which have determined the property in a license?—I would rather that you asked that question of a lawyer. I am not a lawyer. I really cannot tell you in the present chaotic condition of the licensing laws in Ireland, the letter of the law being one thing, and the nearly universal practice being another. I cannot answer you. I cannot say "Yes" or "No" to such a question.

64,849. I suppose you agree with me that custom regulates decisions?—Locally, of course.

64,850. And these decisions became the understood law of the country?—Locally it is so, certainly.

64,851. I think, practically, the majority of the judges were always of the opinion (I except Judge Berry and, perhaps, one or two others), but the decision of the judges from time to time was that the licenses were the property of the licensee?—I have mere personal cognisance of the actions from time to time of the licensing authority in the city of Cork. The licensing of Cork, and certainly one recorder after another, has practically acted as if there was a property in a license.

The witness withdrew.

Mr. DENIS DONOVAN called in and examined.

Mr. D. Donovan.

64,852. (*Chairman.*) You are, I think, the Secretary of the Cork Licensed Vintners' Trade Protection Association?—I am.

Bottom of figures.

64,853. There is no such thing as a licensed victualler in Ireland, is there?—I have never heard of it. The term is generally licensed vintner.

64,854. How long has your association been established?—About [illegible] years.

64,855. Who is the chairman of your association?—He is Alderman [illegible], who was Mayor of Cork for the years [illegible], [illegible], and [illegible].

64,856. You must have a very extensive knowledge of Cork and all its circumstances?—I have.

Rise of Sunday closing in Cork.

64,857. As to the Sunday Closing Act of 1878, what has been the operation of that Act? Cork, of course, is exempted?—Yes, Cork was exempted in 1878.

64,858. The hours were regulated?—The hours were suspended, from [illegible] in the evening to [illegible] in the evening.

64,859. What effect upon the habits of the Cork people has that restriction of two hours produced?—I have just made an analysis of the lists of arrests for four years preceding and for four years succeeding the operation of the Act of 1878, and find that for the four years preceding, 1874, 1875, 1876, and 1877, the average number of arrests per year was [illegible], and in the four years subsequent to Sunday closing, that is, 1879, 1880, 1881, and 1882, the average number was [illegible] per annum.

64,860. You speak for the East Riding of the county of Cork?—Yes, that is the portion of the county surrounding Cork.

64,861. What is the state of drunkenness in the East Riding of Cork, coming down nearer than [illegible], if you have the figures?—I have been able to see the returns of the number of arrests for the half year preceding the operation of the Sunday Closing Act in the East Riding. It has not been very easy to get the returns for the other years previous to the operation of the Act. But for the half year that I mention the number was [illegible], or we might say [illegible] for the whole year. I have been able to strike an average for [illegible] years subsequent to the operation of the Sunday Closing Act, that is, for the years [illegible] to [illegible] inclusive, and I find that the average for the [illegible] years was about [illegible].

64,862. Do you admit that in Cork itself there has been a diminution of drunkenness?—Generally speaking, there has been. I mean for the seven days of the week, taking it all round, there has been a diminution.

64,863. If there has been a diminution, how can you say that it has not been in some measure owing to the restriction of hours, or do you calculate that the restriction of hours has had nothing to do with the diminution?—I do not think it has had anything to do with it. I think it is more or less the change of habits of the people. I do not think you can trace it in any way to restrictive legislation.

64,864. That is your opinion?—Yes, I think so.

Mr. D. [illegible]. 30 May '98.

and they congratulated the city on the diminution of drunkenness.

64,867. Who were the judges who did that?—One was Chief Baron Palles.

64,868. Have you got his words?—I have.

64,869. What were they? I ask you because you state it here, but it does not refer to drunkenness. He congratulated the city, that is all?—It does not exactly apply to drunkenness, it applies more or less to the state of the city.

64,870. To the state of crime?—Yes.

64,871. Can you refer to the judge who did specifically refer to the state of drunkenness?—Yes, Judge O'Brien. I have his words.

64,872. Was that lately?—Yes.

Causes of the diminution of drunkenness.

64,873. In what speech?—On December 1st, 1897, in opening the winter assizes, he said: "There is, with "certain exceptions, a very large decrease in intoxica- "tion applying to almost the whole winter assize "counties, with exceptions, some of which I cannot "easily understand, and you may be pleased to know "that one of these exceptions is the city of Cork."

64,874. My difficulty, which arises on hearing that evidence, is that the judge congratulates the city, and you yourself testify to the diminution of drunkenness in Cork, and yet in Cork we have had the restriction of hours; I want to know why you do not give any credit to the restriction of hours as having produced a diminution of drunkenness?—Taking the number of arrests for the years immediately preceding and succeeding there has at all events been no appreciable result of the legislation.

64,875. The years succeeding do not come down beyond 1883?—No. Comparing a previous period and a corresponding succeeding period there has been no diminution, at all events, of the number of arrests.

64,876. Down to the present day?—Oh, no, I am only speaking of the two corresponding periods.

64,877. It is long ago. 1883 was, after all, a very short time after the passing of the Act?—There has been a diminution of Sunday drunkenness down to a later date, a slight diminution from what it was prior to the Act of 1878.

64,878. You would expect that, would not you?—I may qualify my answer; there has also been a slight diminution of population from the year 1877 down to the year 1886.

64,879. So that the diminution of drunkenness which you attribute to general moral causes has not quite kept pace with the diminution of the population? Is that the right way to state it?—I think there has been a diminution, even taking into account the diminution in the population. There has been a diminution from 1877 down to 1886, but I think it is owing more to a change of habits and tastes, than to anything else.

64,880. You attribute it to some general change of moral habits operating upon the people, and not to any restrictive legislation?—Yes.

Clubs.

64,881. Have the clubs increased?—They have, since the Act of 1878 came into operation.

64,882. We will hear what you have to say, certainly, but I think we have had a great deal about the clubs in Cork. There were seven, I think?—Yes.

64,883. Do you consider that these clubs have sprung up in consequence of restrictive legislation?—I think they have, because the people who supported these clubs were, I am informed, persons who used to frequent public-houses between 7 and 9 o'clock prior to the operation of the Act of 1878.

64,884. Do you think it is better that they should resort to the public-houses than to clubs?—Of course in the clubs they are unlimited as to hours, and that is a great fault in them.

64,885. Are these seven clubs all drinking clubs?—Yes.

64,886. That is to say, they are all clubs where intoxicating liquors are used?—Yes. Intoxicating liquors are sold in all of them.

64,887. (Dean Dickinson.) There are no temperance clubs?—I do not think there is a temperance club in Cork.

64,888. (Chairman.) I did not mean to say drinking clubs in the invidious sense that they only resort there for drinking, but drink is sold to the members?—Yes, in the seven clubs that I mentioned.

64,889. When do they close those clubs?—Some of them are unlimited as to hours. I do not know that any of them have any special limitation of time.

64,890. In their club rules, is there no hour, as in London clubs, at which they are to close?—They do strike an average, I think, but I do not know that they always act up to it.

64,891. Do you mean they remain there all night?—Not all night exactly. They may remain there I think as long as they like.

64,892. Am I to understand you that they close at an hour when the servants of the club find that they can get rid of the customers of the club?—I think that is so.

64,893. Do they ever, to your knowledge, sell off the premises?—There have been a few instances of such a thing, but I do not think it is a very general abuse.

Shebeens.

64,894. The point of your evidence and opinion is, as I gather, that you think that restriction has given rise to an increase in clubs, in club drinking and in shebeens. Would that be correct?—Yes, it is.

64,895. Are there many shebeens in the city of Cork; there are not in the city, I suppose?—Not very many shebeens in the city. There has been no great increase in them, I think.

64,896. In the East Riding of Cork there are a good many I suppose?—Yes, there are a good many shebeens there, particularly in the towns of the East Riding.

64,897. Where whisky is illicitly made?—I do not think so. I do not think whisky is very generally illicitly made in any portion of Cork, either in the Riding or in the city.

64,898. It is sold without a licence; that is the meaning of it?—Yes.

Early Saturday closing.

64,899. As to Saturday night closing; a great number of witnesses have spoken very strongly as to the desirability of earlier Saturday closing, and, in fact, they preferred earlier Saturday closing to any further restriction on Sunday?—It might have been desirable in Cork, speaking of Cork city, at a time when it was customary to pay wages on the Saturday nights, but that custom has more or less gone out of use. All the principal firms of the city now pay on Fridays. Some of them pay on Thursdays.

64,900. You would not argue from that that the houses ought to be closed earlier on the Thursday or the Friday?—No, I would not. Of course the arguments in favour of that are that the working man having his wages in his pocket might be induced to spend a large proportion of it in the public-house on Saturday nights.

64,901. If he had his wages in his pocket on Thursday or Friday night the temptation might be the same, no matter what day of the week it was?—It might. I do not know that there is any increase of drunkenness on Thursday or Friday nights from what there used to be.

64,902. So you think that any restrictions would be service in respect of earlier Saturday closing?—Yes, I think it would.

64,903. At what hour are the wages paid on the Thursday or Friday of which you spoke in Cork?—Generally between two and four in the afternoon, I think, on Fridays, and the same on Thursdays.

64,904. At what hour would the shopping be over in Cork on Saturday night? I suppose the people have pretty early habits in Cork, have they not?—No, the small merchants do not close before 10 o'clock. Some of the drapers close at 7, some at 8, some at 9, some at 10, and some at 11.

64,905. Do you think it would be an undue interference with the habits of the people if there was earlier Saturday closing?—I think so.

Home drinking.

64,906. Are you able to speak, so far as your experience goes (it is a difficult thing to ascertain, I suppose), whether there is an increase of home drinking?—An increase for the past 20 years do you mean?

64,907. Yes?—I really do not know.

64,908. I do not see how you can know?—No, I could give no opinion upon that.

64,909. You think that home drinking would of course be a much greater evil than if the same amount of drink was consumed on licensed premises?—Yes, I think it would be. I am supported in that view by the evidence given by the present Bishop of Waterford before the Select Committee of 1888. Dr. Sheehan was at that time Canon Sheehan, he was a parish priest in Cork City. In a question 7616 on being asked if home drinking increased, would it not be a great evil, he said: "Unquestionably. (Q.) And it would greatly retard you "in the performance of your duties?—(A.) Yes. "(Q.) Would not that be a worse evil than the one you "seek to grapple with?—(A.) I should say that if half the "people brought home drink and took it at home, who "now take it in the public-house, I would not put one "foot beyond another to close the public-houses."

64,910. Is it not too strong a statement to say that if an equal quantity is consumed it is worse for the people if they consume it at home than if they consume it in a public-house. It depends on the quantity. There is no reason why a man should not consume a moderate quantity, and if he consume a moderate quantity it would do him no more hurt in his home than if he drank it in the public-house?—It is not exactly the harm it would do the man himself.

64,911. It is the example to his children?—It is the example he would show to the people surrounding him.

64,912. We all of us drink at home to a certain extent, do not we?—Yes.

64,913. You think if drinking is driven inwards into the house it will be worse for the family?—Yes.

64,914. We have had evidence of a very strong character, I may say, about the general expression of feeling in Ireland as to the advisability of Sunday closing and of earlier Saturday closing, and of the way in which that would recommend itself to the general public and the working men in Ireland. Do you differ from that opinion?—I do.

64,915. Do you know of any great mass meetings which the working men have organised against any proposed further restrictions on Sunday and on Saturday?—Yes, a meeting of the Cork United Trades and Labour Council was held in their hall on April 25th of that year, and the following resolution was unanimously passed: "That we strongly protest against the "Sale of Intoxicating Liquors (Ireland) Bill, at present "before Parliament, and call upon our city and county "members, as well as other Irish representatives, to "oppose the passing of this measure into law."

64,916. What were the provisions of that measure?—The provisions were: Earlier closing on Saturday nights, closing at 9 o'clock; total Sunday closing in the exempted cities, and an increase of the bona-fide [illegible] limit.

64,917. As we are now on that point, the Cork United Trades and Labour Council protested against further restrictions on Saturday and Sunday?—They did. If you wish, I will quote you a passage from the speech of the proposer of the resolution.

64,918. If you think it desirable. Who is the chairman of the meeting?—No, he was the proposer of the resolution, a gentleman named [illegible], a [illegible] maker.

64,919. Was he an influential inhabitant?—He is an influential working man; he is one of the leaders of the workers in the City. "He challenged the statement of "Mr. Maurice Healy that only a small percentage of "the workers of Ireland were opposed to the measure "now before Parliament. Mr. Healy might be speak-"ing what he believed to be the truth, but if a ballot "were taken on the question tomorrow under the "supervision, say, of Government inspectors, he "would guarantee Mr. Healy and the rest of them, "that at all events so far as Cork was concerned, [illegible] "per cent. of the working classes would be in favour "of Sunday and Saturday night closing."

64,920. But what about the other numbers that are required to make up the full percentage, what would be their view?—I do not know. I am only quoting his speech.

64,921. Coming to the municipality of Cork, what action has the corporation taken?—The following resolution against the measure was passed by the Cork Corporation by 22 to 4 at their meeting on the [illegible] April. "That [illegible] as the Sale of Intoxicating "Liquors (Ireland) Bill, which is at present before "Parliament, contains objectionable provisions for the "closing of licensed houses, and the placing on them of "restrictions which are unnecessary and uncalled for, "we earnestly urge on all Irish members to oppose the "passing of this measure into law."

64,922. Have you anything to say on the subject of which we have heard a great deal, the sale by publicans to persons already in a state of drink?—I think before a publican should be punished under the section of the Act of Parliament which regulates that matter, it should be established that the publican had known, at the time of such sale, that the person was under the influence of drink.

64,923. You agree, therefore, with those who think that the word "knowingly" ought to be inserted?—Yes, I do.

64,924. Have you many habitual drunkards in Cork City?—Not a great number I think, as compared with other places.

64,925. I suppose even in a city of the size of Cork those would be pretty well known?—Yes, they make themselves troublesome at times. They make themselves very troublesome to the publicans.

64,926. As a matter of fact, I suppose they frequent the same houses?—Well, I do not know that they do.

64,927. Have they not got their favourite houses?—I do not think they have their favourite houses.

64,928. What was in my mind was, if they frequent a favourite house the publican would know they were habitual drunkards, and might refuse to serve them?—It does not always follow. He may not know them at times.

64,929. At all events you think he should know before he can be punished?—Yes, I think he should know that the person was the worse for drink at any rate.

64,930. And that the police should be in more friendly correspondence with the publicans in informing them when they see a drunken person enter their premises?—Yes. We had two cases in Cork of the following nature—I believe they have been quoted by Mr. [illegible] in his evidence—where the policeman saw drunken persons entering a house, and waited for some time outside, until he thought that these persons would be supplied, and then he went in, and prosecuted the publican for supplying these persons with liquor.

64,931. Even in that case, if the man showed unmistakable signs of drunkenness the publican was clearly wrong in supplying him with drink?—He did not show unmistakable signs of drink, according to the evidence that was before the court. He did not show those unmistakable signs in the presence of the publican or the [illegible].

64,932. How did the constable know that the man was drunk?—It very often happens that such people on entering the premises pull themselves together.

64,933. Would he pull himself together more in the presence of a constable than in the presence of the publican?—He was not exactly in the direct presence of the constable; he was under the constable's eye.

64,934. The constable saw him go in?—Yes.

64,935. When the constable saw him go in, presumably he saw the constable?—He might not have seen the constable.

64,936. He might detain the constable as well as detain the publican, might he not?—I remember the evidence of one of the cases. The constable was about 50 yards away from the house, and he saw this man, and he admitted that he waited outside for some time until he thought that the man would be served.

64,937. We have heard that there are, contrary to the general rule in Ireland, a great number of tied houses in Cork. Do you agree that the tied-house system is not productive of public evil?—I think, so far as the public are concerned, that they do not suffer at the hands of it.

64,938. Who does suffer?—I do not know that anybody does.

64,939. I thought you meant to exclude somebody who did suffer. You think that neither the public nor the tenants suffer?—I think not.

64,940. As to the administration of justice, do you think the present licensing courts are good?—I think it is hard on the trade that in a great many instances charges against publicans are investigated before magistrates who are the open and avowed enemies of the

Mr. R. [illegible].

3rd May '02.

Punishing drunkenness.

Habitual drunkards.

The police and the publicans.

The tied-house system.

Mr. D. [illegible].

14 May '98.

trade, and who cannot bring to the investigation strict impartiality.

64,941. But you must set that against the case, which I suppose does unhappily occur, that the magistrates are the open and avowed friends of the trade. You cannot have one statement on one side without balancing it with the statement on the other. Do you know of any instances in which, while of course there may be people prejudiced against the trade, there are some, even of the class of magistrates, who are prejudiced in favour of the trade?—I do not know that any magistrate is so prejudiced. There might be a prejudice if he had a pecuniary interest in the trade, but outside of that I know of no other prejudice.

Disqualification of justices.

64,942. Do you know many cases in which magistrates have bias, so to speak, natural bias, from the circumstance of being connected with the trade?—You mean outside those who have pecuniary interest in the trade.

64,943. Yes?—I know of no such instances. They have never shown it publicly, whereas the others have done.

64,944. Do you know no magistrates who are in any way connected with the trade?—I know of none of those who show a bias in favour of the trade.

64,945. I am not talking of the bias now, but who are connected with the trade?—Oh yes, there are very large numbers of magistrates in Cork who are connected with the trade.

64,946. Who have direct pecuniary interest in it?—Yes; in fact, I think more than half of them have.

64,947. Do they act on licensing questions?—They are disqualified.

64,948. Do you maintain that while these people are disqualified, those who have the bias the other way are not disqualified?—I maintain that while those who take a very active part in those organisations which have for their object the suppression of all sale of liquor are qualified to act on licensing cases, those who have the pecuniary interests should also be qualified, so long as those who have a pecuniary interest are not interested in the particular application or case before them.

Statistics of drunkenness and the Irish Temperance League.

64,949. As compared with male drunkenness, do you consider female drunkenness has increased, or has decreased, relatively to men?—For what space of time?

64,950. I will take a period as near to the present as possible; comparing it with a year ago, or a few years back?—The figures show a slight increase in female drunkenness, I think.

64,951. You wish to call attention, do you not, to some discrepancy between those figures which you quote and those quoted by the county inspector before this Commission?—Yes. As I am on the question of licensing justices I want to point out that certain justices adjudicated in licensing cases in Cork who were connected with the Irish Temperance League, and I want to show that the Irish Temperance League has for years been trying to mislead public opinion in Cork as to the results of drunkenness.

64,952. The statements that the Irish Temperance League produced were, you think, inaccurate and misleading?—Yes; I think they were grossly misleading. I take the following extract from the report of their Cork branch for the year ending September 30th, 1896, as it appeared in the Cork daily press. I am quoting now from the "Cork Daily Herald": "In October "last, the committee invited a number of influential "citizens to join them, to wait upon the police autho-"rities in order to lay their views before them re-"garding the breaches of the Licensing Acts then very "constantly taking place in the city and county. The "police authorities received the deputation most cor-"dially, and promised to do all in their power to see "that the law was kept. The police court agent has "attended the police court during the year, and the "facts which he has recorded are of the most serious "kind. The convictions are of a character that these facts "cannot be glanced at by any serious thoughtful person "without producing feelings of sadness. The convic-"tions are much larger this year than during the "previous year, 3,[illegible] being the number, while for the "present year the number reached is 4,[illegible], showing an "increase of [illegible]."

64,953. Is this a statement by the Irish Temperance League?—This is an extract from the report of their Cork branch for the year ending September 30, 1896.

64,954. Where does the discrepancy come in between these and any authorised figures?—Mr. Gambell, the county inspector, was examined before this Commission, and he stated that for the year 1895, 1,5[illegible] men and [illegible] women, total 2,[illegible], as compared with 3,[illegible] stated in the extract from the report of the Temperance League, were convicted; and for the year 1896, 1,[illegible] men and [illegible] women, total 2,[illegible], as compared with 4,[illegible] in the report of the Irish Temperance League, were convicted.

64,955. Assuming, as I think we may assume, that it was not a wilful misrepresentation, upon what figures did the Cork branch base their estimate? As you say, between these figures there is a very strange discrepancy. How did it arise?—I do not know exactly how it arose.

64,956. (*Dean Dickinson.*) Did Mr. Gambell speak for the county?—He spoke for Cork City.

64,957. Is he a county Inspector?—He is a county inspector for the East Riding.

64,958. (*Chairman.*) He gave them both separately?—Yes; I am giving the separate figures for the city.

64,959. Are you giving the separate figures of the Cork branch as well as the separate figures given by Mr. Gambell?—Yes; the figures in both cases cover the same area.

64,960. And there is that great discrepancy between them?—There is. I should read another extract from a letter from Mr. Wilkinson, the Secretary of the Irish Temperance League. He wrote to the Cork papers on November [illegible], 1897, and he pointed out the amount of liquor that was consumed by each head in the city of Cork; and he goes on to state what the result of it has been. He says: "The result is, that 2,77[illegible] men and "1,[illegible] women were brought before the magistrates for "drunken offences during the last year. We all know "that these 4,[illegible] are only a few of the worst cases."

64,961. Taking as fair a view as no doubt you are able to take, you cannot account for the discrepancy between the two statements?—I cannot account for it. I do not think they could be justified in making such a statement as that.

64,962. You do not know what their proceedings were?—No, I do not.

64,963. You objected to a gentleman being on the bench who had a bias either one way or the other. Do you know of any notable case of a gentleman with almost [illegible] being on the bench?—I do. In the year 1893, at the annual licensing sessions, these were [illegible] magistrates presided over by a resident magistrate on the bench. On that occasion there were no objections raised by the constabulary to the renewal of any of the licenses. On the contrary, the district inspector of police paid a very high tribute to the manner in which the publicans of the city had conducted their premises during the twelve months. The justices were about to grant certificates in all the cases, when Mr. [illegible], J.P., came on the bench. Mr. [illegible] is a member of the committee of the Irish Temperance League, and a member of the committee of the Church of Ireland Temperance Association.

64,964. You think anybody of such very pronounced opinions as were held by that gentleman should be excluded from the bench?—Exactly.

64,965. Have gentlemen of such pronounced opinions had any effect in reducing the number of licenses in Cork? I think the number of licenses in Cork is pretty numerous, is it not?—Not to any material extent, I think.

64,966. You do not think there is an excessive number of licenses in Cork?—I think there are enough; at least, there are enough to satisfy the wants of the people.

64,967. All I meant was that at all events, though it may be very wrong for a person of very strong pronounced opinions to be on the bench, there has been no miscarriage of justice so far as regards the number of licenses in Cork, and so far as there has been any test of the exercise of the administration of the law by the magistrates?—No; judging it by results, there has been no great decrease.

64,968. As to the form of objection as served by the police on the traders, do you consider that there is any complaint justly attached to that form?—The form of the objection is the following: "Your licence has not "[illegible] conducted in a peaceable and orderly manner "during the year." I think that is very [illegible] and somewhat vague, and scarcely specific enough.

64,969. You think the police should state more specifically the particular [illegible] to which they object?—Yes.

64,970. If there is a complaint made, of course all the particulars and details come out before the court?—Yes; but I think that when the objection is first made the publican should know the nature of the objection, whether it is for permitting drunkenness or permitting gambling, or any other such offence.

64,971. And that the police should not wait for an offence to be committed, and then have the case up before the magistrate?—It involves a great deal of expense on behalf of the party objected to, because it will have the effect of carrying him to two courts; whereas under ordinary circumstances it would be disposed of in one session. I also think that the objector, having once stated the nature of his objection, should not be allowed to travel outside it.

64,972. As to the court, we have had it from a great number of witnesses that the recorder in the city should sit as the sole judge, and that the county court judge should sit outside the city, in the county, either with or without resident magistrates, with no appeal, not necessarily at [illegible] to the high court?—Speaking for the city of Cork, we have the Recorder there at present as the sole licensing authority as far as the granting and transfer of licenses are concerned; and we have no complaint to make regarding him.

64,973. Speaking for the East Riding of Cork, what do you say?—For the East Riding it might be rather dangerous to hand over the power to one man, who very often might be a comparative stranger to the district over which he would have jurisdiction.

64,974. The status of the county court judge would be a very high one, would it not?—It would be a very high one. These ridings comprise as a rule a vast district, and there may be a certain amount of local knowledge wanting in one man—the county court judge.

64,975. Would you object to seeing the resident magistrate sitting side by side with the county court judge in the county?—You mean the resident magistrate and the county court judge alone, without the assistance of the other magistrates?

64,976. Yes?—I prefer the present state of things: that is, where the resident magistrate and the county court judge and the other magistrates sit. At the present time the resident magistrate sits with the county court judge, accompanied by the other magistrates.

64,977. The proposition has been made that the magistrates should be relieved of these duties; that they themselves, or a great many of them at least, would very much like to be relieved from these duties. I have suggested, as an alternative for your consideration, whether you would object to seeing the county court judge sitting with the resident magistrate alone, with no appeal, it might be, to the same going judge?—The appeal ought to be open to objection. It might not be well to appeal to a judge of assize who knows nothing about the wants of the neighbourhood.

64,978. Have you many spirit grocers in Cork?—We have not very many.

64,979. Do you know of any who sell on the premises for consumption?—There is a suspicion attached to one or two.

64,980. You have in Cork one instance, I think, have you not?—I would rather not give the instance.

64,981. You say you could point to one notorious instance. I do not ask for the name, if you do not wish to give us evidence which might possibly lead to the identification of that individual?—There is one instance of a spirit grocer who sells for consumption on the premises.

64,982. And that is [illegible] known?—I think it is generally known.

64,983. Why do not the police interfere?—I cannot understand.

64,984. (*Mr. Grinling.*) Are you sure that he has got a publican's license as well? Because, very often, they hold both a spirit grocer's license and a publican's license?—I do not think he has.

64,985. (*Chairman.*) It is an instance of an abuse, therefore, of the grocer's license?—It is.

64,986. (*Mr. Grinling.*) You would know pretty well all the spirit grocers in Cork. I think in a population of 75,000 there are only two of them?—I have not mixed with them in any way. They are not members, except the members of my association.

64,987. (*Chairman.*) I do not want to ask you much about the quality of the drink. We have had a very great deal of evidence as to that. I suppose you would endorse other witnesses who say that the drink is not adulterated except by water?—Exactly. I should like also to refer to an extract from the report of the city analyst to the public health committee for the quarter ending March 31, 1898. He says: "14 samples "of spirits were examined. They varied in degrees "from 11 to 18 under proof, and gave no evidence of "injurious ingredients foreign to spirits."

64,988. Is it a custom among the Cork publicans to dilute with water?—Their spirits, but not any other drink, as far as I know.

64,989. I suppose that realises a great profit to be made on the sale of the article?—I do not know that it does. As a rule, they buy a good article, and they are only allowed to reduce it down to a certain standard, and that does not leave a very high margin of profit, I think.

64,990. What is the limit to which they may reduce it by dilution?—The usual whisky which the Cork publicans [illegible] is, I think, about five-year-old whisky. I have made inquiries about it, and I find that the amount of water generally placed in ten gallons of five-year-old whisky is from two to three gallons.

64,991. Would that be legal?—Yes, certainly.

64,992. Dilution is not resorted to for the purpose of profit, but is it a feeling on the part of the publican that the proof required is too high, and that it is better in the interest of the consumer that he should drink a less strong article?—Of course, you could not [illegible] the publican to sell without profit, and unless he diluted he would not have any profit at all.

64,993. (*Mr. Grinling.*) At what strength would the publican buy it? Are you talking of proof?—He would buy it at about 10 or 11 over proof, and he would sell it at about 20 under proof.

64,994. In no case would spirits be sold at 25 or 28 over proof. He must dilute it?—He must dilute it, of course; he would have no profit if he did not. If he did not dilute it, and if he sold it at the regular retail market price, he would sell it at an absolute loss.

64,995. (*Chairman.*) Have you any complaint to make of the drinking that goes on in canteens, so far as civilians are concerned?—With regard to these complaints, I do not wish to attribute any blame to the higher military authorities. I think that if there is any infringement of the regulations, it is done entirely by the canteen stewards, and not by the higher officers; it is done without the knowledge or consent of the higher officers.

64,996. Any irregularity on the part of these persons, if brought to the knowledge of the higher military authorities could be at once stopped, no doubt. I received some information regarding the drinking that took place at Fort Elizabeth and Cat Fort last year; and I wrote on the 6th April to the commanding officer of the district. He replied, stating that the practice was contrary to the regulations, and that he would be thankful if I would point out other specific instances of breach. I caused inquiries to be made, and found that the practice was stopped for some time afterwards; but complaints have lately been reaching my ears again regarding the practice.

64,997. I think you yourself personally endeavoured to test whether it was possible to procure drink at these canteens?—It is rather hard to do that.

64,998. But you did it?—I [illegible] watched around the gates, and I have seen civilians going in and coming out, but of course I could not say that they were supplied with drink.

64,999. I think that you yourself obtained drink at one of these places?—That is four years ago.

65,000. Has there been any great change in the system since?—I do not think there has.

65,001. You went there four years ago; was it in company with another civilian?—Yes.

Mr. D. Rahilly [illegible].

1st May '98.

Quality of liquor.

Civilians drinking in canteens.

And yet obtained drink on payment?—

At the Victoria Barracks?—Yes; in Cork.

(Dean Dickinson.) Was it through a soldier? a person with whom I was know a soldier, [illegible] by the soldier, and we went into the [illegible]

(Chairman.) Who paid the money?—I cannot say if it was the civilian or the soldier who paid [illegible]

It all turns upon that, does it not?—I cannot say how that was.

(Mr. Grinling.) Was that after your being to [illegible] offices or before?—Years before.

(Chairman.) Would you increase the [illegible] the law as regards [illegible]?—I think that [illegible] for carrying is very small. That is prohibited [illegible] of 1854.

You think the [illegible] maximum and the [illegible] ought to be altered?—I think it is too small.

How would you increase it? Would you [illegible] the maximum and the minimum?—Yes.

As to persons found upon the premises pro- [illegible] drinking their whisky, are they included [illegible] they punished for being found on the [illegible]?—I think they are included. I should increase [illegible] all round.

If drink were found stored, would you

65,[illegible]. I understand from that that where the houses are closed on Sunday by law except to bonâ fide travellers, the publicans in those houses does, if not the best, say the second best trade on the Sunday of the whole of the days of the week?—In saying that Sunday is a good day, I am not speaking of the houses outside the exempted city of Cork.

65,[illegible]. You cannot speak of the houses outside the exempted city?—Some of the houses outside the exempted city do nothing at all on Sunday, or scarcely anything at all.

65,[illegible]. Perhaps they are not from their surroundings places of resort, and agreeable?—There are some very [illegible] round Cork, and people walk out there on Sundays.

65,[illegible]. Take a place, which I daresay some of us know, outside Cork, a very favourite place of resort, you would not say that the publican in that district does a better trade on the Sunday than on any other day of the week?—I should not exactly say that; but I know that he would do a good trade.

65,[illegible]. I do not say that that is so, I only put a hypothetical case. Do you think that the increase in the bicycle trade has enlarged the facilities of the general body of the working men, so as to extend the limit?—A bicycle is an expensive article, and the majority of the working men cannot afford it.

Adjourned for half-an-hour.

63,040. It is very extraordinary that Cork should have so many. Several of the witnesses who have come up here have said that drunkenness exists to a large extent amongst the women?—I think that more or less applies to a particular section of the women. It applies to some of the women who do [illegible] in [illegible] and [illegible] in the markets. As a rule I think the women are very sober.

63,041. I think I understood you to say that Sunday closing was a failure in the county?—It has been attended with [illegible].

63,042. Did I understand you to say that [illegible] have [illegible] in consequence?—That was in the city. I am only speaking of the city.

63,043. How would there be a reason for the increase of [illegible] when it is one of the exempted cities?—I pointed out at the time that the hours were reduced from 9 to 7 in the evenings and that since then clubs had grown up.

63,044. (Mr. [illegible].) What is the principal employment of women in Cork? Is there any large manufacturing industry there?—There is not, not any particularly large industry.

63,045. We hear of fish curing, which brings a particular class of women to a place which would naturally swell the number of the town by intemperance?—Yes. I wanted to point that out in answer to Mr. Young's question, that it is generally those women who sell fish, or [illegible] the [illegible] that get locked up for drunkenness.

63,046. Is it a fact that much drink is served in Cork by keepers of temperance hotels?—That is true. There is drink sold by them.

63,047. And sales are effected in those hotels—not merely drinking—at any hour at [illegible]?—They are.

63,048. Not only to people who frequent the places, but their friends?—Yes.

63,049. Then the temperance hotels have quite as much to answer for as the trade in Cork in the way of drinking if that is so?—They have.

63,050. They ought not to be the first people to ask a change of the trade, ought they?—They ought not.

63,051. (Mr. [illegible].) I understand that it is admitted that there is a great deal of [illegible] on both sides of the magistrates?—There is [illegible] going on on both sides.

63,052. Do you see your way to advocating a total legal prohibition of it?—It would be very good, I think.

63,053. (Mr. [illegible].) With reference to the suggestion made by Mr. Wilkinson when he gave his evidence here as to the voting on the Sunday Closing Bill in the House of Commons. He made an explanation to account for the somewhat changed aspect of the vote, that one of the political parties in Ireland had been "collared" by the publicans. Do you agree with that statement or do you know anything about it?—I know nothing about such a thing. I read a report of the meeting held by the Dublin Vintners' Association yesterday at which the chairman stated that there was no [illegible] for making such a remark, and as far as I know with reference to the south of Ireland there is no justification also for making such a statement.

63,054. I suppose it is quite untrue that the statement referred to the Parnellites?—It was asserted that the statement did apply to the Parnellites.

63,055. As far as my information goes only one out of that party voted against it?—That is all. I analysed the division list and I found only six Parnellites voted against the Bill last session.

63,056. If the publicans have collared the Parnellites they have done it in an extremely [illegible] way?—They have, and they have made rather a bad bargain.

63,057. You would argue from that that probably they have not done so at all, and that it is not quite a fair way of putting the case?—I never heard of such a thing.

and 60 per cent. of the people against it [illegible] made an [illegible] statement with regard to that. What I mean to convey is this, that 60 per cent. would be in favour of the present system.

63,059. No further restriction?—No further restriction, and that 77 per cent. would be of the contrary way of thinking.

63,060. Then with reference to the magistrates, you have expressed an opinion this morning with reference to the county court judge sitting as the chief magistrate and accompanied by one or two others. Have you taken into consideration the fact that magistrates who have any interest whatever in the trade and who would be [illegible] to the [illegible] are [illegible] to [illegible]?—They are disqualified from sitting.

63,061. Taking that fact into consideration, you would prefer things to be as they are rather than except one man to adjudicate upon and [illegible] the licensing laws?—Yes, that is so, as far as the country districts are concerned. Of course in the city I want to qualify it in this way. In the city at present the trade have no complaint to make against the manner in which the Recorder has acted since his appointment, because he has been very slow to give new licences. In fact, he has only given one new licence for the past seven years.

63,062. Is there any great dissatisfaction expressed by the public outside the trade with reference to the magistrates?—I have never heard of any outside the trade.

63,063. One question about the bona fide traveller. A number of witnesses have expressed an opinion that it would be advisable to extend the limit. As I understand, you the people themselves instead of extending it would prefer the bona fide traveller to be abolished altogether than submit to any [illegible]?—I know there is a very strong feeling amongst the working classes in the city of Cork against the extension of the three miles limit to six miles.

63,064. With reference to the standard of spirits there is a difference between the Irish and Scotch whisky in the standard for buying, is there not?—There is, I think. The Scotch is [illegible] stronger.

63,065. The Irish whisky would run from 4 to 10 under proof?—Yes.

63,066. You are permitted then again to dilute that to 25 under?—Yes, if the publican did not do that he would have no profit at all.

63,067. It is not generally understood that they may dilute to 25 under, but they are permitted to do that if they like?—Exactly.

63,068. (Mr. [illegible].) In reply to his Lordship's question why in your opinion the curtailment of the hours of supply on Sunday had not led to a better state of things you said that you did not think that [illegible] facilities for supplying drink had affected improvement?—There was no immediate improvement at any rate. There has been a slight improvement, but I do not think it has been attributable to the fact that the hours were made a little shorter. I think it is more or less a change of habit.

63,069. You know the city of Cork well?—Yes.

63,070. Would not this change in the habits of the people be brought about by better conditions?—Yes.

63,071. Better dwellings?—Yes.

63,072. Increased religious activity?—Yes.

63,073. New sources of rational amusement and education?—Yes.

63,074. Would not those factors in your opinion be the causes of the great improvement that has taken place of late years in the condition of the people with reference to sobriety and otherwise?—No doubt they have been the causes.

63,075. Another question was asked you as to the habitual drunkard having any [illegible] hours of [illegible], and your reply was that he had not?—I do not think he has any special [illegible] hours of [illegible].

63,076. That would arise from the fact that no [illegible]

Mr. D. [illegible].

31 May [illegible]

[illegible]

The licensing authority.

The bona fide traveller.

[illegible]

[illegible]

The Parnellites and the liquor trade.

Causes of improved drinking habits.

Mr. D. Dorgan.

16 May '98.

65,078. A question was asked you just now about the temperance hotels. Is it within your knowledge that a visitor to a temperance hotel can supply himself with any quantity of alcohol if he thinks proper?—Not supply himself, but he can be supplied, I think, by the keeper of the hotel.

65,079. Of the temperance hotel?—Yes; it is done illicitly of course.

65,080. Illicitly supplied by the keeper of the temperance hotel?—Yes.

65,081. Have you any knowledge or experience of such case as that?—There are a few places that are rather well known.

Temperance hotels.

65,082. Have you any evidence that such is the custom?—There has been a prosecution brought against one of them, but the prosecution failed owing to the fact that they could not prove an absolute sale.

65,083. A prosecution was brought against one but it failed from some technical point?—Yes.

65,084. To take the ordinary temperance hotel where we presume that the proprietor is conducting his house upon true temperance principles there would be nothing to prevent a person visiting them carrying into his room any quantity of alcohol he thought proper?—I do not say that it would apply to all, but it applies to some cases in the city of Cork.

65,085. Would it not apply to all if a person were so minded?—It can be done.

65,086. For instance, have you ever heard of a temperance hotel in Cork where a commercial traveller may go who is under strict injunctions by his firm only to go to a temperance hotel, but he himself is not a teetotaler and therefore he takes drink with him into his room in the temperance hotel. Have you ever heard of a case of that sort?—Plenty of them do that.

Clubs.

65,087. Then as to clubs. The clubs in Cork of course keep open to all hours. There is no uniform time for closing?—There is some regular time but my experience of them is that they never set up to that.

65,088. It is not enforced to?—No, it is not.

65,089. Then your opinion probably would be that the clubs are as much to be blamed, if not more to blame, than the licensed houses for producing drunkenness?—I should say so. So far as the distribution of liquor goes they are very well to do.

65,090. But the licensee has to bear the whole of the blame, whether moral or material, for what is committed by these clubs or irregular unlicensed places?—Yes. With regard to that I may point out that according to the last return of arrests for drunkenness for the city of Cork for Sundays, 65 persons were arrested between the hours of eight in the morning and two in the afternoon, and 43 persons between the hours of two and seven, that is to say, the hours during which the public-houses are allowed to be open. So that it is obvious they must be some other means of supply outside that of public-houses.

Sunday closing.

65,091. Mr. Wilkinson stated in his opinion that if the licensees were consulted one-half of them would vote in favour of Sunday closing. Is that your opinion?—I never heard a licensee advocate Sunday closing, and I do not believe if the question cropped up that any of them would vote in favour of Sunday closing.

65,092. You are Secretary of the Cork Licensed Vintners' Association?—Yes.

65,093. And you are brought directly into contact with the great majority of the licensees?—I am.

65,094. Therefore, if they had any disposition to express that view of the matter, you would certainly have heard of it?—Yes.

65,095. Certainly, half of them could not have expressed that view without it coming to the knowledge of your association?—Not at all.

65,096. And that has never come to the knowledge of your association?—Never.

65,097. Have you any experience in Cork of a paid lecturer of the societies' organisations giving lectures on the question of Sunday closing?—There have been some meetings held on the question of Sunday closing.

65,098. The same witness, Mr. Wilkinson, said that they employed three lecturers to go through Ireland arousing the spirit of the people to approve of Sunday closing. Has there been any house-to-house visitation brought to your knowledge in Cork by these paid lecturers with a view to induce people to vote on the question?—Not within some years.

Mr. D. Dorgan.

65,099. You were asked by his Lordship if you had any knowledge of any meetings of working men held for the purpose of passing a resolution in opposition to Sunday closing?—I never heard of a meeting of working men being held for the purpose of passing a resolution in favour of Sunday closing.

65,100. Did you ever hear of a meeting of working men being held for the purpose of denouncing Sunday closing?—For years the Cork United Trades Association have consistently denounced Sunday closing. They have done so throughout the past year, and they did so, I think, about 10 years ago, and some other time before that.

65,101. How late has such a meeting as that been held?—They denounced it on the 26th of April 1895, and passed a resolution against it in 1888, and sent their president before the Select Committee 1888, to oppose the measure.

65,102. Has there been anything of that kind lately?—There has been in 1895.

65,103. Was that a properly constituted meeting of authorised bodies of men?—Well, I believe it was.

65,104. (Mr. Dickinson.) There are, I think, two temperance hotels in Cork—recognised temperance hotels?—There are more than two.

Temperance hotels.

65,105. I have inquired into the case of some temperance hotels in Dublin, and I have drawn from some of the commercial travellers who have frequented the hotels that they could not be supplied with liquor in the hotels, but that there was nothing to prevent them bringing whisky or anything else they pleased into their own bedrooms, and the two men who told me so told me they did so. How could the proprietor prevent that?—I think it would be very wrong to prevent those people bringing whisky in.

65,106. It would be impossible unless they were searched, and, consequently, men might come out of a temperance hotel the worse for liquor, but that would not prove that the temperance hotel proprietor had supplied them, because they had supplied themselves?—What I wish to explain is this, and that the people themselves took the drink in and used it for their own purposes, but that it was served inside because they could . . . and that it was sold by the hotel-keepers.

65,107. You said that you had tested the case of these houses by going into them. Did you ever go in or test that in any way yourself, or do you know anybody who has tested it by going into a temperance hotel and asking to be supplied there and then with drink?—I will give an instance, if I may.

65,108. A definite case?—Yes. There was a prosecution brought against the keeper of one of the hotels—I forget the name.

65,109. The Metropole?—No. Some four years ago there was a prosecution brought against the keeper, not of the Metropole Hotel, but of another hotel, for keeping drink, and this drink was not found in the possession of the men that were staying in the house, but was found in the room that was confined to the proprietor of the house.

65,110. That was the charge. Was it proved?—The drink was found, not exactly in any particular instance.

65,111. You say there was a prosecution. Was the charge proved?—No, the charge was not proved. His motion was that the drink was kept for the purposes of the lodgers, and that they were entitled to do so.

65,112. Then the prosecution failed?—The prosecution failed.

Returns of Sunday arrests. . . Temperance League.

65,113. With reference to the discrepancy you referred to between the County Inspector's report and the report of the Temperance League, may not this account for that discrepancy. The County Inspector gives the return of arrests for drunkenness simply, whereas the report of the Temperance League includes, as in fact is mentioned in the passage that you quoted, cases that were connected with drink, not of drunkenness simply, but cases of assault, cases brought by the Society for the Prevention of Cruelty to Children, and taking all those additional cases that might account for the increase of the number. The County Inspector's report simply includes those arrested for drunkenness and the report of the Temperance League includes all [illegible] that were in any way connected with or arising out of drink?—I think if they meant to do that in all justice to the trade, they had a right to mention it in their report.

65,114. They do mention it. These are the words of the Report: "All the cases brought before the police courts connected with drink"?—They say drunken offences.

65,115. They say—these are the words: "connected with drink"?—I will read it for you.

65,116. They specify cases?—Mr. Williams in his letter of the [illegible] November 1877 says: "What is "the outcome of this expenditure? One result is that "[illegible] men and [illegible] women were brought before the "magistrates for drunken offences during the last "year."

65,117. What he means by "drunken offences" is, there are offences such as assaults and cruelty to children arising out of drunkenness. It is a somewhat disguised phrase, "drunken offences." He does not mean offences of drunkenness, but offences connected with and springing out of drink?—Even taking it at that, I do not think all the offences arising out of drunkenness would come to that total.

65,118. With reference to the meeting of the corporation of Cork protesting against Sunday closing and earlier Saturday closing, I believe the number of the corporation (including ordinary councillors) of Cork is 56?—Yes.

65,119. And out of that 56 only 29 attended on that occasion?—Twenty-three voted for and six against.

65,120. Twenty-three voted against the Intoxicating Liquor Bill and six in favour; that is to say, only 29 attended that meeting altogether out of 56?—I would not say that. There were some who did not vote.

65,121. I have the figures before me?—There were some who did not vote.

65,122. Twenty-seven were absent altogether?—I would not say they were absent.

65,123. They were not present?—They did not take part in the vote. You can remain in the room and not vote.

65,124. That is not stated in the report. It appears that 23 out of 29 voted against the Sunday Closing Bill, and of those 23 no fewer than 13 were connected with the liquor trade. There were nine publicans amongst those 23; there was one who was a wine and spirit seller; there was one (the cooper) who is a pawnbroker; there was one a commercial traveller engaged in the sale of whisky; there was one a cooper who is employed at Mr. Murphy's brewery and, therefore, is closely connected with the trade; and that makes 13?—May I ask you who is the cooper who is employed at Mr. Murphy's brewery?

65,125. I think his name is M'Carthy?—I think I shall be inclined to doubt it.

65,126. You may be inclined to doubt it if you like, but I am sure if you doubt it you are quite [illegible] in saying so?—I disagree with you. I do not think the man is employed at Mr. Murphy's brewery.

65,127. I cannot undertake to prove that to you, but I find it is stated that he is indirectly employed in the brewery of Mr. Murphy. The point is that 13 out of the 23 are more or less, some of them directly, connected with and interested in the liquor trade?—I have an analysis of the list here and I do not think there are 13 of them.

65,128. Two coopers in the employment of brewers; one commercial traveller, agent for the sale of whisky; the pawnbroker, and nine publicans?—Might I ask you who are the two coopers?

65,129. I cannot remember all their names, one was M'Carthy?—M'Carthy is a baker also.

65,130. I think that somewhat diminishes the value of the vote. It was proposed by a cooper of the name I mentioned—M'Carthy—and it was seconded by Councillor Twomey, who is a publican?—I do not think so.

65,131. I know it?—I have the press report here.

65,132. I have the report here from the Cork paper, which states that Councillor M'Carthy moved the suspension of standing orders, and then moved the resolution that you have read against the Bill of Intoxicating Liquor Bill. Then Councillor Twomey seconded, and I find he is a publican?—I have a report of it also, and I find that Councillor Mooney seconded the resolution.

65,133. Which of the Cork papers tells the truth? I have the "Cork Constitution"?—This is the "Cork Examiner" that I have.

65,134. (Mr. [illegible].) Do you know whether the paper that Dean Dickinson is quoting from is a temperance paper?—I think it has advocated temperance principles.

65,135. (Mr. Gordon.) I think in your evidence-in-chief, and also in answer to several of the honourable Commissioners, you attributed a good deal of the increase of drunkenness in Cork to the clubs, or you were inclined to do so?—I think there is a share of it attributable to them.

65,136. Are we to infer that some of the clubs have grown up in consequence of the restrictions applied by the Sunday Closing Act?—I do infer that.

65,137. We have been furnished with a return of all the clubs, and I have before me a return of all the clubs existing in Cork, the East Riding, and the city of Cork, and I find looking over the list that, with the exception, I think, of three, all these clubs have a very high subscription, that is to say, the members pay one guinea, two guineas, or even higher sums per annum. One can hardly think that that is the class of club you point to?—I think there is very little blame attached to that class of club, but there are some more of them. There are a few there with very small subscriptions.

65,138. My point is that of those which have grown up since 1878 there are only one or two with these small subscriptions?—One or two would do a great deal of harm.

65,139. There is only one on the list that you could say grew up immediately on the passing of the Act. That has been in existence 17 years, and it is called a [illegible] club?—In the time went on the clubs sprang into existence.

65,140. You do not wish to hold out that merely one of two or three clubs any great evil can arise?—There is one statement I wish to make. I have made an analysis of the list of votes in the corporation, and I find that even including the man who is a cooper, M'Carthy, and including the wine and spirit traveller, there were only eleven interested persons took part in that vote in the corporation.

65,141. (Dean Dickinson.) You are not including the clerk in the liquor shop?—I am including him.

65,142. And there are two coopers employed by brewers?—No, there are not two coopers in the list.

The witness withdrew.

Alderman JAMES DEMPSEY called in and examined.

Alderman J. Dempsey.

65,143. (Mr. Gordon.) I understand you are an alderman of the city of Belfast?—Yes.

65,144. And you are hon. president of the Belfast and Ulster Vintners' Association?—Yes.

65,145. Is that a large association?—Yes.

65,146. What number of members have you?—About [illegible], I think. We have a board of management of [illegible], and we have representatives on the board from all the principal towns in Ulster.

65,147. I think you have been connected with the liquor trade for a long period?—Thirty-eight years.

65,148. And you are well acquainted with it generally, and with all the branches of it?—Yes. I have been in all the branches of the trade.

65,149. What is your opinion as to the state of the law?—I consider, as all the authorities who administer it say, I would very much like to have all the laws embodied in one law.

65,150. Decided?—Yes.

65,151. You have, I understand, numerous suggestions you wish to bring before the Commission. The first, I believe, refers to a publican's licence?—Yes. Evidence has been given before the Commission of a system which prevails in Dublin, and that it is suggested as a desirable thing in Cork, and that is to surrender one of two licences in some parts of the city and to give, in lieu of these licences, a new licence in another part of the city. My board is of opinion that such a transaction is not equitable. The removal of such licences, undoubtedly, would benefit the other licence holders in their immediate vicinity, whilst the setting up of a new licence would seriously interfere with the licence holders in the district to which the new licence would be transferred. We hold to the opinion that it would be better to carry out the suggestion of the Government of 1908, and if where licences were redundant, and possibly unprofitable, they should be purchased and extinguished, and that in the case of granting new licences, say in new areas, or where the authority might consider them desirable, there should be a payment made to the [illegible] authority for such new licence.

65,152. Are you prepared to tell us where, in your opinion, the fund is to come from to purchase the licences?—If there was a monopoly for granting new licences it would provide money for extinguishing old licences. It would be a more equitable transaction in our opinion than to carry out the present principle, which seems to be recommended both in Cork and Dublin. I have known a case myself where a licensed house was worth about 150l.; the man practically had no licence of it, and allowed it to get into a dilapidated condition. He built a new house, and got a removal of the licence, and the value of his licensed house to-day is 5,000l., I am told.

65,153. Do you advocate that that profit should go to the community?—The municipality, I think, should have the power to deal with it—the community or municipality.

65,154. They are synonymous expressions?—Yes. We are going to get, under the Local Government Bill, the amount of revenue from licences.

Conditions imposed on licences.

65,155. Then you wish to make some suggestions about the restrictions placed on licences?—This has reference to something that would be extra-judicial, and I understand you have had evidence of that character from some of the recorders themselves. We always complained of this, because they granted licences to persons who were carrying on a wholesale trade, and those persons did not do any bar business, and did not serve any customers for consumption on the premises. The police authorities had power and the year before informed those parties that if they did not open a bar for consumption on the premises they would object to their licences. The consequence was that several of them were forced into establishing public-houses. It was largely due to the putting on of a restriction which had relation, not to supplying customers on the premises, but to enable them to carry on a bottle trade.

65,156. Those restrictions, if they are not illegal, at all events are not included in the statute?—They are not statutory.

Suitability of premises.

65,157. What have you to say as to the suitability of premises?—In none of the statutes is there any definition with reference to the suitability of premises. We look upon it as a very important matter that the suitability of premises should be stated in the statute.

65,158. You have got no definition in Ireland, I understand, of the number of rooms that a house should contain?—There is nothing of that kind. It seems to be entirely a matter for the police, and the police will think suited premises in one part and condemn something like the same premises possibly in another place.

65,159. I understand you do consider that the police have acted fairly with it in your own town of Belfast?—My association has no complaint to make.

Transfers.

65,160. Then with reference to transfers?—This is practically a removal question, and it has a great deal to do with the case I have quoted. My Board would not object to a removal if it was from a bad house to a better house in the same locality or the same street, but to overlap a number of public-houses already existing, and let the man leave the district that the house was originally established for to seek a new trade and possibly interfere with another man's interest, we have a decided objection to. It has been used as a means of increasing the owner's interest in the public-house.

65,161. Do you think transfers should be granted to persons of good character without any trouble or hesitation?—In Ireland the transfers are granted at what is called an [illegible] sessions, whether it is a Recorder's Court or Quarter Sessions, and it is different from England. The same court practically confirms the licence. We think that these transfers should not entail upon the traders so much legal expense as they do in having two courts to appear before, both practically of final decision.

65,162. What is the exact procedure? Do you require a certificate of character for the licence holder?—That comes on on the removal. At the renewal of licences a certificate is procured by the publican signed by six householders as to his character and the orderly conduct of his house, and this certificate is lodged with the clerk of petty sessions. It is then presented to a bench of justices, who sit, I think, two or three days, and it entails an enormous amount of labour on these justices; and I am aware that the clerk of petty sessions and the justices complain of that useless duty.

Registration fee for the renewal of licences.

65,163. There is a registration fee charged, is there not?—There is a registration fee charged by the clerk of the peace of 2s. 6d. That is not so troublesome to manage in Belfast, for the clerk of the peace lives there; but the clerk of the peace for the county lives in Belfast, and it entails a great difficulty over all the counties in getting up the forms and the fees that have to be collected. It has always been a great grievance to the trade, and I have always held the opinion that the collection of it was illegal, that the registration is only required on the grant of a licence, that is, on the original grant, and not on the renewal. In the Act of 3 & 4 William IV., it says in section 10 "And be it "further enacted, that every person who shall obtain a "licence," and so on, and in the same Act, section 12, it says, "And be it further enacted, that every person "who shall obtain or renew." Now the grievance is that the fee is collected on renewal every year annually, and the same form is required to be put in annually.

65,164. You admit that that fee is quite legal under the Act?—I do not.

65,165. It comes in by your own showing. You read—"shall obtain or renew"?—My contention is that the obtaining of this fee should only take place when the first certificate is granted to the incoming publican.

65,166. How do you explain away the word "or"?—This applies to Dublin, and it is with reference to a police tax of 10s. a year paid in Dublin for a superannuation fund for the police. With regard to Dublin, it says:—"And be it further enacted, that every person "who shall obtain or renew under this Act a licence to "sell spirits in any house or premises situate within "the police district of Dublin metropolis, shall, within "ten days next after he shall have so obtained or "renewed such licence, deliver or cause to be "delivered," and so forth, and then it says again— "and such licensed person shall pay or cause to be paid "to the receiver of the police district in the said police "district of Dublin metropolis the sum of ten shillings, "and all sums so paid to the receiver shall go in aid "of the funds of the police district of Dublin metropolis; and if any person who shall have obtained or "renewed a licence under this Act to sell beer and "spirits within the said police district shall not "within the time and in the manner hereinbefore "directed, deliver or cause to be delivered such "same in writing as aforesaid, or shall neglect to pay or "cause to be paid the said sum of ten shillings, every "such person shall forfeit and lose the sum of five "pounds." My contention is that that portion of the statute dealing with the 2s. 6d. fee of the clerk of the peace has only relation to the obtaining of the certificate at the time of its being granted, and that there is no fee necessary in any following year on renewal. It entails a great hardship on the trade. It is not the amount of the fee but the filling up of the forms and completing payment of the fee, and if the forwarding of the form is neglected it passes into a solicitor's hands, who imposes further penalties on the trader for neglect.

65,167. How do you propose to simplify the procedure?—If the fee is charged when the licence is obtained only, it will simplify it. I think the law should be made clearer.

65,168. Then you have some idea about uniformity of licences, have you not?—We have in Ireland a peculiar system of assessing this duty. Some of the [illegible] valuations are old valuations, and some of them are very recent. The old ones are very moderate, and the [illegible] are very high; but in all the cases, whether old or recent, the [illegible] have imposed an additional [illegible] per cent. for the purpose of [illegible] licence duty. I do not know any other case where a [illegible] of licence duty takes place in any other business, only in this. I would not impose the same licence in a rural district as I would in an urban district or in a large city; but if the licence duty produced the same by equalising the duty for all the [illegible], I consider it would be an improvement in the system and would save a great deal of friction, and I believe injustice. All other trades we know of are charged a uniform licence duty, and I do not know how this system has come to be introduced into our trade. In Ireland I should say we pay the [illegible] duty, [illegible], as in England, and we do not think it just at all that we should pay so high a duty for a public-house in a country that has been practically depopulated, or in a country that has been increasing in population so extensively as on the side of the channel.

65,169. You cannot tell me that your own district of Belfast has been depopulated?—I am not speaking in this case of Belfast, but of Ulster and the rest of the country. Only Belfast has been increasing.

65,170. It has increased enormously, I believe?—Very largely.

65,171. During this century it has increased tremendously?—Yes, I think so. It is exceptional in that respect. The rest of the north of Ireland, unless it is Dundalk, has not been increasing, but has been decreasing.

65,172. Then with regard to the question of appeals, you have some suggestions to make as to that?—We agree with the [illegible] made, I think by the Recorder of Belfast and the Recorder of Dublin, and some of the other judges that have given evidence here that there should be an appeal from the recorder. There is not at present an appeal from the recorder. As I explained before, the recorder is the sole judge in cities. In England you have what is practically an appeal to the confirming committee from an ad [illegible] court. We have no such thing as that in Belfast; and as we desire that the authority for dealing with licences, both publicans' licences and spirit grocers' licences, should be assured to the recorder and county court judges, we should desire the right of appeal in all cases to the judges of assize, and it is given to me here so

the two judges of assize which comes, that they should sit together in such a case.

65,173. You endorse the statements of the previous witness with reference to [illegible] taking a place on the magisterial bench?—Yes, there seems to be some abuse in that regard.

65,174. Then with regard to spirit grocers' licences?—The spirit grocers' licences have been granted, and are being granted at almost every court, although the law gives the justices the discretion to [illegible] in granting such licences at the [illegible] sessions. We think that these spirit grocers' licences should in future be granted by the county court judge, and the recorder with the same right of appeal, and that the valuation should be [illegible], and [illegible] is suggested that consumption on the premises should be [illegible] of sale.

65,175. Then with reference to the hours of opening and closing?—The hours are satisfactory in Belfast. There is practically no agitation in Belfast; that has been [illegible] in any sense since [illegible]. I was here when Mr. [illegible] gave his evidence about some vote he [illegible] in [illegible]. As you have referred to the increase of the city, I may say that we have had a very considerable number of English and others come to reside in the city, and the habits of the people are strengthened with reference to their objection to further restriction. The habits of the people are of that character that a vote taken now, in my opinion, would be very much against the vote that was taken even in [illegible]. There is no growth of sentiment or opinion in favour of Sunday closing. I hold that it is directly the other way. The Sunday closing originated in a desire to stop all amusements or out-door recreation. They objected to railway trains; they objected to steamers going to Bangor; in fact, they objected to all Sunday recreation or enjoyment, and the agitation has been altogether abandoned in Belfast. The gentlemen who are so [illegible] on week days close altogether on Sundays, and Belfast would be a very dismal place if the public-houses were closed altogether on Sunday. The public-houses seem to me to be the only places where people can resort under any circumstances in Belfast.

65,176. The Sunday closing has been very beneficial in Scotland. Take Glasgow, for instance, which has a very similar population to Belfast?—No; it is a totally different population to Belfast. We have so many English in Belfast, and we know the feelings of the people very well. If there was not a business on Sundays in Belfast the public-houses would not enter for it. There is a large business to do, and some time ago the police made the following return of the persons who attended 30 public-houses on a Saturday and Sunday in Belfast:—

RETURN showing the Number of Persons who entered 30 Public-houses (four from each District) in each House from 5 p.m. to 11 p.m. on Saturday, [illegible] April [illegible], and from 2 p.m. to 7 p.m. on Sunday, [illegible] April [illegible].

Number of Houses.	Saturday, [illegible] April [illegible].						Sunday, [illegible] April [illegible].					
	5 p.m. to 7 p.m.	7 p.m. to 8 p.m.	8 p.m. to 9 p.m.	9 p.m. to 10 p.m.	10 p.m. to 11 p.m.	Total.	2 p.m. to 3 p.m.	3 p.m. to 4 p.m.	4 p.m. to 5 p.m.	5 p.m. to 6 p.m.	6 p.m. to 7 p.m.	Total.
30	[illegible]	[illegible]	[illegible]	[illegible]	[illegible]	2,114	[illegible]	[illegible]	1,514	[illegible]	[illegible]	[illegible]

We have about [illegible] public-houses, and if this is a correct return, and the [illegible] was multiplied by [illegible], it would represent [illegible] on Sunday. It would have to be taken into consideration that a great number of these people might have gone into more than one public-house. Then on Saturday it would represent [illegible]. The return shows that there is a large demand for refreshments at the periods when the houses are proposed to be closed by the Irish Sunday Closing Act.

65,177. Then with reference to the question of compensation for licences that are suppressed, I think you have something to say, have you not?—In Belfast, with the improvements that have been made, licensed houses have been pulled down, and according to the decisions that we know of, the arbitrator has only awarded three years' compensation for the

estimated profits. The consequence of that has been that it was a matter of the evicted trader endeavouring to get a new licence somewhere else to complete the compensation according to the value of the premises he held. We consider that there should be some alteration in the law in which all the licensed persons being fully compensated for the premises when he is compulsorily evicted.

65,178. For premises acquired by the municipality for the purpose of improvement?—Yes, there is a Bill before Parliament by the Belfast Harbour Commissioners, and I think there will be seven licensed houses pulled down and extinguished under that Bill.

65,179. Then with reference to clubs, I understand you suggest they should be licensed?—I think that my associations have altered their opinion about that and

Alderman J. Dempsey. 15 May '97

changed it to "registered." I do not know whether registration would cover the case or not. In the case of registration of lodging-houses or dairies, or anything else of that kind, the inspecting authority is a local officer, but in [illegible] clubs that are composed of anything, a local officer would not be sufficient, it would require a [illegible] officer.

63,150. You suggest further that the club-houses should be of a certain value?—We suggest it should be 40*l.* in value. The association has struck out that portion about the licence duty in consequence of the word "licensed" being changed to "registered;" but they say that all sale for consumption off the premises should not be permitted in clubs.

63,151. Your association propose further to license confectioners' shops where aërated waters are dispensed?—That is also withdrawn.

63,152. You have departed from that also?—Yes.

63,153. Since when have you come to these alterations?—It was done recently; last week, I think.

63,154. (*Mr. Younger.*) Did you hand the amended statement in?—I am not sure whether it was handed in or not. We intended to hand it in.

Temperance question and elections in Belfast.

63,155. (*Mr. Graham.*) Is there any point in your evidence which I have omitted, and which you would like to state?—We had a statement made with reference to the voting in Belfast at election contests. There was the case quoted here of Mr. Johnston, who is the present member, and his opponent, who was Dr. Seeds, and it was said against us that Dr. Seeds was the vintners' friend, and Mr. Johnston was the temperance advocate. He was then and is now.

63,156. (*Mr. Young.*) He was returned?—Yes. Mr. Johnston was returned. Upon that issue another gentleman came on the scene, a Mr. John Shaw Brown, and while Dr. Seeds and Mr. Johnston would have had a very fair contest, the [illegible] party—the Conservative party—[illegible] Dr. Seeds, and the contest was more between Mr. John Shaw Brown and the Liberals than against Dr. Seeds and Mr. Johnston. Since then we have had another contest which occurred in January 1896, after the death of Sir Edward Harland.

63,157. (*Mr. Graham.*) Are you quoting this to show the influence of the licensed victuallers in Belfast?—I am quoting it to show that those contests have not anything to do with the strength or influence of the temperance vote.

63,158. (*Mr. Younger.*) Evidence has been already laid here to show that it had a bearing on the local opinion about the Sunday Closing Act?—Quite so. The question, as I have tried to explain, was not an issue between the trade and the temperance people. This last election might be cited by us as an issue between ourselves and the temperance people, but we do not even put it forward at that. Sir James Haslett is a strong supporter of the temperance question, and the man who contested with him, a politically unknown man, was a publican. He at present owns one of the licensed public-houses that are put up for sale, so that he was a good friend of the publicans' interest. The poll was Haslett 3,7[illegible]; Turner 2,[illegible]. Sir James Haslett had only a majority of [illegible], but I do not put that forward as being a test question at all. One of my colleagues in the Belfast Corporation, Councillor Taylor, gave evidence here; we do not put this forward either; but we have the evidence of the labour candidates for the town council. There has been no issue in an election between the trade on the one side and the temperance people on the other, and in none of the addresses has there been any reference to Sunday closing question. So that Mr. Wilkinson, we think, has been bringing matters in that do not properly apply. His referral also to a question here with reference to coffee stands. I took some action in that matter myself, because there was a memorial got up by the lodging-house keepers in Belfast, and I think 30 or 40 signatures were attached to it. I have the memorial here, but the signatures unfortunately have been taken off it. I have all about the particulars of the memorial, and it was presented both to the Harbour Commissioners and the Town Council. The result of it was that they revived some of these belonging to the Temperance League. One of them was only revived last year. They held one of their best coffee stands in the centre of what is called Police Square, right opposite the town hall, and for years and years they only paid 1*s.* a year for it. That was increased in September last to

The Temperance League coffee stands.

4*l.* a year, whilst in other parts of the town and in the neighbourhood of the markets they were paying 10*l.* 15*s.*, and [illegible] of them that had been [illegible] attached to each other, and in other parts of the town they pay 3*l.*, 4*l.*, and such sums as that, for the coffee stands. We do not mind if they were purely for the public good, but there is more than that in it. I have here the statement of accounts of the Temperance League, which is carrying on this agitation, which has cost my friends a vast sum of money and expenditure, and has been productive of nothing so far. They have to the credit an amount [illegible] by [illegible] from the [illegible] account of 697*l.* 11*s.* 7*d.* That is for the year [illegible], which backs up my [illegible] position in this matter of the coffee stands is not so much for the public good as for the purpose of making money for the carrying on of a propaganda. Some of the expenditure is, in effect, salaries of officers, and [illegible], special meetings, deputations, and so on. Literature for the League journal, &c., [illegible]; meetings and deputations, [illegible]; salaries of officers, [illegible]; travelling expenses of agents, [illegible]. All this is for running this propaganda that there is no special philanthropy attached to.

Alderman J. Dempsey.

63,189. (*Mr. Graham.*) You mean that they sell coffee for the purposes of profit?—Yes.

63,190. There is no harm in that?—There is no objection to it, but there is objection to their getting coffee stands free of rent and taxes.

63,191. Getting the site?—Yes.

63,192. Are these movable coffee-stands or coffee palaces?—They are put up in the shape of huts in the centre of the street.

63,193. Small pavilions?—I have the memorial to the Harbour Commissioners here, and it says: "The "valuations for such sites are generally very low, and "consequently only small taxes are incurred; whilst "the money for the carrying on of the business is, in "most cases, raised by public subscriptions." I suppose they carry out that part. Then: "On the "other hand we, who are selling similar articles in the "vicinity of these stands, have in the ordinary course "to pay heavy rents as well as taxes, and in many cases "our families are entirely dependent for their support "upon our business, whilst these stands are managed "at the lowest possible expense, only one person as a "rule being employed. We are, therefore, placed at "serious disadvantages in consequence of the unfair "competition to which we are subjected. These hu- "[illegible] at the corners of the streets for which nominal "rents are paid, have publicly stated that these stands "were not only self-supporting, but returned a good "profit, and in some cases a 15 per cent. dividend had "been paid."

63,194. You have been giving us some statistics to prove the strength of your trade in Belfast. If you are so strong you can surely arrange your municipal matters without coming to us?—We should not bring the matter before the Commission at all. It has been brought before the Commission by the temperance party. We do not attach importance to this as a question for the Royal Commission.

63,195. If you do not attach importance to it, why bring it forward?—It has already been brought forward. I do not attach importance to it. It is simply correcting an erroneous impression that we are persecuting these people. We are not doing anything of the sort, and have no disposition to interfere with them.

63,196. (*Dean Dickinson.*) The impression that was left on the Commission by Mr. Wilkinson's testimony was the very one that is contradicted by you now, that the publicans were opposed to the establishment of these coffee stands as producing an unfair competition with them?—No, not on that ground.

63,197. That is the ground you stated?—No.

63,198. The memorial states they were placed in too central places, and were in unfair competition with the trade?—The lodging-house people and refreshment-house people are not publicans. It was the refreshment house people who complained, not the publicans.

63,199. Do you think it is an unfair thing on the part of the Temperance League to establish the coffee stands on commercial principles?—Certainly not.

63,200. Do not you think that purely philanthropic effort would not be at all so likely to be useful as coffee sold on commercial principles giving a fair article for a [illegible] price?—I should not object at all, if they would [illegible] the whole way round. They do not [illegible] on Sundays.

65,[illegible]. What are the publicans? Do they exist as pure philanthropists, or for the purpose of making profit out of their business?—We call them a portion of the Revenue Collecting Department of the State.

65,[illegible]. There is [illegible] principle than you [illegible]?—I do not think so. We are [illegible] like the Inland Revenue department over here.

65,[illegible]. What is the number of that [illegible] as far as you know in Belfast?—I could not answer that question.

65,[illegible]. You have always been an opponent of the [illegible] system?—I do not know. I have not taken any side in it at all.

65,[illegible]. Did you bring an action a few years ago against Sir Charles Cameron for defamation?—I did.

65,[illegible]. What was the subject of the defamation?—I can give you the particulars of it.

65,[illegible]. He spoke of a certain article manufactured by you as a brewer as a debased article?—I will tell you about the case if you wish to have it out. I was supplying, as a brewer, some publicans in a small country town called Holywood, four miles from Belfast. A sample was taken of a cask of porter that was on draught at a public-house belonging to a man named John Anderson. I think a pint was taken, and it was divided into three parts and a portion was sent to Sir Charles Cameron, who was then analyst for the county Down. He sent a report that this sample of porter contained 3 per cent. of alcohol, and, I think, 4·50 of solids. His contention was that it did not contain as much solids as porter supplied to workmen [illegible].

65,[illegible]. He criticised it as a debased article?—He criticised it as not sufficiently strong.

65,[illegible]. Were not these the words he used in his certificate—"a debased article"?—I do not think so.

65,[illegible]. His certificate was upheld by the justices?—The justices fined the publican 5l. It was appealed then to the quarter sessions, and he attended and said that the sample was perfectly sound and free from adulteration; that he had given to a Commission evidence that there ought to be a standard for porter and there is no standard as far as porter is concerned in the trade. There has been a standard [illegible] for spirits but not for porter, and I produced evidence that this was an average [illegible] commercial article.

65,211. The Belfast court at the sessions upheld Sir Charles Cameron's certificate?—I took an action against him on his certificate for libel. He repeated it in several of his grand jury reports, to the injury of my business, and I brought the action and I failed in the action.

65,212. Sir Charles Cameron's certificate was upheld?—He [illegible] himself that there was no adulteration. It was a question of whether there was a standard of gravity for porter or ale, or not, and I am informed there never was a [illegible] of the [illegible] per cent.

65,213. Have you much [illegible] in Belfast?—I could not answer that question. I am no [illegible] [illegible] of [illegible]. There may be more than we know of, but I have no doubt there are some.

65,214. Do you know of them?—I do not know about them personally, but I have seen cases that appear in the newspapers.

65,215. (Mr. Walker.) With reference to this action, the Court held that you had not been injured in any way by the statement of Sir Charles Cameron?—It was [illegible] paid to the first [illegible] and the [illegible] paid now, for these [illegible] in the street?—I [illegible] to say it has gone up from 10s. to 2d. in some cases.

65,219. That was not increased till after [illegible]?—By these people—the [illegible] League.

65,220. After their [illegible], then, the council increased the rent?—Yes, and so did the Harbour Commissioners.

65,221. Is this Temperance League very much in evidence in Belfast?—Only at the annual meeting there.

65,222. Do they publish a paper here?—They do.

65,223. Do you peruse it generally?—Not often. I think it has a very small [illegible] circulation. The [illegible] get it free.

65,224. Do you know that it was stated by a witness that they employed three professional agitators for the purpose of [illegible] up opposition to the licences, and in [illegible] of [illegible]?—That has been the mission of the association since its formation.

65,225. Am I right in saying that the money from the [illegible] of selling coffee or [illegible] drinks in the [illegible] enables them to pay the salaries of these men for persecuting the licensed trade?—So it appears from their own published accounts. Even in one of their principal places in [illegible] Street, they show that at times they sell [illegible], and do not open at all on Sunday.

65,226. The Temperance League did obtain concessions in the [illegible] of [illegible] from the council, which would have been extremely valuable if they had been given to the public in competition?—No doubt of it.

65,227. One word with respect to the removal of licences. I think you expressed an opinion that there should be no removal of licences from one district to another district, because it would seriously interfere with the interests of the already existing licences?—That is the opinion of my association. We have found it out to be [illegible].

65,228. But if it was permitted as the law is in England that the licence should be removed from a congested district to a district without any compensation whatever, you would raise no objection?—We regard the houses in the congested districts as of very little value. We regard a removal to a new district as increasing the value [illegible] to the person interested.

65,230. Would you have any objection to that?—Yes, we should.

65,231. You would have an objection to a licence being transferred from a congested district that had no compensation whatever?—Yes, we object to that. What we say is that if a licence is in a congested district it ought to be purchased and put an end to.

65,232. (Mr. Healy.) With reference to this surrender of licences, is it prevalent in Belfast that one, or two, or three old licences are given up?—No, we have not many cases of the sort—very few cases. In fact, the old parts of the city are the best parts of the city for trade.

65,233. In such a case, where there are two, or three licences are given for a new licence, do I understand you to say you would compensate those that were surrendered?—Certainly.

65,234. In what way?—By the same authority that would receive the money for the new licence, if such a thing were granted.

65,235. I think you referred to a Bill that was brought [illegible]

Alderman J. [illegible]

[illegible] May '99

Licences and [illegible].

[illegible]

Alderman J. Dempsey. 14 May '96.

was that we had no county councils. There was nobody outside the municipalities to manage this business, and they proposed to [illegible] it up.

[illegible]. In your opinion any compensation that is given ought to be of a [illegible] character?—Certainly.

[illegible]. No time limit?—I would not make any [illegible] whatever.

[illegible]. Do you remember the sum allotted that was estimated for that purpose from the 6d. on spirits and 3d. on beer in 1890?—I think in my country it amounted to [illegible] a year.

[illegible]. The Excise collection amounted to 1,[illegible]?—That would include the three kingdoms.

[illegible]. Was any portion of that sum allotted?—It was appropriated to something else; and what we say in Ireland is that in the three countries, I think, it has been admitted there are too many licences or places. I am not going to give evidence about there being too many licences in Ireland. I do not touch that, because it is well known that we are [illegible] in population; but in the country towns the trade, in consequence of the decrease in population, has fallen off enormously, and [illegible] in the matter of reducing the public-houses in those places would be a great boon to the people and the business.

[illegible]. You remember that that sum was allotted for those purposes?—Yes, I am aware of that.

[illegible]. A third portion was to go towards the purchase of those licences—[illegible], for the three kingdoms?—Yes.

[illegible]. Not one farthing of that money has been applied from that day?—Not a farthing. We always regarded the position as that we were deceived, because we did not object to any portion of the proposal of the Chancellor, and he carried his Budget, and it was on the pretence that we should get the money for the [illegible] of licences in Ireland.

Wholesale dealers and the publicans' licence.

[illegible]. With reference to the dealers you spoke of having obtained a wine and spirit licence to sell off the premises. You have told us to-day the police have interfered and almost, if not quite, compelled them to have retail licences and sell on the premises?—Quite so.

[illegible]. Are the police allowed to take any part in compelling people to do a thing of that kind?—It was under the threat that if they would not sell as an ordinary publican their licences would be opposed as [illegible]. They took it up in this way, that the certificate would not be [illegible], that they had conducted their premises in a [illegible] and orderly manner.

[illegible]. Would there be any investigation at the annual licensing sessions with reference to such a case?—One case was decided last week where the police opposed a wholesale dealer's licence, Messrs. [illegible] and [illegible], because they would not sell for consumption on the premises. Their premises are convenient to the [illegible], and they were entirely in the wholesale trade and did not want to bring any ordinary customers amongst their clerks and [illegible]. The magistrates refused the licence, and the police authorities took the case to the Court of Queen's Bench. It was decided last week, and the decision did not appear to have come from the judges, but the wholesale dealers withdrew their claim to have the licence and abandoned the [illegible].

[illegible]. Might I take it that there were any number of old licensed houses in the immediate neighbourhood or in the locality where these licences were granted?—Certainly; it was not for the convenience of the public those licences were granted. It was for the convenience of the wholesale dealers, who wanted to supply private customers in fine and small quantities.

[illegible]. Is it not your opinion this would be a very [illegible] injury on the existing licence-holders?—Undoubtedly, compelling them to sell as publicans.

[illegible]. Then, about the uniformity of licences. I think you observed that there was no other trade or profession in the country in which licences were granted but were granted on the same basis except that of the publican?—I know a distiller pays 10 guineas and a [illegible] no matter what the extent of the trade is.

Scale of licence duties.

[illegible]. There is a stereotyped scale on which those licences are granted?—Yes.

[illegible]. What you complain of is the [illegible] of that in some of the cases where the houses really want improving, and would possibly be improved, the pressure of an [illegible] licence in the licence duty prevents the people from laying out their money.

Ald. J. Dempsey.

[illegible]. Did the Act of 1878 apply to Ireland with reference to the scale of licensing duty?—It was the 1880 Customs Act.

[illegible]. I refer to the Act of Lord Aberdare?—The 1872 Act did apply to Ireland.

[illegible]. The scale of licences going on the basis of [illegible] value did not apply to Ireland?—It did not come in in that Act, but in the Customs and Inland Revenue Act of 1880 where the scale was altered.

[illegible]. It was in the Budget of 1880 that the scale was laid down?—Yes.

[illegible]. Was that scale made applicable to Ireland?—It was, and that is one of the complaints that we make, raised on the licence duty in Ireland upon the same principle as they increased the licence duty in England, and it was not [illegible] because we have not the increasing population or increasing [illegible] that you have got over here.

[illegible]. You mentioned a circumstance with regard to 40 public-houses being [illegible] for the purpose of obtaining a knowledge of how many people entered them. Were those 40 houses a fair criterion of the public-houses in Dublin?—I could not tell you. These were taken by the police officers.

[illegible]. Could you tell us whether the houses selected were the houses of the greatest call or the least call?—They do not say that.

[illegible]. Then the return may have no meaning?—I can only give you the figures that I have. It could not be possibly true that they were all individual callers.

[illegible]. If selected for a certain purpose there is no doubt they were houses of the greatest call?—Possibly. The policeman was posted at the door and entered them in a book.

The clergy and Sunday closing.

[illegible]. (Mr. Roberts.) We have had evidence lately from Ireland as to the strong feeling entertained by the Roman Catholic bishops with reference to the drink traffic. Do you happen to know the view entertained by your bishop in your district?—I know that Mr. [illegible] has been among him pretty often, because he complained about the last visit that Mr. [illegible] paid to him, and told me he would have nothing more to do with him. I do not know what has happened between them particularly. He is not a Sunday closer at all events, and I would say this of all his [illegible] clergymen, that their view of some things would be a very different one if they were allowed to carry it out.

[illegible]. Do you agree with the view of your bishop on this temperance question generally?—I do not know—I have not his views. I do not think I have seen his views in writing.

[illegible]. Is it a fact that you do not now hold a public-house?—It is a fact. I own a public-house but I am not working it.

[illegible]. You are not the tenant?—I am not the tenant.

[illegible]. That would be in accordance with the view of the bishop referred to?—Certainly not. The bishop does not interfere with us that far—no bishop would.

[illegible]. I want to ask you a question as to those coffee stalls. A reference has been made by a Hon. Commissioner to their annoying and injuring the trade. I suppose that would be the view entertained by yourself, would it?—I do not think that they are entitled to take so much credit for philanthropy as they appear to have done before the Commission.

[illegible]. In what way would they, in your opinion, annoy and injure the trade?—They carry on the Sunday closing movement which has had [illegible] [illegible] for the last 20 years or more, and I think it would have ceased in Ireland long ago only for the little investment they have here in coffee stands.

Coffee stalls.

[illegible]. You think the obvious fact is that because people get their wants supplied at those coffee stalls they trade less with the ordinary public-house?—I do not think so.

[illegible]. How would they annoy and injure the trade if that were not so?—I do not know that I used the words "annoy and injure the trade." What I complained about was the [illegible] of the coffee stand.

[illegible] nearly 1,000l., for the purpose of carrying on this Temperance League agitation, which is mainly in the direction of Irish Sunday closing.

[illegible],269. Because they in that way indirectly injure your particular trade—[illegible]. That is why you object to them?—It comes as [illegible] to conflict this thing with them.

[illegible],270. Your objection is mainly a financial one?—We have to show as much life as they do.

[illegible],271. You do not consider the other issues at stake in the matter. You simply regard it from the financial standpoint of your own trade?—We know it is a necessity for us to protect ourselves as best we can.

[illegible],272. You have referred, I think, to a memorial that was presented to the council with reference to the rent, have you not?—Yes.

[illegible],273. Did you give the Commission the names appended to that memorial?—No, but I can do so.

[illegible],274. Have you got the names by you?—I have them, but unfortunately this copy has been mutilated.

[illegible],275. Have you got them now?—I can give the names.

[illegible],276. But have you got them now?—No.

[illegible],277. (Mr. Gordon.) You could send them in?—Yes.

[illegible],278. (Mr. [illegible].) Can you give them now?—No, because the copy I had has got mutilated.

[illegible],279. (Dean [illegible].) Were not some of these signatures proved to have been not genuine?—They were proved with the addresses.

[illegible],280. Were they not proved to be not genuine?—Certainly not. They were always admitted to be genuine from anything I know about them.

[illegible],281. Are you prepared to have that list of names verified?—Certainly, if they are living.

[illegible],282. (Mr. [illegible].) When was the memorial signed?—It is [illegible] years ago.

[illegible],283. How long ago?—In [illegible].

[illegible],284. By how many?—I think there were [illegible] [illegible] to [illegible] of those refreshment-house keepers.

[illegible],285. Were they all refreshment-house keepers?—They were all refreshment-house keepers. Not one was a publican.

[illegible],286. You have not the names by you?—I have not them now. I had them last week.

[illegible],287. May I ask why you are not prepared with them?—This is not the copy I had. In this copy the names are cut off.

[illegible],288. Why would that be?—I could not tell you. It did not come through me. It was not mine.

[illegible],289. Is it not rather strange that you should present a memorial with the names torn off?—I am not presenting it in any way. I had the memorial with the names attached to it, and I thought it was with us; and this is the only copy, and this is not my copy.

[illegible],290. You only discovered this afternoon that the names had been torn off?—I discovered last week I could not get the copy. I knew that I had not got the names.

[illegible],291. Did you write for a copy of the names?—We have not got another copy.

[illegible],292. The names have disappeared altogether?—We can get you the names, and possibly a copy.

[illegible],293. I would only press the matter one point further. Is it not the fact that whether these names represented refreshment-house keepers or not, they were [illegible] to sign by members of your trade?—Possibly that is so, because I have here a document—I was not engaged in this business myself—addressed to Sir [illegible] [illegible], Knight, town clerk of Belfast, and signed by the secretary of the Belfast and Ulster Vintners' Association.

[illegible],294. What does he say?—He says: "I am directed "by the board of management of the above association "to place before the city council our views regarding "the coffee stands [illegible] by the Irish Temperance League "on the public streets—the property of the ratepayers—"at the rent of one shilling per year. On the [illegible] "[illegible] a deputation from our association waited on "the improvement committee, and urged that [illegible] "should be charged on these stands."

[illegible],295. That was a deputation from your body, was it not?—Yes. "The committee, however, passed the "following resolution:—'That the improvement com-"'mittee will be prepared to give similar facilities to "'those enjoyed by the present providers of coffee "'stands to others who will supply similar stands in "'suitable districts, and give equal accommodation and "'advantages to the public.'"

[illegible],296. Does not it appear to be plain from these facts that the agitation against the coffee stalls came directly from your association?—Yes, I agree with you in that.

[illegible],297. And was promoted by them?—Yes.

[illegible],298. I would shortly refer you to the piece of evidence given by Mr. [illegible] last week with reference to yourself. He said: "I think a couple of "weeks ago Mr. Alderman Dempsey moved that the "question of the rent should be reconsidered, and "there was only one other gentleman, the gentleman "who seconded, prepared to support him." Is that so?—That is so. It is a small committee.

[illegible],299. On that occasion you acted, I suppose, for your association?—I would not say for the association. I am not representing the association in the corporation.

[illegible],300. You acted in the interests of your trade?—I acted in the interests of the ratepayers, because I considered it was a very low letting.

[illegible],301. (Dean [illegible].) There was only one gentleman to support you?—Yes.

[illegible],302. (Mr. [illegible].) What mandate had you from the ratepayers to take that action?—I have no mandate on every small item. I took that on my own initiative.

[illegible],303. (Mr. [illegible].) The city of Belfast is greatly on the increase, I understand?—It has increased very largely.

[illegible],304. There are outlying districts from time to time that require a new licence?—On the leading roads.

[illegible],305. Where the city expands a new licence may be required?—On the leading roads before the city extended there were licensed houses.

[illegible],306. Do I understand you to advocate that such a new licence should be put up for tender?—I think that possibly the most convenient way to do it would be for the person who put up the house—the landlord or owner—to seek a licence and propose to pay a sum of money.

[illegible],307. Supposing he did not propose to pay enough?—That would be a matter for the authorities.

[illegible],308. You suggest he should make a payment?—Certainly.

[illegible],309. As Mr. Commissioner asked you the question [illegible] suppressed licences were to be compensated. Would that make a [illegible] for a compensation fund?—I do not think that we have much to deal with in the case of suppressing licences in Belfast.

[illegible],310. I only point out a manner in which it might be done?—It would help to balance the account.

[illegible],311. You suggest a payment should be made in return for a new licence?—Exactly.

[illegible],312. Would it not to a certain extent meet the suppression of licences not required, which I understood you to speak of in your evidence?—I did not say in Belfast that we have such cases.

[illegible],313. I thought you said there was a plethora of licences in some parts of Belfast?—I did not say so. I said that possibly some of the worst houses in the centre of the city were much more valuable than houses in the suburbs.

[illegible],314. Still, if it were intended to reduce the number of licences in a congested district the money would be found by the sale of licences in a new district?—Quite so.

[illegible],315. (Mr. Young.) You do not think that in the rapidly increasing city of Belfast there are too many licences?—I do not think so. What I do say is that in the new districts every new street has either one or two spirit grocers in it.

[illegible],316. Do I understand you to say that you would not allow anyone to transfer a licence from one part of the city to another to a better house?—No. We consider

Alderman J. Dempsey.

[illegible] May '98.

[illegible]

[illegible]

Alderman J. Dempsey.

[illegible] May '98

and a person who does that is gaining very considerable [illegible] and advantage. It is only a house that has got into a very dilapidated state, and possibly the [illegible] between the landlord and tenant are not satisfactory that would be removed at all.

[illegible]. You do not object to a transfer of such a house to a better house in another district?—In the same district we do not object.

[illegible]. Any district?—Yes, we object to it in another district.

[illegible]. Do you think, with reference to the licensing authority, that there should be some local magistrates as well as the county court judge or recorder?—I do not know. It would be an experiment in any case.

[illegible]. May I ask you has your association any authentic account of the meetings said to be held by the Temperance League. It has been said here that there were very influential meetings held in various parts, which showed the tendency of public opinion?—It seems to me that a great deal of the present year's business arises from the subscription of a Mr. [illegible], of [illegible] Street, who it appears gave [illegible] for this agitation.

Sunday closing.

[illegible]. It has been said here that the tendency of opinion in Belfast has run by four [illegible] for Sunday closing. Is that your opinion?—Our opinion is that it is strengthened by agitation on this side of the Channel, because they wish to use the Irish question as a leverage for English Sunday closing. That is our opinion.

[illegible]. Then I think I understood you to say that public opinion rather ran in the other direction. I understood you to say that it was not only the Sabbatarian view of the question, but you said there was an opposition to [illegible] as I, I may take it, theatres and [illegible] and things of that kind on Sundays?—Quite so.

[illegible]. And that, consequently, with those old opinions there was an opposition to public-houses?—Quite so.

[illegible]. Is it your opinion that as that question of Sunday observance passes away you will have the [illegible] view of allowing every one to have their refreshment if they like?—Decidedly. The people are quite able to control and take care of themselves. They are quite as fit on our side of the channel as on this side to use public-houses properly.

[illegible]. You are opposed to Sunday closing as one that has had great experience?—It is not a measure that will at all conduce to improvement in temperance [illegible].

[illegible]. Do you think it would lead to more drinking at home?—It might certainly have that effect.

Alderman J. Dempsey.

[illegible]. I think you object to those licenses which are held by distillers?—I do not object to them, but I object to there being no [illegible] way of these [illegible] carrying on their business than by giving them a publican's license, and they have [illegible] the wholesale dealers' objection to a license like a publican's license—[illegible] of them.

The [illegible] [illegible] [illegible].

[illegible]. Then would you think that the [illegible] license which is held in England should be also given in Ireland by an Act of Parliament?—According to the wholesale section of the trade they seem to desire it, and I do not see why they should not have it, if it suits them.

[illegible]. On payment of the usual license?—Quite so.

[illegible]. (*[illegible]*) Are you not aware that the Sunday closing agitation, or part of it, was carried on largely by Roman Catholic bishops, clergy, and others who are not so very [illegible] on the *Sabbatarian* observance of Sunday?—I am quite sure that all clergymen will join a movement of the sort if they think it will benefit the people.

[illegible]. Not because Sunday was a good day but because they thought whisky was a bad thing and particularly dangerous on Sunday, being a holiday and [illegible] being free from work. It was not on *Sabbatarian* principles at all, but because, being a holiday, workmen had more opportunity of getting drunk and had more temptations to get drunk on Sunday than on any other day?—I do not know that it was that.

[illegible]. And many of the same people who promoted Sunday closing also promoted [illegible] and the opening of [illegible] on Sunday?—I know this for a fact, that the [illegible] movement on Saturdays came in by an observation from my friend Mr. Dwyer, the secretary of the Dublin Licensed Vintners' Association. He said to Mr. Russell, if you are so anxious about temperance on Sunday why not close the houses earlier on Saturday night. Nobody dreamed of it till that observation passed from Mr. Dwyer. He was as much responsible at that time as Mr. Russell, and they were [illegible] here together with Russell in 1878. Mr. Wolff, who is one of the largest employers of labour in Belfast, said to me the other day that he would leave open the public-houses all day on Sunday if they could be closed on Monday; so that you would get variations of everything before this Commission, which would not lead you to a settlement of the question.

The witness withdrew.

Adjourned to [illegible] at [illegible].

ONE HUNDRED AND NINTH DAY.

Queen's Robing Room, House of Lords, Wednesday, May [illegible], 18[illegible].

PRESENT:

THE RIGHT HONOURABLE THE VISCOUNT PEEL, IN THE CHAIR.

The Very Rev. H. H. [illegible], D.D.	[illegible] Johnston, Esq.
Edward [illegible] [illegible], Esq.	John [illegible] Roberts, Esq., M.P.
Alexander [illegible] [illegible], Esq.	Charles Walker, Esq.
[illegible] [illegible], Esq.	[illegible] [illegible], Esq., M.P.
[illegible] [illegible], Esq.	George Young[illegible], Esq.

Mr. Charles M'C[illegible] called in and examined.

Mr. C. M'C[illegible] — Position of witness.

[illegible]. (Chairman.) You are from Ballymena, I think?—Yes.

[illegible]. You are a licensed trader, mostly wholesale, in the town of Ballymena?—Yes.

[illegible]. Have you been long in business?—Nearly [illegible] years.

[illegible]. Not only in Ballymena but throughout Antrim, I suppose, your experience is considerable?—Yes.

[illegible]. Would you desire a simplification of the licensing laws?—I think it would be necessary.

[illegible]. Besides simplification by codification or otherwise, you would like, I suppose, that there should be some changes in the law?—Yes.

Sunday closing and the bonâ fide traveller.

[illegible]. Especially with regard to Sunday closing?—I think Sunday closing is a failure.

[illegible]. In what respect is it a failure?—In most towns there is still a Sunday trade.

[illegible]. Is that for the benefit of the traveller?—Principally. For instance in the coast towns in Antrim there is a large tourist traffic. There is a great number of people come there on Sundays, and it is certainly the best business day of the week.

[illegible]. You would open the public-houses altogether on the Sunday?—For a few hours.

[illegible]. Because they are practically open all day to the bonâ fide traveller?—They are because of the bonâ fide traveller.

[illegible]. You think the bonâ fide traveller should be restricted to getting his refreshments within certain definite hours of the day?—I think it would be well.

[illegible]. Would the publicans interest approve of that, as far as you know?—As far as I know, they would.

[illegible]. It is irksome to them, is it, to be constantly at their business, or having an occasional constantly at the business to which for an odd traveller here and there?—I know they suffer a great deal of inconvenience thereby.

Illicit distilling.

[illegible]. Is there much distillation of [illegible] [illegible] going on in your district?—There is a good deal in both Antrim and Derry, principally in South Derry.

[illegible]. Does the country lend itself to that kind of business? Is it a wild country?—Not so very wild.

[illegible]. I suppose in the mountainous parts of Ireland, where it is very difficult for the police to get at you, there [illegible] illicit distillation [illegible]?—I believe so, but it is not a wild part of the country that I refer to.

[illegible]. What is the reason for the prevalence of illicit distillation in Derry and Antrim?—I do not know how it is, but it seems to have got into that district. It is sold in bottles, and everywhere hawked about the country. It is taken into the houses and sold to women and children, I believe.

[illegible]. You think the evil of that illicit distillation would be greatly remedied or eradicated altogether, do you, if there were Sunday opening?—Yes, I understand, and I have been told often that on Sunday in those districts there is Sunday drinking carried on in the houses.

Mr. C. M'C[illegible] — [illegible] May '[illegible].

[illegible]. You have some guarantee, then, that the liquor sold in a public-licensed house is of good quality, or of fairly good quality in the district?

[illegible]. But you have no security that the stuff that is sold as the produce of illicit distillation is of any quality at all?—No; it is wretched stuff. Licensed traders have told me often that they have seen men coming drunk to their premises from this stuff.

[illegible]. Do you suppose that this illicit liquor gets into the houses, and is sold by the proper licensed publicans?—I have no information to that effect. I have not heard of any traders doing so.

[illegible]. You have not traced this, what you call wretched stuff, to any of the public-houses?—I have never heard of a single instance of it.

[illegible]. Is it adulterated stuff, or simply badly made?—Badly made.

[illegible]. And very raw and new?—Quite new.

The bonâ fide traveller.

[illegible]. Do I understand you that at the resorts, where you would expect the bonâ fide traveller rather to go are there to resort to, there is a Sunday trade ostensibly because of the resort of the bonâ fide traveller?—In some instances there is.

[illegible]. Would you make any difference as to the 3 mile limit?—I think if houses were open for a few hours on Sunday there would be no necessity for bonâ fide traveller clauses.

[illegible]. You would open the public-houses for what hours?—I should say from [illegible] to [illegible] or [illegible].

[illegible]. Outside those hours you would leave the bonâ fide traveller to shift for himself?—He is not so much moving about then. If the houses were open from [illegible] to [illegible] I should say you could increase the limit to [illegible] or [illegible] miles for the bonâ fide traveller, if it were necessary to have a clause.

[illegible]. If the houses were open from [illegible] to [illegible] to all, it would be rather hard to exclude the bonâ fide traveller because he did not travel a certain number of miles?—As it is at present, if he goes 3 miles he can get a drink throughout the day, and I think he would be a more legitimate bonâ fide traveller if the houses were fresh open [illegible] to [illegible].

[illegible]. If the houses are open from [illegible] to [illegible] you do not need any bonâ fide traveller at all, or any distinction?—I would say you might have [illegible] or [illegible] or [illegible] miles; 3 miles would be too short a distance if the houses were open.

[illegible]. (Mr. [illegible].) I think you mean that the bonâ fide traveller should not drink during prohibited hours, and that then the limits should be [illegible]?—That is what I mean.

[illegible]. (Chairman.) Besides opening the houses on Sunday where they are now closed from [illegible] to [illegible] or [illegible], you would allow the bonâ fide traveller to have access to those houses before or after those opening hours?—Yes, if the distance were [illegible] or [illegible] miles.

Mr. C. M'Connell.

22 May '97.

The licensing authority.

63,366. You would put no restriction on the *bona fide* traveller except the limit of travel?—No.

63,367. What do you think of the licensing authority?—I think it does not work satisfactorily in the county.

63,368. You do not object to the recorder in the city?—No.

63,369. Nor to the county court judge in the county?—No. I think that would be the best plan after all.

63,370. What would you do with the magistrates; would you allow the magistrates to sit with the county court judge?—I think it would be better not.

63,371. You would relieve the magistrates altogether of their duties?—I think it would be better.

63,372. As you have a single person, the recorder in the city, and the county court judge in the county, would you have any appeal from their decisions? Perhaps you have not thought that matter over? Are you able to give an opinion?—There is a good deal of confusion at present. For instance those interested in the liquor traffic have to take in the business at all, and persons connected [illegible] and others have every interest in expressing their opinions, and exercising their jurisdiction. We in the trade consider that unfair.

63,373. I gather that you have rather a low opinion of the way in which the law is at present administered outside the jurisdiction of the recorder?—Yes, as it is a very great responsibility to place in the hands of one man, I think it would be better in the hands of the recorder.

63,374. I understand you to hold a very strong opinion of the way in which the law is administered by the magistrates?—I do.

63,375. I do not want to put words into your mouth, but are you of opinion that law is a [illegible] consideration with the magistrates?—In some cases it is.

63,376. I suppose your objection to the magistrates would extend equally to what I may call teetotal magistrates as to a brewer magistrate, or one interested in the trade?—Certainly.

Canvassing.

63,377. Do you agree with previous witnesses who say that there is a good deal of canvassing of magistrates?—Canvassing on both sides.

63,378. And that the magistrates are susceptible; that they yield to the canvass?—The magistrates in the county of Antrim seem to be pretty independent in that way. They cannot prevent persons coming to them, I suppose.

63,379. When you say that law is not so much administered, do you mean to say that the decisions go by the canvass rather than by the requirements of the law?—Undoubtedly influence has a great deal to do with licensing applications.

63,380. That they cannot resist the pressure put upon them?—I do not know.

63,381. Well, that they do not?—I cannot answer that.

63,382. They do not administer the law properly?—There is a feeling that they do not.

63,383. That is your feeling?—It is my feeling.

Renewals to be granted by the Excise only.

63,384. Do you think there should be any simplification or alteration in the annual issue of licenses?—Yes.

63,385. And that the matter should go before the Excise, and if the Excise like to issue a license the license should be granted?—I think that would be the proper way where there is no objection to the renewal of the license.

63,386. What would you have the recorder and the county court judge do, would you have the Excise entirely independent of the county court judge and the recorder?—Not as to the grant of a new license.

63,387. But as to the renewal?—As to the renewal, I would.

63,388. Or a transfer?—Well, as to the transfer, if there is no objection on the part of the police, and nothing against the character of the applicant, I do not think there is any necessity to go before the recorder.

The six householders' certificate.

63,389. Is the form of getting a certificate from six householders a good one or a useless one, in your opinion?—It is entirely useless.

63,390. One witness said that he objected to it, but [illegible] principle, namely, the principle of some exercise of local option. Do you agree with that?—I do not think so. I never would use any one for it at all.

Mr. C. M'Connell.

63,391. You think six householders could be always got together?—Undoubtedly they could.

63,392. To certify to anything?—I am quite sure of it.

63,393. Have you anything to say about the mode of assessing the public duty for a license?—It would be better if there was a uniform license duty.

Illicit distillation.

63,394. (Mr. Young.) You speak of illicit distillation in Ballymena?—Not in Ballymena.

63,395. Where?—In parts of County Antrim along the side of the Bann.

63,396. In what parts of the County Antrim is there illicit distillation?—On the Port Glenone side.

63,397. Have there been any detections there?—Yes, there are, occasionally. The penalty seems to be too small to stamp it out.

63,398. Do you think it applies to Donegal altogether?—Undoubtedly there is a good deal of illicit distillation on both sides of the river Bann.

63,399. The general publichouses do not get this whisky?—No, they do not. I never heard of a single trader having it.

63,400. That illicit distillation is a very infinitesimal matter in County Antrim at all events?—It is larger in South Derry.

63,401. Do you know that of your own knowledge?—I do.

Sunday closing.

63,402. In Ballymena you are all closed on Sundays?—Yes.

63,403. What effect has that had; have you less drinking than you used to have?—We occasionally see drunken people on the streets.

63,404. Where do they get the drink?—I think there are some shebeens in the place. Some of them go out of town perhaps an hour or two in the day, and get drink outside.

63,405. Sunday closing has not had the effect of diminishing the consumption of liquor, I suppose?—No.

63,406. And I suppose you have places in Ballymena where they can always get it?—There is always some place where they can get it, and I have asked the police, and they tell me they have as many arrests for drunkenness on Sunday as on any other day in the week except Saturday, which is the market day, the principal day of the week.

63,407. You think on the whole that it would be better that the publichouses were open on Sundays from 2 to 7 o'clock, or 3 to 8 o'clock?—I think it would be better if they were open three or four or five hours on Sunday.

63,408. Is that the general opinion in Ballymena?—It is.

63,409. How many years is it since you had to close up on Sundays?—In 1878 the Sunday Closing Act was passed.

The *bona fide* traveller.

63,410. I think you said yourself that the failure was in consequence of *bona fide* travellers. You do not quite mean that?—Not entirely that. In the cases here in Antrim, I think the failure is especially due to the *bona fide* traveller. For instance in the summer months, from May, there is a big tourist traffic there, and the houses are closed, but they have to be open for the *bona fide* traveller.

63,411. Do you know how many public-houses you have in Ballymena?—72, I think.

63,412. There has not been an increase of public-houses in the last 10 years?—There have been two or three less within the last 10 years.

63,413. The population is 33,000 in Ballymena?—Oh, no.

63,414. (Mr. Roberts.) 3,000?—About 11,000.

63,415. (Mr. Grindley.) The population is given here in 1881 as 37,915, and in 1891 as 33,468 with 92 public-houses?—That would be the district. As a matter of [illegible]

65,416. (*Mr. Young.*) Are you speaking of the district?—I am speaking of the town now, but I do not know the district you refer to outside Ballymena.

65,417. There has been a decrease of 11 houses during the last 10 years?—A decrease of three or four public-houses in Ballymena during the last 10 years.

65,418. Eleven houses for the district?—There would be, for the district.

65,419. Have you too many public-houses there now?—We have enough, any way, I think.

65,420. (*Mr. Sexton.*) Do you remember the time when the public-houses were closed in Ballymena at an early hour, 10 instead of 11?—I was not in Ballymena at that time.

65,421. You are aware of the fact?—I do not remember the time.

65,422. For a certain number of months the public-houses were closed earlier. Do you know that as a fact?—No, I do not remember that.

65,423. Was not it a fact that some years ago the public-houses were closed in that town at 10 instead of 11 o'clock at night?—Not in my time.

65,424. Do you know that it is a fact?—I never heard of it before.

65,425. About this illegal distillation, following up Mr. Young's question. Can you define where this illicit distillation takes place—could you name the villages in the County Antrim where to your knowledge it takes place?—It is along the shores of the Bann in County Antrim.

65,426. Can you name the place or places?—Coleraine and Derry, and round that way.

65,427. You do not know of any other place where it takes place. You cannot say it takes place anywhere except in that one spot?—For five or six miles round about there.

65,428. That is the only district in which it takes place to your own knowledge?—It takes place on both sides of the Bann in County Antrim and County Derry to my knowledge.

65,429. You have spoken about the canvassing of the magistrates in licensing cases. You said that in your opinion the magistrates of your county are pretty independent but you admit that they are canvassed?—Yes; they are canvassed on both sides.

65,430. I want to ask you a question concerning that, arising out of the application which I believe you made in 1893 for a retail licence in Church Street, Ballymena?—That is in connection with the wholesale licence. It is almost necessary for every wholesale dealer to have a retail licence, in fact every wholesale dealer has a retail licence.

65,431. The premises were carried on as a wholesale trade?—Yes, and they are still.

65,432. Before you acquired it?—Yes.

65,433. And you acquired it as a house, I take it?—Yes.

65,434. And there was an understanding, was there, as to the character of the trade to be carried on in these premises after you had acquired them?—Oh, yes, there was. We got the premises with the intention of carrying on the wholesale business, and we still do that.

65,435. Not with the intention of applying for a seven-day licence, retail?—There was no intention made of that.

65,436. In that case what was the opinion of the chief constable with regard to your application; did he oppose the licence?—On the ground of the increased number of licences, but when we explained what we wanted the licence for, as an accommodation to a wholesale business, the opposition was very slight, and as a matter of fact there has been a similar licence granted since that without the slightest opposition whatever.

65,437. The head constable opposed upon the ground of the unsuitability of the premises, and that such a licence was not required in the neighbourhood?—Yes; that was before we intended to carry it on as a retail public-house, but we did not do so.

65,438. The opinion of the judge coincided apparently

65,439. I am dealing with this particular licence; that is a fact, is it not, that the Head Constable, as representing the police, opposed the grant of the licence, and the judge concurred, but the magistrates granted the licence?—We undertook to carry on the business as a wholesale house without any accommodation in the premises. We have no counter place on the premises at all. We merely wanted the licence as an accommodation to a wholesale business, because in that licence is included a wine licence, and it is a licence that we require for our purposes.

65,440. One further point upon that matter, as to the magistrates; is it a fact that five out of the 10 magistrates who voted in favour of the grant of that licence came from a considerable distance?—Yes; they always do that.

65,441. I am taking it in connection with your statement that the magistrates are canvassed in matters of this kind. Is it a fact, first of all, that one magistrate came from Ballymoney, a distance of 21 miles?—He is at nearly every quarter sessions, the same gentleman.

65,442. And another came from Larne, a distance of 24 miles?—Yes.

65,443. One from Antrim, a distance of 11 miles; another from Cushendall, a distance of 20 miles; and the fifth magistrate came from a place about 11 miles off?—The reason of that is that it is the annual licensing sessions, and these come from their districts, Antrim, or something or other, and that is always the occasion when we have the largest attendance of magistrates.

65,444. I do not wish to imply that your firm in any way canvassed these magistrates, but I suggest, as a matter of fact, these magistrates were asked to attend upon that particular occasion?—I do not know.

65,445. You are not aware of that yourself?—No.

65,446. (*Mr. Young.*) Might I ask you, if you know where there is illicit distillation, do the police not know?—I think the police do not do their duty sufficiently. I think it should be stamped out. I think they hardly exercise enough watch over them.

65,447. (*Mr. Sexton.*) In the district with which you are connected in Antrim, I suppose there is total Sunday closing?—Yes.

65,448. That excludes Londonderry and Donegal?—Yes.

65,449. You have a large number of tourists during the summer months passing through Ballymena going further north?—Yes.

65,450. On the question of illicit distillation without knowing exactly where these stills are, it is a fact, is it not, that the manufacture of it and the consumption of it is prevalent in that county?—It is, indeed.

65,451. Is it your opinion that it is favoured very much by the fact of the closing of all the public-houses on Sunday?—I think it is. It is sold on Sundays.

65,452. Do you think if the public-houses were open a few hours of the day from 2 to 5 that many of these illicit distilleries would be done away with, and the demand for the article itself would go out?—I think that would help to do away with it.

65,453. It would not compete, for instance, with the far-famed Coleraine?—No, certainly not.

65,454. With regard to the population, you do not think that there were 79 licensed houses to 10,000 of the population?—Ballymena is a very large market town. It is one of the busiest market towns in the north.

65,455. Would not that be the Parliamentary division for voting purposes? I take it from the Head Commissioner, when he stated that the population was given as some 57,000, that 57,000 would mean the Parliamentary district for voting purposes?—Yes, of Mid Antrim, of which Ballymena is the centre.

65,456. (*Mr. Fuller.*) You have no doubt as to the existence of these illicit distilleries?—Not the slightest.

65,457. Has there been any prosecution?—There are prosecutions occasionally, but the fines in some cases are too small.

Mr. G. M'Connell.

25 May '98.

Sunday closing.

Mr. C. M'Connell.

15 May '98

65,459. The drunkenness in a great measure might be charged to the consumption of the bogus spirit?—In that part of the country it would.

The bona fide traveller.

65,460. What purpose have you in your mind when you say you would restrict the bona fide traveller to 5 or 6 miles?—I think if the houses were opened the bona fide traveller would be more of a bona fide traveller. It would not be necessary to have the limit so short as 3 miles if the houses were opened a few hours on Sunday.

65,461. Have you in your mind that the bona fide traveller only exists in the middle of the day just for two or three hours, and that for the purpose of obtaining drink?—I think he manœuvres [illegible] to get a drink. At present the distance is 3 miles and the houses are closed.

65,462. Presuming that there was a bona fide traveller at 8 o'clock in the morning would not 5 miles, the present distance, be justifiable for him to obtain refreshment?—I suppose it would.

The licensing authority.

65,463. Do I understand you correctly to express your opinion that the county court judge for the county would be sufficient authority without the assistance of magistrates for licensing purposes?—With the right of an appeal to the judge of assize.

65,464. You have considered that it would not be unadvisable to place the control of this large and valuable trade in the hands of one man?—I think it would be well to have the right of appeal.

65,465. But in the first instance it would be placed entirely in the hands of one man?—I think that would be better than the present system.

65,466. And he an officer appointed by the Crown?—Yes.

65,467. Would the appeal, in your judgment, be sufficient to the judge of assize?—There are generally two judges of assize. There should be an appeal to the two judges of assize.

65,468. Would it be sufficient to the two?—I would not express any further opinion on that.

65,469. If there were three present?—That would be still better, I suppose.

65,470. In reference to the question put to you by Mr. Roberts as to a magistrate going 25 miles to attend a session, I suppose it was his duty to attend?—It was. There is licensing business from all those places.

65,471. There is nothing unusual in the fact that the magistrates in the discharge of their duties do travel a long distance?—They come from all parts of the county.

65,472. Then, in any case, it would not be exceptional?—No.

65,473. (Dean Dickinson.) You said that these public-houses in Ballymena are for the accommodation and convenience of tourists as well as the population?—I was speaking of the usual towns of the county more than Ballymena.

65,474. Tourists do not stop at Ballymena?—They pass through.

65,475. There is nothing to make them stop?—They sometimes stay an hour or so.

Sunday closing.

65,476. You seemed to think that, as regards Antrim, the Sunday Closing Act had proved a failure?—I think so.

is transacted at Ballymena. Sometimes they have to come for that.

65,477. This was a special licensing session?—There is Crown business there as well.

The witness withdrew.

(Chairman.) Perhaps this will be a convenient time for me very shortly to state to the Commissioners a question which arose the other day in reference to the evidence that Mr. Harrington, M.P., gave. It was this. I was examining him, and I asked him this question, "I suppose it is not an injunction to the police from "any superior authority that they must show [illegible] "[illegible]?" His answer was, "I think it is. I "understand that a circular has been issued to the "Dublin Police." I suppose Dean Dickinson [illegible] some more or [illegible] of dissent, for Mr. Harrington says, "I hope if the Reverend Dean disputes my "evidence——"; and the Dean replies, "I do not "dispute it; I deny it." "If you deny it, I hope you "will ask," says Mr. Harrington, "the Commis- "sioner of Police to come here to be examined. [illegible] "I come on information, which I believe to be absolutely "accurate, that a circular has been issued to the police "pointing out to the police that in the opinion of the "superior officer of the police[illegible] [illegible] "him in doing it, and I am making no complaint of [illegible] "but I am explaining what I believe to be the disparity "in the figures between Dublin and elsewhere—[illegible] "policeman ought to have at least five cases a quarter. "That does not mean five cases of drunkenness, or prose- "cutions of publicans, but cases of drunkenness or "prosecutions of publicans, [illegible], and I would "mention the fact to show that that may increase the "number there as well as it would of any other statistic "of prosecutions." "(Q.) Who issued the circular?—(A.) "My information is it was issued by the Commissioner "of Police in Dublin, Mr. Jones." Well, naturally, this being in a certain sense challenged, the Reverend Commissioner, the Reverend Dean, asked if there was any foundation for the statement that a circular had been issued containing the particulars referred to by Mr. Harrington. There had been some little delay because the Dean was unable to obtain authority sufficient to warrant him in producing the actual circular. The Dean has handed me—and I think it right to put it before the other Commissioners—this circular actually issued by the authorities in reference to the particular case to which Mr. Harrington was referring, and I will state everything here, both in fairness to Mr. Harrington and in fairness to the Dean. This is from the Chief Commissioner of Police in Dublin, Mr. Jones, and he says this: "The Inspector's Report "designed to afford the superintendents an opportunity "of calling my attention to slack and inefficient "members of the service; and I hope that the [illegible] "to this a [illegible], and perfunctory preparation of [illegible] "Report, which has been more or less evident in [illegible] "past, will now be abandoned. An Inspection Report "which purports to convey that everything [illegible] "exception is correct, and that every member [illegible] "served out in good order, and answered all questions "satisfactorily is clearly misleading." Then he has a table, or a form, which is issued not to the constables, the force indiscriminately, but to the superintendents of the different districts in Dublin. That form is this: "Table 4. Names of police officers and men who have "made, either by arrests or summonses, less than [illegible] "cases within the past three months. The name, rank "and number. Number of cases made in the past "12 months. Number of cases made in the previous "12 months. Superintendent's remarks"; and [illegible] having one something which is not material [illegible]

Mr. William [illegible] called in and examined.

[illegible] (Chairman.) You are, I think, a [illegible] [illegible] in Londonderry?—Yes.

[illegible]. You, I think, have been connected with the [illegible] for many years?—Yes.

[illegible]. I will not trouble you to go over a good deal of the ground which has been gone over, I think, by Mr. [illegible], and by the last witness. You heard their evidence, I think?—Yes.

[illegible]. I understand you generally agree with what they said?—Yes.

[illegible]. But there are some specific points in your evidence which I should like to dwell upon for a moment. You would say there has been a great [illegible] in the value of licensed property of late?—Yes.

[illegible]. And that license holders are very anxious therefore to preserve [illegible] their property, and are very careful about infringing the [illegible] [illegible]?

[illegible]. There has been a great diminution, has there, in Londonderry, in arrests for drunkenness?—Yes, there has.

[illegible]. To what do you attribute that; to any legislative enactment?—No, I do not attribute it to that. I attribute it to the improvement in [illegible] legislation, and the better [illegible] of the working and artisan classes. That has elevated them considerably in the social scale.

[illegible]. There is less drunkenness?—Yes.

[illegible]. Is there less drinking?—No, the consumption is greater, notwithstanding.

[illegible]. Then it is more evenly distributed. Do more people drink than before, always drinking in reasonable quantities, or what is the cause?—The only cause that I can attribute it to is that there might be more large consumption, home consumption.

[illegible]. But that home consumption not, in your opinion, leading to drunkenness?—No, not visible drunkenness.

[illegible]. You say there are fewer arrests in Londonderry. Is it, or is it not, the fact that the arrests for drunkenness on Sunday in Londonderry have markedly decreased?—Yes.

[illegible]. Do I understand you to say that that diminution of arrests on Sunday is owing not to any legislative enactment, but to the general improvement in the morals and social status of the people?—Certainly.

[illegible]. And not to any restriction in the way of Sunday drinking?—Not the least.

[illegible]. I think we have had the evidence of the County Inspector that proportionately the arrests in Londonderry on the Sunday have gone down to a much greater ratio than on any other day of the week, and yet I understand you to say that that marked diminution of arrests on Sunday in Londonderry is owing, not to the fact of Sunday closing, but to the fact that the general status of the people has improved?—Yes.

[illegible]. (Mr. Younger.) Can you tell us if the same improvement has gone on during the week as on Sunday?—Yes, certainly.

[illegible]. I mean in the arrests. Has there been a week-day improvement as well as a Sunday improvement?—Yes, there has.

[illegible]. (Chairman.) Would you be in favour of making any alteration in the way of Saturday earlier closing?—No, I would not consider a change of the hours advisable. I think the present hours are most satisfactory. The reason of that is that Derry is a very small city. It is principally dependent on the suburbs or part of the county. The labouring class does not get paid there until about half-past 7 o'clock on Saturday evening. Then they have to come in and make their purchases.

[illegible]. A great deal of the shopping must necessarily, according to the habits of the Irish people, go on in the public-houses?—No, not altogether in the public-houses, but the public-houses have groceries and drapery, not in the city, but in the country district. In the city they have a grocery and a spirit counter attached to each other.

[illegible]. Separated by any boundary?—No, not by any boundary. They have an oblong shop, and there may be about six feet between the two counters; and they sell spirits at one counter and groceries at the other counter.

[illegible]. Therefore when the people go to do their shopping on the Saturday night they must needs go into a place where there is a long counter, where drink is sold at one end, and groceries or drapery on the other?—Yes.

[illegible]. I understand you to say that that is so rooted in the habits of the people that it would be unwise to place any restriction upon the present hours?—I think it would be utterly impossible.

[illegible]. Would it be impossible to separate the trades?—Yes, so what I know. It would be impossible to separate the trades.

[illegible]. Sunday closing, of course, is in force in Londonderry?—Yes, and it has been since 1878.

[illegible]. Though it has a larger population than Waterford?—Yes.

[illegible]. Do you think, therefore, it ought to be an exempted city?—I think so.

[illegible]. Would you go so far as to say that if you were to open the houses which are now closed on a Sunday, the effect would be a diminution of drunkenness?—I believe it would. My reason for that is, that [illegible] and beer is the national beverage of the people at the present time, but it is very hard to carry [illegible] home with them on Saturday night, and they take a bottle, or two small bottles of whisky, and sometimes perhaps they will empty one of them before they go into the house, and perhaps empty both. They would not care to take them in to their wives or families. If they were sure that they would get some refreshments on a Sunday I am almost certain that they would not purchase on Saturday night.

[illegible]. If the houses were open on a Sunday, assuming that for a moment, what would you do with the *bonâ fide* traveller? In what respect does the *bonâ fide* traveller present himself to you? Are you in favour of the *bonâ fide* traveller?—I consider him no person at all. He is a nuisance.

[illegible]. When you say continue the evidence of a great many other witnesses, that he is a nuisance. Then why if he is a nuisance should you consider him so carefully? Do I understand you want to make provision for his drink on a Sunday?—Yes, for a genuine *bonâ fide* traveller, but the person who crosses the river in a boat and comes back again, and says he was three miles by road from where he went over in the boat, and it would not be more than 300 yards—I consider that man neither more nor less than a fraud; but a genuine *bonâ fide* traveller I would supply with refreshment, by all means.

[illegible]. You think the traveller who is a fraud exceeds in number the traveller who is *bonâ fide*?—Yes, if you do not know him personally.

[illegible]. Are there more fraudulent travellers than there are *bonâ fide* travellers?—Oh yes, there are.

[illegible]. Notwithstanding that, you would make provision for the *bonâ fide* traveller, and try to separate the fraudulent from the *bonâ fide* traveller?—Yes.

[illegible]. How would you do that?—I could not draw the line there. That would be impossible for me to do.

[illegible]. I was leading up to that, and hoping for a solution of the difficulty, but you do not see any?—No.

[illegible]. Do you think that Sunday closing has increased or decreased the consumption of drink in Derry?—It has not decreased the consumption of drink.

[illegible]. Though you admit there has been a decrease in arrests?—Yes.

[illegible]. Especially on Sunday?—Yes.

[illegible]. You think the quantity of drink has not diminished?—No.

[illegible]. But that there is certainly no increase of drunkenness either at home or in public on the Sunday?—As far as I know. I do not know anything about homes, but in the city there is none.

Mr. W. [illegible]

[illegible]

The mixed trades in public-houses.

Sunday closing.

The *bonâ fide* traveller.

Effect of Sunday closing.

Mr. W. Morris. 26 May '97. Illicit distillation.

45,520. We have heard something from the last witness about illicit distillation. Should you agree with what he said as to illicit distillation—as to there being a considerable amount of illicit distillation going on in the county of Derry, which he especially alluded to?—I do not know anything about the illicit distillation.

45,521. (Mr. Young.) You might, because you are very near Donegal?—I think Donegal is not so bad as it is represented to be.

45,522. (Chairman.) Which do you think is the best county for illicit distillation, so far as you can speak?—I think illicit distillation in any part of Ireland is at a very low ebb at the present time.

45,523. At all events, you say your own county is not the worst?—I believe it is not the worst. I am not conscious of any illicit distillation being carried on there.

45,524. Coming to statistics of illicit distillation, are you able to give us any figures as to seizures and detections?—No, I did not take any interest in that part of the question.

45,525. I thought you did give it to me here?—That is with reference to England and Scotland. I got that from the Licensed Victuallers' Year-Book.

45,526. You wanted to compare the detections for illicit distillation in Ireland with the detections in Scotland and England?—Yes, that is what I meant by that.

45,527. What are the figures? We will take them for what you think they are worth?—Taking six years from [illegible] to 1897 in England, the highest number of detections of illicit distillation in any single one of those years was 18; in Scotland the highest number was 23, whereas the lowest number in Ireland was 1,167. This is a curious thing. That is from the Licensed Victuallers' Year-Book.

45,528. Am I right in drawing the inference from that, that there is more illicit distillation in Ireland than in the other two countries put together?—Ten times as much.

45,529. You wanted to bring that out?—I wanted to point that out.

45,530. I do not want to put any colour upon your evidence, but that is what you were leading up to; that there were more illicit distilleries?—Yes.

45,531. Or do you think it is owing to the fact that the constabulary are more strict in Ireland than in England and Scotland?—The constabulary are very energetic, but after all they are not able to detect one-fourth of the illicit distillation.

45,532. There is a very large amount of illicit distillation in Ireland?—Yes.

45,533. Do you think that is partly caused by restrictive legislation?—I do.

45,534. You have given us the convictions for Scotland, and in Scotland there is universal closing on Sunday; you are still contending that there the number of detections, at all events for illicit distillation, is only 23 at the highest?—Yes.

45,535. Do I understand your argument to be that, though in Scotland there are only 23, with universal Sunday closing, yet in Ireland, with only partial Sunday closing, there is the enormous number of 1,167?—Perhaps the authorities are not so vigilant there as they are in Ireland.

Sunday closing failure.

45,536. However, you think that Sunday closing in Ireland has not succeeded?—I do think it has not succeeded.

45,537. And you think it has not succeeded because a shebeener can carry on his trade, and because a bona fide traveller can get his drink anywhere. Are those two of the reasons why you think it is a failure?—Yes, a shebeener can hoodwink the authorities at any time of the day.

45,538. I think you go so far as to say, if I may quote the words of evidence before me, that Sunday closing is a farce?—Yes.

45,539. Sunday closing being by your admission a farce in Ireland, and the bona fide traveller and the shebeener being mainly instrumental in producing that farcical state of things, why should you not put down the shebeener by the strong arm of the law, and could not you say to the bona fide traveller, "We shall open "the house for your legitimate refreshment in the "middle of the day." Would not that satisfy your wants?—That is the only thing that can be done.

Mr. W. Morris.

45,540. But you would not have publicans' houses open all day for the benefit of a chance stray bona fide traveller?—No, for a few hours, say from 2 to 4, or 5 to 6 or 7.

45,541. Therefore when you say Sunday closing is a farce, the farce could be remedied, in your opinion, by opening the houses on Sunday for the purpose of the bona fide traveller, and anybody else, obtaining legitimate refreshment for two hours, did you say?—Certainly; for a few hours I said.

The six householders' requisition.

45,542. As to the six householders, what do you say as to the character of the six householders who certify?—I think that is a curious mistake. That should be abolished, going about with a blue document to get six respectable householders to sign for a licence. The licence-holder, having an interest in his property, does not require the like of that, and it is very seldom that that is done. I have known it to be signed in the house by the master and his boys, and handed in to the petty sessions clerk as a genuine certificate by so many respectable householders.

45,543. Does the clerk of the petty sessions get any fee?—Yes, 2s. 6d. I think that is a mistake.

45,544. Two shillings and sixpence for the certificate by the six householders together?—Two shillings and sixpence for supplying the paper, the form to get filled up.

45,545. Does he get 2s. 6d. from each householder?—No, he gets it from the licence-holder.

45,546. (Dean Dickinson.) Then he gets 2s. 6d. for not examining the signatures, or for receiving the signatures without examination?—He very seldom sees the paper at all. He has a junior clerk or two or three junior clerks who do the business.

45,547. If a dummy paper were handed in without any signatures at all, he would get the 2s. 6d. all the same?—You have to pay the 2s. 6d. before you get the dummy paper.

Effect of Sunday closing.

45,548. You said that the Sunday closing—speaking generally of Ireland, I think—had been a failure. I will give you the figures of the Sunday arrests for drunkenness in the year before the Sunday Closing Act was passed all over Ireland?—If I referred to all Ireland I made a mistake. I am only talking of my own part of Ireland.

45,549. In your part of Ireland, I will give you that. The arrests for drunkenness on Sunday the year before the Sunday Closing Act were [illegible]. The following year after the Sunday Closing Act they fell to [illegible]. That is nearly the same proportion as I mentioned in the case of [illegible]—an average of [illegible] for every Sunday. Then the total arrests for Sunday drunkenness in Ireland—I want to show you that the Sunday Closing Act has not been a failure in Ireland—in the year previous to the Sunday Closing Act was [illegible], in the year after the Sunday Closing Act it fell to [illegible], and including the five exempted cities, the total number of Sunday arrests in Ireland before the Sunday Closing Act was passed was 7,871, and the following year after the Sunday Closing Act that number fell to [illegible], or about half. That does not seem to show that the Sunday Closing Act has proved a failure. That is not all the complete success you would like, but it has not proved a total failure?—Notwithstanding all that, the consumption of liquor is still going up.

45,550. Yet the consumption of spirits has decreased, but the consumption of beer and porter has increased. The consumption of spirits decreased last year by several thousands of gallons. With reference to illicit distillation, do you not know that 10 or 20 years ago there was a real deal more of illicit distillation than there is now?—Yes.

45,551. And, therefore, there is no increase of illicit distillation due to the Sunday Closing Act, but on the contrary, I do not say due to that Act, but gradually year after year the number of prosecutions for illicit distillation has decreased. It was much worse some years ago?—It was no thanks to legislation putting down illicit distillation. It was the bishops and clergy in my part of Ireland who have been instrumental in that.

63,552. I suppose the same influence would still be continued and increased?—Yes, the same influence does prevail.

63,553. Nobody would say that legislation is the only thing that diminishes crime. There are a great many other things; but legislation does not tend to increase crime, I think?—No, but the people are thinking more of themselves now than they used to do. They are getting higher up in the social scale.

63,554. And, therefore, because they are thinking more of themselves, and of their interests, they are drinking less, you think?—Well, they are better fed, and I presume they can drink more, and not expose themselves so visibly.

63,555. You admit that in proportion as men think of their real interests they drink less?—Well, it is not possible on them if they drink more where they are better fed and better cared for.

63,556. (*Mr. Walker.*) What did you mean when you said, "I am not conscious of any [illegible]"? What had you in your mind when you made that statement?—I have no personal knowledge.

63,557. You wish to say that you yourself took no part in it; that you had nothing to do with [illegible], directly or indirectly.

63,558. Now, I suppose, would any other respectable licensee?—None that I am acquainted with.

63,559. You are personally engaged in the retail trade?—Yes.

63,560. And you express an opinion that notwithstanding Sunday closing the consumption has not decreased?—Yes.

63,561. Is it your opinion that it has considerably increased?—Yes.

63,562. Is it also your opinion that home consumption has very considerably increased?—It must have.

63,563. On Sunday?—Sundays and week nights, or days, as the case may be.

63,564. From your experience have you any reason to believe that home consumption has increased to such an extent as to produce drunkenness, of which there would be or could be no public notice taken?—I would not like to speak with regard to private affairs at all. I should not like to form any opinion on that.

63,565. That has not been a general topic of conversation?—No; but it is the only conclusion one can arrive at when one sees the consumption going up and drunkenness decreasing less.

63,566. Have you ever considered Sunday closing from this point of view; that it was an infringement upon the liberty of the subject?—Undoubtedly; certainly it is an infringement of the liberty of the subject.

63,567. Speaking as a citizen of Londonderry, you are of opinion that Sunday closing absolutely is an infringement of the liberty of the subject?—Undoubtedly.

63,568. (*Mr. Hyslop.*) You have already stated that there is a large diminution in drunkenness in Londonderry?—Yes.

63,569. Is not there a large shipping trade done in Londonderry?—Yes; there is a moderate amount of shipping.

63,570. It is generally understood to be one of the finest bays in Ireland?—The *Foyle* is supposed to be one of the finest rivers in Ireland, with the exception of the Shannon.

63,574. The figures which have been read show that?—Undoubtedly they do. *Mr. W. [illegible]. 6 May '89.*

63,575. You would naturally conclude that Sunday would be the day on which the shebeener would do the greatest amount of trade?—Yes, that is their harvest day, Sunday.

63,576. You have been pleased to state that the clergy and the police have a close eye upon these shebeens?—Yes, but they can hoodwink the police up to their very noses. *Illicit distillation.*

63,577. With regard to private stills, the police, too, are energetic in detecting these places?—Yes, they are obliged to do that.

63,578. May I ask you if the Excise have appointed any detectives?—They have.

63,579. Have they been at all successful in detecting illicit stills?—Well, not in the act of distillation, but I understand that they have got some illicit matter in some of the licensed houses.

63,580. Do you happen to know the number of convictions against license holders during the year?—I do not.

63,581. May we take it that the houses are generally well conducted?—Extra well.

63,582. (*Mr. Roberts.*) You have spoken of the effects of Sunday closing, as far as your opinion goes; Sunday closing goes to only refer to Londonderry?—That is so, to Londonderry and the district. *Sunday closing.*

63,583. And the district immediately around it?—Yes.

63,584. You said that public drunkenness, in your opinion, has decreased, judging by the streets, and your general observation, in your city, since the Act was passed?—Quite so.

63,585. But you also state that, in your opinion, that has been brought about by other causes than Sunday closing?—Certainly.

63,586. You are aware, no doubt, that that opinion is contrary to the opinion expressed by the public authorities?—I am not aware of that.

63,587. However, you give that as your opinion?—Yes, I give that as my honest opinion—what I know to be the fact.

63,588. As one engaged in the trade?—Yes.

63,589. And from a trade standpoint?—Yes.

63,590. What is the opinion of the Bishop of Derry as to Sunday closing?—I could not answer that question.

63,591. You are not aware that he is in favour of it?—I am not.

63,592. I believe you are the clerk of the Derry races, are you not?—Yes. *Occasional licences.*

63,593. From your experience in connection with the racing and football matches, do you consider that occasional licenses are good things to grant?—Yes, and they are necessary.

63,594. Have you ever seen any evil results following from the granting of such occasional licenses?—Never.

63,595. Is it not a fact that disorderly and disgraceful scenes often occur in connection with those fêtes?—I have been connected with the races for 23 years, and I never saw a disorderly crowd there.

Mr. [illegible] in the Chair.

63,596. (*Mr. Bowen.*) Do I understand that that [illegible] is [illegible] on Saturday? *Illicit [illegible].*

Mr. W. [illegible]. 30 May '98.

—the best whisky. They have it stored up in thousands of gallons at [illegible] House.

Sunday closing and the bona fide traveller.

65,599. If the houses were open for a few hours, as you advocate, on Sunday, do you consider that that would dispose of the difficulty of the bona fide traveller?—It would, and, besides, it would allow the legitimate trader to do his business properly, and not be paying a high licence, and a party two or three doors from him selling more on Sunday than he would sell all the week, and paying no duty.

65,600. I mean from the public point of view would it do away with the practical inconvenience of having a bona fide traveller at all; would it be unnecessary to have any provision for a bona fide traveller?—I would not provide for the bona fide traveller if they are open on Sunday; let him take his chance; because you never could discover who the genuine bona fide traveller is.

65,601. Is it the fact that the bona fide traveller is generally an excursionist?—No, not by any means. He is a pest to society in the immediate neighbourhood. That is what the bona fide traveller is stamped as in any part of Ireland.

65,602. You would be glad not to have the trouble?—To be sure. Clear him off altogether from us.

Publicans and back doors.

65,603. (Mr. Young.) On Sundays I suppose many of the publicans supply liquor by the back doors?—I understand they do. I have not any personal knowledge of that, but I understand they do, through the back doors and back yards.

65,604. That is an additional evil from restriction?—Undoubtedly.

65,605. I suppose you have no doubt that that is done in many of the places?—I have not the slightest doubt but that it is done every Sunday.

65,606. I know myself that in several of the other towns it is done?—Certainly, it is done.

65,607. Do you think that arrests form a test with regard to this question of drunkenness, whether it be increased or decreased?—No, not at all. It has not a particle to do with it. You may show as many returns for arrests as you please, but it has nothing to do with the consumption of drink.

65,608. How do you ascertain that the consumption of drink is as large as before?—It is larger than ever.

65,609. How do you arrive at that?—I have already said it goes to house drinking.

65,610. I mean the consumption of drink in your city; you can scarcely say how much is drunk in your city?—I could not give you the exact quantity that is drunk, but I know the drink traffic is as great, or greater than ever, and yet drunkenness is not so great, because any person in the trade detects any person that has the sign of drink on him, we shun him as if he were an unclean animal; keep him away from us; we will not allow him near us at all.

65,611. It is a fact, I suppose, that the publican really does not want drunken men?—Not at all; the publicans want nothing but respectable people to go to him.

Effect of Sunday closing?

65,612. The Sunday closing, you think, has had the effect of inducing people to secure liquor on Saturday for consumption on Sunday?—Yes, they carry it away in bottles on Saturday night, and then perhaps they will drink that before they get home, as I have already stated.

65,613. Many of them do take it home?—A good many do take it home for the next morning, and then there are shebeens through the city, and they have a watch at this corner, and a watch at that corner, and another at the head of the entry, and another at the foot of the entry, and if there is a policeman stationed every ten yards from each other they can hoodwink him, because the place is like a rabbit warren.

65,614. Do you think Sunday closing has had the effect of increasing female drunkenness?—No. We have the most respectable lot of females in the world in Derry, and the most sober lot of women in the world in Derry. There are a class of hardened drunkards that are always in the police courts and in gaol, but outside of that we have the most respectable body of women in the world. Perhaps you might think that extravagant talk, but I positively assure you that it is so.

65,615. I wish the Cork people could say that?—I am sure the Cork people will be able to speak for themselves.

65,616. Do you think that the taking home of whisky on Saturday has not a tendency to the encouragement of drinking?—I think it is a mistake to take it home where there are children. No matter how young they are they are very precocious, and in a small house, where there are only two apartments, a room and a kitchen, there is no place for concealment.

65,617. There may be a less number of arrests in the public street and more drunkenness in private houses?—Certainly.

65,618. Is that your view?—Yes, that is my view.

65,619. Then on the whole you really do think that this Sunday closing has a bad moral effect?—Unquestionably.

Illicit distillation.

65,620. As to the illicit distillation, am I right in supposing that there is less illicit distillation than formerly?—I think you are right enough in fancying that. I believe there is a great deal less of illicit distillation than there was 12 years ago.

65,621. And that the police are very vigilant?—They are.

65,622. I heard you say that the poteen was better whisky than the other?—So I am informed.

65,623. Do you know what it is made from?—Sometimes from molasses, and from sugar; but I think if they got plenty of time to make it, they can make it pure as well as they can make any potstill whisky from malt. Since the duty was taken off malt, malt has been greatly used, though it takes a longer time. They can make poteen from sugar in about 24 hours, or from molasses in the same time, but it would take four days to make it from malt. Malt has to go through the process of fermentation to make it ready for distillation.

65,624. With your knowledge of distillation, do you think the whisky can be better made from molasses or from sugar?—No, quite the contrary; but I am informed by the Inland Revenue authorities that there is no better whisky manufactured than the whisky that is made in the small still, as they call it there, if it is made from malt.

65,625. I understood you to say it is made from molasses?—Molasses and sugar.

65,626. Do you consider that it is better whisky than that which is made from grain in a regular distillery in a scientific way?—No, it could not be better than that; but the illicit whisky that is made from malt is much better than any whisky that is made from a patent still, because it is not whisky at all, it is only a spirit. It has no character. There will come in the world without a character, and it dies the same no matter how long you keep it. That is why it is so much used immediately it is manufactured.

65,627. I will not go into that. It requires scientific knowledge to go into that. At any rate it is your strong opinion that the houses should be open on Sunday?—Certainly.

The witness withdrew.

Mr. Adam Seaton Findlater called in and examined.

Mr. A. S. Findlater.

Position of witness.

65,628. (Mr. Gordon.) I understand that you are a Justice of the Peace for the county of Dublin?—I am.

65,629. And a graduate of Dublin University?—Yes.

65,630. You hold several important posts in that town?—Yes.

65,631. What are they?—I am a member of the Dublin Port and Docks Board; I have been two years a commissioner of Kingstown—three years the chairman, and I am a member also of the Black Rock and Kingstown Drainage Board.

65,632. You have had a long experience, I understand, in the wine and spirit and tea licence grocery trade?—I have, above 27 years.

65,633. On what system is your business carried on?—On the off-licence system; that is to say, our

Mr. A. S. Findlater. — 23 May '97

business as, or is very common in Ireland, supplying wine, spirits, groceries, and tea to the public for consumption in their own homes.

65,634. You have an intimate acquaintance with all the working of the trade?—I have.

65,635. You have read the evidence which the Solicitor-General has given here?—Yes.

65,636. Do you agree with that generally?—Quite so.

65,637. On the whole do you express yourself as fairly satisfied with the existing state of the law?—I do.

65,638. Have you anything to say as to statements that have been made with reference to the abuses of your trade?—From my personal knowledge as to the statements as to abuses, with regard to what I might call false booking, I believe they do not exist.

65,639. Within your knowledge you never heard of such a thing, or found such a thing?—No.

65,640. You think that if such a thing as a false entry of spirits or beer being entered as groceries were attempted, a man could protect himself, if any female members of his family were to order such things?—Quite so.

65,641. Do you say that licenses, such as yours, have been greatly for the public benefit?—I believe they have.

65,642. What have you to say with regard to the transfer of beer licenses under the Beer Licenses (Ireland) Act, 1877?—There is a very inconvenient clause in it, in this way, that the person taking the license must be in occupation for three months. If it so happens that the man dies, and the business has to be carried on by his son, or by his executors, in the strict legal acceptation of the Act of 1877 he could not carry on a beer trade for three months. It is a matter that is to some extent winked at.

65,643. As I understand it, he could carry on the sale of wines and spirits, but not of beer?—Quite so.

65,644. Do you point that out as an anomaly in the present state of the law?—I think it is. It is very hard there on a man who is carrying on practically a business that, if he dies, the business should be interrupted for three months for no reason.

65,645. Then I understand you have another point to which you wish to draw our attention, and that is the practice by the justices of imposing conditions on a license?—Quite so. When the legislature settles the terms of a license, I do not think the licensing authority ought to be able to make special terms. Neither should they make special offences. The law should be settled on a general principle by the legislature.

65,646. I do not think that at present, so far as I am aware, they are entitled to make those conditions on the license?—They are not entitled by law to do so, but they do. I will explain myself. If you go to a licensing authority, and he says "I will not give you a license except under certain terms," you know that you have to go before him again, and though you may legally, during the year that he has granted that license, carry out the rights under that license to the fullest extent, yet if you do not adhere to the conditions under which the license was given to you, having to what that authority was give the license again at the end of the year, you are practically bound by conditions that were never contemplated by the legislature.

65,647. Or you would probably lose your license?—You would not get the renewal.

65,648. Your opinion is that no conditions should be made, except such as are strictly statutory?—Quite so.

65,649. Are there any other points to which you wish to draw the attention of the Commission which I have not put to you?—No; I have come forward practically as representing what we call in Ireland the family grocery trade. They do a class of trade that perhaps is not known on this side, a trade where everything in the way of provisions and tea, and wines, and whisky and spirits are supplied to the householder and sent to his own residence and consumed there.

65,650. Just like the Scotch grocers' license?—Practically.

65,651. It is the same sort of trade. It comes to a great extent in place of the wine merchant?—Quite so. In fact the wine merchant is almost extinct in Ireland.

65,652. That is all you wish to bring forward?—It is.

65,653. (Mr. Young.) You are of opinion that the privileges of the sale of spirituous liquors in grocers' shops are productive of good effects, and you approve of them?—Yes, my experience has been that I have never seen any abuses of them.

Spirit grocers' licenses.

65,654. Are you of opinion that there should be no other qualification for obtaining a spirit grocer's license than the conditions now imposed?—I think without any disadvantage there might be some conditions added. At the present moment there is practically free trade in those licenses, and I do not see that it would do very much harm to have a little restriction; but, as a matter of practice, those licenses have worked for a great number of years, and, as far as I know, without any detriment to the public.

65,655. At the present time you are aware that the only condition is a suitable house and a good character?—Yes.

65,656. You are aware that a license can be obtained by a very large number of people, apart altogether from other considerations?—It could be obtained, undoubtedly.

65,657. If an applicant in a very congested district set towards publichouses sought a license with those conditions he could obtain it?—He could, undoubtedly.

65,658. Do you think that right?—In practice I have never seen any disadvantage on account of it.

65,659. I do not quite want that. Supposing that there were a very large number of public-houses in a street and that there was a suitable house and a good character presented as a reason for obtaining a license, do you think that should be granted?—That is a hypothetical case. I do not think perhaps it ought to be granted in that way, but as a matter of practice the hypothetical case you put does not occur because an off license could not live in the place.

65,660. If they sold other things they could?—No, they could not; because the publican can sell other things as well.

65,661. If they sold tea and various other things they could add this spirit grocer's license now?—Yes.

65,662. The publican has not that advantage?—The publican has the advantage. He can sell tea if he likes.

The licensing authority.

65,663. Are you not of opinion that the licensing authority which grants publicans' licenses should be the sole authority, and that the applicant for a grocer's license should come under the same rules and regulations?—I do not see any objection to it, but in practice the fact has been that there have not been too many of the off-licenses created, because the off-licenses have been regulated by the laws of supply and demand, and as a matter of fact people would not take them out where they would not pay. You may take it from me in this way, that in the whole of Ireland, where publicans' licenses are valuable, if the other license could have lived in competition with it, it would have been demanded and sought for. The off-license only exists where there is a living to be got by it, and where there is a public demand for it on the part of the public who get the goods.

65,664. Under the spirit grocers' license you can sell any quantity up to what extent?—You can sell practically anything under the off-license.

65,665. And with the bottle not corked?—Well, Sale in the people always ask for a cork in the bottles they get bottles. from us; but I believe you could leave the cork out if [illegible] you liked.

65,666. You can sell without the bottle being corked, and you can sell in small quantities?—Yes.

65,667. Do you think it is fair to the fully licensed publican that you should be put into that peculiar position with a few pounds of tea on one side of the house and with this privilege on the other side, and that you may obtain it not in the same way that the publican obtains his license, but in a very different way indeed, and in fact compel the authorities to give it. Do you think that it is fair?—There has never been any complaint of it. The public will come where they get the best value. They get the same thing from us under our license, and they will go where they get the best value, and I think it is to their advantage to get the best value.

65,668. The same observation would apply to the fully licensed trade. It would be like an abolition of

Mr. A. S. Findlater.

[illegible] May '97.

[illegible] limited. As the present time it is a monopoly?—Yes.

65,669. You are not under a very strict monopoly as the spirit grocers' trade and therefore you have peculiar advantages, have not you?—I do not think we have any peculiar advantages.

65,670. You can get a licence wherever you like in any place?—That may be very true, but presuming there is a publican and an off-licensee in a street, what happens? The publican can sell in open vessels to be consumed on the premises or off the premises; we simply sell for consumption off the premises and the public have the choice of buying in either place. Where does the injustice come in? They get the stuff wherever they think they can get the best value.

65,671. The fully licensed publican is under the control, with reference to transfer and everything else, of a tribunal, and you are independent of that tribunal as regards the renewing of the licence and everything else?—There is one thing about it so far as my knowledge goes, that being independent of the tribunal we never do anything that requires to go before the tribunal. That is my general experience.

Spirit grocers and publicans.

65,672. (Mr. Grimshaw.) I suppose your answer to Mr. Young's question would be this, that the two trades are essentially different in character?—Undoubtedly different—two different objects.

65,673. They supply practically a different class of consumer?—Yes.

65,674. And you think there is room for both of them?—Quite so. I may supplement that answer in this way—that a large number of our customers in Dublin I do not suppose were ever inside a public-house in their lives, but still they want to get their supplies and wine sent.

65,675. Those who go to the publican would not go to the off-licence holder for their supplies, and on the other hand the off-licence holder's customers would not go to the publican?—We have both no object in life.

65,676. With reference to the congested district which Mr. Young has pointed to you, I think he had in his mind a parish in Cork or Dublin where there were six or seven public-houses. Would it answer a spirit grocer's while to attempt to start a business there?—He could not live for a month.

65,677. There is no fear of that?—No. The laws of competition come in.

Spirit grocers and magisterial control.

65,678. With reference to this question of magisterial control, the magisterial control of certain off-licences is involved at present, and I should like to ask you whether anything more can be done so far as the public interest is concerned? A man is going to sell a certain article, not in a place of public resort, where no public disorder can take place, and you ensure that the man shall have suitable premises to sell it in, and shall be of good character. Is not that sufficient for the purpose of carrying on any trade of that description?—In practice that has been most distinctly found to be good.

65,679. With reference to your knowledge of Dublin, has there at any time within your knowledge been any private opposition to the spirit grocers' licence as [illegible] by Dublin residents?—None. I never heard of it.

65,680. Notwithstanding that out of 732 spirit grocers' licences in all Ireland you have [illegible] located in Dublin?—Quite so.

65,681. And with these [illegible] you are not aware of any complaint that would come from the residents who would be likely to see the facilities given by these traders?—No.

65,682. Could you give us any idea of how it is that this large number of spirit grocers' licences has arisen in the two towns of Dublin and Belfast?—I do not know anything about Belfast, but with reference to Dublin, I believe that the city is extended a good deal, and it is because they have been a public convenience and necessity. People want to get their supplies reasonably close to their houses.

A rating qualification.

65,683. We have heard of a number of houses carrying on the spirit grocers' trade which have been described as places not suitable for human habitation, and certainly not suitable for carrying on the trade. Would that be due in any way to the low rental or low valuation of the premises do you think?—I think it would be. I would not at all object to one—perhaps it would be an advantage—a margin of valuation necessary.

65,684. At the present time the rating qualification for beer is, with a population of 10,000, [illegible], and under 10,000, [illegible], is it not?—Yes.

Mr. A. S. Findlater.

65,685. And no qualification for wines and spirits?—No.

65,686. You think if there was a reasonable qualification instituted it would do away with the class of houses that we hear of as not suitable for the trade?—Undoubtedly it would do away with what might be called bogus off-licences.

65,687. In all probability the complaints we hear from time to time of drinking on off-premises result from the fact that licences are in the hands of persons who never should have held them?—Yes. I should be very glad to see a [illegible] valuation put on these houses.

Sale in closed vessels of minimum quantity.

65,688. With reference to the quantity of sale in closed vessels, you know in England the law under which the off-licence trader is that he cannot sell less than a quart bottle of spirits nor less than a pint bottle of wine. So far as wines and spirits are concerned, would you see any difficulty on the part of the Irish trade in accepting that change?—Yes. It would not suit Ireland to be confined to the quart and reputed pint. A large proportion of the spirits we sell goes to the public in half-pint bottles and pint bottles, and a small proportion in what are called naggin bottles, that is, a quarter of a pint, and certainly it would absolutely disorganise all our trade in Dublin if we were forced to sell not less than a reputed quart of whisky, and a reputed pint of wine.

65,689. Supposing that the limit, we will say, was half-a-pint for spirits?—I do not think that the law ought to be altered with reference to Ireland in that matter. At the present moment we can sell any quantity we wish. Now, you might say that half a pint is a handy amount to make your sealings, but at the same time, knowing that as a rule the quality of the stuff on account of competition is to my mind better in the off-licensed houses, I think it is a pity to prevent men getting their supplies. Many men go into an off-licensed place and get their supplies, because they think they get, and do get, better quality, and since this Commission has been going on I have watched the trade closely and have seen that lots of people want there and get it, and I think it is unfair to deprive them of it. As for assimilating the law to the English law it would simply disorganise the whole family supplies of the city of Dublin certainly, a place which I know thoroughly.

Suitability of licensed premises.

65,690. One other point with reference to the question of magisterial control. Supposing the second condition, of [illegible] the suitability of premises, was enlarged so as to meet the objection, that a licensed house may be put at the door of a church or a school, and supposing suitability of premises meant suitability of environment, would you object to that?—I would see no objection to that. That is only reasonable.

Hours of opening.

65,691. With regard to the closing hours on Sunday, I understand the general opinion of the off-licensed trade in Dublin is that for a certain time on a Sunday, say before the midday dinner, it is necessary that the off-licensed premises should be opened for the purpose of people getting their dinner beer. Is that your view?—That is my view, but I am not speaking from personal knowledge. My personal belief is that with reference to the dinner beer on a Sunday, I think it is a reasonable thing to give people the opportunity of getting their beer. If you watch on a Sunday those places where off-licensees supply beer in open vessels, I say there is no objection and in fact it is a good system. People will take their jug of beer and drink it with their dinner, and that is supplied by the off-licensed in a satisfactory way. It is true the publican can supply at ten, but I do not see why it should be stopped.

65,692. You think it meets a public necessity, really?—I really think so.

65,693. The last witness gave a very high testimonial to the women of Derry, and I suppose you could say the same with reference to the women of Dublin, as regards this question of female intemperance. Is there any reason to suppose that amongst the females of Dublin—to speak of them in that way—a large amount of intemperance prevails?—It does not to my knowledge. I do not speak of the very lower orders.

Mr. J. S. [illegible] — [illegible]

65,694. If you carried out the principle of largely limiting the number of the spirit grocers' licences, would not it have a tendency to create a monopoly amongst the holders?—Certainly. The first thing it will do is this. It will create a monopoly and ultimately have bad quality. The off-licences exist and compete on the question of quality alone.

65,695. I believe you have taken a certain amount of interest in the evidence that Mr. Daly, the Clerk of the Dublin Police Court, gave here last week?—Yes.

65,696. Mr. Daly suggested that the offence of permitting consumption on the premises by the holders of off-licences should be made liable to compulsory record in cases of conviction. Do you see any objection to that, speaking for the trade?—I think the more severely any breaches of the law are visited on the people that commit them, the better for everybody. I thoroughly agree with Mr. Daly on that.

65,697. Do you believe convictions for that offence can be produced against the majority of the respectable trade?—Certainly not.

65,698. Then, if so, would it not be more equitable to punish the irregular minority who transgress, by increased penalty or forfeiture, rather than force increased restrictions on the trade at large?—I am quite at one with them. It is very hard lines that a person who breaks the law should make severe regulations for those who do not break the law.

65,699. Mr. Daly's great point was this, that he did not think it was fair to increase restrictions on the trade at large without devising special legislation for special offenders. You would agree with that?—Undoubtedly. Before this Commission unfortunately, or fortunately, the people that have been examined are either the publicans or licence-holders like myself who are interested parties on one side, and the police, who are experts. Unfortunately the view of the general public and the person who drinks moderately either at a public-house, or buys his wine or whisky from the holders of licences, like myself, has not been considered, and I think that if he was considered, and his evidence could be given, it would be more important than the evidence of those that are interested.

Conditions upon [illegible] — [illegible]

65,700. (Mr. Solomons.) These restrictions that you complain of as [illegible] to the conditions, I suppose you are aware, are almost invariably imposed in the interest of the applicant?—I do not follow your line of argument.

65,701. An off-licence is applied for—I am speaking of how it works in England, but it may be different with you—and the justices have the intention of granting any licence there; they do not think it is needed for beer on draught, but they say you can get a spirit or bottled wine licence without coming in to sit all [illegible] at a Sessions; we do not object to grant you a beer licence, too, if you will submit to the proper restrictions. The man says he will willingly agree to that, and then he gets a licence, which, if he would not submit to the conditions, he would not get at all. That is my meaning in saying they are imposed in the interest of the applicant?—I do not think so. I think that that practically means for every licensing authority in every licensing district a law for a very small circle of the city. Take a case in point. You go from one county to the other, and step out of licensing jurisdiction to another, and they all have different views and different ideas, and I do not think piecemeal legislation ever [illegible] well.

65,702. You would rather the licence was refused altogether?—I would.

65,703. That does not happen to be the opinion of the applicant?—No, that may be true.

65,704. (Mr. Asburn.) You referred to yourself, as a witness to-day, as an interested party?—I referred to myself as a licence-holder in all the suburbs of Dublin.

65,705. I gather that you appear principally to-day as a representative of the family grocer trade?—Yes. I want to make it clear that the family grocer trade is quite different in Ireland to what it is in England.

65,706. For a long time you have taken an interest in the general interests of the trade?—Certainly, I have.

Mr. J. S. [illegible]
[illegible] May [illegible]

65,707. With regard to your own particular trade, you have a special brand of whisky have you not?—Yes.

65,708. Do you hold a publican's licence?—I do, or our firm does. I do not myself personally. In some of our places we have a publican's licence and in some the off-licence. Personally we were on the off-system.

65,709. You personally hold a publican's licence at one case?—I hold one for the Empire Theatre, but practically any firm, you may take it, holds the publican's licence and the other licence.

65,710. You own a house in the town in which you live?—Yes, that is Kingstown.

65,711. Did you say that you had anything to do with the Empire Music Hall?—Yes.

65,712. What is your connection with that?—I happen to be chairman of the company.

65,713. Would your whisky be sold there?—Yes.

65,714. With its [illegible] as to any other?—That is an ordinary publican's licence.

65,715. You have taken an interest for some time in this inquiry?—Yes, I have. I have not read the evidence all through, because it is rather voluminous.

65,716. I have before me a copy of the "Freeman's Journal" of November 17th, 1897—last year—in which there is a report of the meeting of the Licensed Grocers and Vintners' Association in Dublin?—Yes.

65,717. That would be a publican's association, I take it?—Yes.

65,718. At that meeting you moved a resolution?—I believe I did. I do not remember it.

65,719. Calling upon all the members of the trade to assist in [illegible] witnesses?—I believe I did. I will take it from you that what you say is correct.

65,720. I simply gather from that that you do not only represent the particular family grocery trade here to-day, but that you have been for a long time an active member of the licensed vintners' trade?—You may take it I am interested in all branches of the trade.

65,721. (Mr. Hodges.) With reference to the administration of the licensing laws, you are of opinion that no alteration would be an improvement?—I would not go so far as that. There would be improvements made undoubtedly, but at the same time my evidence-in-chief was to the effect that so far as the off-licence went the system was working very satisfactorily in Dublin.

65,722. I understood you to say you were in favour of the existing law as it stood?—With that reservation, I say so practically.

65,723. There are certain licences you hold under which you are permitted to sell wines and spirits, but you are deprived of the privilege of selling beer?—Yes, beer and wine and spirit licences are, consequently, separate licences.

65,724. By the Beer Licence Act in England you have authority to sell beer only?—Yes.

65,725. No spirits or wines?—Quite so.

65,726. Would there be any anomaly in that, with reference to the wine and spirit trade in Ireland selling beer?—I do not think so. As far as my knowledge of the beer licence legislation on this side is concerned, the English people drink beer in a way we do not on the other side at all.

65,727. Porter?—Porter and whisky, but a beer-house pure and simple could not exist in Dublin.

65,728. (Mr. Grimsley.) You require a separate licence to sell beer in Ireland, the same as the off-trade does in England?—Yes.

65,729. The licence is not a spirit grocer's licence that authorises you to sell beer?—Certainly not, you must have a beer licence.

The witness withdrew.

Mr. [illegible] [illegible] called in and examined.

Mr. [illegible]. — [illegible] May '9[illegible].

[illegible]. (Mr. Gordon.) I understand you are a retired spirit merchant?—Yes.

[illegible]. And you have been for many years connected with the spirit trade?—Yes.

Position of witness.

[illegible]. For how long a period of time?—Thirty years.

[illegible]. You were lately, I believe, chairman of the [illegible] [illegible] Association of Belfast?—Yes.

[illegible]. And also chairman of the Family Grocers' and Spirit Dealers' Association of Belfast?—Yes.

[illegible]. But you now reside on the sea coast?—Yes, recently.

Spirit grocers.

[illegible]. Your evidence is especially with reference to spirit grocers, is it not, and you wish to speak on their behalf?—For the trade generally.

[illegible]. Do you mean the spirit grocers' trade?—For the spirit grocers' trade first, and then I [illegible] something to say upon other portions of the trade, with the permission of the Commission.

[illegible]. You know the whole ramifications of the trade?—[illegible] altogether.

The [illegible] system.

[illegible]. Does the tied-house system prevail much in your town?—Not in the sense of the word as it is used in England. There are young men who get assistance from merchants and from banks.

[illegible]. By merchants, do you mean spirit-dealers and brewers?—In some few cases, but in more cases from other persons who assist them into trade.

[illegible]. What class of persons?—Bankers, and men who would wish to lend money on fair security.

[illegible]. Young men going into the spirit business?—A young man who has served his time to the trade and is known to be sober and prudent will get assistance in many ways to enter the business on his own account.

[illegible]. He would not in consequence of that be strictly tied to purchase his goods at one particular place?—No. There may be a few cases, but I wish the Commission to understand that it is not the rule in Belfast.

[illegible]. You would deprecate any interference with this system, and you think on the whole it is beneficial?—I believe it is [illegible]. The tied-house principle as in England I do not wish to encourage, but what I have [illegible] is encouraging young men without binding them.

[illegible]. Do you consider that the system as [illegible] practised in Belfast is on the whole beneficial?—Very [illegible].

[illegible]. That is your distinct opinion?—Yes.

Spirit grocers of great value in Belfast.

[illegible]. I see you have something to say with regard to the evidence that was given by Mr. T. W. Russell here; you saw it?—Yes.

[illegible]. Under what head?—I consider that the evidence of Mr. T. W. Russell and others reflected upon the spirit grocers, and I think that they were giving evidence from hearsay and did not understand what they were talking about.

[illegible]. I understand he divided the spirit grocers into two different classes, did he not?—Yes.

[illegible]. You, on the other hand, say there are only a few of the larger spirit grocers in Belfast?—There is a very large number, but I think that Mr T. W. Russell wishes to class them as the higher class and the lower class. I suppose he means by the higher class those who supplied the higher class of customers, and by the lower class those who supplied the working class customers in the working-class districts.

[illegible]. Is not that a natural consequence that there should be firms who supply the higher class and the larger quantities?—You might say so, but after all a small shop with a good outside can get customers from high and low.

[illegible]. You think that this class of traders are of great value in Belfast?—I believe that they are a great convenience because they enable a customer to get everything he requires in the one establishment and to have one pass book, and the goods can be sent home at one time without his having a messenger to go to different establishments and paying different accounts.

[illegible]. With regard to the men engaged in the linen and flax business in Belfast, I think you have some opinion that their necessities are largely supplied by this class of trader?—Yes. That is a very important matter and may not be clearly understood, that the men in the flax trade are closed in for long hours in a close atmosphere breathing in flax dust, which affects their lungs very much, and they come out to their meals tired and with no appetite. I have known them to have first to get a glass [illegible] before they could think of taking their food. They drink a little each meal time, and do not buy in large quantities such as would be purchased by richer customers in larger establishments.

Mr. [illegible].

[illegible]. They drink with their meals?—They take spirits before their meals usually.

[illegible]. Is that peculiar to the flax trade?—Yes. There are very few men who have been 40 years in the flax trade that are not very far gone with asthma, and they consider that stimulants are of great assistance to their appetites and to keep them up during their working hours.

[illegible]. (Mr. [illegible].) They take it as a medicine?—They take it for their good, as far as I can understand.

[illegible]. (Mr. Gordon.) You do not give us any statistics as to how many are employed in this trade, but I know it is a large industry?—It is one of the leading industries in Belfast, and a very large number of men are employed in it.

Cause of increase of spirit grocers.

[illegible]. Have you anything to say with reference to the large increase that has taken place in the number of spirit grocers' licences in Belfast of recent years?—Yes. Our population has increased so very much—in some cases districts of [illegible] acres have been covered over with working-men's houses—that it was quite natural there should be an off-licence at the end of each street or block, for the regular licences were not granted.

[illegible]. Your licensing authority in Belfast is the Recorder?—Yes, for the regular licences.

[illegible]. He has not been granting any new public-house licences?—Very few.

[illegible]. So that, in your opinion, these new districts which are arising, along with the increase of population, would be entirely destitute of supply were it not for the spirit grocers' licences—that is your argument?—Yes, but at the same time I agree that in some cases it has been overdone.

[illegible]. The spirit grocers' licences are too numerous?—Yes, in some districts.

Women not supplied by spirit grocers.

[illegible]. What have you to say with reference to the question of women and girls being supplied with drink by the spirit grocers?—After my long experience, I have to say it is purely imaginary. There may be a few solitary cases, but there is nothing at all on which to found an opinion.

[illegible]. You also repudiate any assertion that liquor is supplied under the guise of other goods?—I do most certainly. There could not be anything more suicidal to a trader than to encourage such a thing in his shop. It would lead to bad debts altogether. I have stopped some women's accounts when I have found they were getting goods at a heavy discount, and I have had to inform their husbands of it, and I have put a stop to it myself.

Granting of licences to be in the Recorder's hands.

[illegible]. With reference to the granting of spirit grocers' licences, I understand that you are of opinion that they should be in the hands of the same authority as other licences?—Yes, with power to appeal.

[illegible]. That would be in the hands of the recorder?—Yes.

[illegible]. Would you advocate an appeal from the recorder?—Yes; all men are likely to err, and I would go for an appeal.

[illegible]. To whom would they appeal to?—To the judges of assize.

Sunday closing.

[illegible]. Have you anything to say as to those districts where Sunday closing is in force?—Yes. It is one of the greatest shams that ever came into those districts, generally speaking. I own property in country districts and have been in county towns on Sunday, and I have known the men who own licensed houses sell large quantities of drink to persons [illegible] on the highways and byways on Sundays.

64,770. You mean they sold the drink on Sunday when the houses were closed?—Yes. Barbers would go to a small shop before closing time on Saturday night and purchase a quart, or two quarts, of whisky, keep it [illegible] in the back yard, and supply the men who came in to get their hair dressed or to get shaved. [illegible] would be going at full speed, and nobody could tell how it was going on unless it was ferreted out as I did.

64,771. Then you do not approve of the Sunday closing?—It has done no good. Those who want drink will have it. That is my experience, and we should all like to see improvement, I believe.

64,772. How do you account for the fact that in Scotland it is unanimously agreed that it has done good?—I have some experience of Scotland too and I have seen the Forbes Mackenzie Act broken every Sunday of my life when I was in Scotland, and tickets sold on the fourth story of a Close where it was impossible for the police to detect them.

64,773. There are always evaders of every law, but on the whole the evidence is that it has proved a success?—I am glad to hear it, but my experience was that there was a great abuse and a great amount of drunkenness. There is more difficulty in detecting it, of course, because they put the stock-in-trade down their [illegible] but when they see a policeman coming.

64,774. Have you many shebeens in Belfast?—A few, I believe; I do not know them. I know there are other great classes in illicit trading.

64,775. You mean to say there is a good deal of illicit sale going on in the country districts out of hours?—Yes, I have known men to take a car and drive 4 miles, and the [illegible] have to put the reins round them to get them home, for fear they should fall off.

64,776. You cannot give information as to shebeens?—No, I do not know the number of shebeens in Belfast, but I believe shebeening is carried on. I can tell you how drink is got in Belfast. In one case I know a watchman of some brickfields who had a hut there, and when he got his wages on a Saturday evening he [illegible] went off to a small spirit merchant's place in Belfast, and she laid out the entire amount of his wages in [illegible] and half pints; she brought them up and deposited them under the brick covers in the brickfield, and all the labourers in the locality knew the drink could be got there. They never kept more than one little bottle in the house, or two at a time, and they charged eighteenpence for half a pint of, I suppose, very new whisky, and sixpence for a noggin, and the man that purchased it slipped away along the fields to drink it; and I know, till it came to my knowledge, it was the cause of great [illegible] and annoyance to a respectable [illegible] in the locality there were going about drunk there. The whole thing was charged to him before he knew it; and that was stopped.

64,777. I understand you to say that there is a large capital employed in your trade in Belfast, is there?—In the off-licensed trade there is.

64,778. Can you give us the figures?—Any young man starting cannot enter the trade without fitting up premises and being out of pocket at least [illegible], and it may be [illegible], according to his means, or the extent of the premises he undertakes.

64,779. Can you give us the total sum which is employed in the trade?—I could not give you the correct figures. I can only say it is a very large sum.

64,780. (Mr. Holmes.) How many off-licenses are there in Belfast?—Over 480 off-licenses.

64,781. At an average of [illegible] a place?—Yes; you may safely say that. You cannot fit up a place decently for business without being out [illegible] or more.

64,782. (Mr Gordon.) Have you anything to say as to the valuation of those houses?—They are from [illegible] upwards.

64,783. As to the method of valuing?—I think the method is very good. In a working-class locality a man does not require very large premises. In fact, a man might sell a good article, and a deal of it in a very small house, if he had the trade.

them to be [illegible] their hands with what they call the temperance [illegible]. They consider that no one Government would adopt their views. It seems ridiculous in their eyes, and the same as if they wanted to interfere with vegetarians, or other things that come [illegible] to them.

64,784. That is your opinion?—That is my opinion, indeed. Then I believe that the more you restrict drinking the more the people crave for it. I see more sobriety on the Continent, where brandy can be procured [illegible], than where people are restrained. When men get a chance to drink in a hurry in an illicit way, if there are four altogether, the whole four would buy one after the other, and they would go out with four glasses of whisky each in their stomachs, whereas if not restricted they would have had one small drink and then would go on and have a walk. I may add that I consider there is no remedy for drunkenness except by stopping brewing, distilling, and importing. By changing the channel and allowing the water to run in more freely, I do not think you will ever bring about anything of a better nature. I consider the clergy as a rule are right in their opinion with reference to temperance. They rest their hope in self respect, [illegible], and the grace of God; [illegible] pledging the young people, our present boys and girls, if they can, up to 21 years of age, and then they expect they will become the sober men and women of the time to come.

64,785. (Dean Dickinson.) You say you account for the silence and indifference of the working men to the question of Sunday closing, and so forth, because they believe it would never be carried into effect?—They believe it is an undue interference from outside.

64,786. How do you account for the fact that on the other side very large meetings of working men have been held during the last 10 or 12 years in favour of Sunday closing?—Those who do not use public-houses have interfered largely with the trade, but we say they have no business with the trade when they do not use the public-house.

64,787. But the working men do?—Yes; but one working man, I think, should have no right to dictate to another. The law is quite sufficient to check offenders.

64,788. The working men suffer from the drink traffic and from the consequences of it, and many people suffer from [illegible], and, therefore, they have an interest in the matter?—They may take an interest in it from that point of view, but I have known many of these large meetings to be whipped up by what we call temperance [illegible], who have [illegible] the men to go there, and even promises to be [illegible].

64,789. I have known meetings of working men interrupted by those who have been whipped up on the other side to create a disturbance at those meetings?—Yes, the like of that occurs in every case, but not very often.

64,790. It has, to my personal risk, occasionally. How do you account for the fact that there has been since this Sunday Closing Act a decrease in the consumption of spirits. To take last year, there was a decrease of [illegible] in the consumption of spirits in Ireland, over [illegible] less spent in spirits in Ireland than previously?—I think very few can give a reason for that. Statistics change up and down, and few can tell the reason why.

64,791. Not caused, at all events?—No. I do not think many can.

64,792. There has been a slight decrease in the beer, but a decrease on the previous year of [illegible]; that is to say, that in those two years there has been a decrease of nearly [illegible] in the consumption of intoxicating liquor?—It might be put down to bad times in some cases, scarcity of employment, or strikes. When large bodies of men are idle they can scarcely commit [illegible] in their [illegible].

64,793. Is that all over Ireland?—Sometimes in one part and sometimes another.

64,794. You attribute no part of that decrease to the

Mr. M. Black.

9 May '8[illegible]

Working men and Sunday closing.

Mr. M. [illegible]. — 23 May '97.

Closing Act was passed. Do you attach no value to that fact?—That would arise from the fact of men conducting themselves better and not drinking too much at a time.

[illegible]. It occurred on a sort of [illegible]?—There is a good deal that is shown by statistics that is the result of [illegible]. You cannot tell how it occurs.

The evils of [illegible].

[illegible]. (*Mr. Walker.*) I suppose you have had considerable experience and been brought in contact very much with the working classes of Belfast in particular?—Yes.

[illegible]. And your opinion has been formed from that intercourse that the more you restrict the more injury you do?—Yes. The craving [illegible] on, and the man will drink [illegible] in a shorter time.

[illegible]. And the legally established and properly conducted houses, with sufficient safeguards for the supply of these articles, are much preferable to the [illegible] and irregularly established places?—Yes. I [illegible] that there is no temperance preaching so effective as where the trader refuses a man's money and tells him he will not supply him with any more drink. I consider that that is a proof [illegible] that the establishment is well conducted, and that the welfare of the customer is in the man's mind who conducts the establishment.

[illegible]. Are you secretary to the Belfast Spirit Grocers' Association?—No, I am past chairman of the Licensed Vintners, and also of the Spirit Grocers. I was connected with the Vintners' Association for nearly [illegible] years. I am a property owner and large ratepayer, and have an interest in house property that is licensed, and I have looked into the question carefully.

[illegible]. Why I asked that question is this, that from the position you occupy in connexion with the grocers' association, you certainly no doubt would possess a knowledge of the nature of their business?—Yes.

[illegible]. In your opinion has Sunday closing produced an extra degree of business on Saturday night to the licensed grocer?—I could not say so. If a customer wanted to purchase drink for Sunday he would purchase it of a licensed vintner or spirit grocer.

[illegible]. You cannot answer that question?—I never knew any addition to my trade by the Saturday night purchases—anything I could remark as an addition to it.

[illegible]. We have had it stated here that the consumption has increased and not decreased consequent on Sunday closing, and that there has been more [illegible] consumption. Is that your view?—It may be; but I cannot prove it.

[illegible]. Is that your opinion?—It may be, but I am not positive on that point.

[illegible]. You will not express an opinion upon that?—No. I should say I might make a mistake if I said there was.

[illegible]. You condemn Sunday closing?—Yes. I believe that the houses that are open are the best conducted on the whole, and I think it is a mistake to continue the Sunday Closing Act in the country.

[illegible]. Do I understand you to mean that you approve of Sunday closing?—No, neither in town nor country.

[illegible]. Do I understand you that you are opposed to Sunday closing either in town or country?—I am, decidedly.

[illegible]. Are there any breweries in Belfast?—Yes.

[illegible]. How many?—I think there are three or four.

[illegible]. In your experience, does the firm of [illegible] supply the greater portion of Ireland with beer?—They sell a great deal of stout in Belfast.

Spirit grocers in Belfast.

[illegible]. (*Mr. Roberts.*) I find, from a Parliamentary Return, there were, last year, [illegible] spirit grocers in Belfast?—Yes, and I believe there are more now.

[illegible]. Of these [illegible] have removed their licences during the past 10 years?—Very likely.

[illegible]. I find also, during the last three years, [illegible] persons holding such licences were prosecuted?—Very likely.

[illegible]. And 166 were convicted?—That may be.

[illegible]. No less, in other words, than 75 per cent. were prosecuted during the three years?—That may be.

[illegible]. Now, what is the reason of that?—The over-granting of licences, as many do, is the cause of all the evils, by way of abuse of both the regular licences and off-licences.

Mr. M. [illegible]. — [illegible].

[illegible]. Then, too, many of these licences have been granted?—Yes, where they were not needed.

[illegible]. In that case the magistrates were to blame?—I believe so.

[illegible]. That is your opinion?—Yes.

[illegible]. Have you anything to say as to whether any influence were brought to bear on the magistrates in causing them to grant licences?—There may have been, but I should like to give just a little further explanation with regard to those statistics. When you cut down these men to two men's [illegible] the work upon, as a rule, [illegible] and die away. In the trade the same thing occurs. Where there are three houses where there would be a respectable living for two, the weak man drops out. He is like the drowning man. During the last half-year of his tenancy, when he knows he is bound to go, he catches at any straw and breaks the law without hesitation. He goes away and leaves three or four records behind him, and then after that he is no more in the spirit trade. He may be in the Transvaal or the States. Those records remain against the trade, and the man who is guilty of them has gone away. Then they are used against the respectable persons remaining in the trade as anything which show, as it were, that they are all illicit traders and a disreputable body, whereas it is quite the reverse. I kept an off licence for my son, and I let off two very fine public-houses, and the reason for that was that I believed it was the most select portion of the trade, and my son would not have managed a regular licensed house through reared in the business. He stated that the selling of drink under an off licence was as simple as selling butter-milk, but in the other case there were the usual little accidents that occur at the bar of a dram shop, and I consider he was right.

[illegible]. I can quite understand that being so in your case, but I gather from your evidence that in the last place a great many, too many, of these licences have been granted by these magistrates, and a great deal of undue influence was brought to bear on them to grant them?—I believe you are right in saying that.

That [illegible] in Belfast.

[illegible]. (*Mr. [illegible].*) A word on the subject of your tied-houses in Belfast. I suppose although certain wholesale firms have lent money to licensed persons in Belfast, you differ there from, as in England in this extent, that a great portion of the money is advanced by banks and private individuals to people who carry on this business?—Very much so.

[illegible]. Without any tie of any sort with reference to the supply of liquor?—Yes, only receiving interest and holding the deeds as security.

[illegible]. I suppose you are aware that the Recorder of Dublin, who gave evidence here, suggested that to inquire into advances of that kind was an important element in the granting of a licence as to the suitability of the applicant?—I should think that is going too much into private business.

[illegible]. I was going to ask you whether you would not deprecate any alteration of the law which would allow interference with or inquiry into anything of that kind?—Most decidedly.

[illegible]. As putting difficulties in the way of respectable young men getting reasonable advances?—That is so. The rising young men in our trade have all been assisted and are now respectable traders with good establishments.

[illegible]. And they would have been totally unable to embark in the trade at all unless private lenders had granted them a certain amount of accommodation?—Their start would have been too weak, and they could never have made any headway.

[illegible]. (*Mr. Grinling.*) I think most of the points of your evidence as affects the spirit grocer's licence have been fully gone into, but I should like to clear up a few matters. You are aware that a witness attended here on the 10th of May, representing himself to be the secretary of the Belfast United Trades and Labour Council?—Yes.

[illegible]. Perhaps you know the witness?—I do not know him personally.

[illegible]. I want to ask you if these views are generally accepted by the working classes of Belfast as he explained them to the Commission. One statement he made was this:—"Spirit grocers are regarded with more abhorrence than the public-houses, and the

[illegible]

"general opinion is that they are the most potent agents in the demoralisation of women, and lead to drinking amongst women who go under the cloak of buying groceries and purchasing cheap groceries and purchase drink." Is that a fair statement?—Not at all. That is the statement of a rabid Prohibitionist who knows nothing about the trade and who never entered a house of the kind. He has that opinion and gives expression to it here, but could prove nothing of the sort.

63,834. Is it a fact in your opinion that groceries are sold cheaper in these houses?—It would be ruinous to make two prices. You will have your temperance customer coming into the shop as well as the man who wants liquor. How could you make two prices in your shop? You would destroy your trade. That is altogether imaginary.

63,835. Then he was asked: "You think that is done for an inducement to go and deal there," and he says, "I decidedly do. I think it is to allow women to obtain"?—That is altogether an imaginary statement. The man could prove nothing of the sort. There is nothing connected with the trade that would bear on that.

63,836. Then he is asked:—"Do you believe they get liquor put down to them under the head of other commodities?—(A.) Yes. It is quite a common practice to get liquor put down as 'goods'." I understand you distinctly deny that so far as your experience and knowledge of the trade goes?—Yes. I answered that before, and you heard my opinion on that.

63,837. Then he was asked: "On that head is there anything else you wish to add for the information of the Commission?" and this was his answer: "Yes, I think it would be a great advantage if the spirit grocer's licenses were entirely abolished, and I think it would be also in harmony with public opinion in Belfast. I am certain that at least 90 per cent. of the working men of Belfast would vote for the abolition of the spirit grocer's license." I want to ask you, do you think he could be possibly entitled to speak for 90 per cent. of the working men of Belfast?—He [illegible] I made inquiries with regard to that man, and I find he only came here to speak for himself, and he is known to be a rabid Prohibitionist who would abolish the whole trade.

63,838. You are glad of the opportunity of removing any impression that his evidence might have made on the Commission?—I am pleased to get the opportunity of replying to it.

63,839. (Mr. Young.) You are chairman of the Belfast Spirit Grocers' Association?—I was.

63,840. Is that a large association?—Yes, pretty large.

63,841. They take under their protection simply the spirit grocers?—The off-licensed trade.

63,842. You are of opinion that the granting of the spirit grocer's license should be in the hands of the recorder, and that it would lead to improvement if new licenses were only granted in pursuance of experience[illegible]?—Yes.

63,843. What do you mean by that? Is it not a fact that at the present time these licenses can be got without the discriminating authority of the licensing tribunal, and that they can be got whether they like it or not?—I believe so. A magistrate told me they had no alternative but to grant them.

63,844. Are you of opinion that that should continue?—I am of opinion that it should cease as soon as possible. It is one of the greatest evils we have. I also said to the Chairman that I was in favour of an appeal from the recorder. We find that about [illegible] per cent. of the recorder's decisions are reversed by the judges, and they might err as to licenses as well as in other matters.

63,845. It is your opinion that the granting of spirit grocers' licenses should be under the same authority, and regulated by the same conditions, as the full licenses are?—Yes, new licenses at the annual licensing sessions, and transfers in the ordinary course, but I forgot to mention that we consider having to wait three months for the beer licence and at the same time being empowered to sell spirits, is a great hardship, and that it does not carry any sense with it.

63,846. (Mr. Gordon.) You agree with what was stated by the previous witness on that point?—Very likely.

63,847. (Mr. Young.) Then you want a different mode from the present of licensing spirit grocers?—Yes, I would suggest that it should be in the hands of the recorder, with power to appeal.

63,848. My point is this. Would you like the mode of granting the licence to spirit grocers to be in the same way as granting the full licence?—Yes, I would suggest doing away with the certificate that is required annually and with the fee that is collected annually by the clerk of petty sessions, which I believe he has no claim upon.

Mr. H. [illegible]

13 May '9[illegible]

Licensing authority for spirit grocers.

The witness withdrew.

Mr. J. O'Brien. 20 May '97.

on Sunday morning and [illegible]. I believe it is the [illegible] [illegible] that the publicans of Cork, I [illegible], in [illegible] to them, refuse to supply, that are picked up by the [illegible] that are [illegible] there [illegible] and carried away to these shebeens and [illegible] [illegible].

[illegible] Of your own knowledge you do not know of these shebeens?—Not to my own knowledge.

[illegible] This is only hearsay evidence you are giving as to their existence?—It seems to be agreed, in general, that it is not from any legitimate public-house that the persons who figure in the courts on Sunday morning get their liquor.

[illegible] Have you anything to say as to bogus clubs? —If the present hours are curtailed it will cause the forming up of bogus clubs, because they believe there is every facility for [illegible] six or seven men may form some sort of a club that will be got up for no other than for drinking purposes.

[illegible] Is this the opinion of your council or your own private opinion?—That is the opinion of the council.

Early Saturday closing.

[illegible] Then, with reference to early closing on Saturday night, your opinion, I understand, is the same as it is with reference to Sunday closing, is it not?—Quite so. I believe that if they ever start clubs in the trade society halls it would be ruinous to themselves and their families, for the men are compelled to go up there [illegible] to pay the weekly subscription, and then they may meet a comrade they have not seen for some time, and it is likely, if there are clubs in these society halls, they would sit down there and take more drink than they otherwise would if they went for a walk round the [illegible] and [illegible] home at a reasonable hour.

[illegible] On what day are wages usually paid in Cork?—I think the majority of the trades are paid on Fridays.

[illegible] In some cases on Saturdays?—In some cases on Saturday; but [illegible] o'clock is the latest on Saturday. They generally commence paying at the [illegible] to [illegible] in the building trades, and everything is cleared up by [illegible] o'clock. The majority would be paid on the Saturday morning.

The bonâ fide traveller limit.

[illegible] Have you formed any opinion as to the bonâ fide traveller?—In connection with the proposed extension of the three-mile limit, the council have taken that into consideration. Evidence has been given here by [illegible] witnesses from Cork to the effect that this thing is abused by persons travelling on the tram-cars and the railways, for the purpose of getting liquor outside the three-mile limit. That is not the fact, for the parties who journey out there are generally walk out. There are some picturesque walks round the city [illegible] by [illegible] of families and their children of a Sunday morning. They go down the valley to [illegible], which is a nice walk, and they go in for a refreshing drink, and I have passed there at all times, and I have never seen any drunkenness there. Then another thing, the [illegible] will severely affect the young men of the city. Most of the young men of Cork, even the clerks, and various other bodies, are great sportsmen, and there are seven packs of harriers in the city of

Harriers in Cork.

Cork, and they all meet within the radius of almost seven or eight miles of the city, and at the end of a hard day's running I think it would be very severe if they wound up four miles from Cork and could not get a drink. In fact, I think it would be a great thing, speaking as a follower of those harriers, if liberty were given in the country districts to have the houses open for a couple of hours on the Sunday.

[illegible] Do these packs meet on Sunday?—Sunday is the only day that the worker in Ireland has for recreation purposes unfortunately. There are seven clubs of harriers.

[illegible] (Mr. Younger.) You have regular packs of harriers?—Yes.

[illegible] You do not mean runners?—No.

[illegible] (Dean Dickinson.) Which are you?—I am a follower of the hounds.

[illegible] (Mr. Graham.) Are these really harrier hounds?—Yes. There is the Cork National Hunt Club Hounds, the Cork Southern Hunt Club Harriers, and others, and they all keep separate packs of hounds, and there is a club membership, but at present there are no clubs formed at which liquor is introduced. They are all quite content with the present arrangement to get it outside, and I have known since the [illegible] opened the feeling is that if the Bill is

carried they will have to open clubs, and after a hard day's [illegible] around of [illegible] they will be much more likely to get into the club and stay gambling and drinking there all night.

Mr. J. O'Brien.

Quality of liquor.

[illegible]—Have you anything to say as to the quality of the drink that is sold in Cork?—I do not believe there have been many prosecutions for adulterating liquor in Cork. Most of the liquor drunk in Cork is porter, and that will not bear much adulteration. In fact if you were to go into any house in the city and call for any liquor you like, you will be as safe in getting it as you would in a [illegible] bar. There is very good liquor sold by the vendors in Cork.

[illegible] As to the bars themselves are they pretty well kept?—Very well kept.

Vigilance of the police, &c.

[illegible] Have you any other points you wish to bring before us?—There was some evidence given about the police neglecting their duty, and I do not think it fair that that should remain unchallenged, because so far as the police are concerned in the county they are most vigilant in watching the licensed houses and detecting any breaches of the law that may occur. They have paid great attention to the publicans—perhaps too much—and I believe myself that the restrictions such as are needed in the Bill for the purpose of promoting temperance would never bring it about. Some time ago the temperance movement in Cork was flourishing, but that was at a time when the League of the Cross [illegible] were looked after properly, and care taken to provide concerts and other entertainments for the members. I remember the fact of a large demonstration—one of the largest ever held in Cork—being held to commemorate the death of the great apostle of temperance, Father Mathew, and the gentleman who presided over that temperance demonstration was the president of the Cork Licensed Vintners' Association, the then mayor of Cork, so that that will show you the [illegible] of [illegible] for the vintners. I think they do as much as their neighbours to promote temperance in our city, and I believe it was the unfortunate [illegible] in the late parliamentary party of Ireland that allowed the temperance movement to [illegible] for [illegible]; and if the Catholic clergymen—and I am a Catholic myself—would apply themselves to [illegible] trying to [illegible] by the League of the Cross, [illegible] [illegible] it, and not bother themselves so much about politics, I think we could go along better by moral persuasion to bring about temperance in Ireland than [illegible] restrictive measures, such as the Bill now before Parliament. Then I should like to show the consistency of our council in connection with the opposition to this Bill, as we believe that it would be detrimental to the interests of the trade. In 18[illegible] Alderman Crean, our president, was [illegible] at that time—and he was a [illegible] [illegible]—to come over and give evidence against the Bill. He is at the present day a member of Parliament, representative of the [illegible], and our present president, Mr. [illegible], is also a [illegible], and he has thorough sympathy with the views of the council in the matter. Mr. Maurice Healy, in his

Mr. Healy and Cork.

statement here, said that he represented the [illegible] of Cork with reference to their views on this matter. He did not. Mr. Maurice Healy and Mr. J. F. X. O'Brien, the two city members of Cork, when both seeking election from the representatives of Cork, had to sign a pledge to the representatives of the trade and labour bodies to look after their interests by every means in their power, and we hold that that pledge is good, inasmuch as we have passed a resolution that has been entrusted to their care to carry out. Mr. Maurice Healy is not voicing the opinions of his constituents by coming here to the Commission and stating that [illegible] per cent. of the working classes would not be in favour—he said they would be in favour—of the majority would be in favour of the [illegible] Bill.

[illegible] That is a matter for you to settle with Mr. Maurice Healy, I suppose?—Yes.

[illegible] You wish to contradict the statements he made before us?—Yes.

[illegible] (Mr. Young.) Then really Mr. Maurice Healy did not represent you here?—No.

[illegible] How many members do you represent in Cork in your council? How many comprise the council?—There is one for [illegible] members. The respective trade and labour bodies that have joined our council send any number they like, and then the regulation as to the delegates to represent them is one for [illegible].

[illegible] How many thousands do you represent?—I suppose we represent from [illegible] to [illegible] workers.

...ertain the opinions you ...
...[illegible] us. I am submitted ...
...[illegible] views before you as I ...

...Maurice Healy did not ...ty and the great masses ...have represented them. ...ought to look after our ...sations we passed.

...not know whether you ...tionly in giving his evi... ...to you that the Corpora... ...evented the feelings of ... Are you aware of that? ...en represented a large ...ion the trades.

...a much more representa... ...ationary which elected ...is therefore to be taken ...question than they were. ...?—Indirectly perhaps. ...s to submit him [illegible] to ...ration. He may have

...ention to Mr. Maguire ...t not at all spoken of.

...ly but you have them?—

...were stated that you are

...ployed?—I am employed

...of the Trades Council. ...many members are there ...perhaps we have nearly

...ersons at the meeting to ...ve the number of bodies

...council?—I suppose there ...mbers there.

...? a possible [illegible]?—Out of

...aid that they represented ...—Yes.

...ation of Cork?—I could

...ons of Cork. How many ...ged in manual labour?— ...y the bodies they return ...at consider I should be ...I do not know the exact

...ing it at too high a figure ...[illegible] workmen in Cork? ...that.

...ent that your association ...an [illegible] workmen. You ...to 4,[illegible]?—On the repre... ...return their full repre... ...ing their full quota to our ...stronger representation

...say that this association ...ented the great majority ...—Yes.

...?—They do not pay our ...ation.

...council only represented ...according to the repre... ...tary will return [illegible], and

the point?—Everybody. The only bodies outside are the dock labourers and quay labourers and coal porters, and they form a very big body outside the organised trades, but they generally work in touch with anything the trades council do. If we ever appeal to them for help they are always with us. *Mr. J. O'Brien.* — *15 May '96*

63,908. (*Mr. Roberts.*) As far as this council is concerned, they only directly represent 4,000 men?—No, they represent more than 4,000. *The Trades Council.*

63,909. (*Dean Dickinson.*) Directly?—They represent more. Our council represent the masses in this way. We will take the Bakers' Society. They number 200 members, and they will say we will return 50 members; that will be 2*l*. a year to pay to our council, and though they have only a representation of 50 members on the council they will number 200 in their own society. It is a saving to the respective bodies that they do not return the full number. For every member they return they must pay 1*s*. a year.

63,910. They understate the figures?—Yes.

63,911. (*Mr. Roberts.*) With reference to this body of 2,000 or 4,000 individuals, were they in any way apprised of the business that would be placed before the council on that occasion?—Yes. The meeting previous to the one at which the resolution was coming up for adoption was a specially convened one, not alone of the delegates, but the officers of the respective societies were present. When the notice of motion was given it appeared in the press for a week, and therefore anybody who had the slightest opposition to that resolution had due notice to oppose it before it was carried.

63,912. The trades council is elected every year, is it not?—Yes. It is a curious form. The societies who are affiliated with the council select their own delegates, and they may select them annually, quarterly, or half-yearly.

63,913. It seems rather a loose constitution?—I would not say so. The working man is situated in this way, that he may be working in Cork to-day or may be sent away to County Kerry to-morrow, and therefore they have to elect a substitute. I would not say there was anything loose in that.

63,914. At the last election it was not elected on the question of this Bill?—All matters appertaining to the welfare of the workers. When we are electing officers we do not know the questions that will come up. We are elected to guard their interests. We could not look forward so far that the Bill was going to form one of the questions at the time.

63,915. Should I not be right in saying that so far as that particular meeting went, the delegates present represented nobody but themselves?—No, they represented their bodies.

63,916. Then you have given evidence on a good many points to bring the opinion of the council with reference to licensing questions. I suppose you wish in your evidence to limit your opinion to the contents of the resolution?—That does not deal with the evidence. It embraces it as a whole. *The resolution.*

63,917. The resolution is simply a resolution against the Sale of Intoxicating Liquors (Ireland) Bill?—And the three clauses I have brought forward in my evidence as being directed by the council to lay before you, have been the three-mile limit and the Saturday and Sunday night closing.

63,918. Were you directed at that meeting to bring forward those other subjects?—No. When the resolution was passed those were the points considered, and in a speech by the proposer of the resolution I think he dealt with those points. Mr. James was the mover of it, and he dealt with the clauses that most affected the working classes—the three clauses I have referred to.

Mr. J. O'Brien.

23 May '98.

re-fastened when they come out, and they would not like to find, when they came out, all the public-houses closed. Therefore they would say they would get in the liquor beforehand, and in trade societies where very strong men were had to be taken to prevent such men, such as carters, I do not think liquor in a trade clubroom would be a wise thing, and therefore I think his opinion was to avoid the introduction of liquor into the trade houses on Saturday night.

63,921. Sharing the opinion of that particular meeting of the trades council, you have read the evidence of Mr Gambell given before this Commission?—Yes.

63,922. You are aware of what he stated as to the opinion of the three bishops, of the one member of Parliament, of the mayor of Cork, the president of the Chamber of Commerce, the president of the United Trades of Ireland, the chairman of the Board of Guardians, and some employers of labour and other representative persons, as all for, in favour of Sunday closing, or for diminished hours for the sale of liquor on Sunday. You are aware of all that?—I may be aware of some of the bodies, but I do not vouch for all that Mr Gambell gave in evidence.

63,923. These are public persons and public bodies? —You mentioned the president of the United Trades of Ireland. Had he that gentleman's name?

63,924. I suppose so?—I do not know anybody of that position in Ireland.

63,925. Despite all that body of evidence you are here to say that that particular meeting of the council was not in favour of the Bill now before Parliament?—Quite so.

63,926. And that is your evidence?—Yes.

63,927. (*Mr. Hyslop.*) An attempt has been made to depreciate the importance of that meeting. Will you put in the speech that was delivered by the president on that occasion. It is a very important speech, I understand, and I think it should be placed before the Commission?—Yes. It is the speech of the president of the Cork United Trades' Association [*vide* foot note]. There is another matter I would like to mention, and that is that witnesses from Cork have stated how very much addicted to drink the people are in Cork. I most firmly contradict that, because the working classes in Cork are as sober a body as you can get in Ireland, and I think it most unfair to the women of Cork to hold them up as being terrible drunkards. There are a few, as will appear from the police records, who figure before the magistrates nearly 300 times in the year, such as Mary Glover, and people of her class, but if she is to be held up as any model of the other women of Cork I think it is most unfair. That class, when they come before the magistrates for drunkenness, have two or three days' imprisonment, are released in the morning, and are up again the same night.

Drinking in Cork and habitual drunkards.

63,928. (*Mr. Gordon.*) How often do you say this lady is in gaol?—I am not pressing the particular matter.

63,929. How often during the year has she been in gaol?—From 20 to 30 times she is confined and it would be the 20th or 30th time that she was up before the magistrates. That is on record. The magistrates ask how many times has this lady appeared, and very often it is laughable to read in the papers that it is the 200th time.

[illegible]

63,930. I thought you said she was committed to prison 300 times in the course of the year?—No, that would give a very short time for her to be out of it.

63,931. (*Mr. Wallace.*) You have been sent here by your council?—Quite so.

63,932. Mr. Roberts asked you where you were employed, and you said in the Beamish Brewery?—Yes.

63,933. That does not imply that you were influenced by that fact or by the circumstance that you were employed at the Brewery and that your council sent you here?—There is nothing permanent about my job in Beamish's Brewery. I can be discharged at 6 o'clock in the evening. I have no contract with either Mr. Beamish, or Mr Crawford. I am under the control of Mr. Adams the engineer and as soon as I do not suit him I am sent off.

The Trades Council.

63,934. You are not permanently employed there? —No.

63,935. Now, your council, they representing a very large number of the working classes, are antagonistic to the attempt to further restrict their convenience, or interference with their convenience?—Quite so.

63,936. They regard it in the light of an interference with the liberty of the subject?—Quite so.

63,937. They are not in any way influenced or actuated by any motives or interests associated with the licensed trade, and they are of opinion that any new further restriction of that character is calculated to do harm to their households by their being compelled to take drink home and consume it there?—Quite so.

63,938. And in their view it is calculated to bring about intemperance far more than the legitimately and openly established house?—Quite so.

63,939. As regards delegates, do I understand you that they limit the maximum of delegates to three?—No, there are some societies have seven.

63,940. Is that the maximum?—Yes, I think seven is about the maximum for representatives.

63,941. What is the minimum?—One. They are small bodies that have only 30 members or so.

63,942. Supposing a trade society has 700 members, how many delegates would that society be entitled to send?—It rests with the society to send as many as they like. They may only pay on 40 of that 700. Every member that they return as affiliated to the trades council they will have to pay on, and therefore, as a matter of economy, they do not send their full representation.

63,943. Though they may only send one, yet they really represent the whole society?—Yes. The two that represent them on the council are representative of that body.

63,944. By that means your council does legitimately represent the approximate number of 10,000 workmen in Cork?—Yes.

63,945. (*Dean Dickinson.*) Mr. Maurice Healy's promise or pledge was that he would in every way promote the interests of the working men?—Quite so.

63,946. Is it not conceivable that he may think he is promoting their best interests by the encouragement of temperance and the promotion of that Bill. Is not that conceivable?—We should like to see temperance go ahead; but Mr. Maurice Healy, in his evidence here, appears as if he was speaking on behalf of the masses of Cork at the time, but he could not speak on behalf of that portion which possesses organisation.

63,947. If he thinks the interests of the working classes and the masses would be best promoted by that Bill and by other temperance legislation, then he is keeping his pledge in his own way?—As an individual, not as a duly-elected representative.

63,948. Who is to judge as to the pledge; he himself must be the judge?—Of his own opinions, but not as representing the feelings of the masses at the time. It might be his individual opinion.

63,949. I only know there was a large majority in favour of Sunday closing when the canvass was taken in Cork?—Our council have consistently followed up this matter, and opposed it on all occasions, and therefore I begin to doubt that.

The witness withdrew.

LIST OF APPENDICES.

APPENDIX I.

(Sir Andrew Reed.)

TABLE I.

RETURN of the NUMBER of HOUSES for which LICENSES were held on 1st February 18[illegible], throughout IRELAND, for the SALE by RETAIL of INTOXICATING LIQUORS, showing—1st, Public-houses Licensed for the Sale of Beer, Spirits, &c.; 2nd, Wine Refreshment Houses Licensed for the Sale of Wine for Consumption on the Premises, but not Beer or Spirits; 3rd, Spirit Grocers' Houses having the Spirit License, and also the Beer Retail License; 4th, Spirit Grocers' Houses having the Spirit License only; 5th, Beer Retail Houses having the Beer Retail License only.

Counties, &c.	Number of Public-houses. (1.)	Number of Wine Refreshment Houses. (2.)	Number of Spirit Grocers' Houses having Beer Retail License also. (3.)	Number of Spirit Grocers' Houses having Spirit License only. (4.)	Number of Beer Retail Houses having the Beer Retail License only. (5.)	Total Number of Houses for which Retail Licenses were held. (6.)	Population. (7.)	Ratio of Licensed Premises to Population. (8.)
Antrim	[illegible]	—	[illegible]	[illegible]	[illegible]	[illegible]	[illegible]	1 to [illegible]
Armagh	[illegible]	—	[illegible]	[illegible]	[illegible]	[illegible]	[illegible]	[illegible]
Cavan	[illegible]	—	[illegible]	[illegible]	—	[illegible]	[illegible]	[illegible]
Donegal	[illegible]	—	[illegible]	[illegible]	—	[illegible]	[illegible]	[illegible]
Down	[illegible]	—	[illegible]	[illegible]	[illegible]	[illegible]	[illegible]	[illegible]
Fermanagh	[illegible]	—	[illegible]	[illegible]	—	[illegible]	[illegible]	[illegible]
Londonderry	[illegible]	—	[illegible]	[illegible]	[illegible]	[illegible]	[illegible]	[illegible]
Monaghan	[illegible]	[illegible]	[illegible]	[illegible]	—	[illegible]	[illegible]	[illegible]
Tyrone	[illegible]	—	[illegible]	[illegible]	—	[illegible]	[illegible]	[illegible]
Carlow	[illegible]	—	[illegible]	[illegible]	[illegible]	[illegible]	[illegible]	[illegible]
Dublin	[illegible]	[illegible]	[illegible]	[illegible]	[illegible]	[illegible]	[illegible]	[illegible]
Kildare	[illegible]	—	[illegible]	[illegible]	[illegible]	[illegible]	[illegible]	[illegible]
Kilkenny	[illegible]	—	—	—	—	[illegible]	[illegible]	[illegible]
King's	[illegible]	—	[illegible]	[illegible]	[illegible]	[illegible]	[illegible]	[illegible]
Longford	[illegible]	—	—	[illegible]	—	[illegible]	[illegible]	[illegible]
Louth	[illegible]	[illegible]	[illegible]	[illegible]	[illegible]	[illegible]	[illegible]	[illegible]
Meath	[illegible]	[illegible]	[illegible]	[illegible]	—	[illegible]	[illegible]	[illegible]
Queen's	[illegible]	—	[illegible]	[illegible]	—	[illegible]	[illegible]	[illegible]
Westmeath	[illegible]	[illegible]	[illegible]	[illegible]	[illegible]	[illegible]	[illegible]	[illegible]
Wexford	[illegible]	[illegible]	[illegible]	[illegible]	[illegible]	[illegible]	[illegible]	[illegible]
Wicklow	[illegible]	—	[illegible]	[illegible]	[illegible]	[illegible]	[illegible]	[illegible]
Galway, East Riding	[illegible]	—	—	—	—	[illegible]	[illegible]	[illegible]
Galway, West Riding	[illegible]	—	—	—	—	[illegible]		
Leitrim	[illegible]	—	—	—	—	[illegible]	[illegible]	[illegible]
Mayo	[illegible]	—	[illegible]	[illegible]	[illegible]	[illegible]	[illegible]	[illegible]
Roscommon	[illegible]	[illegible]	[illegible]	[illegible]	—	[illegible]	[illegible]	[illegible]
Sligo	[illegible]	—	[illegible]	[illegible]	—	[illegible]	[illegible]	[illegible]
Clare	[illegible]	—	—	—	—	[illegible]	[illegible]	[illegible]
Cork, East Riding	[illegible]	—	[illegible]	[illegible]	[illegible]	[illegible]	[illegible]	[illegible]
Cork, West Riding	[illegible]	—	[illegible]	—	[illegible]	[illegible]	[illegible]	[illegible]
Kerry	[illegible]	—	—	—	[illegible]	[illegible]	[illegible]	[illegible]
Limerick	[illegible]	[illegible]	—	[illegible]	[illegible]	[illegible]	[illegible]	[illegible]
Tipperary, North Riding	[illegible]	[illegible]	—	[illegible]	[illegible]	[illegible]	[illegible]	[illegible]
Tipperary, South Riding	[illegible]	—	[illegible]	[illegible]	[illegible]	[illegible]	[illegible]	[illegible]
Waterford	[illegible]	—	[illegible]	[illegible]	[illegible]	[illegible]	[illegible]	[illegible]
Dublin Metropolitan Police District	[illegible]	[illegible]	[illegible]	[illegible]	[illegible]	[illegible]	[illegible]	[illegible]
City of Dublin	[illegible]	—	[illegible]	[illegible]	—	[illegible]	[illegible]	[illegible]
City of Cork	[illegible]	—	[illegible]	[illegible]	—	[illegible]	[illegible]	[illegible]
City of Limerick	[illegible]	—	—	[illegible]	—	[illegible]	[illegible]	[illegible]
City of Waterford	[illegible]	—	—	—	[illegible]	[illegible]	[illegible]	[illegible]
Total	[illegible]	[illegible]	[illegible]	[illegible]	[illegible]	[illegible]	[illegible]	1 to [illegible]

TABLE II.

Return showing the Number of Public-houses for which Licenses were held on 1st February, [illegible], for the Sale of Beer, Spirits, &c.

Counties, &c.	(a.) Number for which the Seven-day License was held.	(b.) Number for which the Six-day License was held.	(c.) Number for which the Six-day and Early-closing License was held.	(d.) Number for which the Seven-day and Early-closing License was held.	(e.) Total Number of Public-houses.
Antrim	[illegible]	[illegible]	[illegible]	[illegible]	[illegible]
Armagh	[illegible]	[illegible]	[illegible]	[illegible]	[illegible]
Cavan	[illegible]	[illegible]	[illegible]	[illegible]	[illegible]
Donegal	[illegible]	[illegible]	[illegible]	[illegible]	[illegible]
Down	[illegible]	[illegible]	[illegible]	[illegible]	[illegible]
Fermanagh	[illegible]	[illegible]	[illegible]	[illegible]	[illegible]
Londonderry	[illegible]	[illegible]	[illegible]	[illegible]	[illegible]
Monaghan	[illegible]	[illegible]	[illegible]	[illegible]	[illegible]
Tyrone	[illegible]	[illegible]	[illegible]	[illegible]	[illegible]
Carlow	[illegible]	[illegible]	[illegible]	[illegible]	[illegible]
Dublin	[illegible]	[illegible]	[illegible]	[illegible]	[illegible]
Kildare	[illegible]	[illegible]	[illegible]	[illegible]	[illegible]
Kilkenny	[illegible]	[illegible]	[illegible]	[illegible]	[illegible]
King's	[illegible]	[illegible]	[illegible]	[illegible]	[illegible]
Longford	[illegible]	[illegible]	[illegible]	[illegible]	[illegible]
Louth	[illegible]	[illegible]	[illegible]	[illegible]	[illegible]
Meath	[illegible]	[illegible]	[illegible]	[illegible]	[illegible]
Queen's	[illegible]	[illegible]	[illegible]	[illegible]	[illegible]
Westmeath	[illegible]	[illegible]	[illegible]	[illegible]	[illegible]
Wexford	[illegible]	[illegible]	[illegible]	[illegible]	[illegible]
Wicklow	[illegible]	[illegible]	[illegible]	[illegible]	[illegible]
Galway, East Riding	[illegible]	[illegible]	[illegible]	[illegible]	[illegible]
" West Riding	[illegible]	[illegible]	[illegible]	[illegible]	[illegible]
Leitrim	[illegible]	[illegible]	[illegible]	[illegible]	[illegible]
Mayo	[illegible]	[illegible]	[illegible]	[illegible]	[illegible]
Roscommon	[illegible]	[illegible]	[illegible]	[illegible]	[illegible]
Sligo	[illegible]	[illegible]	[illegible]	[illegible]	[illegible]
Clare	[illegible]	[illegible]	[illegible]	[illegible]	[illegible]
Cork, East Riding	[illegible]	[illegible]	[illegible]	[illegible]	[illegible]
" West Riding	[illegible]	[illegible]	[illegible]	[illegible]	[illegible]
Kerry	[illegible]	[illegible]	[illegible]	[illegible]	[illegible]
Limerick	[illegible]	[illegible]	[illegible]	[illegible]	[illegible]
Tipperary, North Riding	[illegible]	[illegible]	[illegible]	[illegible]	[illegible]
" South Riding	[illegible]	[illegible]	[illegible]	[illegible]	[illegible]
Waterford	[illegible]	[illegible]	[illegible]	[illegible]	[illegible]
Dublin Metropolitan Police District	[illegible]	[illegible]	[illegible]	[illegible]	[illegible]
City of Belfast	[illegible]	[illegible]	[illegible]	[illegible]	[illegible]
" Cork	[illegible]	[illegible]	[illegible]	[illegible]	[illegible]
" Limerick	[illegible]	[illegible]	[illegible]	[illegible]	[illegible]
" Waterford	[illegible]	[illegible]	[illegible]	[illegible]	[illegible]
Total	[illegible]	[illegible]	[illegible]	[illegible]	[illegible]

TABLE III.

Return showing the Number of Persons proceeded against for Drunkenness throughout Ireland during each Year from 1878 to 1897 (excluding the Dublin Metropolitan Police District).

Year.	Number of Persons proceeded against.	Number convicted.	Population (estimated).	Percentage of Convictions to population.	Year.	Number of Persons proceeded against.	Number convicted.	Population (estimated).	Percentage of Convictions to population.
1878	[illegible]	[illegible]	[illegible]	[illegible]	1888	[illegible]	[illegible]	[illegible]	[illegible]
1879	[illegible]	[illegible]	[illegible]	[illegible]	1889	[illegible]	[illegible]	[illegible]	[illegible]
1880	[illegible]	[illegible]	[illegible]	[illegible]	1890	[illegible]	[illegible]	[illegible]	[illegible]
1881	[illegible]	[illegible]	[illegible]	[illegible]	1891	[illegible]	[illegible]	[illegible]	[illegible]
1882	[illegible]	[illegible]	[illegible]	[illegible]	1892	[illegible]	[illegible]	[illegible]	[illegible]
1883	[illegible]	[illegible]	[illegible]	[illegible]	1893	[illegible]	[illegible]	[illegible]	[illegible]
1884	[illegible]	[illegible]	[illegible]	[illegible]	1894	[illegible]	[illegible]	[illegible]	[illegible]
1885	[illegible]	[illegible]	[illegible]	[illegible]	1895	[illegible]	[illegible]	[illegible]	[illegible]
1886	[illegible]	[illegible]	[illegible]	[illegible]	1896	[illegible]	[illegible]	[illegible]	[illegible]
1887	[illegible]	[illegible]	[illegible]	[illegible]	1897	[illegible]	[illegible]	[illegible]	[illegible]

TABLE IV.

Return showing the Number of Persons Proceeded against for Drunkenness within the Metropolitan Police District of Dublin, and the Cities of Belfast, Cork, Limerick and Waterford, during each Year from 1878 to 1897, inclusive.

Year.	Number of Persons proceeded against for Drunkenness. In Metropolitan Police District of Dublin.	In City of Belfast.	In City of Cork.	In City of Limerick.	In City of Waterford.	Year.	Number of Persons proceeded against for Drunkenness. In Metropolitan Police District of Dublin.	In City of Belfast.	In City of Cork.	In City of Limerick.	In City of Waterford.
1878	[illegible]	[illegible]	[illegible]	[illegible]	[illegible]	1888	[illegible]	[illegible]	[illegible]	[illegible]	[illegible]
1879	[illegible]	[illegible]	[illegible]	[illegible]	[illegible]	1889	[illegible]	[illegible]	[illegible]	[illegible]	[illegible]
1880	[illegible]	[illegible]	[illegible]	[illegible]	[illegible]	1890	[illegible]	[illegible]	[illegible]	[illegible]	[illegible]
1881	[illegible]	[illegible]	[illegible]	[illegible]	[illegible]	1891	[illegible]	[illegible]	[illegible]	[illegible]	[illegible]
1882	[illegible]	[illegible]	[illegible]	[illegible]	[illegible]	1892	[illegible]	[illegible]	[illegible]	[illegible]	[illegible]
1883	[illegible]	[illegible]	[illegible]	[illegible]	[illegible]	1893	[illegible]	[illegible]	[illegible]	[illegible]	[illegible]
1884	[illegible]	[illegible]	[illegible]	[illegible]	[illegible]	1894	[illegible]	[illegible]	[illegible]	[illegible]	[illegible]
1885	[illegible]	[illegible]	[illegible]	[illegible]	[illegible]	1895	[illegible]	[illegible]	[illegible]	[illegible]	[illegible]
1886	[illegible]	[illegible]	[illegible]	[illegible]	[illegible]	1896	[illegible]	[illegible]	[illegible]	[illegible]	[illegible]
1887	[illegible]	[illegible]	[illegible]	[illegible]	[illegible]	1897	[illegible]	[illegible]	[illegible]	[illegible]	[illegible]

TABLE V.

Return showing, by Counties, the Number of Persons proceeded against for Drunkenness throughout Ireland during each of the Five Years from 1893 to 1897, inclusive, the Annual Average Number of Persons proceeded against, and the Ratio to the Population.

Counties, &c.	Number of Persons proceeded against for Drunkenness. 1893.	1894.	1895.	1896.	1897.	Average Number of Persons Proceeded against per Annum.	Ratio of Proceedings to Population.	Ratio of Licensed Premises to Population.
Antrim	[illegible]	[illegible]	[illegible]	[illegible]	[illegible]	[illegible]	1 to [illegible]	1 to [illegible]
Armagh	[illegible]	[illegible]	[illegible]	[illegible]	[illegible]	[illegible]	[illegible]	[illegible]
Cavan	[illegible]	[illegible]	[illegible]	[illegible]	[illegible]	[illegible]	[illegible]	[illegible]
Donegal	[illegible]	[illegible]	[illegible]	[illegible]	[illegible]	[illegible]	[illegible]	[illegible]
Down	[illegible]	[illegible]	[illegible]	[illegible]	[illegible]	[illegible]	[illegible]	[illegible]
Fermanagh	[illegible]	[illegible]	[illegible]	[illegible]	[illegible]	[illegible]	[illegible]	[illegible]
Londonderry	[illegible]	[illegible]	[illegible]	[illegible]	[illegible]	[illegible]	[illegible]	[illegible]
Monaghan	[illegible]	[illegible]	[illegible]	[illegible]	[illegible]	[illegible]	[illegible]	[illegible]
Tyrone	[illegible]	[illegible]	[illegible]	[illegible]	[illegible]	[illegible]	[illegible]	[illegible]
Carlow	[illegible]	[illegible]	[illegible]	[illegible]	[illegible]	[illegible]	[illegible]	[illegible]
Dublin	[illegible]	[illegible]	[illegible]	[illegible]	[illegible]	[illegible]	[illegible]	[illegible]
Kildare	[illegible]	[illegible]	[illegible]	[illegible]	[illegible]	[illegible]	[illegible]	[illegible]
Kilkenny	[illegible]	[illegible]	[illegible]	[illegible]	[illegible]	[illegible]	[illegible]	[illegible]
King's	[illegible]	[illegible]	[illegible]	[illegible]	[illegible]	[illegible]	[illegible]	[illegible]
Longford	[illegible]	[illegible]	[illegible]	[illegible]	[illegible]	[illegible]	[illegible]	[illegible]
Louth	[illegible]	[illegible]	[illegible]	[illegible]	[illegible]	[illegible]	[illegible]	[illegible]
Meath	[illegible]	[illegible]	[illegible]	[illegible]	[illegible]	[illegible]	[illegible]	[illegible]
Queen's	[illegible]	[illegible]	[illegible]	[illegible]	[illegible]	[illegible]	[illegible]	[illegible]
Westmeath	[illegible]	[illegible]	[illegible]	[illegible]	[illegible]	[illegible]	[illegible]	[illegible]
Wexford	[illegible]	[illegible]	[illegible]	[illegible]	[illegible]	[illegible]	[illegible]	[illegible]
Wicklow	[illegible]	[illegible]	[illegible]	[illegible]	[illegible]	[illegible]	[illegible]	[illegible]
Galway, East Riding	[illegible]	[illegible]	[illegible]	[illegible]	[illegible]	[illegible]	[illegible]	[illegible]
" West Riding	[illegible]	[illegible]	[illegible]	[illegible]	[illegible]	[illegible]		
Leitrim	[illegible]	[illegible]	[illegible]	[illegible]	[illegible]	[illegible]	[illegible]	[illegible]
Mayo	[illegible]	[illegible]	[illegible]	[illegible]	[illegible]	[illegible]	[illegible]	[illegible]
Roscommon	[illegible]	[illegible]	[illegible]	[illegible]	[illegible]	[illegible]	[illegible]	[illegible]
Sligo	[illegible]	[illegible]	[illegible]	[illegible]	[illegible]	[illegible]	[illegible]	[illegible]
Clare	[illegible]	[illegible]	[illegible]	[illegible]	[illegible]	[illegible]	[illegible]	[illegible]
Cork, East Riding	[illegible]	[illegible]	[illegible]	[illegible]	[illegible]	[illegible]	[illegible]	[illegible]
" West Riding	[illegible]	[illegible]	[illegible]	[illegible]	[illegible]	[illegible]	[illegible]	[illegible]
Kerry	[illegible]	[illegible]	[illegible]	[illegible]	[illegible]	[illegible]	[illegible]	[illegible]
Limerick	[illegible]	[illegible]	[illegible]	[illegible]	[illegible]	[illegible]	[illegible]	[illegible]
Tipperary, North Riding	[illegible]	[illegible]	[illegible]	[illegible]	[illegible]	[illegible]	[illegible]	[illegible]
" South Riding	[illegible]	[illegible]	[illegible]	[illegible]	[illegible]	[illegible]	[illegible]	[illegible]
Waterford	[illegible]	[illegible]	[illegible]	[illegible]	[illegible]	[illegible]	[illegible]	[illegible]
Dublin Metropolitan Police District	[illegible]	[illegible]	[illegible]	[illegible]	[illegible]	[illegible]	[illegible]	[illegible]
City of Belfast	[illegible]	[illegible]	[illegible]	[illegible]	[illegible]	[illegible]	[illegible]	[illegible]
" Cork	[illegible]	[illegible]	[illegible]	[illegible]	[illegible]	[illegible]	[illegible]	[illegible]
" Limerick	[illegible]	[illegible]	[illegible]	[illegible]	[illegible]	[illegible]	[illegible]	[illegible]
" Waterford	[illegible]	[illegible]	[illegible]	[illegible]	[illegible]	[illegible]	[illegible]	[illegible]
Total	[illegible]	[illegible]	[illegible]	[illegible]	[illegible]	[illegible]	[illegible]	[illegible]

TABLE VI.

Return of the Number of Persons Convicted Three Times and upwards of being Drunk, or Drunk and Disorderly, in Ireland during each Year from 1878 to 1897.

Year.	Number Convicted 3 times and less than 5.	Number Convicted 5 times and less than 10.	Number Convicted 10 times and upwards.	Total.	Year.	Number Convicted 3 times and less than 5.	Number Convicted 5 times and less than 10.	Number Convicted 10 times and upwards.	Total.
[illegible]	[illegible]	[illegible]	[illegible]	[illegible]	[illegible]	[illegible]	[illegible]	[illegible]	[illegible]
[illegible]	[illegible]	[illegible]	[illegible]	[illegible]	[illegible]	[illegible]	[illegible]	[illegible]	[illegible]
[illegible]	[illegible]	[illegible]	[illegible]	[illegible]	[illegible]	[illegible]	[illegible]	[illegible]	[illegible]
[illegible]	[illegible]	[illegible]	[illegible]	[illegible]	[illegible]	[illegible]	[illegible]	[illegible]	[illegible]
[illegible]	[illegible]	[illegible]	[illegible]	[illegible]	[illegible]	[illegible]	[illegible]	[illegible]	[illegible]
[illegible]	[illegible]	[illegible]	[illegible]	[illegible]	[illegible]	[illegible]	[illegible]	[illegible]	[illegible]
[illegible]	[illegible]	[illegible]	[illegible]	[illegible]	[illegible]	[illegible]	[illegible]	[illegible]	[illegible]
[illegible]	[illegible]	[illegible]	[illegible]	[illegible]	[illegible]	[illegible]	[illegible]	[illegible]	[illegible]
[illegible]	[illegible]	[illegible]	[illegible]	[illegible]	[illegible]	[illegible]	[illegible]	[illegible]	[illegible]
[illegible]	[illegible]	[illegible]	[illegible]	[illegible]	[illegible]	[illegible]	[illegible]	[illegible]	[illegible]

TABLE VII.

Return showing the Number of Persons Convicted Three Times and upwards of being Drunk, or Drunk and Disorderly, in Ireland during the Year ended 31st December 1897 (as far as known to the Police).

Counties, &c.	Number Convicted 3 times and less than 5.	Number Convicted 5 times and less than 10.	Number Convicted 10 times and upwards.	Total.	Counties, &c.	Number Convicted 3 times and less than 5.	Number Convicted 5 times and less than 10.	Number Convicted 10 times and upwards.	Total.
Antrim	[illegible]	[illegible]	[illegible]	[illegible]	Galway, West Riding	[illegible]	[illegible]	—	[illegible]
Armagh	[illegible]	[illegible]	[illegible]	[illegible]	Leitrim	[illegible]	[illegible]	—	[illegible]
Cavan	[illegible]	[illegible]	—	[illegible]	Mayo	[illegible]	[illegible]	—	[illegible]
Donegal	[illegible]	[illegible]	—	[illegible]	Roscommon	[illegible]	[illegible]	—	[illegible]
Down	[illegible]	[illegible]	[illegible]	[illegible]	Sligo	[illegible]	[illegible]	[illegible]	[illegible]
Fermanagh	[illegible]	[illegible]	[illegible]	[illegible]					
Londonderry	[illegible]	[illegible]	[illegible]	[illegible]	Clare	[illegible]	[illegible]	[illegible]	[illegible]
Monaghan	[illegible]	[illegible]	[illegible]	[illegible]	Cork, East Riding	[illegible]	[illegible]	—	[illegible]
Tyrone	[illegible]	[illegible]	[illegible]	[illegible]	„ West Riding	[illegible]	[illegible]	—	[illegible]
					Kerry	[illegible]	[illegible]	[illegible]	[illegible]
Carlow	[illegible]	[illegible]	—	[illegible]	Limerick	[illegible]	[illegible]	—	[illegible]
Dublin	[illegible]	[illegible]	[illegible]	[illegible]	Tipperary, N. Riding	[illegible]	[illegible]	[illegible]	[illegible]
Kildare	[illegible]	[illegible]	—	[illegible]	„ S. Riding	[illegible]	[illegible]	[illegible]	[illegible]
Kilkenny	[illegible]	[illegible]	—	[illegible]	Waterford	[illegible]	[illegible]	[illegible]	[illegible]
King's	[illegible]	[illegible]	[illegible]	[illegible]					
Longford	[illegible]	[illegible]	—	[illegible]	Dublin Metropolitan Police District	[illegible]	[illegible]	[illegible]	[illegible]
Louth	[illegible]	[illegible]	[illegible]	[illegible]					
Meath	[illegible]	[illegible]	[illegible]	[illegible]	City of Belfast	[illegible]	[illegible]	[illegible]	[illegible]
Queen's	[illegible]	[illegible]	[illegible]	[illegible]	„ Cork	[illegible]	[illegible]	—	[illegible]
Westmeath	[illegible]	[illegible]	[illegible]	[illegible]	„ Limerick	[illegible]	[illegible]	[illegible]	[illegible]
Wexford	[illegible]	[illegible]	—	[illegible]	„ Waterford	[illegible]	[illegible]	[illegible]	[illegible]
Wicklow	[illegible]	[illegible]	[illegible]	[illegible]					
					Total	[illegible]	[illegible]	[illegible]	[illegible]
Galway, East Riding	[illegible]	[illegible]	[illegible]	[illegible]					

TABLE VIII.

Return of the Number of Prosecutions against Persons holding Retail Licences, for Offences against the Intoxicating Liquor Laws, throughout Ireland, in each Year, from [illegible] to 1897 inclusive.
[Including Dublin Metropolitan Police District.]

TABLE IX.

Return showing the Number of Convictions of Licensed Persons throughout Ireland, during each Year from 1893 to 1897, inclusive.

Counties, &c.	1893.	1894.	1895.	1896.	1897.
Antrim	[illegible]	[illegible]	[illegible]	[illegible]	[illegible]
Armagh	[illegible]	[illegible]	[illegible]	[illegible]	[illegible]
Cavan	[illegible]	[illegible]	[illegible]	[illegible]	[illegible]
Donegal	[illegible]	[illegible]	[illegible]	[illegible]	[illegible]
Down	[illegible]	[illegible]	[illegible]	[illegible]	[illegible]
Fermanagh	[illegible]	[illegible]	[illegible]	[illegible]	[illegible]
Londonderry	[illegible]	[illegible]	[illegible]	[illegible]	[illegible]
Monaghan	[illegible]	[illegible]	[illegible]	[illegible]	[illegible]
Tyrone	[illegible]	[illegible]	[illegible]	[illegible]	[illegible]
Carlow	[illegible]	[illegible]	[illegible]	[illegible]	[illegible]
Dublin	[illegible]	[illegible]	[illegible]	[illegible]	[illegible]
Kildare	[illegible]	[illegible]	[illegible]	[illegible]	[illegible]
Kilkenny	[illegible]	[illegible]	[illegible]	[illegible]	[illegible]
King's	[illegible]	[illegible]	[illegible]	[illegible]	[illegible]
Longford	[illegible]	[illegible]	[illegible]	[illegible]	[illegible]
Louth	[illegible]	[illegible]	[illegible]	[illegible]	[illegible]
Meath	[illegible]	[illegible]	[illegible]	[illegible]	[illegible]
Queen's	[illegible]	[illegible]	[illegible]	[illegible]	[illegible]
Westmeath	[illegible]	[illegible]	[illegible]	[illegible]	[illegible]
Wexford	[illegible]	[illegible]	[illegible]	[illegible]	[illegible]
Wicklow	[illegible]	[illegible]	[illegible]	[illegible]	[illegible]
Galway, East Riding	[illegible]	[illegible]	[illegible]	[illegible]	[illegible]
Galway, West Riding	[illegible]	[illegible]	[illegible]	[illegible]	[illegible]
Leitrim	[illegible]	[illegible]	[illegible]	[illegible]	[illegible]
Mayo	[illegible]	[illegible]	[illegible]	[illegible]	[illegible]
Roscommon	[illegible]	[illegible]	[illegible]	[illegible]	[illegible]
Sligo	[illegible]	[illegible]	[illegible]	[illegible]	[illegible]
Clare	[illegible]	[illegible]	[illegible]	[illegible]	[illegible]
Cork, East Riding	[illegible]	[illegible]	[illegible]	[illegible]	[illegible]
„ West Riding	[illegible]	[illegible]	[illegible]	[illegible]	[illegible]
Kerry	[illegible]	[illegible]	[illegible]	[illegible]	[illegible]
Limerick	[illegible]	[illegible]	[illegible]	[illegible]	[illegible]
Tipperary, North Riding	[illegible]	[illegible]	[illegible]	[illegible]	[illegible]
„ South Riding	[illegible]	[illegible]	[illegible]	[illegible]	[illegible]
Waterford	[illegible]	[illegible]	[illegible]	[illegible]	[illegible]
Belfast City	[illegible]	[illegible]	[illegible]	[illegible]	[illegible]
Cork City	[illegible]	[illegible]	[illegible]	[illegible]	[illegible]
Limerick City	[illegible]	[illegible]	[illegible]	[illegible]	[illegible]
Waterford City	[illegible]	[illegible]	[illegible]	[illegible]	[illegible]
Dublin Metropolitan Police District	[illegible]	[illegible]	[illegible]	[illegible]	[illegible]
Totals	[illegible]	[illegible]	[illegible]	[illegible]	[illegible]

TABLE X.

Return of the Number of Arrests for Drunkenness on Sundays in the undermentioned Years within the Metropolitan Police District of Dublin, the Cities of Belfast, Cork, Limerick, and Waterford, and the rest of Ireland, the Arrests being given from 8 a.m. on Sundays till 8 a.m. on Mondays.

—	Dublin Metropolitan Police District.	City of Belfast.	City of Cork.	City of Limerick.	City of Waterford.	Rest of Ireland.	Total.
1 May 1887 to 30 April 1888	[illegible]	[illegible]	[illegible]	[illegible]	[illegible]	[illegible]	[illegible]
„ 1888 „ „ 1889	[illegible]	[illegible]	[illegible]	[illegible]	[illegible]	[illegible]	[illegible]
„ 1889 „ „ 1890	[illegible]	[illegible]	[illegible]	[illegible]	[illegible]	[illegible]	[illegible]
„ 1890 „ „ 1891	[illegible]	[illegible]	[illegible]	[illegible]	[illegible]	[illegible]	[illegible]
„ 1891 „ „ 1892	[illegible]	[illegible]	[illegible]	[illegible]	[illegible]	[illegible]	[illegible]
„ 1892 „ „ 1893	[illegible]	[illegible]	[illegible]	[illegible]	[illegible]	[illegible]	[illegible]
„ 1893 „ „ 1894	[illegible]	[illegible]	[illegible]	[illegible]	[illegible]	[illegible]	[illegible]
„ 1894 „ „ 1895	[illegible]	[illegible]	[illegible]	[illegible]	[illegible]	[illegible]	[illegible]
„ 1895 „ „ 1896	[illegible]	[illegible]	[illegible]	[illegible]	[illegible]	[illegible]	[illegible]
„ 1896 „ „ 1897	[illegible]	[illegible]	[illegible]	[illegible]	[illegible]	[illegible]	[illegible]

TABLE XI.

Return showing the Number of Convictions against Licensed Persons and Keepers of Shebeens for illegally selling Intoxicating Liquors throughout Ireland during each Year from 1888 to 1897, inclusive.

Counties, &c.	1888.	1889.	1890.	1891.	1892.	1893.	1894.	1895.	1896.	1897.
Antrim	[illegible]	[illegible]	—	[illegible]	[illegible]	[illegible]	[illegible]	[illegible]	[illegible]	—
Armagh	[illegible]	[illegible]	[illegible]	[illegible]	[illegible]	[illegible]	[illegible]	[illegible]	[illegible]	[illegible]
Cavan	[illegible]	[illegible]	[illegible]	—	—	[illegible]	[illegible]	—	[illegible]	[illegible]
Donegal	[illegible]	[illegible]	—	[illegible]	[illegible]	[illegible]	—	—	[illegible]	[illegible]
Down	[illegible]	[illegible]	[illegible]	[illegible]	[illegible]	[illegible]	[illegible]	[illegible]	[illegible]	[illegible]
Fermanagh	[illegible]	[illegible]	[illegible]	[illegible]	[illegible]	[illegible]	[illegible]	[illegible]	—	[illegible]
Londonderry	[illegible]	[illegible]	[illegible]	[illegible]	[illegible]	[illegible]	[illegible]	[illegible]	[illegible]	[illegible]
Monaghan	[illegible]	[illegible]	[illegible]	[illegible]	[illegible]	[illegible]	[illegible]	[illegible]	[illegible]	[illegible]
Tyrone	[illegible]	[illegible]	[illegible]	[illegible]	[illegible]	[illegible]	[illegible]	[illegible]	[illegible]	[illegible]
Carlow	[illegible]	—	[illegible]	[illegible]	—	[illegible]	[illegible]	[illegible]	[illegible]	[illegible]
Dublin	[illegible]	[illegible]	[illegible]	[illegible]	[illegible]	[illegible]	[illegible]	[illegible]	[illegible]	[illegible]
Kildare	—	[illegible]	[illegible]	[illegible]	[illegible]	[illegible]	[illegible]	[illegible]	[illegible]	[illegible]
Kilkenny	[illegible]	[illegible]	[illegible]	[illegible]	[illegible]	[illegible]	[illegible]	[illegible]	[illegible]	[illegible]
King's	[illegible]	[illegible]	[illegible]	[illegible]	[illegible]	[illegible]	[illegible]	[illegible]	[illegible]	[illegible]
Longford	—	[illegible]	—	[illegible]	[illegible]	[illegible]	[illegible]	[illegible]	[illegible]	[illegible]
Louth	[illegible]	[illegible]	[illegible]	[illegible]	[illegible]	[illegible]	[illegible]	[illegible]	[illegible]	[illegible]
Meath	[illegible]	[illegible]	[illegible]	[illegible]	[illegible]	[illegible]	[illegible]	—	[illegible]	[illegible]
Queen's	[illegible]	[illegible]	[illegible]	[illegible]	[illegible]	[illegible]	[illegible]	[illegible]	[illegible]	[illegible]
Westmeath	—	—	—	[illegible]	[illegible]	[illegible]	—	—	—	—
Wexford	[illegible]	[illegible]	[illegible]	[illegible]	[illegible]	[illegible]	[illegible]	[illegible]	[illegible]	[illegible]
Wicklow	[illegible]	[illegible]	—	[illegible]	[illegible]	[illegible]	—	[illegible]	[illegible]	[illegible]

TABLE XI.—*continued.*

Counties, &c.	[illegible]	[illegible]	[illegible]	[illegible]	[illegible]	[illegible]	[illegible]	[illegible]	[illegible]	[illegible]
Galway, East Riding	[illegible]	[illegible]	[illegible]	[illegible]	—	[illegible]	[illegible]	[illegible]	[illegible]	[illegible]
" West Riding	[illegible]	[illegible]	[illegible]	[illegible]	[illegible]	[illegible]	[illegible]	[illegible]	[illegible]	[illegible]
Leitrim	[illegible]	[illegible]	[illegible]	—	[illegible]	[illegible]	[illegible]	[illegible]	—	[illegible]
Mayo	[illegible]	[illegible]	[illegible]	[illegible]	[illegible]	[illegible]	[illegible]	[illegible]	[illegible]	[illegible]
Roscommon	[illegible]	[illegible]	[illegible]	[illegible]	—	[illegible]	[illegible]	[illegible]	[illegible]	[illegible]
Sligo	[illegible]	[illegible]	[illegible]	[illegible]	[illegible]	[illegible]	[illegible]	[illegible]	[illegible]	[illegible]
Clare	[illegible]	[illegible]	[illegible]	[illegible]	[illegible]	[illegible]	[illegible]	[illegible]	[illegible]	[illegible]
Cork, East Riding	[illegible]	[illegible]	[illegible]	[illegible]	[illegible]	[illegible]	[illegible]	[illegible]	[illegible]	[illegible]
" West Riding	[illegible]	[illegible]	—	[illegible]	[illegible]	—	[illegible]	[illegible]	[illegible]	[illegible]
Kerry	[illegible]	[illegible]	[illegible]	[illegible]	[illegible]	[illegible]	[illegible]	[illegible]	[illegible]	[illegible]
Limerick	[illegible]	[illegible]	[illegible]	[illegible]	[illegible]	[illegible]	[illegible]	[illegible]	[illegible]	[illegible]
Tipperary, N. Riding	[illegible]	[illegible]	[illegible]	[illegible]	[illegible]	[illegible]	[illegible]	[illegible]	[illegible]	[illegible]
" S. Riding	[illegible]	[illegible]	[illegible]	[illegible]	[illegible]	[illegible]	[illegible]	[illegible]	[illegible]	[illegible]
Waterford	—	[illegible]	[illegible]	—	[illegible]	[illegible]	[illegible]	[illegible]	—	[illegible]
Dublin Metropolitan Police District	[illegible]	[illegible]	[illegible]	[illegible]	[illegible]	[illegible]	[illegible]	[illegible]	[illegible]	[illegible]
City of Belfast	[illegible]	[illegible]	[illegible]	[illegible]	[illegible]	[illegible]	[illegible]	[illegible]	[illegible]	[illegible]
" Cork	[illegible]	—	—	—	—	[illegible]	[illegible]	[illegible]	[illegible]	[illegible]
" Limerick	—	—	—	[illegible]	—	—	—	[illegible]	—	—
" Waterford	[illegible]	[illegible]	[illegible]	[illegible]	[illegible]	[illegible]	[illegible]	[illegible]	[illegible]	[illegible]
Totals	[illegible]	[illegible]	[illegible]	[illegible]	[illegible]	[illegible]	[illegible]	[illegible]	[illegible]	[illegible]

TABLE XII.

RETURN showing the NUMBER of CONVICTIONS against [illegible] in IRELAND during each YEAR from [illegible] to [illegible], inclusive.

Counties, &c.	[illegible]	[illegible]	[illegible]	[illegible]	[illegible]	[illegible]	[illegible]	[illegible]	[illegible]	[illegible]
Dublin	—	—	—	—	—	—	—	1	—	—
Louth	—	—	—	—	—	—	1	—	—	—
Kerry	—	—	—	—	—	—	—	—	1	—
Tipperary, South Riding	—	1	—	—	—	—	—	—	—	—
Dublin Metropolitan Police District	—	1	—	1	1	[illegible]	[illegible]	—	—	1
City of Cork	—	—	—	—	—	—	—	—	—	1
Totals	—	[illegible]	—	1	1	[illegible]	[illegible]	1	1	[illegible]

TABLE XIII.

RETURN for all IRELAND, including the DUBLIN METROPOLITAN DISTRICT, and CITIES of DUBLIN, BELFAST, CORK, LIMERICK and WATERFORD, of the NUMBER of [illegible] for which LICENSES were held on the 1st March [illegible], and 1st February [illegible], for the SALE by RETAIL of INTOXICATING LIQUORS, under the headings given below.

	Number of Public-houses.		Number of Wine [illegible].		Number of Spirit Grocers' Houses.		Number of Beer Retail Houses.	
	[illegible]	[illegible]	[illegible]	[illegible]	[illegible]	[illegible]	[illegible]	[illegible]
All Ireland	[illegible]	[illegible]	[illegible]	[illegible]	[illegible]	[illegible]	[illegible]	[illegible]
Dublin Metropolitan Police District	[illegible]	[illegible]	[illegible]	[illegible]	[illegible]	[illegible]	[illegible]	[illegible]
City of Dublin (within the Municipal Boundary)	[illegible]	[illegible]	[illegible]	[illegible]	[illegible]	[illegible]	[illegible]	[illegible]
City of Belfast	[illegible]	[illegible]	1	—	[illegible]	[illegible]	[illegible]	[illegible]
" " Cork	[illegible]	[illegible]	—	—	[illegible]	[illegible]	[illegible]	4
" " Limerick	[illegible]	[illegible]	—	—	—	—	[illegible]	—
" " Waterford	[illegible]	[illegible]	—	—	—	—	[illegible]	[illegible]

APPENDIX II.

(Sir Andrew Reed.)

Extracts from Official Reports of Experienced Officers in charge of Districts in two large counties in Ireland, who are not to be examined as witnesses by the Royal Commission.

One officer reports:—

[illegible]

[illegible]

[illegible]

Another reports:

[illegible]

[illegible]

Another reports:—

[illegible]

Another reports:—

[illegible]

[illegible]

Another reports:—

[illegible]

friends of mine because I have withstood attempts to draw me about the merits of cases which were coming on. An instance of canvassing. Over two years ago a publican fined his licence for the second time and tried to get a transfer to his wife. Although I opposed this strongly at quarter sessions, it was granted, owing to nearly the whole county bench having been canvassed. As I was walking out of court, I remarked to a J.P. friend: "Well, that was the worst travesty of justice I ever "saw." "What" said he, "granting —— licence "on a transfer?" "Oh," said he, "I did not "know anything about the merits of the case, but "—— wrote to me asking me to vote for the "licence." Up to that I had believed he had voted against the licence. The police do not receive the support they should get from the magistrates. The magistrates only convict with the greatest reluctance. They do not recognise that on the proper regulation of drink traffic depends the good order and peace of the community.

Another reports:—

Publicans prosecuted by us very frequently get their friends to approach justices of the peace on their behalf, it is done indirectly. I have no hesitation in saying that two publicans out of every three prosecuted succeed in approaching certain members of the Bench here. A publican here acting for publicans has occasionally asked for a short adjournment of his case; although in the interval no fresh witness has been noticed to appear in court, there has invariably been a subsequent addition to the Bench on adjournment day.

Five magistrates in this district are certainly open to the influence of outside canvassing, but the majority on the Benches give us support in enforcing the licensing laws. The Benches here are comparatively strong.

Another reports:—

Undoubtedly a system of canvassing and bringing influence to bear on magistrates in favour of publicans when summoned by the police does prevail, but I would say it prevailed more in large towns than in the country, as the magistrates in towns can be better approached than those in the country, they are more in touch with publicans, many of them being personal friends. I would say the system prevailed to a considerable extent, as it is a well-known fact that when licensing cases are for hearing there is usually a larger attendance on the Bench, and the police do not get the benefit. I am quite sure justices are influenced; publicans come and tell their story, it does not lose in the telling, and it naturally makes an impression. I know when I came here first publicans, when caught, had a habit of coming and telling me, and from the short experience I had of them, their stories and the reports of the police were very different. Police do not receive adequate support from justices, and they never will till paid magistrates alone try the cases—men who know nothing of the facts beforehand, and who are perfectly independent.

The law requires (3 & 4 Wm. 4 cap. [illegible]) that the magistrates should consider the fitness and convenience of the house proposed to be licensed. In very many cases this is exactly what they do not do, or if evidence of its unfitness or inconvenience be given, they entirely ignore it. The idea that the interests of the public are considered is a myth. It is the interests alone of the applicant which are looked to as far as my experience goes. In the majority of public-houses in Ireland no accommodation whatever is provided for the public. Many of the houses at present being licensed in the south of Ireland are mere cabins, the Poor Law valuation of some being as low as [illegible]. One house in this district, licensed in [illegible] 1887, has had no value whatever put upon it. The publican interest is a valuable one, and there is great anxiety to obtain a spirit licence. I would, therefore, recommend that a [illegible] standard of valuation be laid down for licensed premises, and that suitable accommodation for the public be insisted upon.

I have stated that there are altogether too many public-houses in all parts of Ireland with which I am acquainted.

Many of the persons holding and obtaining publicans' licences have no capital, and obtain their supplies of drink on credit. I have known some such persons to become bankrupt within a year after commencing business; such persons in order to make a livelihood are almost compelled, not only to sell inferior liquor, but to infringe the licensing laws by permitting excessive drinking on their premises, and by selling during prohibited hours, &c. During the five years ended the 31st December 1887, there were in this [illegible] [illegible] prosecutions against publicans, almost all of this class. As a rule the respectable class of publican—men who have invested considerable capital in their business—conduct their houses properly, and scarcely ever infringe the law. I consider a great injustice is done to the public by granting licences for inferior houses, which, of course, are in the hands of poor persons. It is in such places drunkenness is [illegible] and encouraged. By this means an injustice is also done to the respectable publicans, who conduct their business in a [illegible] manner, as it brings their trade into disrepute. From my experience while serving in county [illegible] [illegible] public-houses most of the crimes which disgraced that county were concocted. It is impossible to estimate the demoralising influence of such houses. If a public-house was intended to be a place for the accommodation of the public, that has been quite ignored, no proper accommodation for the public is provided. Take, for instance, the case of persons who come long distances to fairs and markets; if such persons be rich they can go to a hotel or club, but the public-house is the only accommodation available for ordinary persons. In each house there should be a public room or rooms, with suitable furniture, where persons could be accommodated and obtain rest and refreshment. In wet weather I have seen persons attending fairs and markets suffer great hardship from the want of such accommodation, although the towns to which they had come were full of public-houses. I would recommend that all houses licensed for the sale of drink should sell nothing but drink and other refreshments. I believe much drinking and tippling is encouraged by the fact that other businesses are carried on in connexion, and in the same shop, with the sale of drink. I know instances of the blacksmith being a publican, also the cooper, the draper and the baker, so that it is almost impossible for persons doing ordinary shopping to escape the temptation to drink.

I do not consider that drunkenness can be prevented by Act of Parliament, but I believe it can be very considerably reduced. In my opinion the improper use —almost amounting to abuse—of the machinery provided by law for the granting of publicans' licences is to a large extent responsible for the drunkenness so prevalent in this country. I would not propose that the penalties for drunkenness, drunk and disorderly, &c. already provided should be increased. I consider they are sufficiently severe; but I would suggest that additional restrictions and penalties be imposed on the publican, and that a minimum as well as a maximum penalty be laid down for offences committed by him.

In my opinion during the past 10 years there has been a gradual change in the taste of the people in favour of drinking porter and ale in preference to whisky. The porter and ale supplied to the public in this country is of very good quality, while the whisky to be had in the ordinary public-house is of very inferior quality and maddening in its effects—the poorer class of publicans cannot afford to buy good whisky. I believe a great public benefit would be derived, and drunkenness possibly decreased, by the establishment of houses licensed for the sale of porter and ale only.

APPENDIX III.

([illegible])

CITY OF BELFAST.

TABLE I.

TABLE I.—*continued.*

[illegible]	[illegible]		[illegible]		[illegible]		[illegible]		[illegible]		[illegible]		[illegible]		Remarks.
	M.	F.	M.	F.	M.	F.	M.	F.	M.	F.	M.	F.	M.	F.	
[illegible]	[illegible]	[illegible]	[illegible]	[illegible]	[illegible]	[illegible]	[illegible]	[illegible]	[illegible]	[illegible]	[illegible]	[illegible]	[illegible]	[illegible]	
	[illegible]		[illegible]		[illegible]		[illegible]		[illegible]		[illegible]		[illegible]		
[illegible]	[illegible]		[illegible]		[illegible]		[illegible]		[illegible]		[illegible]		[illegible]		
[illegible]	[illegible]		[illegible]		[illegible]		[illegible]		[illegible]		[illegible]		[illegible]		
[illegible]	[illegible]		[illegible]		[illegible]		[illegible]		[illegible]		[illegible]		[illegible]		
[illegible]	—		—		—		—		[illegible]		—		—		
[illegible]	[illegible]		[illegible]		[illegible]		[illegible]		[illegible]		[illegible]		[illegible]		
[illegible]	[illegible]		[illegible]		[illegible]		[illegible]		[illegible]		[illegible]		[illegible]		
[illegible]	[illegible]		[illegible]		[illegible]		[illegible]		[illegible]		—		—		
[illegible]	—		—		—		—		[illegible]		[illegible]		[illegible]		
[illegible]	[illegible]		—		—		—		—		—		—		
[illegible]	[illegible]		—		—		—		—		—		—		

TABLE II.

A.

[illegible] of Prosecutions—by Arrest and Summons—of Cases of [illegible] in above City on Sundays (between 6 a.m. on Sundays and [illegible] a.m. on Mondays), during the Years 1891 to 1897 inclusive.

I. (By Arrest.)

1891.		1892.		1893.		1894.		1895.		1896.		1897.	
Males.	Females.	Males.	Females.	Males.	Females.	Males.	Females.	Males.	Females.	Males.	Females.	Males.	Females.
[illegible]	[illegible]	[illegible]	[illegible]	[illegible]	[illegible]	[illegible]	[illegible]	[illegible]	[illegible]	[illegible]	[illegible]	[illegible]	[illegible]

II. (By Summons.)

1891.		1892.		1893.		1894.		1895.		1896.		1897.	
Males.	Females.	Males.	Females.	Males.	Females.	Males.	Females.	Males.	Females.	Males.	Females.	Males.	Females.
[illegible]	[illegible]	[illegible]	[illegible]	[illegible]	[illegible]	[illegible]	[illegible]	[illegible]	[illegible]	[illegible]	[illegible]	[illegible]	[illegible]

III. (Total of Tables I. and II.)

1891.		1892.		1893.		1894.		1895.		1896.		1897.	
Males.	Females.	Males.	Females.	Males.	Females.	Males.	Females.	Males.	Females.	Males.	Females.	Males.	Females.
[illegible]	[illegible]	[illegible]	[illegible]	[illegible]	[illegible]	[illegible]	[illegible]	[illegible]	[illegible]	[illegible]	[illegible]	[illegible]	[illegible]

B.

Return showing the Number of Arrests and Prosecutions for Drunkenness in [illegible] on Sundays for 12 Months from May [illegible] to May 1897.

(1.) [illegible] a.m. to [illegible] p.m.	[illegible]
(2.) [illegible] p.m. to 7 p.m.	[illegible]
(3.) 7 p.m. to 12 midnight	[illegible]
(4.) 12 midnight to 8 a.m. (Mondays)	4
Total	[illegible]

TABLE III.

RETURN showing PARTICULARS of PERSONS CONVICTED 100 TIMES and OVER at BELFAST PETTY SESSIONS.

The names are omitted.

No.	Name.	No. of Records.	No.	Name.	No. of Committals.	No.	Name.	No. of Remands.
	Women.		20	. . . . .	201	41	. . . . .	146
1	. . . . .	246	21	. . . . .	213	42	. . . . .	130
2	. . . . .	115	22	. . . . .	204	43	. . . . .	142
3	. . . . .	198	23	. . . . .	221	44	. . . . .	138
4	. . . . .	137	24	. . . . .	205			
5	. . . . .	183	25	. . . . .	220		*Men.*	
6	. . . . .	190	26	. . . . .	235	1	. . . . .	118
7	. . . . .	176	27	. . . . .	212	2	. . . . .	720
8	. . . . .	153	28	. . . . .	193	3	. . . . .	726
9	. . . . .	157	29	. . . . .	159	4	. . . . .	569
10	. . . . .	131	30	. . . . .	196	5	. . . . .	152
11	. . . . .	140	31	. . . . .	177	6	. . . . .	154
12	. . . . .	119	32	. . . . .	164	7	. . . . .	173
13	. . . . .	130	33	. . . . .	201	8	. . . . .	171
14	. . . . .	112	34	. . . . .	261	9	. . . . .	160
15	. . . . .	145	35	. . . . .	215	10	. . . . .	139
16	. . . . .	150	36	. . . . .	209			
17	. . . . .	169	37	. . . . .	150		Total - 44 women	
18	. . . . .	157	38	. . . . .	189		10 men	
19	. . . . .	135	39	. . . . .	205			
			40	. . . . .	252			

Return furnished for years 1894, 1895, 1896, and 1897, and up to present date.

Dated at Police Office, 26th February 1898.

TABLE IV.

NATIONAL SOCIETY for the PREVENTION of CRUELTY to CHILDREN.

The Belfast and District Branch of the above Society has, during the three months ending 31st January [illegible], investigated [illegible] cases of wrongs to children. These cases were drawn from the following towns:—

Belfast	[illegible] cases.	Banbridge	[illegible] cases.	Larne	[illegible] cases.	Newtownards	7 cases.
Bangor	[illegible] cases.	[illegible]	[illegible] cases.	Lisburn	[illegible] cases.	Portadown	[illegible] cases.
Ballymena	[illegible] cases.	Downpatrick	[illegible] cases.	Lurgan	[illegible] cases.	Whiteabbey	[illegible] cases.

TABLE showing CASES in which DRUNKENNESS has been an element.

Description of Case.	Total.	Father's Drunkenness.	Mother's Drunkenness.
Cases involving both parents	80	67	63
Cases involving father only	144	133	—
Cases involving mother only	[illegible]	—	41

Percentage of cases in which drink has been an element, 54·2.

APPENDIX V.

(Mr. C. W. [illegible].)

CITY OF LONDONDERRY.

Area, 2,1[illegible] acres.

Rateable Valuation, [illegible].

TABLE I.

—	1871.	1881.	Males.	Females.	Dwelling-houses.	
					1871.	1881.
Population - -	[illegible]	[illegible]	[illegible]	17,[illegible]	[illegible]	[illegible]

Strength of City Force, [illegible]—being [illegible] persons per constable.

TABLE II.

Licensed Houses.

Years.	Publicans.	Wine Refreshment Houses.	Spirit Grocers.	Beer Retailers.	Wholesale Beer Dealers.	Total.
[illegible]	[illegible]	—	[illegible]	—	—	[illegible]
[illegible]	[illegible]	—	[illegible]	—	[illegible]	[illegible]
[illegible]	*[illegible]	—	[illegible]	—	[illegible]	[illegible]

* Analysis:—

- Number of seven-day licenses - [illegible]
- Number of seven-day early closing - 1
- Number of six-day licenses - [illegible]
- Number of six-day and early closing - [illegible]
- Total - [illegible]

Number of persons per licensed house - 1[illegible].

Tenure of the houses - - - [illegible].

TABLE IV.

Prosecutions against Licensees, for Eleven Years ended 31st December 1897.

—	Nature of Offence.				Total.	Appeal Result.	
	Selling Drink in Prohibited Hours.	Selling to Children.	Permitting Drunkenness, and Selling to Drunken Persons.	Failing to admit a Constable.		Affirmed.	Reversed.
Convicted	[illegible]	1	[illegible]	5	[illegible]	[illegible]	6
Dismissed -	[illegible]	[illegible]	6	1	[illegible]	—	—
				Total -	114	One case pending.	

TABLE V.

Spirits sent for Analysis, for Five Years ended 31st December 1897.

Number of Samples sent for Analysis.	Result of Analysis.			Result of Prosecution.
	Pure.	Watered.	Otherwise Adulterated.	
31	1	30	—	Watering did not exceed 35 per cent.

TABLE VI.

Habitual Drunkards, for Ten Years ended 31st December 1897.

Population, 1891.			Number of Times before the Court during the Year.	Sex.		Totals.
Males.	Females.	Total.		Male.	Female.	
[illegible]	17,[illegible]	[illegible]	Twice - - - -	[illegible]	[illegible]	[illegible]
			3 times - - -	[illegible]	[illegible]	[illegible]
			4 " - - - -	[illegible]	[illegible]	[illegible]
			5 " - - - -	[illegible]	[illegible]	[illegible]
			6 " - - - -	[illegible]	[illegible]	[illegible]
			7 " - - - -	[illegible]	[illegible]	[illegible]
			8 " - - - -	[illegible]	[illegible]	[illegible]
			9 " - - - -	[illegible]	[illegible]	[illegible]
			10 " and upwards -	—	[illegible]	[illegible]
			Totals - -	[illegible]	[illegible]	168

TABLE IX.

[illegible]

Years.	Publicans.	Wine Refreshment Houses.	Spirit Grocers.	Beer Dealers.	Wholesale Beer Dealers.	Totals.
[illegible]	[illegible]	—	[illegible]	—	—	[illegible]
[illegible]	[illegible]	—	[illegible]	—	[illegible]	[illegible]
[illegible]	[illegible]	—	[illegible]	[illegible]	[illegible]	[illegible]

* Analysis:—

[illegible]	[illegible]
[illegible]	—
[illegible]	[illegible]
[illegible]	[illegible]
Total	[illegible]

[illegible] - [illegible]

[illegible] - [illegible]

TABLE X.

[illegible]

Years.	Sundays. [illegible]	Percentage.	Week Days. [illegible]	Percentage.	[illegible]
[illegible]	[illegible]	—	[illegible]	—	[illegible]
[illegible]	[illegible]	—	[illegible]	—	[illegible]
[illegible]	[illegible]	—	[illegible]	—	[illegible]
[illegible]	[illegible]	—	[illegible]	—	[illegible]
[illegible]	[illegible]	—	[illegible]	—	[illegible]
Totals	[illegible]	—	[illegible]	—	[illegible]
[illegible]	[illegible]	—	[illegible]	—	[illegible]
[illegible]	[illegible]	—	[illegible]	—	[illegible]
[illegible]	[illegible]	—	[illegible]	—	[illegible]
[illegible]	[illegible]	—	[illegible]	—	[illegible]
[illegible]	[illegible]	—	[illegible]	—	[illegible]
Totals	[illegible]	[illegible]	[illegible]	[illegible]	[illegible]
[illegible]	[illegible]	—	[illegible]	—	[illegible]
[illegible]	[illegible]	—	[illegible]	—	[illegible]
[illegible]	[illegible]	—	[illegible]	—	[illegible]
[illegible]	[illegible]	—	[illegible]	—	[illegible]
[illegible]	[illegible]	—	[illegible]	—	—
Totals	[illegible]	[illegible]	[illegible]	[illegible]	[illegible]

TABLE XI.

[illegible]

—	[illegible]					Totals.	[illegible]	
	[illegible]	[illegible]	[illegible]	[illegible]	[illegible]		[illegible]	[illegible]
[illegible]	[illegible]	[illegible]	[illegible]	[illegible]	[illegible]	[illegible]	[illegible]	[illegible]
[illegible]	[illegible]	—	[illegible]	—	[illegible]	[illegible]	—	—
					Total	[illegible]		

TABLE XIII.

HABITUAL DRUNKARDS for the Year ended 31st December 1887.

Population in 1881.			Number of Times before the Court during the Year.	Sex.		Total.
Males.	Females.	Total.		Male.	Female.	
[illegible]	[illegible]	[illegible]	Twice	41	6	[illegible]
			3 times	[illegible]	1	[illegible]
			4 "	2	1	[illegible]
			5 "	6	—	[illegible]
			6 "	1	—	1
			7 "	1	—	1
			8 "	1	—	1
			9 "	1	—	1
			10 " and upwards	1	—	1
			Totals	[illegible]	8	[illegible]

CITY AND COUNTY OF LONDONDERRY.

TABLE XIV.

HABITUAL OFFENDERS tried at LONDONDERRY AND ASSIZES for Seven Years ended 31st December 1887.

No.	Offence for which Indicted	Previous Convictions for Drunkenness.	Sex.	
			Males.	Females.
1	Attempted murder	6	1	—
2	Larceny	[illegible]	—	1
3	[illegible]	6	1	—
4	False pretences	11	1	—
5	Larceny	[illegible]	—	1
6	Uttering counterfeit coin	[illegible]	1	—
7	Larceny	[illegible]	1	—
8	Burglary	[illegible]	1	—
9	Larceny	[illegible]	—	1
10	Unnatural offence	[illegible]	1	—
11	Larceny	[illegible]	—	1
12	Housebreaking	[illegible]	1	—
13	Assault	[illegible]	1	—
14	Larceny	17	—	1
15	"	16	1	—
		Totals	10	5

TABLE XV.

VALUATION OF LICENSED HOUSES, AND PREMISES, in connection with RATEABLE VALUE.

—	Population.	Number of Licensed Houses.				Valuation of Premises.							
		Publicans.	Spirit Grocers.	Beer Retailers.	Wholesale Beer Dealers.	Over 50l.	40l. to 50l.	30l. to 40l.	20l. to 30l.	15l. to 20l.	10l. to 15l.	Under 10l.	Total.
City of Londonderry	[illegible]	[illegible]	[illegible]	—	[illegible]	[illegible]	[illegible]	[illegible]	[illegible]	[illegible]	[illegible]	[illegible]	[illegible]
County of Londonderry	[illegible]	[illegible]	[illegible]	1	[illegible]	[illegible]	[illegible]	[illegible]	[illegible]	[illegible]	[illegible]	[illegible]	[illegible]
Totals	[illegible]	[illegible]	[illegible]	1	[illegible]	[illegible]	[illegible]	[illegible]	[illegible]	[illegible]	[illegible]	[illegible]	[illegible]
Number of [illegible] Licenses for [illegible] years ended [illegible] 1887, in connection with Rateable Valuation of Premises						[illegible]	1	1	[illegible]	[illegible]	[illegible]	[illegible]	[illegible]

TABLE XVII.

CLUBS.

Name and Address of Club.	Hours of Opening and Closing.		Number of Members.	Annual Subscription.	Length of Time in Existence.	Members' or "Proprietary".	Special Characteristics.	Intoxicating Liquor sold.
	Week Days.	Sundays.						
				£ s. d.	Years.			
Northern Counties Club, Derry City.	a.m. p.m. 8 to 1	a.m. p.m. 8 to 11	180	1 1 0	7½	Members'	Social club	Yes.
City Club, Derry City - -	a.m. p.m. 10 to 12	p.m. p.m. 1 10	160	2 0 0	6	Do.	Do.	Do.
Coleraine Club, Coleraine -	a.m. p.m. 9 to 12	a.m. p.m. 9 to 12	64	2 2 0	8	Do.	Do.	Do.

TABLE XVIII.

ILLICIT DISTILLATION.

RETURN of SEIZURES and PROSECUTIONS for Seven Years ended 31st December 1897.

Years.	Number of Seizures.	Number of Prosecutions.	Amount of Fines.	Remarks.
			£ s. d.	
1891	—	—	—	
1892	1	—	—	
1893	3	1	—	One dismissed.
1894	—	—	—	
1895	—	—	—	
1896	1	—	—	
1897	17	16	116 0 0	
Totals -	[illegible]	17	116 0 0	

APPENDIX VI.

(Mr. Bell.)

SUMMARY OF RECOMMENDATIONS.

See Question 39,147.

Committing Magistrate.—Should be made a paid official.

Disqualifications.—Should include brewers' agents, near relatives of persons disqualified, and those mainly dependent upon the lower class public in business or other relations.

Court divided.—It should be obligatory on the first act of magistrates to adjudicate again with a resident magistrate detailed by the Under Secretary, and no other magistrate should have a right to adjudicate in the case.

Order by Majority.—Licenses should not be granted, transferred, or renewed by a bare majority.

New Licenses.—The grant should be strictly limited to actual public requirements. Should be granted only for premises in every way suitable, and of a class in [illegible] of the average of those already licensed in the place; should not, unless in special cases, be granted [illegible]; should be granted only to the bona fide tenant of the house and owner of the licence, and only to the sole tenant of the house.

Licensed persons should not sublet any part of premises, nor allow any one to be there after hours, or on Sunday; and should not carry on a mixed business, especially during closing hours.

Suitability of Premises.—Should include facilities for police supervision and should be strictly interpreted.

Undertakings and Conditions.—Any violation of such should be made valid grounds for opposing the renewal of the license.

Alterations of Premises.—Any such improperly made should be sufficient grounds for opposing the renewal of the license.

Applications for New Licenses after Forfeiture.—Any made by a near relative, or the manager of the late licensed person, should be dealt with as if made by the latter.

Transfers.—Should be to actual tenants of houses and owners of licenses. "Brewery licenses" should not be sanctioned; transfers for fraudulent purposes should not be granted, or where an attempt is made to deceive the court.

Renewals.—Should be forbidden when there are in one year two convictions for Sunday trading—one recorded; or three convictions in two years and one of these recorded. Licenses of spirit grocers and beer dealers should be renewed only at the annual licensing petty sessions.

The local constable acting for the district inspector should have power to oppose renewals—"public authority" in s. 16 of Act of 1874 means only the district inspector—s. 77 of Act of 1872.

Forfeiture.—The provisions of s. 30 of the Act of 1872 should apply to endorsements (in title within 5 years), and convictions within 5 years should have full effect for all purposes irrespective of persons concerned and what transfers may have taken place during the period.

Reduction of Number of 7-day Licenses.—Such should be held only by persons not likely to violate the Act. If grounds be given for suspicion the publican should get the option (if the case be not a bad one) of changing his 7-day license for a 6-day one.

Records.—Should be obligatory for the second and every subsequent conviction for Sunday trading; as for sales carried on in a manner difficult to detect; and in every conviction after a clearly perjured defence.

Continuous Offence.—Should not be dealt with as one offence.

Delay in Admit.—Should be included in s. 23 of Act of 1874.

Keeping for Sale.—Should be included at s. 3 of Act of 1874.

Sales at Eating-houses.—Of liquor supplied with food, but not specially charged for, should be distinctly made an offence.

Dancing, &c.—Should not be permitted without sanction of magistrates.

Procuring Liquor.—Without going on premises—private doing so should be included in s. 17 of Act of 1874.

Order and Delivery of Liquor.—Either, if done in closing hours, should be specifically made an offence.

Travellers.—Raise distance 5 miles; restrict the quantity of liquor they may get to drink, and to carry away, to what is reasonable considering the circumstances under which they are travelling.

Drunken and Drunkenness.—The terms in s. 12 of the Act of 1872 should mean a state in which it is palpable to an ordinary person that the person is a good deal under the influence of drink.

Knowingly.—In sec. 14, Act of 1872, should distinctly refer to the woman's character, and in sec. 16 to the fact that the constable was on duty and off his beat. Knowledge on the part of an assistant should in all cases be distinctly stated to be sufficient.

Billiard-rooms.—Should not be open to public after hours—on licensed premises.

Entertainments.—Provision should be made for allowing supper, &c., to be given on licensed premises, by permission of magistrates.

Witness.—It should be distinctly stated that the defendant can claim no privilege if he tender himself as a witness, but must answer all questions relating to the charge.

Occasional Licenses.—Consent should be signed only at petty sessions, or in case of urgency by resident magistrate, all such should be counter-signed by the P.S. clerk.

Appeals.—Police should have the right to appeal against a dismissal—on merits, or without prejudice—and against the renewal of a license.

APPENDIX VII.

[illegible]

[illegible]

[illegible]

[illegible]

APPENDIX VIII.

(*Mrs Crawford.*)

CITY OF DUBLIN.

TABLE I.

Return showing the Number of Children under 13 years of age who entered the Public-Houses indicated on certain Sundays between the Hours of 2 and 3 o'clock.

Reference to Map.	Date.	Length of Observation.	Number of Children with Vessels.	Number of Children without Vessels.	Total.	Remarks.
[illegible]	17 October	[illegible] minutes	[illegible]	—	[illegible]	Those without vessels not counted.
[illegible]	"	[illegible] "	[illegible]	—	[illegible]	
[illegible]	7 November	[illegible] "	[illegible]	—	[illegible]	
[illegible]	"	[illegible] "	[illegible]	—	[illegible]	
[illegible]	14 November	[illegible] "	17	—	17	
[illegible]	21 November	[illegible] "	[illegible]	[illegible]	[illegible]	
[illegible]	"	[illegible] "	[illegible]	[illegible]	[illegible]	" " "
[illegible]	"	[illegible] "	[illegible]	[illegible]	[illegible]	" " "
[illegible]	19 December	[illegible] "	[illegible]	[illegible]	[illegible]	
[illegible]	9 January	[illegible] "	[illegible]	[illegible]	[illegible]	
[illegible]	16 January	[illegible] "	[illegible]	[illegible]	[illegible]	Several drank from the vessels
[illegible]	"	[illegible] "	[illegible]	[illegible]	[illegible]	
[illegible]	13 February	[illegible] "	9	[illegible]	[illegible]	
[illegible]	9 December	[illegible] "	[illegible]	[illegible]	[illegible]	Three sucking. Two with two vessels each, nearly all under 14 years.
[illegible]	"	[illegible] "				
			[illegible]	[illegible]	[illegible]	

SUMMARY (Sundays, 2 to 3).

a. Total number of observations 15
b. Total number of children appearing . . . . . [illegible] { With vessels, [illegible]. Without vessels, [illegible].
c. Average length of observation . . . . . 37 minutes.
d. Average number entering during "a" 41
e. Average number per hour . . . . . [illegible]

TABLE II.

Return showing the Number of Children under 13 years of age who entered the Public-Houses indicated on certain Evenings between the Hours of 6 and 7 o'clock p.m.

Reference to Map.	Date.	Length of Observation.	Number of Children with Vessels.	Number of Children without Vessels.	Total.	Remarks.
[illegible]	14 November	40 minutes	[illegible]	[illegible]	[illegible]	
[illegible]	"	40 "	40	7	47	A boy aged 6 drank some porter from a vessel carried by his sister.
[illegible]	21 November	[illegible] "	19	17	[illegible]	
[illegible]	"	[illegible] "	[illegible]	[illegible]	[illegible]	A girl aged 4 years drank from the vessel she had had filled.
[illegible]	7 December	[illegible] "	7	—	7	
47	19 December	[illegible] "	[illegible]	[illegible]	[illegible]	
[illegible]	"	[illegible] "	[illegible]	[illegible]	[illegible]	
[illegible]	"	[illegible] "	[illegible]	[illegible]	[illegible]	Same child went twice within 5 minutes.
[illegible]	16 December	[illegible] "	[illegible]	[illegible]	[illegible]	
[illegible]	9 January	[illegible] "	[illegible]	[illegible]	[illegible]	
[illegible]	"	[illegible] "	[illegible]	[illegible]	[illegible]	
[illegible]	"	[illegible] "	[illegible]	[illegible]	[illegible]	
[illegible]	"	[illegible] "	[illegible]	[illegible]	[illegible]	
[illegible]	"	[illegible] "	[illegible]	[illegible]	[illegible]	This (January 9) was a very wet evening, and so many of the girls wore shawls or cloaks, it could not be seen whether they carried vessels or not. Except where the vessel was distinctly seen it has not been included.
[illegible]	"	[illegible] "	[illegible]	[illegible]	[illegible]	
[illegible]	"	[illegible] "	[illegible]	[illegible]	[illegible]	
[illegible]	"	[illegible] "	[illegible]	[illegible]	[illegible]	
[illegible]	"	[illegible] "	[illegible]	[illegible]	[illegible]	
[illegible]	"	[illegible] "	[illegible]	[illegible]	[illegible]	* Reference to Map 27.
[illegible]*	"	[illegible] "	[illegible]	[illegible]	[illegible]	† Number of children running in and out, with some in drink, but not counting the house under observation.
[illegible]	"	[illegible] "	[illegible]	[illegible]	[illegible]	

TABLE II.—continued.

Reference to Map.	Date.	Length of Observation.	Number of Children with Vessels.	Number of Children without Vessels.	Total.	Remarks.
[illegible]	9 January	[illegible] minutes	[illegible]	[illegible]	[illegible]	
[illegible]	"	[illegible] "	[illegible]	[illegible]	[illegible]	
[illegible]	"	[illegible] "	[illegible]	[illegible]	[illegible]	
[illegible]	"	[illegible] "	[illegible]	[illegible]	[illegible]	
[illegible]	"	[illegible] "	[illegible]	[illegible]	[illegible]	
[illegible]	"	[illegible] "	[illegible]	[illegible]	[illegible]	
[illegible]	16 January	[illegible] "	[illegible]	[illegible]	[illegible]	
[illegible]	"	[illegible] "	[illegible]	[illegible]	[illegible]	
[illegible]	"	[illegible] "	[illegible]	[illegible]	[illegible]	
[illegible]	"	[illegible] "	[illegible]	[illegible]	[illegible]	
[illegible]	"	[illegible] "	[illegible]	[illegible]	[illegible]	There are four other public-houses in the immediate neighbourhood, into all of which several children were seen to enter with vessels for drink.
[illegible]	"	[illegible] "	[illegible]	[illegible]	[illegible]	
[illegible]	"	[illegible] "	[illegible]	[illegible]	[illegible]	
[illegible]	"	[illegible] "	[illegible]	[illegible]	[illegible]	At [illegible], next door, an equal number, if not more, entered during the hour.
[illegible]	"	[illegible] "	[illegible]	[illegible]	[illegible]	
[illegible]	24 January	[illegible] "	[illegible]	[illegible]	[illegible]	The number of children under 13 in the street with cans was very large, evidently on their way to other public-houses. (Nos. [illegible] are all public-houses.)
[illegible]	"	[illegible] "	[illegible]	[illegible]	[illegible]	
[illegible]	"	[illegible] "	[illegible]	[illegible]	[illegible]	Many went on coming out.
[illegible]	"	[illegible] "	[illegible]	[illegible]	[illegible]	Many drank from the vessels.
[illegible]	"	[illegible] "	[illegible]	[illegible]	[illegible]	" "
[illegible]	"	[illegible] "	[illegible]	[illegible]	[illegible]	
[illegible]	30 January	[illegible] "	[illegible]	[illegible]	[illegible]	Several of these seemed to hide vessels under their shawls or cloaks.
[illegible]	6 February	[illegible] "	[illegible]	[illegible]	[illegible]	
[illegible]	13 February	[illegible] "	[illegible]	[illegible]	[illegible]	
[illegible]	"	[illegible] "	[illegible]	[illegible]	[illegible]	
[illegible]	"	[illegible] "	[illegible]	[illegible]	[illegible]	
[illegible]	"	[illegible] "	[illegible]	[illegible]	[illegible]	
[illegible]	"	[illegible] "	[illegible]	[illegible]	[illegible]	
[illegible]	"	[illegible] "	[illegible]	[illegible]	[illegible]	Numbers of these went out to drink from their jugs and cans, and three out of half-pint bottles. Several had [illegible] to wait on the [illegible]. Most with very little clothing and looking very wretched.
[illegible]	"	[illegible] "	[illegible]	[illegible]	[illegible]	
[illegible]	20 February	[illegible] "	[illegible]	[illegible]	[illegible]	
[illegible]	"	[illegible] "	[illegible]	[illegible]	[illegible]	
[illegible]	"	[illegible] "	[illegible]	[illegible]	[illegible]	
[illegible]	"	[illegible] "	[illegible]	[illegible]	[illegible]	

SUMMARY (Sundays, [illegible]).

a. Total number of observations - - - [illegible]

b. Total number of children entering - - - [illegible] { With vessels, [illegible]. Without vessels, [illegible].

c. Average length of observation - - - [illegible] minutes.

d. Average number entering during "c" - - - [illegible]

e. Average per hour - - - - - [illegible]

TABLE III.

Return showing the Number of Children under 13 years of age who entered the Public-Houses indicated on certain Saturday Afternoons.

Reference to Map.	Date.	Length of Observation.	Number of Children with Vessels.	Number of Children without Vessels.	Total.	Remarks.
[illegible]	[illegible] November	[illegible] minutes	[illegible]	[illegible]	[illegible]	
[illegible]	[illegible] December	[illegible] "	[illegible]	[illegible]	[illegible]	
[illegible]	[illegible] December	[illegible] "	[illegible]	[illegible]	[illegible]	
[illegible]	[illegible] February	[illegible] "	[illegible]	[illegible]	[illegible]	
[illegible]	"	[illegible] "	[illegible]	[illegible]	[illegible]	

SUMMARY (Saturday afternoons).

a. Total number of observations - - - [illegible]

b. Total number of children entering - - - [illegible] { With vessels, [illegible]. Without vessels, [illegible].

c. Average length of observation - - - [illegible] minutes.

TABLE IV.

Return showing the Number of Children under 13 years of age who entered the Public-Houses indicated on several Saturday Nights after 9 o'clock.

Reference to Map.	Date.	Length of Observation.	Number of Children with Vessels.	Number of Children without Vessels.	Total.	Remarks.
[illegible]	10 December	15 minutes	[illegible]	[illegible]	[illegible]	
[illegible]	[illegible] February	42 "	[illegible]	[illegible]	[illegible]	
[illegible]	10 February	[illegible] "	[illegible]	[illegible]	[illegible]	
[illegible]	"	[illegible] "	[illegible]	[illegible]	[illegible]	
[illegible]	"	[illegible] "	[illegible]	17	[illegible]	

SUMMARY (Saturday night after 9 o'clock).

a. Total number of observations - - - - 5

b. Total number of children entering - - - 1[illegible] { With vessels, 1[illegible]. Without vessels, [illegible].

c. Average length of observation - - - - [illegible] minutes.

d. Average number entering during "c" - - - [illegible]

e. Average per hour - - - - - [illegible]

TABLE V.

Return showing the Number of Children under 13 years of age who entered the Public-Houses indicated at Various Hours as mentioned.

Reference to Map.	Date.	Length of Observation.	Hours.	Number of Children with Vessels.	Number of Children without Vessels.	Total.	Remarks.
[illegible]	[illegible] October	[illegible] minutes	[illegible]	31	—	[illegible]	
[illegible]	"	[illegible] "	"	[illegible]	—	[illegible]	
[illegible]	14 November	[illegible] "	[illegible]	[illegible]	[illegible]	[illegible]	
[illegible]	27 November	[illegible] "	[illegible]	[illegible]	14	[illegible]	
[illegible]	12 December	[illegible] "	[illegible]	[illegible]	[illegible]	[illegible]	
[illegible]	[illegible] January	[illegible] "	[illegible]	[illegible]	7	[illegible]	
[illegible]	[illegible] January	[illegible] "	[illegible]	[illegible]	[illegible]	[illegible]	
[illegible]	[illegible] January	[illegible] "	[illegible]	[illegible]	—	[illegible]	
[illegible]	"	[illegible] "	"	7	—	7	
				[illegible]	[illegible]	[illegible]	

SUMMARY (various hours).

a. Total number of observations - - - - [illegible]

b. Total number of children entering - - - 1[illegible] { With vessels, 1[illegible]. Without vessels, [illegible].

c. Average length of observation - - - [illegible] minutes.

d. Average number entering during "c" - - - [illegible]

e. Average per hour - - - - - [illegible]

TABLE VI.

Abstract of Summaries.

—	Sundays between [illegible] p.m. and [illegible] p.m.	Sundays between [illegible] p.m. and [illegible] p.m.	Saturday Afternoons.	Saturdays after 9 p.m.	Various Times.
a. Number of observations - - -	12	[illegible]	[illegible]	5	[illegible]
b. Number of children entering - - -	[illegible]	[illegible]	[illegible]	[illegible]	[illegible]
c. Average length of observation - - -	[illegible] minutes	[illegible] minutes	[illegible] minutes	[illegible] minutes	[illegible] minutes
d. Average number entering during "c" - -	[illegible]	[illegible]	[illegible]	[illegible]	[illegible]
e. Average number entering per hour - -	[illegible]	[illegible]	[illegible]	[illegible]	[illegible]

TABLE VII.

Final Summary.

a. Total number of observations - - - [illegible]

b. Total number of children entering - - - [illegible] { With vessels, [illegible]. Without vessels, 1,[illegible].

c. Average length of observation - - - [illegible] minutes.

d. Average number entering during "c" - - [illegible]

e. Average number entering per hour - - [illegible] { With vessels, [illegible]. Without vessels, [illegible].

APPENDIX DI.

(Judge Curran.)

RETURN showing NUMBER of LICENSED HOUSES and POPULATION in COUNTIES LONGFORD, MEATH, WESTMEATH, and KERRY, and KING'S COUNTY.

TABLE I.

COUNTY LONGFORD.—DISTRICT OF LONGFORD.

RETURN of LICENSED PREMISES, &c., in above District.

No.	Name of Town or Village.	Population.	Total Number of Licensed Houses.	Description of Licenses.				Remarks.
				Seven-day.	Six-day.	Spirit Grocer.	Wholesale Beer dealer.	
1	Longford Town	[illegible]	[illegible]	[illegible]	[illegible]	1	1	
2	[illegible] (village)	[illegible]	[illegible]	[illegible]	—	—	—	
3	[illegible] (village)	[illegible]	[illegible]	[illegible]	—	—	—	
4	[illegible] (village)	[illegible]	[illegible]	[illegible]	1	—	—	
5	[illegible] (village)	[illegible]	[illegible]	[illegible]	—	—	—	
6	[illegible]	—	[illegible]	[illegible]	—	—	—	There is no village. Two country public-houses, one in same locality.
	Totals	[illegible]	[illegible]	[illegible]	[illegible]	1	1	

T. L. M'Causland, D.I.

Longford, [illegible] April 18[illegible].

TABLE II.

Sir,

[illegible], [illegible] April 18[illegible].

[illegible] I beg to give a list of towns and villages in this district, with population, and number of public-houses in each.

I remain, Sir,
Your obedient servant,
[illegible], Head Constable, R.I.C.

J. Adye Curran, Esq.

Name of Town.	Population.	Number of Public-houses.	Remarks.
[illegible]	[illegible]	[illegible]	
[illegible]	About [illegible]	[illegible]	There is [illegible] in country.
[illegible]	[illegible]	[illegible]	
[illegible]	[illegible]	1	
[illegible]	[illegible]	[illegible]	
[illegible]	[illegible]	[illegible]	One is [illegible] in the country.
[illegible]	About [illegible]	[illegible]	A country place.

TABLE III.

LICENSED HOUSES in DISTRICT of [illegible].

[illegible], [illegible] April 18[illegible].

I beg to state that in this district there are in all [illegible] fully licensed, [illegible] partially licensed, houses, and 1 wholesale beer dealer; the population is [illegible]. The houses partially licensed are six-day houses.

In the towns and villages the licensed houses are distributed as follows:—

[illegible]	Population.	Licenses.
[illegible]	[illegible]	[illegible] full, 1 six-day, and 1 beer dealer.
[illegible]	[illegible]	[illegible] full.
[illegible]	[illegible]	1 full, 1 six-day.
[illegible]	[illegible]	4 full.
[illegible]	[illegible]	[illegible] full.

His Honour Judge Curran.

[illegible], [illegible] D.I.

TABLE IV.

COUNTY OF MEATH.

List of the Principal Towns in or about Navan and Kells, with Population and Number of Licensed Houses in each.

Name of Town.	Population.	Number of Licensed Houses.	Remarks.
Navan - - - -	[illegible]	47	
Kells - - - -	[illegible]	[illegible]	
Oldcastle - - -	[illegible]	11	
Duleek - - - -	[illegible]	7	
[illegible] - - -	[illegible]	[illegible]	
[illegible] - - -	[illegible]	[illegible]	

Dated at Kells, [illegible] April [illegible].

His Honour, Judge Curran,
County Court Judge for County Meath.

[illegible],
Head Constable, R.I.C.

TABLE V.

Population and Number of Licensed Houses in following Towns in above County.

No.	Name of Town.	Population of each Town.	Number of Licensed Houses.	Remarks.
1	Trim - - -	1,[illegible]	[illegible]	
2	Athboy - - -	[illegible]	11	
3	Dunshaughlin - -	[illegible]	5	
4	Slane - - - -	[illegible]	6	
	Total - -	[illegible]	[illegible]	

Dated at Trim, [illegible] April [illegible].

His Honour Judge Curran,
County Court Judge.

I certify above return to be correct.

[illegible],
For D.I., sick.

TABLE VI.

COUNTY OF WESTMEATH.

List of the Principal Towns in the County, with Population and Number of Public-houses in each.

Names of the Towns.	Population of each.	Number of existing Public-houses in each.	Remarks.
Mullingar - - -	[illegible]	[illegible]	Population exclusive of public institutions.
Athlone (Westmeath) - - -	[illegible]	[illegible]	Westmeath portion.
Moate - - - -	1,[illegible]	[illegible]	
Castlepollard - - -	[illegible]	[illegible]	
Kilbeggan - - -	[illegible]	[illegible]	
[illegible] - - -	[illegible]	5	
Kinnegad - - -	[illegible]	7	
[illegible] - - -	[illegible]	[illegible]	
Delvin - - - -	[illegible]	[illegible]	
Tyrrellspass - - -	[illegible]	[illegible]	
Ballymore - - -	[illegible]	[illegible]	
Multyfarnham - - -	[illegible]	4	
Killucan - - -	[illegible]	7	
Castletown, G. - - -	[illegible]	4	
Total - - -	14,[illegible]	[illegible]	Average, [illegible] persons per licensed house.

Mullingar, [illegible] April [illegible].

His Honour Judge Curran.

W. W. B. [illegible],
County Inspector.

TABLE VII.

KINGS COUNTY.

LIST of PRINCIPAL TOWNS in above COUNTY, with the POPULATION and NUMBER of PUBLIC-HOUSES at each PLACE.

Name of Town.	Population in 1871.	Number of Public-houses.	Remarks.
Tullamore	4,[illegible]	[illegible]	
Parsonstown	4,[illegible]	44	
Edenderry	1,[illegible]	[illegible]	
Banagher	[illegible]	16	
Clara	[illegible]	11	
Philipstown	[illegible]	[illegible]	
Frankford	[illegible]	[illegible]	

TABLE VIII.

COUNTY OF KERRY.

LIST of PRINCIPAL TOWNS in above COUNTY, showing POPULATION and NUMBER of existing PUBLIC-HOUSES in each.

No.	Name of Town, &c.	Population.	Number of existing Public-houses: Number of Six-day Licenses.	Number of existing Public-houses: Number of Seven-day Licenses.	Total Number of Six-day and Seven-day Licenses.	Remarks.
1	Cahirciveen	[illegible]	[illegible]	[illegible]	[illegible]	
2	Ballinskelligs	[illegible]	—	1	[illegible]	
3	Portmagee	[illegible]	—	[illegible]	[illegible]	
4	Knightstown	[illegible]	—	1	[illegible]	
5	[illegible]	[illegible]	[illegible]	[illegible]	[illegible]	
6	Waterville	[illegible]	—	[illegible]	[illegible]	There are three houses. Ballybrack is 1 mile outside Waterville.
7	Ballybrack	—	—	[illegible]	[illegible]	
8	Castleisland	[illegible]	[illegible]	[illegible]	[illegible]	
9	[illegible]	[illegible]	[illegible]	[illegible]	[illegible]	
10	Knocknagoshel	[illegible]	[illegible]	[illegible]	[illegible]	
11	Dingle	[illegible]	[illegible]	[illegible]	[illegible]	
12	Kenmare	[illegible]	[illegible]	[illegible]	[illegible]	
13	Kilgarvan	[illegible]	—	[illegible]	[illegible]	
14	Sneem	[illegible]	[illegible]	[illegible]	[illegible]	
15	Killarney	[illegible]	[illegible]	[illegible]	[illegible]	
16	Killorglin	[illegible]	[illegible]	[illegible]	[illegible]	
17	Milltown	[illegible]	[illegible]	[illegible]	[illegible]	
18	Castlemaine	[illegible]	[illegible]	[illegible]	[illegible]	
19	Listowel	[illegible]	[illegible]	[illegible]	[illegible]	
20	Tarbert	[illegible]	—	[illegible]	[illegible]	
21	Ballylongford	[illegible]	[illegible]	[illegible]	[illegible]	
22	Ballybunion	[illegible]	—	[illegible]	[illegible]	
23	Tralee	[illegible]	[illegible]	[illegible]	[illegible]	
24	Abbeydorney	[illegible]	[illegible]	—	[illegible]	
25	Ardfert	[illegible]	[illegible]	[illegible]	[illegible]	
26	Ballyheigue	[illegible]	—	[illegible]	[illegible]	
27	Blennerville	[illegible]	[illegible]	[illegible]	[illegible]	
28	Causeway	[illegible]	[illegible]	[illegible]	[illegible]	
29	Fenit	[illegible]	—	[illegible]	[illegible]	One about a mile from Fenit.
30	Spa	[illegible]	—	[illegible]	[illegible]	
31	Kilflynn	[illegible]	—	[illegible]	[illegible]	
	Total	[illegible]	[illegible]	[illegible]	[illegible]	

Dated at Tralee, 22nd April [illegible].

To His Honour John Adye Curran, Q.C.,
County Court Judge,
[illegible], Palmerston Road, Dublin.

FRED J. HALL,
First District Inspector.
For County Inspector, on duty.

APPENDIX XI.

(Mr. F. D. Daly.)

Protection for a Sober Parent against a Drunken or Idle Parent.

On application of any wife, and on proof that her husband is (a) habitually intemperate and drunk, or (b) that he habitually fails, without reasonable excuse, to provide due maintenance for her and for their children, whom he is liable to maintain, or (c) that he habitually and unlawfully assaults her or them, a Court may grant to her an order protecting—

1. Her earnings or separate property.
2. Anything she has purchased or directed to be purchased by the same.
3. The wearing apparel and school requirements of her children or step-children, and their earnings, if any.
4. Tools, instruments, appliances, materials, or anything entrusted to her, and not to her husband.
5. Furniture, bedding, and other articles in use, as household necessaries, in the house.

If a husband or any other person wilfully, or while under the influence of drink, takes away or keeps or damages anything so protected, without the wife's consent, the person so offending shall, on her complaint, be liable to the same procedure and punishment as if he had committed a common assault on her.

In like manner, but only on proof that a wife is habitually intemperate and drunk, a husband may procure a like protecting order, with similar consequences, for—

1. Furniture, bedding, and other articles in use as household necessaries in the house.
2. The wearing apparel or school requirements of children or step-children and their earnings, if any.
3. Tools, instruments, appliances, materials, or anything under his control, and not entrusted to his wife.

APPENDIX XII.

(Mr. W. Wilkinson.)

ARRESTS FOR DRUNKENNESS—IRELAND.

Return giving the Number of Arrests for Drunkenness in Dublin, Cork, Limerick, Waterford, and Belfast on Sundays from 1877 to 1897; also similar returns for the rest of Ireland. Compiled from Official Returns.

Arrests for Drunkenness on Sundays.—Dublin.

—	1877-78.	1878-79.	1879-80.	1880-81.	1881-82.	1882-83.	1883-84.	1884-85.	1885-86.	1886-87.
From 8 a.m. to 2 p.m.	97	No Returns.	47	[illegible]	[illegible]	[illegible]	64	[illegible]	[illegible]	[illegible]
From 2 p.m. to 7 p.m.	[illegible]	"	[illegible]	[illegible]	170	[illegible]	[illegible]	[illegible]	[illegible]	[illegible]
From 7 p.m. to 11 night.	1,126	"	[illegible]	[illegible]	[illegible]	[illegible]	[illegible]	[illegible]	[illegible]	[illegible]
From 11 night to 8 a.m. Monday.	[illegible]	"	[illegible]	[illegible]	[illegible]	47	[illegible]	[illegible]	[illegible]	[illegible]
Total	[illegible]	—	[illegible]	[illegible]	[illegible]	[illegible]	[illegible]	[illegible]	[illegible]	[illegible]
—	1887-88.	1888-89.	1889-90.	1890-91.	1891-92.	1892-93.	1893-94.	1894-95.	1895-96.	1896-97.
From 8 a.m. to 2 p.m.	[illegible]	[illegible]	[illegible]	[illegible]	[illegible]	[illegible]	[illegible]	[illegible]	[illegible]	[illegible]
From 2 p.m. to 7 p.m.	[illegible]	[illegible]	[illegible]	[illegible]	[illegible]	[illegible]	[illegible]	[illegible]	[illegible]	[illegible]
From 7 p.m. to 11 night.	[illegible]	[illegible]	[illegible]	[illegible]	[illegible]	[illegible]	[illegible]	447	[illegible]	[illegible]
From 11 night to 8 a.m. Monday.	[illegible]	[illegible]	[illegible]	[illegible]	[illegible]	[illegible]	[illegible]	[illegible]	[illegible]	[illegible]
Total	[illegible]	[illegible]	[illegible]	[illegible]	[illegible]	[illegible]	[illegible]	[illegible]	[illegible]	[illegible]

Arrests for Drunkenness on Sundays.—Cork.

—	1877-78.	1878-79.	1879-80.	1880-81.	1881-82.	1882-83.	1883-84.	1884-85.	1885-86.	1886-87.
From 8 a.m. to 2 p.m.	[illegible]	No Returns.	[illegible]	[illegible]	[illegible]	14	[illegible]	[illegible]	[illegible]	[illegible]
From 2 p.m. to 7 p.m.	[illegible]	"	[illegible]	[illegible]	[illegible]	47	[illegible]	[illegible]	[illegible]	[illegible]
From 7 p.m. to 11 night.	[illegible]	"	[illegible]	[illegible]	[illegible]	[illegible]	[illegible]	[illegible]	[illegible]	170
From 11 night to 8 a.m. Monday.	[illegible]	"	11	19	[illegible]	[illegible]	14	[illegible]	[illegible]	[illegible]
Total	[illegible]	—	[illegible]	[illegible]	[illegible]	[illegible]	[illegible]	[illegible]	[illegible]	[illegible]

Arrests for Drunkenness—Ireland—continued.

Arrests for Drunkenness on Sundays—Cork—continued.

—	[illegible]	[illegible]	[illegible]	[illegible]	[illegible]	[illegible]	[illegible]	[illegible]	[illegible]	[illegible]
From 8 a.m. to 2 p.m.	[illegible]	[illegible]	[illegible]	[illegible]	[illegible]	[illegible]	[illegible]	[illegible]	[illegible]	[illegible]
From 2 p.m. to 7 p.m.	[illegible]	[illegible]	[illegible]	[illegible]	[illegible]	[illegible]	[illegible]	[illegible]	[illegible]	[illegible]
From 7 p.m. to 12 night.	[illegible]	[illegible]	[illegible]	[illegible]	[illegible]	[illegible]	[illegible]	[illegible]	[illegible]	[illegible]
From 12 night to 8 a.m. Monday.	[illegible]	[illegible]	[illegible]	[illegible]	[illegible]	[illegible]	[illegible]	[illegible]	[illegible]	[illegible]
Total .	[illegible]	[illegible]	[illegible]	[illegible]	[illegible]	[illegible]	[illegible]	[illegible]	[illegible]	[illegible]

Arrests for Drunkenness on Sundays.—Limerick.

—	[illegible]	[illegible]	[illegible]	[illegible]	[illegible]	[illegible]	[illegible]	[illegible]	[illegible]	[illegible]
From 8 a.m. to 2 p.m.	[illegible]	No Returns.	[illegible]	[illegible]	[illegible]	[illegible]	[illegible]	[illegible]	[illegible]	[illegible]
From 2 p.m. to 7 p.m.	[illegible]	"	[illegible]	[illegible]	[illegible]	[illegible]	[illegible]	[illegible]	[illegible]	[illegible]
From 7 p.m. to 12 night.	[illegible]	"	[illegible]	[illegible]	[illegible]	[illegible]	[illegible]	[illegible]	[illegible]	[illegible]
From 12 night to 8 a.m. Monday.	[illegible]	"	[illegible]	[illegible]	[illegible]	[illegible]	[illegible]	[illegible]	[illegible]	[illegible]
Total . .	[illegible]	—	[illegible]	[illegible]	[illegible]	[illegible]	[illegible]	[illegible]	[illegible]	[illegible]

—	[illegible]	[illegible]	[illegible]	[illegible]	[illegible]	[illegible]	[illegible]	[illegible]	[illegible]	[illegible]
From 8 a.m. to 2 p.m.	[illegible]	[illegible]	[illegible]	[illegible]	[illegible]	[illegible]	[illegible]	[illegible]	[illegible]	[illegible]
From 2 p.m. to 7 p.m.	[illegible]	[illegible]	[illegible]	[illegible]	[illegible]	[illegible]	[illegible]	[illegible]	[illegible]	[illegible]
From 7 p.m. to 12 night.	[illegible]	[illegible]	[illegible]	[illegible]	[illegible]	[illegible]	[illegible]	[illegible]	[illegible]	[illegible]
From 12 night to 8 a.m. Monday.	[illegible]	[illegible]	[illegible]	[illegible]	[illegible]	[illegible]	[illegible]	[illegible]	[illegible]	[illegible]
Total . .	[illegible]	[illegible]	[illegible]	[illegible]	[illegible]	[illegible]	[illegible]	[illegible]	[illegible]	[illegible]

Arrests for Drunkenness on Sundays.—Waterford.

—	[illegible]	[illegible]	[illegible]	[illegible]	[illegible]	[illegible]	[illegible]	[illegible]	[illegible]	[illegible]
From 8 a.m. to 2 p.m.	[illegible]	No Returns.	[illegible]	[illegible]	[illegible]	[illegible]	[illegible]	[illegible]	[illegible]	[illegible]
From 2 p.m. to 7 p.m.	[illegible]	"	[illegible]	[illegible]	[illegible]	[illegible]	[illegible]	[illegible]	[illegible]	[illegible]
From 7 p.m. to 12 night.	[illegible]	"	[illegible]	[illegible]	[illegible]	[illegible]	[illegible]	[illegible]	[illegible]	[illegible]
From 12 night to 8 a.m. Monday.	[illegible]	"	[illegible]	[illegible]	[illegible]	[illegible]	[illegible]	[illegible]	[illegible]	[illegible]
Total . .	[illegible]	—	[illegible]	[illegible]	[illegible]	[illegible]	[illegible]	[illegible]	[illegible]	[illegible]

—	[illegible]	[illegible]	[illegible]	[illegible]	[illegible]	[illegible]	[illegible]	[illegible]	[illegible]	[illegible]
From 8 a.m. to 2 p.m.	[illegible]	[illegible]	[illegible]	[illegible]	[illegible]	[illegible]	[illegible]	[illegible]	[illegible]	[illegible]
From 2 p.m. to 7 p.m.	[illegible]	[illegible]	[illegible]	[illegible]	[illegible]	[illegible]	[illegible]	[illegible]	[illegible]	[illegible]
From 7 p.m. to 12 night.	[illegible]	[illegible]	[illegible]	[illegible]	[illegible]	[illegible]	[illegible]	[illegible]	[illegible]	[illegible]
From 12 night to 8 a.m. Monday.	[illegible]	[illegible]	[illegible]	[illegible]	[illegible]	[illegible]	[illegible]	[illegible]	[illegible]	[illegible]
Total . .	[illegible]	[illegible]	[illegible]	[illegible]	[illegible]	[illegible]	[illegible]	[illegible]	[illegible]	[illegible]

APPENDIX [illegible]—IRELAND—continued.

[illegible]—continued.

—	[illegible]	[illegible]	[illegible]	[illegible]	[illegible]	[illegible]	[illegible]	[illegible]	[illegible]	[illegible]
From 8 a.m. to 1 p.m.	[illegible]	No Returns.	[illegible]	[illegible]	[illegible]	[illegible]	[illegible]	[illegible]	[illegible]	[illegible]
From 1 p.m. to 7 p.m.	[illegible]	"	[illegible]	[illegible]	[illegible]	[illegible]	[illegible]	[illegible]	[illegible]	[illegible]
From 7 p.m. to 11 night.	[illegible]	"	[illegible]	[illegible]	[illegible]	[illegible]	[illegible]	[illegible]	[illegible]	[illegible]
From 11 night to 6 a.m. Monday.	[illegible]	"	[illegible]	[illegible]	[illegible]	[illegible]	[illegible]	[illegible]	[illegible]	5
Total - -	[illegible]	—	[illegible]	[illegible]	[illegible]	[illegible]	[illegible]	[illegible]	[illegible]	[illegible]

—	[illegible]	[illegible]	[illegible]	[illegible]	[illegible]	[illegible]	[illegible]	[illegible]	[illegible]	[illegible]
From 1 p.m. to 7 p.m.	[illegible]	[illegible]	[illegible]	[illegible]	[illegible]	[illegible]	[illegible]	[illegible]	[illegible]	[illegible]
From 1 p.m. to 7 p.m.	[illegible]	[illegible]	77	[illegible]	67	[illegible]	[illegible]	[illegible]	[illegible]	[illegible]
From 7 p.m. to 11 night	[illegible]	[illegible]	[illegible]	[illegible]	[illegible]	[illegible]	[illegible]	[illegible]	[illegible]	[illegible]
From 11 night to 6 a.m. Monday.	[illegible]	[illegible]	[illegible]	[illegible]	4	[illegible]	4	11	[illegible]	4
Total - -	[illegible]	[illegible]	[illegible]	[illegible]	[illegible]	[illegible]	[illegible]	[illegible]	[illegible]	[illegible]

[illegible]

APPENDIX XIII.

(Copy of Letter from Sir David Harrel, K.C.B.)

Chief Secretary's Office,
Dublin Castle,
2nd June [illegible]

Sir,

I am directed by the Lords Justices to transmit, for the information of the Royal Commission on Liquor Licensing Laws, the [illegible] copy of a report received from the police and a cutting from the "Freeman's Journal" of the [illegible] May [illegible], on the subject of "Tied houses" in Cork.

I am, sir,
Your obedient servant,
(Signed) D. Harrel.

The Secretary,
Royal Commission on Liquor Licensing Laws.

Enclosure.

District Inspector's Office,
Cork, South,
[illegible] May [illegible].

I beg to report that the facts in the enclosed cutting are quite correct, and the Recorder's remarks on the subject of "Tied houses" are also accurately reported.

Freeman's Journal, [illegible] May [illegible].

"The Recorder of Cork on 'Tied Houses.'

"Our Cork correspondent writes that at the Borough Licensing Sessions yesterday, before the Recorder, a licensing case arose which excited a good deal of interest, in view of the sitting of the Licensing Commission and the evidence which has been given on the subject of 'tied' houses. It was an application by Miss O'Leary, Barrack Street, for transfer of licence held by her sister, Hannah O'Leary.

"The Recorder, in giving his decision, said that he had eight transfers granted there that day, and all were in the occupation of the brewers. There was not one of those transfers or licences in which the person who applied for it was bona fide. They all held their premises as weekly tenants. The practice existed everywhere, and when A. B. was getting a licence they had it before them that they were simply giving it to A. B. as the representative of some brewer. That was a course of dealing which his Honour thought should be brought before the attention of the Commission sitting on Licensing Laws. His Honour proceeded to deal with the facts of the case, and refused the application on the [illegible] and [illegible] of the applicant, and on the objection of the police. He judged her [illegible] and [illegible] on her [illegible] in the proceedings before the Court. He had nothing to say to her character outside that."

The object the Recorder had in view in drawing attention to the system of "Tied houses" was to bring it under the notice of the Licensing Commission, as he stated that, in his opinion, such a practice was never contemplated by the Legislature when the licensing laws were enacted.

B. D. [illegible], D.I.

APPENDIX XIV.

Adulteration of Whisky.

Royal Irish Constabulary Office,
Dublin Castle,
July [illegible], [illegible].

Dear Mr. Peel,

On receipt of your letter of 13th May I asked the officers at Belfast, Cork, Tralee, Limerick, and Londonderry to give me their opinion as to the extent to which whisky is adulterated, and where necessary to have samples taken for analysis.

You will find copies of their replies attached, except in the case of Tralee, which has not yet come in, but which will be forwarded when received.

Yours faithfully,
[illegible] Reed,
Inspector-General.

The Hon. Sidney Peel,
Royal Commission on
Liquor Licensing Laws,
4, Old Palace Yard,
London, S.W.

Belfast.

District Inspector Morell:—

"All the officers here agree that there is little or no adulteration of whisky in Belfast."

Cork.

County Inspector Cambell:—

"A considerable number of samples of whisky have been taken in this riding since May last. In a few instances the liquor was found to be under proof—water having been added—but in no case was there any adulteration."

Limerick.

County Inspector Hayes:—

"From time to time I have had numerous samples taken in different parts of Ireland, and in no instance was it found that there was any adulteration beyond added water. I do not believe there is adulteration to any extent. When in the north of Ireland I had some of the lowest houses tried, and several in Limerick since coming here. I also questioned several of the Food and Drugs Inspectors, and they all said water was the only adulteration found in samples taken by them."

Londonderry.

County Inspector Leathem:—

"Forty-seven samples of whisky were taken in fairs, &c. in May and June 1898. They were genuine, except for being 'under proof' from watering. In one case it amounted to [illegible] per cent., and the publican was fined 10s. and costs."

Royal Irish Constabulary Office,
Dublin Castle,
August [illegible], [illegible].

Dear Mr. Peel,

As promised in the Inspector-General's letter of the [illegible] ultimo, I enclose you the following particulars supplied by the County Inspector, Tralee, relative to adulteration of whisky.

Yours faithfully,
H. Tuthill,
Deputy Inspector-General.

The Hon. Sidney Peel.

Tralee.

County Inspector:—

"I find that out of [illegible] samples of whisky taken in various parts of this county [illegible] were found to be pure, one adulterated with water, and the result in the remainder has not been notified.

"The only way I can account for the absence of the 'bad stuff' is that the publicans are able to dodge the inspectors. I believe they invariably count the stuff as there, but the policeman, who is well known, is not the inspector, does not come across it."

INDEX.

A.

B.

G.

H.

Q

R

U.

V.

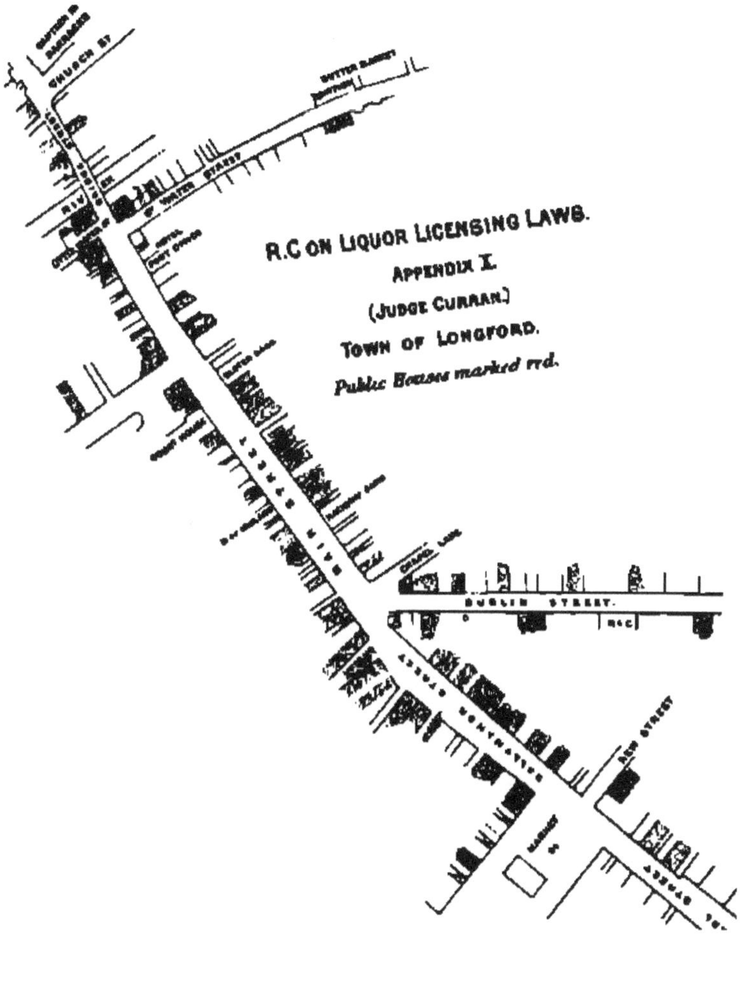
R.C ON LIQUOR LICENSING LAWS.
APPENDIX X.
(JUDGE CURRAN.)
TOWN OF LONGFORD.
Public Houses marked red.
CHURCH ST
WATER STREET
DUBLIN STREET.
NEW STREET